NINTH EDITION

RESPONSIVE WEB DESIGN

WITH HTML 5 & CSS

MINNICK

CENGAGE

Australia • Brazil • Mexico • Singapore • United Kingdom • United States

Responsive Web Design with HTML 5 and CSS, 9th Edition
Jessica Minnick

SVP, Higher Education Product Management: Erin Joyner

VP, Product Management: Mike Schenk

Product Director: Lauren Murphy

Product Team Manager: Kristin McNary

Product Assistant: Tom Benedetto

Director, Learning Design: Rebecca von Gillern

Senior Manager, Learning Design: Leigh Hefferon

Learning Designer: Mary Convertino

Vice President, Marketing – Science, Technology, & Math: Jason Sakos

Senior Marketing Director: Michele McTighe

Marketing Manager: Cassie L Cloutier

Marketing Development Manager: Samantha Best

Director, Content Creation: Juliet Steiner

Senior Manager, Content Creation: Patty Stephan

Content Manager: Christina Nyren

Director, Digital Production Services: Krista Kellman

Digital Delivery Lead: Jim Vaughey

Developmental Editor: Lisa Ruffolo

Production Service/Composition: Lumina Datamatics, Inc.

Design Director: Jack Pendleton

Designer: Erin Griffin

Cover Designer: Heather Marshall, Lumina Datamatics, Inc.

Cover image(s): iStockPhoto.com/koto_feja

For product information and technology assistance, contact us at **Cengage Customer & Sales Support, 1-800-354-9706** or **support.cengage.com**.
For permission to use material from this text or product, submit all requests online at **www.cengage.com/permissions**.

Library of Congress Control Number: 2019957998

ISBN: 978-0-357-42383-7

Cengage
200 Pier 4 Boulevard
Boston, MA 02210
USA

Cengage is a leading provider of customized learning solutions with employees residing in nearly 40 different countries and sales in more than 125 countries around the world. Find your local representative at **www.cengage.com**.

Cengage products are represented in Canada by Nelson Education, Ltd.

To learn more about Cengage platforms and services, register or access your online learning solution, or purchase materials for your course, visit **www.cengage.com**.

Notice to the Reader

Publisher does not warrant or guarantee any of the products described herein or perform any independent analysis in connection with any of the product information contained herein. Publisher does not assume, and expressly disclaims, any obligation to obtain and include information other than that provided to it by the manufacturer. The reader is expressly warned to consider and adopt all safety precautions that might be indicated by the activities described herein and to avoid all potential hazards. By following the instructions contained herein, the reader willingly assumes all risks in connection with such instructions. The publisher makes no representations or warranties of any kind, including but not limited to, the warranties of fitness for particular purpose or merchantability, nor are any such representations implied with respect to the material set forth herein, and the publisher takes no responsibility with respect to such material. The publisher shall not be liable for any special, consequential, or exemplary damages resulting, in whole or part, from the readers' use of, or reliance upon, this material.

Printed at CLDPC, USA, 08-22

Responsive Web Design with HTML 5 & CSS

Ninth Edition

Contents

Appendices

Preface

The Shelly Cashman Series® offers the finest textbooks in computer education. We are proud that our previous web design and development books have been so well received. With each new edition of our HTML and CSS books, we make significant improvements based on web technology and comments made by instructors and students. For *Responsive Web Design with HTML 5 and CSS, Ninth Edition*, the Shelly Cashman Series development team carefully reviewed our pedagogy and analyzed its effectiveness in teaching today's student. Contemporary students read less, but need to retain more. As they develop and perform skills, students must know how to apply the skills to different settings. Today's students need to be continually engaged and challenged to retain what they're learning.

With this web design book, we continue our commitment to focusing on the user and how they learn best.

Objectives of This Textbook

Responsive Web Design with HTML 5 and CSS, Ninth Edition, is intended for a first course that offers an introduction to HTML, CSS, and responsive web design techniques. No experience with webpage development or computer programming is required. The objectives of this book are:

- To teach the fundamentals of how to plan and organize the webpages for a new website

- To thoroughly apply two fundamental webpage technologies to realistic case studies: HTML for structure and CSS for style and layout

- To provide an exercise-oriented approach that reinforces learning by doing

- To introduce students to new web technologies and trends, including responsive web design and mobile-first design strategies

- To demonstrate current techniques for incorporating audio and video and for integrating interactivity using CSS and JavaScript

- To promote curiosity and independent exploration of web resources

- To support current, professional webpage development best practices

- To encourage independent study and support distance learners

The Shelly Cashman Approach

Proven Pedagogy with an Emphasis on Project Planning

Each chapter presents a practical problem to be solved, within a project planning framework. The project orientation is strengthened by the use of the Roadmap, which provides a visual guide for the project. Step-by-step instructions with supporting screens guide students through the steps. Instructional steps are supported by the Q&A, Other Ways, Experimental Steps, and BTW features.

Visually Engaging Book That Maintains Student Interest

The step-by-step tasks with supporting figures create a rich visual experience for the student. Callouts on the screens that present both explanatory and navigational information provide students with information they need when they need to know it.

Supporting Reference Materials (Appendices)

The appendices provide additional information about the details of HTML and CSS so that students can quickly look up information about web design terms, HTML elements, attributes, and valid values as well as CSS properties and values.

End-of-Chapter Student Activities

Extensive end-of-chapter activities provide a variety of reinforcement opportunities for students where they can apply and expand their skills. To complete some of these assignments, you will be required to use the Data Files for Students. Please contact your instructor for information about accessing the required files.

New to This Edition

Fresh, Industry-Leading Website Design Practices

For this edition, the development team made a huge leap forward in bringing up-to-date, forward-thinking website development practices into focus and application.

Custom Fonts

Learn how to integrate custom fonts. You are no longer limited to standard browser fonts. Expand your font options by integrating custom Google fonts.

Design Single- and Multiple-Column Layouts

Learn how to design single-column and multiple-column layouts using the CSS Grid Layout. Create a single-column design for a mobile layout and a multiple-column layout for progressively larger screens.

Interactivity with CSS and JavaScript

Learn how to integrate transforms and animations, which provide interactivity to a webpage. Create a working hamburger icon menu exclusively for a mobile viewport.

Design for Accessibility

Learn how to add closed captions to videos.

Introduction to Bootstrap

Learn how to use Bootstrap, a popular web framework, to create an entire webpage.

All New Projects

This edition contains a wealth of contemporary projects that logically build in complexity and probe for understanding. Our goal is not only to help you teach valid HTML and CSS, but to reveal deeper conceptual issues essential to the field of web development. Using the technologies of today's web developers results in websites that are worthy candidates for an electronic portfolio.

Professional Best Practices

With the advent of today's powerful content management systems and website builder tools, do you still need to learn how to create HTML and CSS files from scratch in a text editor? Professionals in the field answer that question with a united, enthusiastic yes! Mastering these technologies is essential to all web-related careers.

Instructor Resources

The Instructor Resources include both teaching and testing aids and can be accessed via www.cengage.com/login.

Instructor's Manual Includes lecture notes summarizing the chapter sections, figures, and boxed elements found in every chapter, teacher tips, classroom activities, lab activities, and quick quizzes in Microsoft® Word® files.

Figure Files Illustrations for every figure in the textbook in electronic form.

PowerPoint Presentations A multimedia lecture presentation system that provides slides for each chapter. Presentations are based on chapter objectives.

Data Files for Students Includes all the files that are required by students to complete the exercises.

Solutions to Exercises Includes solutions for all end-of-chapter exercises and chapter reinforcement exercises.

Test Bank & Test Engine Test banks include questions for every chapter, featuring objective-based and critical thinking question types. Cengage Learning Testing Powered by Cognero is a flexible, online system that allows you to:

- author, edit, and manage test bank content from multiple Cengage Learning solutions
- create multiple test versions in an instant
- deliver tests from your LMS, your classroom, or wherever you want

Textbook Walk-Through

The Shelly Cashman Series Pedagogy: Project-Based — Step-by-Step — Variety of Assessments

Roadmaps provide a visual guide to each project, showing the students where they are in the process of creating each project.

Step-by-step instructions now provide a context beyond point-and-click. Each step provides information on why students are performing each task, or what will occur as a result.

Q&A boxes anticipate questions students may have when working through the steps and provide additional information about what they are doing right where they need it.

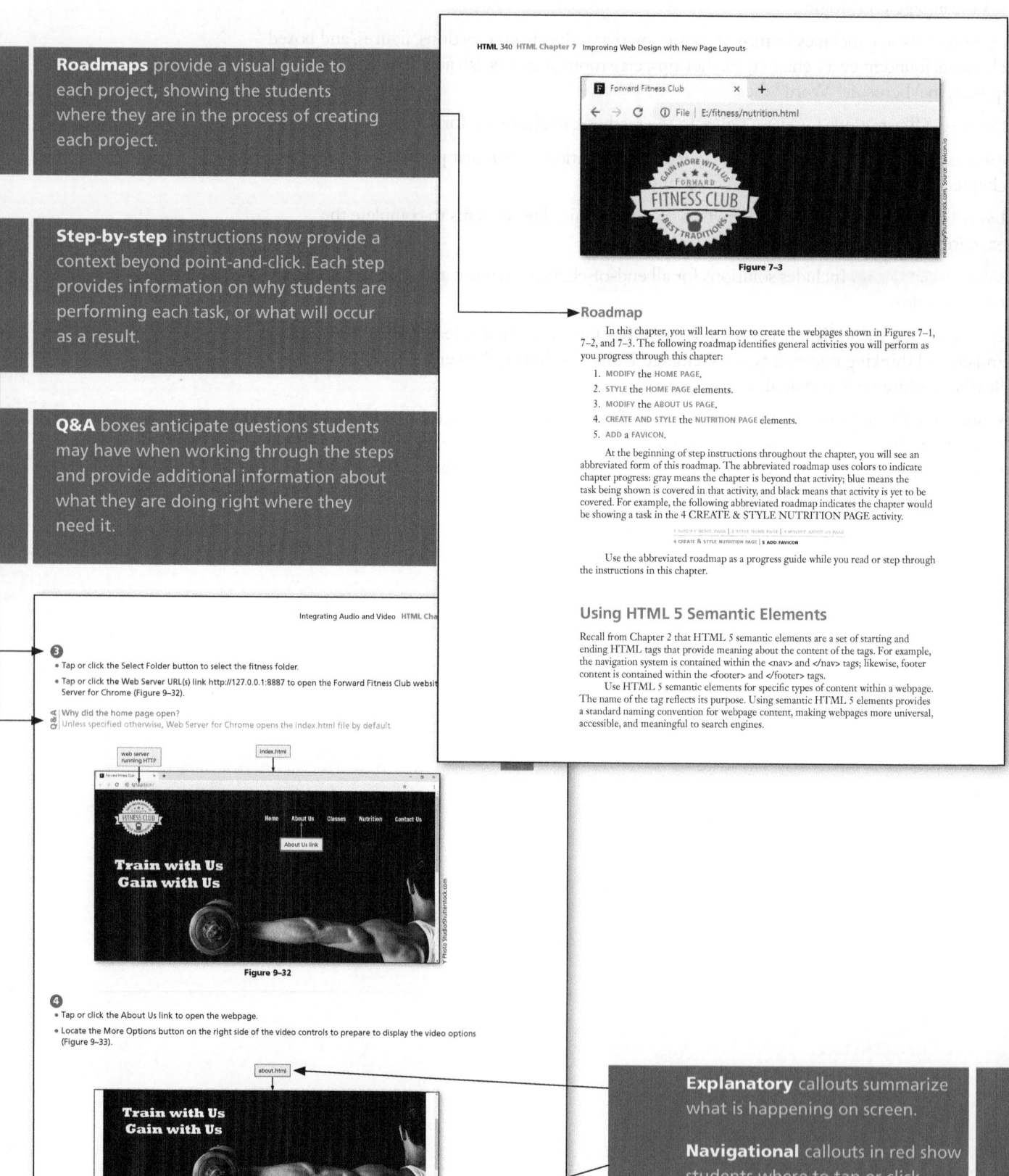

Figure 7–3

Roadmap

In this chapter, you will learn how to create the webpages shown in Figures 7–1, 7–2, and 7–3. The following roadmap identifies general activities you will perform as you progress through this chapter:

1. MODIFY the HOME PAGE.
2. STYLE the HOME PAGE elements.
3. MODIFY the ABOUT US PAGE.
4. CREATE AND STYLE the NUTRITION PAGE elements.
5. ADD a FAVICON.

At the beginning of step instructions throughout the chapter, you will see an abbreviated form of this roadmap. The abbreviated roadmap uses colors to indicate chapter progress: gray means the chapter is beyond that activity; blue means the task being shown is covered in that activity, and black means that activity is yet to be covered. For example, the following abbreviated roadmap indicates the chapter would be showing a task in the 4 CREATE & STYLE NUTRITION PAGE activity.

1 MODIFY HOME PAGE | 2 STYLE HOME PAGE | 3 MODIFY ABOUT US PAGE
4 CREATE & STYLE NUTRITION PAGE | 5 ADD FAVICON

Use the abbreviated roadmap as a progress guide while you read or step through the instructions in this chapter.

Using HTML 5 Semantic Elements

Recall from Chapter 2 that HTML 5 semantic elements are a set of starting and ending HTML tags that provide meaning about the content of the tags. For example, the navigation system is contained within the <nav> and </nav> tags; likewise, footer content is contained within the <footer> and </footer> tags.

Use HTML 5 semantic elements for specific types of content within a webpage. The name of the tag reflects its purpose. Using semantic HTML 5 elements provides a standard naming convention for webpage content, making webpages more universal, accessible, and meaningful to search engines.

Integrating Audio and Video HTML Cha

3
- Tap or click the Select Folder button to select the fitness folder.
- Tap or click the Web Server URL(s) link http://127.0.0.1:8887 to open the Forward Fitness Club website Server for Chrome (Figure 9–32).

Q&A Why did the home page open?
Unless specified otherwise, Web Server for Chrome opens the index.html file by default.

web server running HTTP

index.html

Train with Us Gain with Us

Home About Us Classes Nutrition Contact Us

About Us link

Figure 9–32

4
- Tap or click the About Us link to open the webpage.
- Locate the More Options button on the right side of the video controls to prepare to display the video options (Figure 9–33).

about.html

Train with Us Gain with Us

video controls

More Options button

Figure 9–33

Explanatory callouts summarize what is happening on screen.

Navigational callouts in red show students where to tap or click.

To Add a Linear Gradient

Add a linear gradient to the div element with the id attribute exercises for the tablet viewport. *Why? A gradient background enhances the appearance of the webpage for tablet and desktop displays.* The following steps create a new style rule to apply a linear gradient to the #exercises selector as desired for the tablet viewport.

1

- Place the insertion point at the end of Line 192 and press the ENTER key to insert a new Line 193.

- On Line 193, type `background: linear-gradient(to right, #ccc, #fff);` to add a new declaration (Figure 6–55).

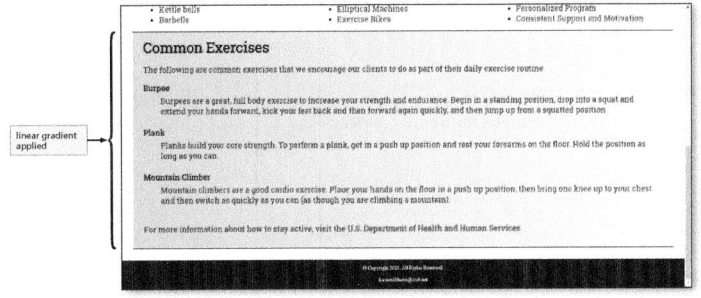

```
185   /* Tablet Viewport: Style rules for main content area */
186   main ul {
187       margin: 0 0 4% 19%;
188   }
189
190   #exercises {
191       border-top: 1px solid #000;
192       border-bottom: 1px solid #000;
193       background: linear-gradient(to right, #ccc, #fff);      ← linear gradient added as a new declaration
194       background-color: #f2f2f2;
195       padding: 1% 2%;
196   }
```

Line 193

Q&A Why am I adding this declaration within the tablet media query?
The Common Exercises div is not displayed on a mobile viewport. Now that you have added this gradient for the tablet viewport, subsequent viewports will inherit the change.

Figure 6–55

2

- Save the styles.css file, and then refresh about.html in your browser to view the changes.

Experiment

- Use Table 6–4 to change the linear gradient to a left to right or to a diagonal gradient, save the styles.css file, and then refresh about.html in your browser.

- Return the background to a linear gradient, save the styles.css file, and then refresh about.html in your browser (Figure 6–56).

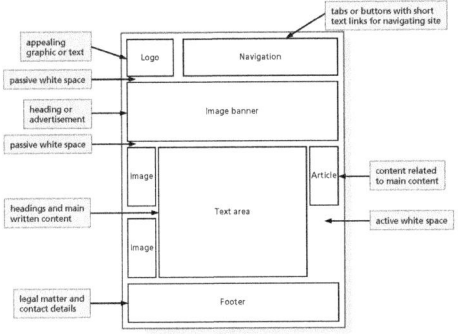

linear gradient applied

Figure 6–56

HTML 14   **HTML Chapter 1**   Introduction to the Internet and Web Design

CONSIDER THIS

Can I redesign a desktop-only website for multiplatform displa
Yes. If your audience is accustomed to the desktop-only website, retrofitting
makes sense because the site remains familiar to users. You also avoid buildi
vantage of design decisions such as color scheme and use media you have a
content and number of pages, redesigning may be a time-consuming proces

Wireframe

Before web designers actually start cre
they sketch the design using a wireframe. A
clearly identifies the location of main webpa
organization logo, content areas, and images
your webpages, use lines and boxes as shown
plenty of white space within your design to i
distinguish among the areas on the webpage
active white space and passive white space. A**ctive white space** is an area on the page
that is intentionally left blank. Typically, the goal of active white space is to help balance
the design of an asymmetrical page. **Passive white space** is the space between content
areas. Passive white space helps a user focus on one part of the page. Proper use of white
space makes webpage content easy to read and brings focus to page elements.

Figure 1–12

CONSIDER THIS

What tools can I use to create a wireframe?
You can use one of several free tools to create a wireframe, including Pencil Project, Mockplus, and Wireframe CC. You can
also use drawing tools in Microsoft Word or PowerPoint or a pen and paper.

Site Map

A **site map** is a planning tool that lists or displays all the pages on a website
and indicates how they are related to each other. In other words, a site map shows
the structure of a website. Begin defining the structure of a website by identifying the
information to provide and then organize that information into divisions using
the organizing method that makes the most sense for the content. For example, if the
website offers three types of products for sale, organize the site by product category.
If the website provides training, organize the site in a step-by-step sequence.

Textbook Walk-Through

Chapter Summary lists the tasks completed in the chapter, grouped into major task categories in an outline format.

Apply Your Knowledge exercise usually requires students to open and manipulate a file to practice the activities learned in the chapter.

Chapter Summary

In this chapter, you learned how to create a CSS file with rules to style HTML elements on a webpage. You linked the CSS file to all of the webpages for the fitness website. The items listed below include all the new concepts and skills you have learned in this chapter, with the tasks grouped by activity.

Using Cascading Style Sheets
Inline, Embedded, and External Style Sheets (HTML 147, HTML 148)
CSS Basics (HTML 149)
CSS Text Properties (HTML 150)
CSS Colors (HTML 151)

Understanding Inline Elements and Block Elements
CSS Box Model (HTML 154)

Creating an External Style Sheet
Create a CSS File (HTML 157)
Create a Style Rule for the Body Element (HTML 157)

Linking an HTML Document to a CSS File
Link HTML Pages to the CSS File (HTML 159)

Creating a Webpage Layout
Set Float and Clear Properties (HTML 161)

Creating Style Rules for Structural Elements
Create Style Rules for the Header, Nav, Main, and Footer Elements (HTML 163–HTML 178)

Modifying the Nav to use an unordered list
Create a Style Rule for the Unordered List within the Nav (HTML 169)

Create a Style Rule for the List Items within the Nav (HTML 170)
Create a Style Rule for the List Item Anchor Elements within the Nav (HTML 170)

Creating Responsive Image
Create a Style Rule for Img Element (HTML 173)
Remove Height and Width Attributes from Img Elements (HTML 174)

Creating Style Rules for ID and Class Attributes
Create a Style Rule for ID Attributes (HTML 179)
Use the Span Element (HTML 184)
Create a Style Rule for Class Attributes (HTML 184)

Creating a CSS Reset
Create a CSS Reset Style Rule (HTML 190)

Adding Comments to CSS Files
Add Comments to a CSS File (HTML 193)

Validating CSS Files
Validate the CSS File (HTML 195)

CONSIDER THIS

What decisions will you need to make when creating your next CSS file?
Use these guidelines as you complete the assignments in this chapter and create your own websites outside of this class.

1. Determine properties for your HTML elements (such as header, nav, main, and footer).
   a. Set webpage width and centering characteristics.
   b. Decide on any necessary text properties to use for font face, size, and style.
   c. Set text and background colors.
   d. Decide if you need borders, and then set the style, size, and color of the border.
   e. Float any content that needs to appear on the same line.
   f. Determine the amount of margins and padding to use.

2. Link the CSS file to your HTML pages and website template.
   a. Add comments to your CSS file, noting the declarations for each selector.
   b. Validate your CSS file to confirm that it does not contain any errors.
   c. View your website in a browser to see the applied styles throughout the development process.
   d. Determine any changes that need to be made and revalidate.

3. Depending on the structure of your website, determine if you should create additional CSS files to accommodate multiple wireframes or different media such as mobile or print. Styling for multiple devices will be covered in later chapters.

CONSIDER THIS

How should you submit solutions to questions in the assignments identified with a ⚙ symbol? Every assignment in this book contains one or more questions identified with a ⚙ symbol. These questions require you to think beyond the assigned presentation. Present your solutions to the questions in the format required by your instructor. Possible formats may include one or more of these options: create a document that contains the answer; present your answer to the class; discuss your answer in a group; record the answer as audio or video using a webcam, smartphone, or portable media player; or post answers on a blog, wiki, or website.

Apply Your Knowledge

Reinforce the skills and apply the concepts you learne

Using Tables
Note: To complete this assignment, you will be required t
instructor for information about accessing the Data Files.

Instructions: In this exercise, you will use your text editor
First, you insert a table element. Next, you add a table capt
data. Then, you create style rules to format the table. Work
folder and the apply08.css file in the apply\css folder from
is shown in Figure 8–67. You will also use professional web
comment, and validate your code.

2025 Sales by Qua

Product	Quarter 1	Quarter 2	Quarter 3	Quarter 4
Tablets	$24,500	$21,525	$20,217	$28,575
Monitors	$12,825	.$12,400	$11,900	$14,233
Laptops	$33,000	$32,750	$31,595	$32,465
Desktops	$21,478	$20,895	$18,200	$21,625

Designed by: Student's Name

Figure 8–67

Perform the following tasks:
1. Open index.html in the chapter08\apply folder from the Data Files in your text editor. Review the page, add a title, modify the comment at the top of the page to include your name and today's date, and replace "Student's Name" with your name in the footer element.

2. Open the apply08.css file from the apply\css folder. Modify the comment at the top of the style sheet to include your name and today's date.

3. In the index.html file, add a `table` element within the `main` element.

4. Nest the following caption element within the `table` element:
   `<caption>2025 Sales by Quarter</caption>`

5. Insert five table rows after the caption and include a comment that specifies the row number. Follow the example below:
   ```
   <tr><!-- Row 1 -->
   </tr>
   ```

Consider This: Plan Ahead box presents a single master planning guide that students can use as they create webpages on their own.

Continued >

Extend Your Knowledge

Extend the skills you learned in this chapter and experiment with new skills. You may need to use additional resources to complete the assignment.

Working with Positions

Instructions: In this exercise, you will create and modify style rules to learn more about how to place elements on a page using positions. An example of page element positions is shown in Figure 5–66.

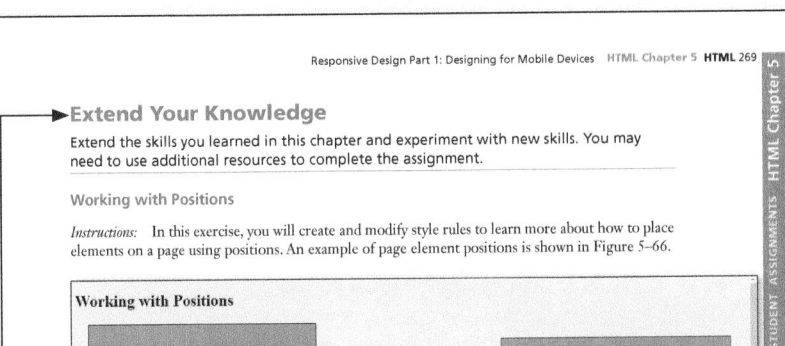

Working with Positions

Sticky
This is an example of an element with a sticky position. Its position is based on the user's scroll position.

Fixed
This is an example of an element with a fixed position. Its position is relative to the viewport.

Relative
This is an example of an element with a relative position. It can move around a little, depending on the viewport, but it is at a position relative to itself.

Absolute
This is an example of an element with an absolute position. It is similar to the fixed position, however, it is positioned relative to the closest parent element.

Figure 5–66

Perform the following tasks:

1. Open your text editor and then open the index.html file in the chapter05\extend folder from the Data Files. Update the comment with your name and today['s date].

2. Open index.html in your browser to view the file.

3. Open the extend05.css file in your text editor. Locate the "sticky" [comment and create a style] rule for the sticky class selector. Add a declaration for the positi[on property and specify a value of] -webkit-sticky. Add a declaration for the position property [with a value of sticky.] Add a declaration for the top property and specify a zero value. [Save your changes. Refresh] your page, and scroll down to view the changes. In the index.ht[ml file, add content to the] element within the sticky div element to briefly explain how to [set a sticky position.]

4. In the extend05.css file, locate the "relative" comment and creat[e a style rule for the relative] class selector. Add a declaration for the position property with a [value of relative. Add] another declaration for the top property and specify a value of [50 pixels. Add a] declaration for the left property with a value of 30 pixels. Save y[our changes. Refresh your] page, and scroll down to view the changes. Return to extend05.[css and change the top and] left property values to a value of your choice. In the index.html [file, add content to the] element within the relative div element to identify the values yo[u used for the top and left] properties and how it affected the relative box.

19. Save your changes and refresh extend06.html in your browser to view the changes.

20. Save your files and submit them in a format specified by your instructor.

21. ⊙ In this exercise, you explored more about gradients and used percentages to set color stops. You also used rgba to set transparency in step 14. Use your browser to research how to set gradient color stops using percentages. Also research how to use the rgba() function to create transparency. Include a description of your findings.

Analyze, Correct, Improve

Analyze a webpage, correct all errors, and improve it.

Modifying Media Queries

Note: To complete this assignment, you will be required to use the Data Files. Please contact your instructor for information about accessing the Data Files.

Instructions: The analyze06.html webpage is a draft website template, but must be corrected and improved for responsive design before presenting it to a client. Use Figure 6–63, Figure 6–64, and Figure 6–65 as a guide to correct these files.

Figure 6–63

Figure 6–64

Continued >

Analyze, Correct, Improve projects call on students to analyze a file, discover errors in it, fix the errors, and then improve the file using the skills they learned in the chapter.

Extend Your Knowledge projects at the end of each chapter allow students to extend and expand on the skills learned within the chapter. Students use critical thinking to experiment with new skills to complete each project.

Textbook Walk-Through

STUDENT ASSIGNMENTS

Analyze, Correct, Improve *continued*

g. Validate the HTML file and correct any errors.

h. Submit the assignment in the format specified by your instructor.

i. ⚪ Use your browser to research screen readers. What are the most popular screen readers? Is there a screen reader extension available for Google Chrome?

In the Lab

Labs 1 and 2, which increase in difficulty, require you to create webpages based on what you learned in the chapter; Lab 3 is ideal for group projects/collaboration.

Lab 1: **Adding Audio to the Strike a Chord Website**

Problem: You work for a local music lesson company called Strike a Chord that provides music lessons for piano, guitar, and violin. The company needs a web presence and has hired you to create their website. You have already created the website and now need to add audio to the Lessons page. Figure 9–39 shows the Lessons page with the audio files.

Figure 9–39

> **In the Lab** Three in-depth assignments in each chapter require students to apply the chapter concepts and techniques to solve problems. One Lab is devoted to independent exploration.

e following tasks:

der and create a new subfolder named media. Copy the Data Files from ur media folder.

l file in your text editor and update the comment with today's date.

after the paragraph element, insert two new blank lines and then add an text, `Piano Spring Performance`.

t, add an audio element with the `controls` attribute.

nt within the audio element that specifies the `piano.mp3` as the source edia folder, and `audio/mp3` as the type.

element that specifies the `piano.ogg` as the source file and `audio`

ment, provide fallback text for legacy browsers that do not support the

---

STUDENT ASSIGNMENTS

In the Lab *continued*

13. Check your spelling. Validate all HTML and CSS files and correct any errors. Save your changes.

14. Submit your assignment in the format specified by your instructor.

15. ⚪ Identify the resource you used to make your video. Identify the resource you used for audio. Identify the resource you used for file conversions.

Consider This: Your Turn

Apply your creative thinking and problem-solving skills to design and implement a solution.

1. Adding Audio to Your Personal Portfolio Website
Personal

Part 1: You have already developed a responsive website for your personal portfolio and now need to add audio to the website.

1. Open your portfolio folder and create a new subfolder named media.

2. Add the `audio` element to one of your webpages. Review your webpages to determine which page will use the audio element.

3. Determine which attributes to include for the `audio` element. Include at least two source files. You may use an existing audio file that you have, you may create an audio file, or you can research the Internet for a free audio resource, such as freemusicarchive.com. Save your audio source files in your portfolio/media folder.

4. Provide fallback text for legacy browsers that do not support the video element.

5. Save and test your files.

6. Validate and correct your HTML file as needed.

7. Submit your assignment in the format specified by your instructor.

Part 2: ⚪ Discuss the reasons you should or should not include audio on your portfolio webpage.

2. Adding a Video to the Dog Grooming Website
Professional

Part 1: You have already created a responsive design website for a dog grooming business, but now need to add a video to the website and make it accessible.

1. Open your groom folder and create a new subfolder named media. Copy the Data Files from chapter09/your_turn2 to your groom/media folder.

2. Open the index.html file in your text editor. Add a video element at the end of the welcome div. Include the controls attribute and a poster attribute that uses the image file of your choice.

3. Nest a source element within the video element that specifies `groom.mp4` as the source file and `video/mp4` as the type.

4. Nest another source element that specifies `groom.webm` as the source file and `video /webm` as the type.

5. Open the media\captions.vtt file in your text editor. Add your name and date to the NOTE. Use Table 9–9 to create a captions file.

> **Consider This: Your Turn** exercises call on students to apply creative-thinking and problem-solving skills to design and implement a solution.

1 Introduction to the Internet and Web Design

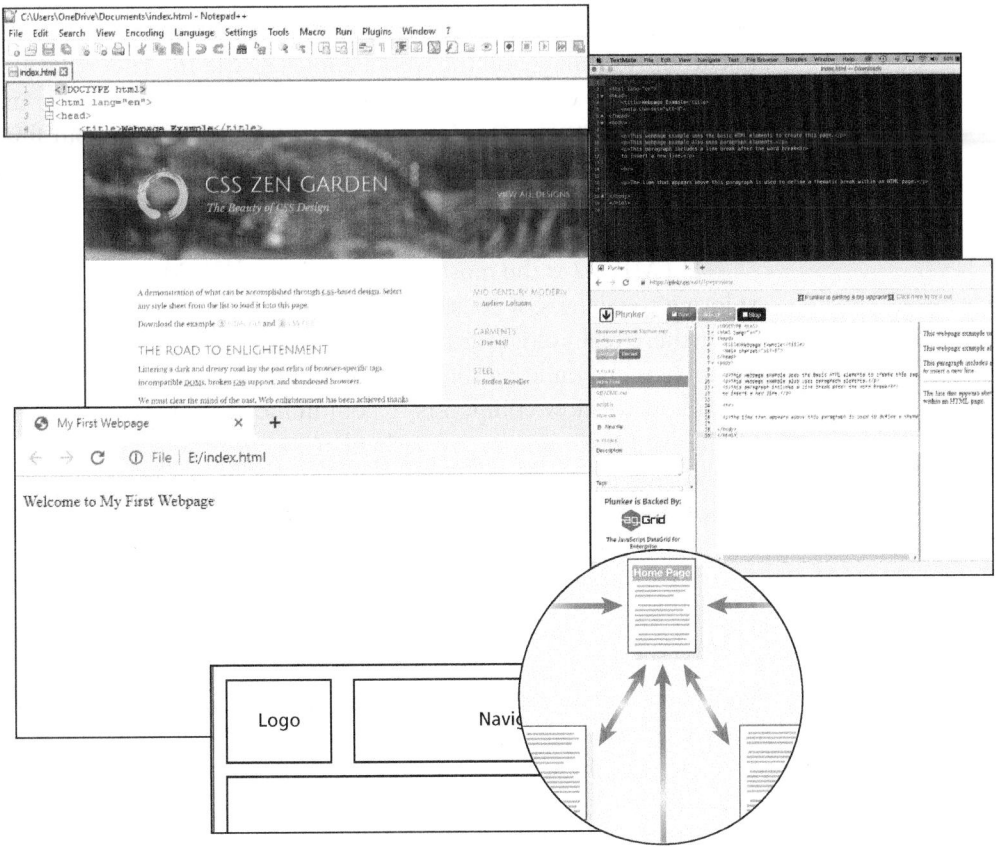

Objectives

You will have mastered the material in this chapter when you can:

- Define the Internet and associated key terms
- Recognize Internet protocols
- Discuss web browsers and identify their main features
- Describe the types and purposes of websites
- Plan a website for a target audience
- Define a wireframe and a site map
- Explain how websites use graphics, navigation tools, typography, and color

- Design for accessibility
- Design for multiplatform display
- Define Hypertext Markup Language (HTML) and HTML elements
- Recognize HTML versions and web programming languages
- Identify web authoring tools
- Download and use a web authoring tool
- Create and view a basic HTML webpage

1 | Introduction to the Internet and Web Design

Introduction

Today, millions of people worldwide have access to the Internet, the world's largest network. Billions of webpages providing information on any subject you can imagine are currently available on the web. People use the Internet to search for information, to communicate with others around the world, and to seek entertainment. Students use the Internet to register for classes, pay tuition, and find out final grades. Businesses and other organizations rely on the Internet and the web to sell products and services. Hypertext Markup Language (HTML) and Cascading Style Sheets (CSS) are two of the technologies that make this possible.

HTML 5.2 is the most recent version of HTML and is called HTML 5. Before exploring the details of creating webpages with HTML 5 and CSS, it is useful to look at how these technologies relate to the development of the Internet and the web. In this chapter, you learn some basics about the Internet and the web, and the rules both follow to allow computers to communicate with each other. You review types of websites and learn how to properly plan a website so that it is appealing and useful to your target audience. You also explore web browsers, HTML, and its associated key terms. Lastly, you create a basic webpage using a text editor.

Project — Create a Basic Webpage

People and organizations create webpages to attract attention to information such as products, services, multimedia, news, and research. Although webpages display content including text, drawings, photos, animations, videos, and links to other webpages, they are created as documents containing only text.

The project in this chapter follows general guidelines and uses a text editor to create the webpage shown in Figure 1–1. Figure 1–1a shows the **code**, meaningful combinations of text and symbols that a web browser interprets to display the webpage shown in Figure 1–1b. Content is displayed in two areas within the web browser. One part of the code indicates that text should be displayed as the webpage title, which appears in the browser tab. Another part of the code specifies that a line of text should appear as a paragraph within the browser window.

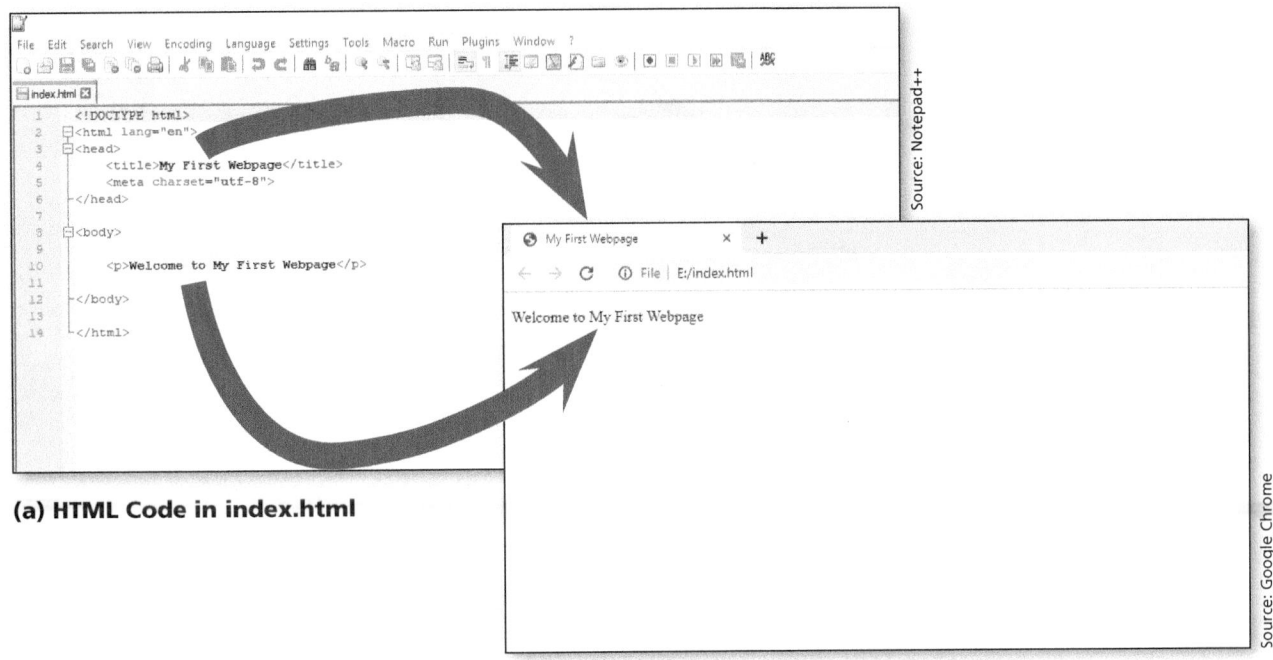

(a) HTML Code in index.html

(b) Webpage in Google Chrome

Figure 1–1

Roadmap

In this chapter, you learn how to create the webpage shown in Figure 1–1. The following roadmap identifies general activities you perform as you progress through this chapter:

1. RUN a TEXT EDITOR and CREATE a BLANK DOCUMENT.

2. ENTER HTML TAGS in the document.

3. ADD TEXT to the webpage.

4. SAVE the WEBPAGE as an HTML document.

5. VIEW the WEBPAGE in a browser.

At the beginning of step instructions throughout the chapter, you see an abbreviated form of this roadmap. The abbreviated roadmap uses colors to indicate chapter progress: gray means the chapter is beyond that activity; blue means the task being shown is covered in that activity; and black means that activity is yet to be covered. For example, the following abbreviated roadmap indicates the chapter would be showing a task in the 4 SAVE WEBPAGE activity.

1 RUN TEXT EDITOR & CREATE BLANK DOCUMENT | 2 ENTER HTML TAGS

3 ADD TEXT | **4 SAVE WEBPAGE** | **5 VIEW WEBPAGE**

Use the abbreviated roadmap as a progress guide while you read or step through the instructions in this chapter.

Exploring the Internet

Every day, millions of people use a computer to connect to the Internet. The **Internet** is a worldwide collection of computers linked together for use by businesses, governments, educational institutions, other organizations, and individuals using modems, phone lines, television cables, satellite links, fiber-optic connections, radio waves, and other communications devices and media (Figure 1–2).

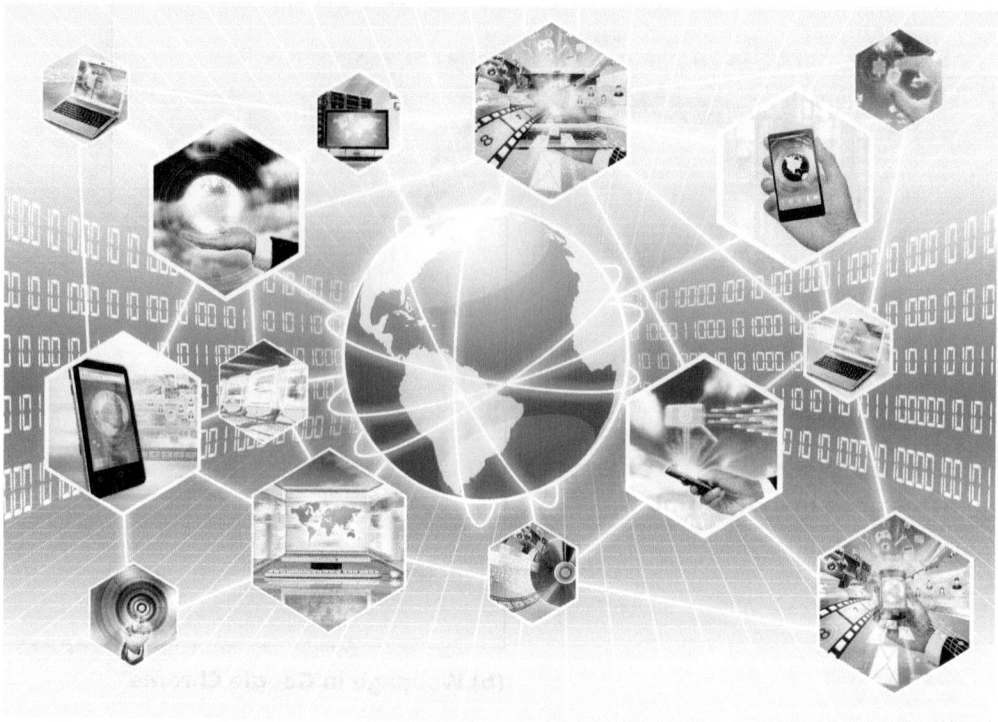

nmedia/Shutterstock.com

Figure 1–2

The Internet was developed in the 1960s by the Department of Defense Advanced Research Projects Agency (ARPA). ARPANET (as the Internet was originally called) had only four nodes and sent its first message in 1969. A **node** is any device, such as a computer, tablet, or smartphone, connected to a **network**, which is a collection of two or more computers linked together to share resources and information. The Internet has billions of nodes on millions of networks. The **Internet of Things** is a term used to describe the ever-growing number of devices connecting to a network, including televisions and appliances. Today, high-, medium-, and low-speed data lines connect networks. These **data lines** allow data (including text, graphical images, audio, and video) to move from one computer to another. The **Internet backbone** is a collection of high-speed data lines that link major computer systems located around the world. An **Internet service provider (ISP)** is a company that has a permanent connection to the Internet backbone. ISPs use high- or medium-speed data lines to allow personal and business computer users to connect to the backbone for access to the Internet. A home Internet connection is generally provided through a cable or fiber-optic line that connects to an ISP.

Billions of people in most countries around the world connect to the Internet using computers in their homes, offices, schools, and public locations such as libraries. In fact, the Internet was designed to be a place in which people could share information and collaborate. Users with computers connected to the Internet can access a variety of popular services, including email, social networking, and the web.

World Wide Web

Many people use the terms Internet and World Wide Web interchangeably, but these terms have different meanings. The Internet is the infrastructure, or the physical networks of computers. The **World Wide Web**, also called the **web**, is the service that provides access to information stored on web servers, the high-capacity, high-performance computers that power the web. The web consists of a collection of linked files known as **webpages**, or pages for short. Because the web supports text, graphics, audio, and video, a webpage can display any of these multimedia elements in a browser.

A **website**, or site for short, is a related collection of webpages created and maintained by a person, company, educational institution, or other organization, such as the U.S. Department of Education (Figure 1–3). Each website contains a **home page**, which is the main page and the first document users see when they access the website. The home page typically provides information about the website's purpose and content, often by including a list of links to other webpages on the website.

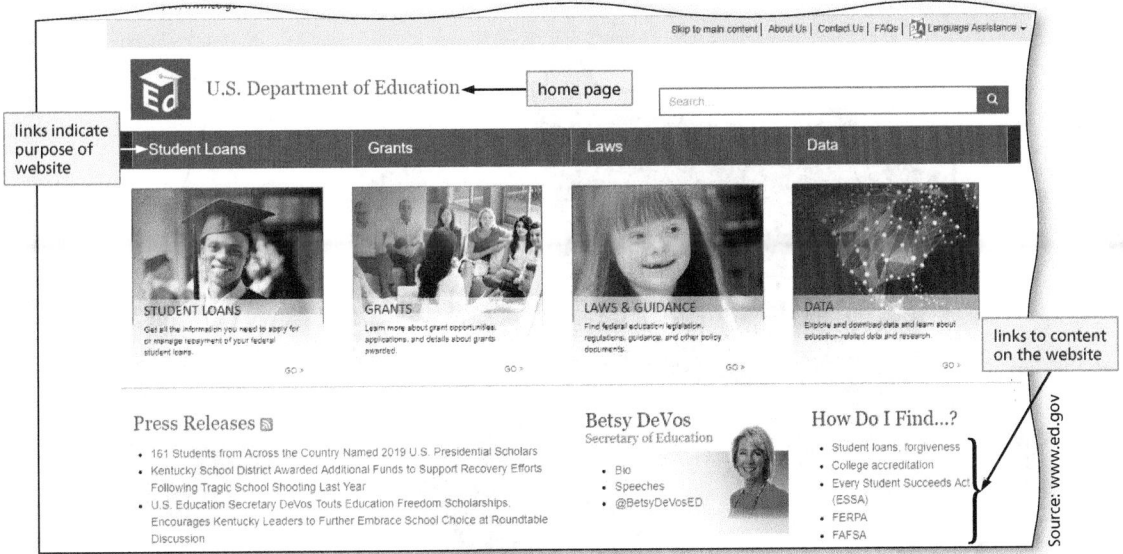

Figure 1–3

Hyperlinks are an essential part of the web. A **hyperlink**, more commonly called a **link**, is an element that connects one webpage to another webpage on the same server or to any other web server in the world. Tapping or clicking a link allows you to move quickly from one webpage to another without being concerned about where the webpages reside. You can also tap or click links to move to a different section of the same webpage.

With hyperlinks, you do not necessarily have to view information in a linear way. Instead, you can tap or click the available links to view the information in a variety of ways, as described later in this chapter. Many webpage components, including text, graphics, and animations, can serve as links. Figure 1–4 shows examples of several webpage components used as hyperlinks.

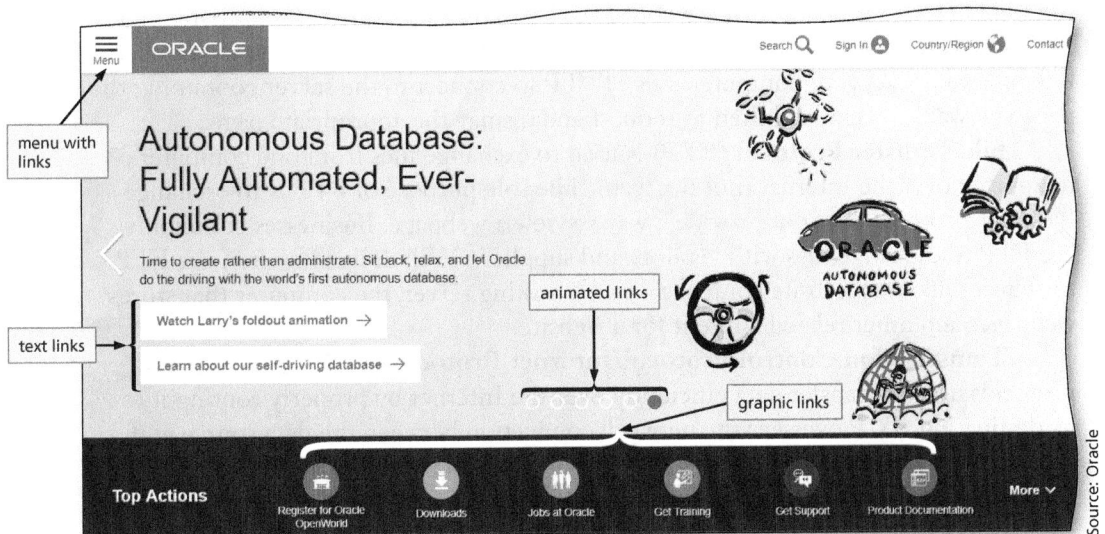

Figure 1–4

Protocols

A computer is also referred to as a client workstation. Client workstations connect to the Internet through the use of a protocol. A **protocol** is a set of rules that defines how a client workstation can communicate with a server. A client workstation uses a protocol to request a connection to a server. The **server** is the host computer that stores resources and files for websites (Figure 1–5).

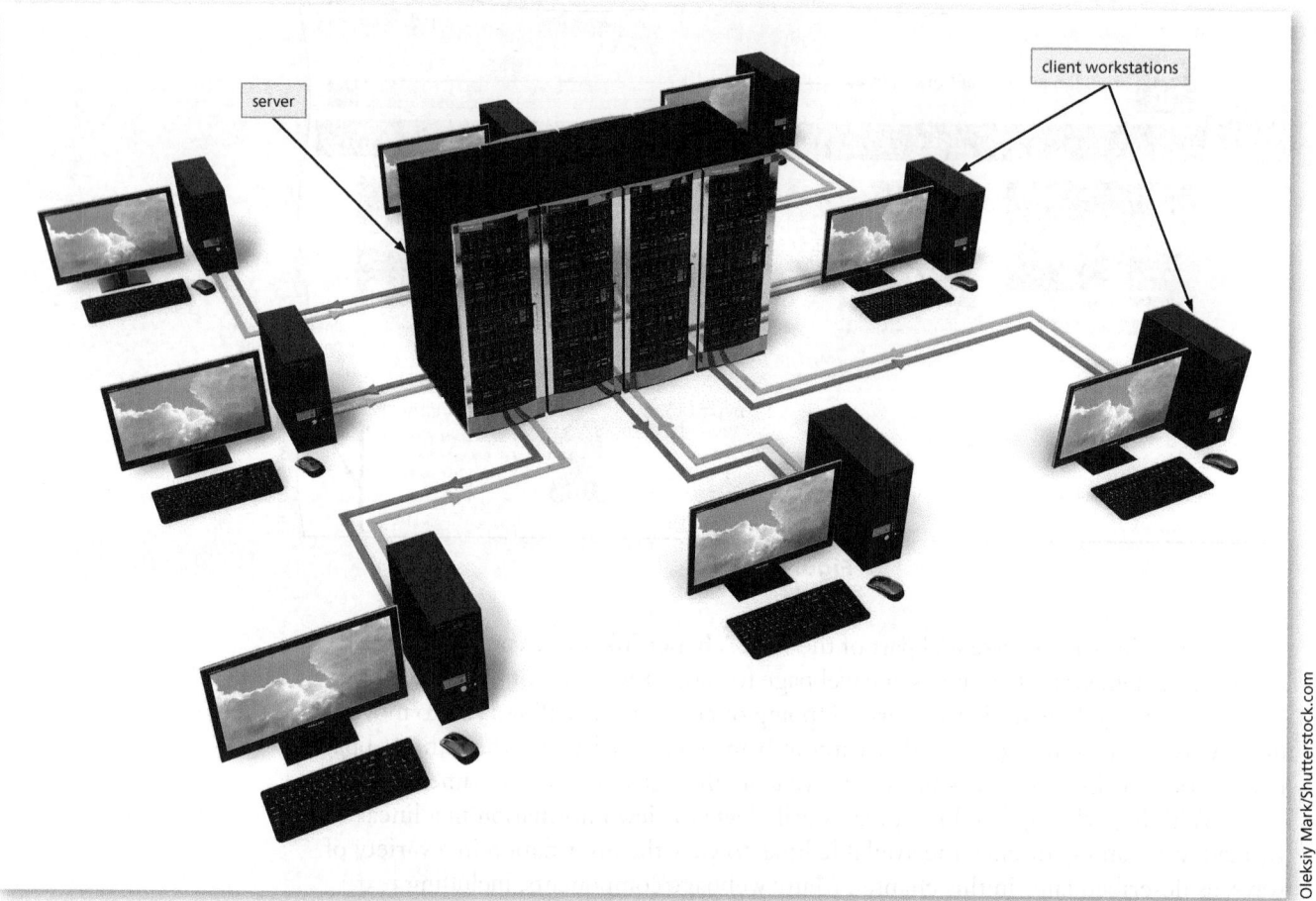

server

client workstations

Oleksiy Mark/Shutterstock.com

Figure 1–5

Hypertext Transfer Protocol (HTTP) is the fundamental protocol used on the web to exchange and transfer webpages. HTTP is a set of rules for exchanging text, graphics, audio, video, and other multimedia files on the web. When you tap or click a link on a webpage, your computer uses HTTP to connect to the server containing the page you want to view, and then to request and display the appropriate page.

File Transfer Protocol (FTP) is used to exchange files from one computer to another over the Internet (not the web). The sole purpose of FTP is to exchange files; this protocol does not provide a way to view a webpage. Businesses commonly use FTP to exchange files with vendors and suppliers. Web designers often use FTP to transfer updated website content to a web hosting server, the computer that stores webpages and other related content for a website.

Transmission Control Protocol/Internet Protocol (TCP/IP) is a pair of protocols used to transfer data efficiently over the Internet by properly routing it to its destination. TCP oversees the network connection between the data source and destination and micromanages the data. When data is sent over the Internet, TCP breaks the data into packets. Each packet contains addressing information, which the IP manages. One way to better understand TCP/IP is through an analogy of the postal system. The tasks TCP performs are similar to those workers or machines perform when handling a bundle of packages in a post office. In this analogy, the packages are addressed to one destination, but are too large to send as a single bundle. TCP breaks up the bundle into manageable pieces and then sends them out for delivery. When each piece arrives at the destination, TCP reassembles the bundle of packages.

Internet Protocol (IP) ensures data is sent to the correct location. In the postal system analogy, the IP part of TCP/IP refers to the street address and zip code to route a piece of mail. Just as people have a unique mailing address, every client workstation and server on the Internet has a unique IP address. An example of an IP address is 192.168.1.5. Every website has a unique IP address, which makes it easy for computers to find websites. However, most people have difficulty in remembering and using IP addresses to access websites. The **Domain Name System (DNS)** was created to resolve this issue. The DNS associates an IP address with a domain name. For example, the DNS associates the IP address 204.79.197.200 with the domain name bing.com.

> **BTW**
> **WhatIsMyIPAddress**
> **.com**
> You can look up the IP address for any domain using WhatIsMyIPAddress.com.

Web Browsers

To access a website and display a webpage, a computer, tablet, or mobile device must have a web browser. A **web browser**, also called a **browser**, is a program that interprets and displays webpages so you can view and interact with them. Computing devices such as smartphones, tablets, laptops, and desktops include their own default browser, but you also have the option to download and use the browser of your choice. Microsoft Edge, Mozilla Firefox, Google Chrome, Apple Safari, and Opera (Figure 1–6) are popular browsers. You use a browser to locate websites, to link from one webpage to another, to add a favorite or bookmark a webpage, and to choose security settings.

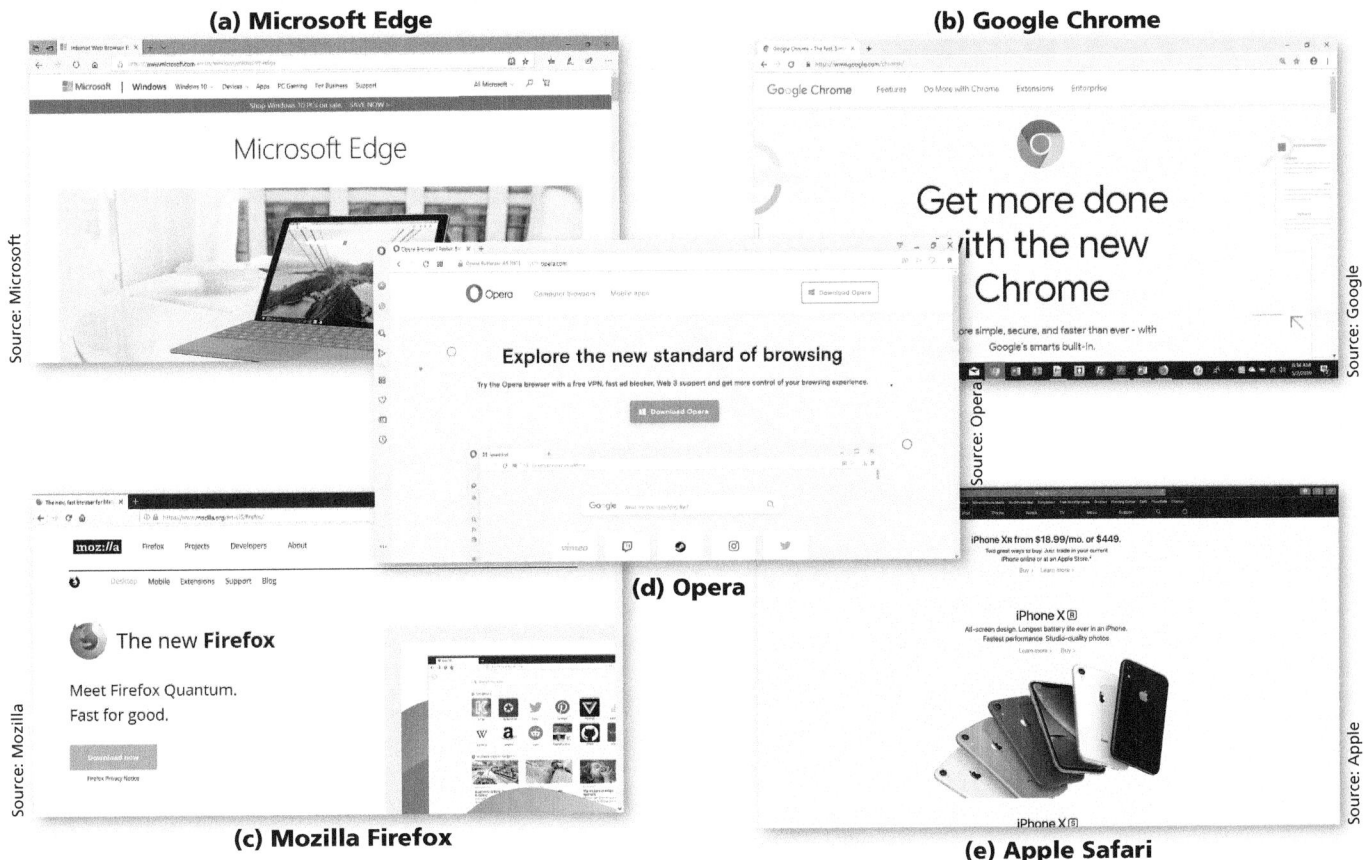

(a) Microsoft Edge

(b) Google Chrome

(d) Opera

(c) Mozilla Firefox

(e) Apple Safari

Source: Microsoft

Source: Google

Source: Opera

Source: Mozilla

Source: Apple

Figure 1–6

BTW
Apple Safari
Apple Safari is only available for download on Apple devices, including iPhones and Mac computers. It previously ran on the Windows operating system, but as of 2018, Apple no longer offers Safari for Windows.

BTW
Browser Interface Updates
The user interface of a browser is updated regularly. If you are using Google Chrome, it may look slightly different from the figures due to recent updates.

Besides varying by publisher, browsers vary by version. Most browsers do not display webpages identically. In fact, older versions of some browsers do not support the most recent HTML 5 standards. As you are designing your website, you must view it using various browsers to ensure that it looks and functions as you intended.

Google Chrome (Figure 1–7) provides tools for visiting webpages and an array of options to customize settings. As with all browsers, you can use Google Chrome to enter a website address in the address bar to display a particular webpage, designate a specific webpage or set of webpage tabs to display when you run the browser, and bookmark frequently visited websites as favorites for easy access. At the time of this writing, Google Chrome is the most popular browser, with more than 60 percent market share worldwide. You can download Google Chrome for free at google.com/chrome. Important features of Google Chrome are summarized in Table 1–1.

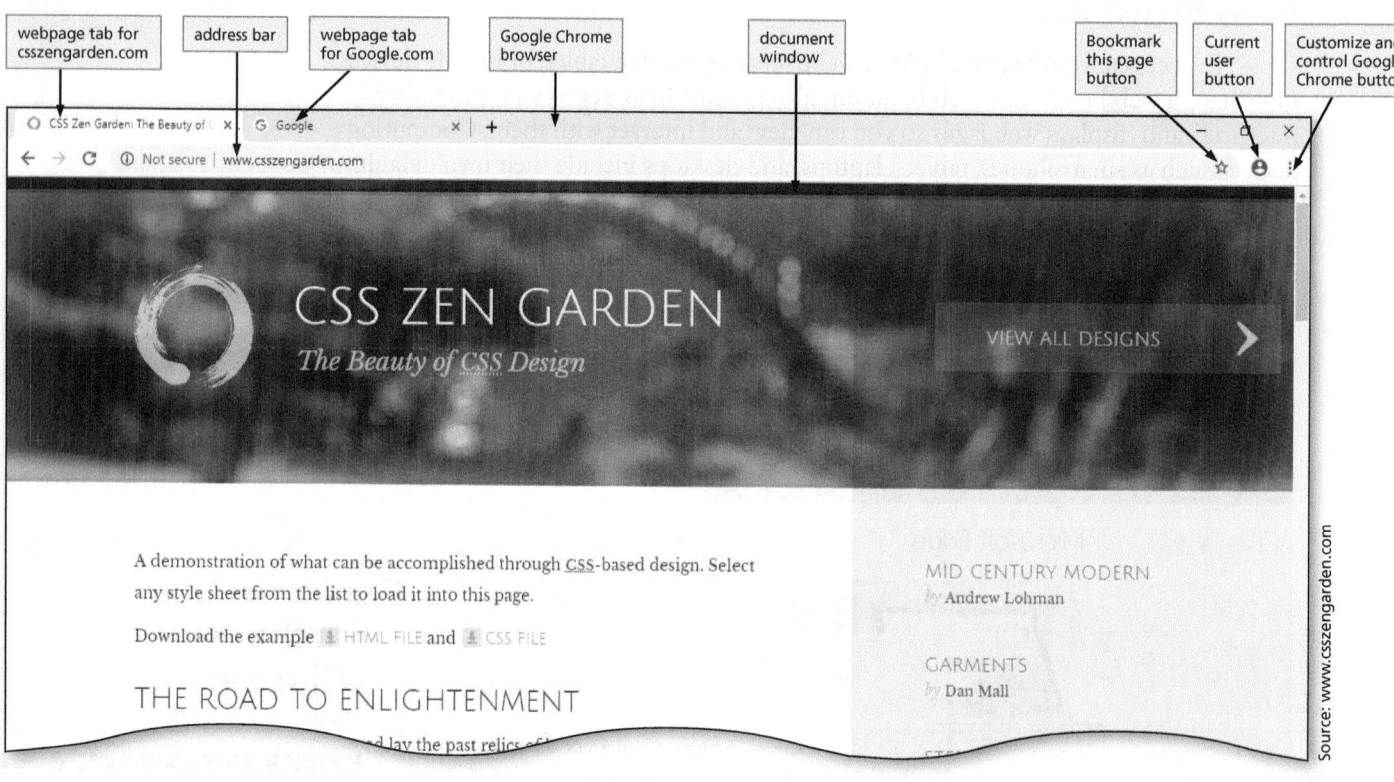

Figure 1–7

Source: www.csszengarden.com

Table 1–1 Features of Google Chrome	
Feature	**Description**
Address bar	Displays the website address of the webpage you are viewing
Webpage tab	Displays the title of the webpage; you can open multiple tabs to view multiple webpages
Current user button	Allows you to sign in to Google and manage your passwords, payments, and addresses
Bookmark this page button	Allows you to save and view your favorite webpages
Customize and control Google Chrome button	Provides access to print, zoom, and history features and lets you view downloads and manage extensions
Document window	Displays the current webpage content

What is the difference between a website's home page and a web browser's home page?
A website's home page is the default page displayed when you enter a web address such as www.cengage.com into the address bar of a browser. As mentioned earlier, this type of home page is the introductory page of a website and provides links to access other parts of the site. A browser also has a home page, which appears when you open a browser or tap or click the Home button in the browser window. You can specify any webpage as the default home page of a browser.

A web address, or **Uniform Resource Locator (URL)**, is the address of a document or other file accessible on the Internet and identifies the network location of a website, such as www.w3.org.com. To access a website using a browser, you type the webpage's URL in the browser's address bar (Figure 1–8).

Figure 1–8

The URL in Figure 1–8 indicates to the browser to use the HTTPS communications protocol to locate the membership.html webpage in the Consortium folder on the w3.org server or domain. A **domain** is an area of the Internet a particular organization or person manages. In this case, w3.org is the name of the domain, with the .org indicating it is registered as a nonprofit organization. The www part of the URL is short for World Wide Web and is a common subdomain used in a URL. The www is not required and can be omitted or replaced with another meaningful name for the subdomain. You can find webpage URLs in a wide range of places, including school catalogs, business cards, product packaging, and advertisements.

How do you use a subdomain within a URL?
A subdomain further identifies an area of content. For example, the URL support.microsoft.com indicates that support is a subdomain name used in the microsoft.com domain or server. This subdomain contains helpful information to support Microsoft products.

Types of Websites

An **Internet site** is another term for a website that is generally available to anyone with an Internet connection. Other types of websites include intranets and extranets, which also use Internet technology, but limit access to specified groups. An **intranet** is a private network that uses Internet technologies to share company information among employees. An intranet is contained within an organization's network, which makes it private and available only to those who need access. Organizations often distribute documents such as policy and procedure manuals, employee directories, company newsletters, product catalogs, and training manuals on an intranet.

An **extranet** is a private network that uses Internet technologies to share business information with select corporate partners or key customers. Companies and other organizations can use an extranet to share product manuals, training modules, inventory status, and order information. An extranet might also allow retailers to purchase inventory directly from their suppliers or to pay bills online.

Companies use websites to advertise or sell their products and services worldwide, as well as to provide technical and product support for their customers. Many company websites also support **electronic commerce (e-commerce)**, which is the buying and selling of goods and services on the Internet. Using e-commerce technologies, these websites allow customers to browse product catalogs, compare products and services, and order goods online. Figure 1–9a shows wayfair.com, a company that uses an e-commerce website to sell and distribute home furnishings. Many e-commerce websites also provide links to order status information, customer service, news releases, and customer feedback tools to solicit comments from their customers.

(a) Wayfair

(b) LMS

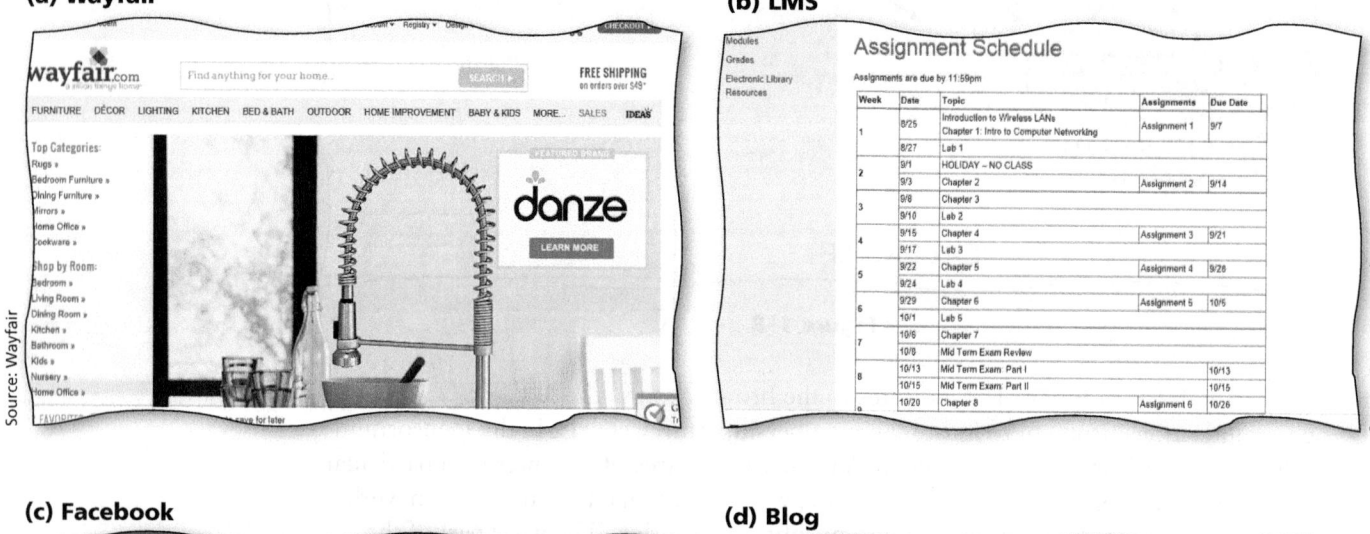

(c) Facebook

(d) Blog

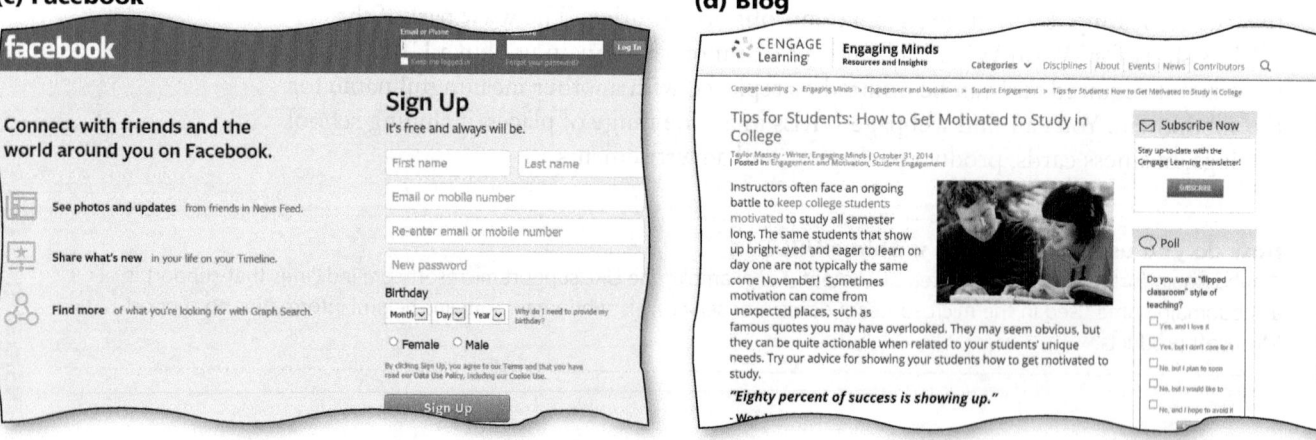

Figure 1–9

Colleges, universities, and other schools use websites to distribute information about areas of study, provide course information, and register students for classes online. Many educational institutions use a **Learning Management System (LMS)** to simplify course management. An LMS is a web-based software application designed to facilitate online learning. Instructors use the LMS to communicate announcements, post questions on reading material, list contact information, and provide access to lecture slides and videos. Students use the LMS to find information related to their courses, including project instructions and grades. Many LMS tools allow instructors to write their own webpage content that provides further information for their students. For example, the LMS webpage in Figure 1–9b is an HTML page written by an instructor to provide an assignment schedule to students.

While organizations create commercial and academic websites, individuals might create personal websites to share information with family and friends. Families and other groups can exchange photographs, video and audio clips, stories, schedules, or other information through websites. Many individual websites allow password protection, which creates a safer environment for sharing information. Another popular type of website is a social media site, such as Facebook, Twitter, or LinkedIn (Figure 1–9c). These websites encourage their users to share information, pictures, videos, and job-related skills. Many business websites also include links to their social media pages.

People use search engine websites to research topics. Popular search engine sites include Google, Bing, and Yahoo!. A news website provides information about current events. Another type of common website is a blog, which is short for weblog. A single person or small group creates and oversees a blog, which typically reflects the author's point of view on a particular topic (Figure 1–9d).

Planning a Website

When visiting a physical retail store, visitors are more likely to make a purchase if the store is clean and well organized and offers quality products and services. Likewise, computer users have several expectations when visiting a website. They expect the website to load quickly in the browser. If a website takes more than a few seconds to load, a visitor is likely to leave and find another site, possibly belonging to a competitor. Website visitors also expect an attractive design and color scheme that enhances the experience of visiting the site and makes it easy to read and view information. They expect a clear navigation system that helps them quickly find the products, services, or information they are seeking. A poor design, distracting color scheme, or confusing website navigation tools also prompt visitors to switch to another website. An attractive, useful, and well-organized website is not created by accident. Building a successful website starts with a solid strategic plan.

Web designers begin planning activities by meeting with key business personnel to ask several important questions to understand the purpose of the website and the goals of the business. If you are a web designer working as a consultant or contractor, you meet with your clients to plan the website. If you are a web designer providing services within an organization, you meet with decision makers and others who are sponsoring the web design project. In either case, you begin by identifying the purpose of the website and goals of the business to help shape the design and type of website you are developing.

Purpose of the Website

The purpose of a commercial business website is related to the goal of selling products or services. A business can take a direct approach and use a website to sell products and services through e-commerce or through information that prompts website users to visit a physical location such as a store or restaurant. As an alternative, a business can take an indirect approach and use a website to generate leads to potential customers, promote the expertise of the business, raise the public profile of the business, or inform and educate its customers. Each purpose demands a different type of website and design. For example, if the purpose of a website is to serve as an online store, the website should allow easy access to product information, reviews, and e-commerce tools. If the purpose of the website is to build a company's reputation, the website should feature articles about the company, its employees, and its products and integrate with social media sites such as Facebook.

Every business needs to have a mission statement that clearly addresses the purpose and goal of the business. For example, the mission statement of a bank might be "Our mission is to provide world-class service while helping our customers achieve their financial goals." The business website should promote the mission statement. Web designers often ask their clients for a copy of the mission statement and use it as the foundation for the website plan. The more you know about the purpose of the website, the more likely you are to be successful with a web development project.

Target Audience

In addition to understanding the website's purpose, you should understand the people who will use the website, also known as the target audience. Knowing the makeup of your target audience — including age, gender, general demographic background, and level of computer literacy — helps you design a website appropriate for them. Figure 1–10 shows the website for The Home Depot, a home improvement store. Its target audience includes people who need supplies for home improvement projects. The home page displays an image customized for the spring season and offers special savings to further entice its target audience to make a purchase. The simple navigation bar near the top of the page makes it easy for a customer to shop, access a specific department, or find inspiration. A search tool above the navigation bar provides quick access to products. Knowing the information that your target audience is searching for means you can design the site to focus on that information, which enhances the shopping and purchasing experience for your audience.

Figure 1–10

Multiplatform Display

Today, users can access a website with computing devices ranging from desktop computers to laptops, tablets, and smartphones. In fact, people are rapidly increasing their use of a mobile device to access websites. According to Pew Research, young people in advanced and emerging economies are likely to have a smartphone and use it to access the Internet and participate in social media. Today, more than 80 percent of Americans own a smartphone, and more than 50 percent of smartphone owners use their phone to access the Internet. In addition, more than 30 percent of those who access the Internet do so exclusively with their smartphones. These trends are only expected to increase. Yet many webpages are designed for a large display screen on a desktop or laptop and do not translate well to the smaller screen of a tablet or smartphone. This problem leads to another question web developers must ask: "How do I consistently reach the people in my target audience when they are using so many difference devices?" The solution is to use **responsive design**, which allows you to create one website that provides an optimal viewing experience across a range of devices. The website itself responds and adapts to the size of screen on the visitor's device. For example, Figure 1–11 shows the responsive design of NASA.gov in desktop, tablet, and mobile screen sizes. Chapter 5 provides much more information about responsive design.

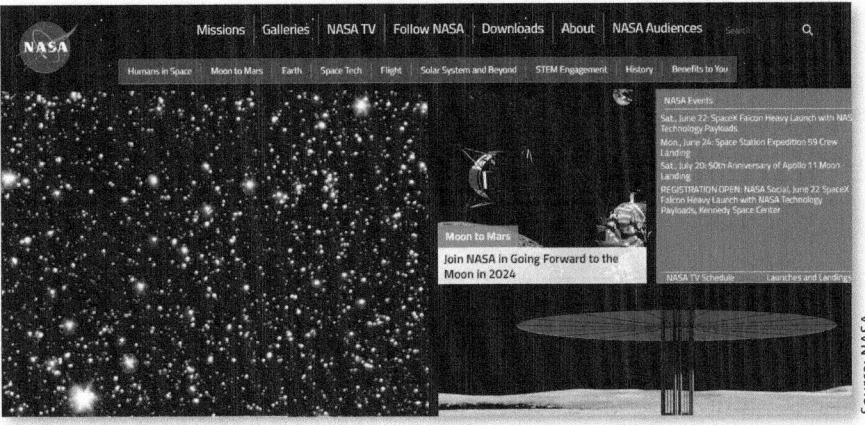

(a) Desktop Display

Source: NASA

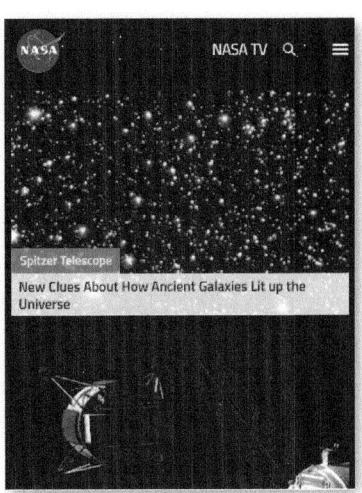

(c) Mobile Display

Source: NASA

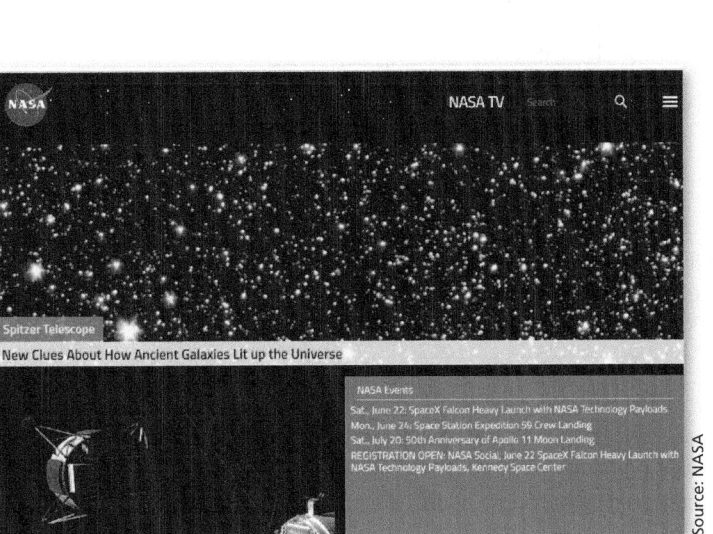

(b) Tablet Display

Source: NASA

Figure 1–11

Can I redesign a desktop-only website for multiplatform display?

Yes. If your audience is accustomed to the desktop-only website, retrofitting the website for tablet and mobile display screens makes sense because the site remains familiar to users. You also avoid building a new site from scratch and you can take advantage of design decisions such as color scheme and use media you have already acquired. However, depending on the site content and number of pages, redesigning may be a time-consuming process.

Wireframe

Before web designers actually start creating the first webpage for a website, they sketch the design using a wireframe. A **wireframe** is a simple, visual guide that clearly identifies the location of main webpage elements, such as the navigation area, organization logo, content areas, and images. When you create a wireframe sketch for your webpages, use lines and boxes as shown in Figure 1–12. Also be sure to incorporate plenty of white space within your design to improve readability and to clearly distinguish among the areas on the webpage. You can use two types of white space: active white space and passive white space. **Active white space** is an area on the page that is intentionally left blank. Typically, the goal of active white space is to help balance the design of an asymmetrical page. **Passive white space** is the space between content areas. Passive white space helps a user focus on one part of the page. Proper use of white space makes webpage content easy to read and brings focus to page elements.

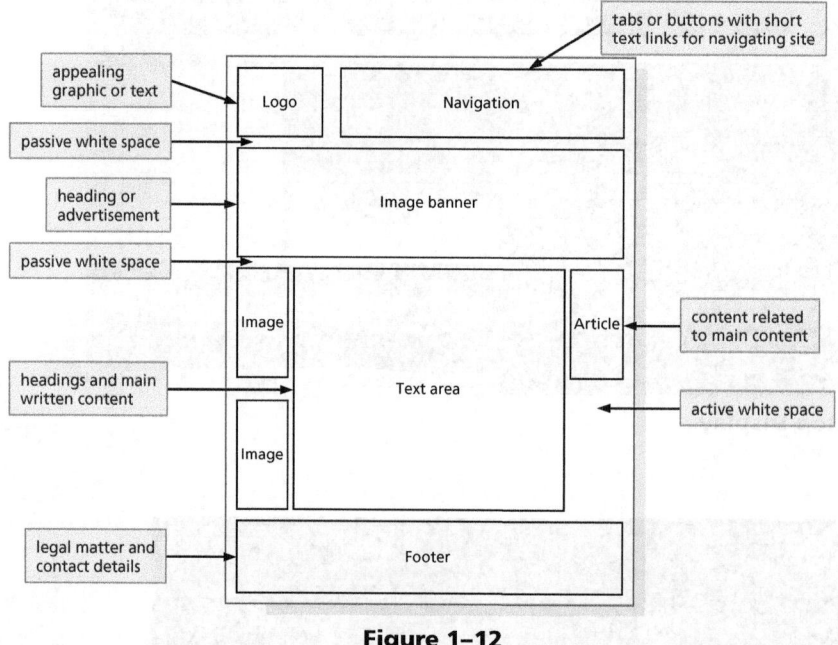

Figure 1–12

What tools can I use to create a wireframe?

You can use one of several free tools to create a wireframe, including Pencil Project, Mockplus, and Wireframe CC. You can also use drawing tools in Microsoft Word or PowerPoint or a pen and paper.

Site Map

A **site map** is a planning tool that lists or displays all the pages on a website and indicates how they are related to each other. In other words, a site map shows the structure of a website. Begin defining the structure of a website by identifying the information to provide and then organize that information into divisions using the organizing method that makes the most sense for the content. For example, if the website offers three types of products for sale, organize the site by product category. If the website provides training, organize the site in a step-by-step sequence.

Next, arrange the webpages according to a logical structure. A website can use several types of structures, including linear, hierarchical, and webbed. Each structure connects the webpages in a different way to define how users navigate the site and view the webpages. You should select a structure for the website based on how you want users to navigate the site and view the content.

A **linear** website structure connects webpages in a straight line, as shown in Figure 1–13. Each page includes a link to the next webpage and another link to the previous webpage. A linear website structure is appropriate if visitors should view the webpages in a specific order, as in the case of training material in which users need to complete Training module 1 before attempting Training module 2. If the information on the first webpage is necessary for understanding information on the second webpage, you should use a linear structure.

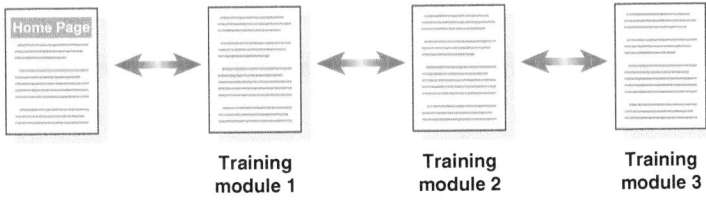

Training module 1   Training module 2   Training module 3

Linear structure

Figure 1–13

In a variation of a linear website structure, each page can include a link to the home page of the website, as shown in Figure 1–14. For some websites, moving from one page to the next page is still important, but you also want to provide users with easy access to the home page at any time. To meet these goals, you provide links from each page to the previous, next, and home pages. In this way, users do not have to tap or click the previous link multiple times to get back to the home page. The home page also includes links to all the pages in the site so users can quickly return to a page.

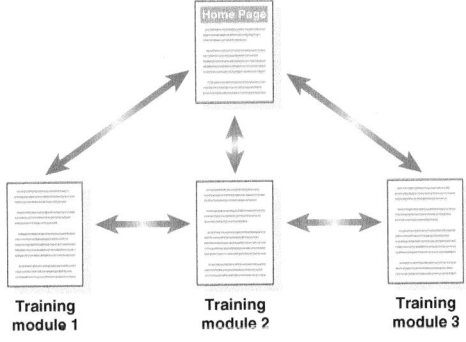

Training module 1   Training module 2   Training module 3

Linear structure with home page links

Figure 1–14

A **hierarchical** website connects webpages in a treelike structure, as shown in Figure 1–15. This structure works well on a site with a main index or table of contents page that links to all other webpages. With this structure, the main index page displays general information and secondary pages include more detailed information. Notice how logically the information in Figure 1–15 is organized. A webpage visitor can go from the home page to any of the three modules. In addition, the visitor can easily find the first page of Training module 3 by way of the Training module 3 link. One of the inherent problems with this structure and the two linear structures, however, is the inability to move easily from one section of pages to another. As an example, to move from Training module 1, page 2, to Training module 3, visitors must tap or click a link to return to Training module 1, introduction, tap or click another link to return to the home page, and then tap or click the Training module 3 link. This is moderately annoying for a site with two webpages, but think what it would be like if Training module 1 had 100 webpages.

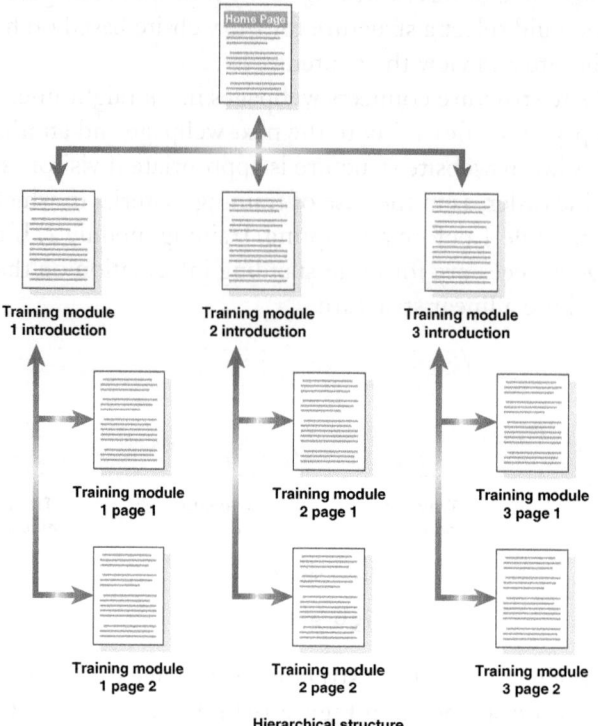

Hierarchical structure

Figure 1–15

To circumvent the problems with the hierarchical model, you can use a webbed model. A **webbed** website structure has no set organization, as shown in Figure 1–16. Visitors can move easily between pages, even if the pages are located in different sections of the website. A webbed structure works best on sites with information that does not need to be read in a specific order and pages that provide many navigation options. The web itself uses a webbed structure, so users can navigate among webpages in any order they choose.

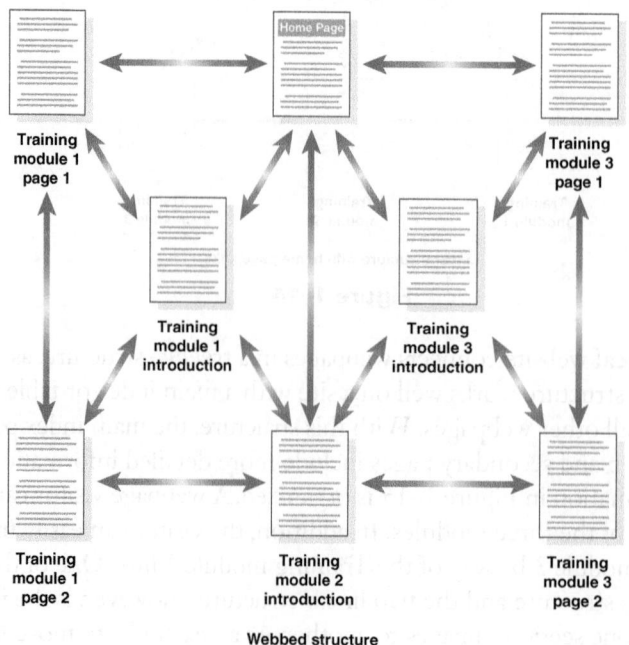

Webbed structure

Figure 1–16

With this model, you most often provide a link to the home page from each page. Many websites use a graphical image (usually the organization's logo) in the upper-left corner of each webpage as the home page link. You will use that technique later in the book.

Most websites use a combination of linear, hierarchical, and webbed structures. Some information on the website might be organized hierarchically from an index page, other information might be accessible from all areas of the site, and still other information might be organized in a linear structure to be read in a specific order. Using a combination of the three structures is appropriate if it helps users navigate the site easily. The goal is to get the right information to the users in the most efficient way possible.

Graphics

Graphics add visual appeal to a webpage and enhance the visitor's perception of your products and services. Be sure to use appropriate graphics on your site, those that communicate your brand, products, and services. For example, the website for Panda Express shown in Figure 1–17 on the left displays a primary graphic that serves as the focal point on the website. The graphic communicates to the user that the new dish is fresh, and the smaller graphics in the webpage on the right offer additional visual stimulation and provide an aesthetically pleasing balance to the page. These graphics are simple, yet effective in catching the user's attention.

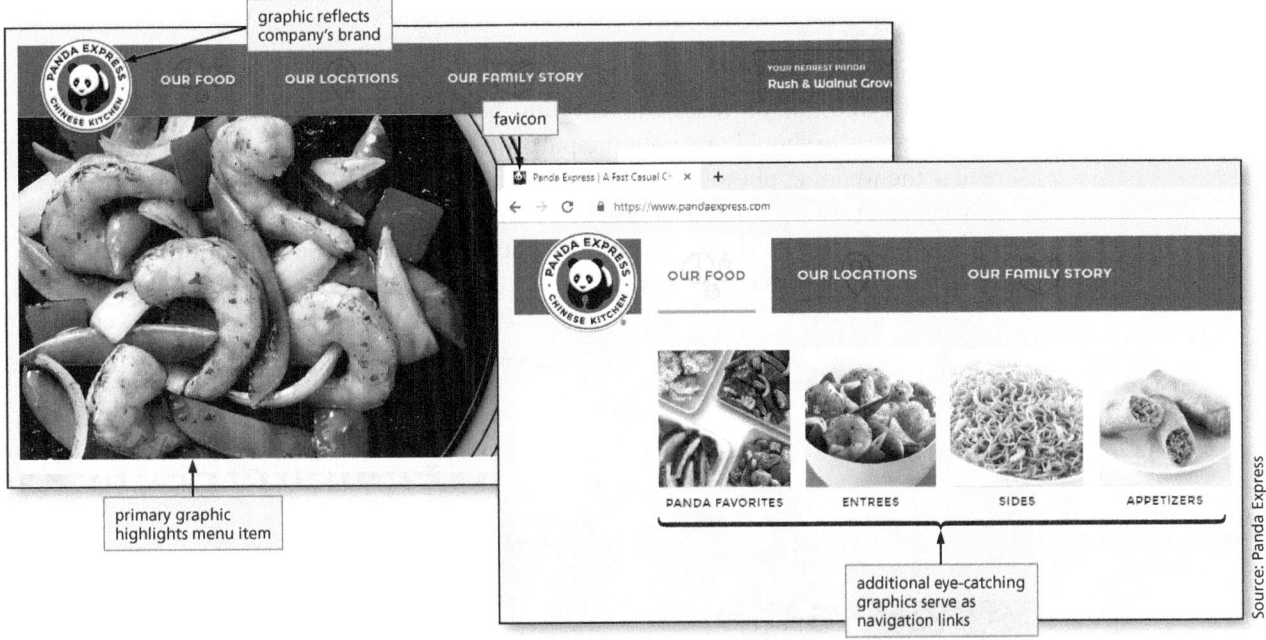

Figure 1–17

Navigation

As mentioned previously, the navigation of your website should be clear and concise. Each webpage should have a designated navigation area with links to other pages in the site, as shown in Figure 1–18. The navigation area should be prominent and easy to use. Incorporating a search box near the navigation area provides another avenue for customers to find the item they want.

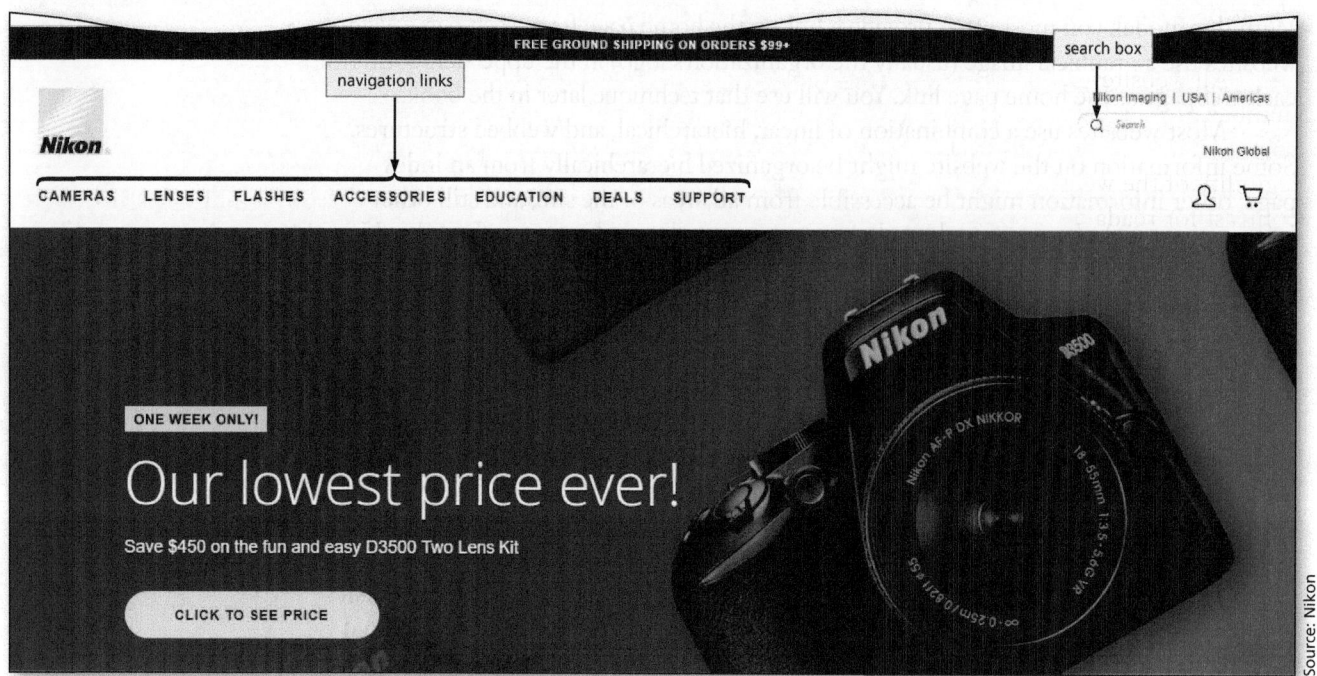

Figure 1–18

Source: Nikon

Typography

The use of effective typography, or fonts and font styles, enhances the visual appeal of a website. Above all, the text must be legible or the website is useless. Typography also should promote the purpose and goal of the website. For example, review the wedding photography website shown in Figure 1–19. The style of the text conveys an attitude of practical elegance mixed with fun. The typography of the title at the top of the page is elegant and whimsical, while the typography of the navigation links is uncluttered and easy to read.

Figure 1–19

Source: K & K Photography

Color

All websites use color, even if the colors are black and white. Select a limited number of coordinated colors that help promote your purpose and brand. The combination of colors, also called a color scheme, contributes to the appeal and legibility of the website. Font and background colors must provide high color contrast for readability, so use dark text on a light background or light text on a dark background. Likewise, avoid a color combination such as a primary red background with yellow text, which is hard on the eyes. Aim to strike a balance among the background color, text color, and the color that represents your brand. Many successful color schemes have one main color, such as medium blue, and add at least one lighter and darker shade of the same color, such as sky blue and navy. Even a single shade can serve as a color scheme. Figure 1–20 displays the home page for the grocery store Publix. The store's logo is green. The site reinforces its brand by integrating the same shade of green throughout the site.

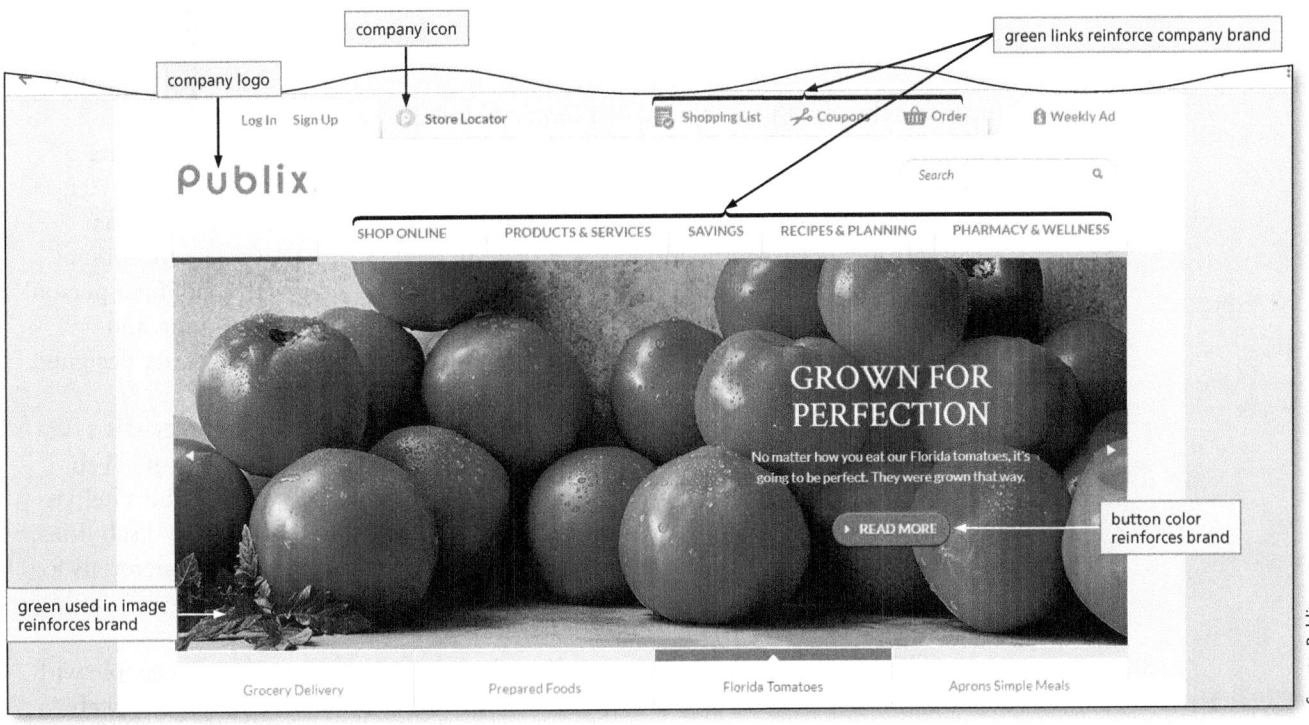

Figure 1–20

Colors convey meanings. For example, green is associated with things that are friendly, fresh, and healthy. Table 1–2 lists colors and their common meanings.

Table 1–2 Common Color Meanings	
Color	**Common Meaning**
Red	Love, romance, anger, energy
Blue	Trust, loyalty, integrity, honesty, dependability
Green	Freshness, friendliness, health, safety, strength.
Yellow	Warmth, cheer, joy, excitement, humor
Orange	Energy, warmth, health
Brown	Nature, wholesomeness, simplicity, friendliness
Black	Elegance, tradition, sophistication, formality
White	Purity, honesty, sincerity, cleanliness

Accessibility

BTW
W3C
The mission of the W3C is "to lead the World Wide Web to its full potential by developing protocols and guidelines that ensure the long-term growth of the Web." Information about the membership process is available at www.w3.org /consortium/membership.

Finally, address accessibility and localization issues. A web designer should create pages for viewing by a diverse audience, including people with physical impairments and global users. Consider the software used by those with physical impairments to work with some web features. For instance, for each graphic you include on the website, always include alternative text so people with sight limitations can use screen-reading software to identify the visual content. To support an international audience, use generic icons that can be understood globally, avoid slang expressions in the content, and build simple pages that load quickly over low-speed connections.

The **World Wide Web Consortium (W3C)** develops and maintains web standards, language specifications, and accessibility recommendations. Several companies that use web technologies participate in work groups with the W3C to develop standards and guidelines for the web. The website for W3C is www.w3.org.

Accessibility Standards for Webpage Developers

According to the W3C, the goal of the web is to be accessible to all people, including those with a disability that limits their ability to perform computer tasks. The U.S. Congress passed the Rehabilitation Act in 1973, which prohibits discrimination against those with disabilities. In 1998, Congress amended this Act to reflect the latest changes in information technology. Section 508 requires that any electronic information developed, procured, maintained, or used by the federal government be accessible to people with disabilities. Disabilities that inhibit a person's ability to use the web fall into four main categories: visual, hearing, motor, and cognitive. This amendment has had a profound effect on how webpages are designed and developed. Visit www.section208.gov for more information.

The summary of Section 508 §1194.22 states, "The criteria for web-based technology and information are based on access guidelines developed by the Web Accessibility Initiative of the World Wide Web Consortium." The guidelines help to include everyone as a potential user of your website, including those with disabilities. The Web Accessibility Initiative (WAI) develops guidelines and support materials for accessibility standards. These guidelines are known as the Web Content Accessibility Guidelines (WCAG) 2.0 and 2.1.

The WCAG specifies how to make web content more accessible to people with disabilities. **Web content** generally refers to the information in a webpage or web application, including text, images, forms, and sounds. All web developers should review the information at the official website at w3.org/WAI/intro/wcag.php for complete information on these guidelines and should apply the guidelines to their webpage development.

The WCAG 2.0 and 2.1 guidelines are organized under four principles: perceivable, operable, understandable, and robust. Anyone who wants to use the web must have content that incorporates the principles as follows:

Perceivable: Information and user interface components must be presentable to users in ways they can perceive. Users must be able to perceive the information being presented. (It cannot be invisible to any of their senses.)

Operable: User interface components and navigation must be operable. Users must be able to operate the interface. (The interface cannot require interaction that a user cannot perform.)

Understandable: Information and the operation of the user interface must be understandable. Users must be able to understand the information as well as the operation of the user interface. (The content or operation cannot be beyond their understanding.)

Robust: Content must be robust enough that it can be interpreted reliably by a wide variety of user agents, including assistive technologies. Users must be able to access the content as technologies advance. (As technologies and user agents evolve, the content should remain accessible.)

If these principles are not applied, users with disabilities may not be able to fully access web content. These guidelines will be addressed throughout this book as you progress through each chapter project.

Planning Checklist

The planning items just discussed are only a few of the basic webpage design issues that you need to consider when developing a website. A more sophisticated website requires additional design considerations and research of the business, its competition, and a complete business analysis. Throughout this book, design issues will be addressed as they relate to the chapter project.

The rest of the chapters in this book employ professional web design practices in addition to the development of webpages. You will learn many design and development techniques, including how to add links, styles, layout, graphics, tables, forms, and multimedia to your webpages.

Table 1–3 serves as a checklist of items to consider when planning a website.

Table 1–3 Checklist for Planning a Website	
Topic	**Web Designer Questions**
Purpose of the website	What is the purpose and goal of the website? What is the organization's mission statement?
Target audience	Describe the target audience (age, gender, demographics). What information is most pertinent to the users?
Multiplatform display	Is the website optimized for mobile devices as well as laptops and desktops?
Site map	How many webpages will be included in the website? How will the webpages be organized? What type of website structure is appropriate for the content?
Wireframe	What features will be displayed on each webpage?
Graphics	What graphics will you use on the website?
Color	What colors will you use within the site to enhance the purpose and brand?
Typography	What font styles will you use within the website?
Accessibility	How will the website accommodate people with disabilities?
Budget	What is the budget for the website?
Project Timeline	What is the project timeline for the website?

Break Point: If you want to take a break, this is a good place to do so. To resume at a later time, continue reading the text from this location forward.

Understanding the Basics of HTML

Webpages are created using **Hypertext Markup Language (HTML),** which is an authoring language used to create documents for the web. HTML consists of a set of special instructions called **tags** to define the structure and layout of content in a webpage. A browser reads the HTML tags to determine how to display the webpage content on a screen. Because the HTML tags define or "mark up" the content on the webpage, HTML is considered a **markup language** rather than a traditional programming language. HTML has evolved through several versions from the initial public release of HTML 1.0 in 1989 to the current version, HTML 5. Each version has expanded the capabilities of the language.

HTML Elements and Attributes

A webpage is a file that contains both content and HTML tags and is saved as an HTML document. HTML tags mark the text to define how it should appear when viewed in a browser. HTML includes dozens of tags that describe the structure of webpages and create links to other content. For instance, the HTML tags <nav> and </nav> mark the start and end of a navigation area, while <html> and </html> indicate the start and end of a webpage. An **HTML element** consists of everything from the start tag to the end tag, including content, and represents a distinct part of a webpage such as a paragraph or heading. For example, <title> Webpage Example </title> is an HTML element that sets the title of a webpage. In common usage, when web designers say "Use a p element to define a paragraph," or something similar, they mean to use a starting <p> tag to mark the beginning of the paragraph and an ending </p> tag to mark the end of the paragraph.

You can enhance HTML elements by using **attributes**, which define additional characteristics, or properties, of the element such as the width and height of an image. An attribute includes a name, such as width, and can also include a value, such as 300, which sets the width of an element. Attributes are included within the element's start tag. Figure 1–21 shows the anatomy of HTML elements in Notepad++, which uses color coding to distinguish parts of the code. For example, Notepad++ displays tags in blue, attribute names in red, attribute values in purple, and content in black.

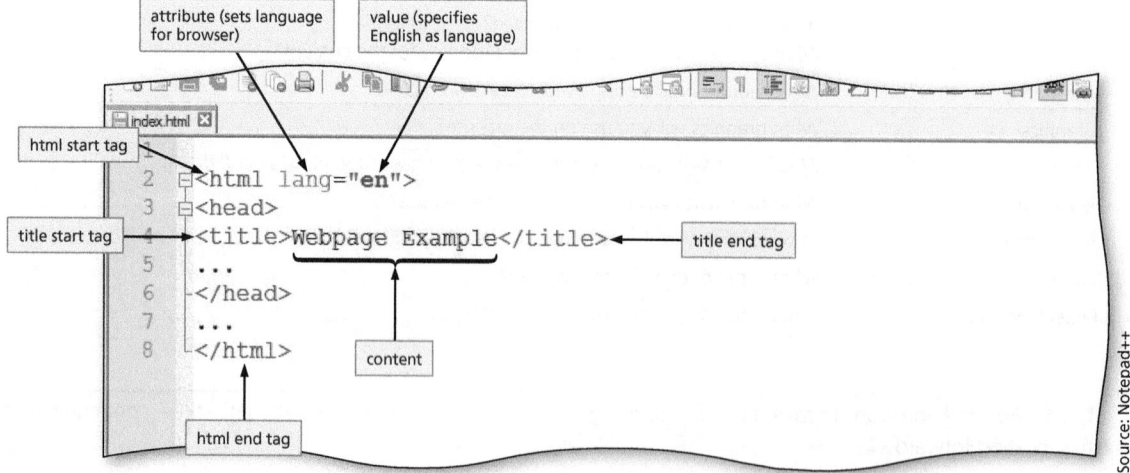

Figure 1–21

HTML combines tags and descriptive attributes that define how a document should appear in a web browser. HTML elements include headings, paragraphs, hyperlinks, lists, and images. Most HTML elements have a start tag and an end tag and follow the same rules, or **syntax**, which determine how the elements should be written so they are interpreted correctly by the browser. These HTML elements are called **paired** tags and use the syntax *<start tag> content </end tag>*, which has the following meaning:

- HTML elements begin with a start tag, or opening tag, such as <title>.
- HTML elements finish with an end tag, or closing tag, such as </title>.
- Content is inserted between the start and end tags. In Figure 1–21, the content for the title tags is Webpage Example.

Some HTML elements are void of content. They are called **empty**, or **void**, tags. Examples of empty tags are <br> for a line break and <hr> for a thematic break. The syntax for empty tags is *<tag>*.

Figure 1–22 shows the HTML code and content needed to create the webpage shown in Figure 1–23.

CONSIDER THIS

What does the hr in <hr> mean?
Prior to HTML 5, the hr meant horizontal rule or reference. It is now called a thematic break and is used to distinguish between various topics on a single webpage.

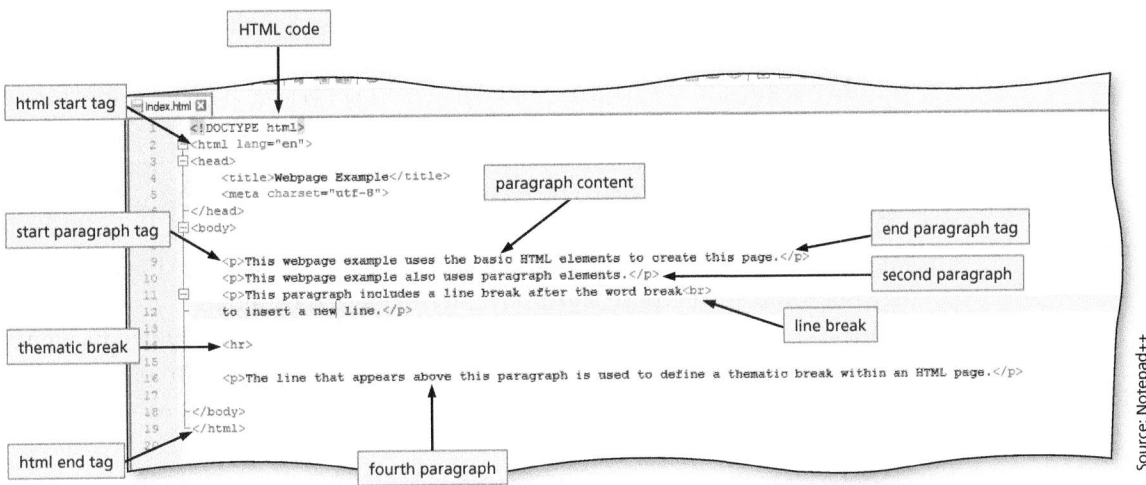

Figure 1–22

Source: Notepad++

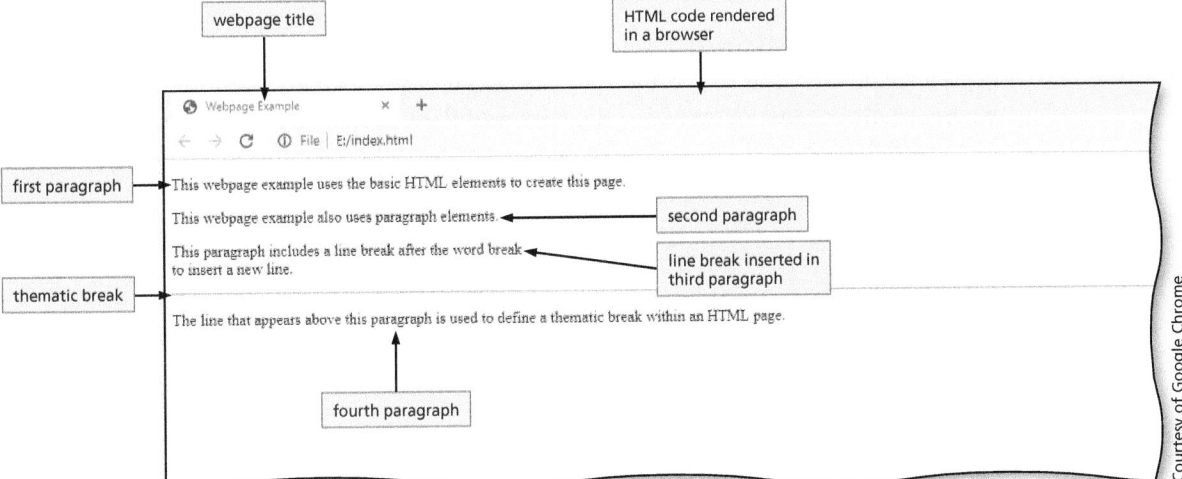

Figure 1–23

Courtesy of Google Chrome

Technologies Related to HTML

Several technologies, listed as follows, have been developed since the introduction of HTML to extend its capabilities. These technologies also use tags to mark up content in a text document.

- **XML** — The W3C introduced **XML (Extensible Markup Language)** in 1998 to exchange and transport data. It does not replace HTML, but rather, can work with HTML by transporting web data obtained through an HTML webpage.

- **XHTML** — **XHTML (Extensible Hypertext Markup Language)** is a rewritten version of HTML using XML and was developed in 2000. Its syntax rules are more strict than HTML. It was created to work with XML-based user agents.

HTML 5

With its debut in 2008, HTML 5 is the most recent version of HTML. HTML 5.2 was introduced in 2017. HTML 5 introduces several new elements such as header, nav, main, and footer to better define the areas of a webpage. They are classified as structural elements because they define the structure of a webpage. These new elements also are considered semantic HTML elements because they provide meaning about the content of the tags. (The term *semantic* refers to the meaning of words or ideas.) For example, <header> is a semantic tag because it defines content that appears at the top of a webpage. The name and purpose of the <header> tag reflect its meaning. On the other hand, <b>, for bold, is not a semantic tag because it defines only how content should look, not what it means.

HTML 5 also provides a more flexible approach to web development. For instance, with HTML 5, you can incorporate audio and video with the use of <audio> and <video> tags. These new features reduce the need for browser plugins, which are small programs that let webpages play sounds or videos, for example. This book shows HTML 5 tags and attributes that are currently supported by modern browsers.

In December 2017, W3C introduced HTML 5.2. This update introduced new features, such as the dialog element. The W3C states that it intends to release annual revisions. At the time of this writing, HTML 5.3 is currently in draft form.

Understanding the Role of Other Web Programming Languages

In addition to HTML, web developers use other web programming languages such as JavaScript and PHP to add interactivity and functionality. Although you can create websites without these languages, they are useful when you need to include features beyond the scope of HTML. You should be aware of these languages as you begin learning about web development.

JavaScript

JavaScript is a popular scripting language used to create interactivity within a web browser. Common uses for JavaScript include creating popup windows and alert messages, displaying the current date, and validating form data. JavaScript is a **client-side scripting language**, which means that the browser processes it on the client computer. JavaScript files are typically named script with an .js file extension.

JavaScript files are referenced within an HTML file through the use of a script element, as in <script src="script.js"></script>. Reference to this file is typically placed above the closing body tag. You will learn more about JavaScript in Chapter 10.

jQuery

jQuery is a library of JavaScript programs designed for easy integration onto a webpage. jQuery makes it easy for web developers to add JavaScript to a webpage. The JS Foundation, formerly known as the jQuery Foundation, (https://js.foundation) is a community of web developers that work together to create JavaScript ecosystem projects. Their mission is to "drive broad adoption and ongoing development of key JavaScript solutions and related technologies." You will learn more about jQuery in Chapter 10.

PHP

PHP (Hypertext Preprocessor) is an open-source scripting language often used for common tasks such as writing to or querying a database located on a central server. PHP is a **server-side scripting language**, which means that the PHP script is processed at the server. The result of the PHP script is often an HTML webpage that is sent back to the client. Pages that contain PHP scripts must have file names that end with the file extension .php.

ASP

ASP (Active Server Pages) is a server-side scripting technology from Microsoft used to accomplish many of the same server-side processing tasks as PHP. Pages that contain ASP scripts must have file names that end with the file extension .asp.

Using Web Authoring Tools

You can create webpages using HTML with a simple text editor, such as Notepad++, Brackets, Atom, Sublime, Visual Studio Code, or TextMate. A **text editor** is a program that allows you to enter, change, save, and print text, which includes HTML tags. Many free text editors are available for download on the web. Text editors such as Atom, Brackets, and Visual Studio Code are cross-platform compatible, meaning they are available for Windows, macOS, and Linux. Notepad++ is only available for Windows. TextMate is only available for macOS. Today's text editors include several built-in tools to help you create HTML, CSS, and JavaScript files. An HTML editor or code editor is a program that provides basic text-editing functions, as well as more advanced features such as color-coding for various HTML tags, menus to insert HTML tags, and a spelling checker. HTML is **platform independent**, meaning you can create, or code, an HTML file in Windows, macOS, or Linux and then view it on any browser.

Text Editors

Notepad++ is a free, open-source text editor. You can use it to create files in several markup, scripting, and programming languages, including HTML, CSS, JavaScript, PHP, Java, C#, and Visual Basic. Notepad++ is only available for the Windows operating system. Visit http://notepad-plus-plus.org to download the program. Figure 1–24 displays the Notepad++ user interface.

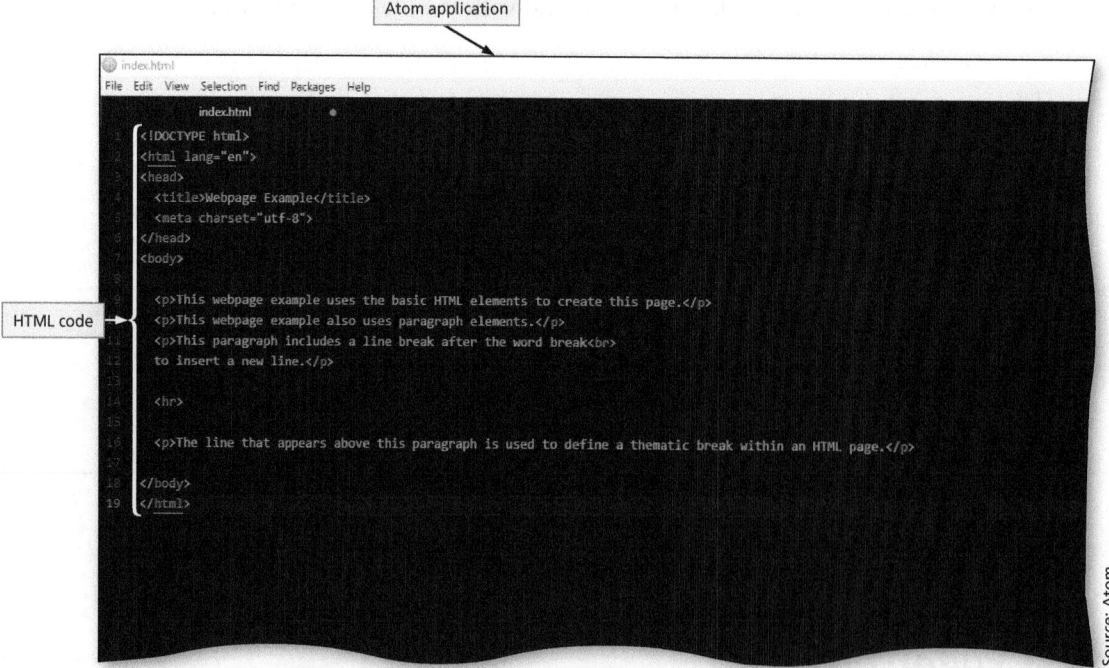

Notepad++
application

C:\Users\OneDrive\Documents\index.html - Notepad++

File Edit Search View Encoding Language Settings Tools Macro Run Plugins Window ?

index.html

```
1   <!DOCTYPE html>
2   <html lang="en">
3   <head>
4       <title>Webpage Example</title>
5       <meta charset="utf-8">
6   </head>
7   <body>
8
9       <p>This webpage example uses the basic HTML elements to create this page.</p>
10      <p>This webpage example also uses paragraph elements.</p>
11      <p>This paragraph includes a line break after the word break<br>
12      to insert a new line.</p>
13
14      <hr>
15
16      <p>The line that appears above this paragraph is used to define a thematic break within an HTML page.</p>
17
18  </body>
19  </html>
```

HTML code

Courtesy of Notepad++

Figure 1–24

Atom is another free, open-source text editor you can use to create webpages. Like Notepad++, you can use Atom to create files in several markup, scripting, and programming languages as well. Atom is available for Windows, macOS, or Linux. Visit atom.io to download the program. Figure 1–25 displays the Atom user interface.

Atom application

index.html

File Edit View Selection Find Packages Help

index.html

```
1   <!DOCTYPE html>
2   <html lang="en">
3   <head>
4       <title>Webpage Example</title>
5       <meta charset="utf-8">
6   </head>
7   <body>
8
9       <p>This webpage example uses the basic HTML elements to create this page.</p>
10      <p>This webpage example also uses paragraph elements.</p>
11      <p>This paragraph includes a line break after the word break<br>
12      to insert a new line.</p>
13
14      <hr>
15
16      <p>The line that appears above this paragraph is used to define a thematic break within an HTML page.</p>
17
18  </body>
19  </html>
```

HTML code

Source: Atom

Figure 1–25

Brackets is another cross-platform text editor you can use on the Windows, macOS, or Linux operating system. With Brackets, you can create files in several formats, including HTML and CSS. Visit brackets.io to download the software. Figure 1–26 displays the Brackets user interface.

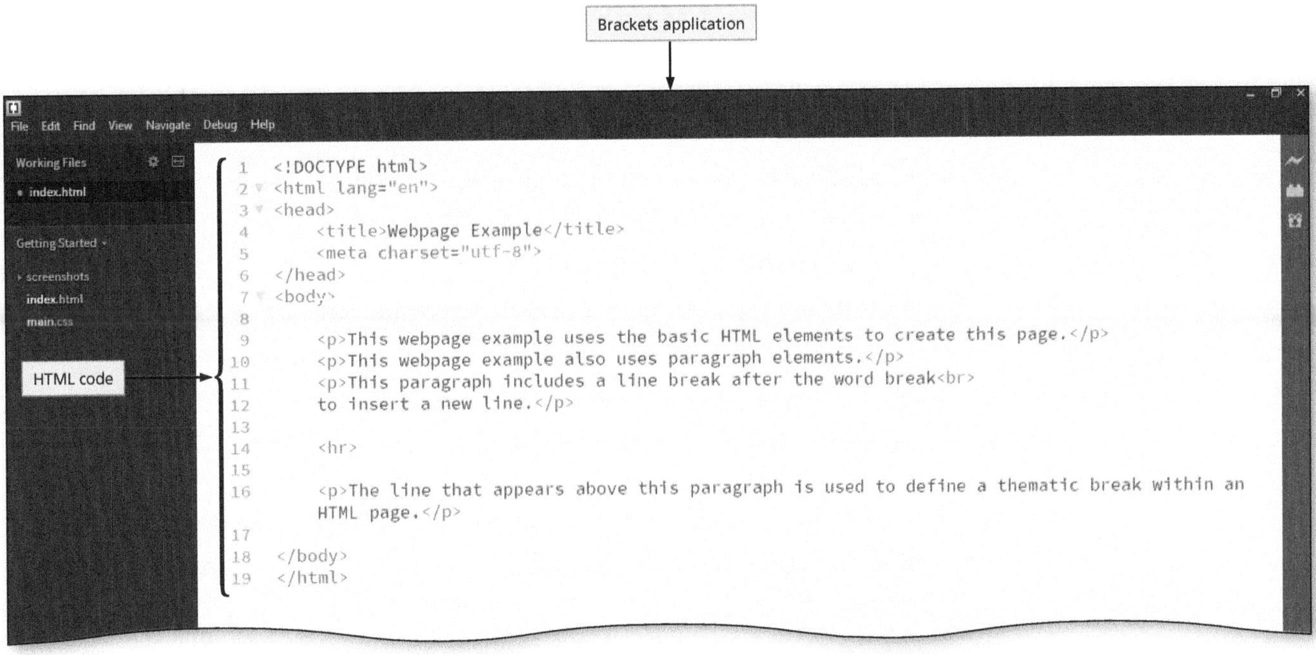

Brackets application

HTML code

Source: Brackets

Figure 1–26

TextMate is a free, open-source text editor available for macOS 10.9 or a later version. You can use it to create files in many formats, including HTML and CSS. Visit macromates.com to download TextMate. Figure 1–27 displays the TextMate user interface.

TextMate application

HTML code

Courtesy of TextMate

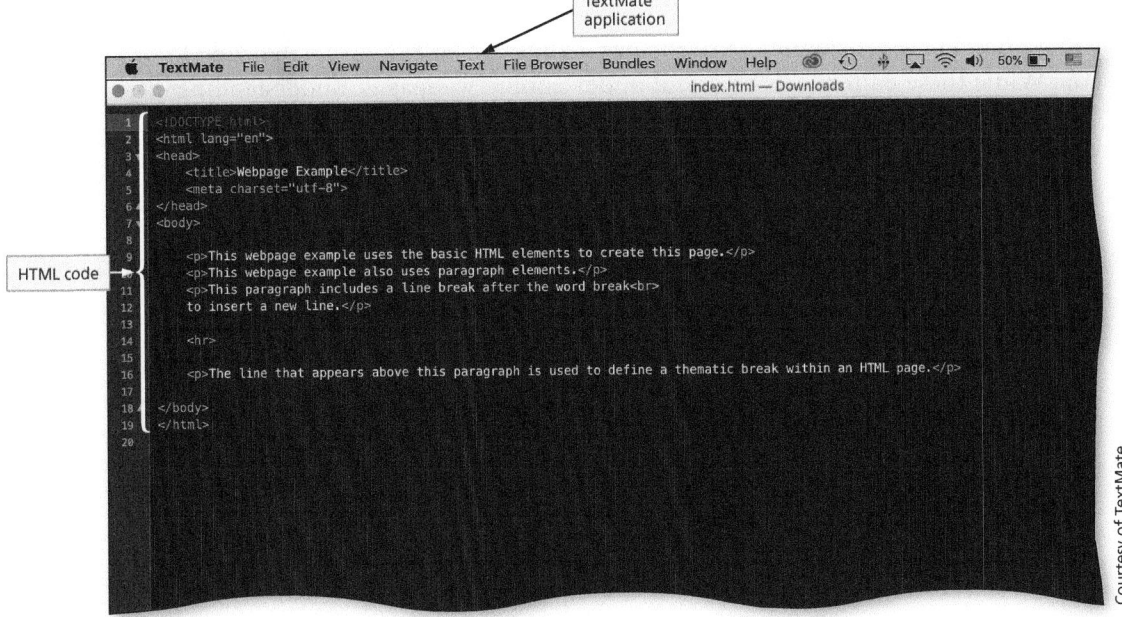

Figure 1–27

To Download and Install a Text Editor

Before you can create your first webpage, you must select a text editor that you will use to create your webpages. Begin by asking whether your instructor has a preferred text editor to use in the course. If not, use a text editor provided by your operating system (such as Notepad or TextEdit) or download one of the HTML text editors previously discussed. If you want to download and install an HTML text editor, you would perform the following steps.

1. Use your browser to access the website for Notepad++, Atom, Brackets, or TextMate.

   - Notepad++ (Windows only): http://notepad-plus-plus.org
   - Atom: https://atom.io/
   - Brackets: http://brackets.io/
   - TextMate (macOS only): https://macromates.com/

2. Navigate the text editor's website to locate the download link.
3. Tap or click the link to download the software.
4. When the download is complete, open the downloaded file to begin the installation.
5. Follow the instructions in the setup wizard to complete the installation.
6. Run the text editor when finished.

WYSIWYG Editors

Many popular software applications also provide features that enable you to develop webpages easily. Microsoft Word and Excel, for example, have a Save As Web Page option that converts a document into an HTML file by automatically adding HTML tags to the document. While these programs provide the capability to save as a webpage, they do not substitute the use of a text editor or a WYSIWYG editor. **WYSIWYG** stands for What You See Is What You Get. WYSIWYG editors provide a graphical user interface to design a webpage, as opposed to the blank page provided in a text editor used to write code. The WYSIWYG editor allows you to drag HTML elements onto the page while the editor writes the code for you. While these editors can be useful in developing webpages, understanding the code means you have the control and flexibility to create webpages that meet your needs.

Adobe Dreamweaver is a popular WYSIWYG editor used by many people and businesses around the world for web development. Several types of web file formats can be developed with Dreamweaver, including HTML, CSS, JavaScript, and PHP. Dreamweaver can be installed on a computer running Windows or macOS. Dreamweaver provides several views for working with a webpage file, including Design view, Code view, Split view, and Live view. Design view shows the design of the webpage, while Code view is similar to a text editor. Split view provides a side-by-side view of the webpage design and code. Live view mimics a browser display. Figure 1–28 shows an example of Dreamweaver in Split view. Dreamweaver is part of Adobe Creative Cloud and is available for purchase as a monthly or annual subscription. Visit www.adobe.com for more information about Adobe Dreamweaver Creative Cloud.

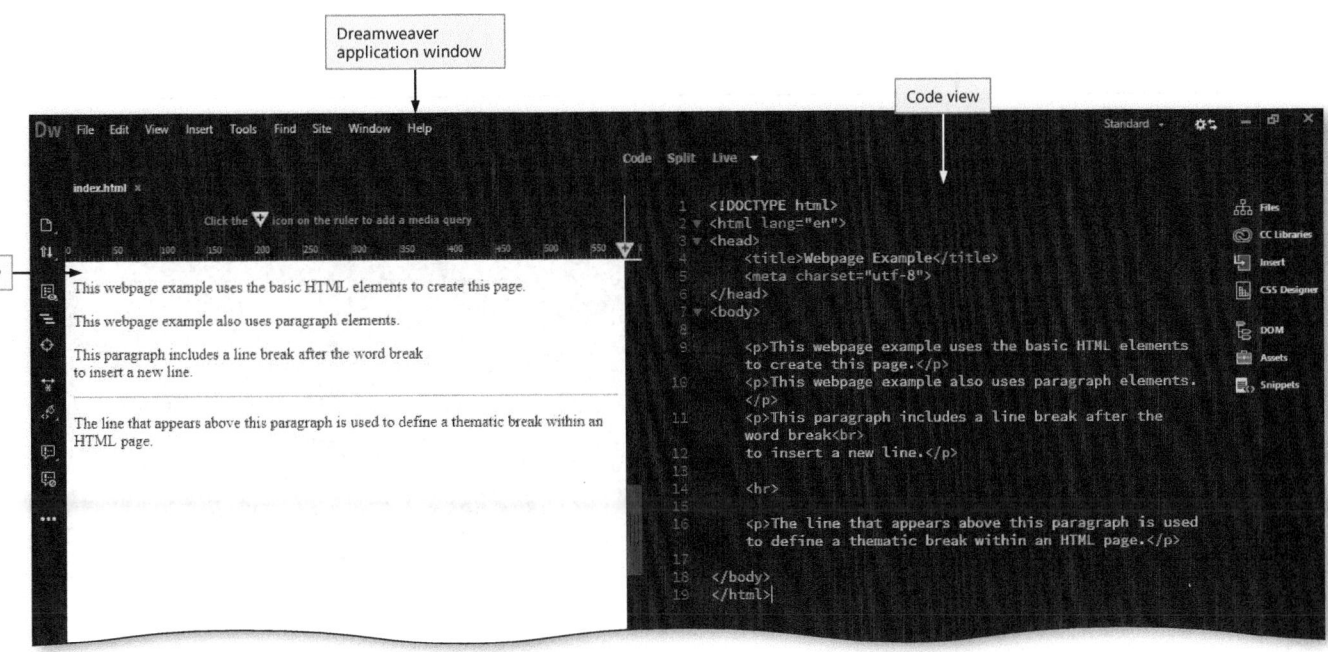

Figure 1–28

Online Code Editors

You can also use one of several free online code editors. No software installation is required. You visit the online code editor's website to type your code and save a file. Plunker is one example of an online code editor. To use Plunker, visit plnkr.co, shown in Figure 1–29. CodePen is another online code editor, available at codepen.io, and is shown in Figure 1–30.

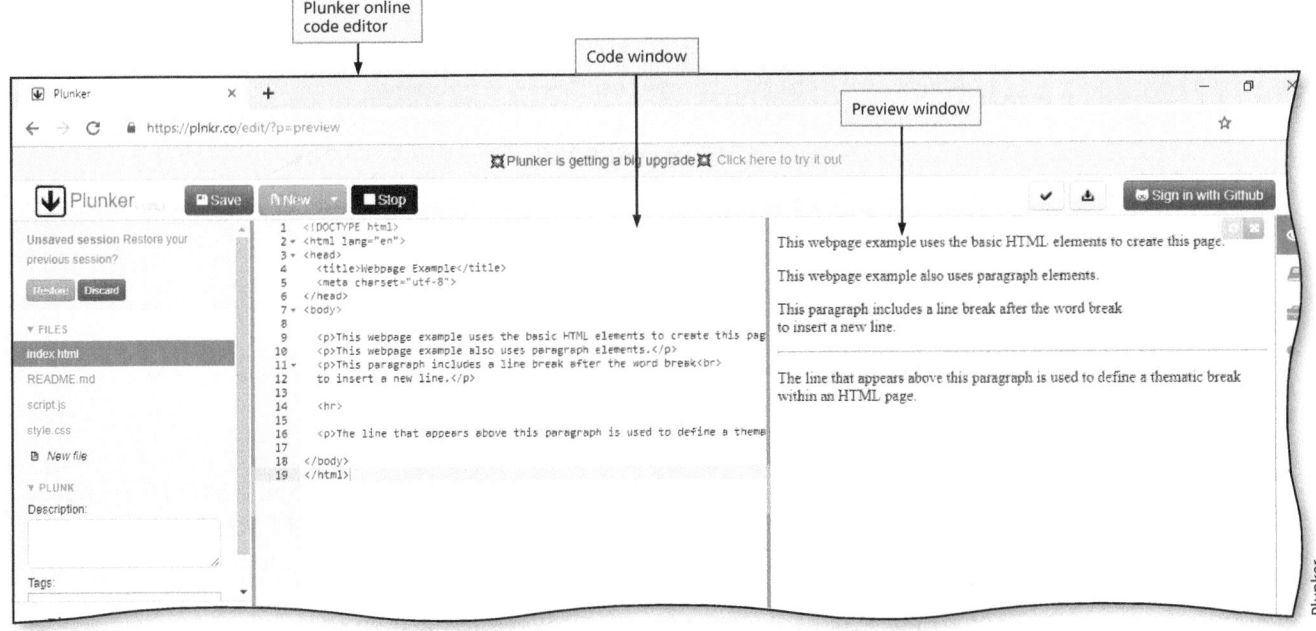

Figure 1–29

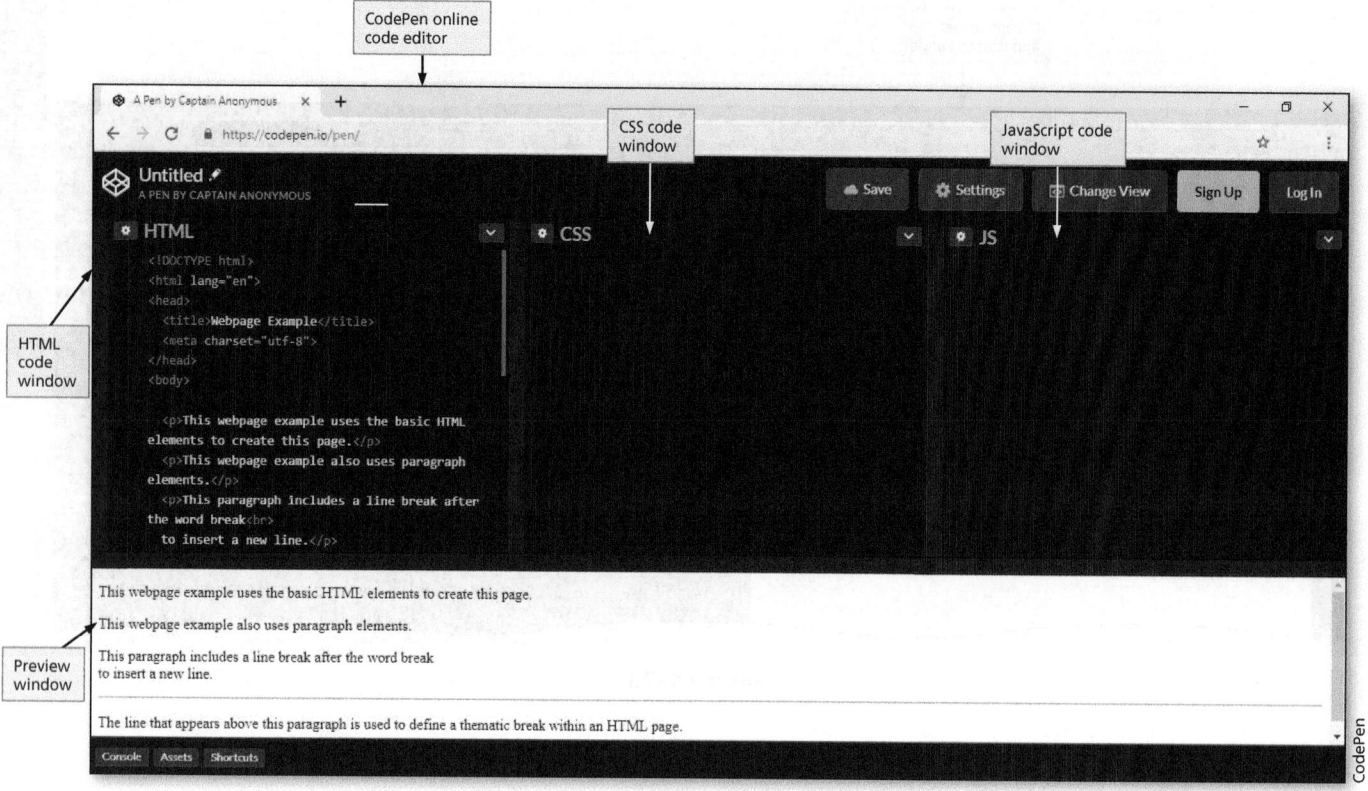

Figure 1–30

Creating a Basic Webpage

Every HTML webpage includes the basic HTML tags shown in Figure 1–31.

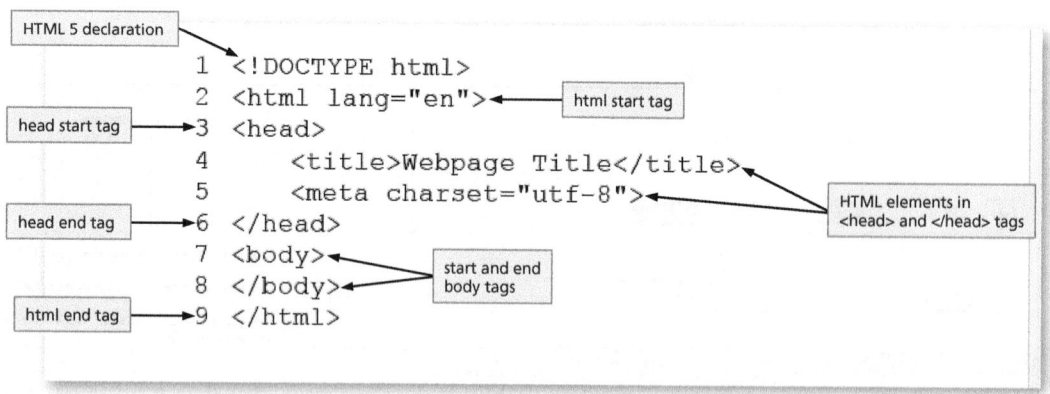

Figure 1–31

The numbers on the left represent line numbers for each line of HTML code. Line 1 shows the tag for declaring an HTML 5 webpage. All HTML 5 webpages must begin with the HTML element **<!DOCTYPE html>**. This is the first line of HTML code for all of your HTML webpages.

Line 2 shows the HTML tag needed to begin an HTML document. The basic opening tag is **<html>** and the closing tag is **</html>**, which always appears on the last line of the webpage. The lang="en" contained within the opening html tag is an attribute that defines the type of language used (English).

Line 3 shows the head tag, which contains the webpage title and other information about the webpage. The opening head tag is **<head>** and the closing tag is **</head>**.

Line 4 shows the webpage title tags, **<title>** and **</title>**. The text contained between these tags is displayed within the web browser tab. The title element belongs within the opening and closing head tags. To make the head section easier to read, web developers customarily indent the tags in the head section, such as the title and meta tags.

Line 5 shows the meta tag. A **meta** tag contains information about the data on the webpage. In this instance, the meta tag designates the type of character set the browser should use, charset="utf-8". The charset is an attribute within the meta tag that specifies the character encoding to be used for the webpage. The **Unicode Transformation Format (UTF)** is a compressed format that allows computers to display and manipulate text. When the browser encounters this meta tag, it displays the webpage properly. UTF-8 is standard for HTML 5 pages and is the preferred encoding standard for email and other applications. The encoding chosen is also important when validating the webpage, which you will do in Chapter 2. Note that the meta tag is a single tag element without opening and closing tags making it an empty element. The meta tag belongs within the opening and closing head tags.

Lines 7 and 8 show the **<body>** and **</body>** tags. All text, images, links, and other content displayed on the webpage are included within the <body> and </body> element.

Do I have to indent certain lines of HTML code?

Indenting lines of code is not required, but it helps improve the readability of the webpage. In Figure 1–31, Lines 4 and 5 are indented to clearly show the elements contained in the <head> and </head> tags. If the code included elements between the <body> and </body> tags, those lines could also be indented to make them easier to read. Using indents is a good web design practice.

Now that you have learned the basic HTML elements, it is time to create your first webpage. The following steps use Notepad++ to create an HTML document. You may complete these steps using a text editor other than Notepad++, but your screens will not match those in the book and your line numbers may vary slightly.

To Start Notepad++ and Create a Blank Document

1 RUN TEXT EDITOR & CREATE BLANK DOCUMENT | 2 ENTER HTML TAGS
3 ADD TEXT | 4 SAVE WEBPAGE | 5 VIEW WEBPAGE

The following steps start Notepad++ based on a typical installation in Windows 10. *Why? Before you can create a webpage, you must open a text editor.* You may need to ask your instructor how to download, install, and start Notepad++ for your computer.

- Tap or click in the Search box on the Windows taskbar.

- Start to type **Notepad++** in the Search box and watch the search results appear in the Best match list (Figure 1–32).

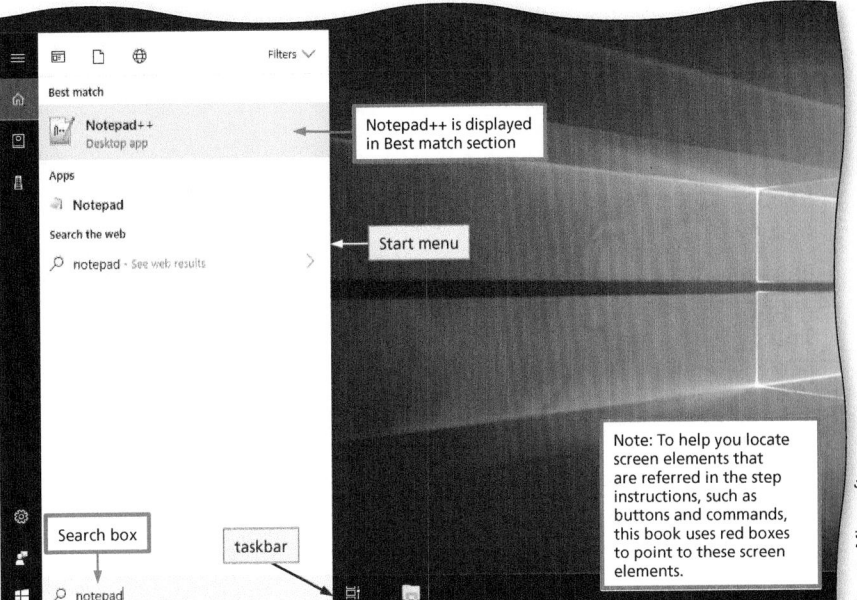

Figure 1–32

Source: Microsoft

BTW
<!DOCTYPE>
Statement
Because the web includes billions of documents, a browser refers to the HTML version and type in the <!DOCTYPE> statement to display a webpage correctly. Previous versions of HTML had complicated <!DOCTYPE> statements.

- Tap or click Notepad++ in the Best match list to start Notepad++ and display a new blank page.
- If the Notepad++ window is not maximized, tap or click the Maximize button next to the Close button on the title bar to maximize the window (Figure 1–33).

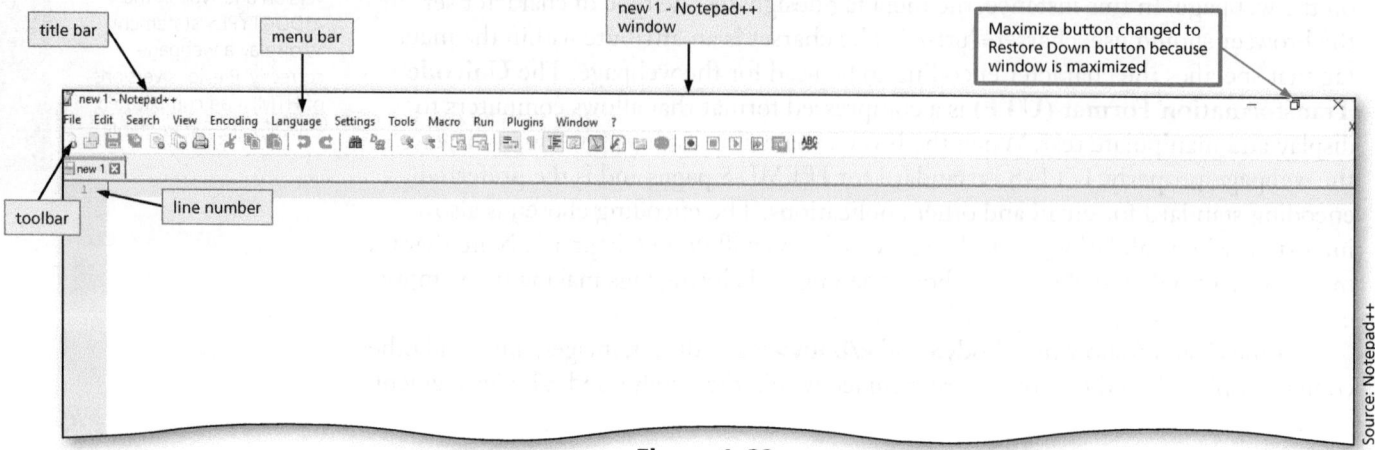

Figure 1–33

Other Ways

1. Double-tap or double-click Notepad++ icon on desktop

CONSIDER THIS

How do I use the touch keyboard with a touch screen?
To display the on-screen touch keyboard, tap the Touch Keyboard button on the Windows taskbar. When finished using the touch keyboard, tap the X button on the touch keyboard to close the keyboard.

To Add Basic HTML Tags to a Document

1 RUN TEXT EDITOR & CREATE BLANK DOCUMENT | 2 ENTER HTML TAGS
3 ADD TEXT | 4 SAVE WEBPAGE | 5 VIEW WEBPAGE

Create your first webpage beginning with the required minimum HTML tags. *Why? An HTML webpage requires several basic HTML tags so it can be displayed properly on a web browser.* The following steps add the required HTML tags to a document.

- On Line 1, type **<!DOCTYPE html>** to declare an HTML 5 document.

- Press the ENTER key and then type **<html lang="en">** to add the opening html tag on Line 2.

- Press the ENTER key and then type **<head>** to add the opening head tag on Line 3 (Figure 1–34).

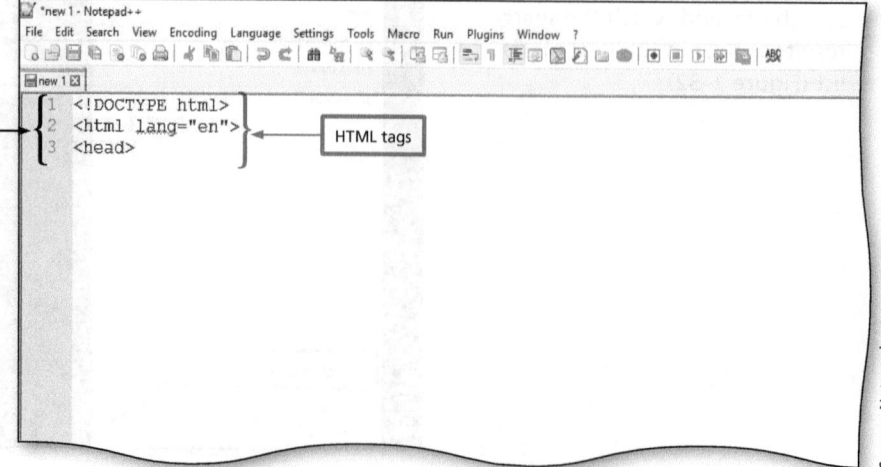

Figure 1–34

Q&A Why is the text "lang" underlined with a wavy red line?
The wavy red line indicates a possible spelling error. Because "lang" is the correct spelling for the language attribute, you can ignore this error.

2

- Press the ENTER key and enter the lines of code as listed in Table 1–4 to add the remaining basic HTML tags (Figure 1–35).

Q&A How should I move from one line to another in the document?
Press the ENTER key after each line to continue to the next line.

Should I indent any lines of code?
Yes. Indent Lines 4 and 5 by pressing the TAB key. Press the SHIFT+TAB keys to return the insertion point to the left margin.

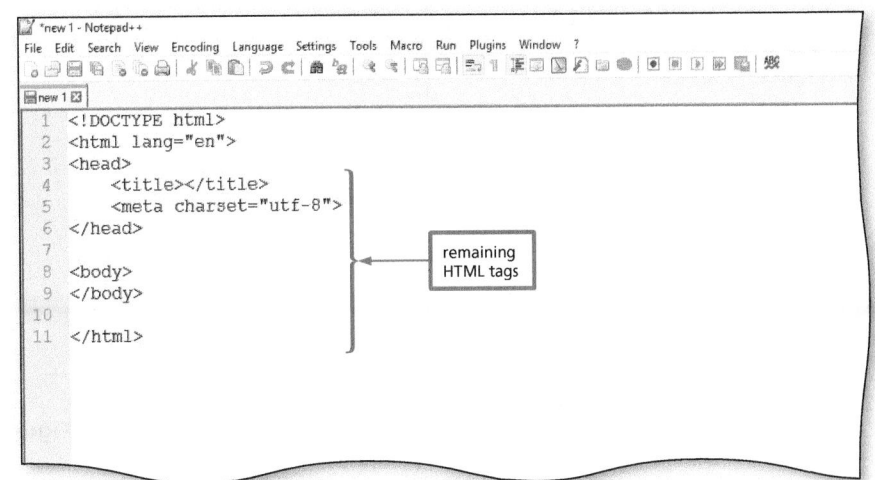

Source: Notepad++

Figure 1–35

Q&A What is the purpose of indenting Lines 4 and 5?
The elements on Lines 4 and 5 are nested elements. When coding a webpage, it is a best practice to indent nested elements, as this helps improve readability for a web developer.

Table 1–4 HTML Tags	
Line Number	HTML Tag
4	<title></title>
5	<meta charset="utf-8">
6	</head>
7	
8	<body>
9	</body>
10	
11	</html>

To Add a Title and Text to a Webpage

1 RUN TEXT EDITOR & CREATE BLANK DOCUMENT | 2 ENTER HTML TAGS
3 ADD TEXT | **4 SAVE WEBPAGE** | **5 VIEW WEBPAGE**

Now that you have added required HTML elements, you are ready to designate a title and add content to the page. *Why? A webpage title appears on the browser tab and usually displays the name of the webpage. After titling a webpage, you add content to the body section.* The following steps add a title and content to the webpage.

- Place the insertion point between the opening and closing title tags to prepare to enter a webpage title.
- Type **My First Webpage** to add a webpage title (Figure 1–36).

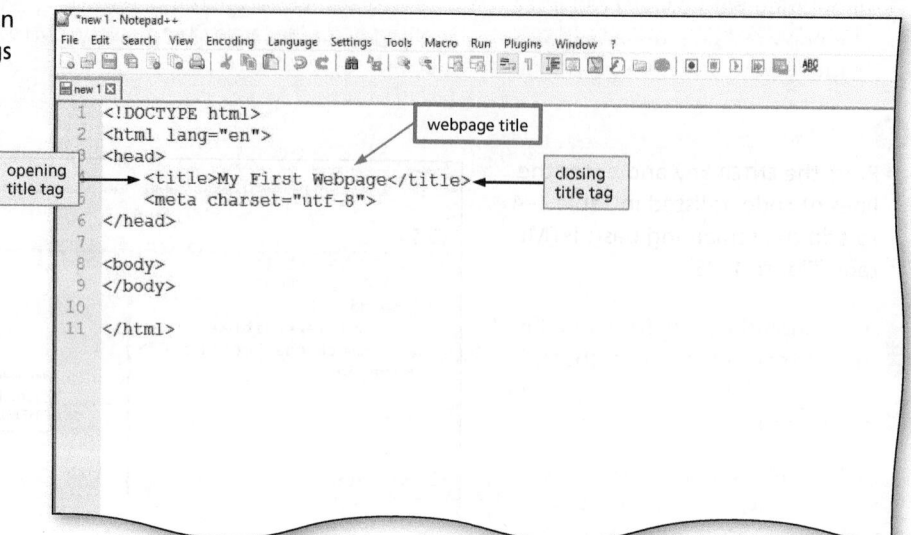

Figure 1–36

Source: Notepad++

2

- Place the insertion point after the opening body tag and press the ENTER key twice to add two new lines.
- Press the TAB key to indent the line.
- Type **<p>Welcome to My First Webpage</p>** to add a paragraph element to the webpage.
- Press the ENTER key to insert a blank line below the paragraph element (Figure 1–37).

Q&A Why did I insert a blank line after the opening body tag and above the closing body tag?
Adding blank lines between elements is a best practice because it helps improve code readability for the developer.

```
1  <!DOCTYPE html>
2  <html lang="en">
3  <head>
4      <title>My First Webpage</title>
5      <meta charset="utf-8">
6  </head>
7
8  <body>
9
10     <p>Welcome to My First Webpage</p>
11
12 </body>
13
14 </html>
```

blank lines → opening body tag
paragraph element
closing body tag

Figure 1–37

Source: Notepad++

To Save a Webpage

1 RUN TEXT EDITOR & CREATE BLANK DOCUMENT | 2 ENTER HTML TAGS
3 ADD TEXT | **4 SAVE WEBPAGE** | **5 VIEW WEBPAGE**

After creating a webpage, you must save it as an HTML file. **Why?** *A text editor can be used to create many types of files; therefore, you must specify that this is an HTML file so a browser can display it as a webpage.* The following steps save the document as an HTML file.

- Tap or click File on the menu bar to display the File menu options.

- Tap or click Save As on the File menu to display the Save As dialog box (Figure 1–38).

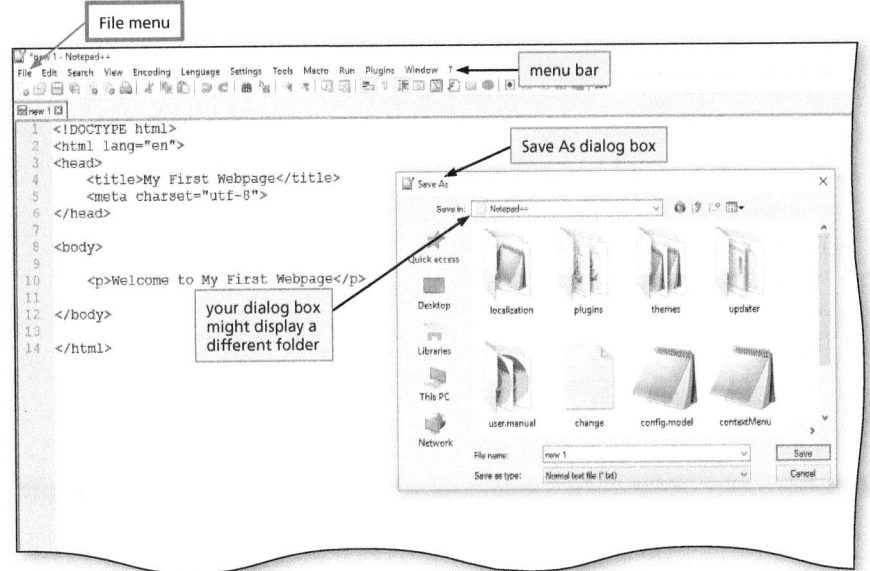

Figure 1–38

Source: Notepad++

- Tap or click the Save in list box and then navigate to your Documents folder.

Q&A Can I save the file in another location on my hard drive or on my flash drive?
Yes. If your instructor specified a different location, use that instead of the Documents folder. You learn about managing website files in Chapter 2.

- In the File name text box, delete the existing text and then type **index** to name the file.

Q&A Why am I using index as the file name?
The file name *index* is the standard name of a home page.

Why am I using all lowercase letters for the file name?
The current convention in web development is to use all lowercase letters for folder and file names.

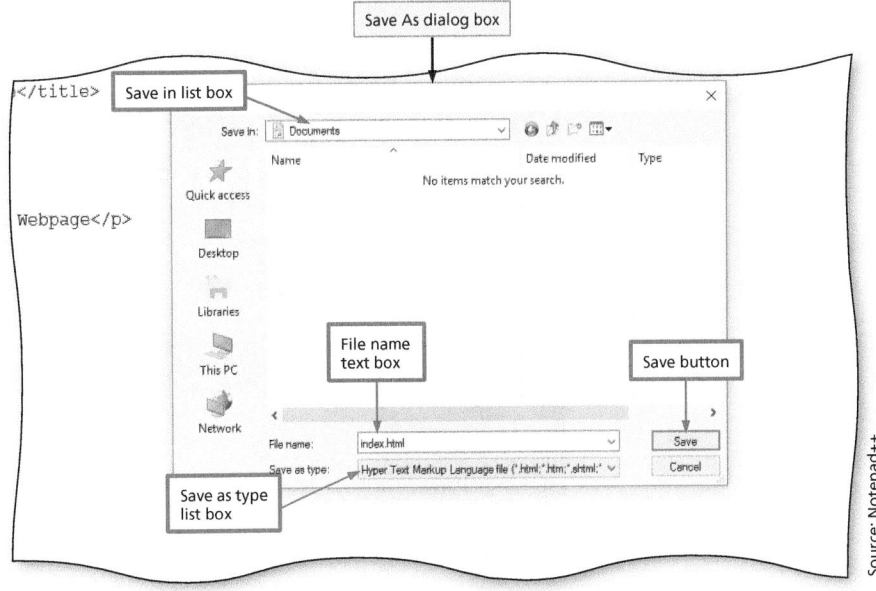

Figure 1–39

Source: Notepad++

- Tap or click the Save as type list box and then tap or click Hyper Text Markup Language file to select the HTML file type (Figure 1–39).

Q&A I am using another text editor and do not have HTML as the Save as type option. What do I do?
If your text editor does not provide a list of Save as type options, then specify the file name as index.html.

- Tap or click the Save button to save the HTML document.

Other Ways
1. Press CTRL+S

To View a Webpage in a Browser

After saving an HTML document, you can view it as a webpage in a web browser. *Why? A web browser reads the HTML code and displays the webpage content.* The following steps display a webpage in a browser.

1

- Tap or click Run on the menu bar to display the Run menu options.
- Tap or click Launch in Chrome to run the Chrome browser and display the webpage (Figure 1–40).

Q&A What should I do if I need to use a different browser?
Tap or click Launch in Firefox or Launch in IE to open the webpage in a different browser.

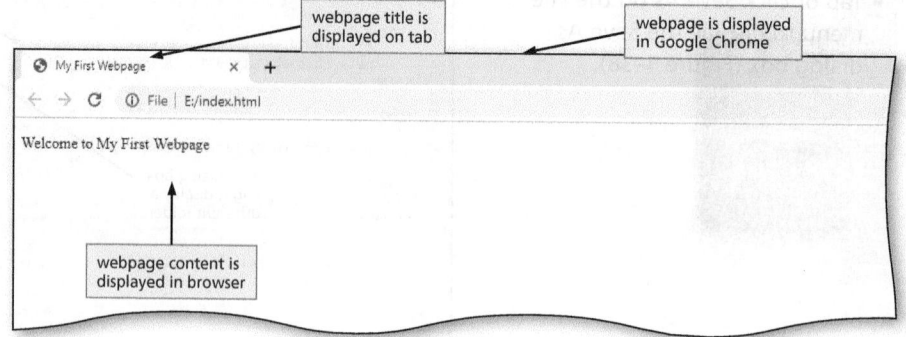

Figure 1–40

Why are the HTML tags not displayed in the browser?
The browser interprets the HTML code and displays only the content that appears within the tags, not the tags themselves.

Why is the content not indented in the browser when I indented it in the text editor?
The browser ignores indents, spaces, and extra blank lines inserted in the HTML file to improve readability.

Using a Different Text Editor

If you completed the previous steps with a text editor other than Notepad++, your screen will look similar to Figure 1–41 for Brackets, to Figure 1–42 for Atom, and to Figure 1–43 for TextMate.

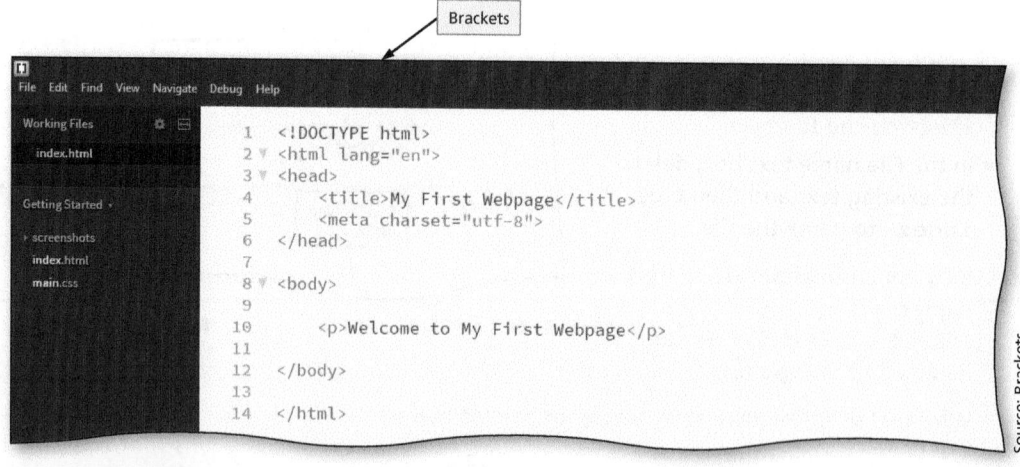

Figure 1–41

Figure 1–42

TextMate

 TextMate   File   Edit   View   Navigate   Text   File Browser   Bundles   Window   Help

```
1    <!DOCTYPE html>
2    <html lang="en">
3 ▼  <head>
4        <title>My First Webpage</title>
5        <meta charset="utf-8">
6 ▲  </head>
7
8 ▼  <body>
9
10       <p>Welcome to My First Webpage</p>
11
12 ▲ </body>
13
14   </html>
```

Source: TextMate

Figure 1–43

Chapter Summary

In this chapter, you learned about the Internet, the web, and associated technologies, including web servers and web browsers. You learned the essential role of HTML in creating webpages and reviewed tools used to create HTML documents. You also learned how to create a basic HTML webpage. The items listed below include all the new concepts and skills you have learned in this chapter, with the tasks grouped by activity.

Creating a Basic Webpage
Start Notepad++ and Create a Blank Document (HTML 31)
Add Basic HTML Tags to a Document (HTML 32)
Add a Title and Text to a Webpage (HTML 33)
Save a Webpage (HTML 34)
View a Webpage in a Browser (HTML 36)

Exploring the Internet
Describe the Internet (HTML 3)
Describe the World Wide Web (HTML 4)
Define Protocols (HTML 6)
Discuss Web Browsers (HTML 7)
Identify Types of Websites (HTML 9)

Planning a Website
Identify the Purpose and Audience of the Website (HTML 11–12)

Design for Multiplatform Display (HTML 13)
Describe a Wireframe and a Site Map (HTML 14)
Consider Graphics, Navigation, Typography, and Color (HTML 17–19)
Design for Accessibility (HTML 20)

Understanding the Basics of HTML
Define Hypertext Markup Language (HTML 21)
Describe HTML Elements (HTML 22)
List Useful HTML Practices (HTML 23)
Identify Technologies Related to HTML (HTML 24)
Explain the Role of Other Web Programming Languages (HTML 24)

Using Web Authoring Tools
Identify Text Editors (HTML 25)
Download and Install a Text Editor (HTML 28)
Describe WYSIWYG and Online Code Editors (HTML 28-30)

What decisions will you need to make when creating your next webpage?
Use these guidelines as you complete the assignments in this chapter and create your own webpages outside of this class.

1. Plan the website.

a. Identify the purpose of the website.

b. Identify the users of the website.

c. Recognize the computing environments of the users.

d. Design a wireframe and a site map.

2. Choose the design components.

a. Identify possible graphics for the website.

b. Determine the types of navigation tools and typography to use.

c. Select a color scheme.

d. Consider accessibility.

Continued >

CONSIDER THIS *continued*

3. Select a webpage authoring tool.

    a. Review available authoring tools.

    b. Determine an authoring tool to use to create the webpages.

4. Create a basic HTML webpage.

    a. Insert the basic HTML tags.

    b. Indent some elements to improve readability.

    c. Add content to the webpage.

    d. Save the file as an HTML document.

    e. Display the webpage in a browser.

CONSIDER THIS

How should you submit solutions to questions in the assignments identified with a symbol?

Every assignment in this book contains one or more questions identified with a symbol. These questions require you to think beyond the assigned presentation. Present your solutions to the questions in the format required by your instructor. Possible formats may include one or more of these options: write the answer; create a document that contains the answer; present your answer to the class; discuss your answer in a group; record the answer as audio or video using a webcam, smartphone, or portable media player; or post answers on a blog, wiki, or website.

Apply Your Knowledge

Reinforce the skills and apply the concepts you learned in this chapter.

Creating a Basic HTML Webpage

Instructions: In this exercise, you will use your text editor to create an HTML webpage. You will add all the necessary basic HTML elements to the page. An example of the completed webpage is shown in Figure 1–44.

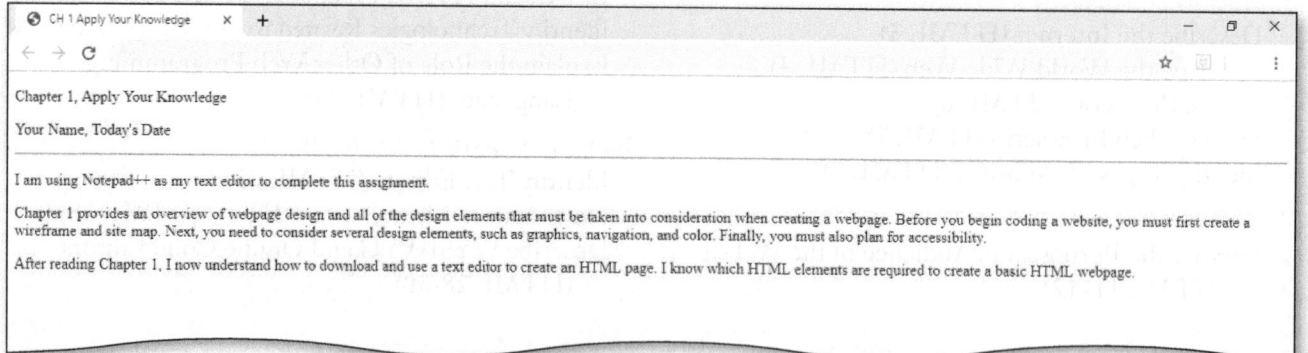

Figure 1–44

Perform the following tasks:

1. Open your text editor and enter all the required HTML elements to create a basic webpage, including the DOCTYPE, html, head, title, meta, and body elements. Use the File Save As feature to save the webpage in the chapter01\apply folder with the name `index.html` to create the webpage.

2. Add the lang attribute to the starting html tag and specify the language as English as follows:
   `<html lang="en">`

3. Add the charset attribute to the meta tag and specify the character set as utf-8.

4. Add the text, `CH 1 Apply Your Knowledge`, to the title element as follows: `<title>CH 1 Apply Your Knowledge</title>`

5. In the body element, nest a paragraph element that includes the following text: `Chapter 1, Apply Your Knowledge`

6. Below the first paragraph element, add another paragraph element that includes your name and today's date.

7. Below the second paragraph, add a thematic break, `<hr>`, followed by two blank lines.

8. Below the thematic break, add another paragraph element that states the name of the text editor you are using to complete this assignment.

9. Below the third paragraph element, add another paragraph element that includes a summary about how to plan a website.

10. Below the fourth paragraph element, add another paragraph element that includes one or two sentences about what you learned in Chapter 1.

11. Indent all nested elements.

12. Add blank lines between paragraph elements three, four, and five.

13. Save your changes and submit the index.html file in a format specified by your instructor.

14. ☀ In Step 2, you specified English as the language for the HTML page. Use your browser to research other languages that you can specify here and note the language attribute value for each.

Extend Your Knowledge

Extend the skills you learned in this chapter and experiment with new skills. You may need to use additional resources to complete the assignment.

Learning More About Web Accessibility

Instructions: In this exercise, you will research web accessibility and use your text editor to discuss your findings. An example of the completed webpage is shown in Figure 1–45.

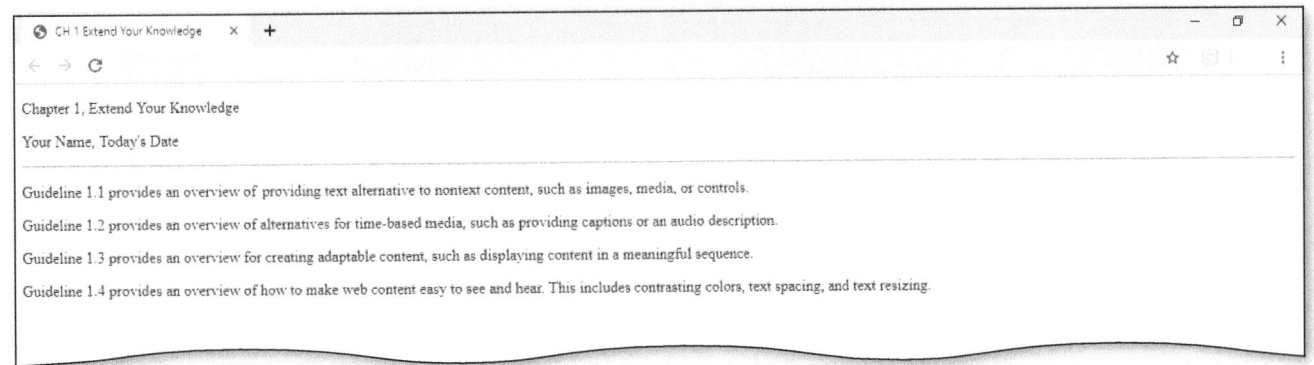

Source: Google Chrome

Figure 1–45

Perform the following tasks:

1. Open w3.org/WAI/standards-guidelines/wcag/ in your browser and read the Introduction section.

2. Above the Introduction, select the link, How to Meet WCAG 2 (Quick Reference), or open www.w3.org/WAI/WCAG21/quickref/ in your browser.

3. Review the various guidelines for Principle 1 – Perceivable, 1.1.1 through 1.4.13.

Continued >

Extend Your Knowledge *continued*

4. Open your text editor and enter all required HTML elements to create a basic webpage, including the DOCTYPE, html, head, title, meta, and body elements. Use the File Save As feature to save the webpage in the chapter01\extend folder with the name `index.html` to create the webpage.

5. Add the lang attribute to the starting html tag and specify the language as English.

6. Add the charset attribute to the meta tag and specify the character set as utf-8.

7. Add the following text to the title element: `CH 1 Extend Your Knowledge`

8. In the body element, nest a paragraph element that includes the following text: `Chapter 1, Extend Your Knowledge`

9. Below the first paragraph element, add another paragraph element that includes your name and today's date.

10. Below the second paragraph, add a thematic break, `<hr>`, followed by two blank lines.

11. Below the thematic break, add a paragraph element that includes a summary of your understanding of Guideline 1.1, followed by two blank lines.

12. Add another paragraph element that includes a summary of Guideline 1.2, followed by two blank lines.

13. Add another paragraph element that includes a summary of Guideline 1.3, followed by two blank lines.

14. Add another paragraph element that includes a summary of Guideline 1.4.

15. Indent all nested elements, and verify you have added blank lines between each paragraph element below the thematic break.

16. Save your changes and submit the index.html file in a format specified by your instructor.

17. ✷ In Step 3, you reviewed guidelines for Principle 1 - Perceivable. Identify the other principles outlined on the How to Meet WCAG 2 (Quick Reference) page.

Analyze, Correct, Improve

Analyze a webpage, correct all errors, and improve it.

Correcting a Webpage

Note: To complete this assignment, you will be required to use the Data Files. Please contact your instructor for information about accessing the Data Files.

Instructions: Open your text editor and then open the index.html file located in the chapter01\analyze folder in the Data Files. The page includes information about HTML; however, the information is incorrect. In addition, the page includes several errors. An example of the corrected page is shown in Figure 1–46.

Your Name, Today's Date

Chapter 1, Analyze, Correct, Improve

HTML stands for Hypertext Markup Language.

You use a text editor to create HTML pages.

HTML 5.2 is the latest version of HTML.

HTML is rendered in a browser, such as Microsoft Edge, Google Chrome, Firefox, Opera, or Safari.

Source: Google Chrome

Figure 1–46

1. Correct

   a. Open the index.html file in your text editor and review the page.

   b. Correct the DOCTYPE tag.

   c. Place the html start tag on a new line and add the appropriate attribute to specify English as the language.

   d. Place the head start tag on a new line, and correct the spelling error.

   e. Indent and correct the title and meta elements within the head element. Specify appropriate text for the title element. Specify the utf-8 character set for the meta element.

   f. Properly close the head element.

   g. Place the starting body tag on a new line.

   h. Use lowercase for all tags, except DOCTYPE.

   i. Correct the <dr> tag to specify a thematic break.

   j. Add the html end tag.

2. Improve

   a. In the body element, place each sentence within its own paragraph element. Review each paragraph element to ensure proper start and end tags.

   b. List each paragraph element on a new line and indent each paragraph element.

   c. Add your name and today's date as the first paragraph element within the body element.

   d. Review and correct each sentence to make the sentence true and insert a blank line between each paragraph.

   e. Place the ending body tag after the last paragraph.

   f. ✳ If you did not make these corrections, would the page still render in a browser? Explain your answer.

In the Lab

Labs 1 and 2, which increase in difficulty, require you to create webpages based on what you learned in the chapter; Lab 3 is ideal for group projects/collaboration.

Lab 1: Creating a Webpage for Strike a Chord

Problem: You work for a local music lesson company called Strike a Chord that provides music lessons for piano, guitar, and violin. The company needs a web presence and has hired you to create their website. You have already created the website plan, wireframe, and site map for the proposed website. You will create a webpage that summarizes the website plan for the company. The webpage is shown in Figure 1–47.

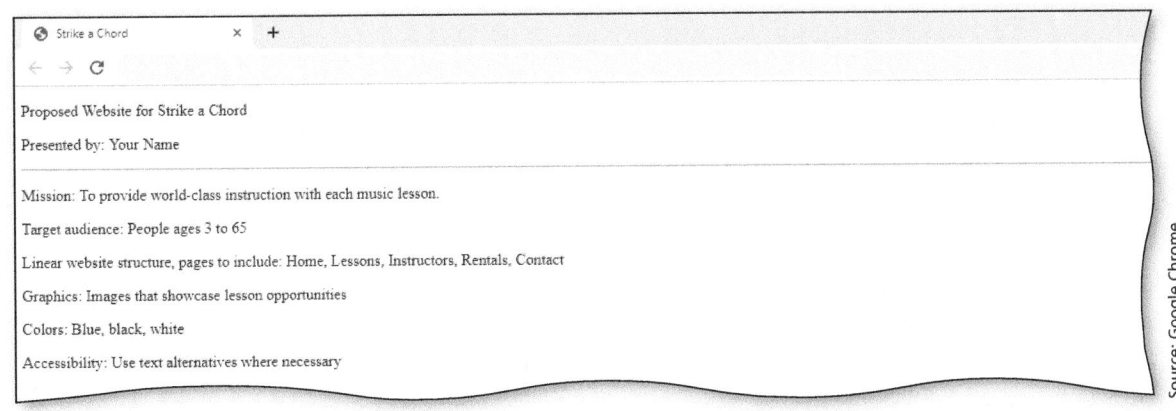

Source: Google Chrome

Figure 1–47

Continued >

In the Lab *continued*

Instructions: Perform the following tasks:

1. Open your text editor and enter all required HTML elements to create a basic webpage, including the DOCTYPE, html, head, title, meta, and body elements. Use the File Save As feature to save the webpage in the chapter01\lab1 folder with the name `plan.html` to create the webpage.

2. Add the lang attribute to the starting html tag and specify the language as English as follows: `<html lang="en">`

3. Add the text, `Strike a Chord`, to the title element as follows: `<title>Strike a Chord</title>`

4. Add the charset attribute to the meta tag and specify the character set as utf-8 as follows: `<meta charset="utf-8">`

5. In the body element, nest a paragraph element that includes the following text: `Proposed Website for Strike a Chord`

6. Below the first paragraph element, add another paragraph element that includes the text `Presented by:` followed by your name.

7. Below the second paragraph, add a thematic break, `<hr>`, followed by two blank lines.

8. Below the thematic break, add the following six paragraph elements:

```
<p>Mission: To provide world-class instruction with each music
lesson.</p>

<p>Target audience: People ages 3 to 65</p>

<p>Linear website structure, pages to include: Home, Lessons,
Instructors, Rentals, Contact</p>

<p>Graphics: Images that showcase lesson opportunities</p>

<p>Colors: Blue, black, white</p>

<p>Accessibility: Use text alternatives where necessary</p>
```

9. Indent all nested elements.

10. Add blank lines between all paragraph elements located below the thematic break.

11. Save your changes and review the plan.html page within a browser.

12. Submit your assignment in the format specified by your instructor.

13. ❈ In Step 8, you created several paragraph elements. What other elements can be used to add content on a page? Research to find your answer.

Lab 2: Creating a Webpage for a Wildlife Rescue Organization

Problem: You volunteer at a local wildlife rescue, a nonprofit organization called Wild Rescues. The organization rescues all kinds of wild animals, rehabilitates them, and then releases them back into the wild. Wild Rescues needs a website to help raise awareness about their mission. The director of Wild Rescues has asked you to build a website for the organization. Create a webpage that outlines the various pages that will be created for the website. The completed webpage is shown in Figure 1–48.

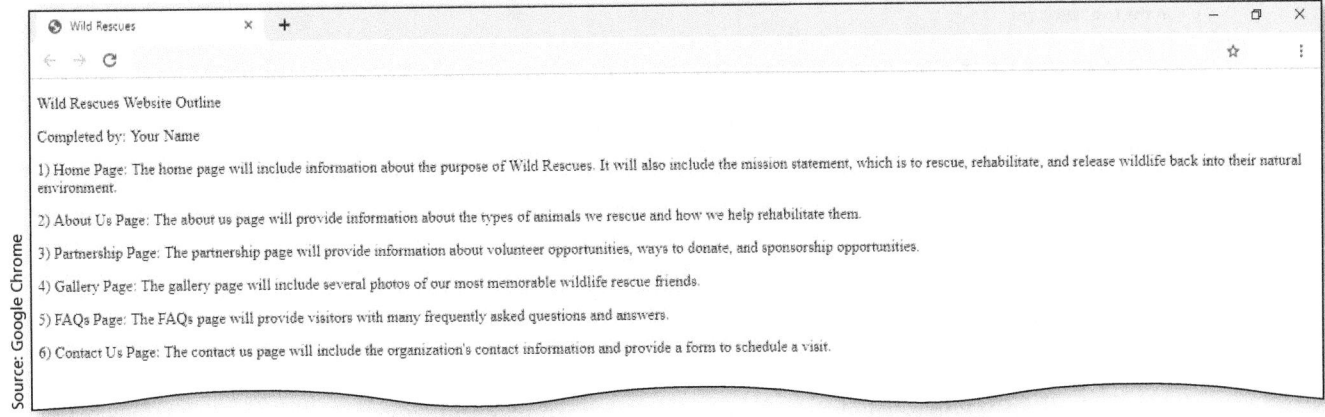

Figure 1–48

Instructions: Perform the following tasks:

1. Open your text editor and enter all required HTML elements to create a basic webpage, including the DOCTYPE, html, head, title, meta, and body elements. Use the File Save As feature to save the webpage in the chapter01\lab2 folder with the name `rescuepages.html` to create the webpage.

2. Add the lang attribute to the starting html tag and specify the language as English.

3. Add the following text to the title element: `Wild Rescues`

4. Add the charset attribute to the meta tag and specify the character set as utf-8.

5. In the body element, nest a paragraph element that includes the following text: `Wild Rescues Website Outline`

6. Below the first paragraph element, add another paragraph element that includes the text, `Completed by:` followed by your name.

7. Below the second paragraph, add two blank lines.

8. Add the following six paragraph elements:

   `1) Home Page: The home page will include information about the purpose of Wild Rescues. It will also include the mission statement, which is to rescue, rehabilitate, and release wildlife back into their natural environment.`

   `2) About Us Page: The about us page will provide information about the types of animals we rescue and how we help rehabilitate them.`

   `3) Partnership Page: The partnership page will provide information about volunteer opportunities, ways to donate, and sponsorship opportunities.`

   `4) Gallery Page: The gallery page will include several photos of our most memorable wildlife rescue friends.`

   `5) FAQs Page: The FAQs page will provide visitors with many frequently asked questions and answers.`

Continued >

In the Lab *continued*

```
6) Contact Us Page: The contact us page will include the
organization's contact information and provide a form to schedule a
visit.
```

9. Indent all nested elements.

10. Add blank lines between all paragraph elements.

11. Save your changes and review the rescuepages.html page within a browser.

12. Submit your assignment in the format specified by your instructor.

13. ✳ In Step 5, you created a paragraph element with text that served as a heading for the webpage. Use your browser to research another HTML element that you can use that would display the text in a larger font size. Include an example. Likewise, in Step 8, you created several paragraph elements to outline the proposed website pages. Use your browser to research another HTML element that you can use to create a numbered outline. Include an example. Your instructor may have you complete this step prior to submitting this assignment.

Lab 3: Creating a Website for Student Clubs and Events

Note: To complete this assignment, you will be required to use the Data Files. Please contact your instructor for information about accessing the Data Files.

Problem: You and several of your classmates have decided to help increase student involvement in school clubs and events by creating a website to promote awareness about the various activities. You will work with three or four classmates to create a website plan, wireframe, and site map for the proposed website.

Instructions:

1. Open the planning.docx document located in the chapter01\lab3 folder in the Data Files and review its contents.

2. Discuss and brainstorm ideas to successfully complete this lab.

3. Work together to create a website plan, a wireframe, and a site map for your proposed website. The website should have a minimum of five pages.

4. ✳ Group collaboration is common when planning a website. It is helpful to designate a project leader, content manager, web designer, and web developer to help manage the project. Discuss these designations within your group to help determine each classmate's role in this project. How did you determine the role for each team member?

Consider This: Your Turn

Apply your creative thinking and problem-solving skills to design and implement a solution.

Note: To complete this assignment, you will be required to use the Data Files. Please contact your instructor for information about accessing the Data Files.

1. Plan a Personal Portfolio Website

Personal

Part 1: As in almost every field, the job market for the best jobs in web development are competitive. One way to give yourself a big edge in a job search is to create an appropriate personal portfolio website to showcase your skills. Plan the website by completing the table in the personal_portfolio_plan.docx document located in the chapter01\your_turn1 folder in the Data Files. Answer the questions with thoughtful, realistic responses. Be sure to sketch the wireframe for your home page and include a site map to list the proposed pages for your website. Submit your assignment in the format specified by your instructor.

Part 2: ✳ What do you want this website to accomplish?

2. Plan a Dog Grooming Website

Professional

Part 1: Your family owns a dog grooming business and needs a website. Your family knows that you are taking a web design class and asks you to create a website for the business. Plan the website by completing the table in the dog_grooming_plan.docx document located in the chapter01\your_turn2 folder in the Data Files. Answer the questions with thoughtful, realistic responses. Be sure to sketch the wireframe for the home page and include a site map to list the proposed pages for the business website. Submit your assignment in the format specified by your instructor.

Part 2: ✳ Use of graphics within this website will help provide visual appeal to potential clients. Where will you obtain graphics used for this website? Are you allowed to use pictures you find on the Internet? Explain your answer.

3. Plan an Information Website About Future Technologies

Research and Collaboration

Part 1: You and several of your classmates have been tasked with creating a website that showcases advancements in technology. This might include, but is not limited to, artificial intelligence, deep learning, robotics, and the Internet of Things (IoT). You will work with three or four classmates to create a website plan, wireframe, and site map for the proposed website. Plan the website by completing the table in the technology_plan.docx document located in the chapter01\your_turn3 folder in the Data Files. Be sure to sketch the wireframe for the home page and include a site map to list the proposed pages for the business website. Submit your assignment in the format specified by your instructor.

Part 2: ✳ Each person in the group should research a current article on advanced technologies and bring it to a group discussion. In the discussion, each person should share their article as well as something they learned from it. Organize your group's findings as requested by your instructor.

2 | Building a Webpage Template with HTML 5

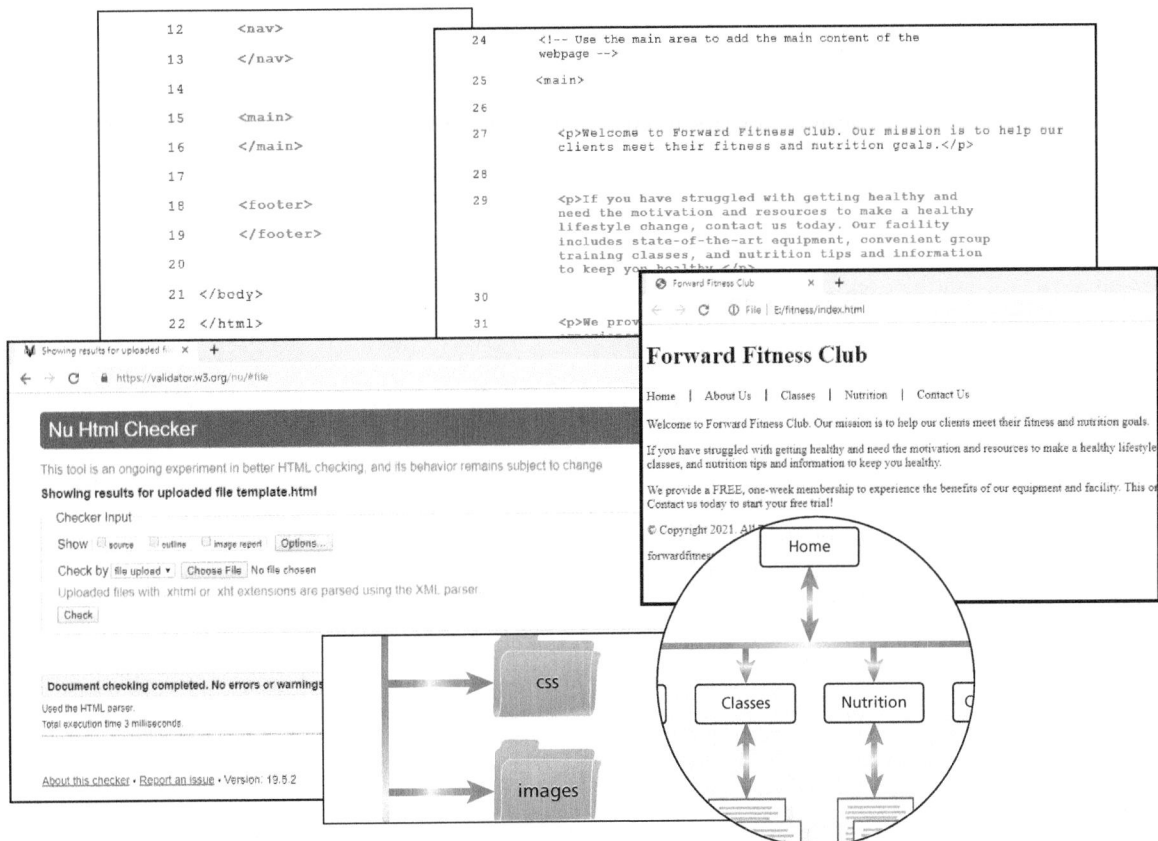

Objectives

You will have mastered the material in this chapter when you can:

- Explain how to manage website files
- Describe and use HTML 5 semantic elements
- Determine the elements to use when setting the structure of a webpage
- Design and build a semantic wireframe
- Create a webpage template
- Insert comments in an HTML document
- Add static content to a webpage template

- Insert symbol codes and other character entities
- Describe and use heading elements
- Describe the benefits of validating web documents
- Validate an HTML template
- Create a home page from an HTML template
- Add unique content to a webpage

2 | Building a Webpage Template with HTML 5

Introduction

Building a website from scratch involves a lot of time and planning, which is one reason that professional web design services are in high demand. Some web designers have their own business and provide their services on contract to clients, who are people or other businesses that want to build or redesign a website. Other web designers work in larger organizations and provide their services to people within the organization, who are called stakeholders. As an introduction to basic website design and development, this book provides a foundation on which to build your web design skills.

As discussed in Chapter 1, before you start building a website, you must plan it, which includes meeting with the clients or stakeholders to discover their needs, the purpose of the website, and their target audience. After developing a plan, you can start constructing the website by creating an HTML document and then adding the required basic HTML elements so visitors can display the webpage in a browser. Next, include HTML 5 elements to define the specific sections or areas of the webpage. This initial HTML document can serve as the template for the site. A **template** is a predefined webpage that contains a specific HTML structure to be used by all pages within the website. This chapter focuses on how to build a webpage template with HTML 5 elements and then use that template to create a home page.

Project — Plan and Build a Website

A local fitness center called Forward Fitness Club opened recently and needs a website to help promote its business. The business owner wants the website to showcase the club's equipment, group fitness classes, nutrition information, and contact information. The owner hired you to plan and design the Forward Fitness Club website.

The project in this chapter follows generally accepted guidelines for planning and building the webpage template shown in Figure 2–1a to produce the home page shown in Figure 2–1b. The template contains code and text including the document title, header, navigation area, and footer, which is repeated on each page of the Forward Fitness Club website. The template also includes comments to remind the web designer about the purpose of each section.

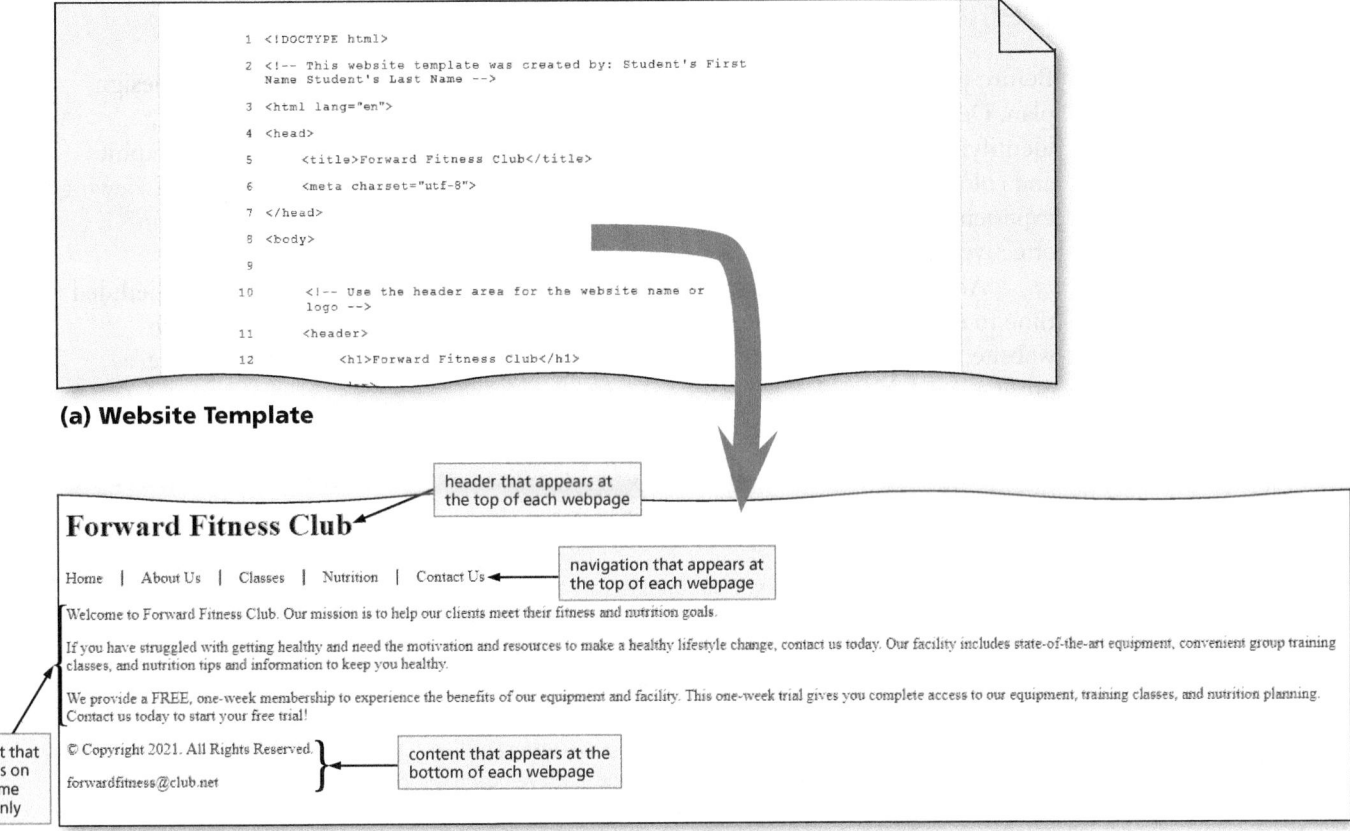

(a) Website Template

(b) Home Page **Figure 2–1**

Roadmap

In this chapter, you will learn how to create the webpage shown in Figure 2–1. The following roadmap identifies general activities you will perform as you progress through this chapter:

1. CREATE WEBSITE FOLDERS to organize files.
2. CREATE a TEMPLATE.
3. ENTER HTML 5 SEMANTIC ELEMENTS in the document.
4. ADD COMMENTS AND CONTENT to the document.
5. VALIDATE the DOCUMENT.
6. CREATE AND VIEW the HOME PAGE.

At the beginning of step instructions throughout the chapter, you will see an abbreviated form of this roadmap. The abbreviated roadmap uses colors to indicate chapter progress: gray means the chapter is beyond that activity; blue means the task being shown is covered in that activity, and black means that activity is yet to be covered. For example, the following abbreviated roadmap indicates the chapter would be showing a task in the 4 ADD COMMENTS & CONTENT activity.

1 CREATE WEBSITE FOLDERS | 2 CREATE TEMPLATE | 3 ENTER HTML 5 SEMANTIC ELEMENTS

4 ADD COMMENTS & CONTENT | **5 VALIDATE DOCUMENT** | **6 CREATE & VIEW HOME PAGE**

Use this abbreviated roadmap as a progress guide while you read or step through the instructions in this chapter.

Designing a Website

Before you begin creating webpages for a website, you must have a solid web design plan. Designing a website includes planning, articulating the website's purpose, identifying the target audience, creating a site map and wireframe, selecting graphics and colors to use in the site, and determining whether to design for an optimal viewing experience across a range of devices. Completing these activities helps ensure an effective design for your website.

After Forward Fitness Club contacted you to develop its website, you scheduled time to meet with the owner and asked several questions to plan and design the website. During the meeting, you learned the needs of the business and website, as outlined in Table 2–1.

Table 2–1 Forward Fitness Club Website Plan	
Purpose of the Website	To promote fitness services and gain new clients. The Forward Fitness Club mission: to facilitate a healthy lifestyle and help our clients meet their fitness and nutrition goals.
Target Audience	Forward Fitness Club customers are adults between the ages of 18 and 50 within the local community.
Multiplatform Display	Forward Fitness Club recognizes the growth in smartphone and tablet usage and wants a single website that provides an optimal viewing experience regardless of whether visitors are using a desktop, laptop, tablet, or smartphone.
Wireframe and Site Map	The initial website will consist of five webpages arranged in a hierarchal structure with links to the home page on every page. Each webpage will include a header area, navigation area, main content area, and footer area.
Graphics	Forward Fitness Club wants to display its fitness equipment and logo to help with local branding. Photos of the facility, members, and staff will increase visual appeal.
Color	Forward Fitness Club wants to use black and white as the primary colors for a clean, sophisticated look.
Typography	To make the content easy to read, the website will use a serif font style for paragraphs, lists, and other body content, while providing contrast by using a sans serif font style for navigation links and headings.
Accessibility	Standard accessibility attributes, such as alternative text for graphics, will be used to address accessibility.

Site Map

Recall that a site map indicates how the pages in a website relate to each other. To create a site map, you first need to know how many pages to include in the website. The owner of Forward Fitness Club has many ideas for the website, including some ambitious ones. To keep the website simple for now while allowing room for growth, you and the owner agree that the initial website will have a total of five webpages titled Home, About Us, Classes, Nutrition, and Contact Us. Because each page will contain links to all pages and accommodate future growth, the website will use a modified hierarchal structure. The webpages will include the following content:

- Home page: Introduces the fitness center and its mission statement
- About Us page: Showcases the facility's equipment and services
- Classes page: Includes a schedule of available group training and fitness classes
- Nutrition page: Provides nutrition tips and simple meal plans
- Contact Us page: Provides a phone number, email address, physical address, and form for potential clients to request additional information about the fitness center's services

Figure 2–2 depicts the site map for the Forward Fitness Club website.

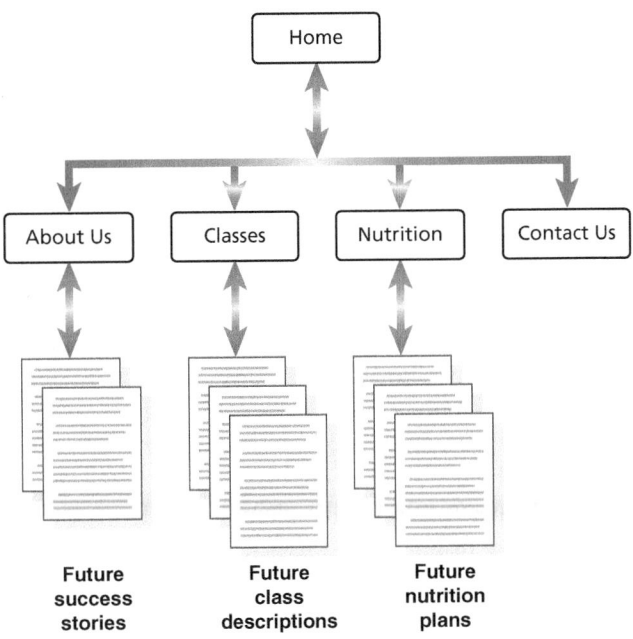

Figure 2–2

Wireframe

In addition to the site map for the Forward Fitness Club website, you have sketched out a webpage wireframe. Recall that a wireframe depicts the layout of a webpage, including its major content areas. Forward Fitness Club wants to promote its brand by including its logo, so each page will contain a designated area called the header for the logo. The header is located at the top of a webpage and identifies the site, often by displaying the business name or logo. For easy navigation, each page also will have a horizontal list of links to the other pages in the site. These page links will appear below the header in the navigation area. An image banner below the navigation area will display a fitness image. The primary page content, or the main content area, will follow the image banner and will contain information that applies to the page, including headings, paragraphs of text, and images. Lastly, the footer will be located below the primary page content and will contain copyright and contact information. Figure 2–3 shows the proposed wireframe with these major content areas.

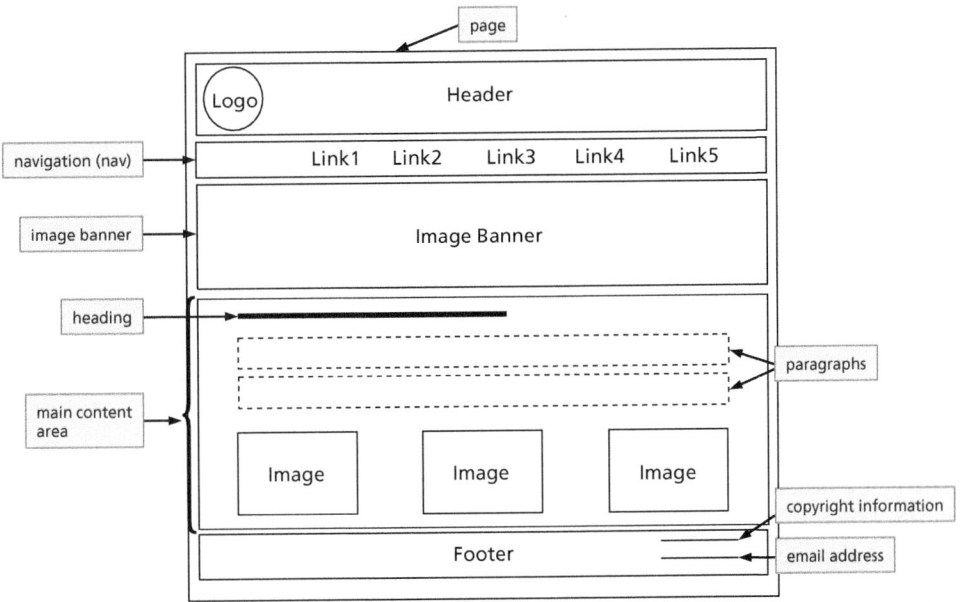

Figure 2–3

What is the difference between a site map and a wireframe?

A site map lists all the webpages in a website that a user can access. It clearly identifies the number of pages in the website and shows how each page is linked to other pages. You can create a site map as an outline in a word processing document or as an image using flowcharting or graphics software.

In contrast, a wireframe shows the visual layout of the webpage to indicate where elements should appear such as the logo, search box, navigation bar, main content, and footer. You typically use graphics software to create a wireframe.

Recall from Chapter 1 that a semantic element provides meaning about the content of the element. For example, you use the **nav** element to define the navigation area. It is a semantic element because its name reflects the purpose of its content, which is to display links to other pages so visitors can navigate the website. Semantic elements reinforce the meaning of the information provided on the webpage. A **semantic wireframe** uses semantic elements to define the structure of a webpage. The wireframe shown in Figure 2–3 uses four semantic elements to define the structure of the Forward Fitness Club webpages: **header, nav, main,** and **footer.**

File Management

Websites use several types of files, including HTML files, image files, media such as audio and video files, and CSS files, which you learn about in Chapter 4. Even a simple website might use hundreds of files. Therefore, each site must follow a systematic method to organize its files. Before you begin to create your first HTML page, start by creating a folder and subfolders to contain and organize your website files as shown in Figure 2–4.

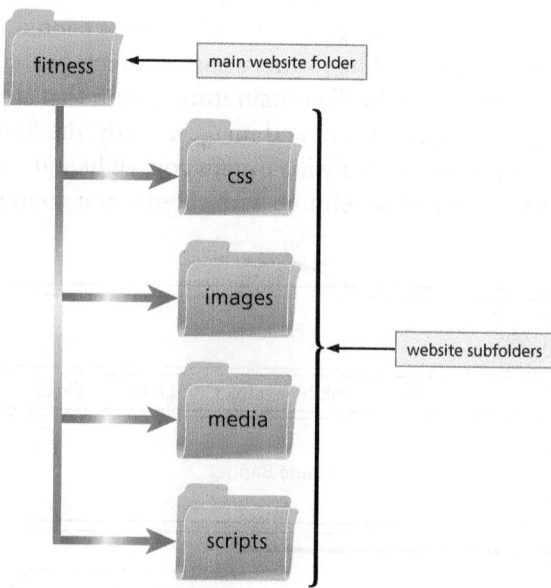

Figure 2–4

The main folder (also called the **root folder**) for the Forward Fitness Club website is the fitness folder. It contains all of the files and other folders for the website. The css folder will contain CSS files, which you create in Chapter 4 to format a webpage and its elements. The images folder will contain the Forward Fitness Club logo, photos, and other images to display on the webpages. The media folder will

contain audio and video files, which you add in Chapter 9. The scripts folder will
contain files related to JavaScript, which you add in Chapter 10.

To Create a Website Folder and Subfolders

1 CREATE WEBSITE FOLDERS | 2 CREATE TEMPLATE | 3 ENTER HTML 5 SEMANTIC ELEMENTS |
4 ADD COMMENTS & CONTENT | 5 VALIDATE DOCUMENT | 6 CREATE & VIEW HOME PAGE

The following steps, which assume Windows 10 is running, create a folder and subfolders for the fitness
website. *Why? Before you can create a website, you should create a folder for the website files.* You may need to ask your
instructor whether you should create the website folder on a portable storage device, such as a USB flash drive.

1

- Tap or click the File Explorer app button on the taskbar to display the File Explorer window.

- Navigate to the desired location for the website folder, such as the Documents folder or your USB flash drive, to prepare to create a new folder.

- Tap or click the New folder button on the Quick Access toolbar to create a new folder.

- Type `fitness` and then press the ENTER key to name the folder (Figure 2–5).

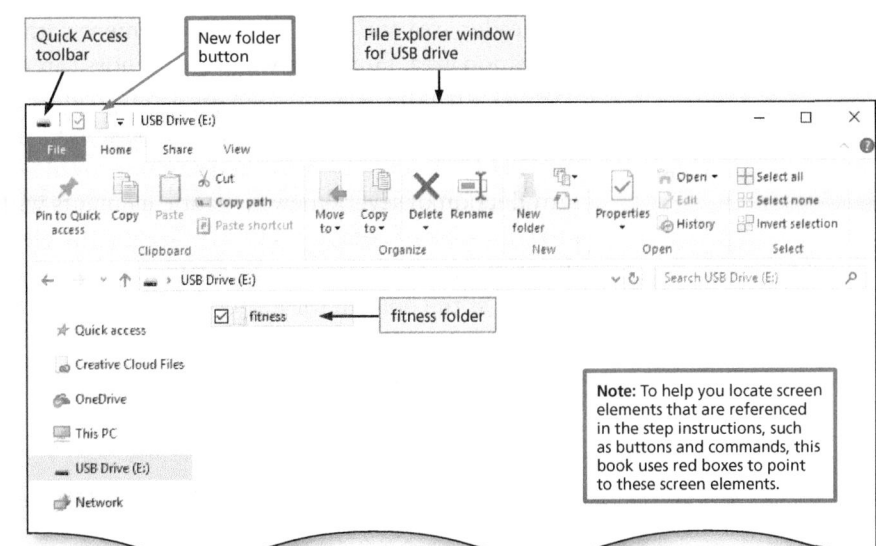

Figure 2–5

2

- Double-tap or double-click the fitness folder to open it.

- Tap or click the New folder button on the Quick Access toolbar to create a new folder.

- Name the new folder `css`.
- Tap or click the New folder button on the Quick Access toolbar to create a new folder.

- Name the new folder `images`.
- Tap or click the New folder button on the Quick Access toolbar to create a new folder.

- Name the new folder `media`.

- Tap or click the New folder button on the Quick Access toolbar to create a new folder.

- Name the new folder `scripts` (Figure 2–6).

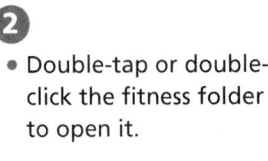
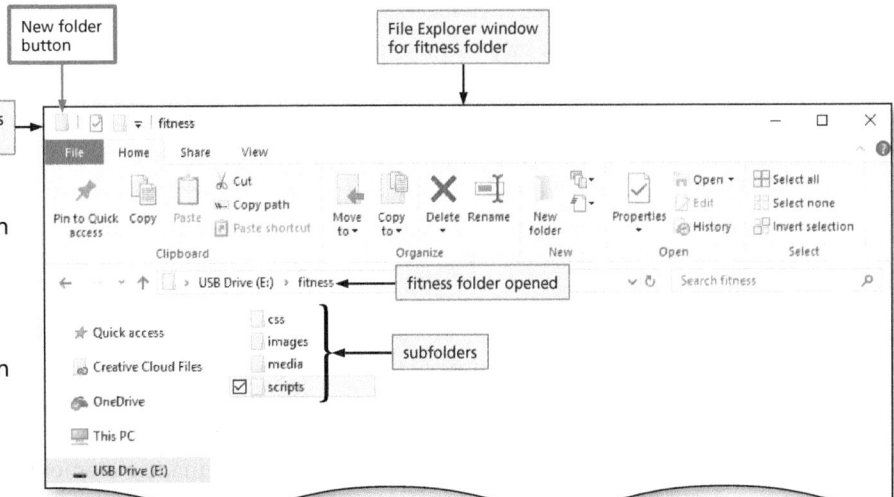

Figure 2–6

Other Ways		
1 Tap or click New folder button (Home tab | New group)	2 Press CTRL+SHIFT+N	3 Press and hold or right-click blank spot in window, tap or click New, tap or click Folder

Using HTML 5 Semantic Elements

As you learned in Chapter 1, you begin a new HTML document by adding the basic required HTML elements to it, such as the **DOCTYPE, html, head,** and **body** elements. Within the **body** element, you next add HTML elements that define the structure of the page. HTML 4.01 introduced the **div** element (with the <div> and </div> tags) to divide a page into separate sections. Each **div** element usually has a unique id attribute to distinguish it from other **div** elements on the page. For example, you might use a **div** element with an id attribute named header for the header area and another **div** element with an id attribute named nav for the navigation area. However, webpage authors can use any name they like to define a **div** id attribute, leading to inconsistency among naming conventions for websites. You will learn more about the div element in Chapter 3.

HTML 5 has transformed and improved website development with the introduction of several new semantic elements with standardized names. Table 2–2 provides a list of common HTML 5 semantic elements. The name of each tag reflects the purpose of the element. For instance, you use the **footer** element to display content at the bottom (or footer) of the webpage. You use the **nav** element to identify the navigation area of a webpage. Because many of the semantic elements help to structure the layout of the page, they are also called structural elements or layout elements.

Table 2–2 HTML 5 Semantic Elements	
Element	**Description**
<header>...</header>	Indicates the header information on the webpage. Header content typically consists of a business name or logo and is commonly positioned immediately after the opening <body> tag.
<nav>...</nav>	Indicates the start and end of a navigation area within the webpage. The **nav** element contains hyperlinks to other webpages within a website and is commonly positioned immediately after the closing </header> tag.
<main>...</main>	Indicates the start and end of the main content area of a webpage. Contains the primary content of the webpage. Only one main element can appear on a page.
<footer>...</footer>	Indicates the start and end of the footer area of a webpage. Contains the footer content of the webpage.
<section>...</section>	Indicates the start and end of a section area of a webpage. Contains a specific grouping of content on the webpage.
<article>...</article>	Indicates the start and end of an article area of a webpage. Contains content such as forum or blog posts.
<aside>...</aside>	Indicates the start and end of an aside area of a webpage. Contains information about nearby content and is typically displayed as a sidebar.

Professional web designers debate whether to use the **div** element or the **main** element to define the main content area of a webpage. Those who favor the **div** element argue that it has widespread browser support. The W3C introduced the **main** element after other semantic elements, and not all browsers or text editors recognize it yet.

Web designers who favor the **main** element do so because **main** is a semantic element while **div** is not. In other words, the name of the **main** element describes its purpose and function. The **div** element relies on its id attribute to provide meaning.

After discussing the pros and cons of the **main** and **div** elements with the owner of the Forward Fitness Club, you decide to use the **main** element for the fitness website. Because it is a new site that does not have to incorporate webpages created with earlier versions of HTML, it will use the new HTML 5 semantic elements, including **header, nav, main,** and **footer,** to lay out the webpages. Although the **div** element achieves the same results in layout, the future of web development includes using the new HTML 5 layout tags, and Forward Fitness wants to create a foundation for this future. Using the semantic HTML 5 elements standardizes naming conventions, making webpages more universal, accessible, and meaningful to search engines.

How can I find out whether my browser supports the new HTML 5 elements?
Most major browsers have embraced several of the new HTML 5 semantic tags. To know whether your preferred browser supports specific tags, visit caniuse.com and enter the name of the semantic element. The site lists the browsers and versions that support the element you entered. This site also provides information about the global usage of major browsers and their share of the market. Currently, the main element is not fully supported by Internet Explorer 11 or earlier.

Another good resource for up-to-date information on HTML 5 is w3schools.com. This site provides a list of HTML elements that are supported in HTML 5. The website also includes a "Try it Yourself" feature, which acts as an online code editor.

Header Element

The **header** element structurally defines the header area of a webpage. The **header** element starts with a <header> tag and ends with a </header> tag. Content placed between these tags appears on the webpage as part of the **header** element. Web designers often place a business name or logo within the **header** element.

Nav Element

The nav element structurally defines the navigation area of a webpage. The **nav** element starts with a <nav> tag and ends with a </nav> tag. The **nav** element usually includes links to other pages within the website.

Main Element

The **main** element structurally defines the **main** content area of a webpage. The main element starts with a <main> tag and ends with a </main> tag. Each page can have only one **main** element because its content should be unique to each page. At the time this book was written, all current major browsers supported the **main** element, with the exception of Internet Explorer 11 and earlier versions. While Internet Explorer 11 will display content within the **main** element, it does not fully support the element. For example, Internet Explorer 11 might not correctly display formatting applied to the **main** element.

Footer Element

The **footer** element structurally defines the bottom, or footer area, of a webpage. The footer element starts with a <footer> tag and ends with a </footer> tag. Common content found within a webpage footer includes copyright information, contact information, social media links, and policy links.

Figure 2–7 identifies the relationship between a coded webpage template with **header, nav, main,** and **footer** elements and the conceptual wireframe design of a webpage.

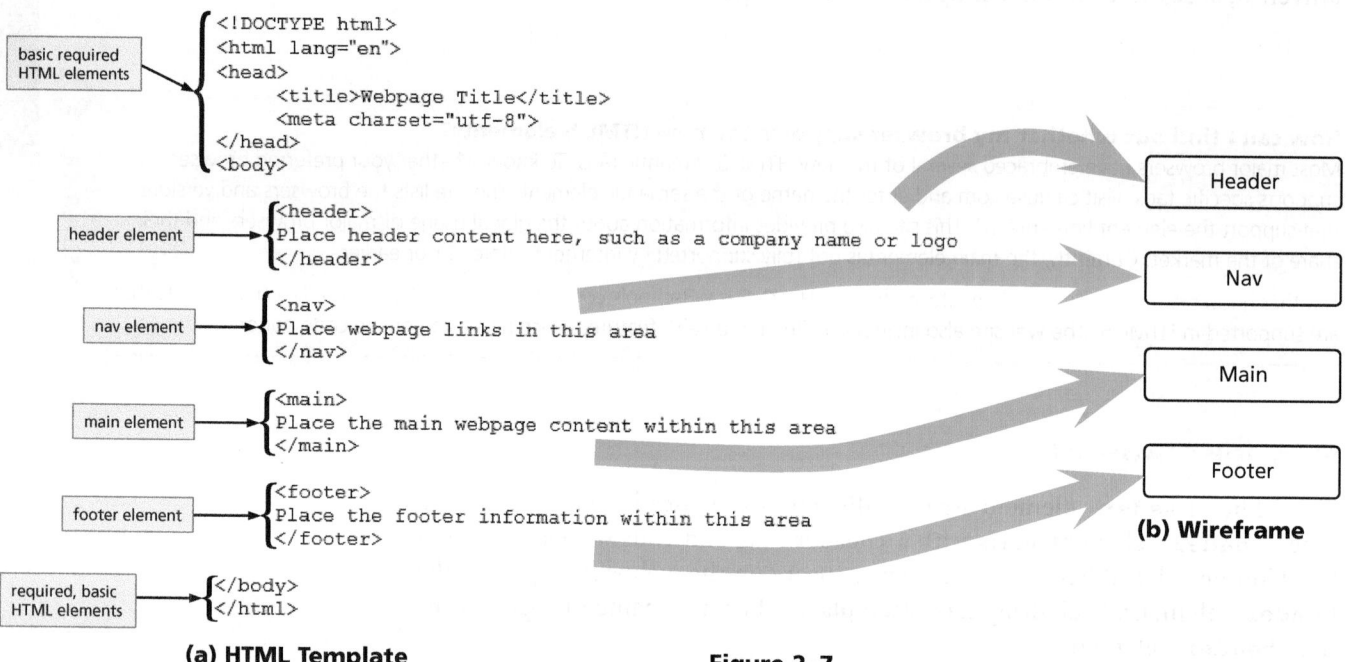

(a) HTML Template

Figure 2–7

Creating a Webpage Template

A hallmark of a well-designed website is that its webpages have the same look and feel. In other words, most pages have the same layout and all the pages share the same color scheme, typography, and style of graphics. In addition, elements work the same way on each page. For example, the navigation bar appears in the same position on each page and uses the same colors, fonts, and font styles. Visitors select a link on the navigation bar the same way, such as by tapping or clicking a page name. The selected link then appears in a contrasting color.

To make sure the webpages in a site share a standard layout, you can create a template, an HTML document that contains elements that should appear on each page. Instead of creating a webpage from scratch, open the template document in a text editor and save it using the name of the new webpage. You can then concentrate on adding content for that particular page rather than re-creating the basic required HTML elements and the structural elements.

For the fitness website, you will create a template that includes the basic required HTML elements (the DOCTYPE declaration and the **html, head, title, meta,** and **body** elements) and the four HTML structural, semantic elements identified in the webpage wireframe shown in Figure 2–3: **header, nav, main,** and **footer.**

BTW

Saving Your Work
It is a good idea to save your HTML file periodically as you are working to avoid the risk of losing your work.

To Create a Webpage Template Document

To create a webpage template, you create an HTML document with the HTML elements that define the webpage structure. Use your preferred text editor to create the template or ask your instructor which text editor to use. The following steps create a basic webpage template.

1
- Open your text editor, tap or click File on the menu bar, and then tap or click New if you need to open a new blank document.
- Tap or click File on the menu bar and then tap or click Save As to display the Save As dialog box.
- Navigate to your fitness folder and then double-tap or double-click it to open it.
- In the File name box, type **template** to name the file.

Q&A | Why is the new file named template instead of index?
Template is the name of the template file you use to create webpages for this website. Use index as the file name for the home page.

- Tap or click the Save as type button and then tap or click Hyper Text Markup Language to select the file format.
- Tap or click the Save button to save the template in the fitness folder.
- On Line 1 of the text editor, type **<!DOCTYPE html>** to define a new HTML 5 document (Figure 2–8).

Q&A | Why does the <!DOCTYPE html> text appear in bold and red in Figure 2–8?
Throughout the book, the new text you add to a file in the current step is shown in bold and red in the accompanying figure.

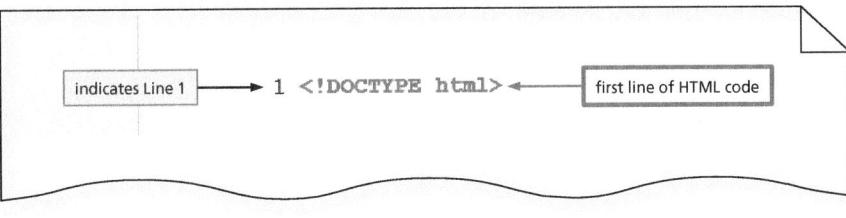

Figure 2–8

2
- Press the ENTER key to add Line 2 and then type **<html lang="en">** to add a starting <html> tag that defines the language as English.

- Press the ENTER key to add Line 3 and then type **<head>** to add a starting <head> tag (Figure 2–9).

Figure 2–9

3
- Add the following HTML elements, also shown in bold and red in Figure 2–10, to complete the template, using the SPACEBAR or TAB key to indent Lines 4 and 5 and using the SHIFT+TAB keys to stop indenting.

```
<title></title>
<meta charset="utf-8">
</head>
<body>
</body>
</html>
```

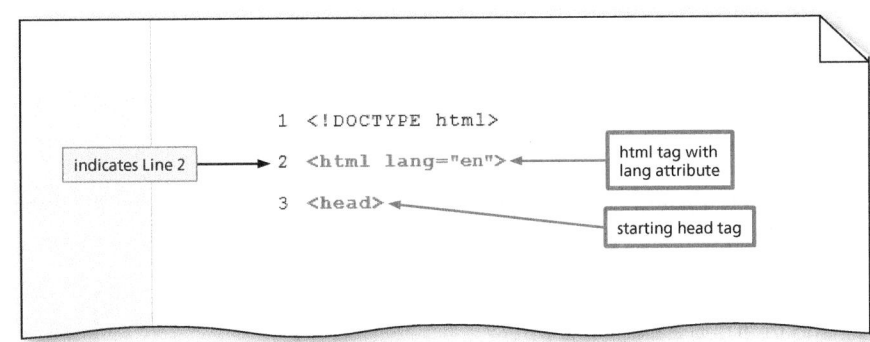

Figure 2–10

4
- Save your changes.

To Add HTML 5 Semantic Elements to a Webpage Template

The wireframe in Figure 2–3 defines four areas to display content for the website. To define these content areas, insert the following HTML 5 elements between the <body> and </body> tags: <header> </header>, <nav> </nav>, <main> </main>, and <footer> </footer>. Recall that the HTML 5 **header** element defines the header area of the webpage. The **nav** element defines the navigation area of the webpage. The **main** element defines the primary content area of the webpage. The **footer** element defines the footer area of the webpage. The following steps insert HTML 5 structural elements within the body tags.

- Place your insertion point after the beginning <body> tag and press the ENTER key twice to insert new Lines 8 and 9.

- On Line 9, press the TAB key and then type **<header>** to add a starting header tag.

- Press the ENTER key to insert a new Line 10 and then type **</header>** to add an ending header tag (Figure 2–11).

Q&A Why is Line 8 blank?
Line 8 is intentionally left blank to improve readability. As you add more HTML elements to a page, including white space helps to clearly identify the areas of a page. Using blank lines between HTML elements is a good design practice.

Will the blank line be noticeable when the page is displayed in a browser?
No. Browsers ignore blank lines when interpreting the code on the page.

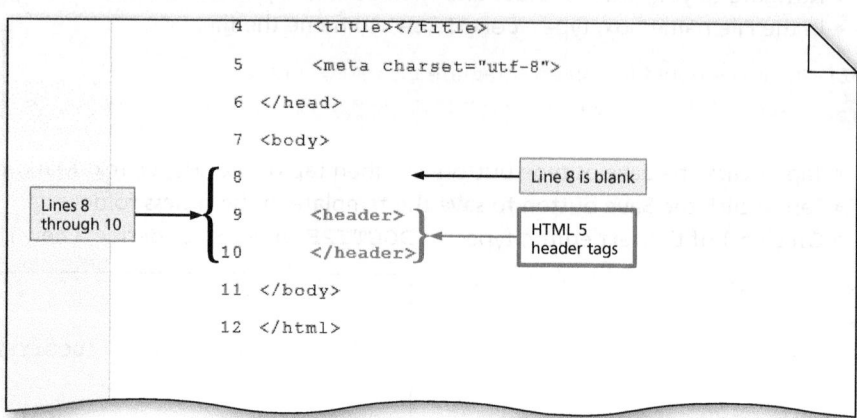

Figure 2–11

2

- Add the following HTML 5 tags, also shown in bold and red in Figure 2–12, to complete the wireframe, indenting each line and inserting a blank line after each ending tag.

<nav>
</nav>
(blank line)
<main>
</main>
(blank line)
<footer>
</footer>

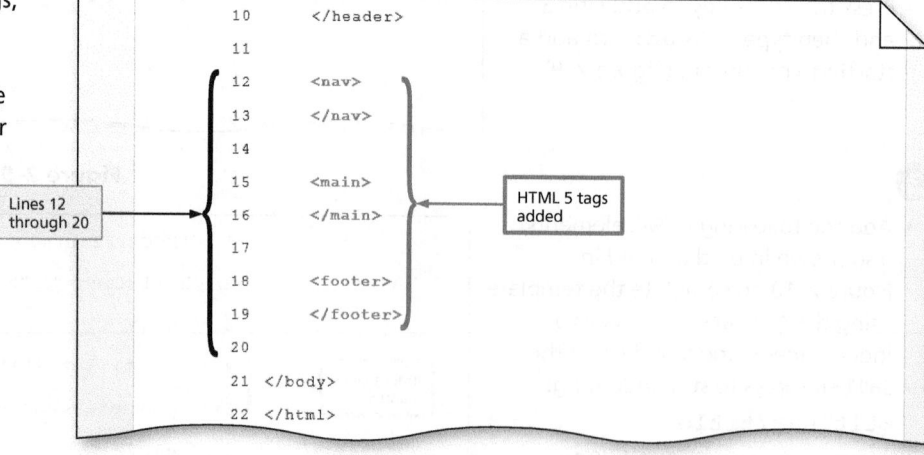

Figure 2–12

3

- Save your changes.

To Add a Title to a Webpage Template

Recall that when a webpage is displayed in a browser, the browser tab displays the document title. To add a document title, type the title text between the starting and ending title tags. The following step adds a webpage title to a template.

- Place your insertion point after the beginning <title> tag and type **Forward Fitness Club** to add a webpage title.

- Save your changes and then view the page in a browser to display the webpage title (Figure 2–13).

Q&A

How do I display the webpage in a browser?

Recall from Chapter 1 that you can use a command in your HTML text editor to display a webpage. For example, in Notepad++, you can tap or click Run on the menu bar and then tap or click Launch in Chrome.

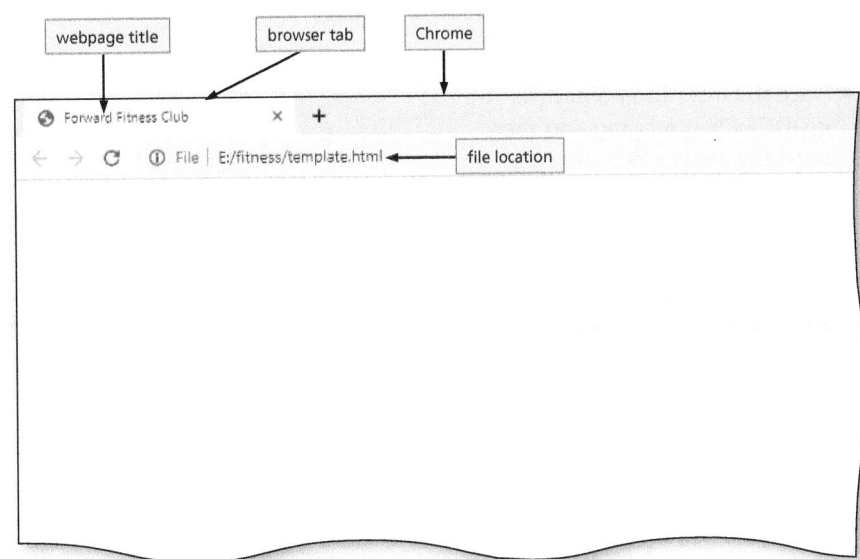

Figure 2–13

Why is the webpage blank when displayed in a browser?

You are creating a webpage template that will be used to create pages for the website. The subsequent webpages will contain content, but you have not added any content yet.

Comments

As you create a webpage template, include comments about the HTML elements you use to define the areas within the webpage. Comments can provide additional information about these areas and the type of information they include, which is especially helpful if you stop working on a partially completed page and then return to it later. Add a comment before a tag using the following syntax:

```
<!-- Place your comment here -->
```

The comment syntax uses the angle brackets, similar to the HTML tags. The next character is an exclamation mark followed by two dashes (--). Add the comment text after the first set of dashes. For example, you use comments to give instructions on how to use the template or to identify the author of the website. Close the comment by adding two dashes, followed by a closing angle bracket. One comment can extend over multiple lines, as shown in the following example:

```
<!-- Student Name
     File Name
     Date
-->
```

If you are using Notepad++, the text you enter scrolls continuously to the right unless you turn on the word wrap feature. **Word wrap** causes text lines to break at the right edge of the window and appear on a new line, so all entered text is visible in the Notepad++ window. When word wrap is enabled, a paragraph of text is assigned a single logical line number even though it may appear to be displayed on multiple physical lines in Notepad++. Word wrap does not affect the way text prints.

BTW
Auto-Fill and Highlighting Features
If you are using Notepad++ or Brackets, you can use the auto-fill feature by starting to type the name of a tag and letting the text editor complete the tag for you. If you are using Notepad++, tap or click the starting <body> tag to highlight the starting and ending tags so you can easily identify them.

BTW
Turning on Word Wrap
To turn on word wrap in Notepad++, select View on the menu bar and then select Word wrap.

To Add Comments to a Webpage Template

When you create a webpage template, including comments provides additional information about how to use the sections of the webpage. You can also use a comment to identify that you are the author of the webpage. *Why? When creating a new webpage from a template, comments provide insight on the type of information to include.* The following steps add comments to a webpage template.

1

- Place the insertion point after the <!DOCTYPE html> tag and then press the ENTER key to insert a new Line 2.

- Type <!-- This website template was created by: *Student's First Name Student's Last Name* --> on Line 2 to add a comment at the beginning of the document that identifies the author (Figure 2–14).

Q&A Should I type "Student's First Name Student's Last Name"?
No. Type your first and last names to identify yourself as the author of the template.

My comment is shown on two lines. Is that okay?
Yes. If your text editor is using word wrap and your document window is not maximized, your comment might wrap to the next line. Note, however, that it is still numbered as Line 2.

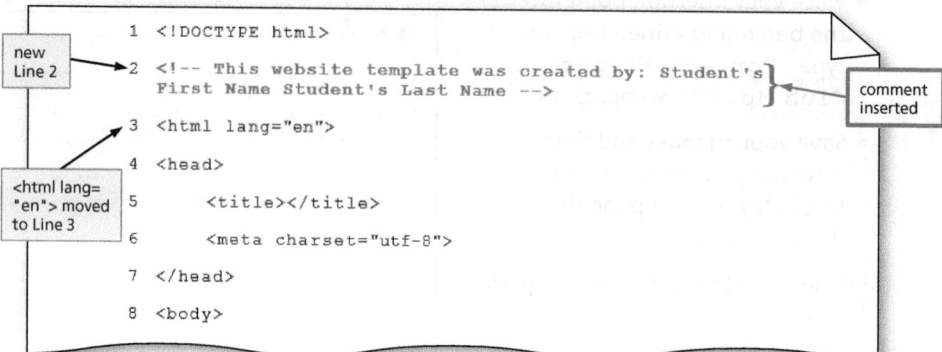

Figure 2–14

2

- Place the insertion point on the blank Line 9 and press the ENTER key to insert a new Line 10.

- On Line 10, press the TAB key and then type <!-- Use the header area for the website name or logo --> to add a comment identifying the type of information to include in the header area (Figure 2–15).

Q&A Do the blank lines affect the HTML elements?
No. inserting blank lines before or after HTML elements does not affect the structure of the webpage.

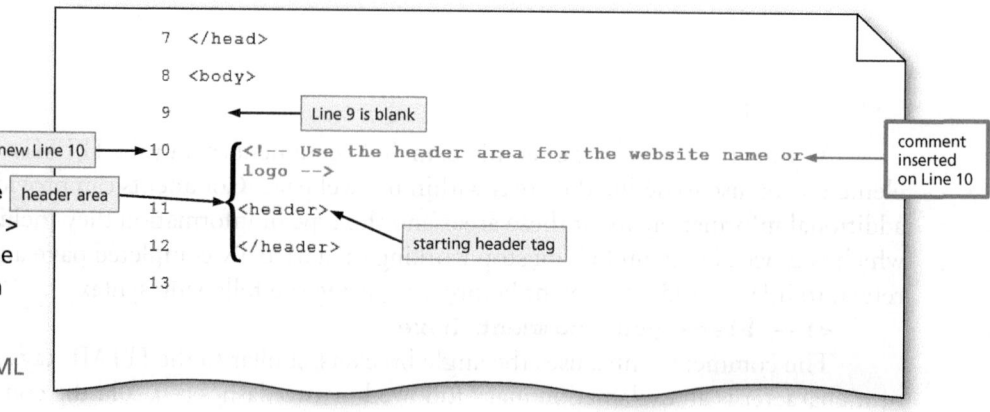

Figure 2–15

3

- Place the insertion point on the blank Line 13 and press the ENTER key to insert a new Line 14.

- On Line 14, type <!-- Use the nav area to add hyperlinks to other pages within the website --> to add a comment above the navigation area (Figure 2–16).

Figure 2–16

4

- Place the insertion point on the blank Line 17 and press the ENTER key to insert a new Line 18.

- On Line 18, type `<!-- Use the main area to add the main content of the webpage -->` to add a comment above the main area.

- Place the insertion point on the blank Line 21 and press the ENTER key to insert a new Line 22.

- On Line 22, type `<!-- Use the footer area to add webpage footer content -->` to add a comment above the footer area (Figure 2–17).

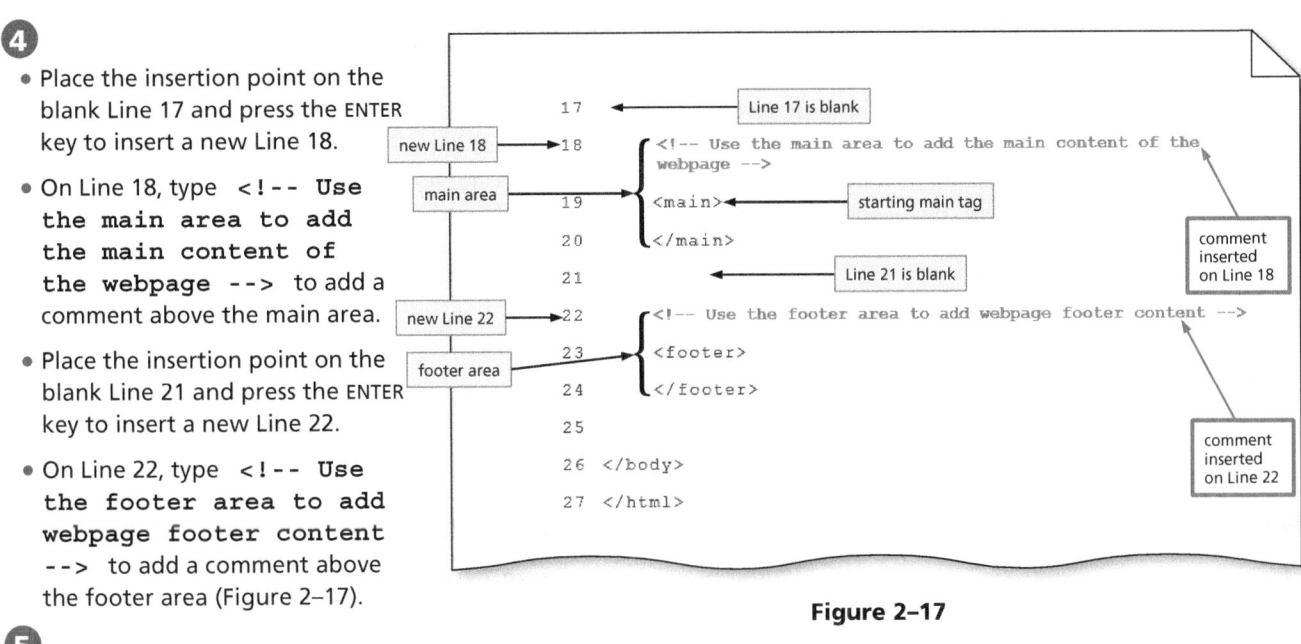

```
17                    Line 17 is blank
new Line 18    18   <!-- Use the main area to add the main content of the
                    webpage -->
main area      19   <main>          starting main tag
               20   </main>                              comment
               21                    Line 21 is blank    inserted
new Line 22    22   <!-- Use the footer area to add webpage footer content -->
footer area    23   <footer>
               24   </footer>
               25                                        comment
               26   </body>                             inserted
               27   </html>                             on Line 22
```

Figure 2–17

5

- Save your changes.

Break Point: If you want to take a break, this is a good place to do so. You can exit the text editor now. To resume at a later time, run your text editor, open the file called template.html, and continue following the steps from this location forward.

Heading Elements

You use **heading elements** to provide a title or heading before a paragraph of text or section of a page. Headings indicate that a new topic is starting and typically identify or summarize the topic. On a webpage, headings appear in a larger font size than normal text, making it easy for users to quickly scan the page and identify its sections. Figure 2–18 shows examples of heading elements on Intel's website. The text in blue, Desktops, Laptops, and Intel® Compute Stick, are all examples of heading elements.

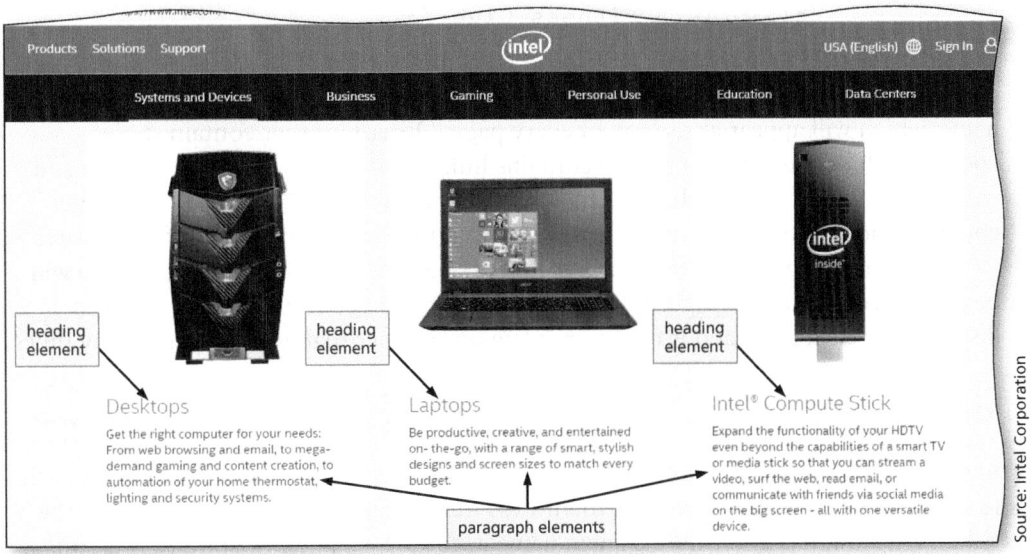

Source: Intel Corporation

Figure 2–18

Heading sizes, or levels, run from 1 (the largest) to 6 (the smallest). Heading level 1 is designed to mark major headings, while heading levels 2 to 6 are for subheadings. The start tag for heading level 1 is <h1> and the end tag is </h1>. The start tag for heading level 2 is <h2>, the end tag is </h2>, and so on. Figure 2–19 displays the size differences among heading levels 1 through 6. In the upcoming steps, you insert a heading element with the header element on the template file for the fitness website.

Example of Heading 1

Example of Heading 2

Example of Heading 3

Example of Heading 4

Example of Heading 5

Example of Heading 6

Figure 2–19

What is the difference between a head element, a header element, and a heading element, and how do I know when to use them?
Recall from Chapter 1 that the *head element* is a required element for an HTML webpage and belongs near the top of the page. A head element is defined by <head> and </head> tags and contains information about the webpage, such as the webpage title and defined character set, not website content. A *header element* is a set of HTML 5 tags (<header> and </header>) that define the header area of a webpage and generally come after the starting <body> tag. Header elements contain webpage content, such as a business name or logo. A *heading element*, h1, h2, h3, h4, h5, or h6, defines headings within a webpage and is generally placed above other webpage content. Heading elements also contain webpage content. A heading element can appear in a header element, a main element, or other HTML elements. A heading level 1 element is defined by <h1> and </h1> tags.

Webpage Content

BTW

Wrapping Content
Inserting text between tags, as in <h1>Spring Courses</h1>, is referred to as "wrapping" because the text, Spring Courses, is wrapped between heading 1 tags.

After inserting the HTML tags and comments for a webpage template, add static content or content that will appear on every webpage, such as the business name or logo, the webpage links, and the footer information. Content is the text or other item that is displayed in a browser. Place content between the starting and ending tags. Following is an example of content added between header tags:

```
<header>
        <h1>Forward Fitness Club</h1>
</header>
```

For the Forward Fitness Club website, the header area contains the business name, which will appear at the top of every page. Other tags that contain static content include the nav area, which contains links to all pages within the website and will remain the same on each page. In addition, the footer area, which contains the copyright notice and an email address, will remain the same throughout the website.

Adding static content to a template saves time. Remember that the template will be used to create the webpages for the website. Because this content is meant to be displayed on each page, add it to the template once rather than to each page many times.

To Add Content to the Header Section

1 CREATE WEBSITE FOLDERS | 2 CREATE TEMPLATE | 3 ENTER HTML 5 SEMANTIC ELEMENTS
4 ADD COMMENTS & CONTENT | 5 VALIDATE DOCUMENT | 6 CREATE & VIEW HOME PAGE

Now that the webpage template structure is complete, you can add static content that will appear on each webpage within the website. The header of each webpage in the fitness website should display the name of the business, Forward Fitness Club. For now, you enter the business name as text. In Chapter 3, you insert an image that displays the business logo, including a graphic and the business name. The following step adds content to the header area of a webpage template.

1

- Place the insertion point after the beginning <header> tag and press the ENTER key to insert a new Line 12.

- On Line 12, press the TAB key and then type **<h1>Forward Fitness Club</h1>** to add the business name to the webpage template (Figure 2–20).

Q&A Do I have to place the content on the line between the beginning and ending <header> tags?
No. This HTML element can also be written on one line as <header><h1>Forward Fitness Club</h1></header>. In this step, you placed the header content on a separate line for improved readability.

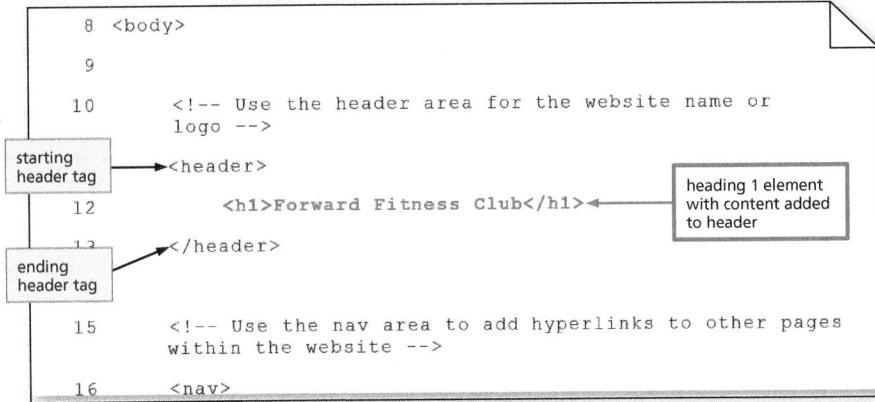

Figure 2–20

Using Symbol Entities

When adding content to a webpage, you often need to insert symbols or characters, such as a copyright symbol, ©. Some symbols such as less than (<) or greater than (>) are reserved for other uses, such as signifying the start and end of HTML tags. Other symbols such as © or € are not included on standard keyboards. Rather than inserting reserved symbols directly or avoiding other special symbols, you can insert a symbol on an HTML webpage by typing its HTML entity name or entity number. Inserting an **HTML character entity** in the code displays a reserved HTML character on the webpage. All character entities start with an ampersand (&) and end with a semicolon (;) to signal to the browser that everything in between is an entity representing a symbol. An **entity name** is an abbreviated name, and an **entity number** is a combination of the pound sign (#) and a numeric code. For example, the entity name for the copyright symbol is **©** and the entity number for the copyright symbol is **©** You can use either an entity's name or number in your HTML code. An entity name is easier to remember than an entity number, though more browsers support entity numbers than names.

Table 2–3 lists common symbols along with their entity names and numbers.

Table 2–3 Common Symbol Entities			
Character	**Description**	**Entity Name**	**Entity Number**
©	Copyright symbol	&copy;	&#169;
®	Registered trademark	&reg;	&#174;
€	Euro	&euro;	&#8364;
&	Ampersand	&amp;	&#38;
<	Less than	&lt;	&#60;
>	Greater than	&gt;	&#62;
	Nonbreaking space		

BTW
More Symbol Entities
For an in-depth listing of character/symbol entities, visit w3schools.com/charsets.

A commonly used character is a nonbreaking space ** ** which forces browsers to display a blank space. You can insert indents, extra spaces, and paragraph breaks to make HTML code easier to read and maintain. When a browser displays the webpage, however, it ignores this extra white space, treating multiple spaces, indents, and paragraph breaks as a single space. For example, when you press the TAB key or use the SPACEBAR to indent header tags and content in the HTML code, a browser displays the header content on the left margin of the webpage with no indent. Likewise, if you insert two spaces between the page names in the nav area, a browser removes the extra spaces when it displays the webpage so only one space appears between the page names. What can you do if you want to display the extra spaces in a browser? You use the nonbreaking space character entity as in the following code:

```
<p>Home     About Us</p>
```

Some characters only use decimal or hexadecimal entity numbers. These number codes are known as dec and hex for short. To use a dec character code, begin with an ampersand (&), followed by a number sign (#), followed by the dec number, and then end with a semicolon (;). For example, to insert a black square, you use the decimal code `&#9632;`. If you want to use a dec entity number to display a black square between navigation links, use the following code:

```
Home   &#25A0;   About us
```

To use a hex character code, begin with an ampersand (&), followed by a number sign (#), followed by a lowercase letter "x", followed by the hex number, and then end with a semicolon (;). For example, to insert a black square using a hex entity number, use `&#x25A0;`.

Today, there are hundreds of HTML character symbols, ranging from currency and math operators, to emojis. Table 2–4 lists some characters and their dec and hex numbers.

Table 2–4			
Character	**Description**	**Dec Number**	**Hex Number**
№	Numero sign	&#8470;	&#x2116;
■	Full block	&#9608;	&#x2588;
▢	White rectangle	&#9645;	&#x25AD;
◆	Black diamond	&#9670;	&#x25C6;
☕	Coffee cup	&#9749;	&#x2615;
★	Black star	&#9733;	&#x2605;

What is the purpose of the UTF-8 character set?

Computers can read many types of character sets. The Unicode Consortium developed Unicode Transformation Format (UTF)-8 to create a standard character set. The UTF-8 has been widely accepted and is the preferred character set for several types of web programming languages, such as HTML, JavaScript, and XML.

CONSIDER THIS

To Add Text and Nonbreaking Spaces to the Nav Section

1 CREATE WEBSITE FOLDERS | 2 CREATE TEMPLATE | 3 ENTER HTML 5 SEMANTIC ELEMENTS

4 ADD COMMENTS & CONTENT | 5 VALIDATE DOCUMENT | 6 CREATE & VIEW HOME PAGE

Next, between the beginning and ending nav tags, add a paragraph element with the name of the links to the other pages. *Why? The nav area is designed to contain hyperlinks to other pages within the website.* To insert two spaces between each page name, use the nonbreaking space character entity ` `. The following steps add content to the nav area of a webpage template.

- Place the insertion point after the beginning `<nav>` tag and press the ENTER key to insert a new Line 17.

- On Line 17, press the TAB key and then type `<p>Home` to add the first webpage link name.

- Press the SPACEBAR once and then type `  &#9475;  ` to add a nonbreaking space, a vertical line, and another nonbreaking space (Figure 2–21).

Q&A Should I insert a closing paragraph tag, </p>, at the end of Line 17?
No. You will first add more content, and then add the closing paragraph tag in Step 3.

What symbol is inserted with entity number 9475?
The name for the character with the dec number 9475 is Box Drawings Heavy Vertical, which is a vertical line.

Why am I adding a nonbreaking space, followed by a vertical line, followed by another nonbreaking space?
The purpose of adding these entities is to provide space and a character between each navigation link. Separating the links provides clear navigation. Otherwise, the words would be very close together.

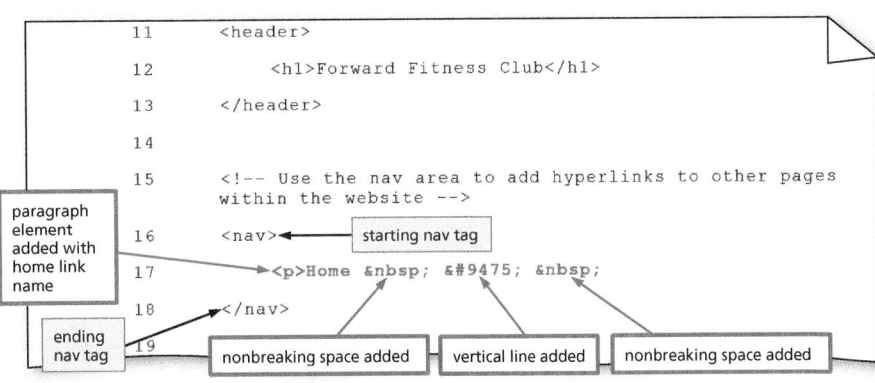

Figure 2–21

2

- Press the ENTER key to insert a new Line 18.
- On Line 18, type **About Us** to add the second webpage link name.
- Press the SPACEBAR once and then type ** ┃ ** to add a nonbreaking space, a vertical line, and another nonbreaking space (Figure 2–22).

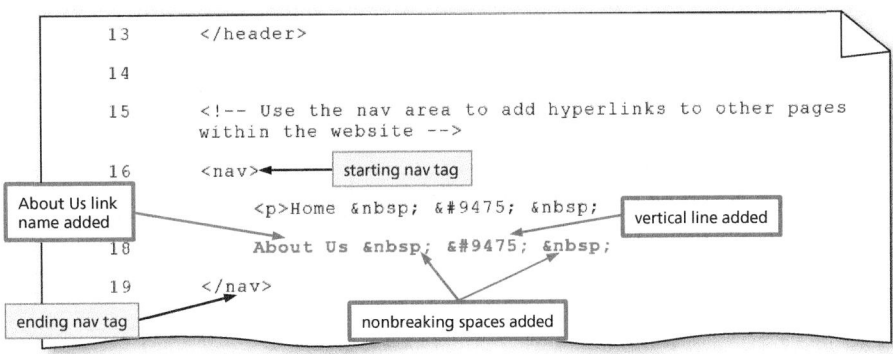

Figure 2–22

3

- Press the ENTER key to insert a new Line 19, type **Classes** to add the third webpage link name, press the SPACEBAR, and then type ** ┃ ** to add a nonbreaking space, a vertical line, and another nonbreaking space.
- Press the ENTER key to insert a new Line 20, type **Nutrition** to add the fourth webpage link name, press the SPACEBAR, and then type ** ┃ ** to add a nonbreaking space, a vertical line, and another nonbreaking space.

```
13      </header>
14
15      <!-- Use the nav area to add hyperlinks to other pages
        within the website -->
16      <nav>
17          <p>Home   &#9475;  
18          About Us   &#9475;  
19          Classes   &#9475;  
20          Nutrition   &#9475;  
21          Contact Us</p>
22      </nav>
```

starting nav tag
ending nav tag
page link names and characters added
closing paragraph tag

Figure 2–23

- Press the ENTER key to insert a new Line 21 and then type **Contact Us</p>** to add the fifth webpage link name (Figure 2–23).

4

- Save your changes.

To Add Content and a Symbol to the Footer Section

The footer section of the website contains a copyright symbol and an email address. *Why? Legal notices and contact information usually appear in the footer of a webpage. You add this content to the footer in the template file so that the content appears on all webpages in the website.* The following steps add content to the footer area of a webpage template.

1

- Place the insertion point after the beginning <footer> tag and press the ENTER key to insert a new Line 30.

- On Line 30, press the TAB key and then type `<p>&copy; Copyright 2021. All Rights Reserved.</p>` to add a paragraph element with the copyright symbol and additional copyright information.

- Press the ENTER key to insert a new Line 31 and then type `<p>forwardfitness@club.net</p>` to add a paragraph element with an email address to the footer section (Figure 2–24).

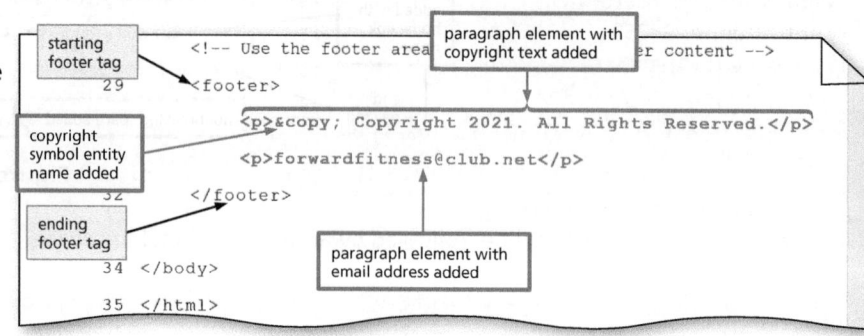

Figure 2–24

2

- Save your changes and then view the page in a browser to display the webpage template (Figure 2–25).

Q&A Why are the header, nav, and footer content areas so close to each other?
To format these areas and add space between each area, you use CSS styles, which you define in Chapter 4.

Where is the main area?
The main area is located after the navigation area and before the footer. Because the main area does not currently have any content, it is not displayed in the browser.

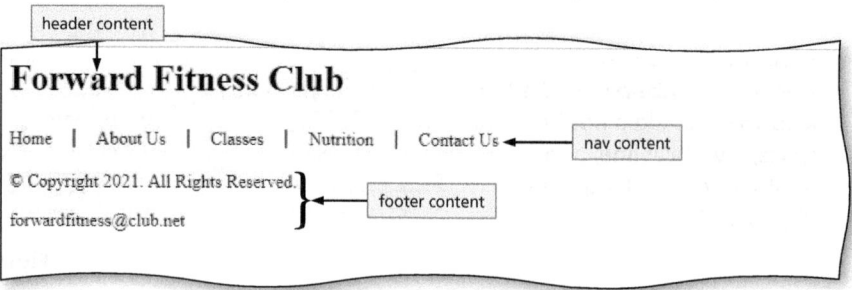

Figure 2–25

Validating HTML Documents

BTW
Common Validation Errors
Common validation errors include not spelling tags or attributes correctly and using uppercase letters (except for DOCTYPE). A single coding error can cause many lines of errors during validation.

After creating an HTML file, you **validate** the document to verify the validity of the HTML code. When you validate an HTML document, you confirm that all of the code is correct and follows the established rules set by the W3C, the organization that sets the standards for HTML. The W3C recommends validating all HTML documents and making validation part of your webpage testing.

Many validation services are available on the web; you can use any of them to make sure that your HTML code follows standards and is free of errors. Some check only for errors, while others flag errors and suggest how to correct them. The W3C has a free online validator that checks for errors, indicates where they are located, and suggests corrections. Keep in mind that a validator looks for coding errors; it cannot make sure that browsers will display the webpage as you intend. To test the design of a webpage, you must display it in all of the popular browsers.

This book uses the online W3C Markup Validation Service (validator.w3.org). This validator checks the markup validity of web documents in HTML and XHTML, along with some other markup languages. The validator scans the DOCTYPE statement to see which version of HTML or XHTML you are using, and then checks to see if the code is valid for that version. You **upload** your HTML file to the validator, which means you transfer a copy of the document to the validation website. The validator reviews each line of code and locates any errors.

If the validator detects an error in your HTML code, it displays a warning such as "Errors found while checking this document as HTML 5!" The W3C validator displays this warning in red in the header bar. A Result line below the header bar shows the number of errors in the document. You can scroll down the page or tap or click the Jump To: Validation Output link to see detailed comments on each error.

BTW
Byte-Order Mark (BOM) Warning
In a common result, the validator finds a BOM in a file encoded for UTF-8. This is a warning rather than an error and does not need to be corrected. However, you can adjust the preferences in your text editor to use UTF-8 without BOM to avoid this warning.

To Validate the Webpage Template

1 CREATE WEBSITE FOLDERS | 2 CREATE TEMPLATE | 3 ENTER HTML 5 SEMANTIC ELEMENTS
4 ADD COMMENTS & CONTENT | **5 VALIDATE DOCUMENT** | **6 CREATE & VIEW HOME PAGE**

Before you use the webpage template to create the necessary webpages for the fitness website, run the template through the W3C validator to check the document for errors. *Why? If the document has any errors, validating gives you a chance to identify and correct them before using the template to create a webpage.* The following steps validate an HTML document.

1

• Open your browser and type **https:// validator .w3.org/** in the address bar to display the W3C Markup Validation Service page.

• Tap or click the Validate by File Upload tab to display the Validate by File Upload information.

• Tap or click the Choose File button to display the Open dialog box.

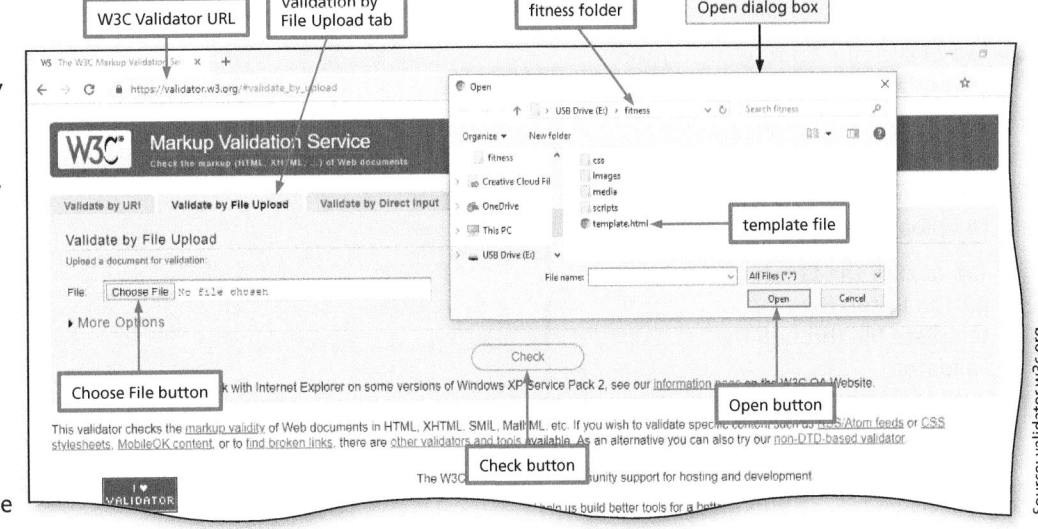

Figure 2–26

Q&A I do not see a Choose File button, but I do have a Browse button. Should I select the Browse button instead?
Yes. The button names and other options may vary slightly depending on your browser.

• Navigate to your fitness folder to find the template.html file (Figure 2–26).

2

• Tap or click the template.html document to select it.

• Tap or click the Open button to upload the selected file to the W3C validator.

• Tap or click the Check button to send the document through the validator and display the validation results page (Figure 2–27).

Nu Html Checker

This tool is an ongoing experiment in better HTML checking, and its behavior remains subject to change

Showing results for uploaded file template.html

Checker Input

Show ☐ source ☐ outline ☐ image report [Options...]

Check by [file upload ▼] [Choose File] No file chosen
Uploaded files with .xhtml or .xht extensions are parsed using the XML parser.

[Check]

Document checking completed. No errors or warnings to show. ◄———— indicates successful validation check

Used the HTML parser.
Total execution time 3 milliseconds.

About this checker • Report an issue • Version: 19.5.2

Source: validator.w3c.org

Figure 2–27

Q&A My results show errors. How do I correct them?

Scroll down the page to display the errors section. Review the errors listed below the validation output. Any line number that contains an error is shown in this section.

To Validate an HTML Document with Errors

1 CREATE WEBSITE FOLDERS | 2 CREATE TEMPLATE | 3 ENTER HTML 5 SEMANTIC ELEMENTS
4 ADD COMMENTS & CONTENT | 5 VALIDATE DOCUMENT | 6 CREATE & VIEW HOME PAGE

If the webpage template was created successfully, you should not receive any errors, but you can review what the validator provides when a document with errors is uploaded to the validator. *Why? When errors are detected on a webpage, the validator provides information about the location of the error so you can identify and correct them.* The following steps insert an error in the template document and then validate the document with the W3C validator.

1

- Return to the template document in your text editor and delete html on Line 1 to remove "html" from the DOCTYPE declaration.

- Save your changes and then return to the W3C Markup Validation Service page in your browser to display the W3C validator.

- If necessary, tap or click the Validate by File Upload tab to display the Validate by File Upload information.

- Tap or click the Choose File button to display the Open dialog box.

- Navigate to the fitness folder, select the template.html file, and then tap or click the Open button to upload the file.

- Tap or click the Check button to run the template file through the validator.

- Scroll down to display the error messages (Figure 2–28).

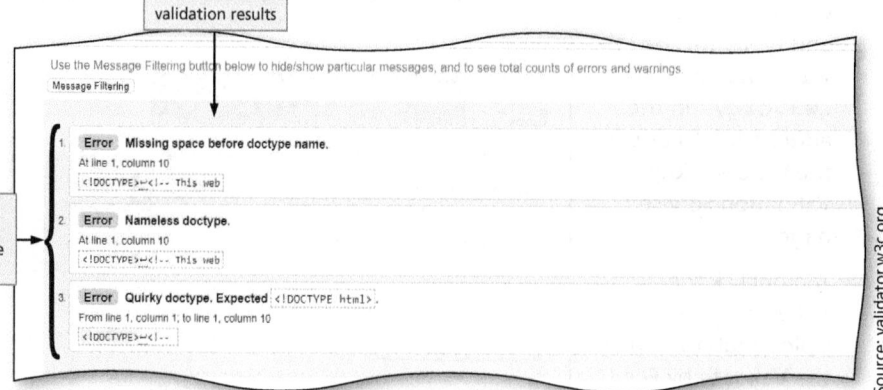

Figure 2–28

Source: validator.w3.org

2

- Scroll down to display the validation errors.

- Review the errors and note the line numbers of the errors in the document (Figure 2–29).

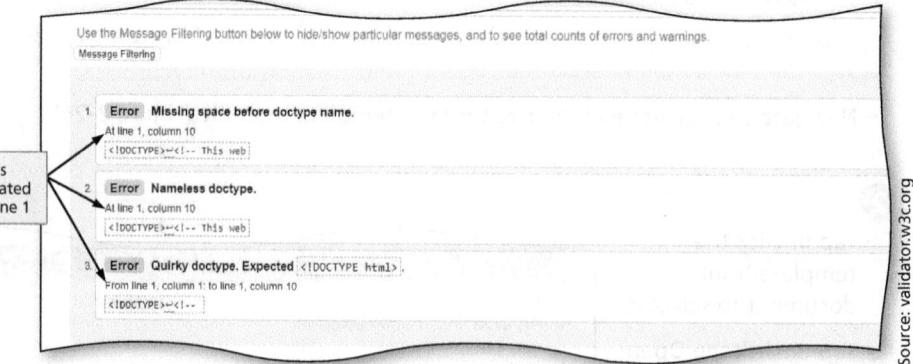

Figure 2–29

Source: validator.w3.org

3

- Return to your text editor and type `html` after the <!DOCTYPE declaration on Line 1 to correct the error.

- Save your changes and validate the document again to confirm it does not contain any errors.

Creating a Home Page Using a Webpage Template

After creating a template for a website, you can save time by using the template to create the webpages in the site. The advantage of starting with a template is that it includes content and HTML elements that appear on every page. By opening the template and then saving it with a new name that corresponds to a page on the site, you save time, ensure consistency across the website, and avoid having to re-create repeating elements such as navigation bars. In the new webpage document, you can focus on developing the parts that are unique to that page.

Now that you have created a template for the Forward Fitness Club website, use it to create the website home page. Recall from Chapter 1 that the home page of a website is usually named index.html. Website home pages use this name for a practical reason. If someone uses a browser to enter a URL that includes the site's domain but does not end with a file name, the browser looks for and displays the index.html page automatically.

When you create the Forward Fitness Club home page from a template, the page includes a document title, HTML structural elements to organize the page, the business name in the header, navigation text, and a copyright notice and business email address in the footer. To complete the home page, you add three paragraphs to the main area. The first paragraph welcomes visitors to Forward Fitness Club and restates the business mission. The second paragraph describes the facility and the benefits of becoming a member. The third paragraph provides a strong call to action, which is an offer or instruction to visitors to contact the business to take advantage of a free one-week trial membership.

To create the paragraphs in the main area, you use the paragraph (<p></p>) element, as you did in the nav area. The paragraph element has the following syntax:

```
<p>content</p>
```

Everything between the <p> and </p> tags is a single paragraph. Browsers add space before and after each paragraph element to separate paragraphs. In contrast, for a line break, browsers do not add space before and after the <br> tag.

To Create a Home Page Using a Webpage Template and Add Content

1 CREATE WEBSITE FOLDERS | 2 CREATE TEMPLATE | 3 ENTER HTML 5 SEMANTIC ELEMENTS
4 ADD COMMENTS & CONTENT | 5 VALIDATE DOCUMENT | 6 CREATE & VIEW HOME PAGE

Create the Forward Fitness Club home page by opening the webpage template and then saving the page with a new name in the root fitness folder. *Why? Using a template saves time in coding because the basic wireframe for the page is already established in the template. As a document for one of the main pages of the site, the home page belongs in the root folder.* You use the fitness template to create all the webpages for the website. The following steps create the home page for the fitness website using the webpage template.

- Tap or click File on the menu bar and then tap or click Save As to display the Save As dialog box.

- In the File name text box, type **index** to name the file.

- Tap or click the Save button to save the index file in the fitness folder.

- Place your insertion point after the beginning <main> tag and press the ENTER key twice to insert two new lines, in this case, Lines 26 and 27.

- On Line 27, press the TAB key and then type `<p>Welcome to Forward Fitness Club. Our mission is to help our clients meet their fitness and nutrition goals. </p>` to add paragraph tags and content to the page (Figure 2–30).

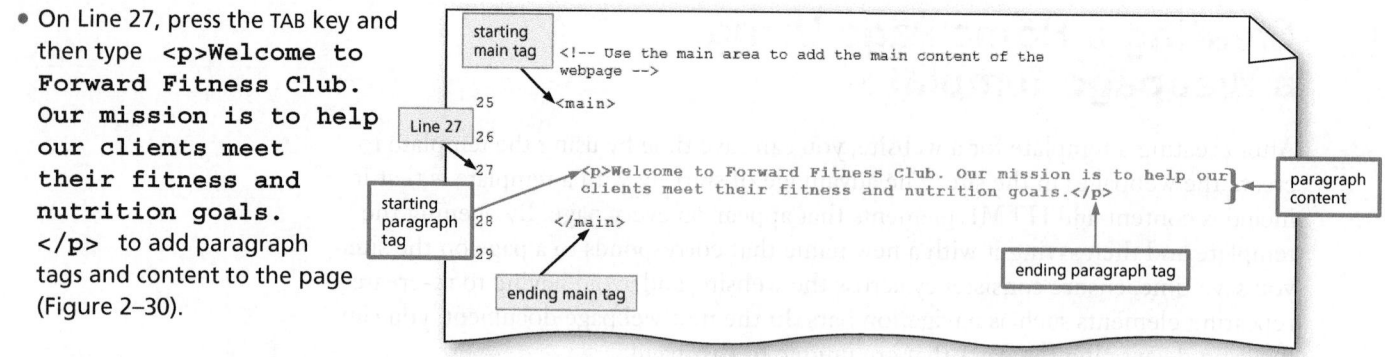

Figure 2–30

2

- Press the ENTER key two times to insert two new lines and then type `<p>If you have struggled with getting healthy and need the motivation and resources to make a healthy lifestyle change, contact us today. Our facility includes state-of-the-art equipment, convenient group training classes, and nutrition tips and information to keep you healthy.</p>` on Line 29 to add a second paragraph to the page.

- Press the ENTER key two times to insert two new lines and then type `<p>We provide a FREE one-week membership so you can experience the benefits of our equipment and facility. This one-week trial gives you complete access to our equipment, training classes, and nutrition planning. Contact us today to start your free trial!</p>` on Line 31 to add a third paragraph to the page (Figure 2–31).

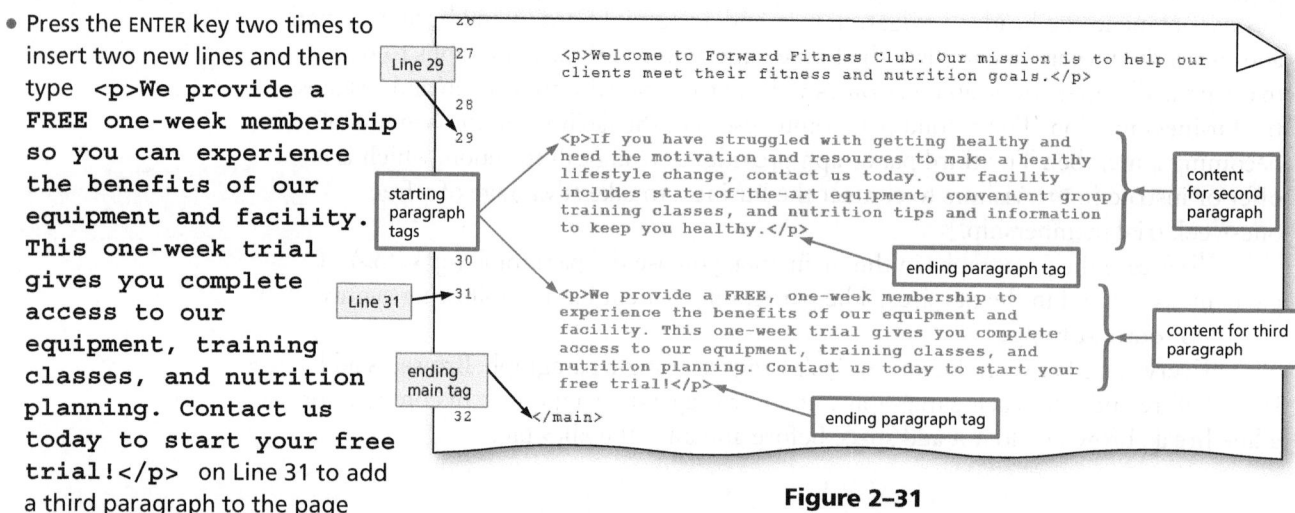

Figure 2–31

- Press the ENTER key to insert a new blank line above the ending `</main>` tag.

- Check the spelling of your document and save your changes.

To Display a Home Page in the Default Browser

1 CREATE WEBSITE FOLDERS | 2 CREATE TEMPLATE | 3 ENTER HTML 5 SEMANTIC ELEMENTS
4 ADD COMMENTS & CONTENT | 5 VALIDATE DOCUMENT | 6 CREATE & VIEW HOME PAGE

After creating the home page or any other page of the website and adding content to it, display it in a browser to view the completed page. ***Why? You should view every page you create in a browser.*** Besides using a command in an HTML editor, such as the Launch in Chrome command on the Run menu in Notepad++, you can open an HTML file from a file viewer such as File Explorer or Finder. When you double-tap or double-click an HTML file, it opens in the default browser on your computer. If you want to open the file in a different browser, you can press and hold or right-click the HTML file, tap or click Open with, and then tap or click an alternate browser. The following steps display the Forward Fitness Club home page in the default browser.

- Run File Explorer and navigate to the fitness folder to display the index .html page.

- Double-tap or double-click the index.html file to display the page in the default browser on your computer (Figure 2–32).

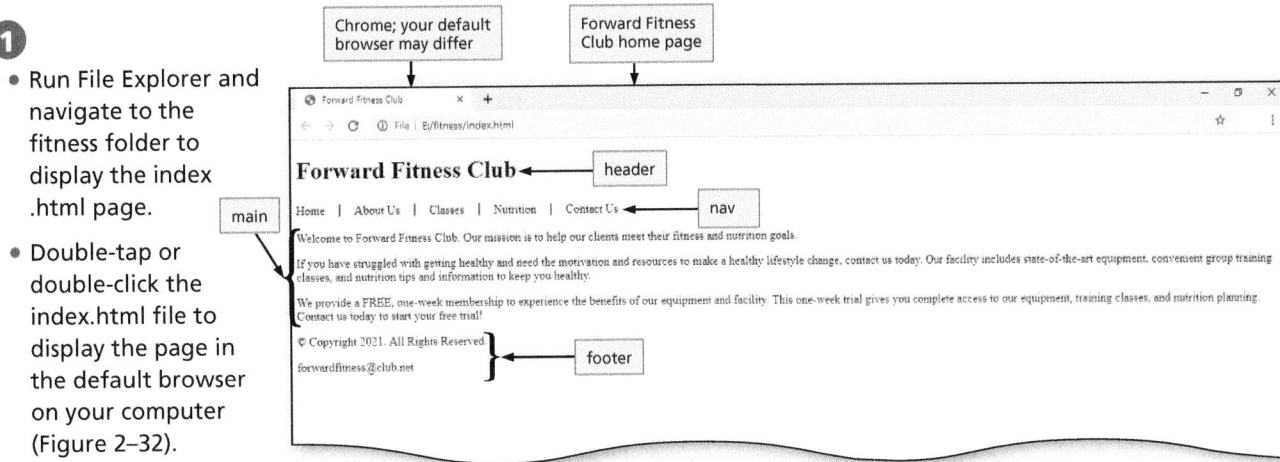

Figure 2–32

Q&A

This page lacks color and looks rather boring. Can I format this page?
Yes, you format the page in Chapter 4, when you learn about CSS.

I clicked the link names in the navigation area, but they do not work. Why not?
The link names are not currently linked to other webpages with a hyperlink. You explore links in Chapter 3.

BTW
Default Browsers
You can make any browser your default browser by adjusting the settings in your operating system. For example, in Windows 10, open the Settings app. In the Find a setting box, type browser, and then select Choose a default web browser. Select your default browser.

- If spelling errors appear in the page, run the spelling checker or edit the text in your HTML text editor and then save your changes.

- Refresh the browser by tapping or clicking the Refresh button on the address bar.

- Close the browser.

- Exit the HTML text editor.

Other Ways

Press and hold or right-click file, tap or click Open with, tap or click browser

Chapter Summary

In this chapter, you learned how to prepare a website by organizing folders for the webpage files, using HTML 5 structural elements to create a webpage template, validating the template, and then creating the home page. The items listed below include all the new concepts and skills you have learned in this chapter, with the tasks grouped by activity.

Designing a Website
Examine the Site Map (HTML 50)
Review the Wireframe (HTML 51)
Create a Website Folder and Subfolders (HTML 53)

Using HTML 5 Semantic Elements
Use the Header Element (HTML 55)
Include the Nav Element (HTML 55)
Use the Main Element (HTML 55)
Insert the Footer Element (HTML 55)

Creating a Webpage Template
Create a Webpage Template Document (HTML 57)
Add HTML 5 Semantic Elements to a Webpage Template (HTML 58)
Add Comments to a Webpage Template (HTML 60)
Add Content to the Header Section (HTML 62)

Using Symbol Entities
Add Text and Nonbreaking Spaces to the Nav Section (HTML 64)

CONSIDER THIS

What decisions will you need to make when creating your next webpage template?
Use these guidelines as you complete the assignments in this chapter and create your own websites outside of this class.

1. Build a wireframe for your website.
   a. Use the wireframe to design an HTML 5 template.
   b. Determine which HTML 5 elements to use in the template.
   c. Identify areas of static content within the wireframe.
2. Create a template.
   a. Create an HTML document with the required elements and the structural elements.
   b. Add comments to the template.
   c. Add static content to the template.
   d. Validate your template and correct any errors.
3. Use the template to create the home page for your website.
   a. Add content to the main area and other areas that do not contain static content.
   b. Validate the home page to confirm that it does not contain any errors.
   c. View the home page in more than one browser.
   d. Identify any changes you need to make.
4. Depending on the structure of your website, determine whether you need to create additional templates to accommodate multiple wireframes.

CONSIDER THIS

How should you submit solutions to questions in the assignments identified with a symbol? Every assignment in this book contains one or more questions identified with a symbol. These questions require you to think beyond the assigned presentation. Present your solutions to the questions in the format required by your instructor. Possible formats may include one or more of these options: create a document that contains the answer; present your answer to the class; discuss your answer in a group; record the answer as audio or video using a webcam, smartphone, or portable media player; or post answers on a blog, wiki, or website.

Apply Your Knowledge

Reinforce the skills and apply the concepts you learned in this chapter.

Creating a Basic HTML Template

Instructions: Providing quick access to validated templates is a good practice. In this exercise, you use a text editor to create an HTML template. You add all necessary, basic HTML elements to the page. Next, you add comments and static content to the page. Finally, you validate the page and correct any errors. There are no Data Files needed to complete this assignment. An example of the completed webpage is shown in Figure 2–33.

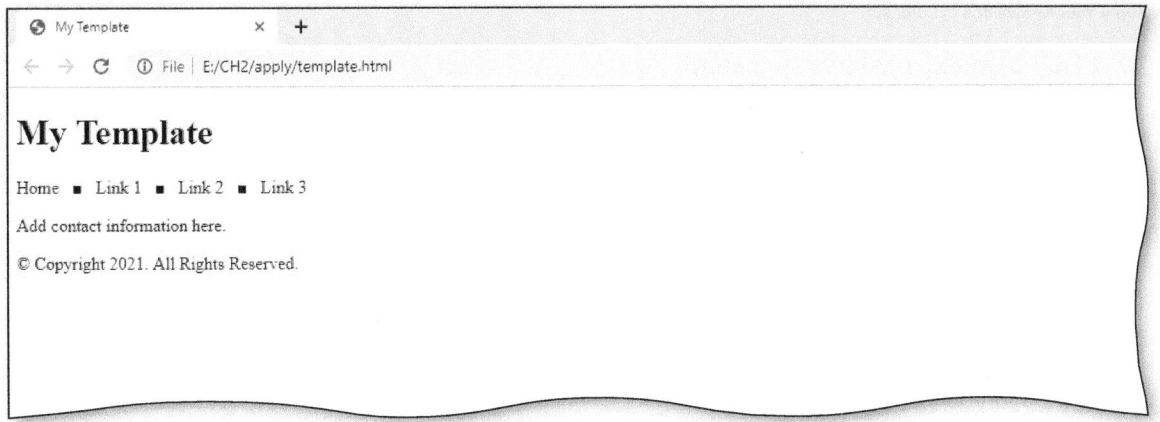

Figure 2–33

Perform the following tasks:

1. Open your text editor and insert all required HTML elements to create a basic webpage, including the DOCTYPE, html, head, title, meta, and body elements. Use the File Save As feature to save the webpage in the chapter02\apply folder with the name `template.html` to create the webpage.

2. Add a multiple-line comment, beginning on Line 2, that includes your name, the file name, and today's date.

```
<!--
     Student Name:
     File Name:
     Date:
-->
```

3. Add the lang attribute to the starting html tag and specify the language as English as follows:
```
<html lang="en">
```

4. Add the charset attribute to the meta tag and specify the character set as UTF-8 as follows:
```
<meta charset="utf-8">
```

5. Add the text, `My Template`, to the title element as follows: `<title>My Template</title>`

6. Nest the following semantic elements within the body element. Add blank lines between each element.

```
<header>
</header>
<nav>
</nav>
<main>
</main>
<footer>
</footer>
```

7. Nest the following heading element within the header element.

```
<h1>My Template</h1>
```

8. Nest the following paragraph element within the nav element.

```
<p>Home   &#9632;  
Link 1   &#9632;  
```

Continued >

Apply Your Knowledge *continued*

```
Link 2   &#9632;  
Link 3</p>
```

9. Nest the following paragraph elements within the footer element.

```
<p>Add contact information here</p>
<p>&copy; Copyright 2021. All Rights Reserved.</p>
```

10. Add a comment above the header that identifies the purpose of the header. Specify if the header content should be static or dynamic. Do the same for the nav, main, and footer elements.

11. Save your changes, upload the template to the W3C validator, and correct any errors.

12. Indent all nested elements.

13. Save your changes and submit the template.html file in a format specified by your instructor.

14. ☀ In step 6, you added several HTML 5 semantic elements to this template. Use your browser to research three other HTML 5 semantic elements and note the purpose for each.

Extend Your Knowledge

Extend the skills you learned in this chapter and experiment with new skills. You may need to use additional resources to complete the assignment.

Updating a Webpage with Semantic Elements

Note: To complete this assignment, you will be required to use the Data Files. Please contact your instructor for information about accessing the Data Files.

Instructions: In this exercise, you will update div elements to use HTML 5 semantic elements, use heading elements, add an article element, and add character codes. An example of the completed webpage is shown in Figure 2–34.

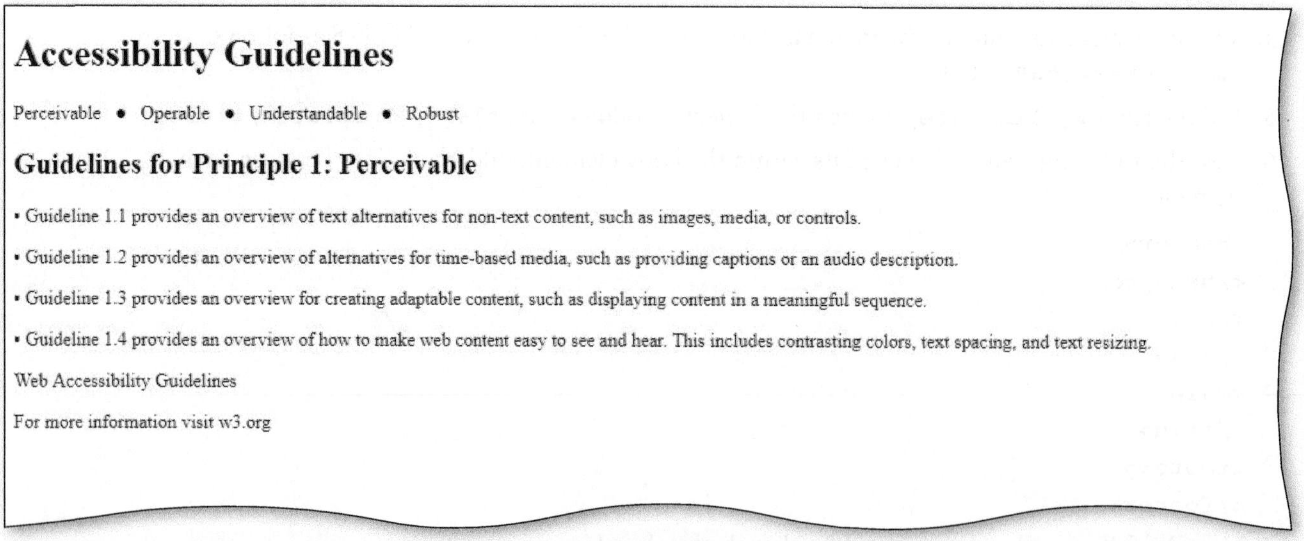

Accessibility Guidelines

Perceivable • Operable • Understandable • Robust

Guidelines for Principle 1: Perceivable

▪ Guideline 1.1 provides an overview of text alternatives for non-text content, such as images, media, or controls.

▪ Guideline 1.2 provides an overview of alternatives for time-based media, such as providing captions or an audio description.

▪ Guideline 1.3 provides an overview for creating adaptable content, such as displaying content in a meaningful sequence.

▪ Guideline 1.4 provides an overview of how to make web content easy to see and hear. This includes contrasting colors, text spacing, and text resizing.

Web Accessibility Guidelines

For more information visit w3.org

Figure 2–34

Perform the following tasks:

1. Open the `extend.html` file from the Data Files and update the comment with your name, the file name, and current date.

2. Add the text, `CH 2 Extend Your Knowledge`, to the title element.

3. Locate all div elements and change them to the appropriate HTML 5 semantic element.

4. Update the paragraph element on Line 15 to use a heading 1 element.

5. Add a nonbreaking space, then a black circle (●), and then another nonbreaking space after the word Perceivable. Do the same for Operable and Understandable.

6. In the main content area, wrap all paragraph elements within one article element and change the first paragraph element to a heading 2.

7. For each paragraph element within the article element, add a black small square (▪) to the beginning of each sentence.

8. Validate your code and correct any errors.

9. Save your changes and submit the extend.html file in a format specified by your instructor.

10. ✸ In step 3, you changed all the div elements to HTML 5 semantic elements. What was the purpose of this step?

Analyze, Correct, Improve

Analyze an external style sheet, correct all errors, and improve it.

Validating an HTML Page

Note: To complete this assignment, you will be required to use the Data Files. Please contact your instructor for information about accessing the Data Files.

Instructions: Open your text editor and then open the analyze.html file from the Data Files. The page includes several errors. An example of the corrected page is shown in Figure 2–35.

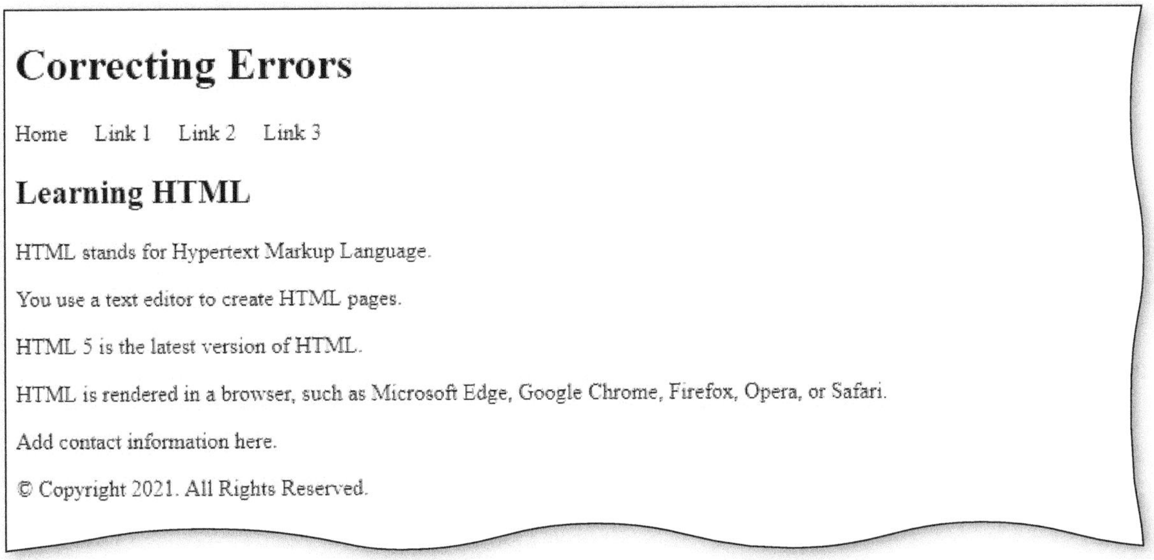

Correcting Errors

Home   Link 1   Link 2   Link 3

Learning HTML

HTML stands for Hypertext Markup Language.

You use a text editor to create HTML pages.

HTML 5 is the latest version of HTML.

HTML is rendered in a browser, such as Microsoft Edge, Google Chrome, Firefox, Opera, or Safari.

Add contact information here.

© Copyright 2021. All Rights Reserved.

Figure 2–35

1. Correct

a. Open the `analyze.html` file in your text editor and review the page.

b. Run the file through the HTML validator, review each error, and correct all errors. Errors may include missing syntax, such as a closing angle bracket or quotation mark, or not properly closing an element.

Continued >

Analyze, Correct, Improve *continued*

c. Use **Analyze** for the webpage title.

d. Continue to run the file through the validator until all errors have been corrected.

2. Improve

a. In the header element, change the nested paragraph element to a heading 1 element.

b. In the nav element, add two nonbreaking spaces after Home, Link 1, and Link 2.

c. In the main element, above the paragraph elements, add a heading 2 element with the following text: **Learning HTML**

d. Add the copyright symbol before the word, Copyright, located within a paragraph element nested within the footer element.

e. Review the document and correct all spelling errors.

f. ✸ What did you notice about the color coding of the file when you first opened it? How many times did you need to run the file through the validator in order to find and correct your errors?

In the Lab

Labs 1 and 2, which increase in difficulty, require you to create webpages based on what you learned in the chapter; Lab 3 is ideal for group projects/collaboration.

Lab 1: Creating a Webpage for Strike a Chord

Problem: You work for a local music lesson company called Strike a Chord that provides music lessons for piano, guitar, and violin. The company needs a web presence and has hired you to create their website. You have already created the website plan, wireframe, and sitemap for the proposed website. Create a webpage template with HTML semantic elements and static content. Next, validate the template, correct any errors, and then use the template to create a home page for Strike a Chord. Finally, add content to the home page. The webpage is shown in Figure 2–36.

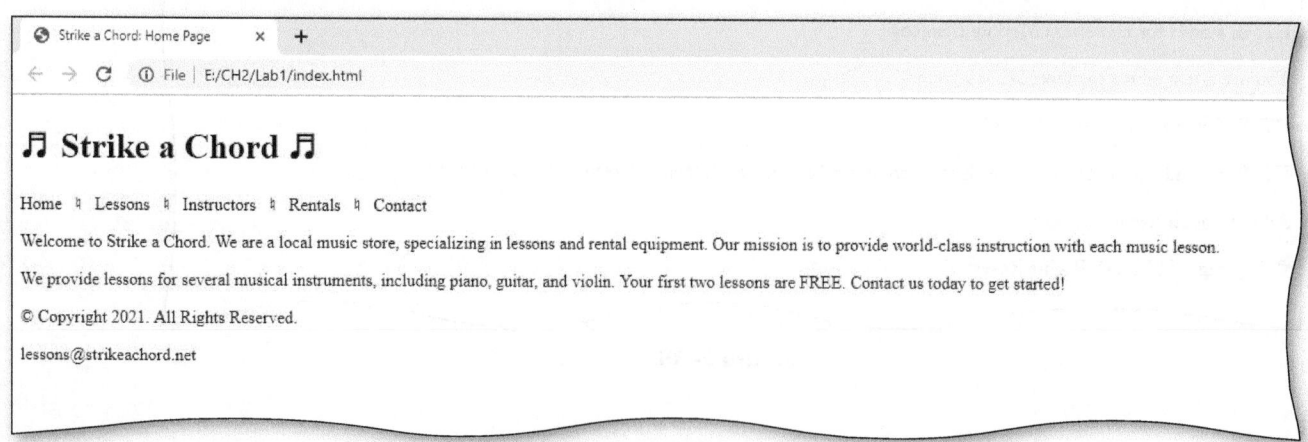

Figure 2–36

Instructions: Perform the following tasks:

1. Create a folder to serve as the root folder for the website and name the folder **music**. Open your text editor and add all required HTML elements to create a basic webpage, including the DOCTYPE, html, head, title, meta, and body elements. Use the File Save As feature to save the webpage in the music folder with the file name **template.html** to create the webpage.

2. Add a multiple-line comment, beginning on Line 2, that includes your name, file name, and today's date.

```
<!--
     Student Name:
     File Name:
     Date:
-->
```

3. Add the lang attribute to the starting html tag and specify the language as English as follows:
```
<html lang="en">
```

4. Add the content, `Strike a Chord: Template`, to the title element as follows:
```
<title>Strike a Chord: Template</title>
```

5. Add the charset attribute to the meta tag and specify the character set as UTF-8 as follows:
```
<meta charset="utf-8">
```

6. Nest the following semantic elements within the body element. Add blank lines between each element.

```
<header>
</header>

<nav>
</nav>

<main>
</main>

<footer>
</footer>
```

7. Nest the following heading element within the header.
```
<h1>&#9836; Strike a Chord &#9836;</h1>
```

8. Nest the following paragraph element within the nav element.
```
<p>Home   &#9838;  
Lessons   &#9838;  
Instructors   &#9838;  
Rentals   &#9838;  
Contact</p>
```

9. Add the following comment above the main element. Ensure that there is a blank line above the comment.
```
<!-- Use the main area to add the main content to the webpage -->
```

10. Nest the following paragraph elements within the footer element.
```
<p>&copy; Copyright 2021. All Rights Reserved.</p>
<p>lessons@strikeachord.net</p>
```

11. Save your changes, upload the template to the W3C validator, and correct any errors.

12. Use your template to create the home page for Strike a Chord. Name the file `index.html`.

13. Update the file name within the comment to index.html. In the title element, replace the word, Template, with `Home Page`.

Continued >

In the Lab *continued*

14. Nest the following paragraph elements within the main element. Add blank lines before and after each paragraph element.

    `<p>Welcome to Strike a Chord. We are a local music store, specializing in lessons and rental equipment. Our mission is to provide world-class instruction with each music lesson.</p>`

    `<p>We provide lessons for several musical instruments, including piano, guitar, bass, and violin. Your first two lessons are FREE. Contact us today to get started!</p>`

15. Indent all nested elements.

16. Save your changes and review the index.html page within a browser.

17. Validate your code and correct any errors.

18. Submit your assignment in the format specified by your instructor.

19. ✸ In steps 7 and 8, you added music symbols. What other music symbol entities are available? Research to find your answer and provide the entity number for at least three other music symbols.

Lab 2: **Creating a Webpage for a Wildlife Rescue**

Problem: You volunteer at a local wildlife rescue, nonprofit organization called Wild Rescues. The organization rescues all kinds of wild animals, rehabilitates them, and then releases them back into the wild. Wild Rescues needs a website to help raise awareness about the organization. The director of Wild Rescues has asked you to build a website for the organization. The website plan, wireframe, and site map has been completed. Create a webpage template with HTML semantic elements and static content. Next, validate the template, correct any errors, and then use the template to create a home page for Wild Rescues. Finally, add content to the home page. The completed webpage is shown in Figure 2–37. (The paw print graphic may have a different appearance in your browser.)

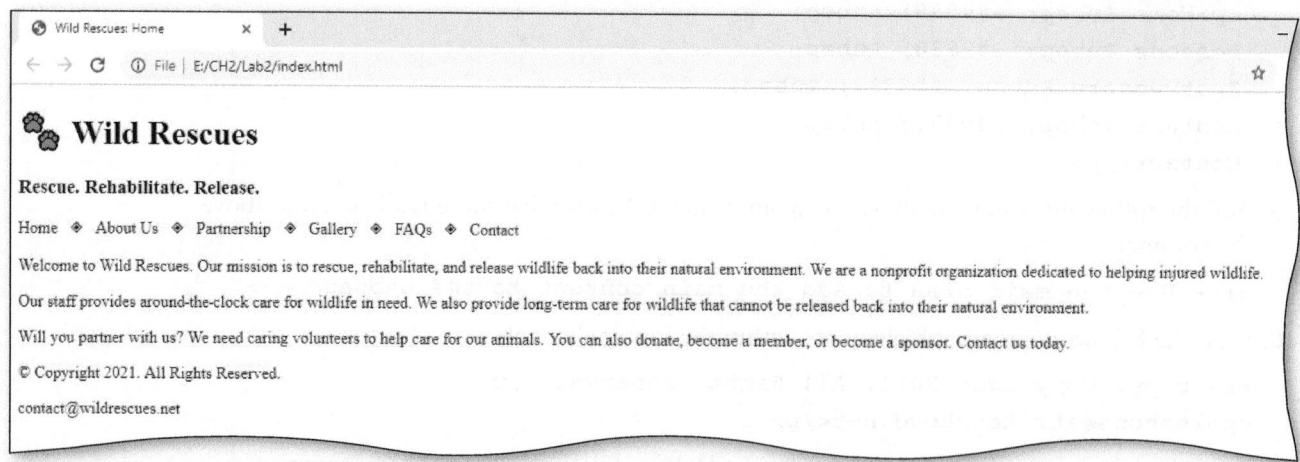

Figure 2–37

Instructions: Perform the following tasks:

1. Create a folder to serve as the root folder for the website and name the folder **rescue**. Open your text editor and add all required HTML elements to create a basic webpage, including the DOCTYPE, html, head, title, meta, and body elements. Use the File Save As feature to save the webpage in the rescue folder with the file name **template.html** to create the webpage.

2. Add a multiple-line comment, beginning on Line 2, that includes your name, file name, and today's date.

```
<!--
      Student Name:
      File Name:
      Date:
-->
```

3. Add the lang attribute to the starting html tag and specify the language as English.

4. Add the content, `Wild Rescues: Template`, to the title element.

5. Add the charset attribute to the meta tag and specify the character set as `utf-8`.

6. Nest the following semantic elements within the body element. Add blank lines between each element.

```
<header>
</header>

<nav>
</nav>

<main>
</main>

<footer>
</footer>
```

7. Within the header element, nest a heading 1 element with the content, `&#128062; Wild Rescues.` Below the heading 1 element, add a heading 3 element with the following content: `Rescue. Rehabilitate. Release.`

8. Nest the following paragraph element within the nav element.

```
<p>Home   &#9672;  
About Us   &#9672;  
Partnership   &#9672;  
Gallery   &#9672;  
FAQs   &#9672;  
Contact</p>
```

9. Add the following comment above the main element. Ensure that there is a blank line above the comment.

```
<!-- Use the main area to add the main content to the webpage -->
```

10. Nest the following paragraph elements within the footer element.

```
<p>&copy; Copyright 2021. All Rights Reserved.</p>
<p>contact@wildrescues.net</p>
```

11. Save your changes, upload the template to the W3C validator, and correct any errors.

12. Use your template to create the home page for Wild Rescues. Name the file `index.html`.

13. Update the file name within the comment to index.html. In the title element, replace the word, Template, with `Home`.

14. Nest the following paragraph elements within the main element. Add blank lines before and after each paragraph element.

```
<p>Welcome to Wild Rescues. Our mission is to rescue, rehabilitate,
and release wildlife back into their natural environment. We are a
```

Continued >

In the Lab *continued*

```
nonprofit organization dedicated to helping injured wildlife.</p>

<p>Our staff provides around-the-clock care for wildlife in need. We
also provide long-term care for wildlife that cannot be released back
into their natural environment.</p>

<p>Will you partner with us? We need caring volunteers to help care
for our animals. You can also donate, become a member, or become a
sponsor. Contact us today.</p>
```

15. Indent all nested elements.

16. Save your changes and review the index.html page within a browser.

17. Validate your code and correct any errors.

18. Submit your assignment in the format specified by your instructor.

19. ✴ In steps 1 through 11, you created and validated an HTML template. What are the benefits of creating a template prior to creating the home page?

Lab 3: Creating a Website for Student Clubs and Events

Problem: You and several of your classmates have decided to help increase student involvement in school clubs and events by creating a website to promote awareness about the various activities. You have already created a website plan, wireframe, and sitemap for the proposed website. Now you need to create a webpage template with HTML semantic elements and static content. Next, validate the template, correct any errors, and then use the template to create a home page for your student club and events website.

Instructions:

1. As a group, determine where you will store your website files, such as a flash drive or cloud storage, and then create a folder to serve as the root folder for the website. Name the folder **student.** Inside of your student folder, create the following subfolders for the website: css, images, media, scripts.

2. Create a template.html file for your website and save it within the student root folder. Add all necessary HTML elements to the template to create an HTML 5 webpage. Your template file should include the following minimum structural elements: header, nav, main, and footer.

3. Add a multiline comment on Line 2 of your template file that identifies the group members, file name, and the current date. Insert a comment above the main element to identify the purpose of the main element and how it should be used.

4. Add static content to your template. Use appropriate text within the title element. Nest a heading element within your header element. If it serves a purpose, you may include a symbol within your heading element. Nest a paragraph element within your nav element that includes text for your future page links. You may include symbols between your text links. Add content to the footer element.

5. Indent all nested elements and add blank lines where appropriate to improve readability.

6. Validate your template file and correct any errors.

7. Use your template file to create your home page. Save the home page with the file name index .html.

8. Add meaningful content to the main element on your home page and change the text in the title element to indicate this page is the home page.

9. ✹ In step 1, you were to identify where your group will save files for this project. What was your decision? What will you do to ensure everyone has access to the files? How often will you backup the project files, in the event that the primary storage option is lost or unavailable?

✹ Consider This: Your Turn

Apply your creative thinking and problem-solving skills to design and implement a solution.

1. Create Template and Home Page for the Personal Portfolio Website

Personal

Part 1:   As in almost every field, the job market for the best jobs in web development are competitive. One way to give yourself a big edge in a job search is to create an appropriate personal portfolio website to showcase your skills. You have already created your website plan, wireframe, and sitemap. Create a folder to serve as the root folder for the website and name the folder portfolio. Create a webpage template with HTML semantic elements and static content. Save the template file within your portfolio folder. Add a multiline comment beginning at Line 2 that includes your name, the file name, and the current date. Add a comment above the main element to note its purpose. In the header, include a heading element for your name, and then add another heading element with your mission statement or tagline. In the nav area, include text for the links you will provide to the other webpages in the website. Validate the template, correct any errors, and then use the template to create a home page for your portfolio. Finally, add content to the main content area on your home page and add at least one character or symbol on your page. Submit your assignment in the format specified by your instructor.

Part 2:   ✹ How will you improve this website? Research other online portfolios for ideas on what you can add to enhance the look of your website.

2. Create Template and Home Page for the Dog Grooming Website

Professional

Part 1:   Your family owns a dog grooming business and needs a website. Your family knows that you are taking a web design class and asks you to create a website for the business. You have already created your website plan, wireframe, and sitemap. Create a folder to serve as the root folder for the website and name the folder groom. Create a webpage template with HTML semantic elements and static content. Save the template file within your groom folder. Add a multiline comment beginning at Line 2 that includes your name, the file name, and the current date. Add a comment above the main element to note its purpose. In the header, include a heading element with the name of the business, then add another heading element with the mission statement or tagline for the business. In the nav area, include text for the links you will provide to the other webpages in the website. Validate the template, correct any errors, and then use the template to create a home page for the business. Finally, add content to the main content area on the home page, and include at least one character or symbol on the page. Submit your assignment in the format specified by your instructor.

Part 2:   ✹ Research websites for dog groomers in your area and review their layout, images, and content. Discuss what you found, what you liked, and how to you might improve the website.

3. Create Template and Home Page for the Future Technologies Website

Research and Collaboration

Part 1:   You and several of your classmates have been tasked with creating a website that showcases advancements in technology. You have already created your website plan, wireframe, and sitemap. As a group, determine where you will store your website files, such as a flash drive or cloud storage,

Continued >

Consider This: Your Turn *continued*

and then create a folder to serve as the root folder for the website. Name the folder tech. Inside of your tech folder, create the following subfolders for the website: css, images, media, scripts. Create a webpage template with HTML semantic elements and static content. Save the template file within your tech folder. Add a multiline comment beginning at Line 2 that includes the names of your group members, the file name, and the current date. Add a comment above the main element to note its purpose. In the header, include a heading element with a title for the home page, then add another heading element with the purpose or tagline for the website. In the nav area, include text for the links you will provide to the other webpages in the website. Validate the template, correct any errors, and then use the template to create a home page for the business. Finally, add content to the main content area on the home page and include at least one character or symbol on the page. Submit your assignment in the format specified by your instructor.

Part 2: ✺ As a group, determine which technological advancement page to focus on next. Each of you research an article for the technology and bring with you to discuss at your next meeting. This will help determine content for your next page. This will also help determine future images to include within your website. Organize your group's findings as requested by your instructor.

3 | Enhancing a Website with Images and Links

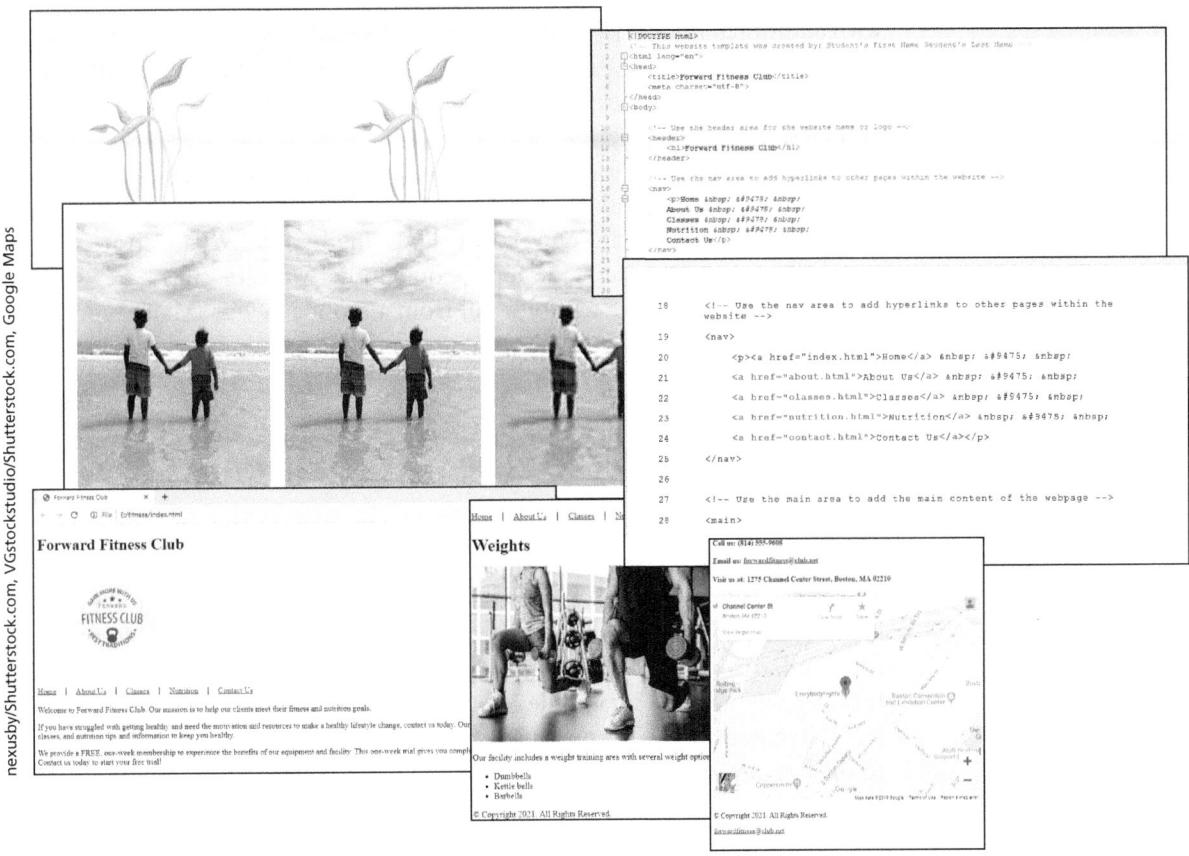

Objectives

You will have mastered the material in this chapter when you can:

- Describe image file formats
- Describe the image tag and its attributes
- Add images to a website
- Explain div elements and attributes
- Use a div element within a webpage
- Describe types of hyperlinks
- Create relative links, absolute links, bookmark links, email links, and telephone links
- Describe the types of lists in an HTML document
- Create an unordered list and a description list
- Embed a map within a webpage
- Test and validate links on a webpage

3 | Enhancing a Website with Images and Links

Introduction

Images are used throughout a website to enhance visual appeal and provide visitors with additional information about a product or service. Other images, such as a business logo, promote the company's presence and brand. Almost all modern webpages contain images, whether they are photos, drawings, logos, or other types of graphics.

One of the most useful and important aspects of the web is the ability to connect (link) one webpage to other webpages — on the same server or on different web servers — located anywhere in the world. Using hyperlinks, a website visitor can move from one page to another, view a page on another website, start a new email message, download a file, or make a phone call from a mobile device. Many types of webpage content, including text, graphics, and animations, can serve as hyperlinks.

Project — Add Images and Links to a Website

Most websites use images to enhance the look and feel of their webpages. In fact, one reason the web is so popular is that its images create immediate visual appeal. However, recall that HTML files are simple text files. To display an image on a webpage, you insert code in an HTML document that references the name and location of the image file, similar to the way you create a hyperlink. When a visitor opens the webpage, the browser retrieves the image file identified in the code and displays it on the webpage.

Because a website consists of many webpages of content, visitors need a way to open one webpage while they are viewing another, or navigate the site. As you know, visitors can navigate a website using hyperlinks, which can link the current page to other pages in the website. Hyperlinks can also link to any other page on the web, to a file other than a webpage, to an email address, to a phone number, or to a network server. A well-designed website includes a list of navigation links specifically designed to let visitors easily access the main pages on the site. Some websites arrange the navigation links in a horizontal list, similar to the one the Forward Fitness Club website uses. Other websites use a vertical list of navigation links. In either case, the navigation links should appear in a location visitors can find easily. Using a **nav** element directly below the **header** element and then inserting the navigation links in the **nav** element ensures that the links appear near the header, where visitors can access them easily. To create a link to a webpage, you insert code in an HTML document that references the webpage by its name and location. When a visitor taps or clicks the link, the browser retrieves the webpage identified in the code.

In Chapter 2, you created a website template for the Forward Fitness Club. You then used the template to create the home page for the website. For this project, you edit the template to add an image in the header area that displays the club's logo and add hyperlinks to the text in the navigation area. You use the template to create two pages for the site: the About Us and Contact Us pages. Finally, you add content to the new pages, including images, lists, and links. Figure 3–1a shows the home page of the fitness site; Figure 3–1b shows the About Us page, which contains text and images; and Figure 3–1c shows the Contact Us page with the fitness club's contact information and contact links.

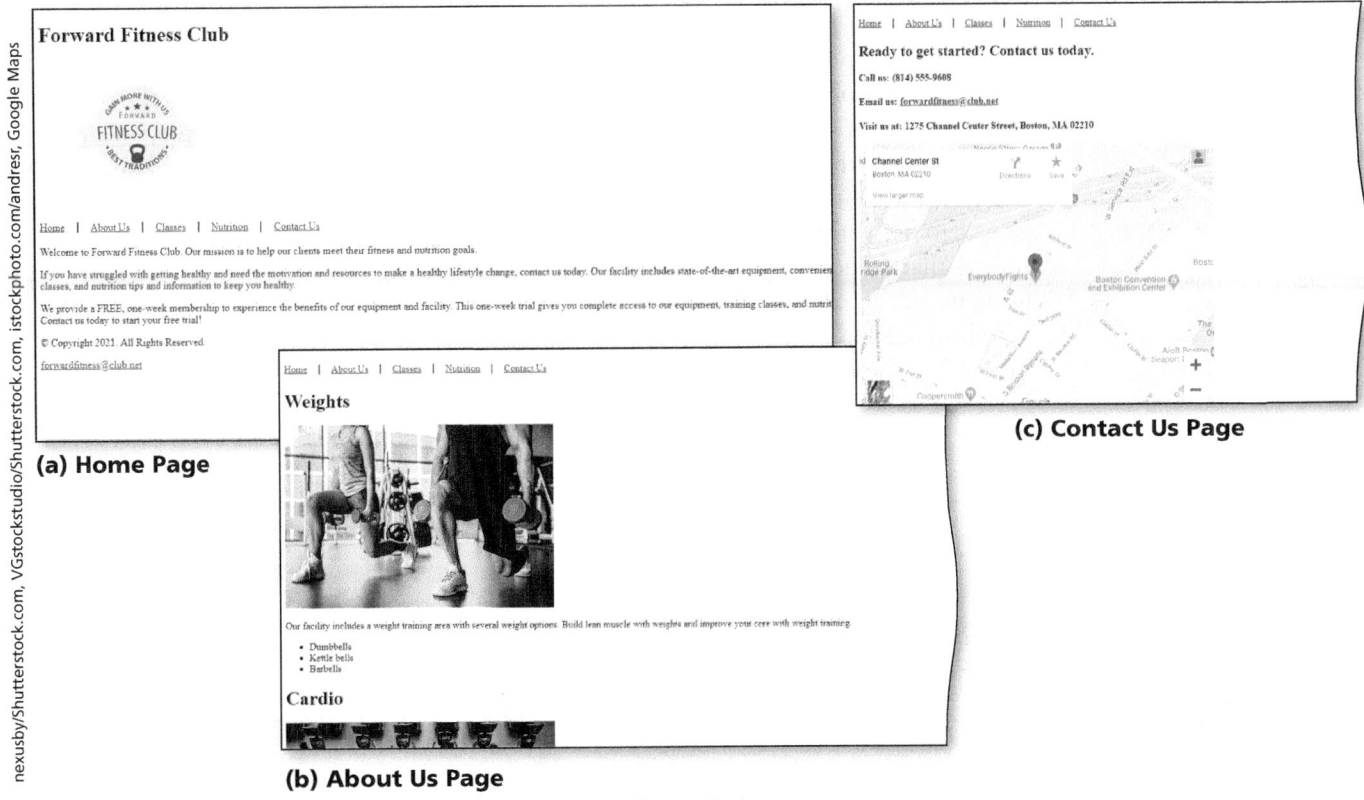

(a) Home Page

(b) About Us Page

(c) Contact Us Page

Figure 3–1

Roadmap

In this chapter, you will learn how to create the webpages shown in Figure 3–1. The following roadmap identifies general activities you will perform as you progress through this chapter:

1. ADD IMAGES to a template and to webpages.
2. ADD DIV ELEMENTS to a template and to webpages.
3. ADD HYPERLINKS to a template and to webpages.
4. ADD LISTS to a webpage.
5. EMBED a MAP on a webpage.
6. VIEW the WEBSITE IN a BROWSER AND TEST the webpage LINKS.
7. VALIDATE the new PAGES.

At the beginning of step instructions throughout the chapter, you will see an abbreviated form of this roadmap. The abbreviated roadmap uses colors to indicate chapter progress: gray means the chapter is beyond that activity; blue means the task being shown is covered in that activity; and black means that activity is yet to be covered. For example, the following abbreviated roadmap indicates the chapter would be showing a task in the 4 ADD LISTS activity.

1 ADD IMAGES | 2 ADD DIV ELEMENTS | 3 ADD HYPERLINKS | 4 ADD LISTS
5 EMBED MAP | 6 VIEW WEBSITE IN BROWSER & TEST LINKS | 7 VALIDATE PAGES

Use the abbreviated roadmap as a progress guide while you read or step through the instructions in this chapter.

Adding Images to a Website

Images include photos, drawings, diagrams, charts, and other graphics that convey visual information. On a webpage, they help break up text and contribute to the design and aesthetics of a website. However, rather than merely decorate a webpage, images should support the purpose of the page or illustrate content. Images can also provide visual representations of a company's products and services. When determining what images to use within your website, choose those that relate directly to the content. Images that do not support the content can be distracting or confusing. For example, using images on a business website that do not pertain to the business may be perceived as unprofessional or may leave the user wondering what the business is actually selling. Figure 3–2 shows the website for Earth Fare, a supermarket dedicated to organic foods. Note the use of the site's logo and photo to demonstrate healthy eating.

Figure 3–2

Source: www.earthfare.com

Image File Formats

When incorporating images into a website, web designers need to consider the file format, image dimensions, and file size. These factors affect the appearance of an image on a webpage and how long it takes the browser to display the image.

Image files are created in several formats; however, when adding images to a webpage, you must use image files in the GIF, PNG, JPG, or SVG format.

GIF stands for Graphics Interchange Format and is pronounced "jiff." GIF is the oldest web file format and supports transparency and frame animation.

To create images that do not display a background color but have a transparent, or clear, background instead, you use a file format that supports transparency, such as GIF.

Figure 3–3 shows an example of an image with and without transparency. GIF files also support short video animation and frame animation. Video animation GIF files typically loop and do not include sound. Frame animation GIF files include a series of drawings that quickly appear in a sequence to give an illusion of movement. Figure 3–4 shows an example of a GIF animation website, giphy.com. Visit this website to see the GIF animation images.

To compress an image, or reduce its file size, the GIF format uses a technique called **lossless compression** that maintains the file's color information. GIF files are 8-bit images that can display up to 256 colors, making the file sizes relatively small. Because of the small color palette in GIF files, they are suitable for icons and line drawings, but not for high-quality pictures or photos.

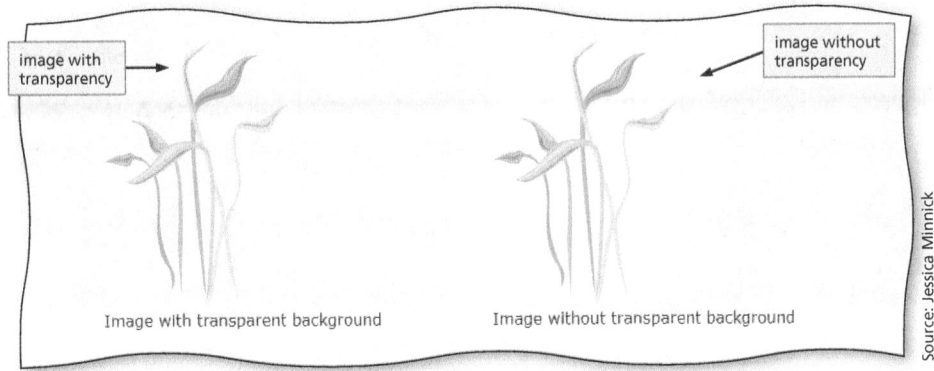

Source: Jessica Minnick

Figure 3–3

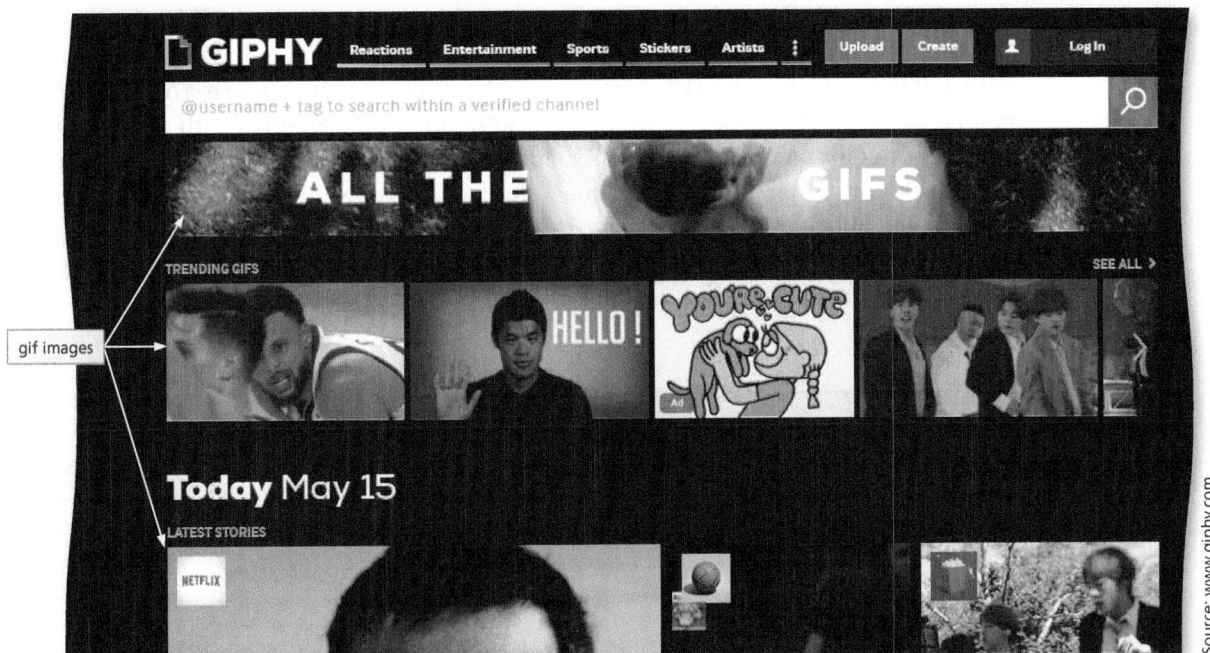

Source: www.giphy.com

Figure 3–4

PNG stands for Portable Network Graphics and is pronounced as "ping." The PNG file format was designed to replace the GIF file format for web graphics. PNG also uses lossless compression and supports 8-bit color images, 16-bit grayscale images, and 24-bit true-color images. PNG8 files are 8-bit images with 256 colors. PNG24 files are 24-bit images that can contain millions of colors. This is one advantage to using PNG compared to GIF: PNG24 can support over 16 million colors, whereas GIF supports only 256 colors. PNG also supports transparency, but not animation. In addition, PNG is not ideal for photographic images, as its lossless compression is not

BTW
Animated GIF
Many of today's mobile devices include access to a bank of GIF images that you can use to send text messages.

as efficient as that of the JPG format. Figure 3–5 shows an example of a website (usa.gov) that contains PNG files.

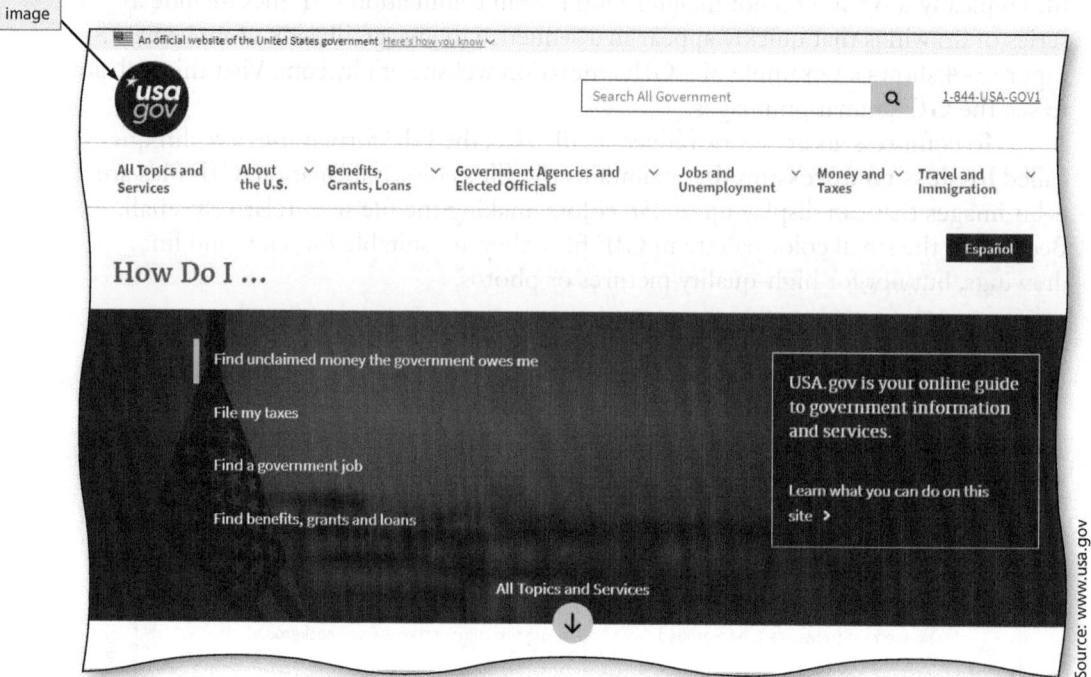

Figure 3–5

JPG or **JPEG** stands for Joint Photographic Experts Group and is pronounced "jay-peg." This is the standard file format for a digital photo, such as one taken with a digital camera. The JPG format is a 24-bit image that supports 16.7 million colors, which is why it is used for digital photos and other pictures with a high level of detail or color complexity, such as shadows. JPG uses a **lossy compression** made exclusively for digital photos. To reduce file size, a lossy compression discards some of the color information in the image, which reduces its original quality. If you include a digital photo in your website, use a JPG or JPEG file format. Figure 3–6 shows a page from the U.S. Capitol website that contains several JPG image files.

Figure 3–6

SVG stands for Scalable Vector Graphics, a format that uses markup language to create two-dimensional graphics, images, and animations. It is a royalty-free graphic format developed by the SVG working group at the W3C. The latest edition of SVG recommended by the W3C is version 1.1, second edition. SVG 2 is currently in development by the W3C SVG Working Group. Use SVG to create shapes such as circles, squares, rectangles, and lines. SVG is supported by all modern desktop and mobile browsers. Certain features may not be supported. To test for browser compatibility, visit caniuse.com/svg. You can create SVG images using the svg element in a text editor or by using drawing software. Figure 3–7a shows an example of the SVG code required to create the rectangle shown on the webpage displayed in Figure 3–7b. An example of an SVG animation game is shown in Figure 3–8.

BTW
Inkscape
Inkscape is a common drawing program used to create SVG files. It is a cross-platform, open-source program, and is available at inkscape.org.

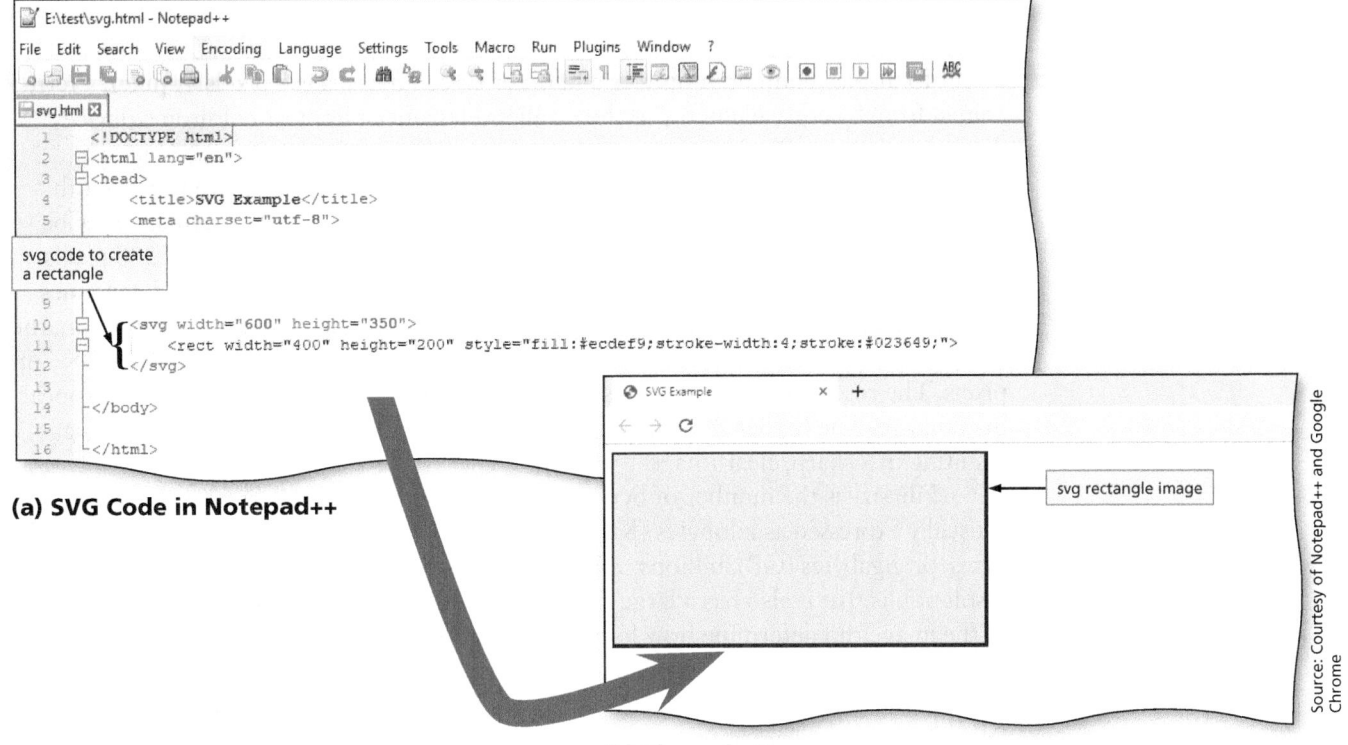

(a) SVG Code in Notepad++

(b) Shape in Browser

Figure 3–7

Source: Courtesy of Notepad++ and Google Chrome

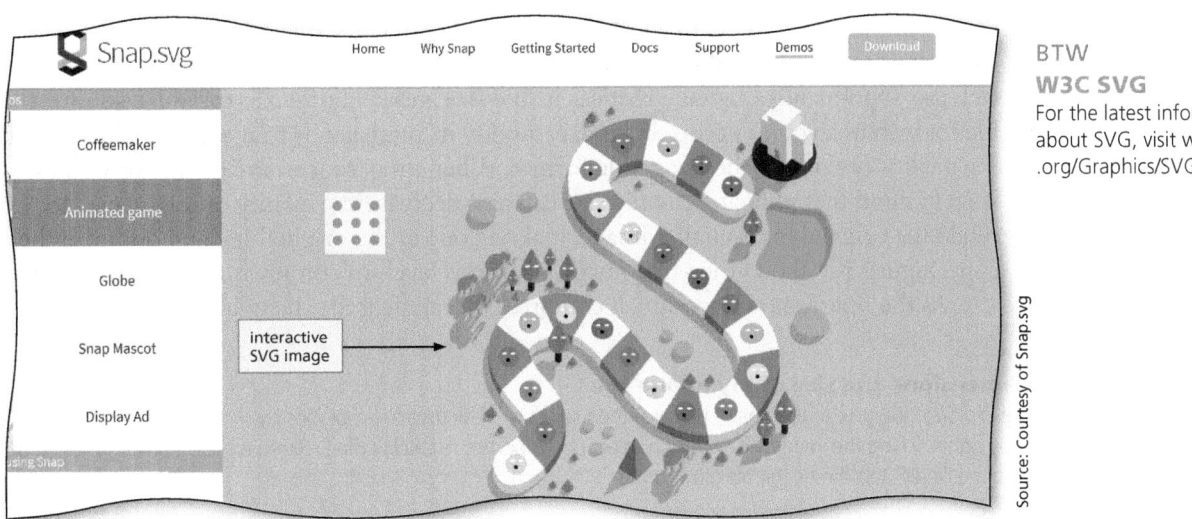

Figure 3–8

Source: Courtesy of Snap.svg

BTW
W3C SVG
For the latest information about SVG, visit www.w3 .org/Graphics/SVG.

Table 3–1 summarizes the pros and cons of each image file format for the web.

Table 3–1 Choosing an Image File Format			
Format	**Pros**	**Cons**	**Use for**
GIF	Small file size; supports transparency and animation	Limited to 256 colors	Line drawings and animations
PNG	Small file size; supports transparency and more than a million colors	Does not support animation	Images that are not digital photos
JPG	Supports more than a million colors	Larger file size	Digital photos
SVG	Flexible; scalable; no files needed because graphics are created with code	Not supported by older browsers and not all modern browsers support all SVG features	Shapes, lines, text, and gradients

Image Dimensions and File Size

BTW
Screen Resolution Statistics
W3Schools.com collects data regarding screen resolutions. See their latest screen resolution information at www.w3schools.com/browsers/browsers_display.asp.

To display content, monitors and other screen devices use pixels. A **pixel**, a term coined from "picture element," is the smallest element of light or color on a device displaying images. Pixels are arranged in rows and columns to compose an image, but are usually so small that you cannot see them, making the image appear smooth and fluid. Webpage images can be measured in pixels. For example, an image may be 200 × 200 pixels, which means it has a height of 200 pixels and a width of 200 pixels.

Monitors and other screen devices have a default resolution, which determines the clarity of the content displayed on the screen. The higher the screen resolution, the sharper text and images appear. A common resolution for today's laptops is 1366 × 768 pixels. The resolution of a device's screen dictates the number of pixels that can appear in an image. The higher the resolution, the greater the number of pixels in the image, resulting in a sharp, clear image.

File size is the number of bytes a file contains, though the size of an image file is usually expressed as kilobytes (KB), thousands of bytes; megabytes (MB), millions of bytes; or gigabytes (GB), billions of bytes. The disadvantage of an image with a high resolution is that it also has a large file size. If a webpage contains an image, the file size of the image can determine how long it takes for the webpage to load in a browser. If a webpage contains several large image files, the page might be slow to load, especially on a mobile device. Today's users expect pages to load as soon as they tap or click a link. The key to reducing page load time is keeping the webpage file small. Though a webpage itself may load quickly, large images on the webpage can take longer to appear.

When you choose a file format for an image, file size is a major factor. For example, JPG files can be large files; a detailed digital photo contains much more data than a simple line drawing in a GIF format. If you are using images with large file sizes, use a photo or graphics editor, such as Adobe Photoshop, to **optimize** the graphic for web use. Optimizing an image reduces its file size and load time. To optimize an image file for web use, you can crop the image, modify its dimensions to make it smaller, adjust the quality, or convert the image file format. When preparing an image file for web use, keep in mind that reducing the file size can also decrease the quality of the image. To retain the original high-quality image, make a copy of the original file and optimize the copy. Figure 3–9 shows the same image at various levels of compression that reduced file size. As the figure shows, too much compression can degrade the quality of the image.

How do I find the dimensions and size of my image file?
In Windows 10, open File Explorer, navigate to the image file, and then select it. View the file properties by clicking the Properties button on the Home tab or by right-clicking the image file and then selecting Properties to display the Properties dialog box. The General tab shows the file size and the Details tab shows the file dimensions.

CONSIDER THIS

Source: Courtesy of Jessica Minnick

Figure 3–9

Another option for optimizing image files is to use an online image file compressor. Several online resources compress image files for a fee or for free. A few examples include:

- Kraken.io
- Compressor.io
- Tingjpg.com
- Jpegmini.com
- Optimizilla, imagecompressor.com

Compressor.io can optimize jpg, png, gif, and svg file formats. Figure 3–10 shows the website for Compressor.io. The home page shows an example of an image with an original file size of 700 KB. After the image was compressed, the file size was reduced by 64 percent to 250 KB.

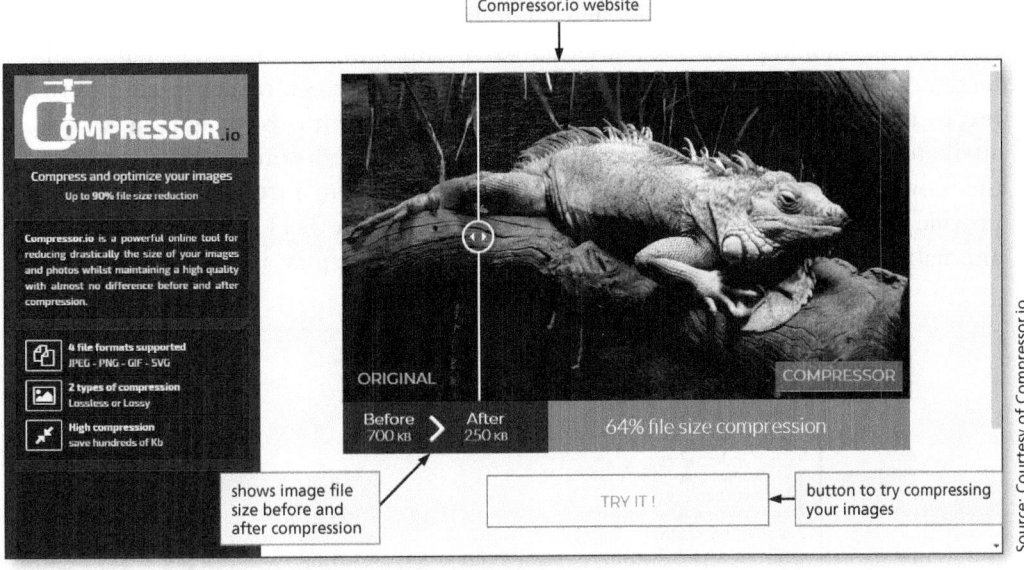

Source: Courtesy of Compressor.io

Figure 3–10

Image File Names

When using images within a website, be sure to give each image file a meaningful file name. Most digital cameras use a default file-naming convention, such as IMG001.jpg, which does not describe the image in the photo. You can rename the file using short, descriptive text that identifies the image. For example, if the image shows a gopher tortoise, use gopher-tortoise.jpg as the file name. Using a short, descriptive, meaningful name for each image file helps improve search engine optimization (SEO). You will learn more about SEO in Chapter 11.

Image Tag and Its Attributes

The **image tag**, <img>, is an empty HTML element used to add an image to a webpage. As an empty element, the image tag does not have an ending tag. It includes many attributes, such as the required file source attribute, **src**, which identifies the image file being inserted. An example of an image element with a source attribute is <img src="logo.png">. This code tells the browser to display the image file named logo.png. Table 3–2 shows a list of common attributes used with the image element.

Table 3–2 Image Element Attributes	
Attribute	**Function**
src	Identifies the file name of the image to display
alt	Specifies alternate text to display when an image is being loaded
	Especially useful for screen readers, which translate information on a computer screen into audio output
	Should briefly describe the purpose of the image in 125 characters or less
height	Defines the height of the image in pixels, which improves loading time
width	Defines the width of the image in pixels, which improves loading time

BTW
**Accessibility,
Principle 1**
For more information about Principle 1, Perceivable, visit https://www.w3.org/WAI/WCAG21/quickref/

You should always use the **alt** attribute in an image tag to specify alternate text in case the image cannot be displayed in a browser. Recall the Web Content Accessibility Guidelines (WCAG) from Chapter 1. Principle 1 is Perceivable and includes several guidelines. Guideline 1.1 addresses text alternatives for any nontext content. You should provide text alternatives for any nontext content, including all images. The alternate text briefly describes the image. Screen readers recite alternate text to address accessibility. An example of an image tag with `src` and `alt` attributes is <img src="fruit-basket.jpg" alt="Basket of fresh fruit">. This code means the browser should retrieve and display the image file named fruit-basket.jpg and provide "Basket of fresh fruit" as the alternate text. Figure 3–11 shows an example of alternative text displayed in a browser that is unable to display an image.

Figure 3–11

Why would a browser not display an image?
A browser might not display an image for many reasons. The image file name specified for the source attribute might be mis-spelled or use incorrect casing. The image file may have been moved or deleted from the server. Finally, the browser might not support the image file format.

When you add an image to a webpage, you can also define the image's height and width. A browser uses these attributes to reserve the amount of space needed for the image. An example of an image element with attributes is shown in Figure 3–12.

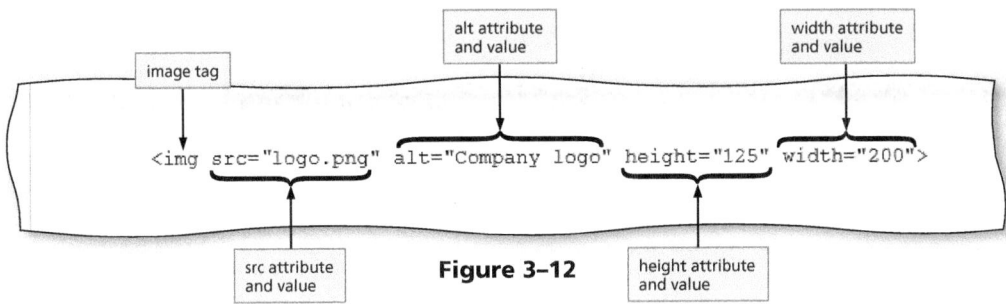

Figure 3–12

A browser interprets the code in Figure 3–12 as follows:

1. First, the browser reads the starting image tag, which indicates the browser should display an image on the webpage.
2. The src="logo.png" attribute and value identify the name of the image to display.
3. The alt="Company logo" attribute and value identify the alternate text to display if the browser cannot display the image.
4. The height="125" attribute and value reserve the height needed to display the image in a browser.
5. The width="200" attribute and value reserve the width needed to display the image in a browser, and the right angle bracket (>) closes the image element.

When specifying values for the **height** and **width** attributes of an image, use the actual dimensions of the image. For example, the code shown in Figure 3–12 is appropriate for an image with a height of 125 pixels and a width of 200 pixels. (You can find the dimensions of an image file by opening it in a graphics editor such as Photoshop, Paint (Windows 10), or Preview (macOS) or by displaying the file's properties using File Explorer or Finder.) If you make the dimensions larger than the actual image, you reduce the quality, which can result in a blurry or distorted image. Making the dimensions smaller than the actual image does not improve the browser's page load time because the image file size remains the same. If you need to use a smaller image, adjust its dimensions in a graphics editor first. Many graphics editors, including Photoshop, let you change the width and height of an image. You can also use Paint, a basic graphics application that comes standard with Windows 10, to resize an image. Be sure to use an option such as "Constrain proportions" or "Maintain aspect ratio" to change each dimension in proportion to the other, which is called maintaining the aspect ratio. Otherwise, you are likely to distort the image. Figure 3–13 shows an example of an image displayed in a browser with its original dimensions and with larger dimensions. The bottom image uses dimensions larger than the file size and does not maintain the aspect ratio, which distorts the image.

Original image dimensions at 600x344

image with original dimensions

Image dimensions at 800x450

image with larger, nonproportional dimensions

Source: Courtesy of Jessica Minnick, Google Chrome

Figure 3–13

Using the **height** and **width** attributes in an image element establishes a fixed size for the image, which can affect the webpage layout. A webpage can have a fixed layout or a fluid layout (also called a flexible or a responsive layout). A webpage with a fixed layout does not change when the browser window is resized or the page is displayed at varying resolutions. In a fixed layout, every element has a predefined height and width. However, as you progress further into this book and begin to design responsively for mobile, tablet, and desktop devices, you will learn how to create fluid layouts and images with CSS. Fluid images adjust their size for optimal display on a desktop, tablet, and mobile device.

CONSIDER THIS

What is the difference between the size of an image and the size of an image file?
The size of an image specifies the height and the width of an image in pixels. An image file size is the amount of storage space needed to save the image on a storage device. An image file size can be measured in kilobytes (KB), megabytes (MB), or gigabytes (GB).

To Copy Files into the Images Folder

1 ADD IMAGES | 2 ADD DIV ELEMENTS | 3 ADD HYPERLINKS | 4 ADD LISTS
5 EMBED MAP | 6 VIEW WEBSITE IN BROWSER & TEST LINKS | 7 VALIDATE PAGES

Before you can add an image to a site, you need to acquire the images and store them in the folder designated for images on your website. *Why? You need to have image files and know where they are stored before you can add them to a webpage. In the following steps, you copy image files to your images folder.* To complete this assignment, you will be required to use the Data Files. Please contact your instructor for information about accessing the Data Files. The following steps copy four image files from the Data Files to the images folder for the fitness site.

- If necessary, insert the drive containing the Data Files into an available port.
- Use File Explorer (Windows) or Finder (Mac) to navigate to the storage location of the Data Files.

- Double-tap or double-click the chapter03 folder, double-tap or double-click the chapter folder, and then double-tap or double-click the images folder to open the images folder and display the image files.

- Tap or click the first file in the list, such as the forward-fitness-logo.png file, hold down the SHIFT key, and then tap or click the last file in the list, such as the personal-trainer.jpg file, to select the images needed for the site (Figure 3–14).

Q&A Why is my file list different?
Your list of files might be sorted in a different order or displayed in a view different from the one shown in Figure 3–14.

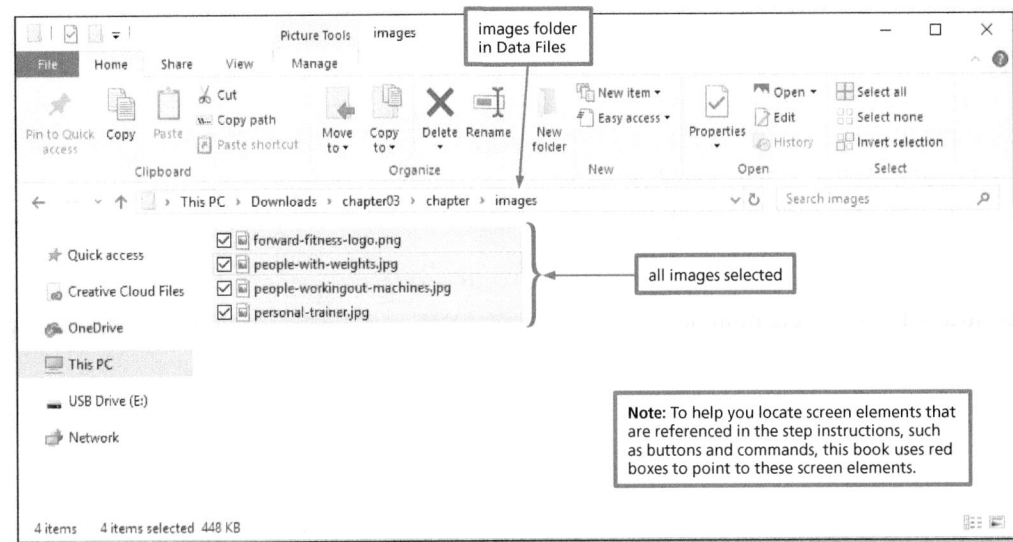

Figure 3–14

Other Ways

1. Press CTRL+A to select all files within the images folder

2

- Press and hold or right-click the selected files, tap or click Copy on the shortcut menu, and then navigate to the images folder in your fitness folder to prepare to copy the files to your images folder.

- Press and hold or right-click a blank area in the open window, and then tap or click Paste on the shortcut menu to copy the files into the images folder.

- Verify that the folder now contains four images (Figure 3–15).

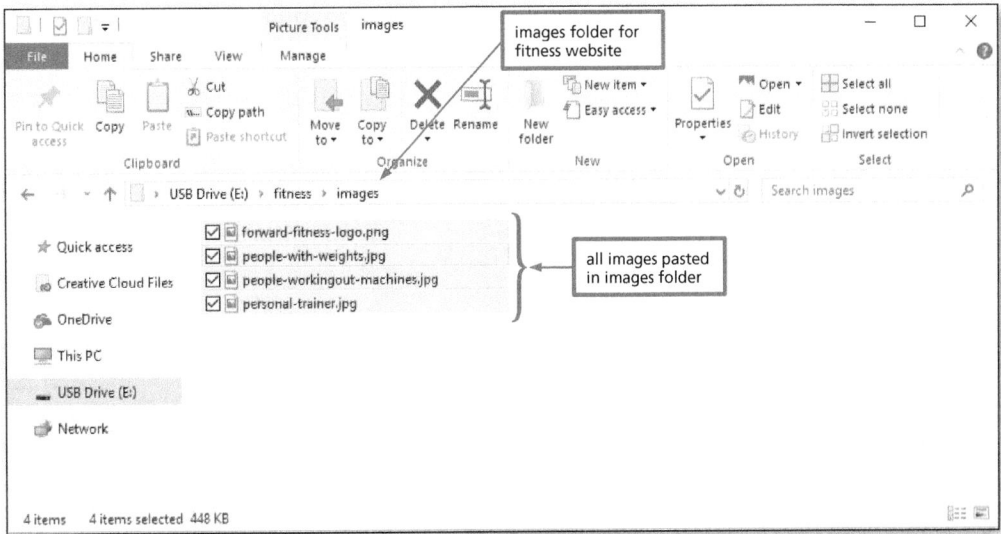

Figure 3–15

Other Ways

1 Select files, tap or click Copy button (Home tab | Clipboard group), navigate to destination folder, tap or click Paste button (Home tab | Clipboard group)

2 Select files, press CTRL+C, navigate to destination folder, press CTRL+V (Mac users: press COMMAND+C and COMMAND+V)

To Add an Image to a Website Template

In the template, the current content in the header area is a heading 1 element with the name of the business, Forward Fitness Club. Add an image below the heading element to display the business logo. *Why? Most businesses use a logo on their webpages to promote their business and brand.* The following steps add a logo image to a website template.

1

- Open your text editor to run the program.

- Tap or click File on the menu bar and then tap or click Open to display the Open dialog box.

- Navigate to your fitness folder to locate the template.html file.

- Tap or click the template.html file to display it in your text editor (Figure 3–16).

template.html file
displayed in text editor

```
1   <!DOCTYPE html>
2   <!-- This website template was created by: Student's First Name Student's Last Name -->
3   <html lang="en">
4   <head>
5       <title>Forward Fitness Club</title>
6       <meta charset="utf-8">
7   </head>
8   <body>
9
10      <!-- Use the header area for the website name or logo -->
11      <header>
12          <h1>Forward Fitness Club</h1>
13      </header>
14
15      <!-- Use the nav area to add hyperlinks to other pages within the website -->
16      <nav>
17          <p>Home   &#9475;  
18          About Us   &#9475;  
19          Classes   &#9475;  
20          Nutrition   &#9475;  
21          Contact Us</p>
22      </nav>
23
24      <!-- Use the main area to add the main content of the webpage -->
25      <main>
26      </main>
27
28      <!-- Use the footer area to add webpage footer content -->
29      <footer>
30          <p>&copy; Copyright 2021. All Rights Reserved.</p>
31          <p>forwardfitness@club.net</p>
32      </footer>
33
34  </body>
35  </html>
```

Source: Courtesy of Notepad++

Figure 3–16

2

- Place your insertion point at the end of Line 12 and press the ENTER key to insert a new Line 13.

- Type `<img src="images/forward-fitness-logo.png" alt="Forward Fitness Club logo" height="220" width="297">` to insert an image element (Figure 3–17).

Q&A Why do I need to type images/ before the name of the logo file?
All images, including the logo, are stored in the images folder, so you must include the folder name in the path to the logo file.

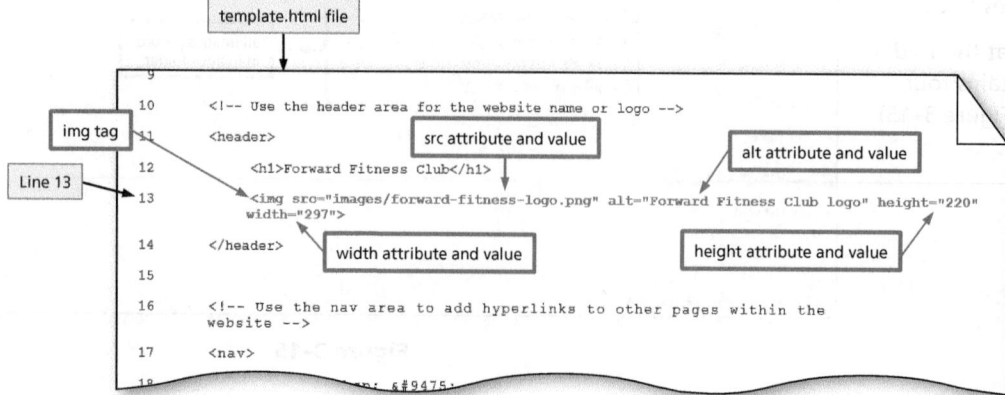

Figure 3–17

- Save your changes.
- Display the page in a web browser to view the image (Figure 3–18).

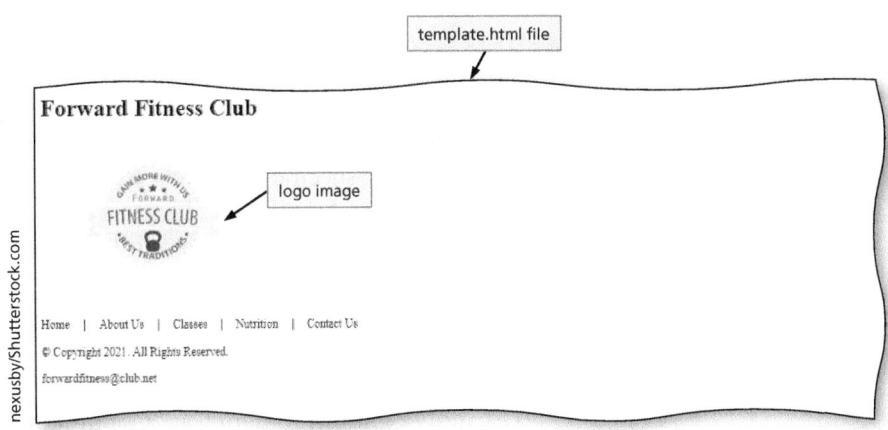

Figure 3–18

To Add an Image to the Home Page

1 ADD IMAGES | 2 ADD DIV ELEMENTS | 3 ADD HYPERLINKS | 4 ADD LISTS
5 EMBED MAP | 6 VIEW WEBSITE IN BROWSER & TEST LINKS | 7 VALIDATE PAGES

Like the template, the current content in the header area of the home page is the name of the business, Forward Fitness Club. Add an image below the heading element to display the business logo. *Why? All of the pages in the fitness website will have a logo in the header. You added an image in the template file, but still need to add it to the index.html document.* The following steps add a logo image to the home page.

- Open index.html in your text editor to edit the file.

- Place your insertion point at the end of Line 12 and press the ENTER key to insert a new Line 13.

- Type `<img src="images/ forward-fitness-logo .png" alt="Forward Fitness Club logo" height="220" width="297">` to insert an image element (Figure 3–19).

Figure 3–19

- Save your changes.

- Open File Explorer (Windows) or Finder (Mac), navigate to the index.html file, and then double-tap or double-click the file to open it in your default browser (Figure 3–20).

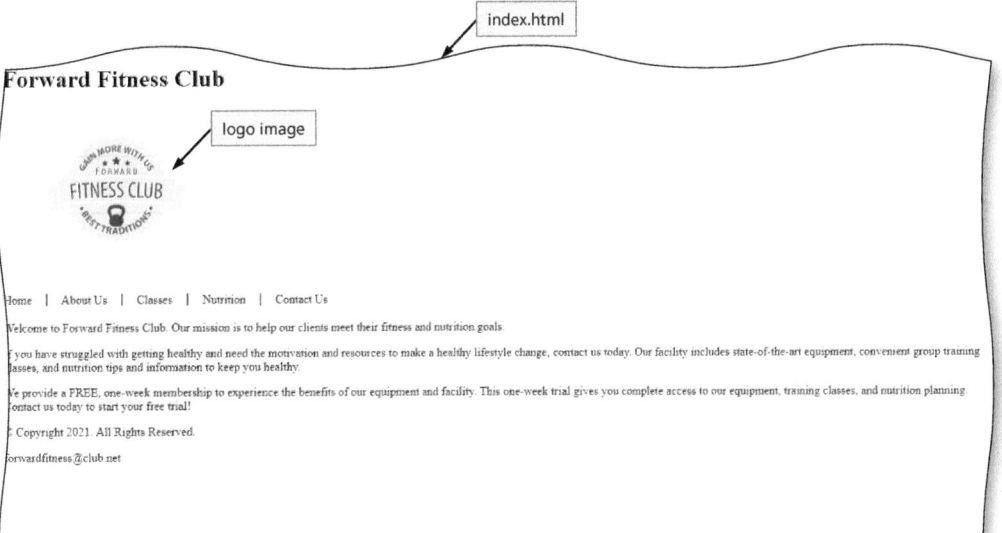

Figure 3–20

Exploring Div Elements

As you have learned, every webpage consists of several essential lines of HTML code used to display and support content in a browser. In addition, you use HTML 5 elements to identify specific areas on a webpage, such as the header, navigation area, main content area, and the footer. These are just a few of the basic HTML elements used to display a webpage. You can use other types of HTML elements to organize and display content on a webpage.

Div Element

Use a **div element** to define an area or a division in a webpage. You insert **div** elements with the <div> and </div> tags. Prior to HTML 5, **div** elements defined specific areas on a webpage, such as the header, navigation area, main content area, and footer. The HTML 5 semantic elements replace the **div** elements for these areas because the new, more meaningful HTML 5 elements better reflect their purpose. However, web designers still use the **div** element on their websites; it is not an obsolete element. One reason is that many well-established websites still have webpages that were created using **div** elements where more semantic HTML 5 elements would now apply. Some people and organizations use older browsers that can read **div** elements but not HTML 5 elements. More commonly, web designers use **div** elements to structure parts of a webpage to which an HTML 5 element does not apply. For example, recall that the **main** element identifies the primary content for the page and that you can have only one **main** element on a webpage. You can also use **div** elements within the **main** element to further divide the primary content area into separate sections, such as the introduction, a long quotation, a list of "See Also" links, and a conclusion. Figure 3–21 shows a wireframe with four **div** elements inside the **main** element.

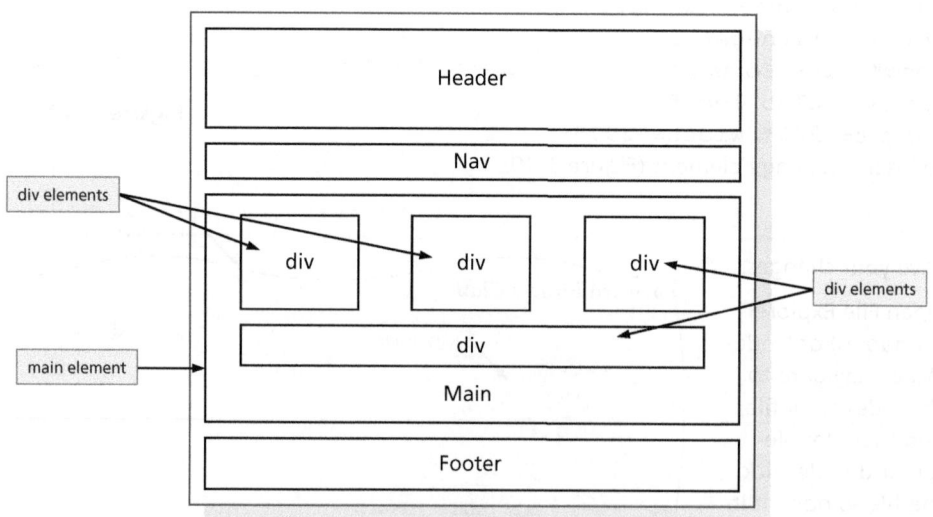

Figure 3–21

Div Attributes

Like other elements, **div** elements have attributes that provide more meaningful information about the element. One div attribute is **id**, which identifies a unique area on a webpage and distinguishes it from other page divisions. For example, <div id="menu"> is a starting div tag with an **id** attribute that has a value of **menu**.

You might use this element to identify a menu of options on the webpage. The `id` attribute value must be unique — no other `div` element on the webpage can have an `id` attribute value of `menu`. Figure 3–22 shows an example of `div` elements used in lieu of HTML 5 semantic elements. Because each `div` element has a different `id` attribute value, browsers interpret the content in those elements as belonging to different areas of the webpage.

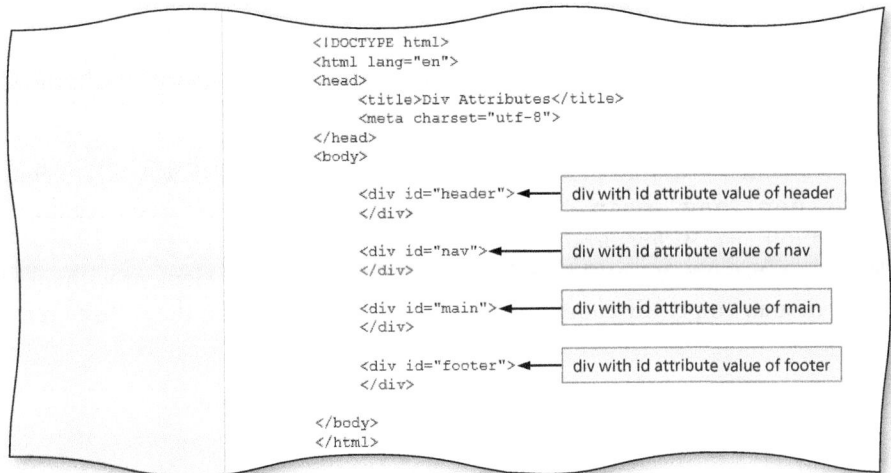

Figure 3–22

To gain flexibility in formatting the webpages on the Forward Fitness Club website, you can add a `div` element to the wireframe and template of the website. The purpose of the new `div` element is to contain all of the other webpage elements, including **header, nav, main,** and **footer.** Containing these HTML 5 elements within a single `div` element prepares the template and future pages for CSS styles, such as one that centers the webpage in a browser window. Figure 3–23 shows the revised wireframe with the `div` element and `id` attribute value defined as **container.**

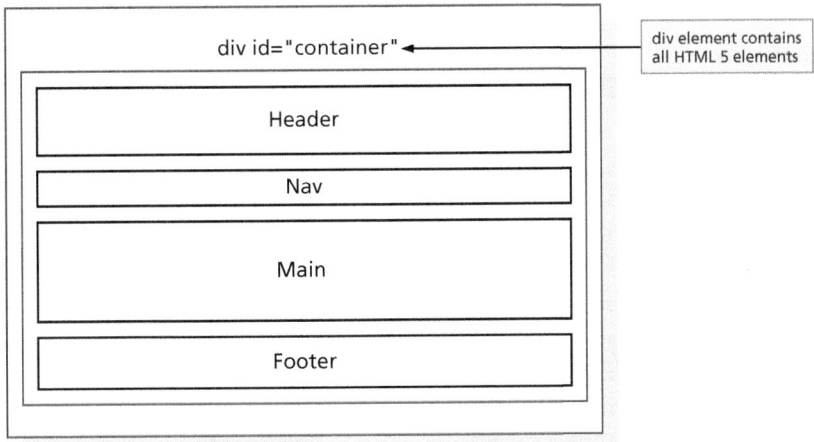

Figure 3–23

Why is "container" the value of the id attribute?

Because this div element will contain all of the webpage elements, it is commonly referred to as the container or the wrapper because it contains or wraps around all of the webpage elements, similar to how a fence wraps around a physical piece of property to contain things on the property.

To Add Div Elements to a Website Template

1 ADD IMAGES | 2 ADD DIV ELEMENTS | 3 ADD HYPERLINKS | 4 ADD LISTS
5 EMBED MAP | 6 VIEW WEBSITE IN BROWSER & TEST LINKS | 7 VALIDATE PAGES

Apply the changes from the Forward Fitness website wireframe to the template. Add a **div** element with an **id** attribute and an attribute value of **container** to contain all of the HTML 5 webpage elements in the fitness template, including **header, nav, main,** and **footer.** In addition, nest an empty div element within the main element for future use. *Why? Because the template will be used to create future pages for the website, edit the template so that all pages use the same layout.* The following steps add a **div** element with an **id** attribute value of **container** and nest an empty div element within the main element on the website template.

1

- If necessary, open the template.html file in your text editor to prepare to insert a div element.

- Place the insertion point after the starting <body> tag and then press the ENTER key two times to create new Lines 9 and 10.

- Press the TAB key to indent the line.

- Type **<div id="container">** to insert a div element with an id attribute and value (Figure 3–24).

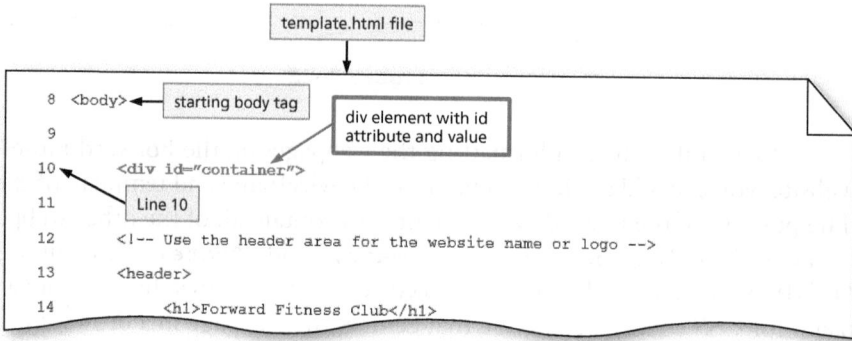

Figure 3–24

2

- Place the insertion point after the ending </footer> tag and press the ENTER key two times to create new Lines 36 and 37.

- Type **</div>** to close the div element (Figure 3–25).

Why is the ending div tag </div> instead of </div id="container">? A div attribute is defined only within the starting div tag. After a div is defined with an attribute, you close it with a </div> tag.

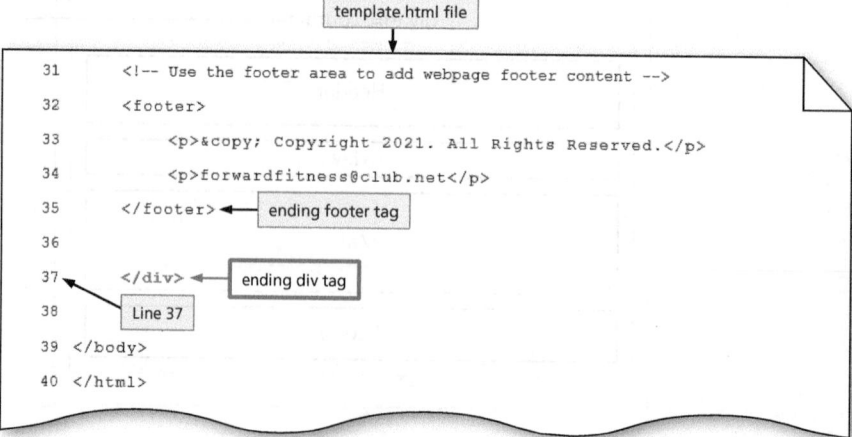

Figure 3–25

3

- Place the insertion point after the starting <main> tag and press the ENTER key two times to create new Lines 29 and 30.

- On Line 30, type **<div>** to add a starting div tag.

- Press the ENTER key and then type **</div>** to add a closing div tag.

- Press the ENTER key to create a new blank Line 32.

- Highlight Lines 12 through 39 to select all elements within the div.

- Press the TAB key to indent all of these elements.

- Save your changes (Figure 3–26).

 Q&A
What is the purpose of indenting elements within the div element?
All of the elements within the div are nested elements. Recall that you indent nested elements as a best coding practice.

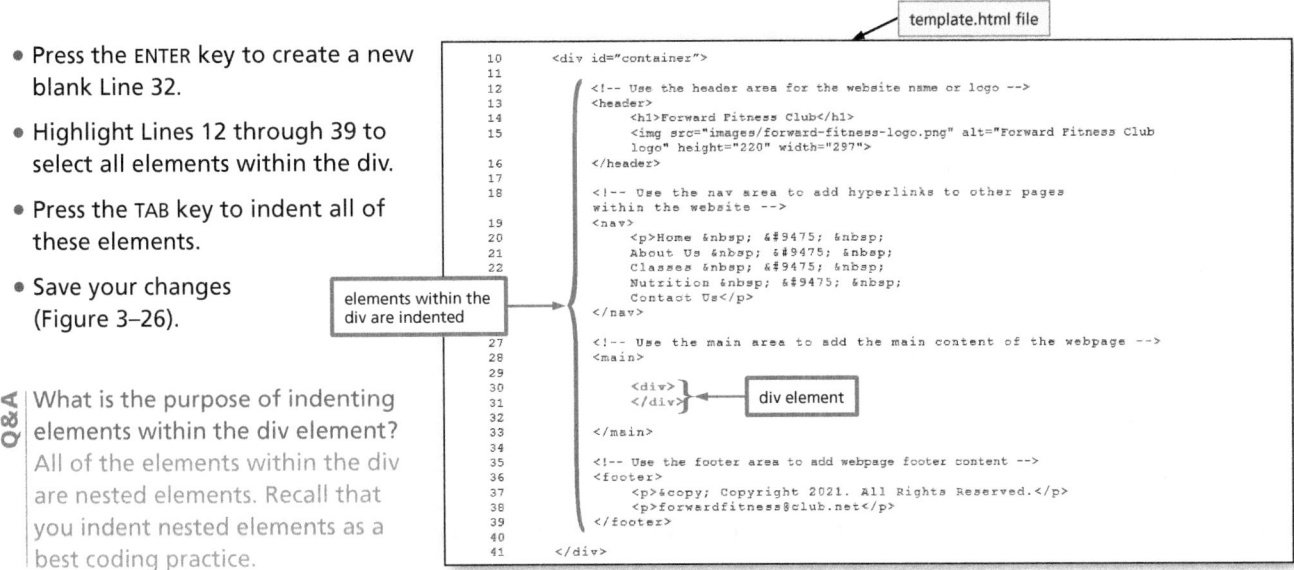

Figure 3–26

To Add a Div Element to the Home Page

1 ADD IMAGES | **2 ADD DIV ELEMENTS** | **3 ADD HYPERLINKS** | 4 ADD LISTS
5 EMBED MAP | **6 VIEW WEBSITE IN BROWSER & TEST LINKS** | **7 VALIDATE PAGES**

You must also edit the home page of the website by adding a **div** element with an **id** attribute and value of **container** to make it consistent with the website template. *Why? All of the pages within the website should use the same general template layout.* The following steps add a **div** element with an **id** attribute and value to the home page.

1

- If necessary, open the index.html file to prepare to insert a div element.

- Place the insertion point after the starting <body> tag and then press the ENTER key two times to create new Lines 9 and 10.

- Press the TAB key to increase the indent.

- Type **<div id="container">** to insert a div element with an id attribute and value (Figure 3–27).

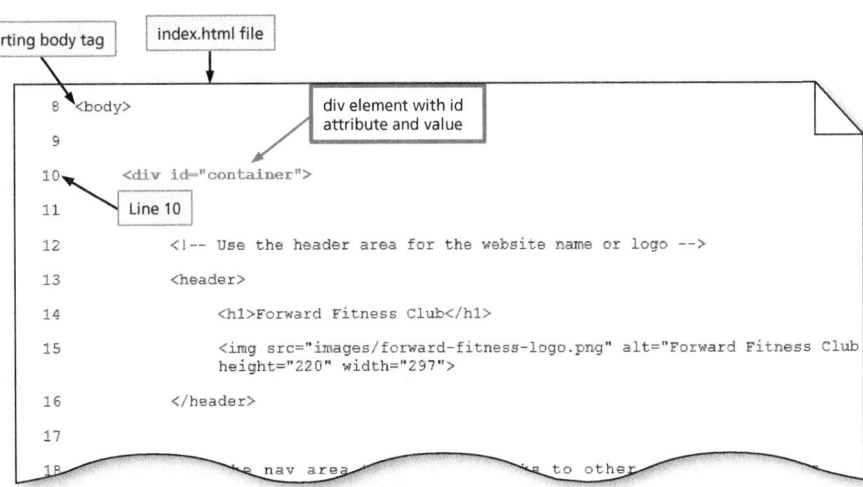

Figure 3–27

2

- Place the insertion point after the ending </footer> tag and then press the ENTER key two times to create new Lines 43 and 44.

- Type **</div>** to close the div element (Figure 3–28).

Figure 3–28

3

- Place the insertion point after the starting `<main>` tag and press the ENTER key two times to create new Lines 29 and 30.

- On Line 30, type `<div id="intro">` to add a starting div tag with an id attribute and value.

- Place your insertion point after the closing paragraph element on Line 36 and then press the ENTER key twice to insert new Lines 37 and 38.

- On Line 38, type `</div>` to close the div element.

- Highlight Lines 32 through 36 and then press the TAB key to indent these paragraph elements.

- Highlight Lines 12 through 46 to select all elements within the div.

- Press the TAB key to indent all of these elements.

- Save your changes (Figure 3–29).

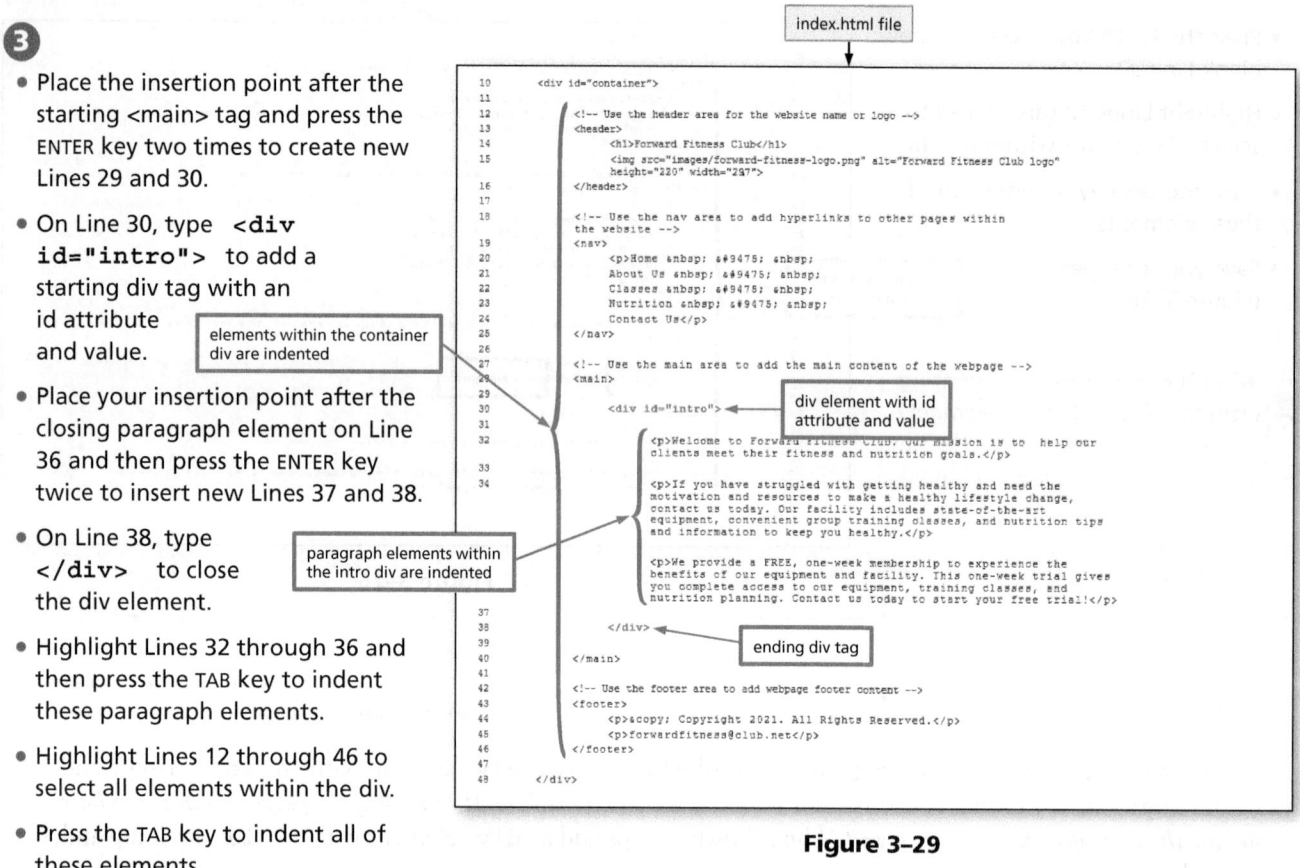

Figure 3–29

Break Point: If you want to take a break, this is a good place to do so. You can exit the text editor now. To resume at a later time, run your text editor, open the file called index.html, and continue following the steps from this location forward.

Adding Links to a Webpage

To allow a user to navigate a website and move from one page to another, web designers must add **hyperlinks**, or links, to a webpage. A **link** is text, an image, or other webpage content that visitors tap or click to instruct the browser to go to a location in a file or to request a file from a server. On the web, links are the primary way to navigate among webpages and websites. Links can reference webpages and other content, including graphics, sound, video, and program files; email addresses; and parts of the same webpage. Text links, also called hypertext links, are the most common type of hyperlink. For example, the text "About Us" in Figure 3–1 links to the About Us page in the Forward Fitness Club website.

When you code text as a hyperlink, it usually appears as underlined text in a color different from the rest of the webpage text. The default hyperlink color is blue. By default, the font color of link text changes to purple when a visitor taps or clicks the link. Most webpages also include image links. For example, the Forward Fitness Club logo in Figure 3–1 links to the home page. When a user taps or clicks the logo image, the browser displays the home page. A business logo often serves as an image link to the home page of a website. Although a hyperlinked image looks the same as other images on the page, some websites display a border around an image to indicate it is a link. As with hyperlink text, the image border is blue by default for unvisited image links and purple for image links visitors have selected.

Anchor Element

You use an **anchor element** to create a hyperlink on a webpage. An anchor element begins with an <a> tag and ends with an </a> tag. Insert the text, image, or other webpage content you want to mark as a hyperlink between the starting and ending anchor tags. Include the **href** attribute (short for "hypertext reference") in the starting anchor tag to identify the webpage, email address, file, telephone number, or other content to access. Recall from Chapter 1 that when you use attributes in HTML code, you insert the attribute name followed by an equal sign and then insert the attribute value between quotation marks, as in *name="value"* where *name* is an attribute name such as href. The value of the `href` attribute is the content to link to, such as a file or a URL. Figure 3–30 shows an example of an anchor `(a)` element with an `href` attribute that links to a home page.

BTW
Anchor Element
An anchor element without an `href` attribute does not create a hyperlink. The element is called an anchor because you use it to anchor content to text or an object on a webpage.

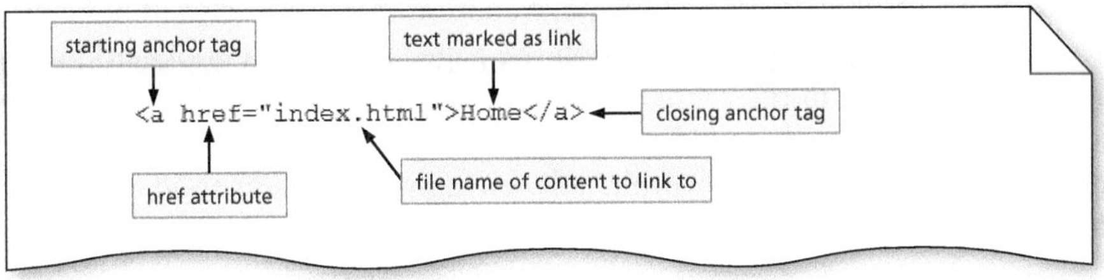

```
           starting anchor tag              text marked as link

              <a href="index.html">Home</a>       closing anchor tag

          href attribute           file name of content to link to
```

Figure 3–30

Relative Links

Hyperlinks that link to other webpages within the same website are known as **relative links**. To create a relative link, use an anchor tag with an `href` attribute that designates the file name of the webpage or the path and the file name of the webpage. Figure 3–30 shows an example of a relative link to the home page named index.html.

Depending on the location of the page or file to be displayed, a relative link may include a file path. Recall that your root fitness folder contains four subfolders: css, images, media, and script. To reference a file in one of the subfolders, you must include the path to the subfolder along with the file name. For example, you would use the following code to create a link to the Forward Fitness logo image file:

```
<a href="images/forward-fitness-logo.png">Forward Fitness
Logo</a>
```

This code means the browser should create a link to the forward-fitness-logo.png file in the images folder using Forward Fitness logo as the link text. To link to the logo in this example, you must include the file path because the logo file is not stored in the fitness root folder.

Absolute Links

Hyperlinks that link to other webpages outside of your website are known as **absolute links**. To create an absolute link, use an `anchor` element with an `href` attribute that designates a website URL. When assigning the attribute for the absolute link, begin with the http:// text, which references the HTTP protocol and indicates the webpage or other resource is located somewhere on the Internet. Next, include the website domain name such as www.cengage.com to link to that domain's home page. Figure 3–31 shows an example of an absolute link to the home page for Google. This code means the browser should create a link to www.google.com using Google as the link text.

BTW
Link Text
When determining the text to use in a link, insert or use text that concisely indicates what appears when visitors tap or click the link. For example, text such as "tap or click here" invites the appropriate action but does not identify what the link is connected to.

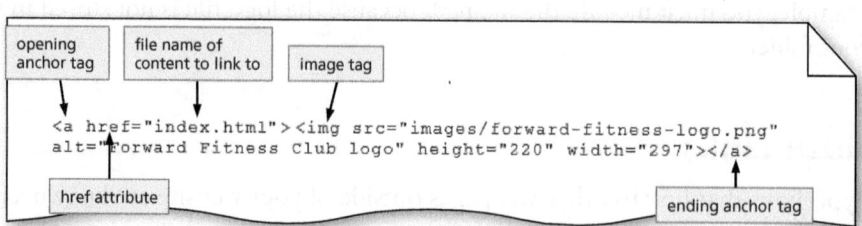

Figure 3–31

Bookmarks

Some webpages contain a lot of content, making the page quite long. This requires excessive scrolling to see all the page content. You can include bookmarks to let website visitors jump to specific areas on the page. To create a bookmark, you insert an id attribute and value in the element where you want to include a bookmark. Next, you create a link to the bookmark. For example, if the webpage has 10 lessons on the page and each lesson is contained within a div element, you insert an id attribute and value for each div. The following code creates a bookmark:

```
<div id="lesson1">
```

The following code creates a link to the bookmark:

```
<a href="#lesson1">
```

When a webpage uses bookmarks, the bookmark links typically appear as a navigation area above the div elements with the id attributes.

Image Links

In addition to text, images can also link to another page within the site, another website, an email address, or a telephone number. To configure an image with a link, place the starting anchor tag before the image element and place the ending anchor tag after the image element. Figure 3–32 shows an example of an image with a relative link to the website's home page. This code means the browser should create a link to the index.html file for the website using the image file named forward-fitness-logo.png as the link object.

```
<a href="index.html"><img src="images/forward-fitness-logo.png"
alt="Forward Fitness Club logo" height="220" width="297"></a>
```

opening anchor tag   file name of content to link to   image tag   href attribute   ending anchor tag

Figure 3–32

Email Links

Hyperlinks that link to an email address are called **email links**. Use **anchor** elements to link to an email address by including the **href** attribute followed by "mailto:" and then the email address. When a user taps or clicks an email link, their default email program runs and opens a new message with the designated email address in the To text box. Figure 3–33 shows an example of an email link. This code means the browser should create an email message addressed to forwardfitness@club .net when someone taps or clicks the "forwardfitness@club.net" link text. Figure 3–34 shows the result of a user tapping or clicking the email link shown in Figure 3–33.

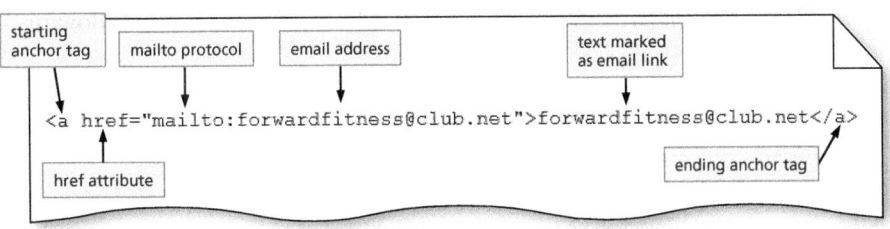

Figure 3–33

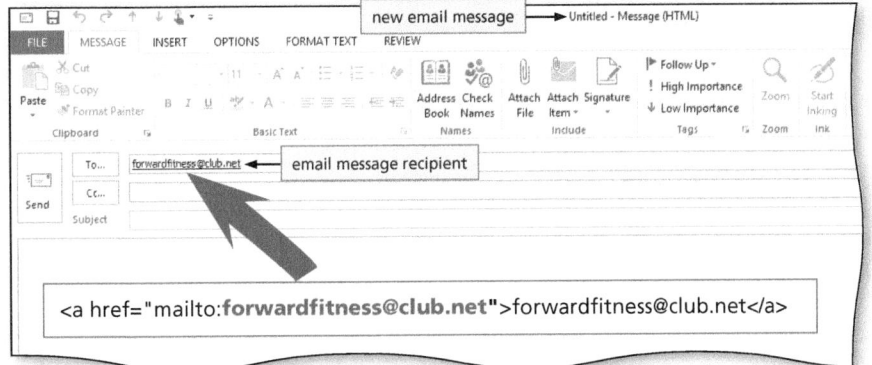

Figure 3–34

BTW
Email Links
You can assign a subject to the email by adding a question mark, followed by subject= as in <a href="mailto:forwardfitness@ club.net?Subject=Free%20 Trial">. Insert %20 instead of a space.

Telephone Links

Hyperlinks that link to a telephone number are called **telephone links** and work primarily on smartphones. Use an **anchor** element to link to a telephone number by including the **href** attribute, followed by "tel:+1*number*" where +1 is the international dialing prefix (in this case, for the United States) and *number* is the phone number, including the area code. Including the international dialing prefix makes the link accurate in any location. When a user taps or clicks a telephone link from a mobile device, a dialog box is displayed, asking whether the user wants to call the phone number. Figure 3–35 shows an example of a telephone link. This code means the browser should dial the phone number 1-800-555-2356 when someone taps or clicks the "Call us today at 800-555-2356" link text.

BTW
Other Links
You also can create links to other locations on the Internet (that is, non-http) such as FTP sites and newsgroups. To link to an FTP site, type ftp:// URL rather than http:// URL. For a newsgroup, type news:newsgroup name, and for any particular article within the newsgroup, type news:article name as the entry.

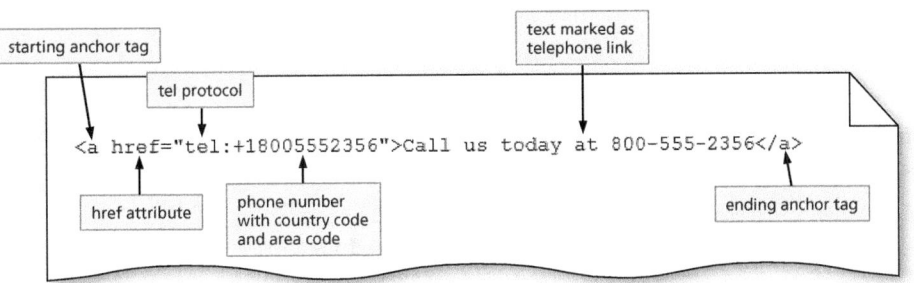

Figure 3–35

To Add Relative Links in a Website Template

1 ADD IMAGES | 2 ADD DIV ELEMENTS | 3 ADD HYPERLINKS | 4 ADD LISTS
5 EMBED MAP | 6 VIEW WEBSITE IN BROWSER & TEST LINKS | 7 VALIDATE PAGES

The **nav** section of the Forward Fitness Club website template and the home page currently contain text and images, but do not yet contain links to the pages in the website. Start by adding a relative link to the logo within the header area of the template. Next, add relative links to the navigation area of the website template to link to the home, About Us, Classes, Nutrition, and Contact Us pages. *Why? If you edit the template to include relative links, future pages created from the template will already have these links established.* The following steps add page links to a website template.

1

- If necessary, open the template .html file in the text editor.
- Place the insertion point before the image element on Line 15 to prepare to insert a starting anchor tag.
- Type **<a href="index .html">** to insert a starting anchor tag (Figure 3–36).

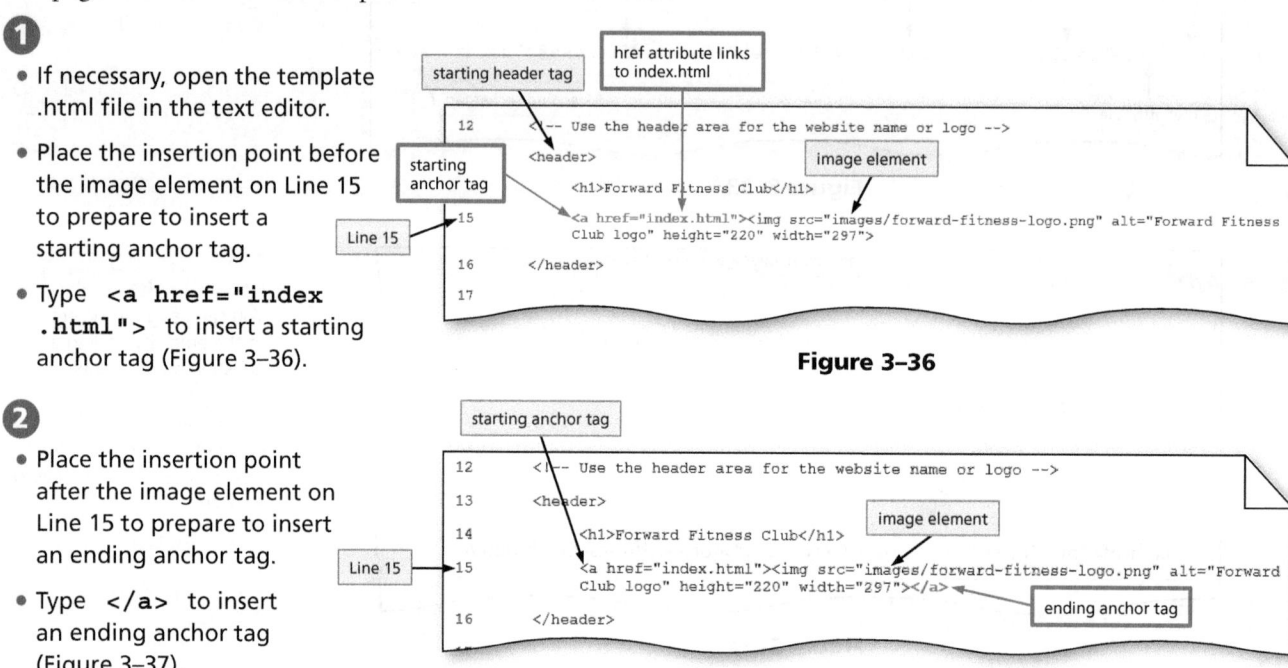

Figure 3–36

2

- Place the insertion point after the image element on Line 15 to prepare to insert an ending anchor tag.
- Type **</a>** to insert an ending anchor tag (Figure 3–37).

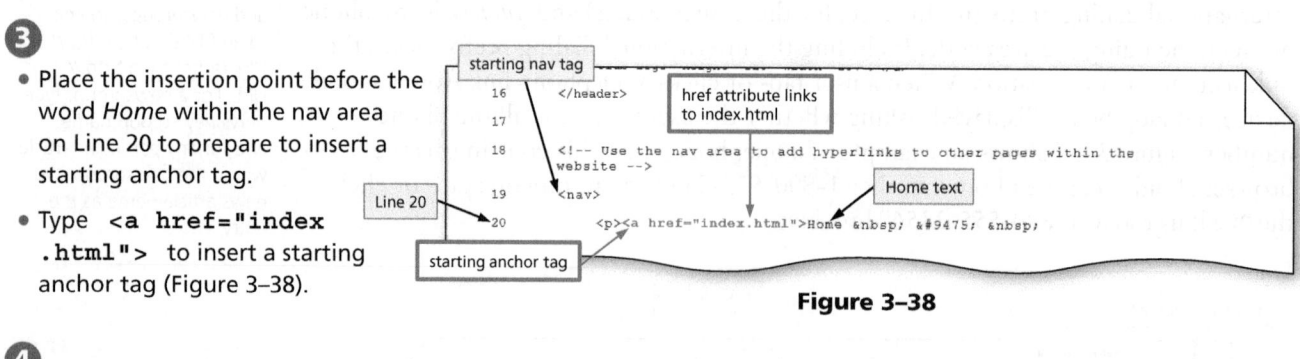

Figure 3–37

Q&A

Why is the ending tag </a> instead of </a href="index.html">?
An href attribute is defined only within the starting anchor tag. After you define an anchor with an attribute, you close the element with an </a> tag.

Why am I adding a link to the logo image?
This is a common practice across websites. On many websites, the company logo links to the home page.

3

- Place the insertion point before the word *Home* within the nav area on Line 20 to prepare to insert a starting anchor tag.
- Type **<a href="index .html">** to insert a starting anchor tag (Figure 3–38).

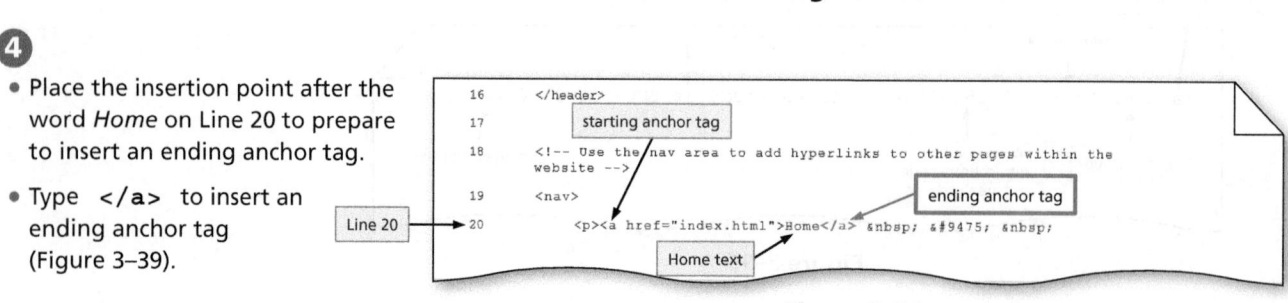

Figure 3–38

4

- Place the insertion point after the word *Home* on Line 20 to prepare to insert an ending anchor tag.
- Type **</a>** to insert an ending anchor tag (Figure 3–39).

Figure 3–39

5

- Place the insertion point before the word *About* on Line 21 to prepare to insert a starting anchor tag.

- Type **<a href="about .html">** to insert a starting anchor tag.

- Place the insertion point after the word *Us* on Line 21 to prepare to insert an ending anchor tag.

- Type **</a>** to insert an ending anchor tag (Figure 3–40).

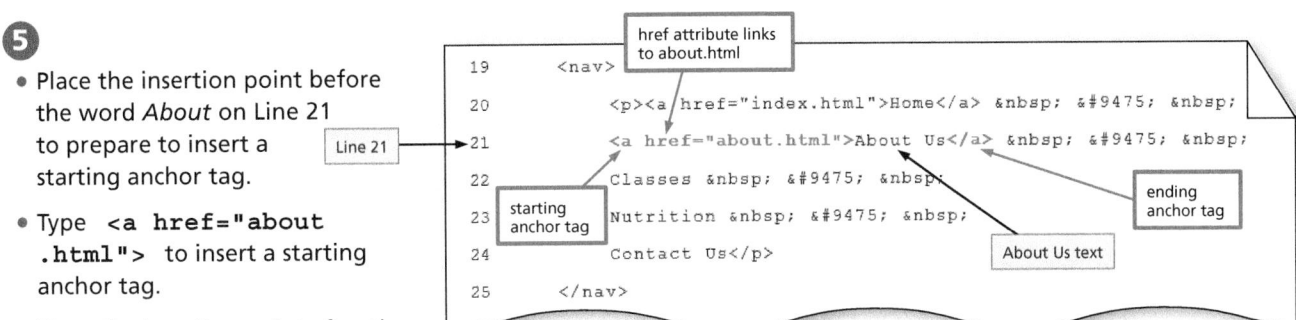

Figure 3–40

Q&A Why do I need to create a link to about.html when I have not yet created the about.html webpage?
You will use this template to create all future pages for this website. Creating the links now saves time coding for pages you create later.

6

- Using the same method as in Steps 3–5, insert anchor elements as shown in Table 3–3 to add hyperlinks to the remaining text within the navigation area (Figure 3–41).

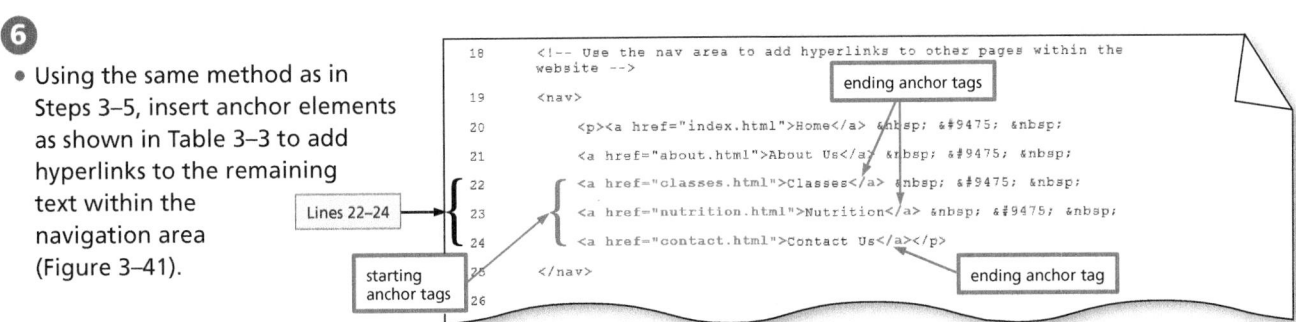

Figure 3–41

Table 3–3 Navigation Anchor Tags

Webpage Link	Anchor Tags
Classes	<a href="classes.html">Classes</a>
Nutrition	<a href="nutrition.html">Nutrition</a>
Contact Us	<a href="contact.html">Contact Us</a>

To Add an Email Link in a Website Template

1 ADD IMAGES | 2 ADD DIV ELEMENTS | 3 **ADD HYPERLINKS** | 4 **ADD LISTS**
5 EMBED MAP | 6 VIEW WEBSITE IN BROWSER & TEST LINKS | 7 VALIDATE PAGES

Next, add an email link to the email address in the footer area of the template. *Why? Visitors can tap or click the link in the footer to quickly send an email message to the Forward Fitness Club.* The following steps insert an email link in a website template.

- Place your insertion point before forwardfitness@ club.net on Line 38, located within the footer area, to prepare to insert an email anchor element.

- Type **<a href="mailto: forwardfitness@club. net">** to insert a starting anchor tag (Figure 3–42).

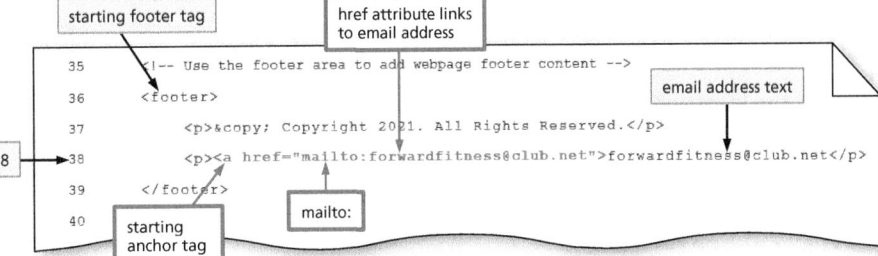

Figure 3–42

- Place the insertion point after the email address to prepare to insert an ending anchor tag.

- Type `</a>` to insert an ending anchor tag (Figure 3–43).

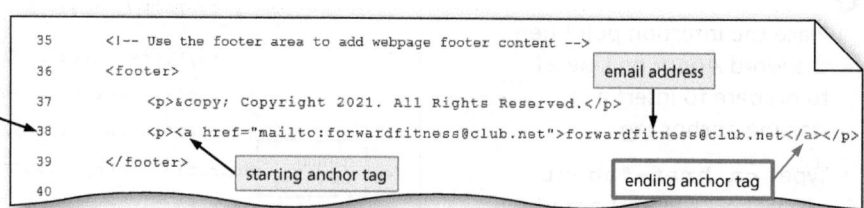

Figure 3–43

Q&A
Is forwardfitness@club.net a valid email address?

No, forwardfitness@club.net is not a valid email address; however, tapping or clicking the email link still runs the default email application on your computer and creates a message addressed to forwardfitness@club.net. If you send a message to this email address, you will receive a delivery failure notice to advise you that the email submission failed.

- Save your changes.

To Add Relative Links in the Home Page

1 ADD IMAGES | 2 ADD DIV ELEMENTS | 3 ADD HYPERLINKS | **4 ADD LISTS**
5 EMBED MAP | 6 VIEW WEBSITE IN BROWSER & TEST LINKS | 7 VALIDATE PAGES

Add relative links to the navigation area of the home page to link to the home, About Us, Classes, Nutrition, and Contact Us pages. *Why? You have already created the home page, so it cannot benefit from the links you added to the template. The home page needs hyperlinks so visitors can navigate from the home page to other pages within the website.* The following steps add relative links to the home page.

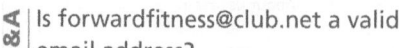

- If necessary, open the index .html file in the text editor.

- Place the insertion point before the image element on Line 15 to prepare to insert a starting anchor tag.

- Type `<a href="index .html">` to insert a starting anchor tag (Figure 3–44).

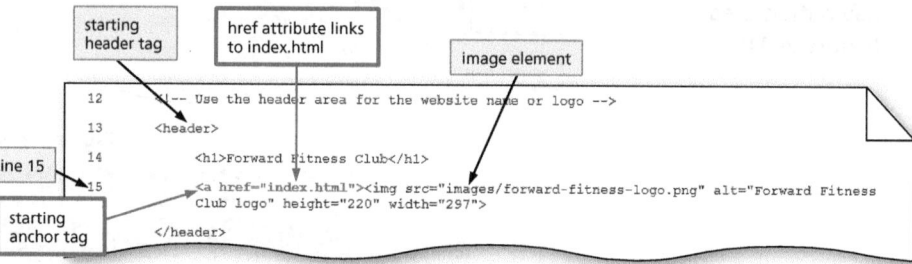

Figure 3–44

- Place the insertion point after the image element on Line 15 to prepare to insert an ending anchor tag.

- Type `</a>` to insert an ending anchor tag (Figure 3–45).

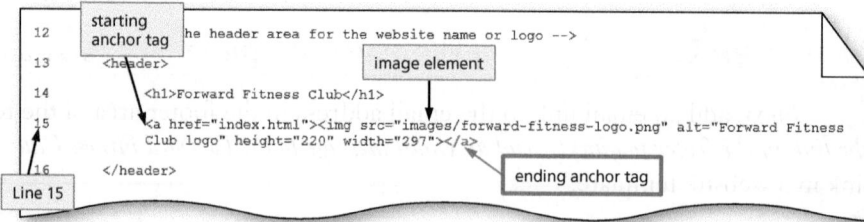

Figure 3–45

- Place the insertion point before the word *Home* within the nav area on Line 20 to prepare to insert a starting anchor tag.

- Type `<a href="index .html">` to insert a starting anchor tag (Figure 3–46).

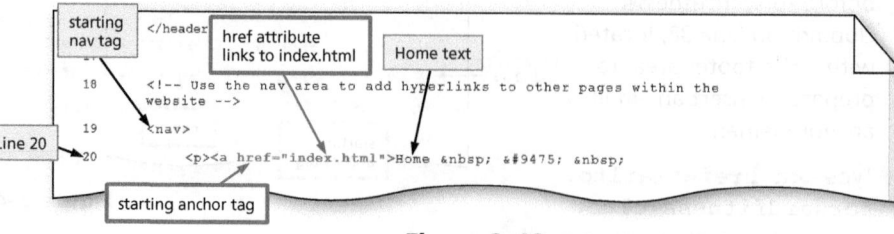

Figure 3–46

- Place the insertion point after the word *Home* on Line 20 to prepare to insert an ending anchor tag.

- Type `</a>` to insert an ending anchor tag (Figure 3–47).

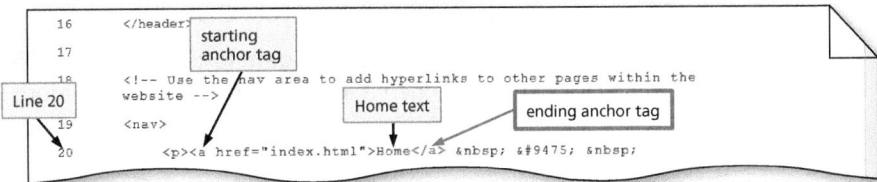

Figure 3–47

- Using the same method as in Steps 3 and 4, insert anchor elements as shown in Table 3–4 to add hyperlinks to the navigation area (Figure 3–48).

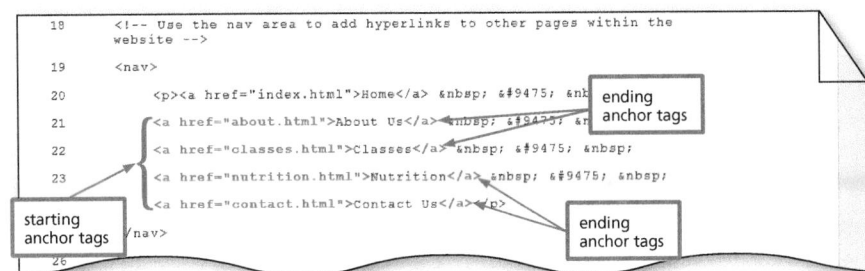

Figure 3–48

Table 3–4 Navigation Anchor Tags	
Webpage Link	**Anchor Tags**
About Us	`<a href="about.html">About Us</a>`
Classes	`<a href="classes.html">Classes</a>`
Nutrition	`<a href="nutrition.html">Nutrition</a>`
Contact Us	`<a href="contact.html">Contact Us</a>`

To Add an Email Link in the Home Page

1 ADD IMAGES | 2 ADD DIV ELEMENTS | 3 **ADD HYPERLINKS** | 4 **ADD LISTS**
5 **EMBED MAP** | 6 **VIEW WEBSITE IN BROWSER & TEST LINKS** | 7 **VALIDATE PAGES**

Next, add an email link to the email address in the footer area of the home page. ***Why?*** *Although you added an email link in the footer of the template, you still need to add an email link to the home page to match the website template.* The following steps add an email link to the home page.

- Place your insertion point before forwardfitness@club.net on Line 45, located within the footer area, to prepare to insert an email anchor tag.

- Type `<a href="mailto: forwardfitness@club .net">` to insert a starting anchor tag that links to an email address.

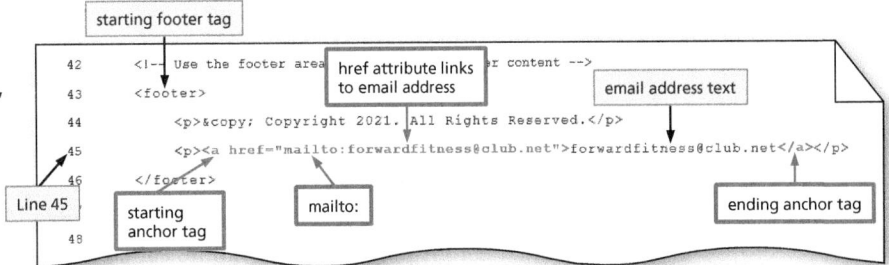

Figure 3–49

- Place the insertion point after the email address on Line 45 to prepare to insert an ending anchor tag.

- Type `</a>` to insert an ending anchor tag (Figure 3–49).

- Tap or click the Save button on the toolbar to save your changes.

- Open File Explorer (Windows) or Finder (Mac), navigate to the index.html file in the fitness folder, and then double-tap or double-click the file to open it in your default browser (Figure 3–50).

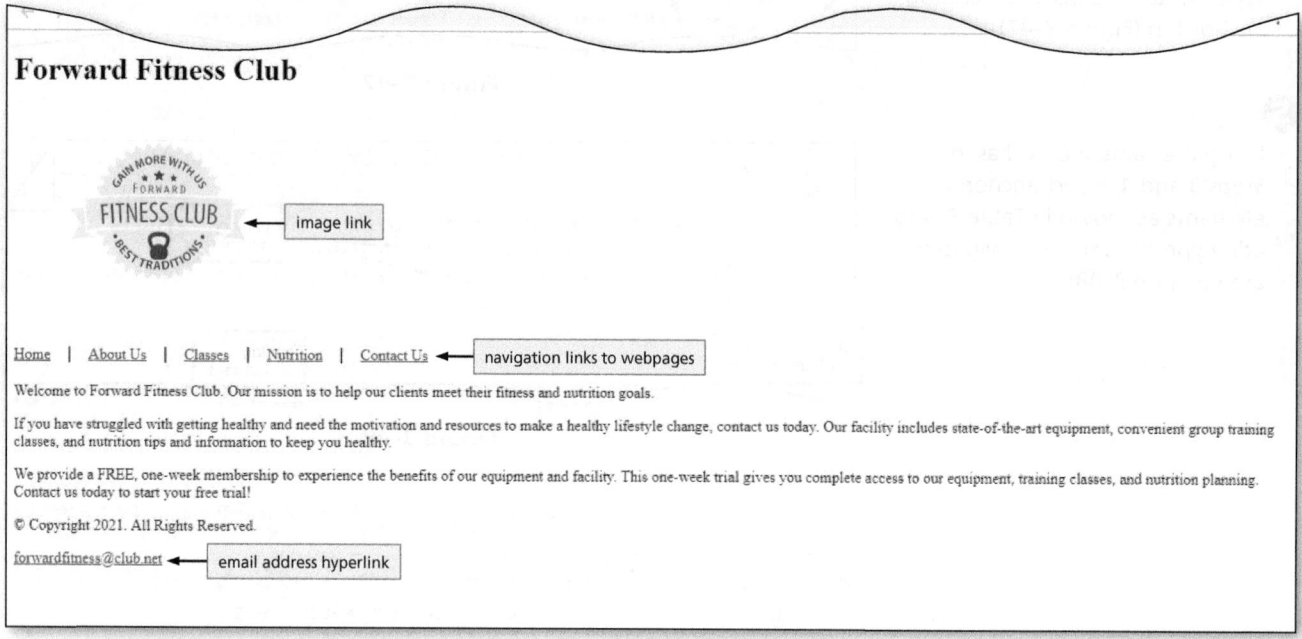

Figure 3–50

Q&A

Why is the Home link purple?

By default, visited links turn purple. The link is purple because the browser is currently displaying the home page.

 **Experiment**

- Tap or click the Home link and the email link, and then close the window for the new email message and close the browser.

Adding Lists

Some HTML elements are designed to group information on a webpage. For example, the `p` element groups text into a paragraph and the `div` element groups elements into an area or section. Lists are another type of grouping element. Lists group related items together in a sequence or collection.

Lists structure text into an itemized format. An **unordered list**, also called a bulleted list, displays a small graphic called a bullet before each item of information. In an unordered list, the bulleted items can appear in any sequence. To mark an unordered list, insert the <ul> tag at the start of the list and the </ul> tag at the end of the list. Mark each item in an unordered list with a set of list item tags (<li> and </li>). The following code creates a bulleted list of two items:

```
<ul>
  <li>First item</li>
  <li>Second item</li>
</ul>
```

An **ordered list**, also called a numbered list, displays information in a series using numbers or letters. An ordered list works well to organize items where sequence matters, such as in a series of steps. To mark an ordered list, insert the <ol> and </ol> tags at the start and end of the list. As with unordered lists, you mark each item in an ordered list with a set of <li> and </li> tags. The following code creates a numbered list of two items:

```
<ol>
   <li>First item</li>
   <li>Second item</li>
</ol>
```

Figure 3–51 shows a webpage with an unordered and an ordered list.

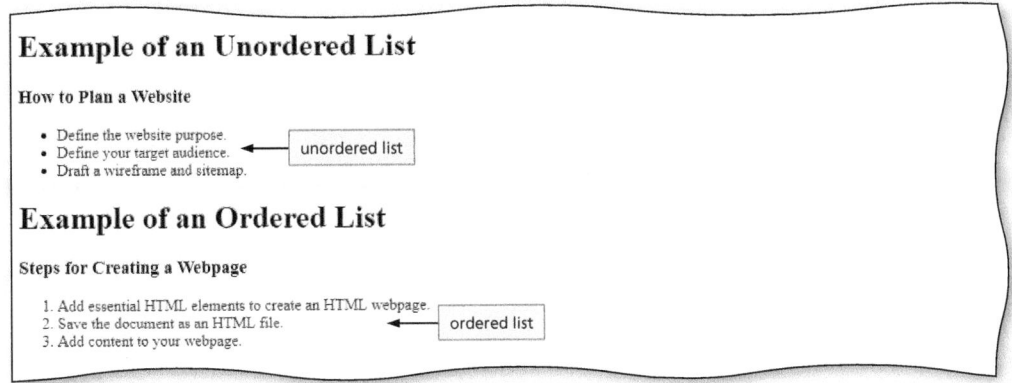

Figure 3–51

Unordered and ordered lists have optional bullet and number types. An unordered list can use one of three bullet options: disc, square, or circle. If no type is identified, the browser displays the default type, a disc. You can also specify an image to use as a bullet. An ordered list can use numbers, letters, or Roman numerals. The default option is to use Arabic numbers, such as 1, 2, and 3. Table 3–5 shows the different values and examples of unordered and ordered list options. Although you can use the `style` attribute to specify the style of bullets and numbers, the recommended method for changing bullet list and number styles is with CSS, which is covered in Chapter 4.

Table 3–5 List Type Attributes	
Value	**Example**
Unordered Lists	
disc (default)	•
square	■
circle	○
Ordered Lists	
1	1. 2. 3.
A	A. B. C.
a	a. b. c.
I	I. II. III.
i	i. ii. iii.

A **description list** contains terms and descriptions. Use a description list to create a glossary or to list questions and answers, for example. A description list includes terms and descriptions or definitions. Define a description list between a pair of <dl> and </dl> tags. Mark each term within a pair of <dt> and </dt> tags. Mark each description or definition between a pair of <dd> and </dd> tags. For each item, the `dt` element must come before the `dd` element. More than one `dd` element can follow a `dt` element. The following code creates a description list of two terms and definitions:

```
<dl>
  <dt>First term</dt>
  <dd>First definition</dd>

  <dt>Second term</dt>
  <dd>Second definition - part 1</dd>
  <dd>Second definition - part 2</dd>
</dl>
```

Figure 3–52 shows an example of a description list.

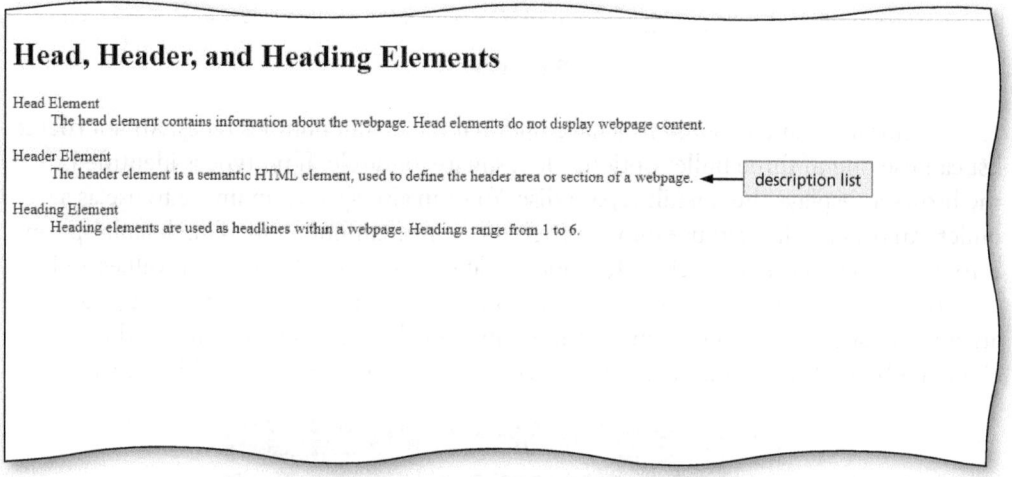

Figure 3–52

To Create the About Us Webpage and Add Content

1 ADD IMAGES | 2 ADD DIV ELEMENTS | 3 ADD HYPERLINKS | 4 ADD LISTS
5 EMBED MAP | 6 VIEW WEBSITE IN BROWSER & TEST LINKS | 7 VALIDATE PAGES

The About Us page provides additional information about the Forward Fitness Club, including pictures of its facility. The page uses div elements, headings, and unordered lists to organize the page content. Use the website template to create the About Us page. *Why? The website template already contains the basic HTML code for the website. Using the template saves time coding.* The following steps create the About Us page for the fitness website using the website template.

- If necessary, reopen the template .html file to create a new webpage using the template file.

- Tap or click File on the menu bar and then tap or click Save As to display the Save As dialog box.

- Type **about** in the File name text box to name the file (Figure 3–53).

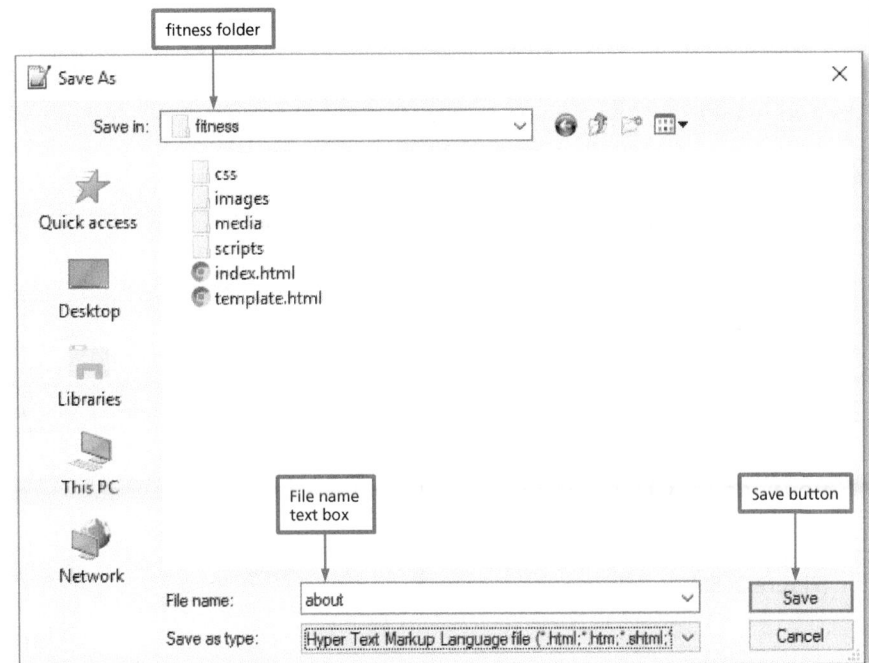

Figure 3–53

- Tap or click the Save button to save the file in the fitness folder.

- On Line 30, within the starting div tag, press SPACEBAR, and then type **id="weights"** to add an id attribute and value.

- To the right of the closing > bracket, press the ENTER key once to insert a new Line 31 (Figure 3–54).

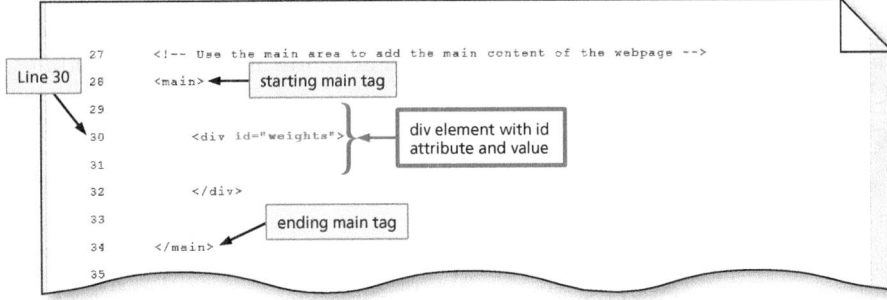

Figure 3–54

3

- Press the ENTER key again to insert a new Line 32.

- On Line 32, press the TAB key and then type **<h1>Weights</h1>** to add a heading 1 element and content to the page.

- Press the ENTER key and then type
<img src="images /people-with-weights .jpg" alt="Two people working out with a weight in each hand" height="300" width="450"> to add an image element to the page (Figure 3–55).

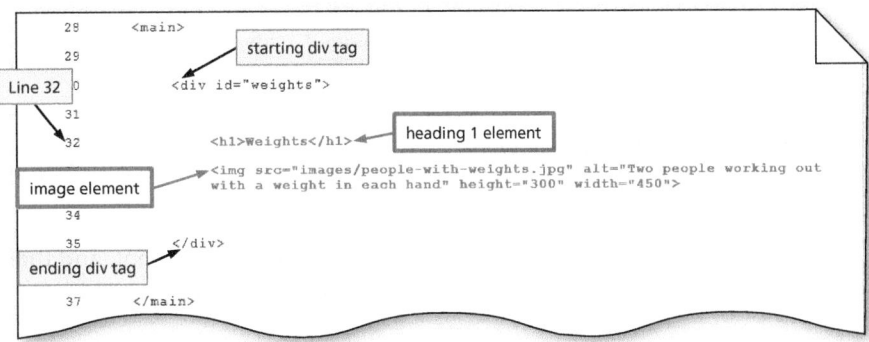

Figure 3–55

Why am I setting 300 as the height and 450 as the width?

These are the actual dimensions of the people-with-weights.jpg image file. In Windows, you can verify the dimensions by pressing and holding or right-clicking the image file, and then selecting Properties on the shortcut menu to display the Properties dialog box for the file. Tap or click the Details tab. The dimensions are listed in the Image section of the Details tabbed page.

4

- Press the ENTER key to insert a new Line 34.

- Type `<p>Our facility includes a weight training area with several weight options. Build lean muscle with weights and improve your core with weight training.</p>` to add a paragraph element to the page (Figure 3–56).

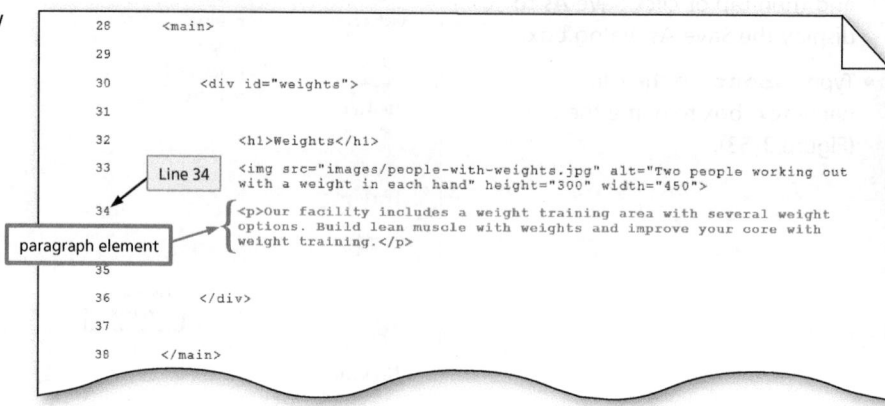

Figure 3–56

To Add Unordered Lists to the About Us Webpage

1 ADD IMAGES | 2 ADD DIV ELEMENTS | 3 ADD HYPERLINKS | 4 ADD LISTS
5 EMBED MAP | 6 VIEW WEBSITE IN BROWSER & TEST LINKS | 7 VALIDATE PAGES

The About Us page should list the types of equipment the Forward Fitness Club provides to its members. You can include these items using unordered lists. *Why? The types of equipment can appear in any order in the lists, so the items are appropriate for unordered lists.* The following steps add headings and unordered lists to the About Us page.

1

- With the insertion point at the end of Line 34, press the ENTER key to insert a new Line 35.

- Type `<ul>` to insert a starting unordered list tag.

- Press the ENTER key, increase the indent, and then type `<li>Dumbbells</li>` to add the first list item.

- Press the ENTER key and then type `<li>Kettle bells</li>` to add the second list item.

- Press the ENTER key and then type `<li>Barbells</li>` to add the third list item.

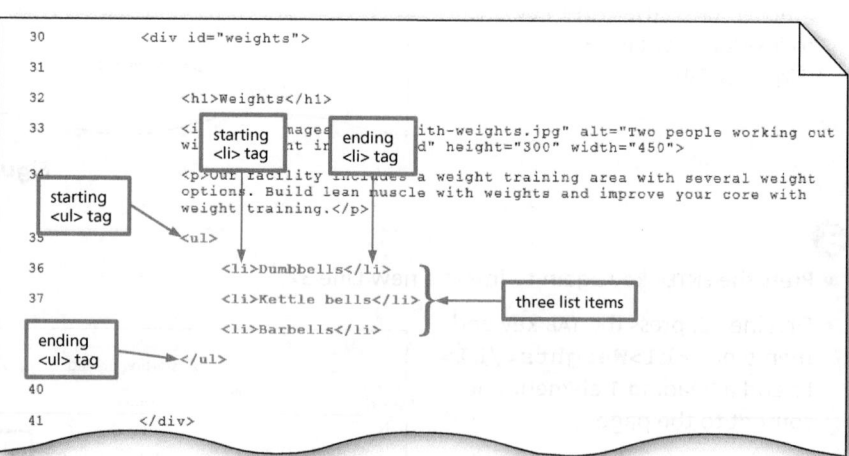

Figure 3–57

- Press the ENTER key, press the SHIFT+TAB keys to decrease the indent, and then type `</ul>` to add the ending unordered list tag (Figure 3–57).

2

- Save your changes.

- Open File Explorer (Windows) or Finder (Mac), navigate to the about.html file, and then double-tap or double-click the file to open it in your default browser.

- If necessary, scroll down to view the main content (Figure 3–58).

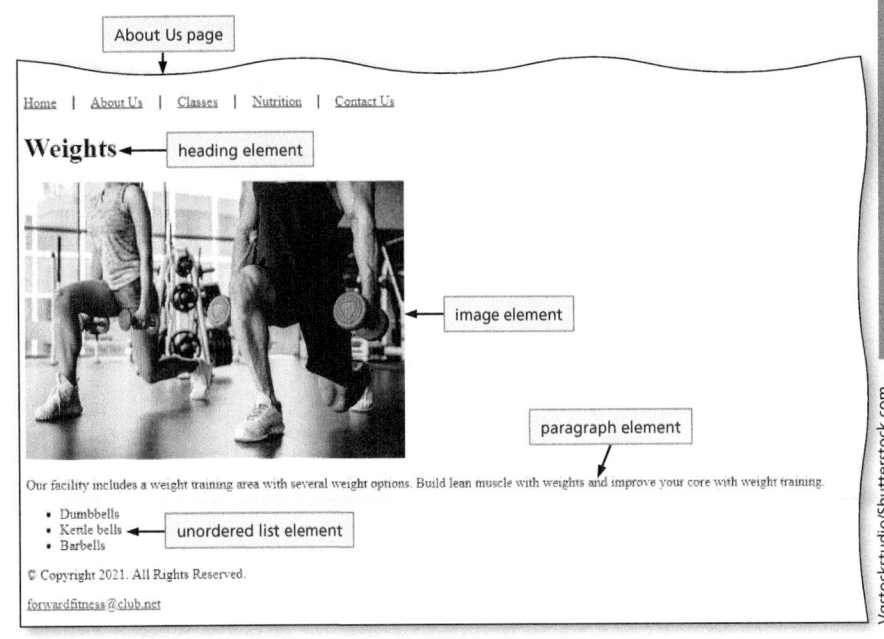

Figure 3–58

3

- Place your insertion point after the closing div tag on Line 41, and then press the ENTER key two times to insert new Lines 42 and 43.

- Type the code shown in Table 3–6 to insert additional div elements with headings, images, and unordered lists (Figure 3–59).

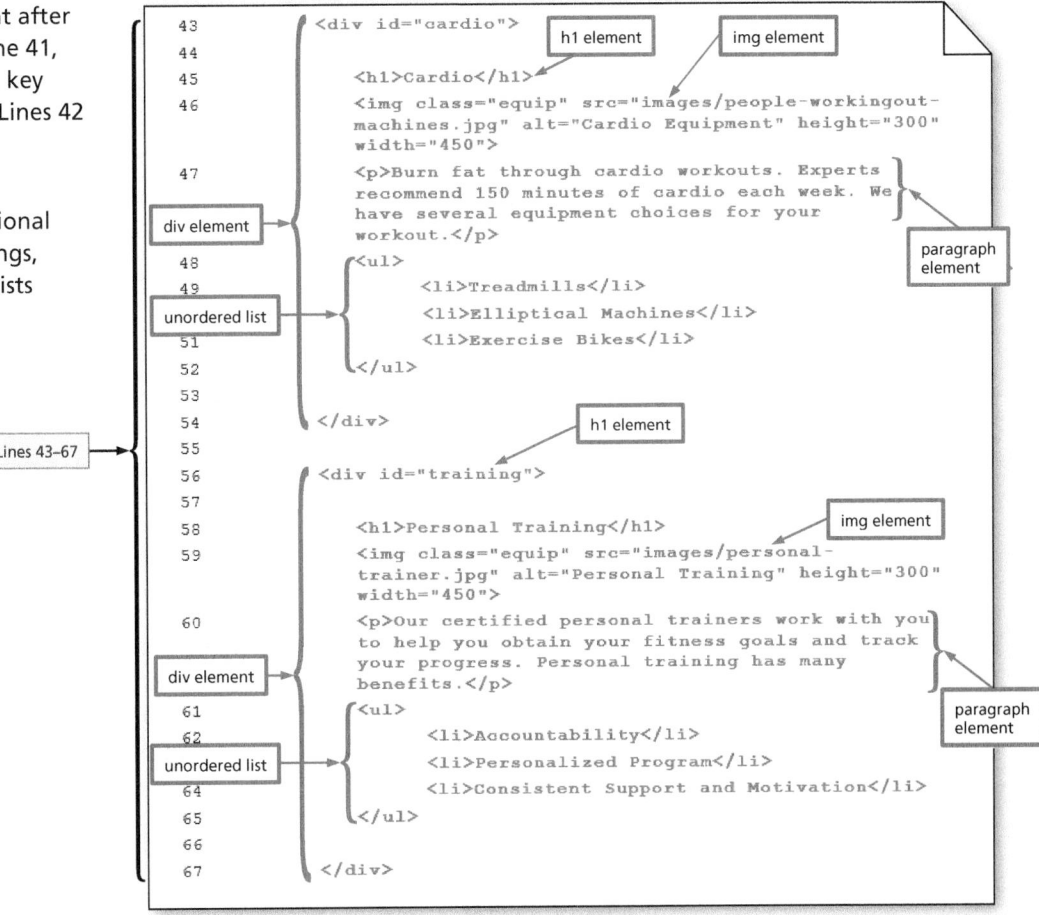

Figure 3–59

Table 3–6 About Us Code for Lines 43–67

Line Number	Code to Insert
43	<div id="cardio">
44	
45	<h1>Cardio</h1>
46	<img class="equip" src="images/people-workingout-machines.jpg" alt="Cardio Equipment" height="300" width="450">
47	<p> Burn fat through cardio workouts. Experts recommend 150 minutes of cardio each week. We have several equipment choices for your workout.</p>
48	<ul>
49	<li>Treadmills</li>
50	<li>Elliptical Machines</li>
51	<li>Exercise Bikes</li>
52	</ul>
53	
54	</div>
55	
56	<div id="training">
57	
58	<h1>Personal Training</h1>
59	<img class="equip" src="images/personal-trainer.jpg" alt="Personal Training" height="300" width="450">
60	<p> Our certified personal trainers work with you to help you obtain your fitness goals and track your progress. Personal training has many benefits.</p>
61	<ul>
62	<li>Accountability</li>
63	<li>Personalized Program</li>
64	<li>Consistent Support and Motivation</li>
65	</ul>
66	
67	</div>

To Add a Description List and Absolute Link to the About Us Webpage

1 ADD IMAGES | 2 ADD DIV ELEMENTS | 3 ADD HYPERLINKS | 4 ADD LISTS
5 EMBED MAP | 6 VIEW WEBSITE IN BROWSER & TEST LINKS | 7 VALIDATE PAGES

The About Us page should also describe the types of exercises the Forward Fitness Club recommends for its members. You can include these descriptions using a description list. Below the description list, include an absolute link to hhs.gov with more information about being active. *Why? The webpage can list the exercises by name followed by a description, which is appropriate for a description list.* The following step adds a description list to the About Us page.

- With the insertion point at the end of Line 67, press the ENTER key two times to insert new Lines 68 and 69.

- Type the code shown in Table 3–7 to insert a div element with a heading 1 element, paragraph elements, and a description list (Figure 3–60).

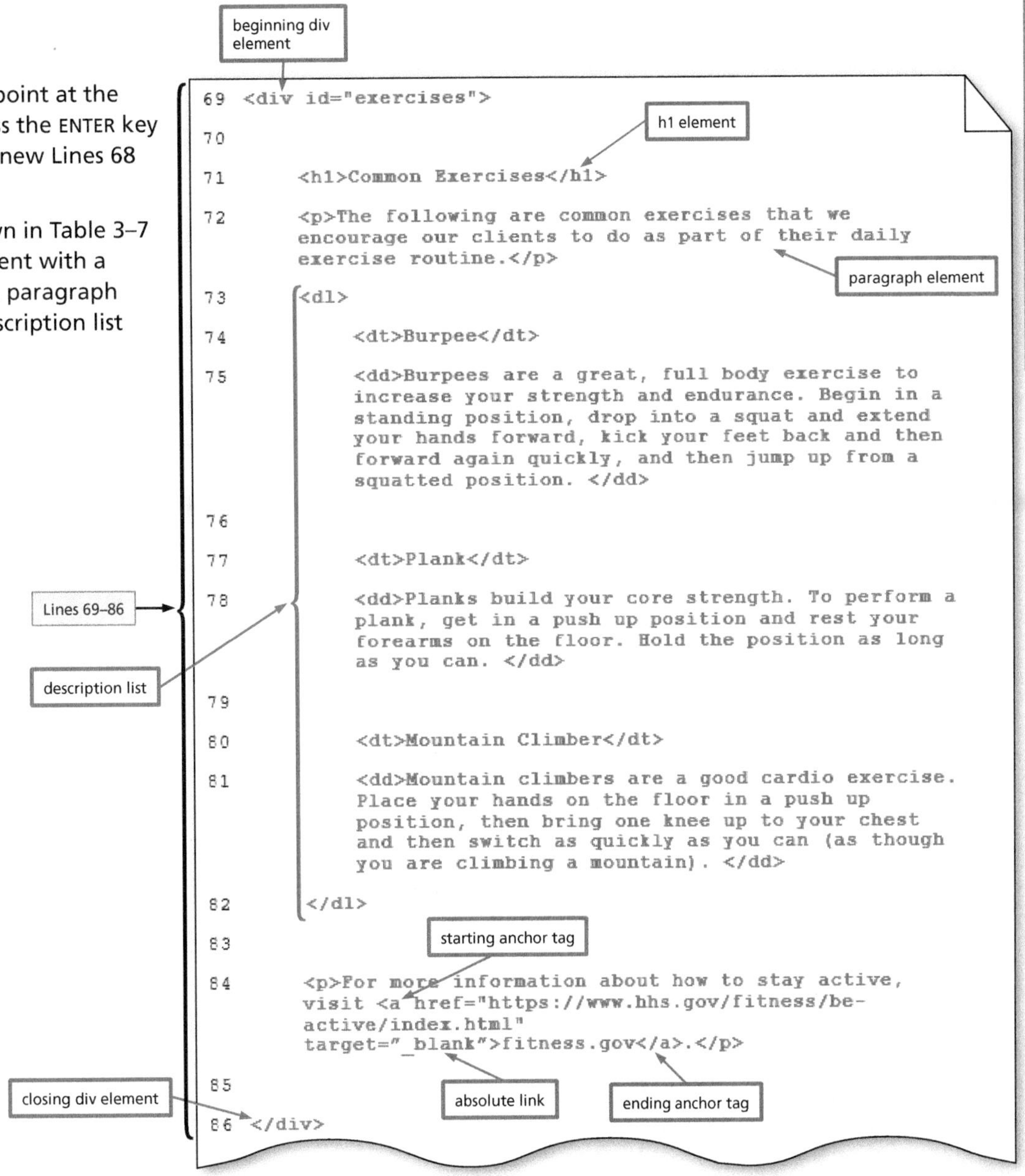

```
69   <div id="exercises">
70
71       <h1>Common Exercises</h1>
72       <p>The following are common exercises that we
         encourage our clients to do as part of their daily
         exercise routine.</p>
73   <dl>
74           <dt>Burpee</dt>
75           <dd>Burpees are a great, full body exercise to
             increase your strength and endurance. Begin in a
             standing position, drop into a squat and extend
             your hands forward, kick your feet back and then
             forward again quickly, and then jump up from a
             squatted position. </dd>
76
77           <dt>Plank</dt>
78           <dd>Planks build your core strength. To perform a
             plank, get in a push up position and rest your
             forearms on the floor. Hold the position as long
             as you can. </dd>
79
80           <dt>Mountain Climber</dt>
81           <dd>Mountain climbers are a good cardio exercise.
             Place your hands on the floor in a push up
             position, then bring one knee up to your chest
             and then switch as quickly as you can (as though
             you are climbing a mountain). </dd>
82   </dl>
83
84       <p>For more information about how to stay active,
         visit <a href="https://www.hhs.gov/fitness/be-
         active/index.html"
         target="_blank">fitness.gov</a>.</p>
85
86   </div>
```

Callouts: beginning div element · h1 element · paragraph element · Lines 69–86 · description list · starting anchor tag · closing div element · absolute link · ending anchor tag

Figure 3–60

Table 3–7 About Us Code for Lines 69–86	
Line Number	**Code to Insert**
69	<div id="exercises">
70	
71	<h1>Common Exercises</h1>
72	<p>The following are common exercises that we encourage our clients to do as part of their daily exercise routine.</p>
73	<dl>
74	<dt>Burpee</dt>
75	<dd>Burpees are a great full-body exercise to increase your strength and endurance. Begin in a standing position, drop into a squat and extend your hands forward, kick your feet back and then forward again quickly, and then jump up from a squatted position. </dd>
76	
77	<dt>Plank</dt>
78	<dd>Planks build your core strength. To perform a plank, get in a push-up position and rest your forearms on the floor. Hold the position as long as you can. </dd>

(*Continued*)

Line Number	Code to Insert
Table 3–7 About Us Code for Lines 69–86 *(Continued)*	
79	
80	<dt>Mountain Climber</dt>
81	<dd>Mountain climbers are a good cardio exercise. Place your hands on the floor in a push-up position, bring one knee up to your chest, and then switch as quickly as you can (as though you are climbing a mountain).</dd>
82	</dl>
83	
84	<p>For more information about how to stay active, visit the <a href="https://www.hhs.gov/fitness/be-active/index.html" target="_blank">U.S. Department of Health and Human Services</a>.</p>
85	
86	</div>

To Save the About Us Webpage and View It in a Browser

The About Us page is finished for now. The following steps save the webpage and view it in your default browser.

1 Check the spelling in your document to find misspelled words and correct them as necessary.

2 Save and close the about.html file.

3 Using File Explorer (Windows) or Finder (Mac), navigate to the about.html file, open the file to display it in your default browser, and then scroll down to display the cardio div element (Figure 3–61).

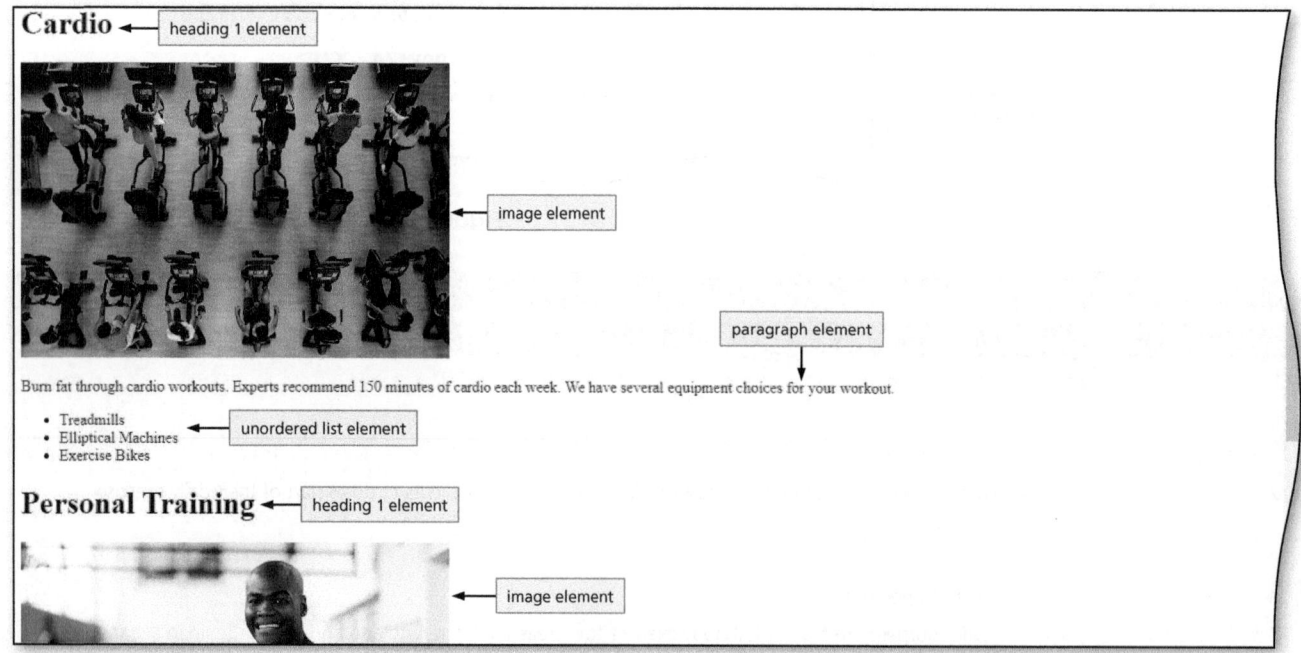

Figure 3–61

istockphoto.com/andresr, michaeljung/Shutterstock.com

④ Scroll down the page and display the description list (Figure 3–62).

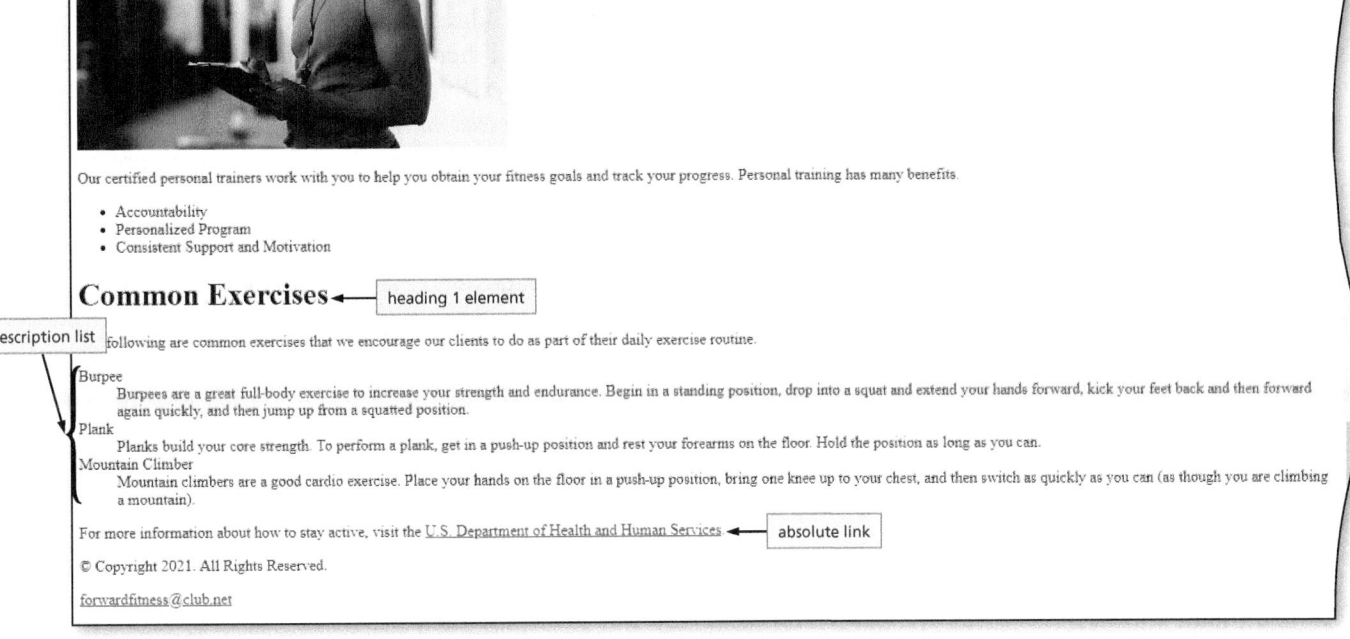

Figure 3–62

⑤ Tap or click the U.S. Department of Health and Human Services link to open the hhs.gov website (Figure 3–63).

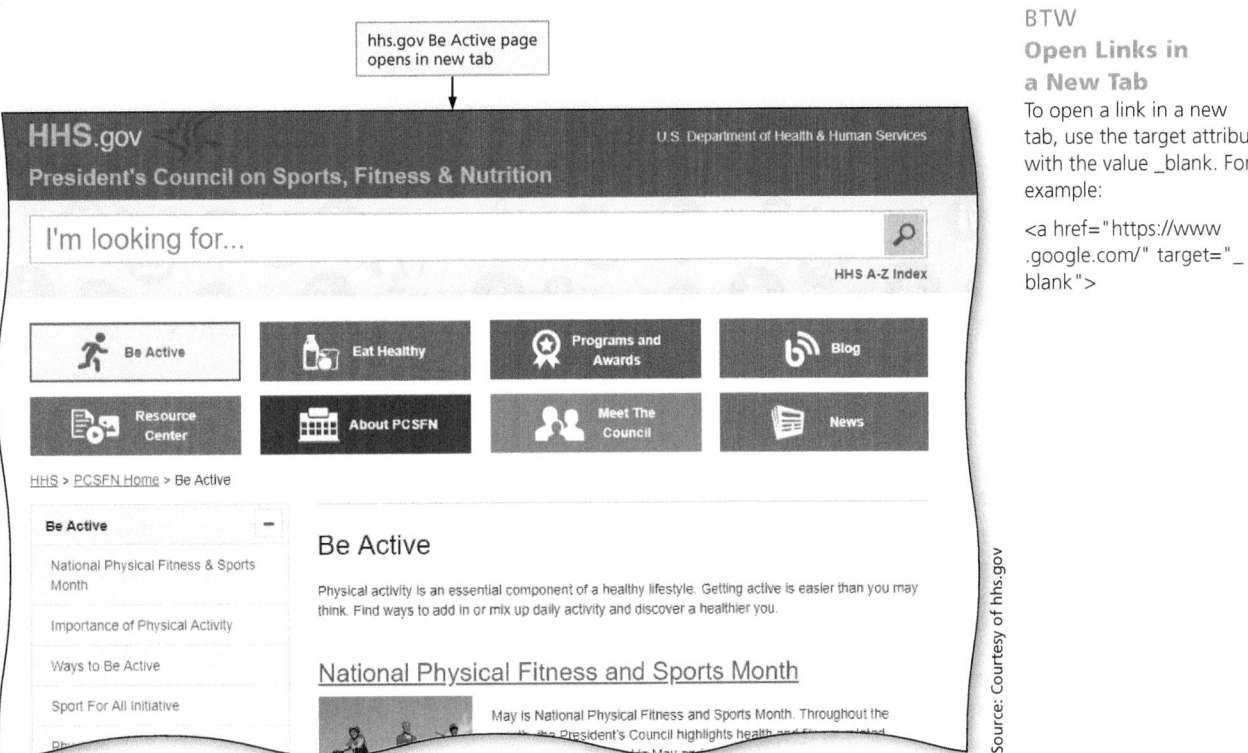

Figure 3–63

BTW

Open Links in a New Tab

To open a link in a new tab, use the target attribute with the value _blank. For example:

<a href="https://www .google.com/" target="_ blank">

To Create the Contact Us Webpage and Add a Heading and Links

The Contact Us page provides an address, a phone number, an email address, and a location map for the Forward Fitness Club. Insert a heading to identify the new information, and then add the phone number, an email address with an email link text, and an address and location map. *Why? Potential customers need to know how to contact the Forward Fitness Club. Including an email link allows visitors to send an email message directly to the Forward Fitness Club. Including a location map allows visitors to see where the club is located.* The following steps create the Contact Us page for the fitness website using the website template.

1
- If necessary, reopen the template.html template file to create a new webpage using the template file.
- Tap or click File on the menu bar and then tap or click Save As to display the Save As dialog box.
- Type `contact` in the File name text box to name the file.
- Tap or click the Save button to save the contact file in the fitness folder.
- On Line 30, within the div element, press SPACEBAR, and then type `id="contact"` to insert an id attribute and value.
- To the right of the closing > bracket, press the ENTER key once to insert a new Line 31. (Figure 3–64).

```
27     <!-- Use the main area to add the main content of the webpage -->
28       <main>          starting main tag
29
30           <div id="contact">
31    Line 30                              div element with id
32           </div>                        attribute and value
33
34       </main>
35                        ending main tag
```

Figure 3–64

2
- Place your insertion point at the end of Line 30 and press the ENTER key twice to insert new Lines 31 and 32.
- On Line 32, press the TAB key, and then type `<h2>Ready to get started? Contact us today.</h2>` to insert a heading 2 element.
- Press the ENTER key to insert a new Line 33 and then type `<h4>Call us: (814) 555-9608</h4>` to insert a heading 4 element.
- Press the ENTER key to insert a new Line 34 and then type `<h4>Email us: <a href="mailto:forwardfitness@club.net">forwardfitness@club.net</a></h4>` to insert a heading 4 element with an email text link.
- Press the ENTER key to insert a new Line 35 and then type `<h4>Visit us at: 1275 Channel Center Street, Boston, MA 02210</h4>` to insert a heading 4 element (Figure 6–65).

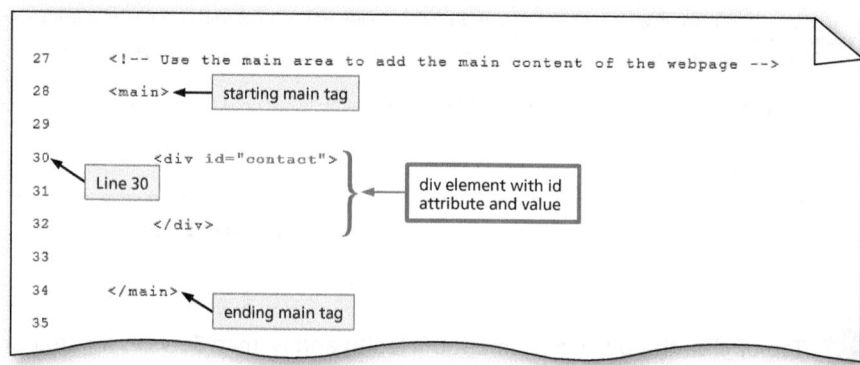

```
28       <main>
                heading elements
30           <div id="contact">
31
32           <h2>Ready to get started? Contact us today.</h2>   link to email address
33           <h4>Call us: (814) 555-9608</h4>
34           <h4>Email us: <a href="mailto:forwardfitness@club.net">forwardfitness@club.net</a></h4>
35           <h4>Visit us at: 1275 Channel Center Street, Boston, MA 02210</h4>
36
37           </div>
38
39       </main>        ending <main> tag
40
```
Lines 32–35

3 Check the spelling in your document to find misspelled words and correct them as necessary.

Figure 3–65

4 Save the contact.html file.

5 In File Explorer (Windows) or Finder (Mac), navigate to the contact.html file, and then open the file in your default browser (Figure 3–66).

contact.html page

Forward Fitness Club

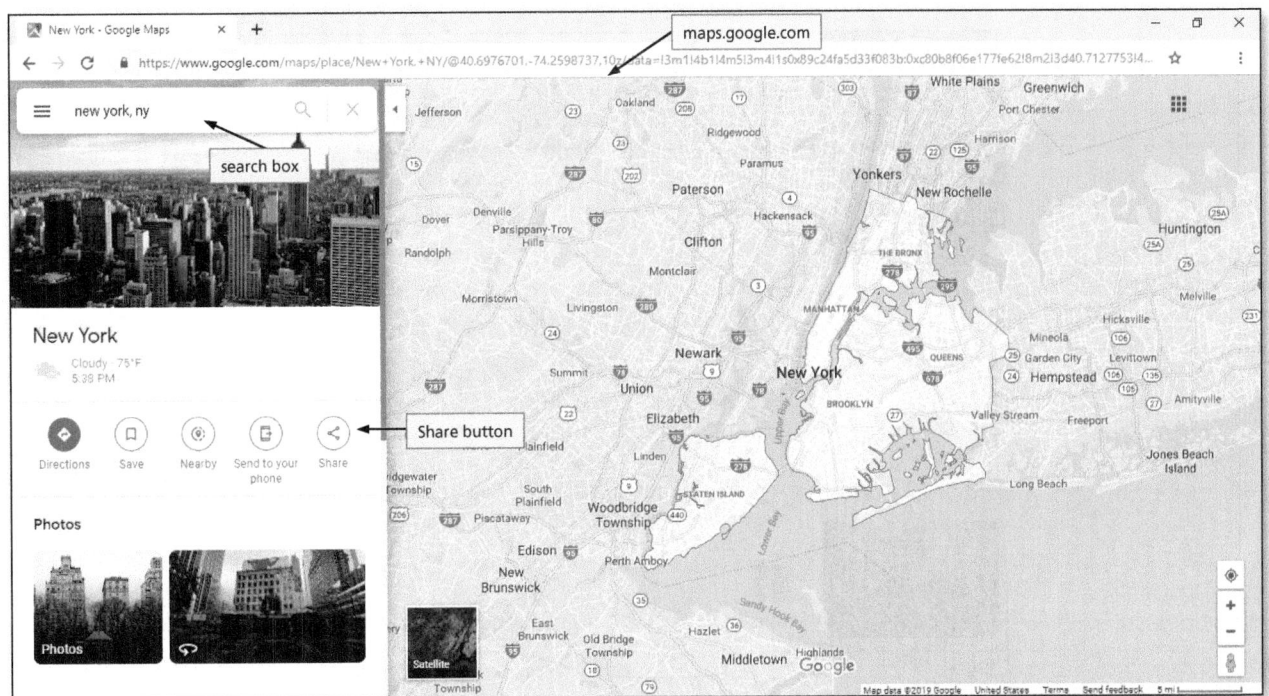

Home | About Us | Classes | Nutrition | Contact Us

Ready to get started? Contact us today.

Call us: (814) 555-9608

Email us: forwardfitness@club.net ◄—— email link

Visit us at: 1275 Channel Center Street, Boston, MA 02210

© Copyright 2021. All Rights Reserved.

forwardfitness@club.net

nexusby/Shutterstock.com

Figure 3–66

Embedding a Map

Many businesses include a location map embedded within their website so visitors have a clear view of the business location. Websites such as maps.google.com and mapquest.com provide online maps. Web developers can visit an online map, enter an address, and then obtain the required code to embed the online map directly within a webpage. For example, when you open maps.google.com in your browser and search for New York, NY, Google Maps displays the online map shown in Figure 3–67.

maps.google.com

Source: maps.google.com

Figure 3–67

To share this location, you select the Share button to open a Share window with several sharing options. You can send a link by selecting the COPY LINK option. You can use this link as the href value within your webpage. When website visitors click the link, the map opens on a new page. Another option is to share the location on Facebook and Twitter. These options are shown in Figure 3–68.

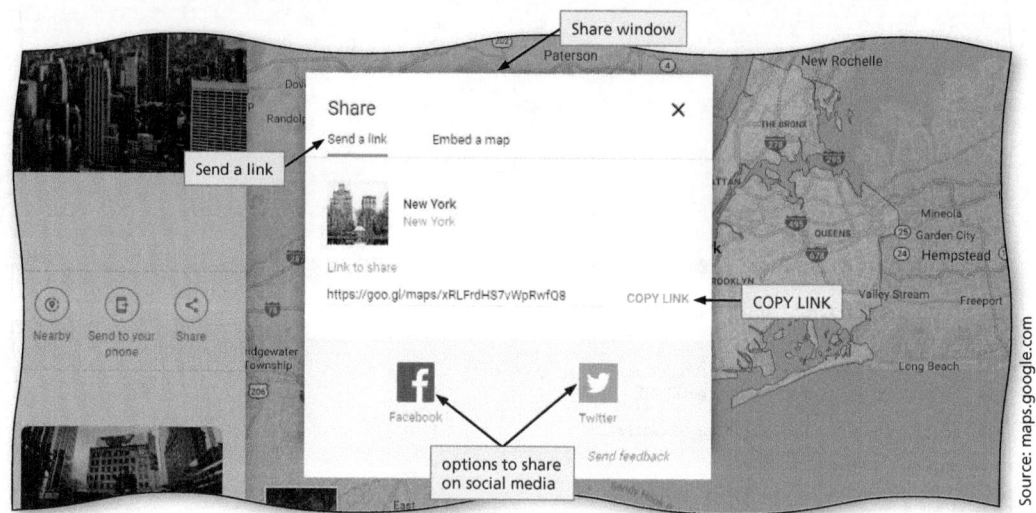

Figure 3–68

The last option is to embed a map. With this option, you select a map size and then tap or click COPY HTML to copy the code needed to embed the map directly within a webpage. The code uses an iframe element, which stands for inline frame. You use the **iframe** element to embed a document within a webpage. The iframe element includes a source attribute for specifying the document to embed on the page. Height and width attributes can also be specified to set the dimensions of the embedded content. The embed a map options are shown in Figure 3–69.

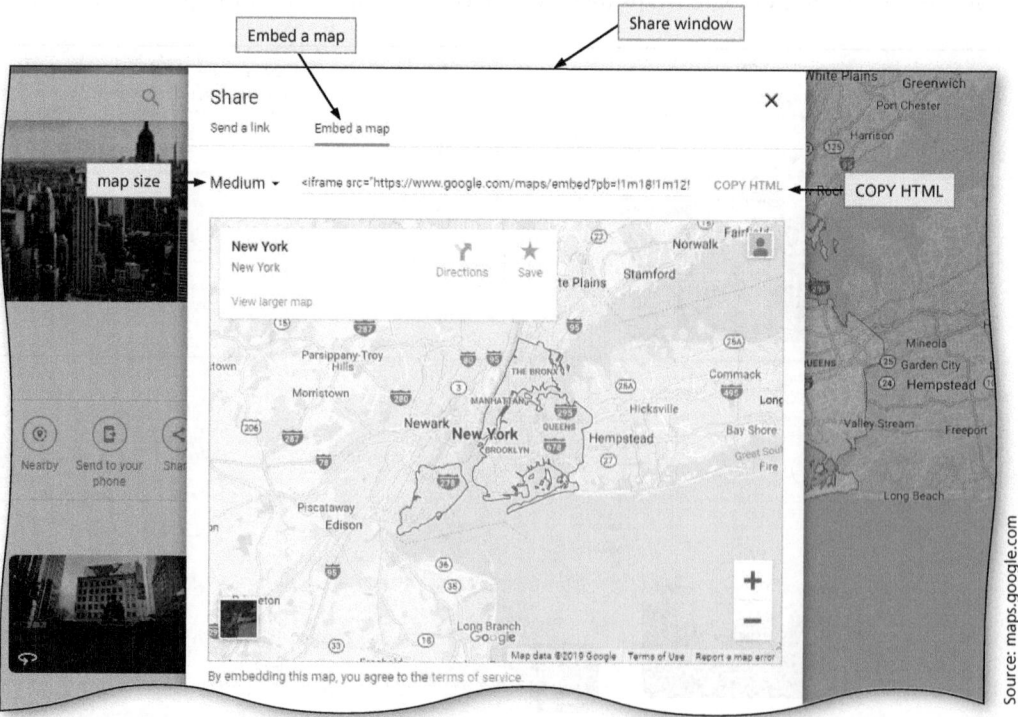

Figure 3–69

I visited maps.google.com and my screen looks different. Why?
Figure 3–67 through Figure 3–69 show what the website looked like at the time this book was written. The user interface for Google Maps may change over time.

To Embed a Map within a Webpage

1 ADD IMAGES | 2 ADD DIV ELEMENTS | 3 ADD HYPERLINKS | 4 ADD LISTS
5 EMBED MAP | **6 VIEW WEBSITE IN BROWSER & TEST LINKS** | 7 VALIDATE PAGES

You have already added contact information to the Contact Us page, but now need to embed a map. *Why? Embedding a map within the webpage allows the visitor to see the location of the business and quickly get directions.* The following steps embed a map on the Contact Us page.

- Open your browser to run the program.
- Type `maps.google.com` to open the Google Maps webpage.
- Type `1275 Channel Center Street, Boston, MA 02210` in the search box to display the location (Figure 3–70).

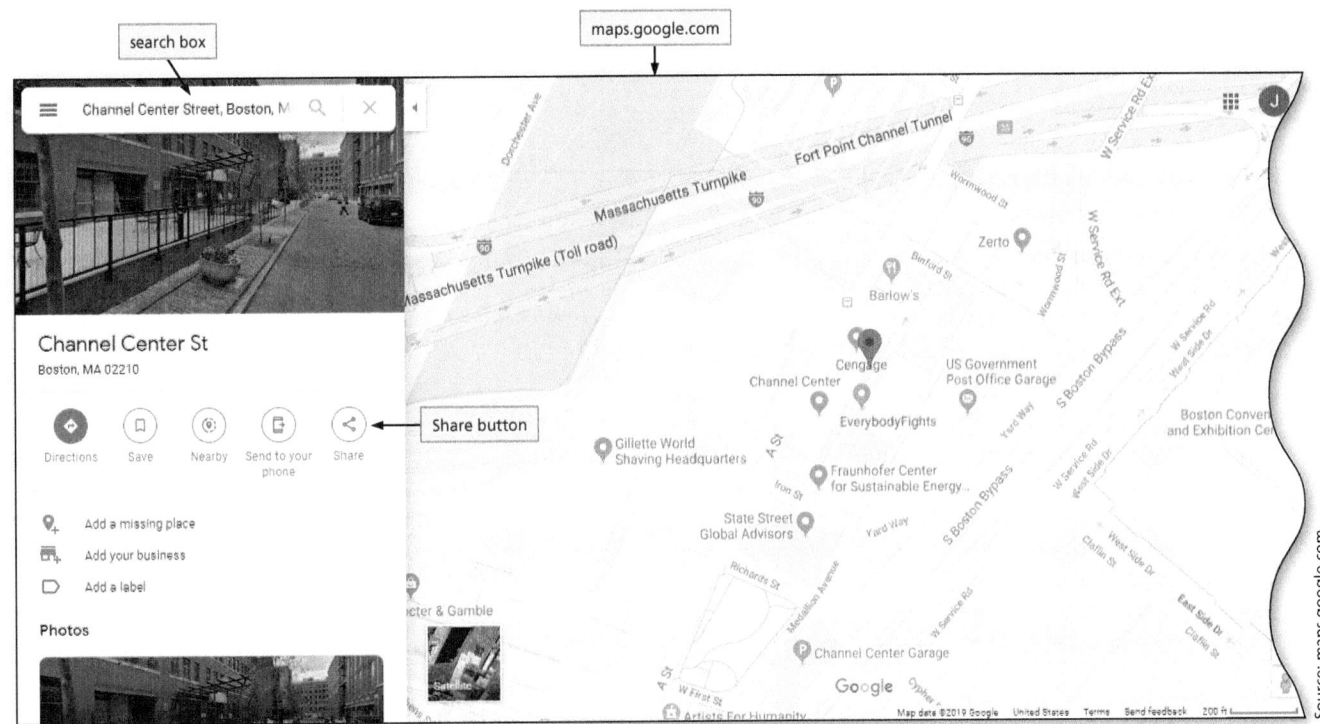

Figure 3–70

Q&A | Is this a real address?
No, this is not a real address. Google Maps shows an approximate map location.

2

- Tap or click the Share button to open the Share window.

- Tap or click Embed a map to display the default medium map.

- Tap or click COPY HTML to copy the iframe code (Figure 3–71).

Q&A I do not see the Share button. What should I do?
The user interface for Google Maps is subject to change. If the Share button is no longer displayed, review your options to determine which button to select. You may need to ask your instructor.

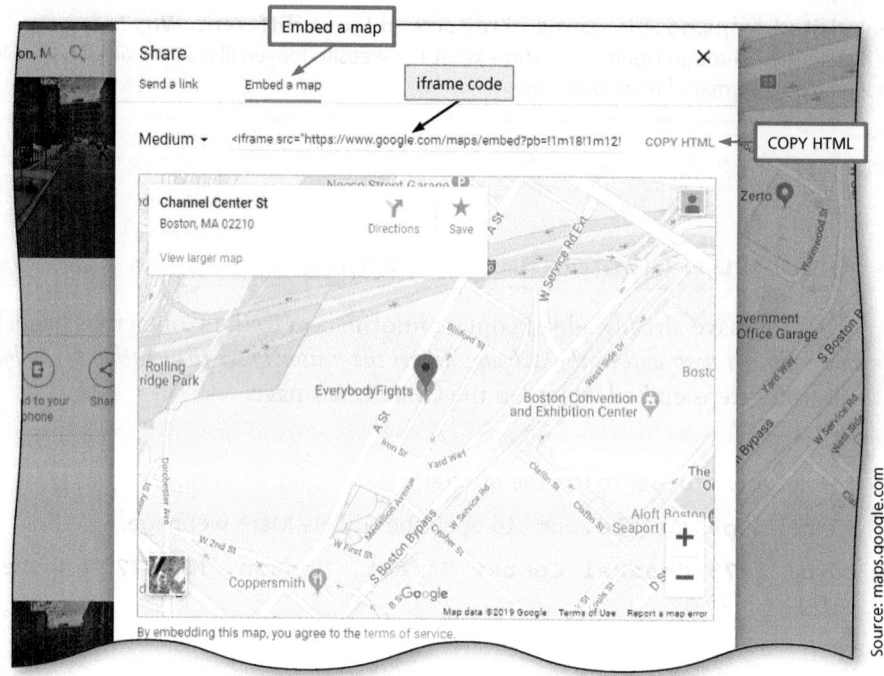

Figure 3–71

3

- If necessary, reopen the contact .html file in your text editor.

- Place your insertion point at the end of Line 35 and press the ENTER key twice to insert new Lines 36 and 37.

- On Line 37, press the CTRL+V keys to paste the iframe code (Figure 3–72).

Q&A The iframe code is very long. Is that normal?
Yes. This is the code that Google Maps generated to create the iframe element for embedding this specific map.

My iframe code is different from the book. Is that okay?
Yes. The auto-generated iframe source value that you copied may not be the same source value in this book.

```
29
30        <div id="contact">
31
32            <h2>Ready to get started? Contact us today.</h2>
33            <h4>Call us: (814) 555-9608</h4>
34            <h4>Email us: <a href="mailto:forwardfitness@club.net">forwardfitness@club.net</a></h4>
35            <h4>Visit us at: 1275 Channel Center Street, Boston, MA 02210</h4>
36
37            <iframe
          src="https://www.google.com/maps/embed?pb=!1m18!1m12!1m3!1d2948.8517572084897!2d-
          71.05362748503984!3d42.34568384400281!2m3!1f0!2f0!3f0!3m2!1i1024!2i768!4f13.1!3m3!1m2!1s
          0x89e37a7do2b67e7b63A0x36ec93427cd9c5f1!2sChannel+Center+St%2C+Boston%2C+MA+02210!5e0!3m
          2!1sen!2sus!4v1558137213400!5m2!1sen!2sus" width="600" height="450" frameborder="0"
          style="border:0" allowfullscreen></iframe>
38
39        </div>
```

Figure 3–72

4

- Save the contact.html file.

- Open the file in your default browser to view the page.

- If necessary, scroll down to view the embedded map (Figure 3–73).

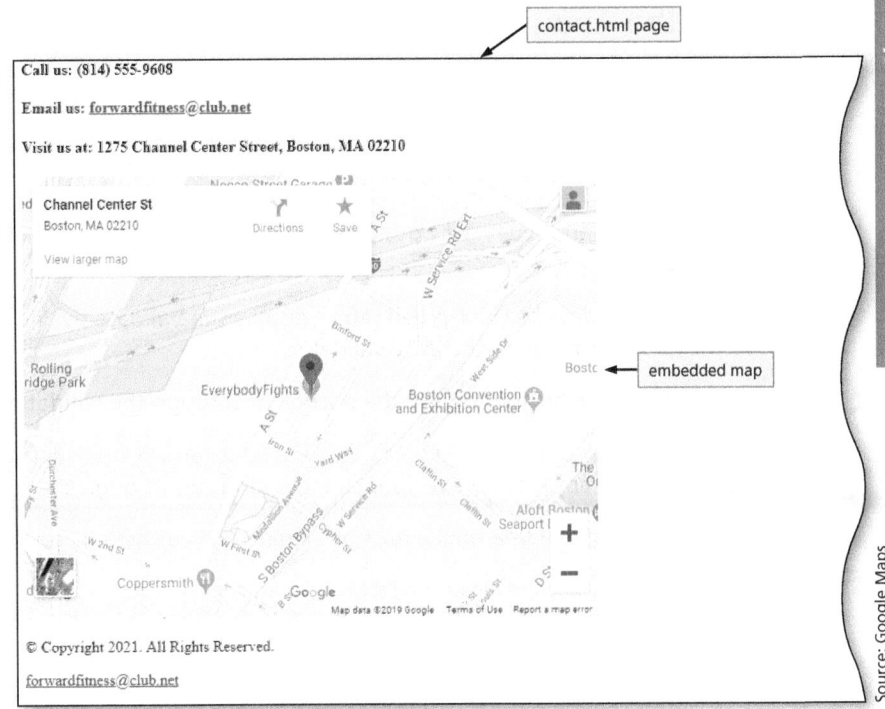

contact.html page

embedded map

Figure 3–73

To Preview a Website in a Browser and Test Page Links

1 ADD IMAGES | 2 ADD DIV ELEMENTS | 3 ADD HYPERLINKS | 4 ADD LISTS

5 EMBED MAP | 6 VIEW WEBSITE IN BROWSER & TEST LINKS | 7 VALIDATE PAGES

Now that you have created three webpages, it is time to test the hyperlinks in a browser. *Why? You need to test your hyperlinks to confirm that your page links work correctly.* The following step displays a webpage in a browser and test hyperlinks.

- If necessary, reopen contact.html in your browser to display the page.

- Tap or click the Home link to display the home page.

- Tap or click the About Us link to display the About Us page (Figure 3–74).

Q&A

Why do I receive an error message when I tap or click the classes and nutrition links?

You have not yet created these pages, but specified their file names in the href attribute. The browser looks for the file specified in the href attribute and displays an error message when it cannot find the file.

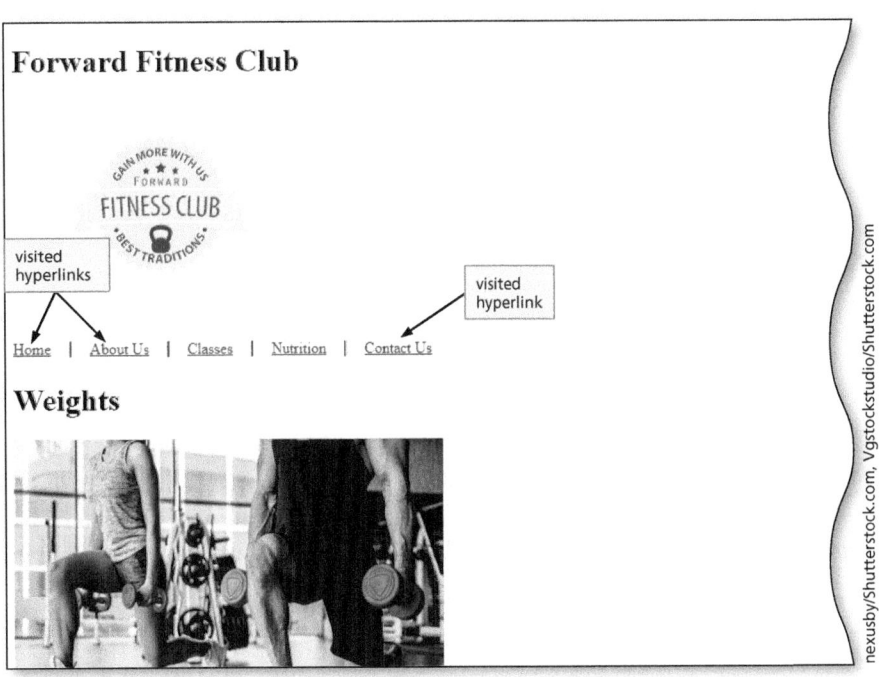

visited hyperlinks

visited hyperlink

Figure 3–74

To Validate the About Us and Contact Us Pages

Every time you create a new webpage, run it through the W3C validator to check the document for errors and correct them. The following steps validate an HTML document.

1 Open your browser and type `http://validator.w3.org/` in the address bar to display the W3C validator page.

2 Tap or click the Validate by File Upload tab to display the Validate by File Upload tab information, and then upload the about.html file to the W3C validator.

3 Tap or click the Check button to send the document through the validator and display the validation results page (Figure 3–75).

4 If necessary, correct any errors, save your changes, and run through the validator again to revalidate the page.

5 Perform Steps 1–4 to validate the contact.html page and correct any errors.

6 Close the browser, and then close the HTML text editor.

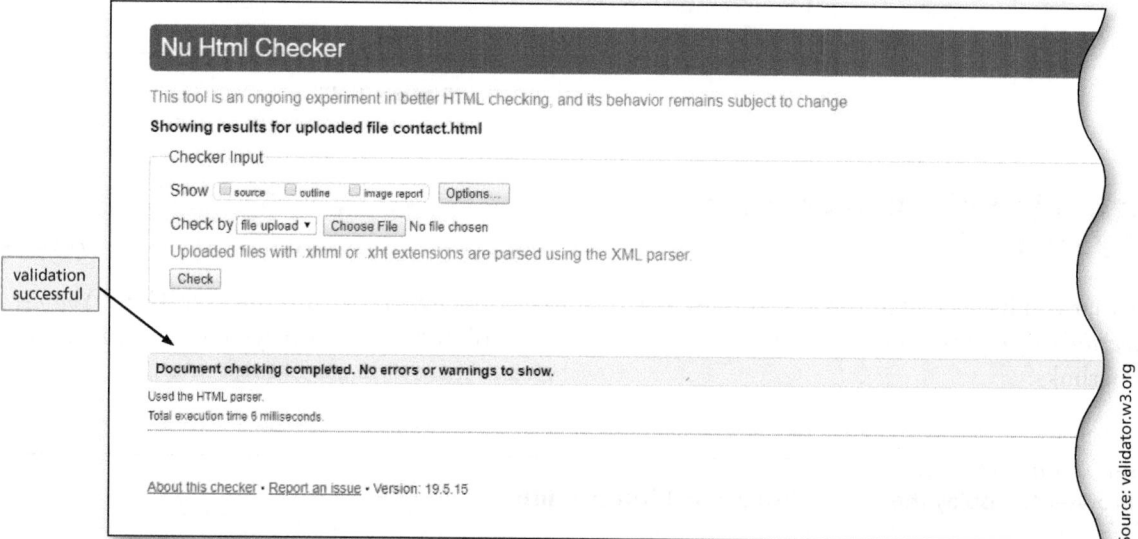

Source: validator.w3.org

Figure 3–75

Q&A I received an error when I validated the contact.html file. The error states that the frameborder attribute on the iframe element is obsolete. What do I do?
You can remove the frameborder attribute and its value of zero from the iframe element.

Chapter Summary

In this chapter, you have learned how to create many types of hyperlinks. You also inserted new HTML elements, including div elements, image elements, headings, and lists. The items listed below include all the new concepts and skills you have learned in this chapter, with the tasks grouped by activity.

What images will you use within your website?
Use these guidelines as you complete the assignments in this chapter and as you create your own webpages outside of this class.

1. Find appropriate images for the website.

   a. Choose images that relate to the website.

   b. For a business website, choose images that illustrate products or services.

   c. Use a logo or other identifying graphic on all pages.

2. Use the correct file format.

   a. Use PNG, GIF, JPG, or SVG images.

   b. Convert all other image files to an appropriate format suitable for web use.

3. Optimize images for web use.

   a. Reduce file size, when necessary, before adding an image to a website.

   b. Use online file compression or photo-editing software to reduce the file size for images.

4. Save all images in the images folder for file organization.

How should you submit solutions to questions in the assignments identified with a symbol?
Every assignment in this book contains one or more questions identified with a symbol. These questions require you to think beyond the assigned presentation. Present your solutions to the questions in the format required by your instructor. Possible formats may include one or more of these options: create a document that contains the answer; present your answer to the class; discuss your answer in a group; record the answer as audio or video using a webcam, smartphone, or portable media player; or post answers on a blog, wiki, or website.

CONSIDER THIS

CONSIDER THIS

Apply Your Knowledge

Reinforce the skills and apply the concepts you learned in this chapter.

Add Images, Lists, and Links to a Webpage

Note: To complete this assignment, you will be required to use the Data Files. Please contact your instructor for information about accessing the Data Files.

Instructions: In this exercise, you will use your text editor to add an image, an ordered list, a description list, and links to an HTML webpage. An example of the completed webpage is shown in Figure 3–76.

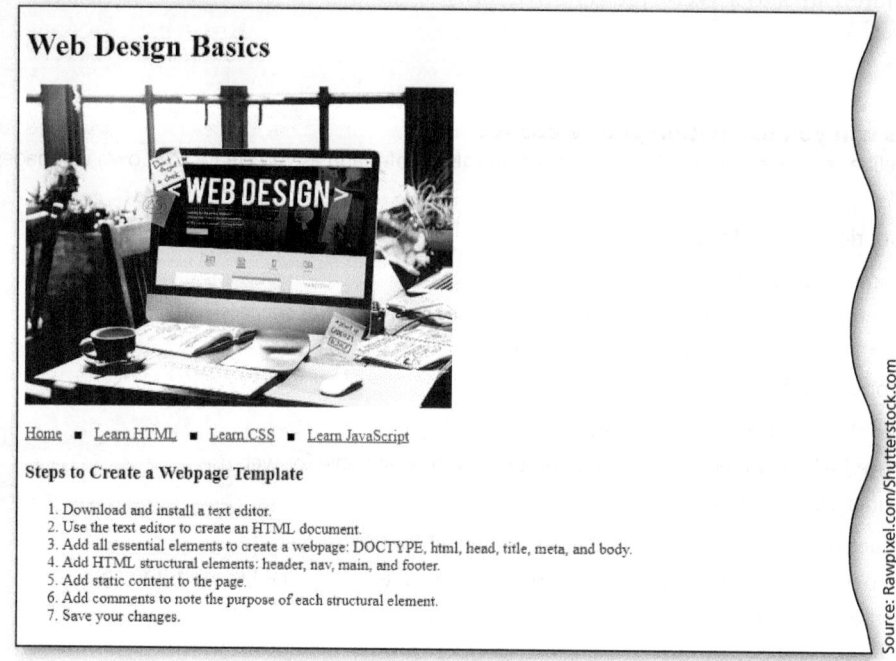

Figure 3–76

Perform the following tasks:

1. Open your text editor and then open the index.html file in the chapter03\apply folder in the Data Files. Update the comment with your name, the file name, and today's date.

2. Nest an img element within the header element below the heading element. Use `images/web-design.jpg` for the value of the src attribute. Add an `alt` attribute with a value of `computer with the text web design`. Add a `height` attribute with a value of `326` and add a `width` attribute with a value of `450`.

3. In the nav element, add a relative link to the text, Home, that links to `index.html`. Add a relative link to the text, Learn HTML, that links to `html.html`. Add a relative link to the text, Learn CSS, that links to `css.html`. Add a relative link to the text, Learn JavaScript, that links to `js.html`.

4. Insert two new blank lines after the starting main tag. Add a `div` element with an `id` attribute value of `template`. Close the div after the paragraph element with the content, Save your changes.

5. Change the first paragraph element within the div to a heading 3 element.

6. Change the remaining paragraph elements within the div to list items and wrap them within an ordered list. If necessary, insert a blank line between the closing ordered list tag and the closing div tag.

7. Insert two new blank lines after the closing div tag. Add a `div` element with an `id` attribute value of `semantic`. Close the div after the paragraph element with the content, Visit W3Schools.com to learn more about HTML semantic elements.

8. Change the first paragraph element within the div to a heading 3 element.

9. Change the paragraph elements with the text, Header, Nav, Main, and Footer, to description term, `<dt> </dt>`, elements.

10. Change the remaining paragraph elements to description definition, `<dd> </dd>`, elements. Do not change the last paragraph element with the text, Visit W3Schools.com to learn more about HTML semantic elements.

11. Wrap the description term elements and description definition elements with a description list element, `<dl> </dl>`. If necessary, insert a blank line between the closing description list tag and the last paragraph element within the div.

12. In the last paragraph element, add an absolute link to the text, W3Schools.com, that links to `https://www.w3schools.com/html/html5_semantic_elements.asp`.

13. Indent all nested elements.

14. Add your name to paragraph element within the footer element.

15. Open the other HTML files, css.html, html.html, and js.html. For each file, update the comment with your name, the file name, and today's date.

16. Add the same image from Step 2, on the same line, to each of these files.

17. Add the same nav links from Step 3 to each of these files.

18. Add your name to the paragraph element within the footer element on each of these files.

19. Validate all HTML files and correct any errors. Open the index.html file in a browser, test the links, and correct any errors. Save your changes and submit the assignment in a format specified by your instructor.

20. ✺ In Step 12, you added an absolute link to W3Schools.com with more information about semantic elements. Use your browser to research HTML semantic elements and provide two other absolute links that could be used here.

Extend Your Knowledge

Extend the skills you learned in this chapter and experiment with new skills. You may need to use additional resources to complete the assignment.

Working with Images and Graphics

Note: To complete this assignment, you will be required to use the Data Files. Please contact your instructor for information about accessing the Data Files.

Instructions: In this exercise, you will examine an image file, change the size of an image, compress an image file, add an image to a website, and then use SVG to create a graphic. You will answer several questions as you complete these tasks. The webpage includes several empty elements and comments that contains questions. You will use the empty elements to answer the questions shown in Figure 3–77.

Continued >

Extend Your Knowledge *continued*

```
19       <p> Software Application   &#9679;  
20       Online Compressor   &#9679;  
21       SVG Resource</p>
22   </nav>
23
24   <main>
25
26       <div id="image">
27
28          <h3>Modifying Images</h3>
29
30          <!-- 1st paragraph element: Use the paragraph element below to explain the importance of using descriptive file names for image files. Use
             complete sentences. -->
31          <p></p>
32
33          <!-- 2nd paragraph element: Use the paragraph element below to identify the application you used to change the size of the image. Use a complete
             sentence. -->
34          <p></p>
35
36          <!-- 3rd paragraph element: Use the paragraph element below to identify the original size of the image, in pixels. Use a complete sentence. -->
37          <p></p>
38
39          <!-- Use image element below to insert the image before compression, html5.jpg -->
40          <img>
41
42          <!-- 4th paragraph element: Use the paragraph element below to identify the online compressor you used to reduce the file size. What was the
             original image file size? What was the reduced image file size? Use complete sentences.  -->
43          <p></p>
44
45          <!-- Use image element below to insert the image after compression, html5_min.jpg -->
46          <img>
47
48          <!-- 5th paragraph element: Use the paragraph element below to note any visual changes that you can see between html5.jpg and html5_min.jpg -->
49          <p></p>
50
51       </div>
```

Source: Notepad++

Figure 3–77

Perform the following tasks:

1. Open your text editor and then open the extend03.html file in the chapter03\extend folder from the Data Files. Update the comment with your name, the file name, and today's date.

2. Open File Explorer (Windows) or Finder (macOS) and then navigate to the chapter03\extend folder from the Data Files. Locate the image file and notice the file name. Change the file name to **html5.jpg**. In the extend03.html file, use the first paragraph element within the main element to explain the importance of using descriptive file names for image files.

3. Open the html5.jpg file in Paint or Preview. Note the current size of the image. Use the software application to resize the image to 500 × 333 pixels. Use your browser to find an online resource to help you complete this task. In Paint, this option is located on the Home tab in the Image group. In Preview, this option is located under the Tools menu tab. Save your changes.

4. In the extend03.html file, use the second paragraph element to identify the application you used to change the size of the image. Use the third paragraph element to identify the original size of the image, in pixels.

5. Add an absolute link to the text, Software Application, located in the nav element, that opens the online resource you used in Step 3. Add the appropriate attribute so that the link opens in a new tab.

6. Open your browser and search for an online image compressor, such as compressor.io or tinyjpg.com. Upload the html5.jpg to the online image compressor and download the compressed file. If the downloaded file is a zip file, extract the zip file to obtain the image file. Save the compressed jpg file within the extend folder and name it **html5_min.jpg**.

7. In the chapter03\extend folder, create a new folder named images. Move html5.jpg and html5_min.jpg to the images folder.

8. In the extend03.html file, use the fourth paragraph element to identify the online image compressor you used to reduce the file size. Include the size of the file before and after the file compression.

9. In the extend03.html file, use the first image element to add the html5.jpg image file to the webpage. Be sure to include all necessary attributes within the img element: src, alt, height, and width. Use **hand writing HTML 5 on glass** for the value of the alt attribute.

10. Use the second image element to add the html5_min.jpg image file to the webpage. Be sure to include all necessary attributes within the img element: src, alt, height, and width. Use **hand writing HTML 5 on glass** for the value of the alt attribute.

11. Save your changes and view extend03.html in a browser. Carefully examine the two images, and then use the fifth paragraph element to describe any noticeable differences between the two images.

12. Add an absolute link to the text, Online Compressor, located in the nav element, that links to the online image compressor you used to complete Step 6. This link should open in a new tab.

13. Use your browser to find a tutorial on how to create an SVG with HTML. In the extend03. html file, create an SVG graphic of your choice using HTML. Add your code below the comment, Insert your SVG code below this comment.

14. Use the sixth paragraph element to provide information about the resource you used to create your SVG image.

15. Add an absolute link to the text, SVG Resource, located in the nav element, that links to the resource you used to complete Step 13. This link should open in a new tab.

16. Save your changes and submit the assignment in a format specified by your instructor.

17. ✳ In this assignment, you added an image to a webpage. Is it possible to use an image as the background of a webpage? If so, how? Research to find your answer.

Analyze, Correct, Improve

Analyze a webpage, correct all errors, and improve it.

Adding Elements to an HTML Webpage

Note: To complete this assignment, you will be required to use the Data Files. Please contact your instructor for information about accessing the Data Files.

Instructions: Open your text editor and then open the analyze03.html file in the chapter03\analyze folder in the Data Files. The page includes content within the main element; however, the content is not wrapped within appropriate elements. The page includes an image but the element is incorrect and is missing several attributes. The page is missing links. An example of the corrected page is shown in Figure 3–78.

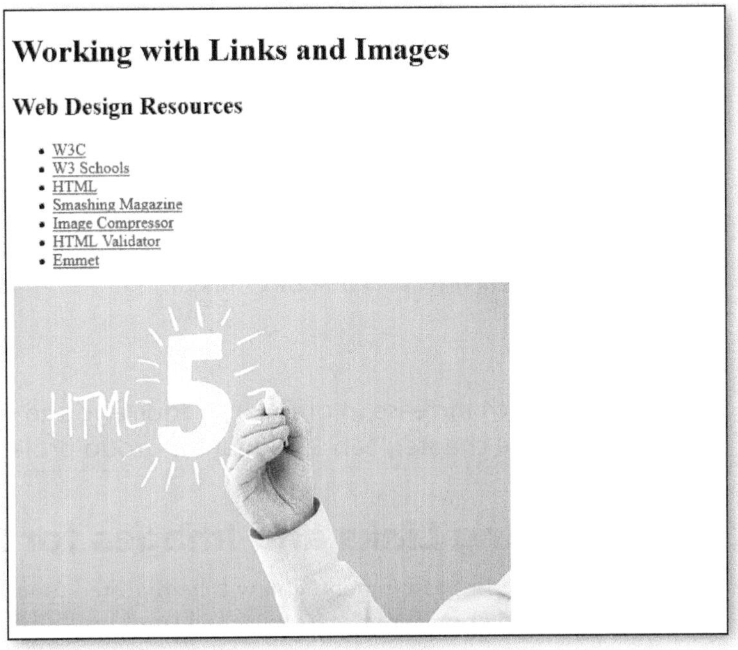

Figure 3–78

Source: istockphoto.com/mrPliskin

Continued >

Analyze, Correct, Improve continued

1. Correct

a. Open the analyze03.html file in your text editor and review the page.

b. Update the comment with your name, the file name, and today's date.

c. Update the title element with the following text: `Chapter 3 Analyze`

d. Wrap the text content, Web Design Resources, within a heading 2 element.

e. Insert a blank line after the heading 2 element.

f. Wrap the remaining text content within an unordered list with seven list items.

g. In the code, insert a blank line after the unordered list.

h. Correct the image element with the correct value for the source attribute. Add the missing alt, height, and width attributes to the image element. Use `hand writing HTML 5` for the value of the alt attribute.

i. Indent all nested elements.

2. Improve

a. In the main element, nest all content within a div element that has an id attribute value of `resources`. Insert a blank line after the starting div tag and above the closing div tag. Indent all nested elements.

b. Link the text, W3C, to `https://www.w3.org/`.

c. Link the text, W3 Schools, to `https://www.w3schools.com/`.

d. Link the text, HTML, to `https://www.html.com/`.

e. Link the text, Smashing Magazine, to `https://www.smashingmagazine.com/`.

f. Link the text, Image Compressor, to an online image compressor of your choice.

g. Link the text, HTML Validator, to W3C's HTML validator.

h. Link the text, Emmet, to `https://emmet.io/`.

i. Update all links to open each website in a new tab.

j. Add your name to the first paragraph element within the footer element.

k. Test all links to confirm they work and that they open in a new tab. Validate the page and correct any errors.

l. Submit the assignment in the format specified by your instructor.

m. ✷ One of the resources listed on the webpage is Emmet. Visit this resource and watch the demo. Provide a brief overview of Emmet.

In the Lab

Labs 1 and 2, which increase in difficulty, require you to create webpages based on what you learned in the chapter; Lab 3 is ideal for group projects/collaboration.

Lab 1: Adding Links and Images for Strike a Chord

Note: To complete this assignment, you will be required to use the Data Files. Please contact your instructor for information about accessing the Data Files.

Problem: You work for a local music lesson company called Strike a Chord that provides music lessons for piano, guitar, and violin. The company needs a web presence and has hired you to create their website. You have already created the website plan, template, and home page in Chapters 1 and 2. You now need to add links, images, and create more webpages for the website. The Lessons and Contact webpages are shown in Figure 3–79.

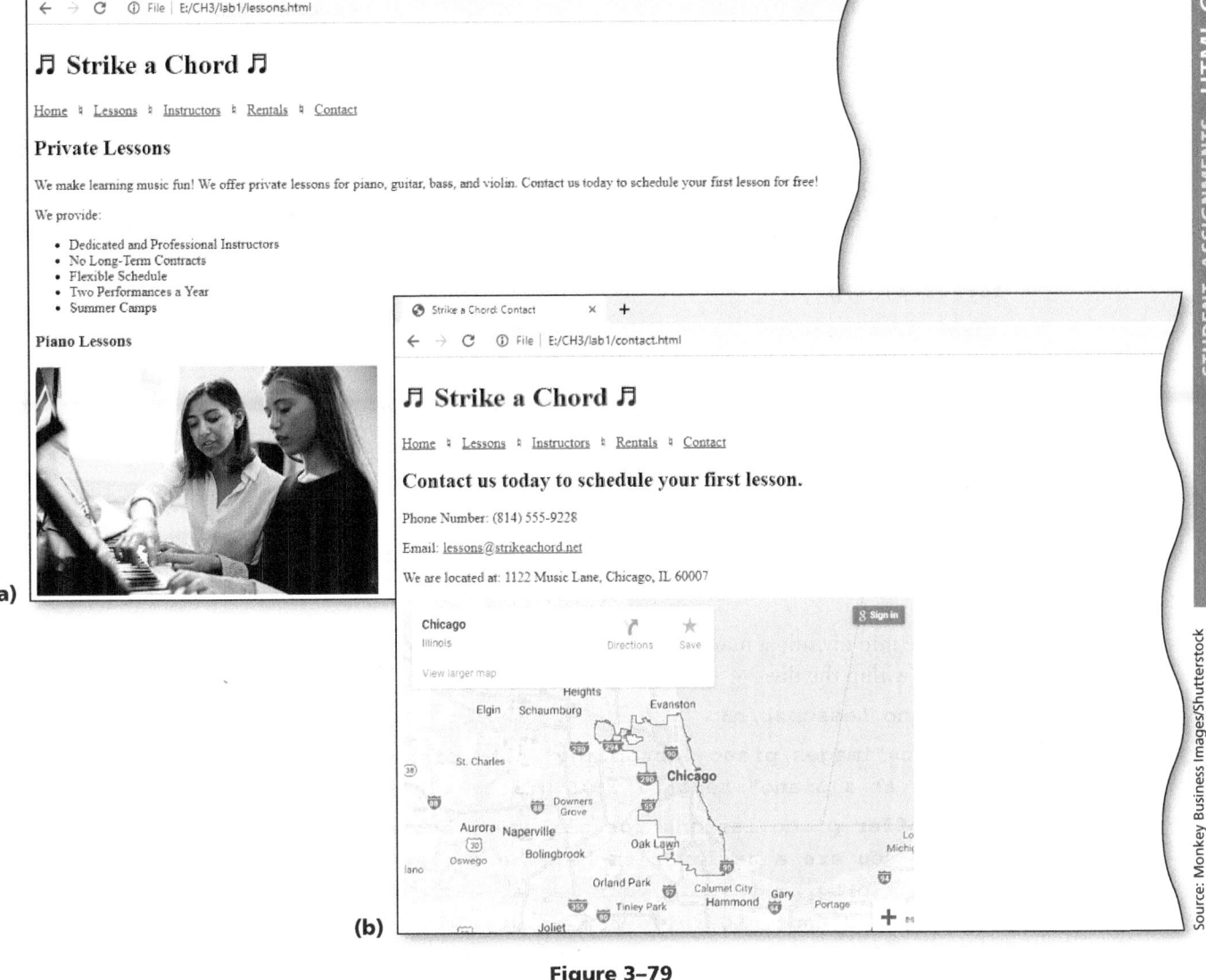

(a)

(b)

Source: Monkey Business Images/Shutterstock.com, Google Chrome, Google Maps

Figure 3–79

Instructions: Perform the following tasks:

1. Use File Explorer (Windows) or Finder (macOS) to navigate to the chapter03\lab1 folder in the Data Files. Copy the images folder to your music website folder created in Chapter 2, Lab 1.

2. Open template.html in your text editor. In the nav element, add a hyperlink to the text, Home, that opens **index.html**. Add a hyperlink to the text, Lessons, that opens **lessons.html**. Add a hyperlink to the text, Instructors, that opens **instructors.html**. Add a hyperlink to the text, Rentals, that opens **rentals.html**. Add a hyperlink to the text, Contact, that opens **contact.html**. Update the nav element in the index.html file to match the template.html file.

3. In the template file, nest an empty div element within the main element.

4. Add an email link to the email address within the footer element on the template.html file and the index.html. Save your changes.

5. In the index.html file, in the main element, wrap the two paragraph elements within a div element with an id attribute value of **intro**. Indent the two paragraph elements. Save your changes.

Continued >

6. Use the template file to create a new page and name the file `lessons.html`.

7. Update the comment with the file name and today's date. In the title element, replace the text, Template, with `Lessons`.

8. Add an id attribute with a value `info` to the div element within the main element. Nest the following elements within the div:

   ```
   <h2>Private Lessons</h2>

   <p>We make learning music fun! We offer private lessons for piano,
   guitar, and violin. Contact us today to schedule your first lesson
   for free! </p>

   <p>We provide:</p>

   <ul>

       <li>Dedicated and Professional Instructors</li>

       <li>No Long-Term Contracts</li>

       <li>Flexible Schedule</li>

       <li>Spring and Winter Performances</li>

       <li>Summer Camps</li>

   </ul>
   ```

9. Below the info div, add a new div element with an id attribute of `piano`. Nest the following elements within the div:

   ```
   <h3>Piano Lessons</h3>

   <img src="images/piano-lesson.jpg" alt="piano teacher and student
   sitting at a piano" height="260" width="400">

   <p>We offer piano lessons for all ages, beginning at age three.
   Whether you are a beginner or have been playing the piano for a while,
   we have a program to suit your needs. Learn new techniques, theory,
   harmony, and tone. Learning how to play the piano helps develop hand-
   eye coordination and self-confidence.</p>
   ```

10. Below the piano div, add a new div element with an id attribute of `guitar`. Nest the following elements within the div:

    ```
    <h3>Guitar Lessons</h3>

    <img src="images/child-guitar.jpg" alt="child with a smile holding a
    guitar" height="260" width="400">

    <p>We teach acoustic guitar, electric guitar, bass guitar, and
    ukulele. We have guitar lessons for beginners, intermediate players,
    and advanced players. Improve your skills with weekly lessons. Learn
    new tips and techniques from experienced instructors. We also have a
    rock band program that you can join!</p>
    ```

11. Below the guitar div, add a new div element with an id attribute of `violin`. Nest the following elements within the div:

    ```
    <h3>Violin Lessons</h3>

    <img src="images/woman-violin.jpg" alt="woman playing the violin"
    height="260" width="400">
    ```

```
<p>We offer violin lessons for all ages, beginning at age six. Our
violin lessons include a variety of music styles, from fiddle to
classical. Our instructors will help you fine-tune techniques and
accomplish your musical goals. We work with you to create a customized
program, tailored to your needs.</p>
```

12. Indent all nested elements. Check your spelling. Validate the file and correct any errors. Save your changes.

13. Use the template file to create a new page and name the file `contact.html`.

14. Update the comment with the file name and today's date. In the title element, replace the text, Template, with `Contact`.

15. Add an id attribute with a value `contact` to the div element within the main element. Nest the following elements within the div:

```
<h2>Contact us today to schedule your first lesson.</h2>

<p>Phone Number: (814) 555-9228</p>

<p>Email: <a href="mailto:lessons@strikeachord.net">lessons@
strikeachord.net</a></p>

<p>We are located at: 1122 Music Lane, Chicago, IL 60007</p>
```

16. Below the last paragraph element added from Step 14, embed an online location map with the location of Chicago, IL.

17. Indent all nested elements. Check your spelling. Validate all HTML files and correct any errors. Save your changes.

18. Open the index.html file in a browser and test your page links. The only links that should currently work are Home, Lessons, and Contact.

19. Submit your assignment in the format specified by your instructor.

20. ✸ Throughout this lab, you added several div elements. What other elements can be used instead of a div element? Research to find your answer.

Lab 2: **Adding Links and Images for a Wildlife Rescue**

Note: To complete this assignment, you will be required to use the Data Files. Please contact your instructor for information about accessing the Data Files.

Problem: You volunteer at a local wildlife rescue, a nonprofit organization called Wild Rescues. The organization rescues all kinds of wild animals, rehabilitates them, and then releases them back into the wild. Wild Rescues needs a website to help raise awareness about the organization. You have already created the website plan, template, and home page in Chapters 1 and 2, Lab 2. You now need to add links, images, and create more webpages for the website. The Home, About Us, and Contact webpages are shown in Figure 3–80.

Continued >

In the Lab *continued*

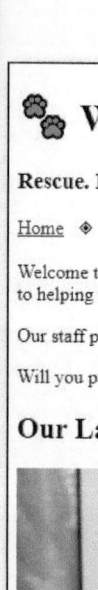
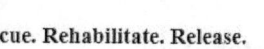

Wild Rescues

Rescue. Rehabilitate. Release.

Home ◆ About Us ◆ Partnership ◆

Welcome to Wild Rescues. Our mission is to
to helping injured wildlife.

Our staff provides around the clock care for

Will you partner with us? We need caring vo

Our Latest Rescue: Baby R:

(a)

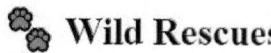

Wild Rescues

Rescue. Rehabilitate. Release.

Home ◆ About Us ◆ Partnership ◆ Gallery ◆ FAQs ◆ Contact

About Us

Wild Rescues is a registered nonprofit wildlife rescue and rehabilitation facility, located in Ocala, Florida. We hel
We help rehabilitate these animals and then release them back into the wild, if possible.

Wild Rescues is a member of the National Wildlife Rehabilitators Association.

(b) We help many animals, suc

Wild Rescues

Rescue. Rehabilitate. Release.

Home ◆ About Us ◆ Partnership ◆ Gallery ◆ FAQs ◆ Contact

You can reach us at:

Office: (814) 555-8989

Email: contact@wildrescues.net

Address: 8989 Rescue Drive, Ocala, FL 34471

© Copyright 2021. All Rights Reserved.

contact@wildrescues.net

(c)

Figure 3–80

Instructions: Perform the following tasks:

1. Use File Explorer (Windows) or Finder (macOS) to navigate to the chapter03\lab2 folder from the Data Files. Copy the images folder to your rescue website folder.

2. Open template.html in your text editor. In the nav element, add a hyperlink to the text, Home, that opens `index.html`. Add a hyperlink to the text, About Us, that opens `about.html`. Add a hyperlink to the text, Partnership, that opens `partnership.html`. Add a hyperlink to the text, Gallery, that opens `gallery.html`. Add a hyperlink to the text, FAQs, that opens `faqs.html`. Add a hyperlink to the text, Contact, that opens `contact.html`. Update the nav element in the index.html file to match the template.html file.

3. In the template file, nest an empty div element within the main element.

4. Add an email link to the email address within the footer element in template.html and index .html. Save your changes.

5. In the index.html file, in the main element, wrap the three paragraph elements within a div element with an id attribute value of `welcome`. Indent the three paragraph elements within the div element. Save your changes.

6. Below the welcome div element, insert a new div element with an id attribute value of `latest`.

7. Nest a heading 2 element with the content, `Our Latest Rescue: Baby Raccoons`, inside the latest div.

8. Below the heading 2 element, add an image element to insert the baby-raccoons.jpg picture. Use `hands holding three baby raccoons` for the alt text and add the proper height and width attributes.

9. Below the image element, add a paragraph element with the text content, `Meet our latest rescues, Fizz, Bandit, and Mohawk. These three little guys were found abandoned near a home.`

10. Indent all nested elements and save your changes.

11. Use the template file to create a new page and name the file, `about.html`.

12. Update the comment with the file name and today's date. In the title element, replace the text, Template, with `About Us`.

13. Add an id attribute with a value `info` to the div element within the main element. Nest the following elements within the div:

    a. Add a heading 2 element with the text content, `About Us`

    b. Below the heading 2 element, add a paragraph element with the following text: `Wild Rescues is a registered nonprofit wildlife rescue and rehabilitation facility, located in Ocala, Florida. We help injured, sick, neglected, and orphaned wildlife. We help rehabilitate these animals and then release them back into the wild, if possible.`

    c. Below the first paragraph element, add a second paragraph element with the following text: `Wild Rescues is a member of the National Wildlife Rehabilitators Association.` Link the text content, National Wildlife Rehabilitators Association, to `https://www.nwrawildlife.org/`, and configure the page to load in a new tab.

    d. Below the second paragraph element, insert two blank lines, and then add an image element to insert the `tortoise.jpg` picture. Use `tortoise eating vegetation` for the alt text and add the proper height and width attributes.

    e. Below the image element, insert two blank lines, and then add a heading 3 element with the following text: `We help many animals, such as:`

    f. Below the heading 3 element, insert an unordered list with the following eight list items: `Raccoons, Squirrels, Fox, Birds, Horses, Deer, Pigs, Reptiles.`

    g. Below the unordered list, insert two blank lines, and then add a paragraph element with the text content `Did you find an injured or orphaned animal? Contact us to see if we can help.` Save your changes.

14. Indent all nested elements and save your changes.

15. Use the template file to create a new page and name the file, `contact.html`.

16. Update the comment with the file name and today's date. In the title element, replace the text, Template, with `Contact`.

17. Add an id attribute with a value `contact` to the div element within the main element. Nest the following elements within the div:

    a. Add a heading 2 element with the following text: `You can reach us at:`

    b. Below the heading 2 element, add a paragraph element with the following text: `Office: (814) 555-8989`

Continued >

In the Lab *continued*

c. Below the paragraph element, add a second paragraph element with the following text and hyperlink content: `Email: <a href="mailto:contact@wildrescues` `.net">contact@wildrescues.net</a>`

d. Below the second paragraph element, add a third paragraph element with the following text: `Address: 8989 Rescue Drive, Ocala, FL 34471`

18. In the third paragraph element, link the text content, 8989 Rescue Drive, Ocala, FL 34471, to an online location map with the location of Ocala, FL. Configure the link to open in a new tab.

19. Indent all nested elements. Check your spelling. Validate all HTML files and correct any errors. Save your changes.

20. Open the index.html file in a browser and test your page links. The only links that should currently work are Home, About, and Contact. Confirm that the address link opens an online location map in a new tab showing Ocala, FL.

21. Submit your assignment in the format specified by your instructor.

22. ✷ In this assignment, you added links within the navigation element. The navigation link text is currently within a paragraph element. Is a paragraph element the best element for navigation links? Research to find your answer and identify another element to use for navigation links.

Lab 3: Adding Links and Images for Student Clubs and Events Website

Note: To complete this assignment, you will be required to use the Data Files. Please contact your instructor for information about accessing the Data Files.

Problem: You and several of your classmates have decided to help increase student involvement in school clubs and events by creating a website to promote awareness about the various activities. You have already created the website plan, template, and home page in Chapters 1 and 2, Lab 3. You now need to add links, images, and create more webpages for the website.

Instructions:

1. Use File Explorer (Windows) or Finder (macOS) to navigate to the chapter03\lab3 folder in the Data Files. Copy the image files to your student\images folder.

2. Open your template.html file and add anchor elements to create text links within the navigation area. Though the other pages do not yet exist, use an appropriate file name for each text link. For example, if you have a navigation link for "Clubs," use clubs.html as the file name. Update the navigation area on your home page to match the navigation area on your template .html file.

3. In the template file, nest an empty div element within the main element.

4. Add an email link to the email address within the footer element in the template.html file and the index.html.

5. In the template.html file, in the footer element, add a paragraph element with the name of your educational institution and link the text to the home page of your educational institution's website. Configure the link to open in a new tab. Update the footer element on your home page to match the footer element on your template.html file. Save your changes.

6. In the index.html file, in the main element, wrap all elements within a div element with an id attribute value of `welcome`. Indent the nested elements within the div element.

7. Nest an image within the welcome div element. You may use one of the image files provided or add your own. Use descriptive alt text and include the proper height and width attributes. If your image is greater than 500 × 500 pixels, use graphic software to resize the image. If the file size is greater than 1 MB, use an online image compressor tool to reduce the file size.

8. Indent all nested elements and save your changes.

9. Review your site map and then use your template to create a new webpage for your website. Save your new webpage with an appropriate file name. For example, if you create a new page for "Clubs," use clubs.html as the file name. As a group, discuss what content will you add to this page.

10. Update the comment and title on the new webpage. Assign an id attribute and value to the div within the main element, then add content to this div. Content should include at least one heading element, at least one paragraph element, an image with all appropriate attributes, and a list (ordered, unordered, or description). Add an absolute link to the webpage that opens another website in a new tab.

11. Indent all nested elements and save your changes.

12. Review your site map and then use your template to create another new webpage for your website. Save your new webpage with an appropriate file name. As a group, discuss what content will you add to this page.

13. Update the comment and title on the new webpage. Assign an id attribute and value to the div within the main element, and then add content to this div. Content should include at least one heading element, at least one paragraph element, an image with all appropriate attributes, and a list (ordered, unordered, or description).

14. Indent all nested elements and save your changes.

15. Review the new pages for spelling errors and correct. Validate your new pages and correct any errors.

16. Submit your assignment in the format specified by your instructor.

17. ✹ In this assignment, you created two lists. How would you assign a specific image to be used as the bullet marker for an unordered list? Research to find your answer.

Consider This: Your Turn

Apply your creative thinking and problem-solving skills to design and implement a solution.

1. Add Images and Links to Your Personal Portfolio Website

Personal

Part 1:   In Chapter 2, you created a webpage template and a home page for your personal portfolio website. You now need to add an image to your home page and template, add page links, create two new pages, add a list, and embed a map.

1. Create a subfolder within your portfolio website folder and name the new folder images. Save a picture of yourself within the images folder. Ensure that the image file has an appropriate file name, such as your name. Use all lowercase and no spaces.

2. Review the image file properties to ensure that the image size and file size are not too large. If your image size is greater than 500 × 500 pixels, use photo-editing software, such as Paint,

Continued >   **HTML** 139

Consider This: Your Turn *continued*

to adjust the image size. Likewise, if the file size is greater than 1 MB, use an online image file compression tool to reduce the file size.

3. Add a picture of yourself within the header element on your home page and your template file. Be sure to include all necessary attributes within the img element; src, alt, height, and width.

4. Open your template.html file and add anchor elements to create text links within the navigation area. Though the other pages do not yet exist, use an appropriate file name for each text link. For example, if you have a navigation link for "About Me," use about.html as the file name. Update the navigation area on your home page to match the navigation area on your template.

5. Add your student email address to the footer element and include an email hyperlink to your email address. Update the footer area on your home page to match the footer area on your template.

6. Review your site map and then use your template to create a new webpage for your website. Save your new page with an appropriate file name. For example, if you create a new page for "About Me," use about.html as the file name.

7. Update the comment and the title element on your new page. Nest a div element with an id attribute and appropriate value within your main element. Add relevant content to the div element and include a list with content relevant to the page. Use at least one ordered list, unordered list, or a description list. If using one list, it should include a minimum of five list items.

8. Create another new webpage using your template file. Use this new page for your contact information. Save the new file with an appropriate file name, such as contact.html.

9. Update the comment and the title element on your new page. Nest a div element with an id attribute and appropriate value within your main element. Add relevant contact information to the div element. Embed an online location map with the location of your educational institution.

10. Review the new pages for spelling errors and correct. Validate your new pages and correct any errors.

11. Submit your assignment in the format specified by your instructor.

Part 2: ✹ Notice how your text and images are all aligned to the left. Use your browser to research how to change the alignment for elements on an HTML webpage.

2. Add Images and Links to Dog-Grooming Website

Professional

Note: To complete this assignment, you will be required to use the Data Files. Please contact your instructor for information about accessing the Data Files.

Part 1: In Chapter 2, you created a webpage template and a home page for your dog-grooming website. You now need to add images to your home page and template, add page links, create two new pages, add a list, and embed a map.

1. Use File Explorer (Windows) or Finder (macOS) to navigate to the chapter03\your_turn2 folder in the Data Files. Copy the images folder to your groom website folder. Review the image file properties to ensure that the image file sizes are not too large. If any file size is greater than 1 MB, use an online image file compression tool to reduce the file size.

2. Add the dog-banner.jpg image file within the header element, below the heading elements, on your home page and your template file. Be sure to include all necessary attributes within the img element; src, alt, height, and width.

3. Open your template.html file and add anchor elements to create text links within the navigation area. Though the other pages do not yet exist, use an appropriate file name for each

text link. For example, if you have a navigation link for "Services," use services.html as the file name. Update the navigation area on your home page to match the navigation area on your template.

4. If necessary, add an email address to the footer element and include an email hyperlink to the email address. Update the footer area on your home page to match the footer area on your template.

5. Nest an empty div element within the main element on the template.html file. In the index.html file, wrap all elements within the main element in a div with an id attribute and appropriate value.

6. Review your site map and then use your template to create a new webpage for your website. Save your new page with an appropriate file name. For example, if you create a new page for "Services," use services.html as the file name.

7. Update the comment and the title element on your new page. Update the div element with an id attribute and appropriate value within your main element. Add relevant content to the div element and include a list with content relevant to the page. Include at least two lists with relevant content. You can use one type of list or a combination of lists; an ordered list, unordered list, or description list. Each list should have a minimum of three list items.

8. Add at least two images to your new page. You may use the images provided with the Data Files or your own images. Be sure to include all necessary attributes within the img element; src, alt, height, and width.

9. Create another new webpage using your template file. Use this new page for contact information for the dog-grooming business. Save the new file with an appropriate file name, such as contact.html.

10. Update the comment and the title element on your new page. Update the div element with an id attribute and appropriate value within your main element. Add relevant contact information to the div element. Embed an online location map with the location of the dog-grooming business. You may use the address of your education institution or a city and state.

11. Review the new pages for spelling errors and correct. Validate your new pages and correct any errors.

12. Submit your assignment in the format specified by your instructor.

Part 2:   ☀ Interview a friend or relative that takes their dog to a groomer on a regular basis. Ask the pet owner what they look for on a dog groomer's website to help them determine whether they would consider taking their dog to the business. Discuss your findings.

3. Add Images and Links to Future Technologies Website

Research and Collaboration

Note: To complete this assignment, you will be required to use the Data Files. Please contact your instructor for information about accessing the Data Files.

Part 1:   You and several of your classmates have been tasked with creating a website that showcases advancements in technology. You have already created the website root folder, tech, template.html file and index.html file. You now need to add image to your home page and template, add page links, create two new pages for your website, add a list, add more images, and include absolute links that open in a new tab.

1. Copy the Data Files from chapter03\your_turn3 to your tech\images folder. Add any other images you want to use for the website to the images folder. Review the image file properties

Continued >

Consider This: Your Turn *continued*

to ensure that the image file sizes are not too large. If any file size is greater than 1 MB, use an online image file compression tool to reduce the file size.

2. Add an image file on your home page. You may use one of the images provided with the data files or your own image. Be sure to include all necessary attributes within the img element; src, alt, height, and width.

3. Open your template.html file and add anchor elements to create text links within the navigation area. Though the other pages do not yet exist, use an appropriate file name for each text link. For example, if you have a navigation link for "AI," use ai.html as the file name. Update the navigation area on your home page to match the navigation area on your template.

4. If necessary, add an email address to the footer element and include an email hyperlink to the email address. Update the footer area on your home page to match the footer area on your template.

5. Nest an empty div element within the main element in the template.html file. In the index.html file, wrap all elements within the main element in a div with an id attribute and appropriate value.

6. Review your site map and then use your template to create a new webpage for your website. Save your new page with an appropriate file name. For example, if you create a new page for "AI," use ai.html as the file name. As a group, discuss what content will you add to this page.

7. Update the comment and the title element on your new page. Update the div element with an id attribute and appropriate value within your main element. Add relevant content to the div element. Provide a definition of the technology as well as several examples. Include a list (ordered, unordered, or description) with content relevant to the page. The list should have a minimum of three list items.

8. Include at least three absolute links that open in a new tab.

9. Add an image to your new page. You may use one of the images provided with the Data Files or your own image. Be sure to include all necessary attributes within the img element; src, alt, height, and width.

10. Use your template.html file to create another webpage for your website. Use this new page to discuss another technology identified in your site map. Save the new file with an appropriate file name.

11. Update the comment and the title element on your new page. Update the div element with an id attribute and appropriate value within your main element. Add relevant content to the div element. Include at least two absolute links that open in a new tab.

12. Review the new pages for spelling errors and correct. Validate your new pages and correct any errors.

13. Submit your assignment in the format specified by your instructor.

Part 2: ✳ In this assignment, you added absolute links to content related to your website. Is it possible to embed a video on your page as well? If so, what element would be used to accomplish this task?

4 Designing Webpages with CSS

Objectives

You will have mastered the material in this chapter when you can:

- Explain the importance of separating design from content
- Describe Cascading Style Sheets (CSS)
- Define inline, embedded, and external styles and their order of precedence
- Describe a CSS rule and its syntax
- Explain the difference between a selector, property, and value
- Create styles that use text and color properties
- Explain the difference between inline and block content

- Describe and use the CSS box model to apply margins, padding, and borders
- Create an external style sheet and link it to an HTML page
- Create responsive images
- Use float and clear properties
- Create and style id and class attributes
- Use a span element
- Add comments to an external style sheet and validate a CSS file

4 | Designing Webpages with CSS

Introduction

Creating a well-designed website that captures your audience's attention is vital in attracting and obtaining new customers. To do so, a web developer can use formatting such as font styles, font colors, white space, and background colors or images to increase the visual appeal of the webpages. Websites developed with HTML 5 alone can be functional, but they lack this important element of visual appeal. To improve the appearance of a website by including color, formatting text, and adding margins, borders, and shadows, for example, you need to apply styles created with **Cascading Style Sheets (CSS)**, a language you use to describe the formatting of a document written in a markup language such as HTML 5. While HTML provides the structural foundation of a webpage, you use CSS styles to determine the formatting for a webpage. By defining CSS styles in a style sheet separate from the HTML code, you can format a webpage in an unlimited number of ways, such as changing the background color of the webpage, increasing the size of text or bolding it, applying margins to a section, and adding borders to elements.

Project — Format Webpages with CSS

In previous chapters, you created a website template and three webpages for the Forward Fitness Club website. You also added content and links to the home page, the About Us page, and the Contact Us page. However, these pages lack formatting to enhance their appearance.

In Chapter 2, you created a website plan to guide the design and development of the Forward Fitness Club website. The plan provides information about the desired typography and colors to enhance the business brand and logo. The plan includes a wireframe, which specifies passive white space between HTML elements. To add these design elements according to your plan, you create and apply CSS styles in an external style sheet, a separate file that contains the styles for the website.

The project in this chapter enhances a website with CSS. You apply styles to the HTML 5 elements on each page to give the site a certain look and feel. After creating a style sheet, you link it to all of the pages in the website, including the template. As you add styles to the style sheet, they immediately format the attached webpages when you open or refresh the pages in a browser. Figure 4–1 shows the home page after it has been enhanced by CSS.

(a) Home Page

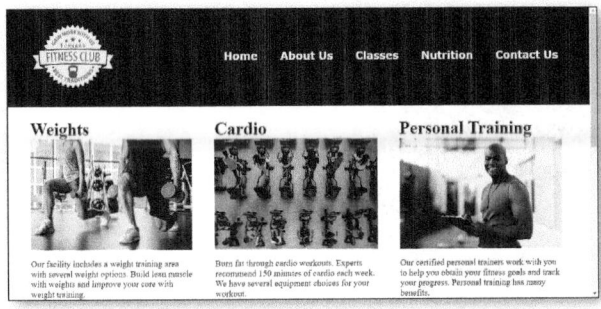

(b) About Us Page

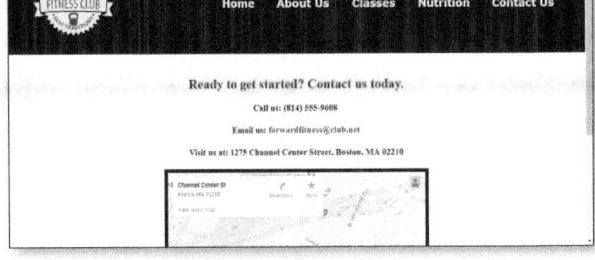

(c) Contact Us Page

Figure 4–1

Roadmap

In this chapter, you will learn how to create the webpage shown in Figure 4–1. The following roadmap identifies general activities you will perform as you progress through this chapter:

1. CREATE a CSS FILE.
2. LINK HTML PAGES TO a CSS FILE.
3. CREATE STYLE RULES.
4. ADD COMMENTS to the CSS file.
5. VALIDATE the CSS FILE.

At the beginning of step instructions throughout the chapter, you will see an abbreviated form of this roadmap. The abbreviated roadmap uses colors to indicate chapter progress: gray means the chapter is beyond that activity; blue means the task being shown is covered in that activity; and black means that activity is yet to be covered. For example, the following abbreviated roadmap indicates the chapter would be showing a task in the 4 ADD COMMENTS activity.

1 CREATE CSS FILE | 2 LINK PAGES TO CSS FILE | 3 CREATE STYLE RULES

4 ADD COMMENTS | **5 VALIDATE CSS FILE**

Use the abbreviated roadmap as a progress guide while you read or step through the instructions in this chapter.

Using Cascading Style Sheets

Although HTML allows web developers to make changes to the structure and content of a webpage, HTML is limited in its ability to define the appearance of one or more webpages. Instead, you use CSS styles to position and format elements on a webpage.

A **style rule**, or **rule-set**, is a rule that defines the appearance of an element on a webpage. You can include CSS styles in a section of an HTML document or in a separate file. In either case, the set of CSS style rules is called a **style sheet**.

Style sheets provide a means to separate style from content. This is ideal for you as a web designer because it gives you the flexibility to easily redesign or rebrand a website. For example, visit the CSS Zen Garden at www.csszengarden.com (Figure 4–2). This website displays an array of styles, all applied to the same HTML page. Review the styles to see how each one changes the webpage. Note that the text content does not change, only the graphics and the styles as defined in the style sheet. If you want the ability to easily redesign a website, keep your content separate from the style.

Figure 4–2

Separating content from style is even more important when you are maintaining a large website. You can define styles in a single CSS style sheet file, and then attach the single file to several webpages to apply the styles to all the attached pages. If you decide to use a different background color on all the webpages in the site, for example, you can make one change to the CSS style sheet to automatically update every page. Not only does this save a lot of time, it also means less maintenance for you or another web developer. If the site contained styles in the HTML code, locating those styles and removing them could be a time-consuming process.

CSS was developed by the W3C and is still evolving. The first version of CSS, CSS 1, was released in 1996. This version of CSS included styles for text, color, alignment, borders, padding, and margins. The second version of CSS, CSS 2, was released two years later in 1998 and included new styles to control the positioning of elements. The third version of CSS, CSS3, was released in 2001. It added many new style features, including shadows, rounded borders, and enhanced text effects.

The CSS Working Group oversees CSS specifications. Instead of releasing new CSS versions, the CSS Working Group now sets standards for CSS levels. The group releases CSS Snapshots, which include updates and revisions to CSS Levels. Visit w3.org/Style/CSS/ for the latest updates to CSS.

Modern browsers support CSS 1 and 2 and many CSS3 features. However, browsers may vary in how they apply CSS styles, so be sure to test and view your site in all the major browsers. Visit www.quirksmode.org to learn which browsers support each CSS style.

The W3C developed CSS as the primary way to format webpages, so you should not use HTML tags to style page content. Tags, such as the <font> tag, have been deemed as obsolete by W3C and should not be used.

Inline Styles

BTW
Deprecated and Unsupported Elements
A **deprecated** element or attribute is one that is outdated. Deprecated elements may become obsolete in the future, though most browsers continue to support deprecated elements for backward compatibility. In addition, many tags and attributes are not supported by HTML 5, as noted in Appendix A. You can also visit w3c.org to find a list of deprecated HTML tags.

CSS supports inline, embedded (or internal), and external styles. With an **inline style**, you add a style to the start tag for an element, such as a heading or paragraph, using the **style attribute**. The style changes the content marked up by a specific pair of tags, but does not affect other content in the document. Because inline styles take precedence over other types of styles and affect the style for individual pieces of content, they are helpful when you need to format only one section of a webpage in a unique way. However, inline styles defeat the purpose and advantages of separating style from content, so they should be used sparingly. An example of an inline style is shown in Figure 4–3. The style rule applies only to the content in this `h1` element, the "Special Note" text. In the starting <h1> tag, you begin writing an inline style using the `style` attribute. The inline style shown in Figure 4–3 defines the font color of the "Special Note" text as navy blue.

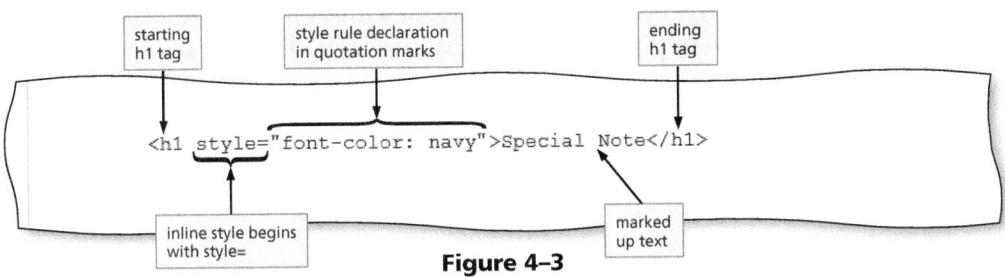

Figure 4–3

Embedded Style Sheets

An **embedded style sheet**, also called an **internal style sheet**, includes the style sheet within the opening <head> and closing </head> tags of the HTML document. Use an embedded style sheet when you want to create styles for a single webpage that are different from the rest of the website. An embedded style sheet takes precedence over an external style sheet. An example of an embedded style sheet is shown in Figure 4–4. In embedded style sheets, you place the style rules between the opening <style> and closing </style> tags. The style rule shown in Figure 4–4 sets the background color for the body section to green for the current webpage only.

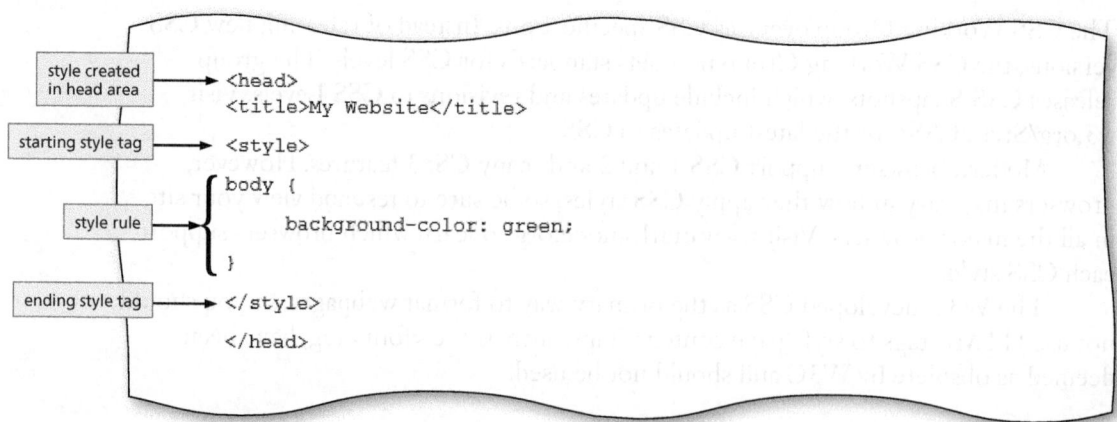

Figure 4–4

External Style Sheets

An **external style sheet**, also called a **linked style sheet**, is a CSS file that contains all of the styles you want to apply to more than one page in the website. An external style sheet is a text file with the **.css** file extension. To apply an external style sheet, you link it (or attach it) to a webpage using a link tag in the head section of the webpage. External style sheets give you the most flexibility to quickly change webpage formats because the styles in an external style sheet are applied to every page linked to that style sheet. Changing the look of an entire website is sometimes called **reskinning** the website. You will create an external style sheet for the Forward Fitness Club's website to enhance the appearance of the `body, header, nav, main,` and `footer` content. An example of a style rule for an external style sheet is shown in Figure 4–5. Like the style rule shown in Figure 4–4, this one sets the background color for the body section to green. Note that external style sheets do not contain any HTML tags.

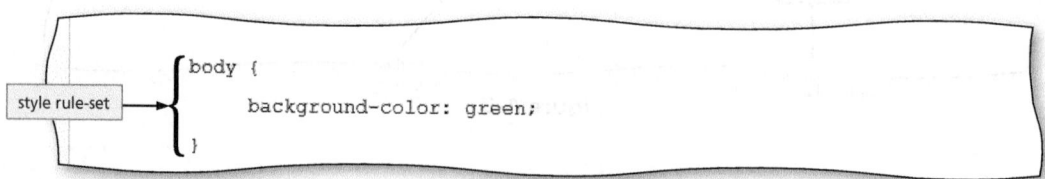

Figure 4–5

Style Sheet Precedence

Style sheets are said to "cascade" because each type of style has a specified level of precedence (or priority) in relationship to the others. For example, suppose you create an inline style to change the text color of an `h1` heading to red. In the `head` section of a webpage, you also create a style in an embedded style sheet to change `h1` headings to blue, and in an external style sheet, you create a style to change `h1` headings to green. What color would `h1` headings be in the webpage with the inline style? They would be red because the style closest to the content takes precedence. In other words, inline styles beat embedded styles, and embedded styles beat external styles.

CSS properties can be inherited from a parent element. This principle is called **inheritance**. For example, paragraphs and headings inherit the font and color rules for the body selector. If a selector has more than one CSS rule, **specificity** determines which CSS rule to apply. The more specific selector is applied. For example, if the value of the background-color property for the body selector is green but the one for p is blue, the p elements will have a blue background because the p selector is more specific than the body selector.

The best practice is to apply inline styles when you want to control the style of content within one pair of HTML tags, an embedded style sheet when you want to change the style of one page, and external or linked style sheets for the styles that apply to many or all pages in the website.

Web designers use external style sheets for most of their styles for many reasons. First, they can create or modify all of the styles in one style sheet file and then link the file to all of the HTML documents. This provides consistency throughout the website and lessens the need for coding beyond the single style sheet. Second, when an HTML document is linked to a CSS file, the page can load in a browser quickly. Third, if web designers need to change the appearance of a particular HTML element, they can do so in one file. The browser applies the change to all of the linked pages, reducing errors and redundancies.

CSS Basics

To write an inline CSS style, you use a style attribute within the HTML element, as shown in Figure 4–3. To write a CSS style rule for an embedded or external style sheet, you write a statement that follows the CSS syntax. Each CSS style rule consists of a selector and a declaration block. See Figure 4–6.

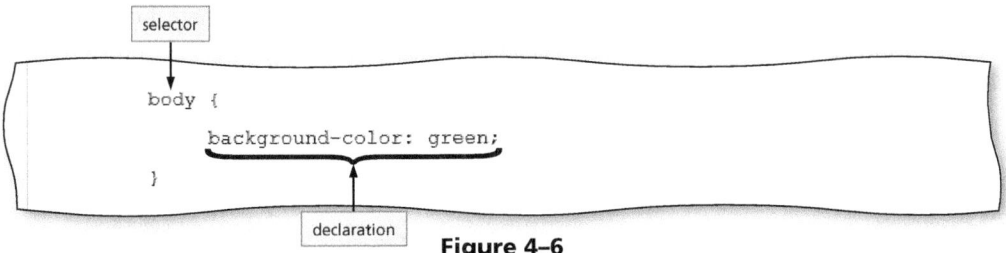

Figure 4–6

The **selector** is the part of the statement that identifies what to style. Any HTML 5 element such as body, header, nav, main, or footer may be a selector. For example, if you want to format the content in the **body** section of a webpage, use **body** as the selector in the style statement. A selector may also be the value of an id or class attribute. For example, if you want to format the content in the **div id="exercises"** section, use **#exercises** as the selector. (You will learn about including a # sign with selectors shortly.)

The **declaration** defines the exact formatting of the style. A declaration consists of a property and a value, separated by a colon and followed by a semicolon (;). The **property** identifies the style quality or characteristic to apply, such as color (text color), background-color, text-align, border-width, or font-size. A declaration includes at least one property to apply to the selected element.

For each property, the declaration includes a related **value** that identifies the particular property value to apply, such as green for color or 150% for font-size. You can use only certain values with each property based on the styles that property can define. The font-color property, for example, can accept navy as a value, but cannot

BTW
Style Rule Syntax
The correct syntax for style rules is to use all lowercase letters for the property name without any spaces. The same is true for values: use all lowercase characters and no spaces.

accept 150% because that is not a valid value for the color property. See Appendix B for a list of properties and valid values.

Figure 4–7 shows the correct syntax for the style rule shown in Figure 4–4 and Figure 4–5. To create a style for an embedded or external style sheet, you first identify the selector, followed by a space and an opening brace. Next, you specify the property, followed by a colon, and then provide a value for the property, followed by a semicolon. Close the rule with a closing brace.

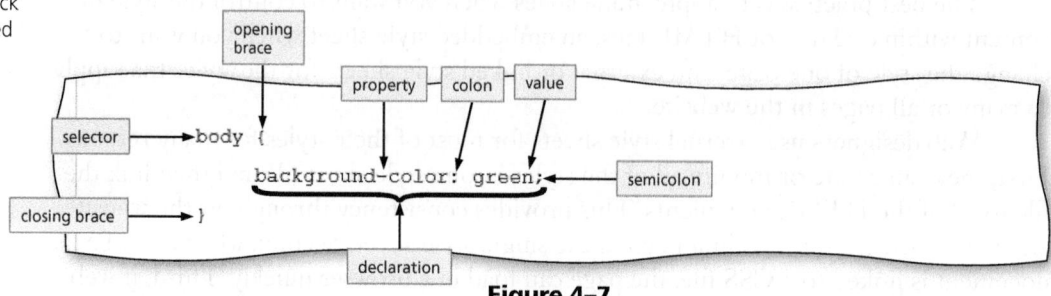

Figure 4–7

CONSIDER THIS

What is the difference between HTML attributes and CSS properties?
You use attributes in HTML elements to define more information for an element. Enter an attribute in an element's start tag as a name="value" pair. For example, in an `img` element, you include an attribute such as `src="logo.png"` to specify the source of the image. In this example, "src" is the attribute name and "logo.png" is the value. In a similar way, a CSS style defines the formatting for one or more elements. A style rule includes a selector and a declaration that consists of a property: value; pair. For example, `h1 {color: blue;}` formats `h1` elements using blue text. Enter a declaration for a selector in a style sheet.

CSS Text Properties

You can use CSS styles to format webpage text in a variety of ways. For example, use the font-family property to define a specific font. Use the font-size property to define a specific font size.

Table 4–1 lists common text properties and values.

Table 4–1 Common Text Properties and Values		
Property	**Description**	**Common Values**
font-family	Specific and general font names	font-family: Cambria, "Times New Roman", serif; font-family: Verdana, Arial, sans-serif; font-family: Georgia, "Times New Roman", serif;
font-size	Absolute or relative size of a font	font-size: 1.5em; font-size: 50%; font-size: x-large; font-size: 14pt;
font-weight	Weight of a font	font-weight: bold; font-weight: bolder; font-weight: lighter;
font-style	Style of a font	font-style: normal; font-style: italic; font-style: oblique;
text-align	Alignment of text	text-align: center; text-align: right; text-align: justify;
color	Color of text	color: red; color: blue; color: green;

Notice that the font-family property includes multiple values. You should provide more than one value for this property in case the browser does not support the primary font. The additional values are called **fallback values**. Specifying two or more font values is known as specifying a **font stack**. If the browser does not support the primary font, it displays the second font family indicated and if the browser does not support the second font family value, the browser uses the next font family. Commas separate each value. The desired value is listed first and the value of serif or sans-serif is listed last. For example, the declaration `font-family: Cambria, "Times New Roman", serif;` means that the browser should use the Cambria font; if the browser cannot use Cambria, it should use Times New Roman, which is listed in quotation marks because the font family name contains more than one word. Finally, if the browser does not support Cambria or Times New Roman, it should use its default serif font.

BTW
Font Names
The W3C recommends quoting font family names that contain spaces, digits, or punctuation characters other than hyphens.

Why would a browser not support certain fonts?
Fonts are installed on a computer, so a computer must have the font installed before a browser can display it. For a list of common web fonts, visit www.w3schools.com/cssref/css_websafe_fonts.asp.

CONSIDER THIS

CSS measures font size using many measurement units, including pixels, points, and ems, and by keyword or percentage. Table 4–2 lists units for measuring font size.

Table 4–2 Font Size Measurement Units			
Unit	**Definition**	**Example**	**Comments**
em	Relative to the default font size of the element	font-size: 1.25em;	Recommended by W3C; sizes are relative to the browser's default font size
%	Relative to the default font size of the element	font-size: 50%;	Recommended by W3C; sizes are relative to the browser's default font size
px	Number of pixels	font-size: 25px;	Depends on screen resolution
pt	Number of points	font-size: 12pt;	Use for printing webpages
keyword	Relative to a limited range of sizes	font-size: xx-small;	Sizes are relative to the browser's default font size, but size options are limited

The em is a relative measurement unit that the W3C recommends for values of the font-size property. The size of an em is relative to the current font size of the element. For example, 1.25em means 1.25 times the size of the current font. If a browser displays paragraphs using 16-point text by default, a font-size property value of 1em is 16 points and 1.25em is 20 points.

Percentage measurements work in a similar way. A font-size property value of 2em and of 200% appear the same when displayed in a browser. Note that no spaces appear in the font-size property value, so 1.25em and 50% are correct, but 1.25 em is not correct.

CSS Colors

One way to help capture a webpage visitor's attention is to use color as a webpage background or for text, borders, or links. HTML uses color names or codes to designate color values. When using a color name, you can specify a word such as aqua or black as a value. Following are 16 basic color names. For more color names, visit www.w3schools.com/colors/colors_names.asp.

aqua	navy
black	olive
blue	purple
fuchsia	red
gray	silver
green	teal
lime	white
maroon	yellow

Color codes are more commonly used in web design. Three common types of color codes used with CSS are hexadecimal, RGB, and HSL.

Hexadecimal values consist of a six-digit number code that corresponds to **RGB (Red, Green, Blue)** color values. When noting color values in CSS, include a number sign (#) before the code. Hexadecimal is a combination of the base-16 numbering system, which includes letters A through F. An example of a hexadecimal color value is 0000ff, which is blue. The first two digits (00) indicate the red value, which is none in this case. The next two digits (00) indicate the green value, which is also none in this case. The last two digits (ff) indicate the blue value. Because ff is the highest two-digit hexadecimal number, 0000ff specifies a pure blue.

RGB notation is used to display colors on a screen, though not in print. RGB blends red, green, and blue color channels to create a color. (A **channel** contains the number of red, green, or blue pixels necessary to create a specified color.) Each color channel is expressed as a number, 0 through 255. For example, the color blue is expressed as rgb(0,0,255). The first number represents the red color channel. The zero represents no pixels from a color channel; in the example, color channels red and green contribute no pixels to the color. The last channel represents the blue color channel; the number 255 represents the truest form of the color channel, in this case, blue. Hexadecimal 0000ff and rgb(0,0,255) are two ways of expressing the same color, pure blue.

The HSL color value notation was introduced with CSS3. It stands for hue, saturation, and lightness. The hue is a degree (0 to 360) on the HSL color wheel. Saturation is indicated as a percentage from 0% to 100% and is used to specify a shade of gray. Lightness is also indicated as a percentage from 0% to 100%. Black is 0% and white is 100%. To use HSL, you use the hsl() function. To create the color red, for example, use the notation hsl(0, 100%, 50%). HSL is supported by modern browsers.

Table 4–3 shows a common list of colors, with the corresponding hexadecimal, RGB, and HSL color codes.

BTW

HWB Colors
HWB (Hue, Whiteness, Blackness) is a new color format under development. It is not currently supported in HTML.

BTW

CMYK Colors
CMYK (Cyan, Magenta, Yellow, and Black) is a new color format under development. CMYK is a standard used for printing. It is not currently supported in HTML.

BTW

Opacity
RGB and HSL color formats also support opacity with the rgba() and hsla() functions.

BTW

Quick Color Picker
W3 Schools provides a quick color picker reference at www.w3schools.com/colors /colors_picker.asp. Here, you can select a color, view various shades of the color, and find the hexadecimal color value.

Table 4–3 Color Values			
Color	Hexadecimal	RGB	HSL
Black	#000000	rgb(0,0,0)	hsl(0, 0%, 0%)
White	#ffffff	rgb(255,255,255)	hsl(0, 0%, 100%)
Red	#ff0000	rgb(255,0,0)	hsl(0, 100%, 50%)
Green	#008000	rgb(0,128,0)	hsl(120, 100%, 25%)
Blue	#0000ff	rgb(0,0,255)	hsl(240, 100%, 50%)
Yellow	#ffff00	rgb(255,255,0)	hsl(60, 100%, 50%)
Orange	#ffa500	rgb(255,165,0)	hsl(39, 100%, 50%)
Gray	#808080	rgb(128,128,128)	hsl(0, 0%, 50%)

To use a color in a style rule declaration, use the color value as the property value. For example, to style a background color as gray, you use the background-color property with a value of #808080, as shown in the following example:

```
background-color: #808080;
```

If a hexadecimal color value repeats the same six characters, you can shorten the value to three characters. For example, the hexadecimal color value for black is #000000, which can be shortened to #000.

Understanding Inline Elements and Block Elements

When you format webpages with CSS, you set rules that describe how the HTML elements should appear in a browser. As you create rules for the elements, review the structure of the HTML document because it plays a part in how a browser displays the element on a webpage.

HTML elements are positioned on the webpage as a block or as inline content. A **block element** appears as a block because it starts and ends with a new line, such as the main element or a paragraph element. Block elements can contain content, other block elements, and inline elements. **Inline elements** are displayed without line breaks, so they flow within the same line. Inline content always appears within block elements. Examples of inline elements include the span element (<span> </span>) and the anchor element (<a> </a>). You use the span element to group inline elements. To format one or more words in a paragraph, for example, include an inline style in the opening span tag that groups the words, as in the following example, which formats only "Warning" in red text.

```
<span style="color: red;">"Warning"</span>
```

An `img` element is also an inline element because it flows in the same line, although it has natural height and width properties unlike other inline elements. Figure 4–8 shows an example of an inline element in a block element.

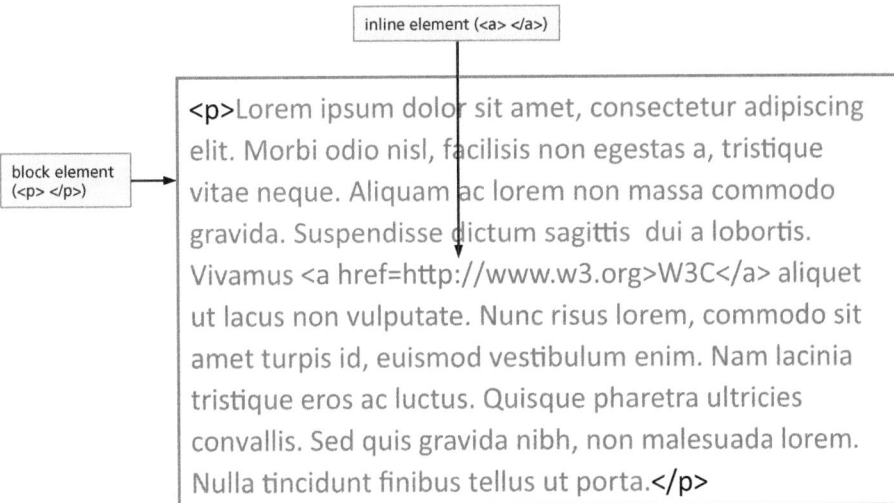

Figure 4–8

Header, nav, main, and footer are all examples of block elements. When you apply CSS styles to these block elements in the website you created for the Forward Fitness Club, you must consider their hierarchical structure to produce the visual effect you intend. Styles applied to elements below or above another element can affect their placement on a webpage. For example, as a block element, the `header` element normally starts on a new line and spans the width of the webpage. A new line also appears after the `header` element. If you want the `nav` element to appear to the right of the header, apply styles to both the `header` element and the `nav` element to accomplish this effect.

CSS Box Model

Each block element such as a header, nav, main, and footer element has a top, right, bottom, and left side. In other words, the element is displayed in a browser as a box with content. The **CSS box model** describes these boxes of content on a webpage. Each content box can have margins, borders, and padding, as shown in Figure 4–9. You refer to the sides of a box in clockwise order: top, right, bottom, and left.

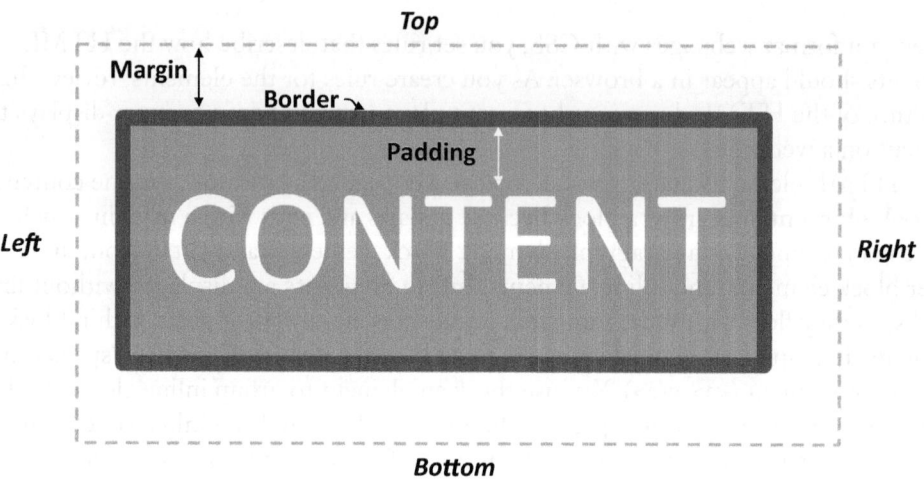

Figure 4–9

The **margin** provides passive white space between block elements or between the top or bottom of a webpage. You can define margins at the top, right, bottom, and left of a block element. Margins are transparent and are measured in ems (em), percentages (%), or pixels (px).

The **border** separates the padding and the margin of the block element. A border can vary in thickness and color and can be defined at the top, right, bottom, and left sides of a block element. A border can also have a style such as solid, dashed, or dotted.

Padding is the passive white space between the content and the border of a block element. Padding is typically measured in ems (em), percentages (%), or pixels (px). By default, padding is set to 0px, so paragraph text, for example, appears at the edges of the block element. You can increase the padding to improve legibility. The box model shown in Figure 4–9 includes more than the default amount of padding. The background color for the padding and content is always the same.

Using CSS, you can specify margin, padding, and border properties for all four sides of a block element. Following are examples of the many ways to specify block element properties.

When you want to use the same amount of margin on all four sides of a block element, specify a single value to the margin property. The following declaration specifies a margin of 2em on the top, bottom, left, and right:

```
margin: 2em;
```

You can also specify different margins for the sides. The following declarations specify a left margin of 2em and a bottom margin of 1em:

```
margin-left: 2em;
margin-bottom: 1em;
```

You can set the top and bottom margins to one value and then set the left and right margins to another value. You do so by including two values in the declaration.

The following shorthand notation sets the top and bottom margins to 1em and the left and right margins to 2em:

```
margin: 1em 2em;
```

You can also use shorthand notation to specify three values for margin. The first value sets the top margin, the second value sets the left and right margins, and the third value sets the bottom margin. The following example sets the top margin to 2em, left and right margins to 1.5em, and bottom margin to 1em:

```
margin: 2em 1.5em 1em;
```

To specify a different value for each side, use shorthand notation to include four values within the declaration. The values move clockwise around the block element. The first value is the top, the second value is the right, the third value is the bottom, and the fourth value is the left. For example, the following declaration specifies a top margin of 1em, right margin of 2em, bottom margin of 1.5em, and left margin of 3em:

```
margin: 1em 2em 1.5em 3em;
```

You can use a similar shorthand notation to set the style, width, and color for all four sides of a block element's border. The property values can appear in any order. The following declaration sets the top, right, bottom, and left borders of a block element to a solid line using a width of 1 pixel and a color of black:

```
border: solid 1px #000000;
```

You can set even more specific property options for the border, such as border-top-width and border-right-color. For example, the following declaration sets only the left border of the block element to a width of 2 pixels:

```
border-left-width: 2px;
```

Table 4–4 lists common CSS box model properties used to style block elements.

Table 4–4 Common CSS Box Model Properties		
Property	**Description**	**Examples**
margin	Sets the amount of space around the block element (top, right, bottom, left)	margin-top: 2em; margin-bottom: 15%; margin: 20px;
padding	Sets the amount of space between content and the border of its block element	padding-left: 1.5em; padding-right: 12%; padding: 10px;
border	Sets the format of the block element's border	border: solid 1px #000000;
border-style	Designates the style of a border	border-top-style: solid; border-top-style: dotted;
border-width	Designates the width of a border	border-top-width: 1px; border-bottom-width: thick;
border-color	Designates the border color	border-top-color: #000000; border-bottom-color: gray;
border-radius	Rounds the corners of a block element's border	border-radius: 10px;
box-shadow	Adds a shadow to a block element's border	box-shadow: 8px 8px 8px #000000;

To have a border appear around the content in a block element, you must specify a border style in a CSS statement. You can include the style value with the border property or use the border-style property with an assigned value.

The border-radius and box-shadow properties are CSS3 properties. As with the other border properties, you can list more than one value to set the top, right, bottom, and left radius values for the border. For the box-shadow property, you must specify the horizontal and vertical offset measurements. In addition, you can set the distance of the shadow's blur, the size of the shadow, and its color. The default color is black.

BTW

CSS Box Properties
Appendix B contains a comprehensive list of the CSS box properties and their acceptable values.

Creating an External Style Sheet

To create style rules that apply to more than one webpage in a website, use an external style sheet. Recall that an external style sheet is a text file that contains the style rules you want to apply to more than one page in the website.

Using an external style sheet involves two steps. First, use a text editor to create and save a document with a .css extension. In the CSS document, create style rules for elements such as body, header, nav, main, and footer to improve the visual appeal of the website. Create rule-sets to add color and borders, apply text properties, align items, and increase white space for padding and margins. Next, link the CSS file to the webpages that should be formatted using the styles defined in the external style sheet.

Selectors

Recall that a style rule begins with a selector, which specifies the element to style. A selector can be an HTML element name, an id attribute value, or a class attribute value. If the selector is an HTML element, you use the element name for the selector. Figure 4–10 shows how a selector in a CSS file selects the content to be styled for an HTML element, an id attribute, and a class attribute for HTML elements in an HTML file.

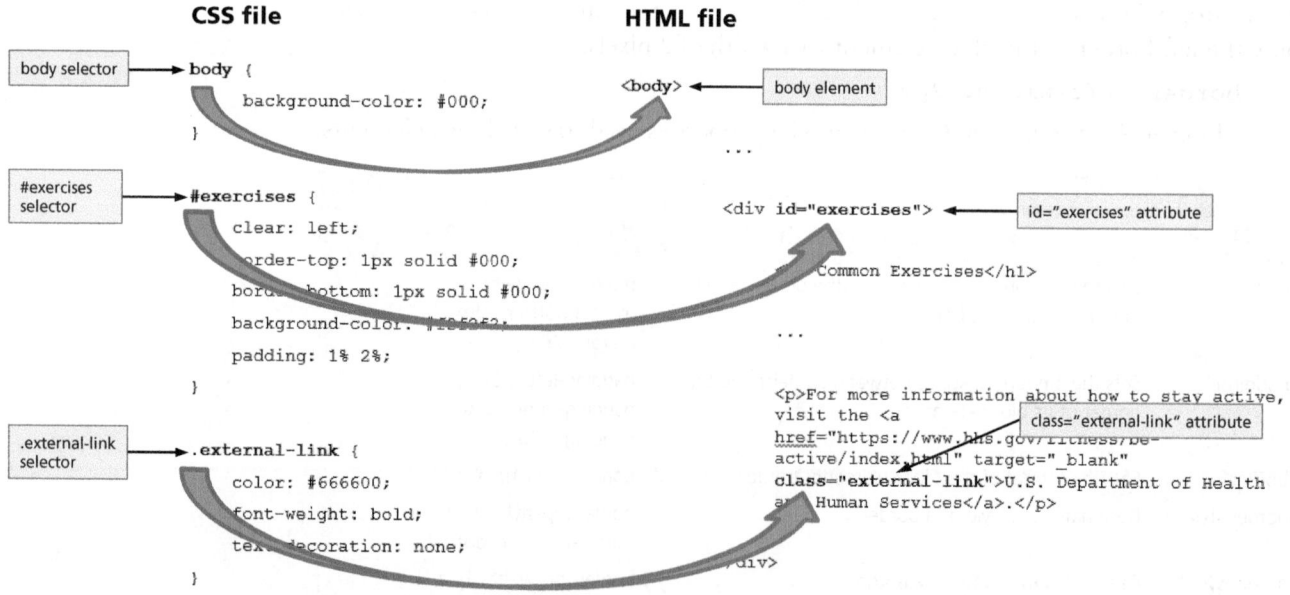

Figure 4–10

For example, to style the header element, use **header** as the name of the selector. To define the style of all p elements so they display white text on a black background, use the following style rule:

```
p {
        color: white;
        background-color: black;
}
```

If you want to apply styles to some p elements but not others, for example, you can create an id or a class selector. An **id selector** uses the id attribute value of an HTML element to select a single element. To create an id selector, you begin the style rule with a number sign (#) followed by the id attribute value. For example, to style the `div id="container"` element, use `#container` as the selector. The following style rule applies a solid 2-pixel border to only the `div id="container"` element:

```
#container {
        border: solid 2px;
}
```

Use a **class selector** to select elements that include a certain class attribute. To create a class selector, you begin the style rule with a period (.) followed by the class attribute value. You will learn more about class selectors later in this chapter. For example, to style class="mobile", use `.mobile` as the selector. The following style rule sets the font size to 1em for all elements that use mobile as their class attribute value:

```
.mobile {
        font-size: 1em;
}
```

If you want to create a style rule that applies to more than one element, you can list more than one selector. For example, the following style rule sets the same font family property and values for the `header, nav,` and `footer` elements:

```
header, nav, footer {
        font-family: Calibri, Arial, sans-serif;
}
```

If you want to create a style rule that applies to an element contained within another element, you list the elements in the order they appear to create the selector in the style rule. This type of selector is called a **descendant selector**. For example, the following style rule sets the list-style property to none for list items in an unordered list included in the navigation area:

```
nav ul li {
        list-style: none;
}
```

The following example is another way to create a style rule that selects all the li elements within the nav parent element:

```
nav > li {
        font-size: 1.5em;
}
```

To Create a CSS File and a Style Rule for the Body Element

1 CREATE CSS FILE | 2 LINK PAGES TO CSS FILE | 3 CREATE STYLE RULES
4 ADD COMMENTS | 5 VALIDATE CSS FILE

To apply styles to the Forward Fitness Club website, you can create them in an external style sheet. *Why? The styles defined in the external style sheet will apply to all the webpages in the website.* To create a CSS file, you use your preferred text editor to create a file and save it as a CSS document. Next, include one or more style rules that apply to all the webpages linked to the CSS document. The first style rule you add sets the background color of the webpages. This rule uses "body" as the selector and the background-color property in the declaration. Because the `body` element contains all the content displayed on a webpage, using "body" as the selector sets the background color of the entire webpage. The following steps create a CSS file and a style rule.

• Open your text editor, tap or click File on the menu bar, and then tap or click New if you need to open a new blank document.

• Tap or click File on the menu bar and then tap or click Save As to display the Save As dialog box.

• Navigate to your fitness folder and then double-tap or double-click the css folder to open it.

• In the File name box, type **styles** to name the file.

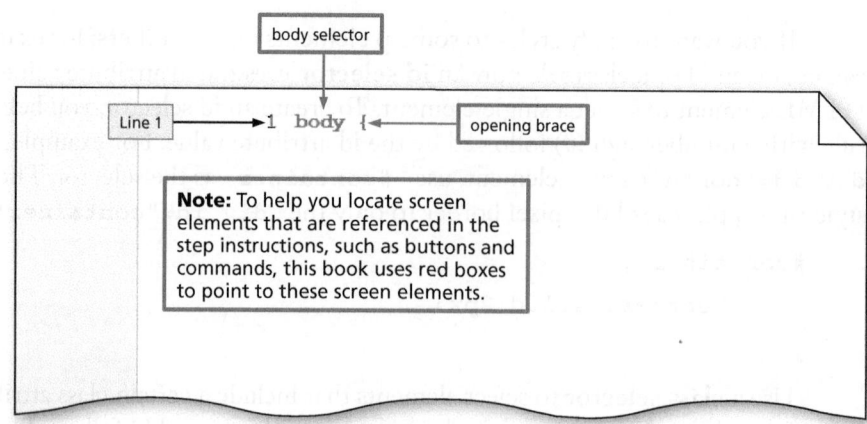

Figure 4–11

Q&A Is "styles" the required file name for the CSS file?
No. You can give a CSS file any meaningful name, but a common name for an external style sheet is styles.css. An external style sheet must end with a .css extension.

• Tap or click the Save as type button, and then tap or click Cascading Style Sheets or CSS to select the file format.

• Tap or click the Save button to save the file in the css folder.

• On Line 1 of the text editor, type **body {** to begin a new style rule for the body element (Figure 4–11).

Q&A Why should I use "body" as the selector?
Using "body" as the selector means the style rule applies to all of the body elements in the webpages linked to the style sheet. In this case, you are creating a style rule that sets the background color for the entire webpage because the body element contains all of the content displayed on a webpage.

• Press the ENTER key to add Line 2, press the TAB key to indent the new line, and then type **background-color: #ccc;** to add a declaration that sets the background color.

• Press the ENTER key to add Line 3, press the SHIFT+TAB keys to decrease the indent, and then type **}** to add a closing brace (Figure 4–12).

Q&A What color does ccc represent?
The color specified by ccc is a light shade of gray. The hexadecimal color code for this shade of gray is cccccc. Because it consists of six "c's," the color code can be shortened to ccc.

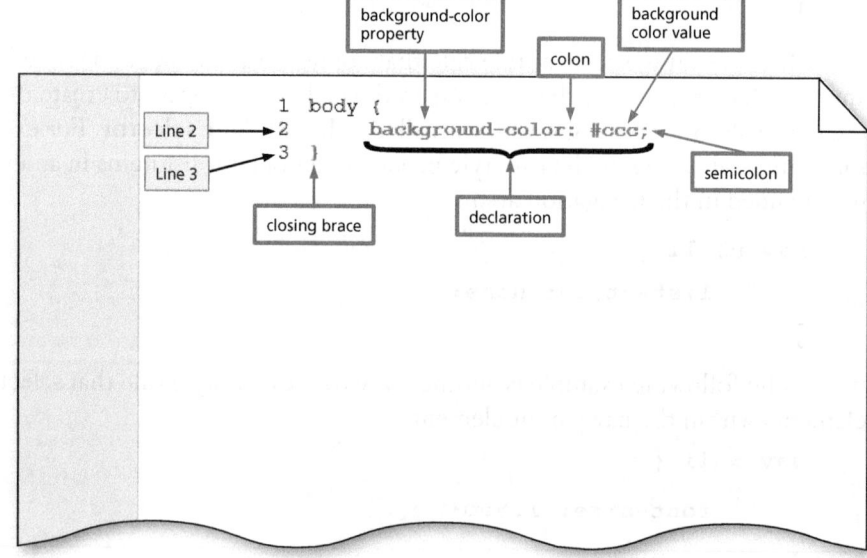

Figure 4–12

• Save your changes.

Linking an HTML Document to a CSS File

After creating a CSS file, link it to all the webpages that will use its styles. Otherwise, the browser will not find and apply the styles in the external style sheet. Insert a **link** element on the HTML page within the <head> and </head> tags, which is the section of an HTML document that provides information to browsers and search engines but is not displayed on the webpage itself.

The **link** element uses two attributes, **rel** and **href.** The **rel** attribute uses the **stylesheet** value to indicate that the document is linked to a style sheet. The **href** attribute value specifies the file path or file name of the CSS file. Following is an example of a link to a style sheet named styles.css and stored in the css folder:

```
<link rel="stylesheet" href="css/styles.css">
```

The **type="text/css"** attribute and value is also commonly used within a **link** element to reference a CSS file. However, with HTML 5, the **type** attribute is not necessary. The W3C says that the use of the **type** attribute within the **link** element is "purely advisory."

To Link HTML Pages to the CSS File

1 CREATE CSS FILE | **2 LINK PAGES TO CSS FILE** | 3 CREATE STYLE RULES
| **4 ADD COMMENTS** | **5 VALIDATE CSS FILE**

To link the styles.css file to an HTML page, you include a link to the style sheet within the **head** section of the document. Next, view the changes to the webpage in a browser. *Why? To apply the CSS style rules to a webpage, you must link the webpage to the CSS file. To view the applied styles, open the home page in a browser.* If you link the website template to the style sheet file, any new pages created from the template will already be linked to the style sheet. The following steps link the home, about, contact, and template HTML documents to the external style sheet file and then view one page in a browser.

- Open index.html in your text editor to prepare to link the page to the CSS file.

- Place the insertion point after the meta element on Line 6 and press the ENTER key to create a new Line 7.

- If necessary, press the TAB key to indent the line and then type **<link rel="stylesheet" href="css/styles.css">** to create a link to the style sheet file (Figure 4–13).

```
1 <!DOCTYPE html>
2 <!-- This website template was created by: Student's First
  Name Student's Last Name -->
3 <html lang="en">
4 <head>
5    <title>Forward Fitness Club</title>
6    <meta charset="utf-8">
7    <link rel="stylesheet" href="css/styles.css">       ← link to
8 </head>                                                   styles.css
```

Line 7 →

Figure 4–13

Q&A Why do I need to include css/ before the name of the file?
The styles.css file is located within the css folder. Because the file is not stored in the same folder as the index.html document, you must include the folder name as well as the file name in the **href** attribute value.

Can I place the link to the style sheet anywhere within the head element or do I have to place it directly after the meta element?
The link to the style sheet can be anywhere within the head element, though placing it below the title element is a best practice.

2

- Save the index.html page to preserve your changes.
- Open about.html in your text editor to prepare to link the page to the CSS file.
- Place the insertion point after the meta element on Line 6 and press the ENTER key to create a new Line 7.
- If necessary, press the TAB key to indent the line and then type `<link rel="stylesheet" href="css/styles.css">` to create a link to the style sheet file.
- Save your changes and close the file.
- Open contact.html in your text editor, place the insertion point after the meta element on Line 6, and then press the ENTER key to create a new Line 7.
- If necessary, press the TAB key and then type `<link rel="stylesheet" href="css/styles.css">` to create a link to the style sheet file.
- Save your changes and close the file.
- Open template.html, place the insertion point after the meta element on Line 6, and then press the ENTER key to create a new Line 7.
- If necessary, press the TAB key and then type `<link rel="stylesheet" href="css/styles.css">` to create a link to the style sheet file.
- Save your changes and close the file.
- View the home page in your default browser to view the page with the linked style sheet (Figure 4–14).

Q&A Why is the background color gray? The example shown at the beginning of the chapter shows a black background. You will change the background to black in future steps. If you use black for the background now, you will not be able to see the black text and other page content.

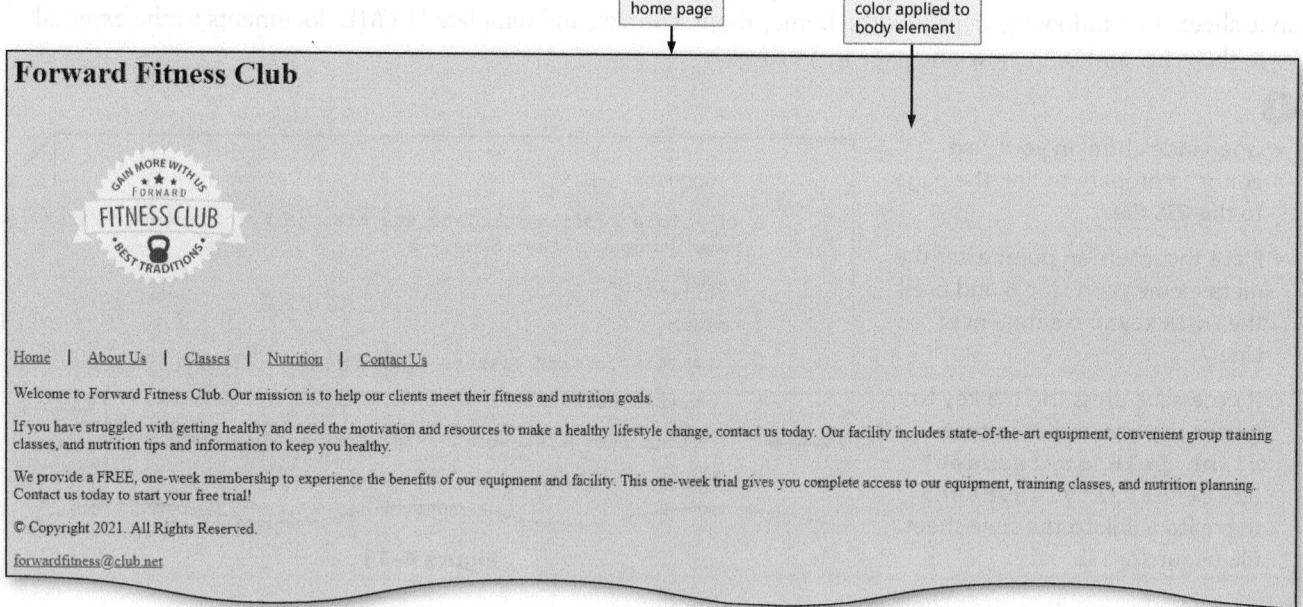

Figure 4–14

CONSIDER THIS

How can I confirm that my style rules have been correctly applied to a webpage?
After creating a CSS file, link it to one of your webpages. Include a complete style rule or add a declaration to a selector, save your changes, and then view the webpage in a browser to view the effects of the new or modified style. If the style is not applied as you intended, return to your CSS file to check for syntax errors, confirm that you saved the CSS file, and check for value errors. It is much easier to find mistakes when you code and test each new style or declaration.

Creating a Webpage Layout

To design a webpage to look the way you want, you cannot use HTML alone. You use CSS to design a webpage layout. With CSS, you can specify where each element should be placed on a webpage. Likewise, you specify how content will appear on each webpage. In Chapters 1 and 2, you learned how to create a website plan and a wireframe. Recall that a wireframe is a sketch of the proposed webpage layout. Figure 4–15 shows the proposed wireframe for the Forward Fitness Club home page.

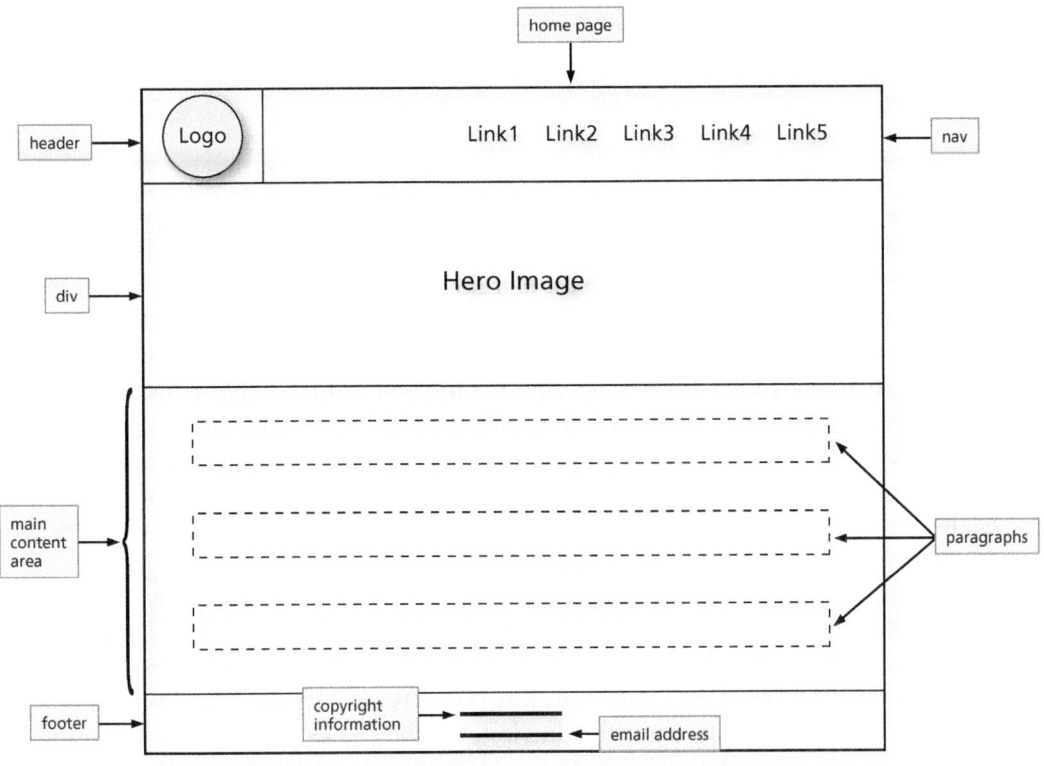

Figure 4–15

To achieve this design, you will create several style rules and use various CSS properties.

Float and Clear Properties

One way to create the layout shown in Figure 4–15 is to use the CSS float property. The **float property** allows you to position an element to the right or left of other elements, while remaining within its parent element. The float property has four valid values: `left, right, inherit,` and `none.` The `left` value floats an element left. The `right` value floats an element right. The `inherit` value floats an element with the same value as its parent element. The `none` value does not float an element and is the default.

To achieve the layout shown in the wireframe (Figure 4–15), float the header element left and float the nav element right. You must also specify a width for each element. Create the following style rules to design the header and nav layout shown in the wireframe:

```
header {
        float: left;
        width: 25%;
}

nav {
        float: right;
        margin: 5em 3em 0 0;
        width: 70%;
}
```

The above style rule for the header floats the header to the left of the nav element and sets its width to 25%. The nav style rule floats the nav to the right of the header; sets its top margin to 5em, right margin to 3em, and top and bottom margins to 0; and specifies a width of 70%. Note the specified widths of each element: 25% and 70%. When added together, their combined width value is 95%. Because these elements share the same vertical space, their combined widths should not exceed 100%. It seems the page allows another 5% to work with; however, it does not. The nav element also includes a right margin value of 3em. Since both margin and padding values take up vertical space within that 100% allotment, you must adjust widths accordingly, so that, all together, width values, padding values, and margin values do not surpass 100%.

If you float an element, neighboring elements will also be affected by the float. Subsequently, the neighboring elements may also appear to float or wrap alongside the element with the specified float. To correct this issue, use the **clear property** to remove the float effect. The valid values for the clear property are `right, left,` and `both.` To clear an element that is floating left, use the `clear: left;` declaration. Likewise, to clear an element that is floating right, use the `clear: right;` declaration. Use the `both` value if elements are floating on both the right and left sides of the text. Apply the clear property to the selector that is affected by the floating element. For example, if you want the main element to appear below the header and nav, create a style rule for the main and use the clear property in one of its declarations.

```
main {
        clear: left;
}
```

When designing layouts such as columns, content can "spill over" to another element and appear outside its parent container. The effect is similar to a cup filling with water that begins to overflow from the cup. To correct this issue, you use the **CSS overflow property** to keep the content within its parent container.

Aligning Webpage Content

One way to align webpage content is to use the text-align property, which applies to block elements. Use the text-align property to set the horizontal alignment for the lines of text in an element. The text-align property can use one of four values: `left` (the default), `center, right,` or `justify.` Use the justify value to align text on the left and right margins by adding white space to the lines of text. Use the center value to center content within an element. For example, the following rule centers an `h1` element:

```
h1 {
        text-align: center;
}
```

Another way to center webpage content is to use the margin property. To center all of the elements so that the page appears centered within a browser window, you create styles to set the left and right margins to auto. You also set the width property to a percentage to specify how much of the page to use for content. For example, if you set the width to 80%, you leave 20 percent of the page for margins. Using "auto" as the property value means that the left and right margins split the available 20 percent equally, leaving 10 percent of the page for the left margin and 10 percent of the page for the right margin. The following declaration specifies the width of the `div id="container"` section as 80 percent of the page and sets the left and right margins to "auto," centering all of the content in that section:

```
container {
        width: 80%;
        margin: 0 auto;
}
```

To Position Elements

1 CREATE CSS FILE | 2 LINK PAGES TO CSS FILE | 3 CREATE STYLE RULES
4 ADD COMMENTS | 5 VALIDATE CSS FILE

Now that you have created a style for the `body` element, return to your CSS file to create style rules for the header, nav, and main elements. To create the layout shown in Figure 4–15, you specify a width of 25% for the header and float it to the left. You specify a width of 70% for the nav and float it to the right. Additionally, you specify a top margin of 5em, right margin of 3em, and bottom and left margins of 0. Finally, you clear the float to the left of the main element. The following steps create style rules for the header, nav, and main to lay out the page elements.

- In the text editor, return to the styles.css file.

- Place the insertion point after the closing brace on Line 3 and press the ENTER key twice to insert new Lines 4 and 5.

- On Line 5, type **header** { to add the header selector and an opening brace (Figure 4–16).

Q&A Why is Line 4 blank?
Reading and reviewing several lines of code can be hard on the eyes. For improved readability, insert blank lines between each style rule.

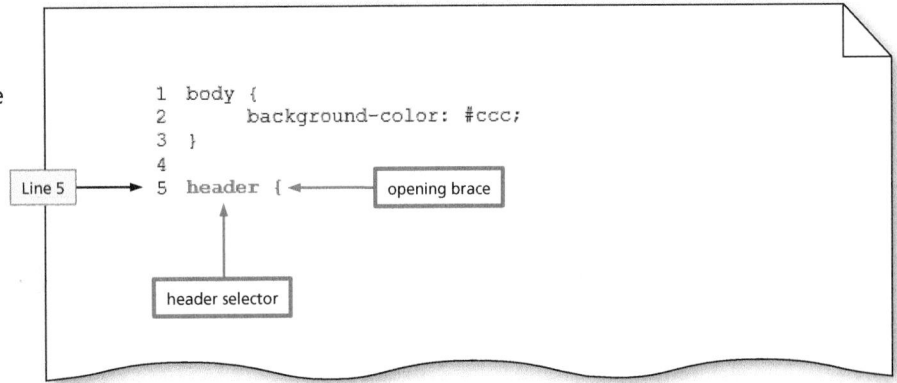

```
1  body {
2          background-color: #ccc;
3  }
4
5  header {
```

Line 5 → 5 header { ← opening brace

header selector

Figure 4–16

2

- Press the ENTER key to add Line 6, press the TAB key to indent the line, and then type **width: 25%;** to add a declaration that sets the width of the element.

- Press the ENTER key to add Line 7 and then type **float: left;** to add a declaration that sets a left float.

- Press the ENTER key to add Line 8, press the SHIFT+TAB keys to decrease the indent, and then type **}** to close the style rule (Figure 4–17).

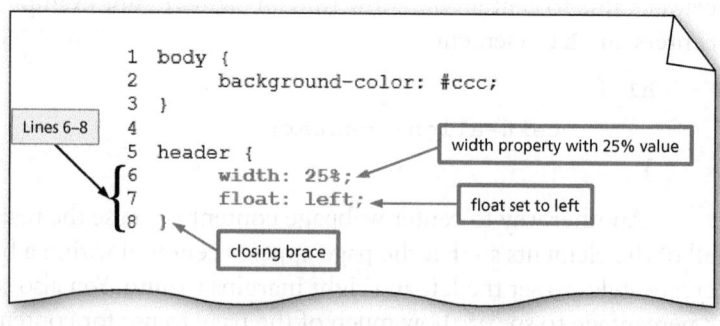

Figure 4–17

Q&A

Why do I need to set the width to 25%?

Currently, the header element on the webpage spans the entire width of the browser window. Setting the width to 25% restricts the width of the header element, allowing room for the nav element to be positioned to the right of the header element.

Do I have to enter each property and value on a separate line?

No. However, listing each property and value on separate lines enhances the readability of the style sheet. A style rule with many declarations is difficult to read unless the declarations are listed on separate lines. Readability helps to find and correct syntax errors.

3

- Press the ENTER key twice to insert new Lines 9 and 10.

- On Line 10, type **nav {** to add the nav selector and an opening brace.

- Press the ENTER key to add Line 11, press the TAB key to indent the line, and then type **width: 70%;** to add a declaration that sets the width of the element.

- Press the ENTER key to add Line 12, and then type **float: right;** to set a right float.

- Press the ENTER key to add Line 13, and then type **margin: 5em 3em 0 0;** to set the margin on all sides of the element.

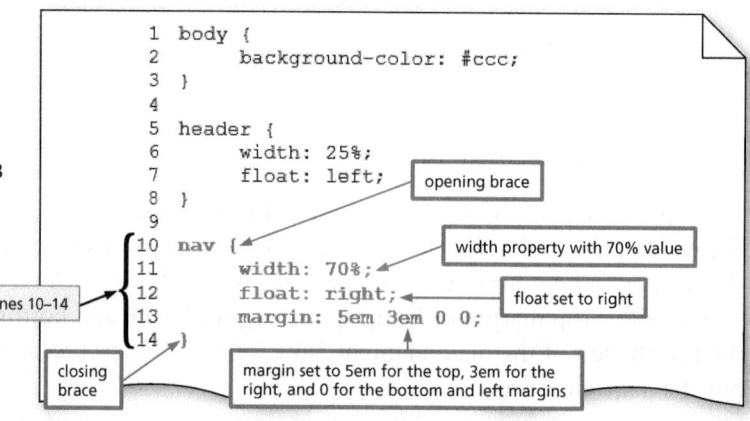

Figure 4–18

- Press the ENTER key to add Line 14, press the SHIFT+TAB keys to decrease the indent, and then type **}** to close the style rule (Figure 4–18).

4

- Press the ENTER key twice to insert new Lines 15 and 16.

- On Line 16, type **main {** to add the main selector and an opening brace.

- Press the ENTER key to add Line 17, press the TAB key to indent the line, and then type **clear: left;** to add a declaration that clears a float to the left.

- Press the ENTER key to add Line 18, press the SHIFT+TAB keys to decrease the indent, and then type **}** to close the style rule (Figure 4–19).

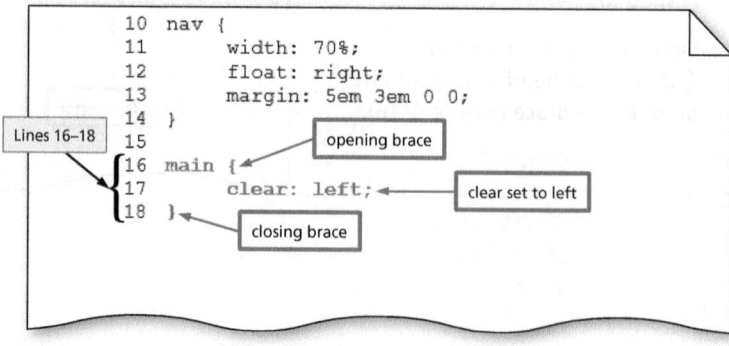

Figure 4–19

- Save your changes.

- View the home page in a browser to see the applied styles (Figure 4–20).

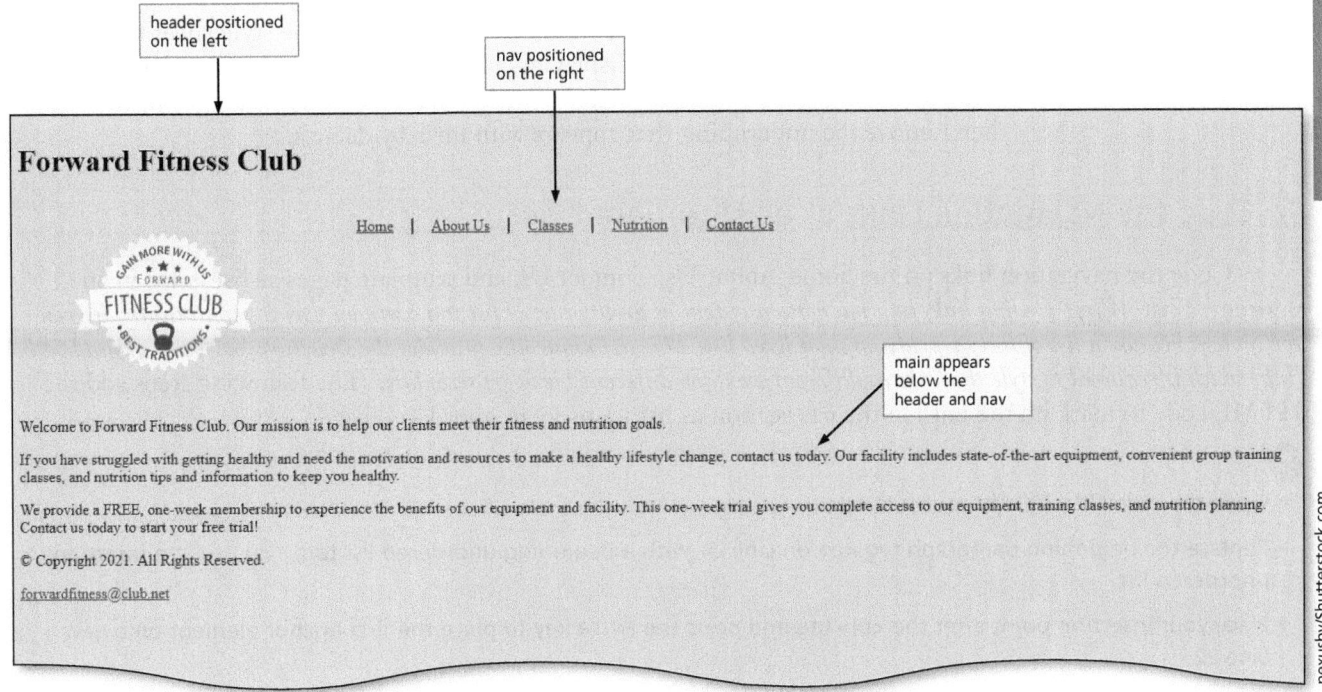

Figure 4–20

Creating Style Rules for Structural Elements

The next formatting task is to create style rules for the HTML 5 structural elements used in the Forward Fitness Center website. Because the header section appears at the top of the webpage, it needs formatting that makes the header contents stand out and attract visitors to the page. You have already completed this task by creating a style rule that sets width and float properties.

The nav section should also be prominent and easy to find on the webpage, so you should format it differently from the other structural elements. Update the nav to use an unordered list, and then create several style rules to format the nav to appear horizontally on the page and remove the bullet markers from each list item.

Because a float was specified for the header and nav, you will need to use the clear property within the main style rule. This will keep the position of the main element below the nav element. Each page contains different content within the main element, so you will create various style rules to style the content for each page.

Finally, create a style rule that formats the footer section by defining the font size, text alignment, and padding of the `footer` element.

BTW
CSS Style Rule Order
Although the styles in a style sheet are not required to follow a specific order, most designers list the styles in the same general order that they will be used on a webpage. In other words, styles that apply to the body, outer container, and sections of the wireframe are typically listed first. Styles that apply to more specific areas of content such as headings, lists, and links are generally listed next.

Use a List for Navigation Links

To make the navigation links more appealing on the webpage, you can format them with CSS. For the Forward Fitness Club website, you will code the navigation links as an unordered list in the HTML document and then add styles in the CSS file to better display and position the navigation system as appropriate for your design.

Format the navigation links by increasing the font size and changing the text color to white, which will create a strong color contrast for the Forward Fitness Club website. Use CSS to create extra space between links to clearly separate the links.

To accomplish this design, first code the navigation links as an unordered list. This is a common web design technique that both semantically describes the content and lets you format each link using CSS. Next, add styles to the style sheet to format the navigation list items without displaying a bullet. You will also apply a background color, text color, and a rounded border to make each link look like a button. You will then remove the underlining that appears with links by default.

To Code the Navigation Links as an Unordered List

Code the navigation links on the home, About Us, Contact Us, and template pages as list items in an unordered list. *Why? Coding links in a navigation system as an unordered list is a common way to semantically describe the content because a list of links is truly an unordered list. This technique also provides the structure, or "box," around each link, which is required to style the links in different ways for different viewport sizes later.* The following steps add the HTML code to mark up the links in the nav section as list items in an unordered list.

- Open the index.html file in your text editor.

- Replace the beginning paragraph tag <p> on Line 21 with a beginning unordered list tag, `<ul>`, to insert an unordered list.

- Place your insertion point after the <ul> tag and press the ENTER key to place the first anchor element on a new Line 22.

- Starting on Line 22, add the li elements and closing ul tag as shown in Figure 4–21 to code the navigation links as list items in an unordered list.

Q&A Do I need to indent the lines of code as I insert the tags?
Yes. Be sure to indent as shown in Figure 4–21 to maintain maximum readability.

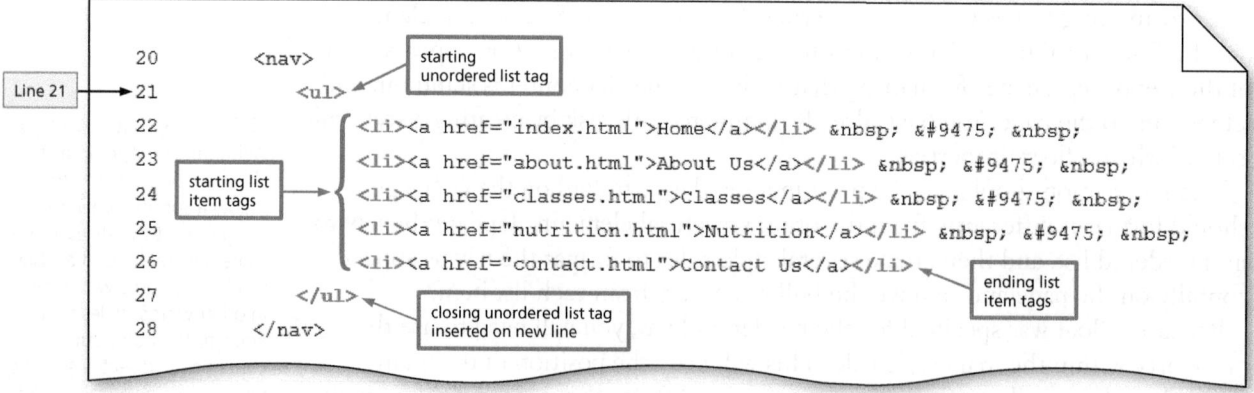

Figure 4–21

- Delete the nonbreaking space characters, , and vertical lines, ┃, after each closing </li> tag (Figure 4–22).

Q&A Why am I deleting the nonbreaking space characters and vertical lines?
You will use CSS to style the padding and margin between these links so you no longer need the nonbreaking spaces or vertical lines to create space between the links.

```
20          <nav>
21              <ul>
22                  <li><a href="index.html">Home</a></li>  ◄── nonbreaking spaces and
                                                                   vertical lines deleted
23                  <li><a href="about.html">About Us</a></li>
24                  <li><a href="classes.html">Classes</a></li>
25                  <li><a href="nutrition.html">Nutrition</a></li>
26                  <li><a href="contact.html">Contact Us</a></li>
27              </ul>
28          </nav>
```

index.html ──►

Figure 4–22

- Copy the unordered list code in the <nav> section, starting with the opening <ul> tag on Line 21 and continuing through the ending </ul> tag on Line 27.
- Open the about.html file in your text editor.
- Select all elements within the <nav>...</nav> tags on Lines 21–25, and then paste the text from index.html containing the links coded as an unordered list (Figure 4–23).

```
20          <nav>
21              <ul>
22                  <li><a href="index.html">Home</a></li>
23                  <li><a href="about.html">About Us</a></li>
24                  <li><a href="classes.html">Classes</a></li>
25                  <li><a href="nutrition.html">Nutrition</a></li>
26                  <li><a href="contact.html">Contact Us</a></li>
27              </ul>
28          </nav>
```

about.html ──►

code pasted
from index.html

Figure 4–23

- Open the contact.html file in your text editor.
- Select all elements within the <nav>...</nav> tags on Lines 21–25, and then paste the text from index.html containing the links coded as an unordered list (Figure 4–24).

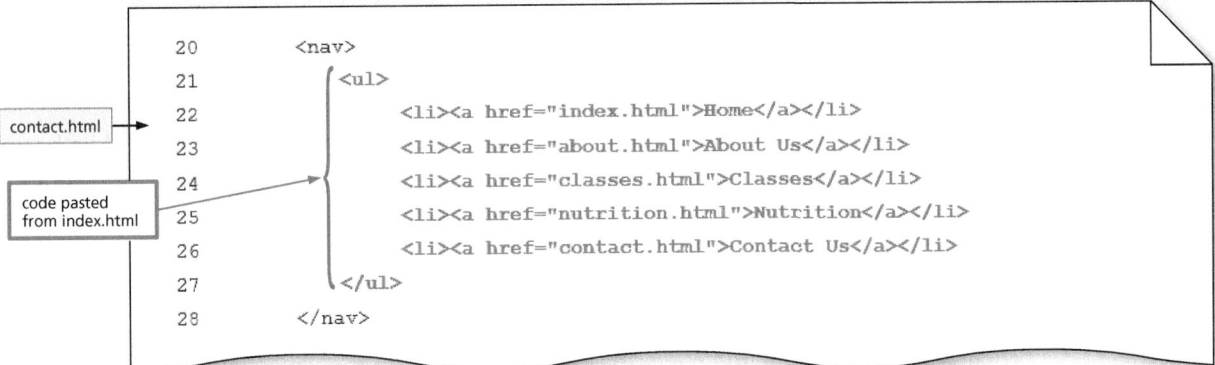

Figure 4–24

- Open the template.html template file in your text editor.
- Select all elements within the <nav>...</nav> tags on Lines 21–25, and then paste the text from index.html containing the links coded as an unordered list (Figure 4–25).

```
20        <nav>
21            <ul>
22                <li><a href="index.html">Home</a></li>
23                <li><a href="about.html">About Us</a></li>
24                <li><a href="classes.html">Classes</a></li>
25                <li><a href="nutrition.html">Nutrition</a></li>
26                <li><a href="contact.html">Contact Us</a></li>
27            </ul>
28        </nav>
```

template.html

code pasted from index.html

Figure 4–25

- Save and view all four HTML files in a browser to verify the list items appear as a bulleted list (Figure 4–26).

Q&A Why does each link appear on its own line in the nav area?

Each link appears on its own line because the list item element is a block element.

Figure 4–26

CSS List Properties

To control the appearance of numbered and bulleted lists, you use the CSS **list-style properties**. By default, unordered lists display a solid bullet before each list item. Likewise, ordered lists display numbers (1, 2, 3, and so on) before each list item. You use the list-style-type property to specify a different type of bullet or a different numbering style to use in a list. For example, the following style rule defines a filled square bullet for an unordered list:

```
ul {

    list-style-type: square;

}
```

The following style rule defines uppercase Roman numerals for an ordered list:

```
ol {

    list-style-type: upper-roman;

}
```

If you want to display an image instead of a bullet, use the list-style-image property. To indicate the file name of the image file, begin the value with "url" followed by the file name or path in parentheses. For example, the following style rule defines the image in the arrow.png file as the bullet for unordered lists:

```
ul {
        list-style-image: url(arrow.png);
}
```

To specify the position of the bullet or number in a list, use the list-style-position property. The default value for this property is **outside**, which displays the list item with a bullet or number outside of the list's content block as in the following text:

1. Lorem ipsum dolor sit amet,
   consectetur adipiscing elit.
2. Morbi odio nisl, facilisis non
   egestas a, tristique vitae neque.

Using **inside** as the value displays the bullet or number inside the list's content block, as in the following text:

1. Lorem ipsum dolor sit amet,
consectetur adipiscing elit.
2. Morbi odio nisl, facilisis non
egestas a, tristique vitae neque.

To Style the Navigation Using CSS

The default marker for each list item in an unordered list is a bullet. Add style rules to remove the bullet from the unordered list and to display the list items as an inline block so that they appear horizontally on the page. ***Why?*** *For a desktop display, you want the links in the navigation bar to appear on a single line, and you do not want to display the bullet marker.* Create three new style rules. First, create a style rule for the unordered list within the nav to remove the bullet and margin, and align text to the right. Next, create a style rule for list item elements within the nav to display them as an inline block and increase the font size. Finally, create a style rule for anchor elements within nav list item elements to display them as a block, change the text color to white, center-align the text, remove the underline, and specify padding. The following steps add three style rules to the style sheet to format the unordered list for the website.

- Open the styles.css file, place the insertion point after the closing brace on Line 14, and then press the ENTER key twice to insert new Lines 15 and 16.

- On Line 16, type **nav ul {** to add the ul selector nested within a nav element and an opening brace.

- Press the ENTER key to add Line 17, press the TAB key to indent the line, and then type **list-style-type: none;** to add a declaration that removes the bullet marker.

- Press the ENTER key to add Line 18, and then type **margin: 0;** to remove margin.

- Press the ENTER key to add Line 19, and then type **text-align: right;** to align the unordered list to the right.

- Press the ENTER key to add Line 20, press the SHIFT+TAB keys to decrease the indent, and then type **}** to close the style rule (Figure 4–27).

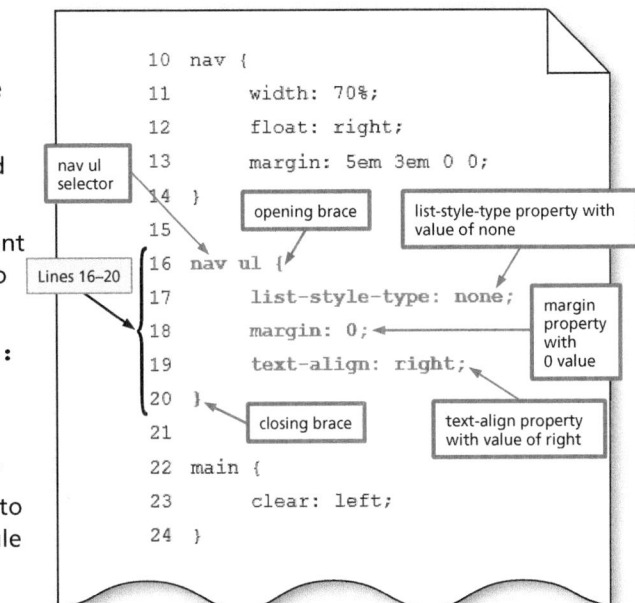

Figure 4–27

Q&A What is the list-style-type property?
The list-style-type property specifies the type of bullet for a list item. If you do not want to display a bullet, specify a value of none to remove the default bullet.

- Press the ENTER key twice to insert new Lines 21 and 22.

- Starting on Line 22, add the style rule for the nav li selector as shown in Figure 4–28 to style the list items within the nav element.

Q&A Why am I using the display property with a value of inline-block?
This will show the list items horizontally on the page instead of vertically.

What does the 1.75em value mean for the font-size property?
Setting the font-size property to 1.75em means the font size of the list item text is 1.75 times larger than the default font size of the browser. If the default size is 1.25em, for example, the font size for list items within the nav element will be 2.1875em.

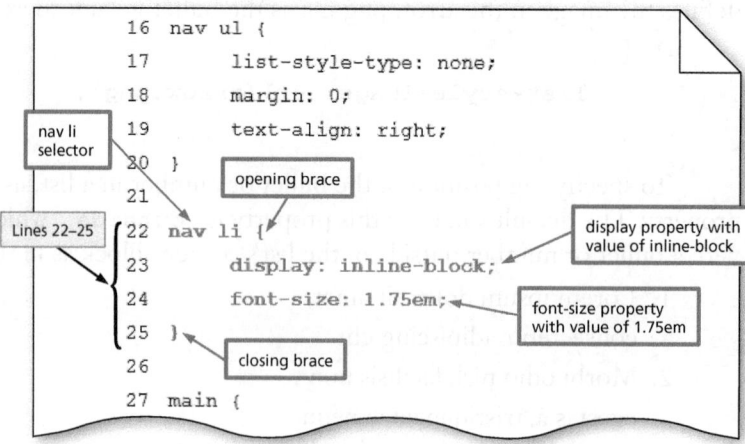

```
16  nav ul {
17      list-style-type: none;
18      margin: 0;
19      text-align: right;
20  }
21
22  nav li {
23      display: inline-block;
24      font-size: 1.75em;
25  }
26
27  main {
```

Figure 4–28

- Press the ENTER key twice to insert new Lines 26 and 27.

- Starting on Line 27, add the style rule for the nav li a selector as shown in Figure 4–29 to style the anchor elements nested within the list items with the nav parent element.

Q&A What is the purpose of the text-decoration property?
The text-decoration property is used to remove the underline from the navigation links.

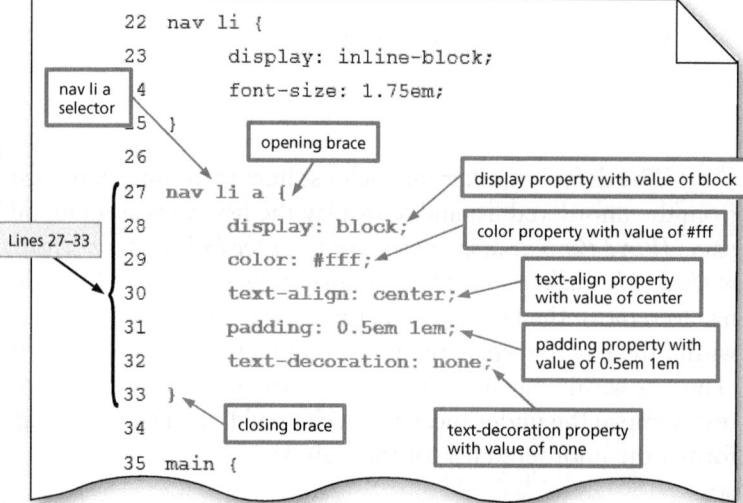

```
22  nav li {
23      display: inline-block;
24      font-size: 1.75em;
25  }
26
27  nav li a {
28      display: block;
29      color: #fff;
30      text-align: center;
31      padding: 0.5em 1em;
32      text-decoration: none;
33  }
34
35  main {
```

Figure 4–29

- Save the styles.css file and view the index.html page in your browser (Figure 4–30).

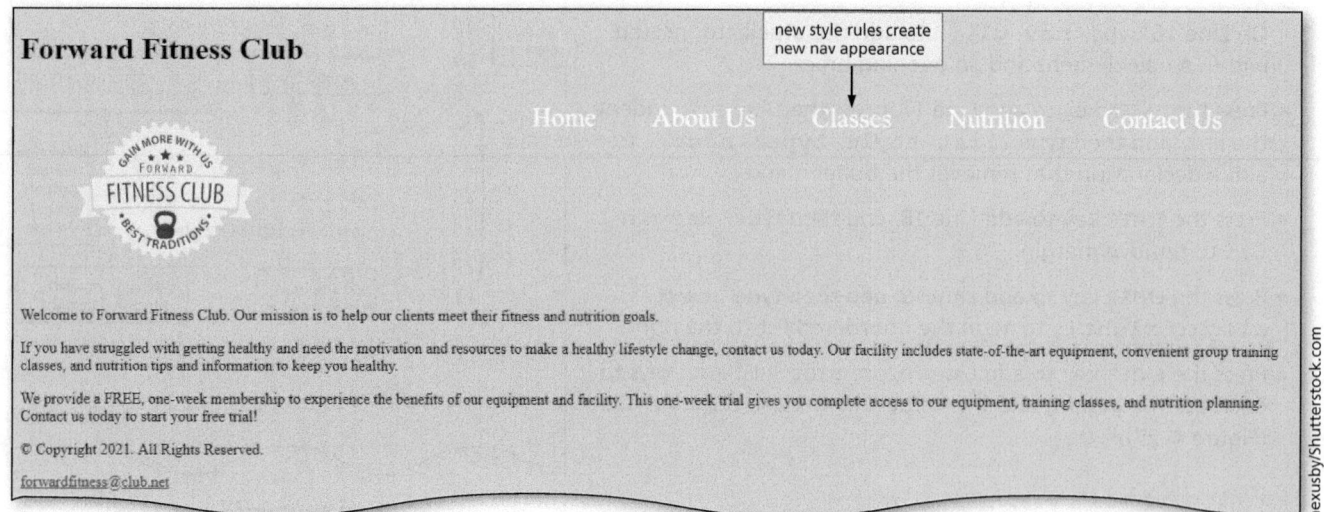

Forward Fitness Club

Home   About Us   Classes   Nutrition   Contact Us

Welcome to Forward Fitness Club. Our mission is to help our clients meet their fitness and nutrition goals.

If you have struggled with getting healthy and need the motivation and resources to make a healthy lifestyle change, contact us today. Our facility includes state-of-the-art equipment, convenient group training classes, and nutrition tips and information to keep you healthy.

We provide a FREE, one-week membership to experience the benefits of our equipment and facility. This one-week trial gives you complete access to our equipment, training classes, and nutrition planning. Contact us today to start your free trial!

© Copyright 2021. All Rights Reserved.

forwardfitness@club.net

nexusby/Shutterstock.com

Figure 4–30

Making Responsive Images

Anyone viewing a webpage within a browser can adjust the width and height of the browser window. To ensure that images on your page adjust to the size of the browser window, you use responsive images in your design, which is major component of a responsive design strategy. You will learn more about responsive design in Chapter 5. A **responsive image** resizes itself to accommodate the size of the browser window. To create responsive images:

1. Delete the height and width attributes and values for the img tags in the HTML files.

2. Add a style rule for the img element in the CSS file to provide the desired flexibility such as the following style: `max-width: 100%;`

By setting the max-width of the image to 100%, the image automatically stretches to fill its parent element, up to 100% of its actual size. The height grows in proportion to the width. Use the `max-width` property instead of the `width` property to constrain the image to 100% of its *actual* size in case the browser window grows even larger. Stretching the image beyond its actual size degrades the quality of the image, even if the webpage is viewed on a very large widescreen monitor.

Figure 4–31 shows an example of a responsive image on the National Oceanic and Atmospheric Administration website. The browser window on the left is wider than the browser window on the right. The same image appears in both windows. Because it is a responsive image, it can grow to accommodate the larger browser window and shrink to accommodate the smaller browser window.

Source: National Oceanic and Atmospheric Administration

Figure 4–31

Recall that the wireframe shown in Figure 4–15 includes a hero image, which appears below the header and navigation elements. A **hero image** is a large banner image strategically placed on the website to capture the visitor's attention. Many of today's websites incorporate hero images within their design. Sometimes, the hero image is a large image displayed near the top of the webpage. Other times, the hero image consumes the entire background of the webpage. Figure 4–31 shows an example of a hero image.

According to the site design, you need to add a hero image to the Forward Fitness Club home page. You will add a div element to contain the image and then use CSS to make the image responsive.

To Add a Hero Image

Add a hero image to the home page of the Forward Fitness Club website. Before you can add the hero image, you need to acquire the hero-image.jpg file from the Data Files and copy it to your fitness/images folder. *Why? Capture the attention of your audience by including visual content to clarify the purpose of the website.* The following steps copy the hero-image.jpg file to the fitness/images folder and add the hero image to the home page of the Forward Fitness Club.

- Use File Explorer (Windows) or Finder (macOS) to navigate to the Data Files.
- Double-tap or double-click the chapter04 folder, double-tap or double-click the chapter folder, and then tap or click the hero-image.jpg file to select it.
- Copy the file to your fitness/images folder.
- If necessary, open the index.htm file in your text editor to prepare to insert a div element.
- Place your insertion point at the end of Line 28 and press the ENTER key twice to insert new Lines 29 and 30.
- On Line 30, type `<!-- Hero Image -->` to insert a comment.
- Press the ENTER key to insert a new Line 31, and then type `<div id="hero">` to add a starting div element with an attribute value of hero.
- Press the ENTER key to insert a new Line 32, press the TAB key to increase the indent, and then type `<img src="images/hero-image.jpg" alt="left arm extended holding a weight">` to add an image element.
- Press the ENTER key to insert a new Line 33, press the SHIFT+TAB keys to decrease the indent, and then type `</div>` to close the div element (Figure 4–32).

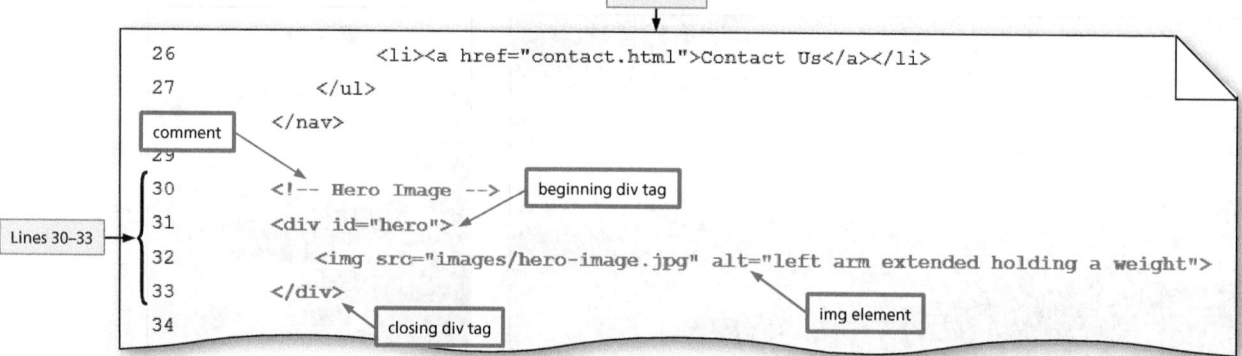

```
index.html

        26              <li><a href="contact.html">Contact Us</a></li>
        27          </ul>
                </nav>
comment     29
Lines 30-33 30      <!-- Hero Image -->          beginning div tag
        31      <div id="hero">
        32          <img src="images/hero-image.jpg" alt="left arm extended holding a weight">
        33      </div>
        34                                                              img element
              closing div tag
```

Figure 4–32

2

- Delete the height and width attributes and values from the logo image on Line 16 (Figure 4–33).

Q&A
Should I delete the closing angle bracket for the img tag?
No. Be careful to delete only the height and width attribute values and not the closing angle bracket (>) for the img tag.

```
index.html

        13      <!-- Use the header area for the website name or logo -->
        14      <header>
        15          <h1>Forward Fitness Club</h1>
        16          <a href="index.html"><img src="images/forward-fitness-logo.png" alt="Forward
                    Fitness Club logo"></a>
        17      </header>                          height and width attributes and
        18                                         values removed from img element
        19      <!-- Use the nav area to add hyperlinks to other pages within the website -->
        20      <nav>
```

Figure 4–33

3

- Switch to the styles.css file, place your insertion point at the end of Line 3, and then press the ENTER key twice to insert new Lines 4 and 5.

- Starting on Line 5, add a style rule for the img selector as shown in Figure 4–34.

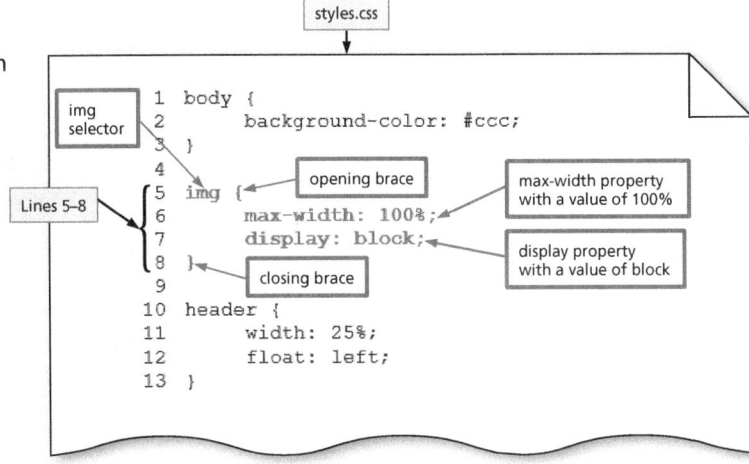

```
1  body {
2          background-color: #ccc;
3  }
4
5  img {
6          max-width: 100%;
7          display: block;
8  }
9
10 header {
11         width: 25%;
12         float: left;
13 }
```

styles.css

img selector → opening brace → max-width property with a value of 100%

Lines 5–8 → display property with a value of block

closing brace

Figure 4–34

4

- Save changes to all files and then open index.html in your browser to view the page (Figure 4–35).

Forward Fitness Club

Home   About Us   Classes   Nutrition   Contact Us

Train with Us
Gain with Us

hero image

nexusby/Shutterstock.com; Y Photo Studio/Shutterstock.com

Figure 4–35

Q&A The hero image is so large that I must scroll down to see it. I also see the gray background color on either side of the image. Will I make more adjustments to the page to fix these flaws?

Yes. You are not done enhancing this webpage. You will make changes in future steps to improve the appearance of the home page.

5

- Resize the window to make it smaller to view how the image decreases in size (Figure 4–36).

Q&A How does the new style change the images on the webpage?

The logo image automatically resizes with the browser window, and the images on the index.html page also resize as the window becomes smaller than their natural size.

The image is responsive, but now my navigation is no longer horizontal. How do I fix this? Resize your window to the size of your desktop display. Do not be concerned about the navigation appearance when the window size is decreased. You will address this in Chapter 5.

hero image decreases in size when the window is narrowed

Figure 4–36

To Remove Height and Width Attributes from img Elements

Remove the height and width attributes from image elements on the About Us, Contact Us, and template pages. *Why? You remove the height and width attributes and use CSS to create a responsive image that grows and shrinks with the size of the browser window.* The following steps delete the height and width attributes from the img tags in the HTML files.

1

- Open the about.html, contact.html, and template.html files in your text editor.
- In the about.html file, delete the height and width attributes and values from the logo img element on Line 16.
- Delete the height and width attributes and values and from the other images on Lines 36, 49, and 62 (Figure 4–37).

Q&A Should I delete the alt attribute within the img tag?

No. Be careful to delete only the height and width attribute values and not the alt attribute for the img tag.

about.html

```
13      <!-- Use the header area for the website name or logo -->
14      <header>
15         <h1>Forward Fitness Club</h1>
16         <a href="index.html"><img src="images/forward-fitness-
           logo.png" alt="Forward Fitness Club logo"></a>
17      </header>
```

```
35      <h1>Weights</h1>
36      <img src="images/people-with-weights.jpg" alt="Two people
        working out with a weight in each hand">
37      <p>Our facility includes a weight training area with several
        weight options. Build lean muscle with weights and improve
        your core with weight training.</p>
```

```
48      <h1>Cardio</h1>
49      <img class="equip" src="images/people-workingout-
        machines.jpg" alt="Cardio Equipment">
50      <p>Burn fat through cardio workouts. Experts recommend 150
        minutes of cardio each week. We have several equipment
        choices for your workout.</p>
```

```
61      <h1>Personal Training</h1>
62      <img class="equip" src="images/personal-trainer.jpg"
        alt="Personal Training">
63      <p>Our certified personal trainers work with you to help you
        obtain your fitness goals and track your progress. Personal
        training has many benefits.</p>
```

height and width attributes and values removed from img element

Figure 4–37

- Switch to the contact.html file.
- Delete the height and width attributes and values from the logo img element on Line 16 (Figure 4–38).

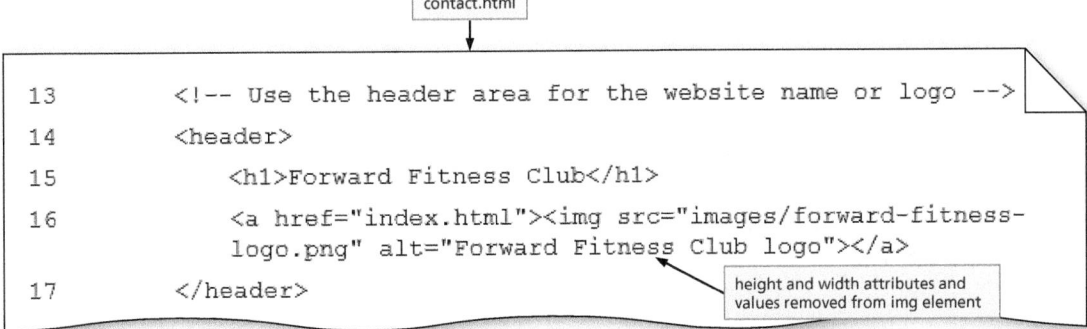

contact.html

```
13      <!-- Use the header area for the website name or logo -->
14      <header>
15         <h1>Forward Fitness Club</h1>
16         <a href="index.html"><img src="images/forward-fitness-
           logo.png" alt="Forward Fitness Club logo"></a>
17      </header>
```

height and width attributes and values removed from img element

Figure 4–38

• Switch to the template.html file.

• Delete the height and width attributes and values from the logo img element on Line 16 (Figure 4–39).

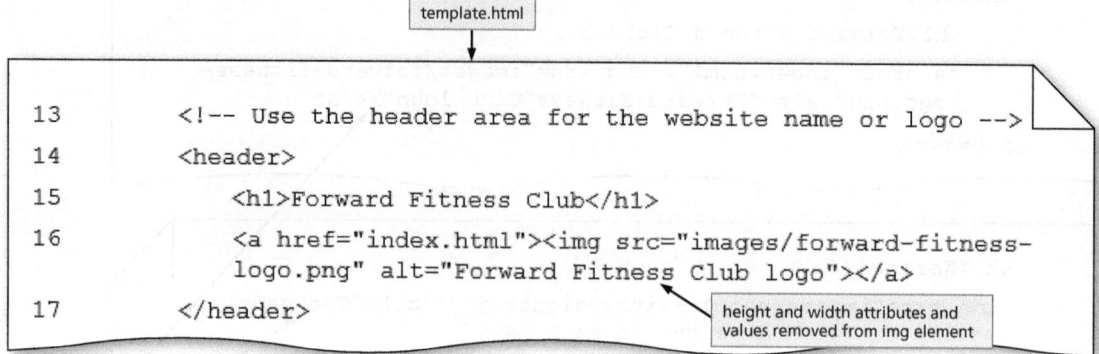

template.html

```
13      <!-- Use the header area for the website name or logo -->
14      <header>
15          <h1>Forward Fitness Club</h1>
16          <a href="index.html"><img src="images/forward-fitness-
            logo.png" alt="Forward Fitness Club logo"></a>
17      </header>
```

height and width attributes and values removed from img element

Figure 4–39

To Modify the Style Rule for the Main Element

1 CREATE CSS FILE | 2 LINK PAGES TO CSS FILE | 3 CREATE STYLE RULES
4 ADD COMMENTS | 5 VALIDATE CSS FILE

You already have a style rule for the main element, but need to modify it to complete its design. *Why? Currently, the style rule for the main selector only has one declaration. Add more declarations to enhance the appearance of the main content on the webpage.* Next, add a declaration to specify the background color and padding, and increase the font size for the main element. You will also remove the clear property. The following steps modify the style rule for the **main** element.

• Switch to the styles.css file, place your insertion point at the end of Line 41, and then press the ENTER key to add Line 42.

• On Line 42, type **background-color: #fff;** to add a declaration that specifies the background color.

• Press the ENTER key to add Line 43, and then type **padding: 2%;** to add a declaration for the padding property.

• Press the ENTER key to add Line 44 and then type **font-size: 1.25em;** to add a declaration that specifies a font size (Figure 4–40).

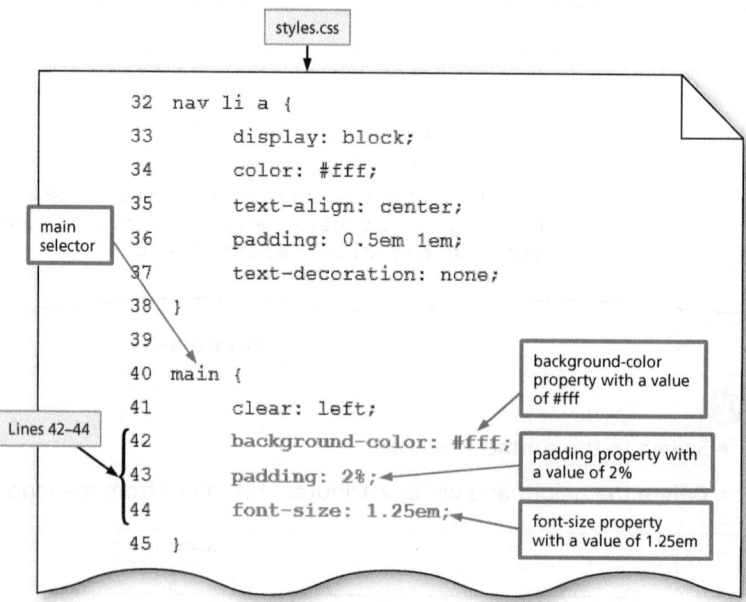

styles.css

```
32  nav li a {
33      display: block;
34      color: #fff;
35      text-align: center;
36      padding: 0.5em 1em;
37      text-decoration: none;
38  }
39
40  main {
41      clear: left;
42      background-color: #fff;
43      padding: 2%;
44      font-size: 1.25em;
45  }
```

main selector

Lines 42–44

background-color property with a value of #fff

padding property with a value of 2%

font-size property with a value of 1.25em

Figure 4–40

• Save your changes.

• View the home page in a browser to see the applied styles. If necessary, scroll down to view the content within the main element (Figure 4–41).

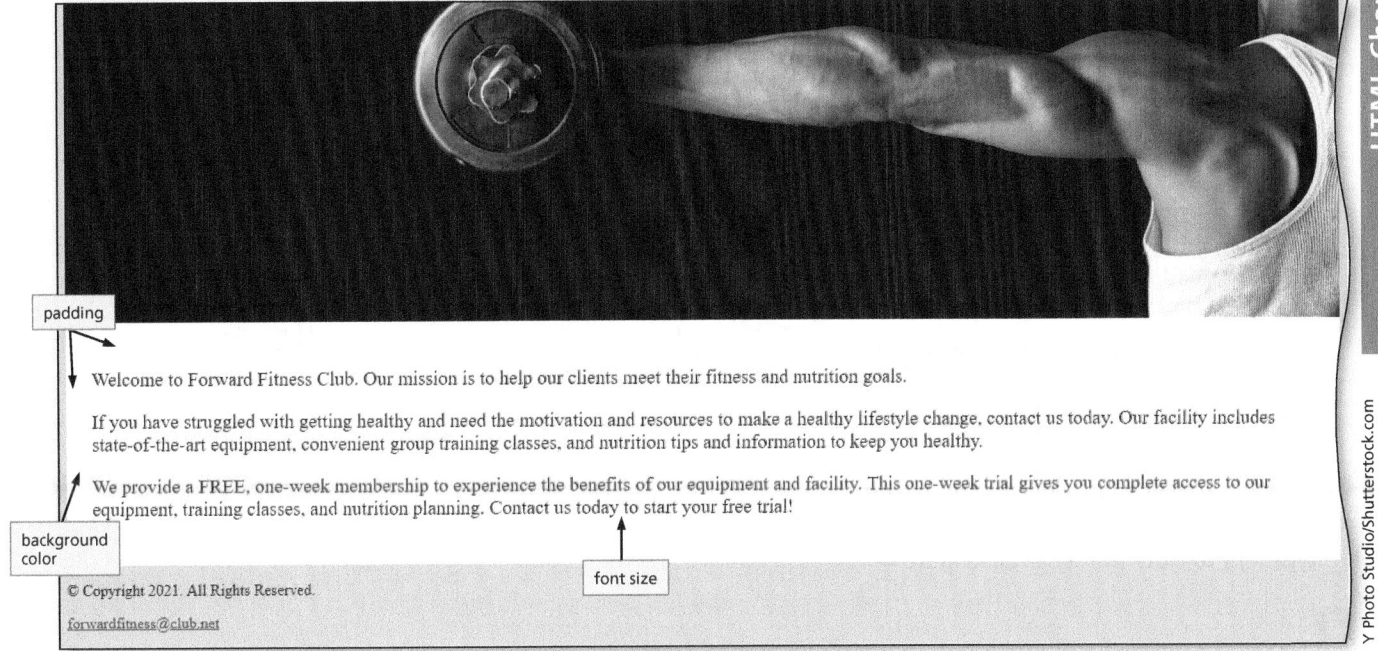

 padding

background color

font size

Figure 4–41

To Create a Style Rule for the Footer Element

The footer is located at the bottom of the webpage below the main area and contains paragraph elements with copyright information and an email address. Create two style rules to style the footer paragraph content and the email link. *Why? The footer section provides supplemental information, so its text should be smaller than the other text on the page. It should also be centered and have some padding to improve its appearance.* The following steps create styles for paragraph elements and links within the footer.

1

- In styles.css, place the insertion point after the closing brace on Line 45 and then press the ENTER key twice to insert new Lines 46 and 47.

- On Line 47, type `footer p {` to add the footer p selector and an opening brace.

- Press the ENTER key to add Line 48, press the TAB key to indent the line, and then type `font-size: 0.75em;` to add a declaration that sets the font size.

- Press the ENTER key to add Line 49 and then type `text-align: center;` to add a declaration for text alignment.

- Press the ENTER key to add Line 50 and then type `color: #fff;` to add a declaration that sets the color.

- Press the ENTER key to add Line 51 and then type `padding: 0 1em;` to add a declaration that sets the padding.

- Press the ENTER key to add Line 52, press the SHIFT+TAB keys to decrease the indent, and then type `}` to close the style rule (Figure 4–42).

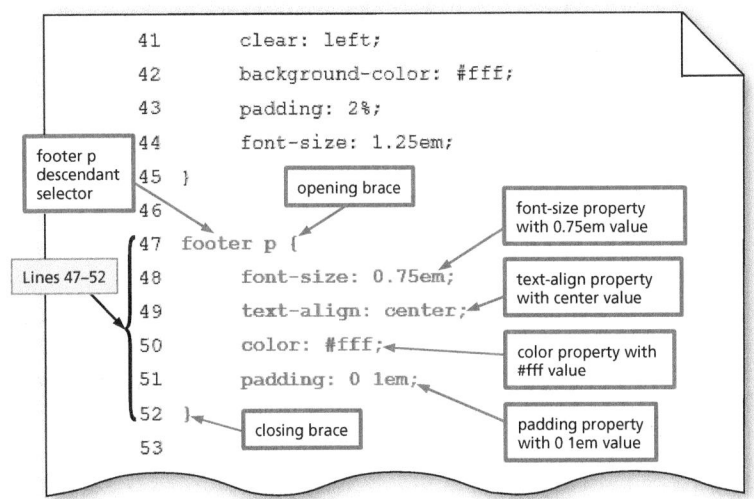

Figure 4–42

- Press the ENTER key twice to insert new Lines 53 and 54.

- On Line 54, type **footer p a {** to add the footer p a selector and an opening brace.

- Press the ENTER key to add Line 55, press the TAB key to indent the line, and then type **color: #fff;** to add a declaration that sets the link color.

- Press the ENTER key to add Line 56, and then type **text-decoration: none;** to add a declaration that removes the underline from the email address.

- Press the ENTER key to add Line 57, press the SHIFT+TAB keys to decrease the indent, and then type **}** to close the style rule (Figure 4–43).

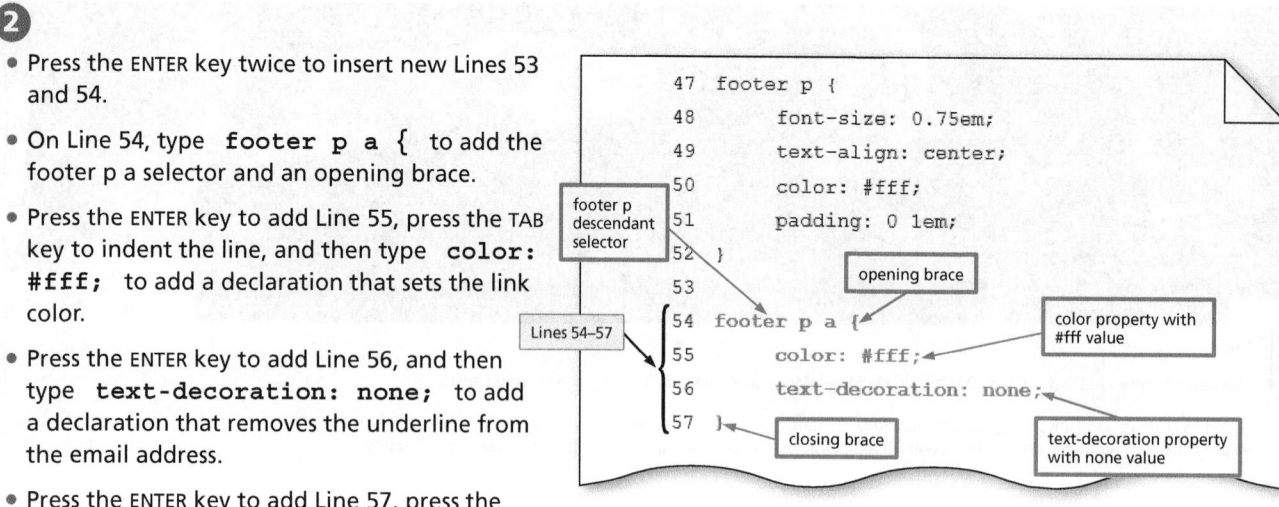

```
47  footer p {
48      font-size: 0.75em;
49      text-align: center;
50      color: #fff;
51      padding: 0 1em;
52  }
53
54  footer p a {
55      color: #fff;
56      text-decoration: none;
57  }
```

footer p descendant selector

opening brace

Lines 54–57

color property with #fff value

text-decoration property with none value

closing brace

Figure 4–43

- Save your changes.

- View the home page in a browser and, if necessary, scroll down to see the applied style (Figure 4–44).

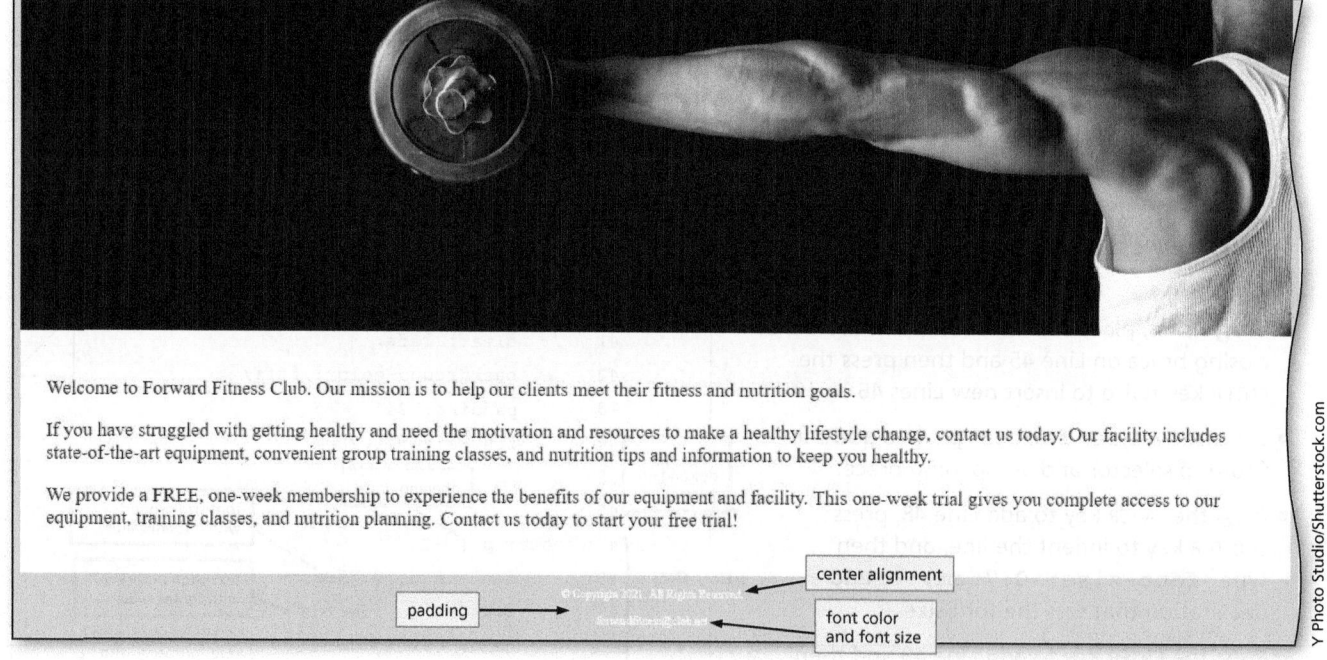

Welcome to Forward Fitness Club. Our mission is to help our clients meet their fitness and nutrition goals.

If you have struggled with getting healthy and need the motivation and resources to make a healthy lifestyle change, contact us today. Our facility includes state-of-the-art equipment, convenient group training classes, and nutrition tips and information to keep you healthy.

We provide a FREE, one-week membership to experience the benefits of our equipment and facility. This one-week trial gives you complete access to our equipment, training classes, and nutrition planning. Contact us today to start your free trial!

© Copyright 2021. All Rights Reserved.

center alignment

padding

font color and font size

Figure 4–44

Break Point: If you want to take a break, this is a good place to do so. You can exit the text editor now. To resume at a later time, run your text editor, open the file called styles.css, and continue following the steps from this location forward.

Creating Style Rules for ID Selectors

In Chapter 3, you created several id attribute values for div elements on every HTML page. Every page includes a primary div with an id attribute value of container, which holds all the webpage content. The About Us page includes several div elements with id attribute values. As discussed earlier in the chapter, you can style an id attribute by using an id selector for a style rule. You will style these id selectors to improve the layout of the content within the main element. The Contact page also includes div id attribute values. You need to create a style rule to format the div element nested within the main element on the Contact page. The following example creates a style rule for an id attribute value of #contact:

```
#contact {
        text-align: center;
}
```

The above style rule will center-align text within an element that has the id attribute value of contact.

1 CREATE CSS FILE | 2 LINK PAGES TO CSS FILE | 3 CREATE STYLE RULES
4 ADD COMMENTS | 5 VALIDATE CSS FILE

To Create Style Rules for IDs on the About Us Page

The content on the About Us page is displayed in a single column. Improve the layout of this page by dividing the page content into three columns. **Why?** *Improving the layout of the webpage will improve the overall appearance and show more content within the same horizontal space.* Create four new style rules. First, create a style rule for the weights, cardio, and training id attributes to adjust their widths, apply a float, and set some margin. Next, create a style rule for the exercises id attribute to clear a float, set top and bottom borders, specify a background color, and set some padding. Create a style rule to format the description terms within the exercises id attribute to make the text bold. Finally, create a style rule for the description definitions within the exercises id attribute to specify some padding. The following steps add four style rules to the style sheet to format div id attributes, description terms, and description definitions on the About Us page.

- In the styles.css file, place the insertion point after the closing brace on Line 45, and then press the ENTER key twice to insert new Lines 46 and 47.

- On Line 47, type **#weights, #cardio, #training {** to add id selectors for weights, cardio, and training and an opening brace.

- Press the ENTER key to add Line 48, press the TAB key to indent the line, and then type **width: 29%;** to add a declaration that specifies a width.

- Press the ENTER key to add Line 49, and then type **float: left;** to add a declaration that specifies a float.

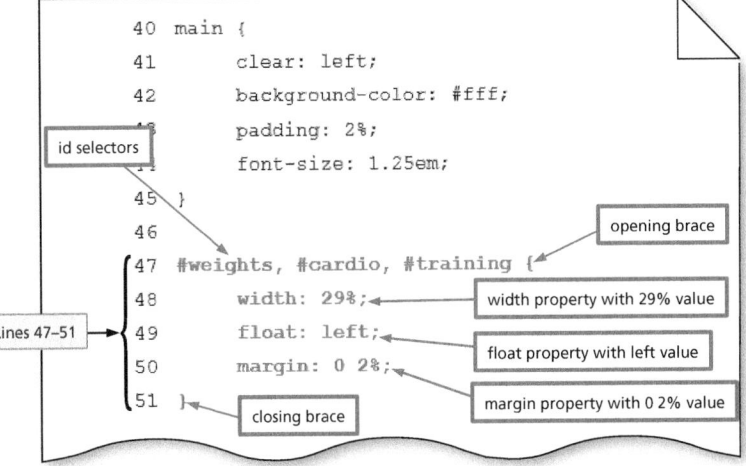

Figure 4–45

- Press the ENTER key to add Line 50, and then type **margin: 0 2%;** to add a declaration that specifies margin.

- Press the ENTER key to add Line 51, press the SHIFT+TAB keys to decrease the indent, and then type **}** to close the style rule (Figure 4–45).

Q&A

Why do I need to use the # symbol before weights, cardio, and training?
To style an id selector, you must begin with the # symbol.

How do you stop content from floating so that it starts on its own line?
To stop floating an element, use the clear property. For example, apply the following declaration to the content that you want to start on its own line, or clear the float: clear: left; (clear left float), clear: right; (clear right float), or clear: both; (clear left and right float).

2

● Press the ENTER key twice to insert new Lines 52 and 53.

● Starting on Line 53, add the style rule for the #exercises id selector as shown in Figure 4–46 to style the exercises id attribute.

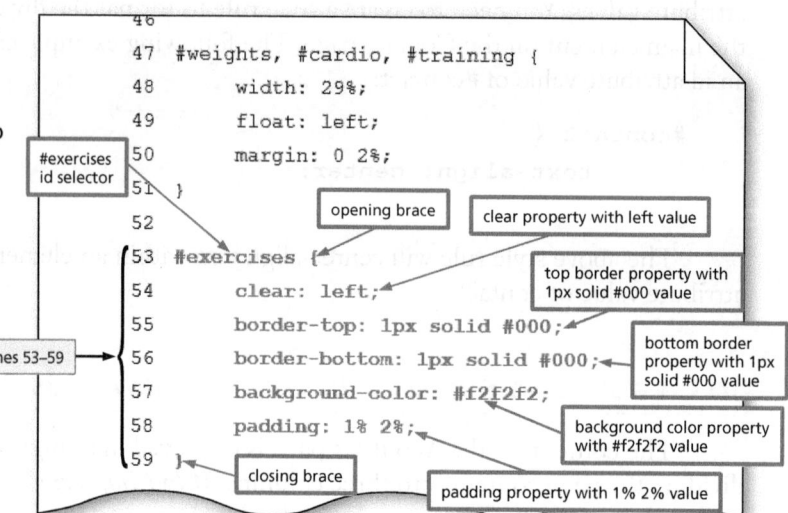

Figure 4–46

3

● Press the ENTER key twice to insert new Lines 60 and 61.

● Starting on Line 61, add the style rules for #exercises dt and #exercises dd selectors as shown in Figure 4–47 to style the description terms and description definitions within the exercises id attribute div element.

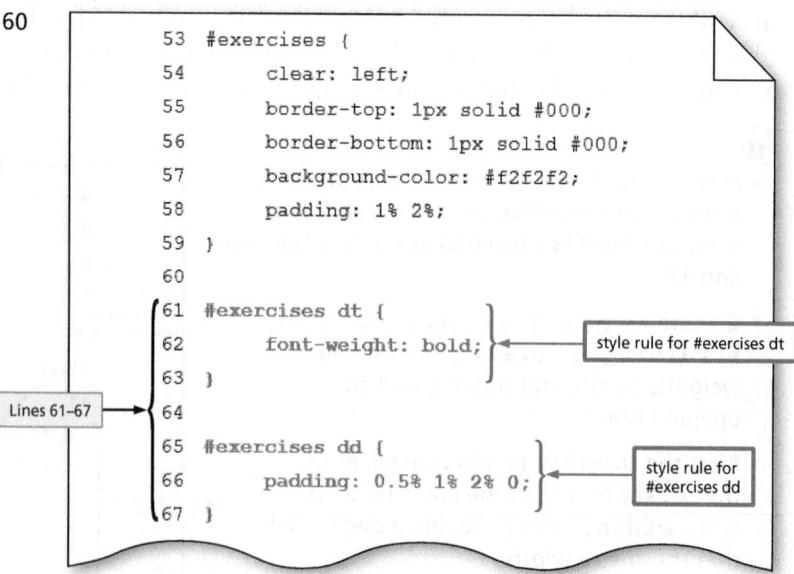

Figure 4–47

4

- Save the styles.css file and view the about.html page in your browser (Figure 4–48).

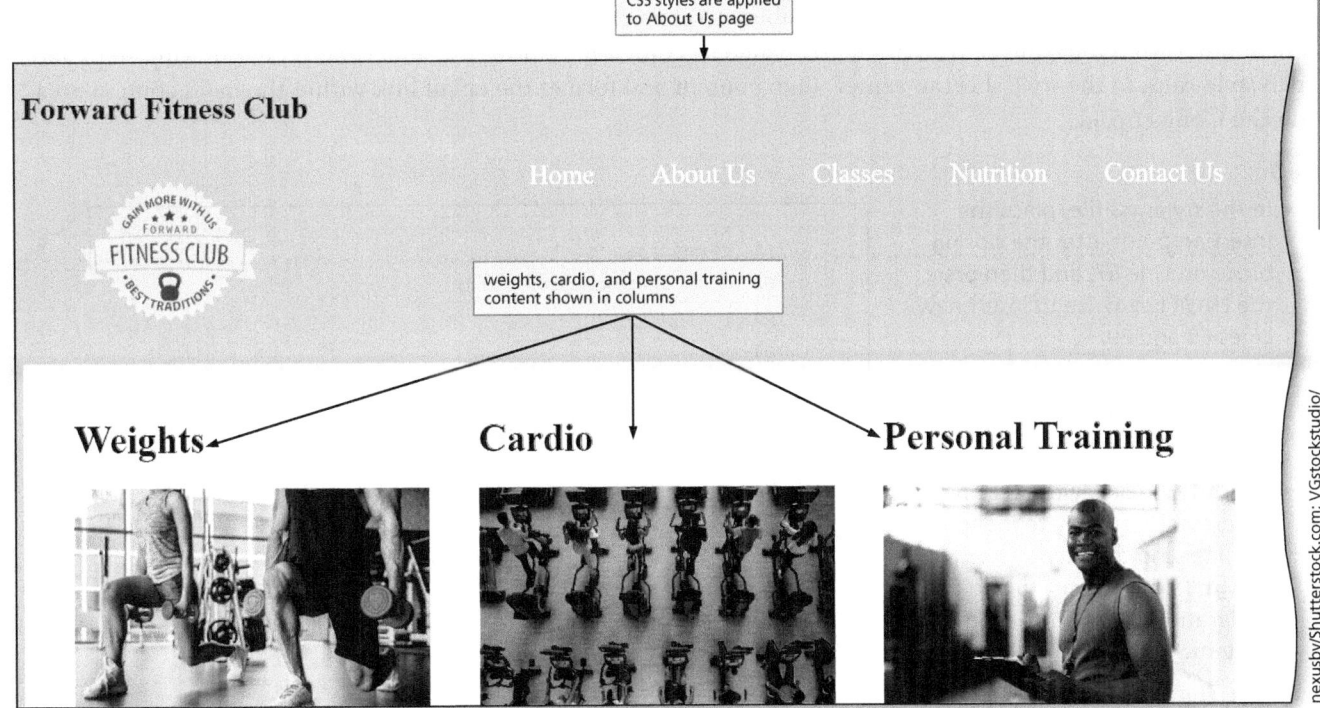

Figure 4–48

5

- Scroll down to view the changes made to the exercises id attribute, description terms, and description definitions (Figure 4–49).

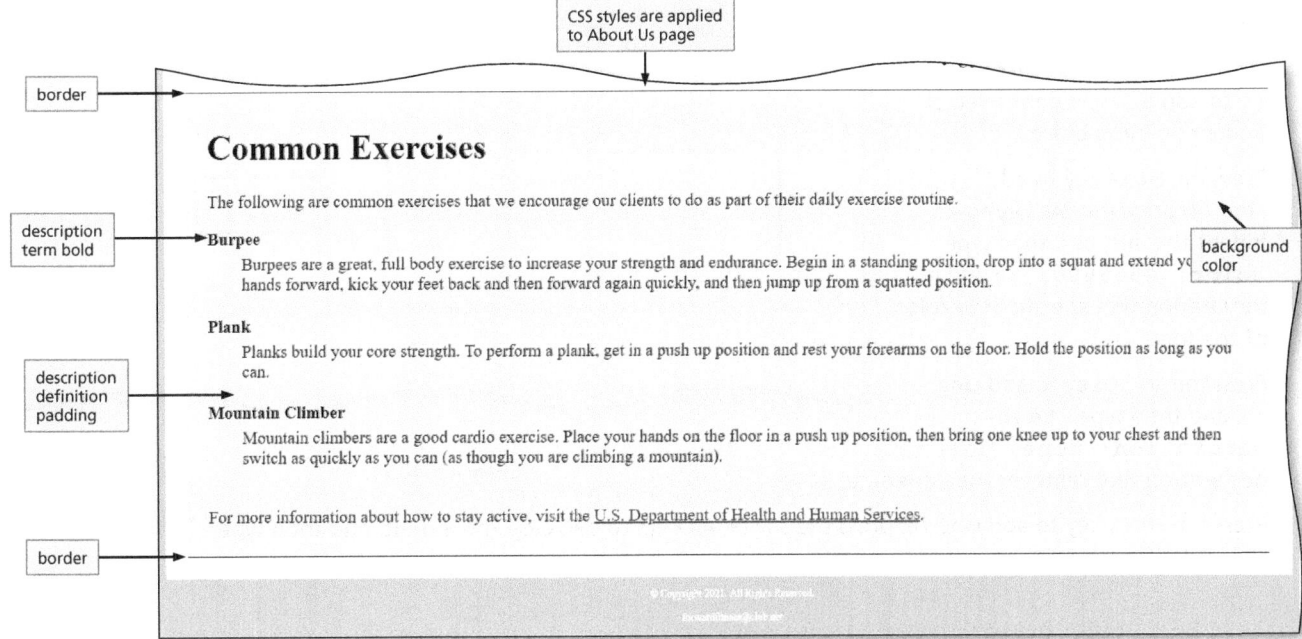

Figure 4–49

To Create Style Rules for IDs on the Contact Page

The content on the About Us page is aligned left. Change the text alignment to center the content within the main element. *Why? Centering the content will improve the overall page appearance.* Create two new style rules. First, create a style rule for the contact id attribute to center-align its content. Then, create a style rule for the email link within the contact id attribute to change its color and remove the underline. The following steps add two style rules to the style sheet to center-align content and format the email link within the main content area on the Contact page.

 1

• In the styles.css file, place the insertion point after the closing brace on Line 67, and then press the ENTER key twice to insert new Lines 68 and 69.

• On Line 69, type **#contact {** to add an id selector for contact and an opening brace.

• Press the ENTER key to add Line 70, press the TAB key to indent the line, and then type **text-align: center;** to add a declaration that center-aligns content.

• Press the ENTER key to add Line 71, press the SHIFT+TAB keys to decrease the indent, and then type **}** to close the style rule (Figure 4–50).

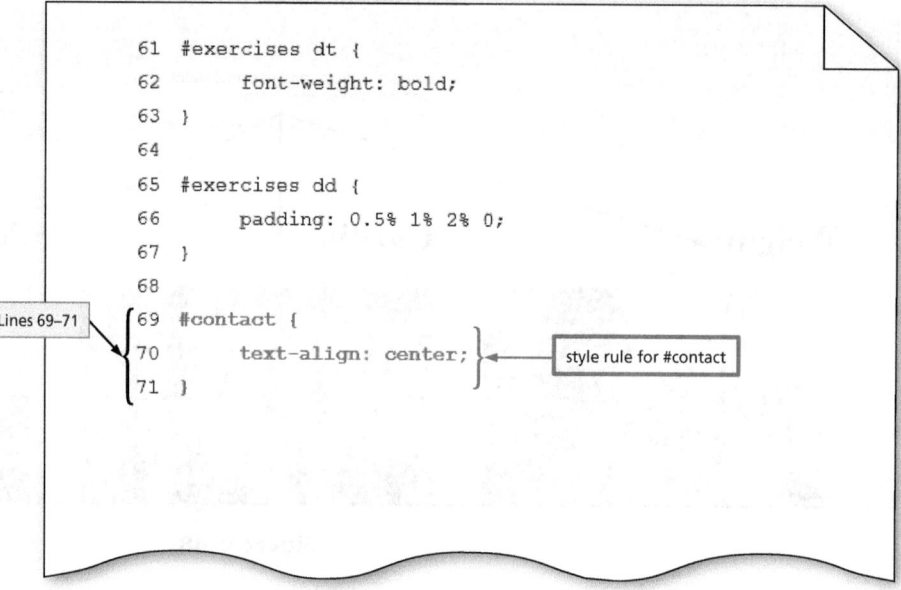

```
61   #exercises dt {
62        font-weight: bold;
63   }
64
65   #exercises dd {
66        padding: 0.5% 1% 2% 0;
67   }
68
69   #contact {
70        text-align: center;        ← style rule for #contact
71   }
```
Lines 69–71

Figure 4–50

 2

• Press the ENTER key twice to insert new Lines 72 and 73.

• On Line 73, type **#contact a {** to add a descendant selector and an opening brace.

• Press the ENTER key to add Line 74, press the TAB key to indent the line, and then type **color: #666600;** to add a declaration that specifies the color of the text.

• Press the ENTER key to add Line 75, and then type **text-decoration: none;** to add a declaration that removes the underline.

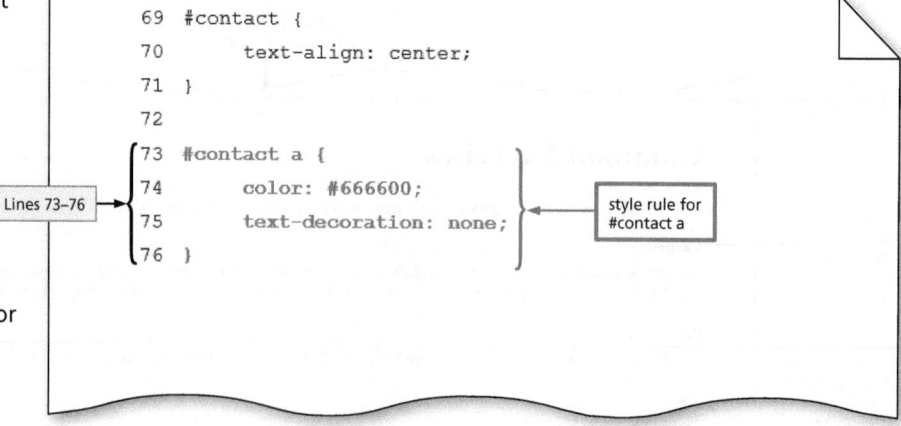

```
69   #contact {
70        text-align: center;
71   }
72
73   #contact a {
74        color: #666600;
75        text-decoration: none;
76   }
```
Lines 73–76

style rule for #contact a

Figure 4–51

• Press the ENTER key to add Line 76, press the SHIFT+TAB keys to decrease the indent, and then type **}** to close the style rule (Figure 4–51).

3
- Save the styles.css file and view the contact.html page in your browser (Figure 4–52).

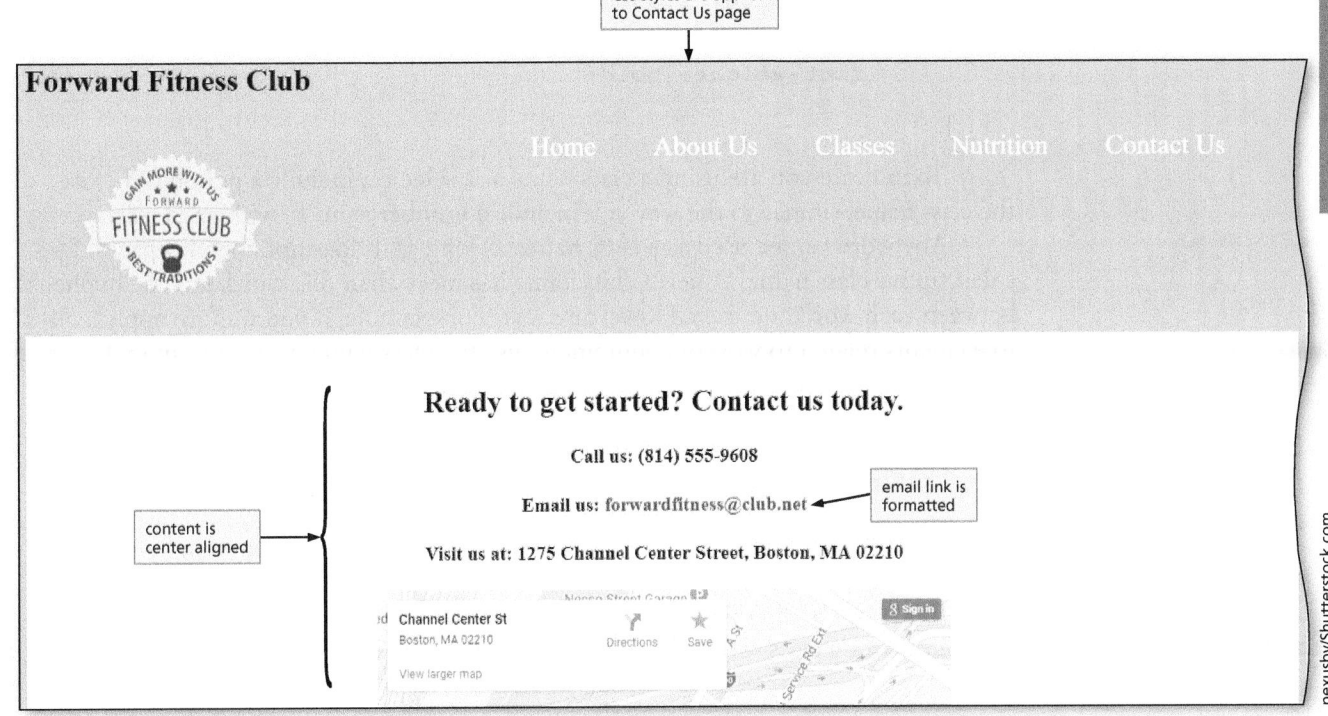

Figure 4–52

Creating Class Attributes

Another commonly used attribute in HTML is the **class** attribute. Unlike the id attribute, a class attribute name can be applied to more than one div or other HTML element on a webpage. Classes provide another level of control over the styling or formatting of specific elements on a webpage. For example, rather than having all paragraphs of text appear with the same formatting, you might want to format call-to-action words different from the other paragraphs of text. To accomplish this, you can wrap the call-to-action words within a span element that uses a class attribute. You use a **span element** to group inline elements together on a webpage. You can then apply specific styling or formatting for the class. Using classes allows you to selectively apply style rules to specific HTML content. For example, if you want to draw the user's attention to specific page content, such as "start your free trial!", you can wrap this text within a span element, include a class attribute, and then create a class selector to style the call-to-action content. The following example shows text wrapped within a span element that includes the class attribute name action:

```
<span class="action">start your free trial!</span>
```

Because the above span element includes a class attribute, you can create a style rule to style the content within the span. For example, the following style rule uses a class selector, .action, that sets the font size to 1.35em, the font color to #666600, and a font weight of bold:

```
.action {
        font-size: 1.35em;
        color: #666600;
        font-weight: bold;

}
```

To indicate you are using a class name as a selector, include a period (.) before the class name, similar to the way you include a number sign (#) with an id selector.

Any word can be used as a class name, as long as it does not contain spaces. Use a descriptive class name. When a class name has more than one word, include hyphens between each word and use all lowercase text. For example, if you want to apply a class to elements related to workout equipment, use the class name, workout-equip. Using names that describe the purpose makes the code easier to read and more flexible.

To Create and Style the action Class

1 CREATE CSS FILE | 2 LINK PAGES TO CSS FILE | 3 CREATE STYLE RULES
4 ADD COMMENTS | 5 VALIDATE CSS FILE

The home page includes the text, "start your free trial!" Enhance this as a call-to-action item by wrapping it in a span element and then assigning a class attribute to the span element to style the text. *Why? Styling the call-to-action text differently from the rest of the paragraph will attract the audience's attention.* The following steps create a span element and a style rule for a class selector.

- Switch to index.html and place your insertion point before the word "start" on Line 44 to prepare to insert a span element.

- Type `<span class="action">` to insert an opening span tag with a class attribute value of action.

- Place your insertion point to the right of the exclamation point after the word trial, and then type `</span>` to insert a closing span tag (Figure 4–53).

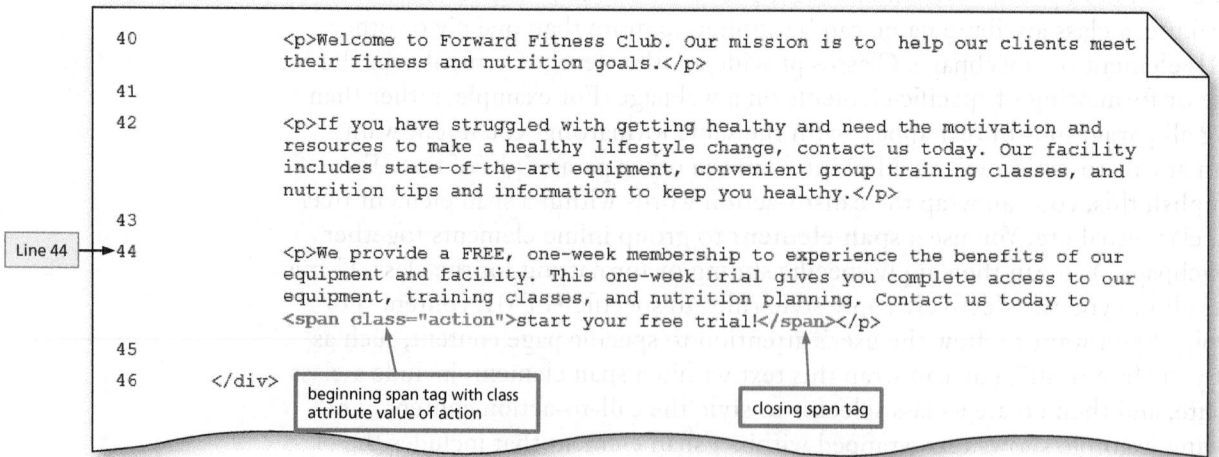

```
40          <p>Welcome to Forward Fitness Club. Our mission is to  help our clients meet
            their fitness and nutrition goals.</p>

41

42          <p>If you have struggled with getting healthy and need the motivation and
            resources to make a healthy lifestyle change, contact us today. Our facility
            includes state-of-the-art equipment, convenient group training classes, and
            nutrition tips and information to keep you healthy.</p>

43

44          <p>We provide a FREE, one-week membership to experience the benefits of our
            equipment and facility. This one-week trial gives you complete access to our
            equipment, training classes, and nutrition planning. Contact us today to
            <span class="action">start your free trial!</span></p>

45

46  </div>
```

Line 44

beginning span tag with class attribute value of action

closing span tag

Figure 4–53

- Switch to styles.css, place your insertion point after the closing brace on Line 45, press the ENTER key twice to insert new Lines 46 and 47, and then type `.action {` to add a class selector and opening brace.

- Press the ENTER key to add Line 48, press the TAB key to increase the indent, and then type `font-size: 1.35em;` to add a declaration for font size.

- Press the ENTER key to add Line 49 and then type `color: #666600;` to add a declaration for the font color.

- Press the ENTER key to add Line 50 and then type `font-weight: bold;` to add a declaration for the font weight.

- Press the ENTER key to add Line 51, press the SHIFT+TAB keys to decrease the indent, and then type `}` to close the style rule (Figure 4–54).

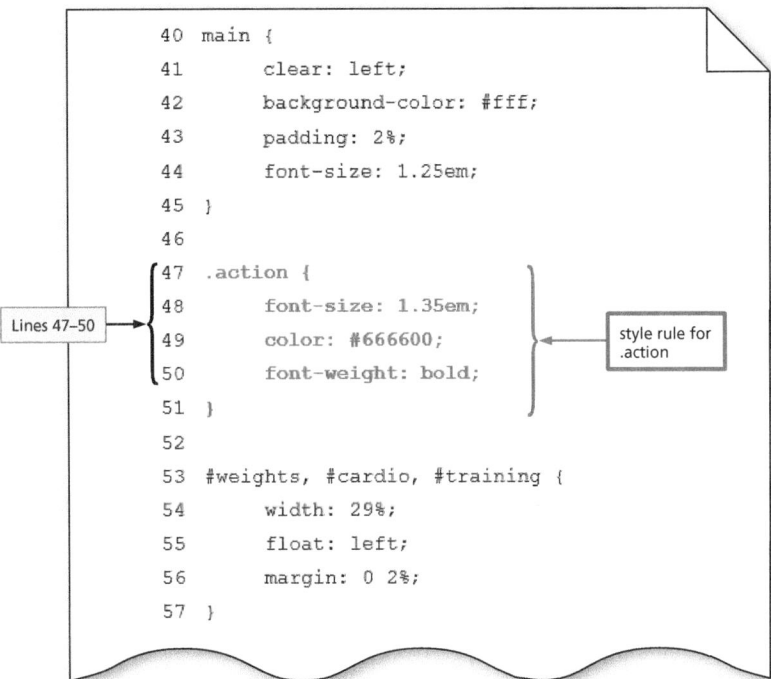

```
40  main {
41      clear: left;
42      background-color: #fff;
43      padding: 2%;
44      font-size: 1.25em;
45  }
46
47  .action {
48      font-size: 1.35em;
49      color: #666600;
50      font-weight: bold;
51  }
52
53  #weights, #cardio, #training {
54      width: 29%;
55      float: left;
56      margin: 0 2%;
57  }
```

Lines 47–50 → {47, 48, 49, 50}

style rule for .action

Figure 4–54

❸

- Save all changes and view index.html in your browser. If necessary, scroll down to view the call-to-action text (Figure 4–55).

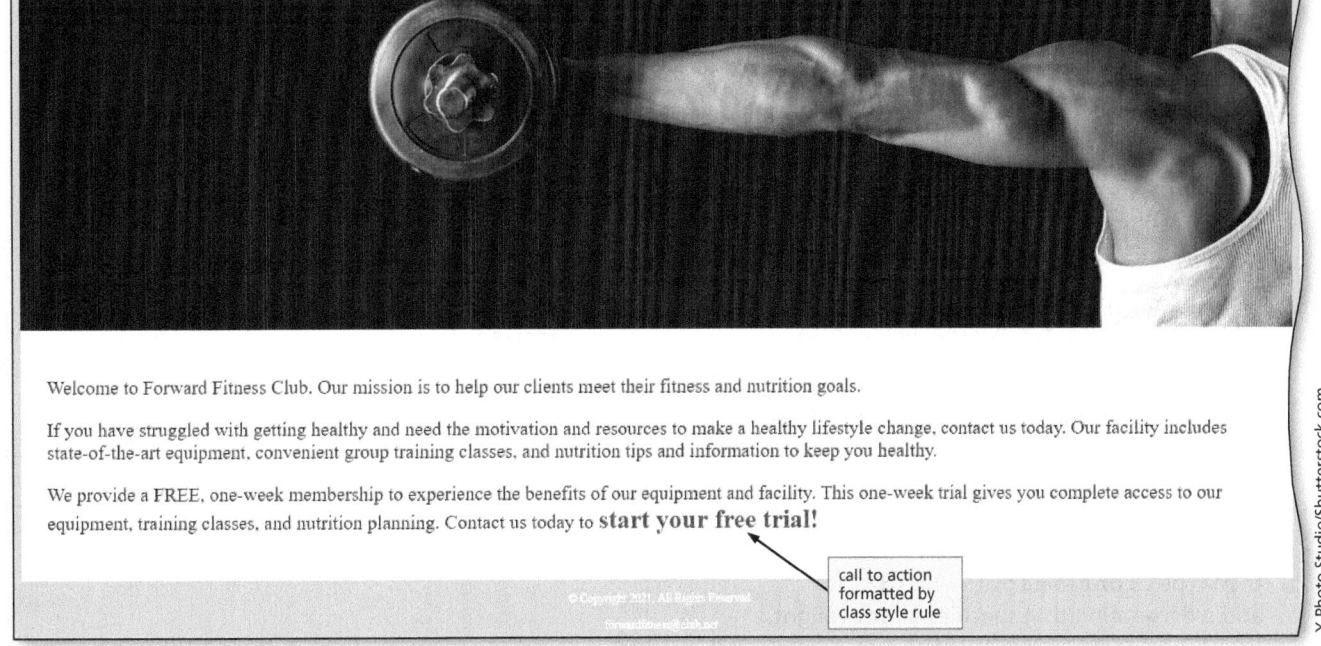

Welcome to Forward Fitness Club. Our mission is to help our clients meet their fitness and nutrition goals.

If you have struggled with getting healthy and need the motivation and resources to make a healthy lifestyle change, contact us today. Our facility includes state-of-the-art equipment, convenient group training classes, and nutrition tips and information to keep you healthy.

We provide a FREE, one-week membership to experience the benefits of our equipment and facility. This one-week trial gives you complete access to our equipment, training classes, and nutrition planning. Contact us today to **start your free trial!**

call to action formatted by class style rule

Figure 4–55

Q&A

Why does the .action selector start with a period?
To style a class, you insert a period before the class name to specify the selector in the CSS file.

Why am I adding the style rule for the class selector after the main style rule?
It is a common practice to keep style rules grouped together based on the HTML page layout. Because the action class is within the main element on the home page, this style rule is placed after the main style rule.

To Create and Style the external-link Class

The About Us page includes an external link to the U.S. Department of Health and Human Services. Add a class attribute to the anchor tag and then create a style rule for a class selector. *Why? Remove the default link format to create a custom look for this external link to improve its appearance.* First, add a class attribute with the value, external-link, to the beginning anchor tag that creates the external link to the U.S. Department of Health and Human Services. Next, create a style rule with external-link as the class selector to format the color, font weight, and to remove the underline from the link. The following steps add a class attribute and a style rule for a class selector.

- Switch to the about.html file, locate the beginning anchor tag on Line 87, place the insertion point before the closing angle bracket (>), and then type `class="external-link"` to add a class attribute to the anchor tag (Figure 4–56).

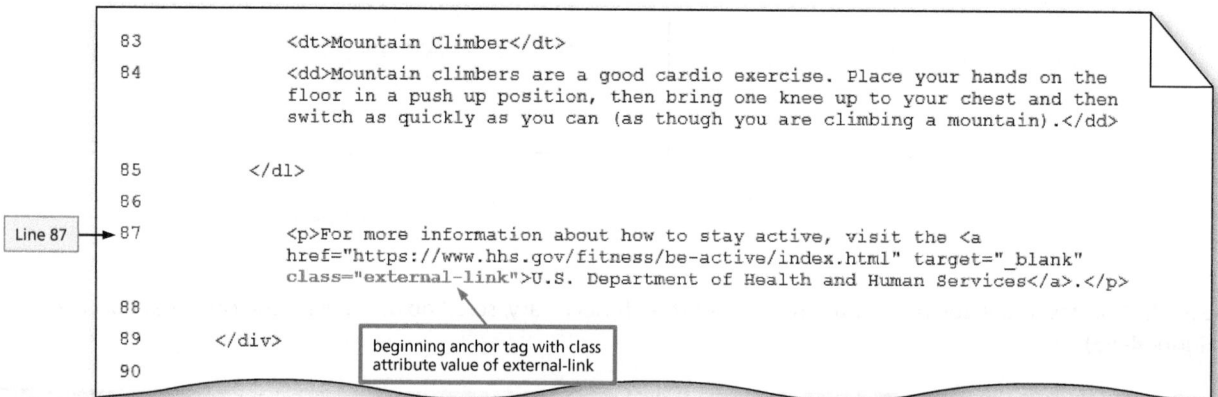

```
83          <dt>Mountain Climber</dt>
84          <dd>Mountain climbers are a good cardio exercise. Place your hands on the
            floor in a push up position, then bring one knee up to your chest and then
            switch as quickly as you can (as though you are climbing a mountain).</dd>

85      </dl>

86

Line 87  → 87      <p>For more information about how to stay active, visit the <a
            href="https://www.hhs.gov/fitness/be-active/index.html" target="_blank"
            class="external-link">U.S. Department of Health and Human Services</a>.</p>

88

89      </div>                    beginning anchor tag with class
90                                attribute value of external-link
```

Figure 4–56

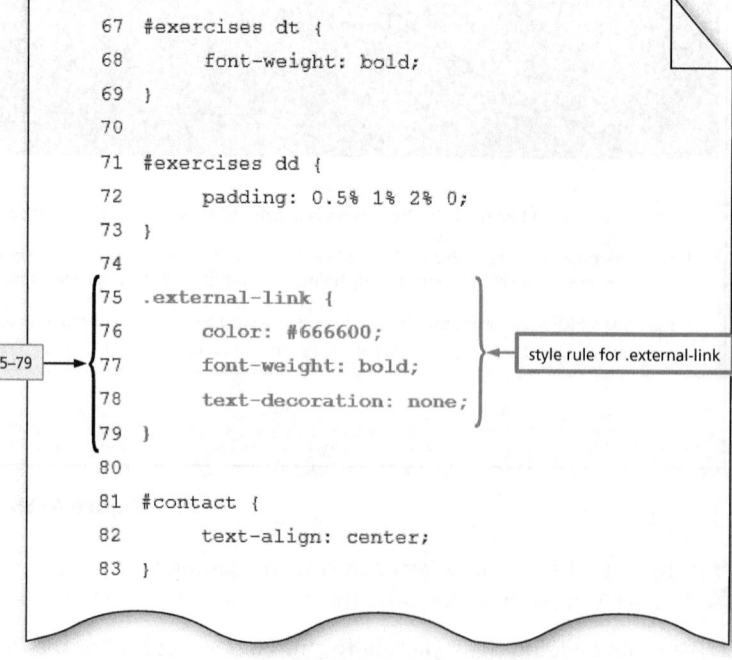

- Switch to the styles.css file, place the insertion point after the closing brace on Line 73, and then press the ENTER key twice to insert new Lines 74 and 75.

- On Line 75, type `.external-link {` to add a class selector for external-link and an opening brace.

- Press the ENTER key to add Line 76, press the TAB key to indent the line, and then type `color: #666600;` to add a declaration that specifies a font color.

- Press the ENTER key to add Line 77 and then type `font-weight: bold;` to add a declaration that specifies a font weight.

- Press the ENTER key to add Line 78 and then type `text-decoration: none;` to add a declaration that specifies a text-decoration.

- Press the ENTER key to add Line 79, press the SHIFT+TAB keys to decrease the indent, and then type `}` to close the style rule (Figure 4–57).

```
67  #exercises dt {
68      font-weight: bold;
69  }

70

71  #exercises dd {
72      padding: 0.5% 1% 2% 0;
73  }

74

75  .external-link {
76      color: #666600;
77      font-weight: bold;          style rule for .external-link
78      text-decoration: none;
79  }

80

81  #contact {
82      text-align: center;
83  }
```

Lines 75–79

Figure 4–57

● Save all changes and view about.html in your browser. If necessary, scroll down to view the external link (Figure 4–58).

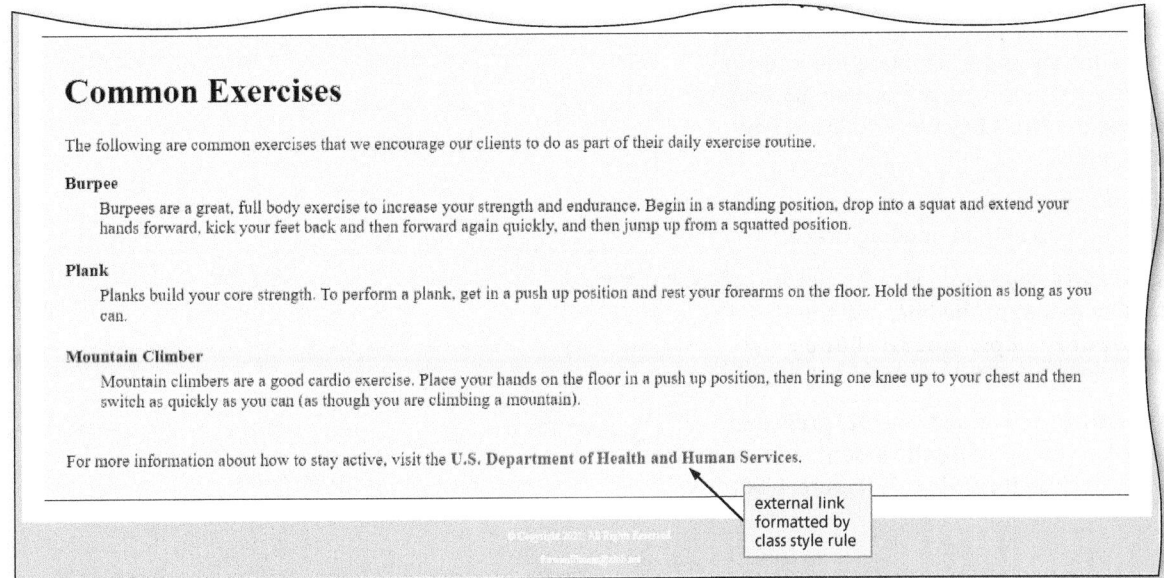

Common Exercises

The following are common exercises that we encourage our clients to do as part of their daily exercise routine.

Burpee
Burpees are a great, full body exercise to increase your strength and endurance. Begin in a standing position, drop into a squat and extend your hands forward, kick your feet back and then forward again quickly, and then jump up from a squatted position.

Plank
Planks build your core strength. To perform a plank, get in a push up position and rest your forearms on the floor. Hold the position as long as you can.

Mountain Climber
Mountain climbers are a good cardio exercise. Place your hands on the floor in a push up position, then bring one knee up to your chest and then switch as quickly as you can (as though you are climbing a mountain).

For more information about how to stay active, visit the **U.S. Department of Health and Human Services.**

external link formatted by class style rule

Figure 4–58

1 CREATE CSS FILE | 2 LINK PAGES TO CSS FILE | **3 CREATE STYLE RULES**
4 ADD COMMENTS | 5 VALIDATE CSS FILE

To Create and Style the map Class

The Contact page includes an embedded map, contained within an iframe element. Add a class attribute to the iframe tag and then create a style rule for a class selector to specify a border. **Why?** *Add a border around the map to improve its appearance and complement the page design.* First, add a class attribute with the value, map, to the beginning iframe tag that creates the embedded map. Next, create a style rule with map as the class selector to format a border. The following steps add a class attribute and a style rule for a class selector.

● Switch to the contact.html file, locate the beginning iframe tag on Line 40, place the insertion point before the closing angle bracket >, and then type **class="map"** to add a class attribute to the iframe tag.

● Delete the text **frameborder="0"** to remove this attribute from the iframe tag.

● Delete the text **style="border:0"** to remove this attribute from the iframe tag (Figure 4–59).

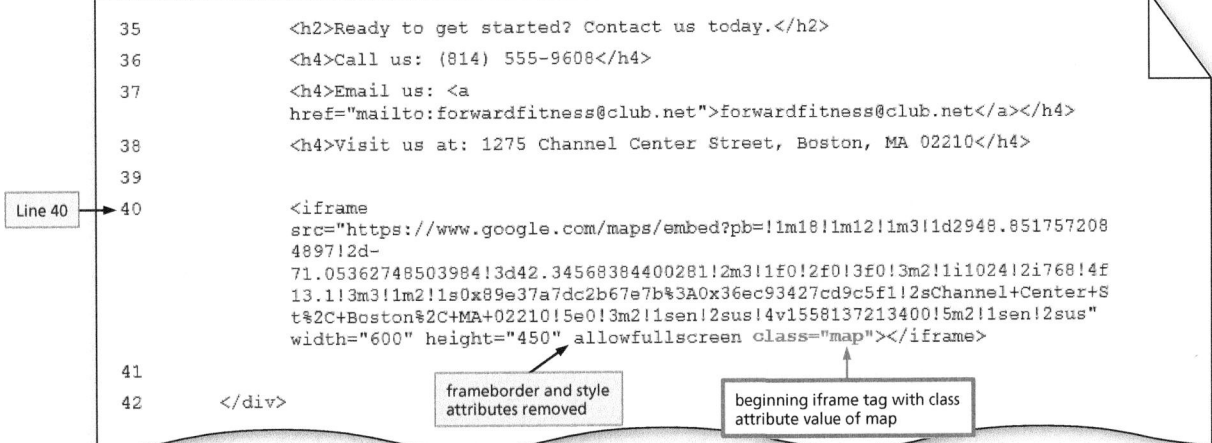

Figure 4–59

Q&A Why do the frameborder and style attributes need to be removed?
These attributes are inline styles that do not allow a border. They must be removed before the style rule can take effect.

2

- Switch to the styles.css file, place the insertion point after the closing brace on Line 88, and then press the ENTER key twice to insert new Lines 89 and 90.

- On Line 90, type `.map {` to add a class selector for map and an opening brace.

- Press the ENTER key to add Line 91, press the TAB key to indent the line, and then type **border: 8px solid #000;** to add a declaration that specifies a border.

- Press the ENTER key to add Line 92, press the SHIFT+TAB keys to decrease the indent, and then type `}` to close the style rule (Figure 4–60).

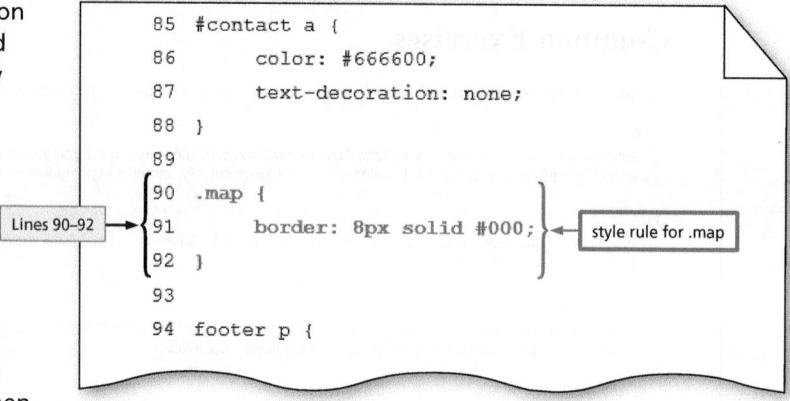

```
85  #contact a {
86      color: #666600;
87      text-decoration: none;
88  }
89
90  .map {
91      border: 8px solid #000;
92  }
93
94  footer p {
```

Lines 90–92

style rule for .map

Figure 4–60

3

- Save all changes and view contact.html in your browser. If necessary, scroll down to view the map (Figure 4–61).

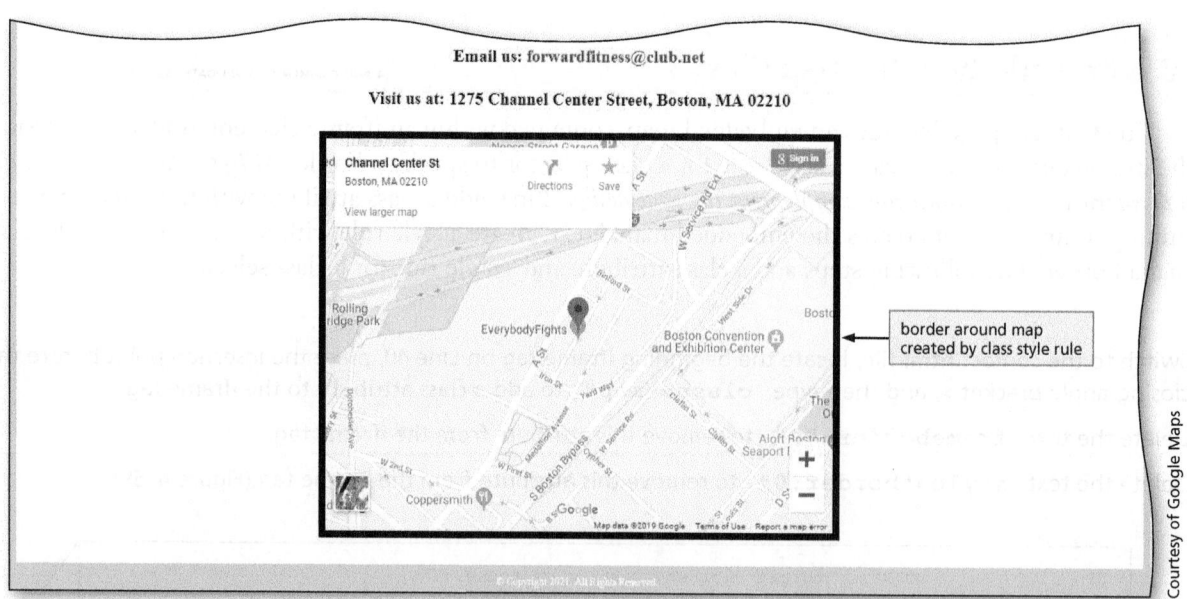

Figure 4–61

Courtesy of Google Maps

CSS Reset

Every browser uses its own default style sheet to display a webpage. Unfortunately, all browsers do not use the same style rules within their style sheets. This can cause the appearance of a webpage to vary slightly when you view the page in different browsers. To help resolve webpage display inconsistencies, you create a style rule known as a CSS reset. A **CSS reset** is a style rule that is applied to the webpage before any other style rule defined within the style sheet. This means that it is the first style rule within a style sheet. The CSS reset style rule includes all major selectors and specifies a zero value for margin, padding, and border. The following is an example of a CSS reset:

```
body, header, nav, footer {
        margin: 0;
        padding: 0;
        border: 0;

}
```

When you view the Forward Fitness Club home page in Google Chrome, you will notice some space on either side of the hero image. When you view the same page in Mozilla Firefox, this space is removed. The change in appearance is due to the different default styles used by these two browsers. Figure 4–62 shows the home page for the Forward Fitness Club in Google Chrome. Figure 4–63 shows the same page in Mozilla Firefox. While the change is subtle, it is an example of an inconsistent appearance when viewing the page on these browsers.

Figure 4–62

Figure 4–63

To Create a CSS Reset

Create a CSS reset style rule that specifies a zero value for margin, padding, and border. *Why? Every browser has its own default style sheet that it uses to display a webpage. You create a CSS reset for a consistent look across all browsers.* Create a style rule for body, header, nav, main, footer, h1, div, and img selectors to specify a zero value for margin, padding, and border. The following steps add a class attribute and a style rule for a class selector.

- Switch to the styles.css file, place the insertion point before the body selector on Line 1, and then press the ENTER key twice to move the body selector to Line 3.

- Place your insertion point on Line 1, and then type `body, header, nav, main, footer, h1, div, img {` to add selectors and an opening brace.

- Press the ENTER key to add Line 2, press the TAB key to indent the line, and then type `margin: 0;` to add a declaration that specifies a zero margin.

- Press the ENTER key to add Line 3, and then type `padding: 0;` to add a declaration that specifies a zero padding.

- Press the ENTER key to add Line 4, and then type `border: 0;` to add a declaration that specifies a zero border.

- Press the ENTER key to add Line 5, press the SHIFT+TAB keys to decrease the indent, and then type `}` to close the style rule (Figure 4–64).

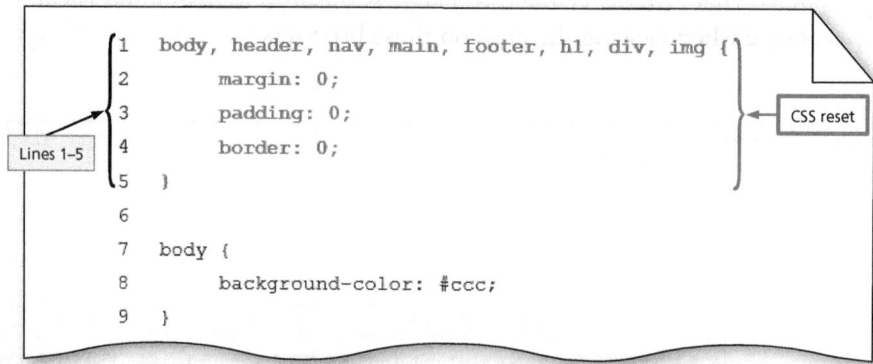

```
1   body, header, nav, main, footer, h1, div, img {
2       margin: 0;
3       padding: 0;
4       border: 0;
5   }
6
7   body {
8       background-color: #ccc;
9   }
```

Lines 1–5

CSS reset

Figure 4–64

- Save all changes and view index.html in your browser (Figure 4–65).

space above heading element is now removed in Google Chrome

space between image and document window is now removed when viewed in Google Chrome

Forward Fitness Club

Home   About Us   Classes   Nutrition   Contact Us

Train with Us Gain with Us

nexusby/Shutterstock.com; Y Photo Studio/Shutterstock.com

Figure 4–65

Improving the Appearance of the Forward Fitness Club Website

The website design at this stage is nearly complete. You can improve a few other elements before this chapter is complete. First, you need to remove all of the heading 1 elements from all the HTML pages. Now that the website includes a logo and a style sheet, this heading element is no longer needed. Second, change the background color for the body element to black to increase the contrast between the background and text.

To Remove the heading 1 Elements

1 CREATE CSS FILE | 2 LINK PAGES TO CSS FILE | 3 CREATE STYLE RULES
4 ADD COMMENTS | 5 VALIDATE CSS FILE

Remove the heading 1 elements within the header element on the home page, About Us page, Contact page, and template. **Why?** *This heading element is no longer needed now that the page is styled and contains a logo within the header element.* The following steps remove the heading 1 element from all HTML files.

- Open index.html in your text editor and delete Line 15 with the heading 1 element to remove the line.

- Open about.html in your text editor and delete Line 15 with the heading 1 element to remove the line.

- Open contact.html in your text editor and delete Line 15 with the heading 1 element to remove the line.

- Open template.html in your text editor and delete Line 15 with the heading 1 element to remove the line (Figure 4–66).

```
heading 1
removed

13        <!-- Use the header area for the website name or logo -->
14        <header>
Line 15   15            <a href="index.html"><img src="images/forward-fitness-logo.png"
                        alt="Forward Fitness Club logo" height="220" width="297"></a>
16        </header>
```

Figure 4–66

- Save all changes and view index.html in your browser (Figure 4–67).

heading 1 element removed

nexusby/Shutterstock.com; Y Photo Studio/Shutterstock.com

Figure 4–67

To Modify a Style Rule

You already have a style rule for the body selector that formats the background color. Likewise, you already have a style rule for list items in the nav to format their appearance. Next, you will modify existing style rules for the body and nav li selectors. *Why? The black background is part of the original design plan. The gray background was used temporarily while style rules were being created for the page. Had the background color been black from the start, you would not have been able to see the page content. Modify the appearance of the nav text to improve the overall look.* The following steps modify style rules for the body and nav li selectors.

 1

- Switch to the styles.css file and on Line 8, change the background-color value to `000` to change the color to black (Figure 4–68).

```
1   body, header, nav, main, footer, h1, div, img {
2       margin: 0;
3       padding: 0;
4       border: 0;
5   }
6
7   body {
8       background-color: #000;
9   }
```

Line 8 → 8

new color value

Figure 4–68

2

- On Line 35, change the font-size value to `1.5em` and then press the ENTER key to insert a new Line 36.

- On Line 36, type `font-family: Verdana, Arial, sans-serif;` to add a font family declaration and font stack.

- Press the ENTER key to insert a new Line 37, and then type `font-weight: bold;` to add a font weight (Figure 4–69).

```
33  nav li {
34      display: inline-bloc
35      font-size: 1.5em;
36      font-family: Verdana, Arial, sans-serif;
37      font-weight: bold;
38  }
```

Line 33 → 33

new font size value

new declaration added for font-family

new declaration added for font-weight

Figure 4–69

3

- Save your changes and open index.html in your browser to view the changes (Figure 4–70).

black background

nav appearance modified

Home   About Us   Classes   Nutrition   Contact Us

Train with Us
Gain with Us

nexusby/Shutterstock.com; Y Photo Studio/Shutterstock.com;
Courtesy of Google Chrome

Figure 4–70

Adding Comments to CSS Files

As you create a CSS file, include comments about each rule to identify its purpose. Comments can provide additional information about the area where the styles are applied or other helpful explanations, such as what the styles do. Add a comment above a selector using the following syntax:

`/* Place your comment here */`

CSS comment syntax specifies a forward slash at the beginning and at the end of the comment. After the first forward slash, insert an asterisk (*) followed by the comment text. For example, the comment text might identify the group of styles or the author of the style sheet. Close the comment by adding another asterisk, followed by a forward slash.

BTW
CSS Comments in Notepad++
When you correctly add comments to a CSS file using Notepad++, the comments appear in green.

To Add Comments to a CSS File

1 CREATE CSS FILE │ 2 LINK PAGES TO CSS FILE │ 3 CREATE STYLE RULES
4 ADD COMMENTS │ **5 VALIDATE CSS FILE**

When you create a CSS file, including comments provides additional information about each style rule. You can also use a comment to identify that you are the author of the style sheet. *Why? When you or another web designer are editing a CSS file, comments provide insight on the purpose of the style rule or its declarations.* The following steps add comments to a CSS file.

- Place the insertion point before the CSS reset on Line 1, and then press the ENTER key twice to place the CSS reset on Line 3.

- On Line 1 type `/*` to add the beginning syntax for a CSS comment.

- Press the ENTER key to create a new Line 2, and then type **`Author:`** followed by your first and last name to add an author name to the comment.

- Press the ENTER key to create a new Line 3, and then type **`Date:`** and include the current date to add the date to the comment.

- Press the ENTER key to create a new Line 4, and then type **`File Name: styles.css`** to add the file name to the comment.

- Press the ENTER key to create a new Line 5, and then type `*/` to close the comment (Figure 4–71).

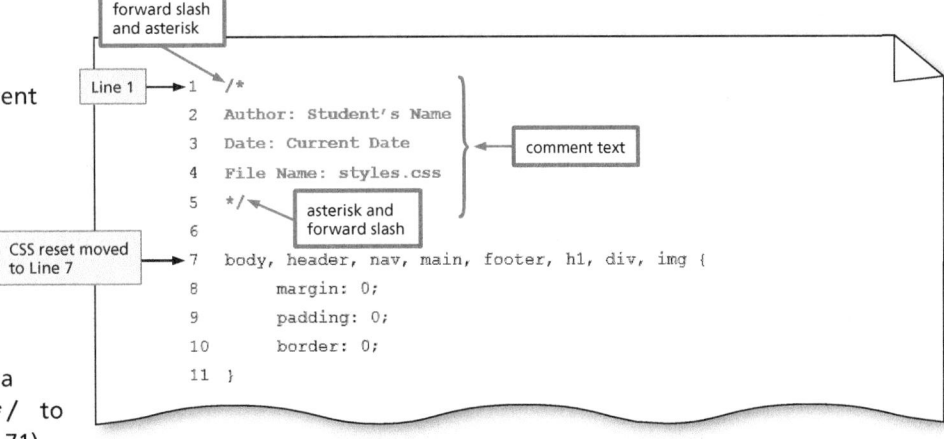

Figure 4–71

◁ | Are comments required in a CSS file?
Q&A | No. Comments are optional, but using comments in a CSS file is a best practice to document the author and date of the last update. Comments also help to organize categories of styles in the style sheet.

2

- Place the insertion point before the CSS reset on Line 7, and then press the ENTER key to place the CSS reset on Line 8.

- On Line 7 type `/* CSS Reset */` to add a comment to indicate that the style rule below the comment is the CSS reset (Figure 4–72).

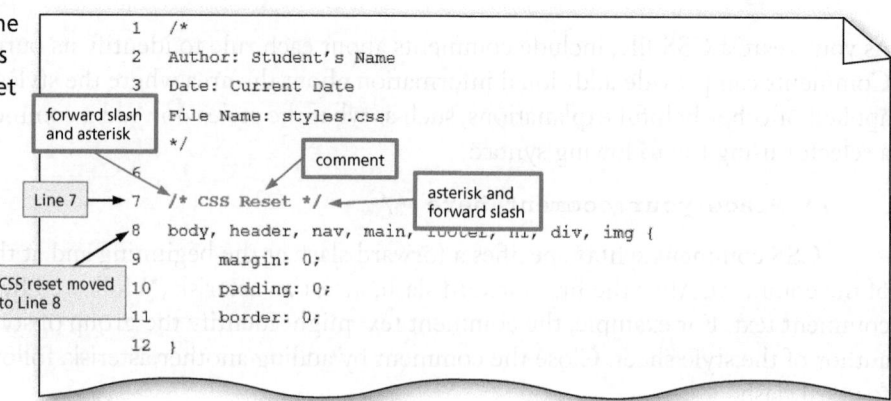

```
1    /*
2    Author: Student's Name
3    Date: Current Date
     File Name: styles.css
     */

7    /* CSS Reset */
8    body, header, nav, main, footer, h1, div, img {
9        margin: 0;
10       padding: 0;
11       border: 0;
12   }
```

forward slash and asterisk
comment
asterisk and forward slash
Line 7
CSS reset moved to Line 8

Figure 4–72

3

- Place the insertion point before the body selector on Line 14, and then press the ENTER key to place the body selector on Line 15.

- On Line 14 type `/* Style rules for body and images */` to add a comment indicating that the following style rules pertain to the body and image elements.

- Place the insertion point before the header selector on Line 24, and then press the ENTER key to place the header selector on Line 25.

- On Line 24 type `/* Style rule for header */` to add a comment indicating that the following style rule pertains to the header element.

```
14   /* Style rules for body and images */
15   body {
16       background-color: #000;
17   }
18
19   img {
20       max-width: 100%;
21       display: block;
22   }
23
24   /* Style rule for header */
25   header {
26       width: 25%;
27       float: left;
28   }
29
30   /* Style rules for navigation area */
31   nav {
32       width: 70%;
33       float: right;
34       margin: 5em 3em 0 0;
35   }
```

Lines 14
comment for body and images
Line 24
comment for header
Line 30
comment for navigation

Figure 4–73

- Place the insertion point before the nav selector on Line 30, and then press the ENTER key to place the nav selector on Line 31.

- On Line 30 type `/* Style for rules for navigation area */` to add a comment indicating that the following style rules pertain to the navigation area (Figure 4–73).

4

- Place the insertion point before the main selector on Line 58, and then press the ENTER key to place the main selector on Line 59.

- On Line 58 type `/* Style rules for main content */` to add a comment indicating that the following style rules pertain to the main content area.

- Place the insertion point before the footer selector on Line 113, and then press the ENTER key to place the footer selector on Line 114.

- On Line 113 type `/* Style rules for footer content */` to add a comment indicating that the following style rules pertain to the footer area (Figure 4–74).

```
Line 58 →  58  /* Style rules for main content */←  comment for
           59  main {                                 main content
           60      clear: left;
           61      background-color: #fff;
           62      padding: 2%;
           63      font-size: 1.25em;
           64  }
```

```
Line 113 → 113  /* Style rules for footer content */← comment for
           114 footer p {                              footer content
           115     font-size: 0.75em;
           116     text-align: center;
           117     color: #fff;
           118     padding: 0 1em;
           119 }
```

Figure 4–74

• Save your changes.

Validating CSS Files

Once you have created a CSS file, you validate it to verify the validity of the CSS code, similar to how you validate an HTML document to make sure it uses proper HTML syntax. When you validate a CSS document, you confirm that all of the code is correct and follows the established rules for CSS. You can use many online validation services to assure that your CSS code follows standards. Validation should always be a part of your web development testing. The validation service used in this book is the W3C Markup Validation Service (jigsaw.w3.org/css-validator/). You start by uploading your CSS file to the validator, which means you copy the file from your computer to the website. The validator reviews each line of code and locates any errors.

If validation detects an error in your CSS code, a warning such as "Sorry! We found the following error(s)!" appears in the header bar. The results also indicate the number of errors and detailed comments regarding each error.

To Validate the CSS File

1 CREATE CSS FILE | 2 LINK PAGES TO CSS FILE | 3 CREATE STYLE RULES
4 ADD COMMENTS | **5 VALIDATE CSS FILE**

After making changes to a CSS file, run the file through W3C's validator to check the document for errors. *Why? If the document has any errors, validating gives you a chance to identify and correct them.* The following steps validate a CSS file.

• Open your browser and type **http://jigsaw.w3.org/css-validator/** in the address bar to display the W3C CSS Validation Service page.

• Tap or click the By file upload tab to display the Validate by file upload information.

• Tap or click the Choose File button to display the Open dialog box.

• Navigate to your css folder to find the styles.css file (Figure 4–75).

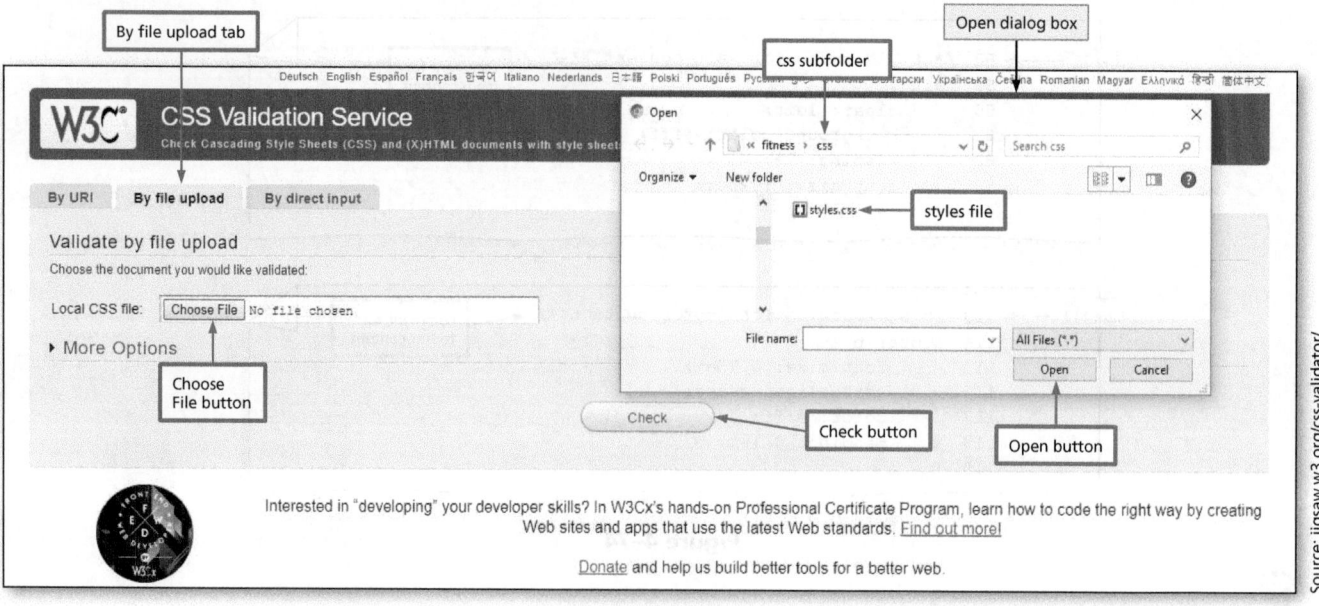

Figure 4–75

2

- Tap or click the styles.css document to select it.

- Tap or click the Open button to upload the selected file to the W3C CSS validator.

- Tap or click the Check button to send the document through the validator and display the validation results page (Figure 4–76).

Q&A My results show errors. How do I correct them?
Review the errors listed below the "Sorry! We found the following errors" message. Any line number that contains an error is shown in this section.

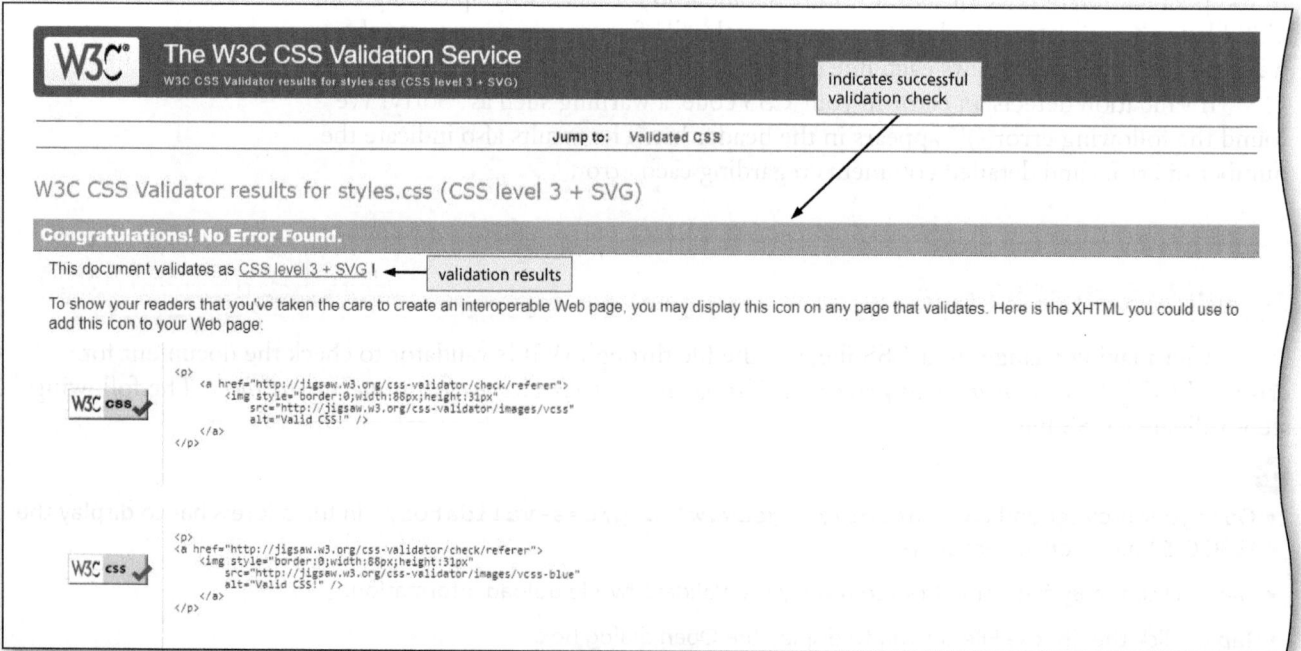

Figure 4–76

To Validate a CSS File with Errors

If you created the CSS file correctly, you should not receive any errors, but you can look at what the validator provides when you upload a style sheet file with errors. *Why? When errors are detected in a CSS file, the validator provides information about the location of each error so you can identify and correct them.* The following steps insert an error in the styles CSS file and then validate the document with the W3C CSS validator.

- Return to the styles.css document in your text editor and delete the colon and semicolon on Line 16 to remove the characters from the background-color property and value.
- Save your changes, and then return to the W3C CSS Validation Service page in your browser to display the W3C CSS validator.
- If necessary, tap or click the By file upload tab to display the Validate by File Upload information.
- Tap or click the Choose File button to display the Open dialog box.
- Navigate to the css folder in the fitness folder, select the styles.css file, and then tap or click the Open button to upload the file.
- Tap or click the Check button to send the revised document through the validator and display the validation results.
- Review the errors and note their line numbers so you can locate them (Figure 4–77).

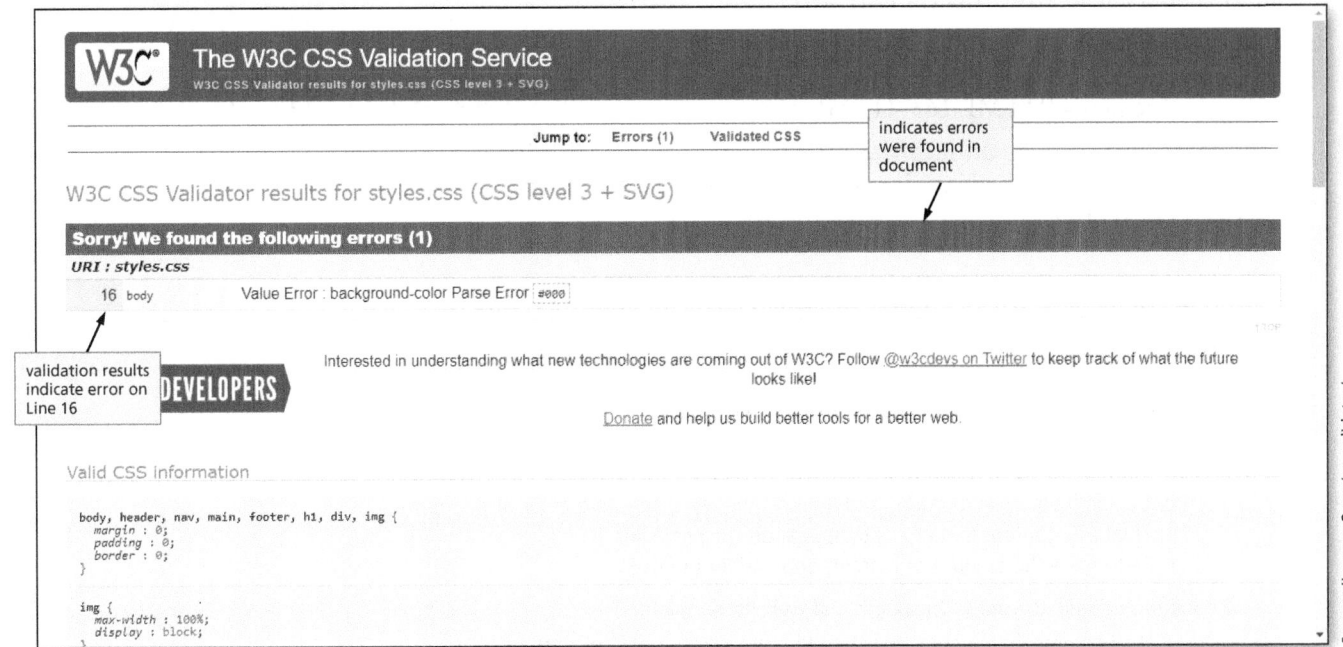

Figure 4–77

Source: jigsaw.w3.org/css-validator/

- Return to your text editor and type **:** after the background-color property and type **;** after the #000 value on Line 16 to correct the errors.
- Save your changes and validate the document again to confirm it does not contain any errors.

Chapter Summary

In this chapter, you learned how to create a CSS file with rules to style HTML elements on a webpage. You linked the CSS file to all of the webpages for the fitness website. The items listed below include all the new concepts and skills you have learned in this chapter, with the tasks grouped by activity.

Using Cascading Style Sheets
Inline, Embedded, and External Style Sheets (HTML 147, HTML 148)
CSS Basics (HTML 149)
CSS Text Properties (HTML 150)
CSS Colors (HTML 151)

Understanding Inline Elements and Block Elements
CSS Box Model (HTML 154)

Creating an External Style Sheet
Create a CSS File (HTML 157)
Create a Style Rule for the Body Element (HTML 157)

Linking an HTML Document to a CSS File
Link HTML Pages to the CSS File (HTML 159)

Creating a Webpage Layout
Set Float and Clear Properties (HTML 161)

Creating Style Rules for Structural Elements
Create Style Rules for the Header, Nav, Main, and Footer Elements (HTML 163–HTML 178)

Modifying the Nav to use an unordered list
Create a Style Rule for the Unordered List within the Nav (HTML 169)

Create a Style Rule for the List Items within the Nav (HTML 170)
Create a Style Rule for the List Item Anchor Elements within the Nav (HTML 170)

Creating Responsive Image
Create a Style Rule for Img Element (HTML 173)
Remove Height and Width Attributes from Img Elements (HTML 174)

Creating Style Rules for ID and Class Attributes
Create a Style Rule for ID Attributes (HTML 179)
Use the Span Element (HTML 184)
Create a Style Rule for Class Attributes (HTML 184)

Creating a CSS Reset
Create a CSS Reset Style Rule (HTML 190)

Adding Comments to CSS Files
Add Comments to a CSS File (HTML 193)

Validating CSS Files
Validate the CSS File (HTML 195)

CONSIDER THIS

What decisions will you need to make when creating your next CSS file?

Use these guidelines as you complete the assignments in this chapter and create your own websites outside of this class.

1. Determine properties for your HTML elements (such as header, nav, main, and footer).
   a. Set webpage width and centering characteristics.
   b. Decide on any necessary text properties to use for font face, size, and style.
   c. Set text and background colors.
   d. Decide if you need borders, and then set the style, size, and color of the border.
   e. Float any content that needs to appear on the same line.
   f. Determine the amount of margins and padding to use.

2. Link the CSS file to your HTML pages and website template.
   a. Add comments to your CSS file, noting the declarations for each selector.
   b. Validate your CSS file to confirm that it does not contain any errors.
   c. View your website in a browser to see the applied styles throughout the development process.
   d. Determine any changes that need to be made and revalidate.

3. Depending on the structure of your website, determine if you should create additional CSS files to accommodate multiple wireframes or different media such as mobile or print. Styling for multiple devices will be covered in later chapters.

CONSIDER THIS

How should you submit solutions to questions in the assignments identified with a symbol? Every assignment in this book contains one or more questions identified with a symbol. These questions require you to think beyond the assigned presentation. Present your solutions to the questions in the format required by your instructor. Possible formats may include one or more of these options: create a document that contains the answer; present your answer to the class; discuss your answer in a group; record the answer as audio or video using a webcam, smartphone, or portable media player; or post answers on a blog, wiki, or website.

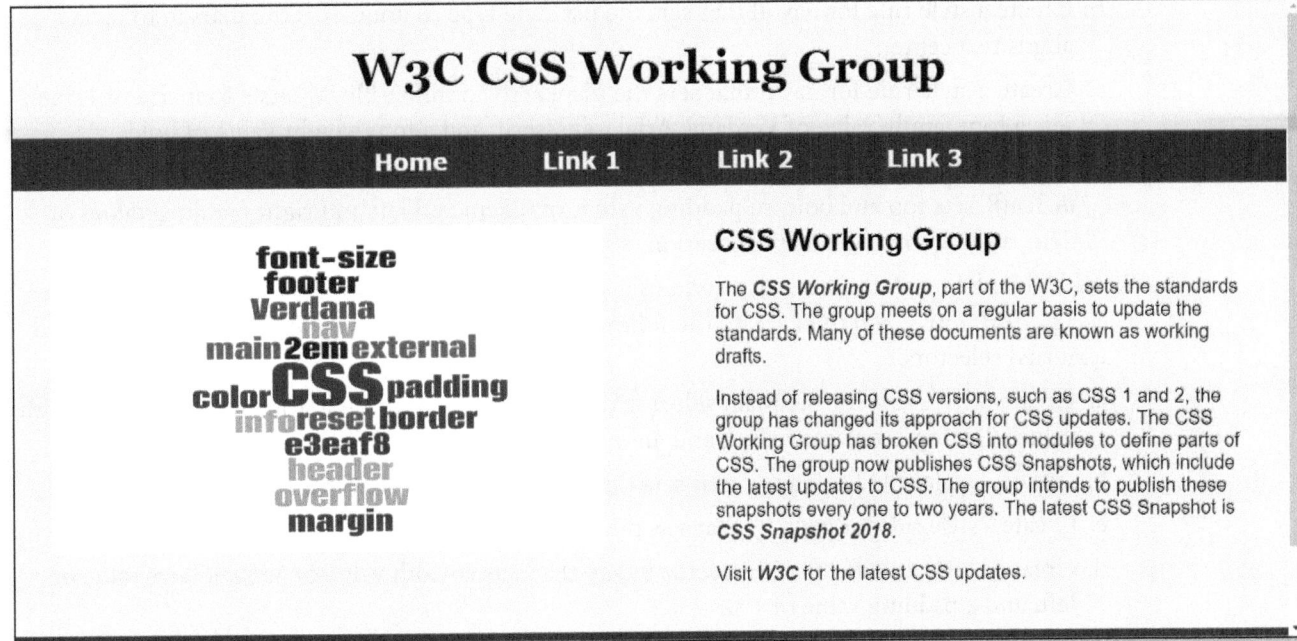

Apply Your Knowledge

Reinforce the skills and apply the concepts you learned in this chapter.

Creating a Style Sheet to Style a Webpage

Note: To complete this assignment, you will be required to use the Data Files. Please contact your instructor for information about accessing the Data Files.

Instructions: In this exercise, you will use your text editor to create a style sheet to format an HTML webpage. An example of the completed webpage is shown in Figure 4–78.

Figure 4–78

Source: Jessica Minnick

Perform the following tasks:

1. Open your text editor and then open the index.html file in the chapter04\apply folder from the Data Files. Update the comment with your name, the file name, and today's date.

2. Update the nav element to use an unordered list instead of a paragraph element for the links. Wrap each anchor within a list item.

3. Create a subfolder named **css** within your chapter04\apply folder. Create a style sheet for your website, name the file **styles.css,** and save it within your css folder. Add a comment at the top of the style sheet that includes your name, the current date, and the name of file.

4. Add the following link element after the meta element in the index.html file:

   `<link rel="stylesheet" href="css/styles.css">`

5. In styles.css, add a blank line after the comment, and then add a new comment with the text **CSS Reset,** followed by a CSS reset style rule that sets the margin, padding, and borders to zero for the following selectors: body, header, nav, main, footer, img, h1, h3.

6. Add a blank line after the CSS reset style rule, add a comment with the text, **Style rule for body and image,** and then create new style rules for the body and img selectors.

   a. Create a style rule for the body selector that sets a background color value of #e3eaf8.

   b. Create a style rule for an img selector that sets a max-width to 100% and displays the images as a block.

Continued >

Apply Your Knowledge *continued*

7. Add a blank line after the img style rule, add a comment with the text `Style rule for header content,` and then create a new style rule for the header h1 descendant selector that aligns text center; sets a font size value of 3em; sets a font family value of Georgia, Times, serif; sets a padding value of 3%; and sets a color value of #101a2d.

8. Add a blank line after the header h1 style rule, add a comment with the text `Style rules for navigation area,` and then create the following style rules for the nav, nav ul, nav li, and nav li a selectors.

   a. Create a style rule for the nav selector that sets the background color to #1d396d.

   b. Create a style rule for nav ul that sets the list style type to none, sets the margin to 0, and aligns text center.

   c. Create a style rule for nav li that sets the display to an inline-block, sets a font size of 1.5em, sets a font family value of Verdana, Arial, sans-serif, and a font weight value of bold.

   d. Create a style rule for nav li a that sets the display to a block, sets a font color value of #e3eaf8, sets top and bottom padding values of 0.5em and left and right padding values of 2em, and removes the text decoration.

9. Add a blank line after the nav li a style rule, add a comment with the text `Style rules for main content,` and then create the following style rules for the main, main p, main h3, and .external selectors.

   a. Create a style rule for the main selector that sets the padding value to 2%, a font family with values Geneva, Arial, sans-serif, and an overflow value of auto.

   b. Create a style rule for main p that sets the font size value to 1.25em.

   c. Create a style rule for main h3 that sets the top padding value to 2% and a font size value to 2em.

   d. Create a style rule for the id selector image that sets a width value of 45%, a float value of left, and a padding value of 1%.

   e. Create a style rule for the id selector group that sets a width value of 45% and a float value of right.

   f. Create a style rule for the class selector `external` that sets the font color to #1d396d, removes the text decoration, sets the font weight value to bold, and sets the font style value to italic.

10. Add a blank line after the external id style rule, add a comment with the text, `Style rules for footer content,` and then create the following style rules for the footer and footer a selectors.

    a. Create a style rule for the footer selector that aligns text center, sets a font size value of 0.85em, sets a background color value of # 1d396d, sets a font color value of # e3eaf8, and sets top and bottom padding values to 1% and right and left padding values to 0%.

    b. Create a style rule for footer a that sets the font color value to # e3eaf8 and removes the text decoration.

11. Include a blank line between each style rule. Save your changes to the styles.css file. Validate styles.css and correct any errors.

12. In index.html, remove the height and width attributes from the word-cloud.png image on Line 35. Save your changes.

13. Add a class attribute with a value of external to all anchor elements on Lines 41, 43, 45, and 47.

14. Add your name to the first paragraph element within the footer element.

15. Validate all HTML files and correct any errors. Save your changes and submit the assignment in a format specified by your instructor.

16. ✳ The page content for this assignment discusses the CSS Working Group. Open the link to W3.org, find the latest highlight or news, and provide a summary of what you read.

Extend Your Knowledge

Extend the skills you learned in this chapter and experiment with new skills. You may need to use additional resources to complete the assignment.

Working with Color Values

Note: To complete this assignment, you will be required to use the Data Files. Please contact your instructor for information about accessing the Data Files.

Instructions: In this exercise, you will create class selectors to style webpage content. You will use hexadecimal, RGB, and HSL color codes in a style sheet, using a browser to find a color converter. The webpage includes empty paragraph elements and comments that contain questions. You will use the empty elements to answer questions noted within the webpage comments. An example of the completed webpage is shown in Figure 4–79.

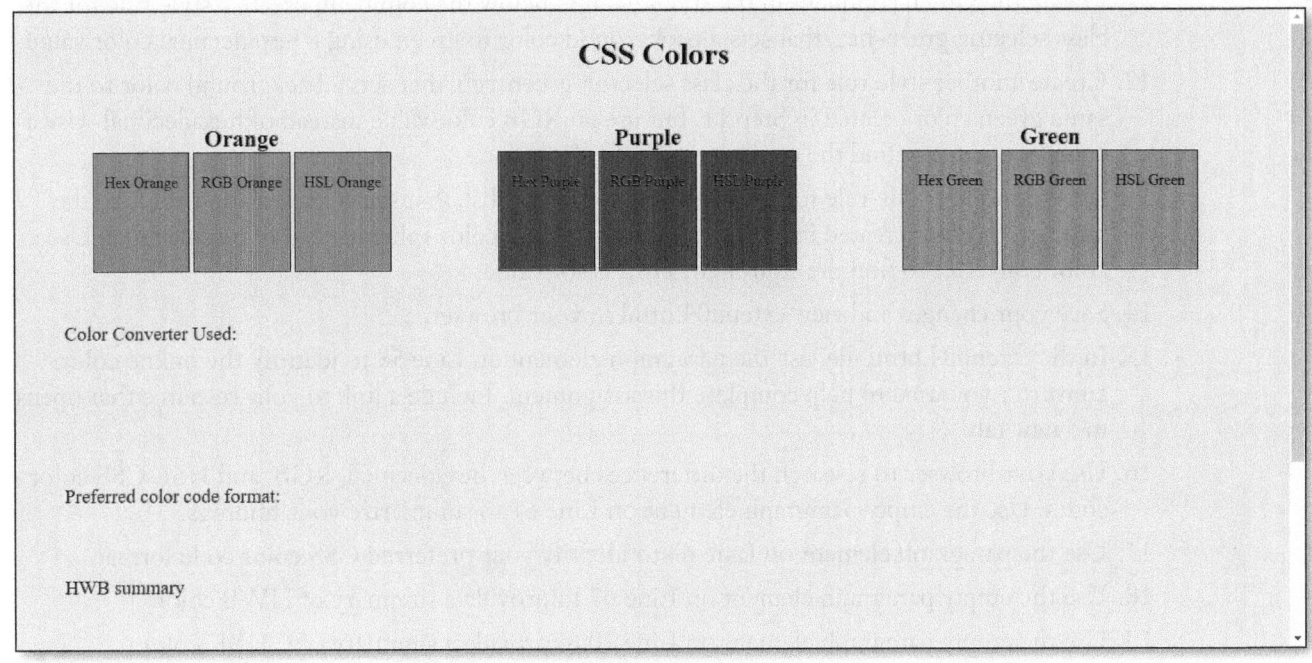

Figure 4–79

Perform the following tasks:

1. Open your text editor and then open the extend04.html file in the chapter04\extend folder from the Data Files. Update the comment with your name, the file name, and today's date. Link the extend04.html file to the style sheet located within the css folder.

2. Use your browser to find a CSS color picker and color converter. Use the color picker to find a shade of orange. Any orange color variation is fine.

3. Open the styles.css file in your text editor. Locate the Orange comment on Line 60. Below the comment, create a style rule for the class selector, orange-hex, that sets a background color to orange using a hexadecimal color value.

4. Create another style rule for the class selector, orange-rgb, that sets a background color to the same orange color created in Step 3, but use an RGB color value instead of hexadecimal. Use a color converter to find the equivalent RGB color value.

5. Create another style rule for the class selector, orange-hsl, that sets a background color to the same orange color created in Step 3, but use an HSL color value instead of hexadecimal. Use a color converter to find the equivalent HSL color value.

Continued >

Extend Your Knowledge *continued*

6. Use the color picker to find a shade of purple. Any purple color variation is fine.

7. Locate the Purple comment in the styles.css file. Below the comment, create a style rule for the class selector, purple-hex, that sets a background color to purple using a hexadecimal color value.

8. Create another style rule for the class selector, purple-rgb, that sets a background color to the same purple color created in Step 7, but use an RGB color value instead of hexadecimal. Use a color converter to find the equivalent RGB color value.

9. Create another style rule for the class selector, purple-hsl, that sets a background color to the same purple color created in Step 7, but use an HSL color value instead of hexadecimal. Use a color converter to find the equivalent HSL color value.

10. Use the color picker to find a shade of green. Any green color variation is fine.

11. Locate the Green comment in the styles.css file. Below the comment, create a style rule for the class selector, green-hex, that sets a background color to green using a hexadecimal color value.

12. Create another style rule for the class selector, green-rgb, that sets a background color to the same green color created in Step 11, but use an RGB color value instead of hexadecimal. Use a color converter to find the equivalent RGB color value.

13. Create another style rule for the class selector, green-hsl, that sets a background color to the same green color created in Step 11, but use an HSL color value instead of hexadecimal. Use a color converter to find the equivalent HSL color value.

14. Save your changes and view extend04.html in your browser.

15. In the extend04.html file, use the paragraph element on Line 58 to identify the online color converter you used to help complete this assignment. Include a link to your resource that opens in a new tab.

16. Use your browser to research the differences between hexadecimal, RGB, and HSL CSS color codes. Use the empty paragraph element on Line 61 to summarize your findings.

17. Use the paragraph element on Line 64 to identify your preferred CSS color code format.

18. Use the empty paragraph element on Line 67 to provide a summary of HWB color.

19. Use the empty paragraph element on Line 70 to provide a summary of CMYK color.

20. Add your name to the first paragraph element within the footer element.

21. Save your changes and validate the HTML and CSS files. Correct any errors.

22. Save your changes and submit the assignment in the format specified by your instructor.

23. ✸ In this assignment, you learned how to use online resources to help select CSS colors. What is the difference between RGB and RGBA?

Analyze, Correct, Improve

Analyze a webpage, correct all errors, and improve it.

Correcting CSS Style Rules

Note: To complete this assignment, you will be required to use the Data Files. Please contact your instructor for information about accessing the Data Files.

Instructions: Open your text editor and then open the chapter04\analyze04.html file from the Data Files. The page is not yet linked to a style sheet, which needs improvement. The page is also missing links. An example of the corrected page is shown in Figure 4–80.

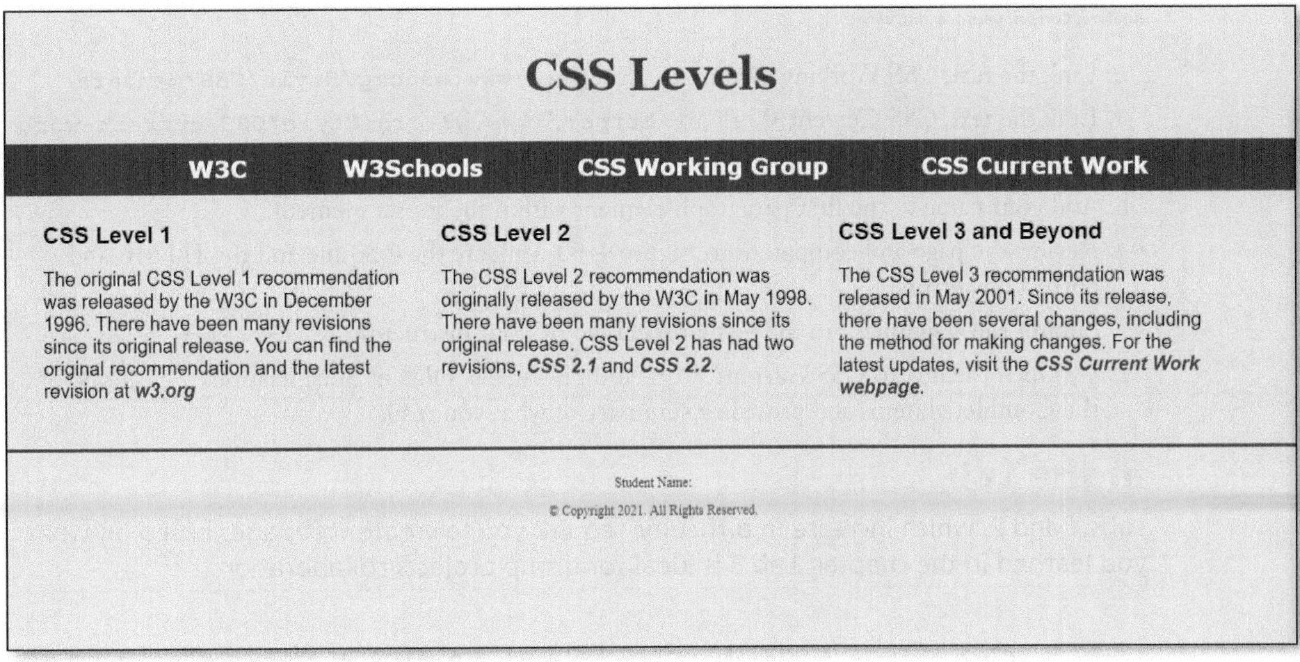

CSS Levels

W3C	W3Schools	CSS Working Group	CSS Current Work

CSS Level 1

The original CSS Level 1 recommendation was released by the W3C in December 1996. There have been many revisions since its original release. You can find the original recommendation and the latest revision at *w3.org*

CSS Level 2

The CSS Level 2 recommendation was originally released by the W3C in May 1998. There have been many revisions since its original release. CSS Level 2 has had two revisions, *CSS 2.1* and *CSS 2.2*.

CSS Level 3 and Beyond

The CSS Level 3 recommendation was released in May 2001. Since its release, there have been several changes, including the method for making changes. For the latest updates, visit the *CSS Current Work webpage*.

Student Name:

Figure 4–80

1. Correct

a. Open the analyze04.html file in your text editor and review the page.

b. Update the comment with your name, the file name, and today's date.

c. Link the analyze04.html file to the style sheet located within the css folder.

d. Review analyze04.html in your browser to view its current layout. Notice how the page does not properly display the webpage content.

e. In the styles.css file, correct the file to list style rules separately, with a space between each style rule for improved readability.

f. Group style rules by area, starting with the body, header, nav, main, and footer. Add a comment before each grouping of style rules.

g. Add a CSS reset as the first style rule.

h. Starting on Line 1, add a comment that includes your name, today's date, and the file name.

i. Correct the style rule for the h1 selector located in the header element to center-align its content.

j. Correct the style rule for the list item elements within the nav to display the list as an inline-block.

k. Update the style rule for the main selector that sets the overflow property to auto.

l. Adjust the width value for the cssl, css2, and css3 id selectors so that they appear next to each other horizontally.

m. Update the style rule for the footer selector to clear a float on the left.

2. Improve

a. Remove the underline from all nav links.

b. Create a style rule for anchor elements within the main element that sets the font color value to #47476b, removes the underline, sets a font weight value of bold, and sets a font style value of italic.

c. In the nav element in analyze04.html, link the text, W3C, to `https://www.w3.org/`.

d. Link the text, W3Schools, to `https://www.w3schools.com/`.

Continued >

Analyze, Correct, Improve *continued*

e. Link the text, CSS Working Group, to `https://www.w3.org/Style/CSS/members`.

f. Link the text, CSS Current Work, to `https://www.w3.org/Style/CSS/current-work`.

g. Update all links to open each website in a new tab.

h. Add your name to the first paragraph element within the footer element.

i. Review the page and compare it to Figure 4–80. Validate the CSS file and the HTML and correct any errors.

j. Submit the assignment in the format specified by your instructor.

k. ✷ Open the link to CSS Current Work and review the Table of Specifications. Select one of the Completed items and provide a summary of what you read.

In the Lab

Labs 1 and 2, which increase in difficulty, require you to create webpages based on what you learned in the chapter; Lab 3 is ideal for group projects/collaboration.

Lab 1: **Creating a Style Sheet for Strike a Chord**

Note: To complete this assignment, you will be required to use the Data Files. Please contact your instructor for information about accessing the Data Files.

Problem: You work for a local music lesson company called Strike a Chord that provides music lessons for piano, guitar, and violin. The company needs a web presence and has hired you to create their website. You have already created the website plan and started creating the HTML pages in Chapters 1 through 3. You now need to create a style sheet to format the website. The Home, Lessons, and Contact webpages are shown in Figure 4–81.

(a)

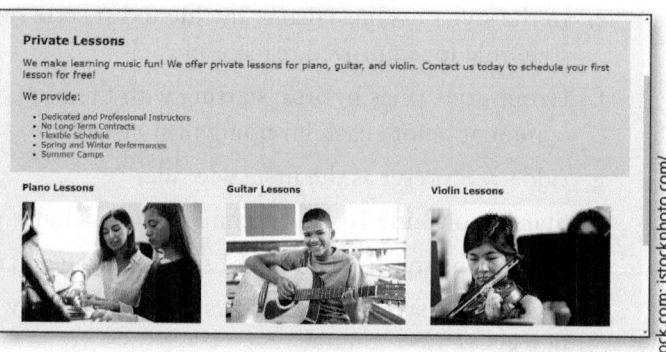

(b)

(c)

Figure 4–81

Instructions: Perform the following tasks:

1. Use File Explorer (Windows) or Finder (macOS) to navigate to the chapter04\lab1 folder in the Data Files. Copy the music-notes.png file to your music\images folder created in Chapter 3 Lab 1.

2. Using File Explorer or Finder, navigate up one level to your music folder and create a new subfolder named css.

3. Open your text editor and create a new file named styles.css. Save the file within your css folder.

4. Add the following link element after the meta element in the index.html, lessons.html, contact.html, and template.html files:

```
<link rel="stylesheet" href="css/styles.css">
```

5. In the styles.css file, add the following comment on Lines 1–5:

```
/*
Author: Student Name
Date: Current Date
File Name: styles.css
*/
```

6. Starting on Line 7, add the following comment and style rule for a CSS reset:

```
/* CSS Reset */
body, header, nav, main, footer, img, h1 {
        margin: 0;
        padding: 0;
        border: 0;
}
```

7. Starting on Line 14, add the following comment and style rule for images:

```
/* Style rule for images */
img {
        max-width: 100%;
        display: block;
}
```

8. Starting on Line 20, add the following comment and style rules for header content:

```
/* Style rules for header content */
header {
        text-align: center;
        font-size: 3em;
        color: #373684;
}

header h1 {
        font-style: italic;
}
```

Continued >

In the Lab *continued*

9. Starting on Line 31, add the following comment and style rules for the navigation area:

```
/* Style rules for navigation area */
nav {
        background-color: #373684;
}

nav ul {
        list-style-type: none;
        margin: 0;
        text-align: center;
}

nav li {
        display: inline-block;
        font-size: 2em;
}

nav li a {
        display: block;
        color: #fff;
        text-align: center;
        padding: 0.5em 1em;
        text-decoration: none;
}
```

10. Starting on Line 55, add the following comment and style rules for main content:

```
/* Style rules for main content */
main {
        padding: 2%;
        background-color: #e5e9fc;
        overflow: auto;
        font-family: Verdana, Arial, sans-serif;
}

main p {
        font-size: 1.25em;
}

.action {
        font-size: 1.75em;
        color: #373684;
        font-weight: bold;
}
```

```
#piano, #guitar, #violin {
      width: 29%;
      float: left;
      margin: 0 2%;
}


#info {
      clear: left;
      background-color: #c0caf7;
      padding: 1% 2%;
}


#contact {
      text-align: center;
}


#contact a {
      color: #4645a8;
      text-decoration: none;
      font-weight: bold;
}


.map {
      border: 5px solid #373684;
}
```

11. Starting on Line 99, add the following comment and style rules for footer content:

```
/* Style rules for footer content */
footer {
      text-align: center;
      font-size: 0.65em;
      clear: left;
}


footer a {
      color: #4645a8;
      text-decoration: none;
}
```

12. Include a blank line between each style rule. Save your changes to the styles.css file. Validate styles.css and correct any errors.

13. In the index.html file, update the nav element to use an unordered list instead of a paragraph element. Remove the nonbreaking spaces and music character codes nested within the nav element. Make the same change to lessons.html, contact.html, and template.html.

Continued >

In the Lab *continued*

14. In the index.html file, add the following comment and div element below the nav element:

```
<!-- Hero Image -->
<div id="hero">
  <img src="images/music-notes.png" alt="colorful music notes">
</div>
```

15. In the index.html file, wrap the text, FREE, (Line 41) within a span element that includes a class attribute with the value action. Save your changes.

16. In the lessons.html file, remove height and width attributes from all image elements. Save your changes.

17. In the contact.html file, remove the frameborder and style attributes from the iframe element. Add a class attribute with the value map to the iframe element. Save your changes.

18. Indent all nested elements. Check your spelling. Validate all HTML files and correct any errors. Save your changes.

19. Open the index.html file in a browser to view the home page, and then navigate to the Lessons and Contact pages to view the design for each page.

20. Submit your assignment in the format specified by your instructor.

21. ✷ In Step 10, you created a style rule for the main selector that included an overflow property. Research this CSS property to find out its purpose. What happens to the look of the Lessons page when this property is removed?

Lab 2: Creating a Style Sheet for a Wildlife Rescue

Note: To complete this assignment, you will be required to use the Data Files. Please contact your instructor for information about accessing the Data Files.

Problem: You volunteer at a local wildlife rescue, a nonprofit organization called Wild Rescues. The organization rescues all kinds of wild animals, rehabilitates them, and then releases them back into the wild. Wild Rescues needs a website to help raise awareness about the organization. You have already created the website plan and started creating the HTML pages in Chapters 1 through 3. You now need to create a style sheet to format the website. The Home, About Us, and Contact webpages are shown in Figure 4–82.

(a)

Figure 4–82 *(Continues)*

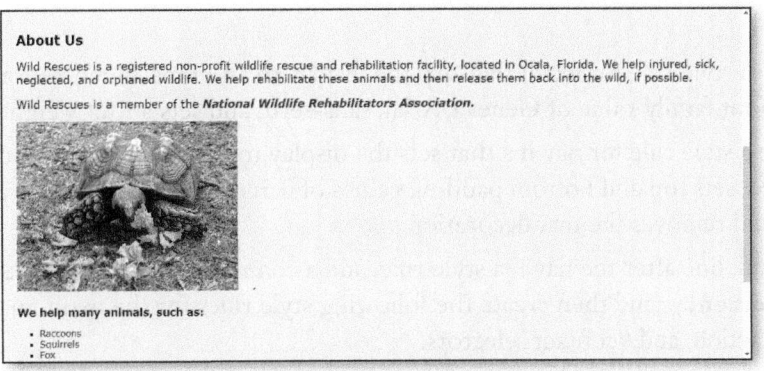

(b)

Courtesy of Jessica Minnick

(c)

Figure 4–82 **(Continued)**

Instructions: Perform the following tasks:

1. Use File Explorer (Windows) or Finder (macOS) navigate to the chapter04\lab2 folder from the Data Files. Copy the baby-hawk.jpg file to your rescue\images folder created in Chapter 3 Lab 2.

2. Using File Explorer or Finder, navigate up one level to your rescue folder and create a new subfolder named `css`.

3. Open your text editor and create a new file named `styles.css`. Save the file within your css folder.

4. In your styles.css file, add one multiline comment that includes your name as the author, the current date, and the file name.

5. Add a blank line after the comment then add a new comment with the text `CSS Reset`, followed by a CSS reset style rule that sets the margin, padding, and borders to zero for the following selectors: body, header, nav, main, footer, img, h1, h3.

6. Add a blank line after the CSS reset style rule, add a comment with the text `Style rules for body and images`, and then create new style rules for the body and img selectors.

   a. Create a style rule for the body selector that sets a background color value of #f6eee4.

   b. Create a style rule for the img selector that sets a max-width to 100% and displays images as a block.

7. Add a blank line after the img style rule, add a comment with the text `Style rules for navigation area`, and then create the following style rules for the nav, nav ul, nav li, and nav li a selectors.

   a. Create a style rule for the nav selector that sets the background color to #2a1f14.

   b. Create a style rule for nav ul that sets the list style type to none, sets the margin to 0, and aligns text center.

Continued >

In the Lab *continued*

   c. Create a style rule for nav li that sets the display to an inline-block, sets a font size of 1.5em, sets a font family value of Geneva, Arial, sans-serif, and sets a font weight value of bold.

   d. Create a style rule for nav li a that sets the display to a block, sets a font color value of #f6eee4, sets top and bottom padding values of 0.5em and left and right padding values of 2em, and removes the text decoration.

8. Add a blank line after the nav li a style rule, add a comment with the text `Style rules for main content`, and then create the following style rules for the main, main p, main h3, main ul, .link, .action, and #contact selectors.

   a. Create a style rule for the main selector that sets the padding value to 2% and a font family with values Verdana, Arial, sans-serif.

   b. Create a style rule for main p that sets the font size value to 1.25em.

   c. Create a style rule for main h3 that sets the top padding value to 2%.

   d. Create a style rule for main ul that sets the list style type value to square.

   e. Create a style rule for the class selector link that sets the font color to #4d3319, removes the text decoration, sets the font weight value to bold, and sets the font style value to italic.

   f. Create a style rule for the class selector action that sets the font size to 1.75em, sets the font weight value to bold, and aligns text center.

   g. Create a style rule for the id selector contact that aligns text center.

9. Add a blank line after the contact id style rule, add a comment with the text `Style rules for footer content`, and then create the following style rules for the footer and footer a selectors.

   a. Create a style rule for the footer selector that aligns text center, sets a font size value of 0.85em, sets a background color value of #2a1f14, sets a font color value of #f6eee4, and sets top and bottom padding values to 1% and right and left padding values to 0%.

   b. Create a style rule for footer a that sets the font color value to #f3e6d8 and removes the text decoration.

10. Include a blank line between each style rule. Save your changes to the styles.css file. Validate styles.css and correct any errors.

11. Add a link to your style sheet in the index.html, about.html, contact.html, and template.html files. Nest the link within the head element, below the meta element.

12. In the index.html file, update the nav element to use an unordered list instead of a paragraph element. Remove the nonbreaking spaces and diamond character codes nested within the nav element. Make the same change to the about.html, contact.html, and template.html files.

13. In the index.html file, remove the two heading elements (h1 and h3) within the header element. Nest an image element within the header. Specify the image source as `baby-hawk.jpg` and alt text value of `rescued baby hawk`. Wrap the image within an anchor element that links to index.html. Make the same change to the about.html, contact.html, and template.html files.

14. Remove the height and width attributes from the baby raccoons image on Line 46. Save your changes.

15. In the about.html file, add a class attribute with the value of link to the anchor element on Line 37. Add a class attribute with the value of action to the paragraph element on Line 53.

16. Remove height and width attributes from the image element on Line 39. Save your changes.

17. In the contact.html file, add a class attribute with the value link to the email and address anchor elements on Lines 37 and 38. Save your changes.

18. Indent all nested elements. Check your spelling. Validate all HTML files and correct any errors. Save your changes.

19. Open the index.html file in a browser to view the home page, and then navigate to the About Us and Contact pages to view the design for each page.

20. Submit your assignment in the format specified by your instructor.

21. ❀ In this assignment, you specified several hexadecimal color values. Find the RGB and HSL color value codes for two hexadecimal colors used in this lab.

Lab 3: Creating a Style Sheet for the Student Clubs and Events Website

Problem: You and several of your classmates have decided to help increase student involvement in school clubs and events by creating a website to promote awareness about the various activities. You have already created the website plan and started creating the HTML pages in Chapters 1 through 3. You now need to create a style sheet to format the website.

Instructions:

1. Open your template.html file and update the nav element to use an unordered list instead of a paragraph element for the links. Wrap each anchor within a list item. Remove any special characters used between navigation links. Make the same change to all HTML files used within your website.

2. Create a style sheet for your website and save it within your css subfolder. Add a comment at the top of the style sheet that includes the names of team members in your group, the current date, and the name of file.

3. Add a CSS reset style rule as the first style rule in the style sheet. Include a comment above the style rule to note its purpose. Include all major selectors used within your website for your CSS reset.

4. Update your HTML files and style sheet to make responsive images. This includes removing height and width attributes from image elements and creating a style rule that sets a max width to 100%. Also display image elements as a block.

5. Link all of your webpages to your style sheet. Nest the link element within the head element, below the meta element.

6. In your style sheet, create a minimum of 12 style rules. Style the nav to remove the bullet marker. Remove the underline from all links. Specify at least one font-family declaration and include fallback values. Include at least one id and one class selector. Use a high color contrast to ensure content is readable. Include comments to note where styles rules for header, nav, main, and footer begin.

7. Validate your style sheet and correct any errors.

8. Review all pages within your website to ensure they appear as intended.

9. Submit your assignment in the format specified by your instructor.

10. ❀ In this assignment, you worked as a group to style your website. How did you determine your color scheme? Find an online resource that helps design a color scheme for your website.

Continued >

Consider This: Your Turn

Apply your creative thinking and problem-solving skills to design and implement a solution.

1. Creating a Style Sheet for Your Personal Portfolio Website

Personal

Part 1: You have already created the website plan and started creating the HTML pages for your personal portfolio website in Chapters 1 through 3. You now need to create a style sheet to format your website.

1. Open your template.html file and update the nav element to use an unordered list instead of a paragraph element for the links. Wrap each anchor within a list item. Remove any special characters used between navigation links. Make the same change to all HTML files used within your website.

2. Create a subfolder named css within your portfolio folder. Create a style sheet for your website and save it within your css folder. Add a comment at the top of the style sheet that includes your name, the current date, and the name of file.

3. Add a CSS reset style rule as the first style rule in the style sheet. Include a comment above the style rule to note its purpose. Include all major selectors used within your website for your CSS reset.

4. Update your HTML files and style sheet to make responsive images. This includes removing height and width attributes from image elements and creating a style rule that sets a max width to 100%. Also display image elements as a block.

5. Link all of your webpages to your style sheet. Nest the link element within the head element, below the meta element.

6. In your style sheet, create a minimum of 12 style rules. Style the nav to remove the bullet marker. Include at least one id and one class selector. Specify at least one font-family declaration and include fallback values. Remove the underline from all links. Use a high color contrast to ensure content is readable. Include comments to note where styles rules for header, nav, main, and footer begin.

7. Validate your style sheet and correct any errors.

8. Review all pages within your website to ensure they appear as intended.

9. Submit your assignment in the format specified by your instructor.

Part 2: ⚙ In this assignment, you used CSS to style your personal portfolio website. Did you try to center an image with the text-align property? Research how to center an image element.

2. Creating a Style Sheet for the Dog Grooming Website

Professional

Note: To complete this assignment, you will be required to use the Data Files. Please contact your instructor for information about accessing the Data Files.

Part 1: You have already created the website plan and started creating the HTML pages for the dog grooming website in Chapters 1 through 3. You now need to create a style sheet to format the website.

1. Open your template.html file and update the nav element to use an unordered list instead of a paragraph element for the links. Wrap each anchor within a list item. Remove any special characters used between navigation links. Make the same change to all HTML files used within your website.

2. Create a subfolder named css within your portfolio folder. Create a style sheet for your website and save it within your css folder. Add a comment at the top of the style sheet that includes your name, the current date, and the name of file.

3. Add a CSS reset style rule as the first style rule on the style sheet. Include a comment above the style rule to note its purpose. Include all major selectors used within your website for your CSS reset.

4. Update your HTML files and style sheet to make responsive images. This includes removing height and width attributes from image elements and creating a style rule that sets a max width to 100%. Also display image elements as a block.

5. Link all of your webpages to your style sheet. Nest the link element within the head element, below the meta element.

6. In your style sheet, create a minimum of 16 style rules. Style the nav to remove the bullet marker. Include at least one id and one class selector. Specify at least one font-family declaration and include fallback values. Use float and clear properties. Use a high color contrast to ensure content is readable. Include comments to note where styles rules for header, nav, main, and footer begin.

7. Validate your style sheet and correct any errors.

8. Review all pages within your website to ensure they appear as intended.

9. Submit your assignment in the format specified by your instructor.

Part 2: ✷ Review the website plan that you created in Chapter 1. Does the wireframe match your design? If not, draft a new wireframe to match your new design.

3. Create a Style Sheet for the Future Technologies Website
Research and Collaboration

Part 1:   You and several of your classmates have been tasked with creating a website that showcases advancements in technology. You have already created the website plan and started creating the HTML pages for the technology website in Chapters 1 through 3. You now need to create a style sheet to format the website.

1. Use File Explorer (Windows) or Finder (macOS) navigate to the chapter04\your_turn3 folder from the Data Files. Copy the tech-banner.png file to your tech\images folder created in Chapter 2 Consider This Your Turn 3.

2. Open your template.html file and update the nav element to use an unordered list instead of a paragraph element for the links. Wrap each anchor within a list item. Remove any special characters used between navigation links. Make the same change to all HTML files used within your website.

3. Create a style sheet for your website and save it within your css folder. Add a comment at the top of the style sheet that includes the name of each team member, the current date, and the name of file.

4. Add a CSS reset style rule as the first style rule in the style sheet. Include a comment above the style rule to note its purpose. Include all major selectors used within your website for your CSS reset.

5. Update your HTML files and style sheet to make responsive images. This includes removing height and width attributes from image elements and creating a style rule that sets a max width to 100%. Also display image elements as a block.

6. Add a hero image to the home page for your website. You may use the tech-banner.png data file or another file that suits your needs.

Continued >

Consider This: Your Turn *continued*

7. Link all of your webpages to your style sheet. Nest the link element within the head element, below the meta element.

8. In your style sheet, create a minimum of 15 style rules. Style the nav to remove the bullet marker. Include at least one id and one class selector. Use a span element. Specify at least one font-family declaration and include fallback values. Use a high color contrast to ensure the content is readable. Include comments to note where styles rules for header, nav, main, and footer begin.

9. Research a CSS property not discussed in Chapter 4 and use it within one of your style rules. Include a comment to note which declaration contains the property you found and its purpose.

10. Validate your style sheet and correct any errors.

11. Review all pages within your website to ensure each appears as intended.

12. Submit your assignment in the format specified by your instructor.

Part 2: ❄ In this assignment, you created a style sheet to format your website. What colors did you use? Why did you choose this color scheme? What is the meaning of the primary color used for the website?

5 | Responsive Design Part 1: Designing for Mobile Devices

Objectives

You will have mastered the material in this chapter when you can:

- Explain the principles of responsive design
- Describe the pros and cons of a mobile website
- Explain the design principles of a mobile website
- Describe a mobile-first strategy
- Define a viewport
- Insert a meta viewport element

- Use a mobile simulator
- Create a sticky element
- Integrate custom fonts
- Use a pseudo-class
- Create a mobile-friendly navigation system
- Add a telephone link
- Make rounded corners

5 | Responsive Design Part 1: Designing for Mobile Devices

Introduction

Prior to the era of mobile devices, websites were almost exclusively accessed by desktop computers. However, the use of mobile devices to connect to the Internet has been rising since 2010. According to statista.com, nearly 50 percent of websites were visited between 2017 and 2018 worldwide using a mobile device. This trend is expected to continue. That means a business must create a website that includes an optimum viewing experience for mobile users. Have you ever visited a website from a mobile device that was not displayed well on a small screen? Webpages that require users to zoom and scroll to read and navigate the website drive visitors away.

The good news is that with a web development approach called responsive design, you have the power to create one website that is displayed well across various screen sizes and browsers on devices ranging from phones and tablets through laptops and traditional desktop displays. **Responsive design** is a website development strategy that strives to provide an optimal user experience of a website regardless of the device used. By applying responsive design principles, the webpage and content respond to the screen size of the user's device to minimize unnecessary scrolling and zooming, making reading and interacting with the site as convenient and intuitive as possible.

Project — Redesign a Website for Mobile Devices

In Chapter 4, you created an external CSS file for the Forward Fitness Club and linked it to each webpage in the fitness website. For this project, you apply responsive web design principles to the fitness website by editing the CSS and HTML files to use a mobile-first responsive design strategy. These enhancements will result in a better experience for mobile device users. You will continue to enhance the site with responsive design for tablet and desktop viewports in Chapter 6.

First, you will modify all the HTML files to add a meta element within the head element to provide support for mobile devices. Next, you will modify the header to keep its position as the user scrolls. You will also learn how to use a mobile device simulator. You will then create a mobile-friendly navigation system and integrate custom fonts. Finally, you will modify and add style rules to design for mobile devices. Figure 5–1 shows the home page, the About Us page, and the Contact Us page of Forward Fitness Club sized for a mobile viewport. Figure 5–1a shows the home page, Figure 5–1b shows the About Us page, and Figure 5–1c shows the Contact Us page.

(a) Home Page

(b) About Us Page

(c) Contact Us Page

nexusby/Shutterstock.com, VGstockstudio/Shutterstock.com, Google Maps

Figure 5–1

Roadmap

In this chapter, you will learn how to create the webpages shown in Figure 5–1. The following roadmap identifies general activities you will perform as you progress through this chapter:

1. ADD a META VIEWPORT ELEMENT to each HTML document.

2. CREATE a STICKY HEADER.

3. ADD CUSTOM FONTS.

4. STYLE PAGES FOR a MOBILE VIEWPORT.

5. STYLE the MAP FOR a MOBILE VIEWPORT.

At the beginning of step instructions throughout the chapter, you will see an abbreviated form of this roadmap. The abbreviated roadmap uses colors to indicate chapter progress: gray means the chapter is beyond that activity; blue means the task being shown is covered in that activity, and black means that activity is yet to be covered. For example, the following abbreviated roadmap indicates the chapter would be showing a task in the 4 STYLE PAGES FOR MOBILE VIEWPORT activity.

1 ADD META VIEWPORT ELEMENT | 2 CREATE STICKY HEADER | 3 ADD CUSTOM FONTS
4 STYLE PAGES FOR MOBILE VIEWPORT | 5 STYLE MAP FOR MOBILE VIEWPORT

Use the abbreviated roadmap as a progress guide while you read or step through the instructions in this chapter.

Exploring Responsive Design

Figure 5–2 shows an example of a website developed using responsive design principles, ethanmarcotte.com. The content appears easy to read and navigate on devices of three sizes: desktop browser, tablet, and phone. If you are working on a desktop computer, you can quickly experience how the webpage responds to different browser sizes by simply resizing your browser window.

(a) Desktop

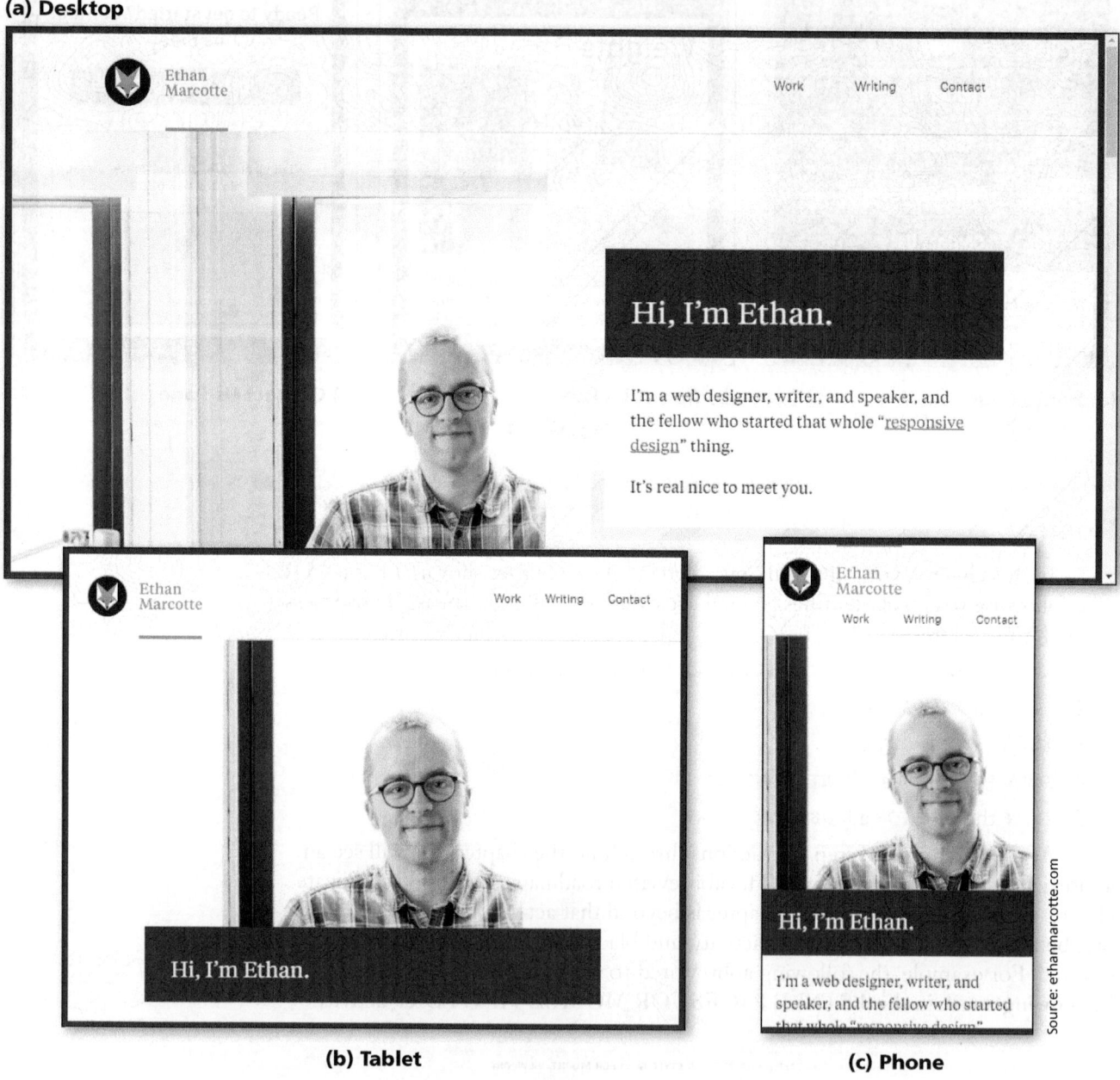

(b) Tablet **(c) Phone**

Source: ethanmarcotte.com

Figure 5–2

Ethan Marcotte is credited with coining the phrase "responsive web design" in a 2010 article he wrote for the web developer community in a magazine called *A List Apart*, alistapart.com. Responsive web design is not a specific set of rules, but is better characterized as a philosophy that is constantly refined as HTML and CSS standards, browsers, and technology evolve and improve. However, most discussions of responsive design highlight the following three concepts:

- Fluid layout: A **fluid layout** or grid applies proportional size measurements to the webpage wireframe and content so that the content stretches, shrinks, and grows as the size of the viewport changes. The **viewport** is the viewing area for the webpage, which is much smaller on a smartphone than on a traditional desktop. On a traditional Windows desktop computer, the viewport is usually the window itself, but the term "viewport" is preferred over "window" because a window on a traditional desktop display might not be maximized to fill the entire screen. Just keep in mind that the viewport refers to the area of the webpage that a user sees at any one time, regardless of device, browser, screen size, screen resolution, window size, or orientation.

- Responsive or flexible images: As previously discussed in Chapter 3, **responsive images** shrink and grow based on the size of the viewport. Responsive images do not have height and width attributes or values in the HTML document. Rather, responsive images use CSS rules to resize the image relative to the wireframe and viewport.

- Media queries: **Media queries** allow the webpage developer to detect the approximate pixel size of the current viewport. The developer can then selectively apply CSS rules that work best for that viewport size. CSS3 standards expanded the capabilities of media queries. Media queries will be further discussed in Chapter 6.

Designing for Mobile Devices

The explosive growth of mobile browsers, including those on phones and tablets, quickly created serious problems for webpage developers because smaller viewports often required excessive zooming and scrolling. Different techniques emerged to address this problem, one of which was to build a completely separate, parallel website optimized for mobile users called a **mobile website**. Mobile websites are often identified with an m. or mo. prefix in the URL such as http://m.phsc.edu/, Pasco-Hernando State College's mobile website. Although the word "mobile" applies to any portable device connected to the Internet such as lightweight laptops, tablets, and phones, in this context, mobile websites are generally focused on providing support for browsers on smartphones.

The mobile website approach helps companies that have large existing websites provide a quick solution for mobile users. An organization's current website may contain a massive number of pages that were developed long ago using unresponsive designs built for traditional desktop browsers. Modifying each of those pages to incorporate responsive techniques is often such a major effort that it may not be considered as a viable solution. The mobile website approach means that developers build a new, parallel website from scratch, specifically designing it for small mobile viewports. This approach can be much faster than converting a large website of nonresponsive pages to modern responsive designs. Today, however, most businesses no longer build separate mobile websites.

The major downside of creating a mobile website is that it multiplies the work required to maintain what becomes two separate websites for the same organization. In contrast, responsive design seeks to optimize the viewing experience for a wide range of devices using *one* website. Therefore, a website developed with responsive design principles from the very beginning is less work to maintain down the road. Creating a website using responsive design is considered a best practice by today's standards.

A **mobile-first strategy** employs responsive design principles, but with an interesting twist. Following a mobile-first strategy, a web developer designs the flexible wireframe and essential content for the smallest viewport *first*, progressively adding more content as the viewport grows. A web developer then uses media queries to add style rules for larger viewports, progressing from tablet to laptop and desktop. See Figure 5–3a. A mobile-first strategy is considered by some to be a more productive and effective way to build a website from scratch because it forces the web developer to focus on the core, essential content first for the smallest viewport. Compare this to Figure 5–3b, the traditional approach, where developers start with a traditional webpage, and then remove or modify nonessential content as the viewport gets smaller. The mobile-first strategy makes the most sense when mobile users are a very high priority for your website and when you have the luxury of building the website from scratch.

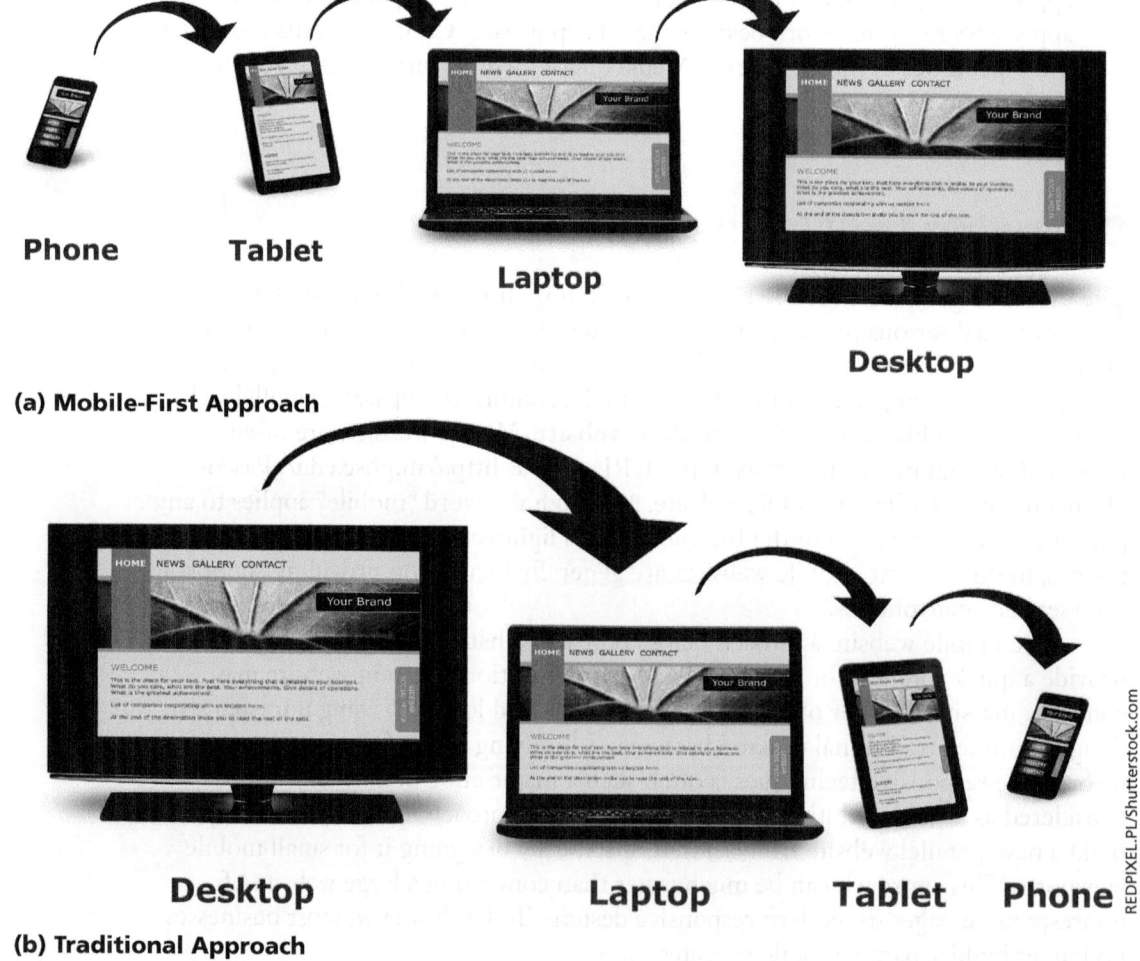

Phone   Tablet

Laptop

Desktop

(a) Mobile-First Approach

Desktop   Laptop   Tablet   Phone

(b) Traditional Approach

REDPIXEL.PL/Shutterstock.com

Figure 5–3

The website development approach you implement depends on many factors, including the current environment, your target audience, available resources, and the time available to tackle the project. Given you are still in the initial stages of developing the Forward Fitness Club website, you will be able to apply a responsive design. Although you already created desktop-sized webpages, you are still in the initial stages of building the Forward Fitness Club website so you can incorporate the mobile-first strategy, which develops an optimum design for a mobile display and focuses on the most essential content.

The following websites provide examples of responsive design. View them using a desktop, tablet, and mobile device to see their responsive design for mobile, tablet, and desktop viewports.

- Intel: www.intel.com
- Microsoft: www.microsoft.com
- Indeed: www.indeed.com
- W3Schools: www.w3schools.com
- Awwwards: www.awwwards.com
- Metropolitan Museum of Art: www.metmuseum.org
- American Red Cross: www.redcross.org

Figure 5–4 shows how the Metropolitan Museum of Art (www.metmuseum.org) website would look on a desktop, tablet, and phone. Notice how the text, pictures, and content are resized and repositioned to work well in all three viewports.

(a) Desktop

(b) Tablet

(c) Phone

Source: metmuseum.org

Figure 5–4

What is the Internet of Things?
The term **Internet of Things (IoT)** refers to the ever-expanding number of devices that connect to the Internet to share information. The IoT includes traditional computers and mobile devices as well as Internet-ready appliances, thermostats, bio-chips, TVs, and any other device that connects to the Internet to retrieve or send information.

Using Responsive Design

BTW
Web Analytics
Web analytics is the study of how users interact with a website. Web analytics provide statistics on how many people visit a website as well as what browsers, devices, and choices the user made while at a website. This data helps a web developer design a site to meet the needs of their desired audience.

A webpage with a fluid layout adjusts the webpage design and content based on the size of the viewport. Responsive designs are based on fluid layouts. Before you create a fluid layout for Forward Fitness Club, however, it is helpful to understand fixed layouts. **Fixed layouts** do not change in width based on the size of the viewport. Fixed layouts use fixed measurement units such as pixels to define the width of the areas of the wireframe that "fix" the width of the content regardless of the size of the viewport. The hernandopa-fl.us website for Hernando County in Florida shown in Figure 5–5 is based on a fixed layout. Note how the text does not wrap and how the images do not resize based on the size of the viewport. Fixed layouts can involve a tremendous amount of horizontal scrolling and require much zooming on small viewports.

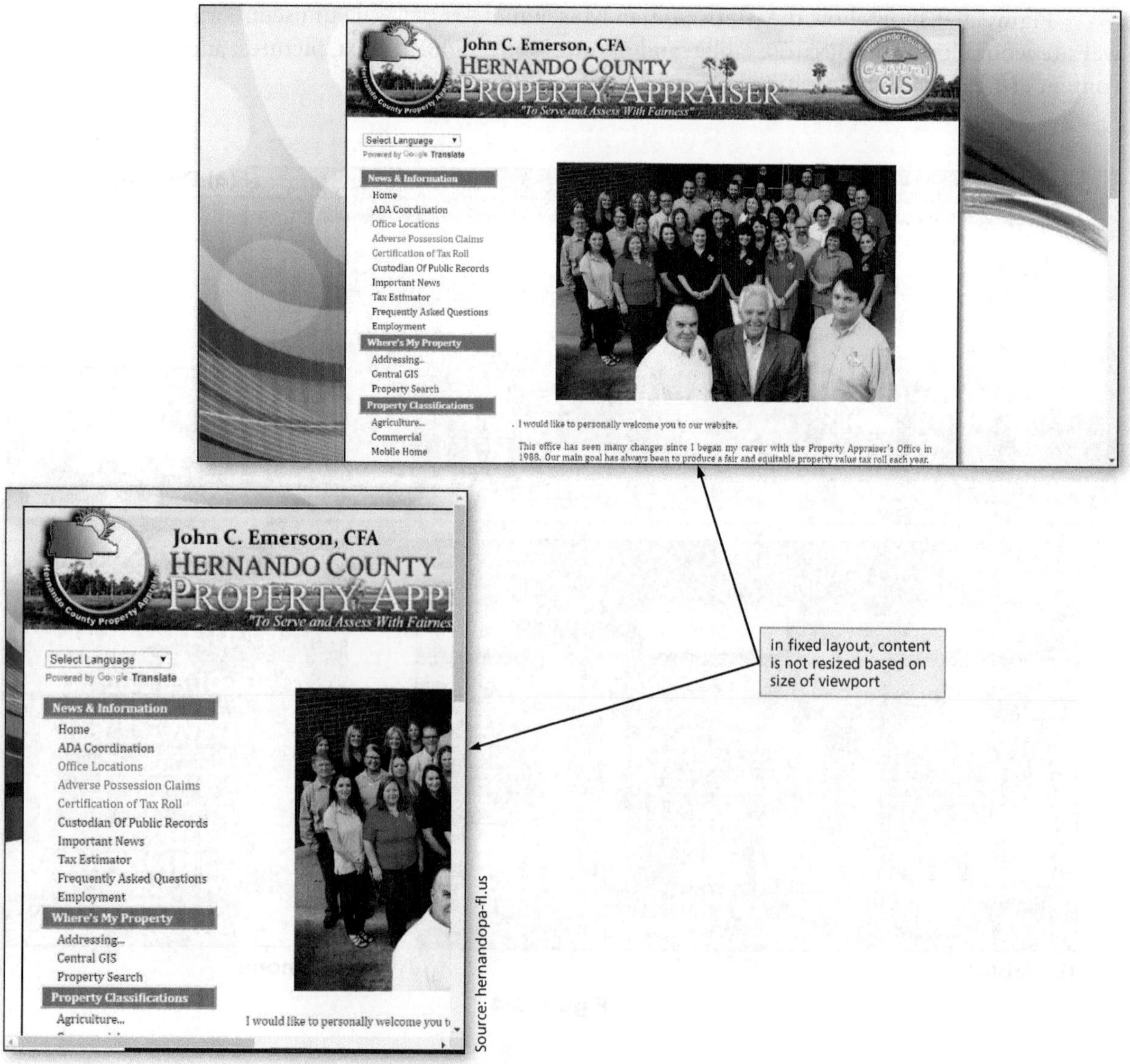

in fixed layout, content is not resized based on size of viewport

Source: hernandopa-fl.us

Figure 5–5

Because so many older websites were built for a single, traditional screen resolution such as 1024 by 768 pixels, the Internet is full of webpages with fixed layouts. In fact, it was not uncommon several years ago to start your wireframe design based on a viewport width of 960 pixels, which generally filled a traditional desktop browser yet allowed for a few pixels of margin on the left and right. Although fixed layouts do not work well for smaller viewports, they may still be appropriate for webpages used in controlled environments such as those created for a specific purpose within an internal company intranet.

You implement fluid layouts by measuring the widths of the wireframe elements and content in relative units such as percentages and ems. Table 5–1 lists the units of measurement you can use in CSS property values as well as the common uses for each. Responsive sites use relative units of measurement.

BTW

Styles and Units of Measurement
Remember that when creating styles that include units of measurement, do not put a space between the value and the unit of measure.

```
font-size: 2em;
/* correct */
font-size: 2 em;
/* incorrect */
```

Table 5–1 Common CSS Units of Measurement

Unit	Description	Relative or Fixed?	Common Uses	CSS Examples

em	An **em** is historically based on the height of the capital letter M of the default font. 1em is typically larger on a desktop browser than on a tablet browser. For example, 1em is usually about 16pt in a desktop browser and about 12pt in a tablet browser.	Relative	Em may be used to scale anything related to textual content such as font size, line sizes, margins, padding. Em sizes are relative to each other. For example, 2em = twice as large as 1em. 0.5em = half as large as 1em.	`p {font-size: 1.0em;`
				`  line-height: 2.0em;`
				`  text-indent: 1.8em;}`
				
				`h1 {font-size: 3.0em;`
				`  margin: 1.0em;`
				`  padding: 1.5em;}`

%	Percentage. The default font size measurement for most browsers on most devices is 100%.	Relative	Developers use % to measure the widths of the wireframe elements and flexible images. Some use % to measure textual content, too.	`#container {width: 80%;}`
				
				`img {width: 100%;}`

px	One **pixel** is equal to one dot on the screen. Different screens have different pixel densities.	Pixels on a device are fixed in size, but the number of pixels varies by device	Pixels are commonly used for textual measurements including padding, borders, and margins. Do not use the px measurement for width measurements, as this creates a fixed, unresponsive layout.	`.advertise {border: 1px` `solid red;}`
pt	points (1pt = 1/72 inch)	Fixed	Points are used to measure font and line sizes in **print** media.	
cm mm in	centimeters millimeters inches	Fixed	These measurements are not commonly used for webpage development.	Because these measurements are fixed and do not scale based on the size of the viewport, they should not be used within a responsive design.
pc	picas (1pc = 12pt)	Fixed	The pica measurement harkens back to the "pica typewriter," which produced a **Courier fixed-width font**, 12pts tall.	

Creating a Fluid Layout

As previously discussed, a fluid layout requires a fluid grid, media queries, and responsive images.

To create a fluid grid, you design a webpage that uses a grid or columns. A mobile viewport should use a single-column design, which is ideal for a smaller viewport. As the viewport's size increases, the number of columns can also increase. The number of columns you use depends on your design and wireframe. Figure 5–6 shows the website w3.org with a three-column design for the desktop and tablet viewports and a single-column design for the mobile viewport.

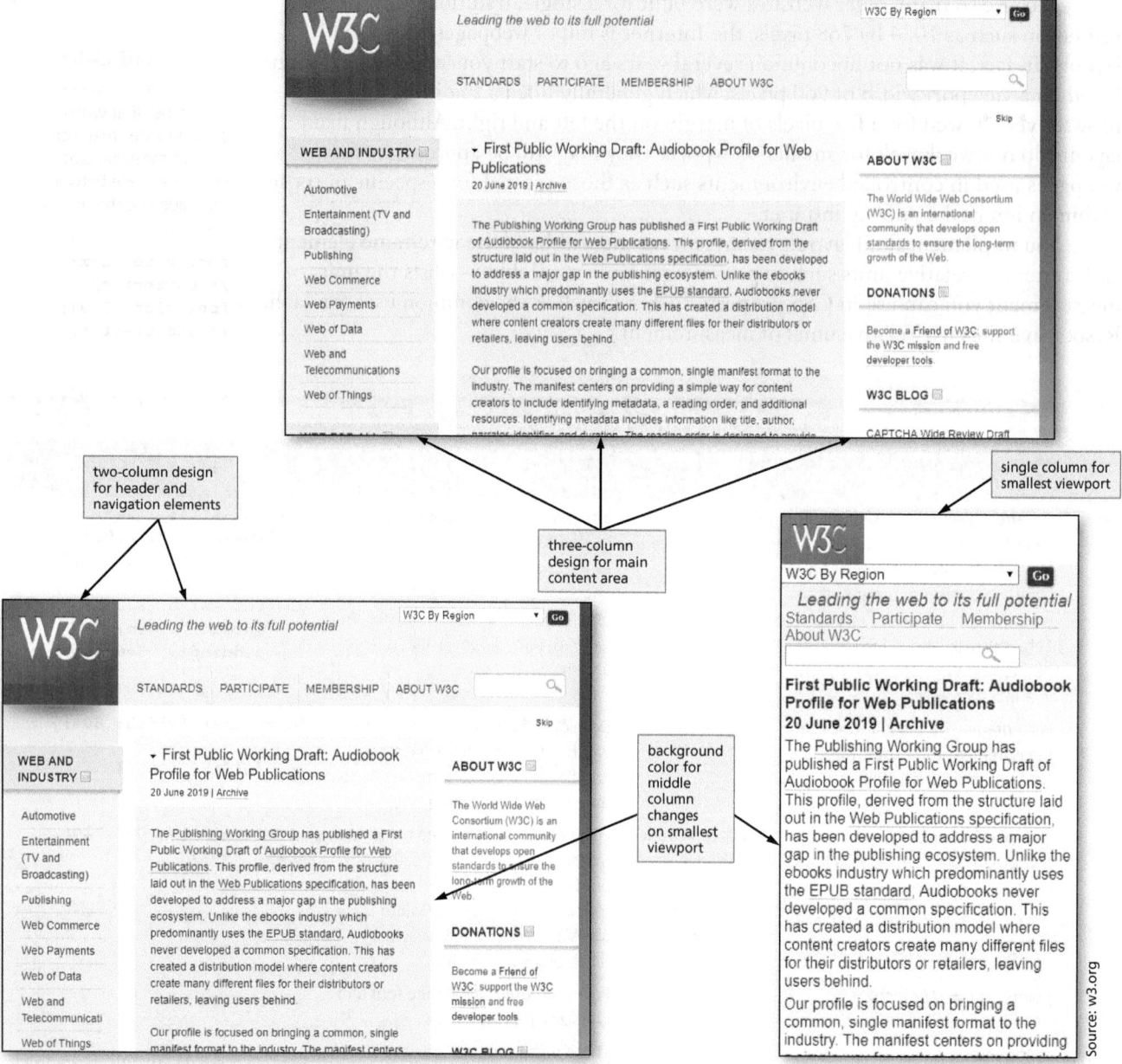

Figure 5–6

In addition to the content stretching or shrinking with the size of the viewport, the smallest viewport in Figure 5–6c hides the first and third columns to give the middle column room to stretch across the entire viewport. The background color of the content in the smallest viewport is also white instead of light blue to make the text easier to read on this smaller device. These formats are automatically applied to the webpage as the viewport changes. The changes are achieved through media queries that detect the size of the viewport and apply the styles that work well for that size.

A media query detects the media type (such as screen or print) and capabilities of the device that the browser is running on (such as the size of the viewport in pixels or its orientation of portrait versus landscape). Based on the information, the media query applies styles that work well for that situation. Several useful examples of how media queries apply styles to resize and reposition content in response to a variety of devices can be found at http://mediaqueri.es/, which is shown in Figure 5–7.

Source: mediaqueri.es

Figure 5–7

When you use responsive images, you allow them to grow and shrink with the viewport. You have already created responsive images for the Forward Fitness Club website by removing the height and width attributes from all image elements. In addition, you have already created a style rule that specifies a maximum width of 100% for images.

Following a Mobile-First Strategy

The responsive web design approach styles content differently depending on the viewport used to view the site. The mobile-first approach focuses on styling content as appropriate for smaller mobile devices. One goal in designing for mobile devices is to prominently display the content accessed most by users. It is also a best practice to use a single-column layout for a mobile display, as this prevents scrolling horizontally. Displaying what mobile device users need and want on a single screen with minimal scrolling creates a more enjoyable experience.

Styles for Content on Mobile Devices

Styling content for mobile devices is different from styling content for a desktop display. Because the screen size is smaller, you must analyze each page to determine the most important content on the page, and then style that content to attract users of mobile devices. If you do not have an existing website, begin by first determining the most essential content for your site.

If you already have page content, you may need to hide some content for a mobile viewport. Think of this approach as similar to moving from a large home to a small condominium. Before the move can take place, you must determine the essential items you want to take with you to the new home and then downsize.

Figure 5–8a depicts a wireframe example for a traditional desktop viewport. Note the multiple column layout and different areas of content. If you were to use all these same areas of content for a mobile design, the wireframe would look like Figure 5–8b.

The mobile layout shown in Figure 5–8b is too long and would require a lot of extra scrolling for a mobile user. An ideal webpage in a mobile viewport limits scrolling. In this example, you need to analyze the page and determine the areas with the most essential content. You then hide the nonessential content areas for a mobile viewport. Figure 5–9 shows how to hide some webpage areas to create a revised mobile wireframe.

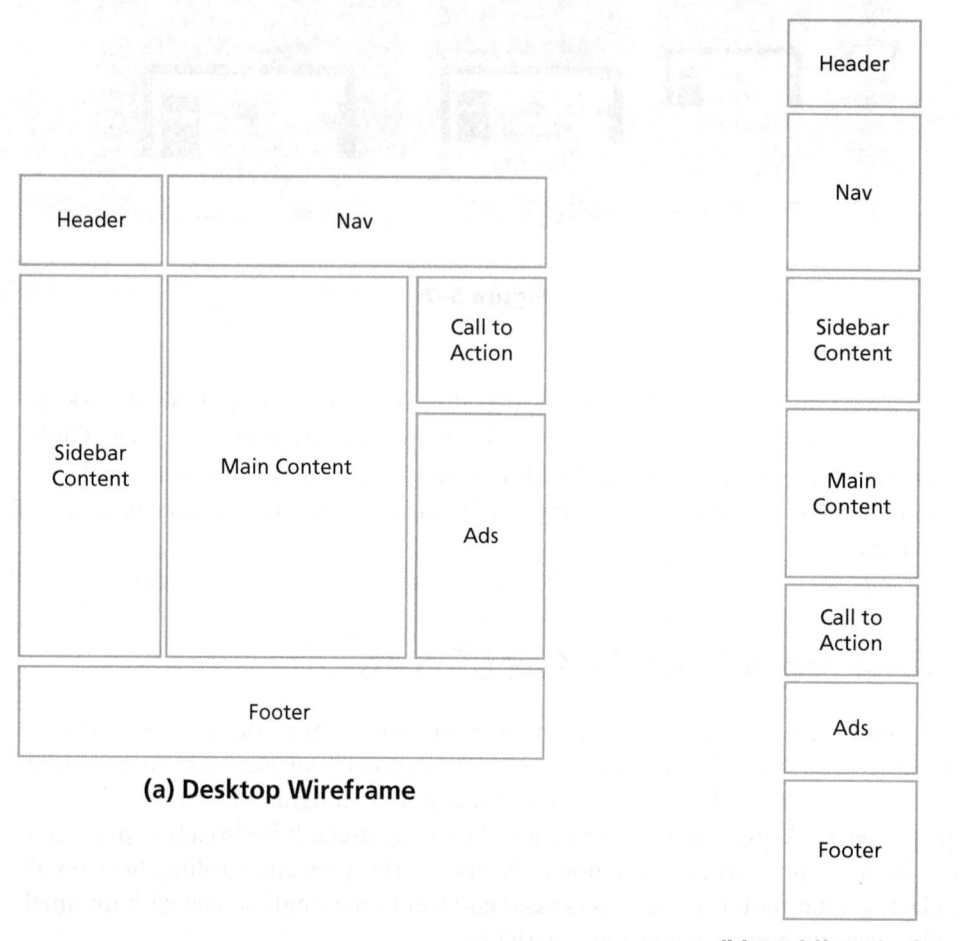

(a) Desktop Wireframe

(b) Mobile Wireframe

Figure 5–8

Optimize the interface to maximize the mobile user experience. The following are some key best practices when designing for mobile viewports.

1. Make use of 100% of the screen space.
2. Design the navigation to be easy and intuitive.
3. Keep load times minimal. Enhance load times by removing bandwidth-intensive content and streamlining your HTML code.
4. Display essential page content and hide nonessential page content.
5. Make the content easy to access and read.
6. Design a simple layout.

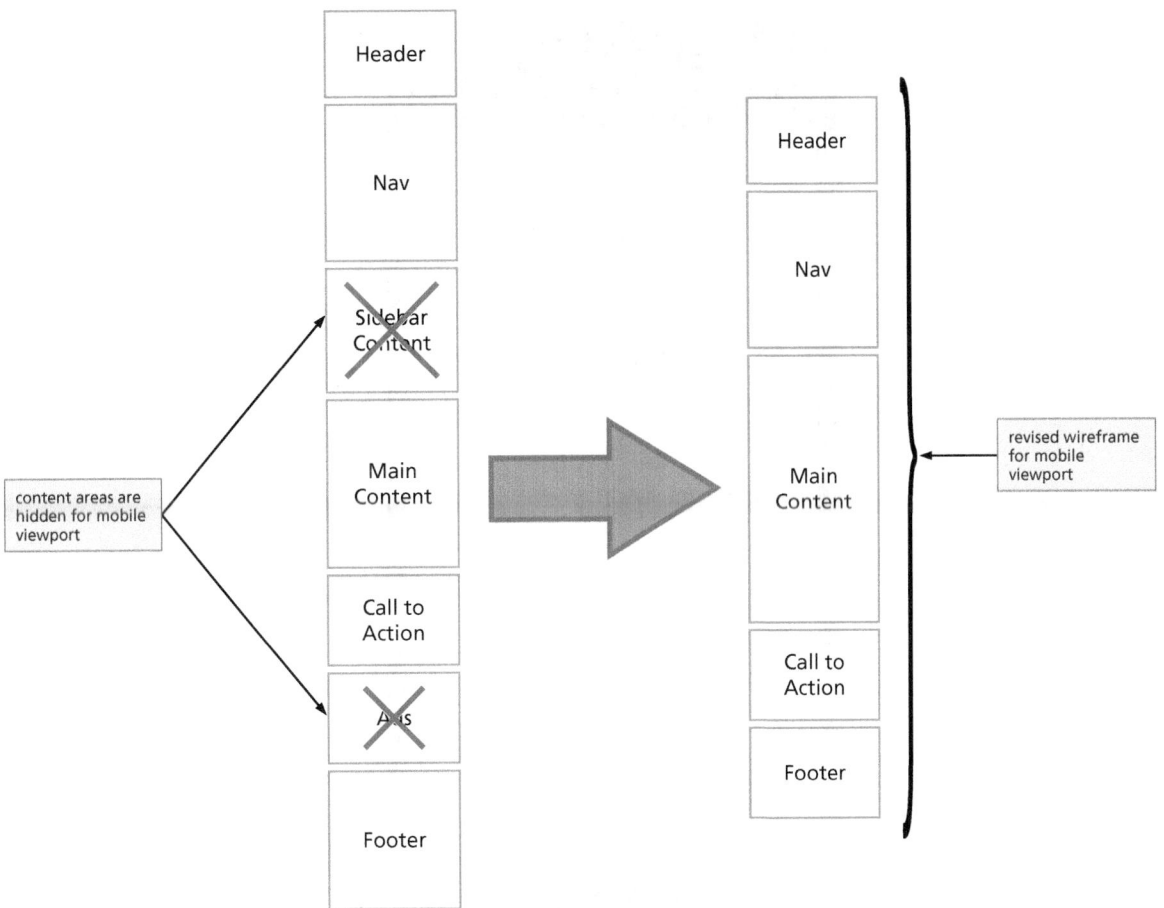

Figure 5–9

Meta Viewport Element

When creating a website with a responsive design, you must include a meta viewport element within every HTML file. The meta viewport element provides the browser with information about the page's dimensions and how to adjust scaling on the webpage. The following is an example of meta viewport element.

```
<meta name="viewport" content="width=device-width, initial-scale=1.0">
```

In the above example, the meta element contains two attributes, name and content. The name attribute has a value of viewport. This lets the browser know that there are instructions about how to control the webpage's dimensions. The content attribute includes two values: width and initial-scale. The width value specifies to use the width of the device. The initial-scale value specifies the beginning zoom level when the page is first displayed.

When you view a website that is missing the meta viewport element from a mobile device, the website will appear quite small. Figure 5–10 shows an example of a webpage that is missing the meta viewport element.

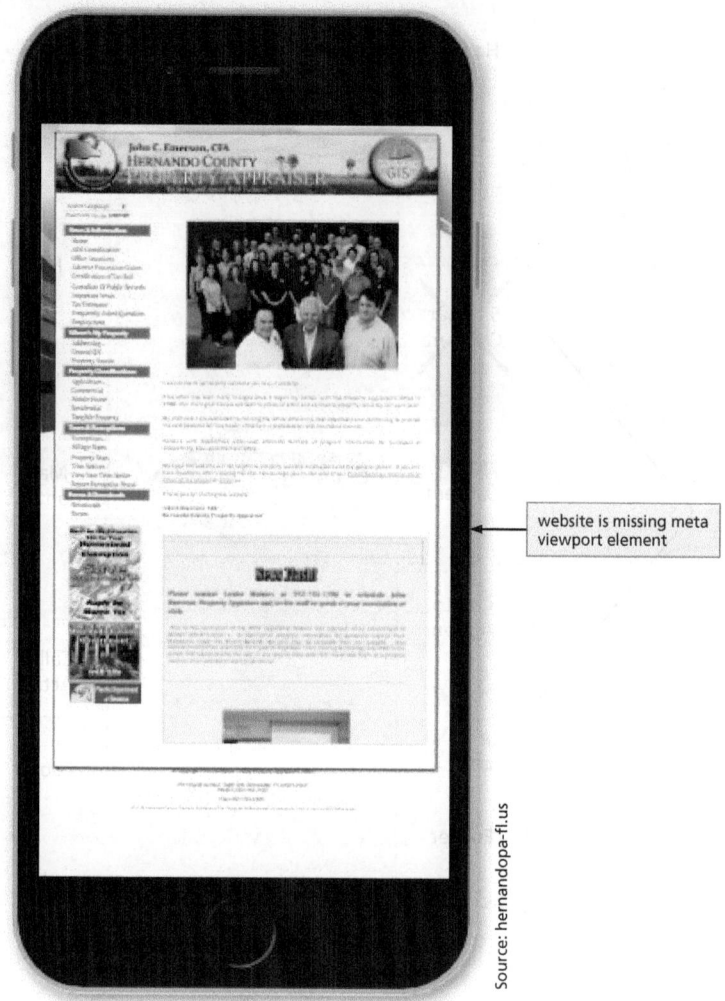

Source: hernandopa-fl.us

website is missing meta viewport element

Figure 5–10

This website is very difficult to read on a mobile device and requires a lot of zooming and scrolling in order to view all the page content.

To Add the Meta Viewport Element for Responsive Design

1 ADD META VIEWPORT ELEMENT | 2 CREATE STICKY HEADER | 3 ADD CUSTOM FONTS
4 STYLE PAGES FOR MOBILE VIEWPORT | 5 STYLE MAP FOR MOBILE VIEWPORT

Add the **meta** viewport element to the **head** section of the home, About Us, Contact Us, and template webpages. *Why? The appropriate meta viewport element helps the webpage initially load in a size that matches the viewport size.* The following steps add the **meta** viewport element to the home, About Us, Contact, and template pages.

- Open index.html, about.html, contact.html, and template.html in your text editor to prepare to modify the files.

- In the index.html file, place the insertion point at the end of Line 7 and then press the ENTER key to insert a new Line 8 just above the closing </head> tag.

- On Line 8, add the tag `<meta name="viewport" content="width=device-width, initial-scale=1">` to insert a meta viewport element for responsive design (Figure 5–11).

```
                    4       <head>

                    5           <link rel="stylesheet" href="css/styles.css">

                    6           <title>Forward Fitness Club</title>

                    7           <meta charset="utf-8">

                    8       <meta name="viewport" content="width=device-width, initial-scale=1">

                    9       </head>
```

index.html

Line 8

new meta
tag added to
head section

Note: To help you locate screen
elements that are referenced in the
step instructions, such as buttons and
commands, this book uses red boxes
to point to these screen elements.

Figure 5–11

- Copy the meta element on Line 8, and then in the about.html file, paste the meta element in the same location, on a new Line 8 just above the closing </head> tag.

- In the contact.html file, paste the meta element in the same location, on a new Line 8 just above the closing </head> tag.

- In the template.html file, paste the meta element in the same location, on a new Line 8 just above the closing </head> tag.

- Save all files.

Mobile Simulator

When designing for a mobile viewport, be sure to view your mobile page frequently throughout the design process. To view a website from an actual mobile device, the page must be published. Constantly publishing a page to view the updated design can be a cumbersome and time-consuming process. An alternative is to use a mobile simulator. A **mobile simulator** displays an example of how a website would appear on a mobile device. Many mobile simulators are available online.

TO OPEN THE GOOGLE CHROME DEVTOOLS

Google Chrome provides several developer tools, including a mobile simulator. You can download Google Chrome for free at google.com/chrome/. These developer tools are known as Chrome DevTools. If you want to open Google Chrome's DevTools, you would perform the following steps.

1. Tap or click the Customize and Control Google Chrome button, located to the right of the address bar.

2. Tap or click More tools.

3. Tap or click Developer tools to open the DevTools.

Another way to open DevTools is to press the F12 key or the CTRL+SHIFT+I keys on your keyboard.

DevTools includes a device mode tool that provides a mobile simulator. Figure 5–12 shows the features of Google Chrome's device mode. Table 5–2 summarizes these features.

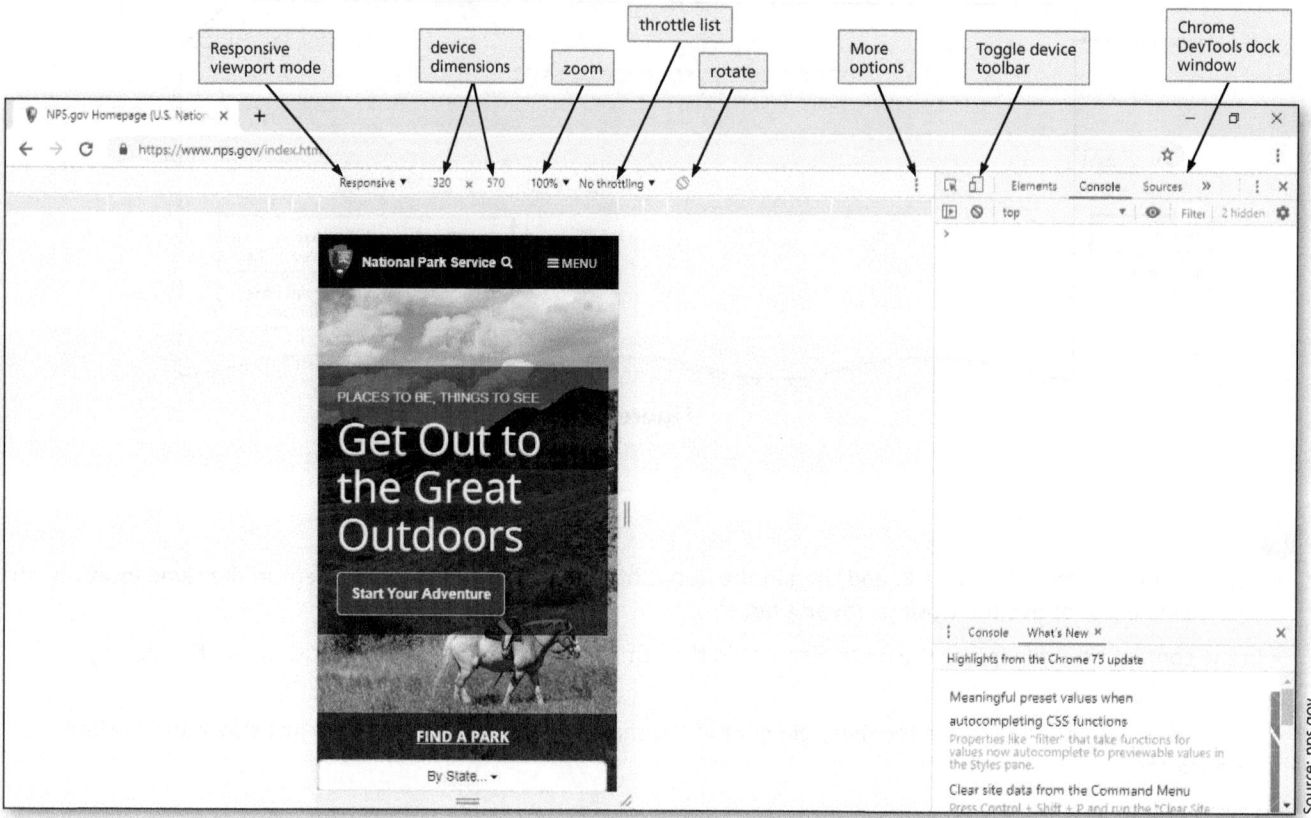

Figure 5–12

Table 5–2 Features of Google Chrome Device Mode	
Feature	**Description**
Responsive viewport mode	Displays a list of specific mobile device options to simulate
Device dimensions	Allows you to enter specific dimensions to simulate
Zoom	Allows you to zoom
Throttle list	Provides simulation options to mimic a mid-tier mobile speed (fast), low-end mobile speed (slow), offline, or none
Rotate	Allows you to toggle the display between portrait and landscape
More options	Displays additional options, such as Show device frame, Show media queries, Show rulers, Capture screenshot, and more
Toggle device toolbar	Toggles the device mode on and off

Using Google Chrome's device mode, you can simulate many types of mobile devices. You can edit the device list to add and remove devices. When you select a specific mobile device to simulate, you can select More options and then select Show device frame. Chrome displays the webpage within the frame of the mobile device selected. Figure 5–13 shows an example of nps.gov with an iPhone 6/7/8 device frame.

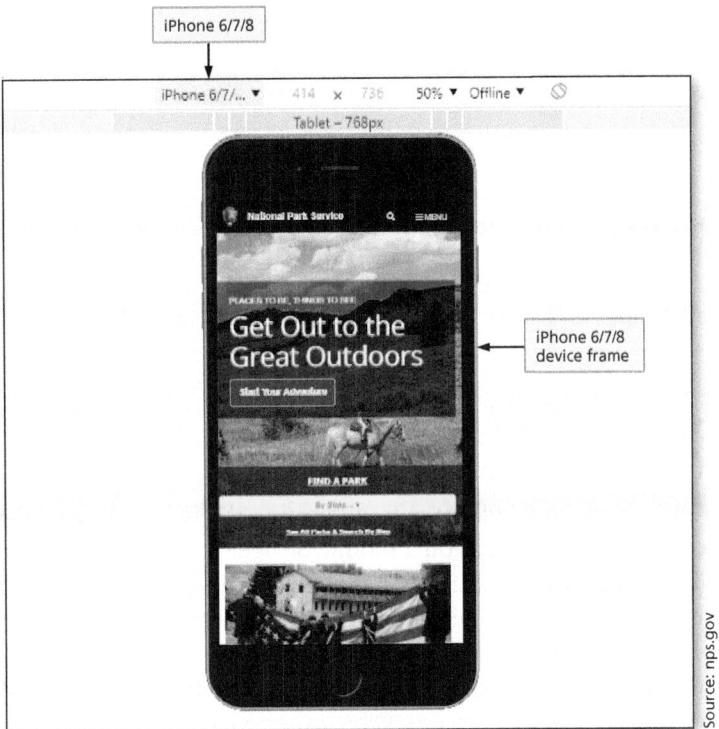

iPhone 6/7/8

iPhone 6/7/8 device frame

Source: nps.gov

Figure 5–13

In addition to displaying various mobile simulation options, you can also use the device mode to quickly set a viewport and view a webpage. Figure 5–14 displays the home page for nps.gov in the Tablet – 768px viewport.

Tablet – 768px viewport

Mobile M – 375px viewport

Mobile S – 320px viewport

Mobile L – 420px viewport

Laptop – 1024px viewport

Laptop L – 1440px viewport

point to a gray bar on the Device toolbar to display its viewport name

Source: nps.gov

Figure 5–14

As shown in Figure 5–14, you can quickly select a viewport for three mobile sizes (small – 320px, medium – 375px, and large – 420px), a tablet viewport at 768 pixels, a laptop viewport at 1,024 pixels, and a larger laptop or desktop at 1,440 pixels from the device toolbar.

BTW

Device Emulators
Device emulators are used to emulate a mobile application on a mobile device.

Mozilla Firefox and Microsoft Edge also provide similar developer tools. As you develop a webpage, use a device simulator to view your webpages and ensure they are displayed as intended.

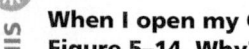

When I open my Google Chrome developer tools, my screen looks different from Figure 5–12 through Figure 5–14. Why?
Figure 5–12 through Figure 5–14 show what the development tools looked like at the time this book was written. The user interface for Google Chrome may change over time.

Steps in a Mobile-First Strategy

When you want to implement a mobile-first strategy with an existing website, you must first analyze each page to determine the most essential content and whether to hide some of the content on a mobile device.

The fitness website already has page content, so you need to analyze each page to select the most essential content and then design the content for a mobile viewport.

To apply a mobile-first strategy, open your CSS file and modify the existing style rules so they apply to a mobile viewport. You will also add new style rules to further improve the site to create an enjoyable experience for mobile device users. When implementing a mobile-first strategy, list styles for the mobile viewport first in the style sheet. You will then create a media query with style rules for tablet, followed by a media query with style rules for desktop. The media queries will include style rules that apply only to tablet and desktop viewports, respectively. (You create media queries in Chapter 6.) An important best practice is to list your viewport styles and media queries in order from the smallest to the largest device.

You will modify the current Forward Fitness website by implementing a mobile-first responsive design strategy. To begin, you will modify and remove certain style rules. In addition, you will only view changes in a mobile viewport. The first task is to add a comment to note where the mobile style rules begin. Then you will modify the header style rule and create a new style rule for the image within the header element.

To Add a Comment for Mobile Styles

Before you create mobile style rules in your CSS file, begin with a comment to signify where the style rules begin. This is a good coding practice and gives a future developer working on the site clear insight about the location of the mobile styles. The following steps add a new comment to note mobile styles in a CSS file.

1 Open styles.css in your text editor, place the insertion point at the end of Line 22 and press the ENTER key twice to insert new Lines 23 and 24.

2 On Line 24, type `/* Style rules for mobile viewport */` to insert a new comment (Figure 5–15).

```
19  img {
20      max-width: 100%;
21      display: block;
22  }
23
24  /* Style rules for mobile viewport */
25
26  /* Style rules for header */
```

Line 24 → 24

new comment inserted

Figure 5–15

Sticky Elements

As you have learned, header content appears at the top of a webpage. Common header content includes the company name or logo. Depending on the design, you may want the company name or logo to remain at the top of the webpage as the user scrolls down. To accomplish this task, you create a fixed or sticky header, known as a **sticky element**. To create a sticky element, you specify a position property with a value of sticky. You also specify a top property with a value of zero. The following is an example of a style rule to create a sticky header.

```
header {

        position: -webkit-sticky;

        position: sticky;

        top: 0;

}
```

In the above example, the position property is used two times; once with the value -webkit-sticky and again with the value sticky. Some browsers require a prefix, such as -webkit-, for certain CSS properties to work. In this case, the -webkit- prefix is required for compatibility with the Safari browser to apply the sticky value for the position property.

What other CSS properties require a prefix?
Several other CSS properties require a prefix, such as transition and animation. Note that this requirement may change over time. At one time, prefixes were required to create CSS gradients, but this is no longer the case. To determine if a prefix is needed for a specific CSS property, visit w3.org or w3schools.com.

CONSIDER THIS

To Create a Sticky Header

1 ADD META VIEWPORT ELEMENT | 2 CREATE STICKY HEADER | 3 ADD CUSTOM FONTS
4 STYLE PAGES FOR MOBILE VIEWPORT | 5 STYLE MAP FOR MOBILE VIEWPORT

You have already created a style rule for the header element but now need to modify it for a mobile viewport and to make it appear as a fixed or sticky element. *Why? The previous design uses a two-column layout for the header and the nav. Use a single-column design for a mobile viewport for a simplified design.* The following steps revise the header style rule and create a new style rule for the header img selector.

- With styles.css open in your text editor, delete the float and width declarations within the header style rule on Lines 27 and 28 to remove them.

- On Line 28, increase the indent if necessary, and then type **position: -webkit-sticky;** to add a new declaration.

- Press the ENTER key to add a new Line 29 and then type **position: sticky;** to add a new declaration.

- Press the ENTER key to add a new Line 30 and then type **top: 0;** to add a new declaration.

- Press the ENTER key to add a new Line 31 and then type **background-color: #000;** to add a new declaration.

- Press the ENTER key to add a new Line 32 and then type **height: 190px;** to add a new declaration (Figure 5–16).

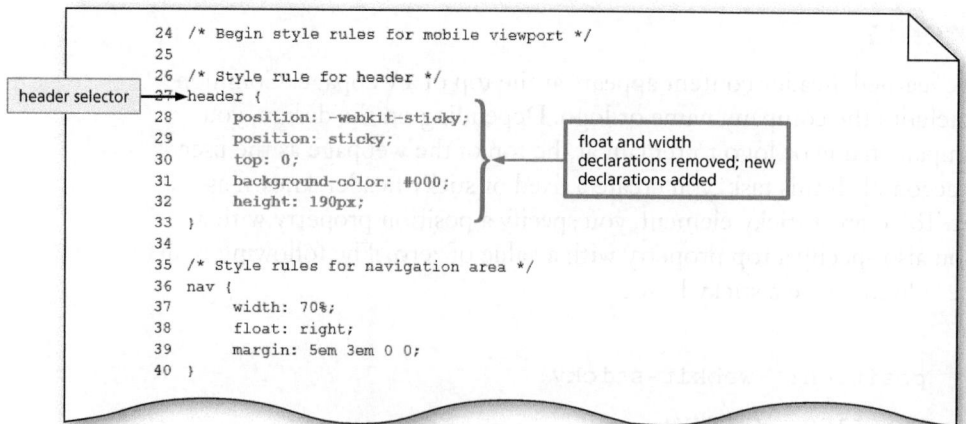

```
24  /* Begin style rules for mobile viewport */
25
26  /* Style rule for header */
27  header {
28      position: -webkit-sticky;
29      position: sticky;
30      top: 0;
31      background-color: #000;
32      height: 190px;
33  }
34
35  /* Style rules for navigation area */
36  nav {
37      width: 70%;
38      float: right;
39      margin: 5em 3em 0 0;
40  }
```

header selector → 27

float and width declarations removed; new declarations added

Figure 5–16

Why do I need to add the position property twice within the same style rule?
You need to design for cross-browser compatibility. The first declaration uses the -webkit- prefix to support Safari browsers. The second declaration specifies a position property for all other major browsers.

Why do I need to specify a black background color for the header when the same background color is already specified for the body?
Since the header element will now be sticky, you need to specify a background color so it does not appear as transparent when the user scrolls down, which will make the logo appear on top of the subsequent elements.

2

- Place your insertion point after the closing brace on Line 33 and press the ENTER key twice to insert new Lines 34 and 35.

- On Line 35, type **header img {** to insert a new selector and opening brace.

- Press the ENTER key to add a new Line 36, press the TAB key to increase the indent, and then type **margin: 0 auto;** to add a new declaration.

- Press the ENTER key to add a new Line 37, press the SHIFT+TAB keys to decrease the indent, and then type **}** to insert a closing brace (Figure 5–17).

```
24  /* Begin style rules for mobile viewport */
25
26  /* Style rule for header */
27  header {
28      position: -webkit-sticky;
29      position: sticky;
30      top: 0;
31      background-color: #000;
32      height: 190px;
33  }
34
35  header img {
36      margin: 0 auto;
37  }
```

Line 35 → 35

style rule created for header img

Figure 5–17

What is the purpose of the new style rule for the image within the header?
This style rule centers the logo on the webpage. The zero value is for the top and bottom margins and the auto value is for the left and right margins. When you specify auto as the value for left and right margins, it centers the content.

- Save your changes.
- Open the index.html file in Google Chrome to view the page.
- Press the F12 key to open the Chrome developer tools (Figure 5–18).

Figure 5–18

Q&A

My DevTools dock appeared on the bottom of the screen. Can I change this?
Yes. You can customize the location of your DevTools dock to be on left side, right side, bottom, or in a separate window. To change the Dock side location, tap or click the Customize and control DevTools button and then select your preferred Dock side location.

Why does the navigation appear to the right and span two lines?
Depending on the size of your monitor, your navigation may or may not appear on two lines. You have made an adjustment to the header element, which affects the nav element because you had previously designed them to be side-by-side in two columns. You will continue to edit the style sheet to improve the appearance of the navigation and the rest of the website.

- Tap or click the Toggle device toolbar to display device mode.
- If necessary, tap or click the Mobile S – 320px (gray) bar (Figure 5–19).

device mode

Mobile S – 320px (gray) bar

Toggle device toolbar

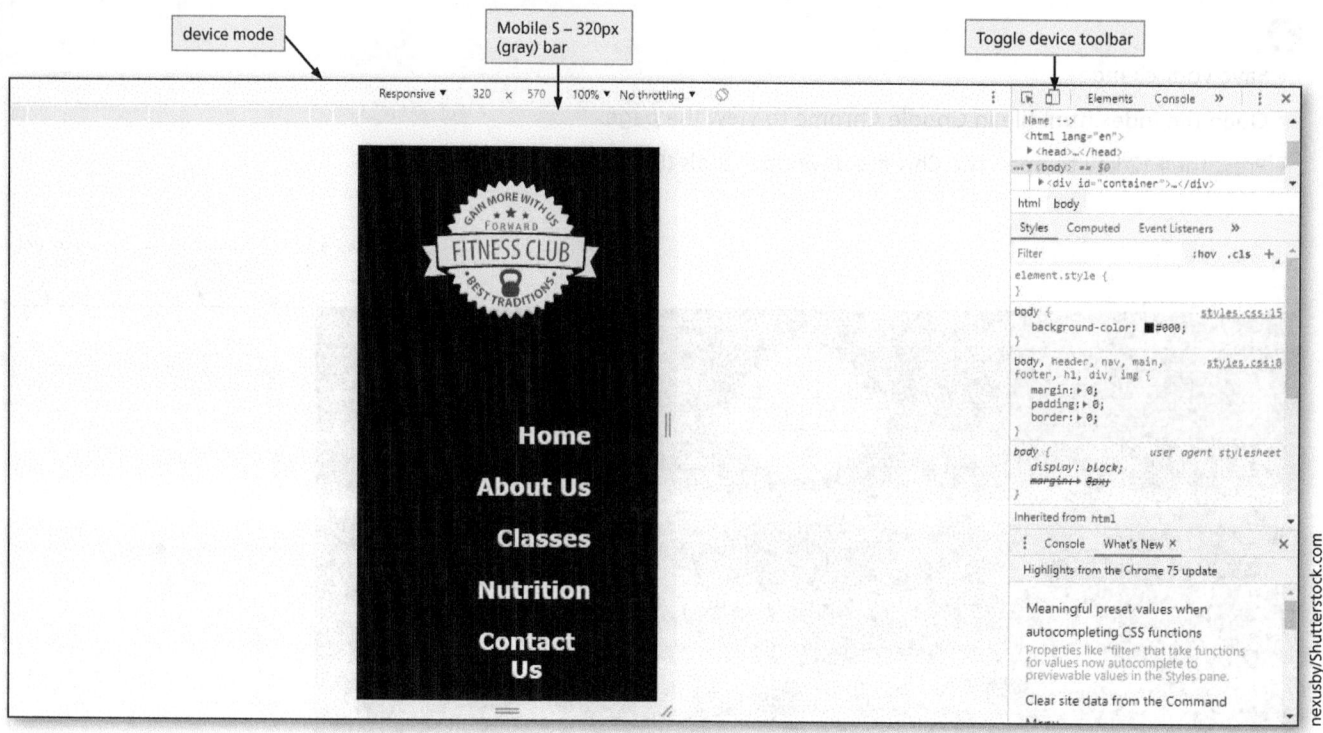

Figure 5–19

 Q&A Why does the navigation appear vertical?
The mobile viewport is more restrictive and does not permit the navigation to appear horizontally with the current style rules. You will edit the navigation in future steps.

5

- Scroll down to display the sticky header, adjusting your browser window as necessary to scroll vertically (Figure 5–20).

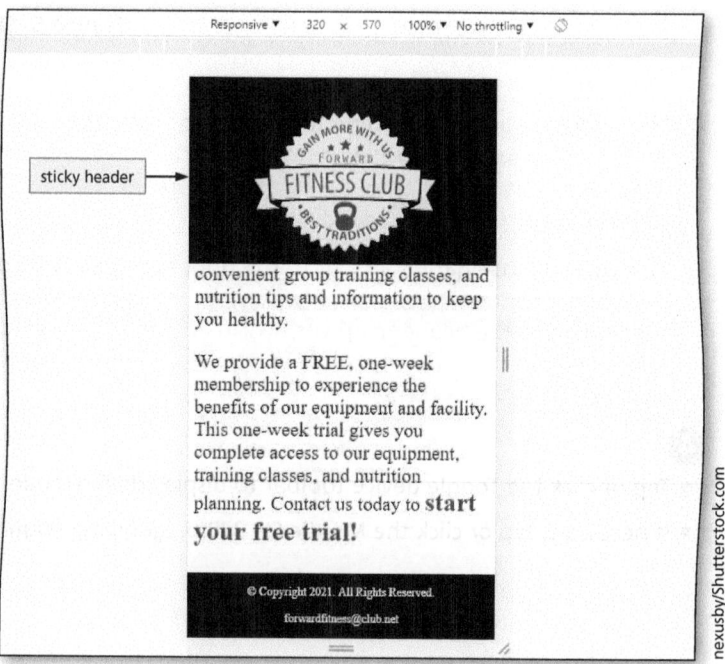

sticky header

Figure 5–20

Other Ways

1. Press the CTRL+SHIFT+I keys

2. Tap or click Customize and control Google Chrome, select More Tools, select Developer tools

Responsive Navigation

The navigation system for a website can look different in each viewport. Many mobile viewport designs use a hamburger button or icon to display or toggle a navigation system. The hamburger button consists of three horizontal, parallel lines. Figure 5–21 shows the hamburger button in the upper-left corner of the w3schools. com mobile viewport.

Figure 5–21

To make the hamburger element functional, you need to write some JavaScript code. You will learn more about how to integrate a hamburger button and make it functional with JavaScript in Chapter 10.

Another mobile design option for a navigation system is to display a vertical navigation bar on the page. This design provides a clear and easy-to-use navigation system in a single column. You can create this design using CSS.

To accomplish this single-column design, you add style rules to the style sheet to format the navigation list items without displaying a bullet. You will also apply a background color, text color, and rounded border to make each link look like a button. You will then remove the underlining that appears with links by default.

To Edit the nav Style Rule for Mobile Viewports

Modify the style rule for the **nav** element to only include padding and margin properties. You will modify the style rule for the unordered list in future steps; however, you must first modify the style rule for the nav selector to use only properties related to padding and margin. The following steps edit the styles for the nav selector in a CSS file.

1 In styles.css, delete the declarations on Lines 41 through 43 to remove the width, float, and margin declarations.

Q&A Why am I removing these properties?

These styles are for a desktop viewport. You need to first style the nav for a mobile viewport. You will design a new nav for tablet and desktop viewports in Chapter 6.

2 On Line 41, indent if necessary, and then type **padding: 1%;** to add a new declaration.

3 Press the ENTER key to insert a new Line 42 and then type **margin-bottom: 1%;** to add a new declaration (Figure 5–22).

4 Save your changes.

```
39  /* Style rules for navigation area */
40  nav {
41      padding: 1%;
42      margin-bottom: 1%;
43  }
44
45  nav ul {
46      list-style-type: none;
47      margin: 0;
48      text-align: right;
49  }
```

Line 41 →41

float, width, and margin declarations removed; new declarations added

Figure 5–22

To Edit the nav ul Style Rule for Mobile Viewports

Recall that you already have a style rule that targets an unordered list within the nav element. This style rule removes the default bullet marker, removes margin, and aligns text right. Edit the style rule to align text center. The following steps modify a nav ul selector and declarations in a CSS file.

1 Locate the nav ul selector that begins on Line 45 to prepare to modify the style rule.

2 Delete the declaration for margin on Line 47 to remove it.

3 If necessary, move the text-align declaration up a line to Line 47. Replace the right value with **center** to change the text-align value.

4 Place your insertion point after the img selector on Line 8, and then type **, ul** to add the ul selector to the CSS reset style rule (Figure 5–23).

5 Save your changes.

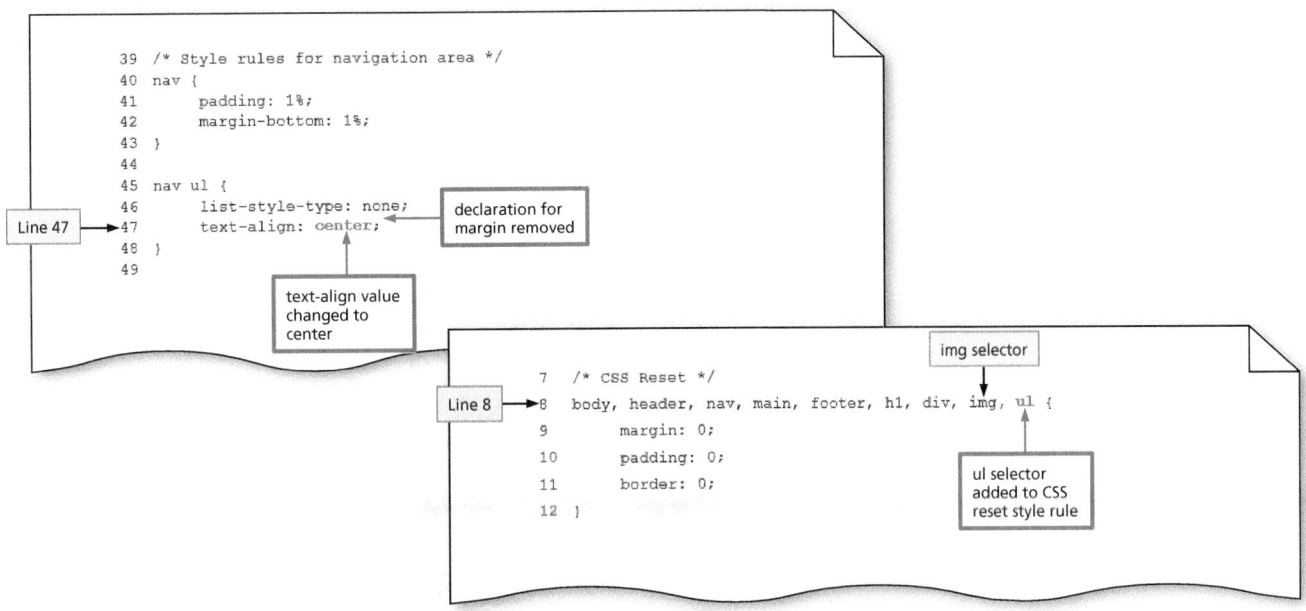

Figure 5–23

To Edit the nav li Style Rule for Mobile Viewports

The current style rule for the nav li selector sets several font properties and sets the display to an inline-block. Remove the display declaration as this pertains to a desktop viewport. In addition, remove the font weight and then add a declaration to apply a top border. The following steps modify the style rule for the nav li selector for mobile displays.

1 Locate the nav li selector that begins on Line 50 to prepare to modify the style rule.

2 Delete the display and font-weight declarations on Lines 51 and 54 to remove these declarations from the style rule.

3 Place your insertion point at the end of Line 52, and then press the ENTER key to insert a new Line 53.

4 On Line 53, type **border-top: 1px solid #fff;**   to add a new declaration (Figure 5–24).

```
39  /* Style rules for navigation area */
40  nav {
41      padding: 1%;
42      margin-bottom: 1%;
43  }
44
45  nav ul {
46      list-style-type: none;
47      text-align: center;
48  }
49
50  nav li {
51      font-size: 1.5em;
52      font-family: Verdana, Arial, sans-serif;
53      border-top: 1px solid #fff;
54  }
```

nav li selector

declaration for display removed

new declaration added for border-top property

declaration for font-weight removed

Figure 5–24

5 Save your changes and open index.html in Google Chrome's device mode to display the webpage in a mobile viewport (Figure 5–25).

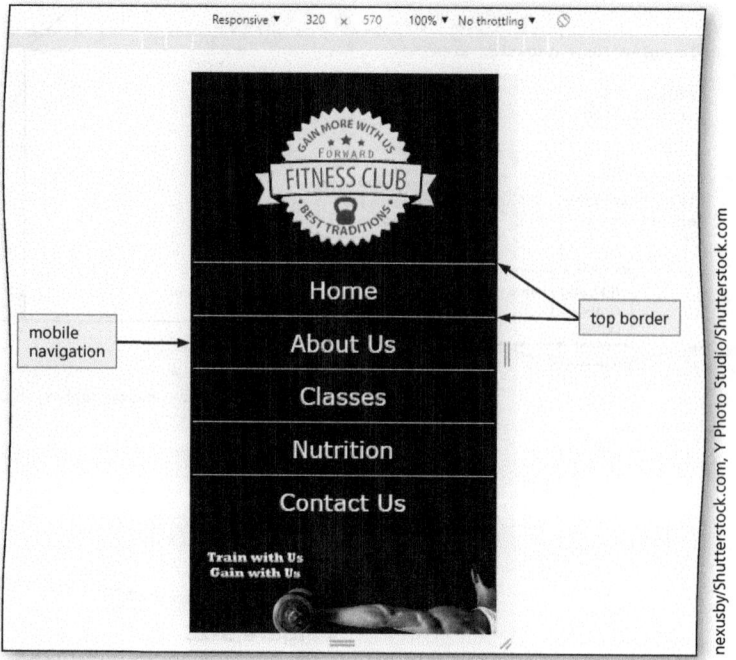

nexusby/Shutterstock.com, Y Photo Studio/Shutterstock.com

Figure 5–25

Q&A
I prefer the look of the hamburger icon. Why did we not add it here?
The hamburger icon requires JavaScript to make it functional. You will add the hamburger icon in Chapter 10.

Custom Fonts

As discussed in Chapter 1, typography is a design element to consider when designing a website. Effective use of typography enhances the visual look and appeal of a website. Today's modern browsers support standard fonts, such as Times New Roman, Arial, Georgia, and Verdana. Traditionally, for a browser to use a specified font, it had to be stored on the local client machine. Today, you can use many custom fonts by downloading them onto your web server or by linking to them in your HTML files. Two popular font solutions include Google Fonts and Adobe Fonts.

Google Fonts is a free web font service provided by Google at fonts.google.com. Google Fonts includes a large selection of custom fonts that you can integrate within your webpage design. Figure 5–26 shows the Google Fonts page.

On the Google Fonts page, you can search for a specific font, type text to see it used with fonts on the page, adjust the font size, and set the background color. In Figure 5–26, the text, Welcome to the Forward Fitness Club, has been typed into the Type something text box, and the Google Fonts page displays the text in several fonts. To use a particular font or set of fonts, you tap or click the Select this font button for each font you want to use. Google Fonts then provides you with a link element to add to the webpages that will use the font, as well as the font family declaration(s) needed for the style sheet. Popular Google Fonts include Crimson Text, Cairo, Karla, and Roboto.

Adobe Fonts provides a similar service at fonts.adobe.com; however, to use Adobe Fonts, you must have a paid subscription to Adobe Creative Cloud.

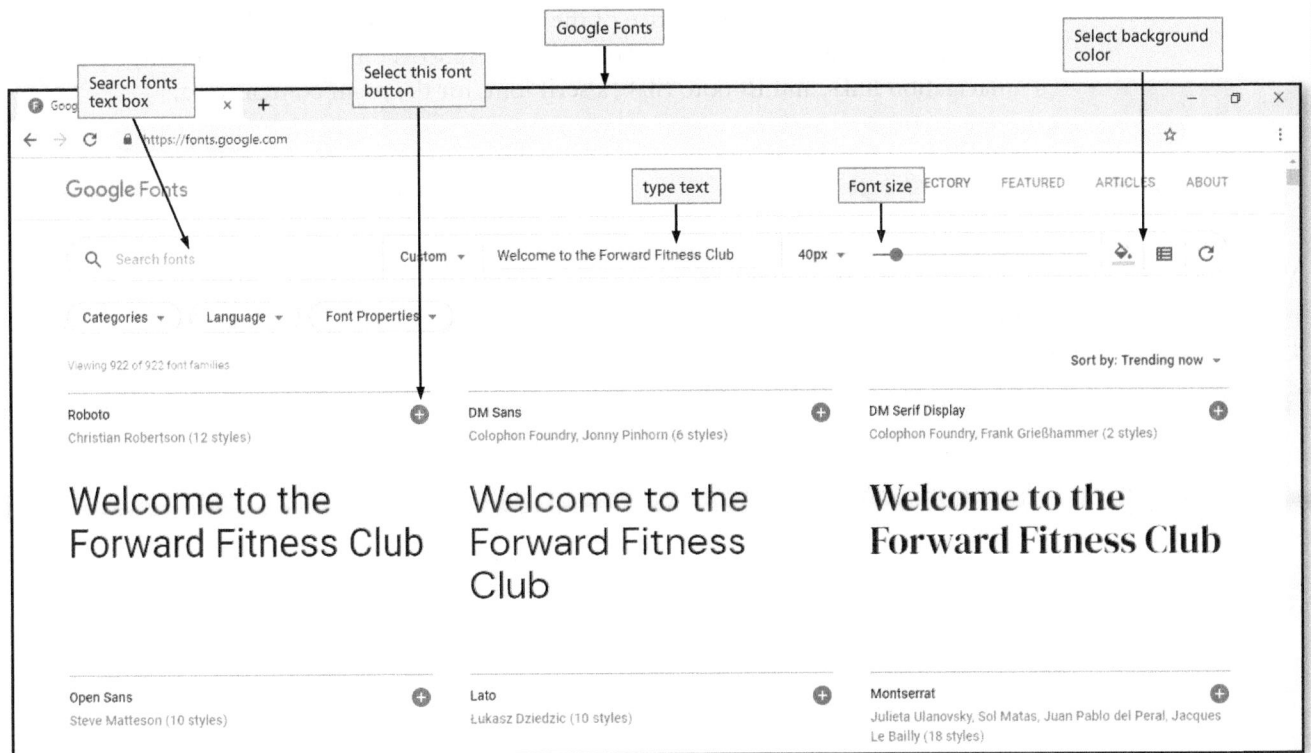

Source: fonts.google.com

Figure 5–26

Determine which font(s) to use within your design as follows:

1. Ensure that the webpage content is legible. If the user cannot easily read the page content, you need to use a different font.

2. Do not use too many different types of fonts. Limit your variety of fonts to three. Use one font for the navigation, another font for main content, and another font for call to action items. A webpage that uses an excessive number of fonts can appear unorganized and unprofessional.

3. Pair a serif font with a sans-serif font. A serif font uses small lines or embellishments at the ends of letters. Times New Roman is a type of serif font. A sans-serif font does not include these extra line details. An example of a sans-serif font is Verdana. Many online resources can help you pair fonts, such as fontpair.co.

Figure 5–27 shows an example of a website that has paired a sans-serif and serif font.

Source: csszengarden.com

Figure 5–27

To enhance the appearance of the Forward Fitness Club website, you will integrate custom Google Fonts. You will use Francois One, a sans-serif font, for the navigation links, and Roboto Slab, a serif font, for the main content area.

To Integrate a Custom Google Font

You will improve the design of the Forward Fitness Club website by integrating custom Google Fonts. You will use the Francois One font for the navigation links and Roboto Slab for the main content. *Why? Using custom fonts improves the overall design of a website.* The following steps integrate a custom Google font within the Forward Fitness Club website.

- Open fonts.google.com in your browser to prepare to search for custom fonts.

- In the Search fonts text box, type **Francois One** to display the Francois One font on the webpage (Figure 5–28).

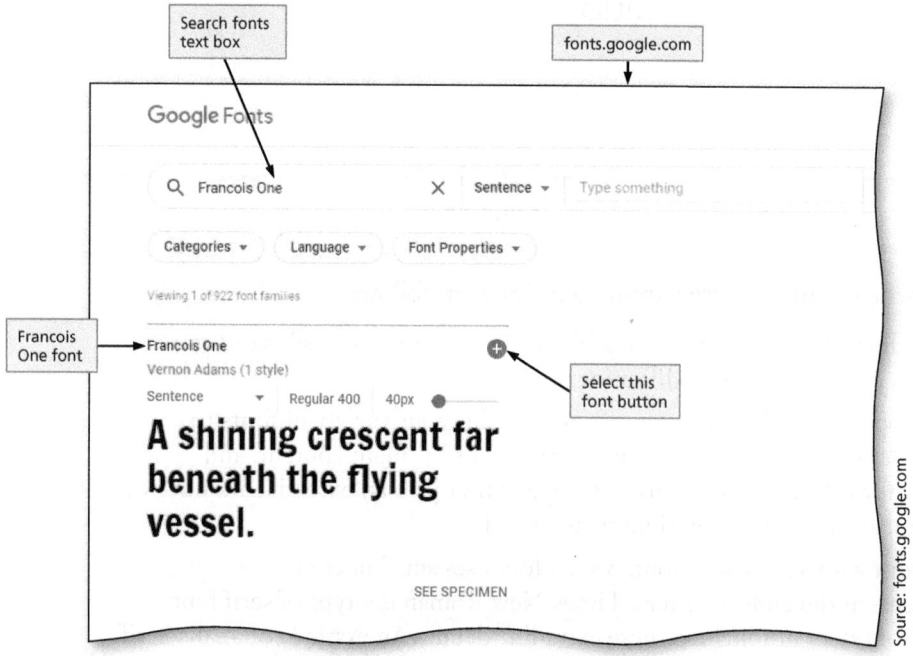

Figure 5–28

Source: fonts.google.com

I cannot find this font. What should I do?
Google Fonts may update their fonts from time to time. If the Francois One font is no longer available, review Google's current fonts to find a similar sans-serif font. Your instructor may have you select another font.

- Tap or click the Select this font button to select the font.

- Return to the Search fonts text box, remove Francois One, and then type **Roboto Slab** to display the Roboto Slab font on the webpage.

- Tap or click the Select this font button to select the font (Figure 5–29).

Figure 5–29

3

- Tap or click the Families Selected collapsible window near the bottom of the webpage to expand the window (Figure 5–30).

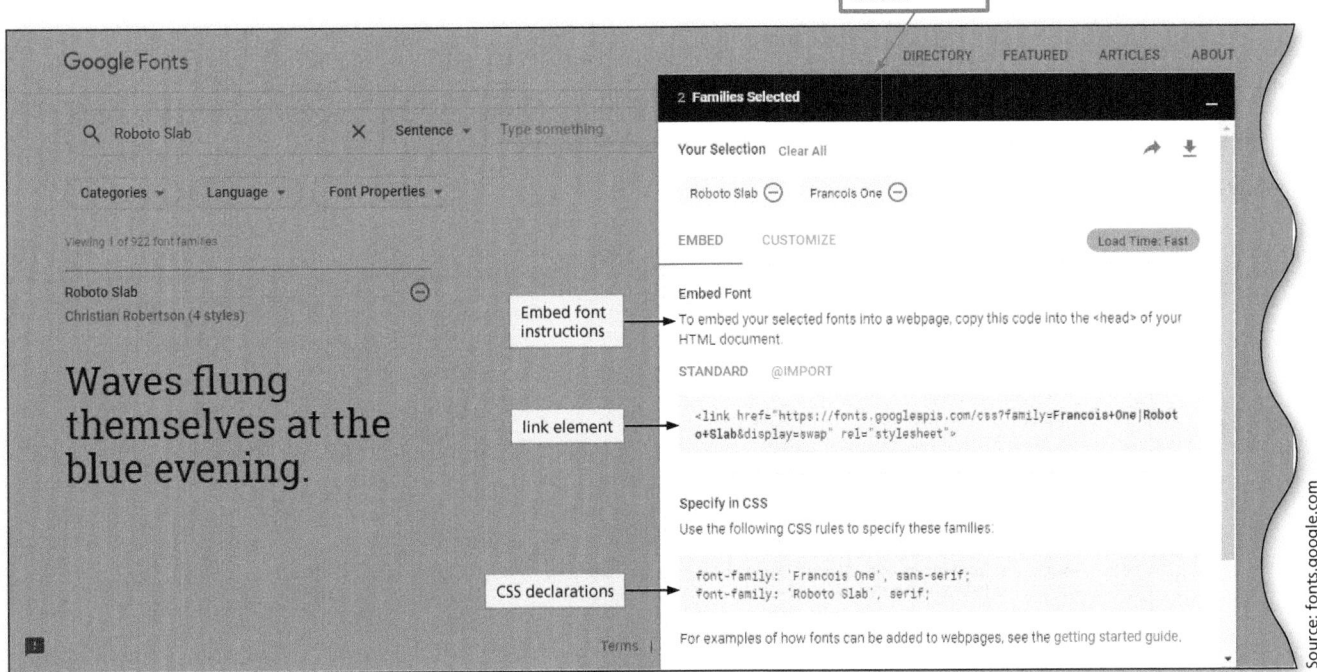

Figure 5–30

4

- Read the Embed Font instructions to understand how to embed these fonts.

- Highlight the link element provided below the text, STANDARD, to select it.

- Press the **CTRL+C** keys to copy the link element and keep your browser window open (Figure 5–31).

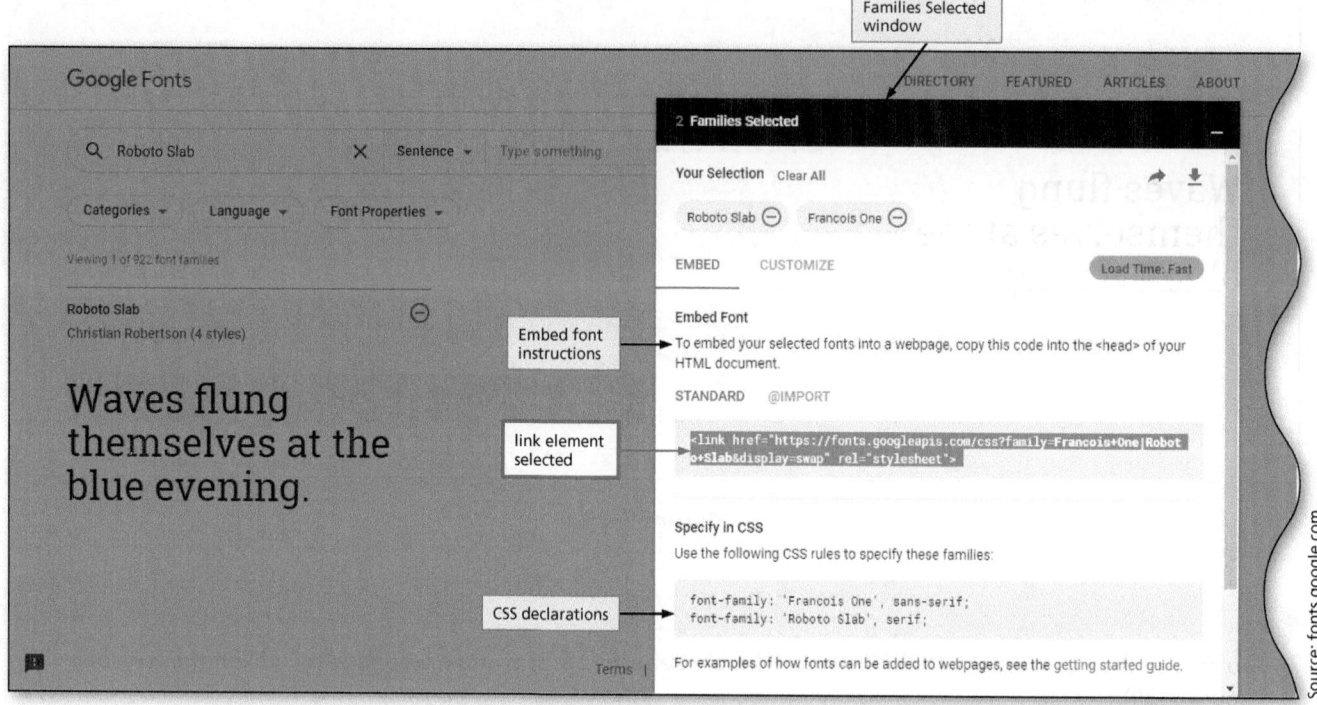

Figure 5–31

5

- Open index.html in your text editor, place your insertion point at the end of Line 8, press the **ENTER** key to insert a new Line 9, and then press the **CTRL+V** keys to paste the link element.

- Save your changes (Figure 5–32).

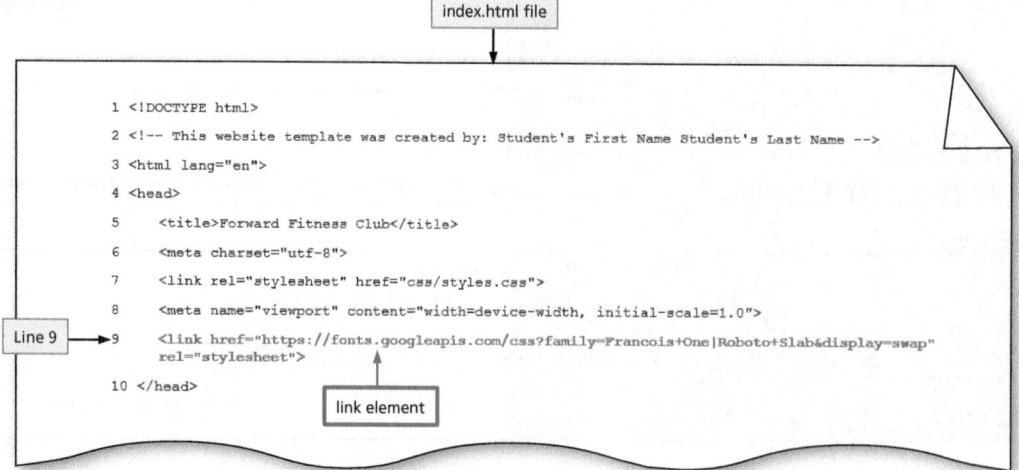

Figure 5–32

- Open about.html in your text editor, place your insertion point at the end of Line 8, press the ENTER key to insert a new Line 9, and then press the CTRL+V keys to paste the link element.

- Save your changes.

- Open contact.html in your text editor, place your insertion point at the end of Line 8, press the ENTER key to insert a new Line 9, and then press the CTRL+V keys to paste the link element.

- Save your changes.

- Open template.html in your text editor, place your insertion point at the end of Line 8, press the ENTER key to insert a new Line 9, and then press the CTRL+V keys to paste the link element.

- Save your changes (Figure 5–33).

template.html file

```
1 <!DOCTYPE html>
2 <!-- This website template was created by: Student's First Name Student's Last Name -->
3 <html lang="en">
4 <head>
5     <title>Forward Fitness Club</title>
6     <meta charset="utf-8">
7     <link rel="stylesheet" href="css/styles.css">
8     <meta name="viewport" content="width=device-width, initial-scale=1.0">
9     <link href="https://fonts.googleapis.com/css?family=Francois+One|Roboto+Slab&display=swap"
        rel="stylesheet">
10 </head>
```

Line 9 → 9

link element

Figure 5–33

Q&A

Why do I need to paste this link element within every webpage?

To use the custom Google fonts, you must provide instructions to the browser about where to obtain the custom fonts. Note how the link element includes a URL to fonts.google.com and then specifies the fonts to display.

- Return to your browser window to display the Google fonts webpage.

- Read the Specify in CSS instructions to understand how to apply these custom fonts in your style sheet.

- In the Families Selected window, select the font-family value, `'Francois One', sans-serif;`, and then press the CTRL+C keys to copy the value. Keep your browser window open.

- Return to your styles.css file in your text editor, find the font-family declaration for the nav li on Line 52, remove the current value (Verdana, Arial, sans-serif;), and then press CTRL+V to paste the new value (Figure 5–34).

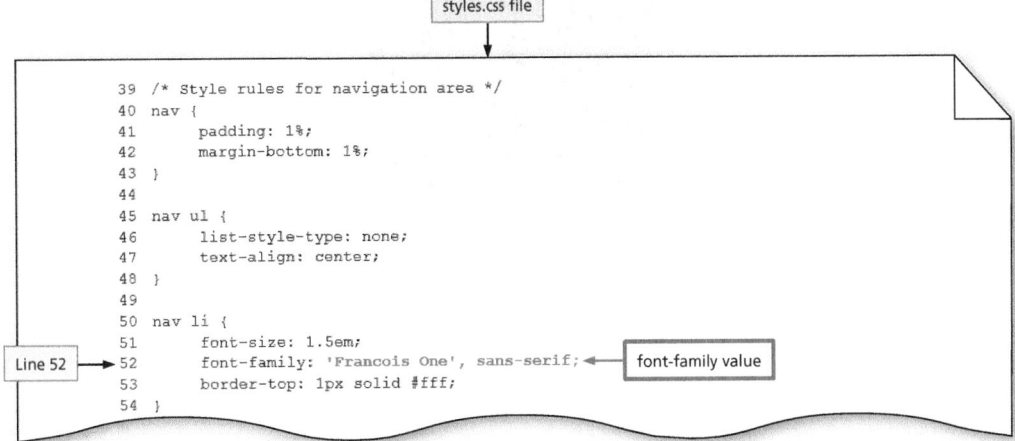

styles.css file

```
39 /* Style rules for navigation area */
40 nav {
41     padding: 1%;
42     margin-bottom: 1%;
43 }
44
45 nav ul {
46     list-style-type: none;
47     text-align: center;
48 }
49
50 nav li {
51     font-size: 1.5em;
52     font-family: 'Francois One', sans-serif;
53     border-top: 1px solid #fff;
54 }
```

Line 52 → 52   font-family value

Figure 5–34

- Return to your browser window to display the Google fonts webpage.

- In the Families Selected window, select the declaration, `font-family: 'Roboto Slab', serif;`, and then press the CTRL+C keys to copy the declaration.

- Return to your styles.css file in your text editor, and then find the style rule for the main selector that begins on Line 65 to prepare to add a new declaration.

- Place your insertion point at the end of Line 69, press the ENTER key to insert a new Line 70, and then press the CTRL+V keys to paste the declaration (Figure 5–35).

```
64  /* Style rules for main content */
65  main {
66      clear: left;
67      background-color: #fff;
68      padding: 2%;
69      font-size: 1.25em;
70      font-family: 'Roboto Slab', serif;    ← font-family
71  }                                            declaration
72
```
Line 70

Figure 5–35

- Save your changes and then open index.html in Google Chrome device mode to view your changes (Figure 5–36).

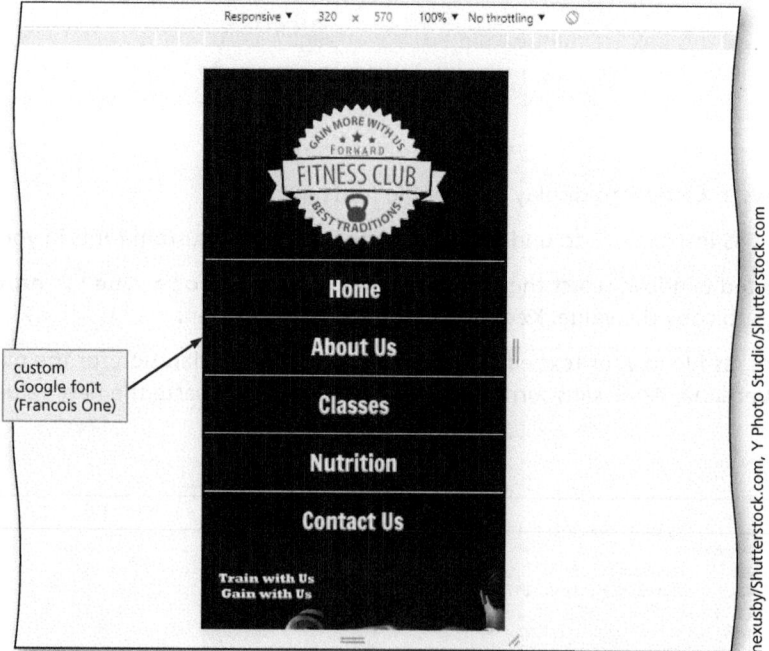

custom
Google font
(Francois One)

nexusby/Shutterstock.com, Y Photo Studio/Shutterstock.com

Figure 5–36

10

- Scroll down to view the custom Google font used for the main element (Figure 5–37).

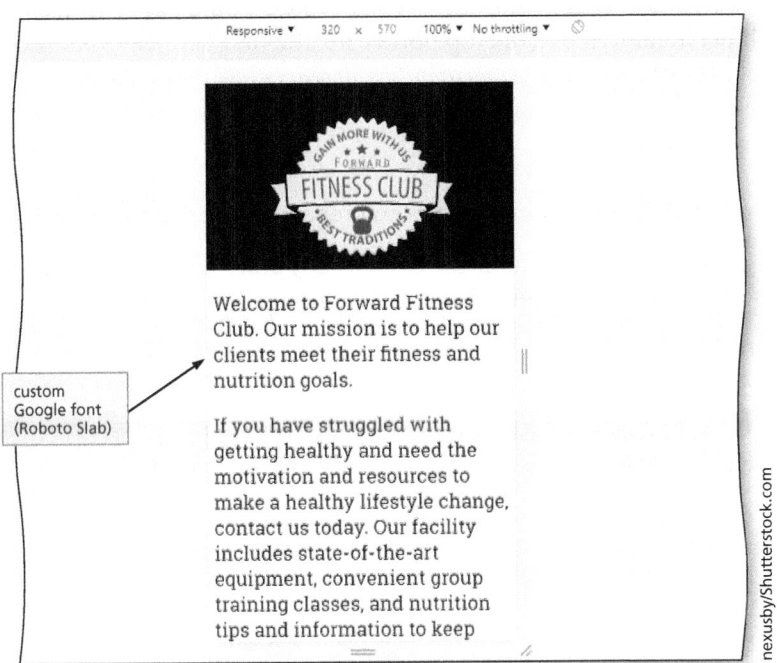

Figure 5–37

Pseudo-Classes

A **pseudo-class** can be used with a selector to specify the state of an element. For example, you can specify a style to apply when a mouse hovers over an element. Likewise, you can specify a style to apply to only a first or last element, such as lists or paragraphs. A pseudo-class consists of a colon, followed by the name of the pseudo-class. The following example creates a style rule for the first list item.

```
li:first-child {
        font-size: 1.25em;
        color: #000066;
}
```

The above style rule will apply to the first list item within a website. Pseudo-classes are grouped into the following categories: dynamic, target, language, UI element states, and structural. Table 5–3 summarizes some common structural pseudo-classes.

Table 5–3 Pseudo-Classes

Pseudo-class	Example	Description
:first-child	li:first-child	Applies to the first list item element
:last-child	li:last-child	Applies to the last list item element
:nth-child(n)	li:nth-child(3)	Applies to the third list item element
:root	:root	Applies to the document's root element
:first-of-type	dt:first-of-type	Applies to every first description term element
:last-of-type	dt:last-of-type	Applies to every last description term element

You will learn more about other pseudo-classes in future chapters. For now, you will learn how to use the first-child pseudo-class to remove the top border for the first list item element within the navigation system for the Forward Fitness Club website.

To Remove the Top Border for the nav li Style Rule

The navigation system on the Forward Fitness home page includes a top border above each list item. Remove the top border for the first list item to improve the overall look. *Why? Because no navigation link appears above the first list item, it does not need a top border.* The following steps create a new style rule that applies to the first child of the nav li selector.

1 Return to styles.css in your text editor to prepare to create a new style rule.

2 Place your insertion point after the closing curly brace on Line 54 and then press the ENTER key twice to insert new Lines 55 and 56.

3 On Line 56, type **nav li:first-child {** to insert a new selector and opening brace.

4 Press the ENTER key to add a new Line 57, press the TAB key to increase the indent, and then type **border-top: none;** to add a new declaration.

5 Press the ENTER key to add a new Line 58, press the SHIFT+TAB keys to decrease the indent, and then type **}** to insert a closing brace (Figure 5–38).

styles.css file

```
50  nav li {
51      font-size: 1.5em;
52      font-family: 'Francois One', sans-serif;
53      border-top: 1px solid #fff;
54  }
55
56  nav li:first-child {
57      border-top: none;
58  }
```

Line 56

style rule created for nav li:first-child

Figure 5–38

6 Save your changes and then open index.html in Google Chrome device mode to view your changes (Figure 5–39).

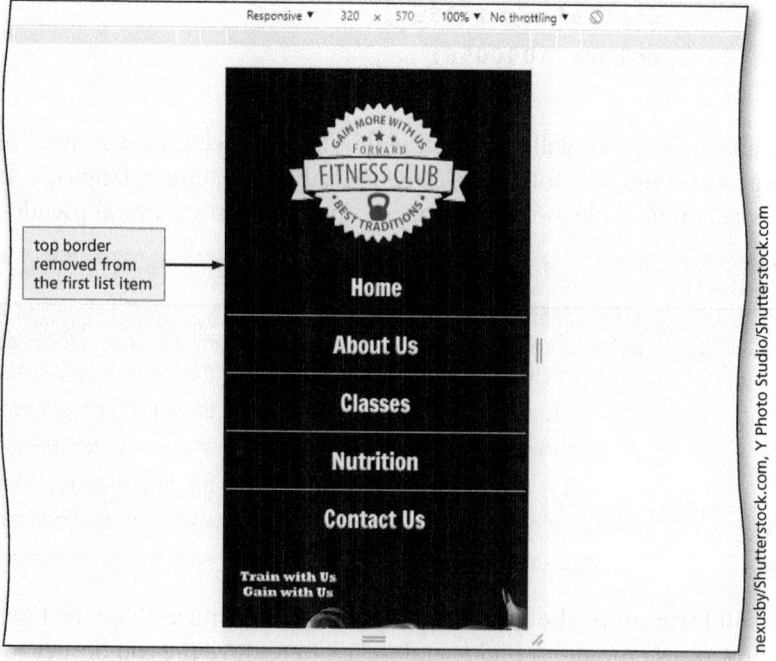

top border removed from the first list item

Responsive ▼   320   ×   570   100% ▼ No throttling ▼

nexusby/Shutterstock.com, Y Photo Studio/Shutterstock.com

Figure 5–39

To Edit the nav li a Style Rule

You have already created a style rule for the nav li a selector. Modify the style rule by removing the text-align property and its value. The following steps modify the style rule for the nav li a selector in a CSS file.

1 Return to styles.css in your text editor and locate the style rule for the nav li a selector, which begins on Line 60, to prepare to edit the style rule.

2 Delete Line 63 to remove the text-align declaration from the style rule (Figure 5–40).

Q&A Why do I need to delete the text-align declaration?
The style rule for the nav ul selector already specifies the text-align property.

```
56  nav li:first-child {
57      border-top: none;
58  }
59
60  nav li a {
61      display: block;
62      color: #fff;
63      padding: 0.5em 1em;
64      text-decoration: none;
65  }
```

nav li a selector → (pointing to line 60)

text-align: center; removed → (pointing to line 62)

Figure 5–40

Break Point: If you want to take a break, this is a good place to do so. To resume at a later time, continue reading the text from this location forward.

Analyze the Home Page for Mobile-First Design

The content on the home page is now styled for a productive viewing experience on a mobile device, but the page content is still best suited to a desktop user. Instead of providing an introductory welcome message, display content a mobile device user wants to find quickly, such as the fitness club's hours and phone number with a telephone link.

You can add this essential information to the home page without removing the content for webpage visitors with a desktop device. To accomplish this task, use a **div** element to contain the content for mobile devices and another **div** element to contain the content for desktop displays. You then add a class attribute to each **div** element; add a class="mobile" attribute and value to the **div** element for the mobile content and add a class="tablet-desktop" attribute and value for the **div** element for the tablet and desktop content. You will then define styles to display the mobile class and hide the tablet-desktop class.

To Modify the Home Page

1 ADD META VIEWPORT ELEMENT | 2 CREATE STICKY HEADER | 3 ADD CUSTOM FONTS
4 STYLE PAGES FOR MOBILE VIEWPORT | 5 STYLE MAP FOR MOBILE VIEWPORT

Modify the home page to add essential content for a mobile user. First, create a new **div** element with a class="mobile" attribute and value, and then add the mobile content within this new **div** element. Next, modify the current <div id="intro"> tag by changing the id to a class and changing the intro value to tablet-desktop. *Why? When following a mobile-first strategy, provide the mobile user with the most important, essential page content and remove or hide the desktop content.* The following steps modify the home page content to follow a mobile-first strategy.

- Open index.html in your text editor to prepare to modify the page.
- Place your insertion point at the end of Line 37 and press the ENTER key twice to insert new Lines 38 and 39.
- On Line 39, press the TAB key to indent and then type `<div class="mobile">` to insert a new div element.
- Press the ENTER key twice to insert new Lines 40 and 41.
- On Line 41, increase the indent if necessary, and then type `<p>Welcome to Forward Fitness Club. Our mission is to help our clients meet their fitness and nutrition goals.</p>` to add a paragraph element.
- Press the ENTER key twice and type `<h3>FREE One-Week Trial Membership!</h3>` on Line 43 to add a heading 3 element.
- Press the ENTER key and type `<p>Call Us Today to Get Started</p>` to add a paragraph element.
- Press the ENTER key and type `<p class="tel-link"><a href="tel:8145559608">(814) 555-9608</a></p>` to add a paragraph element that includes a telephone link (Figure 5–41).

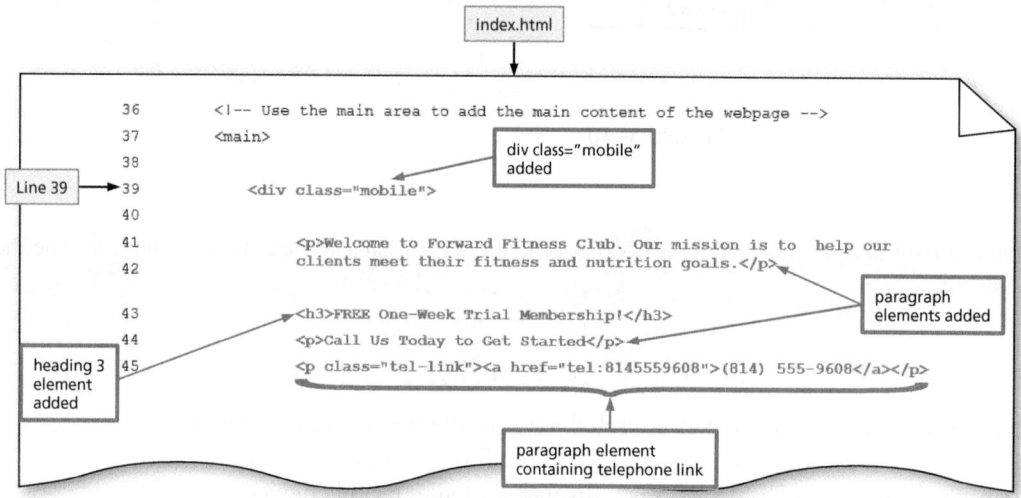

Figure 5–41

- Press the ENTER key twice and then type `<h4>Fitness Club Hours:</h4>` on Line 47 to insert a heading 4 element.
- Press the ENTER key and type `<ul class="hours">` on Line 48 to insert an unordered list with a class attribute.
- Press the ENTER key, increase the indent, and then type `<li>Mon-Thu: 6:00am-6:00pm</li>` on Line 49 to add a list item.
- Press the ENTER key and type `<li>Friday: 6:00am-4:00pm</li>` on Line 50 to add a second list item.
- Press the ENTER key and type `<li>Saturday: 8:00am-6:00pm</li>` on Line 51 to add a third list item.
- Press the ENTER key and type `<li>Sunday: Closed</li>` on Line 52 to add a fourth list item.
- Press the ENTER key, decrease the indent, and then type `</ul>` to close the unordered list.
- Press the ENTER key twice, decrease the indent, and then type `</div>` on Line 55 to close the div element (Figure 5–42).

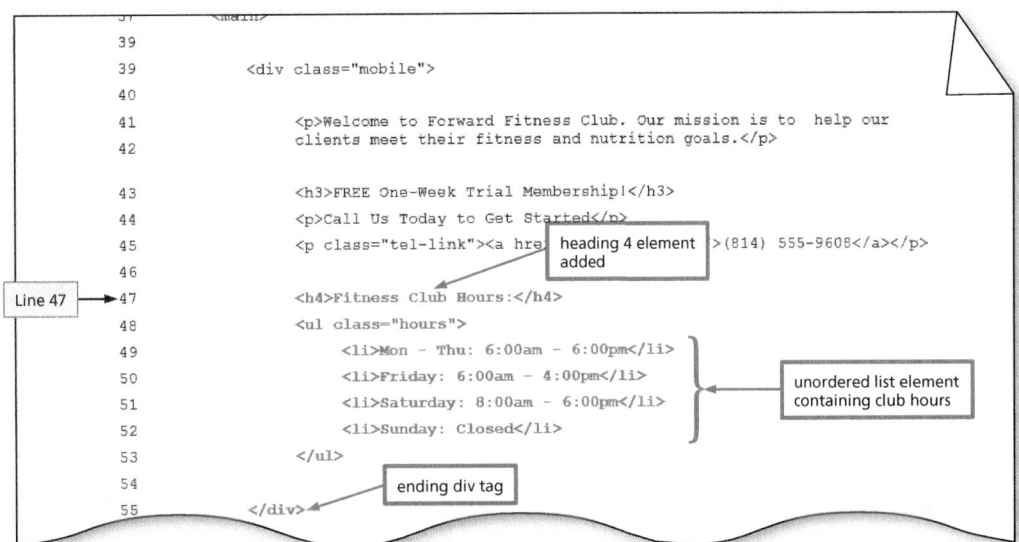

Figure 5–42

❸

- On Line 32, place the insertion point before the closing angle bracket and type `class="tablet-desktop"` to add a class attribute to the div element.
- On Line 57, change the id attribute to `class` and the intro value to `tablet-desktop` (Figure 5–43).

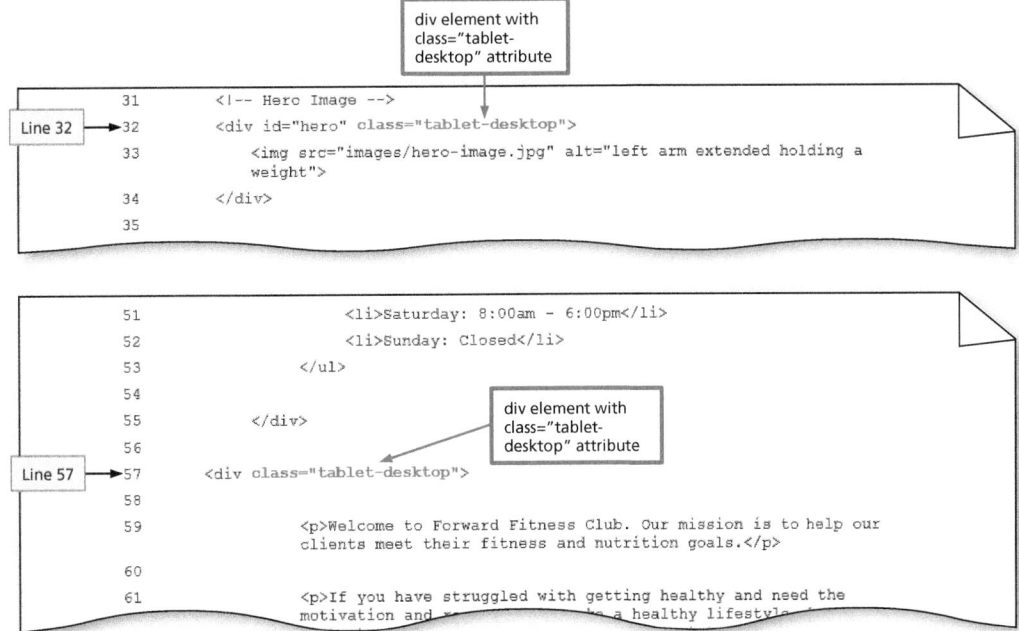

Figure 5–43

- Save your changes.

To Create a Style Rule for the mobile Class

Now that you have a mobile class attribute within the website, create a style rule to display the mobile class as a block element for the mobile viewport. *Why? In the mobile viewport, show the phone number with the link to make it easy for a mobile user to call the business. Use the block value with the display property to display the phone number as a block element.* The following steps create a style rule for the .mobile selector.

- If necessary, reopen styles.css in your text editor to prepare to create a style rule for the mobile class.
- Place your insertion point at the end of Line 65 and press the ENTER key twice to create new Lines 66 and 67.
- On Line 67, type `/* Show mobile class, hide tablet-desktop class */` to insert a comment.
- Press the ENTER key to create a new Line 68 and then type `.mobile {` to add a mobile class selector and opening curly brace.
- Press the ENTER key to create a new Line 69, increase the indent, and then type `display: block;` to add a declaration.
- Press the ENTER key to create a new Line 70, decrease the indent, and then type `}` to close the style rule (Figure 5–44).

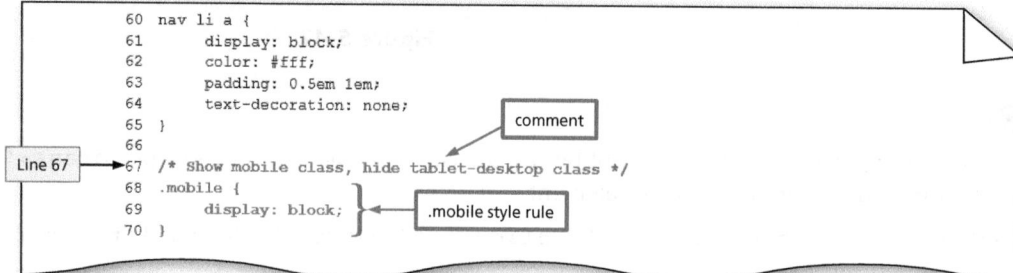

Figure 5–44

- Save your changes.

To Add a Style Rule for the tablet-desktop Class

Create a style rule to hide content in the desktop class. First, insert a .tablet-desktop selector and then set the **display** property to **none**. *Why? You do not want to display tablet or desktop content in the mobile viewport.* The following steps add the style rule for the .tablet-desktop selector.

- Place your insertion point at the end of Line 70 and press the ENTER key twice to create new Lines 71 and 72.
- On Line 72, type `.tablet-desktop {` to add a selector.
- Press the ENTER key, increase the indent, and then type `display: none;` to add a property and value.
- Press the ENTER key, decrease the indent, and then type `}` to close the new style rule (Figure 5–45).

```
67  /* Show mobile class, hide tablet-desktop class */
68  .mobile {
69      display: block;
70  }
71
72  .tablet-desktop {        .tablet-desktop
73      display: none;       style rule
74  }
75
76  /* Style rules for main content */
```
Line 72

Figure 5–45

Rounded Corners

By default, element borders use a 90-degree angle at each corner. You can see the angle when you specify a border all around an element. Likewise, images also have a default 90-degree angle at each corner. You can change this default appearance by applying rounded corners with CSS. The CSS property to round corners is border-radius. The following is an example of a style rule that uses the border-radius property:

```
main {
        border: 1px solid #000;
        border-radius: 5px;
}
```

In the example above, a solid border is applied to the main element. In addition, a border-radius of 5px is applied to each corner. The border radius property allows up to four values, which allows you to specify a different value for each corner. The following example applies a different value to each corner of the main element by specifying four different values:

```
main {
        border: 1px solid #000;
        border-radius: 2px 3px 4px 5px;
}
```

In the example above, 2px is applied to the top-left corner, 3px is applied to the top-right corner, 4px is applied to the bottom-right corner, and 5px is applied to the bottom-left corner. When you specify two values for the border-radius, one value applies to the top-left and bottom-right corners and the other value applies to the top-right and bottom-left corners. The following example uses two values for the border-radius property:

```
main {
        border: 1px solid #000;
        border-radius: 5px 10px;
}
```

In the example above, 5px is applied to the top-left and bottom-right corners, while 10px is applied to the top-right and bottom-left corners. When you specify three values for the border-radius, the first value applies to the top-left, the second value applies to the top-right and bottom-left corners, and the third value applies to the bottom-right corner. The following example uses three values for the border-radius property:

```
main {
        border: 1px solid #000;
        border-radius: 5px 10px 8px;
}
```

The home page for the Forward Fitness Club includes a telephone phone link. Use CSS to make the link appear as a button, making it more intuitive to the user to touch the link in order to make a phone call. Apply rounded corners to improve its appearance as a button.

To Add Style Rules for the tel-link Class

When you added mobile content to the home page, you added a tel-link class to a paragraph element, which contained a telephone link. You now need to create a style rule for the tel-link class to make the phone number stand out by specifying a background color, padding, margins, width, text alignment, and rounded corners. *Why? Style the phone number to appear as a button to indicate that the user can touch it to call the Forward Fitness Club from a mobile device.* The following steps create style rules for the tel-link class.

- Place your insertion point after the closing brace on Line 83 and press the ENTER key twice to insert new Lines 84 and 85.

- On Line 85, type `.tel-link {` to add a selector and opening curly brace.

- Press the ENTER key to insert a new Line 86, increase the indent, and then type `background-color: #404040;` to add a new declaration.

- Press the ENTER key to insert a new Line 87, and then type `padding: 2%;` to add a new declaration.

- Press the ENTER key to insert a new Line 88, and then type `margin: 0 auto;` to add a new declaration.

- Press the ENTER key to insert a new Line 89, and then type `width: 80%;` to add a new declaration.

- Press the ENTER key to insert a new Line 90, and then type `text-align: center;` to add a new declaration.

- Press the ENTER key to insert a new Line 91, and then type `border-radius: 5px;` to add a new declaration.

- Press the ENTER key to insert a new Line 92, decrease the indent, and then type `}` to close the style rule (Figure 5–46).

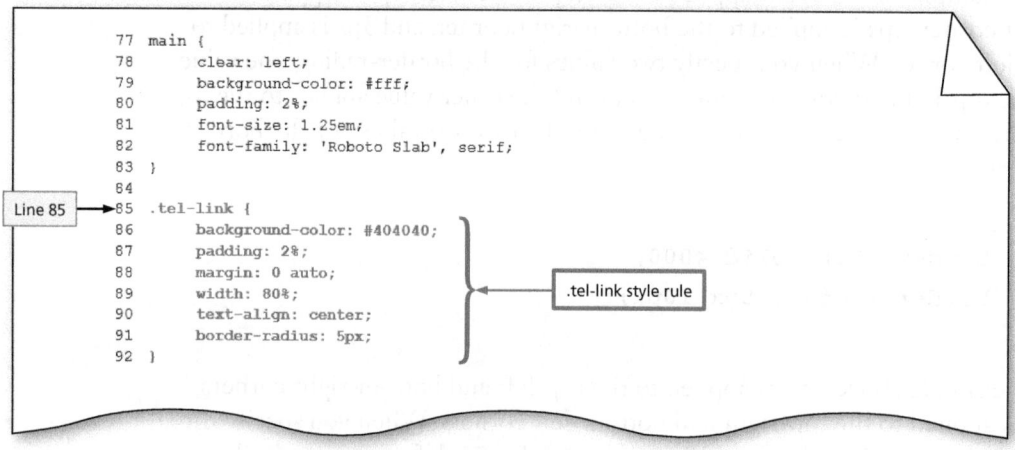

Figure 5–46

Q&A What is the purpose of the new .tel-link style rule?
The purpose of adding the .tel-link style rule is to style the phone number with the telephone link to appear as a button. This helps users recognize that they can touch the button to call the business.

- Press the ENTER key twice to insert new Lines 93 and 94.

- On Line 94, type `.tel-link a {` to add a selector and opening curly brace.

- Press the ENTER key to insert a new Line 95, increase the indent, and then type `color: #fff;` to add a new declaration.

- Press the ENTER key to insert a new Line 96, and then type `text-decoration: none;` to add a new declaration.

- Press the ENTER key to insert a new Line 97, and then type `font-size: 1.5em;` to add a new declaration.

- Press the ENTER key to insert a new Line 98, and then type **display: block;** to add a new declaration.

- Press the ENTER key to insert a new Line 99, decrease the indent, and then type **}** to close the style rule (Figure 5–47).

```
84
85  .tel-link {
86      background-color: #404040;
87      padding: 2%;
88      margin: 0 auto;
89      width: 80%;
90      text-align: center;
91      border-radius: 5px;
92  }
93
94  .tel-link a {          ← Line 94
95      color: #fff;
96      text-decoration: none;    ← .tel-link a style rule
97      font-size: 1.5em;
98      display: block;
99  }
```

Figure 5–47

Q&A

What is the purpose of the new .tel-link a style rule?

The purpose of this style rule is to format the appearance of the telephone link itself.

To Add a Style Rule for the hours Class

When you added mobile content to the home page, you included an unordered list that contained the hours for the Forward Fitness Club. The unordered list element contains a class attribute with the value hours. Style the hours class to add left margin. **Why?** *The ul selector was added to the CSS reset style rule, which removes margin, padding, and borders. Specify some left margin to display the bullet markers.* The following steps create a style rule for the hours class.

1 Place your insertion point after the closing brace on Line 99 and press the ENTER key twice to insert new Lines 100 and 101.

2 On Line 101, type **.hours {** to add a selector and opening curly brace.

3 Press the ENTER key to insert a new Line 102, increase the indent, and then type **margin-left: 10%;** to add a new declaration.

4 Press the ENTER key to insert a new Line 103, decrease the indent, and then type **}** to close the style rule (Figure 5–48).

```
94  .tel-link a {
95      color: #fff;
96      text-decoration: none;
97      font-size: 1.5em;
98      display: block;
99  }
100
101  .hours {          ← Line 101
102      margin-left: 10%;    ← .hours style rule
103  }
```

Figure 5–48

5 Save your changes and open index.html in Google Chrome's device mode to display it in a mobile viewport.

6 Scroll down to view the content in the mobile class, the telephone link, and the unordered list bullet markers, and to confirm that elements within the tablet-desktop class are not displayed (Figure 5–49).

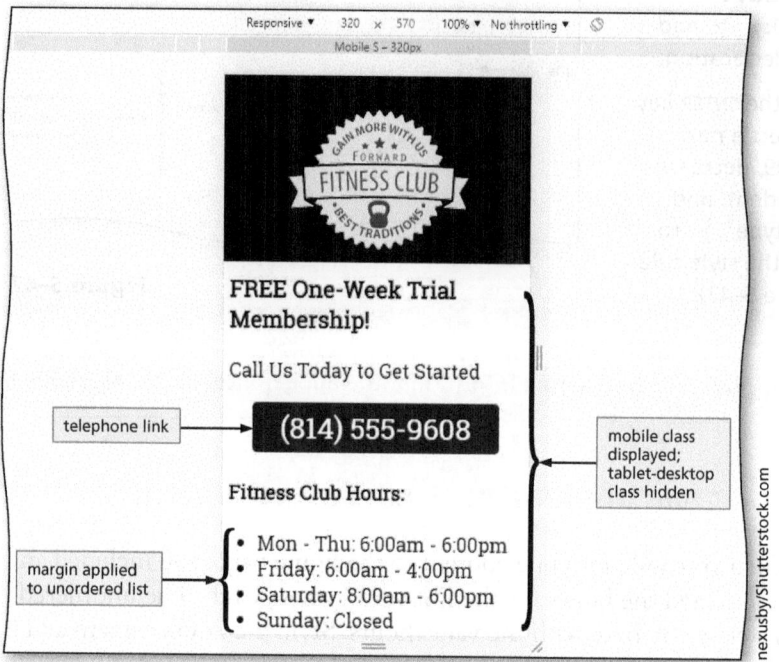

Figure 5–49

To Modify the Style Rule for the main Element

The styles.css file contains a style rule for the main element. Modify the style rule to remove the clear property and value and change the font-size value. Because the header and nav style rules no longer contain a float declaration, you do not need to include a clear property for the main element. Slightly decrease the font size to fit more content within the mobile viewport. The following steps modify the style rule for main element.

1 In styles.css, select and delete Line 78 to remove it from the style rule.

2 On Line 80, change the value for the font-size property to **1.15em** (Figure 5–50).

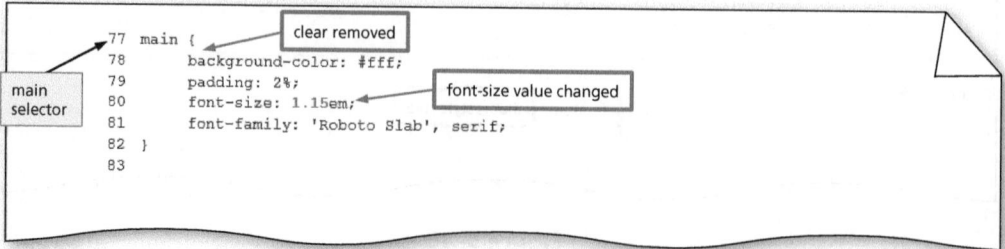

Figure 5–50

3 Save your changes and refresh the index.html page in your browser (Figure 5–51).

Figure 5–51

Analyze the About Us Page for Mobile-First Design

The content on the home page is now styled for an optimum mobile viewing experience, but take a look at the About Us page. Figure 5–52 shows the areas that can be adjusted to better style the content for a mobile viewport.

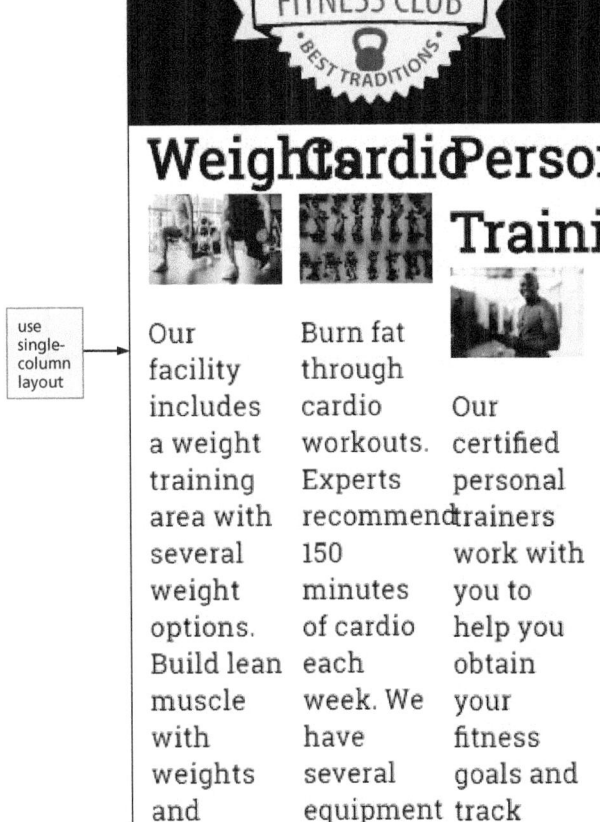

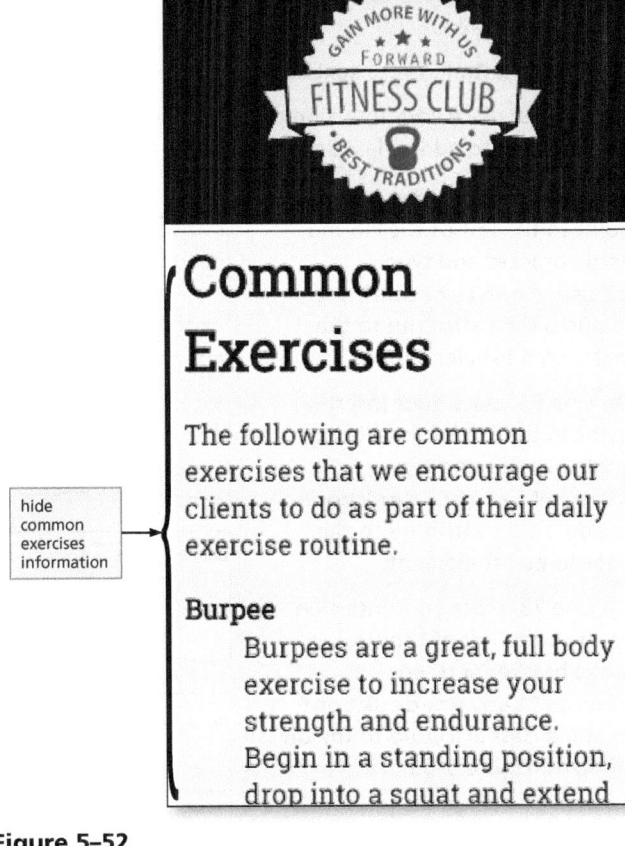

Figure 5–52

The About Us page has more content than the home page. To minimize scrolling, review the page content and determine the most essential information, which describes the equipment and services. In this case, to use as much of the available space as possible, you use a single column layout and hide the unordered lists. Additionally, you can hide other content in the main element, including the common exercise information and the paragraph with the external link. This content is not essential to mobile users, who want to know the basics about the club's equipment and services. You can also improve the appearance of the images on this page by applying rounded corners. This will give the page a cleaner look.

To modify the About Us page for a mobile viewport, add the tablet-desktop class to the unordered list elements within the main element. Next, add the tablet-desktop class to the <div id="exercises"> tag, which contains the common exercises content and the paragraph with the external link. Then, open the styles.css file and modify the style rule for #weights, #cardio, and #training to remove the width and the float and then adjust the margins. Because the exercises div will not be displayed on a mobile viewport, move these style rules below the last footer style rule and then convert them to a comment. You will include the style rules within a media query in Chapter 6. Next, add a class attribute with a value of round to the images within the main element. Finally, create a new style rule that creates rounded corners.

To Modify the About Us Page

1 ADD META VIEWPORT ELEMENT | 2 CREATE STICKY HEADER | 3 ADD CUSTOM FONTS
4 STYLE PAGES FOR MOBILE VIEWPORT | 5 STYLE MAP FOR MOBILE VIEWPORT

Modify the HTML code on the About Us page before you modify the styles.css file so you can see how the changes you make affect the content on the webpage. In about.html, add a class attribute with the value tablet-desktop to the unordered list elements within the main element and to the <div id="exercises"> tag. Then add a class attribute with a value of round to each image element within the main element. *Why? Hide nonessential content for a mobile viewport and improve the overall appearance of the page content.* The following steps modify the About Us page.

- Open about.html in your text editor to prepare to modify the page.

- On Line 39, place your insertion point to the left of the closing angle bracket and type `class="tablet-desktop"` to add a class attribute to the unordered list element.

- On Line 52, place your insertion point to the left of the closing angle bracket and type `class="tablet-desktop"` to add a class attribute to the unordered list element.

- On Line 65, place your insertion point to the left of the closing angle bracket and type `class="tablet-desktop"` to add a class attribute to the unordered list element.

- On Line 73, place your insertion point to the left of the closing angle bracket and type `class="tablet-desktop"` to add a class attribute to the div element (Figure 5–53).

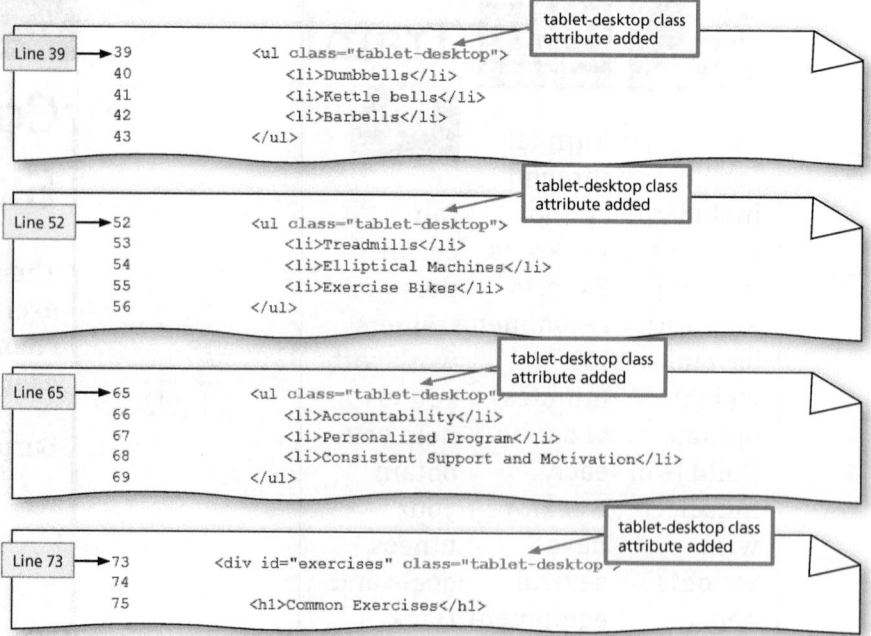

Figure 5–53

②

- On Line 37, place your insertion point to the left of the closing angle bracket and type `class="round"` to add a class attribute to the image element.

- On Line 50, place your insertion point to the left of the closing angle bracket and type `class="round"` to add a class attribute to the image element.

- On Line 63, place your insertion point to the left of the closing angle bracket and type **`class="round"`** to add a class attribute to the image element (Figure 5–54).

③

- Save your changes.

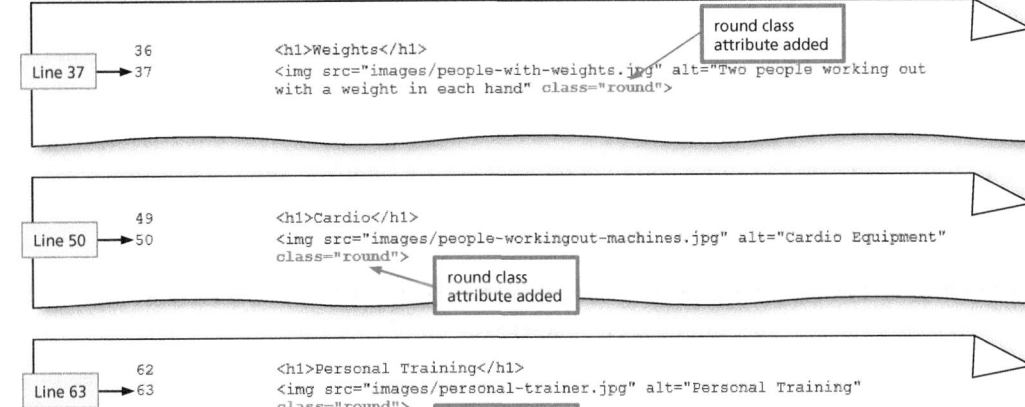

```
                                                              round class
                                                              attribute added
        36              <h1>Weights</h1>
Line 37 ▸37             <img src="images/people-with-weights.jpg" alt="Two people working out
                        with a weight in each hand" class="round">


        49              <h1>Cardio</h1>
Line 50 ▸50             <img src="images/people-workingout-machines.jpg" alt="Cardio Equipment"
                        class="round">
                                            round class
                                            attribute added


        62              <h1>Personal Training</h1>
Line 63 ▸63             <img src="images/personal-trainer.jpg" alt="Personal Training"
                        class="round">
                                          round class
                                          attribute added
```

Figure 5–54

To Add a Style Rule for the round Class

1 ADD META VIEWPORT ELEMENT | 2 CREATE STICKY HEADER | 3 ADD CUSTOM FONTS
4 STYLE PAGES FOR MOBILE VIEWPORT | **5 STYLE MAP FOR MOBILE VIEWPORT**

In the previous steps, you added a class named round to several image elements on the About Us page. Now you can insert a style rule with a new selector named .round that applies to content in the round class. In the style rule, insert a declaration that sets the **`border-radius`** property to **`8px`** for the mobile viewport. *Why? Add rounded corners to the images to improve their appearance on the page.* The following steps create a style rule for the round class.

①

- If necessary, open styles.css to prepare to insert a new style rule.

- Place your insertion point to the right of the closing brace on Line 114 and press the ENTER key twice to insert new Lines 115 and 116.

- On Line 116, type **`.round {`** to begin a new style rule.

- Press the ENTER key to insert a new Line 117, increase the indent, and then type **`border-radius: 8px;`** to insert a property and value.

- Press the ENTER key to insert a new Line 118, decrease the indent, and then type **`}`** to close the style rule (Figure 5–55).

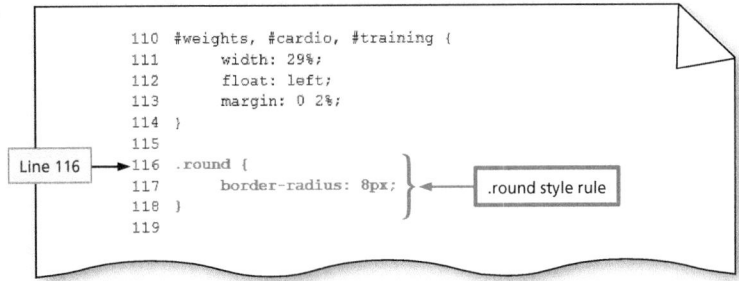

```
110  #weights, #cardio, #training {
111      width: 29%;
112      float: left;
113      margin: 0 2%;
114  }
115
Line 116 ▸116  .round {
117      border-radius: 8px;          .round style rule
118  }
119
```

Figure 5–55

To Modify a Style Rule to Use a Single Column

The styles.css file contains a style rule for #weights, #cardio, and #training div id attributes. Modify the style rule by removing the width and float declarations and values. Then move the #exercises, #exercises dt, #exercises dd style rules to the bottom of the style sheet and convert them to a comment. *Why? Use a single column for a mobile viewport, as this will maximize the allotted space for content. The styles for the #exercises, dt, and dd elements are not needed for the mobile viewport.* The following steps modify the style rule for the #weights, #cardio, and #training div id attributes and remove the style rules for the ul, dt, and dd elements.

- In styles.css, delete the width and float declarations on Lines 111 and 112 to remove them from the style rule, and then delete any blank lines within the style rule.

- Select Lines 118 through 132 and press the CTRL+X keys to cut these style rules.

- Scroll down to the bottom of the style sheet, add a new blank line, and then press the CTRL+V keys to paste the style rules below the style rule for the footer p a selector.

- Place your insertion point before the #exercises selector and then type /* followed by a space to begin a comment.

- Place your insertion point to the right of the closing brace for the #exercises dd style rule, insert a space, and then type */ to close the comment.

- Review the space between the style rule for .round and .external-link. If there is more than one blank line between these style rules, close the gap to leave one blank line (Figure 5–56).

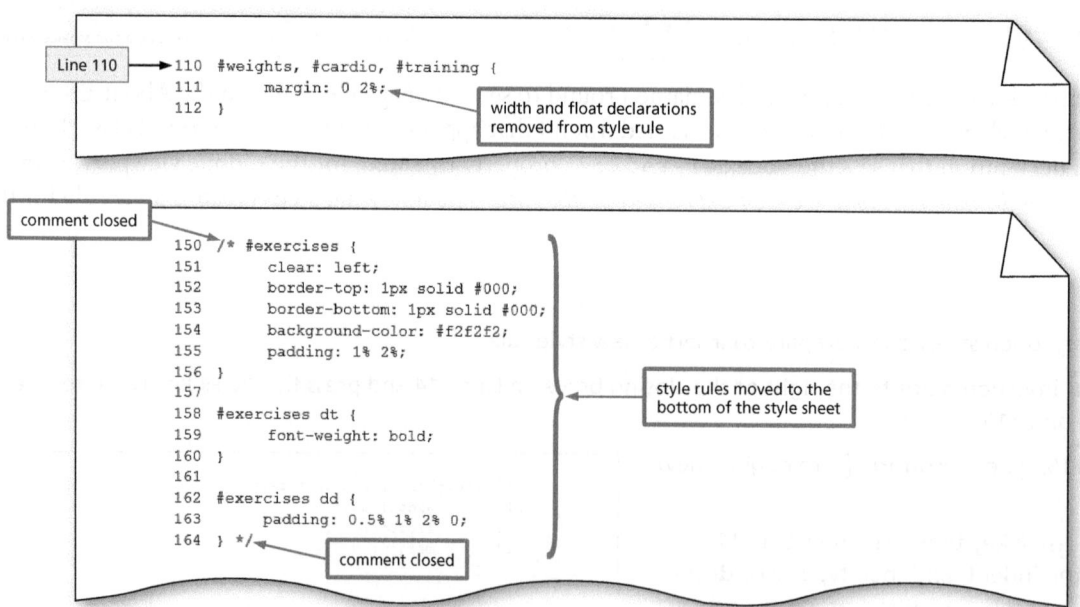

Figure 5–56

Q&A What is the purpose of moving these style rules to the bottom of the style sheet and converting them to comments?

You will need these styles rules for a media query in Chapter 6. Instead of retyping them, you will remove the comment indicators and place the style rules in the media query.

- Save your changes and open about.html in Google Chrome's device mode to display the mobile viewport. If necessary, scroll down to view the changes (Figure 5–57).

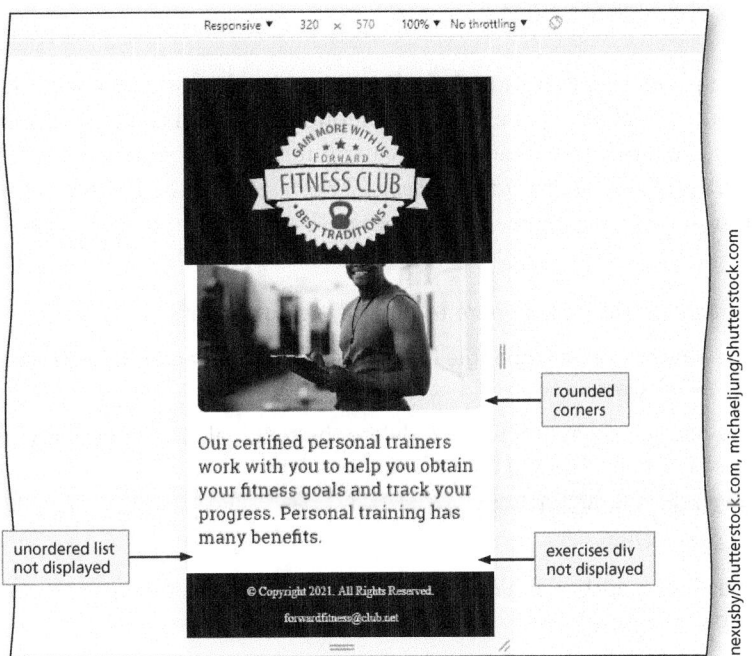

nexusby/Shutterstock.com, michaeljung/Shutterstock.com

Figure 5–57

Analyze the Contact Us Page for Mobile-First Design

Review the Contact Us page to determine how to best style the content for mobile displays. Recall that the Contact Us page includes a telephone number without a telephone link. In addition, the map extends beyond the mobile viewport. Figure 5–58 shows the current appearance of the Contact Us page.

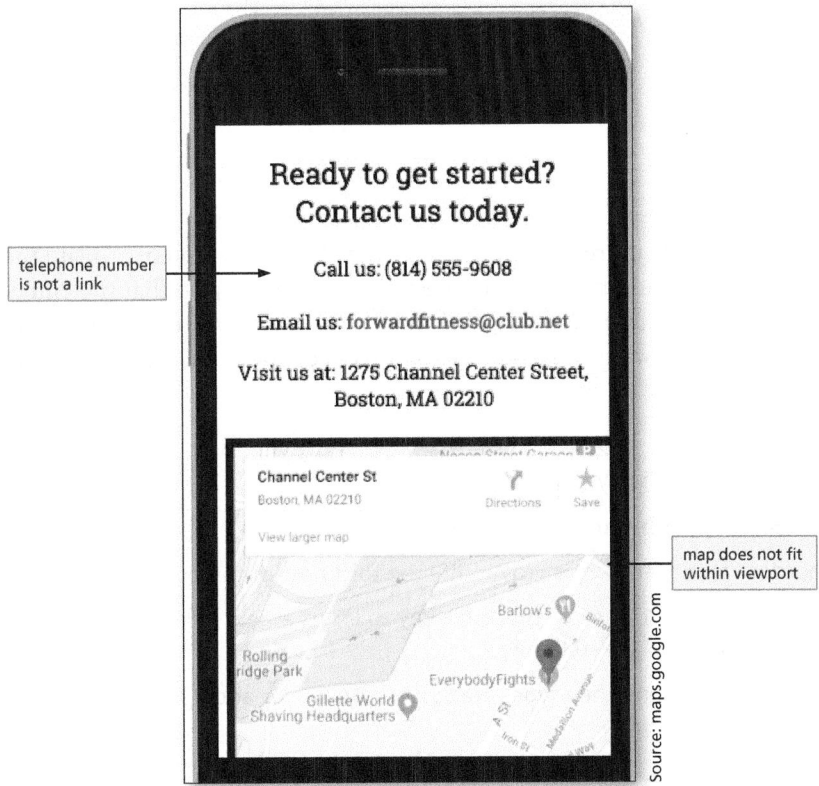

Source: maps.google.com

Figure 5–58

To Modify the Contact Us Page

The Contact Us page includes a phone number; however, the phone number does not include a telephone link, nor is it styled for a telephone link. Update the page to add a telephone link and the tel-link class attribute to apply the tel-link style rule. Modify the email link to add a class attribute with the value contact-email-link. *Why? Add functionality to the mobile viewport by including the telephone link. Mobile users expect this convenience on their mobile devices.* The following steps modify elements on the Contact Us page.

- If necessary, open contact.html in your text editor to prepare to modify the document.

- Place your insertion point before the before the closing angle bracket for the <h4> tag on Line 37 and then type `class="tel-link"` to add the tel-link class.

- Place your insertion point before the phone number on Line 37, delete the text, Call us:, and then type `<a href="tel:8145559608">` to insert an anchor tag with a telephone link.

- Place your insertion point after the last digit in the phone number on Line 37 and then type `</a>` to close the anchor element before the closing tag for </h4>.

- Place your insertion point before the closing anchor angle bracket on Line 38, and then type `class="contact-email-link"` to add a class attribute (Figure 5–59).

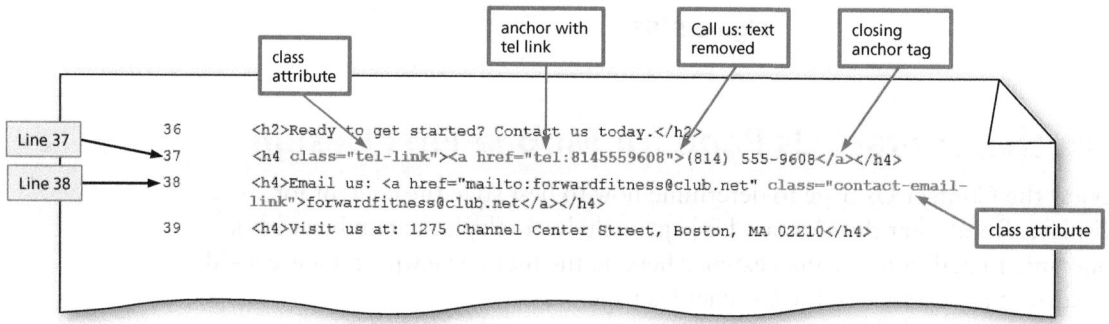

Figure 5–59

To Modify #contact a and .map Style Rules

Now that the contact.html file contains more than one link within the main element, update the #contact a selector to #contact .contact-email-link. In addition, modify the style rule for .map so that the embedded map stays within the mobile viewport. *Why? The telephone and email links should not have the same style applied. The map needs to be within the mobile viewport.* The following steps modify the #contact a selector and add new declarations to the .map style rule in the styles.css file.

- Return to styles.css in your text editor, if necessary.

- Replace the a selector on Line 128 with `.contact-email-link`.

- On Line 134, replace the 8px border value with `2px` to modify the thickness of the border around the map.

- Place your insertion point at the end of Line 134, press the ENTER key to insert a new Line 135, and then type `width: 95%;` to add a new declaration to the style rule.

- Press the ENTER key to insert a new Line 136 and then type `height: 50%;` to add a new declaration to the style rule (Figure 5–60).

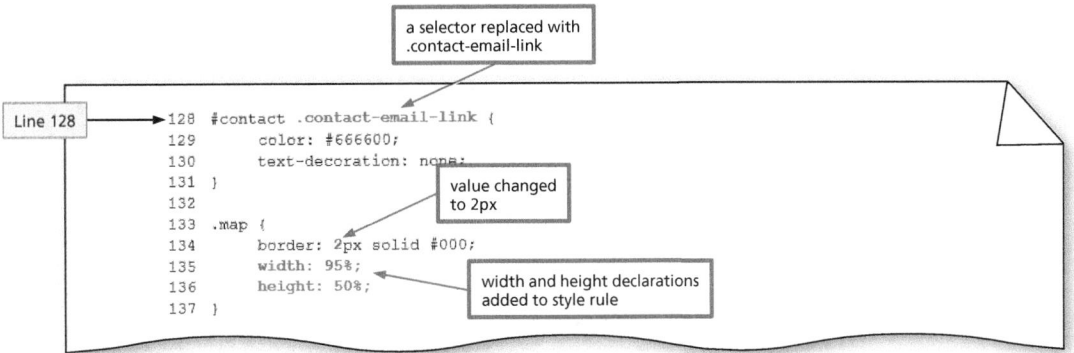

```
                              a selector replaced with
                              .contact-email-link

Line 128  ──▶  128  #contact .contact-email-link {
               129      color: #666600;
               130      text-decoration: none;
               131  }
               132                          value changed
               133  .map {                  to 2px
               134      border: 2px solid #000;
               135      width: 95%;
               136      height: 50%;         width and height declarations
               137  }                        added to style rule
```

Figure 5–60

2

- Save all files and open contact. html in Google Chrome's device mode to display the mobile viewport (Figure 5–61).

nexusby/Shutterstock.com, Google Maps

style rule for tel-link applied

map fits within the mobile viewport

Figure 5–61

Mobile-Friendly Test

Once you have completed your design for a mobile viewport, view and test it on as many smartphone devices as possible. Google Chrome's device mode is helpful during the design process, but testing on an actual device is optimal. You should also check your website for mobile-friendliness. Google has a Mobile-Friendly Test available at search.google.com/test/mobile-friendly. The test page is shown in Figure 5–62.

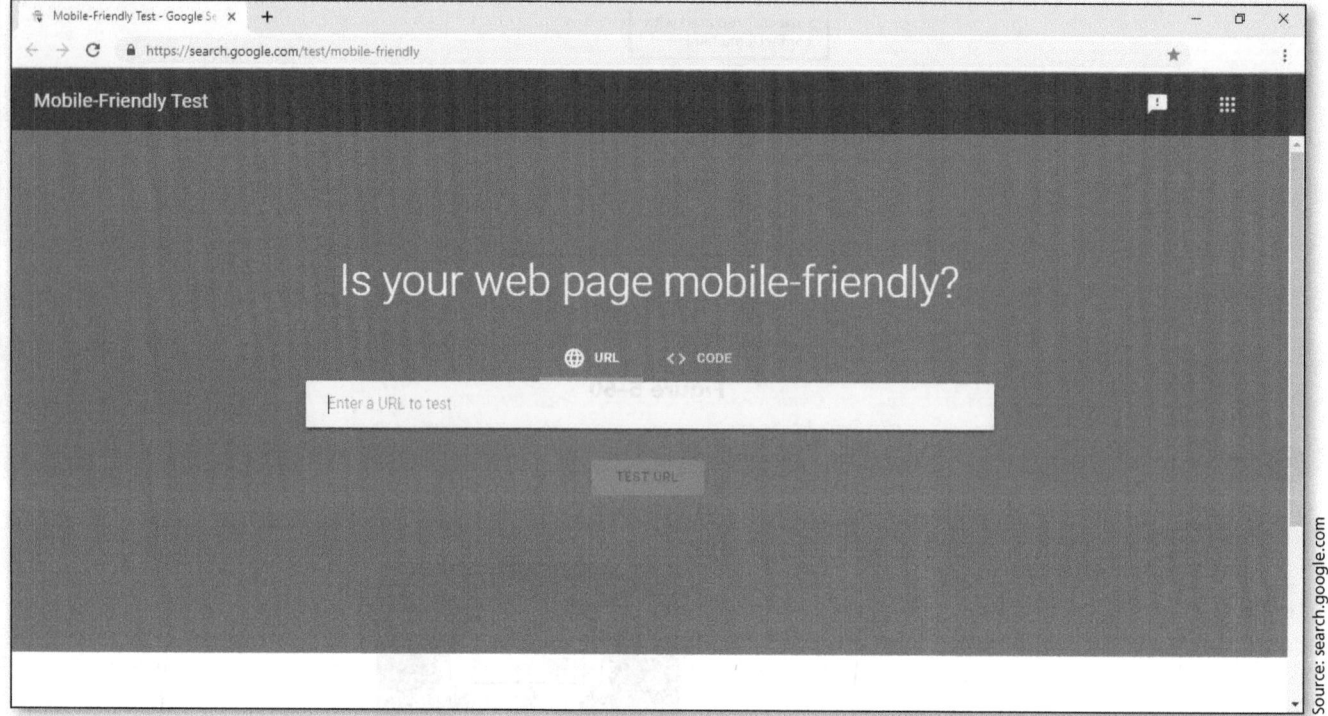

Figure 5–62

To use the mobile-friendly test, you will need to publish your website and provide a link to your URL or copy and paste your HTML code directly within the page. Figure 5–63 shows an example of the test results for the Forward Fitness Club home page.

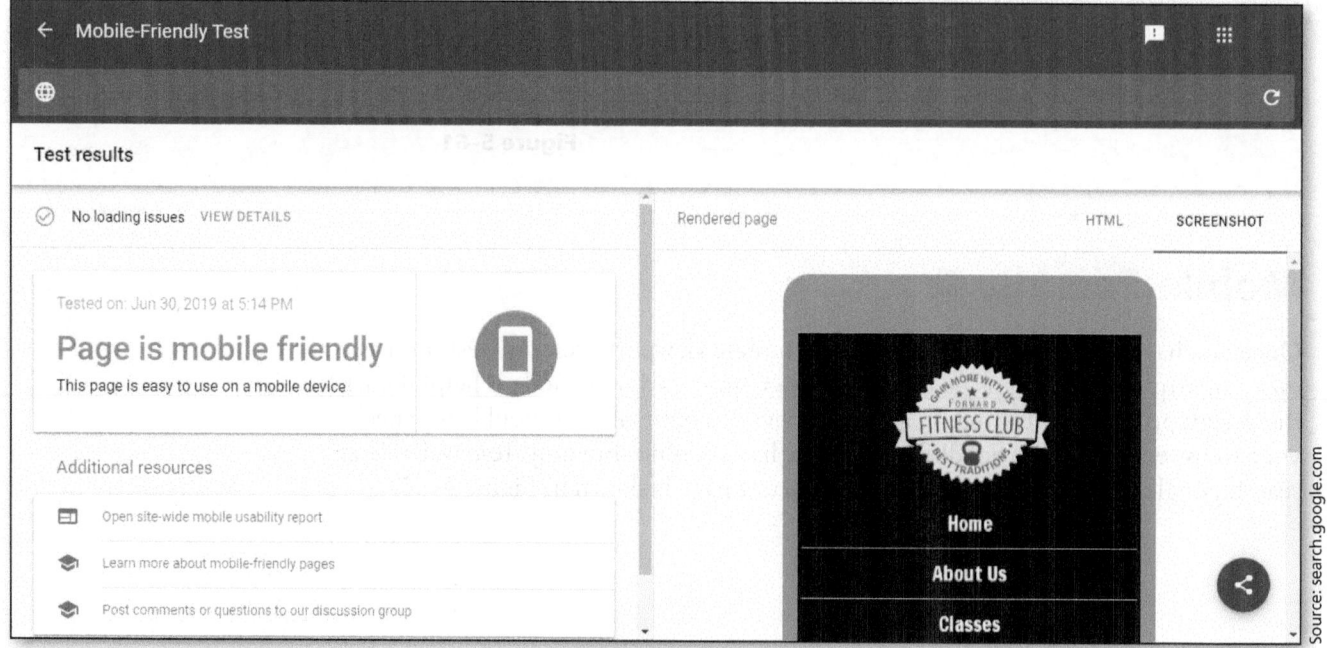

Figure 5–63

Bing also provides a mobile-friendly test checker at bing.com/webmaster/tools/ mobile-friendliness. As shown in Figure 6-64, the test results indicate that the viewport is correct, the page content fits within the device, text is readable, and the links and tap areas are touch-friendly. Note that you will need to publish your website before you can use Bing's mobile-friendly test. Refer to Chapter 11 for website publishing instructions.

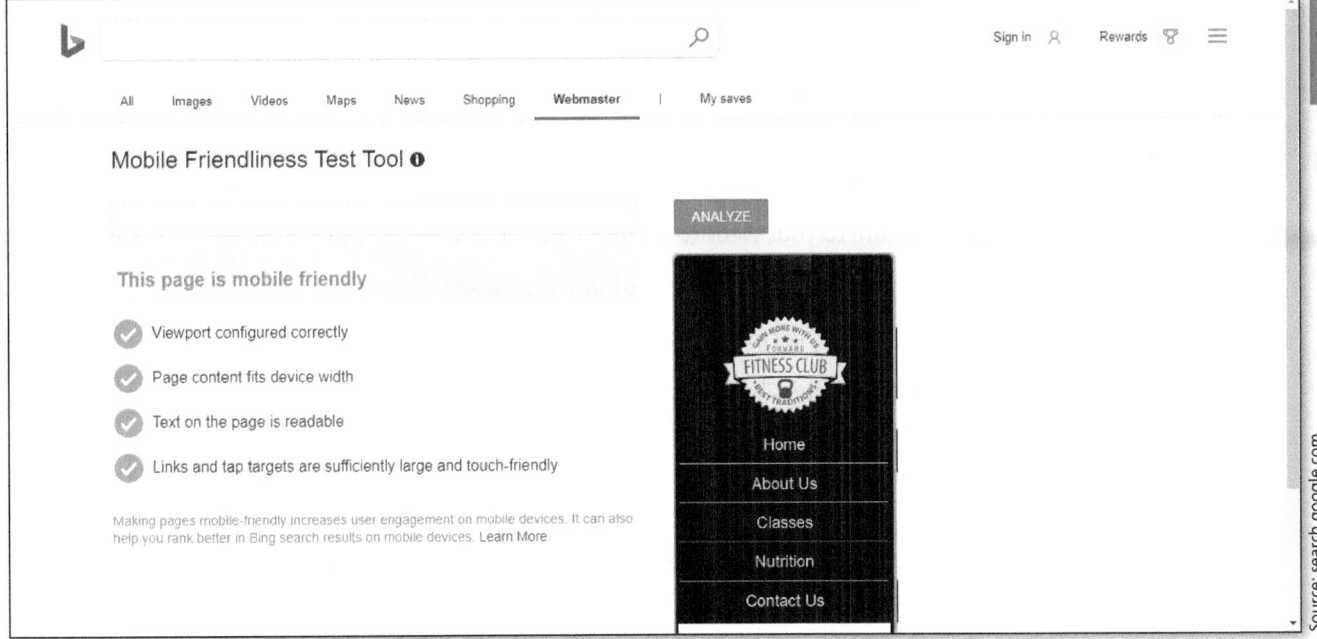

Figure 5–64

To Validate the Style Sheet

Always run your files through W3C's validator to check the document for errors. If the document has any errors, validating gives you a chance to identify and correct them. Validation is also an effective troubleshooting tool during the development process and adds a valuable level of professionalism to your work. The following steps validate a CSS document.

1 Open your browser and type `http://jigsaw.w3.org/css-validator/` in the address bar to display the W3C CSS Validation Service page.

2 Tap or click the By file upload tab to display the Validate by File Upload information.

3 Tap or click the Browse button to display the File Upload dialog box.

4 Navigate to your css folder to find the styles.css file.

5 Tap or click the styles.css document to select it.

6 Tap or click the Open button to upload the selected file to the W3C CSS validator.

7 Tap or click the Check button to send the document through the validator and display the validation results page.

To Validate the HTML Files

Every time you create a new webpage, run it through W3C's validator to check the document for errors. If any errors exist, you need to correct them. Validation is also an effective troubleshooting tool during the development process and adds a valuable level of professionalism to your work. The following steps validate an HTML document.

1 Open your browser and type `http://validator.w3.org/` in the address bar to display the W3C validator page.

2 Tap or click the Validate by File Upload tab to display the Validate by File Upload tab information.

3 Tap or click the Browse button to display the File Upload dialog box.

4 Navigate to your website template folder to find the about.html file.

5 Tap or click the about.html document to select it.

6 Tap or click the Open button to upload it to the W3C validator.

7 Tap or click the Check button to send the document through the validator and display the validation results page.

8 If necessary, correct any errors, save your changes, and run through the validator again to revalidate the page.

9 Follow these steps to validate the contact.html, index.html, and fitness.html pages and correct any errors.

Chapter Summary

In this chapter, you learned how to apply responsive design principles to a website. You modified the fitness website to use a fluid layout, added a meta viewport element, and followed a mobile-first strategy to analyze and modify the webpages in the fitness website. You integrated custom fonts, created a sticky element and a responsive navigation system for a mobile viewport, used a pseudo-class, and added rounded corners. The items listed below include all the new skills you have learned in this chapter, with the tasks grouped by activity.

Adding Meta Viewport Element
Add the Meta Viewport Element for Responsive Design (HTML 228)

Making Sticky Elements
Create a Sticky Header (HTML 233)

Creating a Responsive Navigation
Code the Navigation Links for Mobile Viewports (HTML 238)
Integrate Custom Fonts (HTML 242)
Use a Pseudo-Class (HTML 247)

Following a Mobile-First Strategy
Modify the Home Page (HTML 249)
Create a Style Rule for the mobile Class (HTML 252)
Add a Style Rule for the tablet-desktop Class (HTML 252)
Add Style Rules for the tel-link Class (HTML 254)
Modify the About Us Page (HTML 258)
Create Rounded Corners (HTML 259)
Modify the Contact Us Page (HTML 262)

How will you apply the principles of responsive web design to your website?

Use these guidelines as you complete the assignments in this chapter and create your own webpages outside of this class.

1. Analyze how the principles of responsive design might be applied to your website.

   a. Determine the importance of mobile traffic.

   b. Consider the pros and cons of responsive design versus a mobile website strategy.

   c. Consider mobile-first principles such as focusing on essential content first.

2. Use a fluid layout.

   a. Width measurements should be in flexible units such as % or ems.

   b. Textual content should be measured in ems for maximum flexibility.

3. Use a mobile simulator.

   a. Use a mobile simulator to view your design.

   b. Learn how to effectively use browser developer tools.

4. Test and validate your responsive design.

   a. Check your website to confirm it is mobile-friendly.

   b. Validate both the HTML and CSS.

How should you submit solutions to questions in the assignments identified with a ✳ symbol?

Every assignment in this book contains one or more questions identified with a ✳ symbol. These questions require you to think beyond the assigned presentation. Present your solutions to the questions in the format required by your instructor. Possible formats may include one or more of these options: create a document that contains the answer; present your answer to the class; discuss your answer in a group; record the answer as audio or video using a webcam, smartphone, or portable media player; or post answers on a blog, wiki, or website.

Apply Your Knowledge

Reinforce the skills and apply the concepts you learned in this chapter.

Styling for Responsive Design

Note: To complete this assignment, you will be required to use the Data Files. Please contact your instructor for information about accessing the Data Files.

Instructions: In this exercise, you will use your text editor to design a webpage for a mobile viewport. An example of the completed webpage is shown in Figure 5–65.

Perform the following tasks:

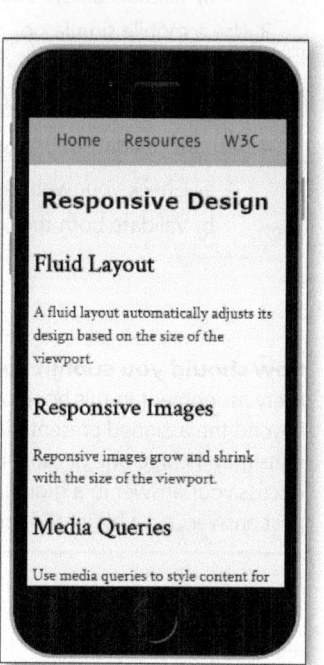

1. Open your text editor and then open the index.html file in the chapter05\apply folder from the Data Files. Update the comment with your name, the file name, and today's date.

2. Link the index.html file to the apply05.css style sheet, located in the css subfolder. Open the file in Google Chrome's device mode to display the page in a mobile viewport.

3. In the index.html file, add a class attribute with the value `tablet-desk` to the second div element within the main element.

4. Add a class attribute with the value `corner` to the image element. Remove the height and width attributes from the image element.

5. In apply05.css, below the body style rule, create a new style rule for the img selector the sets a maximum width of 100% and sets the display value to block.

6. Add two blank lines after the img style rule, add a comment with the text, `Style rules for mobile viewport`.

7. Add two blank lines after the mobile viewport comment, add another comment with the text, `Style rule to hide tablet-desk class`, and then create a style rule that hides the tablet-desk class.

Figure 5–65

8. Add the following declarations to the nav style rule:

   a. Specify a sticky position compatible with all modern browsers. (*Hint*: Use two position declarations and include the -webkit- prefix for the first declaration.)

   b. Specify a top property value of zero.

9. Add a declaration to the nav ul style rule that removes the bullet marker.

10. Add a declaration to the nav li style rule that sets the display to an inline-block.

11. After the main style rule, create a style rule for the corner class that specifies a border radius of 12 pixels.

12. Open fonts.google.com in your browser, search for and select the B612 and Crimson Text fonts. Copy and paste the link element provided by Google Fonts within the head element in the index.html file. In the apply05.css file, update the following style rules:

    a. Update the nav li style rule to use the B612 Google Font.

    b. Update the main style rule to use the Crimson Text Google Font.

13. Validate your HTML and CSS files and correct any errors. Save your changes and submit the assignment in a format specified by your instructor.

14. ✺ The page content for this assignment reviews the basics of responsive web design. Research the CSS grid layout and provide a summary of this relatively new layout.

Extend Your Knowledge

Extend the skills you learned in this chapter and experiment with new skills. You may need to use additional resources to complete the assignment.

Working with Positions

Instructions: In this exercise, you will create and modify style rules to learn more about how to place elements on a page using positions. An example of page element positions is shown in Figure 5–66.

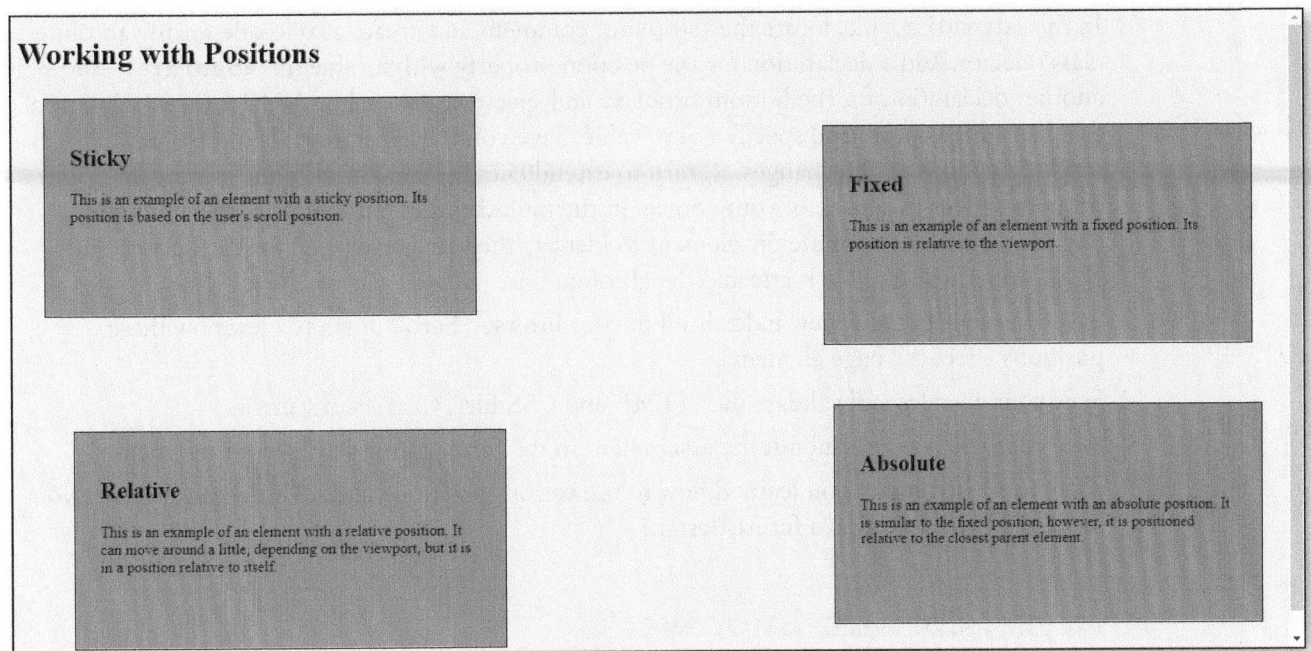

Figure 5–66

Perform the following tasks:
1. Open your text editor and then open the index.html file in the chapter05\extend folder from the Data Files. Update the comment with your name and today's date.

2. Open index.html in your browser to view the file.

3. Open the extend05.css file in your text editor. Locate the "sticky" comment and create a style rule for the sticky class selector. Add a declaration for the position property with a value of `-webkit-sticky`. Add a declaration for the position property with a value of `sticky`. Add a declaration for the top property and specify a zero value. Save your changes, refresh your page, and scroll down to view the changes. In the index.html file, use the empty paragraph element within the sticky div element to briefly explain how to use the sticky position.

4. In the extend05.css file, locate the "relative" comment and create a style rule for the relative class selector. Add a declaration for the position property with a value of `relative`. Add another declaration for the top property and specify a value of 90 pixels. Add another declaration for the left property with a value of 30 pixels. Save your changes, refresh your page, and scroll down to view the changes. Return to extend05.css file and modify the top and left property values to a value of your choice. In the index.html file, use the empty paragraph element within the relative div element to identify the values you used for the top and left properties and how it affected the relative box.

Continued >

Extend Your Knowledge *continued*

5. In the extend05.css file, locate the "fixed" comment and create a style rule for the fixed class selector. Add a declaration for the position property with a value of **fixed**. Add another declaration for the top property and specify a value of 90 pixels. Add another declaration for the right property with a value of 10 pixels. Save your changes, refresh your page, and scroll down to view the changes. Return to extend05.css file and modify the top and right property values to a value of your choice. In the index.html file, use the empty paragraph element within the fixed div element to identify the values you used for the top and right properties and how it affected the fixed box.

6. In the extend05.css file, locate the "absolute" comment and create a style rule for the absolute class selector. Add a declaration for the position property with a value of **absolute**. Add another declaration for the bottom property and specify a zero value. Add another declaration for the right property and specify a zero value. Save your changes, refresh your page, and scroll down to view the changes. Return to extend05.css file and modify the bottom and right property values to a value of your choice. In the index.html file, use the empty paragraph element within the absolute div element to identify the values you used for the bottom and right properties and how it affected the absolute box.

7. Save your changes and view index.html in your browser. Scroll down to view how these positions affect the page elements.

8. Save your changes and validate the HTML and CSS files. Correct any errors.

9. Save your changes and submit the assignment in the format specified by your instructor.

10. ☀ In this assignment, you learned how to use various position values. Which position are you most likely to use within a future design?

Analyze, Correct, Improve

Analyze a webpage, correct all errors, and improve it.

Correcting a CSS File

Note: To complete this assignment, you will be required to use the Data Files. Please contact your instructor for information about accessing the Data Files.

Instructions: Open your text editor and then open the chapter05\ analyze05.html file from the Data Files. The page needs to be redesigned for a mobile viewport. An example of the corrected page is shown in Figure 5–67.

1. Correct

a. Open the analyze05.html file in your text editor and review the page.

b. Update the comment with your name, the file name, and today's date.

c. Review analyze05.html in Google Chrome's device mode to view its current mobile layout. Notice how the page does not properly display the webpage for a mobile viewport.

d. Add the meta viewport element to the analyze05.html file.

e. In the styles.css file, add a comment below the img style rule to indicate where style rules for the mobile viewport begin.

Courtesy of Google Chrome

Figure 5–67

f. Add a declaration to the nav ul style rule to remove the bullet marker.

g. Add a declaration to the nav li style rule to display it as an inline-block.

h. Note the font family values for the header h1 style rule and the main style rule. Both of these declarations use custom Google Fonts; however, the index.html file is not linked to these fonts. Open fonts.google.com in your browser, search for and select these fonts, and then add the link element provided by Google Fonts within the head element of the analyze05.html file.

2. Improve

a. In the analyze05.html file, add a class attribute with the value `tablet-desktop` to the examples div.

b. In the styles.css file, below the mobile viewport comment, add a new comment that indicates that the following style rule hides the tablet-desktop class. Below the comment, add a new style rule that hides the tablet-desktop class.

c. In the analyze05.html file, add a class attribute with a value of `btn` to paragraph elements two, three, and four within the main element.

d. In the styles.css file, below the main p style rule, add a new style rule for the btn class that specifies a background color value of #375f1b, padding value of 2%, top and bottom margin values of 2% and left and right margin values of auto, width value of 80%, text alignment of center, and a border radius of 5 pixels.

e. Below the btn style rule, add a new style rule for anchor elements within the btn class that specifies a color value of #ebf7e3, removes the underline, sets a font size of 1.25em, and displays the content as a block.

f. In the analyze05.html file, add a class attribute with a value of `corner` to the image element.

g. In the styles.css file, below the btn a style rule, add a new style rule for the corner class selector that specifies a border radius of 12px.

h. Review the page in Google Chrome's device mode and compare it to Figure 5–67. Validate the CSS file and the HTML and correct any errors.

i. Submit the assignment in the format specified by your instructor.

j. ✳ You have worked with a several units of measurement, such as pixels, percentages, and ems. Research the vw unit of measurement and provide a summary of it.

In the Lab

Labs 1 and 2, which increase in difficulty, require you to create webpages based on what you learned in the chapter; Lab 3 is ideal for group projects/collaboration.

Lab 1: Styling the Strike a Chord Website for a Mobile Viewport

Problem: You work for a local music lesson company called Strike a Chord that provides music lessons for piano, guitar, and violin. The company needs a web presence and has hired you to create their website. You have already created several pages for the website and made a style sheet, but now you need to design the website for a mobile viewport. The Home, Lessons, and Contact webpages are shown in Figure 5–68.

Continued >

In the Lab *continued*

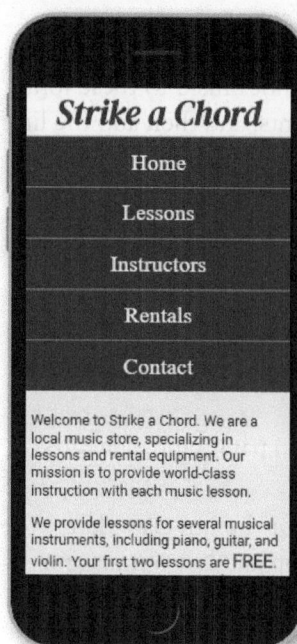

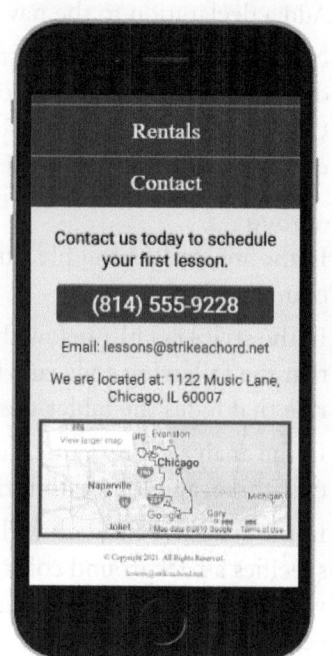

Figure 5–68

Instructions: Perform the following tasks:

1. Navigate to your music folder and open the index.html, lessons.html, contact.html, and template.html files in your text editor and nest the following meta viewport element within the head element.

```
<meta name="viewport" content="width=device-width, initial-scale=1.0">
```

2. In the index.html file, update the heading 1 element by wrapping both music note entity codes within a span element with the class attribute value tab-desk. Copy and paste the revised heading 1 element over the existing heading 1 element in the lessons.html, contact.html, and template.html files. The following shows an example of the music note entity code wrapped within a span element with a class attribute:

```
<span class="tab-desk">&#9836;</span>
```

3. In the index.html, lessons.html, contact.html, and template.html files, add a class attribute with a value of **tab-desk** to the <div id="hero"> tag.

4. In the styles.css file, create a new comment after the img style rule with the following text:

```
Style rules for mobile viewport
```

5. Insert two blank lines below the new comment and add another comment with the following text:

```
Hide tab-desk class
```

6. Add the following style rule below the Hide tab-desk class comment:

```
.tab-desk {
    display: none;
}
```

7. Update the header style rule by changing the font-size value to **1.5em.**

8. Open fonts.google.com in your browser, search for the DM Serif Display font, change its style from Regular 400 to Regular 400 Italic, and then select the font. Search for and select the Roboto font. Copy and paste the link element provided by Google Fonts within the head

element in the index.html, lessons.html, contact.html, and template.html files. In the styles.css file, add the font-family declaration for DM Serif Display to your style rule for header h1. Remove the font-style declaration and italic value from the header h1 style rule. Change the font-family value for the main style rule to use the Roboto value provided by Google Fonts.

9. In the styles.css file, add the ul selector to the CSS reset style rule. Remove the declaration for the margin property in the nav ul style rule. Modify the nav li style rule by changing the display value to `block` and adding the following declaration:

```
border-top: 1px solid #e5e9fc;
```

10. Modify the style rule for .action by changing the font-size value to `1.25em`.

11. Remove the width and float declarations for the #piano, #guitar, #violin style rule.

12. Below the #info style rule, create a new style rule for the #info ul selector that specifies a left margin of 10%.

13. In the lessons.html file, add a class attribute with a value of round to the three image elements.

14. In the styles.css file, below the #info ul style rule, create a new style rule for the round class selector that specifies a border-radius of 8px.

15. In the contact.html file, remove the text, Phone Number:, from the first paragraph element within the main div element. Wrap the phone number within an anchor element that links to the phone number. Add a class attribute with the value `tel-link` to the parent paragraph element that contains the phone number link.

16. In the contact.html file, add a class attribute with the value `email-link` to the anchor element that links to the email address within the main element.

17. In the styles.css file, below the #contact style rule, add the following style rules:

```
.tel-link {
    background-color: #373684;
    padding: 2%;
    margin: 0 auto;
    width: 80%;
    text-align: center;
    border-radius: 5px;
}
.tel-link a {
    color: #fff;
    text-decoration: none;
    font-size: 1.5em;
    display: block;
}
```

18. Change the #contact a selector to `#contact .email-link`.

19. Add a width property with a value of `95%` and a height property of `50%` to the .map style rule.

20. Check your spelling. Validate all HTML and CSS files and correct any errors. Save your changes.

21. Open the index.html file in Google Chrome's device mode to view the home page in a mobile viewport. Navigate to the Lessons and Contact pages to view the mobile design for each page.

22. Submit your assignment in the format specified by your instructor.

23. ✳ In this assignment, you used a custom Google Font. Review the fonts on Google Fonts and find provide another serif and sans-serif pairing for this project.

Lab 2: **Styling the Wild Rescues Website for a Mobile Viewport**

Problem: You volunteer at a local wildlife rescue, a nonprofit organization called Wild Rescues. The organization rescues all kinds of wild animals, rehabilitates them, and then releases them back into the wild. Wild Rescues needs a website to help raise awareness about the organization. You have already created several pages for the website and made a style sheet, but now you need to design the website for a mobile viewport. The Home, About Us, and Contact webpages are shown in Figure 5–69.

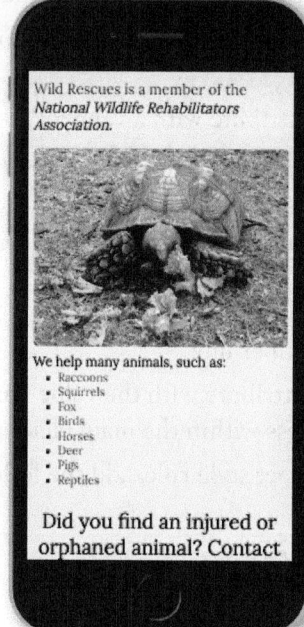

Courtesy of Jessica Minnick

Figure 5–69

Instructions: Perform the following tasks:

1. Navigate to your rescue folder and open the index.html, about.html, contact.html, and template.html files in your text editor and nest the meta viewport element within the head element.

2. In the index.html file, in the header element, wrap the anchor element within a div element with a class attribute value of `tab-desk`. Below this div element (still within the header element), create a new div element with a class attribute value of `mobile`. Nest the following elements within this div:

   ```
   <h1>&#128062; Wild Rescues</h1>
   ```

   ```
   <h3>Rescue. Rehabilitate. Release.</h3>
   ```

3. In the index.html file, copy the new header element and paste it over the existing header element on the about.html, contact.html, and template.html files.

4. In the styles.css file, create a new comment after the img style rule with the following text:

   ```
   Style rules for mobile viewport
   ```

5. Insert two blank lines below the comment created in the step above and add another comment with the following text:

   ```
   Style rules to show mobile class and hide tab-desk class
   ```

6. Add style rules that display the mobile class selector as a block and hide the tab-desk class selector.

7. Insert two blank lines below the tab-desk style rule and add a comment with the text, `Style rules for header area`, and then create one style rule for h1 and h3 selectors within the mobile class that sets the padding to 2% and aligns text center.

8. Add a blank line after the nav li a style rule, add a comment with the text `Style rules for main content`, and then create the following style rules for the main, main p, main h3, main ul, .link, .action, and #contact selectors.

   a. Create a style rule for the main selector that sets the padding to `2%`.

   b. Create a style rule for the main p selector that sets the font size to `1.25em`.

   c. Create a style rule for the main h3 selector that sets the top padding to `2%`.

   d. Create a style rule for the main ul selector that sets the list style type to `square`.

   e. Create a style rule for the link class selector that sets the color to `#4d3319`, removes the underline, sets the font weight to `bold`, and sets the font style to `italic`.

   f. Create a style rule for the action class selector that sets the font size to `1.75em`, the font weight to `bold`, and aligns the text center.

   g. Create a new style rule for the contact id selector that aligns the text center.

9. Open fonts.google.com in your browser, search for and select the Emblema One and Lora fonts. Copy and paste the link element provided by Google Fonts within the head element in the index.html, about.html, contact.html, and template.html files. In the styles.css file, create the following style rules:

   a. Create a style rule for the h1 selector within the mobile class and copy and paste the Google Font CSS declaration for the Emblema font.

   b. Create a style rule for the h3 selector within the mobile class and copy and paste the Google Font CSS declaration for the Lora font.

   c. Copy and paste the Google Font CSS declaration for the Lora font and add it as a new declaration to the main style rule

10. In the styles.css file, add the ul selector to the CSS reset style rule. Remove the declaration for the margin property in the nav ul style rule. Modify the nav li style rule by changing the display value to `block` and add a top border that specifies a solid border width of `0.5px` with the color value `#f6eee4`.

11. In the index.html and about.html files, add a class attribute with a value of `round` to the image elements within the main element.

12. In the styles.css file, below the .action style rule, create a new style rule for the round class selector that specifies a border-radius of 6px.

13. Below the .round style rule, create a new style rule for the #info ul selector that specifies a left margin of 10%.

14. In the contact.html file, remove the text, Office:, from the first paragraph element within the main div element. Wrap the phone number within an anchor element that links to the phone number. Add a class attribute with the values `tel-link` and `round` (*Hint:* "tel-link round") to the parent paragraph element that contains the phone number link.

15. In the styles.css file, below the #contact style rule, add a style rule for the tel-link class selector that sets the background color to #2a1f14, padding to 2%, width to 80%, and top/bottom margins to 0 and right/left margins to auto.

16. Below the tel-link style rule, add a style rule for the anchor selector within the tel-link class that sets the color to #f6eee4, removes the underline, and sets the font weight to bold.

17. Check your spelling. Validate all HTML and CSS files and correct any errors. Save your changes.

Continued >

In the Labs *continued*

18. Open the index.html file in Google Chrome's device mode to view the home page in a mobile viewport. Navigate to the About Us and Contact pages to view the mobile design for each page.

19. Submit your assignment in the format specified by your instructor.

20. ✳ You have learned how to add id and class attributes to an HTML element. Can an HTML element contain both an id and a class value? If so, provide an example of a style rule for the id and the class.

Lab 3: Styling the Student Clubs and Events Website for a Mobile Viewport

Problem: You and several of your classmates have decided to help increase student involvement in school clubs and events by creating a website to promote awareness about the various activities. You have already created several pages for the website and made a style sheet, but now you need to design the website for a mobile viewport.

Instructions:

1. Navigate to your student folder and open all HTML files in your text editor and nest the meta viewport element within the head element.

2. As a team, determine essential page content to show and nonessential content to hide.

3. As a team, discuss and design a mobile viewport layout for your website. Ensure that all page content fits within the mobile viewport.

4. Design a mobile-friendly navigation system.

5. Use two custom Google Fonts.

6. Use at least one structural pseudo class.

7. Apply rounded corners to at least two elements.

8. Add comments in your style sheet to note where mobile style rules begin and add other comments for new style rules as appropriate.

9. Review your files for best coding practices; ensure proper spacing and indents for improved readability.

10. Submit your assignment in the format specified by your instructor.

11. ✳ In this assignment, you used the border-radius property to apply rounded corners. Find another property that you have not yet used and describe its purpose. Provide an example.

Consider This: Your Turn

Apply your creative thinking and problem-solving skills to design and implement a solution.

1. Style Your Personal Portfolio Website for a Mobile Viewport
Personal

Part 1: In Chapters 1 through 4, you created the website plan and started creating and designing your personal portfolio website. You now need redesign your website for a mobile viewport.

1. Add the meta viewport element within the head element of your HTML files.

2. Determine the most essential content on each page and style the HTML elements for a mobile viewport. Use a minimum of two class attributes within your website and create style rules for each class selector. Ensure that all page content fits within the mobile viewport.

3. Design a mobile-friendly navigation system.

4. Use at least one custom Google Font.

5. Apply rounded corners to at least one element within your website.

6. Comment out or remove any style rules that do not pertain to the mobile viewport design.

7. Validate all HTML and CSS files and correct any errors.

8. Review your website with a mobile simulator to ensure it appears as intended.

9. Submit your assignment in the format specified by your instructor.

Part 2: In this assignment, you designed a mobile-friendly navigation system. What resources did you use to accomplish this task?

2. Style the Dog Grooming Website for a Mobile Viewport

Professional

Part 1:   In Chapters 1 through 4, you created the website plan and started creating and designing a website for a dog grooming business. You now need redesign your website for a mobile viewport.

1. Open all HTML files in your text editor and nest the meta viewport element within the head element.

2. Determine essential page content to show and nonessential content to hide. Use CSS to hide nonessential content.

3. Design a mobile viewport layout for your website. Ensure that all page content fits within the mobile viewport.

4. Design a mobile-friendly navigation system.

5. Use two custom Google Fonts.

6. Include a telephone link and style it for a mobile viewport.

7. Apply rounded corners to at least two elements.

8. Add comments in your style sheet to note where mobile style rules begin and add other comments for new style rules as appropriate.

9. Review your files for best coding practices; ensure proper spacing and indents for improved readability.

10. Review your website with a mobile simulator to ensure it appears as intended.

11. Submit your assignment in the format specified by your instructor.

Part 2: In this assignment, you revised your website for a mobile viewport. Open Google Chrome's device mode and review the various windows in the developer tools pane. Locate the Styles section and find the user agent style sheet. Note that the margin has been crossed out. What does this mean?

3. Style the Future Technologies Website for a Mobile Viewport

Research and Collaboration

Part 1: You and several of your classmates have been tasked with creating a website that showcases advancements in technology. You have already created the website plan and started creating the HTML pages for the technology website in Chapters 1 through 4. You now need to create a style sheet to format the website.

1. Open all HTML files in your text editor and nest the meta viewport element within the head element.

2. As a team, determine essential page content to show and nonessential content to hide.

Continued >

Consider this: your turn *continued*

3. As a team, discuss and design a mobile viewport layout for your website. Ensure that all page content fits within the mobile viewport.

4. Design a mobile-friendly navigation system.

5. Use two custom Google Fonts.

6. Use at least one structural pseudo-class.

7. Apply rounded corners to at least two elements.

8. Add comments in your style sheet to note where mobile style rules begin and add other comments for new style rules as appropriate.

9. Review your website with a mobile simulator to ensure it appears as intended.

10. Submit your assignment in the format specified by your instructor.

Part 2: This assignment included a structural pseudo-class. What is a dynamic pseudo-class? Provide an example and explain how to use it.

6 | Responsive Design Part 2: Designing for Tablet and Desktop Devices

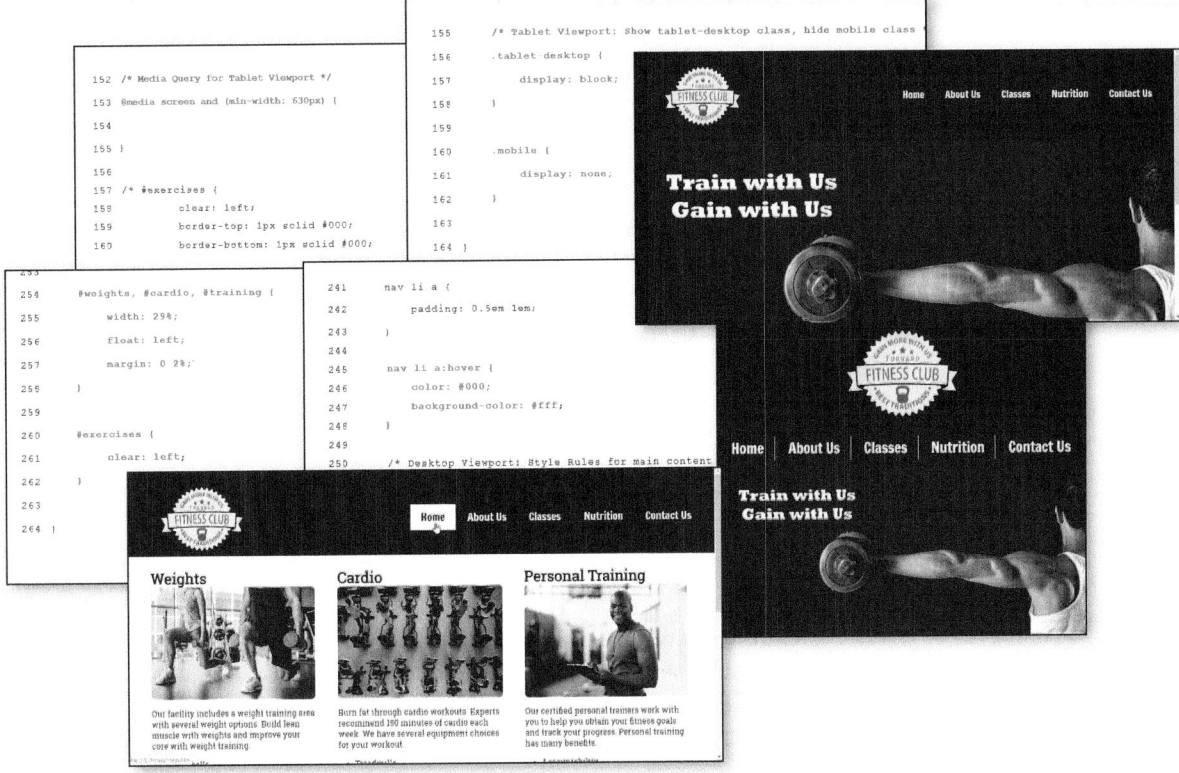

Objectives

You will have mastered the material in this chapter when you can:

- Identify and use media query expressions

- Explain the design principles of a tablet website

- Insert a media query to target tablet viewports

- Create style rules for tablet viewports

- Explain the design principles of a desktop website

- Insert a media query and create style rules to target desktop viewports

- Insert a media query and create a style rule for large desktop viewports

- Create a media query for print

- Identify and modify breakpoints

- Describe and add dynamic pseudo-classes to a website

- Explain linear and radial gradients

- Apply a linear gradient to a webpage for a desktop viewport

6 | Responsive Design Part 2: Designing for Tablet and Desktop Devices

Introduction

As you learned in Chapter 5, the responsive web design approach styles content differently depending upon the type of device used to view the site. The mobile-first approach focuses on styling content appropriately for smaller, mobile devices. It also uses a single-column layout to prevent horizontal scrolling and minimize vertical scrolling. This layout creates a more enjoyable experience for users of mobile devices.

The design process for tablet and desktop displays allows more flexibility with the webpage layout. A tablet design can use a two-column layout, while a desktop design can use a multicolumn layout. Designing layouts for tablet and desktop displays is simplified through the use of media queries. Media queries are essential to responsive web design because they let you customize layouts for various viewport sizes. If you take a mobile-first approach, use media queries to create the desired look for various-sized viewports, such as tablet, laptop, desktop, and larger desktop viewports.

Project — Use Media Queries to Design for Tablet and Desktop Viewports

In Chapter 5, you began to create a responsive design website by styling the Forward Fitness Club website for a mobile viewport. For the Chapter 6 project, you apply responsive web design principles to the Forward Fitness Club website by editing the site's style sheet to include media queries that will apply styles specific to tablet and desktop viewports. These enhancements will result in a better experience for users of tablet and laptop or desktop devices.

First, you will insert a media query to detect a tablet-sized viewport and then add new styles as appropriate for content displayed in that viewport. Next, you will insert a media query to detect a desktop-sized viewport and then add new styles as appropriate for content displayed in that viewport. To add interactivity and visual appeal to webpages displayed in the desktop viewport, you will add pseudo-classes to the style sheet to further style links within the navigation area. You will also add a linear gradient, which is a CSS3 property style, to the background of webpages displayed in the desktop viewport. Finally, you will validate the website and display all viewports in a browser. Figure 6–1 shows the home page of Forward Fitness Club sized for tablet and desktop viewports. Figure 6–1a shows the home page as it appears on a tablet; Figure 6–1b shows the same page as it appears in a desktop browser.

(a) Tablet

(b) Desktop

Figure 6–1

Roadmap

In this chapter, you will learn how to create the webpages shown in Figure 6–1. The following roadmap identifies general activities you will perform as you progress through this chapter:

1. ADD TABLET MEDIA QUERY AND STYLES.
2. ADD DESKTOP MEDIA QUERY AND STYLES.
3. MODIFY VIEWPORT BREAKPOINTS.
4. INSERT AND STYLE PSEUDO-CLASSES.
5. ADD a LINEAR GRADIENT.

At the beginning of step instructions throughout the chapter, you will see an abbreviated form of this roadmap. The abbreviated roadmap uses colors to indicate chapter progress: gray means the chapter is beyond that activity; blue means the task being shown is covered in that activity, and black means that activity is yet to be covered. For example, the following abbreviated roadmap indicates the chapter would be showing a task in the 4 INSERT & STYLE PSEUDO-CLASSES activity.

1 ADD TABLET MEDIA QUERY & STYLES | 2 ADD DESKTOP MEDIA QUERY & STYLES | 3 MODIFY VIEWPORT BREAKPOINTS

4 INSERT & STYLE PSEUDO-CLASSES | **5 ADD LINEAR GRADIENT**

Use the abbreviated roadmap as a progress guide while you read or step through the instructions in this chapter.

Using Media Queries

Recall from Chapter 5 that a **media query** detects the media type (such as screen or print) and the capabilities of the device that the browser is running on (such as the size of the viewport in pixels or its orientation of portrait versus landscape). Based on the information, the media query applies styles that work well for that viewport.

BTW
W3C
Recommendation
The W3C Media Queries recommendation was published in June 2012. Visit w3.org/TR/css3-mediaqueries / to view the recommendation.

In Chapter 5, you created a responsive layout and added style rules for a mobile viewport. These style rules were not included within a media query so that tablet and desktop viewports will use them by default. To add style rules that target tablet or desktop viewports in particular, create a media query for each viewport.

Media queries take responsiveness to an entirely new level. They allow you to apply *different* CSS style rules in response to the environment, such as the media on which the webpage is being viewed (screen or print) or the size of the viewport.

Media queries can apply styles to move, hide, or display content on the page, change text or colors, or add any other styles to make the page easier to read in a particular situation. If you resize a webpage and see the navigation system change or see a multicolumn layout reduce to one column as the viewport narrows to the size of a phone, you know that media queries are working behind the scenes to restyle the webpage in response to the viewport size.

Media queries can be embedded in the `link` tag that connects an external style sheet to an HTML file, or they can be inserted in the external style sheet itself. The following code provides a basic example of a media query inserted into the `link` tag of an HTML page:

```
<link rel="stylesheet" href="css/styles.css" media="screen">
<link rel="stylesheet" href="css/stylesprint.css" media="print">
```

The `media` attribute is used to determine which stylesheet should be applied. In this example, the `styles.css` style sheet found in the `css` folder will be applied if the webpage is displayed on the screen. The `stylesprint.css` stylesheet will be applied if the webpage is printed. This is a common technique to allow developers to style with rich colors and colorful images on the screen, but style with black text on a white background when the same webpage is printed.

Breakpoints

Media queries can do more than detect the current media type. They can also determine the size of the viewport, the viewable portion of the webpage.

To understand the code and syntax of how a media query detects viewport size, you set a **breakpoint** (sometimes called threshold), the point at which you want the webpage to change. The breakpoint is where you apply different styles to the webpage to cause it to change in a way that makes it easier to read and navigate for a particular viewport, such as a user viewing the webpage on a smart phone.

For the Forward Fitness Club website, the media queries should detect and apply style rules based on the three common viewport sizes listed in Table 6–1.

Table 6–1 Common Viewport Breakpoints		
Device	**Minimum Viewport Width**	**Maximum Viewport Width**
Small smartphones	320px	480px
Larger smartphones and tablets	481px	768px
Tablets in landscape orientation, laptops, and small desktop monitors	769px	1279px
Large desktop monitors	1280px	NA

Figure 6–2 shows how the NASA website uses responsive design with many customized layouts. It uses several breakpoints to determine the layout for various viewports. The designs are similar for the small and large smartphone viewports. Viewport widths of 768px and up can use multiple columns.

(a) 320px

(b) 520px

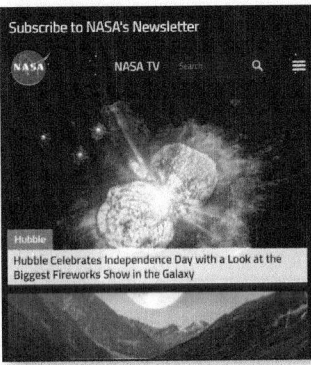

(c) 768px

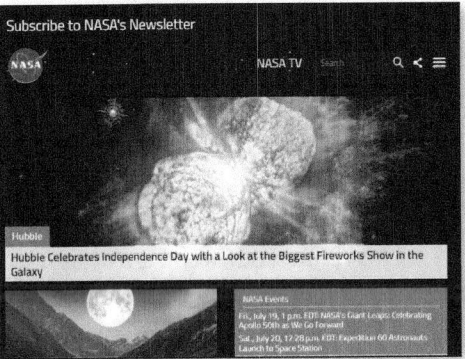

(d) 1000px

(e) 1440px

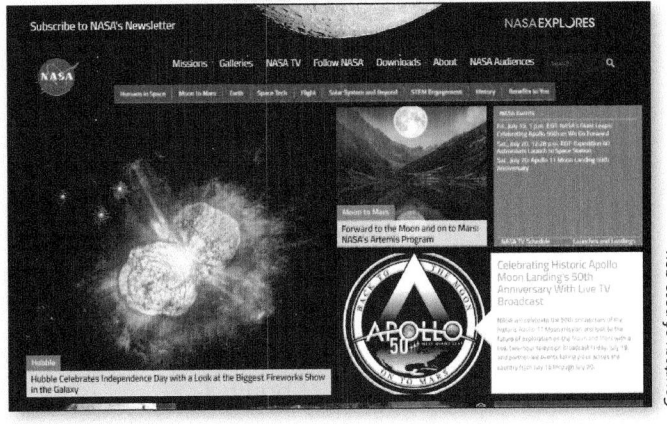

Courtesy of nasa.gov

Figure 6–2

Media Query Expressions

A media query can use a logical expression to test whether a viewport has reached a particular breakpoint. The logical expression includes the name of a **media query feature**, a characteristic of the environment, and a breakpoint value to be tested. If the logical expression evaluates to "true," the media query applies the styles that follow. Following is an example of a media query that includes a media type and a logical expression:

```
<link rel="stylesheet" href="css/styles-mobile.css"
media="screen and (max-width: 480px)">
```

This code directs browsers to use the styles-mobile.css stylesheet in the css folder when screens have a viewport width smaller than or equal to 480px (which is a common maximum viewport size for a phone and thus a common breakpoint for changing styles). In this case, max-width is the feature and 480px is the breakpoint value being tested in the logical condition. A media query can also test for both minimum and maximum breakpoints, as in the following example:

```
<link rel="stylesheet" href="css/styles-tablet.css"
media="screen and (min-width: 481px) and (max-width: 768px)">
```

In this case, the code directs browsers to apply the styles-tablet.css stylesheet in the css folder when screens have a viewport width between 481px and 768px (common breakpoint sizes for tablet devices). When testing for minimum and maximum widths, the word "and" separates each part of the media attribute value. This means that each part must be true to apply the associated styles. The syntax also requires you to surround the logical expression with parentheses and use a colon to separate the media query feature from the value being tested. When writing a media query, follow the requirements of the syntax carefully to make sure the media query works correctly.

At this point, you may be wondering how to select the values to use for breakpoint values, especially when so many new mobile devices of all sizes are constantly being introduced. Table 6–1 shows some common viewport breakpoint values as a starting point. After you understand the overall concept of media queries and how to code them, you can always modify breakpoints and add new media queries to refine your webpage design to look better when new devices hit the market.

A second way to implement media queries is to code them directly into a single CSS file using the `@media` rule. An example of a media query added to an external CSS file might be:

```
@media screen {
  body {
        background-color: #ccc;
  }
}
```

In this case, `@media screen` identifies the media to which the styles will be applied. Although the example shows only one style, a `background-color` applied to the `body,` you could list many style rules within the outer set of curly braces that surround the style rules for that media query. Another application of a media query in a CSS file to apply styles to a printed webpage might look like this:

```
@media print {
  body {
        width: 100%;
        color: #000;
        background-color: #fff;
  }
}
```

In this case, three styles are applied to `body` content when the webpage is printed to allow the content to fill 100% of the printable width of the page, change the text color to black `(#000),` and change the background color of the page to white `(#fff).`

Add logical expressions to media queries in an external CSS file as follows:

```
@media screen and (min-width: 481px) {
  .mobile {
        display: none;
  }
}
```

In this case, `min-width` is the feature of the screen that is tested. If the width is at least `481px,` the style rules will be applied. The `.mobile` selector means that the following styles will be applied to content identified with `class="mobile"` in the HTML document. The style declaration `display: none;` removes the content from the display. This example would hide content meant only for mobile display.

An example with two logical expressions might be:

```
@media all and (min-width: 481px) and (max-width: 768px) {
  body {
        color: #000;
  }
}
```

This media query applies to **all** types of media when both features are true. The viewport width must be at least **481px** but cannot exceed **768px**. The three most common types of media are **screen, print,** and **all**. Table 6–2 lists common media query features that can be used in a logical expression. For a full explanation of media query syntax, media types, and features, see the w3.org website.

Table 6–2 Common Media Query Features

Feature	Description
max-width min-width	Width of the viewport in pixels
max-resolution min-resolution	Resolution of the output device in dots per inch or dots per centimeter
max-height min-height	Height of the viewport in pixels
orientation	Orientation of the device (landscape or portrait)

Adding Media Queries to an External Style Sheet

The style sheet for the Forward Fitness Club website, styles.css, contains several style rules for a mobile display. In a mobile-first strategy, you list the mobile styles first, because these are the default styles. Next, you use media queries to add styles for larger viewports, progressing from tablet to desktop (which includes laptops). Styles created for the smaller viewports apply to larger viewports by default. To modify the appearance of an element for a larger viewport, create a media query for the larger viewport, and then create a new style rule.

For example, the mobile navigation links in the Forward Fitness Club website appear as a column of vertical buttons. To change this appearance for a tablet viewport, create a new style rule for the navigation list items and use the **display** property with a value of **inline** to display the links in a single line, as shown in the following example:

```
@media only screen and (min-width: 481px) {
  nav li {
        display: inline-block;
  }
}
```

This new style rule applies only to viewports with a minimum screen width of 481 pixels. As you continue the responsive design process and create media queries for progressively larger viewports, review the existing style rules for small viewports to know the default settings.

While 481px is a common breakpoint to start style rules for a tablet design, you do not have to start at this breakpoint. It really depends on your design. If you know that the design for the next size viewport requires more space than 481px, you can begin at a higher breakpoint. You can adjust breakpoints as necessary to accommodate your design.

BTW
Using the Keyword "only"
When you write a media query that specifies **@media only screen,** the **only** keyword indicates that older browsers should ignore the media query's style rules.

Designing for Tablet Viewports

The tablet market took off in 2010; however, as the size of smartphones increased, the tablet market started to decline. Tablet devices vary by operating system, manufacturer, and screen size. With so many tablet sizes, it can seem difficult to design a "one size fits all" layout for a tablet device. Luckily, when you use responsive web design and media queries, you do not need to design multiple tablet layouts to accommodate tablet devices. Instead, create one layout to target tablet viewports. If a particular tablet device has a viewport smaller than the minimum size specified in the media query, the layout will default to the mobile viewport layout.

To Create a Media Query for a Tablet Viewport

1 ADD TABLET MEDIA QUERY & STYLES | 2 ADD DESKTOP MEDIA QUERY & STYLES | 3 MODIFY VIEWPORT BREAKPOINTS
4 INSERT & STYLE PSEUDO-CLASSES | 5 ADD LINEAR GRADIENT

You have already completed the mobile style rules and now need to create a media query to target tablet devices. *Why? The media query will adjust the page layout to better display content when viewed on tablet device.* The following steps add a media query to target tablet devices.

1
- Open your text editor to run the program.
- Open styles.css file from the css folder to prepare to insert a media query.
- Tap or click at the end of Line 150 and then press the ENTER key twice to insert two new Lines 151 and 152.
- On Line 152, type `/* Media Query for Tablet Viewport */` to insert a CSS comment that identifies the tablet media query.

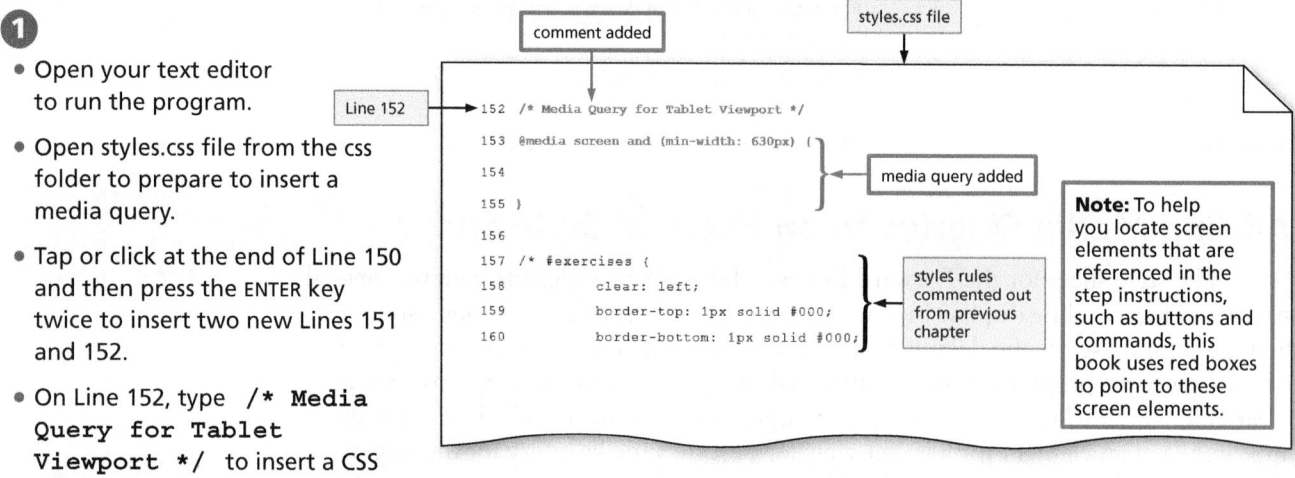

Figure 6–3

- Press the ENTER key to insert a new Line 153.
- On Line 153, type `@media screen and (min-width: 630px) {` to insert a media query.
- Press the ENTER key twice to insert two new Lines 154 and 155.
- On Line 155, type `}` to close the media query (Figure 6–3).

Q&A Why does the media query use `screen and min-width 630px`?
The 630px is a starting breakpoint. In future steps, you will adjust the navigation system to be displayed horizontally instead of vertically. The 630px should provide the needed space for this future change. You can always adjust breakpoints later if necessary.

Page Design for a Tablet Viewport

A tablet viewport is larger than a mobile viewport but smaller than a laptop or desktop viewport. The larger screen provides an opportunity for websites to display more content and use a multicolumn layout. Although tablet users expect to see more content than mobile users, they still expect the website to be touch-friendly, which means links and other touch spots that are easy to tap and text that is large enough to read without zooming.

When designing for a tablet viewport, maintain the same color scheme, typography, and general look of the website. The appearance of the website should look the same from viewport to viewport. The only changes should be layout and placement of content.

To determine the ideal layout for a website's tablet viewport, review the current website in Google Chrome's device mode at 481px to determine where content should be added and whether any content should be hidden. Figure 6–4 shows tablet viewport design suggestions for the home page of the Forward Fitness Center website.

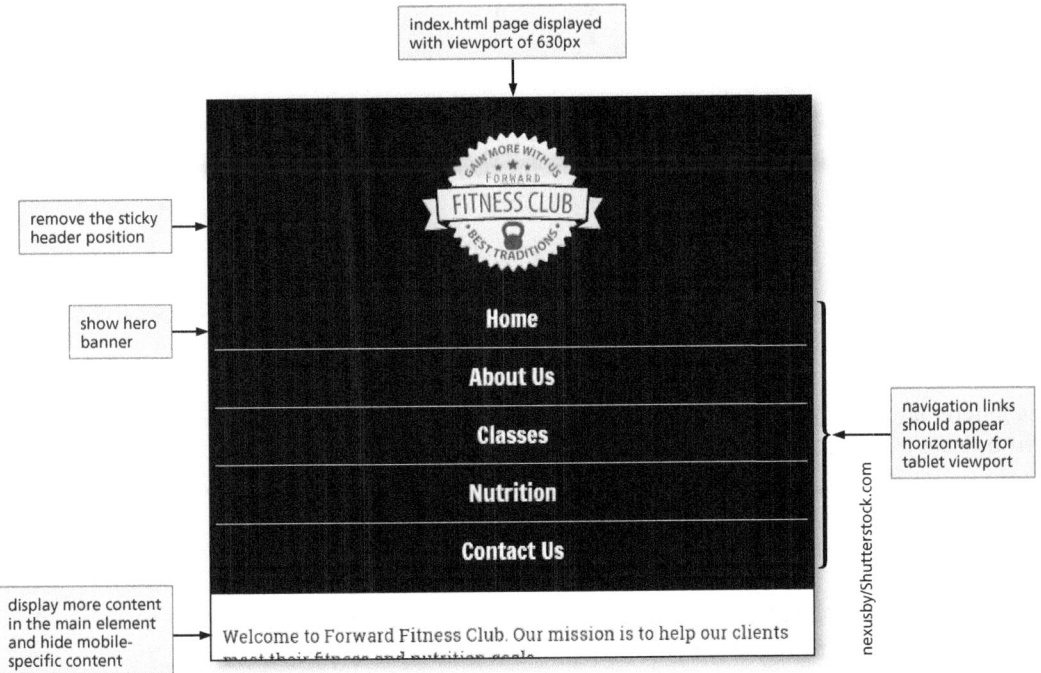

Figure 6–4

To Show and Hide Content for a Tablet Viewport

1 ADD TABLET MEDIA QUERY & STYLES | 2 ADD DESKTOP MEDIA QUERY & STYLES | 3 MODIFY VIEWPORT BREAKPOINTS
4 INSERT & STYLE PSEUDO-CLASSES | 5 ADD LINEAR GRADIENT

The content within the main area of the Forward Fitness Club webpages is ideal for a mobile user. In the HTML documents, this content appears in a `div` element with an attribute and value of `class="mobile"`. Create a new style rule to hide the mobile class in the tablet viewport with a `display` property and value of `none`. Because a tablet screen is larger than a mobile screen, it can display more content. The home page already includes additional content that describes the Forward Fitness Club's equipment and services and provides details about the trial membership. This content appears within a `div` element that contains the attribute `class="tablet-desktop"`. To display this content in a tablet viewport, create a new style rule to show the desktop class with a `display` property and value of `block`. *Why? Change the content to better suit the needs of a tablet device user.* The following steps add style rules to display the tablet-desktop class and to hide the mobile class for a tablet viewport.

1

- Place the insertion point at the end of Line 153 and press the ENTER key twice to insert new Lines 154 and 155.

- On Line 155, indent if necessary, and then type `/* Tablet Viewport: Show tablet-desktop class, hide mobile class */` to insert a comment.

- Press the ENTER key to insert a new Line 156, and then type `.tablet-desktop {` to add a new selector.

- Press the ENTER key to insert a new Line 157, increase the indent, and then type `display: block;` to add a new declaration.

- Press the ENTER key to insert a new Line 158, decrease the indent, and then type `}` to insert a closing brace.

- Press the ENTER key twice to insert new Lines 159 and 160.

- On Line 160, type `.mobile {` to add a new selector.

- Press the ENTER key to insert a new Line 161, increase the indent, and then type `display: none;` to add a new declaration.

- Press the ENTER key to insert a new Line 162, decrease the indent, and then type `}` to insert a closing brace (Figure 6–5).

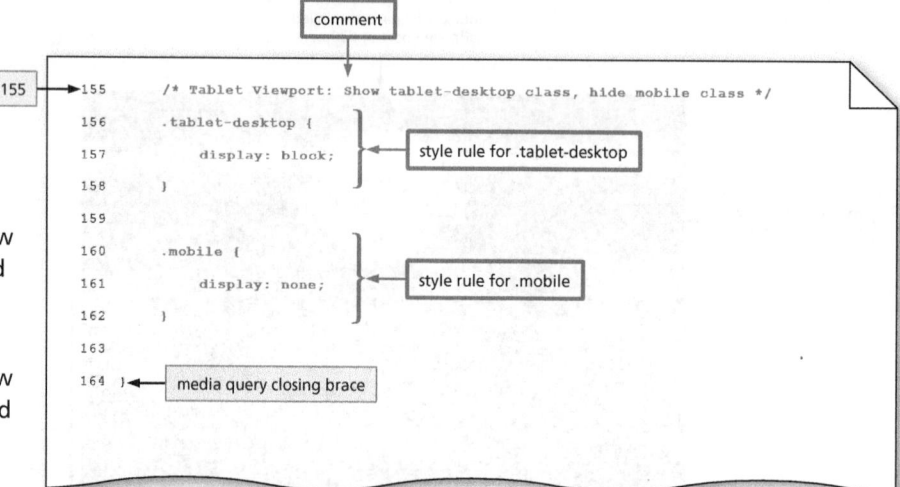

Figure 6–5

2

- Save your changes, open index.html in Google Chrome's device mode, and set the viewport width to 630px to simulate a tablet viewport. Scroll down to view your changes (Figure 6–6).

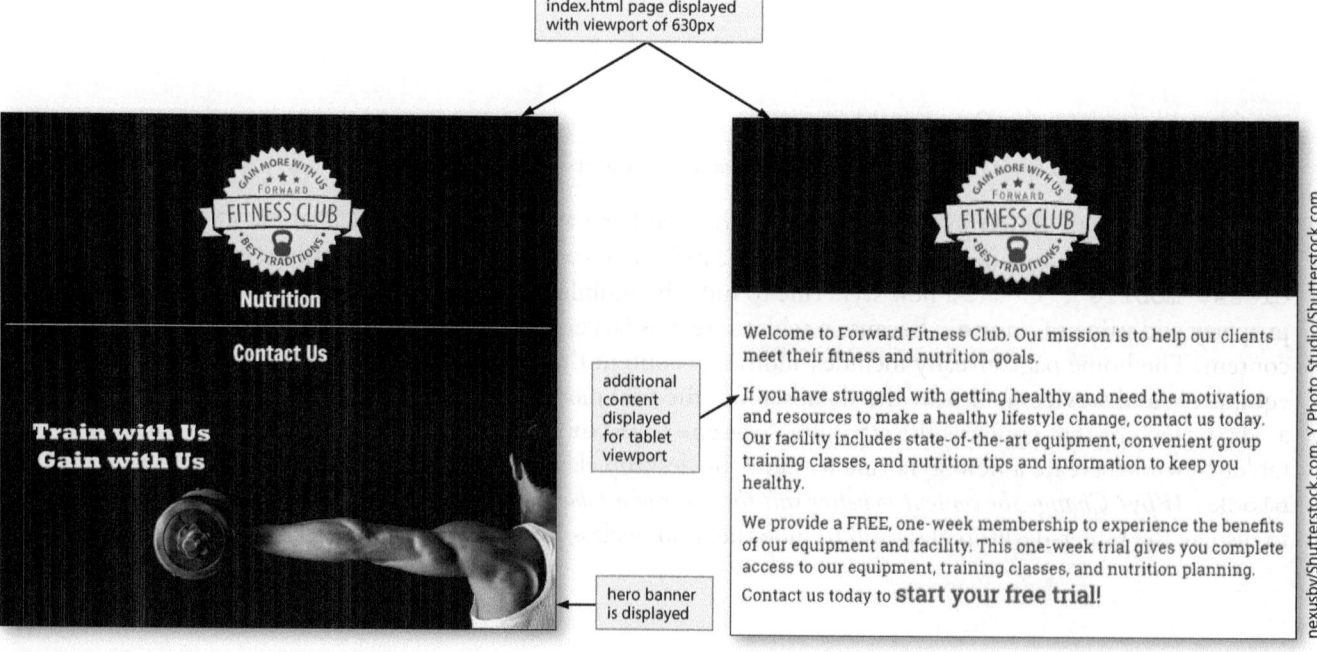

Figure 6–6

To Remove a Sticky Position for the Header for a Tablet Viewport

The purpose of the sticky header was to keep the company name and logo in view for a mobile device user. Because the screen size is larger for a tablet user, you can remove the sticky position. *Why? Improve the layout for a tablet device user by making the header position static.* The following steps remove the sticky position from the header element for a tablet viewport.

- Return to styles.css in your text editor to prepare to edit the file.

- Place your insertion point at the end of Line 162, after the closing curly brace, and then press the ENTER key twice to add new Lines 163 and 164.

- On Line 164, type `/* Tablet Viewport: Style rule for header */` to add a new comment.

- Press the ENTER key to add a new Line 165, and then type `header {` to add a new selector.

- Press the ENTER key to add a new Line 166, increase the indent, and then type `position: static;` to add a new declaration.

- Press the ENTER key to add a new Line 167, and then type `padding-bottom: 2%;` to add a new declaration.

- Press the ENTER key to add a new Line 168, press the SHIFT+TAB keys to decrease the indent, and then type `}` to close the style rule (Figure 6–7).

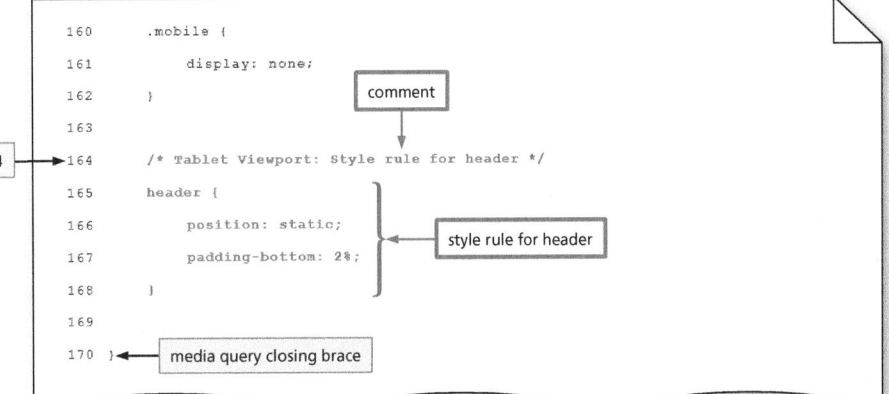

```
160        .mobile {
161            display: none;
162        }
163
164        /* Tablet Viewport: Style rule for header */
165        header {
166            position: static;
167            padding-bottom: 2%;
168        }
169
170    }
```

Line 164 → 164
comment
style rule for header
media query closing brace

Figure 6–7

- Save your changes, refresh index .html in Google Chrome's device mode, and then scroll down to view your changes (Figure 6–8).

Q&A

Does this change also remove the sticky header position for a mobile viewport?
No. Since this style rule is within the media query for the tablet viewport, it will only apply to devices with a minimum width of 630px.

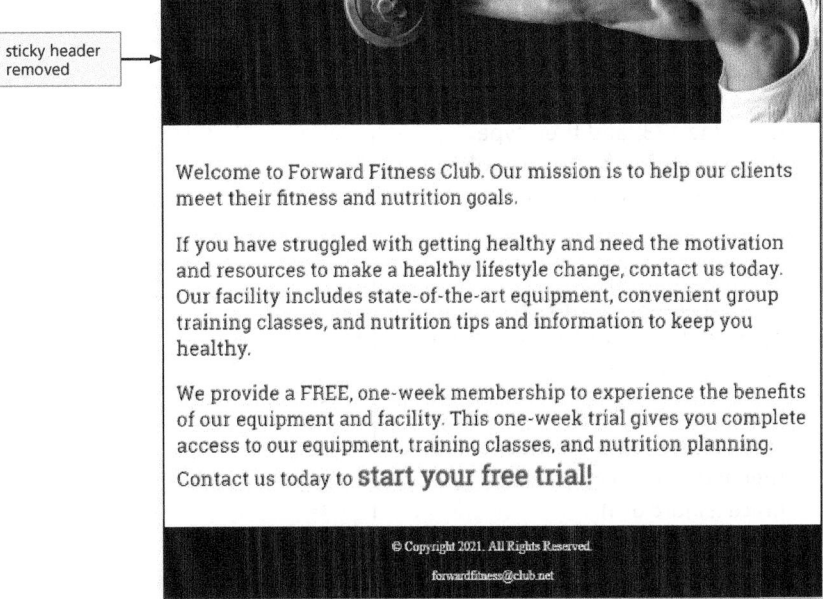

sticky header removed

Welcome to Forward Fitness Club. Our mission is to help our clients meet their fitness and nutrition goals.

If you have struggled with getting healthy and need the motivation and resources to make a healthy lifestyle change, contact us today. Our facility includes state-of-the-art equipment, convenient group training classes, and nutrition tips and information to keep you healthy.

We provide a FREE, one-week membership to experience the benefits of our equipment and facility. This one-week trial gives you complete access to our equipment, training classes, and nutrition planning. Contact us today to **start your free trial!**

© Copyright 2021. All Rights Reserved.
forwardfitness@club.net

Figure 6–8

Navigation Design for a Tablet Viewport

Recall that clear, simple, and easy website navigation is vital in attracting new visitors and keeping current customers. If users have a hard time navigating through a website in any viewport, they are likely to become frustrated and leave the site.

The navigation links in the Forward Fitness website currently appear as a vertical list or column of links. This design is tailored to the navigation needs of a smartphone user. Because a tablet screen is generally larger than a smartphone screen, maintaining a vertical list of navigation links is not necessary. Instead, take advantage of the screen width and align the navigation links in one horizontal line. This frees space for the main content below the navigation area, improving its visibility by displaying it in the middle of the screen.

To accomplish this design, create a style rule to display the navigation list items as a single horizontal line when displayed in a tablet viewport. Add other properties and values that override the defaults already set for the mobile viewport.

To Style the Navigation Area for a Tablet Viewport

1 ADD TABLET MEDIA QUERY & STYLES | **2 ADD DESKTOP MEDIA QUERY & STYLES** | **3 MODIFY VIEWPORT BREAKPOINTS**
4 INSERT & STYLE PSEUDO-CLASSES | **5 ADD LINEAR GRADIENT**

The default style rule for the navigation list items displays them as vertical links with a border between each link. Add a new style rule to display the list items in a single horizontal line and display the border between each link. **Why?** *Improve the webpage layout for a tablet viewport by displaying the navigation horizontally.* Adjust the nav li selector by displaying it as an inline-block, removing the top border, and defining a right border instead. Remove the right border from the last link and modify the padding between each link. The following steps add a style rule to the style sheet to format the nav list items for a tablet viewport.

- Place the insertion point at the end of Line 168 and press the ENTER key twice to insert new Lines 169 and 170.

- On Line 170, type `/* Tablet Viewport: Style rules for nav area */` to insert a comment.

- Press the ENTER key to insert a new Line 171 and type `nav li {` to add a new selector.

- Press the ENTER key to insert a new Line 172, increase the indent, and then type `border-top: none;` to add a new declaration.

- Press the ENTER key to insert a new Line 173, and then type `display: inline-block;` to add a new declaration.

- Press the ENTER key to insert a new Line 174, and then type `border-right: 1px solid #fff;` to add a new declaration.

- Press the ENTER key to insert a new Line 175, decrease the indent, and then type `}` to insert a closing brace (Figure 6–9).

Q&A
How does the inline-block value change the display of the navigation list items?
The inline-block value will display the navigation list items horizontally rather than vertically.

```
164     /* Tablet Viewport: Style rule for header */
165     header {
166         position: static;
167         padding-bottom: 2%;
168     }
169                          ┌─────────────┐
                             │comment added│
                             └─────────────┘
170     /* Tablet Viewport: Style rules for nav area */
171     nav li {
172         border-top: none;
173         display: inline-block;          ┌──────────────────────┐
174         border-right: 1px solid #fff;   │ style rule for nav li for
175     }                                    │ tablet viewport       │
176                                          └──────────────────────┘
177 }   ◄── media query closing brace
```

Line 170

Figure 6–9

- Press the ENTER key twice to insert new Lines 176 and 177.

- On Line 177, type **nav li:last-child {** to add a new selector.

- Press the ENTER key to insert a new Line 178, increase the indent, and then type **border-right: none;** to add new declaration.

- Press the ENTER key to insert a new Line 179, decrease the indent, and then type **}** to close the style rule.

- Press the ENTER key twice to insert new Lines 180 and 181.

- On Line 181, type **nav li a {** to add a new selector.

- Press the ENTER key to insert a new Line 182, increase the indent, and then type **padding: 0.1em 0.75em;** to add new declaration.

- Press the ENTER key to insert a new Line 183, decrease the indent, and then type **}** to close the style rule (Figure 6–10).

Q&A

What is the purpose of the nav li:last-child selector?
Recall that last-child is a structural pseudo-class. It selects the last element within its parent. In this case, the last list item within the navigation is selected and the right border is removed.

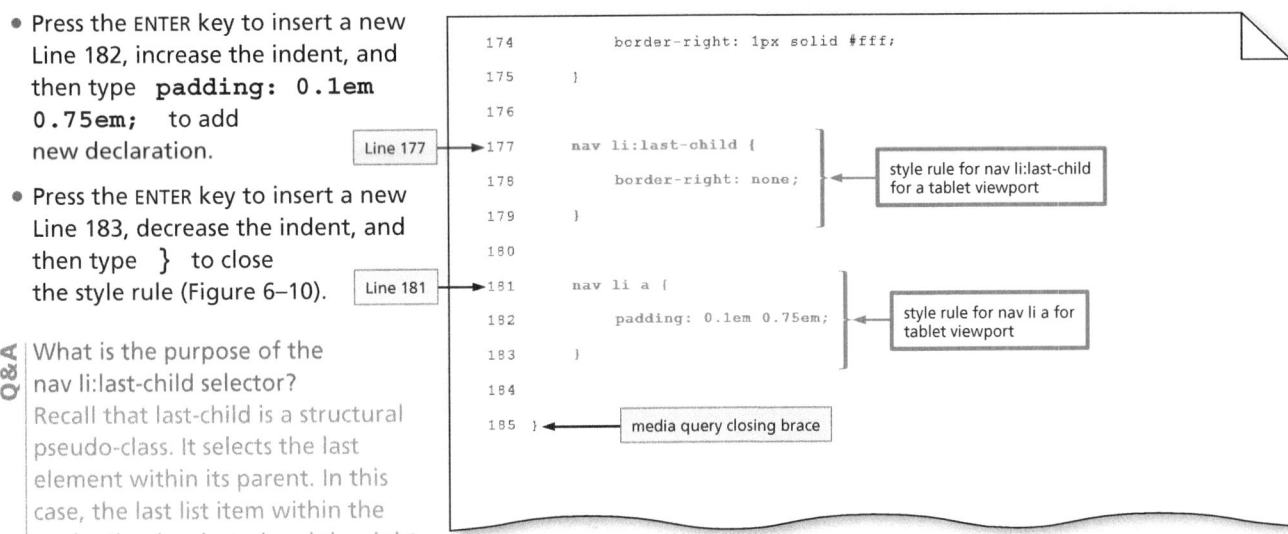

```
174          border-right: 1px solid #fff;
175     }
176
177     nav li:last-child {           ┐ style rule for nav li:last-child
178          border-right: none;      │ for a tablet viewport
179     }                             ┘
180
181     nav li a {                    ┐ style rule for nav li a for
182          padding: 0.1em 0.75em;   │ tablet viewport
183     }                             ┘
184
185 }    ← media query closing brace
```

Line 177 → 177
Line 181 → 181

Figure 6–10

- Save your changes, refresh index.html in your browser, and then adjust the window to the size of a tablet viewport (Figure 6–11).

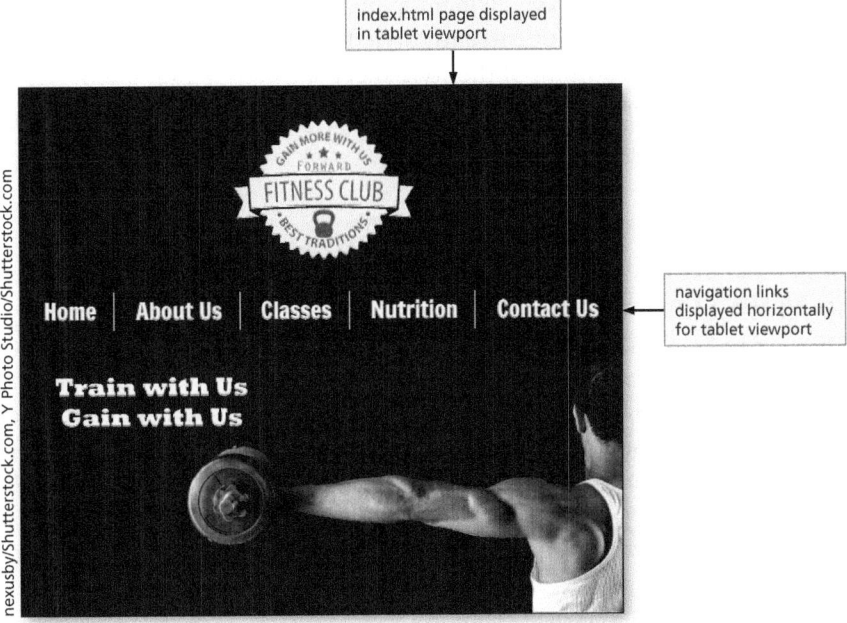

index.html page displayed in tablet viewport

navigation links displayed horizontally for tablet viewport

nexusby/Shutterstock.com, Y Photo Studio/Shutterstock.com

Figure 6–11

About Us Page Design for a Tablet Viewport

The About Us page now displays the content within the tablet-desktop class; however, this content needs to be styled for a tablet viewport to improve its appearance. Figure 6–12 shows the content displayed for a tablet device.

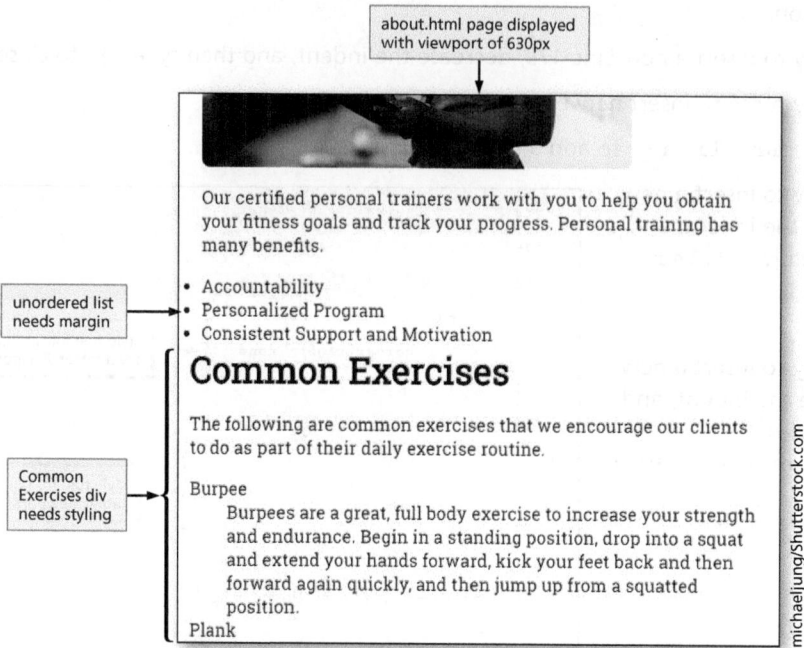

Figure 6–12

The About Us page contains several unordered lists that need some left margin so that the lists appear within their parent div element. Create a new style rule within the tablet viewport media query that applies a left margin to unordered list elements within the main element.

The about.html document also contains descriptions of common exercises within a `div` element with an `id="exercises"` attribute and value, but this content is not currently styled. In Chapter 5, recall that you moved three style rules to the bottom of the style sheet and commented them out for future use. You can now restore these style rules and add them to the tablet media query.

To Style Unordered List Elements within the Main Element for a Tablet Viewport

1 ADD TABLET MEDIA QUERY & STYLES | 2 ADD DESKTOP MEDIA QUERY & STYLES | 3 MODIFY VIEWPORT BREAKPOINTS
4 INSERT & STYLE PSEUDO-CLASSES | 5 ADD LINEAR GRADIENT

The About Us page contains unordered list elements within the main content area. The unordered list elements currently appear outside of their parent div element. Create a new selector for the main ul and then add a style rule to apply margin to the bottom and left of the unordered list.. *Why? Apply left margin to the unordered list elements so that they appear within their parent div elements. Apply bottom margin to include passive white space after each unordered list element.* The following steps add a new style rule to display and format the main ul for a tablet viewport.

1

- Place the insertion point at the end of Line 183 and press the ENTER key twice to insert new Lines 184 and 185.

- On Line 185, type `/* Tablet Viewport: Style rules for main content area */` to insert a comment.

- Press the ENTER key to insert a new Line 186, and then type `main ul {` to add a new selector.

- Press the ENTER key to insert a new Line 187, increase the indent, and then type `margin: 0 0 4% 10%;` to add a new declaration.

- Press the ENTER key to insert a new Line 188, decrease the indent, and then type `}` to insert a closing brace (Figure 6–13).

Why are four values specified for the margin property?

The first value sets the top margin to zero. The second value sets the right margin to zero. The third value sets the bottom margin to 4%. The fourth value sets the left margin to 10%.

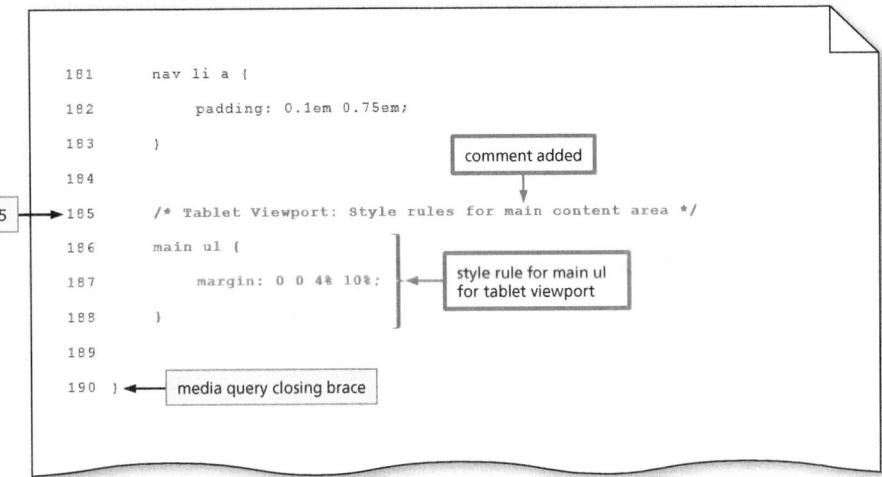

```
181     nav li a {
182         padding: 0.1em 0.75em;
183     }
184
185     /* Tablet Viewport: Style rules for main content area */
186     main ul {
187         margin: 0 0 4% 10%;
188     }
189
190     }
```

comment added

Line 185 →

style rule for main ul for tablet viewport

media query closing brace

Figure 6–13

2

- Save your changes, open about.html in Google Chrome's device mode and set the viewport size to 630px to simulate a tablet viewport, and then scroll the webpage (Figure 6–14).

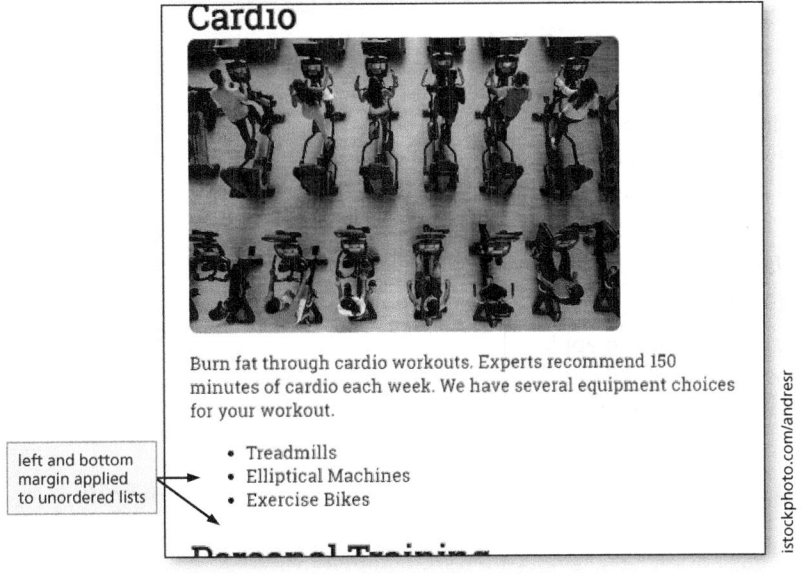

left and bottom margin applied to unordered lists

istockphoto.com/andresr

Figure 6–14

To Restore Previous Style Rules and Move Them into the Tablet Media Query

1 ADD TABLET MEDIA QUERY & STYLES | 2 ADD DESKTOP MEDIA QUERY & STYLES | 3 MODIFY VIEWPORT BREAKPOINTS
4 INSERT & STYLE PSEUDO-CLASSES | 5 ADD LINEAR GRADIENT

In Chapter 4, you created three style rules to style the div element with the id attribute exercises. However, when you styled content for a mobile viewport in Chapter 5, you moved these style rules to the bottom of the style sheet and converted them to a comment. You now need to restore these style rules and move them to the tablet media query. **Why?** *Now that the Common Exercises div content is displayed for a tablet viewport, you need to style the content.* The following steps move the style rules for #exercises, #exercises dt, and #exercises dd into the media query for a tablet viewport.

- Place the insertion point at the beginning of Line 192, just before the /* comment syntax, and then press the DELETE key twice to delete the /* comment syntax.

- Place your insertion point at the end of Line 206 and then press the BACKSPACE key twice to delete the */ comment syntax (Figure 6–15).

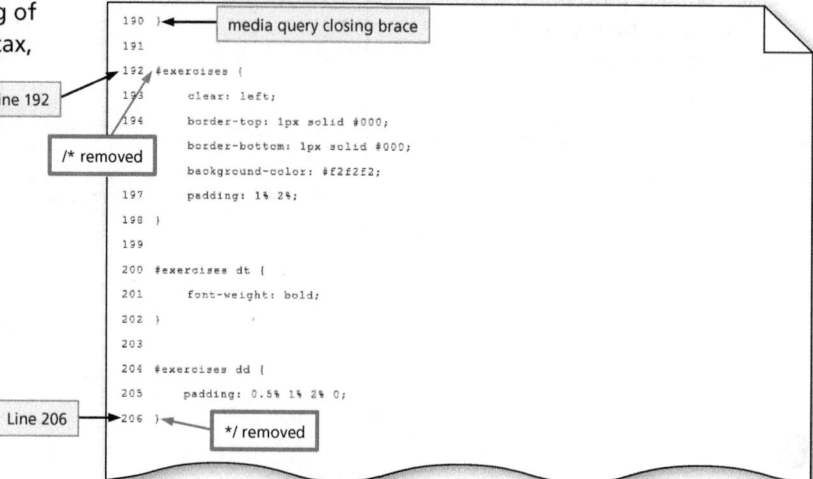

Figure 6–15

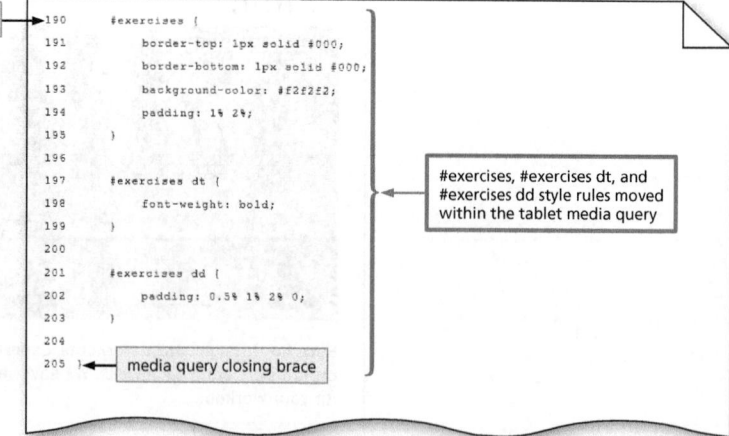

- Select Lines 192 through 206 and press the CTRL+X keys to cut these style rules.

- Place your insertion point at the end of Line 188, after the closing curly brace for the main ul selector style rule, press the ENTER key twice, and then press the CTRL+V keys to paste the style rules.

- Delete the clear: left; declaration from the #exercises style rule to remove it.

- Review the style rules you just pasted and apply indents as necessary to ensure that all style rules are indented within the tablet media query (Figure 6–16).

Figure 6–16

Q&A

Why do I need to move these style rules within the tablet media query?

Because these style rules should apply to a tablet viewport, you place them within the tablet media query. Note that you should never have style rules below a media query.

Why do I need to delete the clear property from the #exercises style rule?

Because the content above the <div id="exercises"> is not floating, the clear property is not needed.

- Save your changes and refresh the about.html page in Chrome to view your changes.
- Scroll down the page to view the content for Common Exercises (Figure 6–17).

style rules are now applied to the Common Exercises div element

Common Exercises

The following are common exercises that we encourage our clients to do as part of their daily exercise routine.

Burpee

Burpees are a great, full body exercise to increase your strength and endurance. Begin in a standing position, drop into a squat and extend your hands forward, kick your feet back and then forward again quickly, and then jump up from a squatted position.

Plank

Planks build your core strength. To perform a plank, get in a push up position and rest your forearms on the floor. Hold the position as long as you can.

Mountain Climber

Mountain climbers are a good cardio exercise. Place your hands on the floor in a push up position, then bring one knee up to your chest and then switch as quickly as you can (as though you are climbing a mountain).

Figure 6–17

Contact Us Page Design for a Tablet Viewport

The Contact Us page is currently designed for a mobile viewport. It displays a telephone link to easily call the Forward Fitness Club. It also displays a smaller map. Figure 6–18 shows the Contact Us page displayed in a tablet viewport.

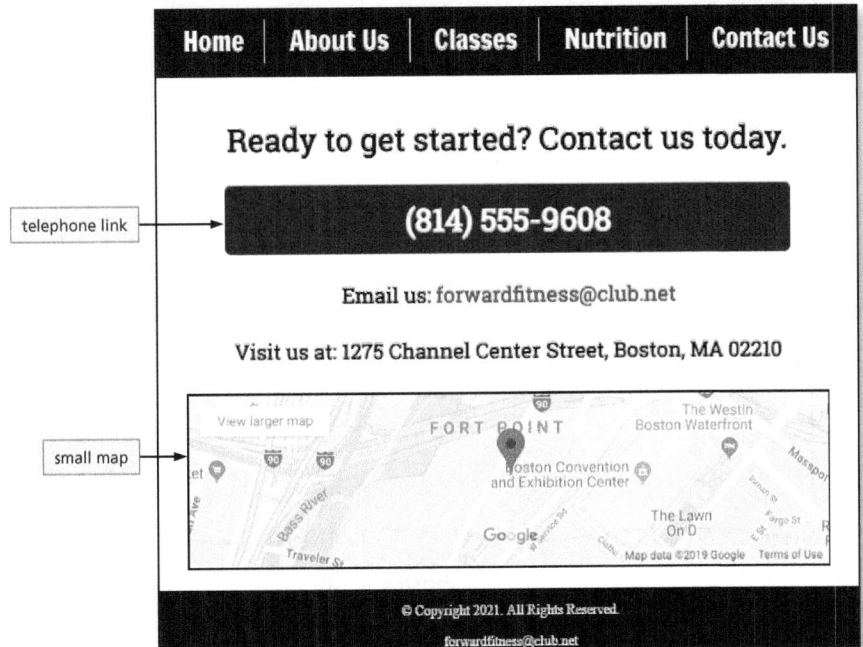

telephone link

small map

Figure 6–18

Because tablet devices cannot make phone calls, the telephone link is unnecessary. Update the Contact Us page by adding another heading 4 element with the phone number, but do not include the telephone link. Apply the tablet-desktop class to the heading 4 element so that it is hidden for a mobile viewport and is displayed for a tablet viewport. You also need to apply the mobile class to the telephone anchor element so that it is displayed only for a mobile viewport.

Because a tablet viewport is larger than a mobile viewport, adjust the height of the map to its original size.

To Modify the Contact Us Page

Add another heading 4 element to the Contact Us page that includes a telephone number without the telephone link, and apply the tablet-desktop class to the element. Next, apply the mobile class to the heading 4 element that contains the telephone link. *Why? A tablet device cannot make a phone call; therefore, you need to hide the telephone link and display only the telephone number.* The following steps create a new heading 4 element with a class attribute value of tel-num on the contact.html page and a style rule for the tel-num class selector.

- Open contact.html in your text editor to prepare to edit the file.

- On Line 37, place your insertion point before the tel-link class value, and then type **mobile** followed by a space to add the mobile class to the element.

- Place your insertion point at the end of Line 37, press the ENTER key to insert a new Line 38, and then type **<h4 class="tablet-desktop tel-num">(814) 555-9608</h4>** to add a heading 4 element (Figure 6–19).

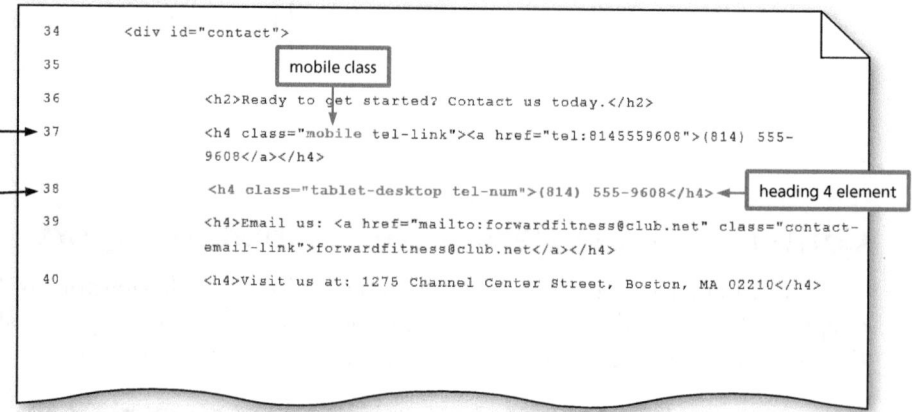

Figure 6–19

- Return to styles.css, place your insertion point at the end of Line 203, and press the ENTER key twice to insert new Lines 204 and 205.

- On Line 205, type **.tel-num {** to add a new selector.

- Press the ENTER key to insert a new Line 206, increase the indent, and then type **font-size: 1.25em;** to add a declaration.

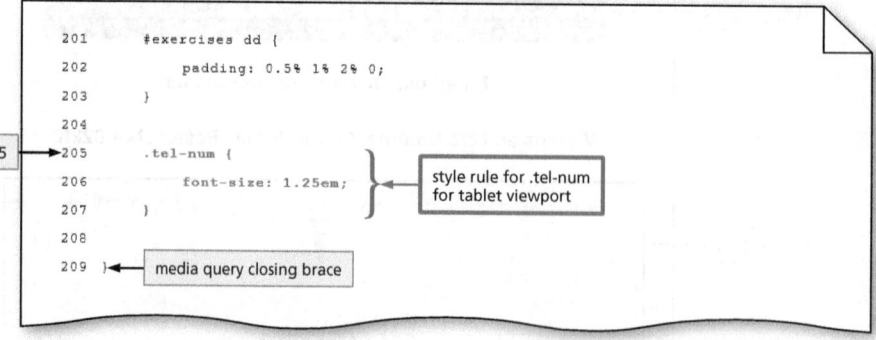

Figure 6–20

- Press the ENTER key to insert a new Line 207, decrease the indent, and then type **}** to close the style rule (Figure 6–20).

3

- Save your changes, open contact.html in Google Chrome's device mode, and then set the viewport size to 630px to simulate a tablet viewport (Figure 6–21).

Figure 6–21

To Style the Map for a Tablet Viewport

The map on the Contact Us page is currently styled for a mobile viewport. Create a new style rule within the tablet media query to use the default height and width of the embedded map. The following steps create a new style rule for the map class selector within the tablet media query.

1 Return to styles.css, place the insertion point at the end of Line 207 and press the ENTER key twice to insert new Lines 208 and 209.

2 On Line 209, type `.map {` to add a new selector.

3 Press the ENTER key, increase the indent, and then type **width: 600px;** to add a declaration.

4 Press the ENTER key to insert a new Line 211, and then type **height: 450px;** to add a declaration.

5 Press the ENTER key to insert a new Line 212, decrease the indent, type `}` to insert a closing brace (Figure 6–22).

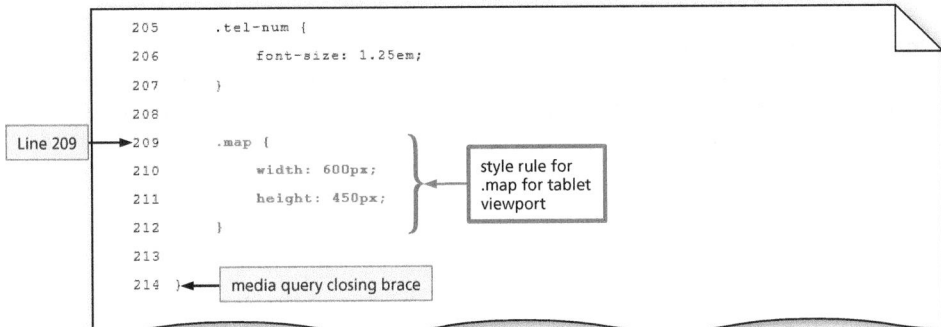

Figure 6–22

6 Save your changes, refresh contact.html in your browser, and then scroll down to view the changes. (Figure 6–23).

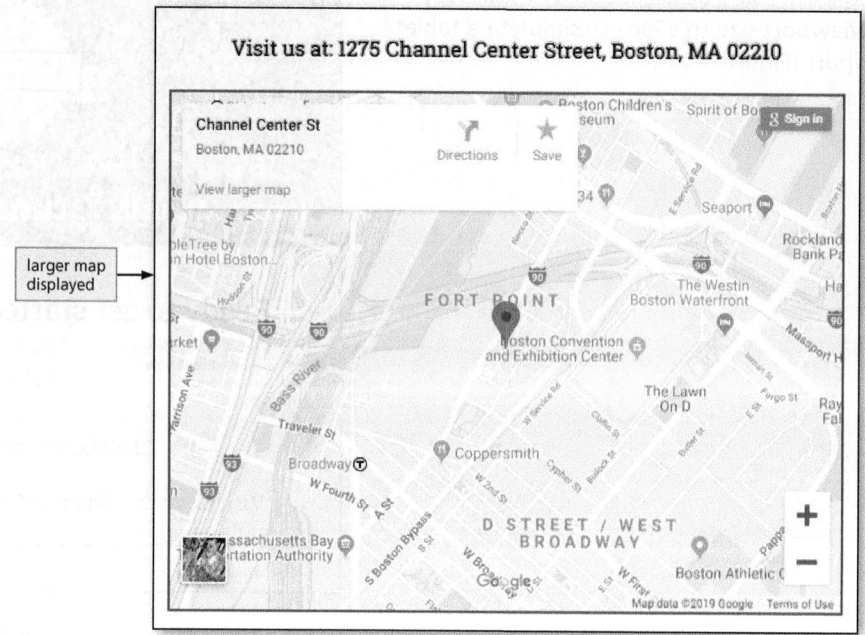

larger map displayed

Figure 6–23

Break Point: If you want to take a break, this is a good place to do so. To resume at a later time, continue reading the text from this location forward.

Designing for Desktop Viewports

You used a simple style sheet in Chapter 4 to create a desktop layout. Now you will create a similar layout using responsive design and create a media query for a desktop viewport. The same desktop design principles apply for responsive design; use simple, intuitive navigation, clear images, and typography and apply the same color scheme. Maintain the same look and feel of the site, but modify the layout to best accommodate the desktop viewport. Because desktop screens are often wider than those for other devices, designing for a desktop viewport also provides an opportunity for a multiple-column layout. One method for multiple-column layouts is shown in this chapter, and another method will be covered in Chapter 7.

CONSIDER THIS

How do I begin designing for a desktop viewport?
Before you modify the layout, review the content on each webpage. Consider the design from the user's point of view. What content do most visitors want to find on the home page? Make sure this content is featured prominently. Balance the tradeoffs of providing additional content such as photos and multimedia with potentially reducing performance.

To Create a Media Query
for a Desktop Viewport

Create a media query for a desktop viewport. **Why?** *The desktop media query will contain styles to alter the website appearance for desktop users.* The following step adds a media query to target desktop viewports.

1

- In styles.css, tap or click at the end of Line 214 and then press the ENTER key twice to insert two new Lines 215 and 216.

- On Line 216, type **/* Media Query for Desktop Viewport */** to insert a CSS comment.

- Press the ENTER key once to insert a new Line 217.

- On Line 217, type **@media screen and (min-width: 769px) {** to insert a media query.

- Press the ENTER key twice to insert new Lines 218 and 219.

- On Line 219, type **}** to insert a closing brace (Figure 6–24).

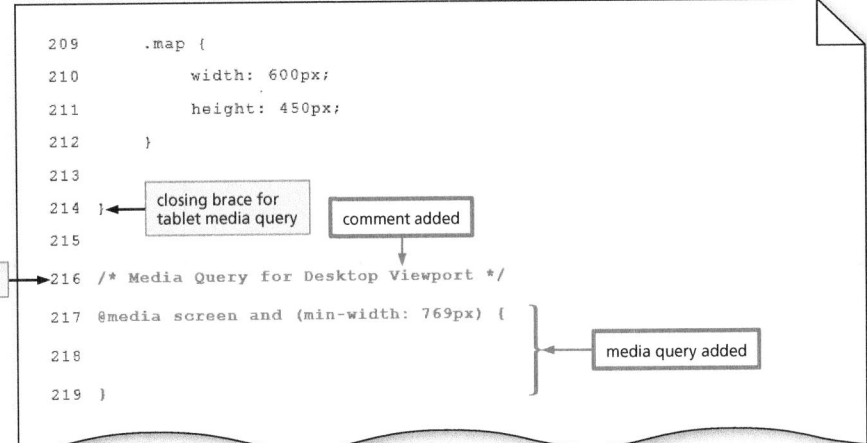

```
209        .map {
210            width: 600px;
211            height: 450px;
212        }
213
214    }          ← closing brace for tablet media query    comment added
215
Line 216 → 216    /* Media Query for Desktop Viewport */
217    @media screen and (min-width: 769px) {
218                                              ← media query added
219    }
```

Figure 6–24

Q&A Why does the media query use **screen and min-width 769px?**

Because 768px is a common breakpoint for tablet devices, set the desktop styles to apply at 769px and above.

To Create a Style Rule for the Header Element in the Desktop Media Query

Create a two-column layout for the header and nav elements, as you did in Chapter 4. Start by creating a style rule for the header element that floats it to the left and sets the width to 25%. The tablet media query specifies bottom padding for the header. Because this style rule is inherited by the desktop media query, remove the bottom padding. The following steps create a style rule for the header selector as desired for a desktop viewport.

1 Place the insertion point at the end of Line 217 and press the ENTER key twice to insert new Lines 218 and 219.

2 On Line 219, indent if necessary, and then type **/* Desktop Viewport: Style rule for header */** to insert a comment.

3 Press the ENTER key to insert a new Line 220 and type **header {** to add a new selector.

4 Press the ENTER key to insert a new Line 221, increase the indent, and then type **width: 25%;** to add a new declaration.

5 Press the ENTER key to insert a new Line 222, and then type **float: left;** to add a new declaration.

6 Press the ENTER key to insert a new Line 223 and then type `padding-bottom: 0;` to add a new declaration.

7 Press the ENTER key to insert a new Line 224, decrease the indent, and then type **}** to insert a closing brace (Figure 6–25).

```
216  /* Media Query for Desktop Viewport */

217  @media screen and (min-width: 769px) {

218
                                                     comment added
219      /* Desktop Viewport: Style rule for header */

220      header {

221          width: 25%;

222          float: left;                            style rule for header

223          padding-bottom: 0;

224      }

225

226  }                media query closing brace
```

Line 219 → 219

Figure 6–25

8 Save your changes, open index.html in your browser, and then maximize the window to view a desktop viewport (Figure 6–26).

index.html page displayed in desktop viewport

header floated to the left

nexusby/Shutterstock.com, Y Photo Studio/Shutterstock.com

Figure 6–26

To Style the Navigation Element for a Desktop Viewport

Style the navigation area to appear as a single unified element, to the right of the header element, with navigation links evenly distributed within the area. The first step to create this layout is to create a style rule that floats the nav to the right, sets its width to 70%, and sets its margin. The following steps create a style rule for the nav selector as desired for a desktop viewport.

1 Place the insertion point at the end of Line 224 and press the ENTER key twice to insert new Lines 225 and 226.

2 On Line 226, type `/* Desktop Viewport: Style rules for nav area */` to insert a comment.

3 Press the ENTER key to insert a new Line 227, and then type `nav {` to add a new selector.

4 Press the ENTER key to insert a new Line 228, increase the indent, and then type `float: right;` to add a new declaration.

5 Press the ENTER key to insert a new Line 229, and then type `width: 70%;` to add a new declaration.

6 Press the ENTER key to insert a new Line 230, and then type `margin: 4em 1em 0 0;` to add a new declaration.

7 Press the ENTER key to insert a new Line 231, decrease the indent, and then type `}` to insert a closing brace (Figure 6–27).

```
221          width: 25%;
222          float: left;
223          padding-bottom: 0;
224      }                          comment added
225
226      /* Desktop Viewport: Style rules for nav area */   ← Line 226
227      nav {
228          float: right;
229          width: 70%;             style rule for the nav
230          margin: 4em 1em 0 0;
231      }
232
233  }   media query closing brace
```

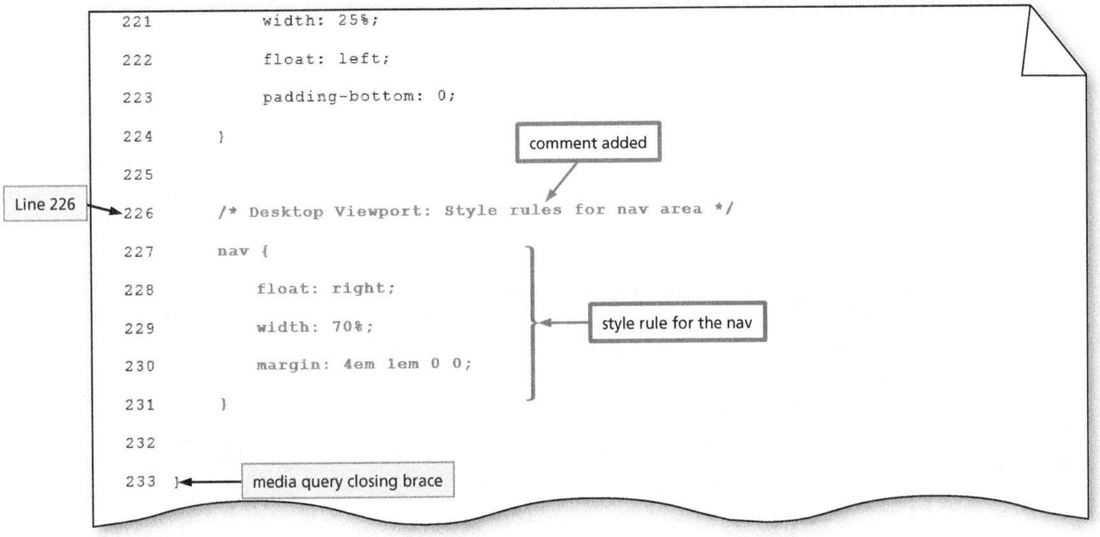

Figure 6–27

To Style the Unordered List in the Navigation Area for a Desktop Viewport

The next step to create a single unified navigation area is to create a new style rule for the unordered list within the nav element. Create a style rule that aligns the text to the right. The following steps add a style rule for the unordered list in the navigation element as desired for a desktop viewport.

1 Place the insertion point at the end of Line 231 and press the ENTER key twice to insert new Lines 232 and 233.

2 On Line 233, type `nav ul {` to add a new selector.

3 Press the ENTER key to insert a new Line 234, increase the indent, and then type `text-align: right;` to add a new declaration.

④ Press the ENTER key to insert a new Line 235, decrease the indent, and then type } to insert a closing brace (Figure 6–28).

```
226     /* Desktop Viewport: Style rules for nav area */

227     nav {

228         float: right;

229         width: 70%;

230         margin: 4em 1em 0 0;

231     }

232

233     nav ul {

234         text-align: right;

235     }

236

237     }
```

Line 233 → 233

style rule for nav ul

media query closing brace

Figure 6–28

⑤ Save your changes and refresh index.html in your browser to view your changes (Figure 6–29).

index.html page displayed
in desktop viewport

desktop viewport
navigation

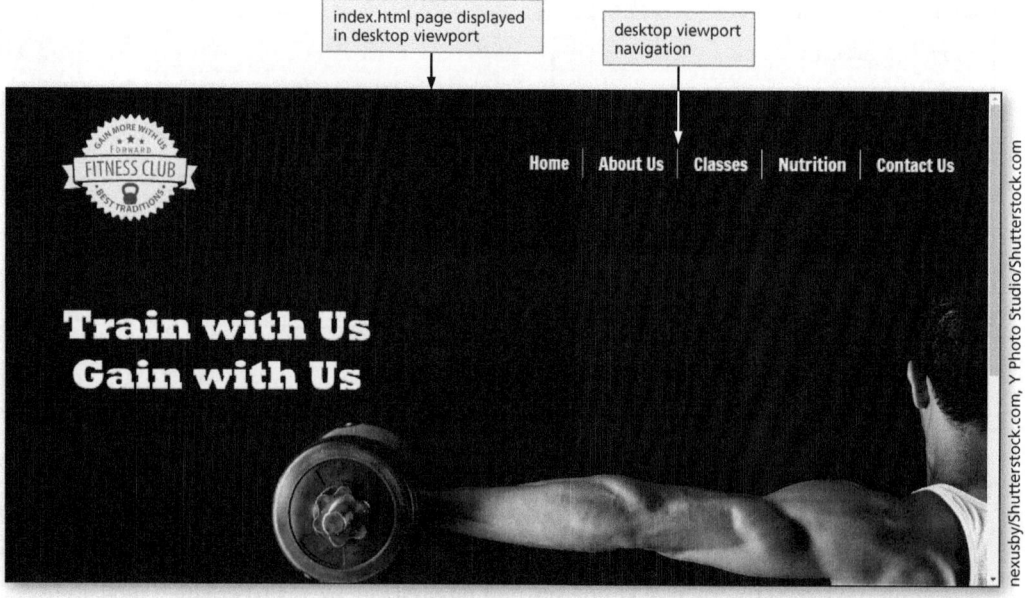

nexusby/Shutterstock.com, Y Photo Studio/Shutterstock.com

Figure 6–29

To Style the List Item Links in the Navigation Area for a Desktop Viewport

The navigation area now appears as a single unified line, although the border needs to be removed. The next step in styling the navigation area is to create a new style rule for the list items and list item links. Create a style rule for the list items within the nav element to remove the border. Next, apply some padding to increase the amount of space around each link. The following steps create a new style rule for the list items and list item links within the navigation element as desired for a desktop viewport.

1 Place the insertion point at the end of Line 235 and press the ENTER key twice to insert new Lines 236 and 237.

2 On Line 237, type `nav li {` to add a new selector.

3 Press the ENTER key to insert new Line 238, increase the indent, and then type `border: none;` to add a new declaration.

4 Press the ENTER key to insert new Line 239, decrease the indent, and then type `}` to insert a closing brace.

5 Press the ENTER key twice to insert new Lines 240 and 241, and then type `nav li a {` to add a new selector.

6 Press the ENTER key to insert a new Line 242, increase the indent, and then type `padding: 0.5em 1em;` to add a new declaration.

7 Press the ENTER key to insert new Line 243, decrease the indent, and then type `}` to insert a closing brace (Figure 6–30).

```
233    nav ul {
234        text-align: right;
235    }
236
237    nav li {
238        border: none;          style rule for nav li
239    }
240
241    nav li a {
242        padding: 0.5em 1em;    style rule for nav li a
243    }
244
245 }   media query closing brace
```
Line 237 →237

Figure 6–30

8 Save your changes and refresh index.html in your browser to view your changes (Figure 6–31).

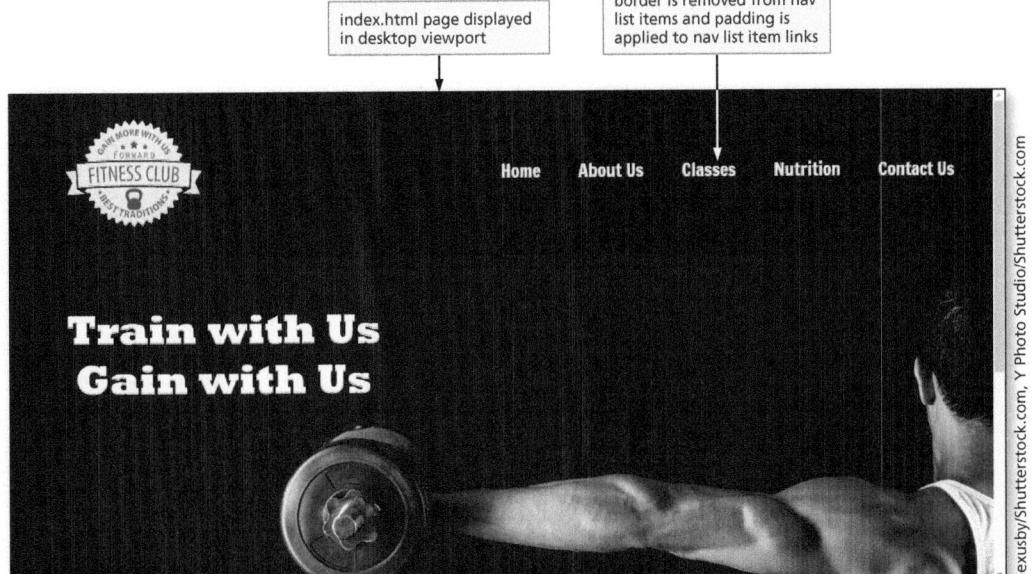

index.html page displayed in desktop viewport

border is removed from nav list items and padding is applied to nav list item links

Figure 6–31

To Style the Main Element for a Desktop Viewport

The appearance of the main content area appears normal on the home page; however, when you view the About Us and Contact Us pages, the page layout appears distorted. This is due to the float properties applied to the header and nav elements. To correct the layout issue, create a new style rule for the main element that specifies a clear property with a value of left. The following steps create a new style rule for the main element as desired for a desktop viewport.

1 Place the insertion point at the end of Line 243 and press the ENTER key twice to insert new Lines 244 and 245.

2 On Line 245, type `/* Desktop Viewport: Style Rules for main content */` to insert a comment.

3 Press the ENTER key to insert a new Line 246, and then type `main {` to add a new selector.

4 Press the ENTER key to insert a new Line 247, increase the indent, and then type `clear: left;` to add a new declaration.

5 Press the ENTER key to insert a new Line 248, decrease the indent, and then type `}` to insert a closing brace (Figure 6–32).

```
241     nav li a {
242         padding: 0.5em 1em;
243     }                              [comment added]
244
Line 245 → 245     /* Desktop Viewport: Style Rules for main content */
246     main {
247         clear: left;      ] ← [style rule for main]
248     }
249
250 }  ← [media query closing brace]
```

Figure 6–32

6 Save your changes and open about.html in your browser to view your changes (Figure 6–33).

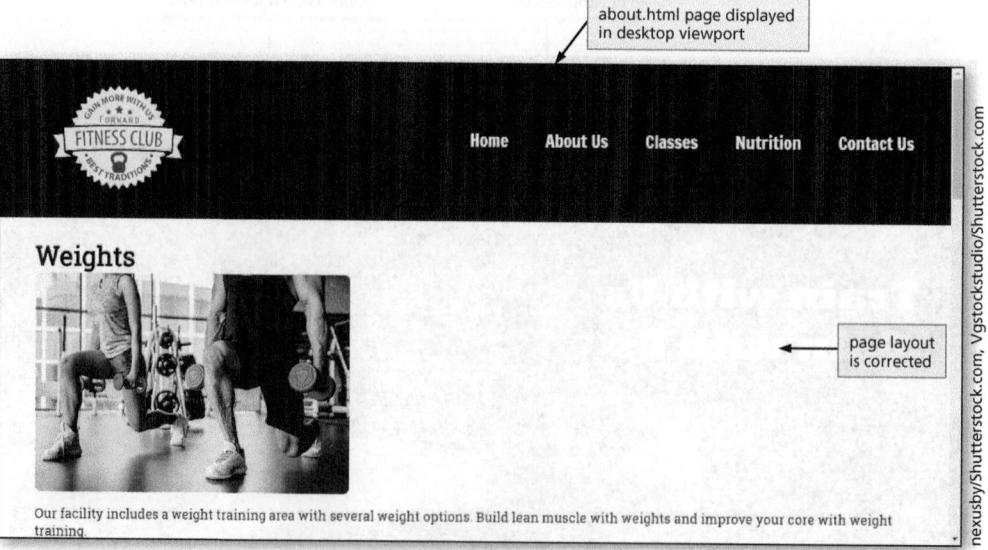

[about.html page displayed in desktop viewport]

[page layout is corrected]

nexusby/Shutterstock.com, Vgstockstudio/Shutterstock.com

Figure 6–33

To Style heading 1 Elements Within the main Element for a Desktop Viewport

Adjust the font size for heading 1 elements in the main element to enhance their appearance to complement a multiple-column layout. The following steps create a new style rule for heading 1 elements within the main element as desired for a desktop viewport.

1 Place the insertion point at the end of Line 248 and press the ENTER key twice to insert new Lines 249 and 250.

2 On Line 250, type **main h1 {** to add a new selector.

3 Press the ENTER key to insert a new Line 251, increase the indent, and then type **font-size: 1.8em;** to add a new declaration.

4 Press the ENTER key to insert a new Line 252, decrease the indent, and then type **}** to insert a closing brace (Figure 6–34).

```
241     nav li a {
242          padding: 0.5em 1em;
243     }
244
245     /* Desktop Viewport: Style Rules for main content */
246     main {
247          clear: left;
248     }
249
250     main h1 {                    ← style rule for main h1
251          font-size: 1.8em;
252     }
253
254 }                                ← media query closing brace
```

Line 250 → 250

Figure 6–34

5 Save your changes and refresh about.html in your browser to view your changes (Figure 6–35).

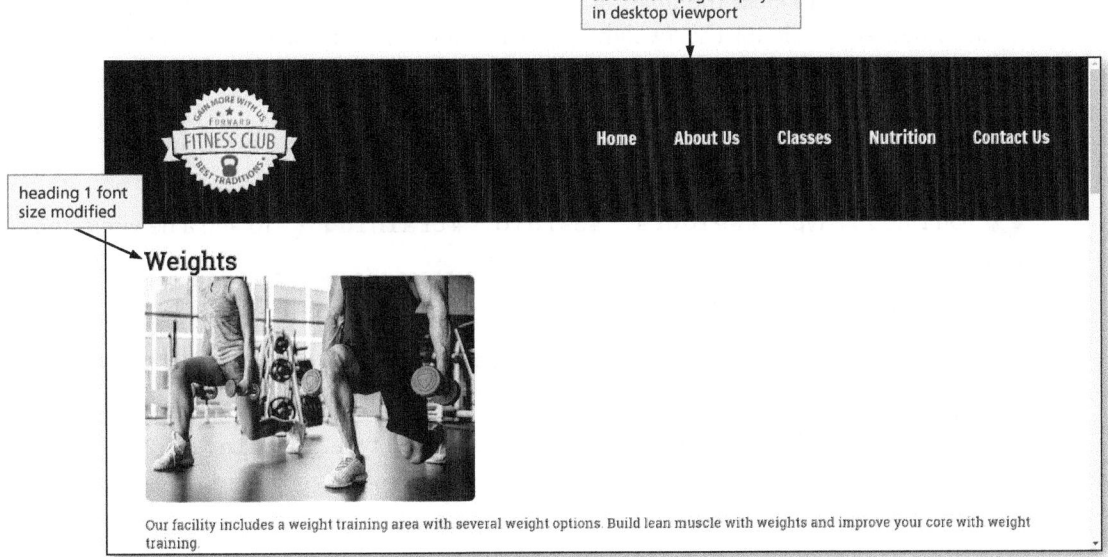

about.html page displayed in desktop viewport

heading 1 font size modified

Figure 6–35

About Us Page Design for a Desktop Viewport

When the About Us page is displayed in a desktop viewport, the Weights, Cardio, and Personal Training div elements appear in a single column. Figure 6–36 shows the About Us page displayed in a desktop viewport.

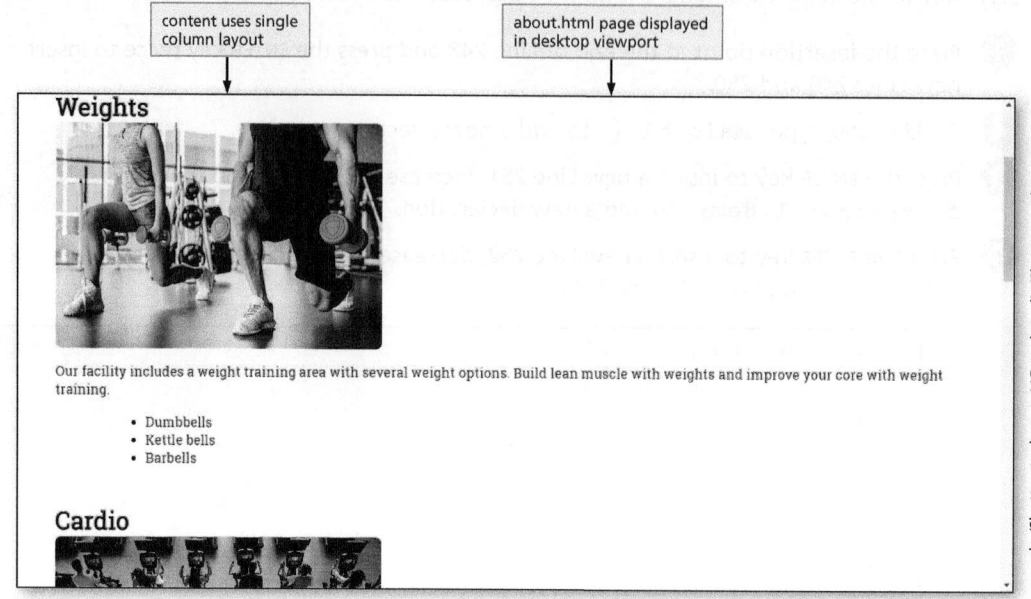

Figure 6–36

Modify the layout to use three columns instead of one column for the main content, similar to what you did in Chapter 4.

To Create a Multiple-Column Layout for a Desktop Viewport

Create a three-column layout for the weights, cardio, and personal training div elements. To make a three-column layout, create a new style rule for the #weights, #cardio, and #training selectors and specify float, width, and margin properties. Create another style rule to clear the float for the exercises div element. The following steps create a new style rule for the #weights, #cardio, and #training selectors as desired for a desktop viewport.

1 Place the insertion point at the end of Line 252 and press the ENTER key twice to insert new Lines 253 and 254.

2 On Line 254, type `#weights, #cardio, #training {` to add a new selector.

3 Press the ENTER key to insert a new Line 255, increase the indent, and then type `width: 29%;` to add a new declaration.

4 Press the ENTER key to insert a new Line 256, and then type `float: left;` to add a new declaration.

5 Press the ENTER key to insert a new Line 257, and then type `margin: 0 2%;` to add a new declaration.

6 Press the ENTER key to insert a new Line 258, decrease the indent, and then type `}` to insert a closing brace.

7 Press the ENTER key twice to insert new Lines 259 and 260, and then type `#exercises {` to add a new selector.

8 Press the ENTER key to insert a new Line 261, increase the indent, and then type `clear: left;` to add a new declaration.

9 Press the ENTER key to insert a new Line 262, decrease the indent, and then type `}` to insert a closing brace (Figure 6–37).

Line 254

```
254        #weights, #cardio, #training {
255            width: 29%;
256            float: left;
257            margin: 0 2%;
258        }
259
260        #exercises {
261            clear: left;
262        }
263
264    }
```

style rule for #weights, #cardio, #training

style rule for #exercises

media query closing brace

Figure 6–37

10 Save your changes and refresh about.html in your browser to view your changes (Figure 6–38).

about.html page displayed in desktop viewport

weights, cardio, and personal training content shown in columns

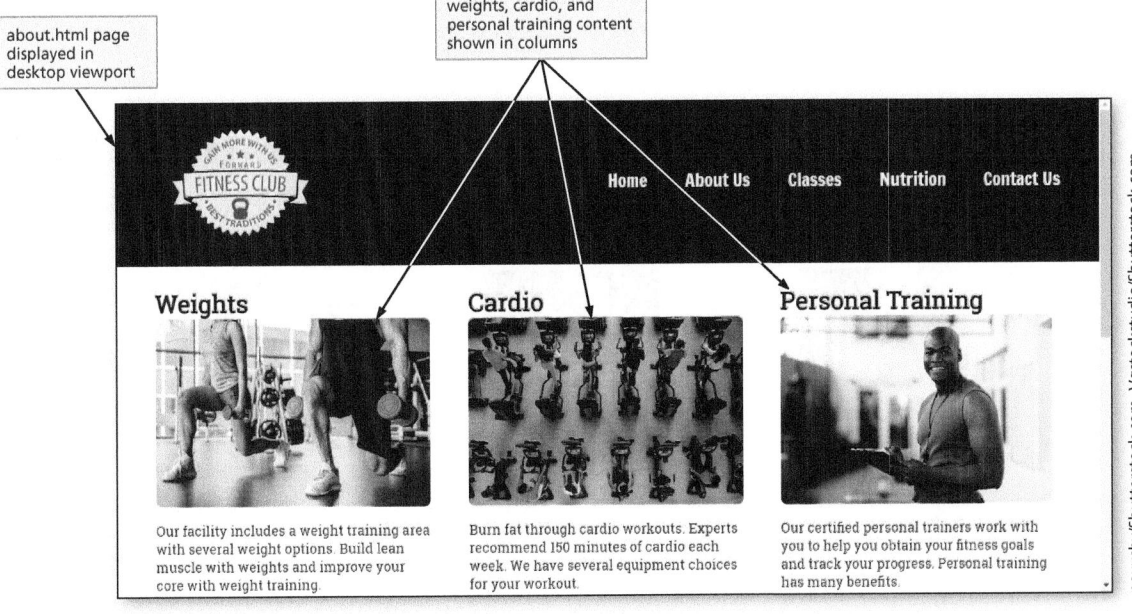

Figure 6–38

nexusby/Shutterstock.com, Vgstockstudio/Shutterstock.com, istockphoto.com/andresr, michaeljung/Shutterstock.com

Media Query for Large Viewports

Today's desktop monitors come in many shapes and sizes. Many can exceed a viewport of 1920 pixels. Given the diverse population of monitors, you determine whether your website layout still looks good when displayed on a larger monitor. You can use Google Chrome's device mode to view your website in viewports up to 2560px or 4K. Figure 6–39 shows NASA's website with a viewport of 2560px.

nasa.gov page displayed
with viewport size of 2560px

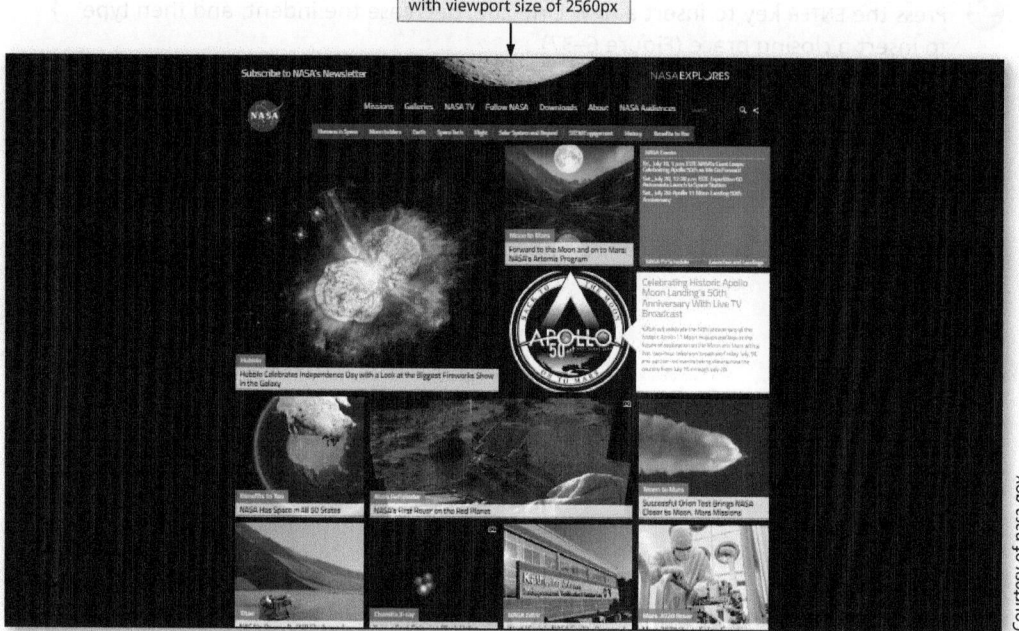

Courtesy of nasa.gov

Figure 6–39

Notice how the website appears in the center of the window with a black background on either side. In this example, NASA's website includes a media query that specifies the width for their website design when the viewport width exceeds 1440px. This keeps the integrity of the website design intact no matter the size of the viewport.

Figure 6–40 shows the Forward Fitness website with a viewport of 2560px.

about.html page displayed
with viewport size of 2560px

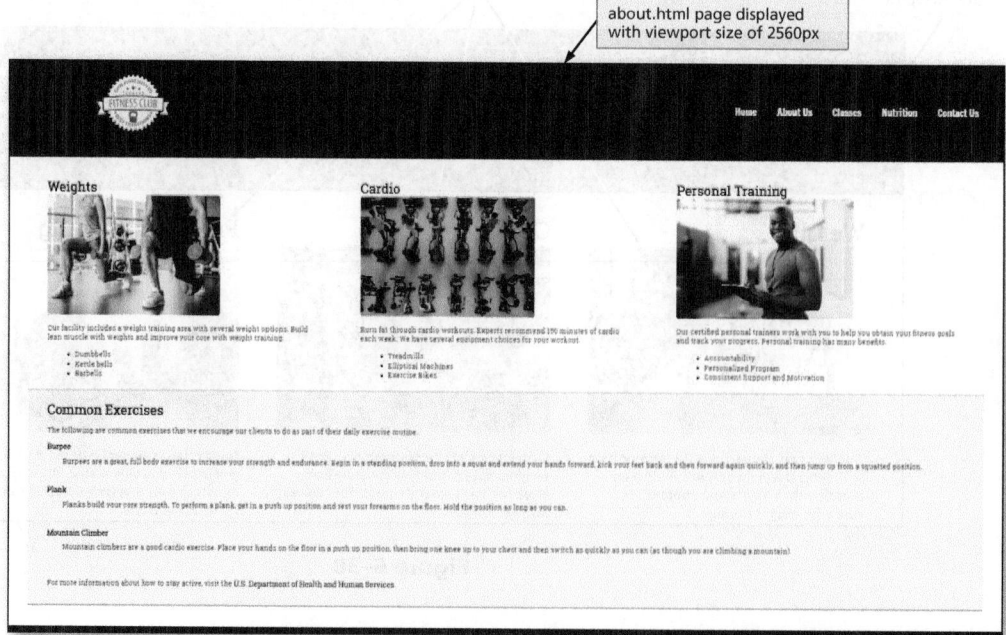

nexusby/Shutterstock.com, Vgstockstudio/Shutterstock.com, istockphoto.com/andresr, michaeljung/Shutterstock.com

Figure 6–40

As the viewport size increases, the layout of the website is degraded. To fix this, create another media query that targets larger viewports and specify a width for the primary div element with the id attribute of container.

To Create a Media Query for Large Desktop Viewports

1 ADD TABLET MEDIA QUERY & STYLES | 2 **ADD DESKTOP MEDIA QUERY & STYLES** | 3 **MODIFY VIEWPORT BREAKPOINTS**
4 **INSERT & STYLE PSEUDO-CLASSES** | 5 **ADD LINEAR GRADIENT**

Create another media query to constrain the width of the website layout. To do this, you create a new media query with a min-width of 1921px. Create a style rule for the #container selector that sets the width to 1920px and sets the left and right margins to auto to center the page. *Why? You want the website layout to look professional on large desktop viewports.* The following steps create a new media query and a style rule for the #container selector.

1

- Return to styles.css in your text editor to prepare to edit the file.

- Place your insertion point at the end of Line 264, press the ENTER key twice to insert new Lines 265 and 266, and then type **/* Media Query for Large Desktop Viewports */** to insert a comment.

- Press the ENTER key to insert a new Line 267, and then type **@media screen and (min-width: 1921px) {** to add a new media query.

- Press the ENTER key twice to insert new Lines 268 and 269, and then type **}** to close the media query (Figure 6–41).

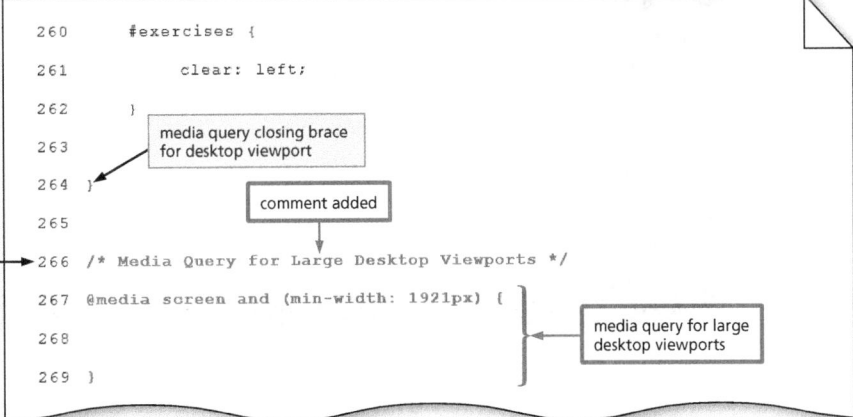

Figure 6–41

2

- Place your insertion point at the end of Line 267 and press the ENTER key twice to insert new Lines 268 and 269.

- On Line 269, type **#container {** to add a new selector.

- Press the ENTER key to insert a new Line 270, increase the indent, and then type **width: 1920px;** to add a declaration.

- Press the ENTER key to insert a new Line 271, and then type **margin: 0 auto;** to add a declaration.

- Press the ENTER key to insert a new Line 272, decrease the indent, and then type **}** to close the style rule (Figure 6–42).

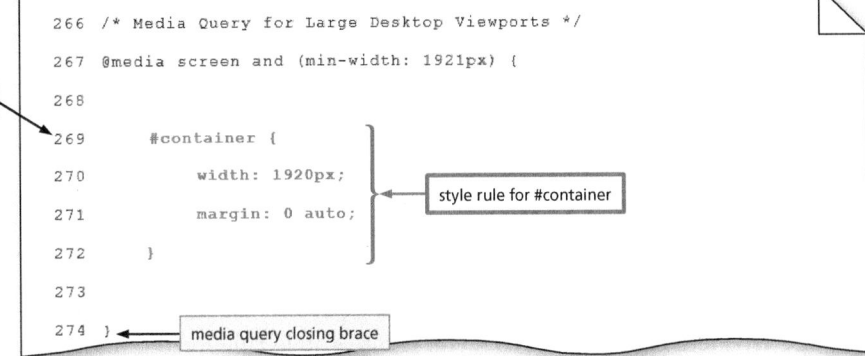

Figure 6–42

Q&A Why am I creating one style rule for #container?
All page elements are within a parent div element with an id attribute value of container.

Why am I setting the top and bottom margin to zero and the left and right margins to auto?
To center the webpage content, you set the left and right margins to auto. Set the top and bottom margin to zero because you do not want a top or bottom margin for #container.

• Save your changes, open about.html in Google Chrome's device mode, and set the viewport size to 2560px to simulate a large desktop viewport (Figure 6–43).

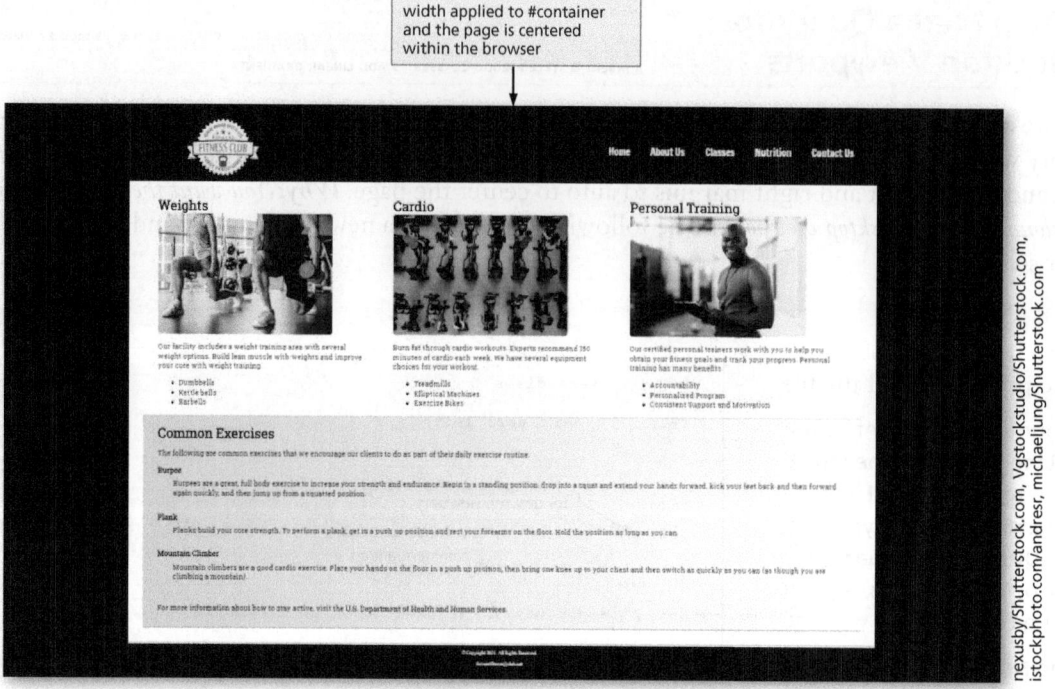

width applied to #container and the page is centered within the browser

Figure 6–43

Media Query for Print

Media queries help make mobile-friendly webpages. They can also be used to create printer-friendly webpages. After a website layout has been configured for various size viewports, the last media query type to be created should be for print. To optimize a webpage for printing, create a media query that specifies the print type. Then, create a style rule for the body selector that sets the background color to white and the font color to black. This removes any extra unnecessary color for printing purposes. After creating the media query for print, add the print type to the tablet and the desktop media queries, so that these layouts will be applied when the page prints. If you do not add the print type to the tablet and desktop media queries, the default mobile style rules will apply to the printed page.

To Create a Media Query for Print

1 ADD TABLET MEDIA QUERY & STYLES | 2 ADD DESKTOP MEDIA QUERY & STYLES | 3 MODIFY VIEWPORT BREAKPOINTS
4 INSERT & STYLE PSEUDO-CLASSES | 5 ADD LINEAR GRADIENT

Create another media query to create a printer-friendly webpage. To do this, you create a new media query and specify the type as print. Next, you create a style rule for the body selector that sets the background color to white and the text color to black. Finally, you add the print type to the tablet and desktop media queries. *Why? Optimize the page in case a user wants to print the page.* The following steps create a new media query and a style rule for the body selector.

1

- Return to styles.css in your text editor to prepare to edit the file.

- Place your insertion point at the end of Line 274, press the ENTER key twice to insert new Lines 275 and 276, and then type `/* Media Query for Print */` to insert a comment.

- Press the ENTER key to insert a new Line 277, and then type `@media print {` to add a new media query.

- Press the ENTER key twice to insert new Lines 278 and 279, and then type `}` to close the media query (Figure 6–44).

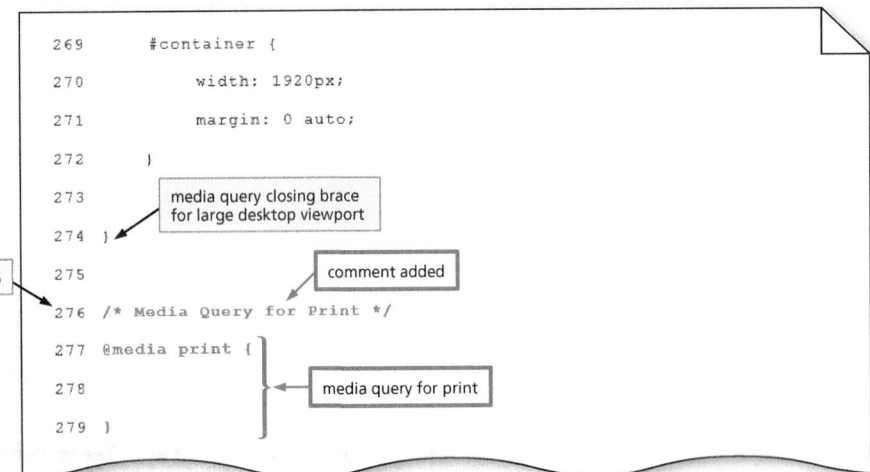

```
269        #container {
270            width: 1920px;
271            margin: 0 auto;
272        }
273
274  }
275
276  /* Media Query for Print */
277  @media print {
278
279  }
```

media query closing brace for large desktop viewport

comment added

Line 276

media query for print

Figure 6–44

2

- Place your insertion point at the end of Line 277 and press the ENTER key twice to insert new Lines 278 and 279.

- On Line 279, increase the indent, and then type `body {` to add a new selector.

- Press the ENTER key to insert a new Line 280, increase the indent, and then type `background-color: #fff;` to add a declaration.

- Press the ENTER key to insert a new Line 281, and then type `color: #000;` to add a declaration.

- Press the ENTER key to insert a new Line 282, decrease the indent, and then type `}` to close the style rule (Figure 6–45).

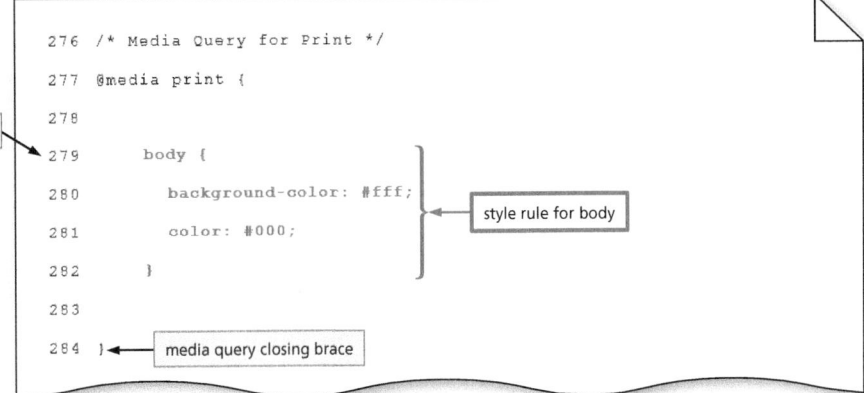

```
276  /* Media Query for Print */
277  @media print {
278
279      body {
280          background-color: #fff;
281          color: #000;
282      }
283
284  }
```

Line 279

style rule for body

media query closing brace

Figure 6–45

3

- On Line 153, place your insertion point after the closing parenthesis, and then type `,print` to add the print type to the tablet media query.

- On Line 217, place your insertion point after the closing parenthesis, and then type `,print` to add the print type to the desktop media query (Figure 6–46).

print type added to tablet media query

```
152  /* Media Query for Tablet Viewport */
153  @media screen and (min-width: 630px), print {
```

Line 153

print type added to desktop media query

```
216  /* Media Query for Desktop Viewport */
217  @media screen and (min-width: 769px), print {
```

Line 217

Figure 6–46

Q&A | Why do I need to add the print type to the tablet and desktop media queries?

If you do not add the print type to the tablet and desktop media queries, the default mobile style rules will apply to the printed page.

4

- Save your changes, open about .html in Google Chrome, maximize the window, and then press the CTRL+P keys to preview the printed webpage (Figure 6–47).

Q&A

Why do the navigation links appear gray?

The print preview link colors may vary from browser to browser. To change the navigation link colors, you can create another style rule for the nav li a selector that sets the color to black.

Why does the Contact Us navigation link appear on the next line? Likewise, why does the Personal Training heading 1 element appear on two lines?

The navigation and the Personal Training text appear on two lines due to printing on a standard 8.5 by 11-inch sheet of paper.

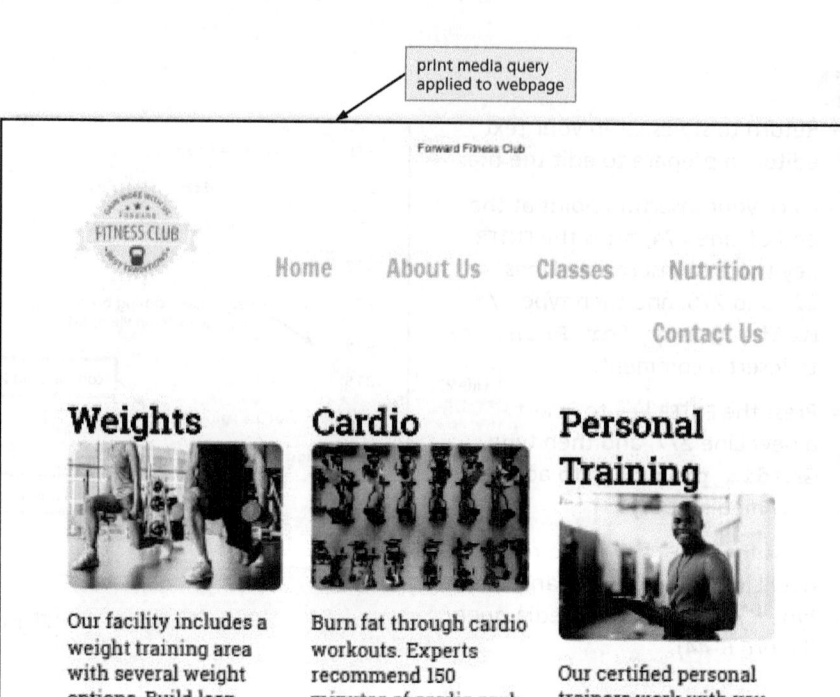

Figure 6–47

nexusby/Shutterstock.com, VGstockstudio/Shutterstock.com, istockphoto.com/andresr, michaeljung/Shutterstock.com

BTW

Browser Developer Tools

Every modern browser provides developer tools that display element dimensions, for example, which are useful when setting breakpoints. You can also use the tools to inspect the HTML, CSS, and other types of code as you view a webpage. For example, you can temporarily remove a CSS declaration to determine its effects on the webpage.

Modifying Breakpoints

Recall that a breakpoint is the point at which you want to apply different styles to the webpage, usually depending on the viewport. Set breakpoints as determined by the content on the page. For example, if the navigation area is displayed on two lines for a desktop viewport, modify a breakpoint to keep the navigation links on the same line. The desktop media query for the Forward Fitness website uses a minimum width of 769px. When you view the About Us page at this viewport size, the navigation is displayed on two lines. In addition, the Personal Training text also appears on two lines. Figure 6–48 shows the home page displayed with a viewport of 769px.

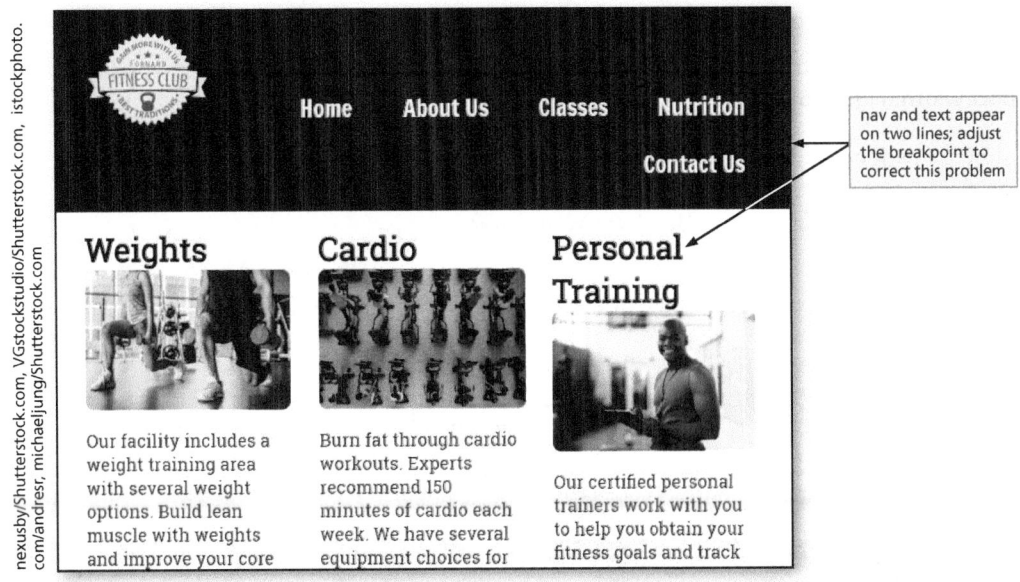

Figure 6–48

To Determine the Viewport Width for the Desktop Viewport

1 ADD TABLET MEDIA QUERY & STYLES | 2 ADD DESKTOP MEDIA QUERY & STYLES | 3 MODIFY VIEWPORT BREAKPOINTS
4 INSERT & STYLE PSEUDO-CLASSES | 5 ADD LINEAR GRADIENT

You have set a standard breakpoint for the desktop media query; however, when the webpage is viewed at 769px, the navigation is displayed on two lines. Likewise, the Personal Training text on the About Us page is also displayed on two lines. To keep the navigation links and heading 1 text on one line, modify the style sheet and adjust the `min-width` size for the desktop media query. *Why? Currently, the breakpoint value is too small for the desktop viewport. Using the correct breakpoint value will correct the two-line problem.* Increase the breakpoint value for the desktop media query to improve the layout of the viewport. Use a browser developer tool to help determine a more suitable breakpoint value. The following steps open the about.html page in Google Chrome's device mode to help determine a more suitable breakpoint for the desktop media query.

1

- Open the about.html file in Google Chrome's device mode to prepare to use the device mode tools.

- Set the viewport size to 769px (Figure 6–49).

Q&A Why does the navigation and Personal Training text appear on two lines?
The current breakpoint is too small to allow these elements to remain on one line.

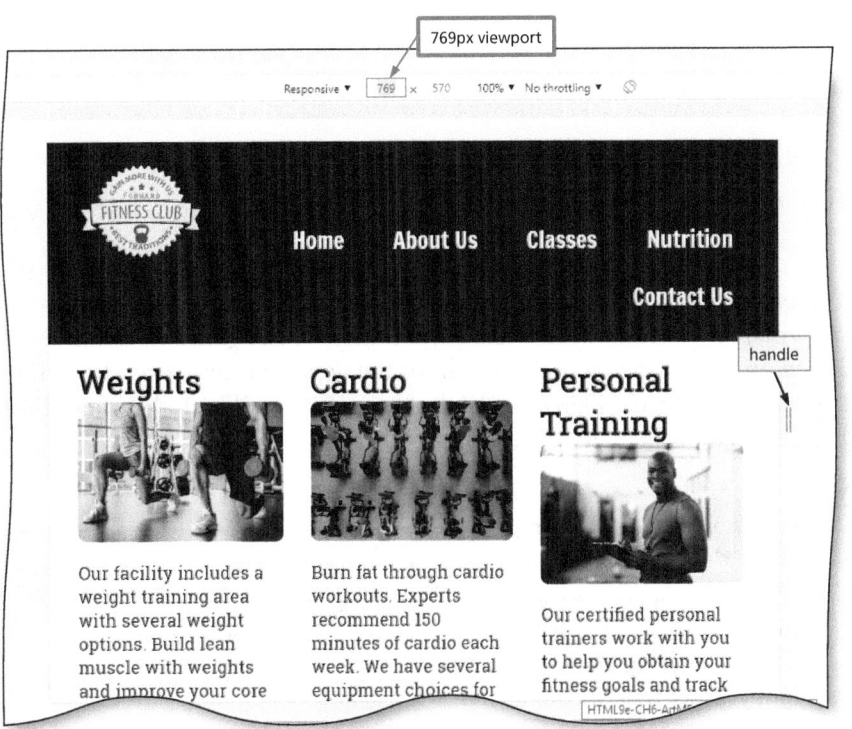

Figure 6–49

- Slowly drag the handle to the right until the navigation and Personal Training text appear on one line. Note the viewport width (Figure 6–50).

Q&A Why should I widen the page until the navigation and Personal Training appear on one line?
This width represents the smallest viewport size that accommodates the navigation links and the Personal Training text to appear link on one line for the desktop viewport.

How can I find the page dimensions if Google Chrome is not installed on my computer?
Most major browsers have built-in development tools that provide information about the HTML and CSS code for the webpage. In Opera, Mozilla Firefox, or Edge, press and hold or right-click a webpage and choose Inspect element on the shortcut menu. In Safari, open Web Inspector using the key combination COMMAND+OPTION+I.

Figure 6–50

nexusby/Shutterstock.com, VGstockstudio/Shutterstock.com, istockphoto.com/ andresr, michaeljung/Shutterstock.com

To Set a New Breakpoint for the Desktop Media Query

1 ADD TABLET MEDIA QUERY & STYLES | 2 ADD DESKTOP MEDIA QUERY & STYLES | 3 MODIFY VIEWPORT BREAKPOINTS

4 INSERT & STYLE PSEUDO-CLASSES | 5 ADD LINEAR GRADIENT

Now that you have determined the minimum width at which the page displays the navigation and Personal Training text on one line, you change the breakpoint width for the desktop media query. *Why? Modify the breakpoint for the desktop media query to keep the navigation links and the Personal Training text on one line each.* Based on your inspection, the width for the desktop viewport is about 1009 pixels. As a best practice, use a width slightly larger than 1009px for the desktop viewport. The following steps modify the breakpoint value for the the desktop media query from 769px to 1015px.

- Return to styles.css to prepare to change the breakpoint value.

- On Line 217, modify the value from 769px to **1015px** to make the desktop viewport width slightly larger than the minimum width (Figure 6–51).

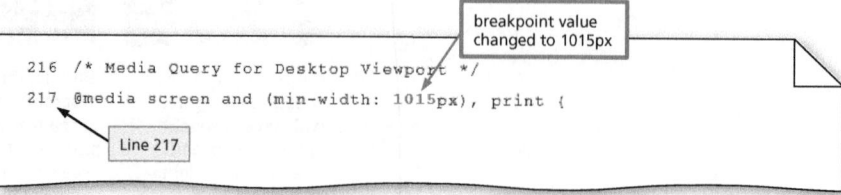

```
216  /* Media Query for Desktop Viewport */
217  @media screen and (min-width: 1015px), print {
```

Figure 6–51

2

- Save the styles.css file to save your changes.

- Refresh the about.html page, select the Mobile S - 320px gray bar to display the mobile viewport, and then slowly move the handle to the right to increase the viewport width to ensure the webpage looks as intended for each viewport (Figure 6–52).

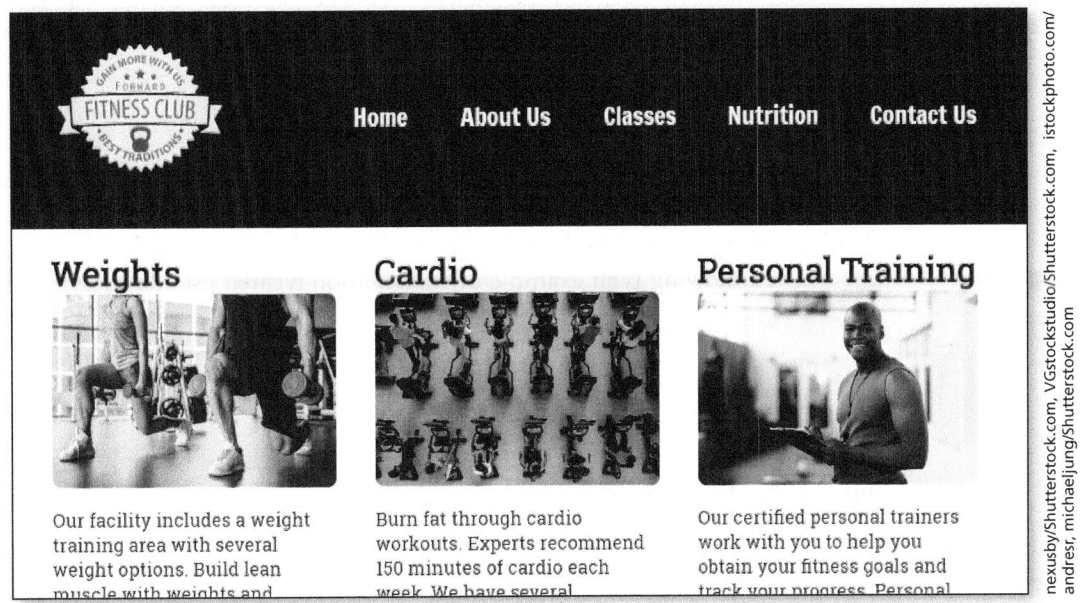

Figure 6–52

nexusby/Shutterstock.com, VGstockstudio/Shutterstock.com, istockphoto.com/ andresr, michaeljung/Shutterstock.com

Break Point: If you want to take a break, this is a good place to do so. To resume at a later time, continue reading the text from this location forward.

Using Dynamic Pseudo-Classes

Have you ever visited a website where the links changed colors when you pointed to (hovered over) them or clicked a link? The link color changes due to the use of dynamic pseudo-classes in the style sheet. **Dynamic pseudo-classes** allow you to change the style of a link based on four link states: link, visited, hover, and active. Table 6–3 describes each link state.

Table 6–3 Dynamic Pseudo-Classes	
Dynamic Pseudo-Class	**Used to Style**
:link	Unvisited link
:visited	Link that has been clicked
:hover	Link when the mouse is hovering over it
:active	Link at the moment it is clicked

You can define a unique style for normal, visited, hover, and active links by creating four separate style rules with **a:link**, **a:visited**, **a:hover**, and **a:active** as the selectors. As you learned in Chapter 4, a pseudo-class is attached to a selector with a colon to specify a state or relation to the selector to give the web developer more control over that selector. Use the following format to construct a style rule for a pseudo-class:

```
selector:pseudo-class {
        property: value;
}
```

The colon (:) is part of the pseudo-class and is placed between the selector and the pseudo-class. The following is an example of a navigation :link pseudo-class:

```
nav a:link {
        color: #fff;
}
```

The selector **nav a:link** identifies the color to apply to a navigation link that has not yet been visited or clicked. In this case, the initial link color is white.

The following is an example of a navigation :visited pseudo-class:

```
nav a:visited {
        color: #000;
}
```

The selector **nav a:visited** identifies the color to apply to a navigation link that has been visited or clicked. In this case, the link color is black.

The following is an example of a navigation :hover pseudo-class:

```
nav a:hover {
        color: #ffff00;
}
```

The selector **nav a:hover** identifies the color to apply to a navigation link while the pointer is hovering over the link. In this case, the link color is yellow. The :hover pseudo-class enhances the interactivity between the user and the webpage.

The following is an example of a navigation :active pseudo-class:

```
nav a:active {
        color: #0066cc;
}
```

The selector **nav a:active** identifies the color to apply to a navigation link when the link is being clicked or when it gains focus. In this case, the link color is blue.

These dynamic pseudo-classes must be used in the following order: link, visited, hover, active. You do not need to use all of the pseudo-classes; however, if you choose to omit a pseudo-class from your design, be sure to maintain the same order of the pseudo-classes in the CSS code.

These dynamic pseudo-classes are more often used in a desktop viewport because mobile and tablet devices are touch devices and do not have a hover option nor an option to click.

BTW
Another Dynamic Pseudo-Class
Another type of dynamic pseudo-class is called :focus. It is typically used to style a form input element when the element is given focus.

To Add Dynamic Pseudo-Classes to a Style Sheet

1 ADD TABLET MEDIA QUERY & STYLES | 2 ADD DESKTOP MEDIA QUERY & STYLES | 3 MODIFY VIEWPORT BREAKPOINTS
4 INSERT & STYLE PSEUDO-CLASSES | 5 ADD LINEAR GRADIENT

Add a new style rule for the hover pseudo-class to style the links within the navigation area for the desktop viewport. *Why? The hover pseudo-class provides an interactive experience for the desktop user.* Create a style rule for list item anchor elements within the navigation and apply the hover pseudo-class. The following steps add a style rule that uses the hover pseudo-class to the desktop media query.

1

- Place the insertion point at the end of Line 243 and press the ENTER key twice to insert new Lines 244 and 245.

- On Line 245, type **nav li a:hover {** to add a new selector.

- Press the ENTER key to insert a new Line 246, increase the indent, and then type **color: #000;** to add a new declaration.

- Press the ENTER key to insert a new Line 247, and then type **background-color: #fff;** to add a new declaration.

- Press the ENTER key to insert a new Line 248, decrease the indent, and then type **}** to insert a closing brace (Figure 6–53).

```
241    nav li a {
242        padding: 0.5em 1em;
243    }
244
245    nav li a:hover {          ← Line 245
246        color: #000;
247        background-color: #fff;    ← style rule for nav li a:hover
248    }
249
250    /* Desktop Viewport: Style Rules for main content */
251    main {
252        clear: left;
253    }
```

Figure 6–53

2

- Save the styles.css file, and then refresh about.html in your browser. If necessary, exit Google Chrome's device mode and then maximize the browser window to view the changes.

- Use a mouse to hover over the Home link to display the link formatting (Figure 6–54).

Q&A
I do not see the hover effect when I mouse over a link. Why?
This might happen for a few reasons. First, exit the device mode and maximize your browser window. Second, if your display width is less than 1015 px, you will not see the hover effect as it applies only to screens wider than 1014 px. Third, save your CSS file and confirm that your style rule is correct and within the correct media query.

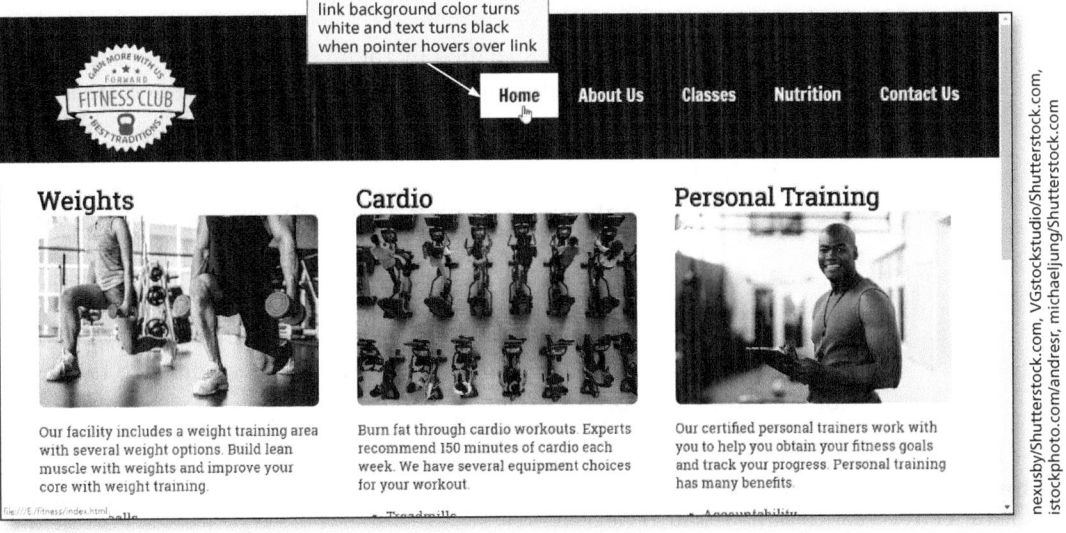

Figure 6–54

BTW
CSS3 Gradients
Before CSS3, web designers created background gradients by tiling gradient images across a page or element. CSS3 gradients offer two significant advantages over this technique: they use fewer resources, meaning they appear more quickly, and remain sharp and clear when users increase or decrease the webpage zoom setting.

Using Gradients

As you have learned, CSS is a powerful tool to format webpages. You have already worked with several CSS properties, but CSS has many more properties to explore.

You can also use CSS to create a gradient. A **gradient** is a gradual transition from one color to another. You can create two types of gradients using CSS: linear and radial.

Linear gradients can transition from several different angles. The default transition is from the top to the bottom. Linear gradients can also transition up, left, right, or diagonally.

To create a linear gradient, use the `linear-gradient` function, linear-gradient(). The following is an example of how to use the linear gradient function:

```
body {
        background: linear-gradient(#fff, #0000ff);
}
```

This example applies a linear gradient that transitions from white at the top to blue at the bottom.

Table 6–4 provides an overview of linear gradients.

Table 6–4 Linear Gradients	
Direction	**Examples**

top to bottom (default)	body {
	        background: linear-gradient: (#fff, #0000ff);
	}

left to right	body {
	        background: linear-gradient: (to right, #fff, #0000ff);
	}

diagonal	body {
	        background: linear-gradient: (to bottom right, #fff, #0000ff);
	}

specified angle	body {
	        background: linear-gradient: (180deg, #fff, #0000ff);
	}

Radial gradients are specified by their center. The color begins in the center and transitions in a radial direction to another color or colors. To create a radial gradient, you must specify at least two colors. The following is an example of a radial gradient:

```
body {
        background: radial-gradient(#ff0000, #fff,
        #0000ff);
}
```

Gradients create interest on a webpage, especially when used as a background. To complete the project for this chapter, add a linear gradient to the #exercises selector for the tablet viewport.

Can multiple colors be used within a gradient?
Yes. You can add as many colors as desired to the gradient.

To Add a Linear Gradient

Add a linear gradient to the div element with the id attribute exercises for the tablet viewport. *Why? A gradient background enhances the appearance of the webpage for tablet and desktop displays.* The following steps create a new style rule to apply a linear gradient to the #exercises selector as desired for the tablet viewport.

 1

- Place the insertion point at the end of Line 192 and press the ENTER key to insert a new Line 193.

- On Line 193, type **background: linear-gradient(to right, #ccc, #fff);** to add a new declaration (Figure 6–55).

```
185  /* Tablet Viewport: Style rules for main content area */
186      main ul {
187          margin: 0 0 4% 10%;
188      }
189
190      #exercises {
191          border-top: 1px solid #000;
192          border-bottom: 1px solid #000;
193          background: linear-gradient(to right, #ccc, #fff);   ← linear gradient added as a new declaration
194          background-color: #f2f2f2;
195          padding: 1% 2%;
196      }
```

Line 193 →

Q&A Why am I adding this declaration within the tablet media query?
The Common Exercises div is not displayed on a mobile viewport.
Now that you have added this gradient for the tablet viewport, subsequent viewports will inherit the change.

Figure 6–55

2

- Save the styles.css file, and then refresh about.html in your browser to view the changes.

Experiment

- Use Table 6–4 to change the linear gradient to a left to right or to a diagonal gradient, save the styles.css file, and then refresh about.html in your browser.

- Return the background to a linear gradient, save the styles.css file, and then refresh about.html in your browser (Figure 6–56).

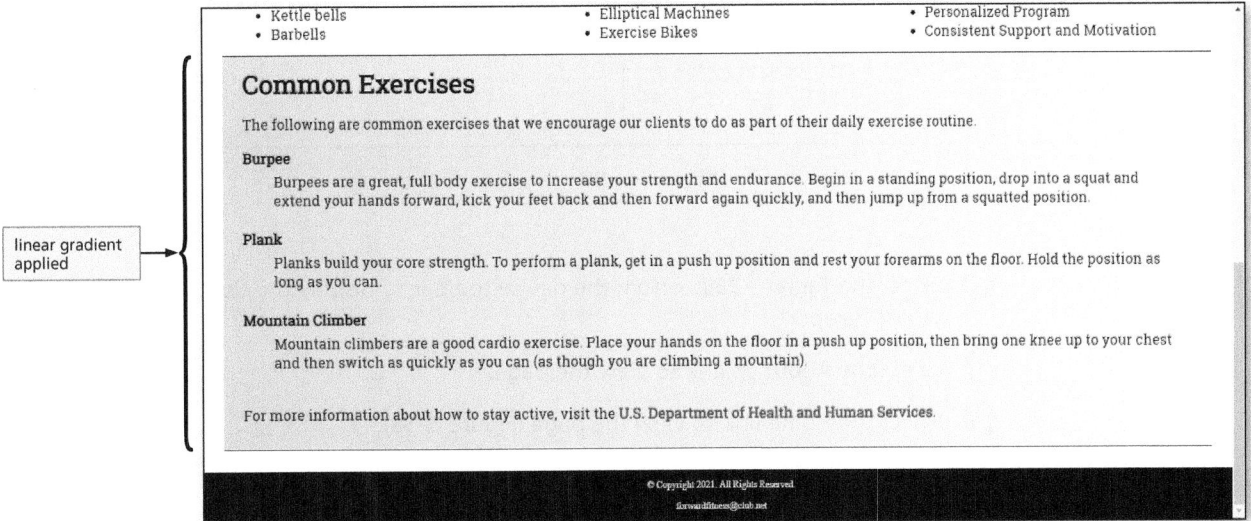

linear gradient applied

Figure 6–56

To Display a Website in Multiple Viewports

Now that you have completed the responsive web design for the Forward Fitness Club website, it is time to view the website from each viewport. You can use Google Chrome's device mode to view and test the website for each viewport. The following steps use Google Chrome's device mode to view the Forward Fitness Club website in a mobile, tablet, and desktop viewport.

1 Open index.html in Google Chrome's device mode, and then select the Mobile - S 320px view (middle gray bar) on the device toolbar.

2 Select the About Us link to view the page.

3 Select the Contact Us link to view the page (Figure 6–57).

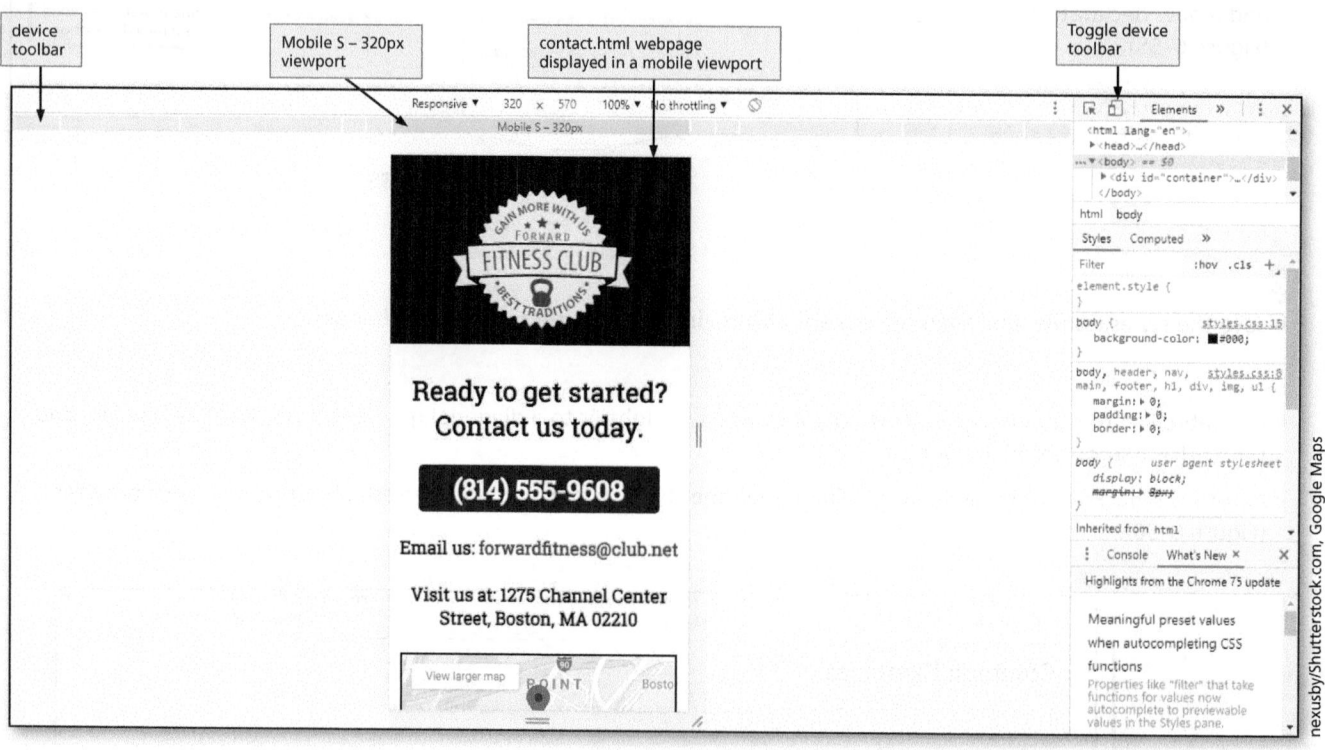

Figure 6–57

4 Select the Tablet – 768px from the device toolbar to display the Contact Us page in a tablet viewport.

5 Select the About Us link to view the page.

6 Select the Home link to view the page (Figure 6–58).

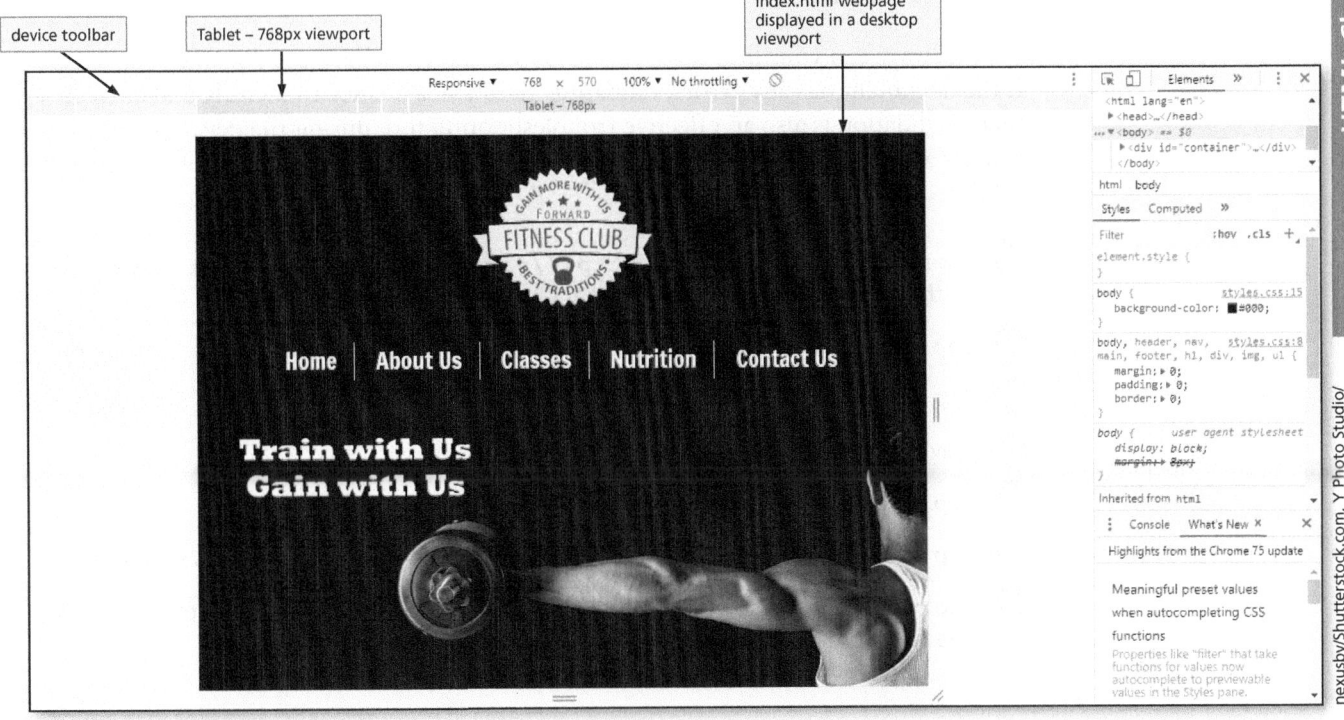

Figure 6–58

7 Select the Laptop – 1024px from the device toolbar to display the Home page in a tablet viewport.

8 Select the Contact Us link to view the page.

9 Select the About Us link to view the page (Figure 6–59).

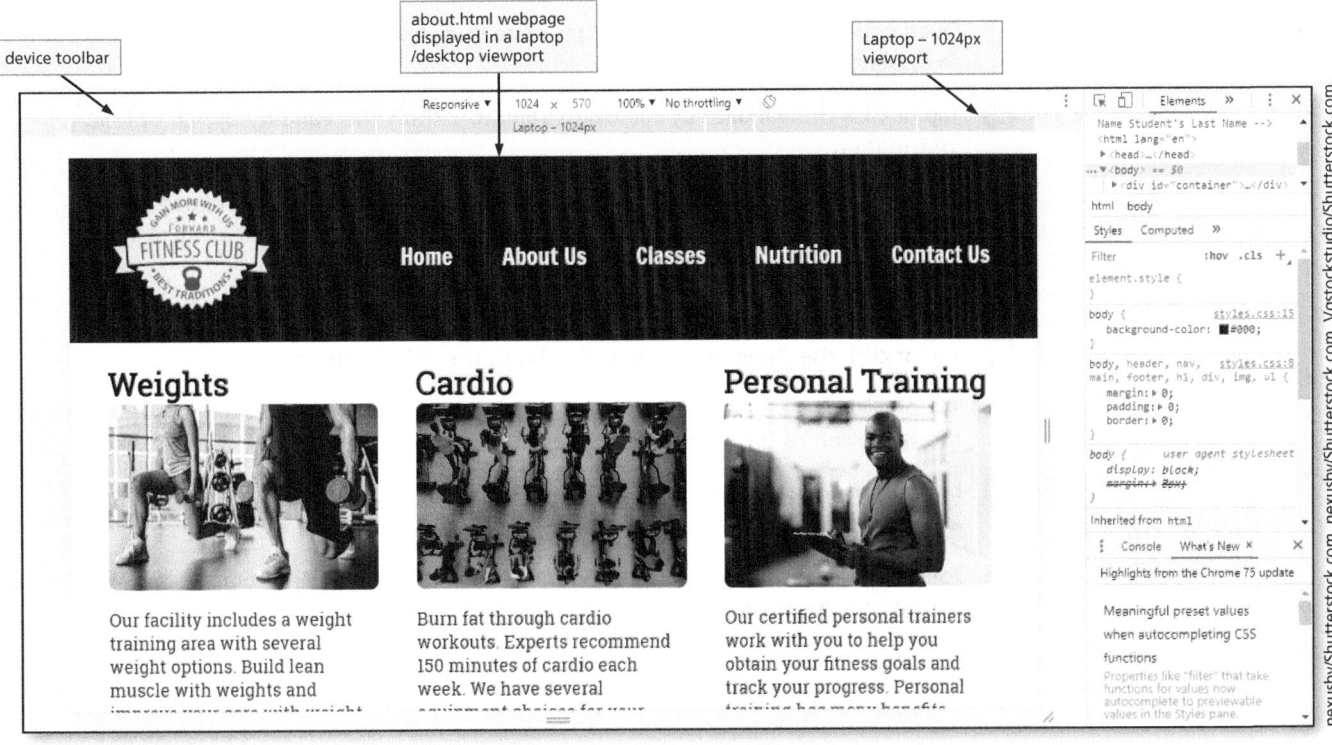

Figure 6–59

To Validate the Style Sheet

Always run your files through W3C's validator to check the document for errors. If the document has any errors, validating gives you a chance to identify and correct them. Validation is also an effective troubleshooting tool during the development process and adds a valuable level of professionalism to your work. The following steps validate a CSS document.

1 Open your browser and type `http://jigsaw.w3.org/css-validator/` in the address bar to display the W3C CSS Validation Service page.

2 Tap or click the By file upload tab to display the Validate by File Upload information.

3 Tap or click the Choose File button to display the Choose File to Upload dialog box.

4 Navigate to your css folder to find the styles.css file.

5 Tap or click the styles.css document to select it.

6 Tap or click the Open button to upload the selected file to the W3C CSS validator.

7 Tap or click the Check button to send the document through the validator and display the validation results page.

To Validate the HTML Files

Every time you create a new webpage, run it through W3C's validator to check the document for errors. If any errors exist, you need to correct them. Validation is also an effective troubleshooting tool during the development process and adds a valuable level of professionalism to your work. The following steps validate an HTML document.

1 Open your browser and type `http://validator.w3.org/` in the address bar to display the W3C validator page.

2 Tap or click the Validate by File Upload tab to display the Validate by File Upload tab information.

3 Tap or click the Browse button to display the Choose File to Upload dialog box.

4 Navigate to your fitness folder to find the about.html file.

5 Tap or click the about.html document to select it.

6 Tap or click the Open button to upload it to the W3C validator.

7 Tap or click the Check button to send the document through the validator and display the validation results page.

8 If necessary, correct any errors, save your changes, and run through the validator again to revalidate the page.

9 Follow these steps to validate the contact.html, index.html, and template.html pages and correct any errors.

Chapter Summary

In this chapter, you learned how to create media queries to target tablet and desktop viewports. You created style rules to format web content displayed on tablet and desktop devices. You modified the media query breakpoints to maintain the integrity of the navigation design. You enhanced the navigation links with pseudo-classes. Finally, you added a linear gradient to the body of the website. The items listed below include all the new skills you have learned in this chapter, with the tasks grouped by activity.

Using Media Queries
Add Media Queries to an External Style Sheet (HTML 285)

Designing for Tablet Viewports
Create a Media Query for a Tablet Viewport (HTML 286)
Show and Hide Content for a Tablet Viewport (HTML 287)
Remove a Sticky Position for the Header for a Tablet Viewport (HTML 289)
Style the Navigation Area for a Tablet Viewport (HTML 290)
Style Unordered List Elements within the Main Element for a Tablet Viewport (HTML 292)
Restore and Move Style Rules within the Tablet Media Query (HTML 294)
Modify the Contact Us Page (HTML 296)
Style the Map for a Tablet Viewport (HTML 297)

Designing for Desktop Viewports
Create a Media Query for a Desktop Viewport (HTML 299)
Style the Header Element for a Desktop Viewport (HTML 299)

Style the Navigation Area for a Desktop Viewport (HTML 300)
Style the Main Element for a Desktop Viewport (HTML 304)
Create a Multiple Column Layout for a Desktop Viewport (HTML 306)

Designing for Large Desktop Viewports
Create a Media Query for Large Desktop Viewports (HTML 309)

Designing for Print
Create a Media Query for Print (HTML 310)

Modifying Breakpoints
Determine the Viewport Width for a Desktop Viewport (HTML 313)
Set a New Breakpoint for the Desktop Media Query (HTML 314)

Using Dynamic Pseudo-Classes
Add Dynamic Pseudo-Classes to a Style Sheet (HTML 316)

Using Gradients
Add a Linear Gradient (HTML 319)

How will you design your tablet and desktop layouts?
Use these guidelines as you complete the assignments in this chapter and create your own webpages outside of this class.

1. Determine the layout of the tablet display.
   a. Restrict the design to one or two columns.
   b. Determine the best navigation design for your audience.
   c. Consider a strategy to focus on essential content.
2. Determine the layout of the desktop display.
   a. Determine number of columns for your layout.
   b. Incorporate active white space between content areas.
3. Test media query viewports.
   a. Use browser developer tools to help determine viewport width.
   b. Modify breakpoints to maintain the tablet design, if necessary.
   c. Modify breakpoints to maintain the desktop design, if necessary.
4. Enhance links with pseudo-classes.
   a. Use a high color contrast between the link color and background color.
   b. Determine which pseudo-classes to use.
5. Evaluate the use of a gradient.
   a. Determine the best location for a gradient.
   b. Determine the type of gradient to use, its direction, and the gradient colors.

How should you submit solutions to questions in the assignments identified with a ⊛ symbol?
Every assignment in this book contains one or more questions identified with a ⊛ symbol. These questions require you to think beyond the assigned presentation. Present your solutions to the questions in the format required by your instructor. Possible formats may include one or more of these options: create a document that contains the answer; present your answer to the class; discuss your answer in a group; record the answer as audio or video using a webcam, smartphone, or portable media player; or post answers on a blog, wiki, or website.

Apply Your Knowledge

Reinforce the skills and apply the concepts you learned in this chapter.

Styling for Responsive Design

Note: To complete this assignment, you will be required to use the Data Files. Please contact your instructor for information about accessing the Data Files.

Instructions: In this exercise, you will use your text editor to add tablet and desktop media queries to a style sheet. You will create style rules for a tablet viewport and a desktop viewport. You then add a style rule for an article element to display the content in two columns for a tablet viewport and three columns for a desktop viewport. You will also apply a linear gradient to the page and use a hover pseudo-class. The completed webpage is shown in Figure 6–60 for a tablet viewport and Figure 6–61 for a desktop viewport. You will also use professional web development practices to indent, space, comment, and validate your code.

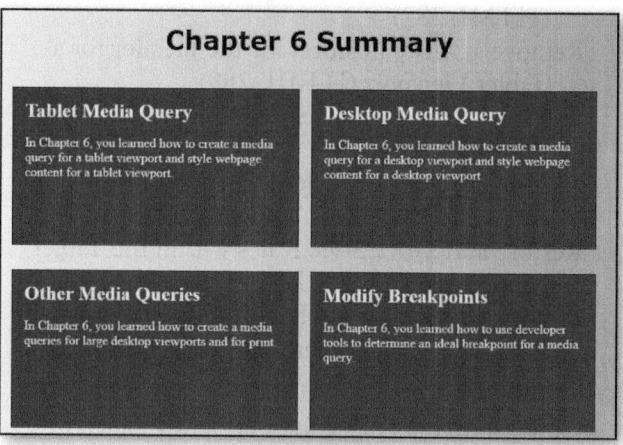

Figure 6–60

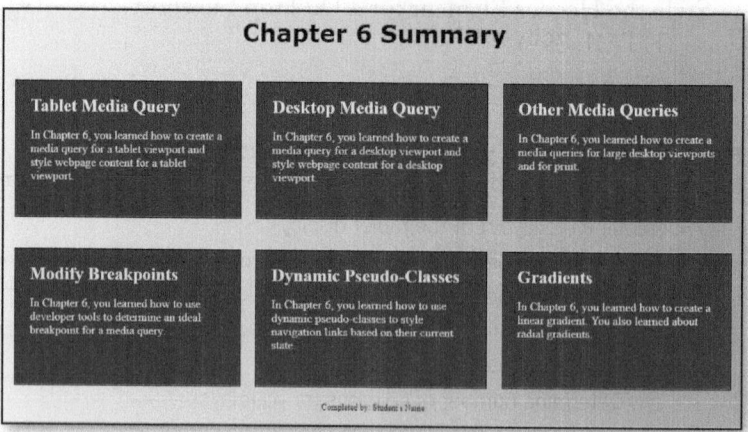

Figure 6–61

Perform the following tasks:
1. Open the index.html file in the chapter06\apply folder from the Data Files in your text editor. Update the comment with your name, the file name, and today's date. Add your name to the paragraph element located within the footer element near the bottom of the page.
2. Open the index.html file in your browser to view the page.
3. Open the apply06.css file from the apply\css folder. Modify the comment at the top of the style sheet to include your name, today's date, and the file name.
4. In the apply06.css file, below the last style rule, add a new comment with the text, **Media Query for Tablet Viewport**. Below the comment, add a media query to target screen and print for a tablet viewport. Use a **min-width: 481px**.
5. In the tablet media query, create a new style rule for the article element that sets the width to **43%**, floats the element to the **left**, and sets a height of **160px**.
6. In the tablet media query, create a new style rule for the footer selector that clears a float on the **left**.

7. In the apply06.css file, below the tablet media query, add a comment with the text, `Media Query for Desktop Viewport.` Below the comment, add a media query to target a desktop viewport screen with a minimum width of `900px`.

8. In the desktop media query, create a style rule for an article selector that sets the width to `27%` and the height to `140px`.

9. In the desktop media query, create another style rule for the article selector with a hover pseudo-class that sets the background color to `#ffe5dc` and the color to `#a22c02`.

10. Modify the style rule for the body selector by specifying a background with a linear gradient that uses a direction of `to left,` first color value of `#fe9972,` and second color value of `#ffe5dc.` Remove the declaration for the background color from the style rule.

11. Save your changes and view the index.html file in your browser. Use Google Chrome's device mode to display the page in a mobile, tablet, and desktop viewport. Exit device mode to view and test the hover pseudo-class.

12. Validate your HTML and CSS files and correct any errors. Save your changes and submit the assignment in a format specified by your instructor.

13. ☀ In steps 4 and 7, you created media queries to target tablet and desktop viewports by using min-width and a value. Describe how you could use max-width and provide the value you would use for each media query.

Extend Your Knowledge

Extend the skills you learned in this chapter and experiment with new skills. You may need to use additional resources to complete the assignment.

Exploring Gradients

Note: To complete this assignment, you will be required to use the Data Files. Please contact your instructor for information about accessing the Data Files.

Instructions: In this exercise, you will explore how to work with different kinds of gradients. You will discover how to create various linear gradients, angled gradients, gradients with multiple colors, repeating gradients, gradients that use transparency, and radial gradients. The completed webpage is shown in Figure 6–62.

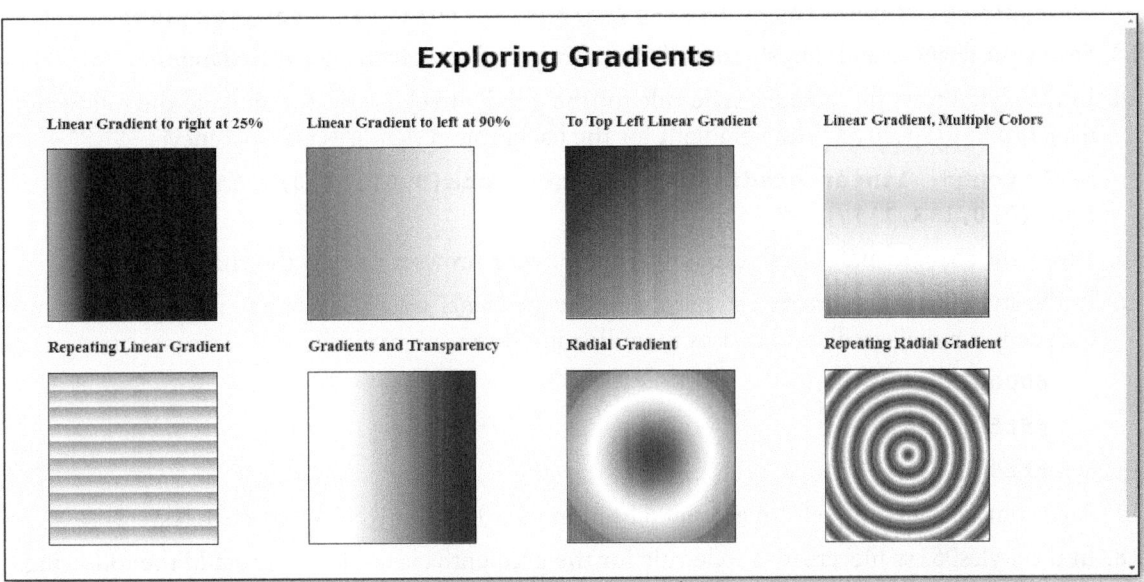

Figure 6–62

Continued >

Extend Your Knowledge *continued*

Perform the following tasks:

1. Open your text editor and then open the extend06.html file in the chapter06\extend folder from the Data Files. Update the comment with your name, the file name, and today's date. Add your name to the paragraph element located within the footer element near the bottom of the page.

2. Open extend06.html in your browser to view the webpage. Maximize the browser window to use a desktop viewport.

3. Open the styles06.css file from the extend\css folder. Modify the comment at the top of the style sheet to include your name, today's date, and the file name.

4. Below the Gradient style rules comment, create a style rule for the gradient1 class selector and add the following declaration to specify a linear-gradient for the background:

```
background: linear-gradient(to right, #67afcb, #1a3e4c 25%);
```

5. Save your changes and refresh extend06.html in your browser to view the changes.

6. In the styles06.css file, create a style rule for the gradient2 class selector and add a declaration to specify a linear-gradient to the left, use `#d4f7ec` and `#448d76` for color values, and use `90%` as the color stop.

7. Save your changes and refresh extend06.html in your browser to view the changes.

8. In the styles06.css file, create a style rule for the gradient3 class selector and add a declaration to specify a linear-gradient to the top left, and use `#efddfd` and `#36065b` for color values.

9. Save your changes and refresh extend06.html in your browser to view the changes.

10. In the styles06.css file, create a style rule for the gradient4 class selector and add a declaration to specify a linear-gradient that uses the following four color values:

```
#e6e6ff
#70dbdb
#ffffcc
#cc6699
```

11. Save your changes and refresh extend06.html in your browser to view the changes.

12. In the styles06.css file, create a style rule for the gradient5 class selector and add the following declaration to specify a repeating linear-gradient for the background:

```
background: repeating-linear-gradient(#df80ff 10%, #ccffff 20%);
```

13. Save your changes and refresh extend06.html in your browser to view the changes.

14. In the styles06.css file, create a style rule for the gradient6 class selector and add the following declaration to specify a linear-gradient for the background that uses transparency:

```
background: linear-gradient(to right, rgba(0,0,153,0) 25%,
rgba(0,0,153,1));
```

15. Save your changes and refresh extend06.html in your browser to view the changes.

16. In the styles06.css file, create a style rule for the gradient7 class selector and add a declaration to specify a radial-gradient that uses the following three color values:

```
#0000ff
#fff
#ff0000
```

17. Save your changes and refresh extend06.html in your browser to view the changes.

18. In the styles06.css file, create a style rule for the gradient8 class selector and add the following declaration to specify a repeating radial-gradient for the background:

```
background: repeating-radial-gradient(#0000ff, #fff, #ff0000 15%);
```

19. Save your changes and refresh extend06.html in your browser to view the changes.

20. Save your files and submit them in a format specified by your instructor.

21. ✳ In this exercise, you explored more about gradients and used percentages to set color stops. You also used rgba to set transparency in step 14. Use your browser to research how to set gradient color stops using percentages. Also research how to use the rgba() function to create transparency. Include a description of your findings.

Analyze, Correct, Improve

Analyze a webpage, correct all errors, and improve it.

Modifying Media Queries

Note: To complete this assignment, you will be required to use the Data Files. Please contact your instructor for information about accessing the Data Files.

Instructions: The analyze06.html webpage is a draft website template, but must be corrected and improved for responsive design before presenting it to a client. Use Figure 6–63, Figure 6–64, and Figure 6–65 as a guide to correct these files.

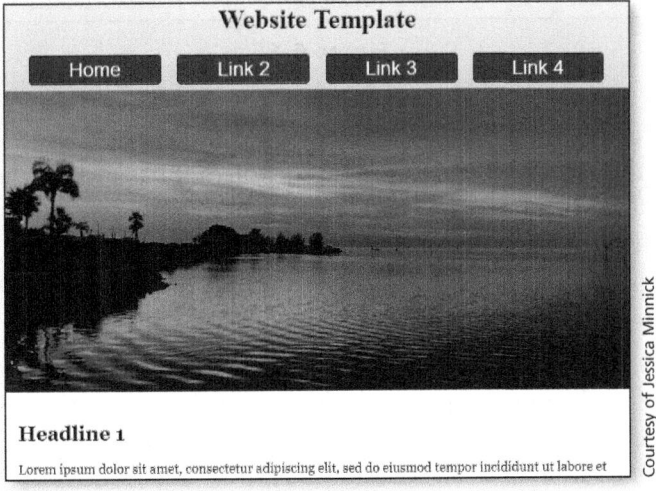

Courtesy of Jessica Minnick

Figure 6–63

Courtesy of Jessica Minnick

Figure 6–64

Continued >

Analyze, Correct, Improve *continued*

Courtesy of Jessica Minnick

Figure 6–65

1. Correct

a. Open your text editor, open the analyze06.html file in the chapter06\analyze folder from the Data Files, and then modify the comment at the top of the page to include your name and today's date. Add your name to the paragraph element located within the footer element near the bottom of the page.

b. Open the styles06.css file from the analyze\css folder. Modify the comment at the top of the style sheet to include your name, today's date, and the file name.

c. Open analyze06.html in Google Chrome's device mode and resize the page to the current breakpoint for the tablet media query, which is 481px. Note how the navigation links appear on two lines. Use Google Chrome's device mode to determine a more suitable breakpoint that shows the navigation links on the same line.

d. In the styles06.css file, modify the tablet media query with a more suitable breakpoint value that displays the navigation links on the same line.

e. Open analyze06.html in a browser and simulate a tablet or desktop viewport. Note that the image does not display in either viewport.

f. In the styles06.css file, within the tablet media query, add a new comment two lines below the opening media query brace that indicates that the following style rule shows the tablet-desktop class. Below the comment, add a new style rule for the tablet-desktop class that sets the display as a block.

2. Improve

a. In the styles06.css file, modify the body style rule to use a linear gradient for the background with color values `#e5e0fa` and `#29157e`. Remove the declaration that specifies a background color.

b. Within the desktop media query, add a new comment two lines below the opening media query brace that indicates that the following style rule is for the header element when displayed in a desktop viewport. Below the comment, add a style rule for the header selector that sets the width to `25%` and floats it to the `left`.

c. Within the desktop media query, add a new style rule below the navigation comment that aligns text to the right for unordered list elements within the nav element.

d. Within the desktop media query, below the style rule for nav li a, add a new style rule for the nav li a selector that uses the hover pseudo-class. Set the color to `#4424d6` and the background color to `#e5e0fa.`

e. In the analyze06.html file, add the class attribute `col-content` to the three div elements nested within the main element.

f. In the styles06.css file, within the desktop media query, below the style rule for main, add a new style rule for the col-content class selector that sets a width of `30%`, sets a float to the `left`, and padding of `1.5%` on all sides.

g. In the styles06.css file, below the last media query, add a new comment with the text, `Media Query for Large Desktop Viewport.` Below the comment, create a new media query that targets a screen with minimum width of `1441px.` Inside the media query, create a style rule for the #container selector that sets the width to `1440px`, the top and bottom margins to zero, and the left and right margins to `auto.`

h. Save your changes and review analyze06.html in Google Chrome's device mode, view the page at 768px, 1024px, and 1920px, and compare it to Figures 6-63, 6-64, and 6-65. Exit device mode to view and test the hover pseudo-class.

i. Validate the CSS and the HTML files and correct any errors.

j. Submit the assignment in the format specified by your instructor.

k. ✸ Identify other ways to style a pseudo-class and provide an example.

In the Lab

Labs 1 and 2, which increase in difficulty, require you to create webpages based on what you learned in the chapter; Lab 3 is ideal for group projects/collaboration.

Lab 1: Creating Media Queries for the Strike a Chord Website

Problem: You work for a local music lesson company called Strike a Chord that provides music lessons for piano, guitar, and violin. The company needs a web presence and has hired you to create their website. You have already created the mobile layout, but now need to add media queries for tablet, desktop, and print layouts. Figure 6–66 shows the home page in the tablet viewport and Figure 6–67 shows the Lessons page in the desktop viewport.

Figure 6–66

Continued >

In the Lab *continued*

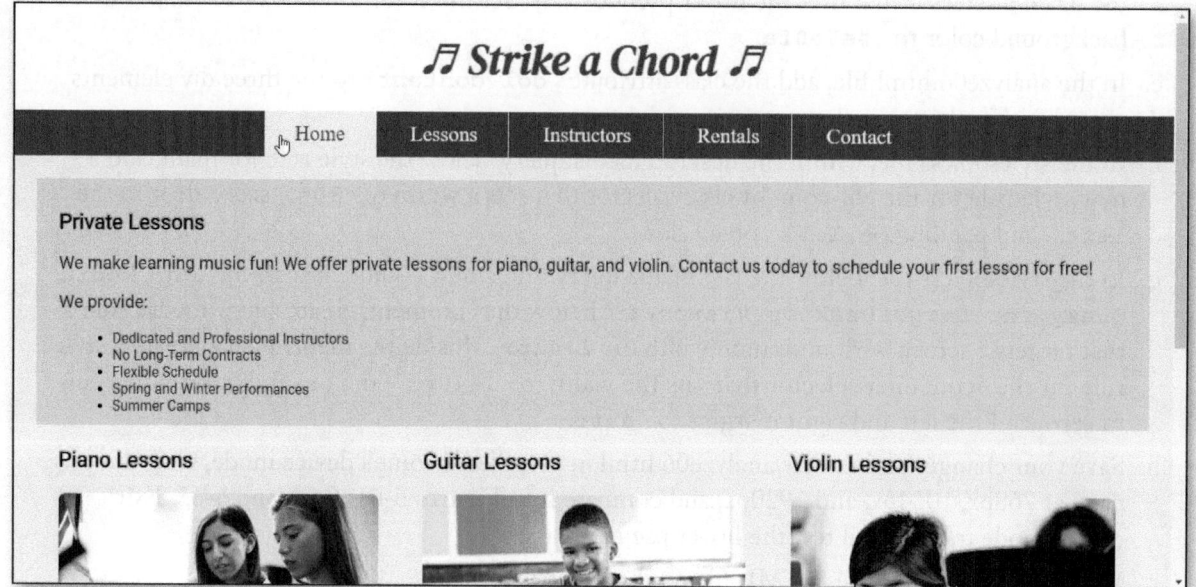

Figure 6–67

Instructions: Perform the following tasks:

1. Open the styles.css file in your text editor and add the following comment and media query below the last style rule on the document:

```
/* Media Query for Tablet Viewport */
@media screen and (min-width: 550px), print {

}
```

2. Within the tablet media query, add the following comments and style rules:

```
/* Tablet Viewport: Show tab-desk class, hide mobile class */
.tab-desk {
    display: block;
}
.mobile {
    display: none;
}
/* Tablet Viewport: Style rule for header content */
span.tab-desk {
    display: inline;
}
```

3. Within the tablet media query, add a new comment with the text, `Tablet Viewport: Style rules for nav area`. Below the comment, add a new style rule for the nav li selector that sets the top border to **none**, display to an `inline-block`, font size to `1.5em`, and a right border property with `1px solid #e5e9fc` as its values.

4. Below the style rule you created in step 3, add another style rule for the nav li selector that uses the last-child pseudo-class and removes the right border.

5. Below the style rule you created in step 4, add another style rule for the nav li a selector that sets the top and bottom padding to `0.25em` and the left and right padding to `0.5em`.

6. In the contact.html file, add `mobile` to the existing class attribute within the paragraph element on Line 37. (*Hint*: class="tel-link mobile")

7. Insert the following paragraph element after Line 37:

   `<p class="tab-desk">(814) 555-9228</p>`

8. In the styles.css file, within the tablet media query, add a new comment with the text, `Tablet Viewport: Style rule for map`. Below the comment, add a new style rule for the map class selector that sets the width to `500px` and the height to `450px`.

9. Below the tablet media query, add a new comment with the text, `Media Query for Desktop Viewport`. Below the comment, add a new media query that targets a screen with a minimum width of 769px and print.

10. Within the desktop media query, add a new comment with the text, `Desktop Viewport: Style rule for header`. Below the comment, add a style rule for the header selector that sets the padding to `2%`.

11. Within the desktop media query, below the header style rule, add a new comment with the text, `Desktop Viewport: Style rules for nav area`. Below the comment, add a style rule for the nav li a selector that sets the padding to `0.5em` on the top and bottom and `1.5em` on the left and right. Add another style rule for the nav li a selector that uses the hover pseudo-class and sets the color to `#373684` and the background color to `#e5e9fc`.

12. Within the desktop media query, below the nav area style rules, add a new comment with the text, `Desktop Viewport: Style rules for main content`. Below the comment, add a style rule for the following selectors:

    a. #info ul selector that sets the left margin to `5%`

    b. main h3 selector that sets the font size to `1.5em`

    c. #piano, #guitar, and #violin selectors that sets the width to `29%`, a float to the `left`, top/bottom margin value of `0`, and left/right margin value of `2%`

13. Below the desktop media query, add a new comment with the text, `Media Query for Print`. Below the comment, add a new media query that targets print.

14. Within the print media query, add a style rule for the body selector that sets the background color to `#fff` and the color to `#000`.

15. Use good coding practices by including indents and spacing between style rules.

16. Check your spelling. Validate all HTML and CSS files and correct any errors. Save your changes.

17. Open the index.html file in Google Chrome's device mode to view the home page in a tablet viewport. Navigate to the Lessons and Contact pages to view the tablet design for each page.

18. Open the index.html file in Google Chrome's device mode to view the home page in a desktop viewport. Navigate to the Lessons and Contact pages to view the desktop design for each page.

19. Submit your assignment in the format specified by your instructor.

20. ✴ In step 2, you created a style rule for the selector span.tab-desk. What was the purpose of this style rule? What happens when you remove it? Why is there no space between span and .tab-desk for this selector? Research to find your answer.

Continued >

In the Lab *continued*

Lab 2: **Creating Media Queries for the Wild Rescues Website**

Problem: You volunteer at a local wildlife rescue, a nonprofit organization called Wild Rescues. The organization rescues all kinds of wild animals, rehabilitates them, and then releases them back into the wild. Wild Rescues needs a website to help raise awareness about the organization. You have already created the mobile layout, but now need to add media queries for a tablet, desktop, and print. Style the website shown in Figure 6–68 for the tablet viewport. Style the website shown in Figure 6–69 for the desktop viewport. Style the website shown in Figure 6–70 for a large desktop viewport.

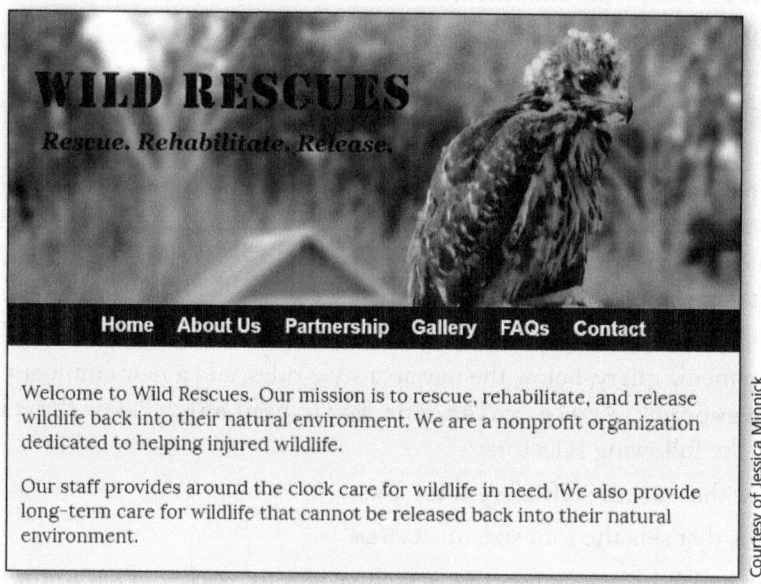

Figure 6–68

Figure 6–69

Figure 6–70

Instructions: Perform the following tasks:

1. Open the styles.css file in your text editor. Below the last style rule, add a comment with the text, `Media Query for Tablet Viewport`.

2. Below the comment, add a media query that targets a screen with a minimum width of 620px and print.

3. Add the following comments to the tablet media query:

   a. `Tablet Viewport: Show tab-desk class, hide mobile class`

   b. `Tablet Viewport: Style rules for nav area`

4. Add the following style rules below the Show tab-desk class, hide mobile class comment:

   a. Style rule for the tab-desk class selector that sets the display to a `block`.

   b. Style rule for the mobile class selector that sets the display to `none`.

5. Add the following style rules below the style rules for nav area comment:

   a. Style rule for the nav li selector that removes the top border, sets the display to an `inline-block`, and sets the font size to `1.25em`.

   b. Style rule for the nav li a selector that sets the padding to `0.5em`.

6. In the contact.html file, add `mobile` to the existing class attribute within the paragraph element on Line 44.

7. Insert a new Line 45 and add a paragraph element with the tab-desk class. Wrap the phone number, `(814) 555-9228`, within the paragraph element.

8. In the styles.css file, below the tablet media query, add a comment with the text, `Media Query for Desktop Viewport`.

9. Below the comment, add a media query that targets a screen with a minimum width of 1000px and print.

Continued >

In the Lab *continued*

10. Within the desktop media query, add a comment with the text, `Desktop Viewport: Style rules for nav area`. Add the following style rules below the comment.

   a. Style rule for the nav li selector that sets the font size to `1.5em`

   b. Style rule for the nav li a selector that sets the top and bottom padding to `0.5em` and the left and right padding to `1.5em`

   c. Style rule for the nav li a selector with a hover pseudo-class that sets the color to `#2a1f14` and the background color to `#f6eee4`

11. Within the desktop media query, add a comment with the text, `Desktop Viewport: Style rules for main content`. Below the comment, add a style rule for the #info ul selector that sets the left margin to `5%`.

12. In the index.html, about.html, contact.html, and template.html files, wrap all of the elements between the body tags within a single, parent div element with an id attribute of `wrapper`. Indent all nested elements.

13. In the styles.css file, below the tablet media query, add a comment with the text, `Media Query for Large Desktop Viewports`.

14. Below the comment, add a media query that targets a screen with a minimum width of 1921px. Add the following style rules to the large desktop media query:

   a. Style rule for the body element that sets the background to a linear gradient with the color values `#f6eee4` and `#78593a`

   b. Style rule for the #wrapper selector that sets the width to `1920px`, top and bottom margin to `0`, and left and right margins to `auto`

   c. Style rule for the main selector that sets the background color to `#f6eee4`

15. Below the large desktop media query, add a comment with the text, `Media Query for Print`. Below the comment, add a media query that targets print.

16. In the print media query, add a style rule for the body selector that sets the background color to white and the font color to black.

17. Check your spelling. Validate all HTML and CSS files and correct any errors. Save your changes.

18. Open the index.html file in Google Chrome's device mode to view the home page in a tablet viewport. Navigate to the About Us and Contact pages to view the tablet design for each page.

19. Open the index.html file in Google Chrome's device mode to view the home page in a desktop viewport. Navigate to the About Us and Contact pages to view the desktop design for each page. Exit device mode to view and test the hover pseudo-class.

20. Open the index.html file in Google Chrome's device mode to view the home page in a large desktop viewport (at least 1950px). Navigate to the About Us and Contact pages to view the large desktop design for each page.

21. Submit your assignment in the format specified by your instructor.

22. ✺ In step 14, you created a style rule for a gradient. Discuss at least three different ways this gradient could be applied.

Lab 3: Creating Media Queries for the Student Clubs and Events Website

Problem: You and several of your classmates have decided to help increase student involvement in school clubs and events by creating a website to promote awareness about the various activities. You have already created several pages for the website and designed it for a mobile viewport, but now you need to add media queries to design for tablet, desktop, large desktop, and print.

Instructions:

1. Open the styles.css file in your text editor and add media queries for tablet, desktop, large desktop, and print.

2. As a team, determine the design and breakpoint for each viewport.

3. Hide any mobile-specific content and show any tablet or desktop-specific content.

4. Use at least one dynamic pseudo-class in your desktop media query.

5. Apply a gradient.

6. Use a two-column layout for at least one page.

7. Add comments in your style sheet to note where each media query begins and add other comments for new style rules as appropriate.

8. View and test each viewport design and adjust breakpoints where necessary. Exit device mode to view and test the hover pseudo-class.

9. Review your files for best coding practices; ensure proper spacing and indents for improved readability.

10. Submit your assignment in the format specified by your instructor.

11. ✸ In this assignment, you needed to determine at least three different breakpoints for your media queries. What breakpoints did you use and why?

Consider This: Your Turn

Apply your creative thinking and problem-solving skills to design and implement a solution.

1. Styling Your Personal Portfolio Website for Tablet and Desktop Viewports

Personal

Part 1: In Chapter 5, you designed your personal portfolio website for a mobile viewport. You now need to design for tablet and desktop viewports.

1. Add a minimum of two media queries to your style sheet; one for tablet and at least one for desktop.

2. Hide any mobile-specific content and show any tablet or desktop-specific content.

3. Use at least one dynamic pseudo-class in your desktop media query.

4. Add comments in your style sheet to note where each media query begins, and add other comments for new style rules as appropriate.

5. View and test each viewport design and adjust breakpoints where necessary. Exit device mode to view and test the hover pseudo-class.

6. Review your files for best coding practices; ensure proper spacing and indents for improved readability.

7. Validate all HTML and CSS files and correct any errors.

8. Submit your assignment in the format specified by your instructor.

Part 2: ✸ Use your browser to research tips for creating a portfolio website. Provide a summary of your findings.

2. Styling the Dog Grooming Website for Tablet, Desktop, and Print Viewports

Professional

Part 1: In Chapter 5, you designed your dog grooming business website for a mobile viewport. You now need to design it for tablet, desktop, large desktop, and print viewports.

Continued >

Consider This: Your Turn *continued*

1. Add four media queries to your style sheet; one for tablet, one for desktop, one for a large desktop, and one for print.

2. Hide any mobile-specific content and show any tablet or desktop-specific content.

3. Use at least one dynamic pseudo-class in your desktop media query.

4. Use a gradient for a background.

5. Use a multiple-column layout on at least one page.

6. Add comments in your style sheet to note where each media query begins and add other comments for new style rules as appropriate.

7. View and test each viewport design and adjust breakpoints where necessary. Exit device mode to view and test the hover pseudo-class.

8. Review your files for best coding practices; ensure proper spacing and indents for improved readability.

9. Validate all HTML and CSS files and correct any errors.

10. Submit your assignment in the format specified by your instructor.

Part 2: ✳ In this assignment, you specified a gradient for a background. Research the background-repeat property and provide a summary of its use.

3. Styling the Future Technologies Website for Tablet, Desktop, and Print Viewports
Research and Collaboration

Part 1: You and several of your classmates have been tasked with creating a website that showcases advances in technology. You have already designed the website for a mobile viewport and now need to design it for tablet, desktop, large desktop, and print viewports.

1. Add four media queries to your style sheet; one for tablet, one for desktop, one for a large desktop, and one for print. As a team, determine the design and breakpoint for each viewport.

2. Hide any mobile-specific content and show any tablet or desktop-specific content.

3. Use at least three dynamic pseudo-classes in your desktop media query.

4. Use a gradient.

5. Use a multiple-column layout on at least one page.

6. Add comments in your style sheet to note where each media query begins and add other comments for new style rules as appropriate.

7. View and test each viewport design and adjust breakpoints where necessary. Exit device mode to view and test the hover pseudo-class.

8. Review your files for best coding practices; ensure proper spacing and indents for improved readability.

9. Validate all HTML and CSS files and correct any errors.

10. Submit your assignment in the format specified by your instructor.

Part 2: ✳ So far, you have learned about and used structural and dynamic pseudo-classes. What other categories of pseudo-classes exist? Identify at least two.

7 | Improving Web Design with New Page Layouts

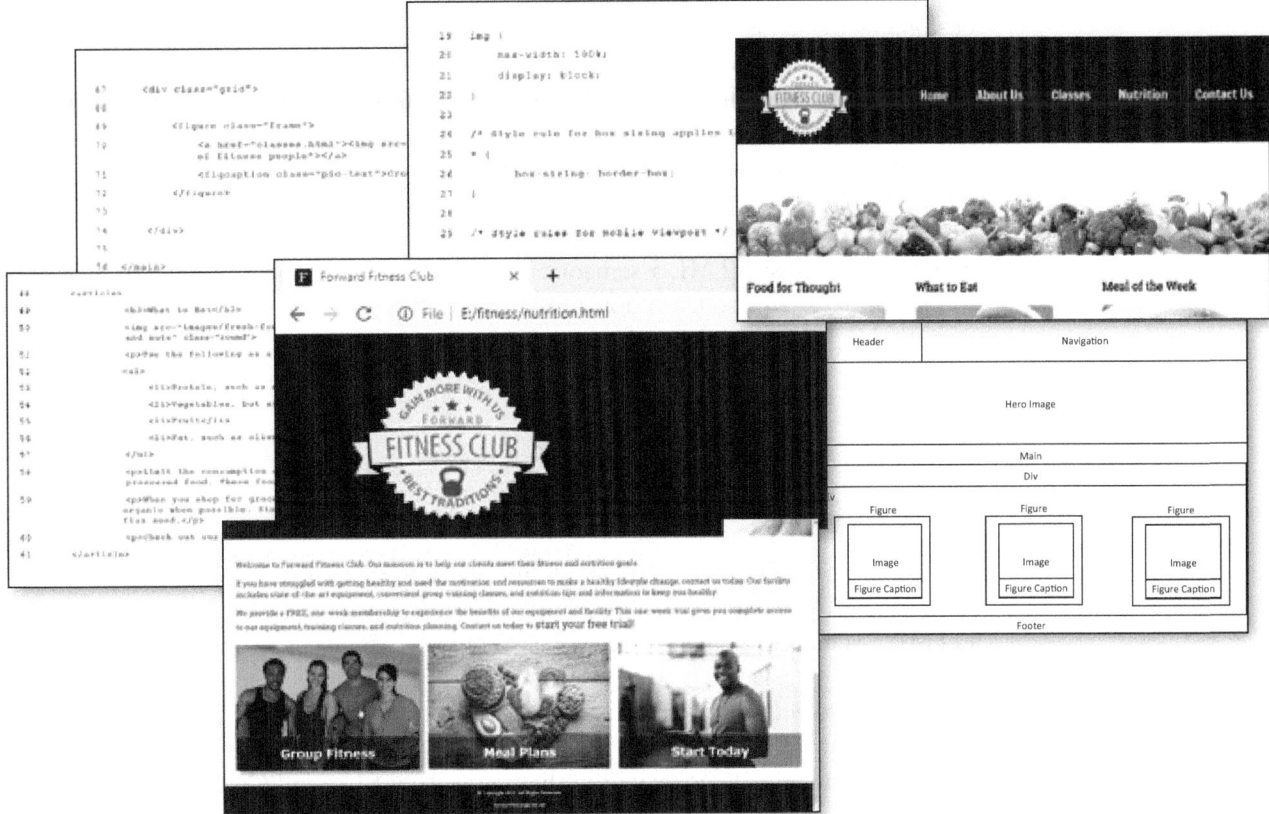

Objectives

You will have mastered the material in this chapter when you can:

- Describe and use article, aside, and section elements
- Describe and use figure and figcaption elements
- Describe and use the CSS grid layout
- Describe and use the opacity property
- Describe and use the box sizing property
- Describe and use the text shadow property

- Describe and use the box shadow property
- Insert and style figure and figcaption elements
- Insert a section element
- Insert and style an article element
- Insert and style an aside element
- Describe and add a favicon to a webpage

7 | Improving Web Design with New Page Layouts

Introduction

Web design involves a daily pursuit of perfection in layout, function, and efficiency. Every site you create expresses your personal creativity while balancing your customers' demands with content and design that capture and hold the attention of your dynamic audience. To meet these requirements, you must constantly re-evaluate your content and design and apply new technologies and innovations to keep your audience engaged and your customers elated.

As you have learned, HTML 5 provides tools for improving webpage design, including semantic elements for specific types of content. You have already integrated four semantic elements in a website: header, nav, main, and footer. In this chapter, you will discover other HTML 5 semantic elements and learn how to integrate them into webpages. You will also learn how to use other CSS properties to further improve your current design for mobile, tablet, and desktop viewports.

Project — Use HTML 5 Structural Elements to Redesign a Website

In Chapters 5 and 6, you discovered how to create a responsive design website. In Chapter 7, you continue to improve the website structure by integrating more HTML 5 semantic elements. You will also improve the website design with more CSS properties.

The project in this chapter enhances a website with new HTML 5 semantic elements to structure new content. To complete this task, you integrate additional HTML 5 semantic elements within the home, About Us, and Contact Us pages. You also update and create style rules for the new and existing elements. Next, you create a wireframe for the Nutrition page, a new webpage in the site. Create the Nutrition page using HTML 5 semantic elements and create new style rules to format the page content. You apply styles to the HTML 5 elements on each page to give the site an enhanced look and feel. Figure 7–1 shows the home page for the mobile, tablet, and desktop viewports after the improvements are applied. Figure 7–2 shows the Nutrition page for the mobile, tablet, and desktop viewports after the page is created and styled. Figure 7–3 shows the favicon added to the website.

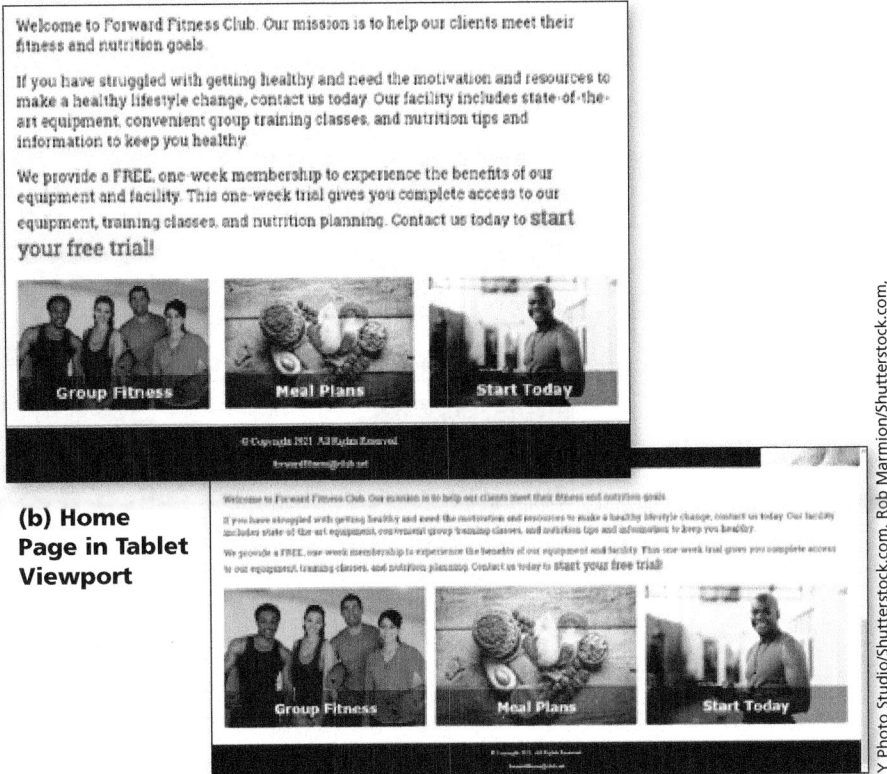

(a) Home Page in Mobile Viewport

(b) Home Page in Tablet Viewport

(c) Home Page in Desktop Viewport

Figure 7–1

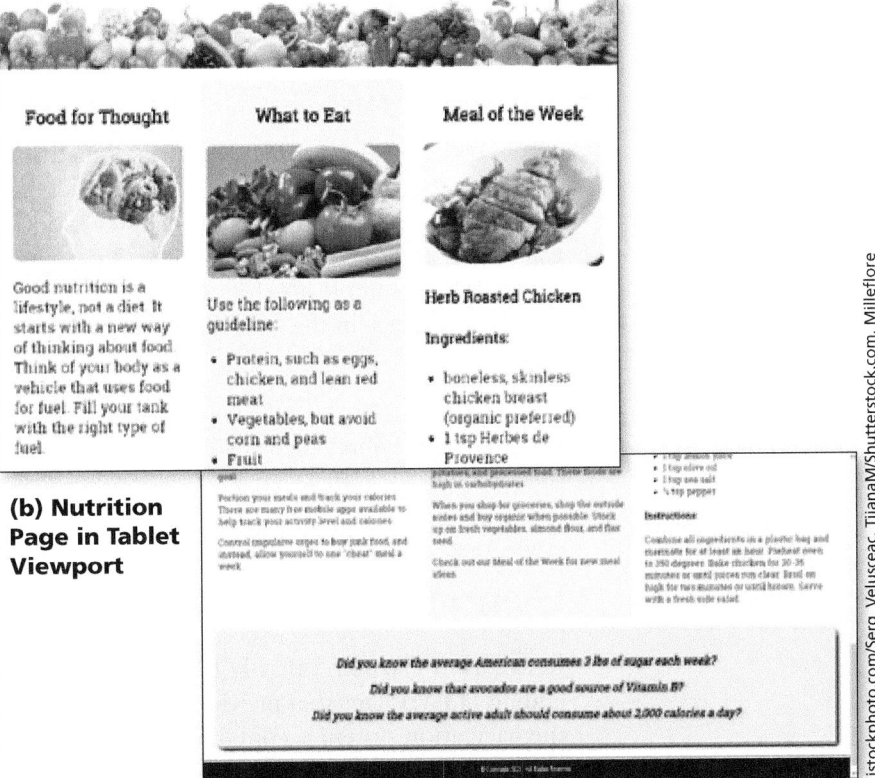

(a) Nutrition Page in Mobile Viewport

(b) Nutrition Page in Tablet Viewport

(c) Nutrition Page in Desktop Viewport

Figure 7–2

Figure 7–3

Roadmap

In this chapter, you will learn how to create the webpages shown in Figures 7–1, 7–2, and 7–3. The following roadmap identifies general activities you will perform as you progress through this chapter:

1. MODIFY the HOME PAGE.
2. STYLE the HOME PAGE elements.
3. MODIFY the ABOUT US PAGE.
4. CREATE AND STYLE the NUTRITION PAGE elements.
5. ADD a FAVICON.

At the beginning of step instructions throughout the chapter, you will see an abbreviated form of this roadmap. The abbreviated roadmap uses colors to indicate chapter progress: gray means the chapter is beyond that activity; blue means the task being shown is covered in that activity, and black means that activity is yet to be covered. For example, the following abbreviated roadmap indicates the chapter would be showing a task in the 4 CREATE & STYLE NUTRITION PAGE activity.

1 MODIFY HOME PAGE | 2 STYLE HOME PAGE | 3 MODIFY ABOUT US PAGE
4 CREATE & STYLE NUTRITION PAGE | **5 ADD FAVICON**

Use the abbreviated roadmap as a progress guide while you read or step through the instructions in this chapter.

Using HTML 5 Semantic Elements

Recall from Chapter 2 that HTML 5 semantic elements are a set of starting and ending HTML tags that provide meaning about the content of the tags. For example, the navigation system is contained within the <nav> and </nav> tags; likewise, footer content is contained within the <footer> and </footer> tags.

Use HTML 5 semantic elements for specific types of content within a webpage. The name of the tag reflects its purpose. Using semantic HTML 5 elements provides a standard naming convention for webpage content, making webpages more universal, accessible, and meaningful to search engines.

The Forward Fitness Club website contains the following semantic elements: header, nav, main, and footer. HTML 5 includes several other types of semantic elements. You will learn about and use many new semantic elements to complete this project. Table 7–1 lists other HTML 5 semantic elements.

Table 7–1 HTML 5 Semantic Elements

Element	Description
<article> ... </article>	Indicates the start and end of an article area of a webpage; contains content such as forum or blog posts
<aside> ... </aside>	Indicates the start and end of an aside area of a webpage; contains information about nearby content and is typically displayed as a sidebar
<details> ... </details>	Indicates the start and end of a details area of a webpage; contains additional information that the user can display or hide Note that this element is not supported by all major browsers at the time of this publication.
<figure> ... </figure>	Indicates the start and end of a figure area of a webpage; contains pictures and images
<figcap> ... </figcaption>	Indicates the start and end of a figure caption area of a webpage; defines a caption for a figure element
<section> ... </section>	Indicates the start and end of a section area of a webpage; contains a specific grouping of content on a webpage
<summary> ... </summary>	Indicates the start and end of a summary area of a webpage; contains a visible heading for the details element on a webpage Note that this element is not supported by all major browsers at the time of this publication.
<time> ... </time>	Indicates the start and end of a time area of a webpage; contains a date/time on a webpage

Article Element

The **article element**, as described by the W3C, represents "a self-contained composition in a document, page, application, or site and that is, in principle, independently distributable or reusable, e.g. in syndication. This could be a forum post, a magazine or newspaper article, a blog entry, a user-submitted comment, an interactive widget or gadget, or any other independent item of content." The article element starts with an <article> tag and ends with an </article> tag. Content placed between these tags will appear on a webpage as part of the article element. Articles may be nested within other HTML elements, such as the main element, or other article elements. Articles are commonly used to contain news articles, blog and forum posts, or comments. The article element is supported by the major modern browsers. The following is an example of three article elements nested within a main element.

```
<main>
    <article>
        <h1>Article 1 Title</h1>
        <p>Information about article 1</p>
    </article>
    <article>
        <h1>Article 2 Title</h1>
        <p>Information about article 2</p>
    </article>
```

```
<article>
        <h1>Article 3 Title</h1>
        <p>Information about article 3</p>
</article>
</main>
```

An example wireframe that uses the article element is shown in Figure 7–4. An example of a webpage that uses article elements is shown in Figure 7–5.

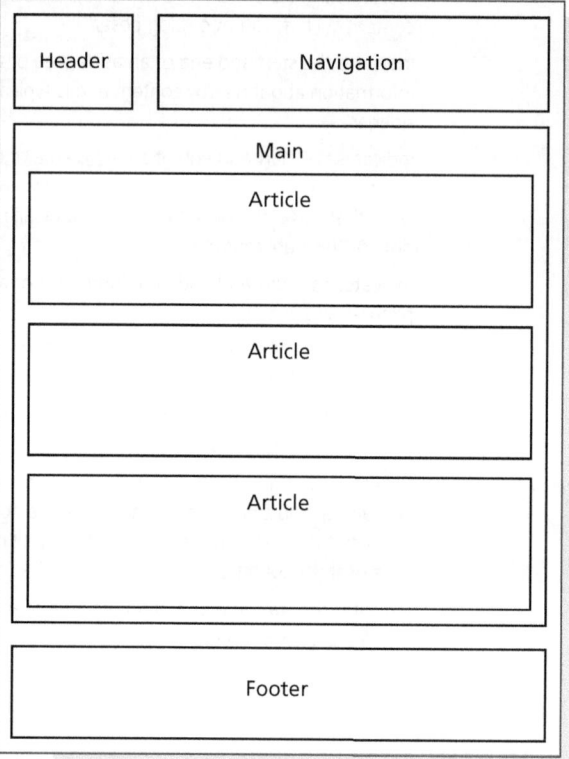

Figure 7–4

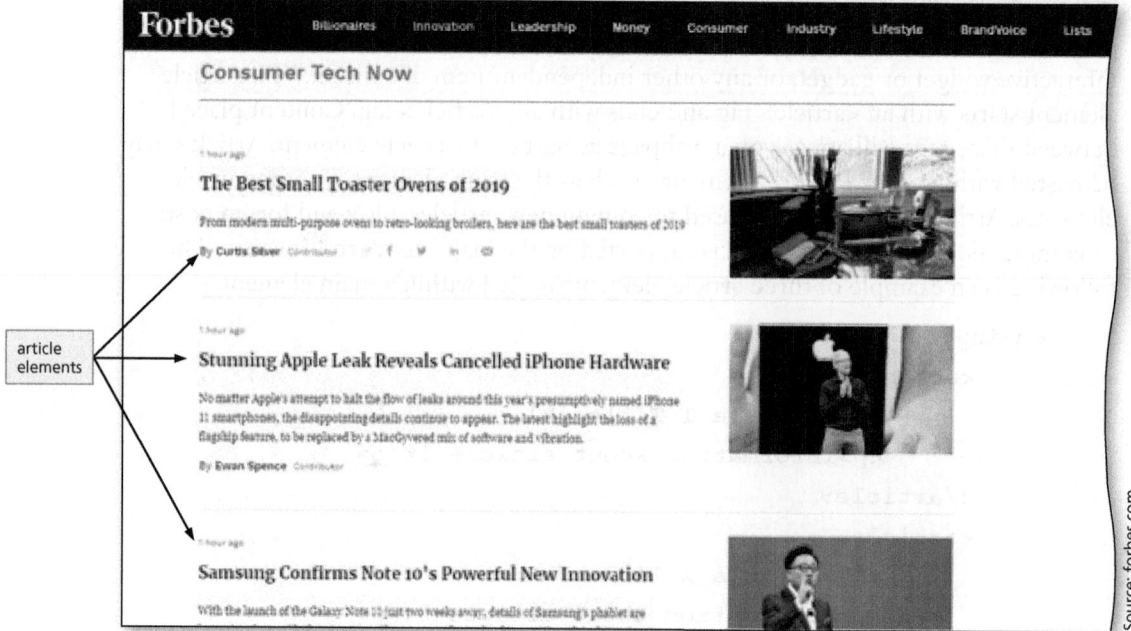

Figure 7–5

Aside Element

The **aside element**, as described by the W3C, is an element that "represents a section of a page that consists of content that is tangentially related to the content around the aside element, and which could be considered separate from that content." The aside element is used as a sidebar and contains additional information about a particular item mentioned within another element, such as an article or section element. For example, if an article on a webpage contains a recipe and a list of ingredients, you could include an aside element with more information about one of the key ingredients, such as its origin or where to purchase it. Aside elements can be nested within article elements or within main or section elements. Aside elements are commonly used for pull-out quotes, glossary terms, or related links. The following is an example of an aside element nested within an article element.

```
<article>
    <h1>Recipe</h1>
    <p>Recipe ingredients and instructions</p>
    <aside>
      <p>More information about a specific ingredient</p>
    </aside>
</article>
```

An example wireframe that uses the aside element is shown in Figure 7–6. An example of a webpage that uses an article element is shown in Figure 7–7.

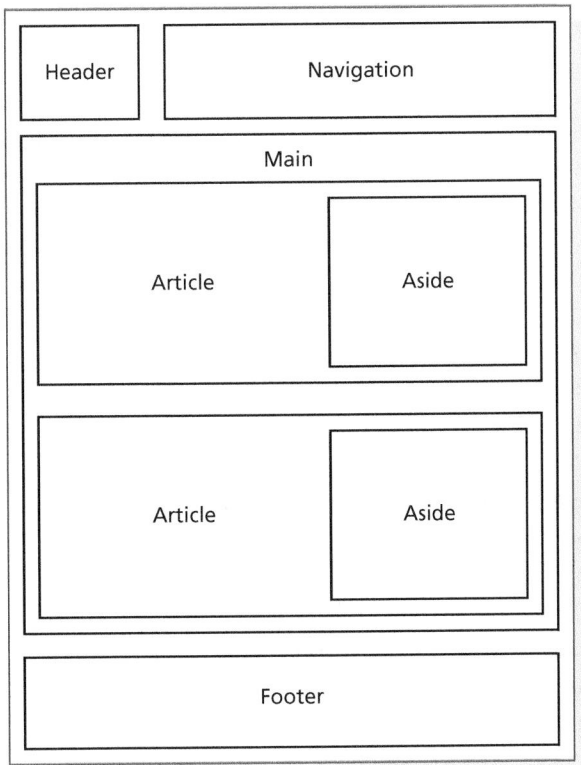

Figure 7–6

Figure 7–7

Source: foodnetwork.com

Section Element

The **section element**, as described by the W3C, is an element that "represents a generic section of a document or application. A section, in this context, is a thematic grouping of content. The theme of each section should be identified, typically by including a heading." The section element defines different parts of a webpage document, such as an introduction, new products, or service information. For example, in a webpage that contains a list of tutorials, Tutorials 1-3, each tutorial can be placed within a section and include a heading element with an appropriate title, Tutorial 1, Tutorial 2, Tutorial 3, followed by the tutorial content. Be sure to include a heading element within a section element or the page will receive a warning from the W3C HTML validator. Use a section element for content that naturally contains a heading. The W3C encourages designers to use article elements for other types of subdivided content. The W3C also states that the section element "is not a generic container element. When an element is needed only for styling purposes or as a convenience for scripting, authors are encouraged to use the div element instead. A general rule is that the section element is appropriate only if the element's contents would be listed explicitly in the document's outline." The following is an example of a several section elements nested within an article element.

```
<article>
    <h1>Tutorials: Cooking Basics</h1>
    <p>Watch our tutorials to learn the basics of good
        cooking.</p>
    <section>
      <h1>Tutorial 1</h1>
      <p>Assembling basic kitchen tools.</p>
    </section>
    <section>
      <h1>Tutorial 2</h1>
      <p>Cooking with essential spices.</p>
    </section>
    <section>
      <h1>Tutorial 3</h1>
      <p>Following food prep basics.</p>
    </section>
</article>
```

An example wireframe that uses the section element is shown in Figure 7–8. An example of a webpage that uses a section element is shown in Figure 7–9.

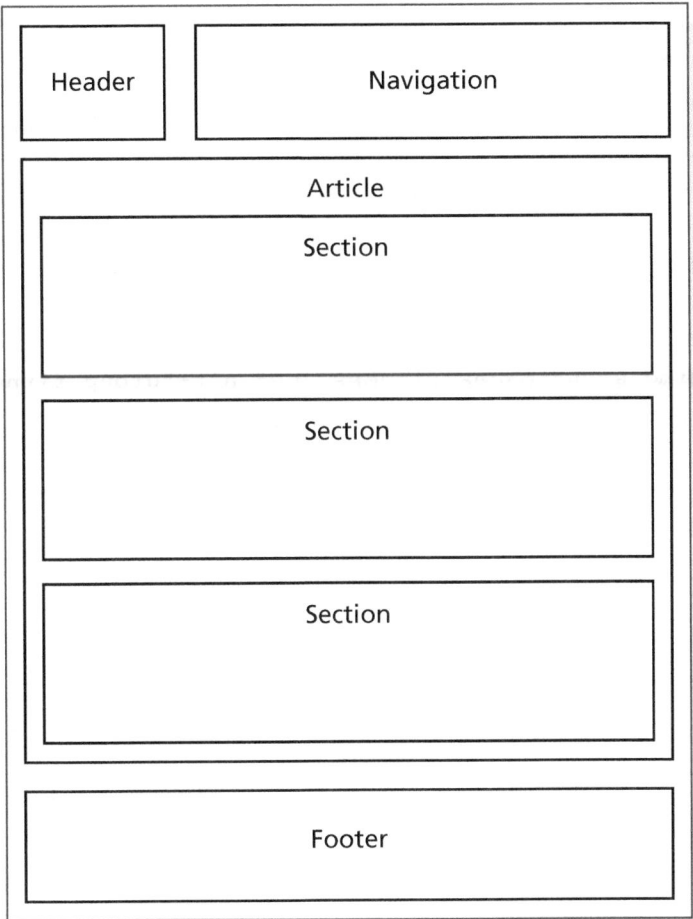

Figure 7–8

Figure 7–9

Figure and Figure Caption Elements

The **figure element** is used to group content, such as illustrations, diagrams, and photos. According to the W3C, the figure element "represents some flow content, optionally with a caption, that is self-contained and is typically referenced as a single unit from the main flow of the document." Though the figure element is commonly used to contain images, it can also be used to display a chart, graph, or other graphic. Do not confuse the figure element with the img element. The figure element is a semantic element with self-contained content. A figure element can contain one or more img elements.

The figure element may contain an optional **figure caption** element, which is used to provide a caption for the figure element. The figure caption element uses a <figcaption> tag as the starting tag and a </figcaption> tag as the ending tag. The following is an example of the figure element and the figure caption element.

```
<figure>
        <img src="images/fitness.jpg" alt="group fitness">
        <figcaption>Group Fitness</figcaption>
</figure>
```

An example wireframe that uses the figure and figure caption elements is shown in Figure 7–10. An example of a webpage that uses these elements is shown in Figure 7–11.

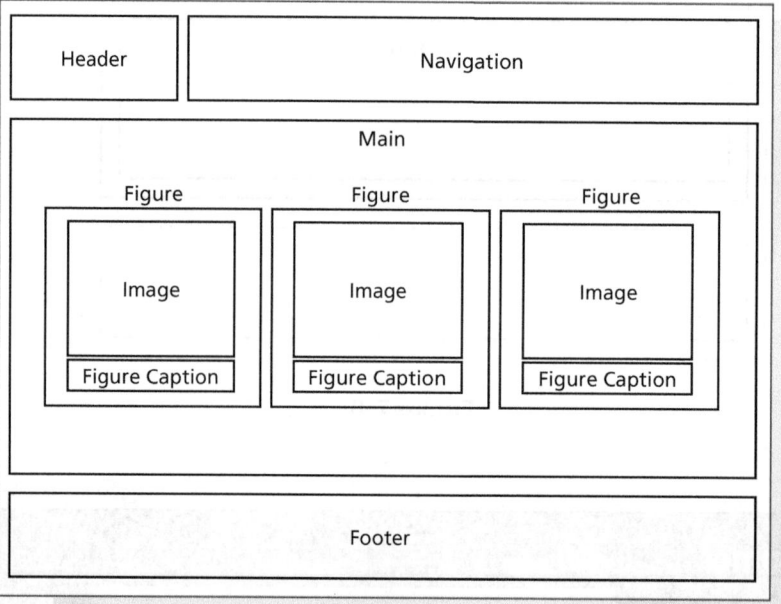

Figure 7–10

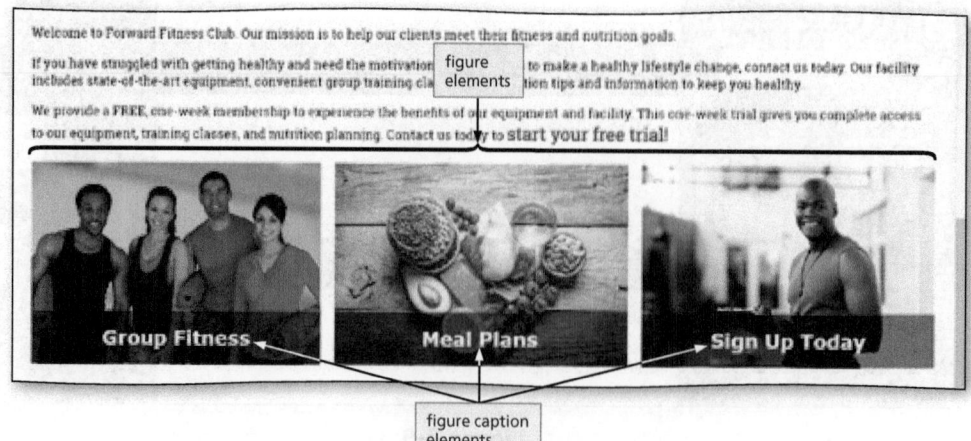

Figure 7–11

Rob Marmion/Shutterstock.com, Oleksandra Naumenko/Shutterstock.com, michaeljung/Shutterstock.com

Can I use figure and figure caption elements to wrap image elements separately?
Yes. You can wrap each image element within separate figure and figure caption elements.

Improving Design with CSS

You have learned how to style webpages using CSS and how to use responsive web design to create a website that is optimized for a variety of viewports. You have used many CSS properties but have really only scratched the surface of the power of CSS. There are many more CSS properties to explore.

CSS Grid Layout

In Chapters 5 and 6, you used responsive web design to optimize the layout for the Forward Fitness Club website across viewports of various sizes. As discussed in Chapter 5, a single-column layout is best for a mobile viewport design. However, as the viewport size increases, a multiple-column layout can be used.

In Chapter 6, you designed a multiple-column layout for a desktop viewport. To accomplish this design, you used CSS float, width, and clear properties. This is just one method to create a multiple-column layout. Another method for creating a multiple column layout is known as the **CSS grid layout**. The CSS grid layout is a newer webpage design model used to create a single or multiple-column layout by controlling the size and position of boxes of content on a webpage. The CSS grid layout was created by the W3C Working Group to lay out boxes of content into rows and columns, making a more reliable pattern of responsive element-sizing behaviors. Web developers can use the CSS grid layout to design a multiple-column layout with better accuracy than float, width, and clear properties. Table 7–2 shows several CSS grid layout properties.

Table 7–2 CSS Grid Layout Properties

Property	Description	Example
grid-template-columns	Specifies the number of columns within a grid	grid-template-columns: auto auto auto; (creates a three-column layout)
grid-template-rows	Specifies the size of rows within a grid	grid-template-rows: 200px 400px;
grid-column-start	Specifies the start of a grid	grid-column-start: 1;
grid-column-end	Specifies the ending of a grid	grid-column-end: 3;
grid-column-gap	Specifies the column gap between each box of content	grid-column-gap: 50px;
grid-row-gap	Specifies the row gap between each box of content	grid-row-gap: 40px;
grid-gap	Shorthand for grid-row-gap and grid-column-gap	grid-gap: 20px 80px; (20px is the row gap; 80px is the column gap)

To use the CSS grid layout, you first create a container for the grid within the HTML document and then you create a style rule to display the container as a grid or as an inline-grid. The following example creates a div element with a class attribute of grid and a style rule to display the div as a grid:

HTML element:

```
<div class="grid">

    <p>Lorem ipsum dolor sit amet, consectetur adipiscing
    elit, sed do eiusmod tempor incididunt ut labore et
    dolore magna aliqua. Ut enim ad minim veniam, quis
    nostrud exercitation ullamco laboris nisi ut aliquip
    ex ea commodo consequat.</p>

    <p>Lorem ipsum dolor sit amet, consectetur adipiscing
    elit, sed do eiusmod tempor incididunt ut labore et
    dolore magna aliqua. Ut enim ad minim veniam, quis
    nostrud exercitation ullamco laboris nisi ut aliquip
    ex ea commodo consequat.</p>

    <p>Lorem ipsum dolor sit amet, consectetur adipiscing
    elit, sed do eiusmod tempor incididunt ut labore et
    dolore magna aliqua. Ut enim ad minim veniam, quis
    nostrud exercitation ullamco laboris nisi ut aliquip
    ex ea commodo consequat.</p>

</div>


CSS style rule:
.grid {
    display: grid;
}
```

Next, you create a style rule to specify the number of columns you want to use in the grid layout. To do this, add the CSS `grid-template-columns` property to the style rule and specify the number of columns using the value auto as many times as necessary to create the multiple-column layout. For example, if you want a three-column layout, then specify the auto value three times, as shown in the following example:

```
.grid {
    display: grid;
    grid-template-columns: auto auto auto;
}
```

BTW
W3C Working Group
For the latest information about the CSS Working Group and the CSS grid layout, visit www.w3.org/TR/css-grid-1.

BTW
CSS Flexbox Layout
The CSS Flexbox Layout is another layout module used to create a multiple column layout. To learn more about the CSS Flexbox, visit www.w3schools.com/css/css3_flexbox.asp.

Using the auto value allows the column to grow and shrink, depending on the size of the viewport. Other values for the grid-template-columns property are shown in Table 7–3.

Table 7–3 CSS grid-template-columns Property Values

Property	Description
auto	Column size adjusts based on the size of the viewport
max-content	Column size is based on the largest element within the column
min-content	Column size is based on the smallest element within the column
length	Column size is based on a legal length value

The CSS grid layout is supported by all modern browsers.

Opacity

Figure 7–11 also demonstrates the use of opacity. Opacity refers to the transparency of an element. One way to add opacity within a webpage is to use the CSS **opacity** property, which specifies the amount transparency of an element. Opacity's default value is 1, which does not make the element transparent. An opacity value of 0.50 makes an element 50 percent transparent and an opacity value of 0 makes an element completely transparent. Major modern browsers support the opacity property. The following example specifies an opacity of 50 percent for the background color of the main element:

```
main {
        background-color:#ff0000;
        opacity: 0.5;
}
```

When you specify opacity for the background of an element, any nested elements will inherit the transparency. To avoid this, use RGBA for the color value. Another way to add opacity is through the use of the rgba() function. Recall the RGB color notation from Chapter 4. To specify the color blue using RGB, use rgb(0,0,255). The numbers 0,0,255 represent the color blue. The rgba() function is similar, except that it takes four numbers and the fourth specifies the opacity of the color. The following example specifies a blue background color for the main element with an opacity value of 50 percent:

```
main {
        background-color: rgba(0,0,255,0.5);
}
```

CSS Shadows

The **box-shadow** property is another CSS property that applies a shadow to an element, such as a div or an img element. This property requires a minimum of two values: the h-shadow value, which designates the horizontal offset of the shadow, and the v-shadow, which designates the vertical offset of the shadow. Optional values include a blur radius and a color. Below is an example of a style rule that applies a text shadow to an img element.

```
img {
        text-shadow: 5px 10px 8px #ccc;
}
```

In this example, a box shadow with a horizontal offset of 5px, a vertical offset of 10px, a blur of 8px, and a light gray color is applied to an img element.

The **text-shadow** property is another CSS property that applies a shadow to text. This property requires a minimum of two values: the h-shadow value, which designates the horizontal offset of the shadow, and the v-shadow, which designates the vertical offset of the shadow. Optional values include a blur radius and a color. Below is an example of a style rule that applies a text shadow to a heading 1 element.

```
h1 {
        text-shadow: 2px 2px #292933;
}
```

In this example, a text shadow with a horizontal offset of 2px, a vertical offset of 2px, and a dark gray color is applied to an h1 element.

CSS Box Sizing

When you create a wireframe, you use boxes to create the layout of webpage and note the location of the header, nav, main, footer, and other page content areas. Each of these elements can vary in size. Their size depends upon specified CSS box model properties (padding and borders) along with height and width properties. Two elements with the same height and width properties can still appear as two different sizes if they use different padding and border values. You can correct this issue with the CSS **box-sizing** property with a value of border-box. The box-sizing property allows any specified padding or border to be included within the element's total size. The following example applies the box-sizing property to a div element:

```
div {
        box-sizing: border-box;
}
```

In today's web development environment, it is a common practice to apply box-sizing to all webpage elements. To quickly and easily apply a style rule to all elements, you use the asterisk (*) to select all elements. The following examples applies the box-sizing property to all elements:

```
* {
        box-sizing: border-box;
}
```

Redesigning the Home Page

BTW
Web Content Strategist
A web content strategist is responsible for developing strategies for displaying content on a webpage. A web content strategist analyzes current content, performs in-depth research, and then drafts recommendations for new content ideas in order to attract new clients.

Improve the look of the home page by adding figure and figcaption elements with pictures to provide more visual content for potential clients.

Start by reviewing the existing wireframe for each viewport to determine how to improve it. You decide to keep the same wireframe for the home page mobile viewport because it is basic, is adaptable, and works well in the limited space of the mobile viewport. However, you can modify the wireframes for tablet and desktop viewports because the additional space allows you to include extra content, such as images within a figure element. You draft new wireframes for the tablet and desktop viewports, which integrate a div for a banner image and a figure element, as shown in Figures 7–12 and 7–13.

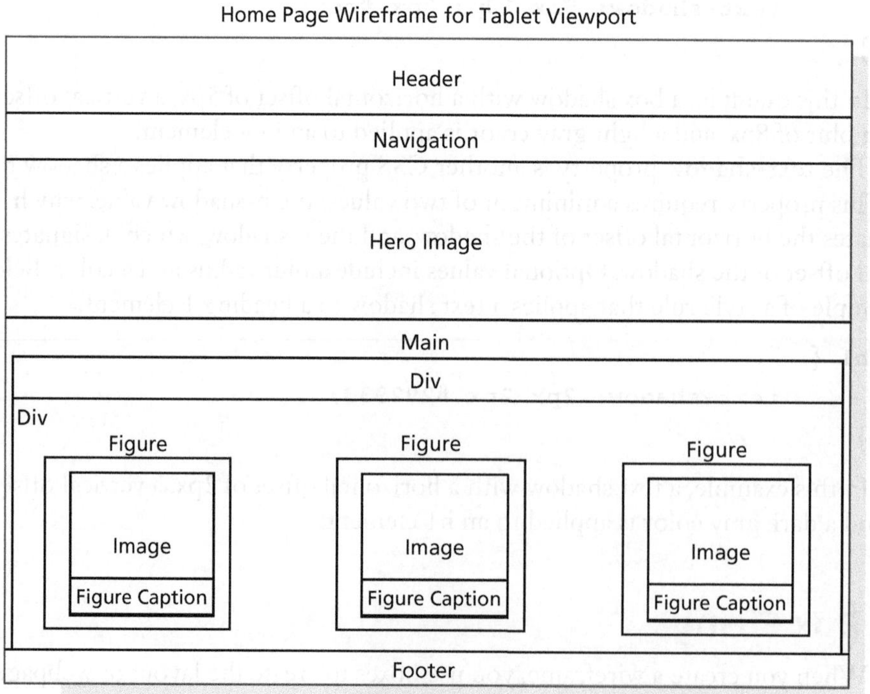

Home Page Wireframe for Tablet Viewport

Figure 7–12

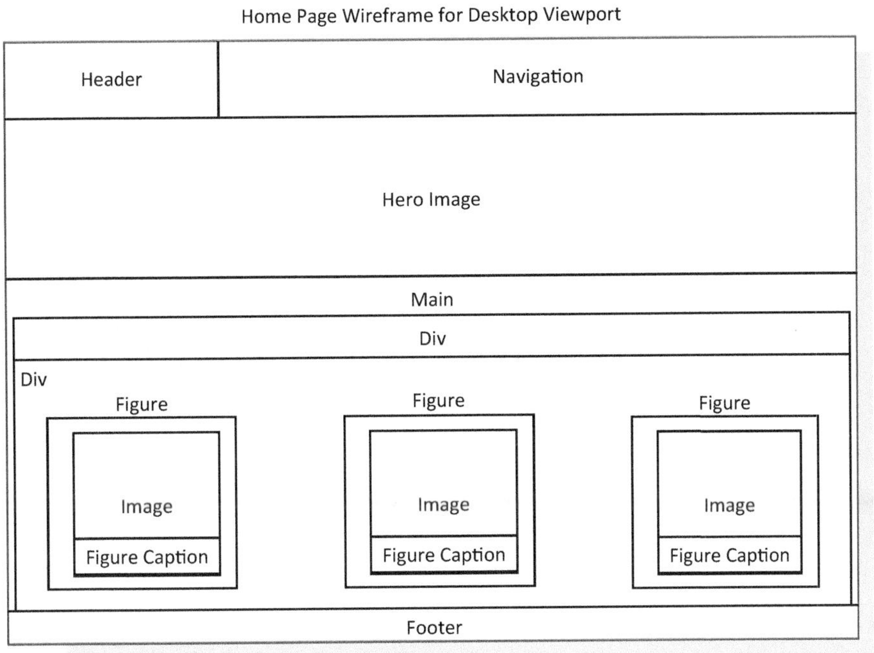

Home Page Wireframe for Desktop Viewport

Header	Navigation

Hero Image

Main

Div

Div

Figure	Figure	Figure
Image	Image	Image
Figure Caption	Figure Caption	Figure Caption

Footer

Figure 7–13

To Add a New div Element to the Home Page

Modify the home page by adding a new div element to contain figure elements. To complete this assignment, you will be required to use the Data Files. Please contact your instructor for information about accessing the Data Files. Next, open the index. html file in your text editor and insert a **div** element with the class attribute and value of grid. The following steps add a **div class="grid"** element to the home page.

1. If necessary, insert the drive containing the Data Files into an available port.

2. Use File Explorer (Windows) or Finder (Mac) to navigate to the storage location of the Data Files.

3. Navigate to chapter07\chapter\images folder and copy the 10 image files to your fitness\images folder.

4. Open index.html in your text editor, tap or click at the end of Line 65, and then press the ENTER key twice to insert new Lines 66 and 67.

5. On Line 67, type **<div class="grid">** to insert a div tag.

6. Press the ENTER key twice to insert new Lines 68 and 69 and then type **</div>** to insert a closing div tag (Figure 7–14).

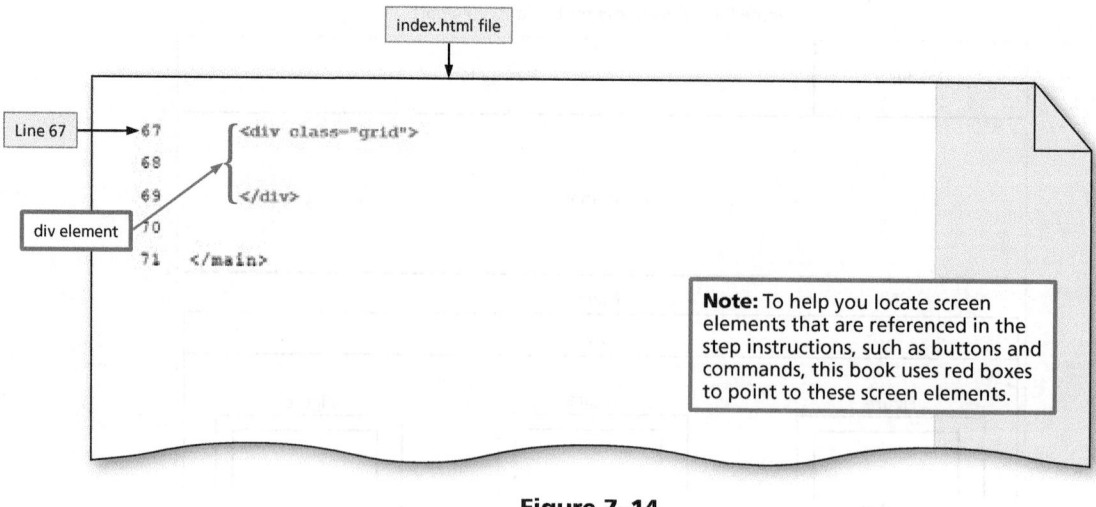

Figure 7–14

To Add figure Elements to the Home Page

1 MODIFY HOME PAGE | 2 STYLE HOME PAGE | 3 MODIFY ABOUT US PAGE
4 CREATE & STYLE NUTRITION PAGE | 5 ADD FAVICON

Insert three figure elements within the `div class="grid"` element. Each figure element will contain an image and a figcaption element. *Why? Use figure elements to contain new images for the home page.* Add three figure elements within the grid div and then nest an img and figcaption element within each figure element. Link the img elements to the Classes, Nutrition, and Contact Us pages. The following steps add figure, img, figcaption, and anchor elements to the home page.

- Tap or click at the end of Line 67, and then press the ENTER key twice to insert new Lines 68 and 69.

- On Line 69, type `<figure class="frame">` to insert a starting figure tag.

- Press the ENTER key to insert a new Line 70, increase the indent, and then type `<a href="classes.html"><img src="images/fitness-group.jpg" alt="group of fitness people"></a>` to insert a link and an image element.

- Press the ENTER key to insert a new Line 71, and then type `<figcaption class="pic-text">Group Fitness</figcaption>` to insert a figcaption element.

- Press the ENTER key to insert a new Line 72, decrease the indent, and then type `</figure>` to insert a closing figure tag (Figure 7–15).

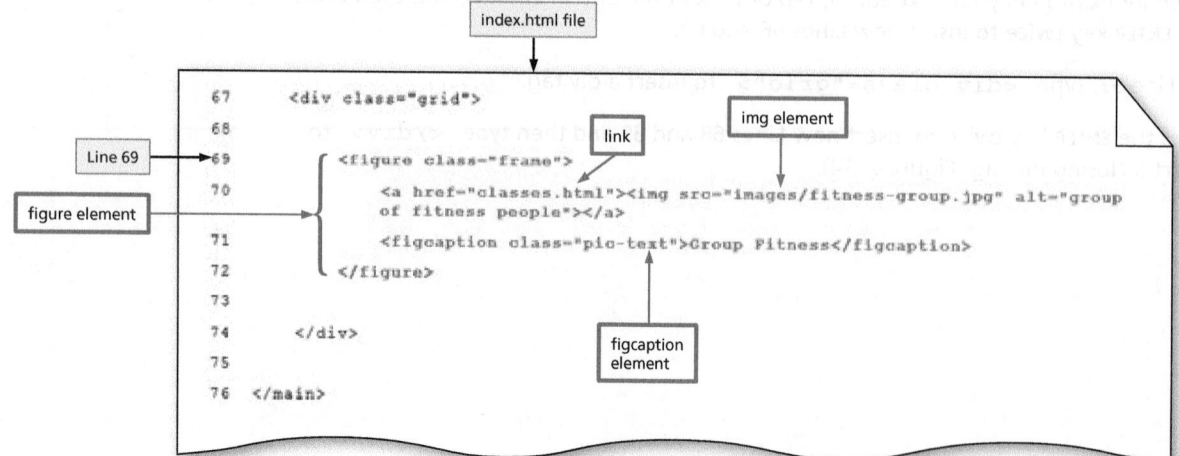

Figure 7–15

2

- Press the ENTER key twice to insert new Lines 73 and 74.

- On Line 74, type **<figure class="frame">** to insert a starting figure tag.

- Press the ENTER key to insert a new Line 75, increase the indent, and then type **<a href="nutrition. html"><img src="images/ food-heart.jpg" alt="healthy food in the shape of a heart"></ a>** to insert a link and an image element.

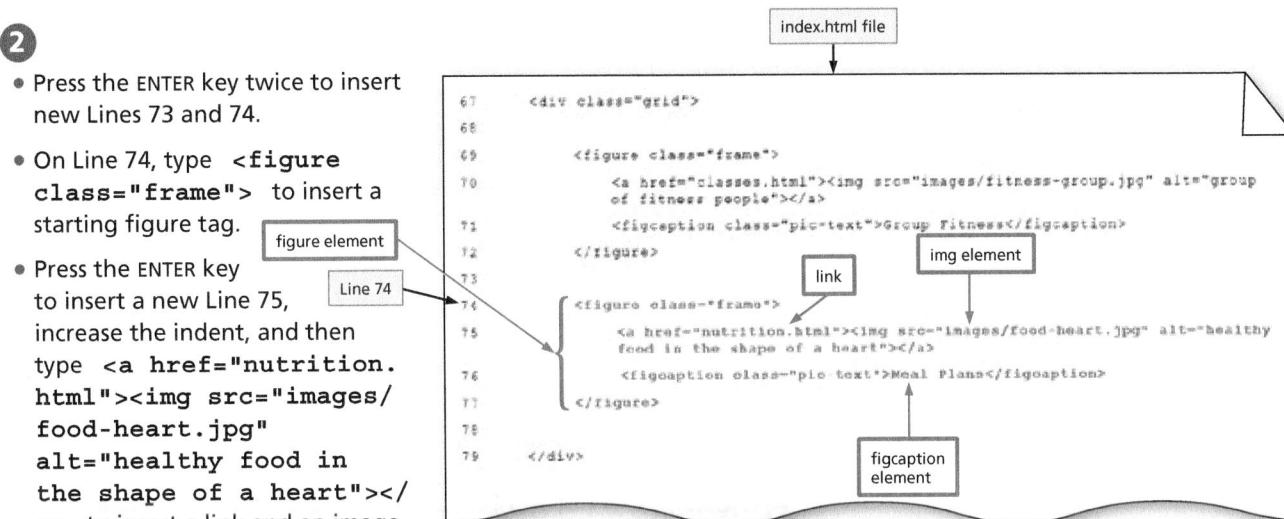

Figure 7–16

- Press the ENTER key to insert a new Line 76, and then type **<figcaption class="pic-text">Meal Plans</figcaption>** to insert a figcaption element.

- Press the ENTER key to insert a new Line 77, decrease the indent, and then type **</figure>** to insert a closing figure tag (Figure 7–16).

3

- Press the ENTER key twice to insert new Lines 78 and 79.

- On Line 79, type **<figure class="frame">** to insert a starting figure tag.

- Press the ENTER key to insert a new Line 80, increase the indent, and then type **<a href= "contact.html"> <img src="images/ personal-trainer. jpg" alt="personal trainer with a clipboard"></a>** to insert a link and an image element.

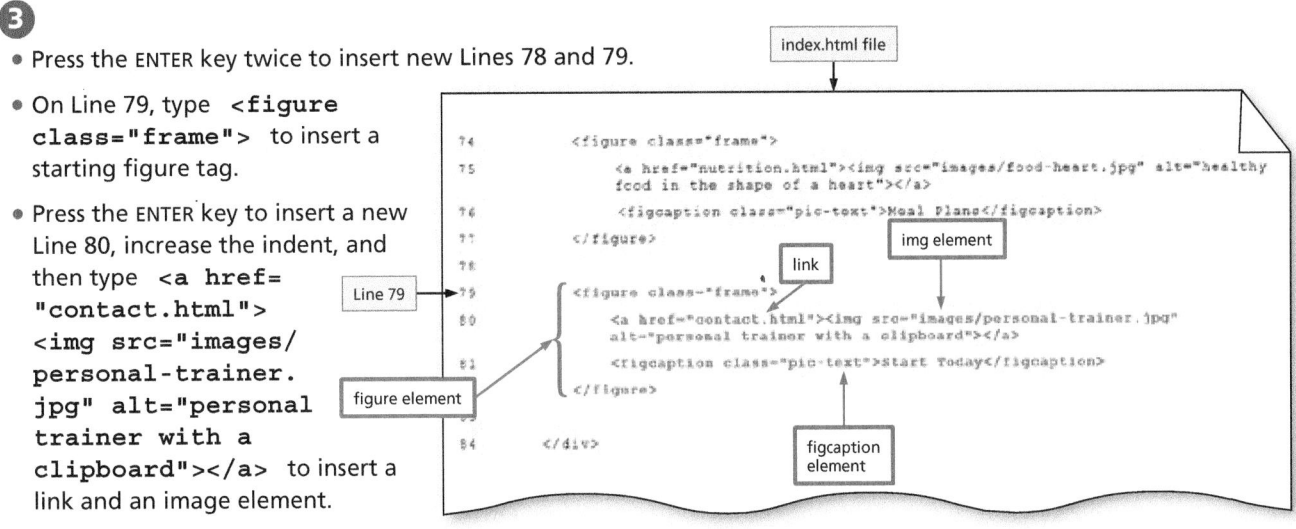

Figure 7–17

- Press the ENTER key to insert a new Line 81, and then type **<figcaption class= "pic-text">Start Today</figcaption>** to insert a figcaption element.

- Press the ENTER key to insert a new Line 82, decrease the indent, and then type **</figure>** to insert a closing figure tag (Figure 7–17).

4

- Save your changes, open index. html in your browser, and scroll down to view the new images (Figure 7–18).

figcaption element → Meal Plans

images within figure elements

figcaption element → Start Today

Figure 7–18

To Update the Style Sheet for the New Design in a Mobile Viewport

1 MODIFY HOME PAGE | 2 STYLE HOME PAGE | 3 MODIFY ABOUT US PAGE
4 CREATE & STYLE NUTRITION PAGE | 5 ADD FAVICON

Update the CSS reset style rule in the style sheet to add the figure and figcaption selectors. Modify and create new style rules for the mobile viewport. *Why? The figure and figcaption elements need to be added to the CSS reset for the default style rule to apply. Remove the sticky property to allow for more page content within the viewport. Create style rules to style the new page content.* The following steps update the CSS reset, modify the header style rule, and create new style rules for the mobile viewport.

1

- Open the styles.css file in your text editor to prepare to edit it.

- On Line 8, before the opening curly brace, type `, figure, figcaption` to add the figure and figcaption elements to the CSS reset style rule (Figure 7–19).

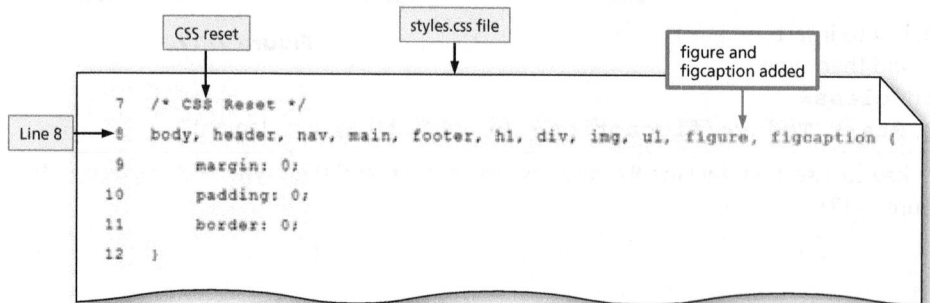

CSS reset   styles.css file   figure and figcaption added

```
7    /* CSS Reset */
8    body, header, nav, main, footer, h1, div, img, ul, figure, figcaption {
9        margin: 0;
10       padding: 0;
11       border: 0;
12   }
```

Line 8 →

Figure 7–19

- Remove Lines 28 and 29 to delete the sticky position declarations from the header style rule (Figure 7–20).

Q&A Why am I deleting the sticky position?
Now that you have added more content to the page, remove the sticky header to allow more space in the mobile viewport to adequately display the new images.

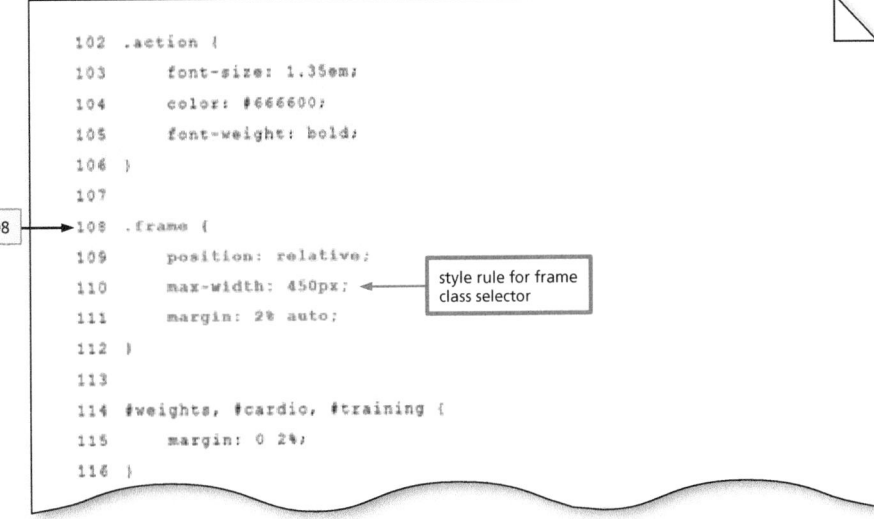

```
24    /* Style rules for mobile viewport */
25
26    /* Style rule for header */
27    header {
28        top: 0;
29        background-color: #000;
30        height: 190px;
31    }
```

position declarations are removed from the header style rule

header style rule

Figure 7–20

- Tap or click at the end of Line 106, and then press the ENTER key twice to insert new Lines 107 and 108.

- On Line 108, type **.frame {** to insert a new selector.

- Press the ENTER key to insert a new Line 109, increase the indent, and then type **position: relative;** to add a declaration.

- Press the ENTER key to insert a new Line 110, and then type **max-width: 450px;** to add a declaration.

- Press the ENTER key to insert a new Line 111, and then type **margin: 2% auto;** to add a declaration.

- Press the ENTER key to insert a new Line 112, decrease the indent, and then type **}** to close the style rule (Figure 7–21).

```
102    .action {
103        font-size: 1.35em;
104        color: #666600;
105        font-weight: bold;
106    }
107
108    .frame {
109        position: relative;
110        max-width: 450px;
111        margin: 2% auto;
112    }
113
114    #weights, #cardio, #training {
115        margin: 0 2%;
116    }
```

Line 108

style rule for frame class selector

Figure 7–21

Q&A What is the purpose of this style rule?
This style rule applies to the frame class, which is an attribute of the figure element. The maximum width is set to 450px, since this is the width of the img elements within each figure element. The position is set to relative to help achieve a text-overlay effect that you will complete in the next set of steps. The margin is set to apply some space between each figure element within a mobile viewport and to center the images on the page.

- Press the ENTER key twice to insert new Lines 113 and 114.

- On Line 114, type **.pic-text {** to insert a new selector.

- Press the ENTER key to insert a new Line 115, increase the indent, and then type **position: absolute;** to add a declaration.

- Press the ENTER key to insert a new Line 116, and then type **bottom: 0;** to add a declaration.

- Press the ENTER key to insert a new Line 117, and then type **background: rgba(0, 0, 0, 0.5);** to add a declaration.

- Press the ENTER key to insert a new Line 118, and then type `color: #fff;` to add a declaration.
- Press the ENTER key to insert a new Line 119, and then type `width: 100%;` to add a declaration.
- Press the ENTER key to insert a new Line 120, and then type `padding: 20px;` to add a declaration.
- Press the ENTER key to insert a new Line 121, and then type `text-align: center;` to add a declaration.
- Press the ENTER key to insert a new Line 122, and then type `font-family: Verdana, Arial, sans-serif;` to add a declaration.
- Press the ENTER key to insert a new Line 123, and then type `font-size: 1.5em;` to add a declaration.
- Press the ENTER key to insert a new Line 124, and then type `font-weight: bold;` to add a declaration.
- Press the ENTER key to insert a new Line 125, decrease the indent, and then type `}` to close the style rule (Figure 7–22).

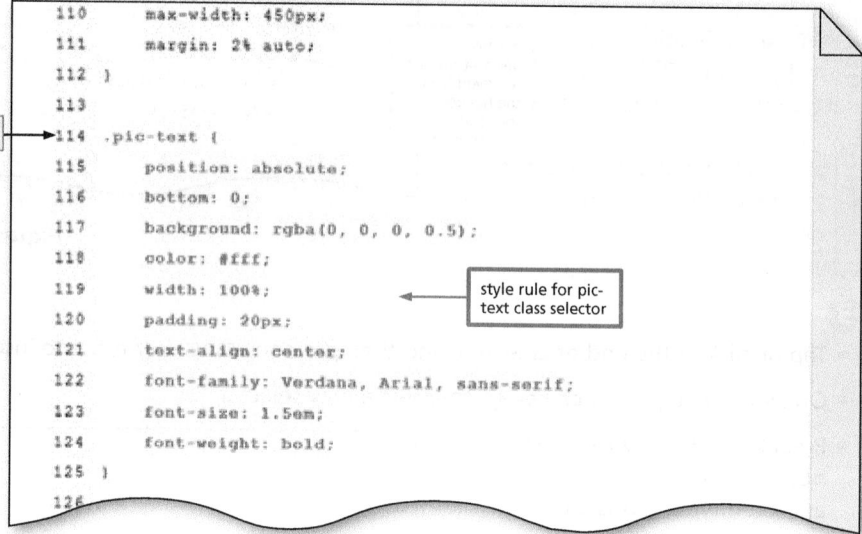

```
110      max-width: 450px;
111      margin: 2% auto;
112  }
113
114  .pic-text {                          ← Line 114
115      position: absolute;
116      bottom: 0;
117      background: rgba(0, 0, 0, 0.5);
118      color: #fff;
119      width: 100%;                      ← style rule for pic-
120      padding: 20px;                      text class selector
121      text-align: center;
122      font-family: Verdana, Arial, sans-serif;
123      font-size: 1.5em;
124      font-weight: bold;
125  }
126
```

Figure 7–22

Q&A What is the purpose of the position and bottom declarations?

The position declaration with a value of absolute will place the figcaption text at the bottom of the image element since the figure element has a position of relative. The bottom property specifies to place the figcaption at the bottom of the figure element. Together, these two declarations will overlay the figcaption text at the bottom of the image.

What does the background value of rgba(0,0,0,0.5) mean?

The background value used is the rgba() function. The three zeros specify the color black. The 0.5 value sets the transparency to 50 percent, which will make the figcaption background transparent.

5

- Save your changes, open the index.html file in Google Chrome's device mode, set a mobile viewport, and scroll down to view your changes (Figure 7–23).

Q&A Why does the figcaption extend the width of the figure element?

This is a box sizing issue that can be corrected by creating a style rule with the box-sizing property set to border-box, which will keep the figcaption contained within the figure element.

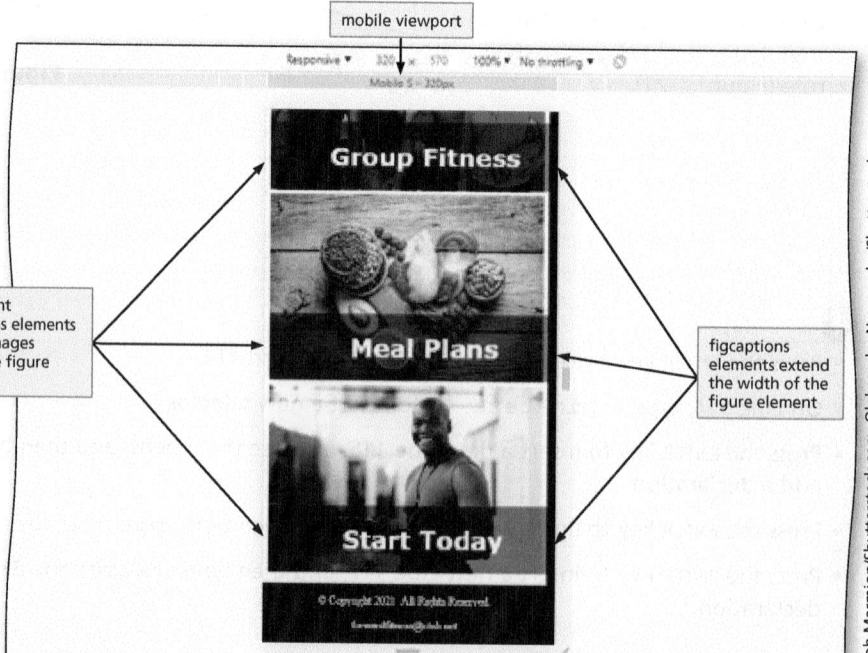

Figure 7–23

6

- Place your insertion point at the end of Line 22, and then press the ENTER key twice to insert new Lines 23 and 24.

- On Line 24, type `/* Style rule for box sizing applies to all elements */` to add a new comment.

- Press the ENTER key to insert a new Line 25, and then type `*{` to insert a new selector.

- Press the ENTER key to insert a new Line 26, increase the indent, and then type `box-sizing: border-box;` to add a declaration.

```
19   img {
20       max-width: 100%;
21       display: block;
22   }
23
24   /* Style rule for box sizing applies to all elements */
25   * {
26       box-sizing: border-box;
27   }
28
29   /* Style rules for mobile viewport */
```

comment added

Line 24

style rule for box sizing applies to all elements

- Press the ENTER key to insert a new Line 27, decrease the indent, and then type `}` to close the style rule (Figure 7–24).

Figure 7–24

Q&A

What is the * selector?
The * selector applies to all elements.

What is the purpose of this style rule?
The box sizing style rule will apply to all elements. It includes any specified padding or borders within the overall size of an element.

 7

- Save your changes, refresh the index.html file in Google Chrome's device mode, and then scroll down to view your changes (Figure 7–25).

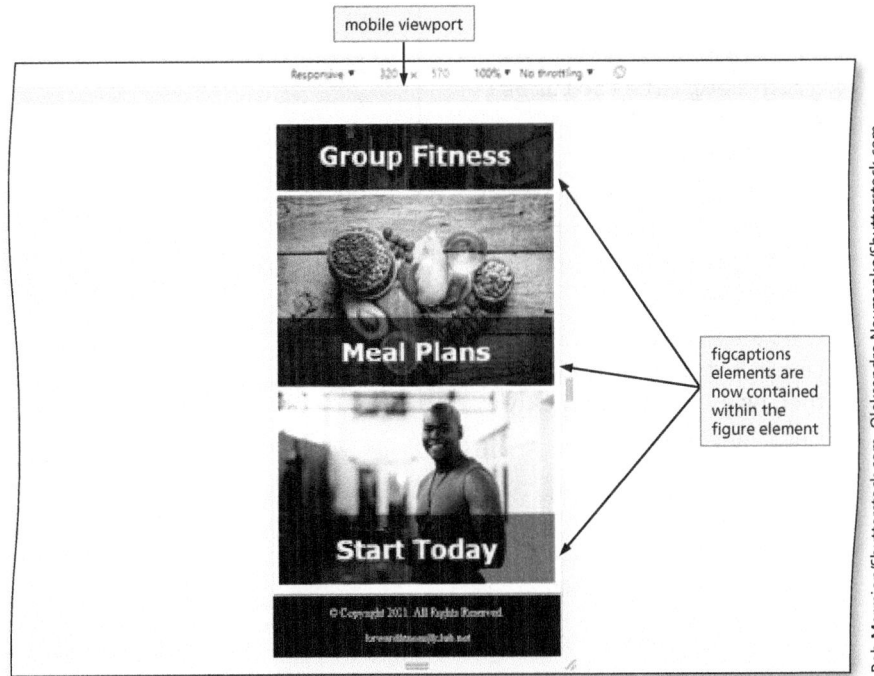

mobile viewport

figcaptions elements are now contained within the figure element

Figure 7–25

To Use the CSS Grid in a Tablet Viewport

1 MODIFY HOME PAGE | 2 STYLE HOME PAGE | 3 MODIFY ABOUT US PAGE | 4 CREATE & STYLE NUTRITION PAGE | 5 ADD FAVICON

Update the style sheet for the tablet viewport to use the CSS grid and create a multiple-column layout. *Why? Style the new figure elements to appear horizontally in a tablet viewport instead of vertically.* First, modify the header style rule within the tablet media query by removing the position declaration. Next, in the tablet media query, add new style rule for the grid class selector and set the display to grid, set the grid columns to three, and specify the grid gap. Then, create a style rule for the pic-text class selector that sets the font size to 1em and sets the padding to 10px. The following steps create two new style rules for the tablet viewport.

- In styles.css, remove the position declaration on Line 188 to delete it from the header style rule (Figure 7–26).

Q&A Why do I need to remove this declaration?
This declaration cleared the sticky header inherited from the mobile viewport. Now that the header position is no longer sticky, this declaration is unnecessary.

```
186    /* Tablet Viewport: position declaration removed for header */
187    header {
188        padding-bottom: 2%;
189    }
```
header style rule

Figure 7–26

2

- Tap or click at the end of Line 209, and then press the ENTER key twice to insert new Lines 210 and 211.

- On Line 211, type `.grid {` to insert a new class selector.

- Press the ENTER key to insert a new Line 212, increase the indent, and then type **display: grid;** to insert a declaration.

- Press the ENTER key to insert a new Line 213, and then type **grid-template-columns: auto auto auto;** to insert a declaration.

- Press the ENTER key to insert a new Line 214, and then type **grid-gap: 20px;** to insert a declaration.

- Press the ENTER key to insert a new Line 215, decrease the indent, and then type `}` to close the style rule (Figure 7–27).

```
206    /* Tablet Viewport: Style rules for main content area */
207    main ul {
208        margin: 0 0 4% 10%;
209    }
210
211    .grid {
212        display: grid;
213        grid-template-columns: auto auto auto;
214        grid-gap: 20px;
215    }
```
Line 211
style rule for grid class selector

Figure 7–27

Q&A What is the purpose of the style rule for the grid class selector?
Recall that the new div element on the home page includes a class attribute value of grid. This style rule instructs the browser to display this div as a grid with three columns (noted by the three auto values) and 20px of gap between each column.

- Save your changes, refresh the index.html file in Google Chrome's device mode, set the viewport to tablet, and then scroll down to view your changes (Figure 7–28).

Q&A Why does the figcaption appear so large over the image?
The figcaption appears this size due to the inherited font size and padding from the .pic-text style rule for the mobile viewport. You will correct this in Step 4.

tablet viewport

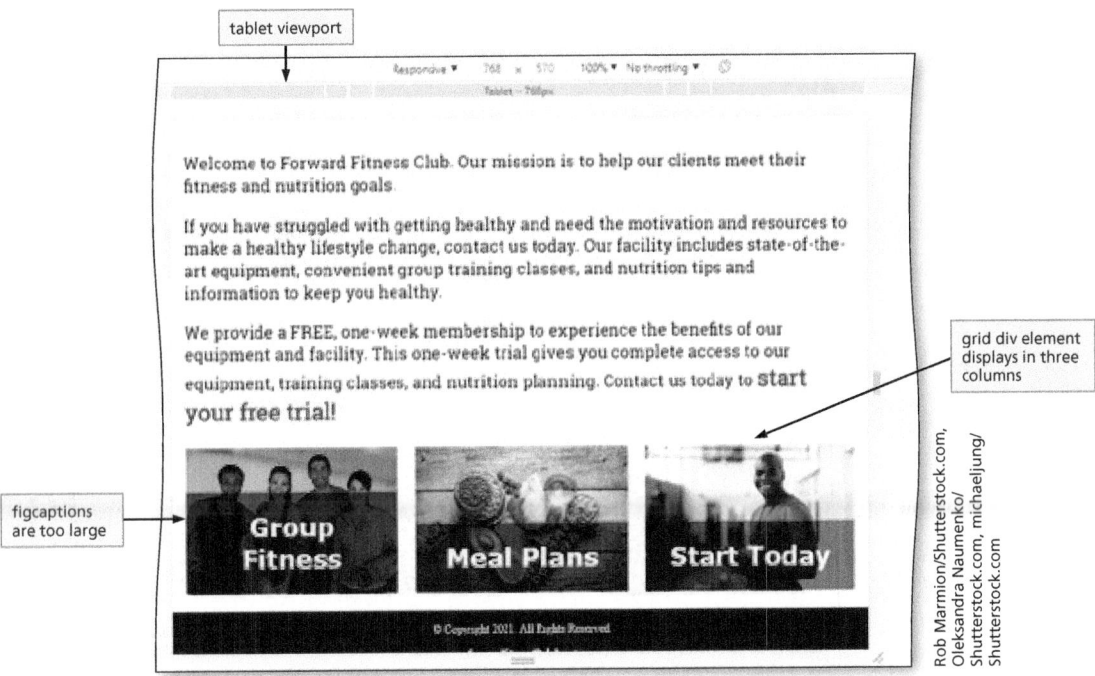

grid div element displays in three columns

figcaptions are too large

Rob Marmion/Shutterstock.com, Oleksandra Naumenko/ Shutterstock.com, michaeljung/ Shutterstock.com

Figure 7–28

 4

- In styles.css, tap or click at the end of Line 215, and then press the ENTER key twice to insert new Lines 216 and 217.

- On Line 217, type   `.pic-text {`   to insert a new class selector.

- Press the ENTER key to insert a new Line 218, increase the indent, and then type   **`font-size: 1em;`** to insert a declaration.

- Press the ENTER key to insert a new Line 219, and then type **`padding: 10px;`**   to insert a declaration.

- Press the ENTER key to insert a new Line 220, decrease the indent, and then type   `}`   to close the style rule (Figure 7–29).

```
211      .grid {
212          display: grid;
213          grid-template-columns: auto auto auto;
214          grid-gap: 20px;
215      }
216
217      .pic-text {
218          font-size: 1em;
219          padding: 10px;
220      }
```

Line 217

style rule for pic-text class selector

Figure 7–29

5

- Save your changes, refresh the index.html file in Google Chrome's device mode, set the viewport to tablet, and then scroll down to view your changes (Figure 7–30).

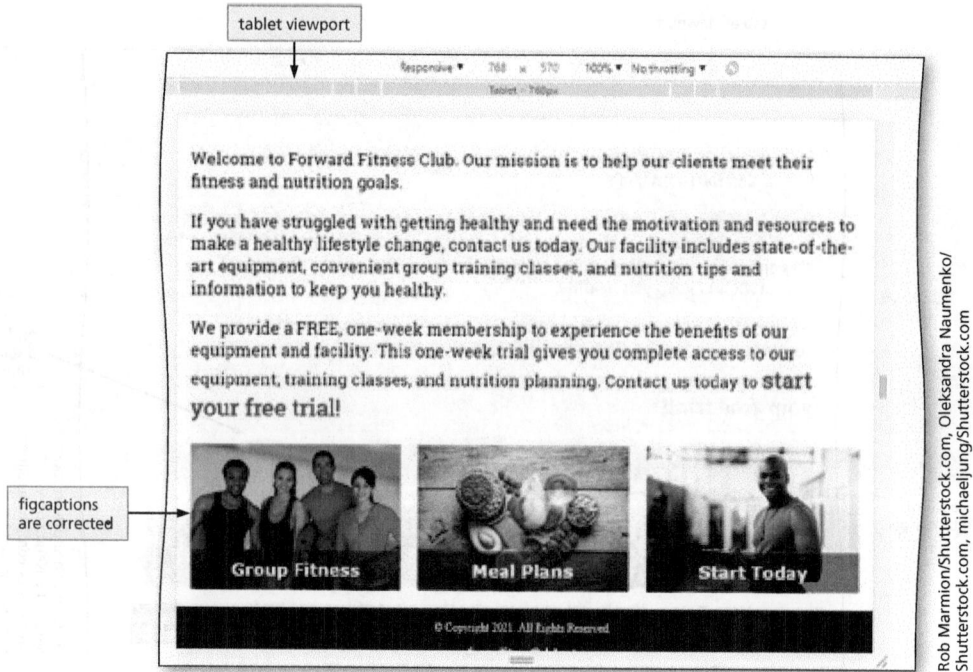

Rob Marmion/Shutterstock.com, Oleksandra Naumenko/
Shutterstock.com, michaeljung/Shutterstock.com

Figure 7–30

To Add New Style Rules in a Desktop Viewport

1 MODIFY HOME PAGE | 2 STYLE HOME PAGE | 3 MODIFY ABOUT US PAGE |
4 CREATE & STYLE NUTRITION PAGE | 5 ADD FAVICON

Update the style sheet for the desktop viewport to style the new class attributes on the home page. Increase the font size and padding for the figcaption text. Apply some opacity to images within the figure elements. Use the hover pseudo-class to remove the opacity and apply a box shadow to the figure elements. *Why? These changes will improve the appearance of the figcaptions and add interactivity to the webpage.* First, in the desktop media query, create a style rule for the pic-text class selector that sets the font size to 1.5em and padding to 20px. Next, create a new style rule for the frame class selector that sets the opacity to 90 percent. Finally, create a style rule for the frame class selector with the hover pseudo-class that sets the opacity to 1 and applies a box shadow. The following steps create three new style rules for the desktop viewport.

- In styles.css, tap or click at the end of Line 290, and then press the ENTER key twice to insert new Lines 291 and 292.

- On Line 292, type `.pic-text {` to insert a new class selector.

- Press the ENTER key to insert a new Line 293, increase the indent, and then type `font-size: 1.5em;` to insert a declaration.

- Press the ENTER key to insert a new Line 294, and then type `padding: 20px;` to insert a declaration.

- Press the ENTER key to insert a new Line 295, decrease the indent, and then type `}` to close the style rule (Figure 7–31).

```
288      main h1 {
289         font-size: 1.8em;
290      }
291
292      .pic-text {
293         font-size: 1.5em;
294         padding: 20px;
295      }
```

Line 292

style rule for pic-text class selector within the desktop media query

Figure 7–31

2

- Save your changes, open the index.html file in your browser in a normal desktop viewport to view your changes, and then scroll down to view your changes (Figure 7–32).

desktop viewport

figcaption text and padding increased

Figure 7–32

3

- In styles.css, tap or click at the end of Line 295, and then press the ENTER key twice to insert new Lines 296 and 297.
- On Line 297, type **.frame {** to insert a new class selector.
- Press the ENTER key to insert a new Line 298, increase the indent, and then type **opacity: 0.9;** to insert a declaration.
- Press the ENTER key to insert a new Line 299, decrease the indent, and then type **}** to close the style rule.
- Press the ENTER key twice to insert new Lines 300 and 301.
- On Line 301, type **.frame:hover {** to insert a new class selector with a hover pseudo-class.
- Press the ENTER key to insert a new Line 302, increase the indent, and then type **opacity: 1;** to insert a declaration.
- Press the ENTER key to insert a new Line 303, and then type **box-shadow: 8px 8px 10px #808080;** to insert a declaration.
- Press the ENTER key to insert a new Line 304, decrease the indent, and then type **}** to close the style rule (Figure 7–33).

```
292     .pic-text {
293         font-size: 1.5em;
294         padding: 20px;
295     }
296
297     .frame {
298         opacity: 0.9;
299     }
300
301     .frame:hover {
302         opacity: 1;
303         box-shadow: 8px 8px 10px #808080;
304     }
305
306     #weights, #cardio, #training {
```

Line 297

style rules for .frame and .frame:hover

Figure 7–33

- Save your changes, refresh the index.html file in your browser, and then hover over one of the images within a figure element to view your changes (Figure 7–34).

desktop viewport

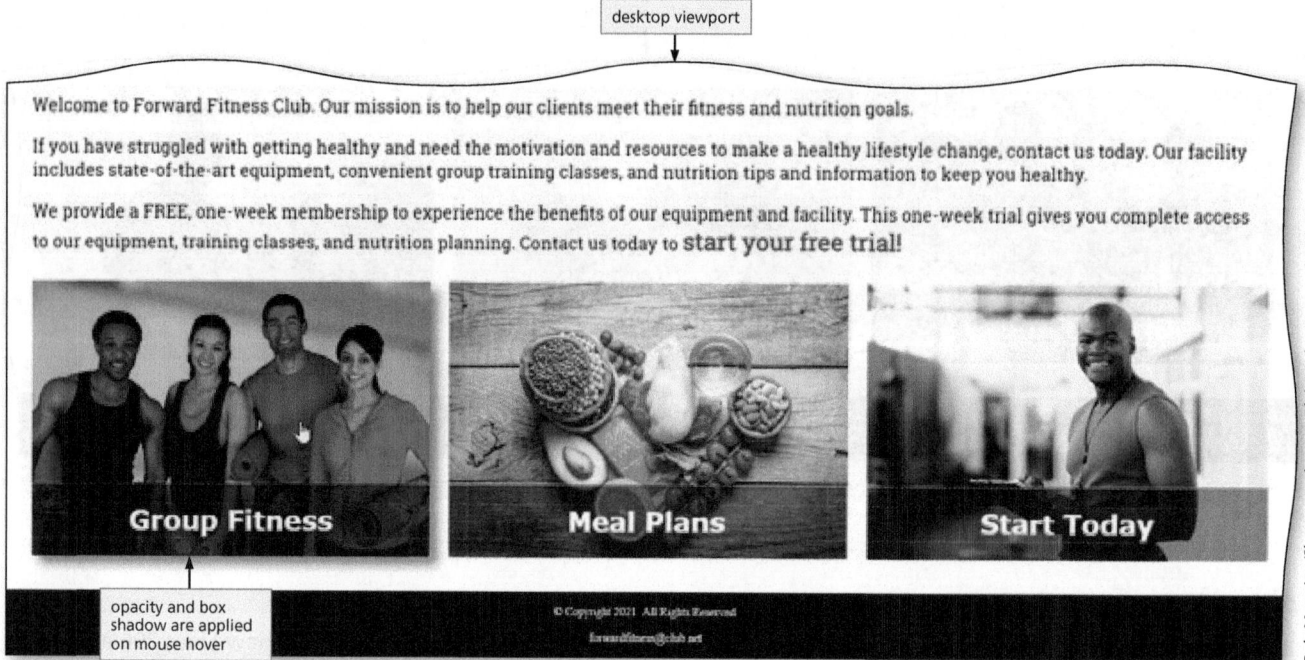

Welcome to Forward Fitness Club. Our mission is to help our clients meet their fitness and nutrition goals.

If you have struggled with getting healthy and need the motivation and resources to make a healthy lifestyle change, contact us today. Our facility includes state-of-the-art equipment, convenient group training classes, and nutrition tips and information to keep you healthy.

We provide a FREE, one-week membership to experience the benefits of our equipment and facility. This one-week trial gives you complete access to our equipment, training classes, and nutrition planning. Contact us today to start your free trial!

Group Fitness   **Meal Plans**   **Start Today**

opacity and box shadow are applied on mouse hover

© Copyright 2021 All Rights Reserved

forwardfitness@club.net

Figure 7–34

To Apply a Text Shadow

Create a style rule that applies a text shadow to the heading 3 element within the mobile div. Modify the style rule for the action class to also apply a text shadow. ***Why?*** *Use of a text shadow improves the overall look of a website and gives dimension to text to make it stand out.* First, create a new style rule for heading 3 elements within the mobile class to apply a text shadow. Then, update the style rule for the action class to apply a text shadow. The following steps create one new style rule and modify a style rule within the style sheet.

- In styles.css, tap or click at the end of Line 85, and then press the ENTER key twice to insert new Lines 86 and 87.

- On Line 87, type `.mobile h3 {` to insert a new selector.

- Press the ENTER key to insert a new Line 88, increase the indent, and then type `text-shadow: 5px 5px 8px #ccc;` to insert a declaration.

- Press the ENTER key to insert a new Line 89, decrease the indent, and then type `}` to close the style rule (Figure 7–35).

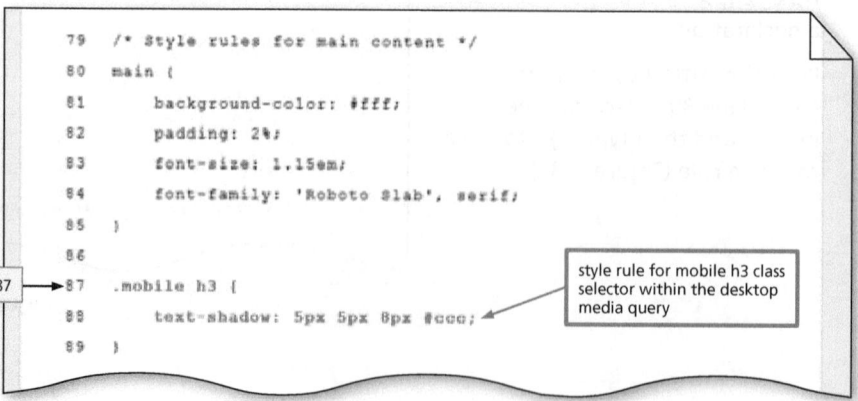

```
79    /* Style rules for main content */
80    main {
81        background-color: #fff;
82        padding: 2%;
83        font-size: 1.15em;
84        font-family: 'Roboto Slab', serif;
85    }
86
87    .mobile h3 {
88        text-shadow: 5px 5px 8px #ccc;
89    }
```

Line 87

style rule for mobile h3 class selector within the desktop media query

Figure 7–35

2

- Tap or click at the end of Line 114, and then press the ENTER key to insert a new Line 115.

- On Line 115, type `text-shadow: 5px 5px 8px #ccc;` to insert a new declaration (Figure 7–36).

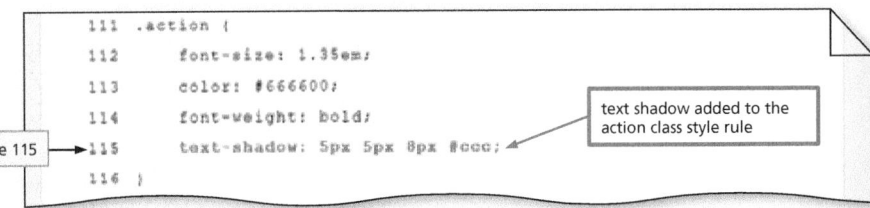

```
111   .action {
112       font-size: 1.35em;
113       color: #666600;
114       font-weight: bold;
115       text-shadow: 5px 5px 8px #ccc;
116   }
```

Line 115 → 115

text shadow added to the action class style rule

Figure 7–36

3

- Save your changes, open the index.html file in Google Chrome's device mode, set a mobile viewport, and then scroll down to view your changes (Figure 7–37).

mobile viewport

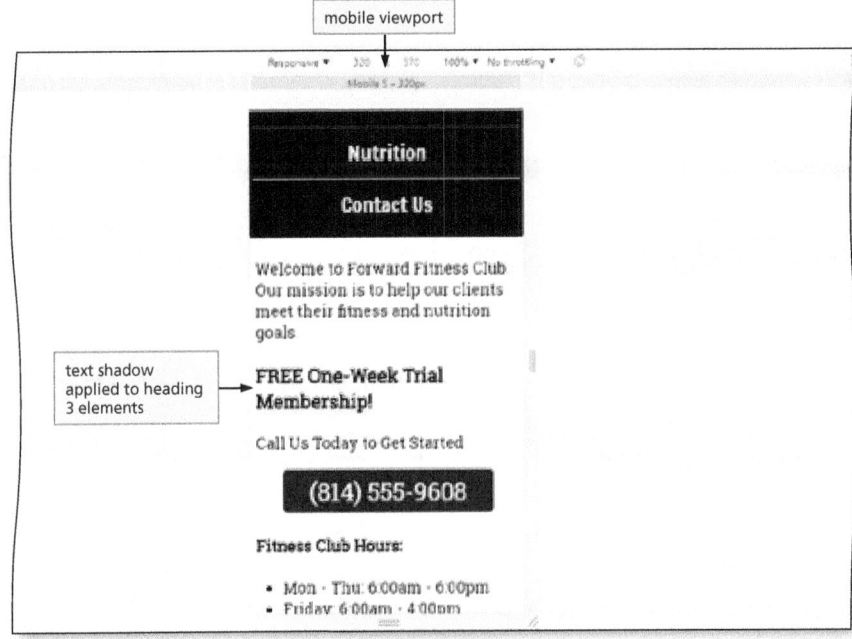

text shadow applied to heading 3 elements

Figure 7–37

4

- Change the viewport to desktop to view your changes (Figure 7–38).

desktop viewport

Welcome to Forward Fitness Club. Our mission is to help our clients meet their fitness and nutrition goals.

If you have struggled with getting healthy and need the motivation and resources to make a healthy lifestyle change, contact us today. Our facility includes state-of-the-art equipment, convenient group training classes, and nutrition tips and information to keep you healthy.

We provide a FREE, one-week membership to experience the benefits of our equipment and facility. This one-week trial gives you complete access to our equipment, training classes, and nutrition planning. Contact us today to **start your free trial!** ◄—

text shadow applied to heading 3 element

© Copyright 2021. All Rights Reserved.

forwardfitness@club.net

Figure 7–38

Updating the About Us Page

The home page now displays new visual content to enhance the overall design of the Forward Fitness Club home page. Next, revise the About Us page to integrate additional HTML 5 semantic elements.

The About Us page contains groups of content that are currently wrapped within div elements. These groups of content include the Weights group, the Cardio group, the Personal Training group, and the Common Exercises group. Use a section element instead of a div element to group each of these areas together.

To Add Section Elements to the About Us Page

1 MODIFY HOME PAGE | 2 STYLE HOME PAGE | 3 MODIFY ABOUT US PAGE | 4 CREATE & STYLE NUTRITION PAGE | 5 ADD FAVICON

Add section elements to the About Us page to group content. *Why? Group content to improve semantic design and search engine results.* Replace each div element with a section element for the Weights group, the Cardio group, the Personal Training group, and the Common Exercises group. The following steps add section elements to the About Us page.

1

- Open about.html in your text editor to prepare to modify it.

- On Line 34, replace div with **section**.

- On Line 45, replace div with **section**.

- On Line 47, replace div with **section**.

- On Line 58, replace div with **section** (Figure 7–39).

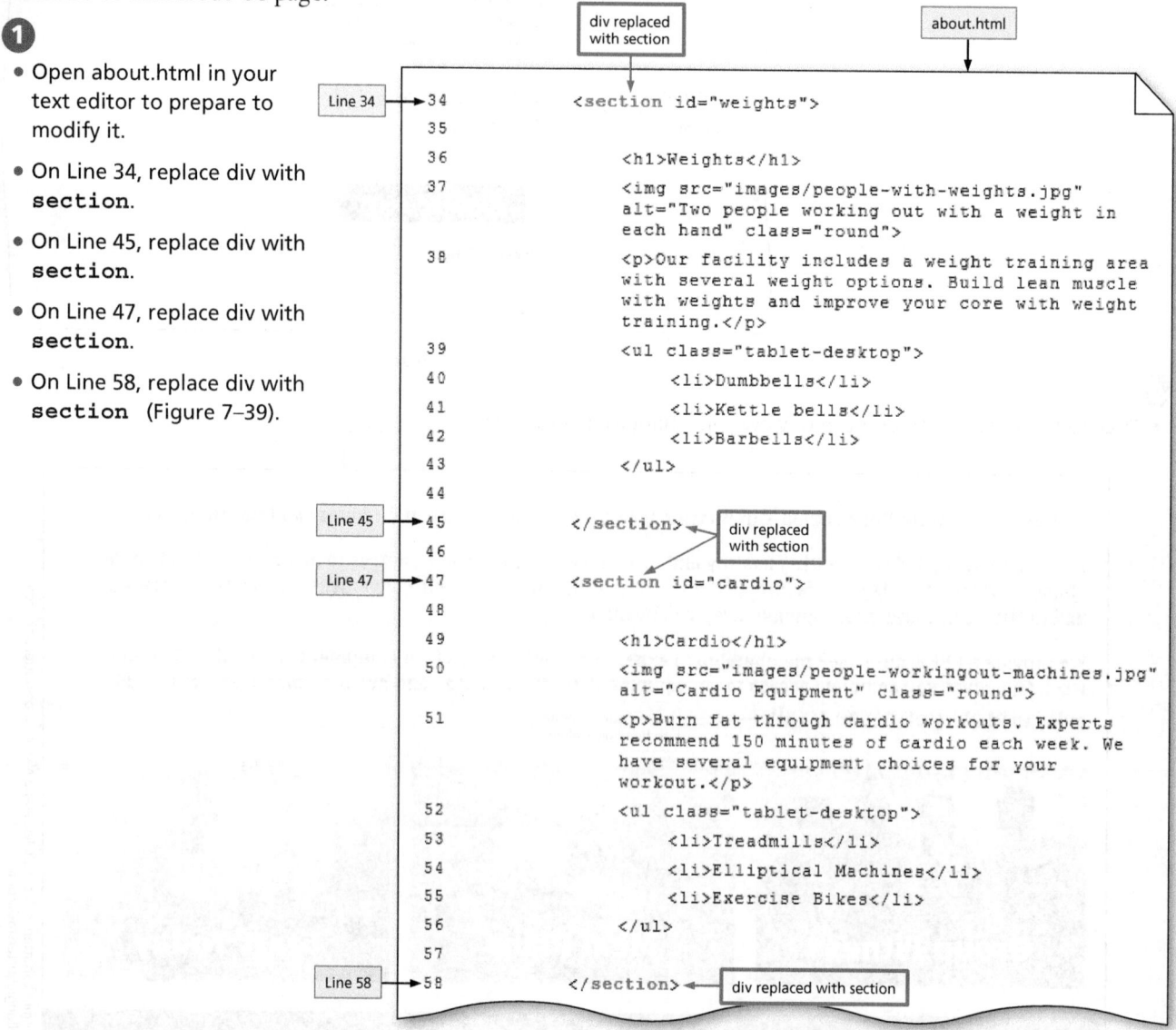

Figure 7–39

2

- On Line 60, replace div with **section**.
- On Line 71, replace div with **section** (Figure 7–40).

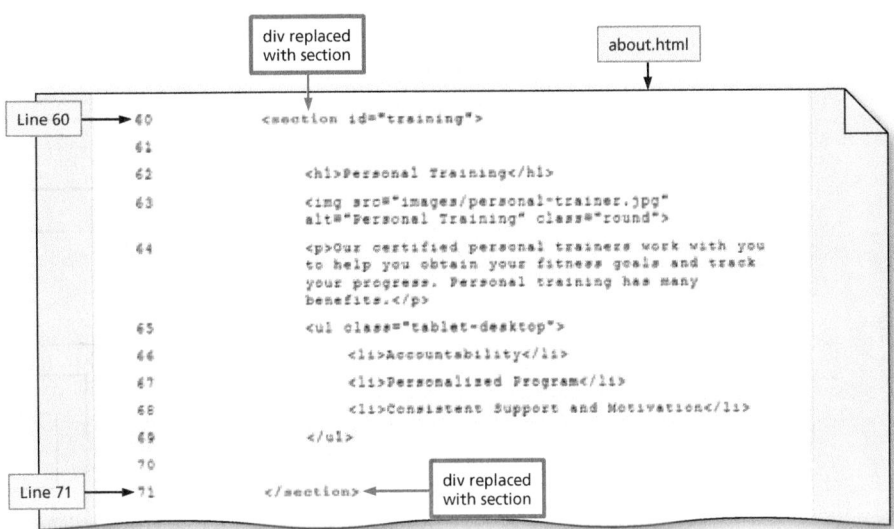

Figure 7–40

3

- On Line 73, replace div with **section**.
- On Line 90, replace div with **section** (Figure 7–41).

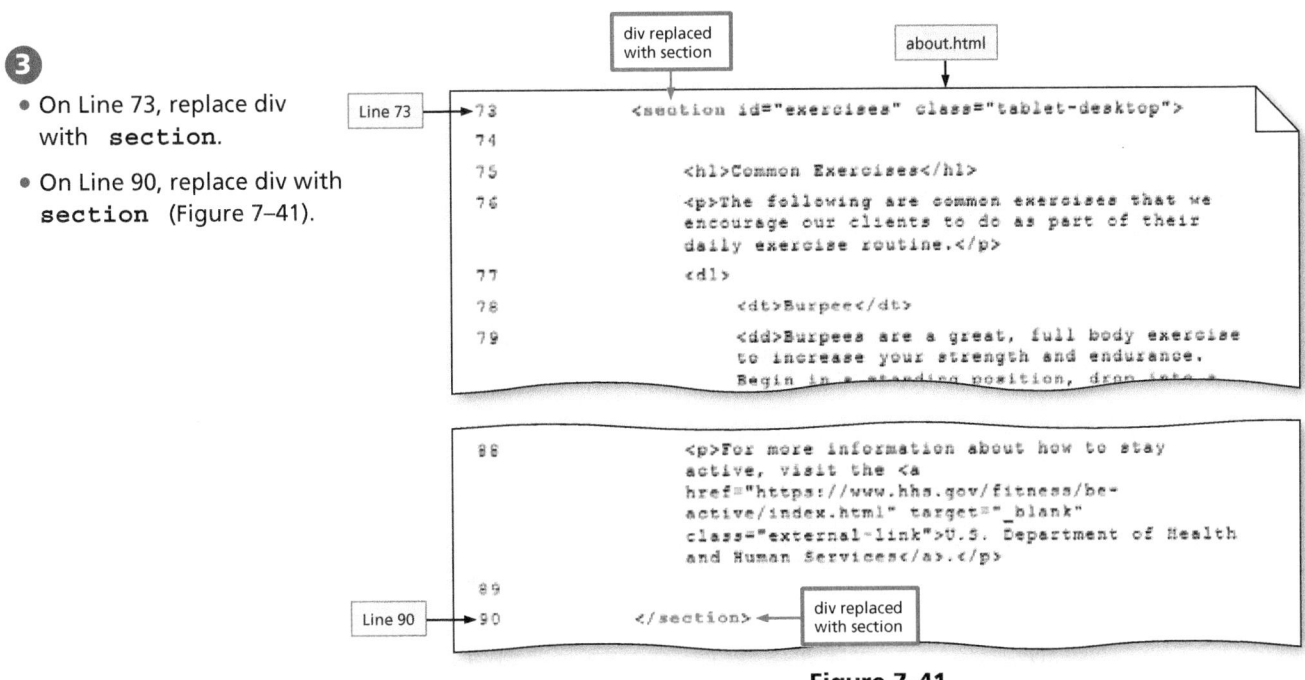

Figure 7–41

Break Point: If you want to take a break, this is a good place to do so. You can exit the text editor now. To resume at a later time, run your text editor, open the file called styles.css, and continue following the steps from this location forward.

Creating the Nutrition Page

The home, About Us, and Contact Us pages have been created for the Forward Fitness Club. Next, you create the Nutrition page, which provides tips for good nutrition, guidelines for a healthy diet, and a featured recipe of the week. To have the new page follow the same design as the other pages in the site, use the template.html file to create the new page and then add HTML 5 semantic elements. Style the page to be consistent with the other pages.

You drafted a wireframe for the Nutrition page in tablet and desktop viewports, which use article and aside elements, as shown in Figures 7–42 and 7–43. This page uses a three-column layout for tablet and desktop viewports. The mobile layout will remain the same as the other pages, a single-column layout.

Nutrition Page Wireframe for Tablet and Desktop Viewports

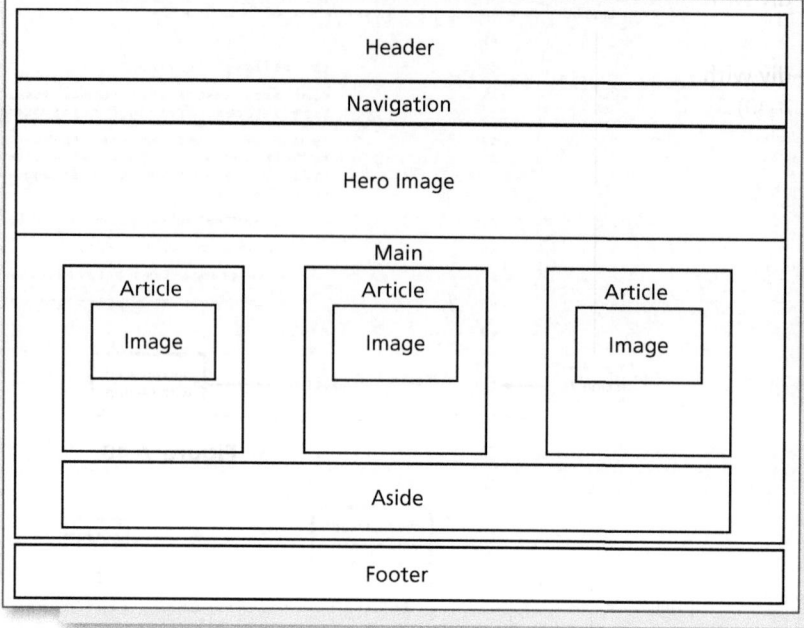

Figure 7–42

Nutrition Page Wireframe for Desktop Viewport

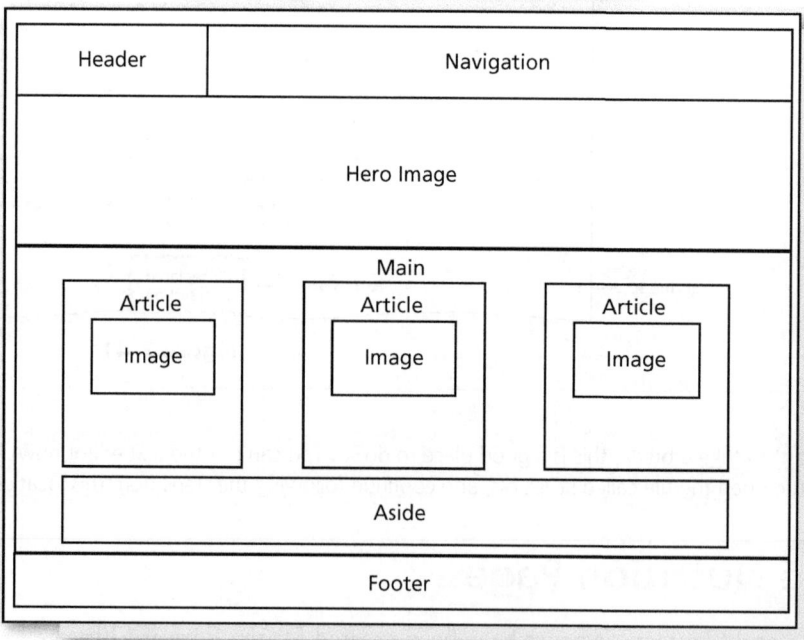

Figure 7–43

CSS Grid Spans

Use the CSS grid layout to create the three-column layout for tablet and desktop viewports. As shown in Figures 7–42 and 7–43, the main element uses a three-column layout; however, the aside element spans all three columns. As a web developer, there may be times when you want certain elements to span several grid columns. This task can be completed with the grid-column property in CSS. To design this layout, assign a class attribute with a value of your choice to the aside element. Create a style rule for the class that spans the element across three columns. The following is an example of how to create a span:

```
.grid-item {
    grid-column: 1 / span 3
}
```

In the above example, a style rule is created for the grid-item class selector. The style rule includes a declaration that sets the grid column to 1 and to span the column over three columns (1 / span 3). Once you create the Nutrition page, you will add new style rules to the style sheet, including a style rule that spans one column over several columns.

BTW
CSS Multiple Column Layout
You can also create columns using the CSS property, column-count. The value you use for this property indicates the desired number of columns. Other properties you can use with the column-count property include column-gap, column-width, and column-rule.

To Create the Nutrition Page

Use the template.html file to create the Nutrition page. After creating the page, insert a hero image. The following steps create the Nutrition page.

1 Open template.html in your text editor, and then save the page as nutrition.html in your fitness folder.

2 Update the comment with your name and today's date, tap or click at the end of Line 29, and then press the ENTER key twice to insert new Lines 30 and 31.

3 On Line 31, type `<!-- Nutrition Hero Image -->` to insert a comment.

4 Press the ENTER key to insert new Line 32, and then type `<div id="hero">` to insert a div tag.

5 Press the ENTER key to insert new Line 33, increase the indent, and then type `<img src="images/hero-veggies.jpg" alt="fresh vegetables">` to insert an image.

6 Press the ENTER key to insert new Line 34, decrease the indent, and then type `</div>` to close the div element (Figure 7–44).

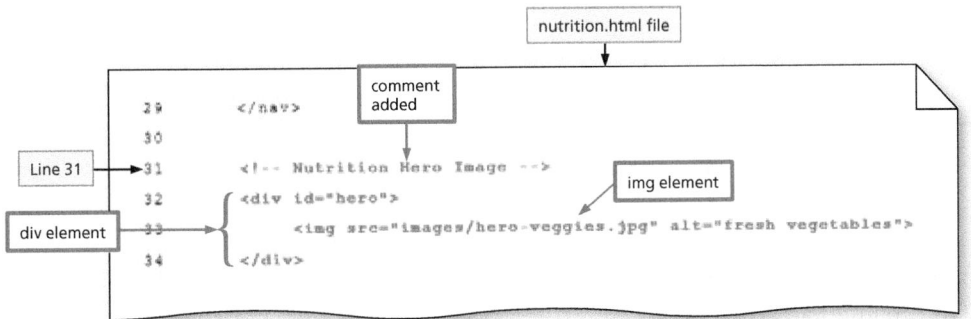

Figure 7–44

To Add article and aside Elements to the Nutrition Page

Add a class attribute value of grid to the **main** element, insert three article elements within the **main** element, and then add content to each. Below the last article element, insert an aside element with additional content. To complete this assignment, you will be required to use the Data Files. Please contact your instructor for information about accessing the Data Files. *Why? The article elements will contain new page content, including tips, guidelines, and recipes.* In each article element, add a heading element, an image element, paragraph elements, and unordered list elements. Below the last article element, add an aside element with new content. The following steps add article elements and an aside element to the Nutrition page.

- In nutrition.html, add a class attribute with a value of **grid** to the main tag on Line 37.
- Tap or click at the end of Line 37, and then press the ENTER key twice to insert new Lines 38 and 39.
- On Line 39, type **<article>** to insert an article tag.
- Press the ENTER key to insert a new Line 40, increase the indent, and then type **<h3>Food for Thought</h3>** to insert a heading 3 element.
- Press the ENTER key to insert a new Line 41, and then type **<img src="images/food-thought.jpg" alt="food for thought image" class="round">** to insert an image element.
- Open the nutritionText.txt file located in the chapter07\chapter folder provided with your Data Files, select Lines 2 through 5, and then press CTRL+C to copy Lines 2 through 5.
- In the nutrition.html file, place your insertion point at the end of Line 41, press the ENTER key to insert a new Line 42, and then press CTRL+V to paste the new content.
- If necessary, indent Lines 42 through 45 to align with the img element on Line 41.
- Place your insertion point at the end of Line 45, press the ENTER key to insert a new Line 46, decrease the indent, and then type **</article>** to insert an ending article tag (Figure 7–45).

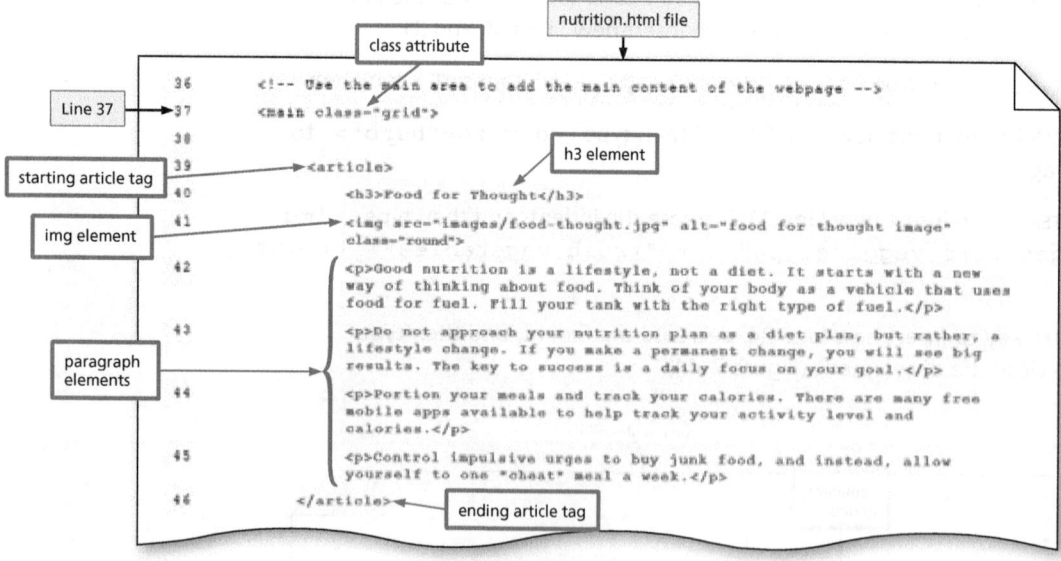

Figure 7–45

- Press the ENTER key twice to insert new Lines 47 and 48.
- On Line 48, type **<article>** to insert an article tag.
- Press the ENTER key to insert a new Line 49, increase the indent, and then type **<h3>What to Eat</h3>** to insert a heading 3 element.

- Press the ENTER key to insert a new Line 50, and then type `<img src="images/fresh-food.jpg"`
  `alt="fresh vegetables, fruit, eggs, and nuts" class="round">` to insert an image element.

- In the nutritionText.txt file, select Lines 8 through 17, and then press CTRL+C to copy Lines 8 through 17.

- In the nutrition.html file, place your insertion point at the end of Line 50, press the ENTER key to insert a new Line 51, and then press CTRL+V to paste the new content.

- If necessary, indent Lines 51 through 60 to align with the img element on Line 50.

- If necessary, indent the list item elements on Lines 53 through 56.

- Place your insertion point at the end of Line 60, press the ENTER key to insert a new Line 61, decrease the indent, and then type `</article>` to insert an ending article tag (Figure 7–46).

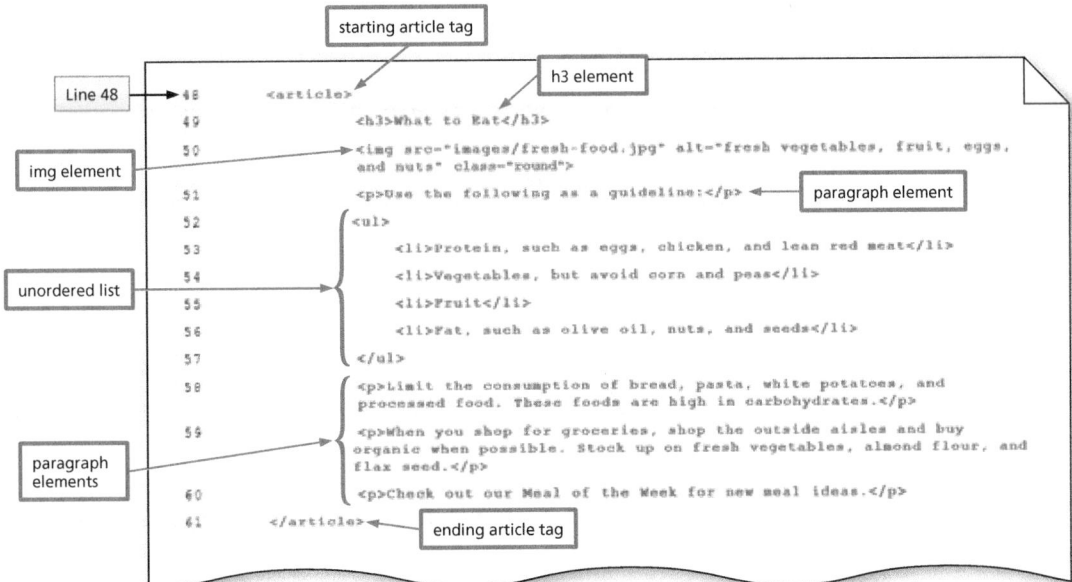

Figure 7–46

 3

- Press the ENTER key twice to insert new Lines 62 and 63.

- On Line 63, type `<article>` to insert an article tag.

- Press the ENTER key to insert a new Line 64, increase the indent, and then type `<h3>Meal of the Week</h3>` to insert a heading 3 element.

- Press the ENTER key to insert a new Line 65, and then type `<img src="images/food-chicken.jpg"`
  `alt="herb roasted chicken" class="round">` to insert an image element.

- In the nutritionText.txt file, select Lines 20 through 31, and then press CTRL+C to copy Lines 20 through 31.

- In the nutrition.html file, place your insertion point at the end of Line 65, press the ENTER key to insert a new Line 66, and then press CTRL+V to paste the new content.

- If necessary, indent Lines 66 through 77 to align with the img element on Line 65.

- If necessary, indent the list item elements on Lines 69 through 74.

- Place your insertion point at the end of Line 77, press the ENTER key to insert a new Line 78, decrease the indent, and then type `</article>` to insert an ending article tag (Figure 7–47).

Q&A What does ¼ represent?

This is an HTML entity used to display ¼ on a webpage.

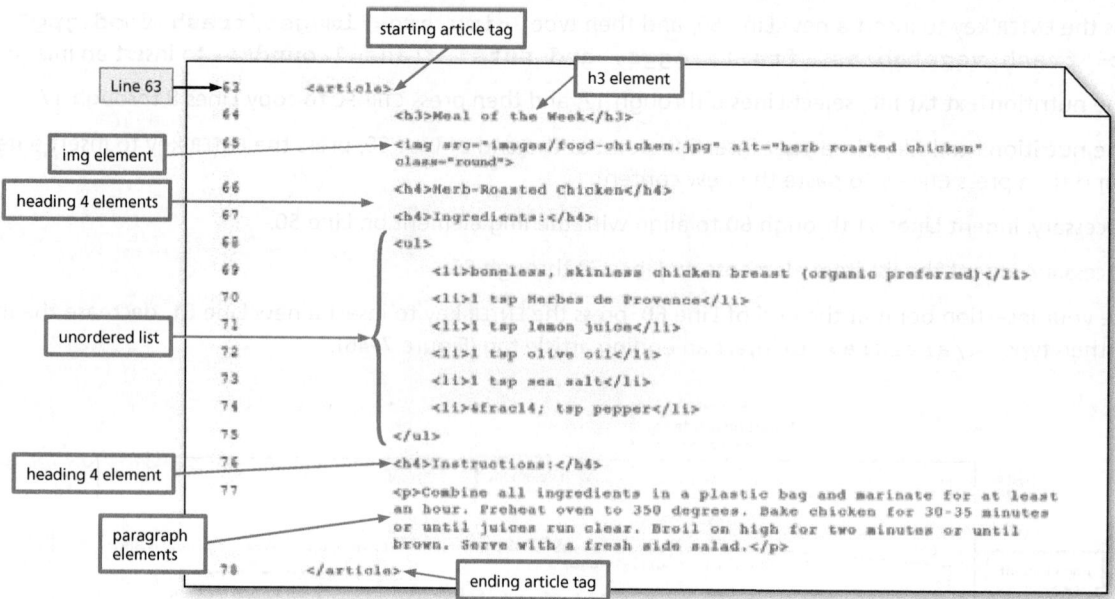

Figure 7–47

 4

- Tap or click at the end of Line 78, and then press the ENTER key twice to insert new Lines 79 and 80.

- On Line 80, type `<aside class="tablet-desktop grid-item4">` to insert an aside tag with two class attribute values.

- Press the ENTER key to insert a new Line 81, increase the indent, and then type `<p>Did you know the average American consumes 3 lbs of sugar each week?</p>` to insert a paragraph element.

- Press the ENTER key to insert a new Line 82, and then type `<p>Did you know that avocados are a good source of Vitamin B?</p>` to insert a paragraph element.

- Press the ENTER key to insert a new Line 83, and then type `<p>Did you know the average active adult should consume about 2,000 calories a day?</p>` to insert a paragraph element.

- Press the ENTER key to insert a new Line 84, decrease the indent, and then type `</aside>` to close the aside element.

- Delete the div element and blank line on Lines 86–88 (Figure 7–48).

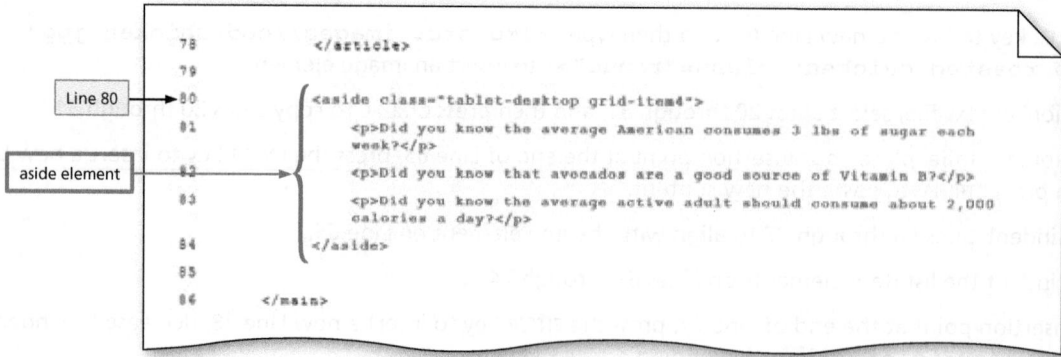

Figure 7–48

5

- Save your changes, open nutrition.html in your browser, and then adjust the window to the size of a desktop viewport to view the page (Figure 7–49).

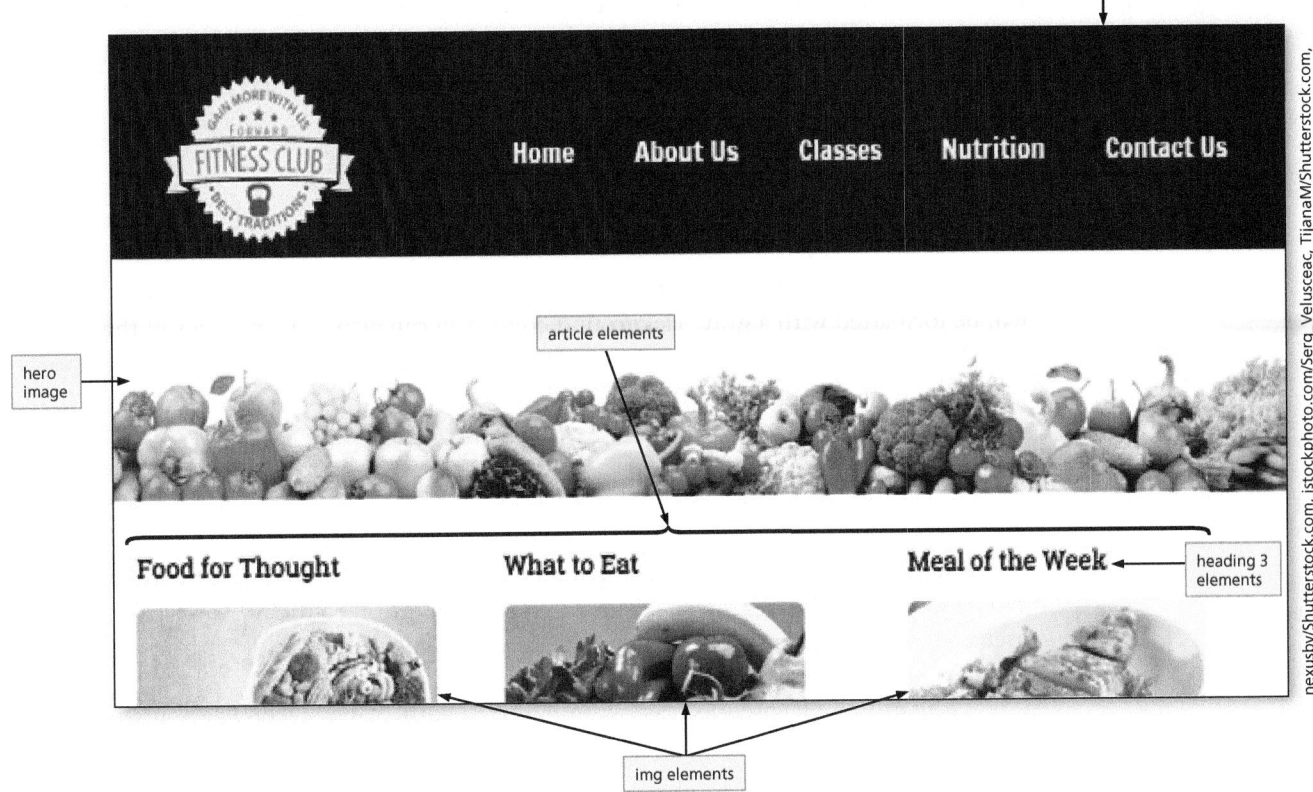

nutrition.html displayed in a browser, desktop viewport

article elements

hero image

heading 3 elements

img elements

nexusby/Shutterstock.com, istockphoto.com/Serg_Veluseac, TijanaM/Shutterstock.com, Milleflore Images/Shutterstock.com, verchik/Shutterstock.com

Figure 7–49

6

- Scroll down to view the article elements and the aside element (Figure 7–50).

Q&A Why does the aside element appear below the first article element?

Because the main element contains the grid class attribute, the article and aside elements are styled as a three-column grid. The aside element is the fourth child element within the main, so it appears within the first column. You will correct this problem in future steps.

nutrition.html displayed in a browser, desktop viewport

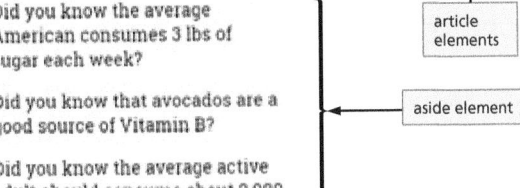

Portion your meals and track your calories. There are many free mobile apps available to help track your activity level and calories.

Control impulsive urges to buy junk food, and instead, allow yourself to one "cheat" meal a week.

When you shop for groceries, shop the outside aisles and buy organic when possible. Stock up on fresh vegetables, almond flour, and flax seed.

Check out our Meal of the Week for new meal ideas.

Combine all ingredients in a plastic bag and marinate for at least an hour. Preheat oven to 350 degrees. Bake chicken for 30-35 minutes or until juices run clear. Broil on high for two minutes or until brown. Serve with a fresh side salad.

Did you know the average American consumes 3 lbs of sugar each week?

Did you know that avocados are a good source of Vitamin B?

Did you know the average active adult should consume about 2,000 calories a day?

article elements

aside element

Figure 7–50

Structural Pseudo-Class, nth-of-type()

In Chapter 5, you learned how to use the first-child structural pseudo-class. In Chapter 6, you learned how to use dynamic pseudo-classes, such as link, active, and hover. The nth-of-type() selector is another kind of structural pseudo-class. It is used to select specific elements within a parent element. For example, if you have a table with 20 rows, you may want to apply a different background color to all odd or all even rows. You would use the nth-of-type() pseudo-class to accomplish this task. The following is an example of the nth-of-type() pseudo-class.

```
p:nth-of-type(odd) {
    background-color: #ccc;
}
```

In the above example, every odd paragraph element within its parent container will be formatted with a gray background color. You can also use a number in the parentheses to specify a specific paragraph out of a group of paragraph elements. The following example uses a number with the nth-of-type() pseudo-class.

```
p:nth-of-type(5) {
    background-color: #ccc;
}
```

In the above example, the fifth paragraph element within its parent container will be formatted with a gray background color. In addition to the nth-of-type() pseudo-class, there are three other, similar pseudo-classes; nth-child(), nth-last-child(), and nth-last-of-type().

The nth-child() pseudo-class is similar to the nth-of-type(); however, it will apply to every specified element on the webpage, regardless of its parent.

The nth-last-child() pseudo-class applies to every specified element, beginning with the last element.

The nth-last-of-type() pseudo-class applies to every specified element within its parent, beginning with the last element.

To Style the Nutrition Page for a Mobile Viewport

1 MODIFY HOME PAGE | 2 STYLE HOME PAGE | 3 MODIFY ABOUT US PAGE
4 CREATE & STYLE NUTRITION PAGE | 5 ADD FAVICON

Style the Nutrition page for a mobile viewport. Create a style rule to apply padding to the article elements. Create a style rule to center-align the heading 3 elements within each article element. Create another style rule that center-aligns each image within its parent article element. Create another style rule that applies a background color to just the second article element within the main parent element. Create a final style rule that applies left margin to the unordered lists within the article elements. ***Why? These style rules format the new article elements and improve the appearance for a mobile viewport.*** The following steps create five style rules for a mobile viewport.

1

- If necessary, reopen styles.css to prepare to modify it.

- On Line 8, before the opening curly brace, type **, section, article, aside** to add the section, article, and aside elements to the CSS reset style rule (Figure 7–51).

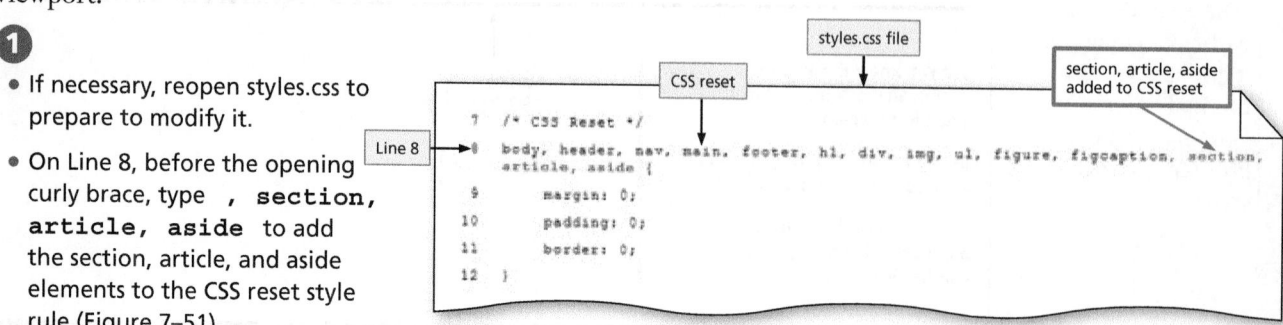

Figure 7–51

2

- Tap or click at the end of Line 89, and then press the ENTER key twice to insert new Lines 90 and 91.

- On Line 91, type **article { ** to insert a new selector.

- Press the ENTER key to insert a new Line 92, increase the indent, and then type **padding: 2%;** to insert a declaration.

- Press the ENTER key to insert a new Line 93, decrease the indent, and then type **}** to close the style rule (Figure 7–52).

```
87    .mobile h3 {
88        text-shadow: 5px 5px 8px #ccc;
89    }
90
91    article {          ← article style rule
92        padding: 2%;
93    }
```
Line 91

Figure 7–52

3

- Press the ENTER key twice to insert new Lines 94 and 95.

- On Line 95, type **article h3 { ** to insert a new selector.

- Press the ENTER key to insert a new Line 96, increase the indent, and then type **text-align: center;** to insert a declaration.

- Press the ENTER key to insert a new Line 97, decrease the indent, and then type **}** to close the style rule (Figure 7–53).

```
91    article {
92        padding: 2%;
93    }
94
95    article h3 {          ← article h3 style rule
96        text-align: center;
97    }
```
Line 95

Figure 7–53

4

- Press the ENTER key twice to insert new Lines 98 and 99.

- On Line 99, type **article img { ** to insert a new selector.

- Press the ENTER key to insert a new Line 100, increase the indent, and then type **margin: 0 auto;** to insert a declaration.

- Press the ENTER key to insert a new Line 101, decrease the indent, and then type **}** to close the style rule (Figure 7–54).

```
95 article h3 {
96     text-align: center;
97 }
98
99 article img {          ← article img style rule
100    margin: 0 auto;
101 }
```
Line 99

Figure 7–54

5

- Press the ENTER key twice to insert new Lines 102 and 103.

- On Line 103, type **article ul { ** to insert a new selector.

- Press the ENTER key to insert a new Line 104, increase the indent, and then type **margin-left: 10%;** to insert a declaration.

- Press the ENTER key to insert a new Line 105, decrease the indent, and then type **}** to close the style rule (Figure 7–55).

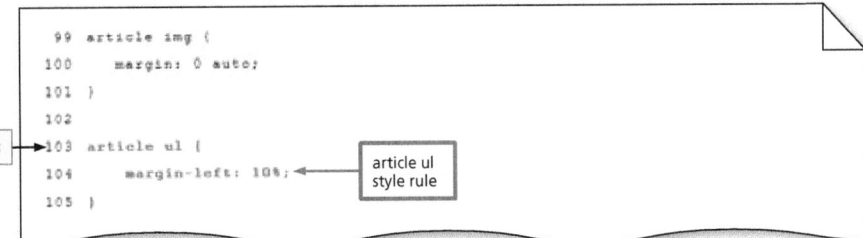
```
99 article img {
100    margin: 0 auto;
101 }
102
103 article ul {          ← article ul style rule
104    margin-left: 10%;
105 }
```
Line 103

Figure 7–55

6

- Press the ENTER key twice to insert new Lines 106 and 107.
- On Line 107, type `article:nth-of-type(2){` to insert a new selector.
- Press the ENTER key to insert a new Line 108, increase the indent, and then type `background-color: rgba(204, 204, 204, 0.3);` to insert a declaration.
- Press the ENTER key to insert a new Line 109, decrease the indent, and then type `}` to close the style rule (Figure 7–56).

Q&A

What is the purpose of the nth-of-type(2) pseudo-class?
This pseudo-class will select and style the second article element within the main element.

What color is rgba(204, 204, 204, 0.3)?
The value, 204, 204, 204 is a light gray and the last value, 0.3, sets the transparency to 30 percent.

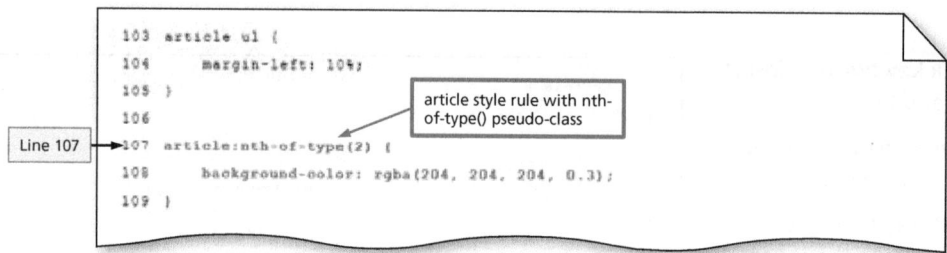

```
103  article ul {
104      margin-left: 10%;
105  }
106
107  article:nth-of-type(2) {
108      background-color: rgba(204, 204, 204, 0.3);
109  }
```

Line 107

article style rule with nth-of-type() pseudo-class

Figure 7–56

7

- Save your changes, open nutrition.html in Google Chrome's device mode, and then set the viewport to mobile to view the page (Figure 7–57).

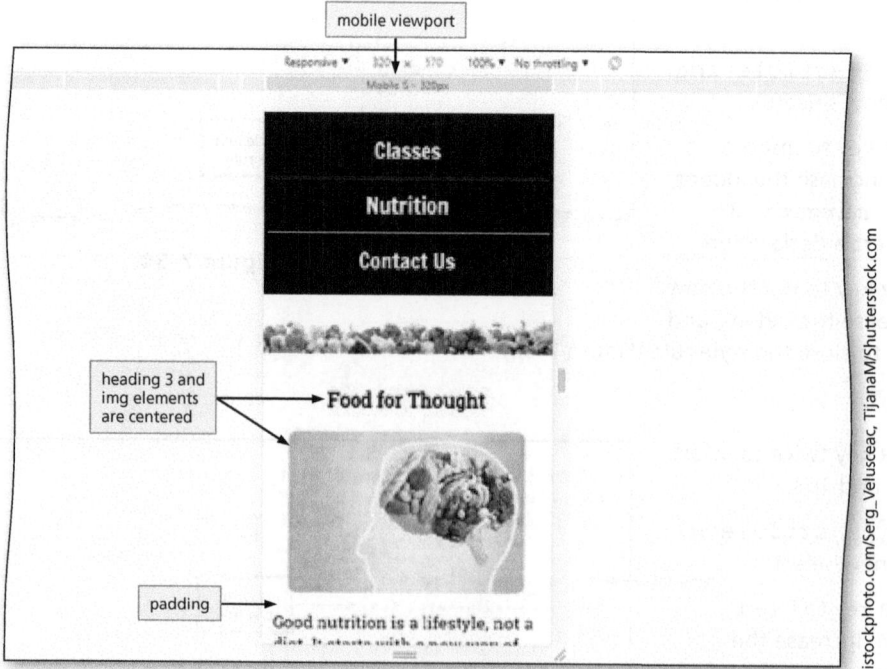

mobile viewport

heading 3 and img elements are centered

padding

Figure 7–57

8

- Scroll down to view the second and third article elements (Figure 7–58).

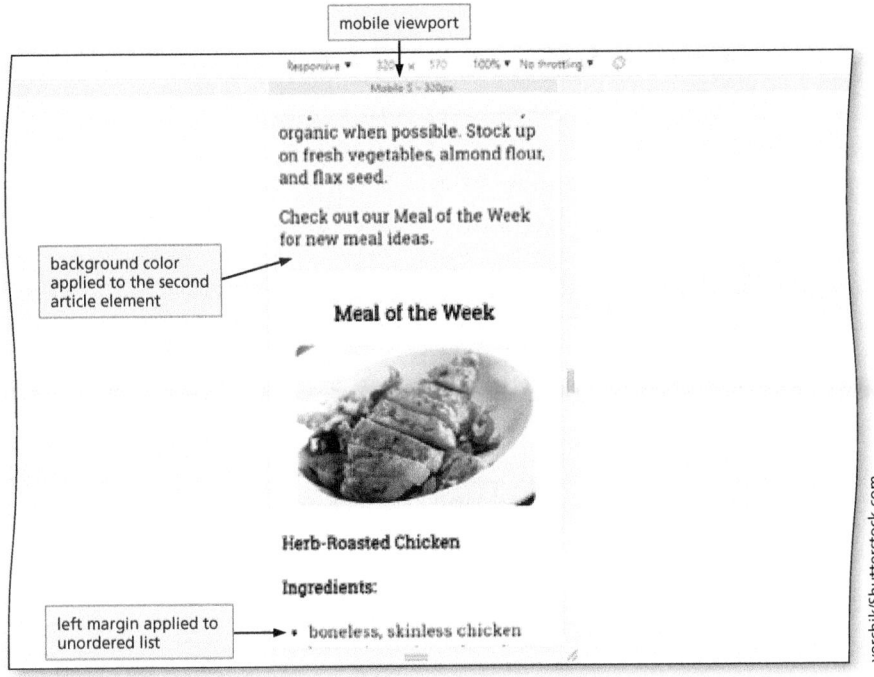

mobile viewport

background color applied to the second article element

Meal of the Week

Herb-Roasted Chicken

Ingredients:

left margin applied to unordered list

verchik/Shutterstock.com

Figure 7–58

To Style the Nutrition Page for a Tablet Viewport

1 MODIFY HOME PAGE | 2 STYLE HOME PAGE | 3 MODIFY ABOUT US PAGE
4 CREATE & STYLE NUTRITION PAGE | **5 ADD FAVICON**

The wireframe for the Nutrition page uses a three-column layout with an aside element below that spans the three columns. Create a new style rule to style the aside element. Then, create another style rule that spans the three columns. *Why? Format the aside element to stand out and capture the user's attention, and then style it so that it appears across all three columns.* Update the style sheet for the tablet viewport to format the aside element on the Nutrition page. The following steps add two new style rules for the tablet viewport.

- In styles.css, tap or click at the end of Line 245, and then press the ENTER key twice to insert new Lines 246 and 247.

- On Line 247, type `aside {` to insert a new selector.

- Press the ENTER key to insert a new Line 248, increase the indent, and then type `text-align: center;` to insert a declaration.

- Press the ENTER key to insert a new Line 249, and then type `font-size: 1.25em;` to insert a declaration.

- Press the ENTER key to insert a new Line 250, and then type `font-style: italic;` to insert a declaration.

- Press the ENTER key to insert a new Line 251, and then type `font-weight: bold;` to insert a new declaration.

- Press the ENTER key to insert a new Line 252, and then type `padding: 2%;` to insert a new declaration.

- Press the ENTER key to insert a new Line 253, and then type `background-color: rgba(204, 204, 204, 0.5);` to insert a new declaration.

- Press the ENTER key to insert a new Line 254, and then type `box-shadow: 5px 5px 8px #000;` to insert a new declaration.

- Press the ENTER key to insert a new Line 255, and then type **text-shadow: 5px 5px 5px #b3b3b3;** to insert a new declaration.

- Press the ENTER key to insert a new Line 256, and then type **border-radius: 0 15px;** to insert a new declaration.

- Press the ENTER key to insert a new Line 257, decrease the indent, and then type **}** to close the style rule (Figure 7–59).

Q&A

What color is rgba(204, 204, 204, 0.5)?
The value, 204, 204, 204, is a light gray and the last value, 0.5, sets the transparency to 50 percent.

Why does the border-radius property have two values?
The first value, 0, specifies no value for the top-left and bottom-right corners. The second value, 15px, rounds the top-right and bottom-left corners.

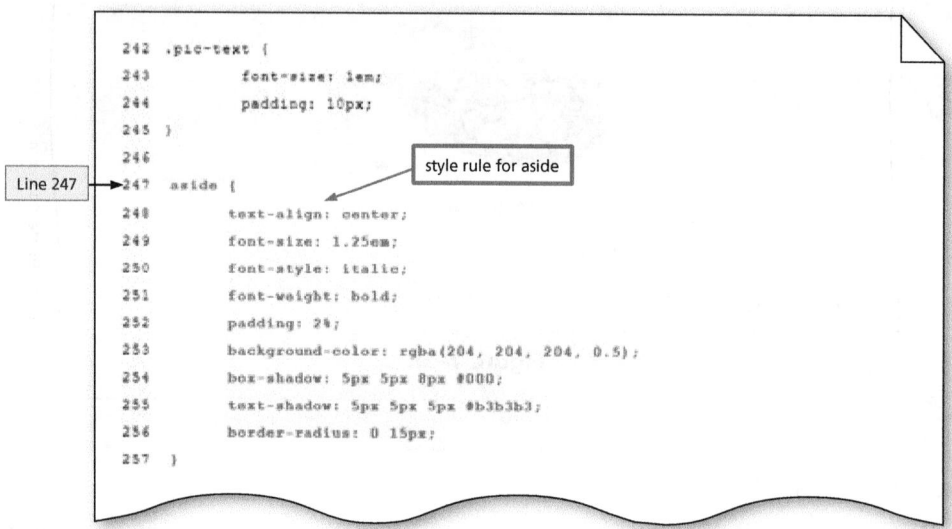

Figure 7–59

2

- Press the ENTER key twice to insert new Lines 258 and 259.

- On Line 259, type **.grid-item4 {** to insert a new selector.

- Press the ENTER key to insert a new Line 260, increase the indent, and then type **grid-column: 1 / span 3;** to insert a declaration.

- Press the ENTER key to insert a new Line 261, decrease the indent, and then type **}** to close the style rule (Figure 7–60).

Q&A

What is the purpose of the declaration, grid-column: 1 / span 3?
This declaration gives instructions to span the grid-item4 class three columns.

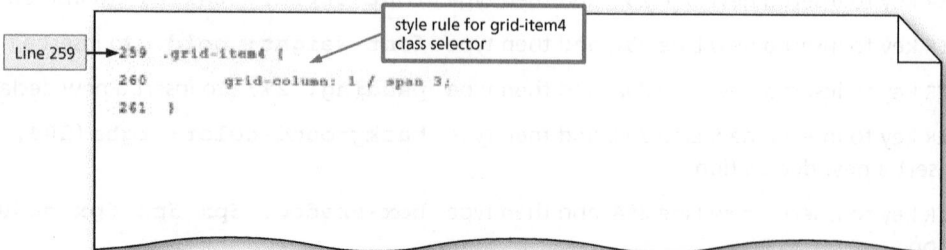

Figure 7–60

③

- Save your changes, refresh nutrition.html, and then adjust the device mode to a tablet viewport.
- Scroll down to view the article elements (Figure 7–61).

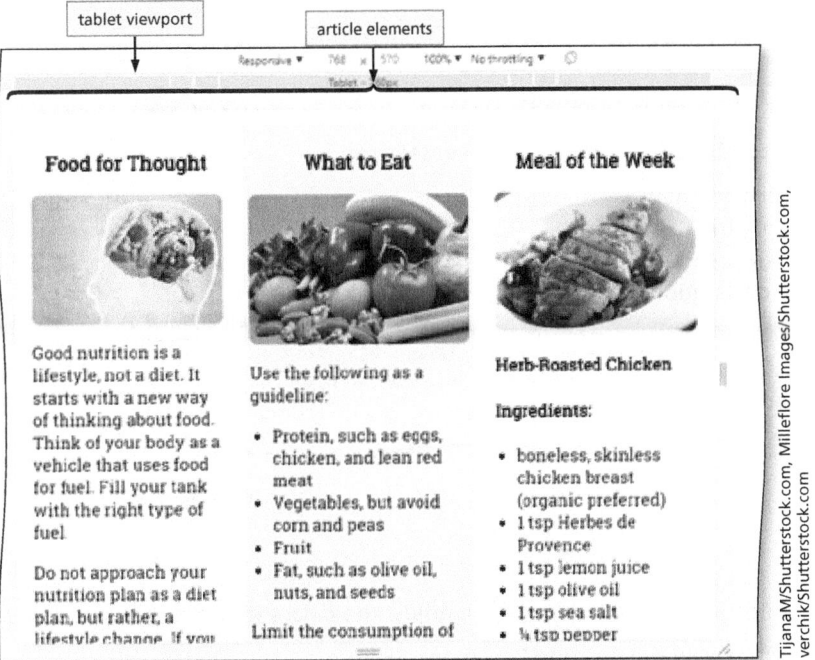

Figure 7–61

④

- Scroll down to view the aside element (Figure 7–62).

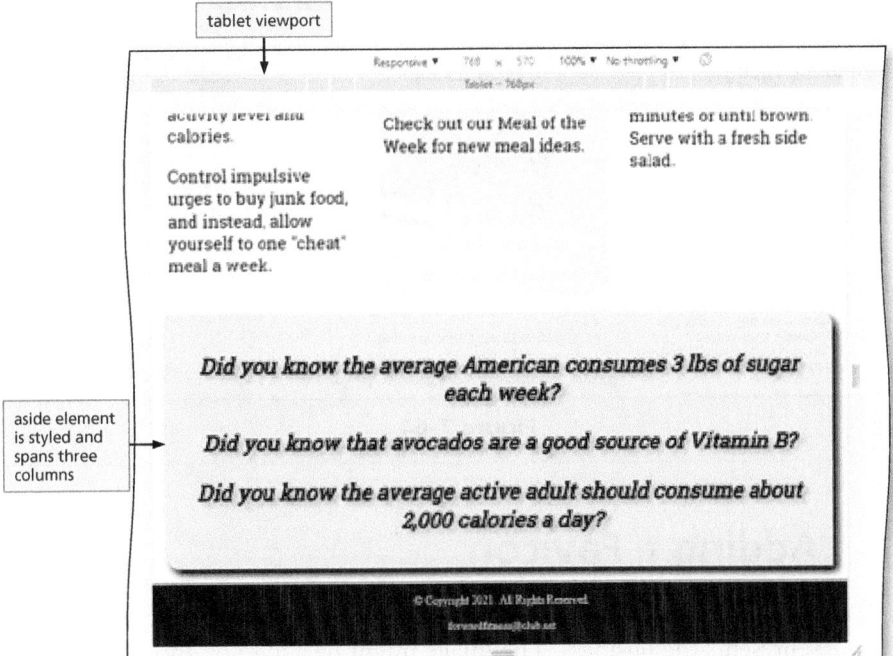

Figure 7–62

To Style the Nutrition Page for a Desktop Viewport

Create a new style rule to style to increase the size of the heading 3 elements within the article elements. *Why? The font size should be larger for a desktop viewport.* The following steps add a new style rule for the desktop viewport.

 1

- In styles.css, tap or click at the end of Line 331, and then press the ENTER key twice to insert new Lines 332 and 333.

- On Line 333, type **article h3 {** to insert a new selector.

- Press the ENTER key to insert a new Line 334, increase the indent, and then type **font-size: 1.75em;** to insert a declaration.

- Press the ENTER key to insert a new Line 335, decrease the indent, and then type **}** to close the style rule (Figure 7–63).

```
329      main h1 {
330          font-size: 1.8em;
331      }
332
333      article h3 {          article h3 style rule
334          font-size: 1.75em;
335      }
```
Line 333 →

Figure 7–63

2

- Save your changes, refresh nutrition.html, and then adjust the device mode to a desktop viewport.

- If necessary, scroll down to view the heading 3 elements (Figure 7–64).

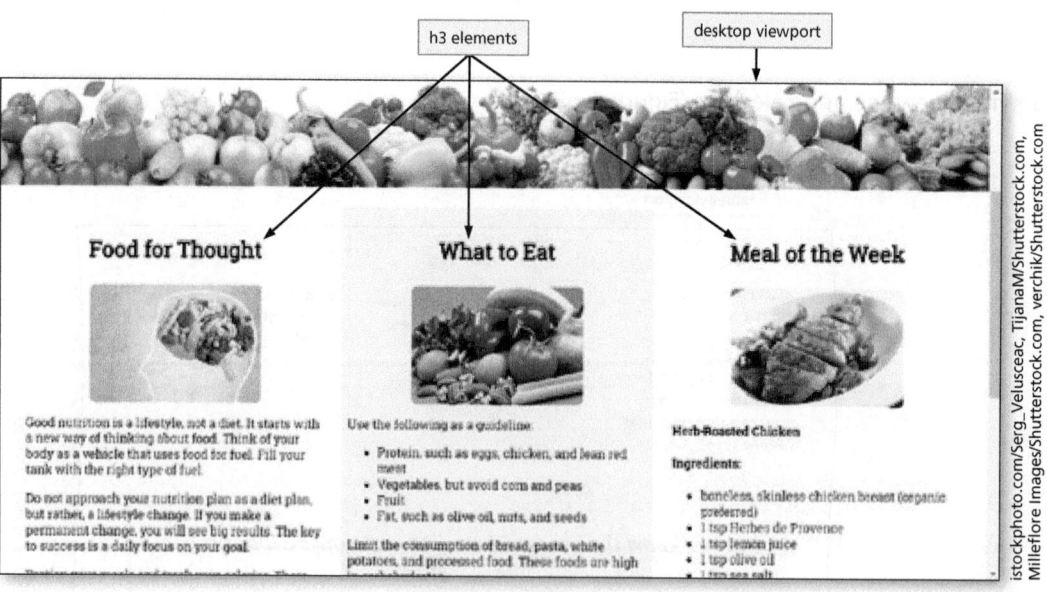

istockphoto.com/Serg_Velusceac, TijanaM/Shutterstock.com, Milleflore Images/Shutterstock.com, verchik/Shutterstock.com

Figure 7–64

Adding a Favicon

Today, most websites use a **favicon**, a small image that appears on the browser tab that represents the business. The image might be a logo or another graphic that identifies the business brand. Favicons help improve search engine optimization, which will be further discussed in Chapter 11. An example of a favicon is shown in Figure 7–65.

Google's favicon

Figure 7–65

In addition to appearing on the browser tab, favicons are used for webpage bookmarks and favorites. When you save a webpage as a bookmark or favorite, the favicon appears near the bookmark or favorite. An example of a favicon used with a bookmark is shown in Figure 7–66.

Firefox Bookmarks

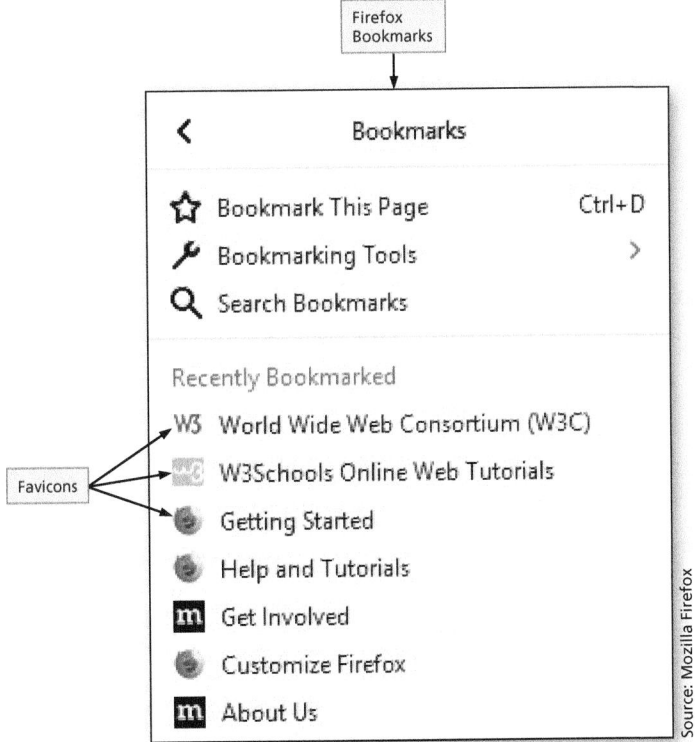

Favicons

Figure 7–66

Favicons can be PNG, GIF, or ICO files. The ICO file format, short for icon, was originally developed for Microsoft Windows. Today's modern browsers display any of these file formats.

When creating favicon files, you can use many recommended image sizes, based upon the favicon's use. An ideal image size for the favicon for website use is 32 x 32, the current standard for most modern desktop browsers.

To add a favicon to a webpage, add a link element within the head element. The following example shows the link element needed to add a favicon to a webpage:

```
<link rel="icon" type="image/png" sizes="32x32"
href="images/favicon-32.png">
```

The rel attribute is the relationship and its value is icon. The type attribute specifies that the favicon is a PNG image. The sizes attribute value identifies the file size. The href attribute provides a path to the actual file.

Favicons are also for bookmarks and favorites on smartphone devices and tablets. If the smartphone uses Apple iOS, you can include a link that gives the favicon rounded corners by adding the following link within the head element:

```
<link rel="apple-touch-icon" sizes="180x180" href="images/
apple-touch-icon.png">
```

```
Likewise, include the following link element to accommodate
Android smartphone devices:
```

```
<link rel="shortcut icon" sizes="192x192" href="images/
android-chrome-192.png">
```

When adding a favicon to a webpage, you typically include more than one link element within the head. One link specifies the 32 x 32 image, another for iOS, and another link for Android. These are not the only options, though. You can also include link elements to additional favicons with various image sizes.

Many free favicon generators are available online, such as favicon.io. You can upload your image or create a text favicon.

Add a favicon to the Forward Fitness Club website. The favicon is a black square with a white "F" that uses the same Roboto Slab font as the website.

To Add a Favicon to a Website

1 MODIFY HOME PAGE | 2 STYLE HOME PAGE | 3 MODIFY ABOUT US PAGE
4 CREATE & STYLE NUTRITION PAGE | 5 ADD FAVICON

Add a favicon to every HTML file for the Forward Fitness Club, including the template.html file. *Why? Improve the overall appearance of the website by adding a favicon.* The following steps add a favicon to each HTML file for the Forward Fitness Club website.

1

- If necessary, reopen the nutrition.html file in your text editor to prepare to modify the file.

- Place your insertion point at the end of Line 9 and press the ENTER key to insert a new Line 10.

- On Line 10, type `<link rel="shortcut icon" href="images/favicon.ico">` to insert a link element.

- Press the ENTER key to insert a new Line 11, and then type `<link rel="icon" type="image/png" sizes="32x32" href="images/favicon-32.png">` to insert another link element.

- Press the ENTER key to insert a new Line 12, and then type `<link rel="apple-touch-icon" sizes="180x180" href="images/apple-touch-icon.png">` to insert another link element.

- Press the ENTER key to insert a new Line 13, and then type `<link rel="icon" sizes="192x192" href="images/android-chrome-192.png">` to insert another link element (Figure 7–67).

Q&A | What is the purpose of including these four link elements?
The first link element uses an ICO file as the shortcut icon if the user creates a shortcut. The second link element is displayed in the browser tab. The third link element is for iOS devices. The fourth element is for Android devices.

nutrition.html file

```
 4   <head>
 5       <title>Forward Fitness Club</title>
 6       <meta charset="utf-8">
 7       <link rel="stylesheet" href="css/styles.css">
 8       <meta name="viewport" content="width=device-width, initial-scale=1.0">
 9       <link href="https://fonts.googleapis.com/css?family=Francois+One|
         Roboto+Slab&display=swap" rel="stylesheet">
10       <link rel="shortcut icon" href="images/favicon.ico">
11       <link rel="icon" type="image/png" sizes="32x32" href="images/favicon-32.png">
12       <link rel="apple-touch-icon" sizes="180x180" href="images/apple-touch-
         icon.png">
13       <link rel="icon" sizes="192x192" href="images/android-chrome-192.png">
14   </head>
```

Line 10 → 10

link elements

Figure 7–67

2

- Save your changes and open nutrition.html in your browser to view the favicon (Figure 7–68).

Q&A I opened the nutrition.html file in Microsoft Edge and my favicon does not appear. Why?
In order to view the favicon in Microsoft Edge, you must first publish the website or use a local web server.

favicon

Figure 7–68

nexusby/Shutterstock.com, istockphoto.com/Serg_Velusceac, TijanaM/Shutterstock.com, Millefiore Images/Shutterstock.com, verchik/Shutterstock.com, Source: favicon.io

3

- Return to the nutrition.html file in your text editor, highlight Lines 10–13, and then press the CTRL+C keys to copy the link elements.

- Open the about.html file in your text editor to prepare to modify the file.

- Place your insertion point at the end of Line 9, and then press the ENTER key to insert a new Line 10.

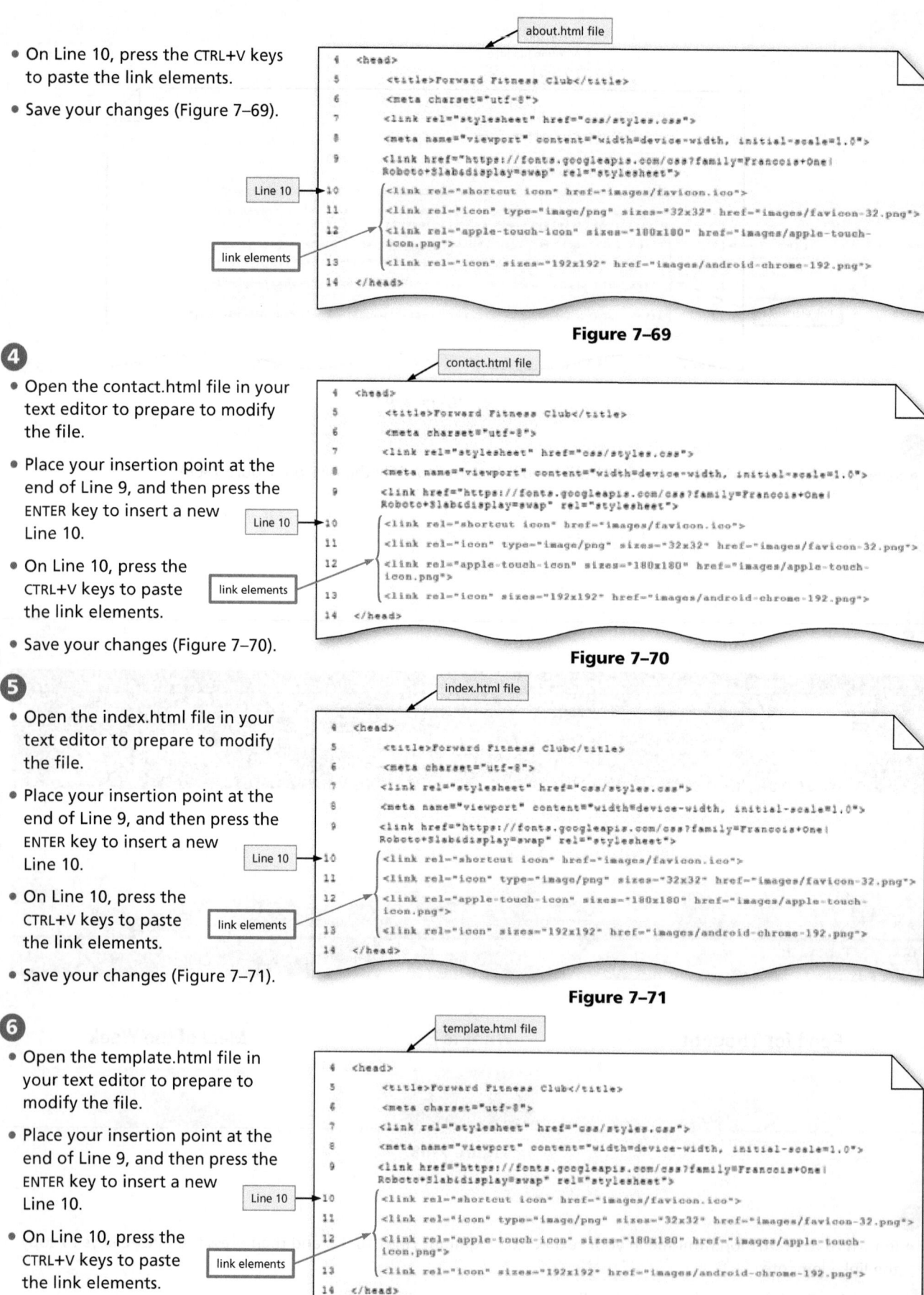

- On Line 10, press the CTRL+V keys to paste the link elements.
- Save your changes (Figure 7–69).

```
about.html file

4    <head>
5        <title>Forward Fitness Club</title>
6        <meta charset="utf-8">
7        <link rel="stylesheet" href="css/styles.css">
8        <meta name="viewport" content="width=device-width, initial-scale=1.0">
9        <link href="https://fonts.googleapis.com/css?family=Francois+One|
         Roboto+Slab&display=swap" rel="stylesheet">
10       <link rel="shortcut icon" href="images/favicon.ico">
11       <link rel="icon" type="image/png" sizes="32x32" href="images/favicon-32.png">
12       <link rel="apple-touch-icon" sizes="180x180" href="images/apple-touch-
         icon.png">
13       <link rel="icon" sizes="192x192" href="images/android-chrome-192.png">
14   </head>
```

Line 10 → 10

link elements

Figure 7–69

4

- Open the contact.html file in your text editor to prepare to modify the file.
- Place your insertion point at the end of Line 9, and then press the ENTER key to insert a new Line 10.
- On Line 10, press the CTRL+V keys to paste the link elements.
- Save your changes (Figure 7–70).

```
contact.html file

4    <head>
5        <title>Forward Fitness Club</title>
6        <meta charset="utf-8">
7        <link rel="stylesheet" href="css/styles.css">
8        <meta name="viewport" content="width=device-width, initial-scale=1.0">
9        <link href="https://fonts.googleapis.com/css?family=Francois+One|
         Roboto+Slab&display=swap" rel="stylesheet">
10       <link rel="shortcut icon" href="images/favicon.ico">
11       <link rel="icon" type="image/png" sizes="32x32" href="images/favicon-32.png">
12       <link rel="apple-touch-icon" sizes="180x180" href="images/apple-touch-
         icon.png">
13       <link rel="icon" sizes="192x192" href="images/android-chrome-192.png">
14   </head>
```

Line 10 → 10

link elements

Figure 7–70

5

- Open the index.html file in your text editor to prepare to modify the file.
- Place your insertion point at the end of Line 9, and then press the ENTER key to insert a new Line 10.
- On Line 10, press the CTRL+V keys to paste the link elements.
- Save your changes (Figure 7–71).

```
index.html file

4    <head>
5        <title>Forward Fitness Club</title>
6        <meta charset="utf-8">
7        <link rel="stylesheet" href="css/styles.css">
8        <meta name="viewport" content="width=device-width, initial-scale=1.0">
9        <link href="https://fonts.googleapis.com/css?family=Francois+One|
         Roboto+Slab&display=swap" rel="stylesheet">
10       <link rel="shortcut icon" href="images/favicon.ico">
11       <link rel="icon" type="image/png" sizes="32x32" href="images/favicon-32.png">
12       <link rel="apple-touch-icon" sizes="180x180" href="images/apple-touch-
         icon.png">
13       <link rel="icon" sizes="192x192" href="images/android-chrome-192.png">
14   </head>
```

Line 10 → 10

link elements

Figure 7–71

6

- Open the template.html file in your text editor to prepare to modify the file.
- Place your insertion point at the end of Line 9, and then press the ENTER key to insert a new Line 10.
- On Line 10, press the CTRL+V keys to paste the link elements.
- Save your changes (Figure 7–72).

```
template.html file

4    <head>
5        <title>Forward Fitness Club</title>
6        <meta charset="utf-8">
7        <link rel="stylesheet" href="css/styles.css">
8        <meta name="viewport" content="width=device-width, initial-scale=1.0">
9        <link href="https://fonts.googleapis.com/css?family=Francois+One|
         Roboto+Slab&display=swap" rel="stylesheet">
10       <link rel="shortcut icon" href="images/favicon.ico">
11       <link rel="icon" type="image/png" sizes="32x32" href="images/favicon-32.png">
12       <link rel="apple-touch-icon" sizes="180x180" href="images/apple-touch-
         icon.png">
13       <link rel="icon" sizes="192x192" href="images/android-chrome-192.png">
14   </head>
```

Line 10 → 10

link elements

Figure 7–72

How can I make my own favicon?
You can use many online resources to create your own favicon. You can also use graphic software, such as Adobe PhotoShop, Paint 3D, or Paint.

To Validate the Style Sheet

Always run your files through W3C's validator to check the document for errors. If the document has any errors, validating gives you a chance to identify and correct them. Validation is also an effective troubleshooting tool during the development process and adds a valuable level of professionalism to your work. The following steps validate a CSS document.

1 Open your browser and type `http://jigsaw.w3.org/css-validator/` in the address bar to display the W3C CSS Validation Service page.

2 Tap or click the By file upload tab to display the Validate by File Upload information.

3 Tap or click the Choose file button to display the File Upload dialog box.

4 Navigate to your css folder to find the styles.css file.

5 Tap or click the styles.css document to select it.

6 Tap or click the Open button to upload the selected file to the W3C CSS validator.

7 Tap or click the Check button to send the document through the validator and display the validation results page.

To Validate the HTML Files

Every time you create a new webpage, run it through W3C's validator to check the document for errors. If any errors exist, you need to correct them. Validation is also an effective troubleshooting tool during the development process and adds a valuable level of professionalism to your work. The following steps validate an HTML document.

1 Open your browser and type `http://validator.w3.org/` in the address bar to display the W3C validator page.

2 Tap or click the Validate by File Upload tab to display the Validate by File Upload tab information.

3 Tap or click the Choose File button to display the Open dialog box.

4 Navigate to your website template folder to find the nutrition.html file.

5 Tap or click the nutrition.html document to select it.

6 Tap or click the Open button to upload it to the W3C validator.

7 Tap or click the Check button to send the document through the validator and display the validation results page.

8 If necessary, correct any errors, save your changes, and run through the validator again to revalidate the page.

9 Follow these steps to validate the about.html, contact.html, index.html, and fitness.html pages and correct any errors.

Chapter Summary

In this chapter, you learned how to use the HTML 5 figure, figcaption, section, article, and aside semantic elements. You added these elements to the webpages in the website, and then created and modified style rules in the style sheet to format the new elements and adapt to the website design. You used a CSS grid layout to create multiple columns. You created style rules to add opacity, box shadows, and text shadows. Finally, you added a favicon to a website.

Redesigning the Home Page
Add figure Elements to the Home Page
(HTML 352)
Add figcaption Elements to the Home Page
(HTML 352)
Style figure and figcaption Elements (HTML 354)
Apply Box Sizing to All Elements (HTML 357)
Apply a Three-Column Layout Using CSS Grid
Layout (HTML 357)
Apply Opacity and Box Shadows with the hover
Pseudo-class (HTML 361)
Apply a Text Shadow (HTML 362)

Updating the About Us Page
Add Section Elements to the About Us Page
(HTML 364)

Creating the Nutrition Page
Create the Nutrition Page (HTML 367)
Add a Hero Image to the Nutrition Page
(HTML 367)
Add article and aside Elements to the
Nutrition Page (HTML 368)
Style the Nutrition Page for a Mobile Viewport
(HTML 372)
Style Only the Middle Column for the Nutrition
Page (HTML 374)
Create a Three-Column Layout for the Nutrition
Page in a Tablet Viewport (HTML 375–376)
Style the aside Element to Span Three Columns
(HTML 376)

Adding a Favicon to a Website
Add a Favicon to All Webpages (HTML 380)

How will you improve the design of your website?

Use these guidelines as you complete the assignments in this chapter and create your own webpages outside of this class.

1. Determine the best layout for each viewport.

   a) Design a wireframe for mobile, tablet, and desktop viewports.

   b) Determine what images you will use and whether to display them on a mobile viewport.

   c) Decide how to use the hover pseudo-class for desktop viewports.

2. Determine how many columns are needed.

   a) Draft a wireframe to determine the number of columns needed for each page.

   b) Determine which method you will use to create columns within a website.

3. Enhance the website design with CSS properties.

   a) Determine the best use of the opacity property.

   b) Determine the best use of the text-shadow property.

   c) Determine the best use of the box-shadow property.

5. Create a favicon.

   a) Determine how you will create your favicon.

   b) Determine which image sizes you will need for your favicon.

How should you submit solutions to questions in the assignments identified with a symbol? Every assignment in this book contains one or more questions identified with a symbol. These questions require you to think beyond the assigned presentation. Present your solutions to the questions in the format required by your instructor. Possible formats may include one or more of these options: create a document that contains the answer; present your answer to the class; discuss your answer in a group; record the answer as audio or video using a webcam, smartphone, or portable media player; or post answers on a blog, wiki, or website.

Apply Your Knowledge

Reinforce the skills and apply the concepts you learned in this chapter.

Using HTML 5 Semantic Elements

Note: To complete this assignment, you will be required to use the Data Files. Please contact your instructor for information about accessing the Data Files.

Instructions: In this exercise, you will use your text editor to add and style HTML 5 semantic elements. You insert section, article, and aside elements in an HTML document. You then add a style rule to format each element. You will create a two-column layout for a tablet viewport and a three-column layout for a desktop viewport using the CSS grid layout. You will also apply a box shadow to the aside element. Finally, you will add a favicon. You will also use professional web development practices to indent, space, comment, and validate your code. The completed webpage, as displayed in a mobile viewport, is shown in Figure 7–73. The completed webpage, as displayed in a tablet viewport, is shown in Figure 7–74. The completed webpage, as displayed in a desktop viewport, is shown in Figure 7–75.

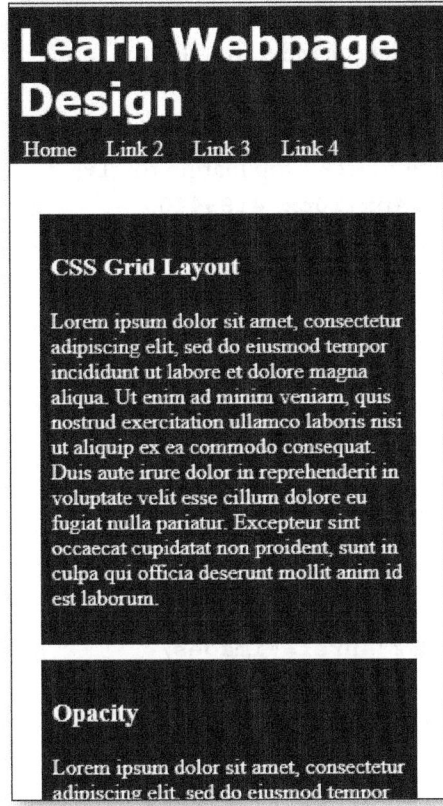

Figure 7–73

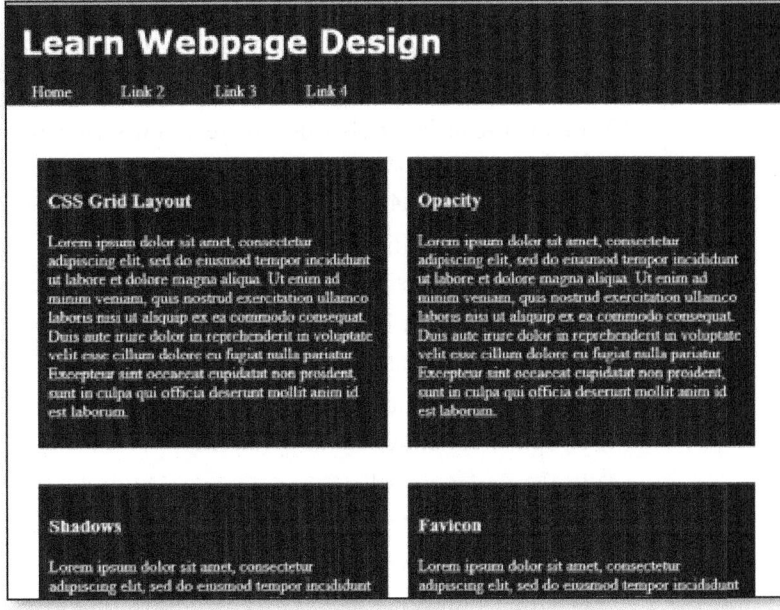

Figure 7–74

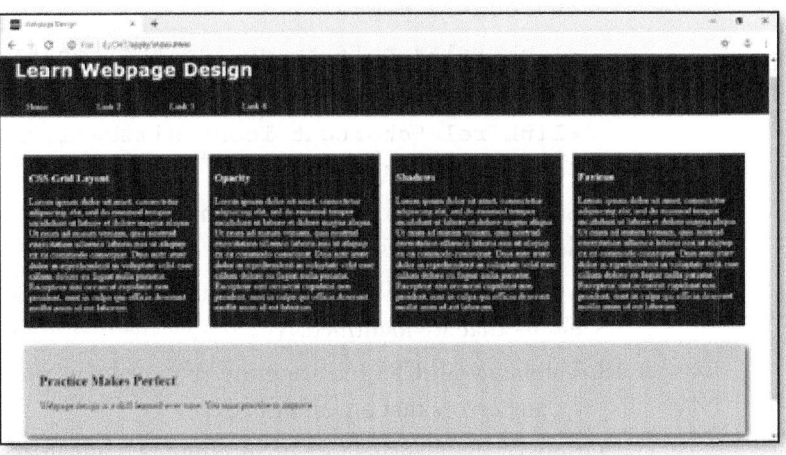

Figure 7–75

Source: favicon.io

Continued >

Apply Your Knowledge *continued*

Perform the following tasks:

1. Open the index.html file in the chapter07\apply folder from the Data Files in your text editor. Update the comment with your name, the file name, and today's date. Add your name to the paragraph element located within the footer element near the bottom of the page.

2. Open the index.html file in your browser to view the page.

3. Open the apply07.css file from the apply\css folder. Modify the comment at the top of the style sheet to include your name, today's date, and the file name.

4. In the index.html file, within the main element, replace the first div element with an article element and add a class attribute with a value of **grid**. Be sure to update the closing div tag as well, just above the closing main tag.

5. Replace the next four div elements with section elements.

6. Replace the last div element with an aside element.

7. In the apply07.css file, add **section**, **article**, and **aside** to the CSS reset.

8. In the style rules for the mobile viewport, below the main style rule, add a new style rule for the section element that sets the background color to **#183440**, the color to **#fff**, top margin to **4%**, and padding to **3%**.

9. Below the section style rule, create a new style rule for the article element that sets the top margin to **1%** and padding to **2%**.

10. Below the article style rule, create a new style rule for the aside element that sets the background color to **rgba(24, 52, 64, 0.3)**, padding to **2%**, top margin to **1%**, color to **#183440**, and a box shadow with values of **4px 4px 10px #183440**.

11. In the tablet media query, create a new style rule for the grid class selector that sets the display to a **grid**, sets grid template columns to two columns, and sets a grid gap of **20px**.

12. In the tablet media query, create a new style rule for the aside element that creates one grid column that spans two columns.

13. In the desktop media query, create a new style rule for the grid class selector that sets grid template columns to four columns.

14. In the desktop media query, create a new style rule for the aside element that creates one grid column that spans four columns.

15. In the index.html file, add the following link elements within the head element, just above the closing head tag:

```
<link rel="icon" type="image/png" sizes="32x32" href="images/
favicon-32.png">

<link rel="apple-touch-icon" sizes="180x180" href="images/apple-touch-
icon.png">

<link rel="shortcut icon" sizes="192x192" href="images/android-
chrome-192.png">
```

16. Save all files and open the index.html in your browser. View the webpage in mobile, tablet, and desktop viewports.

17. Validate your HTML document using the W3C validator found at validator.w3.org and fix any errors that are identified.

18. Validate your CSS file using the W3C validator found at http://jigsaw.w3.org/css-validator/ and fix any errors that are identified.

19. Submit the files in a format specified by your instructor.

20. ✻ In this assignment, you created two-column and three-column layouts using the CSS grid layout. What other method can you use to create columns?

Extend Your Knowledge

Extend the skills you learned in this chapter and experiment with new skills. You may need to use additional resources to complete the assignment.

Exploring Column Layouts

Note: To complete this assignment, you will be required to use the Data Files. Please contact your instructor for information about accessing the Data Files.

Instructions: In this exercise, you research other ways to create a column layout for a webpage and then use the Data Files provided to create the column layout. You will also use an online favicon generator to create your own favicon. An example of the completed webpage is shown in Figure 7–76.

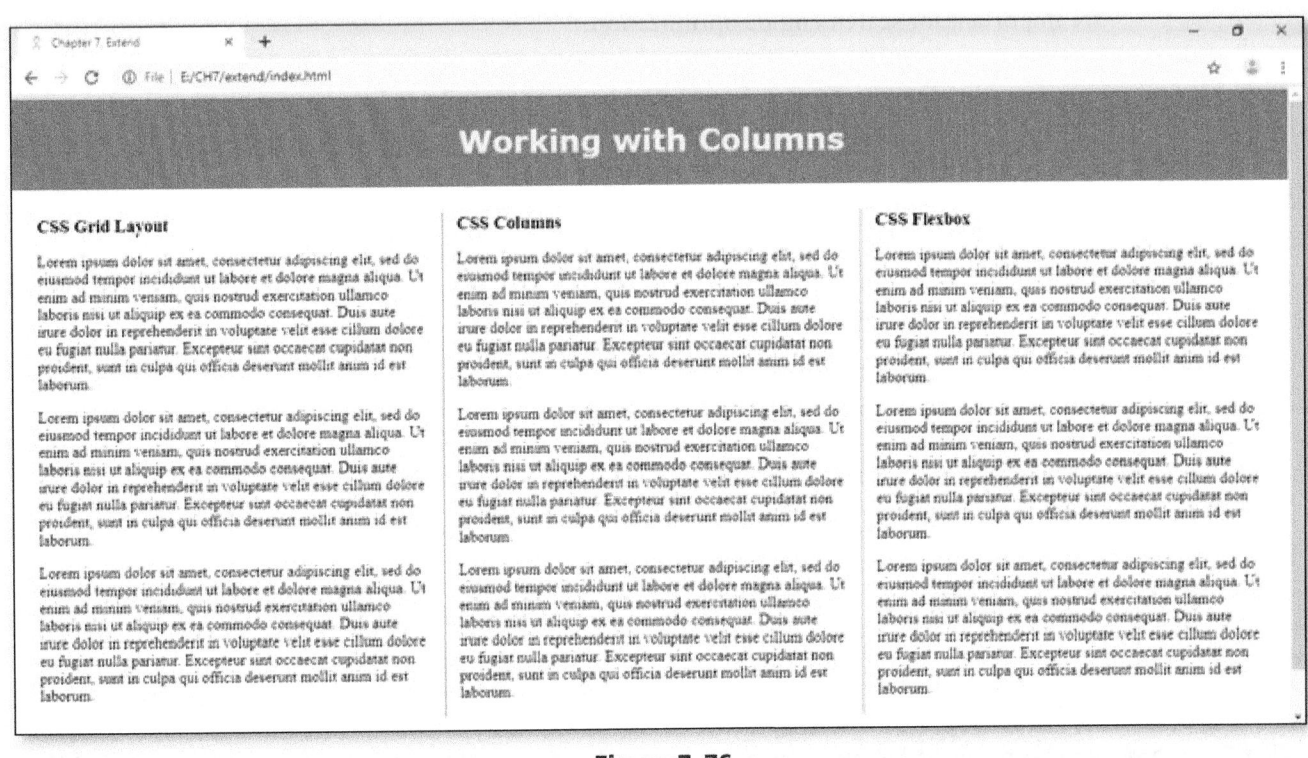

Figure 7–76

Source: favicon.io

Perform the following tasks:

1. Open your text editor and then open the extend07.html file in the chapter07\extend folder from the Data Files. Update the comment with your name and today's date. Add your name to the paragraph element located within the footer element near the bottom of the page.

2. Open extend07.html in your browser to view the webpage. Maximize the browser window to use a desktop viewport.

3. Open the styles07.css file from the extend\css folder. Modify the comment at the top of the style sheet to include your name, today's date, and the file name.

4. Use your browser to research different ways to create a multiple-column layout for webpage design.

5. Use the extend07.html and styles07.css files to create the three-column layout. Use Figure 7–76 as guide. Do not use the CSS grid layout or CSS width, float, and clear properties.

Continued >

Extend Your Knowledge *continued*

6. Use the first empty paragraph element within the aside element to summarize the method you used to create your columns. Identify the resource you used and include a link to the resource that opens in a new tab.

7. Use your browser to find an online favicon generator and create your own favicon. Save your favicon files in the extend\images folder. Include the proper link elements within the extend07.html file.

8. Use the second paragraph element within the aside element to note the resource you used to create your favicon. Include a link to the resource that opens in a new tab.

9. Validate your HTML and CSS files. Correct any errors.

10. Submit your answers in the format specified by your instructor.

11. ✳ In this exercise, you created your own favicon. Use your browser to research why favicons are important for search engine optimization.

Analyze, Correct, Improve

Analyze a website, correct all errors, and improve it.

Improving an HTML Document with Semantic Markup

Note: To complete this assignment, you will be required to use the Data Files. Please contact your instructor for information about accessing the Data Files.

Instructions: Work with the analyze07.html file in the analyze folder and the styles07.css file in the analyze\css folder from the Data Files. The analyze07.html webpage contains generic `div` elements for content and needs to be revised to use HTML 5 semantic elements. You then create new style rules to format the semantic elements. Use Figure 7–77 as a guide to correct these files.

Figure 7–77

Source: favicon.io

1. Correct

    a. Open the analyze07.html file in your editor from the Data Files and then modify the comment at the top of the page to include your name and today's date. Add your name to the paragraph element located within the footer element near the bottom of the page.

    b. Open the styles07.css file in your editor from the Data Files and then modify and correct the comment at the top of the document to include your name and today's date.

    c. In the analyze07.html file, review the current div elements used to structure content and replace them with header, nav, main, section, article, aside, and footer HTML 5 semantic elements. Do not replace the `div id="container"` element.

    d. Add a class attribute with the value of grid to every `article` element.

    e. In the styles07.css file, add missing HTML 5 semantic elements to the CSS reset style rule.

2. Improve

    a. In the styles07.css file, add a declaration to the section style rule that sets the background color to `#9d4502`.

    b. Add another declaration to the section style rule that sets the top and bottom margin to `1%` and the left and right margin to `0`.

    c. Add a declaration to the aside style rule that specifies a text shadow with the values `4px 4px 8px #fc7307`. Add another declaration to the aside style rule that specifies a box shadow with the values `4px 4px 10px #183440`.

    d. In the tablet media query, add a style rule for the grid class selector that sets the display to a `grid`, creates three columns with the grid template columns property, and sets the grid gap to `20px`.

    e. In the tablet media query, add a style rule for the aside element that creates one grid column that spans three columns.

    f. Review the various favicons in the analyze07\images folder. Add four link elements within the head to add a favicon, favicon shortcut, and favicons for iOS and Android.

    g. Validate your CSS file using the W3C validator found at http://jigsaw.w3.org/css-validator/ and fix any errors that are identified.

    h. Validate your HTML webpage using the W3C validator found at validator.w3.org and fix any errors that are identified.

    i. ✸ Use your browser to research the Bootstrap grid system and summarize your findings.

In the Lab

Labs 1 and 2, which increase in difficulty, require you to create webpages based on what you learned in the chapter; Lab 3 requires you to dive deeper into a topic covered in the chapter.

Lab 1: Integrating HTML 5 Semantic Elements for the Strike a Chord Website

Note: To complete this assignment, you will be required to use the Data Files. Please contact your instructor for information about accessing the Data Files.

Problem: You work for a local music lesson company called Strike a Chord that provides music lessons for piano, guitar, and violin. The company needs a web presence and has hired you to

Continued >

In the Lab *continued*

create their website. You have already developed a responsive web design website and now need to integrate additional HTML 5 semantic elements and create a new page. The Instructors page, displayed in mobile, tablet, and desktop viewports, and the favicon is shown in Figure 7–78.

(a) Mobile Viewport

(b) Tablet Viewport

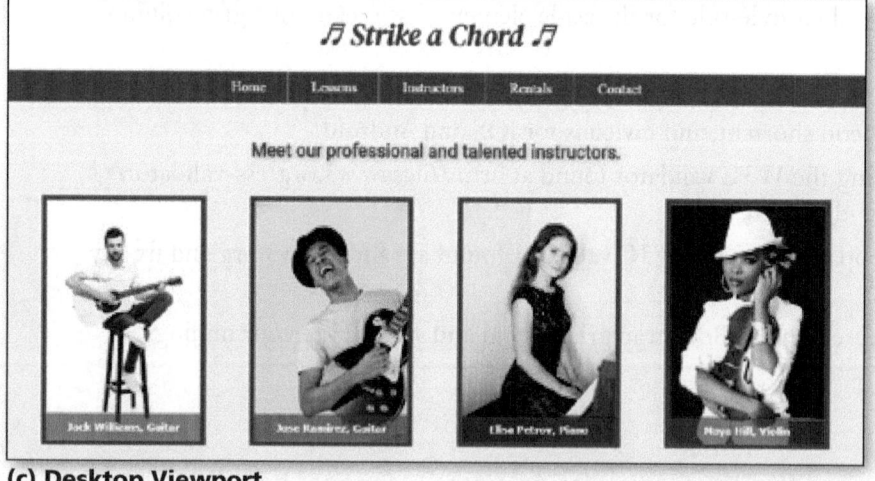

(c) Desktop Viewport

(d) Favicon

Figure 7–78

Instructions: Perform the following tasks:

1. Copy the image files in the chapter07\lab1 folder from the Data Files to your music\images folder.

2. Open the lessons.html file in your text editor and then replace all of the div elements with `section` elements.

3. Use the template.html file to create a new HTML file and name the file instructors.html. Add the current date to the comment near the top of the page and update the file name.

4. In the nutrition.html file, update the title by replacing the word Template with `Instructors`.

5. In the `main` element, add a class attribute with a value of grid.

6. In the **main** element, replace the **div** element with an **aside** element, and then add a paragraph with the following text:

   Meet our professional and talented instructors.

7. Add a **figure** element below the **aside** element. Nest the following elements within the **figure** element:

   a. Add the guitar-instructor picture and use **guitar instructor** for the alt text.

   b. Add a figcaption below the picture and include the text **Jack Williams, Guitar.**

8. Add another **figure** element and nest the following elements:

   a. Add the electric-guitar-instructor picture and use **electric guitar instructor** for the alt text.

   b. Add a figcaption below the picture and include the text **Jose Ramirez, Guitar.**

9. Add another **figure** element and nest the following elements:

   a. Add the piano-instructor picture and use **piano instructor** for the alt text.

   b. Add a figcaption below the picture and include the text **Elisa Petrov, Piano.**

10. Add another **figure** element and nest the following elements:

    a. Add the violin-instructor picture and use **violin instructor** for the alt text.

    b. Add a figcaption below the picture and include the text **Maya Hill, Violin.**

11. In the styles.css file, add the **section, aside, figure,** and **figcaption** elements to the CSS reset.

12. Below the img style rule, add the following comment and style rule:

    ```
    /* Style rule for box sizing applies to all elements */
    * {
    box-sizing: border-box;
    }
    ```

13. Create a style rule for the **aside** element within the mobile viewport and include the following declarations:

    a. **text-align: center;**

    b. **font-size: 1.5em;**

    c. **font-weight: bold;**

    d. **color: #373684;**

    e. **text-shadow: 3px 3px 10px #8280cb;**

14. Create a style rule for the **figure** element within the mobile viewport, and include the following declarations:

    a. **position: relative;**

    b. **max-width: 275px;**

    c. **margin: 2% auto;**

    d. **border: 8px solid #373684;**

15. Create a style rule for the **figcaption** element within the mobile viewport, and include the following declarations:

    a. **position: absolute;**

    b. **bottom: 0;**

    c. **background: rgba(55, 54, 132, 0.7);**

    d. **color: #fff;**

    e. **width: 100%;**

Continued >

In the Lab *continued*

    f. `padding: 5% 0;`

    g. `text-align: center;`

    h. `font-family: Verdana, Arial, sans-serif;`

    i. `font-size: 1.5em;`

    j. `font-weight: bold;`

16. In the tablet media query, create a style rule for the `grid` class selector that sets the display to a `grid,` sets the grid template columns to a two-column layout, and sets the grid gap to `20px.`

17. Create a style rule for the aside element that sets the grid column value to `1 / span 2.`

18. In the desktop media query, create a style rule for the grid class selector that sets the grid template columns to a four-column layout.

19. Create a style rule for the figcaption element that sets the font size to 1em.

20. Create a style rule for the aside element that sets the grid column value to `1 / span 4.`

21. Add the following link elements within the head element on all of the HTML files, including the template.html file:

    ```
    <link rel="shortcut icon" href="images/favicon.ico">

    <link rel="icon" type="image/png" sizes="32x32" href="images/
    favicon-32.png">

    <link rel="apple-touch-icon" sizes="180x180" href="images/apple-
    touch-icon.png">

    <link rel="icon" sizes="192x192" href="images/android-chrome-192.png">
    ```

22. Validate your HTML and CSS files and correct any errors.

23. Review your files for best coding practices; ensure proper spacing and indents for improved readability.

24. Save all files, open the instructors.html page within a browser, and view the page in all three viewports, as shown in Figure 7–78.

25. Submit your assignment in the format specified by your instructor.

26. ✺ In this assignment, you add HTML 5 semantic elements. Research the time semantic element, identify its use, and then discuss its attribute and the different ways in which time can be displayed.

Lab 2: Integrating HTML 5 Semantic Elements for the Wild Rescues Website

Note: To complete this assignment, you will be required to use the Data Files. Please contact your instructor for information about accessing the Data Files.

Problem: You volunteer at a local wildlife rescue, a nonprofit organization called Wild Rescues. The organization rescues all kinds of wild animals, rehabilitates them, and then releases them back into the wild. Wild Rescues needs a website to help raise awareness about the organization. You have already developed a responsive web design website and now need to integrate additional HTML 5 semantic elements and create a new page. The Gallery page, displayed in mobile and tablet viewports, is shown in Figure 7–79. The Gallery page, as displayed in desktop and large desktop viewports is shown in Figure 7–80. Figure 7–80 also shows the favicon.

(a) Mobile Viewport

(b) Tablet Viewport

Figure 7–79

Source: favicon.io, courtesy of Jessica Minnick

(a) Desktop Viewport

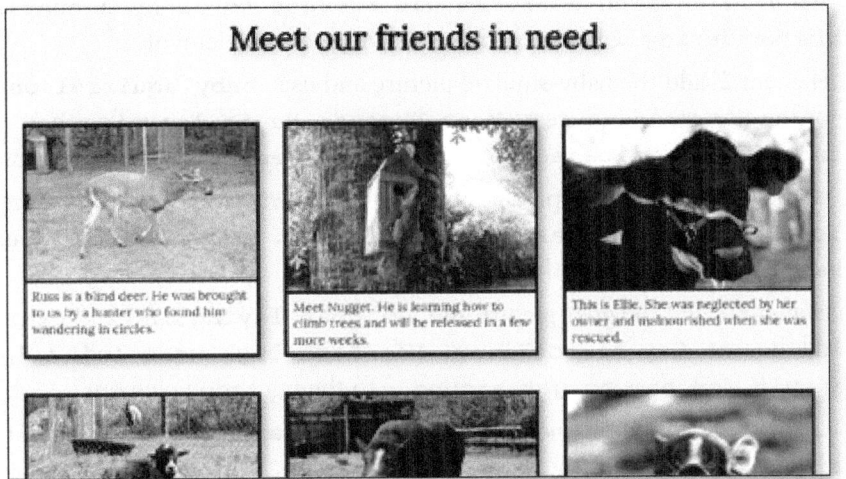

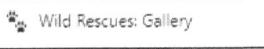

(c) Favicon

(b) Large Desktop Viewport

Source: favicon.io, courtesy of Jessica Minnick

Figure 7–80

Continued >

In the Lab *continued*

Instructions: Perform the following tasks:

1. Copy the image data files in the chapter07\lab2 folder from the Data Files your rescue\images folder.

2. Use the template.html file to create a new HTML file, and name the file gallery.html. Add the current date to the comment near the top of the page and update the file name.

3. In the gallery.html file, update the title by replacing the word Template with `Gallery`.

4. In the `main` element, add a class attribute with a value of grid.

5. In the `main` element, replace the `div` element with an `aside` element and then add a paragraph with the following text:

   `Meet our friends in need.`

6. Add 12 `figure` elements below the `aside` element. Add a comment for each figure element to note figure element 1, figure element 2, and so on. Follow the example below:

   ```
   <figure> <!-- Figure Element 1 -->
   </figure>
   ```

7. Nest an `img` and a `figcaption` within the `figure` element, and then add the following images and figcaption content to each img and figcaption element:

   a. In figure element 1, add the blind-deer picture and use `blind deer` for the alt text. Add the text `Russ is a blind deer. He was brought to us by a hunter who found him wandering in circles.` to the figcaption element.

   b. In figure element 2, add the baby-squirrel picture and use `baby squirrel on a tree house` for the alt text. Add the text `Meet Nugget. He is learning how to climb trees and will be released in a few more weeks.` to the figcaption element.

   c. In figure element 3, add the cow picture and use `face of a cow` for the alt text. Add the text `This is Ellie. She was neglected by her owner and malnourished when she was rescued.` to the figcaption element.

   d. In figure element 4, add the goat picture and use `goat laying in the grass` for the alt text. Add the text `Say hi to Vinny. His back legs were injured, making it difficult for him to get around.` to the figcaption element.

   e. In figure element 5, add the pig picture and use `pig standing` for the alt text. Add the text `Rosie was just a baby when she arrived. Now she has babies.` to the figcaption element.

   f. In figure element 6, add the baby-pig picture and use `pig standing` for the alt text. Add the text `Squirt is one of Rosie's babies.` to the figcaption element.

   g. In figure element 7, add the house picture and use `face of a horse` for the alt text. Add the text `Muffin has come a long way. She was very thin when she was rescued.` to the figcaption element.

   h. In figure element 8, add the hawk picture and use `baby hawk` for the alt text. Add the text `Poor Harley was rescued when he was just three weeks old. He is getting big and will be released in about a month.` to the figcaption element.

   i. In figure element 9, add the bearded-dragon picture and use `bearded dragon` for the alt text. Add the text `Gizmo was abandoned by his owner and is available for adoption.` to the figcaption element.

   j. In figure element 10, add the bird picture and use `cockatoo` for the alt text. Add the text `Peaches was also abandoned by his owner. He loves to talk.` to the figcaption element.

   k. In figure element 11, add the hedgehog picture and use `hedgehog` for the alt text. Add the text `Sonny was just a baby when he was brought to us for rehabilitation.` to the figcaption element.

   l. In figure element 12, add the tortoise-pyramid picture and use `tortoise with shell pyramiding` for the alt text. Add the text `Poor Victor has "shell pyramiding," a form of bone disease.` to the figcaption element.

8. In the styles.css file, add the `aside, figure`, and `figcaption` elements to the CSS reset.

9. Below the .round style rule, add the following style rules:

   a. Add a new style rule for the `aside` element that aligns the text `center`, sets the font size to `1.5em`, sets the font weight to `bold`, and sets a text shadow value to `4px 4px 10px #c5a687`.

   b. Add a new style rule for the `figure` element that sets a border value to `4px solid #2a1f14`, sets a box shadow value to `6px 6px 10px #c5a687`, sets a maximum width of `400px`, and sets a margin value of `2% auto`.

   c. Add a new style rule for the `figcaption` element that sets the padding to `2%` and a top border value to `4px solid #2a1f14`.

10. In the tablet media query, below the style rule for nav anchor elements, add the following style rules:

   a. Add a style rule for the grid class selector that sets the display to a `grid`, sets the grid template columns to a two-column layout, and sets the grid gap to `10px`.

   b. Add a style rule for the aside element that sets the grid column value to `1 / span 2`.

11. In the desktop media query, add a declaration to the nav li a:hover style rule that sets the opacity to 0.5.

12. In the desktop media query, below the last style rule, add the following style rules:

   a. Add a style rule for the grid class selector that sets the grid template columns to a three-column layout, and sets the grid gap to `30px`.

   b. Add a style rule for the aside element that sets the grid column value to `1 / span 3`, and set the font size to `2em`.

13. In the large desktop media query, below the last style rule, add the following style rules:

   a. Add a style rule for the grid class selector that sets the grid template columns to a four-column layout.

   b. Add a style rule for the aside element that sets the grid column value to `1 / span 4`, and set the font size to `3em`.

14. Add the following link elements within the head element on all of the HTML files, including the template.html file:

```
<link rel="shortcut icon" href="images/favicon.ico">

<link rel="icon" type="image/png" sizes="32x32" href="images/favicon-32.png">

<link rel="apple-touch-icon" sizes="180x180" href="images/apple-touch-icon.png">

<link rel="icon" sizes="192x192" href="images/android-chrome-192.png">
```

15. Validate your HTML and CSS files and correct any errors.

16. Save all files, open the gallery.html page within Google Chrome's device mode, and view the page in a mobile, tablet, desktop, and large desktop viewports. Exit device mode, view the page in the desktop viewport, and use your mouse to hover over a navigation link to see the opacity effect.

17. Review your files for best coding practices; ensure proper spacing and indents for improved readability.

Continued >

In the Lab *continued*

18. Submit your assignment in the format specified by your instructor.

19. ✸ In this assignment, you created style rules for the aside, figure, and figcaption elements. Discuss at least three different declarations you would use to improve the appearance of these elements.

Lab 3: Integrating HTML 5 Semantic Elements for the Student Clubs and Events Website

Problem: You and several of your classmates have decided to help increase student involvement in school clubs and events by creating a website to promote awareness about the various activities. You have already developed a responsive web design website and now need to integrate additional HTML 5 semantic elements and create a new page.

Instructions: Perform the following tasks:

1. As a team, review your current pages to determine where you can replace div elements with article, section, or aside elements, and then update those elements as appropriate. Add these elements to the CSS reset style rule.

2. As a team, review and discuss where you can integrate figure elements and at least one figcaption element. Add these elements to the CSS reset style rule.

3. As a team, discuss and create a new page for your website. Use your template.html file to create the new page. Add the current date to the comment near the top of the page, and update the file name and the text within the title element.

4. Style your new elements or create and style class attributes to style the new element content.

5. Integrate and use the CSS grid layout within your website. Include a style rule that spans an element across at least two grid columns.

6. Use the opacity property or rgba() function in your style sheet.

7. Use at least one text shadow and at least one box shadow within your website.

8. Create and add a favicon to all HTML pages within the website.

9. Validate your HTML and CSS files and correct any errors.

10. Save and view all files with Google Chrome's device mode, and view the new page in a mobile, tablet, desktop and large desktop viewports. Test your links to ensure they work.

11. Review your files for best coding practices; ensure proper spacing and indents for improved readability.

12. Submit your answers in the format specified by your instructor.

13. ✸ In this assignment, you worked with your team to create a new page for your website. Discuss the steps you took to create your new page.

Consider This: Your Turn

Apply your creative thinking and problem-solving skills to design and implement a solution.

1. Improving the Design of Your Personal Portfolio Website
Personal

Part 1: In Chapter 6, you completed your personal portfolio website for a responsive design. In this exercise, you update the website as follows:

1. Review your current pages to determine where you can replace div elements with article, section, or aside elements, and then update those elements as appropriate. Add these elements to the CSS reset style rule.

2. Your header element contains your picture. Wrap your picture within a figure element and place your mission statement or tag line within a figcaption element. Update all pages to include this change, including your template file. Add the figure and figcaption elements to the CSS reset style rule.

3. Create a new page for your website. Use your template file to create the new page. Add the current date to the comment near the top of the page, and update the file name and the text within the title element.

4. Add content to your new page. Use your CSS file to style your new elements and/or create and style class attributes to style the new element content.

5. Integrate and use the CSS grid layout within your website.

6. Use at least one text shadow or one box shadow within your website.

7. Validate your HTML and CSS files and correct any errors.

8. Save and view all files with Google Chrome's device mode, and view the new page in a mobile, tablet, desktop, and large desktop viewports. Test your links to ensure they work.

9. Review your files for best coding practices; ensure proper spacing and indents for improved readability.

10. Submit the assignment in the format specified by your instructor.

Part 2: ✷ Use your browser to research the HTML 5 details and summary semantic elements. Discuss where you could integrate these elements with your site and why.

2. Improving the Design of the Dog Grooming Website

Professional

Note: To complete this assignment, you will be required to use the Data Files. Please contact your instructor for information about accessing the Data Files.

Part 1: In Chapter 6, you completed a responsive design website for a dog grooming website. In this exercise, you update the site as follows:

1. Review your current pages to determine where you can replace div elements with article, section, or aside elements, and then update those elements as appropriate. Add these elements to the CSS reset style rule.

2. Review where you can integrate figure elements and at least three figcaption elements. Add these elements to the CSS reset style rule.

3. Create a new page for your website. Use your template.html file to create the new page. Add the current date to the comment near the top of the page, and update the file name and the text within the title element. Pictures of dog groomers are provided with the chapter07\your_turn2 Data Files folder if you want to use them on your new page.

4. Add content to your new page. Use your CSS file to style your new elements and/or create and style class attributes to style the new element content.

5. Integrate and use the CSS grid layout within your website. Include a style rule that spans an element across at least two grid columns.

6. Use the opacity property or rgba() function in your style sheet.

7. Use at least one text shadow or one box shadow within your website.

8. Create and add a favicon to all HTML pages within the website.

9. Validate your HTML and CSS files and correct any errors.

Continued >

Consider This: Your Turn *continued*

10. Save and view all files with Google Chrome's device mode, and view the new page in a mobile, tablet, desktop, and large desktop viewports. Test your links to ensure they work.

11. Review your files for best coding practices; ensure proper spacing and indents for improved readability.

12. Submit the assignment in the format specified by your instructor.

Part 2: ✳ In this assignment, you may have created and styled an aside element. Use your browser to research different ideas for styling the aside element. Provide a screen shot of the designs you found and a link to each resource.

3. Improving the Design of the Future Technologies Website
Research and Collaboration

Part 1: In Chapter 6, you completed a responsive design website for the future technologies website. In this exercise, you will work with your group to update the website as follows:

1. As a team, review your current pages to determine where you can replace div elements with article, section, or aside elements, and then update those elements as appropriate. Add these elements to the CSS reset style rule.

2. As a team, review and discuss where you can integrate figure elements and at least two figcaption elements. Add these elements to the CSS reset style rule.

3. As a team, discuss and create a new page for your website. Use your template.html file to create the new page. Add the current date to the comment near the top of the page, and update the file name and the text within the title element. Pictures of new technology are provided with the chapter07\your_turn3 Data Files folder if you want to use them on your new page.

4. Add content to your new page. Use your CSS file to style your new elements and/or create and style class attributes to style the new element content.

5. Integrate and use the CSS grid layout within your website. Include a style rule that spans an element across at least two grid columns.

6. Use the opacity property or rgba() function in your style sheet.

7. Use at least one text shadow and at least one box shadow within your website.

8. Create and add a favicon to all HTML pages within the website.

9. Validate your HTML and CSS files and correct any errors.

10. Save and view all files with Google Chrome's device mode, and view the new page in a mobile, tablet, desktop and large desktop viewports. Test your links to ensure they work.

11. Review your files for best coding practices; ensure proper spacing and indents for improved readability.

12. Submit the assignment in the format specified by your instructor.

Part 2: ✳ Each person in the group should research different layout design strategies for the website and present them to the group for a discussion. In the discussion, the group should review each strategy and make a decision to apply the most popular layout strategy. Organize your group's findings as requested by your instructor.

8 Creating Tables and Forms

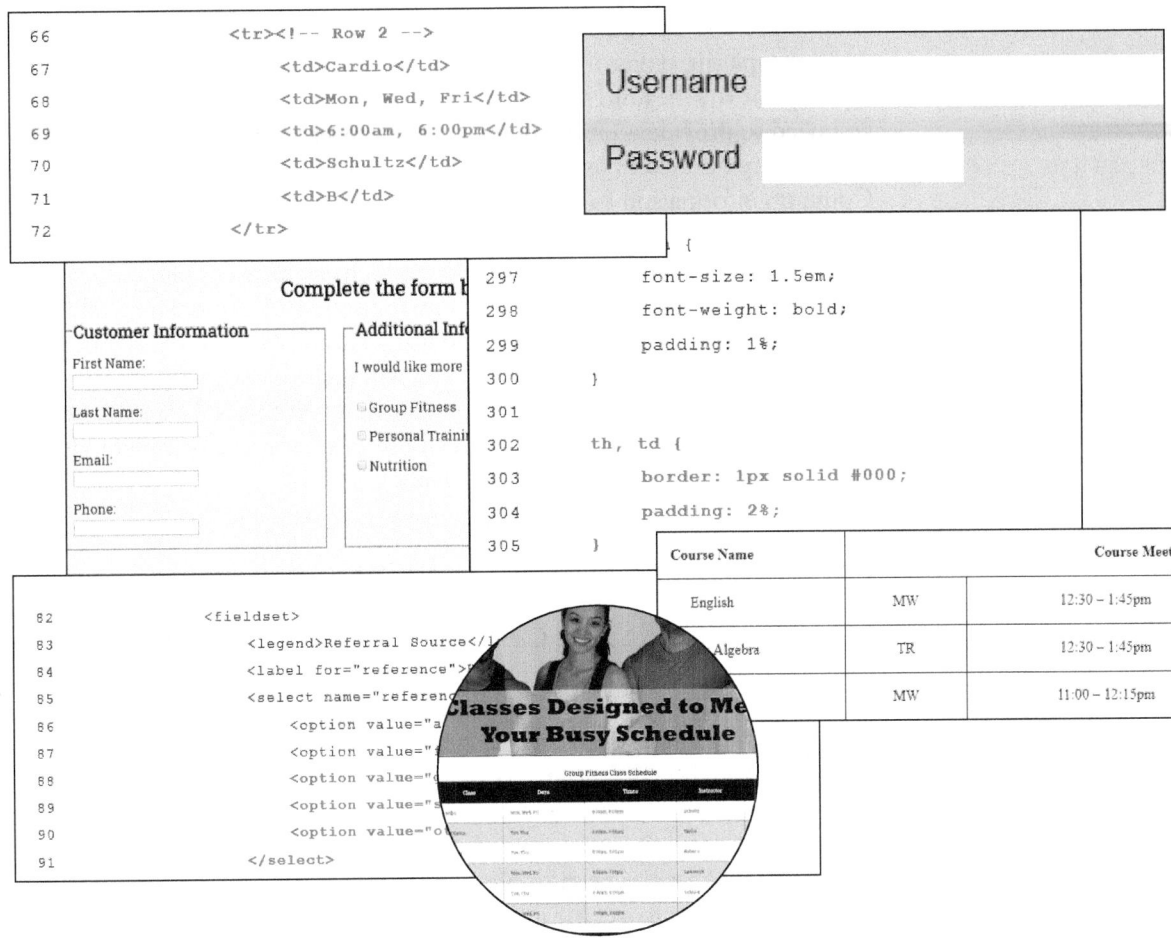

Objectives

You will have mastered the material in this chapter when you can:

- Define table elements
- Describe the steps used to plan, design, and code a table
- Create a table with rows and data
- Insert a table caption
- Style a table for tablet and desktop viewports
- Describe form controls and their uses
- Use the form and input elements
- Create text input controls, labels, and check boxes
- Create a selection menu with multiple options
- Use the textarea element
- Create a Submit button

8 | Creating Tables and Forms

Introduction

Content you can organize into categories is often best presented in a table format. A **table** presents related information in rows and columns, and is especially useful when comparing types of data or listing topics and details. Tables can use column headings or row headings to identify categories or topics. Tables are also helpful when you need to provide a lot of content in a compact form.

Many businesses use **forms** to collect information about their customers. Common information to collect includes a customer's first and last names, address, email address, and phone number. Websites provide forms so visitors can create an account, register for an event, or make a purchase, for example.

In this chapter, you will learn how to use HTML to create a table and a form on a webpage. After creating the table using several HTML elements, you format the table using CSS. To create the form, you will include several controls on a webpage, including check boxes, a drop-down menu, and text boxes. You will also learn how to add a Submit button that customers can use to submit the completed form. Finally, you will learn to style the form elements using CSS.

Project—Create a Table and a Form

In Chapter 8, you create the Classes page, which contains information about the classes offered at the Forward Fitness Club. The classes are offered on various days and times during the week, led by an instructor, and held in a room at the club. You create and style a table to display a class schedule in a compact format for tablet and desktop viewports. You display a brief version of the class schedule as a list for the mobile viewport because the table does not adapt well to fit on the screens of mobile devices.

In addition, you add a form to the Contact Us page. The goal of the projects completed thus far has been to present content *to* website visitors. In this chapter, you will learn how to get information *from* website visitors by adding a form for user input. The form collects information about potential new clients and provides the information to the Forward Fitness Club owners for follow-up. You then style the form for mobile, tablet, and desktop viewports.

The project in this chapter improves a website by including a table and a form. To perform these tasks, you first create the Classes page and insert a table. Next, you complete the table by adding a table caption, table header, table rows, and table data. In the style sheet, you add style rules for the table elements for tablet and desktop viewports. For the mobile viewport, you add a short version of the class information to the new Classes page. Next, you create a form on the Contact Us page, and then apply styles to the form for mobile, tablet, and desktop viewports. Figure 8–1 shows the new Classes page for mobile, tablet, and desktop viewports. Figure 8–2 shows the form on the Contact Us page for mobile, tablet, and desktop viewports.

(a) Classes Page in Mobile Viewport

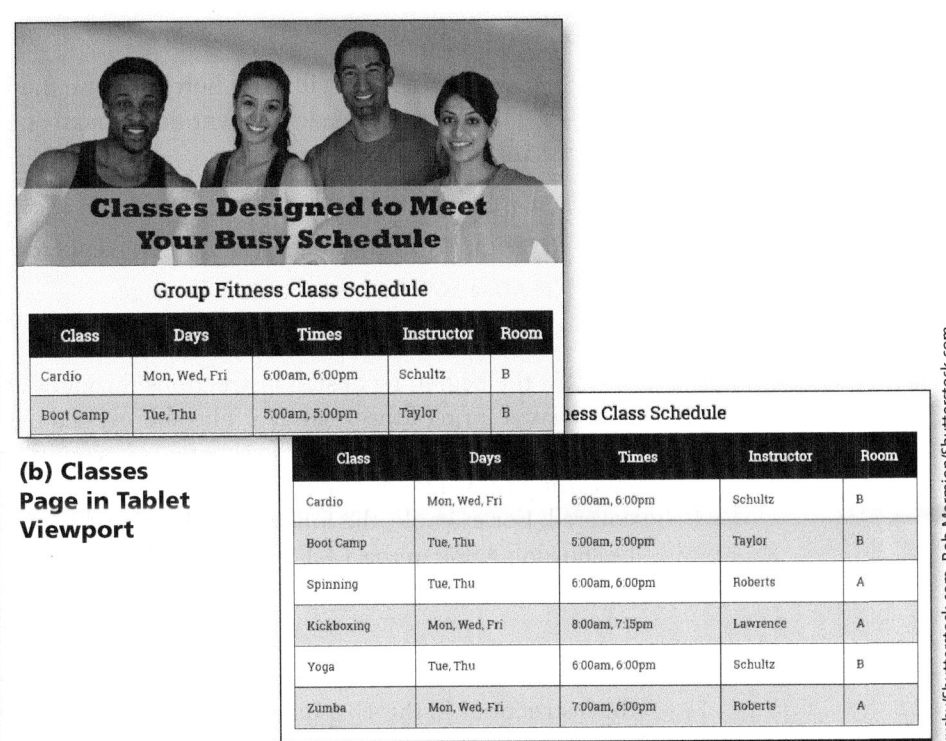

(b) Classes Page in Tablet Viewport

(c) Classes Page in Desktop Viewport

Figure 8–1

(a) Contact Us Page in Mobile Viewport

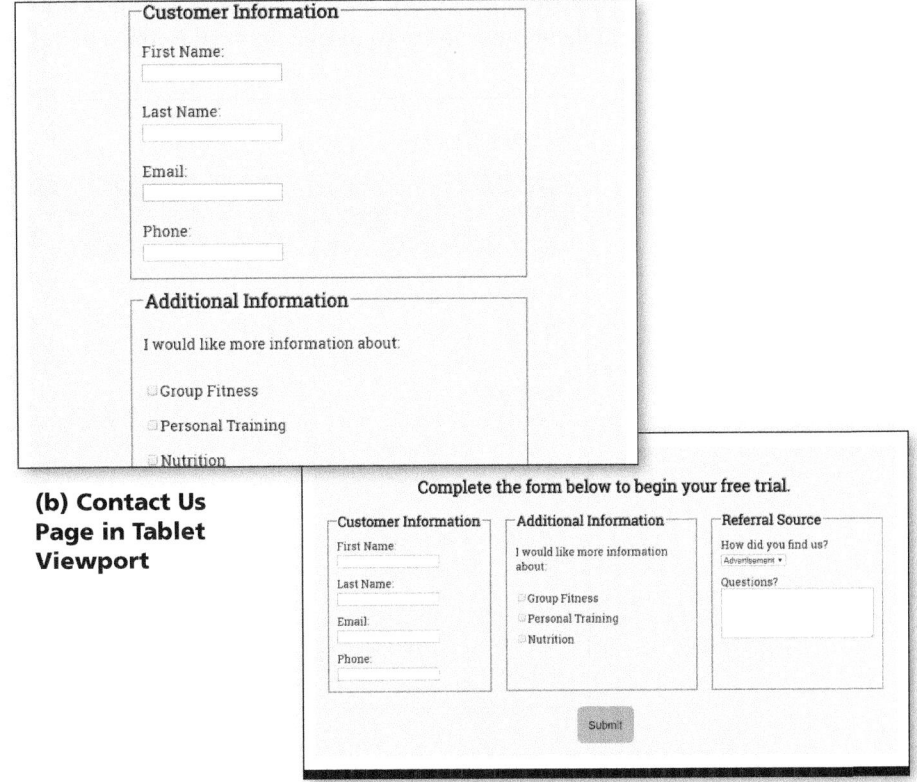

(b) Contact Us Page in Tablet Viewport

(c) Contact Us Page in Desktop Viewport

Figure 8–2

Roadmap

In this chapter, you will learn how to create the webpages shown in Figures 8–1 and 8–2. The following roadmap identifies general activities you will perform as you progress through this chapter:

1. CREATE the CLASSES PAGE AND its TABLE.
2. STYLE the TABLE for tablet and desktop viewports.
3. CREATE a FORM on the Contact Us page.
4. STYLE the FORM for mobile, tablet, and desktop viewports.

At the beginning of step instructions throughout the chapter, you will see an abbreviated form of this roadmap. The abbreviated roadmap uses colors to indicate chapter progress: gray means the chapter is beyond that activity; blue means the task being shown is covered in that activity, and black means that activity is yet to be covered. For example, the following abbreviated roadmap indicates the chapter would be showing a task in the 3 CREATE FORM activity.

1 CREATE CLASSES PAGE & TABLE | 2 STYLE TABLE
3 CREATE FORM | **4 STYLE FORM**

Use the abbreviated roadmap as a progress guide while you read or step through the instructions in this chapter.

Discovering Tables

Tables compare data or outline a detailed topic, such as a schedule or menu in a compact format. For example, Figure 8–3 shows how the University of Tampa uses a table on its website to display its final exam schedule.

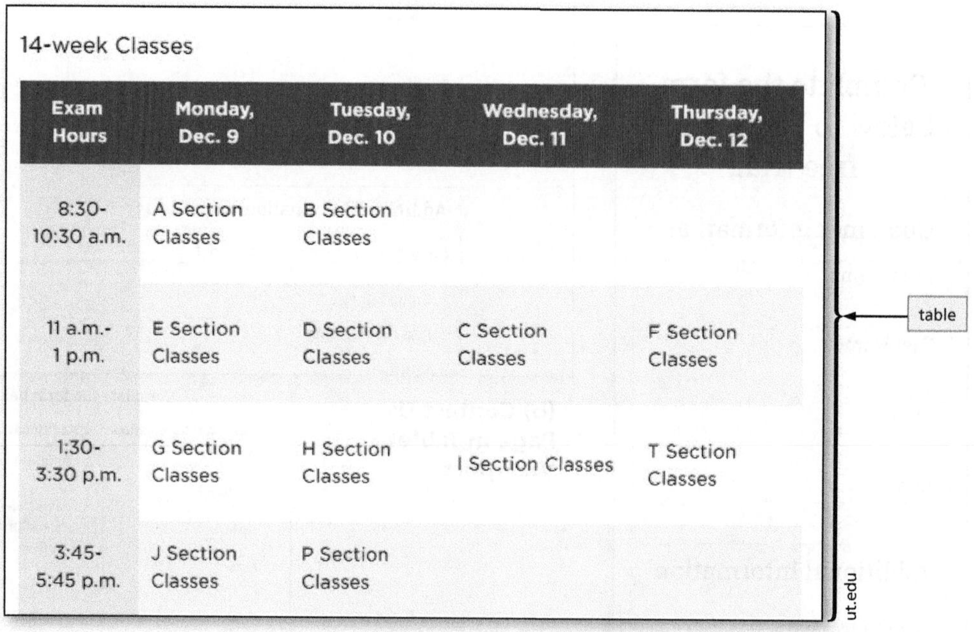

14-week Classes				
Exam Hours	**Monday, Dec. 9**	**Tuesday, Dec. 10**	**Wednesday, Dec. 11**	**Thursday, Dec. 12**
8:30-10:30 a.m.	A Section Classes	B Section Classes		
11 a.m.-1 p.m.	E Section Classes	D Section Classes	C Section Classes	F Section Classes
1:30-3:30 p.m.	G Section Classes	H Section Classes	I Section Classes	T Section Classes
3:45-5:45 p.m.	J Section Classes	P Section Classes		

table

ut.edu

Figure 8–3

A table consists of rows, columns, and cells, much like a spreadsheet. A **row** is a horizontal line of information. A **column** is a vertical line of information. A **cell** is the intersection of a row and a column and usually contains data. Figure 8–4 shows examples of these three elements.

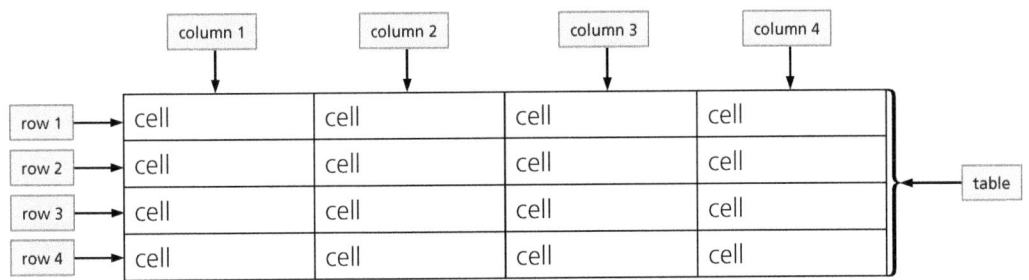

Figure 8–4

A cell can be one of two types: a header cell or a data cell. A **header cell** displays text as bold and center-aligned. For example, you use header cells to display column headings that identify the information in each column. A **data cell** displays normal, left-aligned text and contains information appropriate for the column and row. You should understand the differences among table row, header cell, and data cell elements so you can use HTML to create a table that matches your design.

Creating a Table with HTML Elements

Table 8–1 lists the HTML elements you use to create a table.

Table 8–1 HTML Table Elements

Element	Indicates the start and end of:	Contains:
<table> ... </table>	Table within a webpage	All related table elements
<tr> ... </tr>	Table row within a table	Table data cells
<th> ... </th>	Table header cell	Table header content
<td> ... </td>	Table data	Table cell content
<caption> ... </caption>	Table caption	Table caption or title
<thead> ... </thead >	Table header area	Grouped header content
<tbody> ... </tbody >	Table body area	Grouped body content
<tfooter> ... </tfooter >	Table footer area	Grouped footer content

To create a table on a webpage, start with the <table> and </table> tags and then add table rows and table data within those tags. The following is an example of code used to create the table shown in Figure 8–5, which consists of four rows and four columns.

```
<table>
  <tr>
      <td>Semester 1</td>
      <td>Semester 2</td>
      <td>Semester 3</td>
      <td>Semester 4</td>
  </tr>
  <tr>
      <td>English I</td>
      <td>English II</td>
      <td>Spanish I</td>
      <td>Spanish II</td>
  </tr>
```

```
<tr>
    <td>College Algebra</td>
    <td>College Geometry</td>
    <td>Calculus</td>
    <td>Trigonometry</td>
</tr>
<tr>
    <td>Physical Science</td>
    <td>Biology</td>
    <td>Humanities</td>
    <td>World History</td>
</tr>
</table>
```

td elements

Semester 1	Semester 2	Semester 3	Semester 4
English I	English II	Spanish I	Spanish II
College Algebra	College Geometry	Calculus	Trigonometry
Physical Science	Biology	Humanities	World History

tr elements

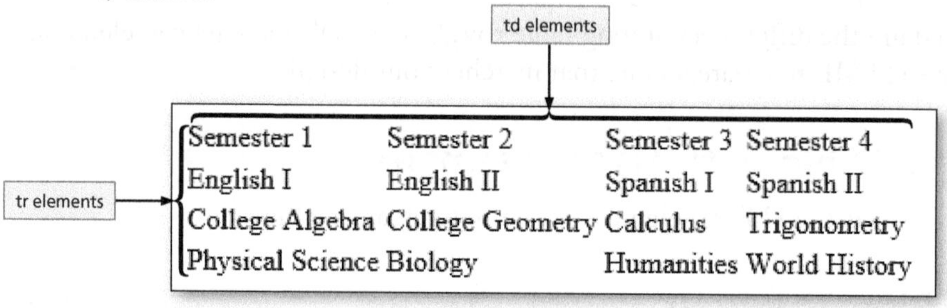

Figure 8–5

The <table> tag indicates the beginning of the table. Likewise, the </table> tag indicates the end of a table. Each table row is indicated by a starting <tr> tag and an ending </tr> tag. The table shown in Figure 8–5 has four table row elements. Each table row element contains table data elements, indicated by a starting <td> tag and an ending </td> tag. The number of table data elements in each table row element determines the number of columns in the table. In this example, four table data elements are used within each table row element, which means this table consists of four columns.

The table shown in Figure 8–5 does not have any applied style rules, so typical table formatting, such as borders and spacing, is not included by default. You specify properties, such as borders, margins, and padding in a style sheet.

Table Borders, Headers, and Captions

BTW
WCAG and Tables
For a web accessibility tutorial with tables, visit w3.org/WAI/tutorials/tables/.

In addition to columns and rows, tables also include features such as borders, headers, and captions. A **table border** is the line that defines the perimeter of the table. You display table borders using a style rule in a style sheet. A **table header** is a heading cell, which is formatted with bold, centered text that indicates the purpose of the row or column. Headers are typically used to identify row or column content. Nonvisual browsers also use headers to identify table content. The Web Content Accessibility Guideline (WCAG) 1.3.1 addresses the importance of using table headers within a table. Screen readers speak one cell at a time and will include a reference to the cell's table header. Define a table header with a starting <th> tag and an ending </th> tag.

A **table caption** is descriptive text that serves as a title or identifies the table's purpose. The table caption text appears above a table, spans its length, and is center-aligned by default. Define a table caption with a starting <caption> tag and an ending </caption> tag. When using a table caption, insert it after the starting <table> tag. A table can have only one caption.

Tables can include headers and captions individually or in combination. The purpose for the table dictates which of these features you use. Figure 8–6 shows a table created with the following code, which includes a table caption and table headers. The figure also shows a table border as defined by an external style sheet.

```
<table>
  <caption>College Course Recommendations by Semester</caption>
  <tr>
      <th>Semester 1</th>
      <th>Semester 2</th>
      <th>Semester 3</th>
      <th>Semester 4</th>
  </tr>
  <tr>
      <td>English I</td>
      <td>English II</td>
      <td>Spanish I</td>
      <td>Spanish II</td>
  </tr>
  <tr>
      <td>College Algebra</td>
      <td>College Geometry</td>
      <td>Calculus</td>
      <td>Trigonometry</td>
  </tr>
  <tr>
      <td>Physical Science</td>
      <td>Biology</td>
      <td>Humanities</td>
      <td>World History</td>
  </tr>
</table>
```

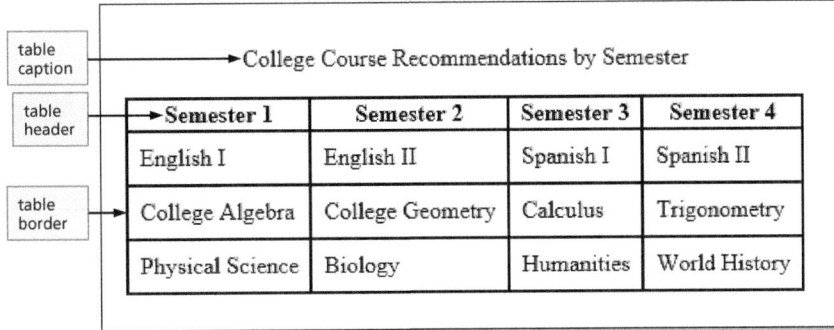

Figure 8–6

What is the difference between the <th> and the <thead> tags?
The table header element uses the <th> and </th> tags to create table header cells. A header cell contains a header title, such as a column or row title, which describes the column or row content. The table head element uses the <thead> and </thead> tags to group table header content within a table and is used with the table body and table footer elements to identify each part of a table. When you use the table head, table body, and table footer elements, users can scroll the table body content separate from the table head and table footer. For a large table that spans more than one page, users can also print the table head at the top of the page and the table footer at the bottom.

CONSIDER THIS

Table Element Attributes

You can use three primary attributes within a table: id, colspan, and rowspan.

As with div elements, use the id attribute to specify a unique id for a table when necessary.

If you need to span text or other content across two or more columns, use the colspan attribute. The following is an example of how to construct a table using the colspan attribute to span text across three columns:

```
<table>
   <tr>
      <th>Course Name</th>
      <th colspan="3">Course Meeting</th>
   </tr>
   <tr>
      <td>English</td>
      <td>MW</td>
      <td>12:30 - 1:45pm</td>
      <td>Room 205</td>
   </tr>
   <tr>
      <td>College Algebra</td>
      <td>TR</td>
      <td>12:30 - 1:45pm</td>
      <td>Room 112</td>
   </tr>
   <tr>
      <td>Biology</td>
      <td>MW</td>
      <td>11:00 - 12:15pm</td>
      <td>Room 315</td>
   </tr>
</table>
```

The table, as displayed in a browser, is shown in Figure 8–7.

Course Name	Course Meeting		
English	MW	12:30 – 1:45pm	Room 205
College Algebra	TR	12:30 – 1:45pm	Room 112
Biology	MW	11:00 – 12:15pm	Room 315

Figure 8–7

Likewise, if you need to span content across two or more rows, use the rowspan attribute. The following is an example of how to construct a table using the rowspan attribute to span text across three rows:

```
<table>
   <tr>
      <th>Instructor</th>
      <td>G. Williams</td>
   </tr>
   <tr>
      <th rowspan="3">Office Hours</th>
      <td>MW: 11 - 2pm</td>
   <tr>
      <td>TR: 9:30am - 2pm</td>
   </tr>
   <tr>
      <td>F: Web Conference</td>
   </tr>
</table>
```

The table, as displayed in a browser, is shown in Figure 8–8.

<table>
<tr><th>Instructor</th><td>G. Williams</td></tr>
<tr><th rowspan="3">Office Hours</th><td>MW: 11 - 2pm</td></tr>
<tr><td>TR: 9:30am - 2pm</td></tr>
<tr><td>F: Web Conference</td></tr>
</table>

Figure 8–8

Use of Tables

Using tables for web design and page layout was quite popular in the late 1990s; however, this was a misuse of the table elements. Tables are meant to display data in rows and columns and should not be used to design a layout for a webpage.

Before you add a table, you must first determine whether it is necessary on the webpage. As general rule, use a table when it will help organize information so that that it is easier for the user to read. Tables are also useful if the webpage needs to display a structured, organized list of information. Figures 8–9a and 8–9b show examples of information displayed as text in a bulleted list and a table. The bulleted list (Figure 8–9a) provides the schedule information, but the table (Figure 8–9b) presents the same information more clearly.

BTW

Avoid Using Tables for Layout

Many legacy webpages use tables to lay out content in columns or sections. If you assume the responsibility of such a website, analyze the site, draft a wireframe, and then redesign the site using HTML 5 semantic elements. Create the site in a test environment before you publish it.

- Work Schedule
    - T. Anderson: M 12-5pm, T 2-7pm, W Off, R 8-12pm, F 8-12pm
    - E. Davis: M 8-12pm, T 8-12pm, W 12-5pm, R Off, F 2-7pm
    - J. Smith: M 8-12pm, T 12-5pm, W 8-12pm, R 2-7pm, F Off
    - S. Watson: M 12-7pm, T Off, W 2-7pm, R 12-5pm, F 12-5pm

(a) Schedule as Bulleted List

Work Schedule

Employee	Mon	Tue	Wed	Thu	Fri
T. Anderson	12 – 5pm	2 – 7pm	Off	8 – 12pm	8 – 12pm
E. Davis	8 – 12pm	8 – 12pm	12 – 5pm	Off	2 – 7pm
J. Smith	8 – 12pm	12 – 5pm	8 – 12pm	2 – 7pm	Off
S. Watson	12 – 7pm	Off	2 – 7pm	12 – 5pm	12 – 5pm

(b) Schedule as Table

Figure 8–9

Planning the Table

To create effective tables, you must plan the information that will appear in columns and rows and then create a design that presents the information clearly. Before writing any HTML code, sketch the table on paper or in an electronic document to see how many rows and columns you need and determine whether the table needs headers or a caption. Conceptualizing the table first saves time when you are determining which HTML table elements to use to create the table. Because you enter the content of a table row by row in an HTML document, you also need a sketch of the finished table to create the table accurately as you are coding.

When planning a table for responsive web design, give careful consideration to the mobile viewport. Because the screen on a mobile viewport is much smaller than a tablet or desktop viewport, tables with several columns are not conducive for mobile viewports. You might need to display only the most important table content in another form, such as a list.

Before adding a table to the Forward Fitness Club website, create the webpage that will contain the table, a schedule for the group classes the club offers.

BTW
**HTML Entities
in Tables**
You often use symbols, such as dollar signs ($) and ampersands (&) in tables to save space. To create these symbols on a webpage, use HTML entities, such as $ for a dollar sign and & for an ampersand.

To Create the Classes Page

Use the template.html file to create the Classes page, and then insert a hero image on the page. To complete this assignment, you will be required to use the Data Files. Please contact your instructor for information about accessing the Data Files. The following steps create the Classes page.

1 Copy the image file from the chapter08\fitness folder provided with the Data Files to the fitness\images folder.

2 Open the template.html file in your text editor, and then save the page as classes.html in your fitness folder.

③ Update the comment with your name and today's date, tap or click at the end of Line 33, and then press the ENTER key twice to insert new Lines 34 and 35.

④ On Line 35, type `<!-- Classes Hero Image -->` to insert a comment.

⑤ Press the ENTER key to insert a new Line 36, and then type `<div id="hero" class="tablet-desktop">` to insert a div tag.

⑥ Press the ENTER key to insert a new Line 37, increase the indent, and then type `<img src="images/classes-hero-image.jpg" alt="group of fitness people">` to insert an image.

⑦ Press the ENTER key to insert a new Line 38, decrease the indent, and then type `</div>` to insert a closing div tag (Figure 8–10).

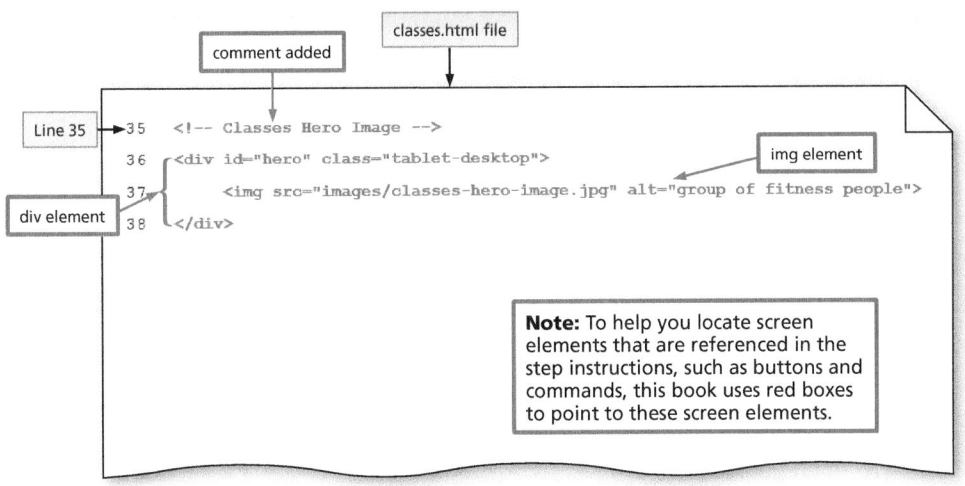

Figure 8–10

To Add a div Element to the Classes Page

Create a **div** element on the Classes page to provide separate content for a mobile user. The following step adds a **div** element to the Classes page.

① In the classes.html file, tap or click at the end of Line 41 and press the ENTER key twice to insert new Lines 42 and 43.

② On Line 43, increase the indent, and then type `<div class="mobile">` to insert a div tag.

③ Press the ENTER key twice to insert new Lines 44 and 45.

④ On Line 45, increase the indent, and then type `<h3>Group Fitness Classes </h3>` to insert a heading element.

⑤ Press the ENTER key to insert a new Line 46 and then type `<p>Boot Camp: TR 5am &amp; 5pm</p>` to insert a paragraph element.

⑥ Press the ENTER key to insert a new Line 47 and then type `<p>Cardio: MWF 6am &amp; 6pm</p>` to insert a paragraph element.

⑦ Press the ENTER key to insert a new Line 48 and then type `<p>Kickboxing: MWF 8am &amp; 7:15pm</p>` to insert a paragraph element.

8 Press the ENTER key to insert a new Line 49 and then type `<p>Spinning: TR 6am &amp; 6pm</p>` to insert a paragraph element.

9 Press the ENTER key to insert a new Line 50 and then type `<p>Yoga: TR 6am &amp; 6pm</p>` to insert a paragraph element.

10 Press the ENTER key to insert a new Line 51 and then type `<p>Zumba: MWF 7am &amp; 6pm</p>` to insert a paragraph element.

11 Press the ENTER key twice to insert new Lines 52 and 53, decrease the indent, type `</div>`, and then press the ENTER key once to insert a new blank line 54 (Figure 8–11).

Q&A What does & represent?

The & code is an HTML entity used to display an ampersand (&) on a webpage.

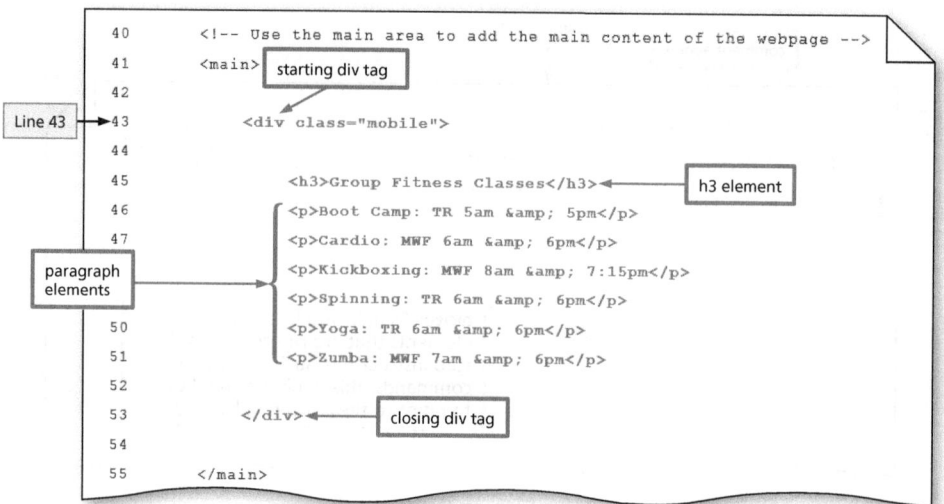

Figure 8–11

12 Save your changes, open classes.html in Google Chrome's device mode, select the mobile viewport, and then scroll down the page to view the main content (Figure 8–12).

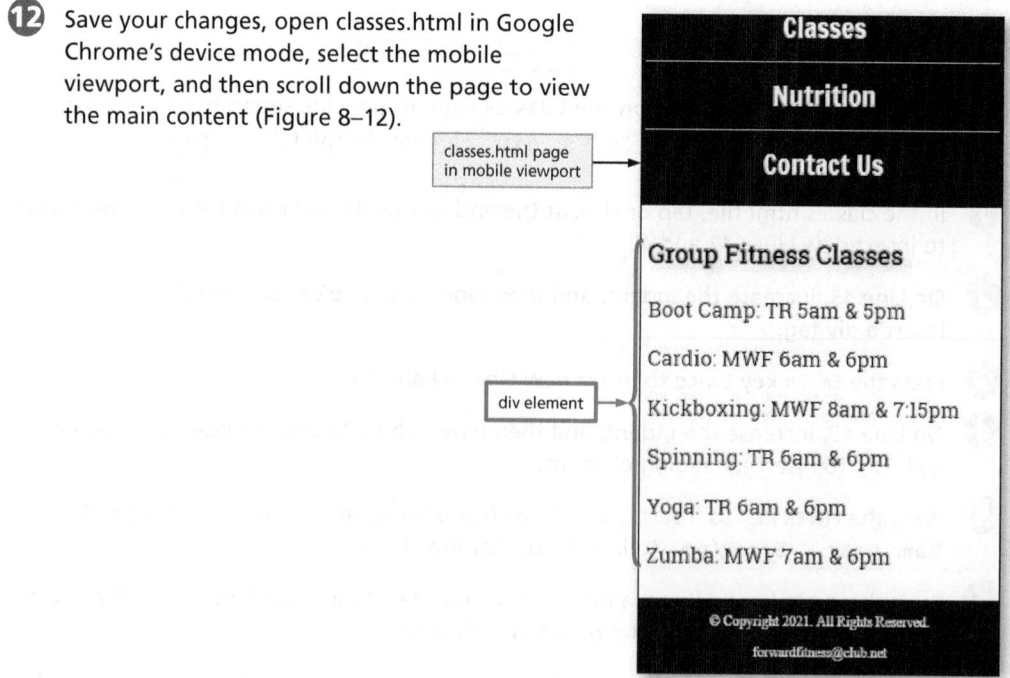

Figure 8–12

To Add a Table to the Classes Page

Next, insert a table within a new **`div class="desktop"`** element to display information about the classes offered at the Forward Fitness Club. *Why? Only the elements specified as belonging to the mobile class will appear in a mobile viewport. The table will be displayed for all other viewports.* After inserting a new **`div`** element to contain the table, insert a starting table tag and a **`caption`** element. Insert table rows, table headers, and table data elements followed by an ending table tag. The following steps add a **`div`** and **`table`** element to the Classes page.

1

- Tap or click at the end of Line 53, and then press the ENTER key twice to insert new Lines 54 and 55.

- On Line 55, type **`<div class="tablet-desktop">`** to insert a div tag.

- Press the ENTER key twice to insert new Lines 56 and 57, increase the indent, and then type **`<table><!-- Start Table -->`** to insert a starting table tag and a comment.

- Press the ENTER key to insert a new Line 58, increase the indent, and then type **`<caption>Group Fitness Class Schedule</caption>`** to insert a table caption element.

- Press the ENTER key to insert a new Line 59, and then type **`<tr><!-- Row 1 -->`** to insert a starting table row tag and a comment.

- Press the ENTER key to insert a new Line 60, increase the indent, and then type **`<th>Class</th>`** to insert a table header element (Figure 8–13).

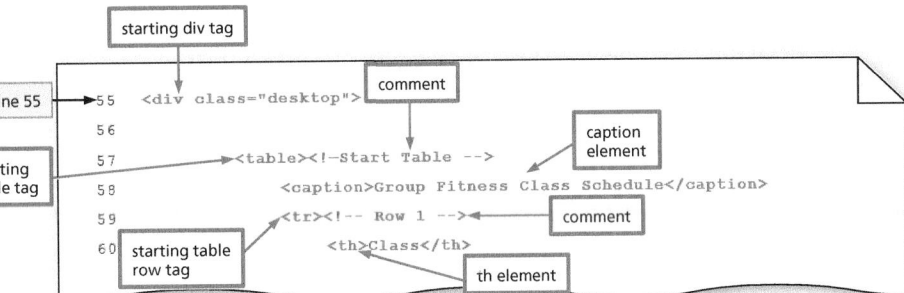

Figure 8–13

Where will the "Class" content appear in the table?
The text "Class" will appear in the first row of the table, also called the header row, as indicated by the comment on Line 54. Because it is specified as a `th` element, "Class" will be bold and centered.

2

- Press the ENTER key to insert a new Line 61, and then type **`<th>Days</th>`** to insert a table header element.

- Press the ENTER key to insert a new Line 62, and then type **`<th>Times</th>`** to insert a table header element.

- Press the ENTER key to insert a new Line 63, and then type **`<th>Instructor</th>`** to insert a table header element.

- Press the ENTER key to insert a new Line 64, and then type **`<th>Room</th>`** to insert a table header element.

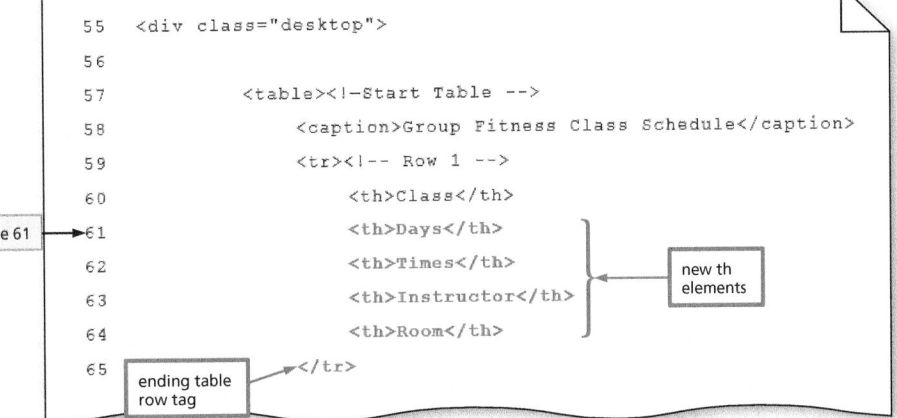

Figure 8–14

- Press the ENTER key to insert a new Line 65, decrease the indent, and then type **`</tr>`** to insert a closing table row tag (Figure 8–14).

What does the table consist of so far?
At this point, the table has one row (the header row) and five columns, one each for Class, Days, Times, Instructor, and Room.

3

- Press the ENTER key to insert a new Line 66, and then type `<tr><!-- Row 2 -->` to insert a starting table row tag and a comment.

- Press the ENTER key to insert a new Line 67, increase the indent, and then type `<td>Cardio</td>` to insert a table data element.

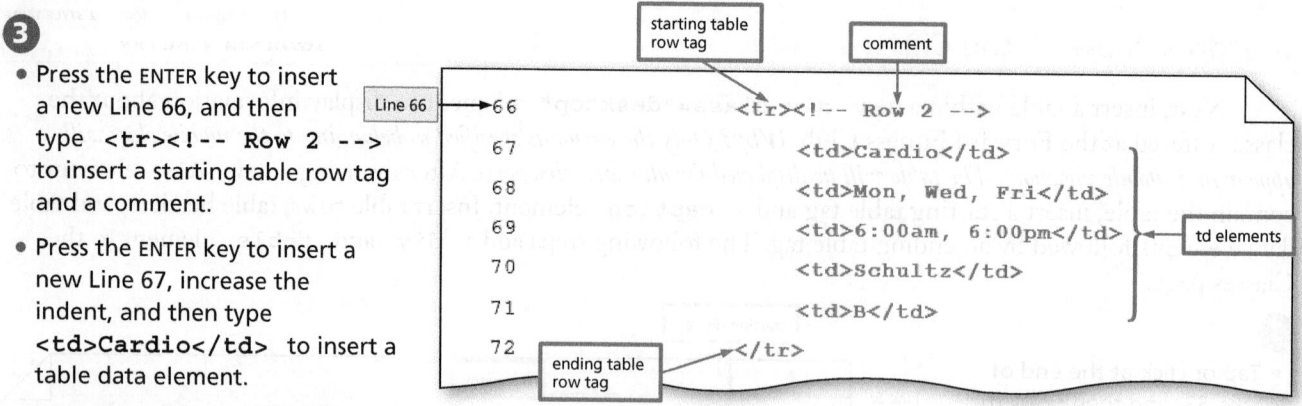

Figure 8–15

- Press the ENTER key to insert a new Line 68, and then type `<td>Mon, Wed, Fri</td>` to insert a table data element.

- Press the ENTER key to insert a new Line 69, and then type `<td>6:00am, 6:00pm</td>` to insert a table data element.

- Press the ENTER key to insert a new Line 70, and then type `<td>Schultz</td>` to insert a table data element.

- Press the ENTER key to insert a new Line 71, and then type `<td>B</td>` to insert a table data element.

- Press the ENTER key to insert a new Line 72, decrease the indent, and then type `</tr>` to insert a closing table row tag (Figure 8–15).

Q&A | What did I add to the table in this step?
You added the second row of the table, which contains details about the Cardio class.

4

- Press the ENTER key to insert a new Line 73, and then type `<tr><!-- Row 3 -->` to insert a starting table row tag and a comment.

- Press the ENTER key to insert a new Line 74, increase the indent, and then type `<td>Boot Camp </td>` to insert a table data element.

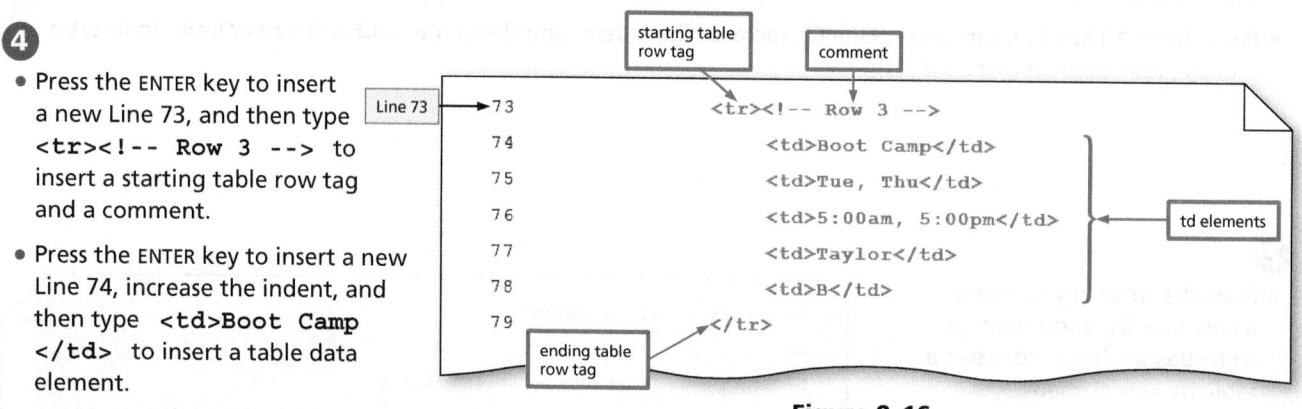

Figure 8–16

- Press the ENTER key to insert a new Line 75, and then type `<td>Tue, Thu</td>` to insert a table data element.

- Press the ENTER key to insert a new Line 76, and then type `<td>5:00am, 5:00pm</td>` to insert a table data element.

- Press the ENTER key to insert a new Line 77, and then type `<td>Taylor</td>` to insert a table data element.

- Press the ENTER key to insert a new Line 78, and then type `<td>B</td>` to insert a table data element.

- Press the ENTER key to insert a new Line 79, decrease the indent, and then type `</tr>` to insert a closing table row tag (Figure 8–16).

Q&A | What did I add to the table in this step?
You added the third row of the table, which contains details about the Boot Camp class.

5

- Press the ENTER key to insert a new Line 80, and then type `<tr><!-- Row 4 -->` to insert a starting table row tag and a comment.

- Press the ENTER key to insert a new Line 81, increase the indent, and then type `<td>Spinning</td>` to insert a table data element.

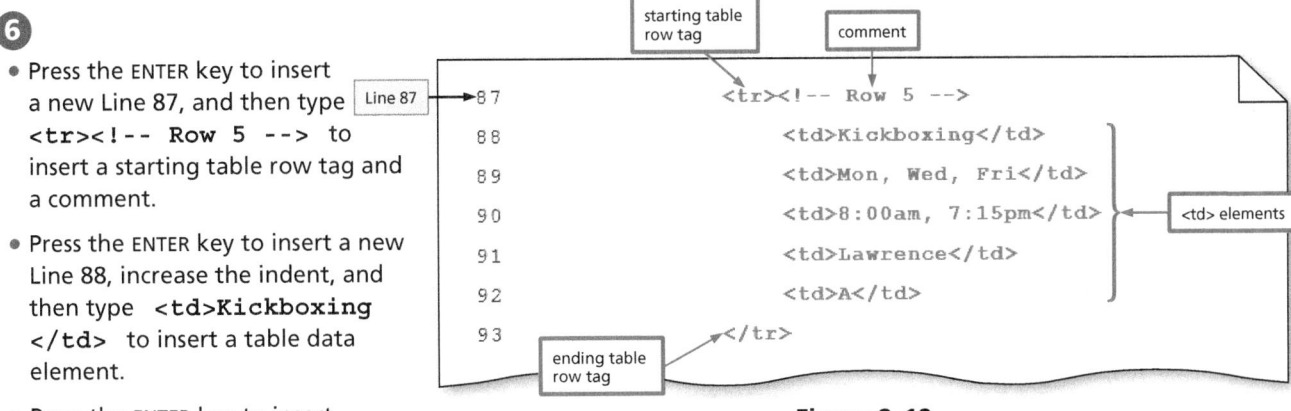

Figure 8–17

- Press the ENTER key to insert a new Line 82, and then type `<td>Tue, Thu</td>` to insert a table data element.

- Press the ENTER key to insert a new Line 83, and then type `<td>6:00am, 6:00pm</td>` to insert a table data element.

- Press the ENTER key to insert a new Line 84, and then type `<td>Roberts</td>` to insert a table data element.

- Press the ENTER key to insert a new Line 85, and then type `<td>A</td>` to insert a table data element.

- Press the ENTER key to insert a new Line 86, decrease the indent, and then type `</tr>` to insert a closing table row tag (Figure 8–17).

Q&A What did I add to the table in this step?
You added the fourth row of the table, which contains details about the Spinning class.

6

- Press the ENTER key to insert a new Line 87, and then type `<tr><!-- Row 5 -->` to insert a starting table row tag and a comment.

- Press the ENTER key to insert a new Line 88, increase the indent, and then type `<td>Kickboxing </td>` to insert a table data element.

- Press the ENTER key to insert a new Line 89, and then type `<td>Mon, Wed, Fri</td>` to insert a table data element.

```
87        <tr><!-- Row 5 -->
88            <td>Kickboxing</td>
89            <td>Mon, Wed, Fri</td>
90            <td>8:00am, 7:15pm</td>
91            <td>Lawrence</td>
92            <td>A</td>
93        </tr>
```

Figure 8–18

- Press the ENTER key to insert a new Line 90, and then type `<td>8:00am, 7:15pm</td>` to insert a table data element.

- Press the ENTER key to insert a new Line 91, and then type `<td>Lawrence</td>` to insert a table data element.

- Press the ENTER key to insert a new Line 92, and then type `<td>A</td>` to insert a table data element.

- Press the ENTER key to insert a new Line 93, decrease the indent, and then type `</tr>` to insert a closing table row tag (Figure 8–18).

7

- Press the ENTER key to insert a new Line 94, and then type `<tr><!-- Row 6 -->` to insert a starting table row tag and a comment.

- Press the ENTER key to insert a new Line 95, increase the indent, and then type `<td>Yoga</td>` to insert a table data element.

- Press the ENTER key to insert a new Line 96, and then type `<td>Tue, Thu</td>` to insert a table data element.

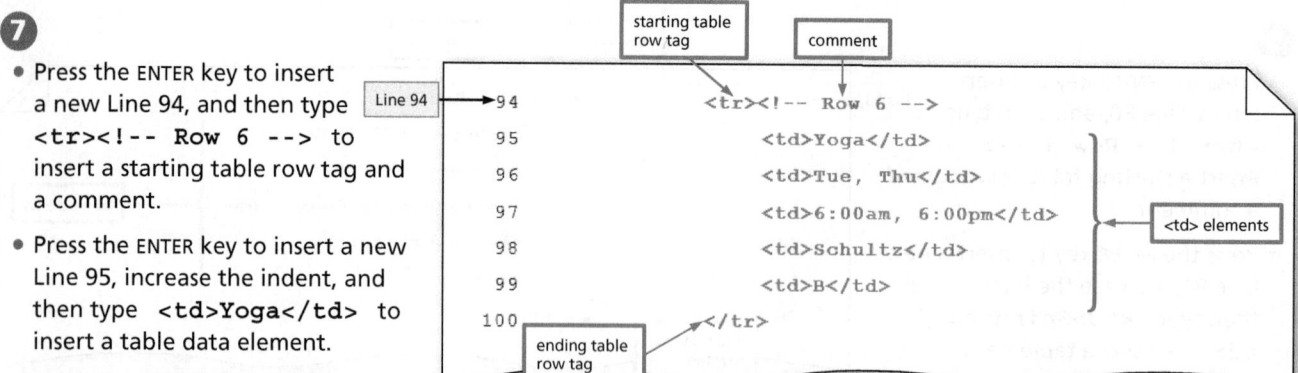

Figure 8–19

- Press the ENTER key to insert a new Line 97, and then type `<td>6:00am, 6:00pm</td>` to insert a table data element.

- Press the ENTER key to insert a new Line 98, and then type `<td>Schultz</td>` to insert a table data element that spans two rows.

- Press the ENTER key to insert a new Line 99, and then type `<td>B</td>` to insert a table data element.

- Press the ENTER key to insert a new Line 100, decrease the indent, and then type `</tr>` to insert a closing table row tag (Figure 8–19).

8

- Press the ENTER key to insert a new Line 101, and then type `<tr><!-- Row 7 -->` to insert a starting table row tag and a comment.

- Press the ENTER key to insert a new Line 102, increase the indent, and then type `<td>Zumba</td>` to insert a table data element.

- Press the ENTER key to insert a new Line 103, and then type `<td>Mon, Wed, Fri </td>` to insert a table data element.

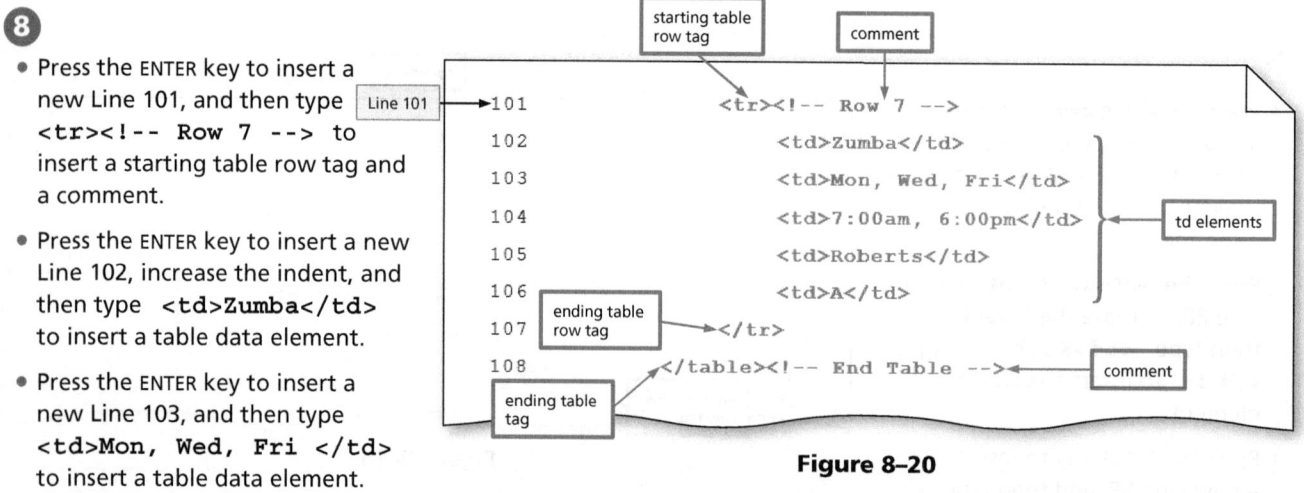

Figure 8–20

- Press the ENTER key to insert a new Line 104, and then type `<td>7:00am, 6:00pm</td>` to insert a table data element.

- Press the ENTER key to insert a new Line 105, and then type `<td>Roberts</td>` to insert a table data element.

- Press the ENTER key to insert a new Line 106, and then type `<td>A</td>` to insert a table data element.

- Press the ENTER key to insert a new Line 107, decrease the indent, and then type `</tr>` to insert a closing table row tag.

- Press the ENTER key to insert a new Line 108, decrease the indent, and then type `</table>` `<!-- End Table-->` to insert a closing table tag and comment (Figure 8–20).

Q&A What did I add to the table in the last three steps?
You added the rows 5, 6, and 7 of the table, which contain details about the Kickboxing, Yoga, and Zumba classes.

9

- Press the ENTER key twice to insert new Lines 109 and 110, decrease the indent, and then type `</div>` to insert a closing div tag.

- Save your changes, refresh classes.html in Google Chrome's device mode, select the tablet viewport, and then scroll down to view the table (Figure 8–21).

Q&A

Why do the columns appear to run together?
You have not applied styles to the table. In later steps, you will apply borders, margins, and padding so that each column and data cell appear separately.

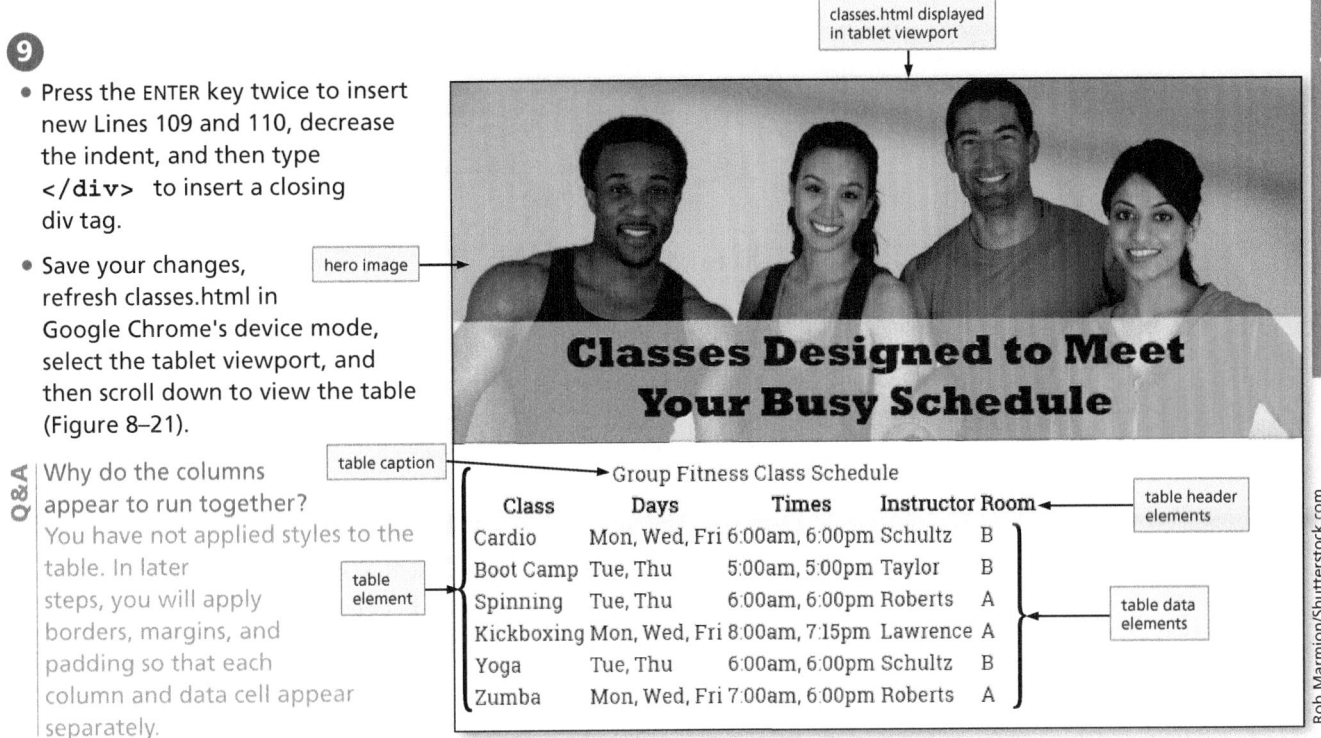

Figure 8–21

Styling Table Elements

After creating a table, style it by adding new style rules to the style sheet for the website. You can specify style rules for each table element. Table 8–2 lists common CSS properties and examples for styling tables.

Table 8–2 Common CSS Table Properties		
Property	**Example**	**Explanation**

background-color	th {
	    background-color: #ccc;
	}
		Displays the table header with a light gray background

	tr:nth-child(even) {
	    background-color: #ccc;
	}
		Applies a light gray background to even rows within the table

border	table, th, td {
	    border: 0.1em solid #000;
	}
		Displays the table, table header, and data cells with a thin solid black border

border-collapse	table {
	    border-collapse: collapse;
	}
		Collapses borders in the table so that adjacent cells share borders

color	caption {
	    color: #003300;
	}
		Displays the table caption in dark green text

height	td {
	    height: 2em;
	}
		Sets the height of a table data cell to 2em

margin	table {
	    margin-top: 2em;
	}
		Applies a 2em top margin to the table

(Continued)

Table 8–2 Common CSS Table Properties *(Continued)*

Property	Example	Explanation
padding	caption, th, td { padding: 1em; }	Applies 1em of padding to the table caption, header, and data cells
text-align	td { text-align: center; }	Aligns the table data in the center of the cell
vertical-align	td { vertical-align: center; }	Aligns the table data vertically in the middle of the cell
width	table { width: 80%; }	Sets the width of the table to 80% of the page width

When a border is applied to table elements, by default, each cell has its own border, making the table appear to use double lines between each table data cell. This type of border is called a separated border. Figure 8–22 shows a table with the default border applied.

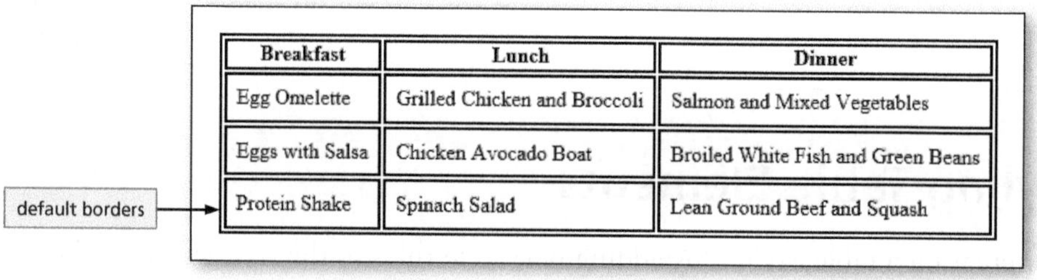

Breakfast	Lunch	Dinner
Egg Omelette	Grilled Chicken and Broccoli	Salmon and Mixed Vegetables
Eggs with Salsa	Chicken Avocado Boat	Broiled White Fish and Green Beans
Protein Shake	Spinach Salad	Lean Ground Beef and Squash

Figure 8–22

If you want to display a table with single, consolidated borders as shown in Figure 8–23, use the `border-collapse` property with a value of `collapse`. This type of border is called a collapsed border.

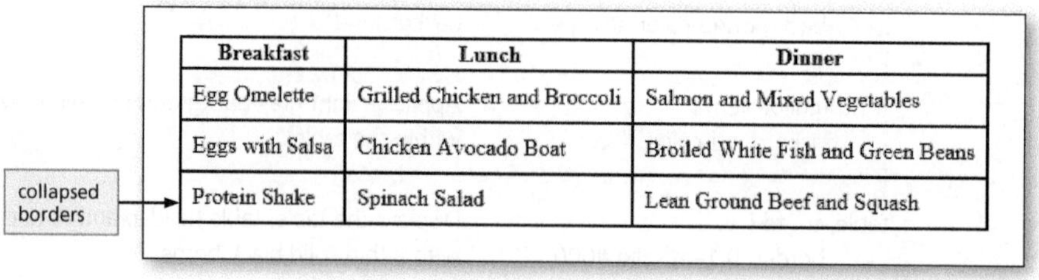

Breakfast	Lunch	Dinner
Egg Omelette	Grilled Chicken and Broccoli	Salmon and Mixed Vegetables
Eggs with Salsa	Chicken Avocado Boat	Broiled White Fish and Green Beans
Protein Shake	Spinach Salad	Lean Ground Beef and Squash

Figure 8–23

BTW
Converting a Table to a Chart
If your table contains numeric information, such as financial data or compares information among categories, consider converting your table to a chart for the mobile viewport.

Styling Tables for Responsive Web Design

It can be difficult to style a table for a mobile viewport, especially when the table consists of several columns. Many times, viewing a table requires extra horizontal and vertical scrolling by the user. Other times, the table is so small that it is difficult to read. Determine whether you can format the table so it is still easy to read in a mobile viewport. If the table is too large or complex to format, you can display the content in a different format such as a list or a chart in a mobile viewport.

To Style a Table for a Tablet Viewport

Create new style rules to style the table for the tablet viewport. *Why? Format the table to clearly present its information in a tablet viewport.* First, create a style rule for the **table** element to specify borders, including collapsed borders, to center the table on the page, and to set a width. Next, create a style rule for the caption element and specify a font size, font color, and padding. Create a style rule for **th** and **td** elements to specify borders and padding for the table header and data cells. Create a separate style rule for the **th** element to format the table header with a dark background color and light font color. Finally, create a style rule to apply a background color to every odd row within the table.

Add these new style rules to the end of the media query for the tablet layout so the rules will apply to webpages displayed in a tablet viewport. The following steps create style rules for table elements in the tablet viewport.

- Open the styles.css file in your text editor to prepare to edit it.
- Tap or click at the end of Line 286, and then press the ENTER key twice to insert new Lines 287 and 288.
- On Line 288, type **/* Tablet Viewport: Style rules for table */** to insert a new comment.
- Press the ENTER key to insert a new Line 289, and then type **table {** to insert a new selector.
- Press the ENTER key to insert a new Line 290, increase the indent, and then type **border: 1px solid #000;** to insert a new declaration.
- Press the ENTER key to insert a new Line 291, and then type **border-collapse: collapse;** to insert a new declaration.
- Press the ENTER key to insert a new Line 292, and then type **margin: 0 auto;** to insert a new declaration.
- Press the ENTER key to insert a new Line 293, and then type **width: 100%;** to insert a new declaration.
- Press the ENTER key to insert a new Line 294, decrease the indent, and then type **}** to insert a closing brace (Figure 8–24).

Q&A

What is the result of setting the left and right margins to a value of auto?
Specifying left and right margins of auto centers the table on the page.

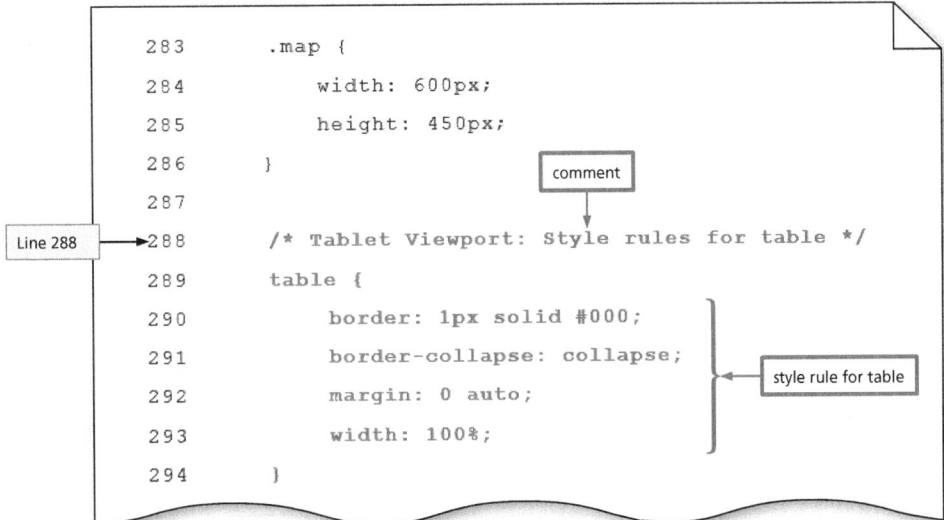

Figure 8–24

- Save your changes and refresh classes.html in your browser (Figure 8–25).

Q&A Why does the border appear only around the sides of the table?

The style rule you created applies to the table only. You will style the `th` and `td` elements in future steps.

Figure 8–25

Labels in figure: table border; table is centered on the page; table width is 100% within the main element; Rob Marmion/Shutterstock.com

Table shown in figure:

Group Fitness Class Schedule

Class	Days	Times	Instructor	Room
Cardio	Mon, Wed, Fri	6:00am, 6:00pm	Schultz	B
Boot Camp	Tue, Thu	5:00am, 5:00pm	Taylor	B
Spinning	Tue, Thu	6:00am, 6:00pm	Roberts	A
Kickboxing	Mon, Wed, Fri	8:00am, 7:15pm	Lawrence	A
Yoga	Tue, Thu	6:00am, 6:00pm	Schultz	B
Zumba	Mon, Wed, Fri	7:00am, 6:00pm	Roberts	A

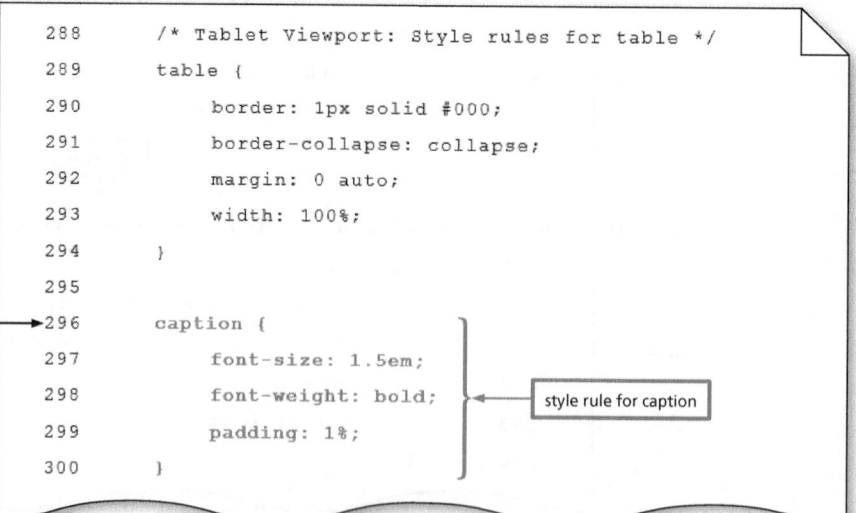

3

- In the styles.css file, tap or click at the end of Line 294, if necessary, and then press the ENTER key twice to insert new Lines 295 and 296.

- On Line 296, type **caption {** to insert a new selector.

- Press the ENTER key to insert a new Line 297, increase the indent, and then type **font-size: 1.5em;** to insert a new declaration.

- Press the ENTER key to insert a new Line 298, and then type **font-weight: bold;** to insert a new declaration.

- Press the ENTER key to insert a new Line 299, and then type **padding: 1%** to insert a new declaration.

- Press the ENTER key to insert a new Line 300, decrease the indent, and then type **}** to insert a closing brace (Figure 8–26).

```
288        /* Tablet Viewport: Style rules for table */
289        table {
290            border: 1px solid #000;
291            border-collapse: collapse;
292            margin: 0 auto;
293            width: 100%;
294        }
295
296        caption {
297            font-size: 1.5em;
298            font-weight: bold;
299            padding: 1%;
300        }
```

Labels in figure: Line 296; style rule for caption

Figure 8–26

4

• Save your changes and refresh classes.html in your browser (Figure 8–27).

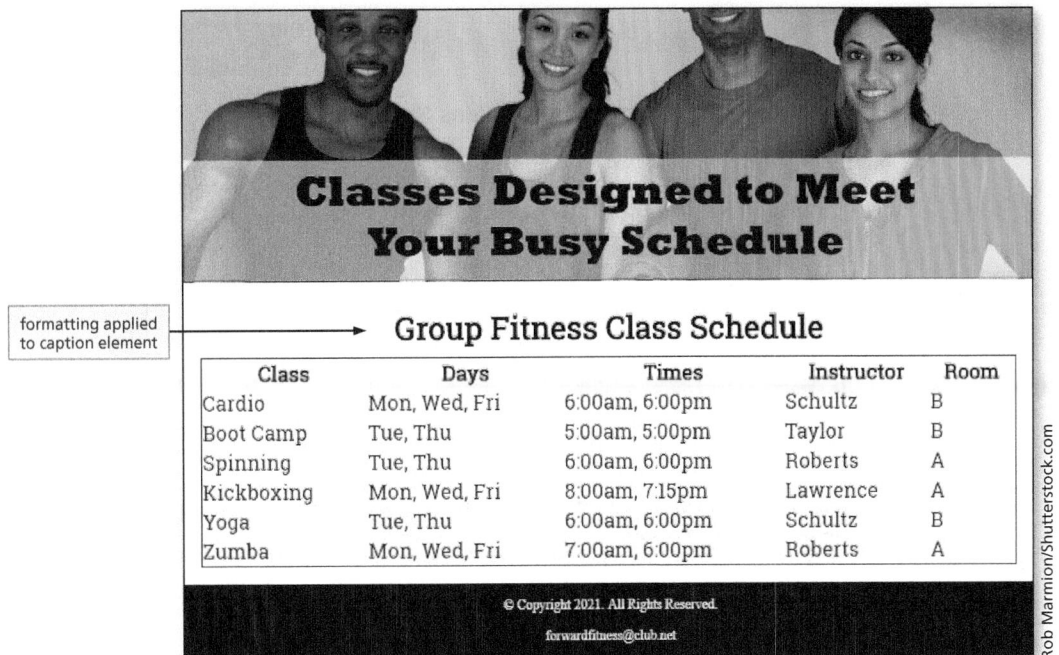

formatting applied to caption element →

Group Fitness Class Schedule

Class	Days	Times	Instructor	Room
Cardio	Mon, Wed, Fri	6:00am, 6:00pm	Schultz	B
Boot Camp	Tue, Thu	5:00am, 5:00pm	Taylor	B
Spinning	Tue, Thu	6:00am, 6:00pm	Roberts	A
Kickboxing	Mon, Wed, Fri	8:00am, 7:15pm	Lawrence	A
Yoga	Tue, Thu	6:00am, 6:00pm	Schultz	B
Zumba	Mon, Wed, Fri	7:00am, 6:00pm	Roberts	A

© Copyright 2021. All Rights Reserved.
forwardfitness@club.net

Rob Marmion/Shutterstock.com

Figure 8–27

5

• In the styles.css file, tap or click at the end of Line 300, if necessary, and then press the ENTER key twice to insert new Lines 301 and 302.

• On Line 302, type **th, td {** to insert two selectors.

• Press the ENTER key to insert a new Line 303, increase the indent, and then type **border: 1px solid #000;** to insert a new declaration.

• Press the ENTER key to insert a new Line 304, and then type **padding: 2%;** to insert a declaration.

• Press the ENTER key to insert a new Line 305, decrease the indent, and then type **}** to insert a closing brace (Figure 8–28).

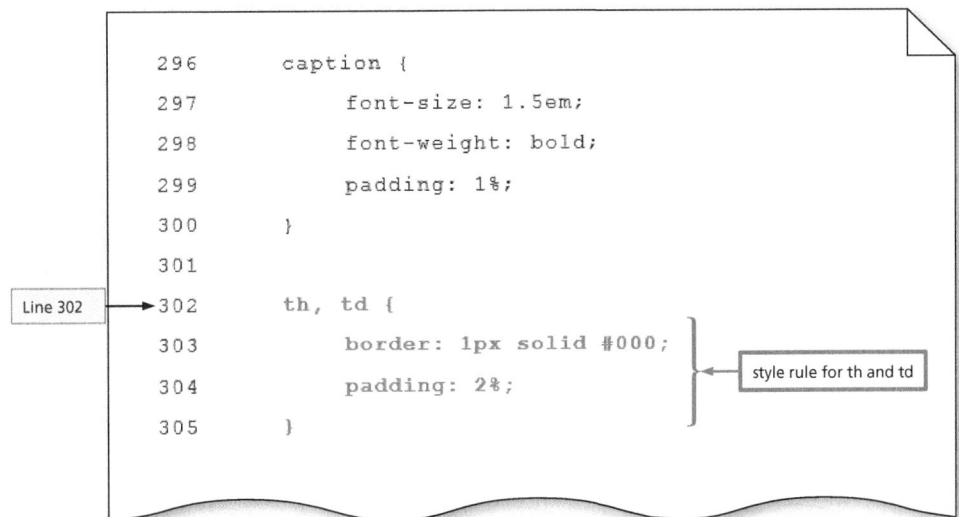

```
296        caption {
297             font-size: 1.5em;
298             font-weight: bold;
299             padding: 1%;
300        }
301
302        th, td {
303             border: 1px solid #000;
304             padding: 2%;
305        }
```

Line 302 → 302

style rule for th and td

Figure 8–28

6
- Save your changes and refresh classes.html in your browser (Figure 8–29).

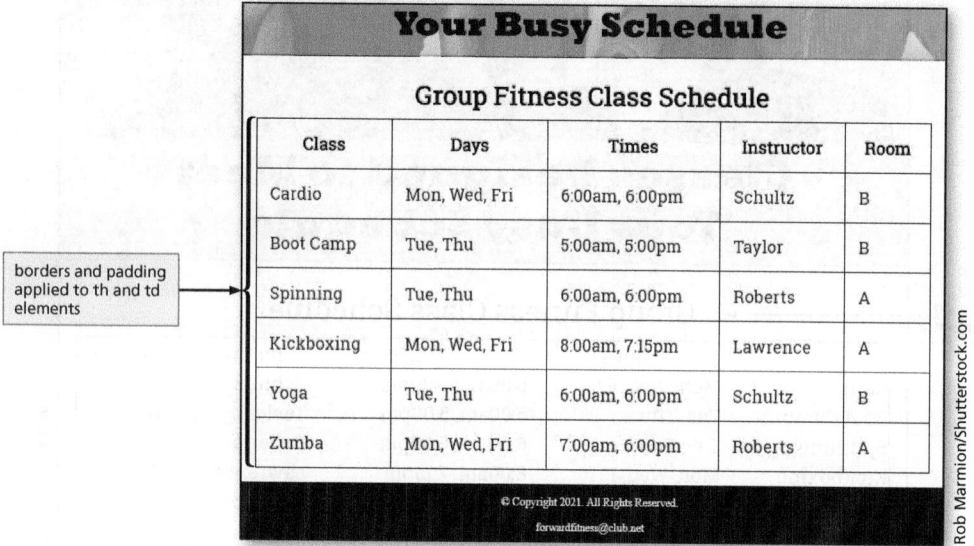

Figure 8–29

7
- In the styles.css file, tap or click at the end of Line 305, if necessary, and then press the ENTER key twice to insert new Lines 306 and 307.
- On Line 307, type `th {` to insert a new selector.
- Press the ENTER key to insert a new Line 308, increase the indent, and then type `background-color: #000;` to insert a new declaration.
- Press the ENTER key to insert a new Line 309, and then type `color: #fff;` to insert a new declaration.
- Press the ENTER key to insert a new Line 310, and then type `font-size: 1.15em;` to insert a new declaration.
- Press the ENTER key to insert a new Line 311, decrease the indent, and then type `}` to insert a closing brace (Figure 8–30).

Q&A Why do I need to create another style rule for the `th` element?
The previous style rule applied to both the `th` and the `td` elements. This style rule applies only to the `th` element and uniquely formats the table header elements to have a black background and white text.

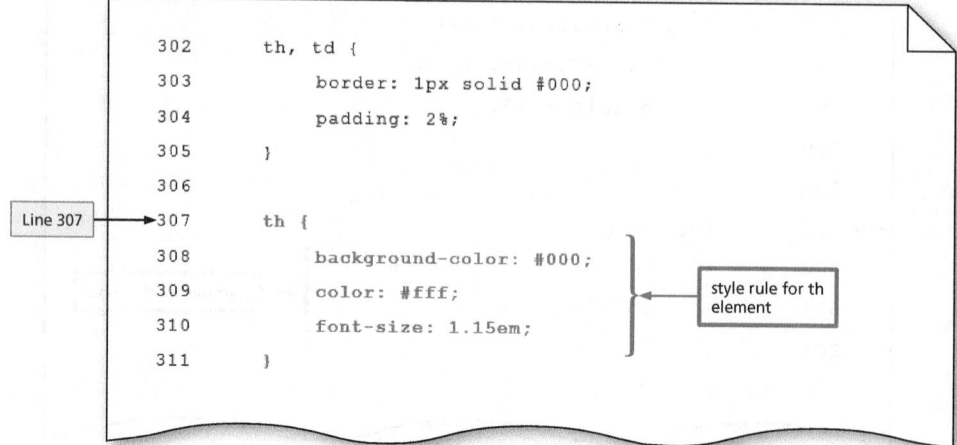

Figure 8–30

8
● Save your changes and refresh classes.html in your browser (Figure 8–31).

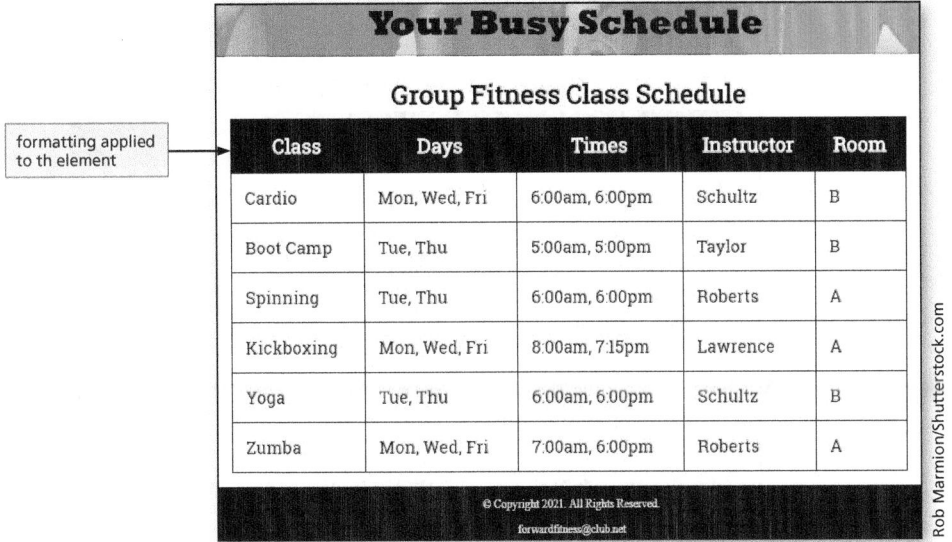

formatting applied
to th element

Figure 8–31

9
● In the styles.css file, tap or click at the end of Line 311, if necessary, and then press the ENTER key twice to insert new Lines 312 and 313.

● On Line 313, type `tr:nth-child(odd) {` to insert a new selector.

● Press the ENTER key to insert a new Line 314, increase the indent, and then type `background-color: #ccc;` to insert a new declaration.

● Press the ENTER key to insert a new Line 315, decrease the indent, and then type `}` to insert a closing brace (Figure 8–32).

Q&A | What is the purpose of the nth-child(odd) pseudo-class?
The nth-child(odd) pseudo-class is used to apply a background color to the odd rows or alternating rows.

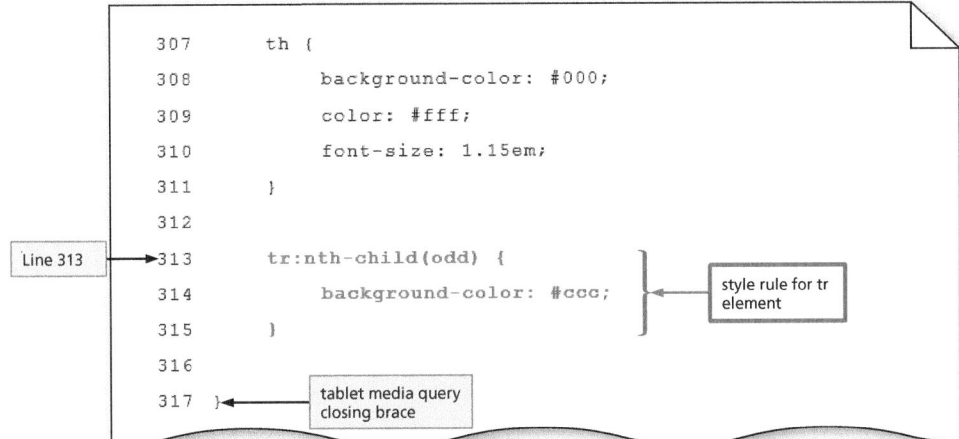

```
307      th {
308          background-color: #000;
309          color: #fff;
310          font-size: 1.15em;
311      }
312
313      tr:nth-child(odd) {
314          background-color: #ccc;
315      }
316
317  }
```

Line 313

style rule for tr
element

tablet media query
closing brace

Figure 8–32

- Save your changes and refresh classes.html in your browser (Figure 8–33).

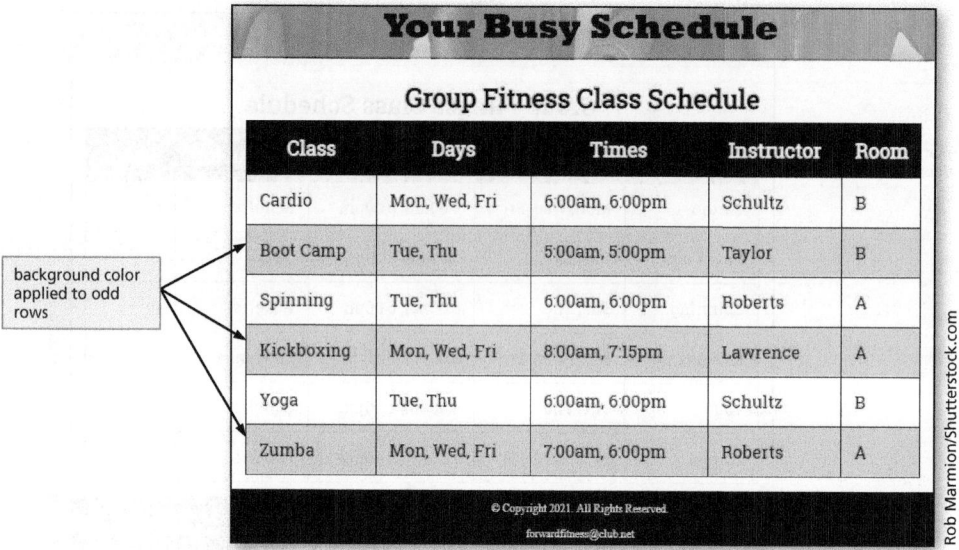

Figure 8–33

To Style a Table for a Large Desktop Viewport

Create a new style rule to style the table for a large desktop viewport. ***Why?*** *Format the table to restrict the width to 80 percent for a large desktop viewport.* Add a new style rule to the large desktop media query to format the table width to 80 percent. The following steps create a new style rule for the large desktop viewport.

- In the styles.css file, tap or click at the end of Line 398, and then press the ENTER key twice to insert new Lines 399 and 400.
- On Line 400, type **table {** to insert a new selector.
- Press the ENTER key to insert a new Line 401, increase the indent, and then type **width: 80%;** to insert a new declaration.
- Press the ENTER key to insert a new Line 402, decrease the indent, and then type **}** to insert a closing brace (Figure 8–34).

```
392   /* Media Query for Large Desktop Viewports */
393   @media screen and (min-width: 1921px) {
394
395       #container {
396           width: 1920px;
397           margin: 0 auto;
398       }
399
400       table {
401           width: 80%;
402       }
403
404   }
```

Line 400 → 400

style rule for table → 401

large desktop media query closing brace → 404

Figure 8–34

Experiment

- By default, table captions are positioned above a table. To see what the caption looks like at the bottom of the table, add the caption-side property with a value of bottom to the caption style rule. Save your changes and then refresh classes.html in your browser. After you view the effect, remove the caption-side property from the caption style rule.

- Save your changes, refresh classes.html in Google Chrome's device mode, and set the viewport to 4K or a large viewport (Figure 8–35).

table width is 80% for a large desktop viewport

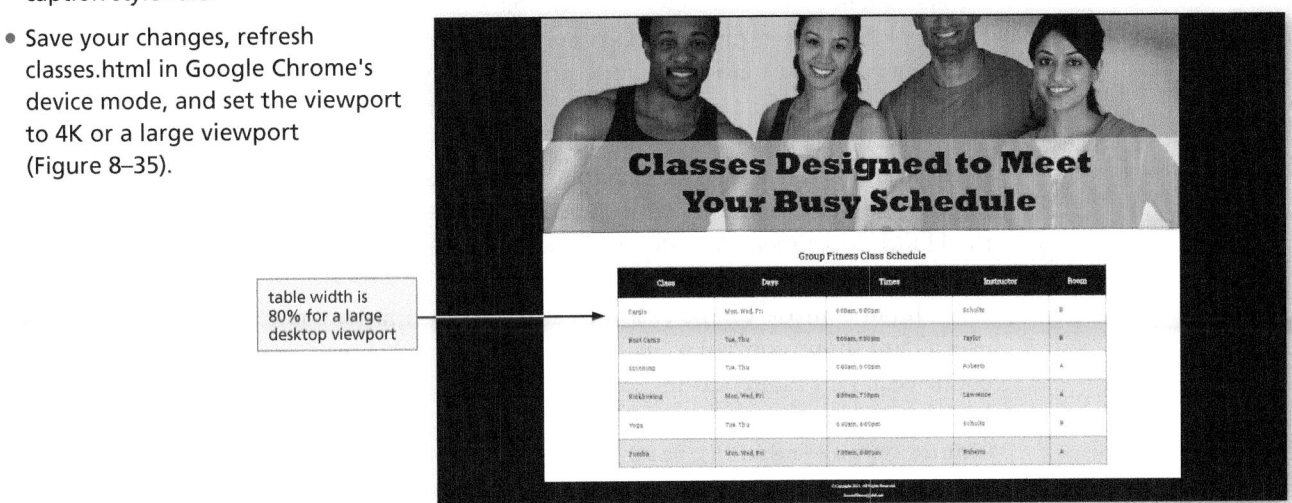

Figure 8–35

Break Point: If you want to take a break, this is a good place to do so. You can exit the text editor now. To resume at a later time, run your text editor, open the file called styles.css, and continue following the steps from this location forward.

Creating Webpage Forms

Forms provide a structured way to collect information from webpage visitors, such as a visitor's first name, last name, address, email, and telephone number. Visitors often complete webpage forms to register for an account or to make a purchase. Businesses use forms to gather visitor or customer information and store it in a database for future use. Figure 8–36 shows the Sign Up form on Facebook.com. Visitors complete the form to create a new Facebook account.

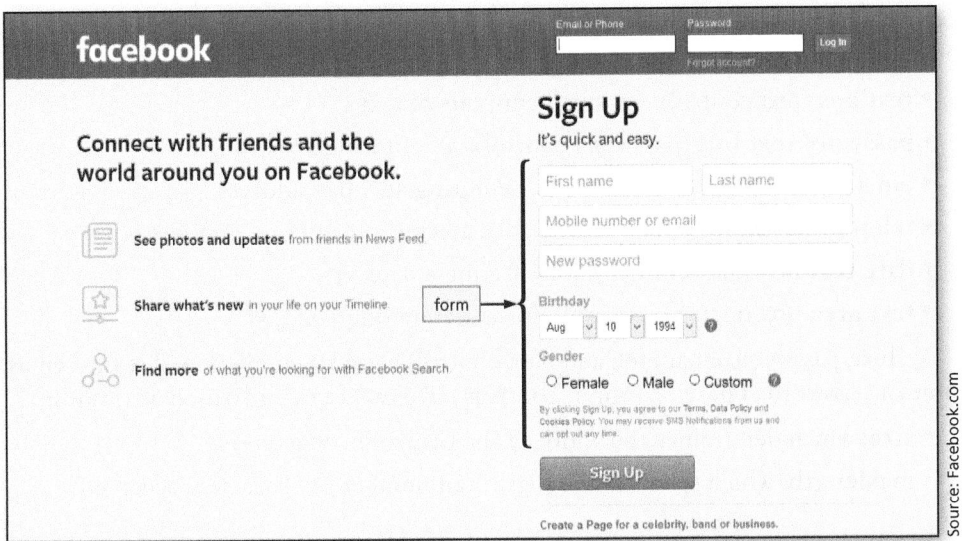

Figure 8–36

Form Controls

BTW
**HTML Forms
and JavaScript**
A **script** is a program that
runs in a browser to add
functionality to a webpage.
You can use JavaScript to
write scripts commonly used
to validate HTML forms.
Because JavaScript runs on
the user's computer, it is a
client-side scripting language.
Using JavaScript, you can
create pop-up messages and
alerts, validate a form, and
perform other beneficial tasks
within a webpage.

A form consists of a starting <form> tag and an ending </form> tag. All form elements are contained with the <form> and </form> tags. Input controls are used within the form element to collect visitor information. An **input control** is an interactive mechanism in which users enter text or make selections on a form. For example, on the Facebook Sign Up form, the text boxes requesting a visitor's first name and last name are input controls. A **label** is text describing the type of information to enter with an input control. On the Facebook Sign Up form, "Birthday" is a label.

You define most controls in an HTML form by using the `type` attribute of the `input` element. For example, to add a text box to a form, you include an `input` element beginning with `input type="text"` in the `form` element in the HTML document. You define a few other controls using separate elements, such as the `textarea` and `select` elements.

Input controls can be classified as data or text input controls. A webpage visitor uses a **data input control** to make a selection or perform a command. A data input control can be a radio button (`input type="radio"`), a check box (`input type="checkbox"`), a Submit button (`input type="submit"`), a Reset button (`input type="reset"`), or a selection menu (`select` element). A **text input control** accepts text, such as names, dates, and passwords, and is often called an input field. Table 8–3 lists input types for an input control.

Regardless of the specific type, each input control has attributes that are used more frequently than the others:

- **name**, which identifies the specific information that is being sent when the form is submitted for processing. All controls have a name.
- **id**, which provides a unique ID for the element. Use the `id` attribute to link a label element with an input control or other form element.
- **value**, which specifies the value of an `input` element and varies depending on input type. For text, password, and hidden controls, the `value` attribute defines the default value. For checkbox, radio, and image controls, it specifies the data submitted with the form when the control is selected. For button, reset, and submit controls, the `value` attribute defines the text on the button. All controls except textarea also have a `value` attribute. For a textarea field, no `value` attribute is possible because of the variability of the input.

Common input controls used with a form include text, password, email, tel, date, textarea, checkbox, radio, select, submit, and reset. Text input controls include the following types:

- **text box** (text control), for small amounts of text
- **password text box** (password control), for entering a password
- **email text box** (email control), for entering an email address
- **telephone text box** (tel control), for entering a telephone number
- **date text box** (date control), for entering a date
- **text area box** (textarea control), for larger amounts of text

Text, password, email, tel, and date controls accept a single line of text, such as a name or password. These text input controls have two frequently used attributes:

- **size**, which determines the width of the control in characters
- **maxlength**, which specifies the maximum number of characters accepted

Table 8–3 Input Types

Input Type	Description	Code Example
button	Creates a button; typically used to run a script when clicked	`<input type="button" onclick="alert('Good Morning!')" value="My Button">`
checkbox	Creates a check box that the user can select	`<input type="checkbox" name="fruit" value="banana">`
color	Creates a field for the user to select a color	`<input type="color" name="item-color">`
date	Creates an input field used to contain a date; the field may appear as a date picker, depending on the browser	`<input type="date" name="birthday">`
datetime	Creates an input field for a date and time with a time zone	`<input type="datetime" name="bdaydatetime">`
datetime-local	Creates an input field for a date and time without a time zone	`<input type="datetime-local" name="bddatetime">`
email	Creates an input field for an email address	`<input type="email" name="email" id="email">`
file	Creates a file-select field and a Browse button	`<input type="file" name="doc">`
hidden	Creates a control that is hidden from the user but contains information to process the form	`<input type="hidden" name="ship">`
image	Creates a graphical button instead of the default button	`<input type="image" name="reset" src="reset.png" alt="Reset">`
month	Creates an input field for a month and year; the field may appear as a date picker, depending on the browser	`<input type="month" name="bdaymth">`
number	Creates an input field for a numeric value	`<input type="number" name="cost">`
password	Creates a single-line field for a relatively small amount of text and masks the entered text as asterisks or bullets	`<input type="password" name="pw" id="pw">`

radio	Creates a radio button to allow the user to select one option	`<input type="radio" name="state" value="AL">`
		`<input type="radio" name="state" value="AK">`
		`<input type="radio" name="state" value="AZ">`

range	Creates an input field for a value within a range; the field may appear as a slider control, depending on the browser	`<input type="range" name="survey" min="0" max="10">`
reset	Resets the form	`<input type="reset" value="Reset Form">`
search	Creates an input field used as a search field	`<input type="search" name="search">`
submit	Submits a form for processing	`<input type="submit" value="Submit Form">`
tel	Creates an input field for a telephone number	`<input type="tel" name="phone" id="phone">`
text	Creates a single-line field for text	`<input type="text" name="fName" id="fName">`
time	Creates an input field for a time without a time zone; the field may appear as a time picker, depending on the browser	`<input type="time" name="time">`
url	Creates an input field for a URL	`<input type="url" name="page">`
week	Creates an input field for a week and year; the field may appear as a date picker, depending on the browser	`<input type="week" name="week">`

For example, the first line of the following code creates a 25-character text box for the user's username and the second line creates an eight-character text box for the user's password:

```
<label>Username <input name="username" type="text"
    size="25"></label>
<label>Password <input name="password" type="password"
    size="8"></label>
```

Figure 8–37 shows an example of the code when rendered in a browser. Because each **input** element uses the **size** attribute, a user can enter a last name longer than 25 characters and a password longer than eight characters. If the **input** elements used the **maxlength** attribute instead of **size**, a user could only enter up to 25 characters for the username and up to eight characters for the password.

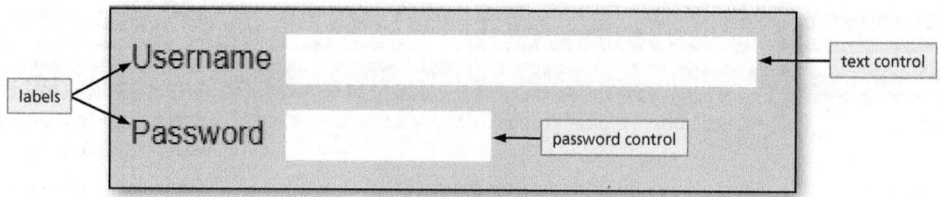

Figure 8–37

The maximum length of the text box may exceed the size of the text box that appears on the form. For example, consider a size of three characters and a maximum length of nine characters. If a webpage visitor enters more than three characters, the characters scroll to the left, allowing the visitor to enter a maximum of nine characters.

A **password control** is like a text control because it provides a text box for a single line of input—the password a visitor enters. However, as the visitor enters the password, the characters appear as asterisks or bullets, one per character. This feature helps protect the visitor's password from being observed by others as it is entered.

An **email control** is a text box where visitors enter an email address. Some browsers validate that the email address is in the proper format before submitting the form for processing. If the email address is not in the proper format, the browser displays a message asking the user to correct the data. A **tel control** is a text box where visitors enter a telephone number. A **date control** is a text box that accepts a date. Some browsers display a calendar when a visitor taps or clicks a date control.

A **textarea control** creates a text box that allows multiple lines of input. Textarea controls are useful to collect more than a single line of text from a webpage visitor, such as a product review. To create a textarea control, you use the `textarea` element instead of the `input` element. The `textarea` element has two primary attributes, which set the size of the textarea control:

rows, which specifies the number of rows, or lines, in the textarea control

cols, which sets the width of the textarea control as the number of columns, with each column containing one character.

The following is an example of HTML code defining a textarea control:

```
<label>Please tell us more about your shopping experience
       with us today.</label>
<textarea name="feedback" rows="5" cols="100"></textarea>
```

Figure 8–38 shows an example of the label and textarea control when rendered in a browser. This textarea control provides five lines of 100 characters each to let visitors describe their shopping experience.

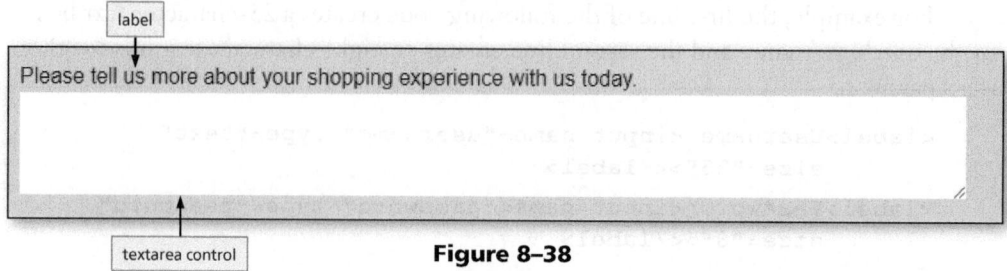

Figure 8–38

A **checkbox control** allows a webpage visitor to select items from a list of one or more choices. Each choice appears with a graphical box, which can be checked (selected or on) or unchecked (deselected or off). By default, all check boxes are deselected. To set a particular check box to be preselected as the default, use the `checked` attribute and value `(checked="checked")` within the <input> tag. The following is sample code for four checkbox controls that might appear on a form for a college website where potential students select their career fields of interest.

```html
<input type="checkbox" id="webdev" value="Web Development"
       name="field">
<label for="webdev">Web Development</label>

<input type="checkbox" id="program" value="Programming"
       name="field">
<label for="program">Programming</label>

<input type="checkbox" id="network" value="Networking"
       name="field">
<label for="network">Networking</label>

<input type="checkbox" id="appdev" value="Application
       Development" name="field">
<label for="appdev">Mobile App Development</label>
```

Figure 8–39 shows an example of the labels and checkbox controls when rendered in a browser. Users can select more than one item in a check box list. For example, a user could select both Web Development and Programming when selecting a field of interest from the website form.

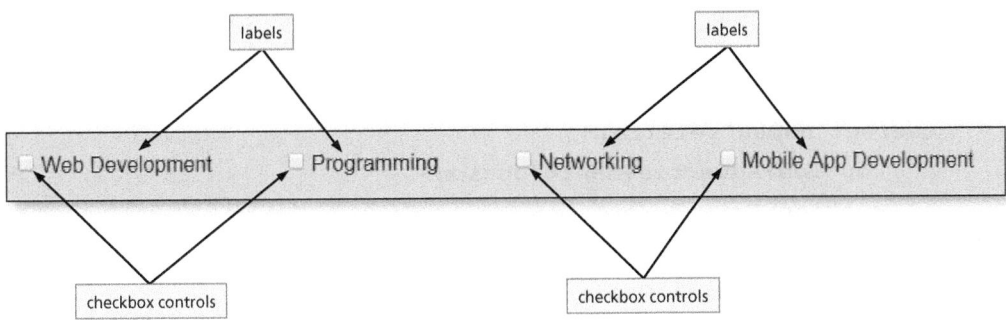

Figure 8–39

A **radio control** limits the webpage visitor to only one choice from a list of choices. Each choice has a **radio button**, or option button, which typically appears as an open circle. When the visitor selects one of the radio buttons, all other radio buttons in the list are automatically deselected. By default, all radio buttons are deselected. To set a particular button as the default, you use the `checked` attribute and value within the <input> tag as you do with the checkbox control. The following example is similar to the previous checkbox control example, except it uses the radio controls on a website form:

```html
<input type="radio" id="webdev" value="Web Development"
       name="field">
<label for="webdev">Web Development</label>

<input type="radio" id="program" value="Programming"
       name="field">
<label for="program">Programming</label>

<input type="radio" id="network" value="Networking"
       name="field">
<label for="network">Networking</label>

<input type="radio" id="appdev" value="Application
       Development" name="field">
<label for="appdev">Mobile App Development</label>
```

BTW
Radio Buttons
Antique car radios were operated by a row of large black plastic buttons. Push one button, and you would get one preset radio station. You could push only one button at a time. Radio buttons on forms work the same way as the antique radio buttons—one button at a time. With check boxes, more than one option can be selected at a time.

Figure 8–40 shows an example of the labels and radio controls when rendered in a browser. A potential student will only be able to select one program of interest when using radio controls.

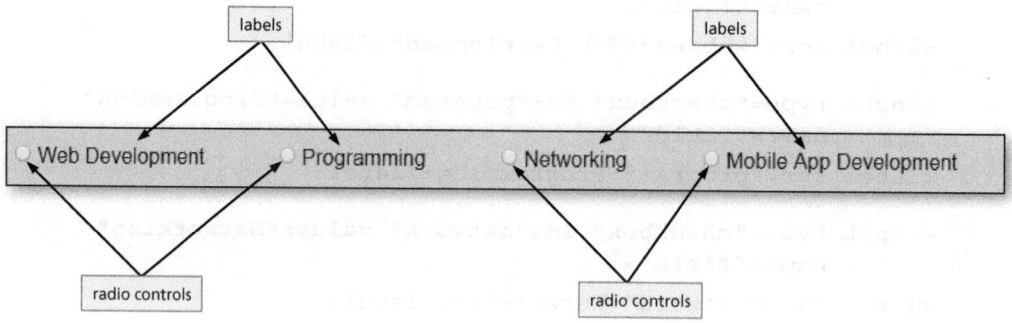

Figure 8–40

A **select control** creates a selection menu from which the visitor makes one or more choices. This prevents the visitor from having to type information into a text or textarea control. A select control is suitable when a limited number of choices are available. It appears on a form as a text box with a list arrow. The user taps or clicks the list arrow to view all the choices in the menu. The default choice appears first in the menu and is highlighted to indicate that it is selected.

Instead of using the `type` attribute of the `input` element, you define a select control using the `select` and `option` elements. The following is sample code for a select control:

```
<select name="referral">
    <option>Advertisement</option>
    <option>Friend</option>
    <option>Google</option>
    <option>Social Media</option>
</select>
```

Figure 8–41 shows an example of the select control when rendered in a browser. This selection menu contains four options—Advertisement, Friend, Google, and Social Media—with "Advertisement" appearing as the selected option.

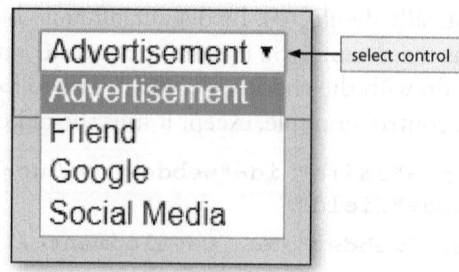

Figure 8–41

The **submit control** and the **reset control** create the Submit and Reset buttons. The **Submit button** sends the form information to the appropriate location for processing. When a webpage visitor taps or clicks the Submit button on the form, the name of each control and the value of its data are sent to the server to be processed.

The **Reset button** clears any input entered in the form, resetting the input controls to their defaults. A webpage form must include a submit control, and must also include a reset control. You use the `value` attribute to specify the text that appears on the button. The submit and reset controls are created with the following code:

```
<input type="submit" value="Submit">
<input type="reset" value="Reset">
```

Some forms can be divided into various sections using a **fieldset element**, which is used to group related form elements. Each fieldset may include a **legend**, which is used as a caption for the fieldset. Figure 8–42 shows an example of a form that includes fieldsets, legends, and several input controls, including text, email, tel, checkbox, date, select, and textarea.

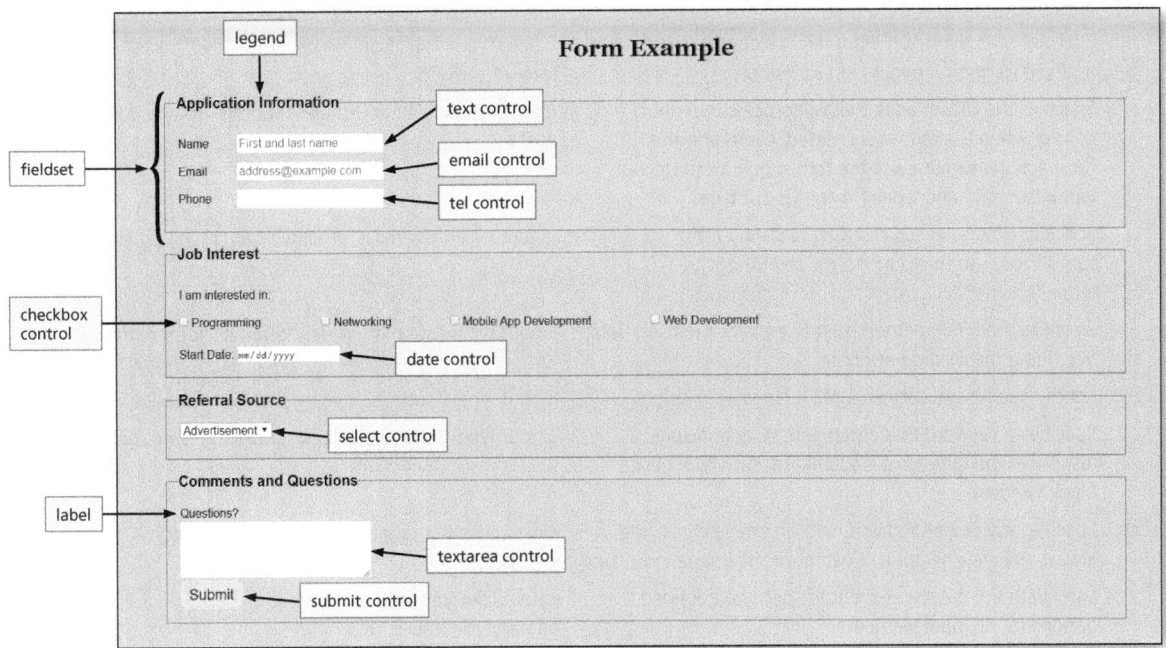

Figure 8–42

Form Labels

Form labels identify the type of information to enter into or select from an input control. You add a label to a form using the `label` element. To connect a label to its control, include the `for` attribute with the same value as the input control's `id` value. The following code creates a label and a text box for a visitor's first name:

```
<label for="fName">First Name:</label>
<input type="text" name="fName" id="fName">
```

Attributes of HTML Tags Used to Create Forms

Many of the HTML tags used to create forms have several attributes. Table 8–4 lists common form attributes, including several HTML 5 attributes for the input elements. However, many of these attributes are not supported by all major browsers, so be sure to test them first.

Table 8–4 Common Form Attributes

Attribute	Description	Code Example
accept-charset	Specifies the character set used for the form submission	`<form accept-charset="UTF-8">`
action	Specifies where to submit the form data (a URL)	`<form method="POST" action="form.php">`
autocomplete	Specifies whether a form or input field should use autocomplete; when enabled, the browser can complete input fields based on information entered in previous input fields	`<form autocomplete="on">`
autofocus	Specifies that an input field should have focus when the page is displayed, which places the insertion point within a specific input field	`<input type="text" name="fName" id="fName" autofocus>`
disabled	Specifies that the input field is disabled and not available for user input	`<input type="radio" name="terms" value="Accept" disabled>`
enctype	Specifies the encoding of the form for submitting data	`<form enctype="app/urlencoded">`
form	Specifies which form an input field belongs to when multiple forms are used within a website	`<input type="text" name="fName" id="fName" form="form1">`
formaction	Specifies the URL of a file that will process the input control when the form is submitted, overriding the form action attribute; use the formaction attribute with type="submit" and type="image" input types	`<input type="submit" value="Submit" formaction="process.asp">`
formenctype	Specifies how to encode form data during form submission; use the formenctype attribute with type="submit" and type="image" input types	`<input type="submit" formenctype="multipart/form-data">`
formmethod	Specifies the HTTP method used to transfer the form data, overriding the method attribute	`<input type="submit" value="Submit" formmethod="post">`
formnovalidate	Specifies to not validate an input element	`<input type="submit" value="Submit" formnovalidate>`
formtarget	Specifies a keyword that determines how to display a response when the form is submitted, such as a new, blank window	`<input type="submit" value="Submit" formtarget="_blank">`
height and width	Specifies the height and width for an image input type; always specify a height and width for the image input type	`<input type="image" src="btn1" alt="button 1" height="25" width="30">`

list	Used with the datalist element to specify predefined options for an input element	`<input list="music">`
		`<datalist id="music">`
		`<option value="Country">`
		`<option value="Classical">`
		`<option value="Hip Hop">`
		`<option value="Rock">`
		`</datalist>`

max and min	Specifies the maximum and minimum values for an input element	`<input type="number" name="survey" min="1" max="10">`
maxlength	Specifies the maximum number of characters allowed within the input field	`<input type="text" name="fName" id="fName" maxlength="15">`
method	Specifies the HTTP method used to submit the form data	`<form method="POST">`
multiple	Specifies that user may input more than one value within an input element; used with email and file input types	`<input type="email" name="email" id="email" multiple>`
novalidate	A form attribute that specifies not to validate form data when the submit button is clicked	`<form novalidate>`
pattern	Specifies a regular expression for checking an input element value; used with text, search, url, tel, email, and password input types	`<input type="password" name="pw" id="pw" pattern="[A-Za-z]{8}">`
placeholder	Specifies a hint of the type of information expected within an input field	`<input type="email" name="email" id="email" placeholder="youremail@domain.com">`
readonly	Specifies that the input field is a read-only field and cannot be modified	`<input type="text" name="ssn" id="ssn" value="555123654" readonly>`

Table 8–4 (continued)

Attribute	Description	Code Example
required	Specifies that an input field is required	`<input type="text" name="fName" id="fName" required>`
size	Specifies the size (length) of an input field	`<input type="text" name="fName" id="fName" size="20">`
step	Specifies the legal number intervals for an <input> element	`<input type="number" name="math" step="5">`
target	Specifies the target address in the action attribute	`<form target="_blank">`
value	Specifies the value for an input field.	`<option value="Colorado">`

Form Processing

After creating a form on a webpage, you need to identify how to process the form and when to submit it. Use the **action** attribute of the <form> tag to specify the action the browser takes when submitting the form. Browsers can send information entered in forms to a database on a web server or sent by email to an email address. Many websites use form processing software tools available from the web server or website hosting provider.

The **method** attribute of the <form> tag specifies how to send the data entered in the form to the server to be processed. HTML provides two primary ways to send form data: the get method and the post method. The **get method** appends the name-value pairs to the URL indicated in the action attribute. You need to be cautious when using the get method. Some web servers limit the size of a URL, so you run the risk of truncating relevant information when using the get method. The following is an example of a form tag with the get method and specified action:

```
<form method="GET" action="formInfo.php">
```

The **post method** sends a separate data file with the name-value pairs to the URL (or email address) indicated in the action attribute. The post method is the more common method because it can be used to send sensitive form data and does not have a size limitation. The following is an example of a form tag with the post method and specified action:

```
<form method="POST" action="formInfo.php">
```

Since form data processing involves web server and programming tasks that are beyond the scope of this book, the information entered in the form created in this chapter will not contain a **method** or an **action** attribute, and therefore, no data will be submitted to a web server or email address.

BTW
Security
Security is an important consideration when using web forms, especially when you are collecting credit card information. Search the web for specific information concerning the usage of the SSL-encrypted HTTPS protocol versus the unencrypted HTTP protocol.

How do I send the form data to my email address?
To send form data to an email address, use the action attribute with a value of mailto: followed by your email address within the form tag. Also include the method attribute with a value of post. An example is <form action="mailto:myemail@domain.com" method="POST">

CONSIDER THIS

To Add a Form, Fieldset, Legend, Labels, and Text Input Controls to the Contact Us Page

Insert a form on the Contact Us page to collect information from prospective clients. *Why? The Forward Fitness Club wants to create a database of prospective clients and use it to market their services. Most of this client data can come from the form on the Contact Us page.* Start by including a new div element with a heading that alerts visitors to the form. Add the starting <form> tag to the page, and then insert label elements and input text controls. Finally, insert the ending </form> tag to complete the form. The following steps add a form to the Contact Us page.

1

- Open contact.html in your text editor to prepare to modify the document.
- Tap or click at the end of Line 48 and press the ENTER key twice to insert new Lines 40 and 50.
- On Line 50, type `<div id="form">` to insert a new div tag.
- Press the ENTER key twice to insert new Lines 51 and 52.
- On Line 52, increase the indent, and then type `<h2>Complete the form below to begin your free trial.</h2>` to insert a heading 2 element.
- Press the ENTER key twice to insert new Lines 53 and 54, and then type `<form class="form-grid">` `<!-- Start Form -->` to insert a starting form tag and a comment.
- Press the ENTER key twice to insert new Lines 55 and 56.
- On Line 56, increase the indent, and then type `<fieldset>` to insert a beginning fieldset tag.
- Press the ENTER key to insert a new Line 57, increase the indent, and then type `<legend>Customer Information</legend>` to insert a legend for the fieldset.
- Press the ENTER key to insert a new Line 58, and then type `<label for="fName">First Name:</label>` to insert a label element.
- Press the ENTER key to insert a new Line 59, and then type `<input type="text" name="fName" id="fName" required>` to insert an text input control (Figure 8–43).

Q&A

What is the effect of the code I entered?

The form contains a fieldset with a First Name: label and a text box. The `fName` value for the `for` attribute in the `label` element matches the `fName` value for the `id` attribute in the `input` element to bind the controls together. The required attribute means that this field must be completed before the user can submit the form.

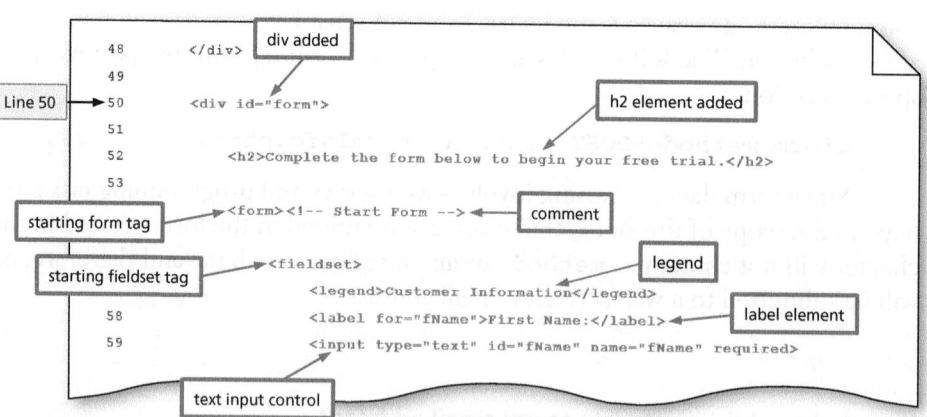

Figure 8–43

2

- Press the ENTER key twice to insert new Lines 60 and 61, and then type `<label for="lName">Last Name:</label>` to insert a label element.
- Press the ENTER key to insert a new Line 62, and then type `<input type="text" name="lName" id="lName" required>` to insert an text input control.
- Press the ENTER key to insert a new Line 63, decrease the indent, and then type `</fieldset>` to insert an ending fieldset tag.
- Press the ENTER key twice to insert new Lines 64 and 65, decrease the indent, and then type `</form>` to insert an ending form tag (Figure 8–44).

Q&A What is the difference between the `name` and the `id` attributes?

The `name` attribute identifies the information being sent when the form is submitted for processing. The `id` attribute is a unique identifier used for this specific form element and can be used by scripts.

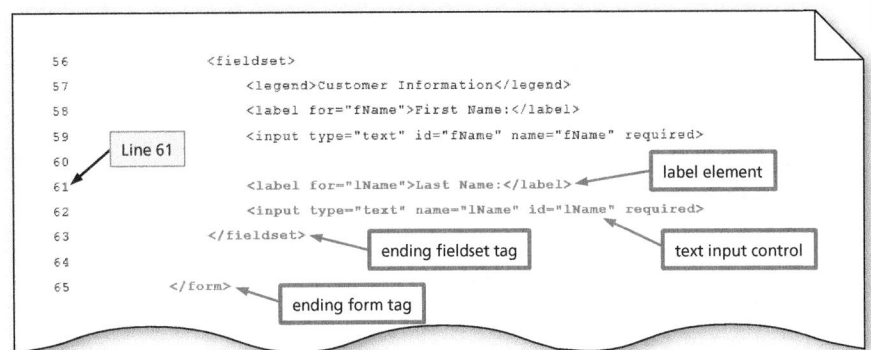

```
56              <fieldset>
57                  <legend>Customer Information</legend>
58                  <label for="fName">First Name:</label>
59                  <input type="text" id="fName" name="fName" required>     ← label element
60
61          Line 61
62                  <label for="lName">Last Name:</label>
63                  <input type="text" name="lName" id="lName" required>     ← text input control
64              </fieldset>     ← ending fieldset tag
65          </form>     ← ending form tag
```

Figure 8–44

③

- Save your changes, open contact.html in your browser with a standard desktop viewport and scroll down if necessary to display the form (Figure 8–45).

Q&A Why do the first name and last name labels and input elements appear on the same line?

You need to set a style rule to display these elements as block elements so they appear on separate lines. You will add style rules in later steps.

Figure 8–45

To Add email and tel Input Controls to a Form

1 CREATE CLASSES PAGE & TABLE | 2 STYLE TABLE
3 CREATE FORM | **4 STYLE FORM**

Add email and tel input controls to collect the customer's email address and telephone number. *Why? Using these input controls instead of text controls makes it easier for visitors to enter the appropriate information.* First, add a new label and an **input** element with an **email** type. Then, add a new label and an **input** element with a **tel** type. The following steps add email and tel input controls to the form on the Contact Us page.

①

- Tap or click at the end of Line 62 and press the ENTER key twice to insert new Lines 63 and 64.

- On Line 64, type `<label for="email">Email:</label>` to insert a label element.

- Press the ENTER key to insert a new Line 65, and then type `<input type="email" name="email" id="email" required>` to insert an email input control (Figure 8–46).

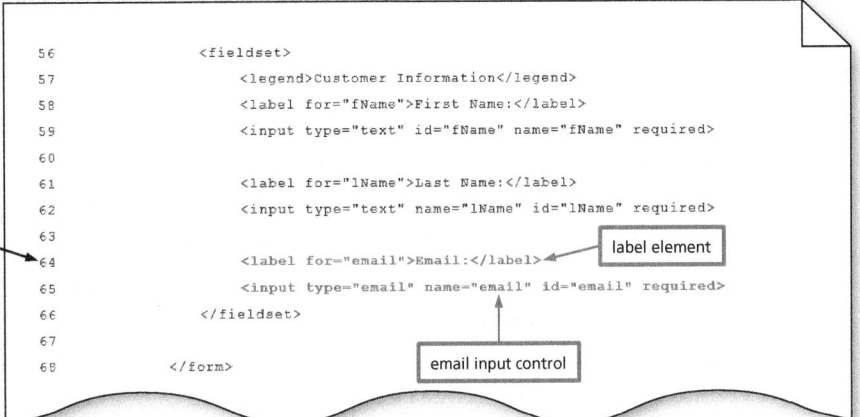

```
56              <fieldset>
57                  <legend>Customer Information</legend>
58                  <label for="fName">First Name:</label>
59                  <input type="text" id="fName" name="fName" required>
60
61                  <label for="lName">Last Name:</label>
62                  <input type="text" name="lName" id="lName" required>
63
64                  <label for="email">Email:</label>     ← label element
65                  <input type="email" name="email" id="email" required>
66              </fieldset>
67
68          </form>     ← email input control
```

Figure 8–46

- Press the ENTER key twice to insert new Lines 66 and 67, and then type `<label for="phone">Phone:</label>` to insert a label element.

- Press the ENTER key to insert a new Line 68, and then type `<input type="tel" id="phone" name="phone" required>` to insert a tel input control (Figure 8–47).

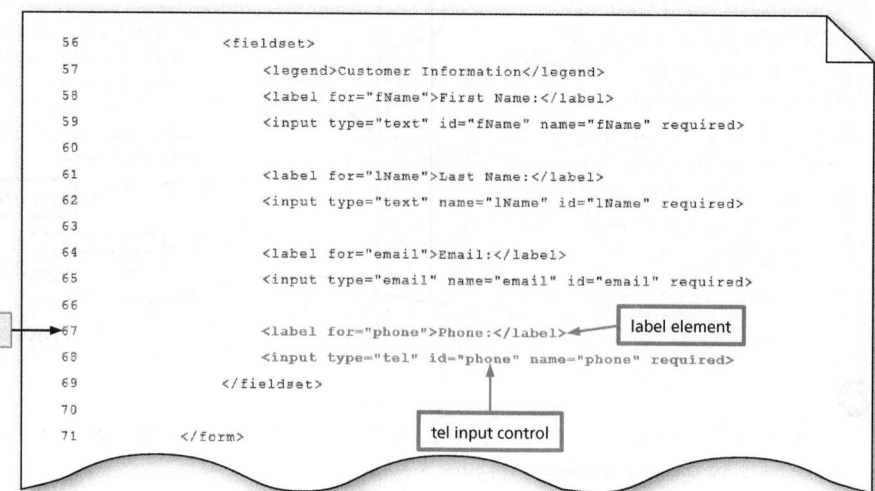

```
56          <fieldset>
57              <legend>Customer Information</legend>
58              <label for="fName">First Name:</label>
59              <input type="text" id="fName" name="fName" required>
60
61              <label for="lName">Last Name:</label>
62              <input type="text" name="lName" id="lName" required>
63
64              <label for="email">Email:</label>
65              <input type="email" name="email" id="email" required>
66
67              <label for="phone">Phone:</label>        ← label element
68              <input type="tel" id="phone" name="phone" required>
69          </fieldset>
70
71      </form>
```

Line 67

tel input control

Figure 8–47

- Save your changes and refresh contact.html in your browser (Figure 8–48).

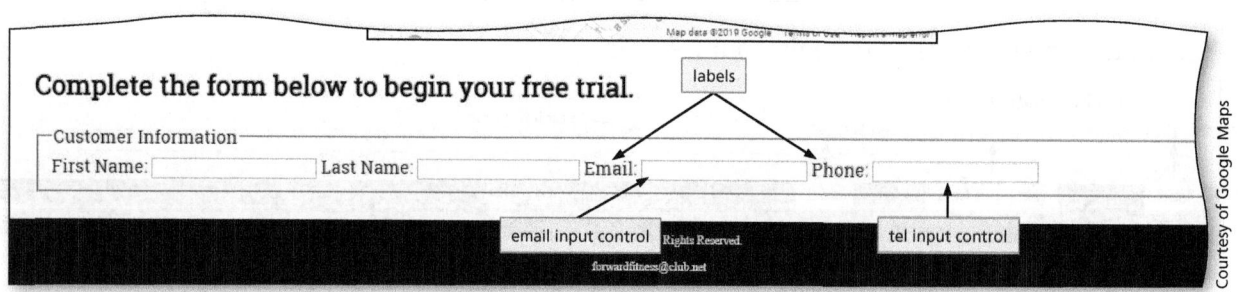

Complete the form below to begin your free trial.

labels

Customer Information
First Name: [____]   Last Name: [____]   Email: [____]   Phone: [____]

email input control

tel input control

Figure 8–48

To Add Checkbox Controls to a Form

1 CREATE CLASSES PAGE & TABLE | 2 STYLE TABLE
3 CREATE FORM | **4 STYLE FORM**

Add checkbox controls to collect information from customers about their primary interest in the fitness club. *Why? Using checkbox controls lets customers select more than one interest.* First, add a new fieldset and legend to group the new form elements together. Next, add a new paragraph element to introduce the checkbox controls. Next, insert checkbox input elements nested within label elements. The following steps add checkbox controls to the form on the Contact Us page.

- Tap or click at the end of Line 69 and press the ENTER key twice to insert new Lines 70 and 71.

- On Line 71, type `<fieldset>` to insert a starting fieldset tag.

- Press the ENTER key to insert a new Line 72, increase the indent, and then type `<legend>Additional Information</legend>` to insert a legend element.

- Press the ENTER key to insert a new Line 73, and then type `<p>I would like more information about:</p>` to insert a paragraph element.

- Press the ENTER key twice to insert new Lines 74 and 75, and then type `<label for="grpfit"><input type="checkbox" name="interest" id="grpfit" value="Group Fitness">Group Fitness</label>` to insert a label element and a checkbox input element.

- Press the ENTER key twice to insert new Lines 76 and 77, and then type `<label for="prtrain"><input type="checkbox" name="interest" id="prtrain" value="Personal Training">Personal Training</label>` to insert a label element and a checkbox input element.

- Press the ENTER key twice to insert new Lines 78 and 79, and then type `<label for="nutr"><input type="checkbox" name="interest" id="nutr" value="Nutrition">Nutrition</label>` to insert a label element and a checkbox input element.

- Press the ENTER key to insert a new Line 80, decrease the indent, and then type `</fieldset>` to insert a closing fieldset tag (Figure 8–49).

Q&A Why am I nesting the checkbox input elements within a label?
Nesting the checkbox input elements within label elements will provide the control needed to style them with CSS.

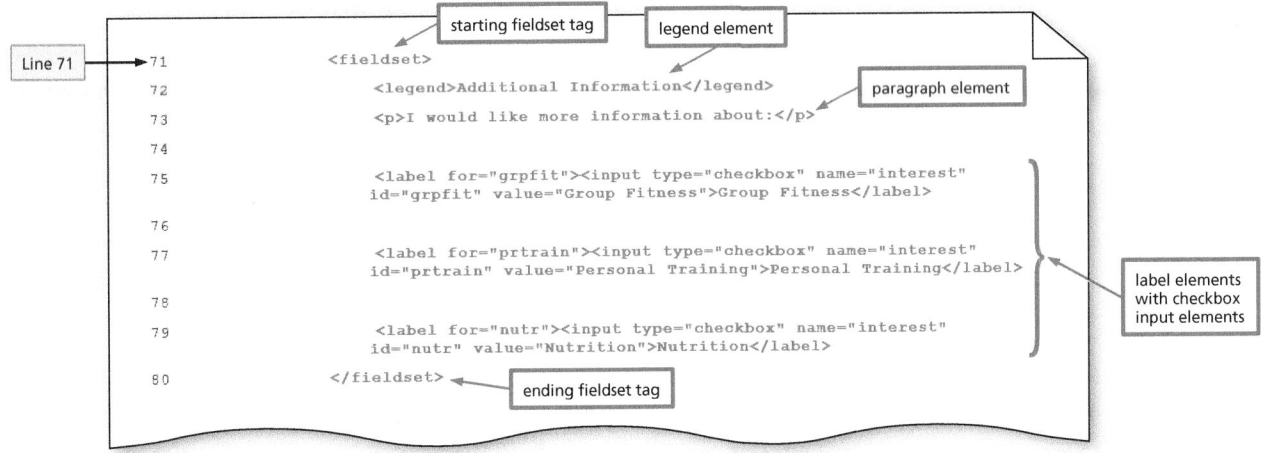

Figure 8–49

2

- Save your changes and refresh contact.html in your browser (Figure 8–50).

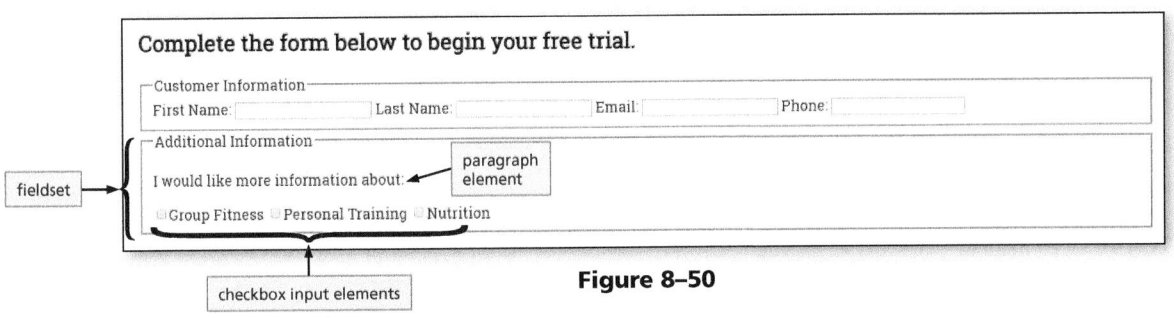

Figure 8–50

To Add a select Element to a Form

1 CREATE CLASSES PAGE & TABLE | 2 STYLE TABLE
3 CREATE FORM | 4 STYLE FORM

Add a `select` element to learn how customers discovered the Forward Fitness Club. *Why? A select element lets users select from a list of options, restricting them to a valid option.* First, add a new fieldset and legend to group the new form elements together. Next, add a new label element for the referral source. Then, create a `select` element with five `option` elements. The following steps add a `select` element to the form on the Contact Us page.

1

- Tap or click at the end of Line 80 and press the ENTER key twice to insert new Lines 81 and 82.

- On Line 82, type `<fieldset>` to insert a new starting fieldset tag.

- Press the ENTER key to insert a new Line 83, increase the indent, and then type `<legend>Referral Source</legend>` to insert a legend element.

- Press the ENTER key to insert a new Line 84 and then, type `<label for="reference">How did you find us?</label>` to insert a label element.

- Press the ENTER key to insert a new Line 85, and then type `<select name="reference" id="reference">` to insert a starting select tag.

- Press the ENTER key to insert a new Line 86, increase the indent, and then type `<option value="ad">Advertisement</option>` to insert an option element.

- Press the ENTER key to insert a new Line 87, and then type `<option value="friend">Friend</option>` to insert an option element (Figure 8–51).

Q&A

What is the effect of the code I entered?
The selection menu now includes two options: Advertisement and Friend. You add three other options in the next step.

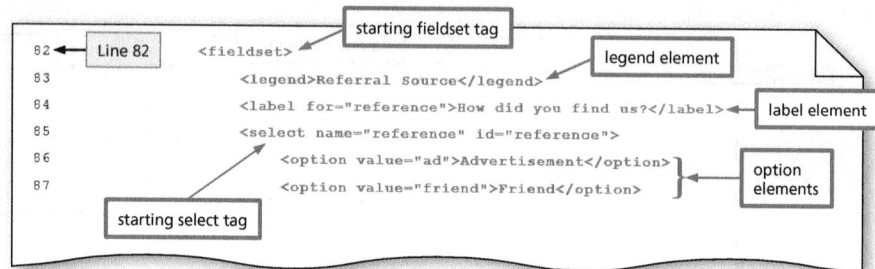

Figure 8–51

2

- Press the ENTER key to insert a new Line 88, and then type `<option value="google">Google</option>` to insert an option element.

- Press the ENTER key to insert a new Line 89, and then type `<option value="social">Social Media</option>` to insert an option element.

- Press the ENTER key to insert a new Line 90, and then type `<option value="other">Other</option>` to insert an option element.

- Press the ENTER key to insert a new Line 91, decrease the indent, and then type `</select>` to insert a closing select tag.

- Press the ENTER key to insert a new Line 92, decrease the indent, and then type `</fieldset>` to insert an ending fieldset tag (Figure 8–52).

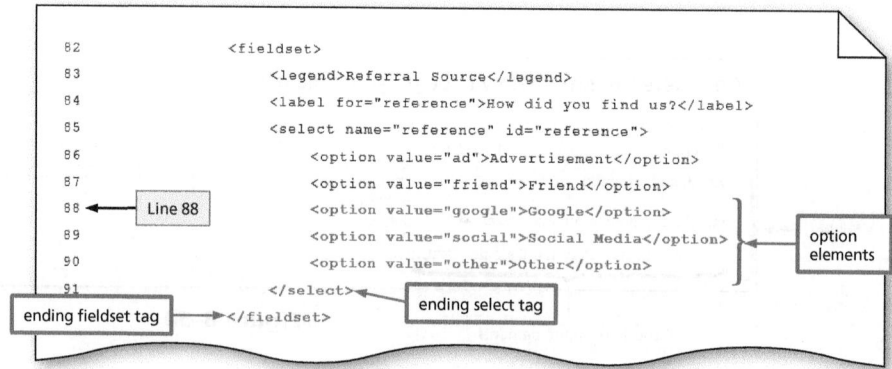

Figure 8–52

- Save your changes, refresh contact.html in your browser, and then tap or click the new select control (Figure 8–53).

Q&A

Does the order of the options matter?
Yes. The first option in the list appears in the select control before a visitor taps or clicks the control. The first option also appears as selected when a visitor taps or clicks the control.

Complete the form below to begin your free trial.

Customer Information
First Name: _____ Last Name: _____ Email: _____ Phone: _____

Additional Information

I would like more information about:

☐ Group Fitness ☐ Personal Training ☐ Nutrition

fieldset →

Referral Source

How did you find us? [Advertisement ▼]   ← select element

Advertisement
Friend
Google
Social Media
Other

label element

option elements

© Copyright 2021. All Rights Reserved.

Figure 8–53

1 CREATE CLASSES PAGE & TABLE | 2 STYLE TABLE
3 CREATE FORM | 4 STYLE FORM

To Add a textarea Element to a Form

Add a `textarea` element to the form to provide an opportunity for customers to ask questions. *Why? Customers can enter more than one line of text in a textarea control.* The following steps add a label and a `textarea` element to the form on the Contact Us page.

1

- Tap or click at the end of Line 91 and press the ENTER key twice to insert new Lines 92 and 93.

- On Line 93, type
`<label for="questions">Questions?</label>`
to insert a label element.

- Press the ENTER key to insert a new Line 94, and then type
`<textarea id="questions" name="questions" rows="5" cols="35"></textarea>` to insert a textarea element (Figure 8–54).

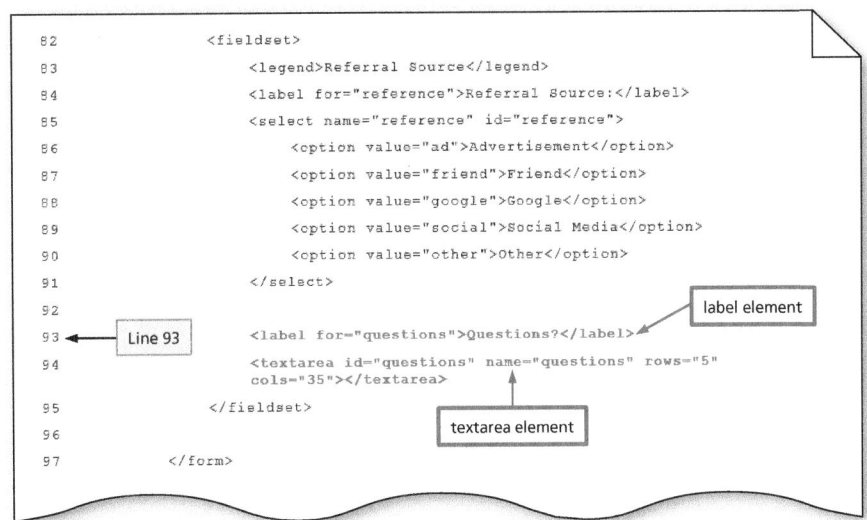

```
82              <fieldset>
83                  <legend>Referral Source</legend>
84                  <label for="reference">Referral Source:</label>
85                  <select name="reference" id="reference">
86                      <option value="ad">Advertisement</option>
87                      <option value="friend">Friend</option>
88                      <option value="google">Google</option>
89                      <option value="social">Social Media</option>
90                      <option value="other">Other</option>
91                  </select>
92
93                  <label for="questions">Questions?</label>
94                  <textarea id="questions" name="questions" rows="5"
                        cols="35"></textarea>
95              </fieldset>
96
97          </form>
```

Line 93 →

label element

textarea element

Figure 8–54

Q&A What do the rows and cols attributes mean?
The rows and cols attributes set the size of the textarea control. In this case, the textarea control provides five 35-character lines where visitors can enter questions.

2

- Save your changes and refresh contact.html in your browser (Figure 8–55).

Q&A Why does the textarea element appear to the right of the select element?
You need to create a style rule to display the textarea element as a block so it is positioned below the select element.

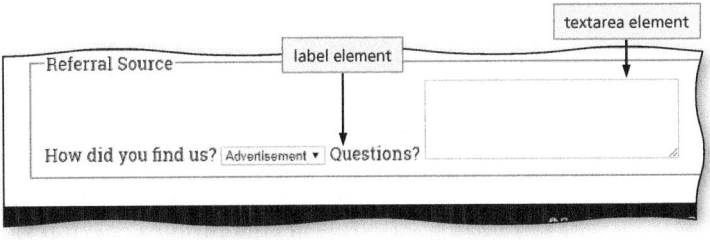

textarea element

label element

Referral Source

How did you find us? [Advertisement ▼] Questions?

Figure 8–55

To Add a Submit Button to a Form

After adding text input controls and other form elements to a form, insert a submit control so that visitors can submit the form with their responses. *Why? Every form requires a submit control to send the information to a web server for processing if specified.* The following steps add a submit control to the form on the Contact Us page.

- Tap or click at the end of Line 95 and press the ENTER key twice to insert new Lines 96 and 97.

- On Line 97, type `<input type="submit" id="submit" value ="Submit" class="btn">` to insert a submit input type (Figure 8–56).

What is the purpose of the btn class?
The btn class will be used to specify a style rule for the submit button.

Do I have to use Submit as the value for submit controls?
No. You can use other values, such as Send or OK. The value you specify appears as text on the button.

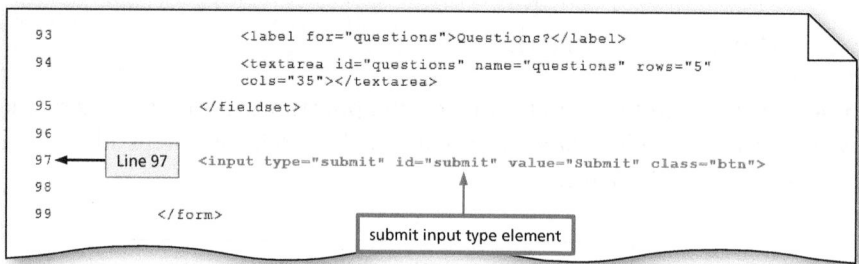

Figure 8–56

- Save your changes and refresh contact.html in your browser (Figure 8–57).

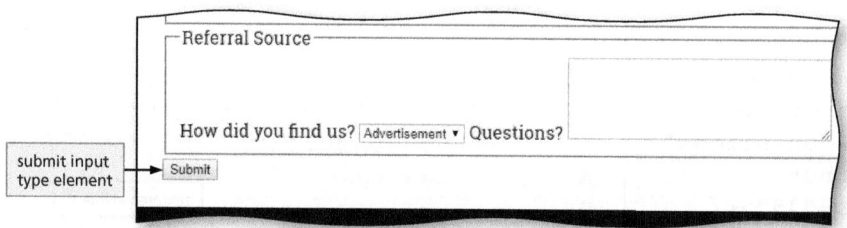

Figure 8–57

Styling Forms

You apply CSS styles to forms for the same reason you style other webpage elements: to improve the appeal and usefulness of the form and its controls. For example, you position labels and form controls so users can quickly and clearly understand what type of information to provide in each control. As with tables, consider forms in the context of responsive design. Start with a simple, basic form for the mobile viewport. This form requests only the most essential information. You can modify the appearance and the content of the form for the tablet and desktop viewports. For example, you can change a form that is long and narrow in a mobile viewport so it is wider and arranges controls in columns in a desktop viewport. You can also include controls to collect optional information, such as product feedback, in tablet and desktop viewports.

To Style a Form for a Mobile Viewport

Now that the form is complete, you can style the form for a mobile viewport. First, create a style rule for the form div to set some top margin, specify a background color, and set some padding. Next, create a style rule to center-align the heading 2 element within the form div. Create a style rule that sets the bottom margin for the fieldsets and controls. **Why?** *To avoid horizontal scrolling, display the form elements as blocks so that each element appears on its own line.* Create another style rule to format the fieldset legend elements. Create another style rule to display the label elements as a block and add some top padding. The following steps create style rules for form elements in a mobile viewport.

1

- Open styles.css to prepare to modify it.

- Tap or click at the end of Line 184 and press the ENTER key twice to insert new Lines 185 and 186.

- On Line 186, type **#form {** to add a new selector.

- Press the ENTER key to insert a new Line 187, increase the indent, and then type **margin-top: 2%;** to insert a declaration.

- Press the ENTER key to insert a new Line 188, and then type **background-color: #f2f2f2;** to insert a declaration.

- Press the ENTER key to insert a new Line 189 and then type **padding: 2%;** to insert a declaration.

- Press the ENTER key to insert a new Line 190, decrease the indent, and then type **}** to insert a closing brace.

- Press the ENTER key twice to insert new Lines 191 and 192.

- On Line 192, type **#form h2 {** to add a new selector.

- Press the ENTER key to insert a new Line 193, increase the indent, and then type **text-align: center;** to insert a declaration.

- Press the ENTER key to insert a new Line 194, decrease the indent, and then type **}** to insert a closing brace (Figure 8–58).

Q&A Why did I enter the #form style rule after the .map style rule in the style sheet?
The .map style rule is the last style rule in the main content area for the mobile viewport. Since the form div is within the main content element, you place this style rule in the area for style rules that pertain to the main element.

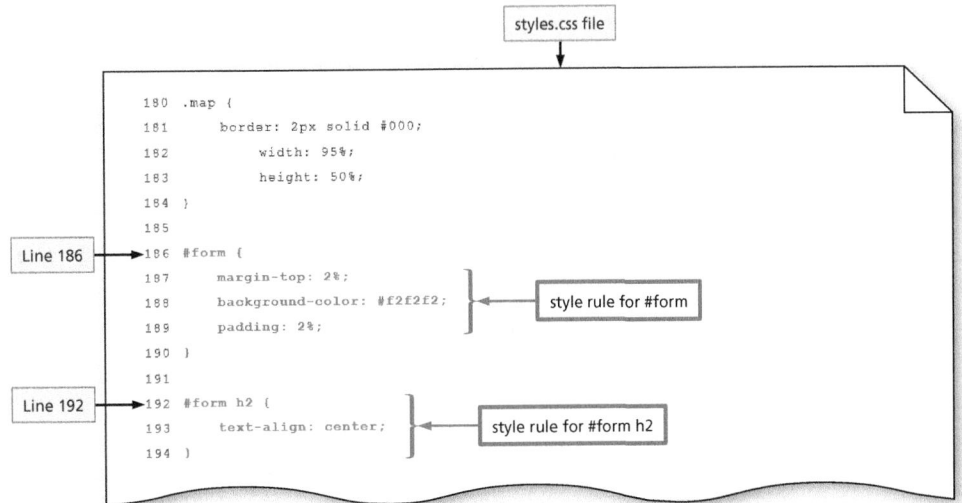

Figure 8–58

2

- Press the ENTER key twice to insert new Lines 195 and 196.

- On Line 196, type `/* Style rules for form elements */` to insert a comment.

- Press the ENTER key to insert a new 197, and then type `fieldset, input, select, textarea {` to add a new selector.

- Press the ENTER key to insert a new Line 198, increase the indent, and then type `margin-bottom: 2%;` to insert a declaration.

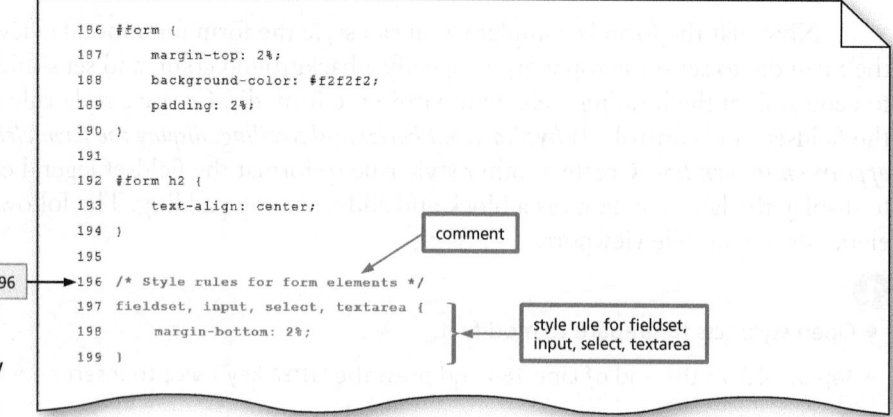

```
186  #form {
187      margin-top: 2%;
188      background-color: #f2f2f2;
189      padding: 2%;
190  }
191
192  #form h2 {
193      text-align: center;
194  }
195
196  /* Style rules for form elements */
197  fieldset, input, select, textarea {
198      margin-bottom: 2%;
199  }
```

comment

Line 196

style rule for fieldset, input, select, textarea

Figure 8–59

- Press the ENTER key to insert a new Line 199, decrease the indent, and then type `}` to insert a closing brace (Figure 8–59).

Why does the style rule use fieldset, input, select, textarea as the selectors?

Since this style rule needs to apply to the fieldset, input, select, and textarea elements, you need to specify all as selectors.

 3

- Press the ENTER key twice to insert new Lines 200 and 201.

- On Line 201, type `fieldset legend {` to insert a new selector.

- Press the ENTER key to insert a new Line 202, increase the indent, and then type `font-weight: bold;` to insert a declaration.

- Press the ENTER key to insert a new Line 203, and then type `font-size: 1.25em;` to insert a new declaration.

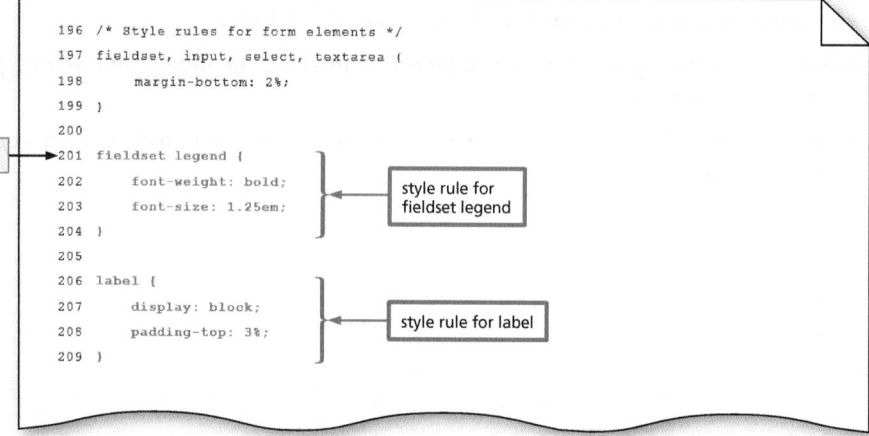

```
196  /* Style rules for form elements */
197  fieldset, input, select, textarea {
198      margin-bottom: 2%;
199  }
200
201  fieldset legend {
202      font-weight: bold;
203      font-size: 1.25em;
204  }
205
206  label {
207      display: block;
208      padding-top: 3%;
209  }
```

Line 201

style rule for fieldset legend

style rule for label

Figure 8–60

- Press the ENTER key to insert a new Line 204, decrease the indent, and then type `}` to insert a closing brace.

- Press the ENTER key twice to insert new Lines 205 and 206.

- On Line 206, type `label {` to insert a new selector.

- Press the ENTER key to insert a new Line 207, increase the indent, and then type `display: block;` to insert a declaration.

- Press the ENTER key to insert a new Line 208, and then type `padding-top: 3%;` to insert a declaration.

- Press the ENTER key to insert a new Line 209, decrease the indent, and then type `}` to insert a closing brace (Figure 8–60).

Why do I need to display the label elements as a block?

By default, label elements are inline elements. Display them as block elements so that they appear above their respective input, select, and textarea elements.

- Press the ENTER key twice to insert new Lines 210 and 211.

- On Line 211, type **form #submit {** to insert a new selector.

- Press the ENTER key to insert a new Line 212, increase the indent, and then type **margin: 0 auto;** to insert a declaration.

- Press the ENTER key to insert a new Line 213, and then type **border: none;** to insert a declaration.

```
206  label {
207      display: block;
208      padding-top: 3%;
209  }
210
211  form #submit {
212      margin: 0 auto;
213      border: none;
214      display: block;
215      padding: 2%;
216      background-color: #b3b3b3;
217      font-size: 1em;
218      border-radius: 10px;
219  }
```

Line 211 → (points to line 211)

style rule for form #submit → (points to lines 211-219)

Figure 8–61

- Press the ENTER key to insert a new Line 214, and then type **display: block;** to insert a declaration.

- Press the ENTER key to insert a new Line 215, and then type **padding: 2%;** to insert a declaration.

- Press the ENTER key to insert a new Line 216, and then type **background-color: #b3b3b3;** to insert a declaration.

- Press the ENTER key to insert a new Line 217, and then type **font-size: 1em;** to insert a declaration.

- Press the ENTER key to insert a new Line 218, and then type **border-radius: 10px;** to insert a declaration.

- Press the ENTER key to insert a new Line 219, decrease the indent, and then type **}** to insert a closing brace (Figure 8–61).

Q&A | What is the purpose of this style rule?
This style rule formats the Submit button by centering it within the form, changing its default background color, giving it rounded corners, and removing its default border.

- Save your changes, open contact.html in Google Chrome's device mode, select the mobile viewport, and then scroll down to view the form. (Figure 8–62).

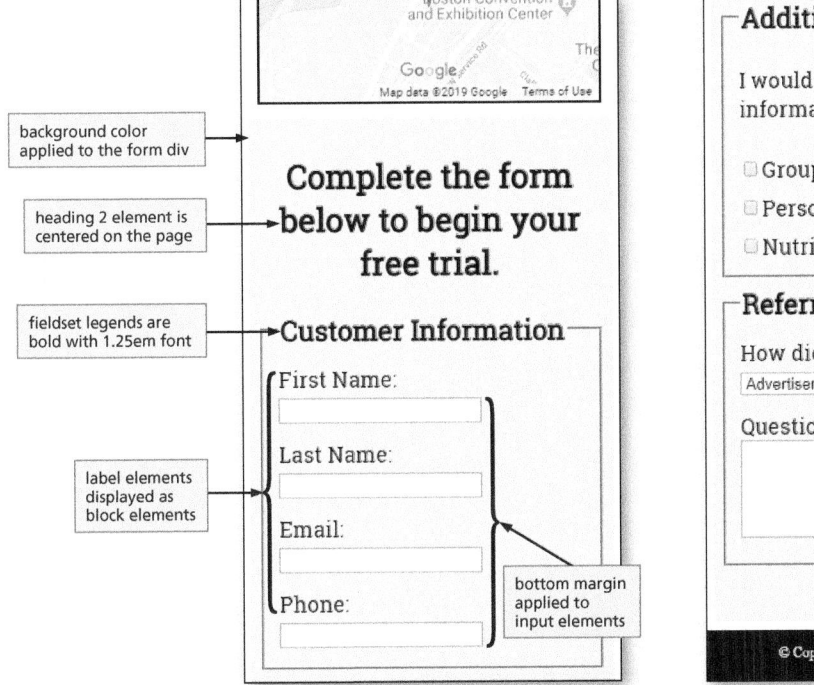
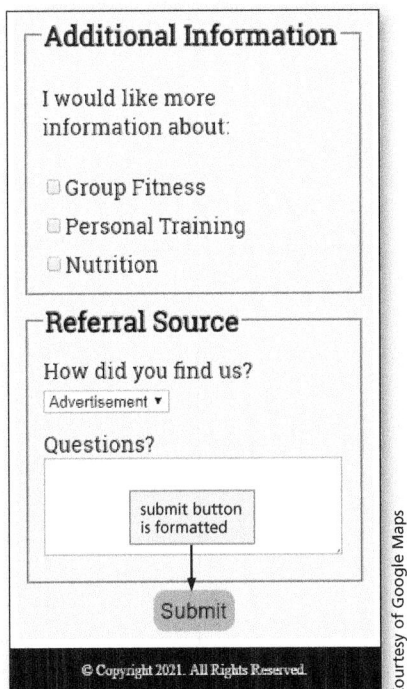

background color applied to the form div

heading 2 element is centered on the page

fieldset legends are bold with 1.25em font

label elements displayed as block elements

bottom margin applied to input elements

submit button is formatted

Courtesy of Google Maps

Figure 8–62

To Style a Form for a Tablet Viewport

Now that you have styled the form for a mobile viewport, you can also style the form for a tablet viewport. **Why?** *The current styles work best for the form in a mobile viewport. Optimize the form for the best viewing experience by a tablet user.* In the tablet media query, create a style rule for the form element that sets the width to 70 percent and centers the form on the page. The following steps create new style rules for the form element within the tablet media query of the styles.css file.

- In the styles.css file, tap or click at the end of Line 350 and press the ENTER key twice to insert new Lines 351 and 352.

- On Line 352, type `/* Tablet Viewport: Style rule for form element */` to add a comment.

- Press the ENTER key to insert a new Line 353, and then type `form {` to add a new selector.

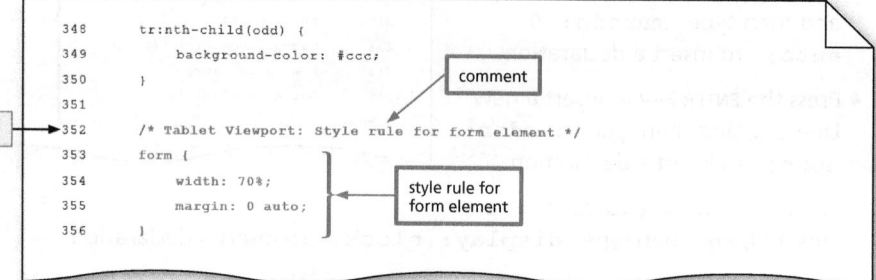

Figure 8–63

- Press the ENTER key to insert a new Line 354, increase the indent, and then type `width: 70%;` to insert a declaration.

- Press the ENTER key to insert a new Line 355, and then type `margin: 0 auto;` to insert a declaration.

- Press the ENTER key to insert a new Line 356, decrease the indent, and then type `}` to insert a closing brace (Figure 8–63).

Q&A What is the purpose of this style rule?
This style rule centers the form on the page and sets the form width to 70 percent.

- Save your changes, refresh contact.html in your browser, and select the tablet viewport, and then scroll down if necessary to view the changes (Figure 8–64).

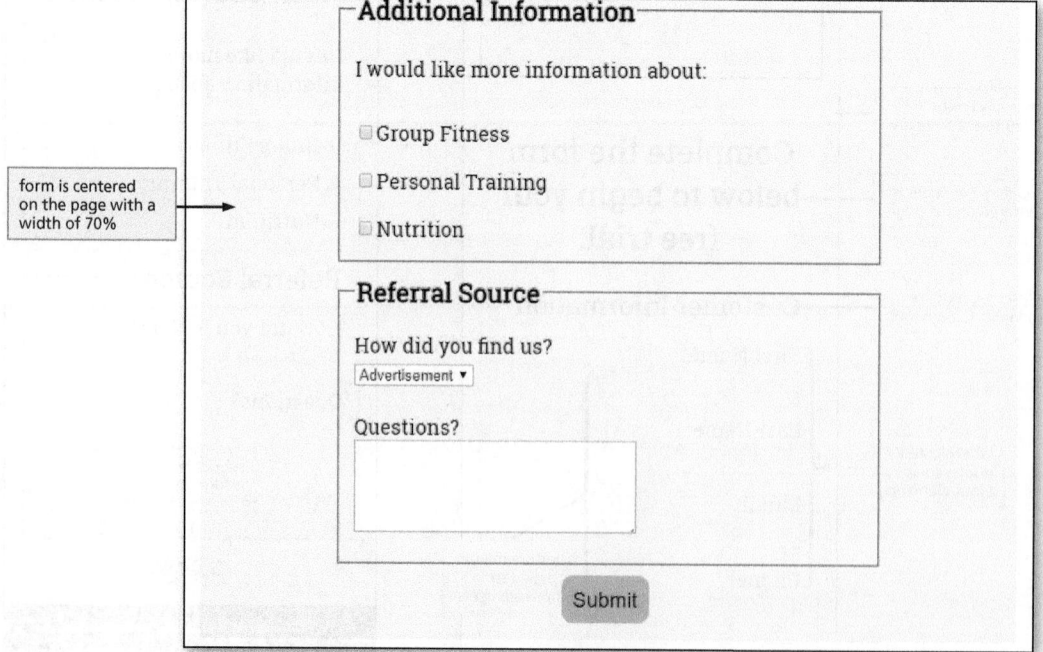

Figure 8–64

To Style a Form for a Desktop Viewport

Now that you have styled the form for a mobile and tablet viewports, you can style the form for a desktop viewport. *Why? The desktop viewport provides more space to modify the form layout to use to three columns.* First, create a style rule that sets the form width to auto. Next, create a style rule for the form-grid class selector that sets the display to a grid with three columns and sets the grid gap to 20px. Finally, create a style rule for the btn class selector that spans the Submit button across the three columns. The following steps create style rules for a form elements within the desktop media query of the styles.css file.

1

- Tap or click at the end of Line 429 and press the ENTER key twice to insert new Lines 430 and 431.

- On Line 431, type `/* Desktop Viewport: Style rules for form elements */` to add a comment.

- Press the ENTER key to insert a new Line 432, and then type `form {` to add a new selector.

- Press the ENTER key to insert a new Line 433, increase the indent, and then type `width: auto;` to insert a declaration.

- Press the ENTER key to insert a new Line 434, decrease the indent, and then type `}` to insert a closing brace.

- Press the ENTER key twice to insert new Lines 435 and 436.

- On Line 436, type `.form-grid {` to add a new selector.

- Press the ENTER key to insert a new Line 437, increase the indent, and then type `display: grid;` to insert a declaration.

- Press the ENTER key to insert a new Line 438, and then type `grid-template-columns: auto auto auto;` to insert a declaration.

- Press the ENTER key to insert a new Line 439, and then type `grid-gap: 20px;` to insert a declaration.

- Press the ENTER key to insert a new Line 440, decrease the indent, and then type `}` to insert a closing brace.

- Press the ENTER key twice to insert new Lines 441 and 442.

- On Line 442, type `.btn {` to insert a new selector.

- Press the ENTER key to insert a new Line 443, increase the indent, and then type `grid-column: 1 / span 3;` to insert a declaration.

- Press the ENTER key to insert a new Line 444, decrease the indent, and then type `}` to insert a closing brace (Figure 8–65).

Q&A How do these style rules change the appearance of the form?

In a desktop viewport, the form width will widen up to 100%, the form fieldsets will appear in a three-column layout, and the Submit button will appear below centered below the fieldsets.

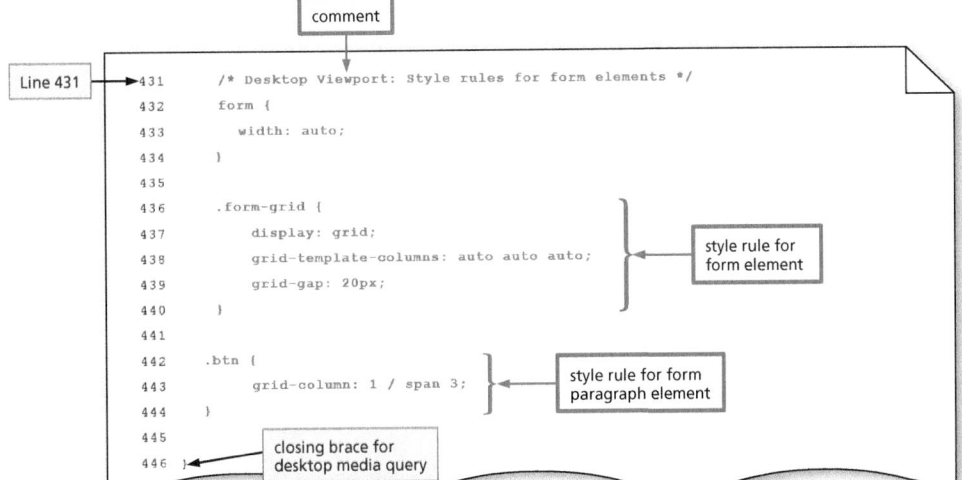

```
431     /* Desktop Viewport: Style rules for form elements */
432     form {
433         width: auto;
434     }
435
436     .form-grid {
437         display: grid;
438         grid-template-columns: auto auto auto;
439         grid-gap: 20px;
440     }
441
442     .btn {
443         grid-column: 1 / span 3;
444     }
445
446  }
```

comment

Line 431

style rule for form element

style rule for form paragraph element

closing brace for desktop media query

Figure 8–65

2

- Save your changes, refresh contact.html in your browser, and display the webpage in a desktop viewport (Figure 8–66).

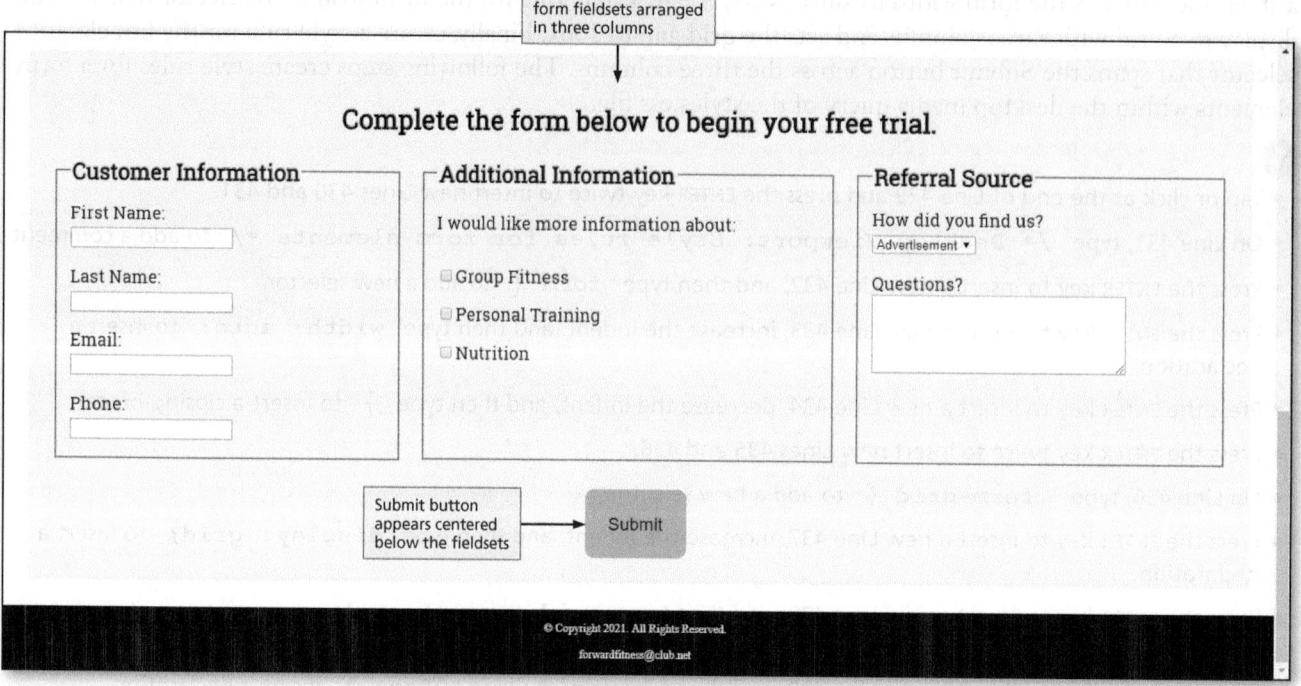

Figure 8–66

To Validate the Style Sheet

Always run your files through W3C's validator to check the document for errors. If the document has any errors, validating gives you a chance to identify and correct them. Validation is also an effective troubleshooting tool during the development process and adds a valuable level of professionalism to your work. The following steps validate a CSS document:

1 Open your browser and type `http://jigsaw.w3.org/css-validator/` in the address bar to display the W3C CSS Validation Service page.

2 Tap or click the By file upload tab to display the Validate by file upload information.

3 Tap or click the Browse button to display the Choose File to Upload dialog box.

4 Navigate to your css folder to find the styles.css file.

5 Tap or click the styles.css document to select it.

6 Tap or click the Open button to upload the selected file to the W3C CSS validator.

7 Tap or click the Check button to send the document through the validator and display the validation results page.

8 If necessary, correct any errors, save your changes, and run through the validator again to revalidate the page.

To Validate the HTML Files

Every time you create a new webpage or modify an existing webpage, run it through W3C's validator to check the document for errors. If any errors exist, you need to correct them. Validation is also an effective troubleshooting tool during the development process and adds a valuable level of professionalism to your work. The following steps validate an HTML document.

1 Open your browser and type **http://validator.w3.org/** in the address bar to display the W3C validator page.

2 Tap or click the Validate by File Upload tab to display the Validate by File Upload information.

3 Tap or click the Choose File button to display the Open dialog box.

4 Navigate to your fitness folder to find the classes.html file.

5 Tap or click the classes.html document to select it.

6 Tap or click the Open button to upload it to the W3C validator.

7 Tap or click the Check button to send the document through the validator and display the validation results page.

8 If necessary, correct any errors, save your changes, and run through the validator again to revalidate the page.

9 Follow these steps to validate the contact.html page and correct any errors.

Chapter Summary

In this chapter, you learned how to include tables and forms on webpages. You created a table that displays related information and then formatted it using CSS properties you have used before and one new property specific to tables. You also learned about webpage forms and form controls, including the HTML elements, attributes, and values for creating the controls you need. Finally, you used CSS styles to format a form for mobile, tablet, and desktop viewports. The items listed below include all the new skills you have learned in this chapter, with the tasks grouped by activity.

Discovering Tables
Add a Table to the Classes Page (HTML 411)

Styling Table Elements
Style a Table for a Tablet Viewport (HTML 417)
Style a Table for a Large Desktop Viewport (HTML 422)

Creating Webpage Forms
Add a Form and Form Controls to the Contact Us Page (HTML 432)
Add email and tel Input Controls to a Form (HTML 433)

Add Checkbox Controls to a Form (HTML 434)
Add a select Element to a Form (HTML 435)
Add a textarea Element to a Form (HTML 437)
Add Submit Button to a Form (HTML 438)

Styling Forms
Style a Form for a Mobile Viewport (HTML 439)
Style a Form for a Tablet Viewport (HTML 442)
Style a Form for a Desktop Viewport (HTML 443)

CONSIDER THIS

How will you improve the design of your website?

Use these guidelines as you complete the assignments in this chapter and create your own webpages outside of this class.

1. Determine if a table is right for your webpage.

   a) Determine if the information is best presented in a tabular format.
   b) Determine the number of rows and columns needed for the table.
   c) Determine whether or not the table can be easily displayed within a mobile viewport of if another format is needed to summarize the content for a mobile viewport.

2. Determine how to style the table elements.

   a) Determine how to style the table caption to make it stand out.
   b) Determine how to style each table element for mobile, tablet, and desktop viewports.

3. Determine the type of information your form should collect.

   a) Identify the different input types needed within your form.
   b) Determine the attributes needed for each input element.
   c) Determine what other form elements to use within your form.

4. Style the form for mobile, tablet, and desktop viewports.

   a) Determine the alignment and look of the form elements for a mobile viewport and then style.
   b) Determine the alignment and look of the form elements for a tablet viewport and then style.
   c) Determine the alignment and look of the form elements for a desktop viewport and then style.

5. Determine the action and method used to submit the form.

   a) Evaluate web server software capabilities to determine the best action and method for the form submission.
   b) Determine security measures needed to encrypt confidential data.

CONSIDER THIS

How should you submit solutions to questions in the assignments identified with a symbol?

Every assignment in this book contains one or more questions identified with a symbol. These questions require you to think beyond the assigned presentation. Present your solutions to the questions in the format required by your instructor. Possible formats may include one or more of these options: create a document that contains the answer; present your answer to the class; discuss your answer in a group; record the answer as audio or video using a webcam, smartphone, or portable media player; or post answers on a blog, wiki, or website.

Apply Your Knowledge

Reinforce the skills and apply the concepts you learned in this chapter.

Using Tables

Note: To complete this assignment, you will be required to use the Data Files. Please contact your instructor for information about accessing the Data Files.

Instructions: In this exercise, you will use your text editor to create a table and apply table styles. First, you insert a table element. Next, you add a table caption, table rows, table headers, and table data. Then, you create style rules to format the table. Work with the index.html file in the apply folder and the apply08.css file in the apply\css folder from the Data Files. The completed webpage is shown in Figure 8–67. You will also use professional web development practices to indent, space, comment, and validate your code.

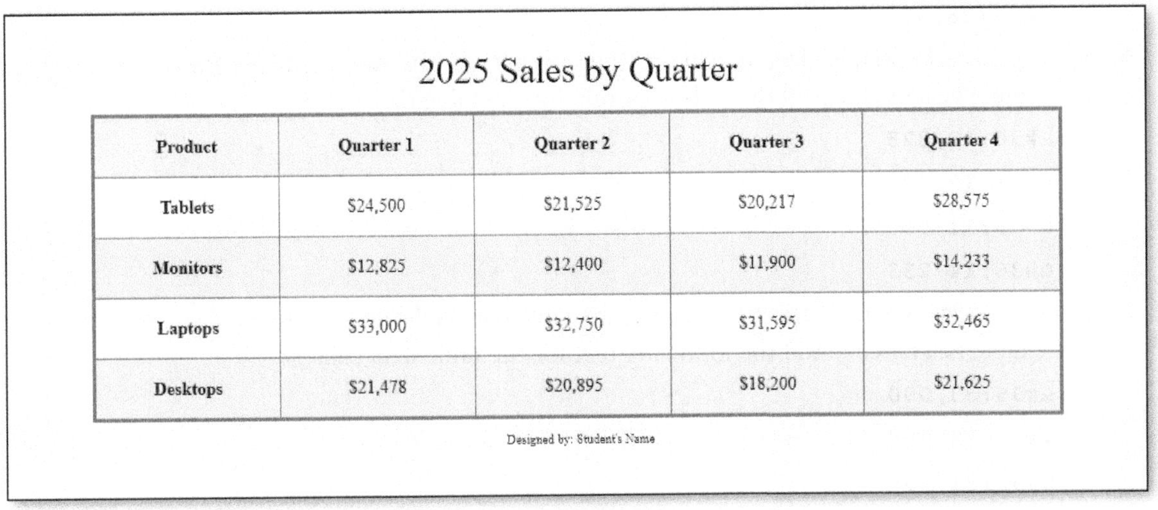

2025 Sales by Quarter

Product	Quarter 1	Quarter 2	Quarter 3	Quarter 4
Tablets	$24,500	$21,525	$20,217	$28,575
Monitors	$12,825	$12,400	$11,900	$14,233
Laptops	$33,000	$32,750	$31,595	$32,465
Desktops	$21,478	$20,895	$18,200	$21,625

Designed by: Student's Name

Figure 8–67

Perform the following tasks:

1. Open index.html in the chapter08\apply folder from the Data Files in your text editor. Review the page, add a title, modify the comment at the top of the page to include your name and today's date, and replace "Student's Name" with your name in the footer element.

2. Open the apply08.css file from the apply\css folder. Modify the comment at the top of the style sheet to include your name and today's date.

3. In the index.html file, add a `table` element within the `main` element.

4. Nest the following caption element within the `table` element:

   `<caption>2025 Sales by Quarter</caption>`

5. Insert five table rows after the caption and include a comment that specifies the row number. Follow the example below:

   `<tr><!-- Row 1 -->`

   `</tr>`

Continued >

Apply Your Knowledge *continued*

6. In row 1, insert five table header cells and use the following text for column titles:

   ```
   Product

   Quarter 1

   Quarter 2

   Quarter 3

   Quarter 4
   ```

7. In row 2, insert one table header cell and four table data cells. Add the text, **Tablets**, to the table header cell. Add the following text for the table data cells:

   ```
   &#36;24,500

   &#36;21,525

   &#36;20,217

   &#36;28,575
   ```

8. In row 3, insert one table header cell and four table data cells. Add the text, **Monitors**, to the table header cell. Add the following text for the table data cells:

   ```
   &#36;12,825

   &#36;12,400

   &#36;11,900

   &#36;14,233
   ```

9. In row 4, insert one table header cell and four table data cells. Add the text, **Laptops**, to the table header cell. Add the following text for the table data cells:

   ```
   &#36;33,000

   &#36;32,750

   &#36;31,595

   &#36;32,465
   ```

10. In row 5, insert one table header cell and four table data cells. Add the text, **Desktops**, to the table header cell. Add the following text for the table data cells:

    ```
    &#36;21,478

    &#36;20,895

    &#36;18,200

    &#36;21,625
    ```

11. In the apply08.css file, create the following style rules:

    a. Create a style rule for the table element that sets the width to **80%**, top and bottom margins to **0**, left and right margins to **auto**, and sets a border with the values **3px solid #71881b**.

    b. Create a style rule for table, tr, th, and td selectors that collapses the border and sets the padding to **2%**.

    c. Create a style rule for the caption element that sets the font size to **2em**, padding to **2%**, and top margin to **2%**.

    d. Create a style rule for th and td selectors that sets a border with the values **1px solid #7188bb**.

    e. Create a style rule for td that center-aligns its text.

    f. Create a style rule for tr that sets the background color to **#d3e788** for odd rows.

12. Add a comment above each style rule to note its purpose.

13. Save all of your changes and open the index.html in your browser.

14. Validate your HTML document using the W3C validator found at validator.w3.org and fix any errors that are identified.

15. Validate your CSS file using the W3C validator found at http://jigsaw.w3.org/css-validator/ and fix any errors that are identified.

16. Submit the files in a format specified by your instructor.

17. ✸ In Steps 7 through 10, you coded a table header as the first element within rows two through five. What was the purpose of using the table header elements here? What steps would you take to style these table header elements to left-align the text?

Extend Your Knowledge

Extend the skills you learned in this chapter and experiment with new skills. You may need to use additional resources to complete the assignment.

Creating a Table from a Visual Example

Instructions: In this exercise, you will create the table shown in Figure 8–68. You will also use professional web development practices to indent, space, comment, and validate your code.

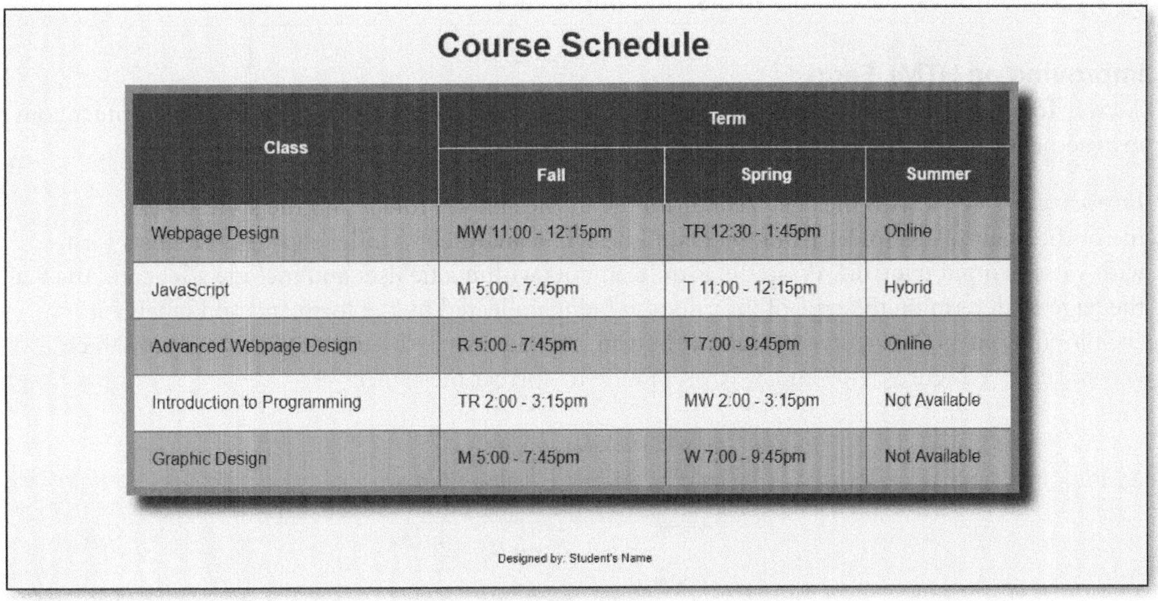

Course Schedule

Class	Term		
	Fall	Spring	Summer
Webpage Design	MW 11:00 - 12:15pm	TR 12:30 - 1:45pm	Online
JavaScript	M 5:00 - 7:45pm	T 11:00 - 12:15pm	Hybrid
Advanced Webpage Design	R 5:00 - 7:45pm	T 7:00 - 9:45pm	Online
Introduction to Programming	TR 2:00 - 3:15pm	MW 2:00 - 3:15pm	Not Available
Graphic Design	M 5:00 - 7:45pm	W 7:00 - 9:45pm	Not Available

Designed by: Student's Name

Figure 8–68

Perform the following tasks:

1. Create a folder named **extend08**. In the extend08 folder, create a subfolder named **css**.

2. Create a new HTML file and name it **extend08.html**. Add all the necessary HTML elements to create a basic webpage. Include a comment on Line 2 with your name and today's date.

3. In the extend08.html file, create a table with seven rows and four columns. Include a caption with the text, **Course Schedule**. Use the skills you have learned in this chapter to create the table shown in Figure 8–68. Note that you will need to properly use thead and tbody elements, as well as rowspan and colspan attributes.

4. Create a new style sheet, name it **styles08.css**, and save it within the extend08\css folder. Include a comment at the top of the style sheet with your name and today's date. Link extend08.html to the styles08.css file.

Continued >

Extend Your Knowledge *continued*

5. Use the styles08.css file to create style rules to design the table as shown in Figure 8–68. The table uses the following hexadecimal color codes: ffe5dc (body background color), fd4d0c (table border color), 792101 (box shadow color), a22c02 (table data border color), fe9772 (odd rows background color).

6. Apply a box shadow to the table.

7. Apply a sans-serif font to the page.

8. Add appropriate comments above each style rule to note its purpose.

9. Save all of your changes and open extend08.html in your browser.

10. Validate your HTML document using the W3C validator found at validator.w3.org and fix any errors that are identified.

11. Validate your CSS file using the W3C validator found at http://jigsaw.w3.org/css-validator/ and fix any errors that are identified.

12. Submit the files in a format specified by your instructor.

13. ❋ In this exercise, you discovered how to use colspan and rowspan attributes. Identify the resources you used to complete this assignment.

Analyze, Correct, Improve

Analyze a website, correct all errors, and improve it.

Improving an HTML Form

Note: To complete this assignment, you will be required to use the Data Files. Please contact your instructor for information about accessing the Data Files.

Instructions: Work with the analyze08.html file in the analyze folder and the styles08.css file in the analyze\css folder from the Data Files. The analyze08.html webpage contains a form with various input controls. Wrap the form elements within a fieldset and include a legend. Analyze the page to determine the type of information being collected by the form and add labels for each input control. Next, create a submit button, and then style the form for mobile and tablet viewports. Use Figures 8–69 and 8–70 as a guide to correct these files.

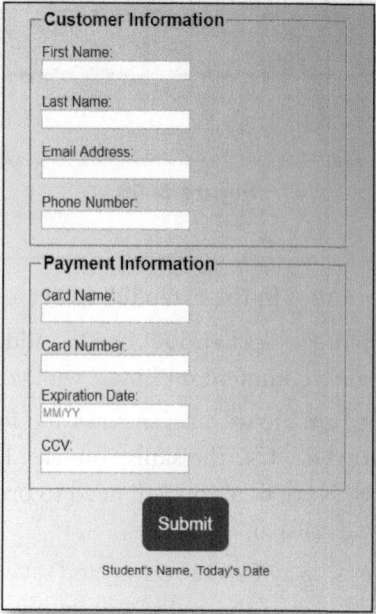

Figure 8–69

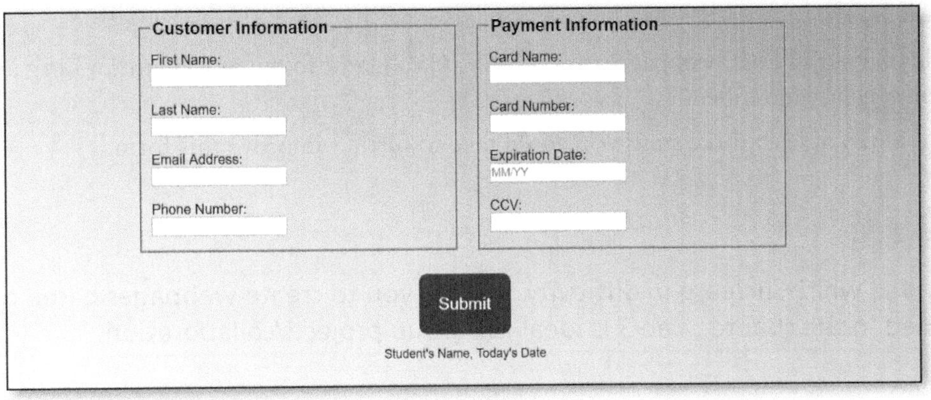

Figure 8–70

1. Correct

a. Open the analyze08.html file in your text editor from the Data Files. Modify the comment at the top of the page to include your name and today's date and then link the file to styles08.css. Indent all nested elements and place input elements on their own line. Add blank lines between elements as appropriate to improve readability.

b. Open the styles08.css file in your text editor from the Data Files and then modify and correct the comment at the top of the document to include your name and today's date.

c. Review the form elements within the analyze08.html file and add labels to all input controls. Be sure to include the `for` attribute.

d. Wrap the form elements within two separate fieldset elements. Analyze the input elements to determine where the fieldsets should start and stop. Use Figures 8–69 and 8–70 as a reference.

e. Include a legend for each fieldset element. Use Figures 8–69 and 8–70 as a reference.

2. Improve

a. In the analyze08.html file, add a submit button below the second fieldset and include the class attribute with a value of btn.

b. Add a placeholder attribute with a value of `MM/YY` to the expDate input.

c. Add the following style rules for a mobile viewport.

   • Create a style rule for the fieldset and input elements that sets the bottom margin to `2%`.

   • Create a style rule for the fieldset legend that sets the font size to `1.25em` and makes the font `bold`.

   • Create a style rule for the btn class selector that removes the border, sets the top and bottom margin to zero and the left and right margin to `auto`, sets the display to a `block`, sets the padding to `5%`, sets the background color to `003399`, sets the font size to `1.25em`, sets the border radius to `10px`, and sets the color to white (fff).

d. Add the following style rules to the tablet media query.

   • Create a style rule for the form element that sets the width to `80%`, sets the top and bottom margins to zero, and the left and right margins to `auto`.

   • Create a style rule for the grid class that sets the display to a grid, sets the grid template columns value to `auto auto`, and sets the grid gap to `20px`.

   • Create a style rule for the btn class that sets the grid column value to `1 / span 2` and padding to `3%`.

e. Save all of your changes and open the analyze08.html in your browser.

f. Validate your CSS file using the W3C validator found at http://jigsaw.w3.org/css-validator/ and fix any errors that are identified.

Continued >

Analyze, Correct, Improve *continued*

g. Validate your HTML webpage using the W3C validator found at validator.w3.org and fix any errors that are identified.

h. ❋ Identify at least three steps you could take to further improve this form.

In the Lab

Labs 1 and 2, which increase in difficulty, require you to create webpages based on what you learned in the chapter; Lab 3 is ideal for group projects/collaboration.

Lab 1: **Adding a Table and Form to the Strike a Chord Website**

Problem: You work for a local music lesson company called Strike a Chord that provides music lessons for piano, guitar, and violin. The company needs a web presence and has hired you to create their website. You have already developed a responsive website and now need to add a table and a form to the website. Use the template.html file to create the Rentals page and add a table to the page. Update the Contact page by adding a form. Figure 8–71 shows the Rentals page in mobile, tablet, and desktop viewports and Figure 8–72 shows the Contact page in mobile, tablet, and desktop viewports.

(a) Mobile Viewport

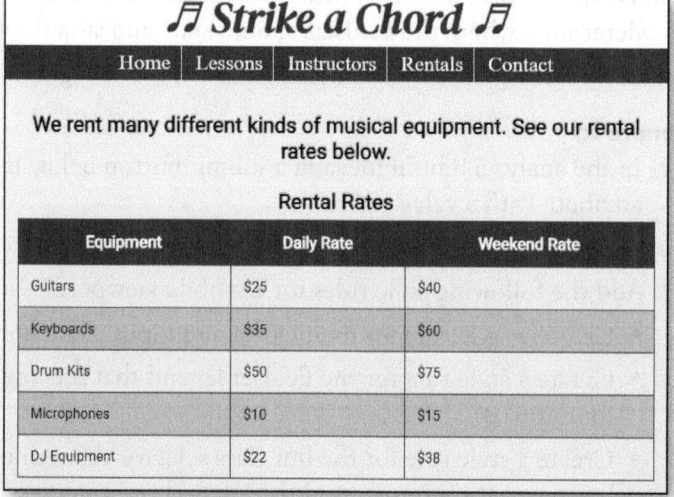

(b) Tablet Viewport

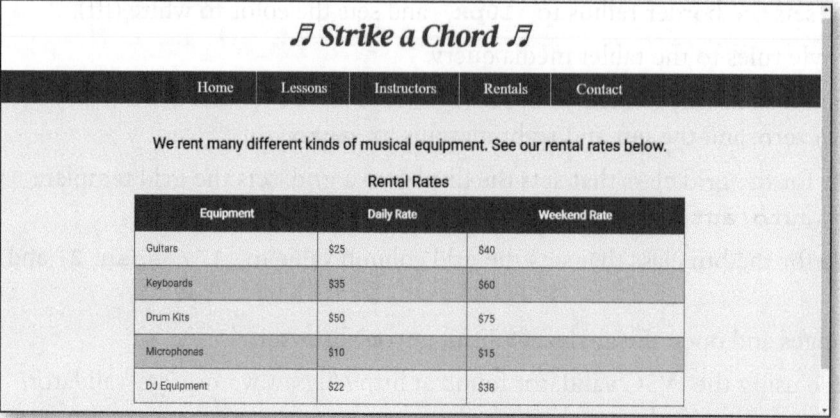

(c) Desktop Viewport

Figure 8–71

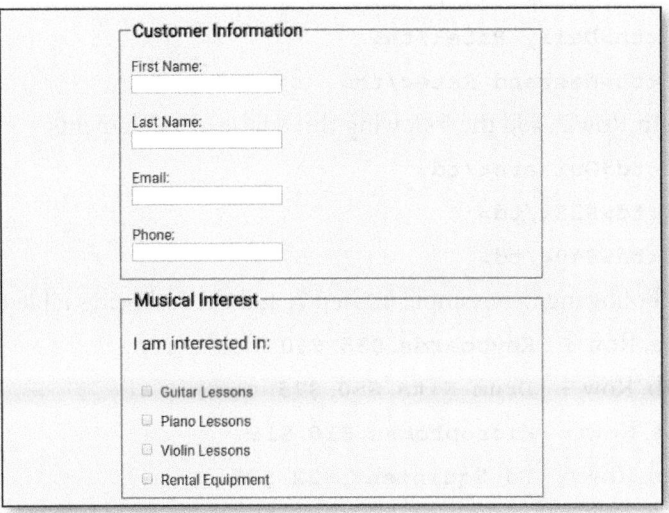

(a) Mobile Viewport

(b) Tablet Viewport

(c) Desktop Viewport

Figure 8–72

Instructions: Perform the following tasks:

1. Open the template.html file in your text editor and use it to create a new page with the file name, `rentals.html`. Update the comment with the file name and today's date. In the title element, replace the word Template with `Rentals`.

2. In the rentals.html file, add an id attribute with a value of `rental` to the empty div element nested within the main element.

3. Insert a heading 2 element within the rental div that contains the following text:

   We rent many different kinds of musical equipment. See our rental rates below.

4. Below the heading 2 element, insert a table element. Add a caption element with the text **Rental Rates**.

5. Insert six rows within the table and include a comment for each row to note the row number. Follow the example below:

   ```
   <tr><!-- Row 1 -->

   </tr>
   ```

Continued >

In the Lab *continued*

6. In Row 1, add the following three table header elements:

```
<th>Equipment</th>
<th>Daily Rate</th>
<th>Weekend Rate</th>
```

7. In Row 2, add the following three table data elements:

```
<td>Guitars</td>
<td>$25</td>
<td>$40</td>
```

8. Following the example in Step 7, add the following table data elements to the remaining rows:

 a. Row 3: `Keyboards, $35, $60`

 b. Row 4: `Drum Kits, $50, $75`

 c. Row 5: `Microphones, $10, $15`

 d. Row 6: `DJ Equipment, $22, $38`

9. In the styles.css file, locate the mobile style rule for #contact and add `#rental h2` as another selector for this style rule.

10. Below the mobile style rule for .map, add the following comment:

```
/* Style rules for table */
```

11. Below the comment, add the following style rules:

```
table {
    border: 1px solid #373684;
    border-collapse: collapse;
    margin: 0 auto;
    width: 100%;
}

caption {
    font-size: 1.5em;
    font-weight: bold;
    padding: 1%;
}

th, td {
    border: 1px solid #373684;
    padding: 2%;
}

th {
    background-color: #373684;
    color: #fff;
    font-size: 1.15em;
}
}
```

```
tr:nth-child(odd) {
    background-color: #b7b7e1;
}
```

12. Within the desktop media query, below the last style rule, add a new comment with the text **Desktop Viewport: Style rules for table.** Below the comment, add a style rule for the table selector that sets the width to **70%**.

13. In the contact.html file, insert a new div element with an id attribute value of **form** below the contact div within the main element. Insert a heading 2 element within the form div and include the text, **Complete the form below and one of our staff members will contact you.** Insert a form element with a class attribute value of **form-grid** below the heading 2 element. Include a comment to note where the form begins. Follow the example below.

```
<form class="form-grid"><!-- Start Form -->
</form>
```

14. Nest two fieldsets within the form element. Include a legend for each fieldset. Use the text **Customer Information** for the first fieldset legend, and use the text **Musical Interest** for the second fieldset legend.

15. Add the following label and input elements to the first fieldset:

```
<label for="fName">First Name:</label>
<input type="text" name="fName" id="fName">

<label for="lName">Last Name:</label>
<input type="text" name="lName" id="lName">

<label for="email">Email:</label>
<input type="email" name="email" id="email">

<label for="phone">Phone:</label>
<input type="tel" id="phone" name="phone">
```

16. Add the following paragraph, label, and input elements to the second fieldset:

```
<p>I am interested in:</p>

<label for="guitarles"><input type="checkbox" name="interest"
id="guitarles" value="Guitar Lessons">Guitar Lessons</label>

<label for="piano"><input type="checkbox" name="interest"
id="pianoles" value="Piano Lessons">Piano Lessons</label>

<label for="violin"><input type="checkbox" name="interest"
id="violinles" value="Violin Lessons">Violin Lessons</label>

<label for="rent"><input type="checkbox" name="interest"
id="rent" value="Rental Equipment">Rental Equipment</label>
```

17. Below the second fieldset, add a submit button with the following attributes:

```
type="submit"
id="submit"
value="Submit"
class="btn"
```

Continued >

In the Lab *continued*

18. In the styles.css file, insert a comment with the text `Style rules for form elements` above the comment for the footer style rules. Then create the following style rules for a mobile viewport:

   a. Create a style rule for the fieldset and input selectors that sets the bottom margin to `2%`.

   b. Create a style rule for the fieldset legend selector that sets the font weight to `bold` and font size to `1.25em`.

   c. Create a style rule for the label selector that sets the display to a `block` and sets the top padding to `3%`.

   d. Create a style rule for the form #submit selector that sets the top and bottom margin to zero, left and right margins to `auto`, display to `block`, padding to `3%`, background color to `b7b7e1`, and the font size to `1em`.

19. In the styles.css file, within the tablet media query, insert a comment with the text `Tablet Viewport: Style rule for form element` below the .map style rule. Then, create a style rule for the form selector that sets the width to `70%` and sets top and bottom margin to zero, and left and right margins to `auto`.

20. In the styles.css file, within the desktop media query, insert a comment with the text `Desktop Viewport: Style rules for form elements` below the table style rule. Then create the following style rules:

   a. Create a style rule for the form-grid class selector that sets the display to a `grid`, sets the grid template columns value to `auto auto`, and sets the grid gap to `20px`.

   b. Create a style rule for the btn class selector that sets the grid column value to `1 / span 2`.

21. Use good coding practices by including indents and spacing between style rules.

22. Check your spelling. Validate all HTML and CSS files and correct any errors. Save your changes.

23. Open the rentals.html file in Google Chrome's device mode to view the table on the Rentals page in mobile, tablet, and desktop viewports.

24. Open the contact.html file in Google Chrome's device mode to view the form on the Contact page in mobile, tablet, and desktop viewports.

25. Submit your assignment in the format specified by your instructor.

26. ✳ In this assignment, you created a form with several input elements. What other elements could you use to improve this form? Provide a code example.

Lab 2: Adding a Table and Form to the Wild Rescues Website

Problem: You volunteer at a local wildlife rescue, a nonprofit organization called Wild Rescues. The organization rescues all kinds of wild animals, rehabilitates them, and then releases them back into the wild. Wild Rescues needs a website to help raise awareness about the organization. You have already developed a responsive website and now need to add a table and a form to the website. Use the template.html file to create the Partnership page and add a table to the page. Update the Contact page by adding a form. Figure 8–73 shows the Partnership page in in mobile and desktop viewports. Figure 8–74 shows the form on the Contact page in mobile, tablet, and desktop viewports.

We are grateful for the support from our community partners. We have many sponsorship opportunities.

Sponsorship Levels

Green: $200

Blue: $400

Red: $600

Purple: $800

Silver: $1,000

Gold: $1,500

Each sponsorship supports our animals and operations. Business recognition is given at every

(a) Mobile Viewport

Sponsorship Opportunities

Sponsorship Level	Dollar Amount	Details	Sponsorship Benefits
Green	$200	The green sponsorship helps us maintain green pastures for our grazing friends.	Recognition on our website.
Blue	$400	The blue sponsorship helps us provide food for the animals.	Recognition on our website and our brochure.
Red	$600	The red sponsorship helps us provide medical care for the animals.	Recognition on our website and our brochure. Business logo displayed on a banner at our facility.
Purple	$800	The purple sponsorship helps us maintain homes for the animals.	Recognition on our website and our brochure. Business logo displayed on a banner at our facility. Business name and logo displayed at the annual community event.
Silver	$1,000	The silver sponsorship supports our monthly expenses.	Recognition on our website and our brochure. Business logo displayed on a banner at our facility. Business name and logo displayed at the annual community event. Recognition plaque with business name prominently displayed within the facility.
Gold	$1,500	The gold sponsorship supports our operation costs.	Recognition on our website and our brochure. Business logo displayed on a banner at our facility. Business name and logo displayed at the annual community event. Recognition plaque with business name prominently displayed within the facility. Display table at the annual community event. Recognition in all media releases.

(b) Desktop Viewport

Figure 8–73

(a) Mobile Viewport

Contact Information
First Name:

Last Name:

Name of Business:

Email:

Phone:

Additional Information

I would like more information about:

○ Volunteering
○ Sponsorship Opportunities
○ Wildlife
○ Other, please specify below.

(b) Tablet Viewport

Contact Information
First Name:

Last Name:

Name of Business:

Email:

Phone:

Additional Information

I would like more information about:

○ Volunteering
○ Sponsorship Opportunities
○ Wildlife

(c) Desktop Viewport

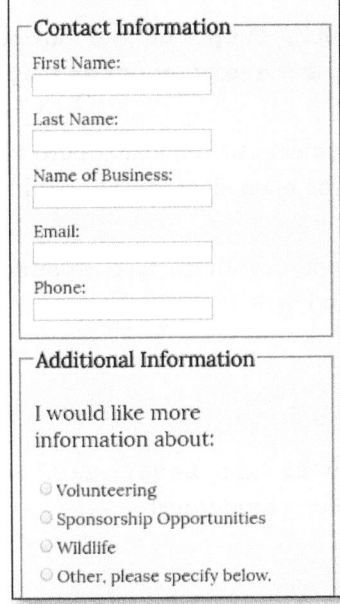

Complete the form below and we will contact you soon.

Contact Information
First Name:

Last Name:

Name of Business:

Email:

Phone:

Additional Information

I would like more information about:

○ Volunteering
○ Sponsorship Opportunities
○ Wildlife
○ Other, please specify below.

What questions do you have for us?

Submit

Figure 8–74

Continued >

In the Lab *continued*

Instructions: Perform the following tasks:

1. Open the template.html file in your text editor and use it to create a new page with the file name **partnership.html**. Update the comment with the file name and today's date. In the title element, replace the word Template with **Partnership**.

2. In the partnership.html file, nest a heading 2 element within the main element (above the empty div element) that contains the following text:

   We are grateful for the support from our community partners. We have many sponsorship opportunities.

3. Add a class attribute with the value **mobile-tablet** to the empty div element. Nest the following elements within this div element:

   a. Heading 3 element with the text **Sponsorship Levels.**

   b. Paragraph element with the text **Green: $200.**

   c. Paragraph element with the text **Blue: $400.**

   d. Paragraph element with the text **Red: $600.**

   e. Paragraph element with the text **Purple: $800.**

   f. Paragraph element with the text **Silver: $1,000.**

   g. Paragraph element with the text **Gold: $1,500.**

   h. Paragraph element with the text **Each sponsorship supports our animals and operations. Business recognition is given at every sponsorship level. Contact us today to become a sponsor.**

4. Insert a new div element below the mobile-tablet div element. Add an id attribute with a value of **partner** to the empty div element nested within the main element. Then, add a class attribute with a value of **desktop** to the div element.

5. Nest a table within the partner div element. Include a caption with the text **Sponsorship Opportunities.** Insert seven rows within the table and include a comment for each row to note the row number. Follow the example below:

   ```
   <tr><!-- Row 1 -->
   </tr>
   ```

6. In Row 1, add four table header elements and use **Sponsorship Level, Dollar Amount, Details,** and **Sponsorship Benefits** as the column header text.

7. Add the following table data to rows two through seven:

Green	$200	The green sponsorship helps us maintain green pastures for our grazing friends.	Recognition on our website.
Blue	$400	The blue sponsorship helps us provide food for the animals.	Recognition on our website and our brochure.
Red	$600	The red sponsorship helps us provide medical care for the animals.	Recognition on our website and our brochure. Business logo displayed on a banner at our facility.
Purple	$800	The purple sponsorship helps us maintain homes for the animals.	Recognition on our website and our brochure. Business logo displayed on a banner at our facility. Business name and logo displayed at the annual community event.

Silver	$1,000	The silver sponsorship supports our monthly expenses.	Recognition on our website and our brochure. Business logo displayed on a banner at our facility. Business name and logo displayed at the annual community event. Recognition plaque with business name prominently displayed within the facility.
Gold	$1,500	The gold sponsorship supports our operation costs.	Recognition on our website and our brochure. Business logo displayed on a banner at our facility. Business name and logo displayed at the annual community event. Recognition plaque with business name prominently displayed within the facility. Display table at the annual community event. Recognition in all media releases.

8. In the styles.css file, locate the mobile style rule for .mobile and add the mobile-tablet class selector as another selector for this style rule. Locate the mobile style rule for .tab-desk and add the desktop class selector as another selector for this style rule.

9. In the desktop media query, modify the first comment within the query to, Desktop Viewport: Show desktop class`, hide mobile-tablet class.` Below the .desktop style rule, create a new style rule for the mobile-tablet class selector that sets the display to **none**.

10. In the desktop media query, add the following comment after the style rule for aside:

    `/* Style rules for table */`

11. Below the comment, add the following style rules:

    a. Create a style rule for the table selector that specifies a border with values of **1px solid #2a1f14,** collapses the border, and sets top and bottom margins to zero and left and right margins to **auto.**

    b. Create a style rule for the caption selector that specifies a font size of **1.5em,** font weight of **bold,** and sets the padding to **1%.**

    c. Create a style rule for th and td selectors that specifies a border with values of **1px solid #2a1f14,** and sets the padding to **1%.**

    d. Create a style rule for the th selector that sets the background color to **2a1f14,** the color to white (fff), and the font size to **1.15em.**

    e. Create a style rule for the tr selector that sets the background color to **#deccba** for odd rows.

12. In the contact.html file, insert a new div element with an id attribute value of **form** below the contact div within the main element. Insert a heading 2 element within the form div and include the text **Complete the form below and we will contact you soon.** Insert a form element with a class attribute value of **form-grid** below the heading 2 element. Include a comment to note where the form begins. Follow the example below.

    `<form class="form-grid"><!-- Start Form -->`

    `</form>`

13. Nest two fieldsets within the form element. Include a legend for each fieldset. Use the text **Contact Information** for the first fieldset legend, and use the text **Additional Information** for the second fieldset legend.

Continued >

In the Lab *continued*

14. Add the following label and input elements to the first fieldset:

   a. Insert a label element with the for attribute value `fName` and include the text, `First Name:` between the label tags. Below the label, insert an input element and specify the type attribute as `text`, name attribute as `fName`, and id attribute as `fName`.

   b. Insert a label element with the for attribute value `lName` and include the text `Last Name:` between the label tags. Below the label, insert an input element and specify the type attribute as `text`, name attribute as `lName`, and id attribute as `lName`.

   c. Insert a label element with the for attribute value `bName` and include the text `Name of Business:` between the label tags. Below the label, insert an input element and specify the type attribute as `text`, name attribute as `bName`, and id attribute as `bName`.

   d. Insert a label element with the for attribute value `email` and include the text `Email:` between the label tags. Below the label, insert an input element and specify the type attribute as `email`, name attribute as `email`, and id attribute as `email`.

   e. Insert a label element with the for attribute value `phone` and include the text `Phone:` between the label tags. Below the label, insert an input element and specify the type attribute as `tel`, name attribute as `phone`, and id attribute as `phone`.

15. Add the following elements to the second fieldset, below the legend:

   a. Insert a paragraph element with the text `I would like more information about:`.

   b. Insert a label element with the for attribute value `vol`. Nest an input element within the label element and specify the type attribute as `radio`, name attribute as `info`, id attribute as `vol`, and value as `Volunteering`. Add the text `Volunteering` after the input element and before the closing label tag.

   c. Insert a label element with the for attribute value `sponsor`. Nest an input element within the label element and specify the type attribute as `radio`, name attribute as `info`, id attribute as `sponsor`, and value as `Sponsorship Opportunities`. Add the text `Sponsorship Opportunities` after the input element and before the closing label tag.

   d. Insert a label element with the for attribute value `wild`. Nest an input element within the label element and specify the type attribute as `radio`, name attribute as `info`, id attribute as `wild`, and value as `Wildlife`. Add the text, `Wildlife`, after the input element and before the closing label tag.

   e. Insert a label element with the for attribute value `other`. Nest an input element within the label element and specify the type attribute as `radio`, name attribute as `info`, id attribute as `other`, and value as `Other`. Add the text `Other, please specify below.` after the input element and before the closing label tag.

   f. Insert a label element with the for attribute value `questions` and include the text `What questions do you have for us?` between the label tags. Below the label, insert a textarea element and specify the name attribute as `questions`, the id attribute as `questions`, the rows attribute to `5`, and the cols attribute to `35`.

16. Below the second fieldset, add a submit button with the following attributes:

   `type="submit"`

   `id="submit"`

   `value="Submit"`

   `class="btn"`

17. In the styles.css file, locate the style rule for #contact within the style rules for mobile. Add `#form h2` as another selector for this style rule.

18. Insert a comment with the text **Style rules for form elements** above the comment for the footer style rules. Then create the following style rules for a mobile viewport:

   a. Create a style rule for the fieldset, input, and textarea selectors that sets the bottom margin to **2%**.

   b. Create a style rule for the fieldset legend selector that sets the font weight to **bold** and font size to **1.25em**.

   c. Create a style rule for the label selector that sets the display to a **block** and sets the top padding to **2%**.

   d. Create a style rule for the form #submit selector that sets the top and bottom margin to zero, left and right margins to **auto**, display to **block**, padding to **2%**, background color to **78593a**, color to **f6eee4**, the font size to **1.25 em**, and the border radius to **10px**.

19. In the styles.css file, within the tablet media query, insert a comment with the text **Tablet Viewport: Style rule for form element** below the aside style rule. Then, create a style rule for the form selector that sets the width to **70%** and sets top and bottom margin to zero, left and right margins to **auto**.

20. In the styles.css file, within the desktop media query, insert a comment with the text **Desktop Viewport: Style rules for form elements** below the table row style rule. Then create the following style rules:

   a. Create a style rule for the form selector that sets the width to **auto**.

   b. Create a style rule for the form-grid class selector that sets the display to a **grid**, sets the grid template columns value to **auto auto**, and sets the grid gap to **20px**.

   c. Create a style rule for the btn class selector that sets the grid column value to **1 / span 2**.

21. Use good coding practices by including indents and spacing between style rules.

22. Check your spelling. Validate all HTML and CSS files and correct any errors. Save your changes.

23. Open the partnership.html file in Google Chrome's device mode to view the table on the Partnership page in mobile, tablet, and desktop viewports.

24. Open the contact.html file in Google Chrome's device mode to view the form on the Contact page in mobile, tablet, and desktop viewports.

25. Submit your assignment in the format specified by your instructor.

26. ☀ Research the date type input control. Is this input type supported by all major browsers? Note your findings.

Lab 3: Adding a Table and Form to the Student Clubs and Events Website

Problem: You and several of your classmates have decided to help increase student involvement in school clubs and events by creating a website to promote awareness about the various activities. You have already created a responsive design website and now you need to add a table and form to the website.

Instructions:

1. Add a table with a minimum of five columns and six rows. As a team, discuss how the table will be used and determine which page will contain the table. Include at least one rowspan or colspan. Create a new page if necessary.

Continued >

In the Lab *continued*

2. Design the table as a team. Use your stylesheet to format your table for all viewports. Determine if the table is suitable for a mobile viewport. If not, hide the table for mobile and use an alternate method to display the content.

3. As a team, design and build a form. Create a new page if necessary. Decide what input controls you will use and how you will style the form elements for mobile, tablet, and desktop viewports. At a minimum, update the HTML and CSS files to do the following:

   a. Add a form to the page of your choice.

   b. Add text input controls, include appropriate attributes, and make at least two fields required.

   c. Add a select and textarea element.

   d. Add a form element not used within the chapter project.

   e. Add a submit button.

   f. Style the form elements for mobile, tablet, and desktop viewports.

4. Use Google Chrome's device mode to view and the table and form for each viewport.

5. Review your files for best coding practices; ensure proper spacing and indents for improved readability. Add comments when adding new style rules.

6. Submit your assignment in the format specified by your instructor.

7. ✺ Research the requirements to submit a form to a server for processing and provide a summary of your findings.

Consider This: Your Turn

Apply your creative thinking and problem-solving skills to design and implement a solution.

1. Adding a Table and Form to Your Personal Portfolio Website
Personal

Part 1: You have already developed a responsive website for your personal portfolio and now need to add a table and a form to the website.

1. Add a table to one of your webpages. Use the table to list your work experience or to showcase your technological proficiencies. Use a minimum of four rows and three columns for your table.

2. Determine whether to show or hide the table for a mobile viewport. If you hide the table from the mobile viewport, use a list to display your table content for a mobile viewport.

3. Update the CSS file to:

   a. Style the table element for mobile, tablet, and desktop viewports.

   b. Refine your style sheet as desired.

   c. Add comments to note all changes and updates.

4. Add a form to your website. Use a minimum of five form elements, including a Submit button.

5. Use your style sheet to create rules for your form elements. Style for mobile, table, and desktop viewports.

6. Review your files for best coding practices; ensure proper spacing and indents for improved readability.

7. Validate all HTML and CSS files and correct any errors.

8. Submit your assignment in the format specified by your instructor.

Part 2: ✺ List at least three pros and three cons of using a table.

2. Adding a Table and Form to the Dog Grooming Website

Professional

Part 1:   You have already developed a responsive website for your personal portfolio and now need to add a table and a form to the website.

1. Add a table to one of your webpages. Use a minimum of six rows and three columns for your table.

2. Determine whether to show or hide the table for a mobile viewport. If you hide the table from the mobile viewport, use a list or other element to display your table data for a mobile viewport.

3. Update the CSS file to:

    a.   Style the table element for mobile, tablet, and desktop viewports.

    b.   Style alternating rows differently.

    c.   Refine your style sheet as desired.

    d.   Add comments to note all changes and updates.

4. Add a form to your website. Include a minimum of six form elements, including a Submit button. Include at least two fieldsets and two legends.

5. Use your style sheet to create rules for your form elements. Style for mobile, table, and desktop viewports.

6. Review your files for best coding practices; ensure proper spacing and indents for improved readability.

7. Validate all HTML and CSS files and correct any errors.

8. Submit your assignment in the format specified by your instructor.

Part 2:   ⚙ Research TSL/SSL (Transport Layer Security/Secure Sockets Layer) and then provide a summary of your findings and a link to your resource.

3. Adding a Table and Form to the Future Technologies Website

Research and Collaboration

Part 1:   You and several of your classmates have been tasked with creating a website that showcases advances in technology. You have already created already design the website for a mobile viewport and now need to design it for tablet, desktop, large desktop, and print viewports.

1. Add a table to one of your webpages. As a group, determine the best use of a table within the website. Use a minimum of eight rows and five columns for your table. Use at least one rowspan or colspan within your table.

2. Determine whether to show or hide the table for a mobile viewport. If you hide the table from the mobile viewport, use a list or other element to display your table data for a mobile viewport.

3. Update the CSS file to:

    a.   Style the table element for mobile, tablet, and desktop viewports.

    b.   Style alternating rows differently.

    c.   Refine your style sheet as desired.

    d.   Add comments to note all changes and updates.

4. Add a form to your website. Include a minimum of eight form elements, including a Submit button. Include at least two fieldsets and two legends. Add the required attribute to at least two input elements. Add a placeholder attribute to at least one input element.

Continued >

Consider This: Your Turn *continued*

5. Use your style sheet to create rules for your form elements. Style for mobile, table, and desktop viewports.

6. Review your files for best coding practices; ensure proper spacing and indents for improved readability.

7. Validate all HTML and CSS files and correct any errors.

8. Submit your assignment in the format specified by your instructor.

Part 2: ✳ Research PHP and discuss how it is used with web form processing. Provide an example of its syntax.

9 | Integrating Audio and Video

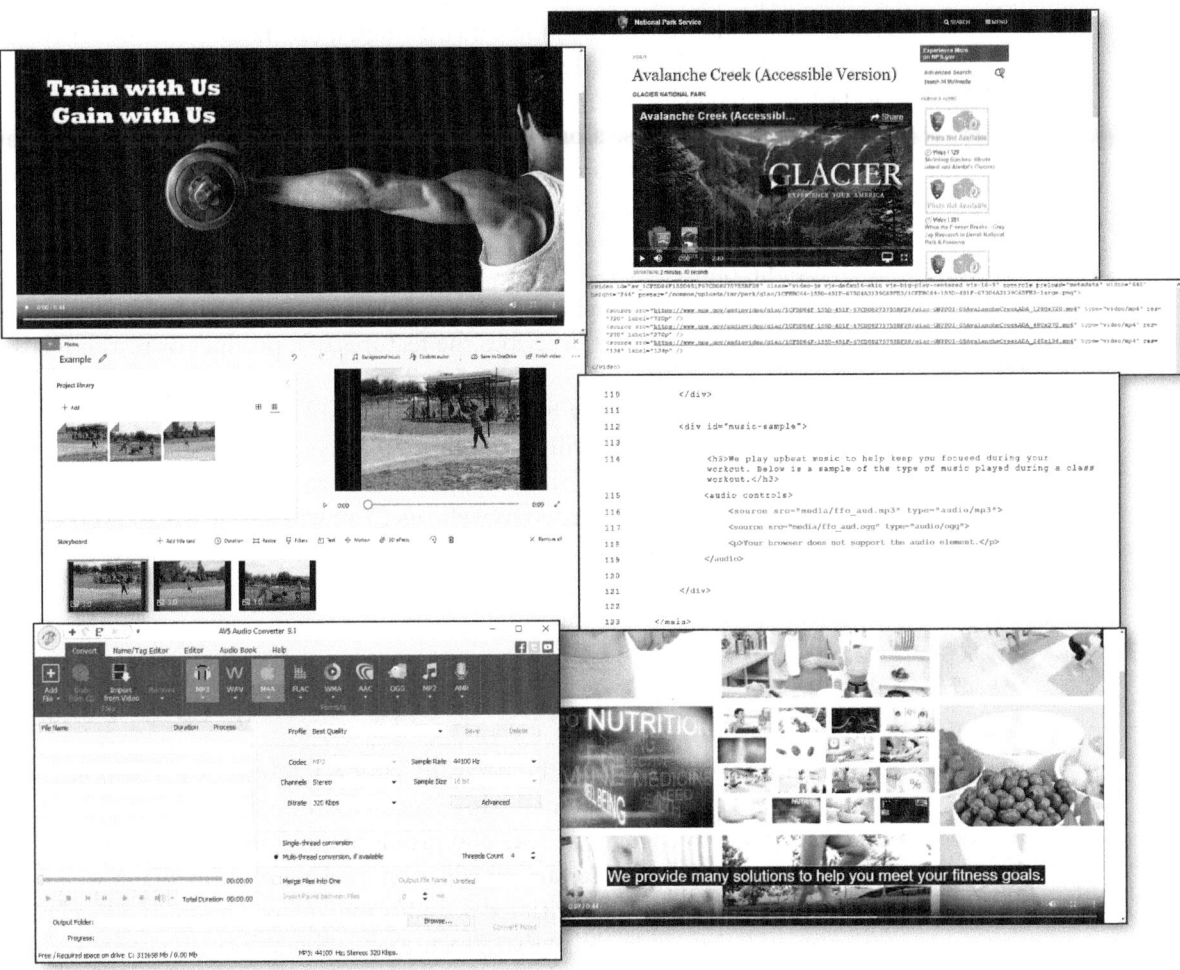

Objectives

You will have mastered the material in this chapter when you can:

- Describe the benefits and limitations of multimedia in websites
- Identify audio formats
- Identify video formats
- Describe a plug-in
- Understand codecs
- Understand and create audio elements

- Understand and create video elements
- Identify common audio attributes
- Identify common video attributes
- Understand the source element
- Test audio elements
- Test video elements
- Make videos accessible

9 | Integrating Audio and Video

Introduction

A website provides several creative opportunities to capture the attention of your audience. Many websites use multimedia (digital media such as audio, video, and animation) to enrich the user experience and provide interactivity. For example, websites include videos to share news updates, promote products and services, or demonstrate how to use a product. Videos add visual appeal and can pack a huge amount of information into a few seconds. According to a recent study by Forrester Research, consumers prefer videos to text, find them more memorable, and stay on websites that include videos longer than websites that do not.

Audio on webpages can set a mood or tone and further entice a user to make a purchase. Audio can also provide information more quickly or effectively than text, such as a guided tour that describes the features of a product or testimonials from customers that support a product or service.

In this chapter, you will learn how to use HTML 5 to embed audio and video on an HTML webpage. You will learn how to use the **audio** element and its attributes to add audio to a webpage. Similarly, you will learn how to use the **video** element and its attributes to add a video to webpage. You will also learn about the various audio and video file formats and which formats to use for the web. Finally, you will learn how to make videos accessible.

Project — Add Audio and Video to a Webpage

In this chapter, you enhance the Forward Fitness Club website by adding audio to the Classes page to improve the user experience. Additionally, you insert a video in the About Us page to engage the user and promote the club.

This chapter provides an introduction to using multimedia in web development, focusing on two forms of multimedia: audio and video. The finished webpages contain relevant audio and video clips that provide valuable multimedia content for visitors of the Forward Fitness Club website.

The project in this chapter improves a website by integrating HTML 5 **audio** and **video** elements. To perform these tasks, you first copy the media files to your media folder. Next, you add an **audio** element to a webpage. Then, you add a **video** element to a webpage. Finally, you make the video accessible by integrating captions. In the style sheet, you add style rules for the **video** element for tablet and desktop viewports. Figure 9–1 shows the Classes page with the embedded audio and controls. Figure 9–2 shows the video on the About Us page.

Boot Camp	Tue, Thu	5:00am, 5:00pm	Taylor	B
Spinning	Tue, Thu	6:00am, 6:00pm	Roberts	A
Kickboxing	Mon, Wed, Fri	8:00am, 7:15pm	Lawrence	A
Yoga	Tue, Thu	6:00am, 6:00pm	Schultz	B
Zumba	Mon, Wed, Fri	7:00am, 6:00pm	Roberts	A

We play upbeat music to help keep you focused during your workout. Below is a sample of the type of music played during a class workout.

▶ 0:00 / 2:21 ━━━━━ 🔊

Classes Page

Figure 9–1

About Us Page

Figure 9–2

Roadmap

In this chapter, you will learn how to create the webpages shown in Figures 9–1 and 9–2. The following roadmap identifies general activities you will perform as you progress through this chapter:

1. INSERT the AUDIO ELEMENT.
2. INSERT the VIDEO ELEMENT.
3. STYLE the VIDEO ELEMENT.
4. MAKE the VIDEO ACCESSIBLE.

At the beginning of step instructions throughout the chapter, you will see an abbreviated form of this roadmap. The abbreviated roadmap uses colors to indicate chapter progress: gray means the chapter is beyond that activity; blue means the task being shown is covered in that activity; and black means that activity is yet to be covered. For example, the following abbreviated roadmap indicates the chapter would be showing a task in the 2 INSERT VIDEO ELEMENT activity.

1 INSERT AUDIO ELEMENT | 2 INSERT VIDEO ELEMENT

3 STYLE VIDEO ELEMENT | 4 MAKE VIDEO ACCESSIBLE

Use the abbreviated roadmap as a progress guide while you read or step through the instructions in this chapter.

Using Multimedia

The popularity of the web is due in part to its ability to display webpages that include graphic images, audio, and video. These additions can boost the visual appeal of a website and make the browsing experience more enjoyable and interactive. Sometimes, however, multimedia can distract from the website message. When deciding whether to include multimedia, remember the purpose of the website. If the multimedia content enhances that purpose, it should be included. If the multimedia content distracts from the purpose of the website, then you should reconsider using it.

Multimedia is the combination of text, images, sound, and video to express an idea or convey a message. Because most people have broadband Internet connections that can transfer data quickly, multimedia webpages that include large graphics, audio, and video are common. Figure 9–3 shows an example of multimedia used on the ted.com.

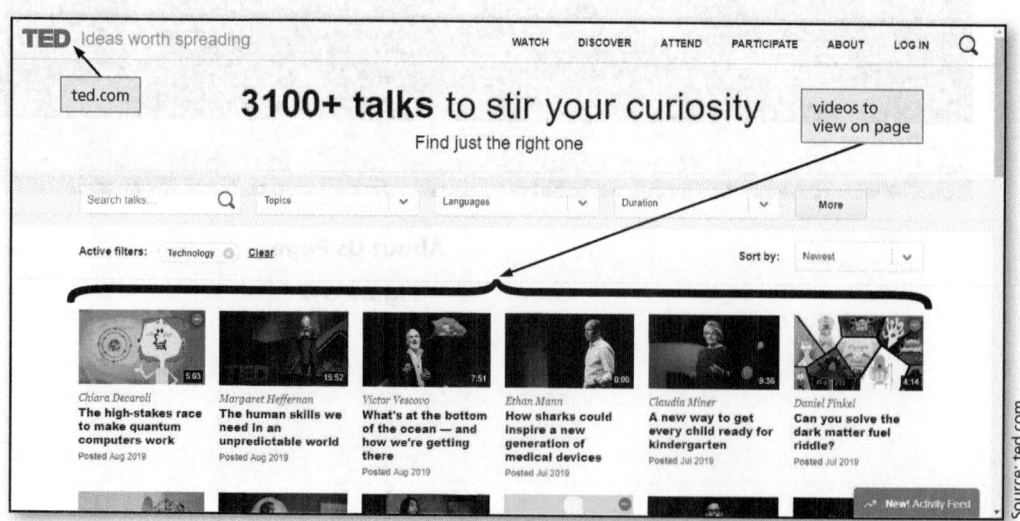

Figure 9–3

Many websites use videos to advertise products, to entertain visitors, or to provide instruction. For example, you may be able to review a medical procedure online before having the procedure done yourself. You can view clips of movies or hear segments of audio recordings from webpages that provide content in those formats. **Podcasts**, a series of audio or video clips that are released in a sequence, are popular in home, academic, and corporate settings. Figure 9–4 shows an example of podcasts on the National Public Radio website.

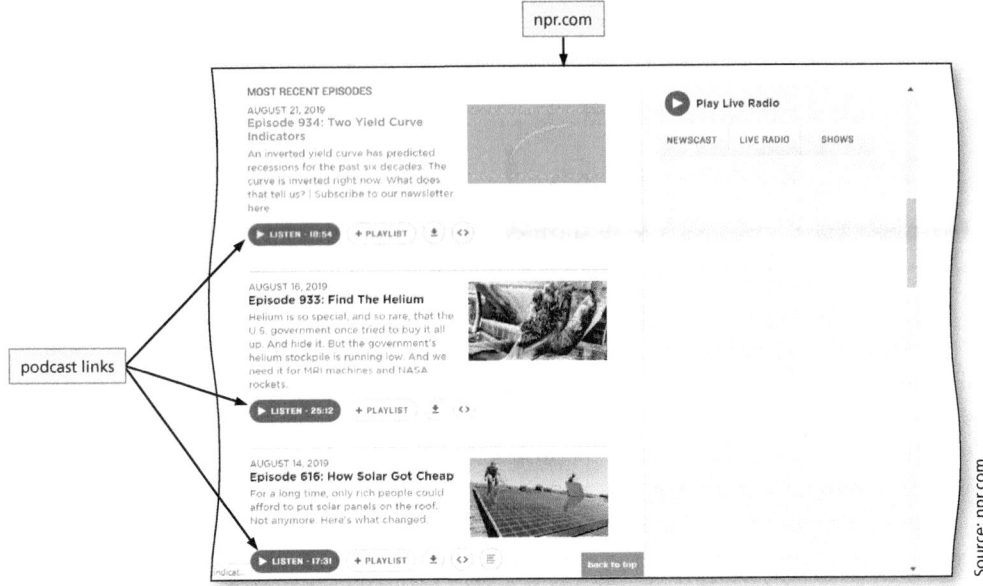

Figure 9–4

Creating Multimedia Files

You can obtain multimedia files by creating them yourself or by finding files that are already available. If you create your own multimedia files, you do not have to be concerned with copyright or licensing agreements. On the other hand, the multimedia files might not have the same quality and effectiveness as professional content. You can create your own audio files using a microphone and software designed to edit digital files, such as Audacity, a free, open-source audio editor, and Adobe Audition, which can be purchased as part of the Adobe Creative Cloud. If you do use any portion of files that have been professionally developed, such as those from an online multimedia provider, be certain that you understand and follow the copyright and licensing requirements.

For video files, you can use a digital camcorder, a digital camera, or even a smartphone to create clips that can be included on a webpage. Photos is a video editor that comes standard with the Windows 10 operating system (Figure 9–5). This application can be used to create a multimedia video. Movie Maker 10 is available as a free app through the Microsoft Store, with an option to upgrade features for a nominal fee. Corel VideoStudio Ultimate has simple and more advanced menu system options that novice movie editors and professionals alike can use comfortably. CyberLink PowerDirector is another software option that allows you to create professional-quality videos.

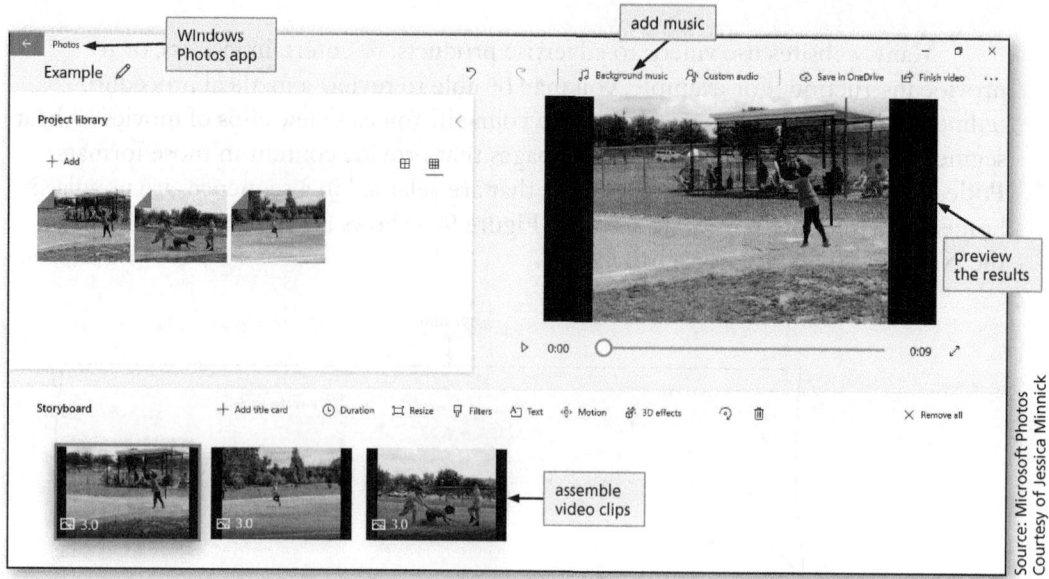

Figure 9–5

The Apple operating system, macOS, includes iMovie, which is another application used for creating and editing videos. iMovie comes standard on the macOS. It is also available as a free app for the Apple iPad and iPhone. Final Cut Pro X is a video editor for the macOS that offers professional-level editing. Final Cut Pro X is available for purchase from Apple.

Adobe Premiere Pro is another highly rated application for movie editing that can be used on either the macOS or Windows operating systems. As with many multimedia software products, Adobe Premiere Pro lets novice users create professional-quality video. Adobe Premiere can be purchased with an Adobe Creative Cloud subscription. Figure 9–6 shows the Adobe Premiere Pro Creative Cloud application.

Figure 9–6

Many audio- and video-editing applications offer a free trial period. You might try downloading a free trial of the software, if available, and using it to create or edit a movie. You could also try a few different programs to see how they work. Most multimedia software operates in a similar fashion and has a user-friendly help utility that guides you through the process of editing. Most products also provide templates and effects that enhance the creative aspects of presenting multimedia.

To find multimedia resources on the web, search for "public domain audio or video." These resources are available free of copyright restrictions. Websites that provide stock photos often provide music, sound, and video files for a fee. Before using any content, be sure to understand and follow the copyright license agreements that accompany any multimedia content that you find on the web.

BTW

Online Resources
Shutterstock provides audio and video files for a fee. Free Music Archive has many audio files available under the Creative Commons license.

Can I use any images, audio, or video I find on the Internet to create a multimedia file?
In general, no, you cannot use any file you find. However, as a student, you are permitted to use some for academic purposes. This is known as Fair Use. For more information about copyright laws, visit copyright.gov.

Embedded vs. External Multimedia

Embedding media is similar to inserting inline images. The embedded media files appear within the webpage along with the audio or video player controls. Visitors use the controls to play or stop the media. Because the media file is embedded directly into the webpage, you can complement the audio or video clip resource with surrounding text or graphical images. Before HTML 5, the **object** element was used to insert embedded content, including multimedia. HTML 5 introduced two new elements, **audio** and **video**, to use as an alternative to the **object** element. Figure 9–7 shows an example of how the National Park Service uses the **video** element on its webpage.

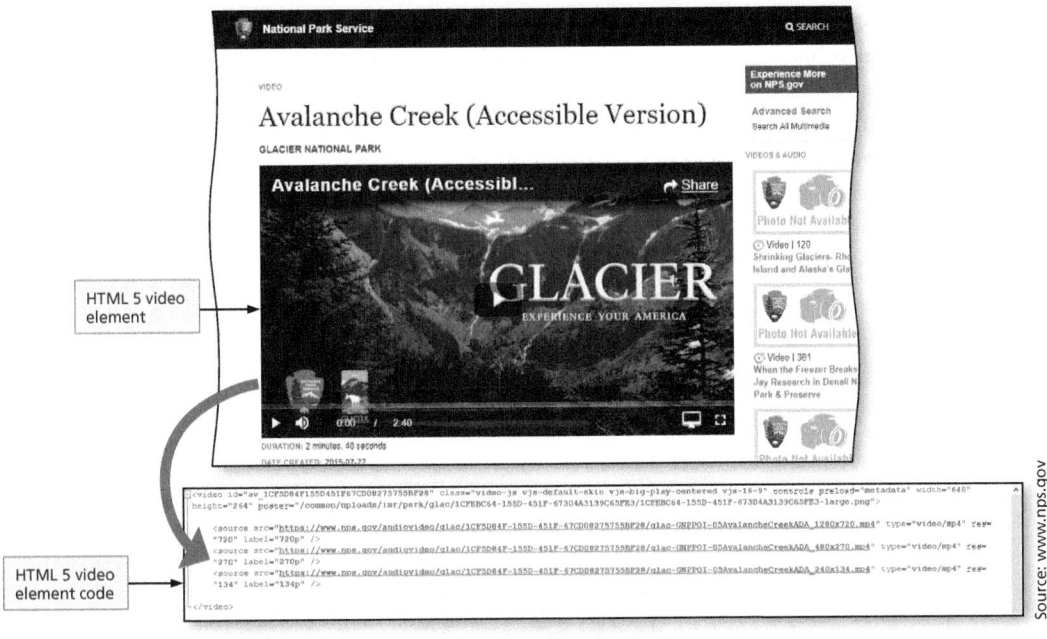

HTML 5 video element

HTML 5 video element code

Source: www.nps.gov

Figure 9–7

To access external media files, website visitors click a link. They can then decide whether to link directly to the external source or download the file. Unlike embedded media, the external media is displayed out of context with the webpage that contains the link. Using external links is a common web development practice. For example, sites that provide many video resources, such as YouTube, use external media files and the **embed** element, which defines a container for an external application or interactive content (also called a plug-in). Figure 9–8 shows an example of an embedded YouTube video on the Mashable website.

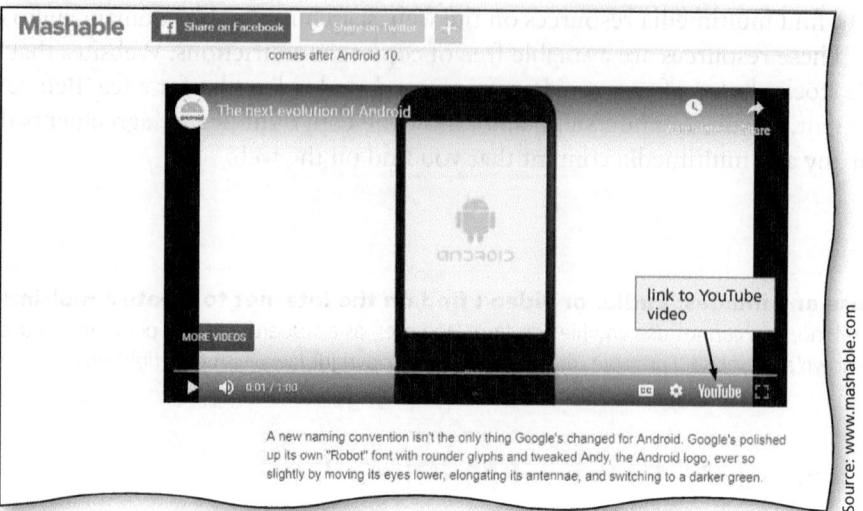

Source: www.mashable.com

Figure 9–8

Media Players and Plug-Ins

As you know, browsers can display text and the graphics formats discussed in earlier chapters without using external software. To play an audio or video file, however, some browsers need the help of an application called a media player or an extension. A **media player** is computer software that plays multimedia files. Most software media players support an array of media formats, including audio and video files. This chapter uses an .mp3 audio file and an .mp4 video file. The Google Chrome browser can play files in both formats. Windows Media Player, included as part of Windows, also plays both audio and video. The Mac operating system comes with QuickTime Player for playing movies, while iTunes can be downloaded for Windows or macOS to play a variety of media formats.

A **browser extension** (also called a plugin) is extra software added to the browser (or other program) to provide a capability that is not inherent to the browser. More than 1,000 extensions are available for Google Chrome that allow users to customize their Google Chrome browser experience. Popular browser extensions include Grammarly, AdBlocker Ultimate, McAfee SiteAdvisor, HTTPS Everywhere, and Adobe Acrobat. Figure 9–9 shows the home page for Google Chrome extensions, where you can search for extensions to add to your Google Chrome browser.

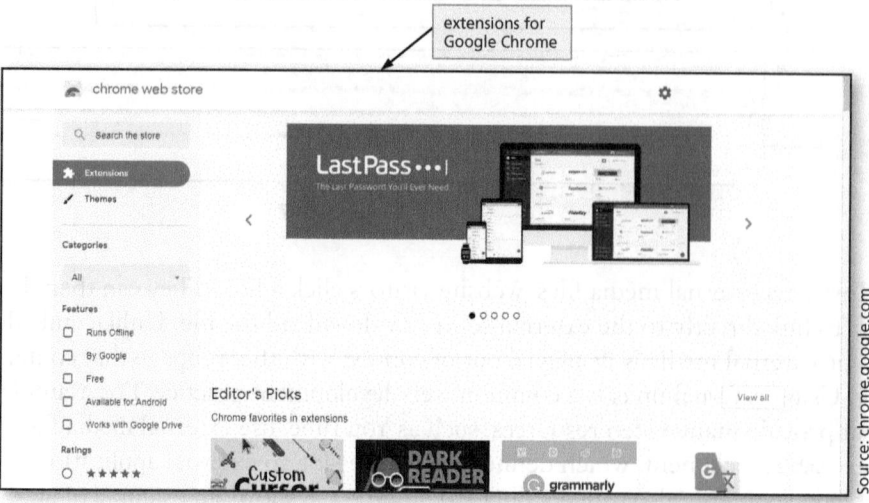

Source: chrome.google.com

Figure 9–9

As you will see in the following section, the various audio and video formats can be played on a variety of players. For embedded multimedia, use a format supported by multiple players.

HTML 5 and Multimedia

HTML 5 introduced built-in media support via the `audio` and `video` elements. Using these elements, web developers can easily embed media into HTML documents. This chapter teaches you how to use the HTML 5 `audio` and `video` elements. Additional multimedia types discussed in this chapter include Flash, Java applets, and the HTML `object` element.

Flash

Flash, or Adobe Flash Player, has been used within websites for more than 20 years. Using Flash, you can create animations or movie files. Flash files have the .swf file extension and require the browser to have a Flash plug-in. Incorporating Flash animation was popular on websites before using smartphones and tablets became widespread. Some websites were developed exclusively with Flash. However, many of today's websites use Flash sparingly, if at all, partly because the iPhone and iPad, which run the iOS operating system, do not support Flash. Adobe announced that it will end the support for Flash in December 2020. Instead, many web developers have embraced JavaScript to incorporate additional interactivity within their websites. Figure 9–10 shows an example of an interactive Flash video used on the National Parks Service website.

BTW
Chrome Extensions
To view the current extensions installed on Google Chrome, select the Customize and control Google Chrome button, select Settings, and then select Extensions.

Figure 9–10

Java Applets

A **Java applet** is a small program created with Java, a programming language. A Java applet can be embedded within a webpage, though the browser must have Java installed and enabled. Java applets were very popular in the late 1990s; however, their use in today's modern websites is in decline.

Object Element

You can use the `object` element to embed plug-ins on a webpage, including Flash Players, PDF readers, and Java applets. Use the `param` element to define parameters for plug-ins embedded with an `object` element. The following is an example of the `object` element.

```
<object data="audio.wav">
  <param name="autoplay" value="true">
</object>
```

In this example, an audio file named audio.wav is embedded on the webpage. The autoplay parameter is set to true, meaning the audio starts playing when the webpage opens. Recently, some browsers have disabled audio files from playing automatically.

BTW
Parameters
Many other object parameters are available that are not discussed in this chapter. Review online other parameters that might be effective for you to use in your web development.

Integrating Audio

Adding audio to a webpage can help set a desired mood or tone. It can also be a distraction to some users, so you must first determine if the audio is appropriate for the webpage and its audience. Audio integrated within a webpage should have a distinct purpose and should provide added value or instruction. You should also consider the time it takes for the browser to load the audio file. If your audience includes users with dial-up connections rather than broadband access, they will likely experience a delay, especially if the audio files are large. Keep in mind that using audio or video on a mobile device requires a data plan if the device is not connected to a wireless network. One popular way that websites use audio is to provide links to music files that visitors can play or download. Figure 9–11 shows list of music files to listen to on the Pandora.com website.

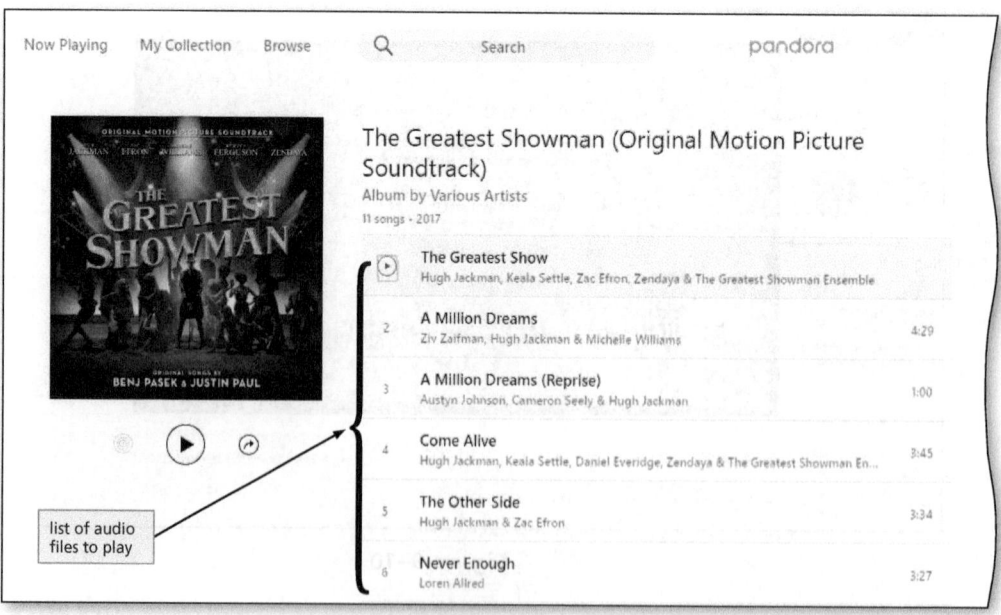

Figure 9–11

Source: Pandora.com

Audio File Formats

Table 9–1 lists the most common audio file formats. The HTML 5 `audio` element supports only three audio file formats: .mp3, .ogg, and .wav. These supported formats are indicated with an asterisk in Table 9–1. However, you can use audio converter software to convert files from one audio format to a supported format. Audio files for the web often use file compression techniques to reduce the size of the file, though they can also diminish the sound quality.

Table 9–1 Common Audio File Formats

File Format	File Extension	Description
AAC	.aac	AAC stands for Advanced Audio Coding. The AAC file format was developed by Apple and works with macOS.
MIDI	.mid .midi	Musical Instrument Digital Interface (MIDI) Limited to electronic musical instruments (such as synthesizers) and other electronic equipment Files can be much smaller than in other formats
MP3*	.mp3	One of the most popular formats for music players Compresses files to approximately one-tenth the size of uncompressed files
MP4	.mp4	Common video format that can also be used for audio files
Ogg*	.ogg	Maintained by Xiph.Org Foundation
RealAudio	.rm .ram	Designed for streaming audio on low bandwidths
WAV*	.wav	Standard audio format for Windows Commonly used for storing uncompressed CD-quality sound files Compression is available to reduce file size

File Compression and Codecs

When embedding an audio or video file onto a webpage, you should keep the file size small and compress the file when necessary. A **codec** is a compression technology used to compress images, audio, and video files. The word codec is short for code /decode because it consists of an encoder, which compresses the file, and a decoder, which decompresses the file. An audio editor uses a codec to reduce the size of an audio file, while maintaining enough quality to play the audio file on a computer. Although codecs improve the page load time, compressing a media file too much results in a loss of sound quality. On the other hand, if you do not compress a media file enough, the file may take too long to download into a browser. Figure 9–12 shows an example of audio converter software that uses a codec to compress files.

conversion format
options

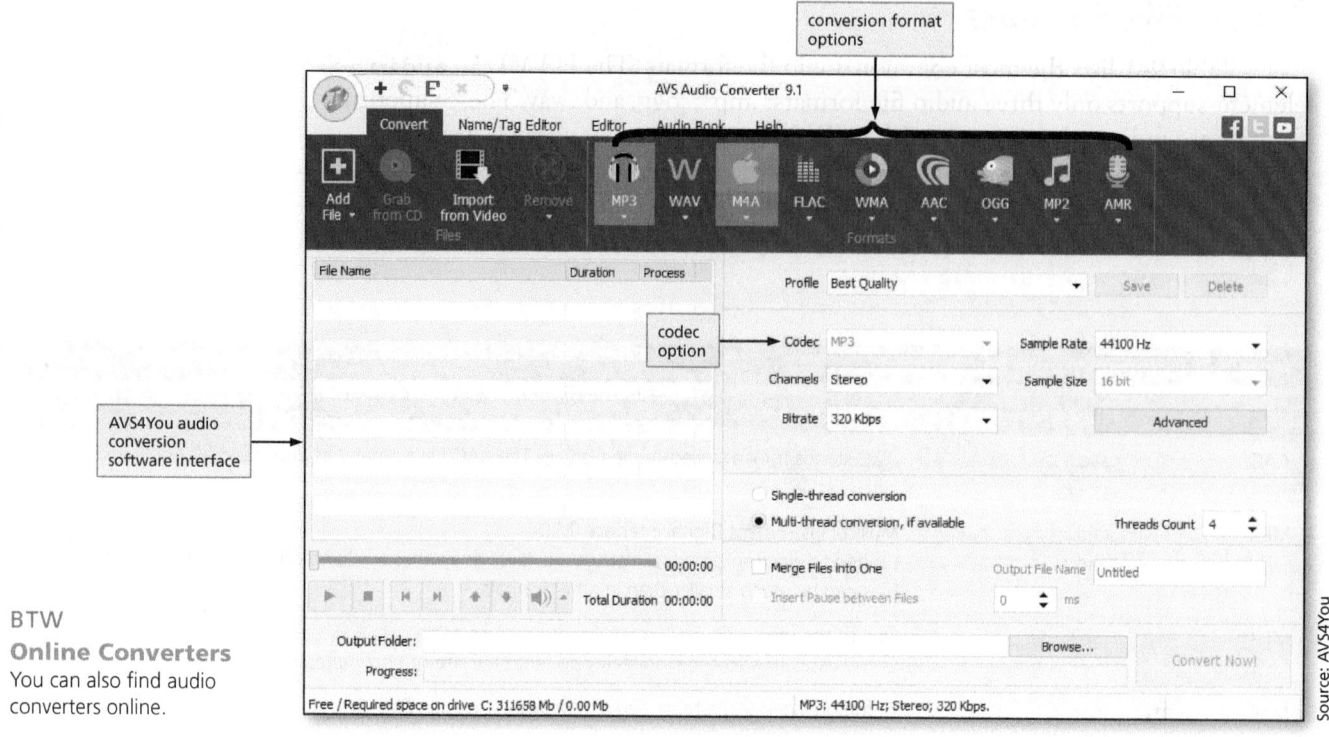

AVS4You audio
conversion
software interface

codec
option

BTW
Online Converters
You can also find audio
converters online.

Figure 9–12

HTML 5 audio Element

One of the most long-awaited features in HTML 5 was the `audio` element, which you use to define sound, such as music or other audio streams. Table 9–2 shows the attributes and values that can be used with the `audio` element.

The following sample code shows how to use the `audio` element to insert an audio file named music.mp3. Because browsers that do not support the `audio` element ignore the <audio> tag, you should insert text content within the audio element to alert users, as the paragraph element does in the following code.

```
<audio controls autoplay>
   <source src="music.mp3" type="audio/mp3">
   <p>Your browser does not support the audio element.</p>
</audio>
```

Table 9–2 Audio Element Attributes

Attribute	Value	Description
autoplay	autoplay	Specifies that the audio will automatically start playing
controls	controls	Specifies that audio controls should be displayed (such as a play/pause button)
loop	loop	Specifies that the audio will start playing every time it is finished
muted	muted	Specifies that the audio should be muted
preload	auto metadata none	Specifies whether and how the audio should be loaded when the page loads
src	*URL*	Specifies the URL of the audio file

In this example, an audio file named music.mp3 is embedded on the webpage. The first line shows the beginning `audio` tag and includes two attributes: `controls` and `autoplay`. The `controls` attribute specifies to display the audio controls, such as play/pause and volume control. The `autoplay` attribute specifies to start playing the audio file once the page is loaded in the browser. Note, however, that some major browsers, such as Google Chrome and Mozilla Firefox, have disabled the setting that plays audio and video automatically. The second line uses the `source` tag with two attributes, `src` and `type`. The `src` attribute specifies the location of the audio file. The `type` attribute specifies the type of audio file, in this instance, MP3. The third line is a `paragraph` element with fallback text to let the user know that their browser does not support the audio element. The sentence "Your browser does not support the audio element" appears in a legacy browser that does not support HTML 5. The fourth line includes the ending `audio` tag.

Prior to HTML 5, the `object` element was used to add audio to a webpage. The object element requires at least one data or type attribute. The data attribute specifies the resource file, while the type attribute specifies the type of media, such as Flash. Only one `data` attribute can be specified within one `object` element. In addition, you need to include the `param` element in the `object` element to specify additional parameters, such as `autoplay`. However, many of the attributes for the object element and the parameter element are not supported in HTML 5. You can add the object element as a fallback in case visitors to your website are using a legacy browser, such as Internet Explorer 8. Microsoft discontinued support for Internet Explorer 8, 9, and 10 in 2016.

The `controls` attribute adds audio controls, such as play, pause, and volume. It can be set up in any of the three following ways:

```
<audio controls="controls">
<audio controls>
<audio controls="">
```

Similarly, the autoplay attribute can be set up in any of these ways:

```
<audio autoplay>
<audio autoplay="autoplay">
<audio autoplay="">
```

To enable the `audio` element to work in all browsers, use `source` elements inside the `audio` element. The `source` elements can link to the same or different audio files as appropriate. Including the `source` elements accommodates visitors who use any of the five major browsers. The browser will use the first recognized format. The following is an example of an `audio` element with multiple `source` elements:

```
<audio controls="controls" autoplay="autoplay">
  <source src="music.mp3" type="audio/mp3">
  <source src="music.ogg" type="audio/ogg">
  <source src="music.wav" type="audio/wav">
  <p>Your browser does not support the audio element.</p>
</audio>
```

In this example, if the browser cannot play MP3 files, it checks to determine whether it can play Ogg files. If it can, it plays the music.ogg file. If it cannot play Ogg files, it checks to determine whether it can play WAV files. If it can, it plays the music.wav file. Otherwise, it does not play any audio. If the browser cannot play the audio, then it does not support HTML 5. Because WAV files are typically large, it is best to use MP3 and Ogg to improve load time. Table 9–3 lists the three audio file formats supported by the `audio` element and identifies whether each file format is also supported by the five major browsers. While most of these browsers support more than the audio file formats listed in Table 9–3, at this time, the **audio** element only supports three.

Other attributes include the **preload** attribute, which tells the browser to begin downloading the audio file immediately when it encounters the **audio** element. However, if you use the **autoplay** attribute, which also begins downloading immediately, you do not need to also use the **preload** attribute. The **loop** attribute restarts the audio immediately once it has finished playing. According to the Web Content Accessibility Guidelines (WCAG 2.1), section 1.4.2, if audio on a webpage starts to play automatically for more than 3 seconds, display controls for a user to pause or stop the audio.

BTW
Audio Clip
Many web design sites discuss the use of audio clips in web development. Search for ideas of how you can most effectively use an audio clip.

Table 9–3 Audio File Browser Support					
Audio File Format	Edge	Google Chrome	Mozilla Firefox	Apple Safari	Opera
MP3	•	•	•	•	•
Ogg		•	•		•
Wav		•	•	•	•

To Add Audio to the Classes Page

1 INSERT AUDIO ELEMENT | 2 INSERT VIDEO ELEMENT
3 STYLE VIDEO ELEMENT | 4 MAKE VIDEO ACCESSIBLE

Insert an **audio** element on the Classes page of the Forward Fitness Center website to add sound to the page. *Why? The audio file provides an example of the music played during a class training session.* Include two file sources to accommodate all browsers and include the controls attribute to display controls on the webpage. The following steps add audio to the Classes page.

1
- Copy the files from the chapter09\fitness\media folder provided with the Data Files to the fitness\media folder.
- Open classes.html in your text editor and update the comment with today's date.
- Tap or click at the end of Line 110, and then press the ENTER key twice to insert new Lines 111 and 112.
- On Line 112, type **<div id="music-sample">** to add a new div tag.
- Press the ENTER key twice to insert new Lines 113 and 114.
- On Line 114, increase the indent, and then type **<h3>We play upbeat music to help keep you focused during your workout. Below is a sample of the type of music played during a class workout.</h3>**
- Press the ENTER key to insert a new Line 115, and then type **<audio controls>** to insert a starting audio tag (Figure 9–13).

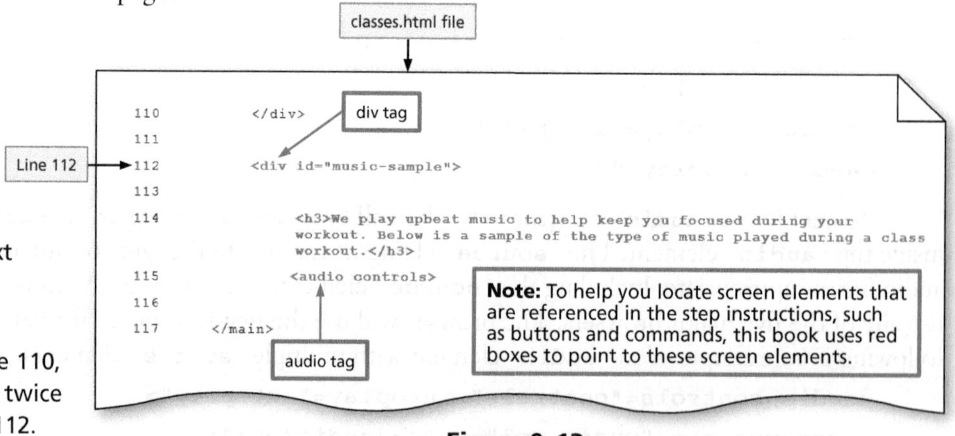

Figure 9–13

Q&A What is the purpose of the **controls** attribute?
The **controls** attribute specifies to display the audio controls within the browser, which allows the user to play or pause the music and adjust the volume.

2

- Press the ENTER key to insert a new Line 116, increase the indent, and then type `<source src="media/ffc_aud.mp3" type="audio/mp3">` to insert a source element.

- Press the ENTER key to insert a new Line 117, and then type `<source src="media/ffc_aud.ogg" type="audio/ogg">` to insert a source element.

- Press the ENTER key to insert a new Line 118, and then type `<p>Your browser does not support the audio element.</p>` to insert a paragraph element.

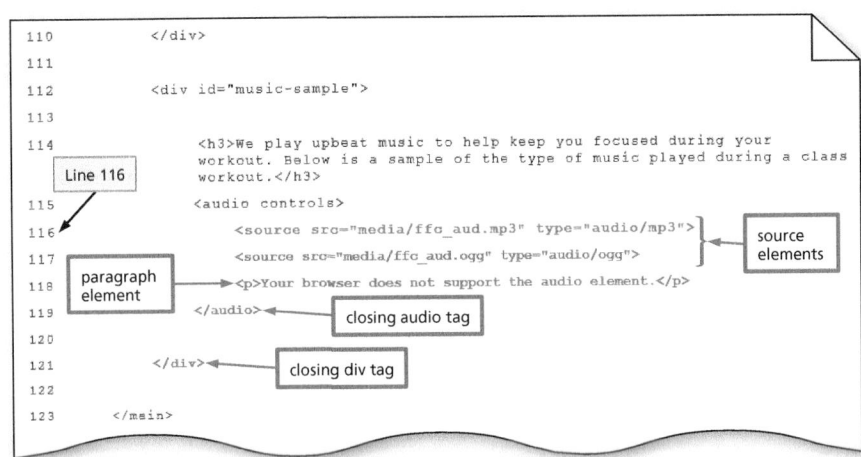

```
110        </div>
111
112        <div id="music-sample">
113
114            <h3>We play upbeat music to help keep you focused during your
               workout. Below is a sample of the type of music played during a class
               workout.</h3>
115            <audio controls>
116                <source src="media/ffc_aud.mp3" type="audio/mp3">
117                <source src="media/ffc_aud.ogg" type="audio/ogg">
118            <p>Your browser does not support the audio element.</p>
119            </audio>
120
121        </div>
122
123    </main>
```

Line 116 · paragraph element · source elements · closing audio tag · closing div tag

Figure 9–14

- Press the ENTER key to insert a new Line 119, decrease the indent, and then type `</audio>` to insert a closing audio tag.

- Press the ENTER key twice to insert new Lines 120 and 121.

- On Line 121, decrease the indent, and then type `</div>` to close the div element (Figure 9–14).

Q&A

Why do I need to include two source elements?
To accommodate all major browsers, you specify two audio source files, MP3 and Ogg. These file formats are supported by the audio element.

Why did I not add a WAV source file?
WAV files are typically very large. To reduce page loading time, use only MP3 and Ogg file formats.

Will the webpage display the paragraph element?
The webpage displays the paragraph element only if the browser does not support the `audio` element.

 3

- Save your changes, open classes.html in your browser, adjust the window to the size of a desktop viewport, and then scroll down to view the audio controls (Figure 9–15).

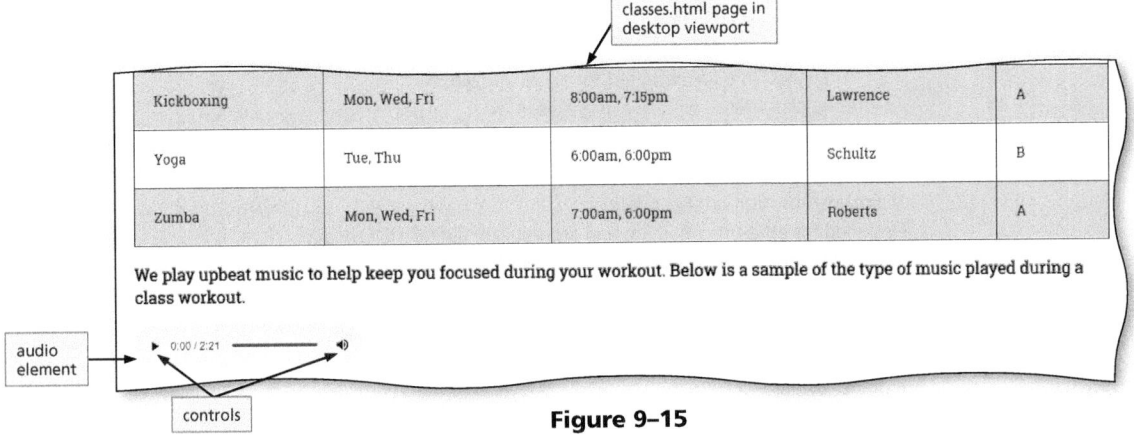

classes.html page in desktop viewport

Kickboxing	Mon, Wed, Fri	8:00am, 7:15pm	Lawrence	A
Yoga	Tue, Thu	6:00am, 6:00pm	Schultz	B
Zumba	Mon, Wed, Fri	7:00am, 6:00pm	Roberts	A

We play upbeat music to help keep you focused during your workout. Below is a sample of the type of music played during a class workout.

▶ 0:00 / 2:21 ━━━━━ ◀)

audio element · controls

Figure 9–15

Ⓟ Experiment

- The autoplay attribute automatically plays the audio file when the page loads. To see how this works, add the autoplay attribute to the audio tag, save your changes, and then refresh classes.html in your browser.
- Remove the controls attribute from the audio element to view the page without controls, save your changes, and then refresh classes.html in your browser.
- Remove the autoplay attribute, add the controls attribute to the audio tag, and then save your changes.

Q&A My controls do not look like the controls in Figure 9–15. Why?
Figure 9–15 shows the controls in Google Chrome. If you are using a different browser, your controls may look different.

Break Point: If you want to take a break, this is a good place to do so. You can exit the text editor now. To resume at a later time, run your text editor, open the file called about.html, and continue following the steps from this location forward.

Integrating Video

Video is used widely on today's websites, as it is a powerful visual communication tool to capture the attention of your target audience. Make sure you can identify the best uses for video, video file formats, encoding, the video element, and making videos accessible so video enhances, rather than distracts from, your websites.

Video File Formats

Table 9–4 lists the most commonly used video file formats. The HTML 5 `video` element supports only three of these video file formats: .mp4, .ogg, and .webm. The supported formats are indicated with an asterisk in Table 9–4.

Table 9–4 Common Video File Formats		
File Format	**File Extension**	**Description**
AVI	.avi	Audio/Video Interleaved Developed by Microsoft to use with Windows Can contain both audio and video data
Flash	.swf .flv	Small Web Format / Flash Video Can contain audio, video, or animations Requires Adobe Flash Player
MPEG-4 MP4*	.mp4	Moving Picture Experts Group Can be highly compressed, resulting in small file size Based on QuickTime format; used for audio and video Creates quicker, faster, high-quality media Supported by all browsers
Ogg*	.ogg	Theora Ogg Maintained by Xiph.org Foundation Designed for efficient streaming and high-quality digital multimedia
QuickTime	.mov	Developed by Apple for both Windows and Mac operating systems File compression can result in smaller file size Requires QuickTime Player or Adobe Flash Player, which are easily downloaded
RealVideo	.rm .ram	Proprietary video format developed by Real Media Requires RealPlayer
WebM*	.webm	Developed by Google, Mozilla, Adobe, and Opera Royalty-free, open format
Windows Media	.wmv	Developed by Microsoft Originally designed for Internet streaming applications Requires Windows Media Player or RealPlayer

If you want to use an unsupported video file format with the `video` element, use video converter software to convert the file to a supported format. The `video` element does not work in legacy browsers, so consider your audience before using the `video` element. If necessary, you can use the object element as a fallback. The H.264 codec is a common codec used for video today. Using it is currently considered as a best practice for video compression.

HTML 5 video Element

Until the HTML 5 `video` element was introduced, browsers did not have a standard for playing video on a webpage. Most videos were shown through a plug-in (such as Adobe Flash). The problem with plug-ins is that browsers may have different plug-ins or only recognize specific video formats. This problem became more complicated with the introduction of mobile smartphones. The HTML 5 `video` element solves this problem and provides a standard way to play web videos in today's modern browsers and mobile devices.

You can use three HTML elements to incorporate video: `embed`, `object`, and `video`. You would have to add all three elements and use different video formats to make sure your video can play in all browsers and browser versions (Internet Explorer, Chrome, Firefox, Safari, and Opera) and on all hardware (PC, macOS, Android Tablet, Android Smartphone, iPad, and iPhone).

The purpose of the `embed` element is to embed multimedia files with in HTML pages. The `embed` element is an HTML 5 element used to insert a plug-in, such as a Flash video. The following is an example of the embed element:

```
<embed src="media/video.swf">
```

You can also use the `object` element to embed multimedia elements in HTML pages. Use the object element as fallback to display a video in legacy browsers that do not support HTML 5.

Using the video Element

Use the `video` element to specify a video, such as a movie clip or other video stream, on a webpage. Table 9–5 lists the attributes and values that can be used with the `video` element.

Table 9–5 Video Element Attributes		
Attribute	**Value**	**Description**
autoplay	autoplay	Specifies that the video will start playing as soon as it is ready
controls	controls	Specifies that video controls should be displayed (such as a play/pause button)
height	*pixels*	Sets the height of the video player
loop	loop	Specifies that the video will start playing every time it is finished
muted	muted	Specifies that the audio output of the video should be muted
poster	*URL*	Specifies an image to be shown while the video is downloading, or until the user clicks the play button
preload	auto metadata none	Specifies whether and how the video should be loaded when the page loads
src	*URL*	Specifies the URL of the video file
width	*pixels*	Sets the width of the video player

The following sample code shows how to use the **video** element to insert a video file named advertisement.mp4 in a webpage. Because browsers that do not support the **video** element ignore the <video> tag, you should insert text content within the video element to alert users, as the paragraph element does in the following code.

```
<video width="320" height="240" controls="controls">
   <source src="advertisement.mp4" type="video/mp4">
   <p>Your browser does not support the video element.</p>
</video>
```

In this example, the code sets the dimensions of the video (320 pixels by 240 pixels) and displays the playback controls. The browser plays the advertisement.mp4 file, which is an MP4 video file. If the browser does not support the **video** element, the user is alerted.

It is a good idea to include width and height attributes when you are not designing a responsive website. If you set the width and height, the space required for the video is reserved when the page is loaded. However, without these attributes, the browser does not know the size of the video and cannot reserve the appropriate space for it. The effect is that the page layout will change when the video loads. If you are designing a responsive website, do not include width and height attributes. Instead, use CSS to set the height to **auto** and the **max-width** attribute to 100%, as this will allow the video to automatically resize to fit the user's viewport.

As with the **audio** element, the **controls** attribute adds video controls including play, pause, and volume. It can be set up in any of the three following ways:

```
<video controls="controls">
<video controls>
<video controls="">
```

You can use the **src** attribute in the **video** element itself, as shown in the sample below:

```
<video controls autoplay src="advertisement.mp4">
   <p>Your browser does not support the video element.</p>
</video>
```

Also, as you did with the **audio** element, you should specify **source** elements within the **video** element. The **video** element allows multiple **source** elements, which can link to different video files. Including the **source** elements accommodates visitors who use any of the five major browsers. The browser will use the first recognized format. The following is an example of a **video** element with multiple **source** elements:

```
<video controls="controls" autoplay="autoplay">
   <source src="advertisement.mp4" type="video/mp4">
   <source src="advertisement.ogg" type="video/ogg">
   <source src="advertisement.webm" type="video/webm">
   <p>Your browser does not support the video element.</p>
</video>
```

In this example, if the browser cannot play MP4 files, it checks to determine whether it can play Ogg files. If it cannot play the advertisement.ogg file, it checks to determine whether it can play WebM files. If it cannot play MP4, Ogg, or WebM files, then the browser does not support the HTML 5 **video** element. Table 9–6 lists the three video file formats supported by the **video** element and identifies whether or not each file format is supported by the five major browsers. While most of these browsers support more than the video file formats listed in Table 9–6, at this time, the **video** element only supports three.

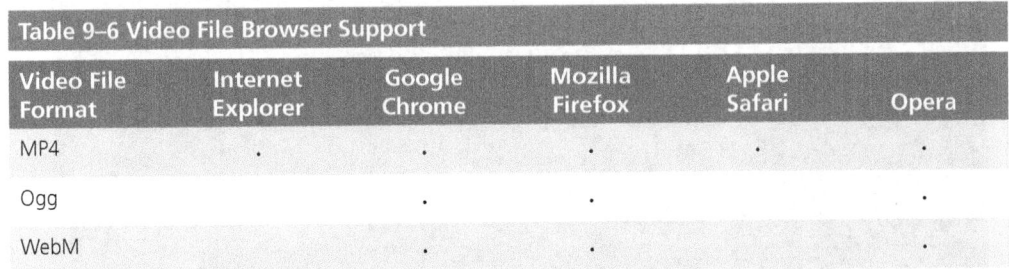

Table 9–6 Video File Browser Support					
Video File Format	Internet Explorer	Google Chrome	Mozilla Firefox	Apple Safari	Opera
MP4	·	·	·		·
Ogg		·	·		·
WebM		·	·		·

BTW
Video Clips
Video clips can have a large file size depending on the length and the quality of the clip. Search for rules-of-thumb for file sizes when video clips are incorporated into a website.

To Add Video to the About Us Page

1 INSERT AUDIO ELEMENT | 2 INSERT VIDEO ELEMENT
3 STYLE VIDEO ELEMENT | 4 MAKE VIDEO ACCESSIBLE

Next, insert a video on the About Us page to highlight its services. *Why? You can use a video to promote the benefits of joining the Forward Fitness Club.* Include two file sources to accommodate all browsers. Also include attributes to specify a poster image (an image the browser displays when the video is not playing) and to display controls on the webpage. The following steps add video to the About Us page.

- Open about.html in your text editor and update the comment with today's date.

- Tap or click at the end of Line 36, and then press the ENTER key twice to insert new Lines 37 and 38.

- On Line 38, increase the indent, and then type `<video controls poster="images /hero-image.jpg">` to insert a starting video tag.

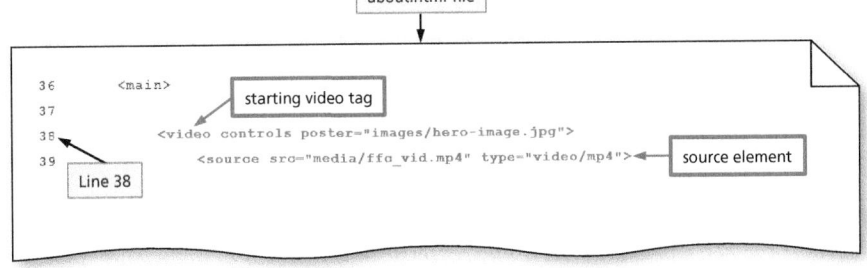

Figure 9–16

- Press the ENTER key to insert a new Line 39, increase the indent, and then type `<source src="media /ffc_video.mp4" type="video/mp4">` to insert a source element (Figure 9–16).

Q&A What is the purpose of the poster attribute?
The poster attribute specifies an image to display before the user chooses to play the video.

2

- Press the ENTER key to insert a new Line 40, and then type `<source src="media/ffc_video.webm" type="video/webm">` to insert a source element.

- Press the ENTER key to insert a new Line 41, and then type `<p>Your browser does not support the video element.</p>` to insert a paragraph element.

- Press the ENTER key to insert a new Line 42, decrease the indent, and then type `</video>` to insert a closing video tag (Figure 9–17).

Q&A Why do I need to include two source elements?
The MP4 video file format is supported by modern browsers. Include the WebM video file format for earlier versions of Opera. The Ogg file format was not used as these files are larger than MP4 and WebM files.

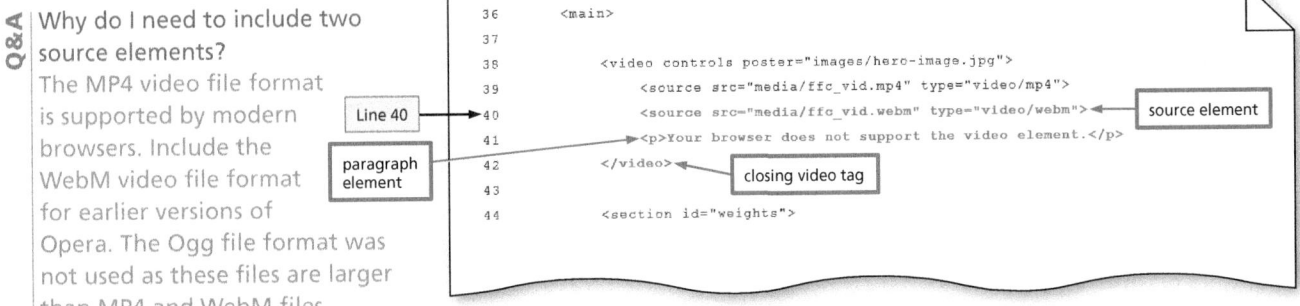

Figure 9–17

③

- Save your changes, open about.html in your browser, and then adjust the window to the size of a desktop viewport (Figure 9–18).

Q&A Why does the video show the hero image from the home page? The hero image is used as the poster image before the video is played.

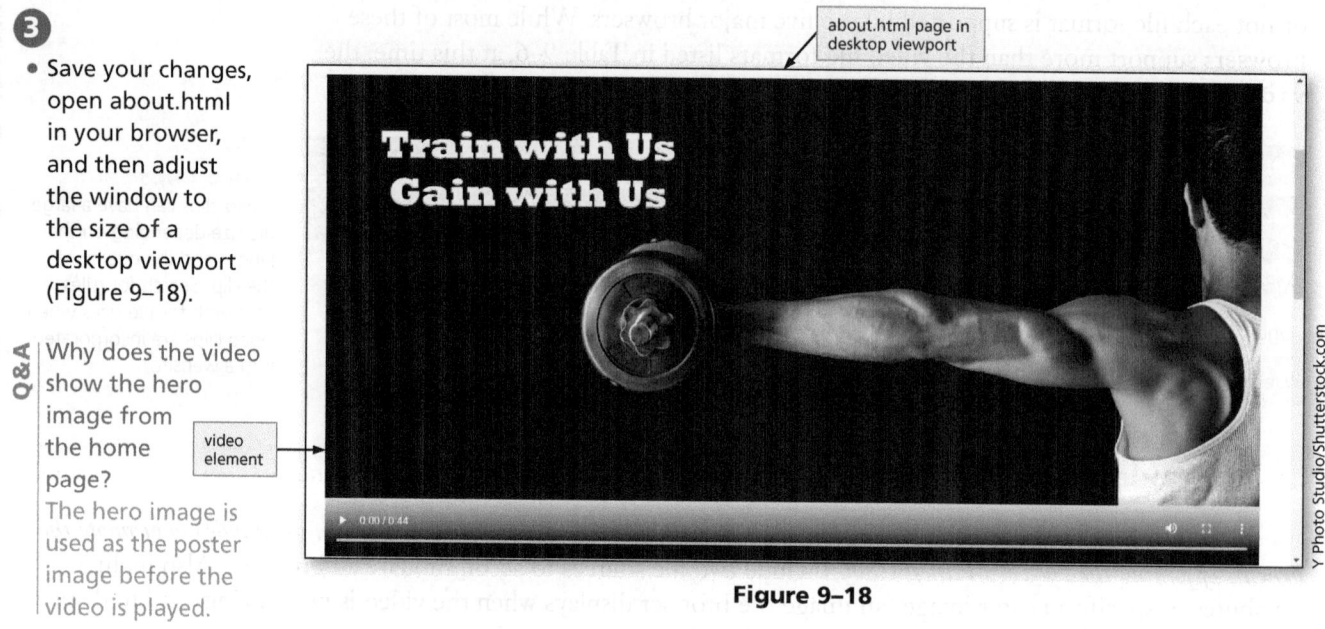

about.html page in desktop viewport

video element

Figure 9–18

Y Photo Studio/Shutterstock.com

To Style the Video

You have added a video to the About Us page, but need to format the video to improve its appearance on the webpage. Start by adding the audio and video selectors to the CSS reset style rule. Then, add the video selector to the img style rule. Finally, create a new style rule for the video selector to specify margin. *Why? Format the video to appear vertically centered on the page and incorporate more white space between the video and the section elements on the page.* The following steps format the video by adding the video selector to two existing style rules and by creating a new style rule in the styles.css file.

①

- Open styles.css in your text editor and update the comment with today's date.

- Tap or click after the aside selector on Line 8 and then type **, audio, video** to add the audio and video selectors to the CSS reset style rule.

- Tap or click after the img selector on Line 19, and then type **, video** to add the video selector to this style rule.

- Tap or click at the end of Line 85, press the ENTER key twice to insert new Lines 86 and 87, and then type **video {** to insert a new selector.

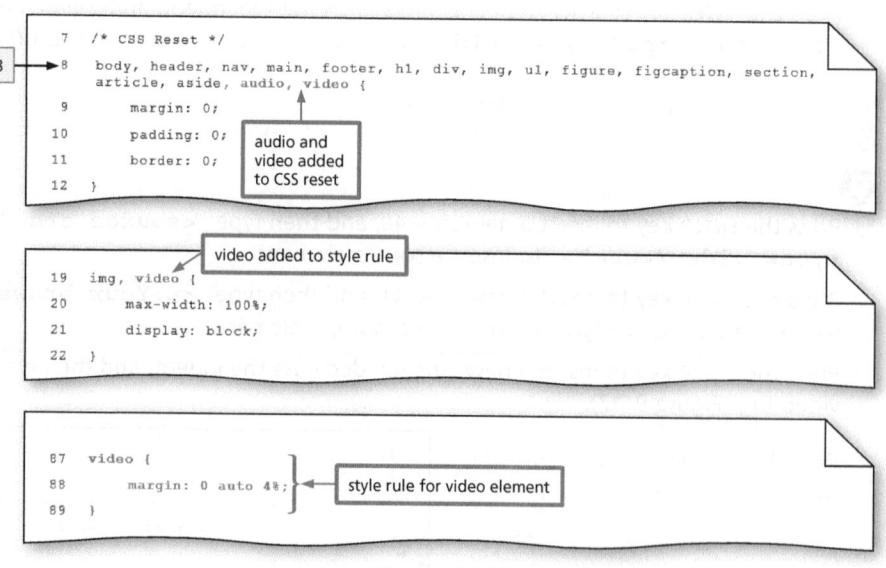

```
 7    /* CSS Reset */
 8    body, header, nav, main, footer, h1, div, img, ul, figure, figcaption, section,
      article, aside, audio, video {
 9        margin: 0;
10        padding: 0;
11        border: 0;
12    }
```

Line 8

audio and video added to CSS reset

```
19    img, video {
20        max-width: 100%;
21        display: block;
22    }
```

video added to style rule

```
87    video {
88        margin: 0 auto 4%;
89    }
```

style rule for video element

Figure 9–19

- Press the ENTER key to insert a new Line 88, increase the indent, and then type **margin: 0 auto 4%;** to insert a declaration.

- Press the ENTER key to insert a new Line 89, decrease the indent, and then type **}** to insert a closing brace (Figure 9–19).

2

- Save your changes and refresh about.html in your browser (Figure 9–20).

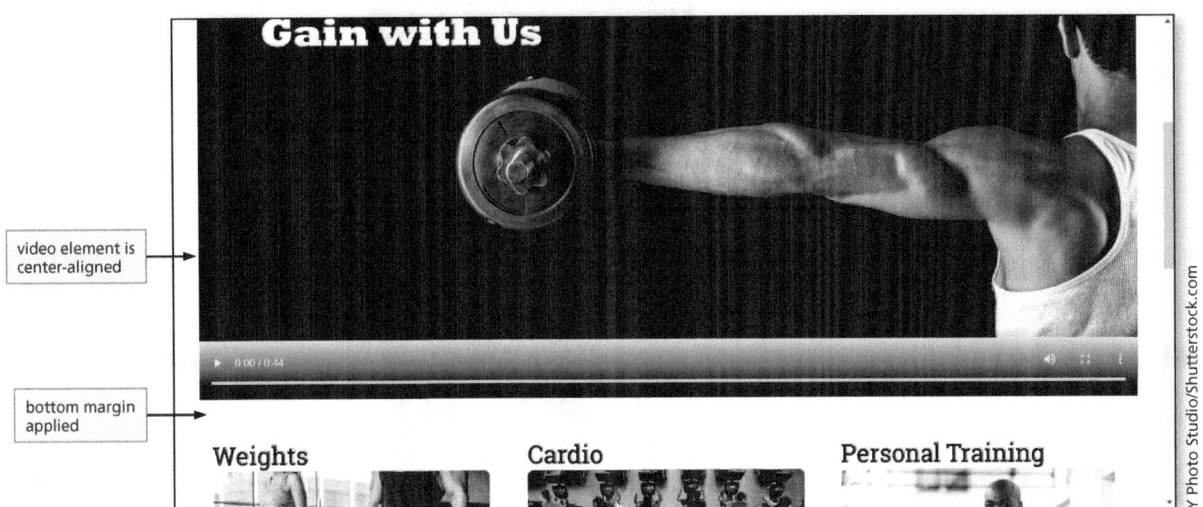

video element is
center-aligned →

bottom margin
applied →

Figure 9–20

3

- Adjust your browser to a tablet viewport (Figure 9–21).

about.html displayed in
tablet viewport

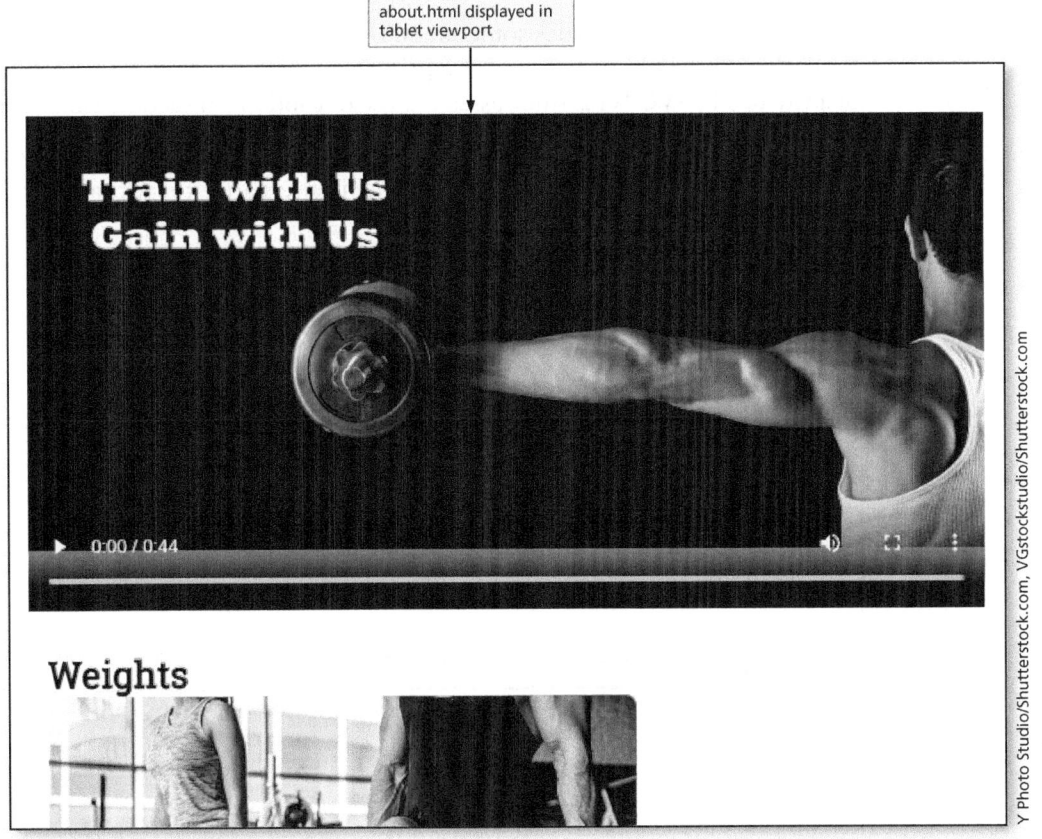

Figure 9–21

- Adjust your browser to a mobile viewport (Figure 9–22).

Figure 9–22

Making Videos Accessible

When a video includes someone speaking, include captions to make it accessible for deaf and hard of hearing users. **Captions** are text appearing over the bottom portion of a video. The WCAG 2.1 discusses the use of captions in section 1.2.2. It states:

"Captions are provided for all prerecorded audio content in synchronized media, except when the media is a media alternative for text and is clearly labeled as such."

An example of a video that uses captions is shown in Figure 9–23.

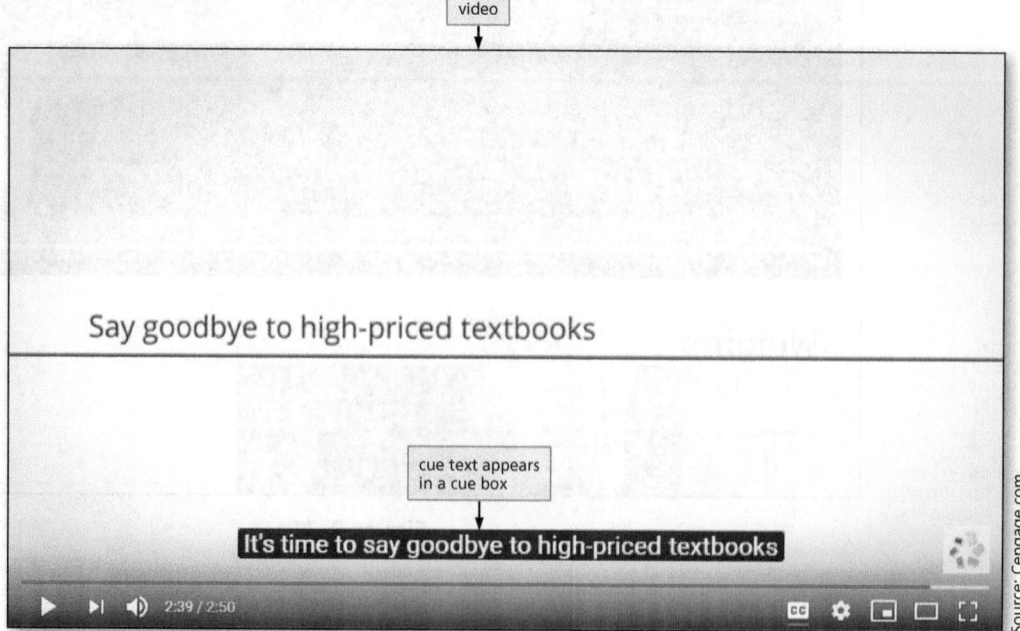

Figure 9–23

The caption text, also known as **cue text**, displays the words being spoken in the video or describes a sound in the video, such as water splashing or an audience laughing. Cue text appears within a cue box on the video. To create captions, you use the **WebVTT** format. WebVTT, which stands for Web Video Text Track, is the W3C standard used to create captions for video content. The file is created with a text editor and saved with an extension of .vtt. The HTML **track** element is used to insert the captions file within the webpage. An example of a WebVTT file is shown in Figure 9–24.

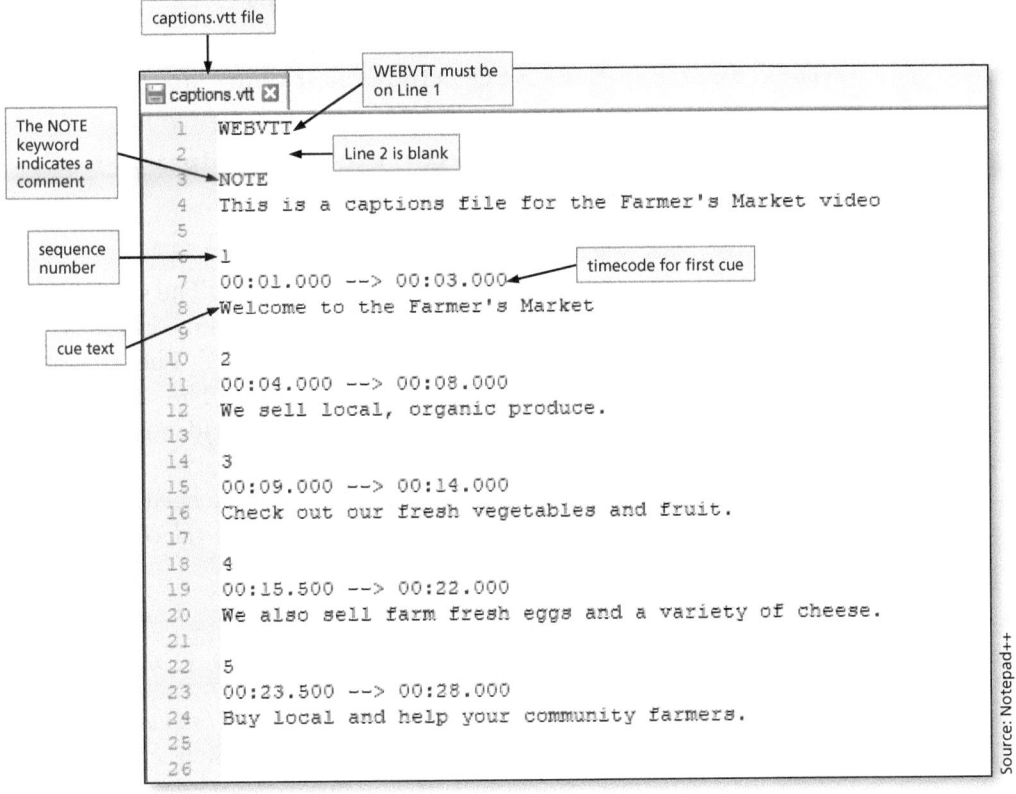

Figure 9–24

As shown in Figure 9–24, the first line must be WEBVTT. Line 2 must be blank. If you want to include a comment, use the keyword NOTE, followed by the file comments on the next line. The number 1 on Line 6 is the first sequence number. This denotes the first caption to be displayed. Line 7 denotes the timecode when the caption should appear on the video. The time format is minutes, seconds, and milliseconds (00:01.000). The timecode can also be in hours, minutes, seconds, and milliseconds (00:00:01.000). The timecodes shown on Line 7 indicate that the first caption, known as a WebVTT cue or cue text, will appear on the video after one second of the video playing. The caption will automatically be removed when the video time meets three seconds. The text on Line 8 is the caption that will appear on video. The number 2 on Line 10 is the next sequence number. This denotes the second caption. Line 11 denotes the timecode in which the caption should appear on the video. The second caption will appear on the video starting at four seconds. The caption will automatically be removed when the video time meets eight seconds. The text on Line 12 is the caption that will appear on video. There must be a blank line between each sequence, as this defines the end of a sequence.

In addition to captions, you should also include a **descriptions** file, which can be read by screen readers. This makes the video accessible to visually impaired users.

Like the captions file, a description file is also created with the WebVTT format. Creating the file is very similar to creating a captions file, but instead of writing caption text, you include text that describes the images on the video within a timecode. For more information about the WebVTT format, visit w3.org/TR/webvtt1/.

To add a captions file or descriptions file, you nest the **track** element within the video element, below the video source elements. The following is an example of a track element nested within a video element.

```
<video width="320" height="240" controls>
        <source src="video.mp4" type="video/mp4">
        <source src="video.webm" type="video/webm">
        <track src="captions.vtt" kind="captions" srclang="en"
        label="English">
        <track src="descriptions.vtt" kind="descriptions"
        srclang="en" label="English">
</video>
```

In this example, the first track element includes three attributes. The src attribute is required with the track element as it specifies the source of the captions.vtt file. The kind attribute specifies the kind of text track that is being used. The **srclang** attribute specifies the language used by the track element. The **label** attribute specifies the title of the text track. The second track element identifies the descriptions file to be used for the video.

In order to make the video on the About Us page accessible, you need to create a captions file and then insert a track element to add the captions to the video.

To Create a Captions File

1 INSERT AUDIO ELEMENT | 2 INSERT VIDEO ELEMENT
3 STYLE VIDEO ELEMENT | 4 MAKE VIDEO ACCESSIBLE

Create a captions file for the video. *Why? The video must be accessible in order to meet WCAG standards.* Use the captions.vtt file provided with the Data Files to create the captions file. The following steps create a captions file.

1

- Open the captions.vtt file in your text editor.

- On Line 1, type **WEBVTT** to note that the file format is WebVTT.

- Press the ENTER key twice to insert Lines 2 and 3. On Line 3, type **NOTE** to start a comment.

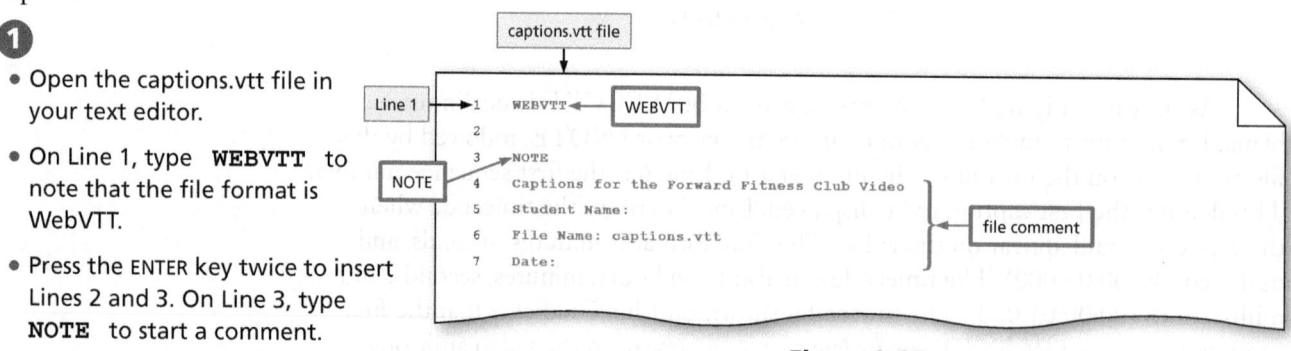

Figure 9–25

- Press the ENTER key to insert Line 4, and then type **Captions for the Forward Fitness Club Video** to insert comment.

- Press the ENTER key to insert Line 5, and then type **Student Name:** followed by your name to add your name to the comment.

- Press the ENTER key to insert Line 6, and then type **File Name: captions.vtt** to insert comment.

- Press the ENTER key to insert Line 7, and then type **Date:** followed by today's date to add today's date to (Figure 9–25).

- Press the ENTER key twice to insert Lines 8 and 9.

- On Line 9, type **1** to add the first sequence number.

- Press the ENTER key to insert Line 10, and then type **00:00.000 --> 00:02.500** to add the timecode.

- Press the ENTER key to insert Line 11, and then type **Welcome to the Forward Fitness Club.** to insert cue text.

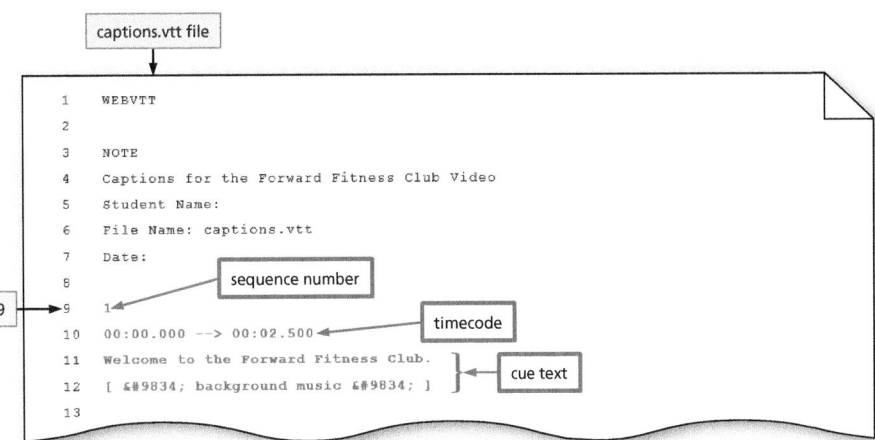

Figure 9–26

- Press the ENTER key to insert Line 12, and then type **[♪ background music ♪]** to insert cue text.

- Press the ENTER key to insert a blank Line 13 (Figure 9–26).

Q&A

What is the purpose of the 1 on Line 9?
The 1 on Line 9 indicates the first caption to display over the video.

What is the purpose of the timecode on Line 10?
The timecode specifies at what time in the video to display the cue text. The first caption will begin at 0 seconds and is displayed until 2.5 seconds of the video has elapsed.

What character entity is 9834?
Character entity 9834 is a music note.

- Using the same method as Step 2, insert the remaining sequence numbers, timecodes, and cue text as shown in Table 9–7 for the captions file (Figure 9–27).

Table 9–7 Content to Enter in Captions File	
Line Number	**Code to Insert**
14	2
15	00:05.000 --> 00:09.000
16	We provide many solutions to help you meet your fitness goals.
17	
18	3
19	00:15.000 --> 00:20.000
20	We offer a variety of group fitness classes.
21	
22	4
23	00:24.500 --> 00:27.500
24	Meet with our nutrition specialist.
25	
26	5
27	00:29.500 --> 00:33.000
28	We provide delicious, weekly recipes.
29	
30	6
31	00:35.500 --> 00:39.000
32	Our friendly staff is here to help and support you.

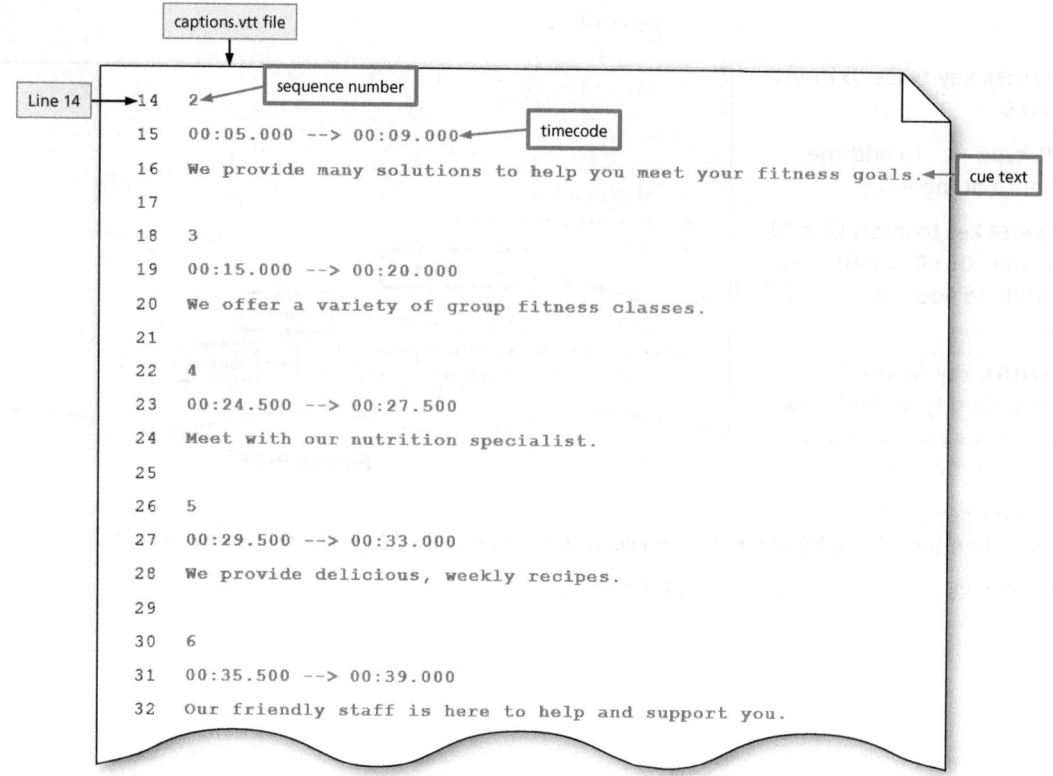

Figure 9–27

4

- Save your changes.

To Add a Track Element

Now that you have a captions file, add it to the video by nesting a track element within the video element. *Why? You use the track element to add captions and descriptions to a video.* The descriptions.vtt file is provided within the Data Files. The following steps add two track elements to the video element.

- If necessary, reopen about.html in your text editor to prepare to edit the file.

- Tap or click at the end of Line 40, press the ENTER key to insert a new Line 41, and then type `<track src="media/captions. vtt" kind="captions" srclang="en" label="Captions">` to add a track element that specifies the captions.vtt file.

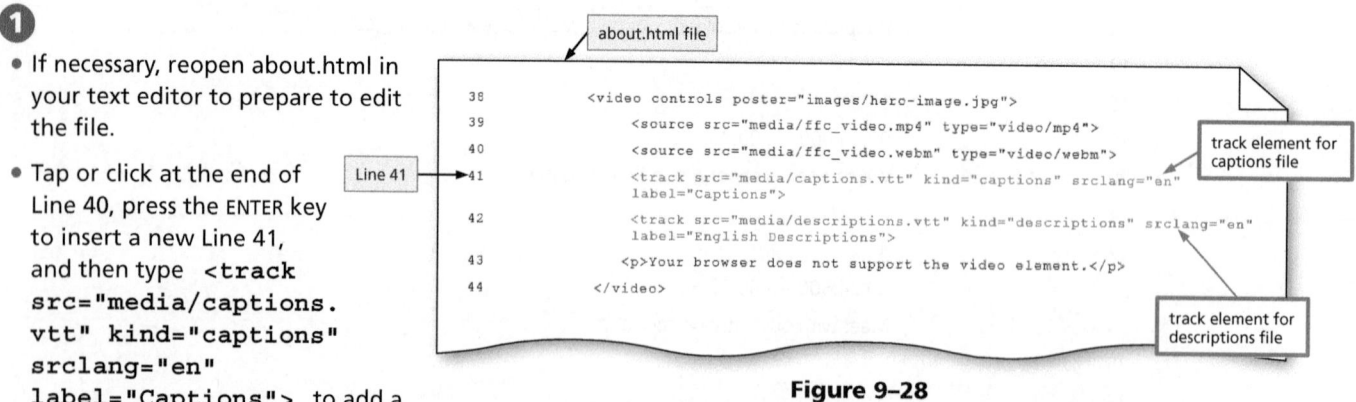

Figure 9–28

- Press the ENTER key to insert a new Line 42, type `<track src="media/descriptions.vtt" kind="descriptions" srclang="en" label="English Descriptions">` to add a track element that specifies the descriptions.vtt file, and then save your changes (Figure 9–28).

Why do I need to add two track elements?
The first track element specifies the captions to show over the video. The second track element specifies the descriptions file to be used by a screen reader for a visually impaired user.

In order to view captions on a video, you need to publish the website or use a local web server. Web Server for Chrome is an app available for download at chrome.google.com/webstore/. Web Server for Chrome is a simple solution to run a local website using HTTP, and is shown in Figure 9–29.

Figure 9–29

Download and install Web Server for Chrome to follow the next steps to display the captions on the video.

To View Video Captions Using Web Server for Chrome

Open the Forward Fitness Club website using Web Server for Chrome and then navigate to the About Us page to view the video and captions. *Why? You must either publish the website or view it with a local web server in order to see the video captions.* Assuming that Web Server for Chrome is installed on your local machine, the following steps open the Forward Fitness Club website using Web Server for Chrome.

1

- Open Web Server for Chrome (Figure 9–30).

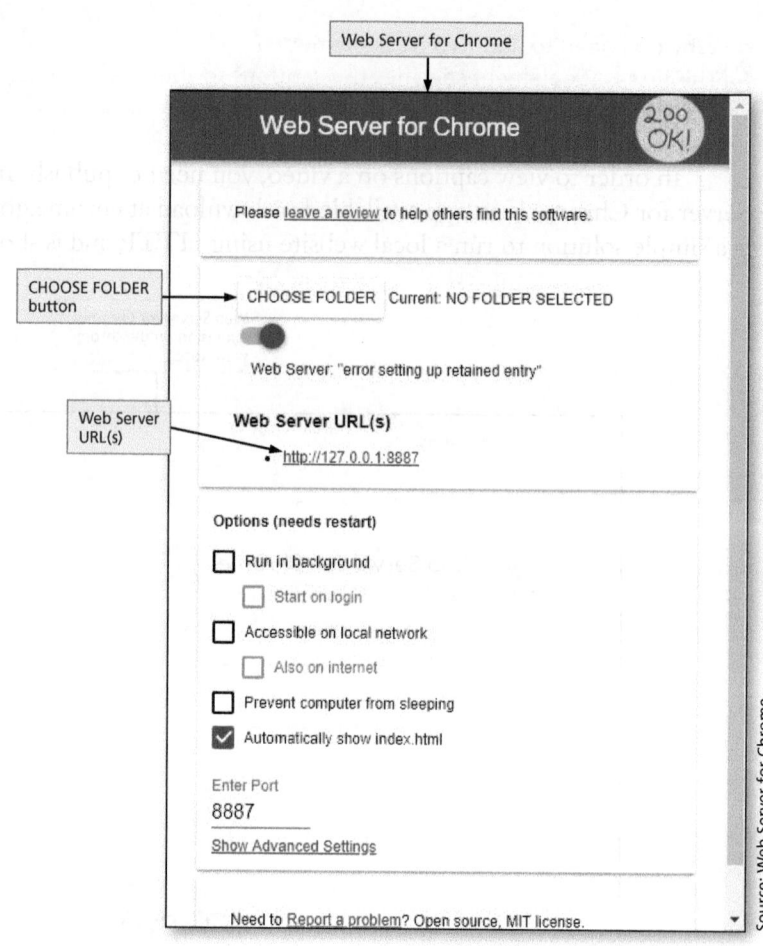

Figure 9–30

2

- Tap or click the Choose Folder button, navigate to your fitness folder, and then double-tap or double-click the fitness folder to open it (Figure 9–31).

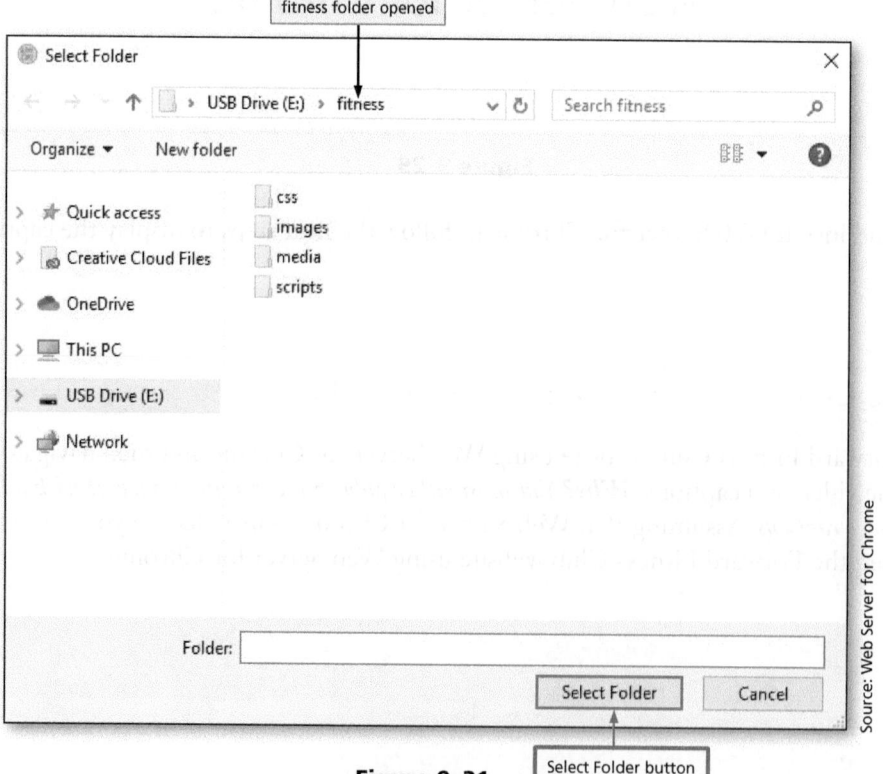

Figure 9–31

3

- Tap or click the Select Folder button to select the fitness folder.
- Tap or click the Web Server URL(s) link http://127.0.0.1:8887 to open the Forward Fitness Club website using Web Server for Chrome (Figure 9–32).

Q&A | Why did the home page open?
Unless specified otherwise, Web Server for Chrome opens the index.html file by default.

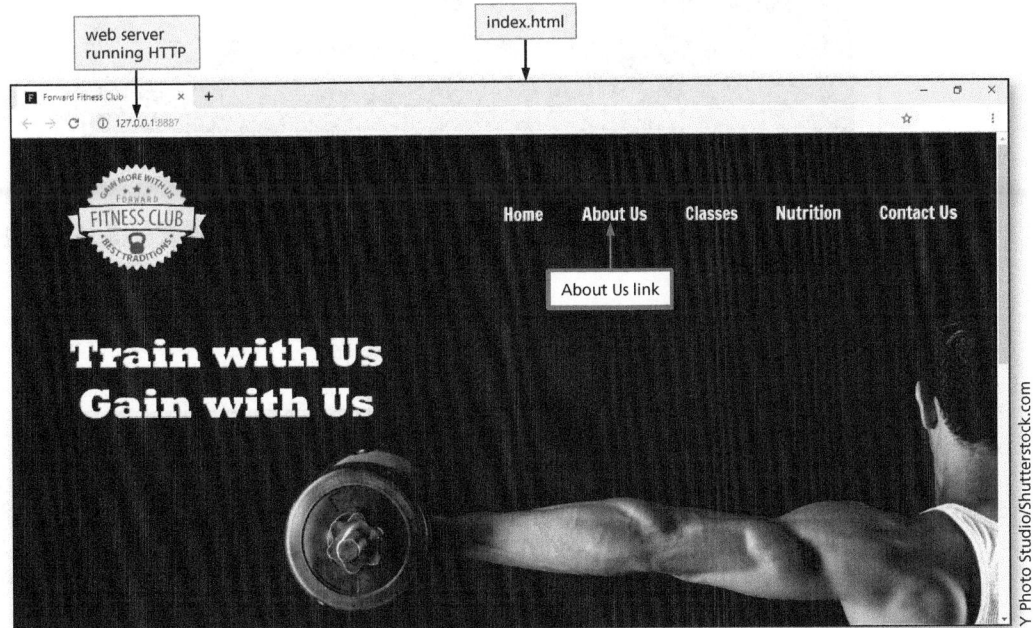

Figure 9–32

4

- Tap or click the About Us link to open the webpage.
- Locate the More Options button on the right side of the video controls to prepare to display the video options (Figure 9–33).

Figure 9–33

5

• Tap or click the More Options button to display the video options (Figure 9–34).

Figure 9–34

6

• Tap or click the Captions option to display the Captions menu (Figure 9–35).

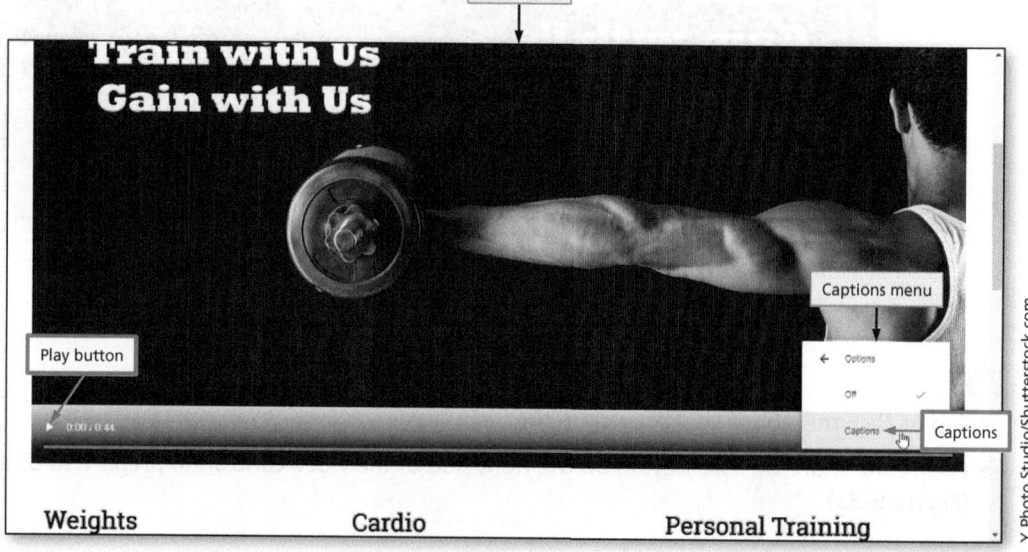

Figure 9–35

7

• Tap or click Captions to turn on captions.

• Tap or click the Play button on the video controls to play the video and display the captions (Figure 9–36).

Figure 9–36

To Validate the Style Sheet

Always run your files through W3C's validator to check the document for errors. If the document has any errors, validating gives you a chance to identify and correct them. Validation is also an effective troubleshooting tool during the development process and adds a valuable level of professionalism to your work. The following steps validate a CSS document.

1. Open your browser and type `http://jigsaw.w3.org/css-validator/` in the address bar to display the W3C CSS Validation Service page.

2. Tap or click the By file upload tab to display the Validate by file upload information.

3. Tap or click the Browse button to display the Choose File to Upload dialog box.

4. Navigate to your css folder to find the styles.css file.

5. Tap or click the styles.css document to select it.

6. Tap or click the Open button to upload the selected file to the W3C CSS validator.

7. Tap or click the Check button to send the document through the validator and display the validation results page.

8. If necessary, correct any errors, save your changes, and run through the validator again to revalidate the page.

To Validate the HTML Files

Every time you create a new webpage or modify an existing webpage, run it through W3C's validator to check the document for errors. If any errors exist, you need to correct them. Validation is also an effective troubleshooting tool during the development process and adds a valuable level of professionalism to your work. The following steps validate an HTML document.

1. Open your browser and type `http://validator.w3.org/` in the address bar to display the W3C validator page.

2. Tap or click the Validate by File Upload tab to display the Validate by File Upload information.

3. Tap or click the Browse button to display the Choose File to Upload dialog box.

4. Navigate to your fitness folder to find the classes.html file.

5. Tap or click the classes.html document to select it.

6. Tap or click the Open button to upload it to the W3C validator.

7. Tap or click the Check button to send the document through the validator and display the validation results page.

8. If necessary, correct any errors, save your changes, and run through the validator again to revalidate the page.

9. Follow these steps to validate the about.html page and correct any errors.

Chapter Summary

In this chapter, you learned how to integrate audio and video elements within a website. You used HTML 5 audio element to insert three audio source elements and specified that it automatically play and display controls. You also learned how to use the HTML 5 video element and insert a video onto a webpage and coded for cross-browser compatibility. You used CSS styles to format a video for all viewports. Finally, you made the video accessible to all visitors and tested the video in a web server. The items listed below include all the new skills you have learned in this chapter, with the tasks grouped by activity.

Integrating Audio
Add Audio to the Home Page (HTML 478)

Integrating Video
Add Video to the About Us Page
(HTML 483)
Style the Video (HTML 484)

Making a Video Accessible
Create a Captions File (HTML 448)
Add a Track Element with Captions (HTML 490)
Add a Track Element with Descriptions
(HTML 490)
View Video Captions (HTML 491)

How will you use multimedia?

Use these guidelines as you complete the assignments in this chapter and create your own webpages outside of this class.

1. Determine if audio has a defined purpose for your website.

   a) Determine if the audio should automatically play when the page loads.

   b) Determine the best page for the audio.

2. Determine if a video can enhance your website.

   a) Determine the ideal placement of your video to make it stand out.

   b) Determine how to style the video for mobile, tablet, and desktop viewports.

3. Determine how to best obtain multimedia for your website.

   a) Identify tools and software necessary to create your own video.

   b) Identify public domain content available for use.

   c) Learn how to use multimedia and converter software.

4. Determine how to make your videos accessible.

   a) Identify the timecodes for captions.

   b) Identify the timecodes for descriptions.

How should you submit solutions to questions in the assignments identified with a symbol?

Every assignment in this book contains one or more questions identified with a ✳ symbol. These questions require you to think beyond the assigned presentation. Present your solutions to the questions in the format required by your instructor. Possible formats may include one or more of these options: create a document that contains the answer; present your answer to the class; discuss your answer in a group; record the answer as audio or video using a webcam, smartphone, or portable media player; or post answers on a blog, wiki, or website.

Apply Your Knowledge

Reinforce the skills and apply the concepts you learned in this chapter.

Adding Audio to a Webpage

Instructions: In this exercise, you will use your text editor to add audio to a webpage. Insert three audio elements and include two source elements for each audio file. Work with the index.html file in the apply folder and audio files in the apply\media folder from the Data Files. The completed webpage is shown in Figure 9–37. You will also use professional web development practices to indent, space, comment, and validate your code.

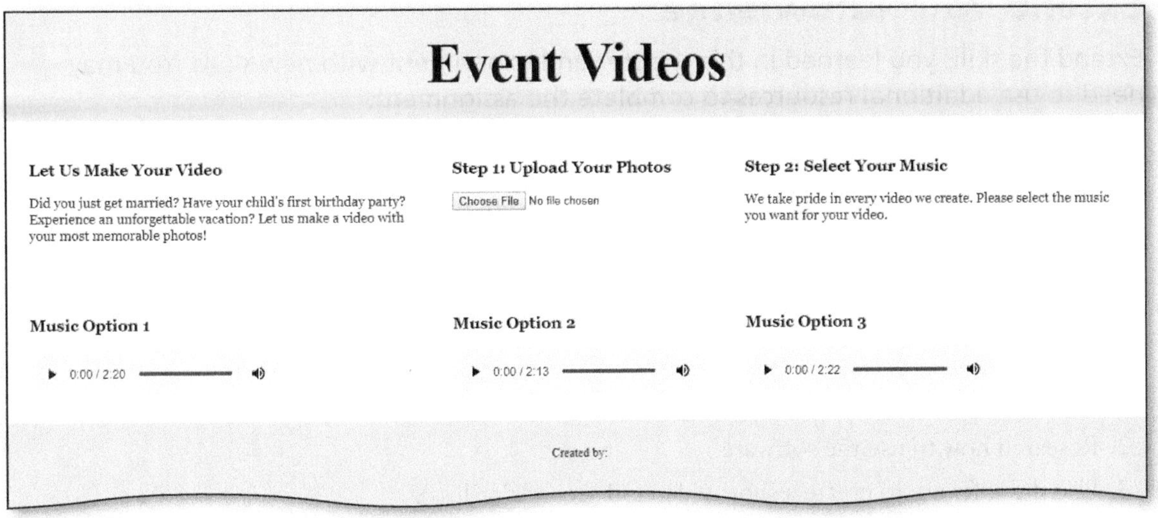

Figure 9–37

Perform the following tasks:

1. Open index.html in your text editor, review the page, add a title, modify the comment at the top of the page to include your name and today's date, and replace "Student's Name" with your name in the footer element.

2. Insert an **audio** element below the **h3** element, Music Option 1.

3. Add the controls attribute to the audio element.

4. Insert two **source** elements within the **audio** element and use the two audio-happy audio files contained within the apply\media folder.

5. Insert another **audio** element below the **h3** element, Music Option 2.

6. Add the controls attribute to the audio element.

7. Insert two **source** elements within the **audio** element and use the two audio-rock audio files contained within the apply\media folder.

8. Insert another audio element below the **h3** element, Music Option 3.

9. Add the controls attribute to the audio element.

10. Insert two **source** elements within the **audio** element and use the two audio-tech audio files contained within the apply\media folder.

11. Include a paragraph element within each **audio** element that advises legacy browser users that their browser does not support the **audio** element.

Continued >

Apply Your Knowledge *continued*

12. Save all of your changes and open the index.html in your browser.

13. Validate your HTML document using the W3C validator found at validator.w3.org and fix any errors that are identified.

14. Submit the files in a format specified by your instructor.

15. ✺ In this exercise, you specified two source files, one of which was an Ogg file. Use your browser to research free resources available to convert an audio file to the Ogg format. Summarize your findings and provide a link to at least three different resources.

Extend Your Knowledge

Extend the skills you learned in this chapter and experiment with new skills. You may need to use additional resources to complete the assignment.

Using Multimedia Software

Instructions: In this exercise, you use multimedia software to create a short video. If you use a Windows 10 computer, you can use Microsoft Photos. If you use macOS and have iMovie on your system, use iMovie to complete this project. You may also use your browser to research other online multimedia options.

Perform the following tasks:

1. Open Microsoft Photos, macOS iMovie, or another multimedia software application.

2. Research how to use the software.

3. Use the software to create a short video (30 seconds or less).

4. Your video should include, at a minimum, images, sound, and captions or titles.

5. Save the movie in the MP4 file format. Compress the file if it is larger than 15 MB.

6. View your video in your preferred video player.

7. Submit the video in a format specified by your instructor.

8. ✺ In this exercise, you learned how to use multimedia software. Describe the next steps you would take to convert the video file you created to another file format.

Analyze, Correct, Improve

Analyze a webpage, correct all errors, and improve it.

Adding a Video File and Captions File

Note: To complete this assignment, you will be required to use the Data Files. Please contact your instructor for information about accessing the Data Files.

Instructions: The index.html webpage includes a video element; however, no video source is specified. The video also needs captions and descriptions files added for accessibility. Figure 9–38 provides an example of the corrected video on a webpage.

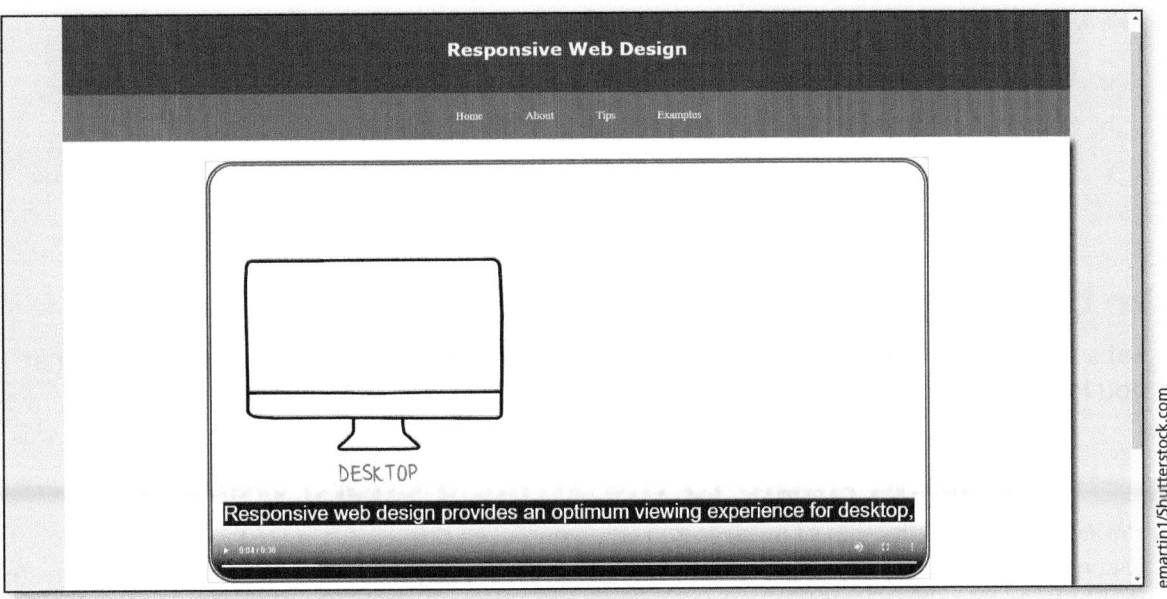

Figure 9–38

emartin1/Shutterstock.com

1. Correct

a. Open your text editor, open the index.html file in the chapter09\analyze folder from the Data Files, and then modify the comment at the top of the page to include your name and today's date. Add your name to the paragraph element located within the footer element near the bottom of the page.

b. Open index.html in your browser and notice the empty video element. Review the files provided in your media folder and add at least two video source files with appropriate attributes. Include a paragraph element that advises legacy browser users that their browser does not support the video element.

c. Add the poster attribute that uses the image within the images folder and add the controls attribute to the video element.

d. Save your changes, and then view the video in your browser.

2. Improve

a. Create a captions file for the video. Open the captions.vtt file provided in the chapter09/analyze folder from the Data Files. Add your name and date to the NOTE. Use the captions.vtt file to create captions for the video. Use seven sequence numbers. Review the video to help determine appropriate timecodes.

b. Save your changes to the captions.vtt file. In the index.html file, use the track element to add the captions file to the video element. Include the following attributes: src, kind, srclang, and label.

c. Use Web Server for Chrome to review the video with captions, and make additional adjustments to the caption timecodes as necessary. Review the video again with captions to ensure that the captions match the speaker's words.

d. Open the descriptions.vtt file provided in the chapter09/analyze folder from the Data Files and add your name and date to the NOTE.

e. Add descriptive text to Line 11 to describe the page for a visually impaired person. Describe what is happening in the video.

f. Save your changes to the descriptions.vtt file. In the index.html file, use the track element to add the descriptions file to the video element. Include the following attributes: src, kind, srclang, and label.

Continued >

Analyze, Correct, Improve *continued*

g. Validate the HTML file and correct any errors.

h. Submit the assignment in the format specified by your instructor.

i. ✷ Use your browser to research screen readers. What are the most popular screen readers? Is there a screen reader extension available for Google Chrome?

In the Lab

Labs 1 and 2, which increase in difficulty, require you to create webpages based on what you learned in the chapter; Lab 3 is ideal for group projects/collaboration.

Lab 1: **Adding Audio to the Strike a Chord Website**

Problem: You work for a local music lesson company called Strike a Chord that provides music lessons for piano, guitar, and violin. The company needs a web presence and has hired you to create their website. You have already created the website and now need to add audio to the Lessons page. Figure 9–39 shows the Lessons page with the audio files.

Figure 9–39

Instructions: Perform the following tasks:

1. Open your music folder and create a new subfolder named media. Copy the Data Files from chapter09/lab1 to your media folder.

2. Open the lessons.html file in your text editor and update the comment with today's date.

3. In the piano section, after the paragraph element, insert two new blank lines and then add an h4 element with the text, `Piano Spring Performance`.

4. Below the h4 element, add an audio element with the `controls` attribute.

5. Nest a source element within the audio element that specifies the `piano.mp3` as the source file, located in the media folder, and `audio/mp3` as the type.

6. Nest another source element that specifies the `piano.ogg` as the source file and `audio/ogg` as the type.

7. Below the source element, provide fallback text for legacy browsers that do not support the audio element.

8. In the guitar section, after the paragraph element, insert two new blank lines and then add an h4 element with the text, `Guitar Winter Performance`.

9. Below the h4 element, add an audio element with the `controls` attribute.

10. Nest a source element within the audio element that specifies the `guitar.mp3` as the source file and `audio/mp3` as the type.

11. Nest another source element that specifies the `guitar.ogg` as the source file and `audio /ogg` as the type.

12. Below the source element, provide fallback text for legacy browsers that do not support the audio element.

13. In the violin section, after the paragraph element, insert two new blank lines and then add an h4 element with the text, `Violin Spring Performance`.

14. Below the h4 element, add an audio element with the `controls` attribute.

15. Nest a source element within the audio element that specifies the `violin.mp3` as the source file and `audio/mp3` as the type.

16. Nest another source element that specifies the `violin.ogg` as the source file and `audio /ogg` as the type.

17. Below the source element, provide fallback text for legacy browsers that do not support the audio element.

18. Check your spelling. Validate your HTML file and correct any errors. Save your changes.

19. Open the lessons.html file in your browser and test the audio.

20. Submit your assignment in the format specified by your instructor.

21. ⚙ Research the Internet to locate free resources for audio files and provide a summary of your findings. Include at least three resource links.

Lab 2: **Adding a Video to the Wild Rescues Website**

Problem: You volunteer at a local wildlife rescue, a nonprofit organization called Wild Rescues. The organization rescues all kinds of wild animals, rehabilitates them, and then releases them back into the wild. Wild Rescues needs a website to help raise awareness about the organization. You have already created the website and now need to add a video with captions. The video, with captions, is shown in Figure 9–40.

romakoma/Shutterstock.com

Figure 9–40

Continued >

In the Lab *continued*

Instructions: Perform the following tasks:

1. Open your rescue folder and create a new subfolder named media. Copy the Data Files from chapter09/lab2 to your rescue/media folder.

2. Open the about.html file in your text editor. Replace the image element on Line 53 with a paragraph element that includes the following text:

   `Watch the video below to meet our new, rescued friends.`

3. Insert two new lines below the paragraph element you added in Step 2. Add a video element with the controls attribute and a poster attribute that uses the baby-hawk.jpg image file.

4. Nest a source element within the video element that specifies `wildrescues.mp4` as the source file and `video/mp4` as the type.

5. Nest another source element that specifies `wildrescues.webm` as the source file and `video/webm` as the type.

6. Open the media\captions.vtt file in your text editor. Add your name and date to the NOTE. Use Table 9–8 to create a captions file.

Table 9–8 Captions for the Wild Rescues Video	
Line Number	**Code to Insert**
9	1
10	00:03.200 --> 00:07.200
11	These baby raccoons were found abandoned near a home.
12	
13	2
14	00:08.900 --> 00:11.700
15	Nugget is learning how to climb trees.
16	
17	3
18	00:13.800 --> 00:16.500
19	Princess was neglected by her owner.
20	
21	4
22	00:18.900 --> 00:20.500
23	Sox is an orphan.
24	
25	5
26	00:24.000 --> 00:26.000
27	Frank was found abandoned.
28	
29	6
30	00:29.000 --> 00:31.500
31	Prince's hooves are in bad shape.

7. In about.html, use the track element to add the captions file to the video element. Include the following attributes: src, kind, srclang, and label.

8. Use the track element to add the descriptions file to the video element. Include the following attributes: src, kind, srclang, and label.

9. Below the source element, provide fallback text for legacy browsers that do not support the video element.

10. Open the styles.css file in your text editor. Add the video selector to the CSS Reset style rule. Add the video selector to the img style rule as well.

11. Save your changes. Use Web Server for Chrome to launch the website and then navigate to the About Us page. Turn the captions on and view the video with captions.

12. Check your spelling. Validate all HTML and CSS files and correct any errors. Save your changes.

13. Submit your assignment in the format specified by your instructor.

14. ✳ In this assignment, you added a video element and made it accessible by including captions and descriptions files. Is it possible to style captions? Research to find your answer and include an example of your findings.

Lab 3: Adding Audio and Video to the Student Clubs and Events Website

Problem: You and several of your classmates have decided to help increase student involvement in school clubs and events by creating a website to promote awareness about the various activities. You have already created the website and now need to further enhance it with audio and video.

Instructions:

1. As a team, discuss the best page to integrate audio. You may create an audio file or research the Internet for royalty-free audio resources.

2. Save the audio file within your media folder and create two audio files, using MP3 and Ogg file formats. Compress any audio files larger than 12 MB. Add the audio element with controls to a webpage within your website. Provide fallback text for legacy browsers that do not support the audio element.

3. As a team, discuss the best page to integrate video. Take pictures and video of your campus and use them to create a video to use within your website. You can use Microsoft Photos, Apple iMovie, or another software application of your choice.

4. The video should include at least five pictures or video clips. Add music and voice audio to your video. Keep the video brief, 45 seconds or less.

5. Save your video as an MP4 file. Find an online converter and create a WebM file as well.

6. Compress your video files if they are larger than 12 MB.

7. Use the video element to add your video to a webpage within your website. Include the controls and poster attributes. Include two source elements. Provide fallback text for legacy browsers that do not support the video element.

8. Create captions and descriptions files. Start files for your captions and descriptions are provided in the Data Files chapter09/lab3 folder.

9. Use the track element to add the captions and descriptions files to the video element. View your video with captions using Web Server for Chrome or by publishing your website.

10. Review the captions to ensure that the timecodes are accurate and make any necessary adjustments.

11. Open the styles.css file in your text editor. Add the video selector to the CSS Reset style rule. Add the video selector to the img style rule as well.

12. Review your files for best coding practices; ensure proper spacing and indents for improved readability.

Continued >

STUDENT ASSIGNMENTS

In the Lab *continued*

13. Check your spelling. Validate all HTML and CSS files and correct any errors. Save your changes.

14. Submit your assignment in the format specified by your instructor.

15. ✹ Identify the resource you used to make your video. Identify the resource you used for audio. Identify the resource you used for file conversions.

Consider This: Your Turn

Apply your creative thinking and problem-solving skills to design and implement a solution.

1. Adding Audio to Your Personal Portfolio Website
Personal

Part 1: You have already developed a responsive website for your personal portfolio and now need to add audio to the website.

1. Open your portfolio folder and create a new subfolder named media.

2. Add the `audio` element to one of your webpages. Review your webpages to determine which page will use the audio element.

3. Determine which attributes to include for the `audio` element. Include at least two source files. You may use an existing audio file that you have, you may create an audio file, or you can research the Internet for a free audio resource, such as freemusicarchive.com. Save your audio source files in your portfolio/media folder.

4. Provide fallback text for legacy browsers that do not support the video element.

5. Save and test your files.

6. Validate and correct your HTML file as needed.

7. Submit your assignment in the format specified by your instructor.

Part 2: ✹ Discuss the reasons you should or should not include audio on your portfolio webpage.

2. Adding a Video to the Dog Grooming Website
Professional

Part 1: You have already created a responsive design website for a dog grooming business, but now need to add a video to the website and make it accessible.

1. Open your groom folder and create a new subfolder named media. Copy the Data Files from chapter09/your_turn2 to your groom/media folder.

2. Open the index.html file in your text editor. Add a video element at the end of the welcome div. Include the controls attribute and a poster attribute that uses the image file of your choice.

3. Nest a source element within the video element that specifies `groom.mp4` as the source file and `video/mp4` as the type.

4. Nest another source element that specifies `groom.webm` as the source file and `video /webm` as the type.

5. Open the media\captions.vtt file in your text editor. Add your name and date to the NOTE. Use Table 9–9 to create a captions file.

Table 9–9 Captions for the Dog Grooming Video	
Line Number	**Code to Insert**
9	1
10	00:05.000 --> 00:09.400
11	All of our grooming packages include a relaxing bath.
12	
13	2
14	00:12.300 --> 00:14.700
15	Nails are carefully trimmed.
16	
17	3
18	00:16.700 --> 00:19.900
19	Our groomers cut and style with precision.
20	
21	4
22	00:23.600 --> 00:26.300
23	We offer several grooming packages.
24	
25	5
26	00:28.000 --> 00:32.000
27	Let us pamper your pet today.

6. Use the track element to add the captions file to the video element. Include the following attributes: src, kind, srclang, and label.

7. Use the track element to add the descriptions file to the video element. Include the following attributes: src, kind, srclang, and label.

8. Below the source element, provide fallback text for legacy browsers that do not support the video element.

9. Open the styles.css file in your text editor. Add the video selector to the CSS Reset style rule. Add the video selector to the img style rule as well.

10. Save your changes. Use Web Server for Chrome to launch the website. Turn the captions on and view the video with captions.

11. Check your spelling. Validate all HTML and CSS files and correct any errors. Save your changes.

12. Submit your assignment in the format specified by your instructor.

13. ✴ Identify the steps you would take to accommodate legacy browsers if you included a Flash video on the Dog Grooming website.

3. Adding Audio and Video to the Future Technologies Website
Research and Collaboration

Part 1:   You and several of your classmates have been tasked with creating a website that showcases advances in technology. You have already created a responsive design website and now need to add audio and video to the website.

1. As a team, discuss the best page to integrate audio. You may create an audio file or research the Internet for royalty-free audio resources.

2. Save the audio file within your media folder and create two audio files, using the MP3 and Ogg file formats. Compress any audio files larger than 12 MB. Add the audio element with controls

Continued >

Consider This: Your Turn *continued*

to a webpage within your website. Provide fallback text for legacy browsers that do not support the audio element.

3. As a team, discuss the best page to integrate video. Find or take pictures and/or video of technologies and use them to create a video to use within your website. You can use Microsoft Photos, Apple iMovie, or another software application of your choice.

4. The video should include at least five pictures or video clips. Add music and voice audio to your video. Keep the video brief, 45 seconds or less.

5. Save your video as a MP4. Find an online converter and create a WebM file as well.

6. Compress your video files if they are larger than 12 MB.

7. Use the video element to add your video to a webpage within your website. Include the controls and poster attributes. Include two source elements. Provide fallback text for legacy browsers that do not support the video element.

8. Create captions and descriptions files. Start files for your captions and descriptions are provided in the Data Files chapter09/your_turn3 folder.

9. Use the track element to add the captions and descriptions files to the video element. View your video with captions using Web Server for Chrome or by publishing your website.

10. Review the captions to ensure that the timecodes are accurate and make any necessary adjustments.

11. Open the styles.css file in your text editor. Add the video selector to the CSS Reset style rule. Add the video selector to the img style rule as well.

12. Review your files for best coding practices; ensure proper spacing and indents for improved readability.

13. Check your spelling. Validate all HTML and CSS files and correct any errors. Save your changes.

14. Submit your assignment in the format specified by your instructor.

15. ✳ As a group, discuss the benefits of uploading a video file to YouTube and then linking the YouTube video to a website. List the steps you would take accomplish this task.

10 | Creating Interactivity with CSS and JavaScript

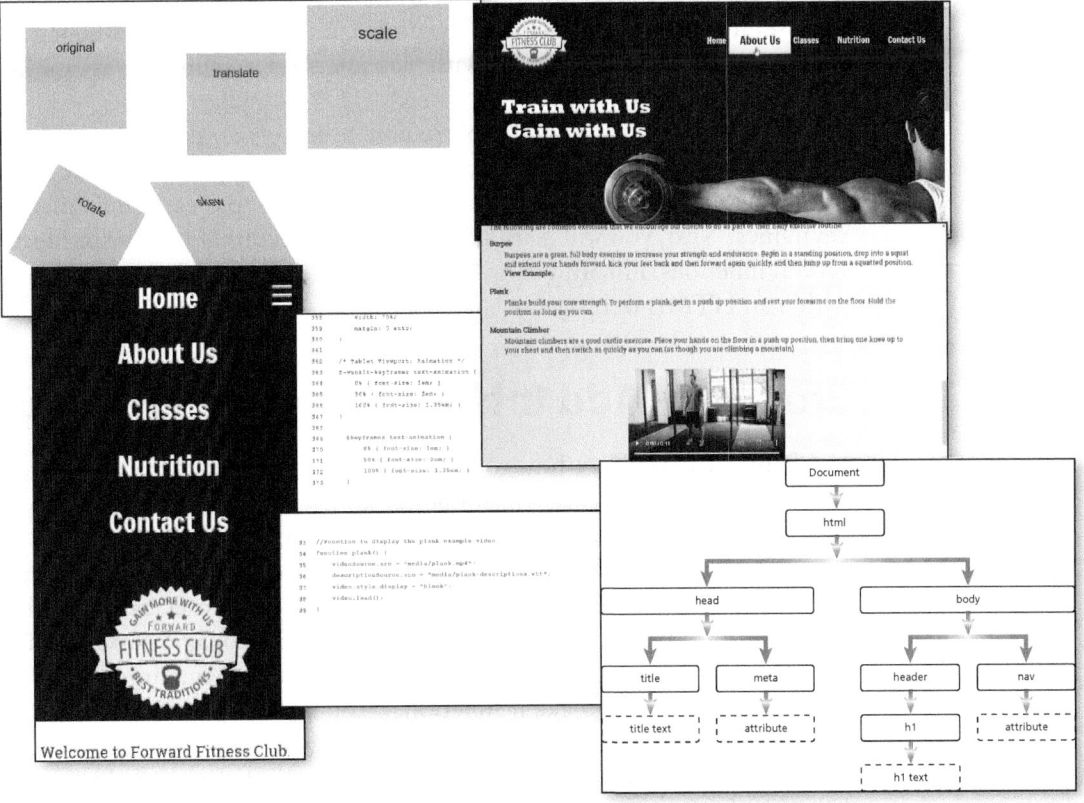

Objectives

You will have mastered the material in this chapter when you can:

- Use the CSS transform property
- Create animations with CSS keyframes
- Understand JavaScript
- Describe JavaScript code
- Understand and use the script element
- Understand where JavaScript code may be written

- Create an external JavaScript file
- Create JavaScript functions
- Understand events
- Use an onclick event handler

10 | Creating Interactivity with CSS and JavaScript

Introduction

Most modern websites include some form of interactivity. Interactivity is commonly integrated within a website using CSS and JavaScript, a web programming language used to enhance a website and create interactivity. An effective way to create interesting and useful webpages is to include dynamic content to make the webpage interactive. One way to engage and interact with customers on a webpage is to use JavaScript code to display messages.

In this chapter, you will explore how to integrate animation on a webpage using CSS and JavaScript. You will learn how to use the CSS transform property to make elements move on a webpage. You will also use CSS to create an animation using keyframes. Next, you will learn how to create an external JavaScript file and write several functions. Finally, you will learn how to reference the external JavaScript file within an HTML webpage.

Project — Add Interactivity to a Webpage

In Chapter 10, you learn how to use CSS to create interactivity and animations. This chapter also provides a basic introduction to JavaScript and discusses how to use JavaScript to enhance a webpage through interactivity.

The project in this chapter improves a website by adding interactivity to webpages using both CSS and JavaScript. To perform these tasks, you first use the CSS transform property to animate elements on a webpage. Next, you use CSS to create animation using keyframes. Then, you create a hamburger menu icon and use JavaScript code to make it functional. You also use JavaScript code to dynamically change a video on the About Us page. Finally, you use JavaScript code to dynamically change text within the Contact Us page. Figure 10–1 shows the home page with the CSS transform property applied. Figure 10–2 shows a still of the animation on the home page. Figure 10–3 shows the hamburger menu icon as displayed in a mobile viewport. Figure 10–4 shows the video displayed as a result of a JavaScript function.

Roadmap

In this chapter, you will learn how to create the webpages shown in Figures 10–1, 10–2, 10–3, and 10–4. The following roadmap identifies general activities you will perform as you progress through this chapter:

1. CREATE CSS TRANSFORM.
2. CREATE CSS ANIMATION.
3. CREATE a HAMBURGER MENU.
4. CREATE a JAVASCRIPT FILE.
5. CREATE AND CALL JAVASCRIPT FUNCTIONS.

Home Page with CSS Transform Property

Figure 10–1

nexusby/Shutterstock.com, Y Photo Studio/Shutterstock.com

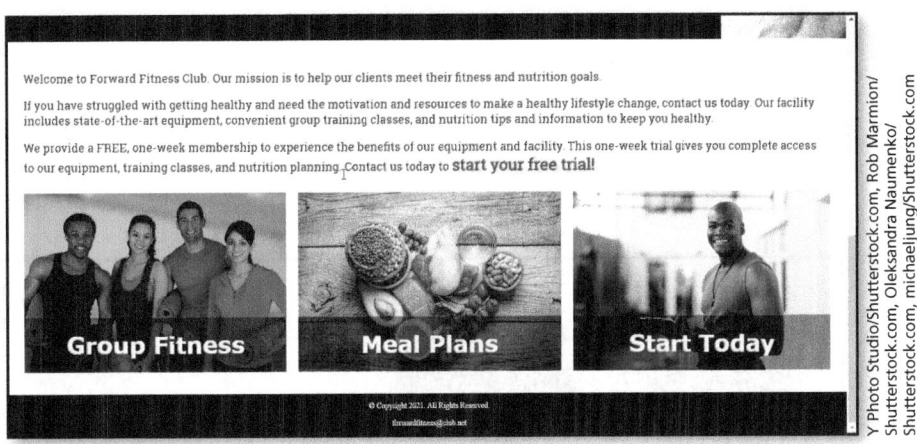

Welcome to Forward Fitness Club. Our mission is to help our clients meet their fitness and nutrition goals.

If you have struggled with getting healthy and need the motivation and resources to make a healthy lifestyle change, contact us today. Our facility includes state-of-the-art equipment, convenient group training classes, and nutrition tips and information to keep you healthy.

We provide a FREE, one-week membership to experience the benefits of our equipment and facility. This one-week trial gives you complete access to our equipment, training classes, and nutrition planning. Contact us today to **start your free trial!**

Group Fitness   **Meal Plans**   **Start Today**

© Copyright 2021. All Rights Reserved.
fitness@club.net

Home Page with Animated Captions

Figure 10–2

Y Photo Studio/Shutterstock.com, Rob Marmion/Shutterstock.com, Oleksandra Naumenko/Shutterstock.com, michaeljung/Shutterstock.com

nexusby/Shutterstock.com, Rob Marmion/Shutterstock.com

Welcome to Forward Fitness Club. Our mission is to help our clients meet their fitness and nutrition goals

FREE One-Week Trial Membership!

Call Us Today to Get Started

(814) 555-9608

Fitness Club Hours:

- Mon - Thu: 6:00am - 6:00pm
- Friday: 6:00am - 4:00pm
- Saturday: 8:00am - 6:00pm
- Sunday: Closed

**Home Page with
Hamburger Menu Icon**

Figure 10–3

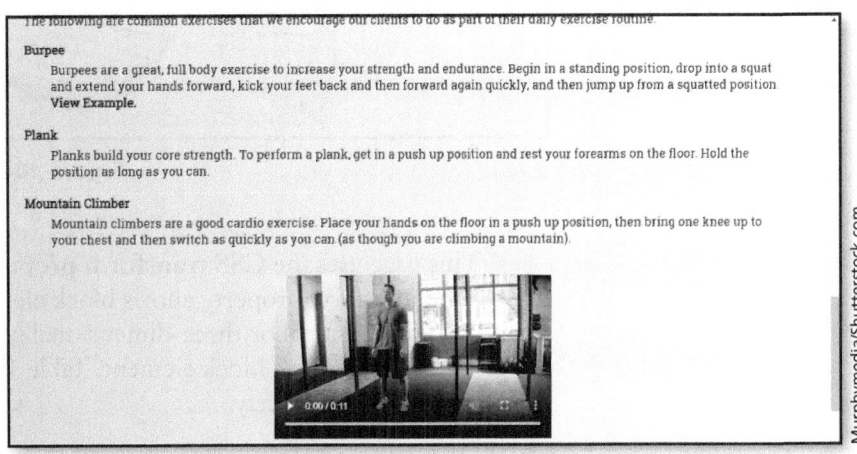

The following are common exercises that we encourage our clients to do as part of their daily exercise routine.

Burpee

Burpees are a great, full body exercise to increase your strength and endurance. Begin in a standing position, drop into a squat and extend your hands forward, kick your feet back and then forward again quickly, and then jump up from a squatted position. **View Example.**

Plank

Planks build your core strength. To perform a plank, get in a push up position and rest your forearms on the floor. Hold the position as long as you can.

Mountain Climber

Mountain climbers are a good cardio exercise. Place your hands on the floor in a push up position, then bring one knee up to your chest and then switch as quickly as you can (as though you are climbing a mountain).

0:00 / 0:11

Murphymedia/Shutterstock.com

JavaScript Displaying Video

Figure 10–4

At the beginning of step instructions throughout the chapter, you will see an abbreviated form of this roadmap. The abbreviated roadmap uses colors to indicate chapter progress: gray means the chapter is beyond that activity; blue means the task being shown is covered in that activity, and black means that activity is yet to be covered. For example, the following abbreviated roadmap indicates the chapter would be showing a task in the 2 CREATE CSS ANIMATION activity.

1 CREATE CSS TRANSFORM | **2 CREATE CSS ANIMATION** | **3 CREATE HAMBURGER MENU**
4 CREATE JAVASCRIPT FILE | **5 CREATE & CALL JAVASCRIPT FUNCTIONS**

Use the abbreviated roadmap as a progress guide while you read or step through the instructions in this chapter.

Using CSS to Create Interactivity

CSS began as a simple way to add color and design a webpage, but today, it has evolved to become so much more. CSS can be used to move elements on a webpage, change the color of an element, or change the appearance of an element. To see a demonstration of how CSS is used to create interactivity, open your browser to emporiumpies.com/pies, which is shown in Figure 10–5.

emporiumpies.com

Figure 10–5

This page uses the CSS **transform property** to rotate the pies 180 degrees in 3D. The transform property allows block elements to be transformed or changed within two-dimensional or three-dimensional space. You can use a transform to rotate, scale, skew, or translate a block element. Table 10–1 lists the methods that can be used with the transform property.

Table 10–1 Transform Property Values

Method	Description	Example
matrix( )	A 2D transformation; accepts six values	transform: matrix(1, 0.5, -0.5, 1, 10, 0)
rotate( )	A 2D rotation; rotates an element a specified number of degrees clockwise or counter-clockwise	transform: rotate(10deg)
rotateX( )	A 3D rotation; rotates an element a specified number of degrees on the elements X-axis	transform: rotateX(40deg)
rotateY( )	A 3D rotation; rotates an element a specified number of degrees on the elements Y-axis	transform: rotateY(30deg)
rotateZ( )	A 3D rotation; rotates an element a specified number of degrees on the elements Z-axis	transform: rotateX(20deg)
scale( )	A 2D scale transformation; resizes an element	transform: scale(1.5)
scaleX( )	A 2D scale transformation; resizes an element on its X-axis	transform: scaleX(1.5)
scaleY( )	A 2D scale transformation; resizes an element on its Y-axis	transform: scaleY(1.5)
skew( )	A 2D skew transformation; moves the top and bottom or left and right sides a specified number of degrees	transform: skew(10deg, 10deg)
skewX( )	A 2D skew transformation for the X-axis of an element	transform: skewX(20deg)
skewY( )	A 2D skew transformation for the Y-axis of an element	transform: skewY(30deg)
translate( )	A 2D translation; moves the block element from its original position on the webpage	transform: translate(30px, 40px)
translateX( )	A 2D translation; moves the block element from its original position on the webpage	transform: translateX(30px)
translateY( )	A 2D translation; moves the block element from its original position on the webpage	transform: translateY(40px)

Figure 10–6 shows an example of several transforms.

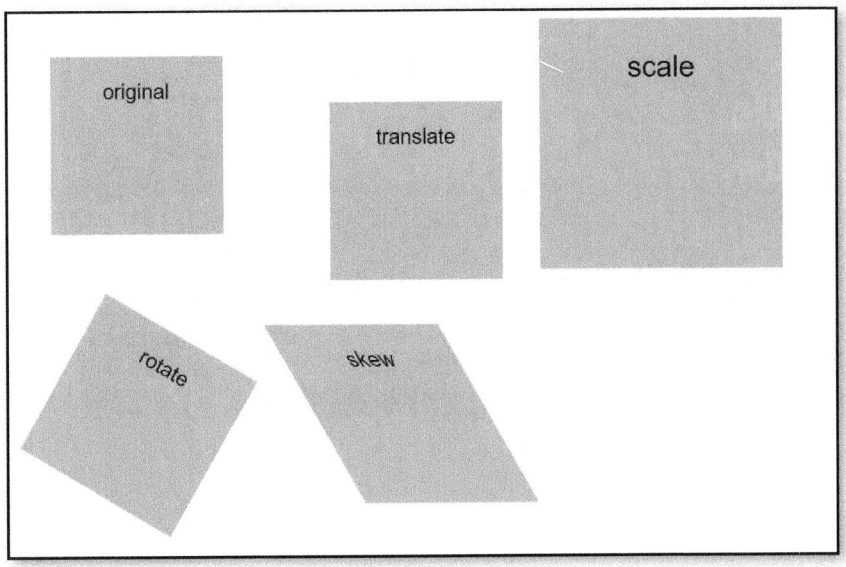

Figure 10–6

As Figure 10–6 demonstrates, the translate method moves the element from its original position. The scale method increases the size of the original element. The rotate method rotates the element 30 degrees clockwise. The skew method skews the sides of the element.

BTW
Experimenting with Transforms
You can further experiment with transforms at w3schools.com/cssref/css3_pr_transform.asp.

To Apply a CSS Transform to a Webpage

Apply a transform scale method to the navigation links for a desktop viewport and apply a translate method to the figure elements on the home page. *Why? Applying a transform to a website adds interactivity to a webpage and improves the user experience.* The following steps add the transform property to the style sheet.

- Open styles.css in your text editor and update the comment with today's date.

- Scroll down to the desktop media query and locate the style rule for nav li a:hover on Line 393.

- Tap or click at the end of Line 395, press the ENTER key to insert a new Line 396, and then type **transform: scale(1.3);** to insert a new declaration.

- Save your changes (Figure 10–7).

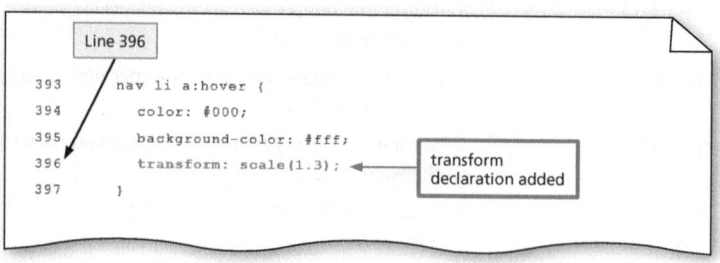

Figure 10–7

Q&A What is the result of adding this new declaration?
When the user hovers over a navigation link, the size of the link will increase.

- Open index.html in your browser, adjust the window to the size of a desktop viewport, and then hover over the navigation links to view the transform effect (Figure 10–8).

Figure 10–8

- Return to styles.css in your text editor.

- Tap or click at the end of Line 423, press the ENTER key to insert a new Line 424, and then type **transform: translateY(10px);** to insert a new declaration.

- Save your changes (Figure 10–9).

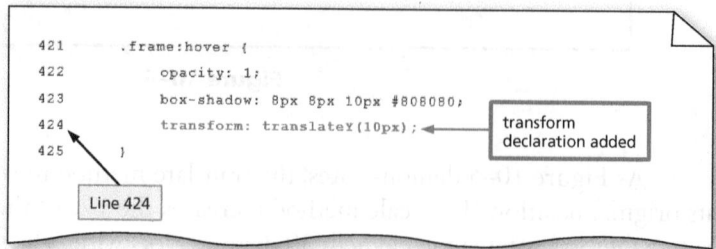

Figure 10–9

4

- Refresh index.html in your browser, and then hover over the images in the main content area to view the transform effect (Figure 10–10).

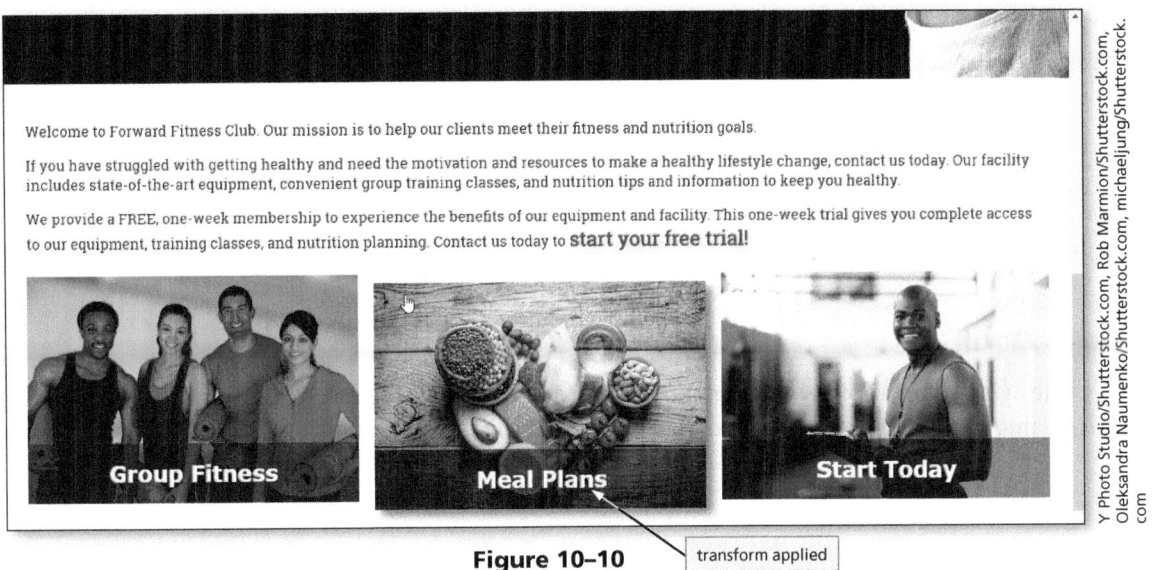

Figure 10–10   transform applied

Y Photo Studio/Shutterstock.com, Rob Marmion/Shutterstock.com, Oleksandra Naumenko/Shutterstock.com, michaeljung/Shutterstock.com

You can add interactivity to a webpage in other ways. CSS also provides a method to create animations on a webpage. Animations allow you to move elements on a page or change their appearance. To see a demonstration of how CSS is used to create animation, open your browser to supremo.co.uk/typeterms/. This page is shown in Figure 10–11.

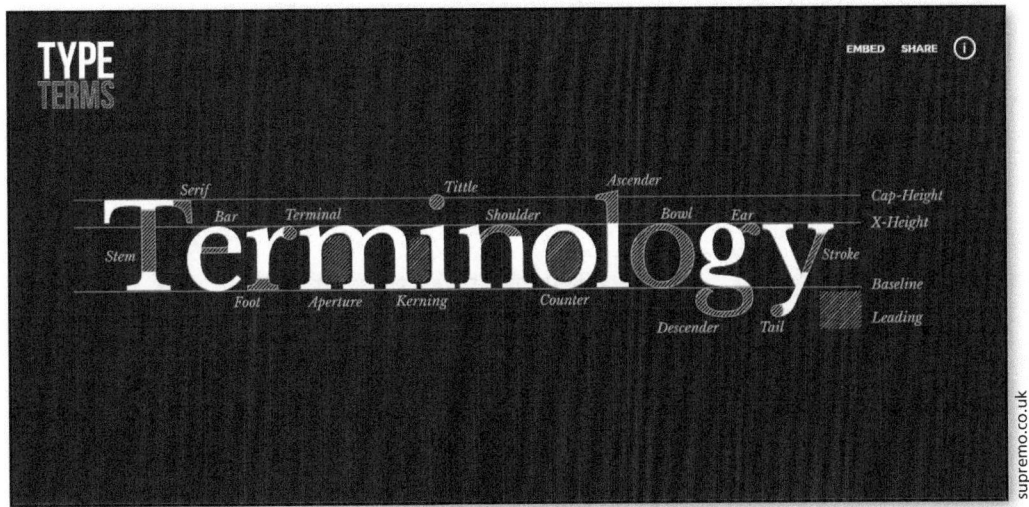

Figure 10–11

supremo.co.uk

When you tap or click a type term, CSS animation is used to move elements and display new content. To add an animation with CSS, you create it with an @keyframes rule. The @keyframes rule specifies the name of the animation as well as the animation parameters. The following is an example of an @keyframes rule.

```
@keyframes my-animation {
        0% { opacity: 0; }
        100% { opacity: 1; }
}
```

In the example above, my-animation is the name of the animation. When the animation begins, at 0%, the opacity is set to 0. When the animation ends, at 100%, the opacity is set to 1. Older versions of the Apple Safari browser require the prefix @-webkit- before keyframes. For browser compatibility, create two @keyframes rules; the first with the @-webkit- prefix, and the second without the prefix. Refer to the following example.

```
@-webkit-keyframes my-animation {
    0% { opacity: 0; }
    100% { opacity: 1; }
}
@keyframes my-animation {
    0% { opacity: 0; }
    100% { opacity: 1; }
}
```

After creating the animation, you can apply it to an existing style rule or create a new style rule. Table 10–2 lists the various animation properties that can be used to apply an animation.

Table 10–2 Animation Properties

Property	Description	Example

animation-delay	Specifies a time delay, in seconds, before the animation begins	`figure {`
		`    animation-delay: 2s;`
		`}`

animation-direction	Specifies the direction of an animation; forwards or reverse	`figure {`
		`    animation-direction: reverse;`
		`}`

animation-duration	Specifies the time it should take for the animation to complete; time is in seconds	`div {`
		`    animation-duration: 5s;`
		`}`

animation-fill-mode	Specifies the element style when the animation is not taking place	`div {`
		`    animation-fill-mode: backwards;`
		`}`

animation-iteration-count	Specifies the number of times an animation should take place	`article {`
		`    animation-iteration-count: 3;`
		`}`

animation-name	Specifies the name of the @keyframes animation	`article {`
		`    animation-name: my-animation;`
		`}`

animation-play-state	Specifies if the animation is in progress or paused	`article {`
		`    animation-play-state: paused;`
		`}`

animation-timing-function	Specifies the speed of the animation	`section {`
		`    animation-timing-function: ease-in;`
		`}`

animation	Shorthand property for the above properties	`section {`
		`    animation: my-animation 5s ease-in;`
		`}`

To apply the my-animation to an element, add new declarations to an existing style rule or create a new style rule. Include a declaration that uses the -webkit- prefix for browser compatibility. For example, if you want to apply the my-animation to a figure element, create the following style rule:

```
figure {
        -webkit-animation-duration: 5s;
        animation-duration: 5s;
        -webkit-animation-name: my-animation;
        animation-name: my-animation;
}
```

In this style rule, the my-animation is applied to the figure element with a duration of five seconds.

BTW
GitHub
GitHub is an online repository used by developers to share code. The W3C uses GitHub to track any issues related to CSS property recommendations.

To Add Animation to a Webpage

1 CREATE CSS TRANSFORM | 2 CREATE CSS ANIMATION | **3 CREATE HAMBURGER MENU**
4 CREATE JAVASCRIPT FILE | **5 CREATE & CALL JAVASCRIPT FUNCTIONS**

Use CSS to create an animation and then apply the animation to elements on the home page. *Why? Adding animation to a webpage grabs the user's attention and improves the user experience.* The following steps add an animation to the style sheet.

- Return to styles.css in your text editor, tap or click at the end of Line 360 and press the ENTER key twice to insert new Lines 361 and 362.

- On Line 362, type `/* Tablet Viewport: Animation */` to insert a new comment.

- Press the ENTER key to insert a new Line 363, and then type `@-webkit-keyframes text-animation {` to create a new @keyframes rule with the webkit prefix.

- Press the ENTER key to insert a new Line 364, increase the indent, and then type `0% { font-size: 1em; }` to specify the start of the animation.

- Press the ENTER key to insert a new Line 365, and then type `50% { font-size: 2em; }` to specify the middle of the animation.

- Press the ENTER key to insert a new Line 366, and then type `100% { font-size: 1.35em; }` to specify the end of the animation.

- Press the ENTER key to insert a new Line 367, decrease the indent, and then type `}` to close the animation (Figure 10–12).

Q&A

What is the purpose of the webkit prefix?
The webkit prefix is needed to accommodate later versions of Apple Safari.

What does this animation do?
When the animation begins (at 0%), the font size will be 1em, grow to 2em halfway through the animation (at 50%), and then scale down to 1.35em at the end of the animation (at 100%).

```
356      /* Tablet Viewport: Style rule for form element */
357      form {
358          width: 70%;
359          margin: 0 auto;
360      }
361
362      /* Tablet Viewport: Animation */
363      @-webkit-keyframes text-animation {
364          0% { font-size: 1em; }
365          50% { font-size: 2em; }
366          100% { font-size: 1.35em; }
367      }
```

Line 362

animation with -webkit- prefix

Figure 10–12

2

- Press the ENTER key twice to insert new Lines 368 and 369, and then type **@keyframes text-animation {** to create a new @keyframes rule.

- Press the ENTER key to insert a new Line 370, increase the indent, and then type **0% { font-size: 1em; }** to specify the start of the animation.

- Press the ENTER key to insert a new Line 371, and then type **50% { font-size: 2em; }** to specify the middle of the animation.

- Press the ENTER key to insert a new Line 372, and then type **100% { font-size: 1.35em; }** to specify the end of the animation.

- Press the ENTER key to insert a new Line 373, decrease the indent, and then type **}** to close the animation (Figure 10–13).

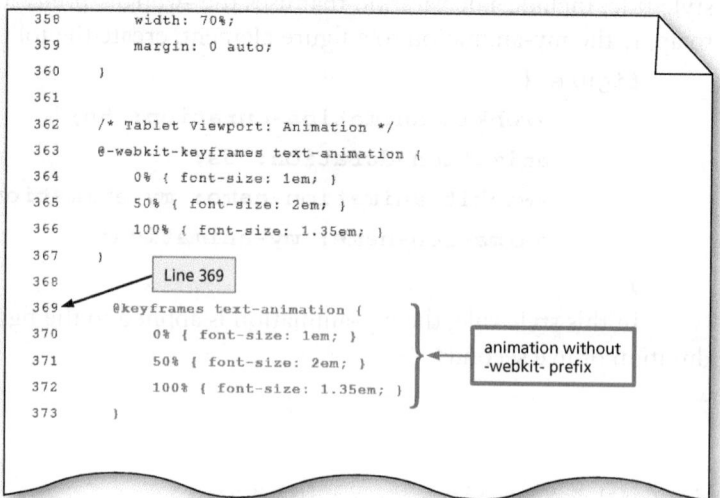

```
358        width: 70%;
359        margin: 0 auto;
360    }
361
362    /* Tablet Viewport: Animation */
363    @-webkit-keyframes text-animation {
364        0% { font-size: 1em; }
365        50% { font-size: 2em; }
366        100% { font-size: 1.35em; }
367    }
368
369        @keyframes text-animation {
370        0% { font-size: 1em; }
371        50% { font-size: 2em; }
372        100% { font-size: 1.35em; }
373    }
```

Line 369

animation without -webkit- prefix

Figure 10–13

Q&A Why did I need to create the same animation again?
The first animation uses the webkit prefix to support older versions of Apple Safari. This animation will be read by all other major browsers.

3

- Press the ENTER key twice to insert new Lines 374 and 375, and then type **figcaption {** to add a new selector.

- Press the ENTER key to insert a new Line 376, increase the indent, and then type **-webkit-animation-name: text-animation;** to add a new declaration.

- Press the ENTER key to insert a new Line 377, and then type **animation-name: text-animation;** to add a new declaration.

- Press the ENTER key to insert a new Line 378, and then type **-webkit-animation-delay: 3s;** to add a new declaration.

- Press the ENTER key to insert a new Line 379, and then type **animation-delay: 3s;** to add a new declaration.

- Press the ENTER key to insert a new Line 380, and then type **-webkit-animation-duration: 5s;** to add a new declaration.

- Press the ENTER key to insert a new Line 381, and then type **animation-duration: 5s;** to add a new declaration.

- Press the ENTER key to insert a new Line 382, decrease the indent, and then type **}** to close the animation (Figure 10–14).

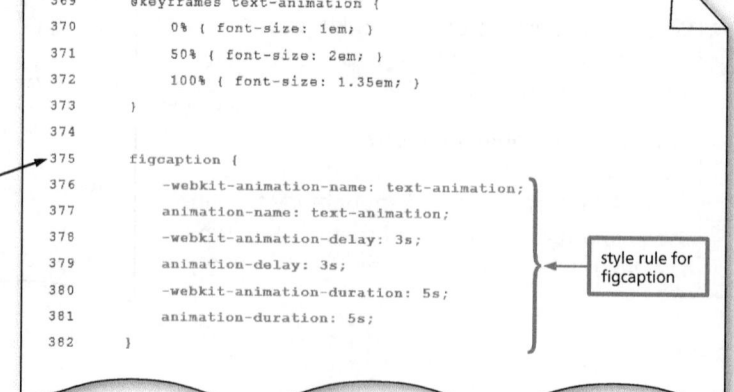

```
369        @keyframes text-animation {
370        0% { font-size: 1em; }
371        50% { font-size: 2em; }
372        100% { font-size: 1.35em; }
373    }
374
375    figcaption {
376        -webkit-animation-name: text-animation;
377        animation-name: text-animation;
378        -webkit-animation-delay: 3s;
379        animation-delay: 3s;
380        -webkit-animation-duration: 5s;
381        animation-duration: 5s;
382    }
```

Line 375

style rule for figcaption

Q&A What is the purpose of this style rule?
This style rule applies the text-animation to the figcaption. It delays the animation by three seconds. Once the animation begins, it will take five seconds to complete.

Figure 10–14

④
- Save your changes.

- Refresh index.html in your browser, scroll down the page to view the figure and figcaption elements, and then wait three seconds for the animation to begin (Figure 10–15).

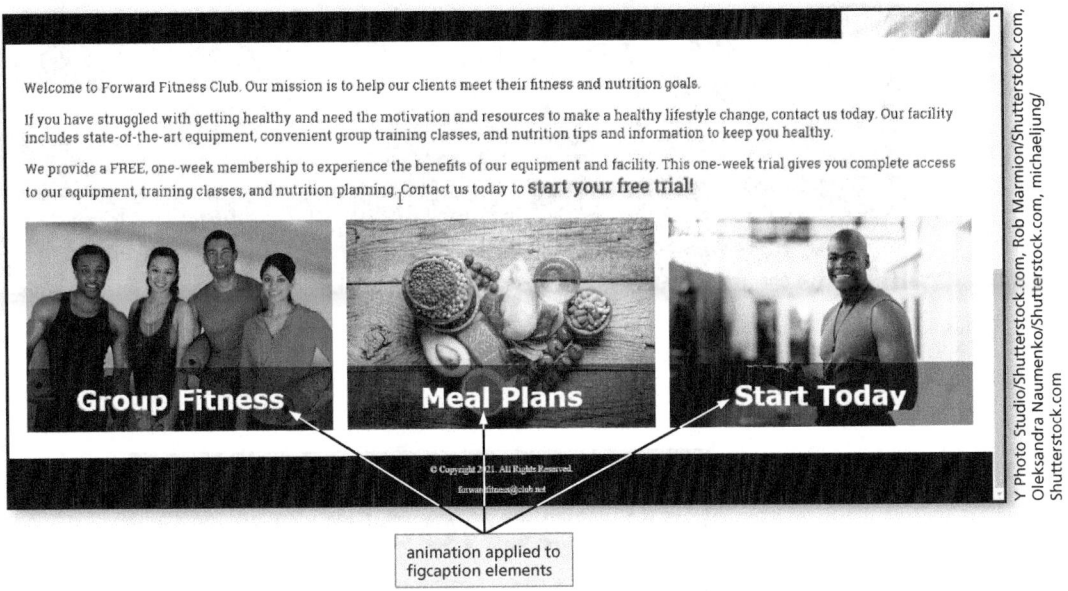

animation applied to
figcaption elements

Figure 10–15

Incorporating JavaScript

JavaScript is scripting language used to provide various types of functionality to webpages, such as the ability to interact with the user. In a web environment, web developers use a scripting language to control webpages. This includes providing user feedback, validating form data, and creating dynamic content based on user actions. JavaScript is a **client-side scripting** language, which means that the browser (i.e., the client) interprets and renders the JavaScript.

JavaScript was developed in the 1990s by Brendan Eich at Netscape and was originally known as Mocha and then LiveScript. During this same period, the Sun Microsystems Java technology was gaining in popularity. A marketing deal was struck with Sun Microsystems to adopt the Java name and change LiveScript to JavaScript. However, JavaScript and Java are not the same. Java is a more complex programming language, commonly used to create large business applications and native mobile applications for the Android operating system.

Most modern websites use some form of JavaScript within their website. JavaScript provides additional interactivity between the webpage and the user. Developers can use JavaScript to validate form information, send an alert to a user, change HTML content, show or hide content, animate elements, and much more. Efficient use of JavaScript can significantly improve and enrich the user experience. Figure 10–16 demonstrates how JavaScript is used to create a slide show on the home page for Boyne Mountain Resort.

Many mobile websites integrate an icon commonly known as the hamburger icon for use as a menu button. The hamburger icon consists of three horizontal, parallel lines, as shown in Figure 10–17, and uses JavaScript to display a menu and allow users to select an option.

BTW
Server-Side Scripting
Server-side scripting entails using a programming language to write a script that is performed by a web server. Server-side scripting processes data for a database. Common server-side scripting languages include ASP.NET, PHP, Python, and Ruby.

JavaScript
slide show

Figure 10–16

Source: boynemountain.com

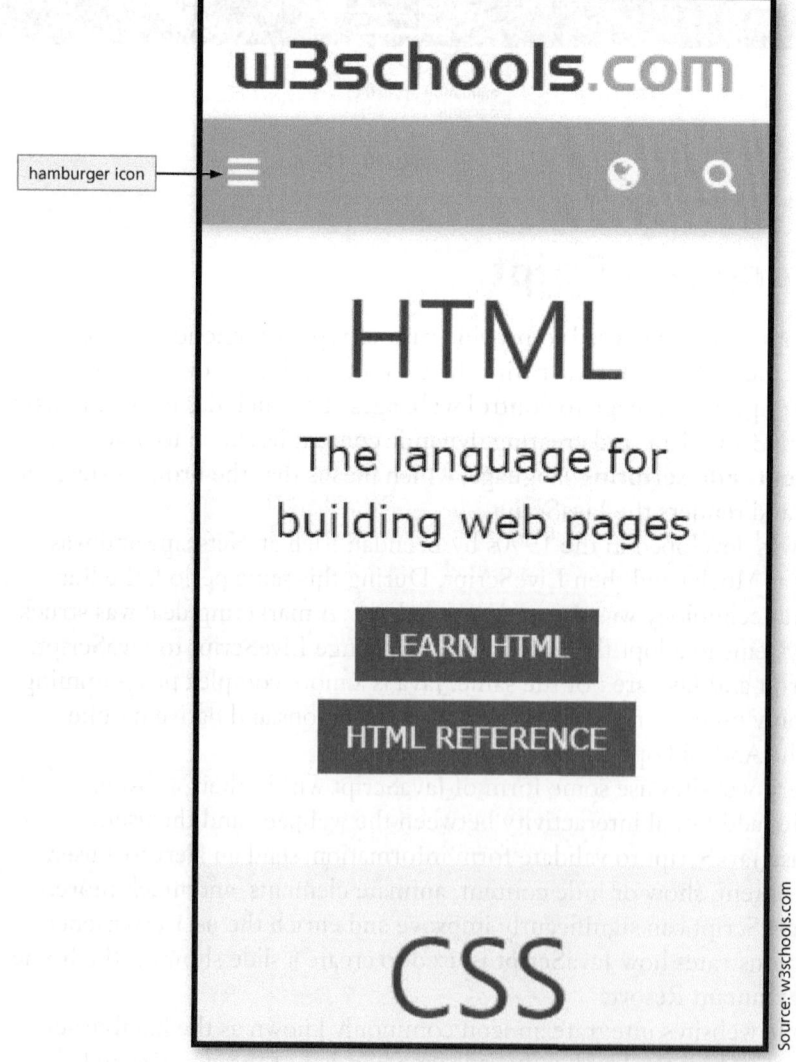

hamburger icon

Figure 10–17

Source: w3schools.com

Figure 10–18 shows how JavaScript is used on the Snap.svg demo page. Users select the type of coffee to make and then watch the animation of the coffee maker. The legend next to the coffee maker lets the user know the ingredients and amounts.

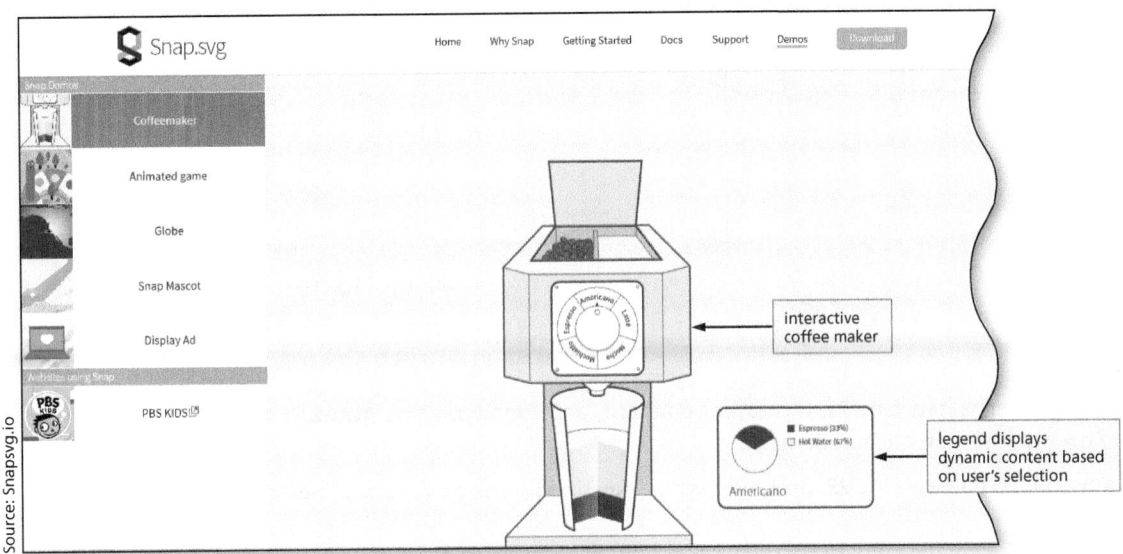

Source: Snapsvg.io

Figure 10–18

You can integrate JavaScript into webpages in many ways. You must first determine the types of interactivity you want to provide into your website and then determine whether JavaScript is the best approach to accomplish the interactivity.

You will replace the current navigation bar used for the mobile viewport of the Forward Fitness Club website with a hamburger menu. The following steps create the hamburger menu icon on all of the webpages for the Forward Fitness Club website. Later, you will use JavaScript to make the hamburger functional.

How do I find errors in my JavaScript code?

Carefully review your code for syntax errors. Check to ensure that you have correctly ended statements with a semicolon. Check for missing parentheses, braces, and periods. To troubleshoot JavaScript errors, you can use browser developer tools. In Google Chrome, display the developer tools (press the F12 key), and then open the console window. Trigger an event to call a JavaScript function. The console window will display any errors in red and provide you with the line number of the error.

CONSIDER THIS

To Create a New Nav Element for a Mobile Viewport

1 CREATE CSS TRANSFORM | 2 CREATE CSS ANIMATION | **3 CREATE HAMBURGER MENU**
4 CREATE JAVASCRIPT FILE | **5 CREATE & CALL JAVASCRIPT FUNCTIONS**

Add a new nav element to the HTML webpages. *Why? The new nav element will be used to display a hamburger menu for a mobile viewport.* To create a hamburger menu, begin by adding a new nav element to the index.html file. The following steps add a new nav element to all of the HTML webpages.

1

- Open the index.html file in your text editor to prepare to edit the file.
- Tap or click at the end of Line 17, and then press the ENTER key twice to insert new Lines 18 and 19.
- On Line 19, type `<!-- Mobile Nav -->` to insert a new comment.
- Press the ENTER key to insert a new Line 20, and then type `<nav class="mobile-nav">` to insert a starting nav tag.

- Press the ENTER key to insert a new Line 21, increase the indent, and then type `<div id="menu-links">` to insert a starting div tag (Figure 10–19).

Why am I adding another nav element?
This new nav element will be used to contain the hamburger icon and will only be displayed for mobile viewports.

What is the purpose of the div element?
The div element will contain the navigation links for the hamburger menu.

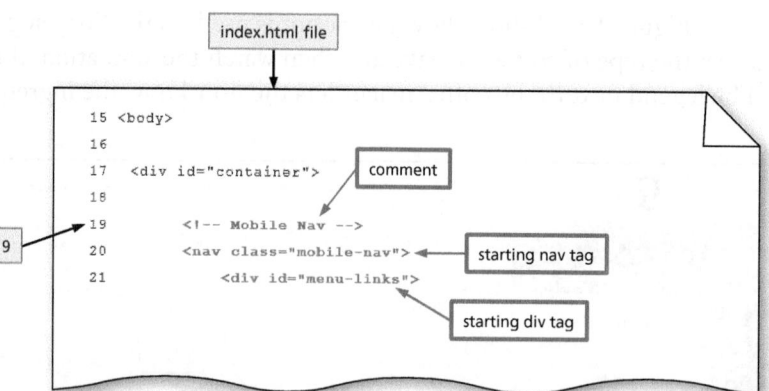

Figure 10–19

2

- Press the ENTER key to insert a new Line 22, increase the indent, and then type `<a href="index.html">Home</a>` to insert an anchor element.

- Press the ENTER key to insert a new Line 23, and then type `<a href="about.html">About Us</a>` to insert an anchor element.

- Press the ENTER key to insert a new Line 24, and then type `<a href="classes.html">Classes</a>` to insert an anchor element.

- Press the ENTER key to insert a new Line 25, and then type `<a href="nutrition.html">Nutrition</a>` to insert an anchor element.

- Press the ENTER key to insert a new Line 26, and then type `<a href="contact.html">Contact Us</a>` to insert an anchor element.

- Press the ENTER key to insert a new Line 27, decrease the indent, and then type `</div>` to insert a closing div tag (Figure 10–20).

Why do I need to add these anchor elements when they already exist on the page?
These anchor elements will be used to create the hamburger menu. Once the hamburger menu is complete, these links will only be displayed when the user taps the hamburger icon. The other nav element will not be displayed for mobile viewports.

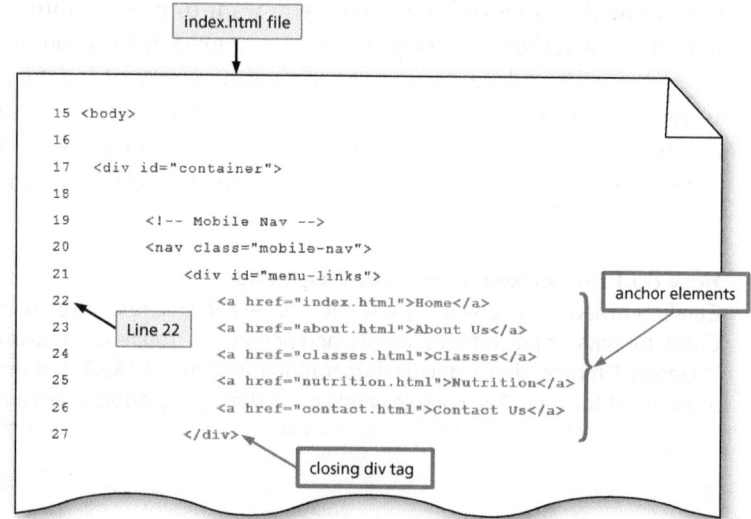

Figure 10–20

3

- Press the ENTER key to insert a new Line 28, and then type `<a class="menu-icon">` to insert a starting anchor tag.

- Press the ENTER key to insert a new Line 29, increase the indent, and then type `<div>&#9776;</div>` to insert a new div element.

- Press the ENTER key to insert a new Line 30, decrease the indent, and then type `</a>` to insert a closing anchor tag.

- Press the ENTER key to insert a new Line 31, decrease the indent, and then type `</nav>` to insert a closing nav tag (Figure 10–21).

What is the purpose of this anchor element?
This anchor element will be used to toggle the hamburger menu on and off.

What character is represented by 9776?
The 9776 entity code is the hamburger (three lines) icon.

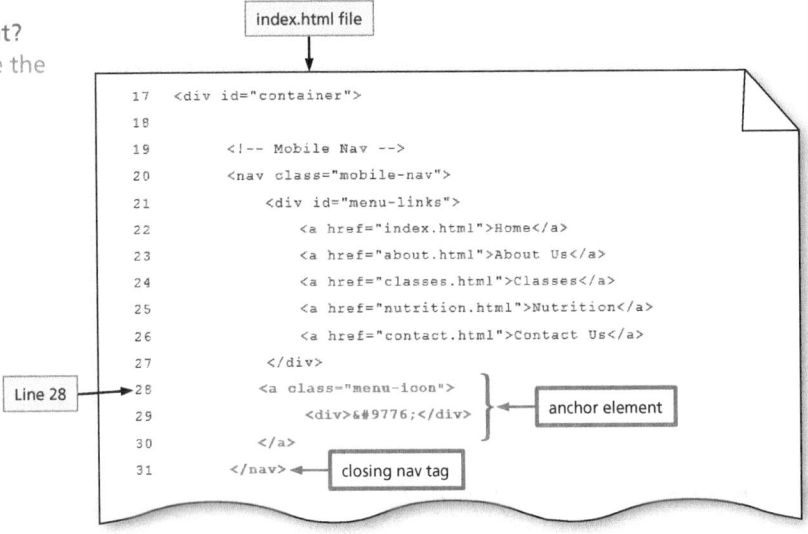

```
17    <div id="container">
18
19        <!-- Mobile Nav -->
20        <nav class="mobile-nav">
21            <div id="menu-links">
22                <a href="index.html">Home</a>
23                <a href="about.html">About Us</a>
24                <a href="classes.html">Classes</a>
25                <a href="nutrition.html">Nutrition</a>
26                <a href="contact.html">Contact Us</a>
27            </div>
28            <a class="menu-icon">
29                <div>&#9776;</div>
30            </a>
31        </nav>
```

Figure 10–21

4

• Save your changes.

• Open the index.html file in Google Chrome's device mode, and then tap or click the Mobile – S 320px (gray) bar to view the page in a mobile viewport (Figure 10–22).

Figure 10–22

Why are the new nav links blue?
The new nav links are blue because a style rule has not yet been created for them.

Why can I see the new nav links and the old vertical nav bar?
You will modify the old nav element in future steps by adding the tablet-desktop class attribute, which will hide the vertical nav bar.

5

• Select Lines 19 through 31 and then press CTRL+C to copy these lines of code.

• Open the about.html file in your text editor, tap or click at the end of Line 17, and then press the ENTER key twice to insert new Lines 18 and 19.

• On Line 19, press CTRL+V to paste the lines of code (Figure 10–23).

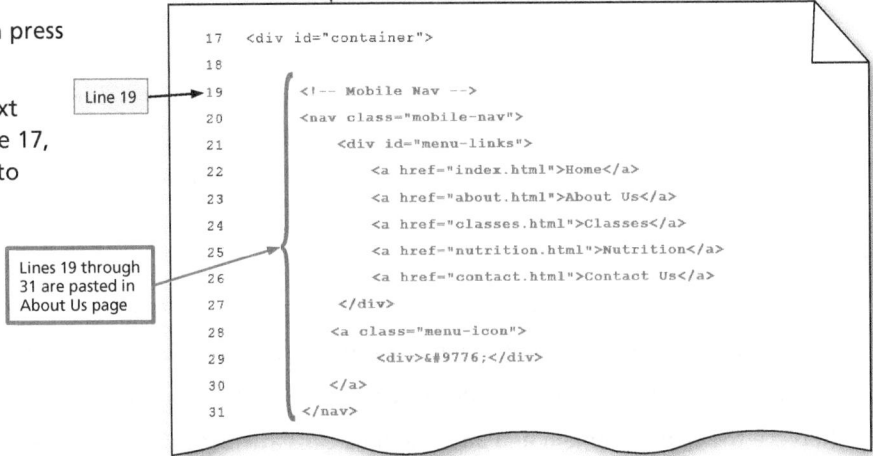

```
17    <div id="container">
18
19        <!-- Mobile Nav -->
20        <nav class="mobile-nav">
21            <div id="menu-links">
22                <a href="index.html">Home</a>
23                <a href="about.html">About Us</a>
24                <a href="classes.html">Classes</a>
25                <a href="nutrition.html">Nutrition</a>
26                <a href="contact.html">Contact Us</a>
27            </div>
28            <a class="menu-icon">
29                <div>&#9776;</div>
30            </a>
31        </nav>
```

Figure 10–23

6

- Open the classes.html file in your text editor, tap or click at the end of Line 17, and then press the ENTER key twice to insert new Lines 18 and 19.

- On Line 19, press CTRL+V to paste the lines of code.

- Open the nutrition.html file in your text editor, tap or click at the end of Line 17, and then press the ENTER key twice to insert new Lines 18 and 19.

- On Line 19, press CTRL+V to paste the lines of code.

- Open the contact.html file in your text editor, tap or click at the end of Line 17, and then press the ENTER key twice to insert new Lines 18 and 19.

- On Line 19, press CTRL+V to paste the lines of code.

- Open the template.html file in your text editor, tap or click at the end of Line 17, and then press the ENTER key twice to insert new Lines 18 and 19.

- On Line 19, press CTRL+V to paste the lines of code (Figure 10–24).

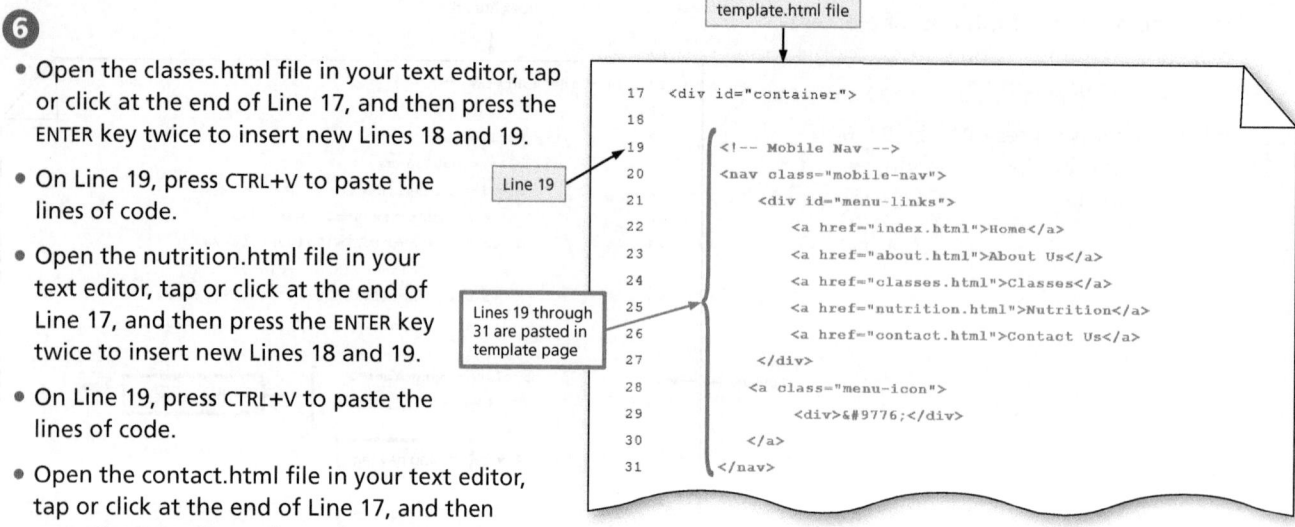

```
17    <div id="container">
18
19        <!-- Mobile Nav -->
20        <nav class="mobile-nav">
21            <div id="menu-links">
22                <a href="index.html">Home</a>
23                <a href="about.html">About Us</a>
24                <a href="classes.html">Classes</a>
25                <a href="nutrition.html">Nutrition</a>
26                <a href="contact.html">Contact Us</a>
27            </div>
28            <a class="menu-icon">
29                <div>&#9776;</div>
30            </a>
31        </nav>
```

template.html file

Line 19

Lines 19 through 31 are pasted in template page

Figure 10–24

7

- Return to the index.html file in your text editor to prepare to modify the file.

- On Line 34, within the header tag, type `id="ffc-logo"` to add an id attribute.

- Add the same id attribute to the header tag for the about.html, classes.html, nutrition.html, contact.html, and template.html files (Figure 10–25).

Q&A | What is the purpose of this id attribute?
This id attribute will be used by JavaScript in future steps.

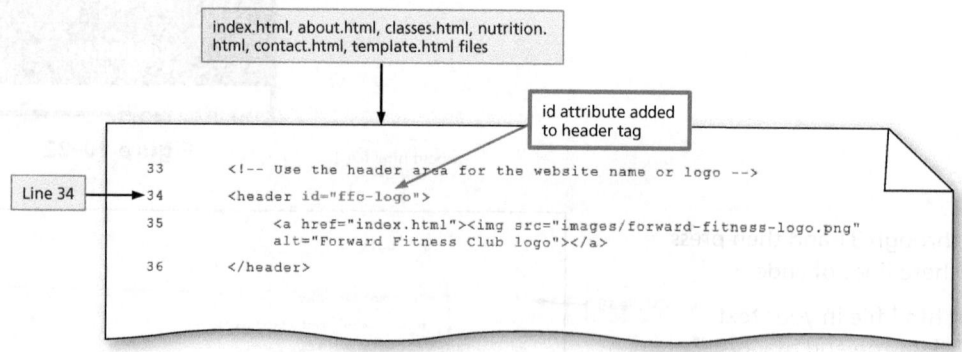

index.html, about.html, classes.html, nutrition. html, contact.html, template.html files

id attribute added to header tag

```
33    <!-- Use the header area for the website name or logo -->
34    <header id="ffc-logo">
35        <a href="index.html"><img src="images/forward-fitness-logo.png"
                alt="Forward Fitness Club logo"></a>
36    </header>
```

Line 34

Figure 10–25

8

- Return to the index.html file in your text editor to prepare to modify the file.

- On Line 38, replace the existing comment with the text `Tablet, Desktop Nav` to modify the comment.

- On Line 39, within the nav tag, type `class="tablet-desktop"` to add a class attribute.

- Replace the same comment and add the same class attribute to the nav tag on Line 39 for the about.html, classes. html, nutrition.html, contact.html, and template.html files (Figure 10–26).

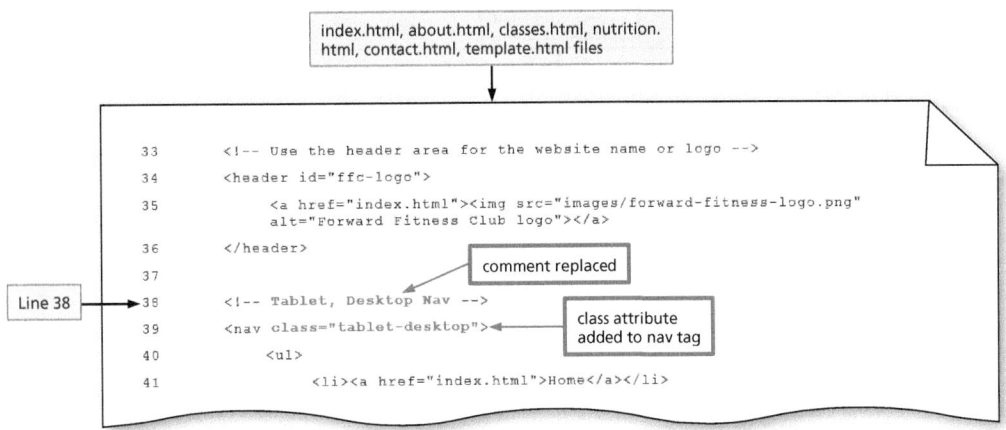

index.html, about.html, classes.html, nutrition.
html, contact.html, template.html files

```
33        <!-- Use the header area for the website name or logo -->
34        <header id="ffc-logo">
35            <a href="index.html"><img src="images/forward-fitness-logo.png"
               alt="Forward Fitness Club logo"></a>
36        </header>
37
38        <!-- Tablet, Desktop Nav -->
39        <nav class="tablet-desktop">
40            <ul>
41                <li><a href="index.html">Home</a></li>
```

comment replaced

Line 38

class attribute
added to nav tag

Figure 10–26

To Style the New Nav Element for a Mobile Viewport

1 CREATE CSS TRANSFORM | 2 CREATE CSS ANIMATION | 3 CREATE HAMBURGER MENU
4 CREATE JAVASCRIPT FILE | 5 CREATE & CALL JAVASCRIPT FUNCTIONS

Now that you have added the hamburger icon, style it for a mobile viewport. *Why? Show the hamburger icon and hide the new nav links. You will use JavaScript in future steps to toggle the links to be displayed.* Create a style rule for the menu-links id to format the appearance of the navigation links when displayed. Create a style rule to format the appearance and the position of the hamburger icon. The following steps create new style rules for a mobile viewport in the styles.css file.

- If necessary, reopen the styles.css file in your text editor to prepare to edit the file.
- On Line 42, replace the text, navigation area, with **hamburger menu**.
- Tap or click at the end of Line 42, and then press the ENTER key to insert a new Line 43.
- On Line 43, type **.mobile-nav a {** to add a new selector.
- Press the ENTER key to insert a new Line 44, increase the indent, and then type **color: #fff;** to insert a new declaration.
- Press the ENTER key to insert a new Line 45, and then type **font-family: 'Francois One', sans-serif;** to insert a new declaration.
- Press the ENTER key to insert a new Line 46, and then type **text-align: center;** to insert a new declaration.
- Press the ENTER key to insert a new Line 47, and then type **font-size: 2em;** to insert a new declaration.
- Press the ENTER key to insert a new Line 48, and then type **text-decoration: none;** to insert a new declaration.
- Press the ENTER key to insert a new Line 49, and then type **padding: 3%;** to insert a new declaration.
- Press the ENTER key to insert a new Line 50, and then type **display: block;** to insert a new declaration.
- Press the ENTER key to insert a new Line 51, decrease the indent, and then type **}** to close the style rule.
- Press the ENTER key to insert a new, blank Line 52 (Figure 10–27).

Q&A
Why is the selector .mobile-nav a?
This selector targets anchor elements in the mobile-nav class.

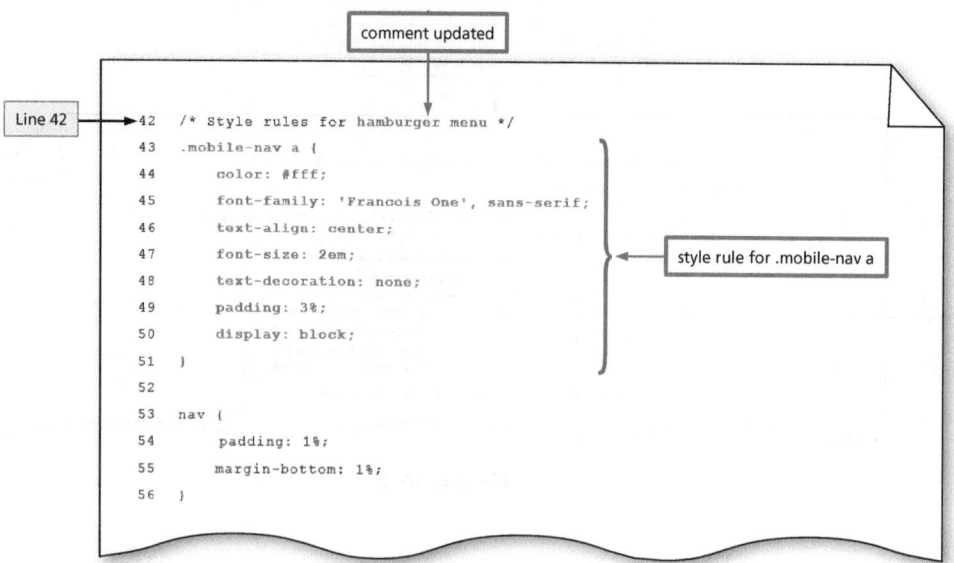

Figure 10–27

❷
- Save your changes.
- Open the index.html file in Google Chrome's device mode and, if necessary, tap or click the Mobile – S 320px (gray) bar to view the page in a mobile viewport (Figure 10–28).

Q&A

Why are the navigation links displayed?
The navigation links are displayed by default. In future steps, you will hide them and then use JavaScript to display them when the hamburger icon is touched.

Why is the hamburger icon displayed below the navigation links?
The hamburger icon does not yet have a style rule to position it. You will create a style rule to move it so that it appears in the top-right corner of the mobile viewport.

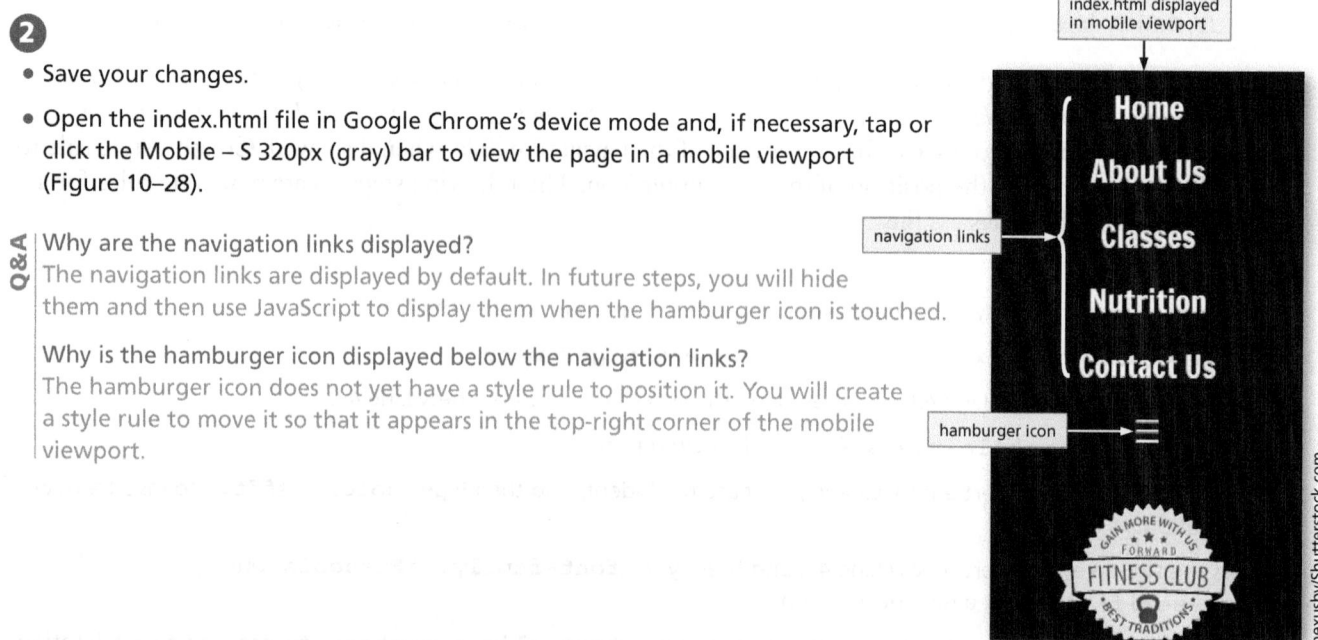

Figure 10–28

❸
- Tap or click at the end of Line 51, and then press the ENTER key twice to insert new Lines 52 and 53.
- On Line 53, type `.mobile-nav a.menu-icon {` to add a new selector.
- Press the ENTER key to insert a new Line 54, increase the indent, and then type `display: block;` to insert a new declaration.
- Press the ENTER key to insert a new Line 55, and then type `position: absolute;` to insert a new declaration.
- Press the ENTER key to insert a new Line 56, and then type `right: 0;` to insert a new declaration.
- Press the ENTER key to insert a new Line 57, and then type `top: 0;` to insert a new declaration.
- Press the ENTER key to insert a new Line 58, decrease the indent, and then type `}` to close the style rule (Figure 10–29).

Q&A Why is the selector .mobile-nav a.menu-icon?
This selector targets the hamburger icon within a div element with the class attribute menu-icon. This div is nested within an anchor element, which is contained in the mobile-nav class.

Line 53

```
45        font-family: 'Francois One', sans-serif;
46        text-align: center;
47        font-size: 2em;
48        text-decoration: none;
49        padding: 3%;
50        display: block;
51    }
52
53    .mobile-nav a.menu-icon {
54        display: block;
55        position: absolute;
56        right: 0;
57        top: 0;
58    }
59
60    nav {
61        padding: 1%;
```

style rule for .mobile-nav a.menu-icon

Figure 10–29

4

- Save your changes.
- Refresh the index.html file in Google Chrome's device mode to view the changes (Figure 10–30).

index.html displayed in mobile viewport

hamburger icon

Figure 10–30

5

- Locate the comment on Line 87.
- Add the text **and menu-links id** to the end of the comment to modify the comment.
- Locate the style rule for the .tablet-desktop class on Line 92.
- Place the insertion point after .tablet-desktop and then type **, #menu-links** to add a new selector to this style rule (Figure 10–31).

 Q&A Why do I need to add the #menu-links selector to this style rule?
This style rule sets the display to none. When the page opens, you do not want the links displayed. Instead, you will use JavaScript to display the navigation links when the user taps the hamburger icon.

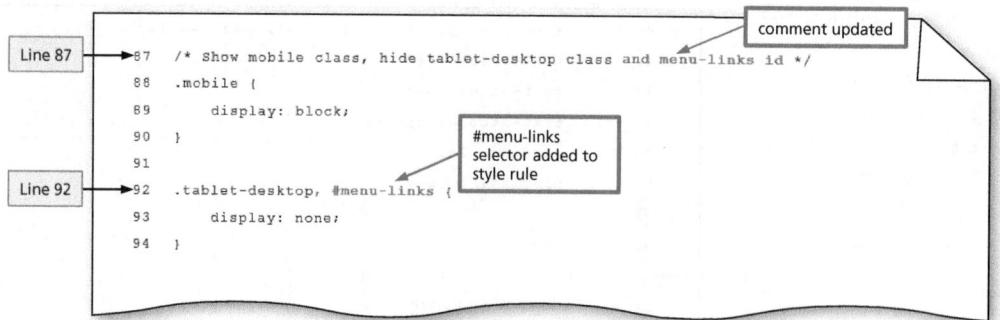

Line 87 → 87 /* Show mobile class, hide tablet-desktop class and menu-links id */   comment updated
88 .mobile {
89   display: block;
90 }
91
Line 92 → 92 .tablet-desktop, #menu-links {   #menu-links selector added to style rule
93   display: none;
94 }

Figure 10–31

6

- Locate the style rule for the .mobile class on Line 263, located within the tablet media query.

- Place the insertion point after .mobile and then type
  , .mobile-nav
  to add a new selector to this style rule (Figure 10–32).

```
255  /* Media Query for Tablet Viewport */
256  @media screen and (min-width: 630px), print {
257
258      /* Tablet Viewport: Show tablet-desktop class, hide mobile class */
259      .tablet-desktop {
260          display: block;
261      }
262
263      .mobile, .mobile-nav {
264          display: none;
265      }
```

Line 263 → 263   .mobile-nav selector added to style rule

Figure 10–32

Q&A Why do I need to add the .mobile-nav selector to this style rule?
This style rule sets the display to none for tablet viewports. This ensures that the hamburger icon will be displayed only for a user with a mobile viewport.

7

- Save your changes.

- Refresh the index.html file in Google Chrome's device mode to view the changes (Figure 10–33).

Q&A When I click the hamburger icon, nothing happens. Why?
To have the hamburger icon toggle the navigation links on and off, you must first write the required JavaScript code.

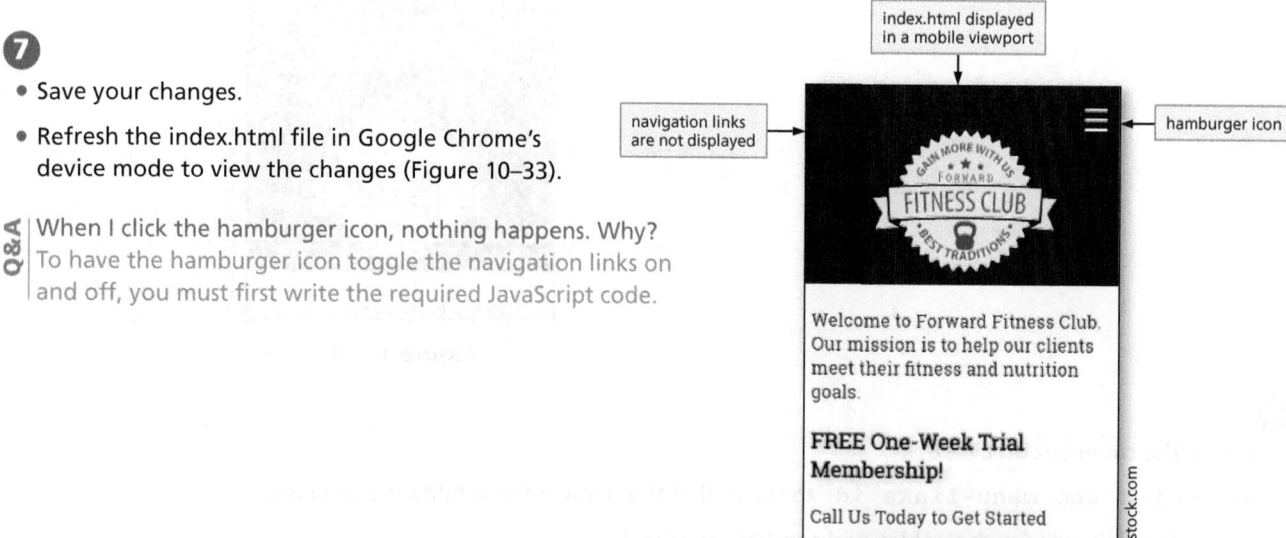

index.html displayed in a mobile viewport

navigation links are not displayed

hamburger icon

Welcome to Forward Fitness Club. Our mission is to help our clients meet their fitness and nutrition goals.

FREE One-Week Trial Membership!

Call Us Today to Get Started

(814) 555-9608

Fitness Club Hours:

nexusby/Shutterstock.com

Figure 10–33

8

- Switch to a tablet viewport to display the tablet navigation (Figure 10–34).

index.html displayed in tablet viewport

hamburger icon is not displayed

navigation links are displayed → Home | About Us | Classes | Nutrition | Contact Us

Train with Us
Gain with Us

nexusby/Shutterstock.com, Y Photo Studio/Shutterstock.com

Figure 10–34

To Modify Previous Navigation Style Rules for a Mobile Viewport

1 CREATE CSS TRANSFORM | 2 CREATE CSS ANIMATION | 3 CREATE HAMBURGER MENU
4 CREATE JAVASCRIPT FILE | 5 CREATE & CALL JAVASCRIPT FUNCTIONS

You have finished styling the hamburger menu and navigation links but need to do some housekeeping regarding the previous style rules created for the navigation links for the mobile viewport. *Why? As a developer, you should always keep your code clean and remove unnecessary code.* Move the mobile style rules for the nav, nav ul, and nav li a to the tablet media query. Move two declarations from the nav li for mobile to the nav li style rule for tablet. Remove the nav li and nav li:first-child style rules for mobile. The following steps modify style rules for mobile and tablet viewports in the styles.css file.

- If necessary, reopen the styles.css file in your text editor to prepare to edit the file.

- Select the nav and nav ul style rules on Lines 60 through 68, and then press CTRL+X to cut these style rules.

- If necessary, move the nav li style rule up to Line 60.

- Locate the comment, Tablet Viewport: Style rules for nav area, located within the tablet media query on Line 262.

- Tap or click at the end of Line 262, and then press the ENTER key to insert a new Line 263.

- On Line 263, press CTRL+V to paste the style rules. If necessary, indent the style rules.

- Tap or click at the end of Line 271, and then press the ENTER key to insert a new, blank Line 272, if necessary (Figure 10–35).

Q&A Why do I need to move these style rules to the tablet media query?
Now that you have created a hamburger menu, these style rules are no longer relevant to the mobile viewport, but they are needed for the tablet viewport.

```
        262      /* Tablet Viewport: Style rules for nav area */
Line 263 →263      nav {
        264          padding: 1%;
        265          margin-bottom: 1%;
        266      }
        267
        268      nav ul {
        269          list-style-type: none;
        270          text-align: center;
        271      }
        272
        273      nav li {
        274          border-top: none;
        275          display: inline-block;
        276          border-right: 1px solid #fff;
        277      }
```

nav and nav ul style rules moved to tablet media query

Figure 10–35

- Locate the nav li style rule above the tablet media query on Line 60.

- Select the font-size: 1.5em; and font-family: 'Francois One', sans-serif; on Lines 61 through 62 and then press CTRL+X to cut these style rules.

- If necessary, move the border-top declaration up to Line 61.

- Scroll down to the tablet media query and locate the nav li style rule that begins on Line 271.

- Select the border-top: none; declaration on Line 272, and then press CTRL+V to replace the declaration with the copied declarations. If necessary, indent the declarations (Figure 10–36).

Q&A Why do I need to move these declarations to the nav li style rule in the tablet media query?
Now that you have created a hamburger menu, these style rules are no longer relevant to the mobile viewport, but they are needed for the tablet viewport.

```
        260      /* Tablet Viewport: Style rules for nav area */
        261      nav {
        262          padding: 1%;
        263          margin-bottom: 1%;
        264      }
        265
        266      nav ul {
        267          list-style-type: none;
        268          text-align: center;
        269      }
        270
Line 271 →271      nav li {
        272          font-size: 1.5em;
        273          font-family: 'Francois One', sans-serif;
        274          display: inline-block;
        275          border-right: 1px solid #fff;
        276      }
```

declaration for top border is removed; declarations moved to nav li in tablet media query

Figure 10–36

- Scroll back up to the mobile nav li style rule, select Lines 60 through 66, and then press the DELETE key to remove the nav li and the nav li:first-child style rules.

- If necessary, move the nav li a style rule up to Line 60 (Figure 10–37).

Q&A | Why did I delete these style rules?
These style rules are not needed for the new hamburger menu.

```
53    .mobile-nav a.menu-icon {
54        display: block;
55        position: absolute;
56        right: 0;
57        top: 0;
58    }
59
60    nav li a {
61        display: block;
62        color: #fff;
63        padding: 0.5em 1em;
64        text-decoration: none;
65    }
66
67    /* Show mobile class, hide tablet-desktop class and menu-links id */
68    .mobile {
69        display: block;
70    }
```

Line 60 → 60

mobile style rules for nav li and nav li:first-child are deleted

Figure 10–37

- Select Line 63, and then press the DELETE key to remove the padding declaration.

- If necessary, move the text-decoration declaration up to Line 63.

- Select Lines 61 through 63, and then press the CTRL+X keys to cut the three declarations out of the nav li a style rule.

- Select Lines 60 through 62, and then press the DELETE key to remove the nav li a style rule.

- If necessary, move the Show mobile class comment up to Line 60 (Figure 10–38).

```
53    .mobile-nav a.menu-icon {
54        display: block;
55        position: absolute;
56        right: 0;
57        top: 0;
58    }
59
60    /* Show mobile class, hide tablet-desktop class and menu-links id */
61    .mobile {
62        display: block;
63    }
```

Line 60 → 60

declarations for mobile style rule nav li a are cut and style rule is deleted

Figure 10–38

- Scroll down to the tablet media query and locate the nav li a style rule that begins on Line 267.
- Tap or click at the end of Line 268, press the ENTER key to insert a new Line 269, and then press the CTRL+V keys to paste the three declarations within the nav li a style rule.
- If necessary, indent the declarations (Figure 10–39).

```
263    nav li:last-child {
264        border-right: none;
265    }
266
267    nav li a {
268        padding: 0.1em 0.75em;
269        display: block;
270        color: #fff;
271        text-decoration: none;
272    }
273
274    /* Tablet Viewport: Style rules for main content area */
275    main ul {
276        margin: 0 0 4% 10%;
277    }
```

Line 269 → 269

declarations moved to nav li a style rule in tablet media query

Figure 10–39

- Save your changes.
- Refresh the index.html file in Google Chrome's device mode and select the mobile viewport to view the hamburger menu icon (Figure 10–40).

index.html displayed in mobile viewport

hamburger icon

nexusby/Shutterstock.com

Figure 10–40

7

• Switch to a tablet viewport to display the tablet navigation (Figure 10–41).

BTW
jQuery Animations
You can use the jQuery animate( ) method to create animations on a webpage. Visit w3schools.com/jquery /jquery_animate.asp for a demonstration.

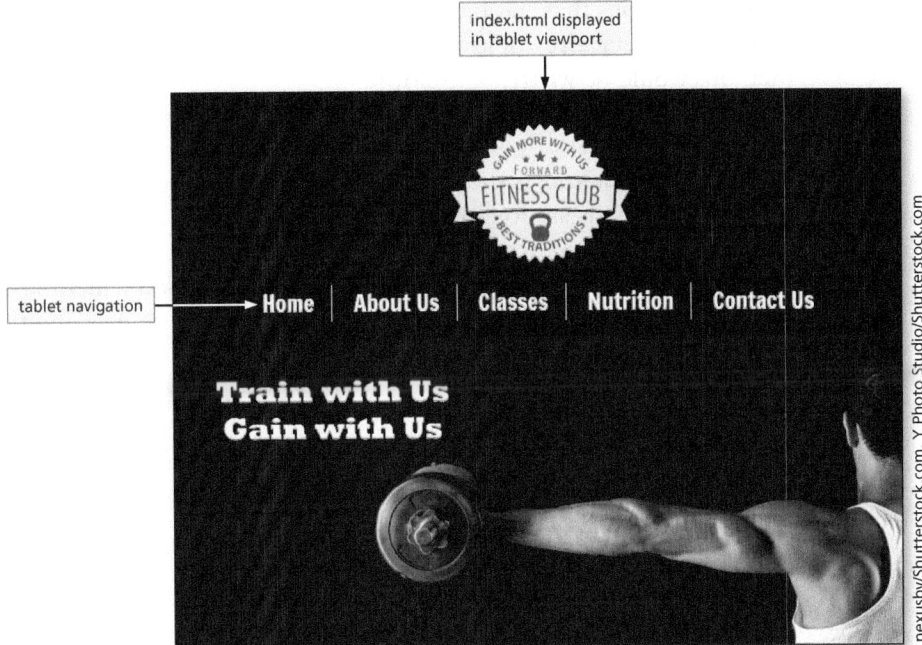

index.html displayed in tablet viewport

tablet navigation

Home | About Us | Classes | Nutrition | Contact Us

nexusby/Shutterstock.com, Y Photo Studio/Shutterstock.com

Figure 10–41

Break Point: If you want to take a break, this is a good place to do so. You can exit the text editor now. To resume at a later time, run your text editor, open index.html, and continue following the steps from this location forward.

JavaScript Terminology

To use JavaScript effectively, you should be familiar with its basic terminology, including statements, objects, properties, methods, arguments, functions, and variables.

A JavaScript **statement** is a line of programming instructions to be executed by the client (the browser). JavaScript statements end with a semicolon. The following is an example of a JavaScript statement:

```
document.write("Good Morning");
```

An **object** in JavaScript is anything that can be treated as its own entity. Examples of objects include a document (the webpage), an HTML element, or webpage content. Developers can also create objects. For example, a developer might create an array object, used to hold customer information, such as first name, last name, address, and email address.

Properties can be assigned to JavaScript objects. **Properties** are attributes that describe an object's characteristics. As shown in the following example, an object name and its property are separated by a period.

```
video.style.display = "block";
```

In this example, the video object is stated first followed by a period, followed by the style property, which indicates a style is to be applied. After the style property, another period is inserted, followed by the display property. In this example, the video's display property is set to block. A value can be assigned to the property, or the property can return a value. The equal sign in this example is an assignment operator. It assigns a value to the video's display property.

Methods are actions that an object can perform. For example, methods associated with the `document` object might be `write` and `open`. An object and one of its methods would be written as follows:

```
document.write();
```

In this code, `document` is the object and `write` is a method of the `document` object. Methods are followed by parentheses, which may be empty, or may contain an argument.

An **argument** or parameter is a value given to a method. Some methods require arguments, and others do not. For example, given a `document` object and the `write()` method, include the argument "Good Morning" to describe the content to display for the document as follows:

```
document.write("Good Morning");
```

In this case, the argument "Good Morning" describes the text content to display on the document.

A **function** is a set of JavaScript statements that perform a specific task. For example, you could create a function that calculates the sales tax for items purchased. A function must include a name and statements that specify a task to be performed. Following is an example of a function.

```
function myFunction() {
    statement 1;
    statement 2;
    statement 3;
}
```

A **variable** is a container that holds a value. JavaScript uses variables to store values temporarily in internal memory. A variable's value can change, depending on the results of an expression or data entered by a user in a form. Variables must have a unique name and must follow the same naming conventions as user-defined functions. The following is an example of a variable.

```
var promo = "Save today with promo code SAVE25";
```

When defining a variable, begin with the keyword var, followed by the variable name. In this example, promo is the variable name. The equal sign assigns this variable a text string, Save today with promo code SAVE25.

Variables can be defined locally or globally. Local variables are created within a function. These variables can only be used by the function in which they are defined. Global variables are created outside of a function. They are typically defined near the top of an external JavaScript file. Global variables may be used by any function within the JavaScript file.

Most JavaScript user-defined functions are called or invoked using event handlers. An **event** is the result of an action, such as a mouse click or a webpage loading into the browser. An **event handler** is how JavaScript associates an action with a function. JavaScript event handlers make webpages more dynamic and interactive by allowing JavaScript code to execute only in response to a user action, such as a mouse click. Table 10–3 lists common event handlers.

Table 10–3 Event Handlers

Event Handler	Description
onabort	User stopped loading the page
onblur	User left the object
onchange	User changed the object
onclick	User clicked the object
onerror	Script encountered an error
onfocus	User made an object active
onload	Object finished loading
onmouseover	Mouse moved over an object
onmouseout	Mouse moved off an object
onselect	User selected contents of an object
onsubmit	User submitted a form
onunload	User left the page

BTW
AngularJS
AngularJS is a popular JavaScript framework used by developers. It extends HTML and creates its own elements, which are called directives. You can use the directives in expressions to tie data to HTML. AngularJS is popular for building web applications.

Writing JavaScript Code

Keep the following syntax rules and guidelines in mind when writing JavaScript code. First, JavaScript is case sensitive, which means that it distinguishes between upper- and lowercase letters. If you create a variable named foodGroup, JavaScript will not recognize this variable if it is written as FoodGroup.

Like HTML and CSS, you can incorporate comments in JavaScript code. Use two slashes for a one-line comment and use the slash and asterisk for multiline comments, as follows:

```
// Single line comment syntax
/* Multiple line
comment syntax */
```

Using semicolons to end JavaScript statements is a common practice by programmers. Although it is not always necessary, it is a good best practice. The only time the semicolon is necessary is when multiple statements appear on the same line. The semicolon is used to separate each statement, similar to how a period separates one sentence from another. The following statements are all valid:

```
foodOne = squash
foodTwo = pepper;
foodOne = squash; foodTwo = pepper;
```

You can write JavaScript within a script element on an HTML page or as a separate JavaScript file with the filename extension .js. When JavaScript is written within an HTML page, the code may be within the **head** element or the **body** element, depending upon the developer and the task at hand. The following is an example of how to write a JavaScript statement within an HTML document using the script tags.

```
<script>
    JavaScript statements;
</script>
```

Using an external JavaScript file is a best practice. When you create JavaScript as an external .js file, you reference the file using a script element. If the JavaScript file is needed during the page loading time, place the script element within the **head** element of the HTML document. If the JavaScript file is not needed for page loading, place the script element above the closing **body** tag on the HTML file. Specify the external .js file as the file source, as shown in the following example:

```
<script src="scripts/myscripts.js"></script>
```

DOM Methods

DOM stands for Document Object Model. Recall that every element on an HTML page is an object. The HTML DOM consists of all the HTML elements, attributes, and text. Together, all of these items are objects on the page. Figure 10–42 shows an example of an HTML DOM tree.

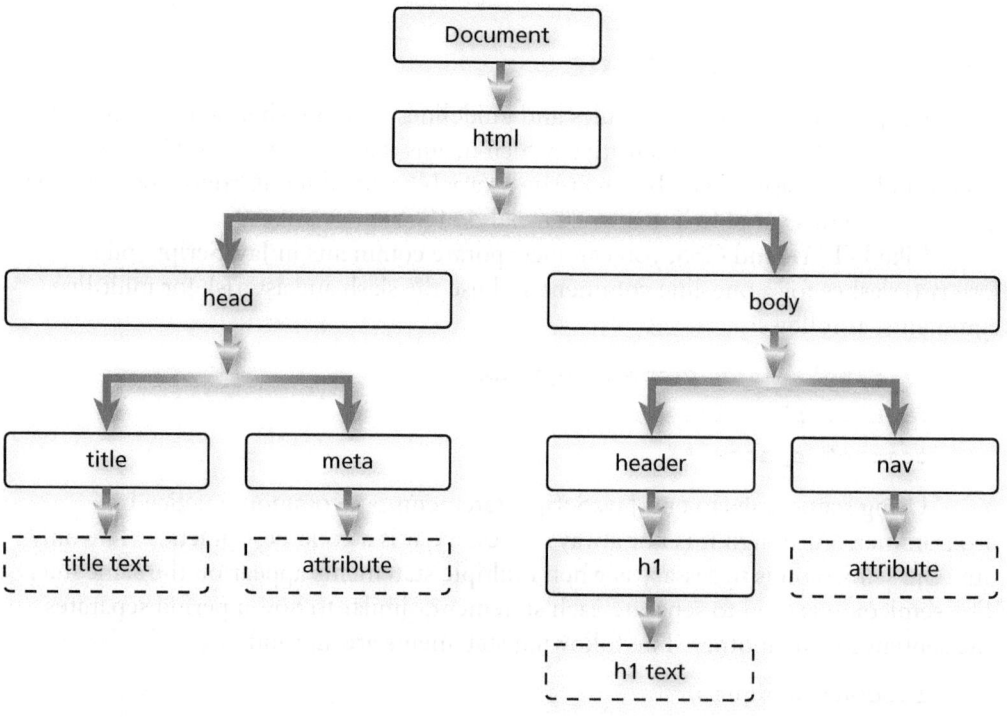

Figure 10–42

Each item in the DOM tree is also known as a node. Any of these objects can be accessed using JavaScript DOM methods. Using a DOM method, you can use JavaScript to manipulate an HTML element. One common DOM method is getElementById( ). The following provides an example of the getElementById( ) method:

```
var logo = document.getElementById("ffc-logo");
```

In this statement, the logo variable is assigned to document. getElementById("ffc-logo"). The document is the object (the webpage) and getElementById( ) is the method. The ("ffc-logo") is the id attribute of the HTML element. The contents of this element are then held within the variable. Table 10–4 lists other common DOM methods.

Table 10–4 DOM Methods

Method	Description
getElementsByClassName( )	Returns all HTML elements with the specified class name
getElementsByName( )	Returns all HTML elements with the specified name value attribute
getElementsByTagName( )	Returns all HTML elements with the specified tag name
querySelector( )	Returns the first HTML element with the specified CSS selector
querySelectorAll( )	Returns a list of all HTML elements with the specified CSS selector

The addEventListener( ) method is commonly used to "listen" for a specific event and then call a function. The following is an example of the addEventListener( ) method:

```
window.addEventListener("load", runPage, false);
```

In this example, the addEventListener( ) method is attached to the window object. When the window loads (load being the event), the runPage function is called.

Using if/else Statements

One common JavaScript statement used within a function is the if/else statement. An if/else statement assesses a specified condition. If the condition is true, then a specific block of code is executed. If the condition is false, a different block of code is executed. Consider the following analogy. If I have a text editor (condition is true), I can create a JavaScript file. If I do not have a text editor (condition is false), I cannot create a JavaScript file. The following is an example of an if/else JavaScript statement, used within a function.

```
function day() {
    var day = document.getElementById("date");
    if (day === "Saturday") {
        document.write("I love Saturdays");
    } else {
        document.write("I wish it was Saturday");
    }
}
```

In this example, a function named day is created. It consists of a variable named day that is assigned to the date id attribute on the document. The if condition tests to see if the day is Saturday. The use of the three equal signs (===) is a strict equal that compares the value and the data type to ensure both match. If the condition is true, the text, I love Saturdays, is written on the document. If the condition is false, the text, I wish it was Saturday is written on the document.

jQuery

A developer often needs to use the same code for a project. In this case, it is ideal to group sets of code into a library. One commonly used library is jQuery, a JavaScript library that can significantly reduce the amount of code (and time) needed to complete a web project. For more information about jQuery, visit jquery.com or w3schools.com/jquery.

You have already created the hamburger icon for the mobile viewport. Now use JavaScript to make the hamburger icon functional. Create a JavaScript file and write a JavaScript function that toggles the navigation menu on and off when the hamburger icon is selected.

BTW

Node.js
Node.js provides the ability to use JavaScript on a server. It can open, read, and write server files and can add and modify data in a database. It can also generate dynamic content and collect data.

BTW

camelCase
Camel case is commonly used with JavaScript. Camel case applies to two or more words put together. The first letter is lowercase, and the first letter of the next word is capitalized. For example, you would use firstName as a variable name.

To Create a JavaScript File

Create a JavaScript file to write your JavaScript code and then add a script element with the JavaScript source file to all of the webpages. *Why? The HTML files need to know the location of the JavaScript file in order to use it.* Once you have created the JavaScript file, add a comment to the page. The following steps create a JavaScript file and add a script element to all of the HTML webpages.

- Open your text editor, tap or click File on the menu bar, and then tap or click New if you need to open a new blank document.

- Tap or click File on the menu bar and then tap or click Save As to display the Save As dialog box.

- Navigate to your fitness/scripts folder, and then double-tap or double-click the scripts folder to open it.

- In the File name box, type **script** to name the file.

- Tap or click the Save as type button, and then tap or click JavaScript (.js) to select the file format.

- Click the Save button to save the new file.

- On Line 1 of the script.js file, type **/*** to start a new comment.

- Press the ENTER key to insert Line 2, increase the indent, and then type **Student Name:** and add your name.

- Press the ENTER key to insert Line 3, and then type **File Name: script.js** to add the file name.

- Press the ENTER key to insert Line 4, type **Date:** , and then type today's date.

- Press the ENTER key to insert Line 5, decrease the indent, and then type ***/** to close the comment (Figure 10–43).

Q&A My text editor does not have a Save as type to select the file format. How do I save the file as a JavaScript file?
Name the file script.js to specify to JavaScript file format.

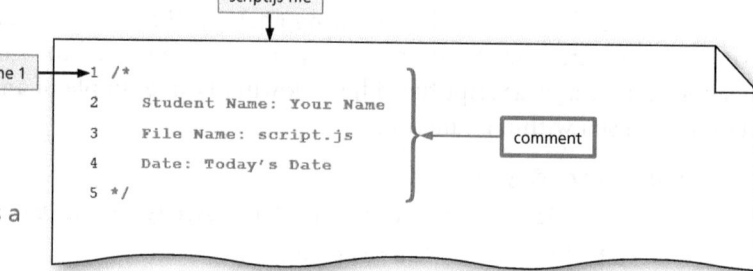

Figure 10–43

- Save your changes.

- Open the index.html file in your text editor, tap or click at the end of Line 112, and then press the ENTER key twice to insert new Lines 113 and 114.

- On Line 114, type **<script src="scripts/script.js"></script>** to insert a script element (Figure 10–44).

Q&A What is the purpose of the script element?
The script element connects the HTML file to find the JavaScript file.

Why am I inserting the script element above the closing body tag?
When a webpage is loaded in a browser, the browser also loads any scripts within the head element before rendering the body element. To improve the page-loading process, if the JavaScript file is not needed during the page-loading process, place the script element above the closing body tag. When the JavaScript file is needed as the page loads, place the script element within the head element.

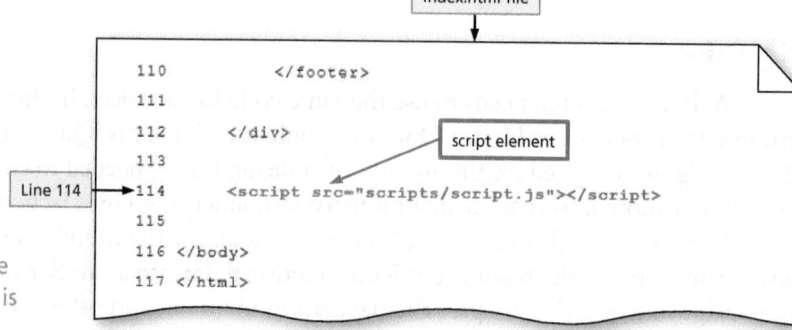

Figure 10–44

3

- Save your changes.

- Open the about.html file in your text editor, tap or click at the end of Line 126, and then press the ENTER key twice to insert new Lines 127 and 128.

- On Line 128, type `<script src="scripts/script.js"></script>` to insert a script element (Figure 10–45).

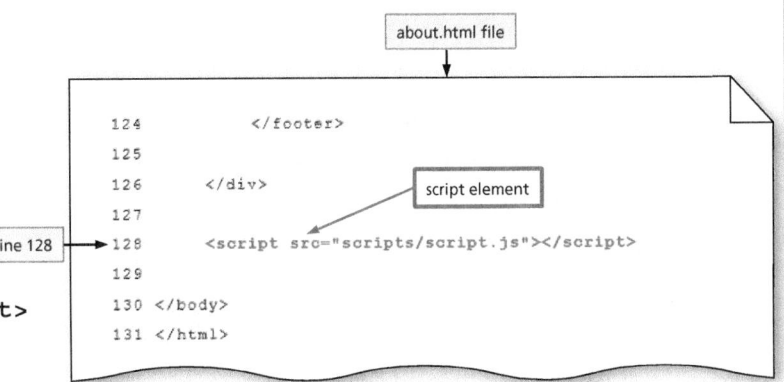

about.html file

```
124        </footer>
125
126    </div>                    script element
127
128        <script src="scripts/script.js"></script>    ← Line 128
129
130 </body>
131 </html>
```

Figure 10–45

4

- Save your changes.

- Open the classes.html file in your text editor, tap or click at the end of Line 145, and then press the ENTER key twice to insert new Lines 146 and 147.

- On Line 147, type `<script src="scripts/script.js"></script>` to insert a script element.

- Save your changes.

- Open the nutrition.html file in your text editor, tap or click at the end of Line 112, and then press the ENTER key twice to insert new Lines 113 and 114.

- On Line 114, type `<script src="scripts/script.js"></script>` to insert a script element.

- Save your changes.

- Open the contact.html file in your text editor, tap or click at the end of Line 125, and then press the ENTER key twice to insert new Lines 126 and 127.

- On Line 127, type `<script src="scripts/script.js"></script>` to insert a script element.

- Save your changes.

- Open the template.html file in your text editor, tap or click at the end of Line 59, and then press the ENTER key twice to insert new Lines 60 and 61.

- On Line 61, type `<script src="scripts/script.js"></script>` to insert a script element (Figure 10–46).

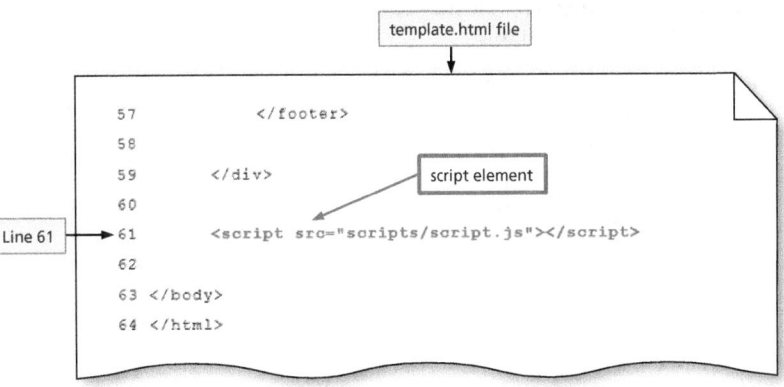

template.html file

```
57        </footer>
58
59    </div>                    script element
60
61        <script src="scripts/script.js"></script>    ← Line 61
62
63 </body>
64 </html>
```

Figure 10–46

BTW
JSON
JSON stands for JavaScript Object Notation. It is used to send text data from a client to a server.

To Create the hamburger( ) Function

1 CREATE CSS TRANSFORM | 2 CREATE CSS ANIMATION | 3 CREATE HAMBURGER MENU
4 CREATE JAVASCRIPT FILE | 5 CREATE & CALL JAVASCRIPT FUNCTIONS

The hamburger menu is almost ready. You now need to create a JavaScript function to make the hamburger menu functional. *Why? JavaScript programming is needed to display and hide the navigation links for a mobile viewport.* Use the external JavaScript file, script.js, to write a function that displays the navigation links when the hamburger icon is selected. The following steps create the hamburger( ) function on the script.js file.

1

- If necessary, reopen the script.js file in your text editor to prepare to modify it.

- Tap or click at the end of Line 5, and then press the ENTER key twice to insert new Lines 6 and 7.

- On Line 7, type **//Hamburger menu function** to insert a new, single-line comment.

- Press the ENTER key, and then on Line 8, type **function hamburger() {** to begin a new function.

- Press the ENTER key twice to insert new Lines 9 and 10.

- On Line 10, type **}** to close the function (Figure 10–47).

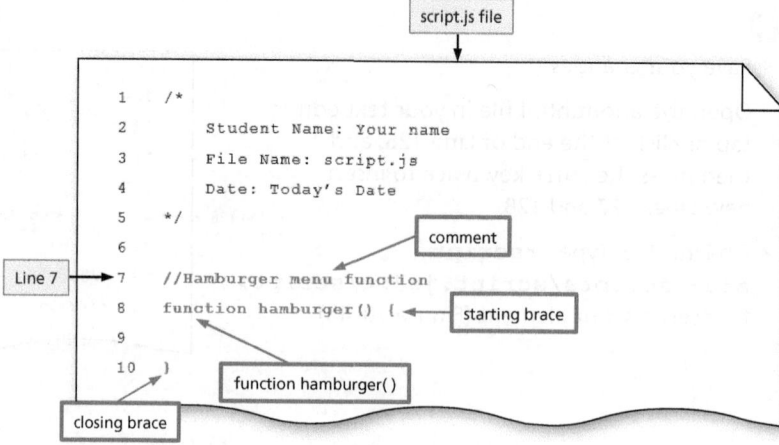

Figure 10–47

Q&A | What is the purpose of this step?
This step creates the hamburger function. You will add statements within the function in future steps.

2

- On Line 9, increase the indent, and then type **var menu = document. getElementById("menu-links");** to define a local variable.

- Press the ENTER key to insert a new Line 10, and then type **var logo = document.getElementById("ffc-logo");** to define another local variable (Figure 10–48).

Q&A | What is the purpose of these variables?
The menu variable is assigned to the menu-links id on the HTML document. The logo variable is assigned to the ffc-logo id on the HTML document.

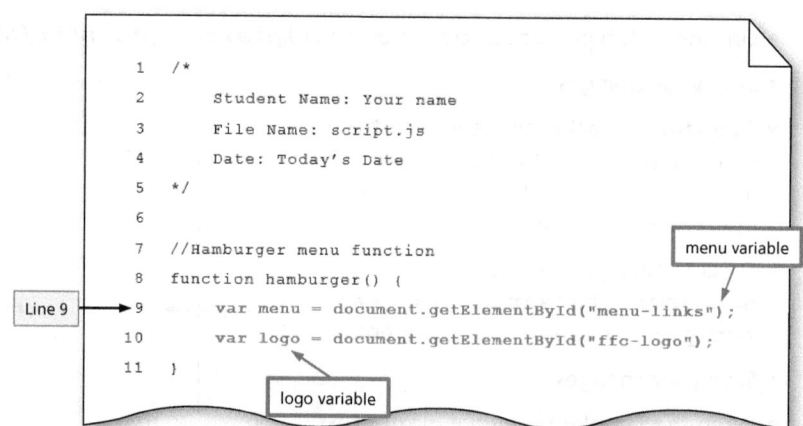

Figure 10–48

3

- Press the ENTER key to insert a new Line 11, and then type **if (menu.style.display === "block" && logo.style.display === "none") {** to insert an if statement.

- Press the ENTER key to insert a new Line 12, increase the indent, and then type **menu.style.display = "none";** to insert a statement.

- Press the ENTER key to insert a new Line 13, and then type **logo.style.display = "block";** to insert a statement.

- Press the ENTER key to insert a new Line 14, decrease the indent, and then type **}** to close the if statement (Figure 10–49).

Q&A | What is the purpose of the if statement?
The if statement checks to see if a condition is met. In this instance, the if statement is checking to see if the menu variable (i.e., the menu-links id) is set to display as a block. In addition, the if statement is also checking to see if the logo variable (i.e., the ffc-logo id) is set to display none. If both conditions are met, then the menu display will be set to none and the logo display will be set to block.

Q&A What does the double ampersand (&&) represent?
The double ampersand (&&) represents "and."

Why does the if statement use three equal signs (===)?
The three equal signs represent a strict comparison operator, which means that the value must be the same data type and the same value.

```
1    /*
2         Student Name: Your name
3         File Name: script.js
4         Date: Today's Date
5    */
6
7    //Hamburger menu function
8    function hamburger() {
9         var menu = document.getElementById("menu-links");
10        var logo = document.getElementById("ffc-logo");
11        if (menu.style.display === "block" && logo.style.display === "none") {
12             menu.style.display = "none";
13             logo.style.display = "block";
14        }
15   }
```

Line 11 → 11

if statement

Figure 10–49

4

- At the end of Line 14, press the SPACEBAR to insert a space, and then type **else {** to insert an else statement.

- Press the ENTER key to insert a new Line 15, increase the indent, and then type **menu.style.display = "block";** to insert a statement.

- Press the ENTER key to insert a new Line 16, and then type **logo.style.display = "none";** to insert a statement.

- Press the ENTER key to insert a new Line 17, decrease the indent, and then type **}** to close the else statement.

- Save your changes (Figure 10–50).

Q&A What is the purpose of the else statement?
The else statement executes when the condition for the if statement is not met. When the else statement is executed, then the menu display will be set to block and the logo display will be set to none.

```
7    //Hamburger menu function
8    function hamburger() {
9         var menu = document.getElementById("menu-links");
10        var logo = document.getElementById("ffc-logo");
11        if (menu.style.display === "block" && logo.style.display === "none") {
12             menu.style.display = "none";
13             logo.style.display = "block";
14        } else {
15             menu.style.display = "block";
16             logo.style.display = "none";
17        }
18   }
```

Line 14 → 14

else statement

Figure 10–50

To Call the hamburger( ) Function

Now that you have created the JavaScript function to make the hamburger menu functional, use an event to invoke, or call, the hamburger function. *Why? JavaScript functions must be called in order to use them.* Add an onclick event to the anchor element that contains the hamburger icon. Set the onclick event to call the hamburger function. The following steps add an onclick event to each HTML webpage.

- If necessary, reopen the index.html file in your text editor to prepare to modify it.

- Tap or click to the left of the closing angle bracket of the anchor tag on Line 28, and then type `onclick="hamburger()"` to add an onclick event.

- Perform the same step for the about.html, classes.html, nutrition.html, contact.html, and template.html files.

- Save all of your changes (Figure 10–51).

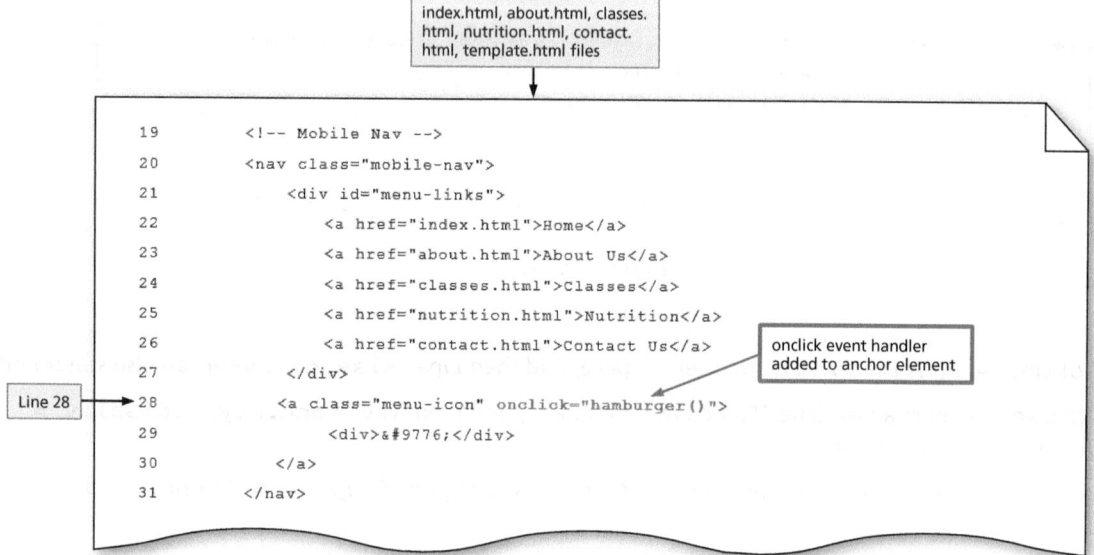

Figure 10–51

- Open the index.html file in Google Chrome's device mode and tap or click the Mobile – S 320px (gray) bar to view the page in a mobile viewport.

- Tap or click the hamburger icon to display the navigation links (Figure 10–52).

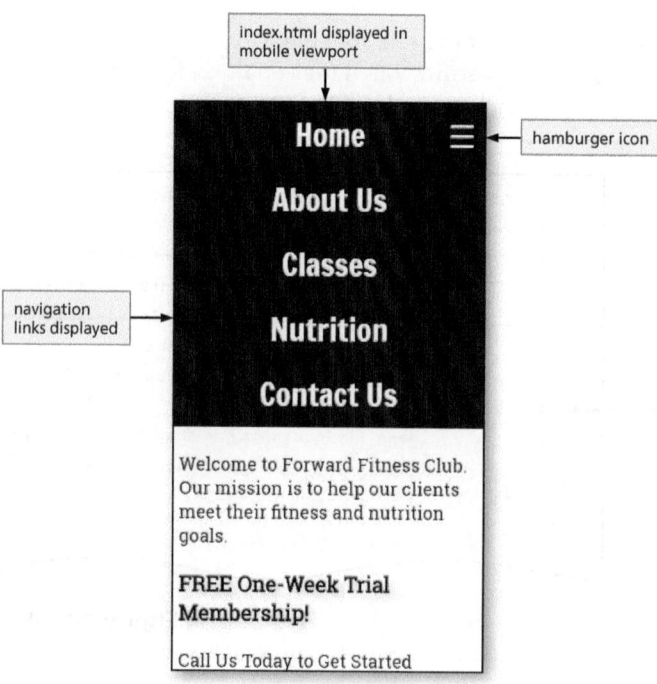

Figure 10–52

3

- Tap or click the hamburger icon to hide the navigation links (Figure 10–53).

4

- Display each page within the website and test the hamburger icon on each page to ensure that it works on all pages within the website.

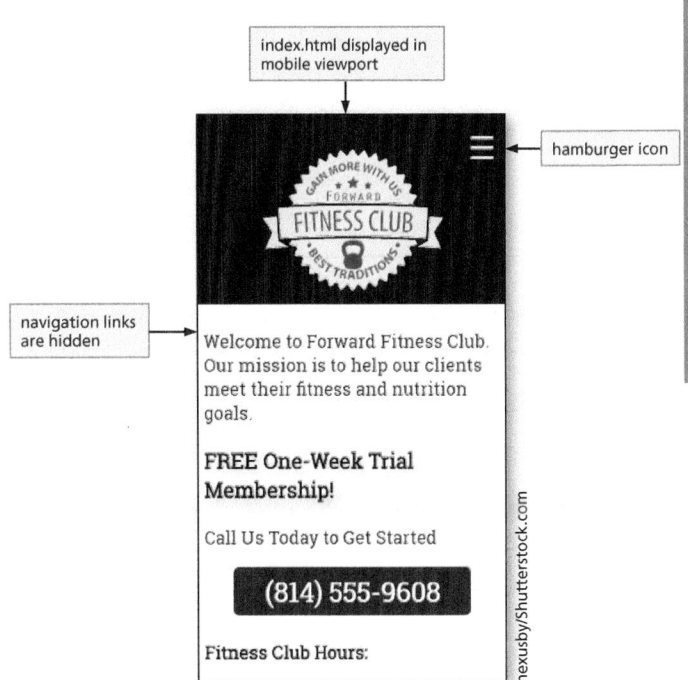

Figure 10–53

Break Point: If you want to take a break, this is a good place to do so. You can exit the text editor now. To resume at a later time, run your text editor, open index.html, and continue following the steps from this location forward.

To Add and Style a Video Element on the About Us Page

1 CREATE CSS TRANSFORM | 2 CREATE CSS ANIMATION | 3 CREATE HAMBURGER MENU
4 CREATE JAVASCRIPT FILE | 5 CREATE & CALL JAVASCRIPT FUNCTIONS

The About Us page includes three common exercises. Improve this page by adding the option for the user to view a video demonstration of each exercise. *Why? Providing a video demonstration improves the user experience, as it provides a clear visual example of how to perform the exercise.* Create a video element on the About Us page and include a source and track element. Then, use CSS to hide the video element until the user makes a selection to view the video. In future steps, you will use JavaScript to write functions to dynamically display an exercise demonstration video. The following steps create a video element in the about.html file and a style rule in the styles.css file.

- Copy the six files from the chapter10\fitness folder provided with the Data Files to your fitness\media folder.

- Open the about.html file in your text editor, tap or click at the end of Line 112, and then press the ENTER key twice to insert new Lines 113 and 114.

- On Line 114, type `<video controls id="example">` to insert a video tag.

- Press the ENTER key to insert a new Line 115, increase the indent, and then type `<source id="vid-src" src="vid" type="video/mp4">` to insert a source element.

- Press the ENTER key to insert a new Line 116, and then type `<track id="despsrc" src="des" kind="descriptions" srclang="en" label="English Descriptions">` to insert a source element.

- Press the ENTER key to insert a new Line 117, and then type `<p>Your browser does not support the video element.</p>` to insert a paragraph element.

- Press the ENTER key to insert a new Line 118, decrease the indent, and then type `</video>` to insert a closing video tag (Figure 10–54).

Q&A Why do the src attributes for the source and track elements not point to files?
You will use JavaScript functions to dynamically set files as the src values for the source and track elements.

Why is there not another track element for captions?
The exercise video demonstrations do not contain any sound; therefore, captions are not needed.

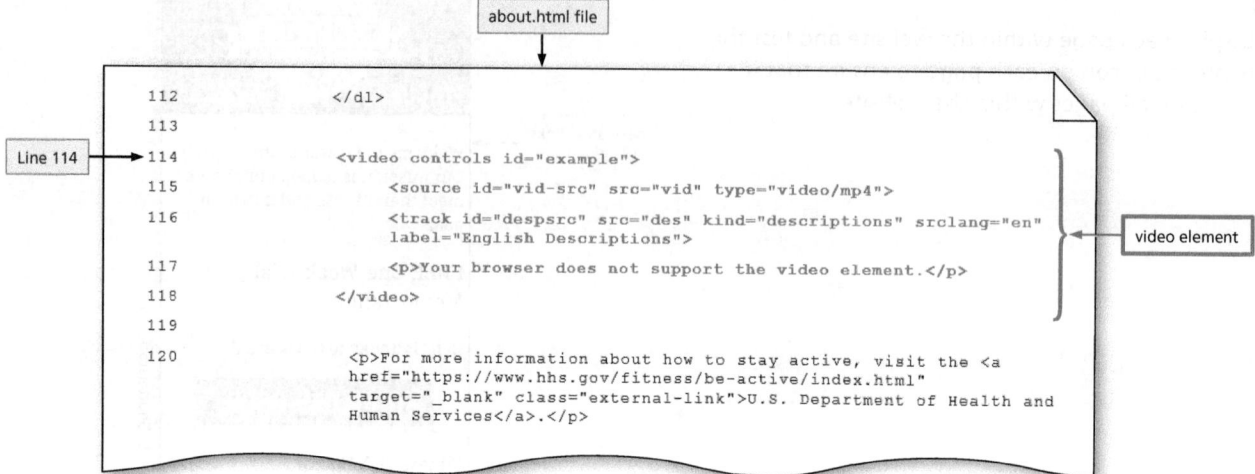

about.html file

```
112             </dl>
113
114            <video controls id="example">
115                <source id="vid-src" src="vid" type="video/mp4">
116                <track id="despsrc" src="des" kind="descriptions" srclang="en"
                   label="English Descriptions">
117                <p>Your browser does not support the video element.</p>
118            </video>
119
120            <p>For more information about how to stay active, visit the <a
               href="https://www.hhs.gov/fitness/be-active/index.html"
               target="_blank" class="external-link">U.S. Department of Health and
               Human Services</a>.</p>
```

Line 114 → 114

video element

Figure 10–54

 2

- If necessary, reopen the styles.css file in your text editor to prepare to modify it.

- Tap or click at the end of Line 320, and then press the ENTER key twice to insert new Lines 321 and 322.

- On Line 322, type **#example {** to add a new selector.

- Press the ENTER key to insert a new Line 323, increase the indent, and then type **display: none;** to add a declaration.

- Press the ENTER key to insert a new Line 324, decrease the indent, and then type **}** to close the style rule (Figure 10–55).

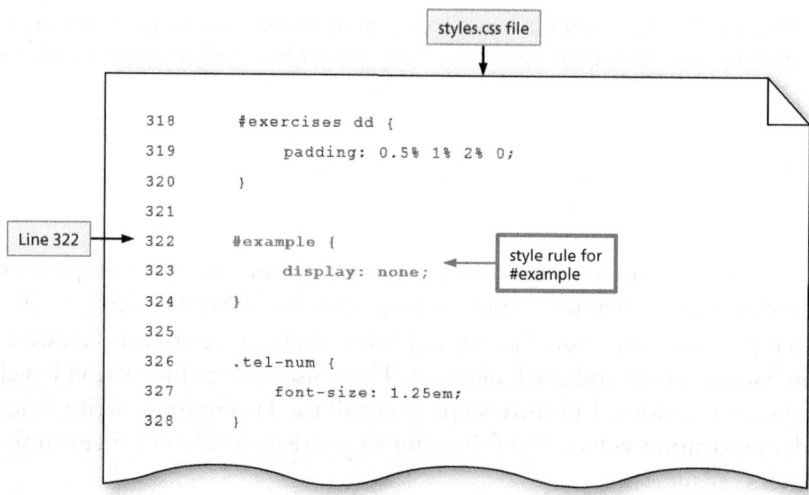

styles.css file

```
318        #exercises dd {
319            padding: 0.5% 1% 2% 0;
320        }
321
322        #example {
323            display: none;
324        }
325
326        .tel-num {
327            font-size: 1.25em;
328        }
```

Line 322 → 322

style rule for #example

Figure 10–55

Q&A What is the purpose of this style rule?
The example id is an attribute within the video element. You set the display to none so that the video element does not appear on the page. You will create a JavaScript function in future steps to dynamically display a video.

3

- Save your changes to the about.html and styles.css files.

- Open the about.html file in your browser to view the page in a desktop viewport (Figure 10–56).

BTW
React
React is a popular JavaScript library created by Facebook that developers use to create user interface components and applications. It extends HTML and creates its own elements referred to as directives. For more information about React, visit reactjs.org.

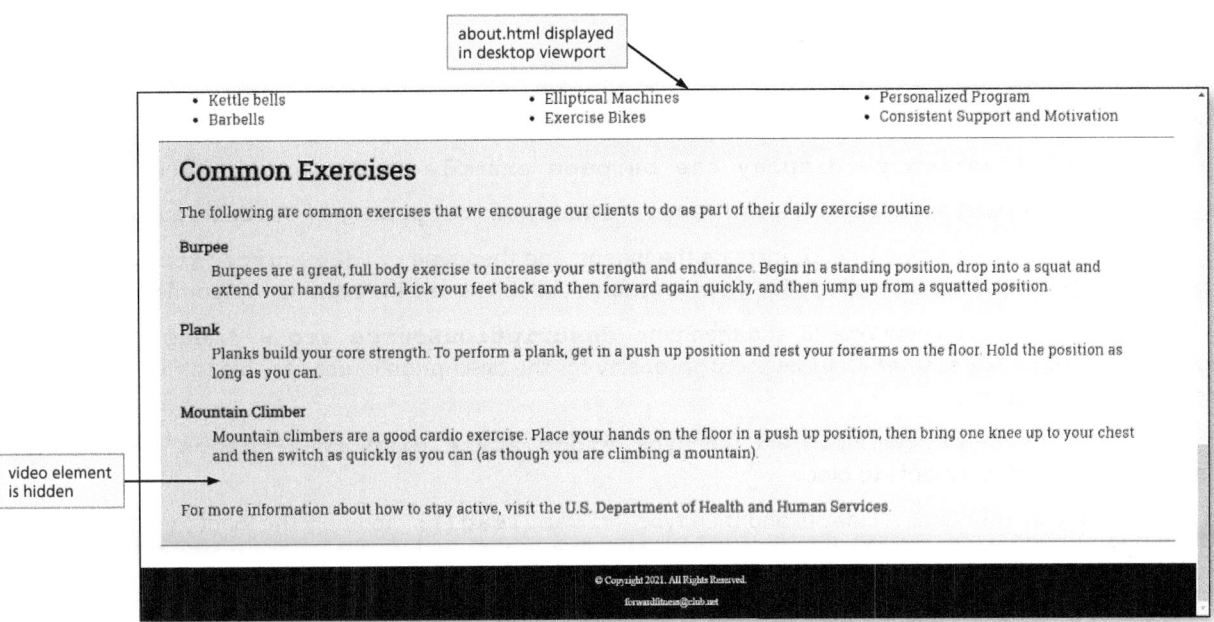

about.html displayed
in desktop viewport

- Kettle bells
- Barbells

- Elliptical Machines
- Exercise Bikes

- Personalized Program
- Consistent Support and Motivation

Common Exercises

The following are common exercises that we encourage our clients to do as part of their daily exercise routine.

Burpee

Burpees are a great, full body exercise to increase your strength and endurance. Begin in a standing position, drop into a squat and extend your hands forward, kick your feet back and then forward again quickly, and then jump up from a squatted position.

Plank

Planks build your core strength. To perform a plank, get in a push up position and rest your forearms on the floor. Hold the position as long as you can.

Mountain Climber

Mountain climbers are a good cardio exercise. Place your hands on the floor in a push up position, then bring one knee up to your chest and then switch as quickly as you can (as though you are climbing a mountain).

video element
is hidden

For more information about how to stay active, visit the U.S. Department of Health and Human Services.

© Copyright 2021. All Rights Reserved.
forwardfitness@club.net

Figure 10–56

To Create and Call the burpees( ) Function

1 CREATE CSS TRANSFORM | 2 CREATE CSS ANIMATION | 3 CREATE HAMBURGER MENU
4 CREATE JAVASCRIPT FILE | 5 CREATE & CALL JAVASCRIPT FUNCTIONS

Now that the About Us page contains a video element, create a JavaScript function to load the burpees. mp4 video when an onclick event is triggered. *Why? Display an example video of how to perform burpees when the user clicks an element to trigger the onclick event.* Use the external JavaScript file, script.js, to write a function that displays a video demonstration of burpees within the video element and then use the onclick event in the about. html file to call the function. The following steps create the burpees( ) function in the script.js file and specify an onclick event in the about.html file.

1

- If necessary, reopen the script.js file in your text editor to prepare to modify it.

- Tap or click at the end of Line 5, and then press the ENTER key twice to insert new Lines 6 and 7.

- On Line 7, type `//Global variables` to insert a new comment.

- Press the ENTER key to insert a new Line 8, and then type `var video = document.getElementById("example");` to define a global variable.

- Press the ENTER key to insert a new Line 9, and then type `var videoSource = document.getElementById("vid-src");` to define another global variable.

- Press the ENTER key to insert a new Line 10, and then type `var descriptionSource = document.getElementById("despsrc");` to define a global variable (Figure 10–57).

Q&A

What are global variables?

Global variables can be used by any function within the same JavaScript file. You will create three functions and each will use these global variables. Rather than defining the variables as local variables within the function three separate times, define them one time as a global variable.

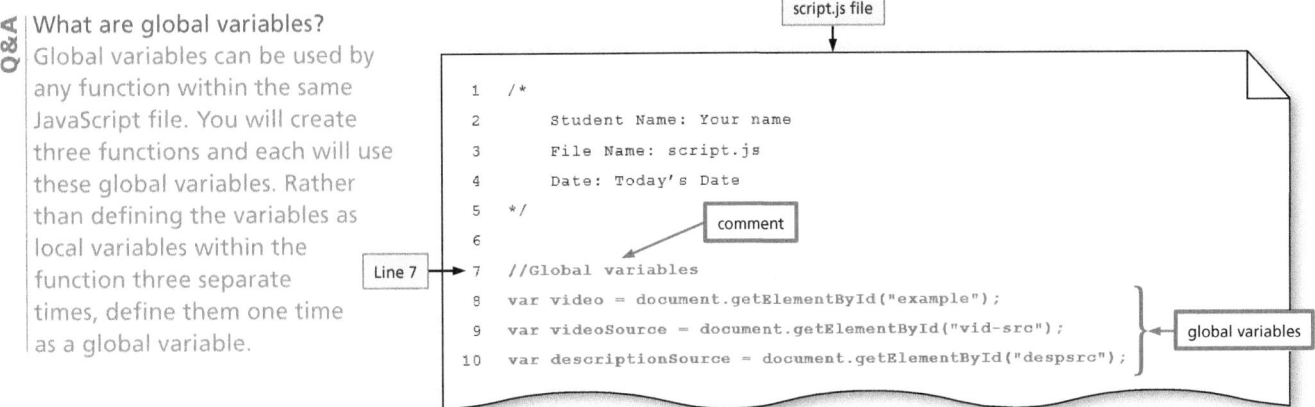

script.js file

```
1   /*
2       Student Name: Your name
3       File Name: script.js
4       Date: Today's Date
5   */
6
7   //Global variables
8   var video = document.getElementById("example");
9   var videoSource = document.getElementById("vid-src");
10  var descriptionSource = document.getElementById("despsrc");
```

comment

Line 7

global variables

Figure 10–57

- Tap or click at the end of Line 23, and then press the ENTER key twice to insert new Lines 24 and 25.
- On Line 25, type **//Function to display the burpees example video** to insert a new comment.
- Press the ENTER key to insert a new Line 26, and then type **function burpees() {** to begin a new function.
- Press the ENTER key to insert a new Line 27, increase the indent, and then type **videoSource.src = "media/burpees.mp4";** to set the src property for the videoSource variable to the burpees.mp4 video file.
- Press the ENTER key to insert a new Line 28, and then type **descriptionSource.src = "media/burpees-descriptions.vtt";** to set the src property for the descriptionSource variable to the burpees-descriptions.vtt file.
- Press the ENTER key to insert a new Line 29, and then type **video.style.display = "block";** to set the display style for the video variable to block.
- Press the ENTER key to insert a new Line 30, and then type **video.load();** to apply the load() method to the video variable.
- Press the ENTER key to insert a new Line 31, decrease the indent, and then type **}** to close the function (Figure 10–58).

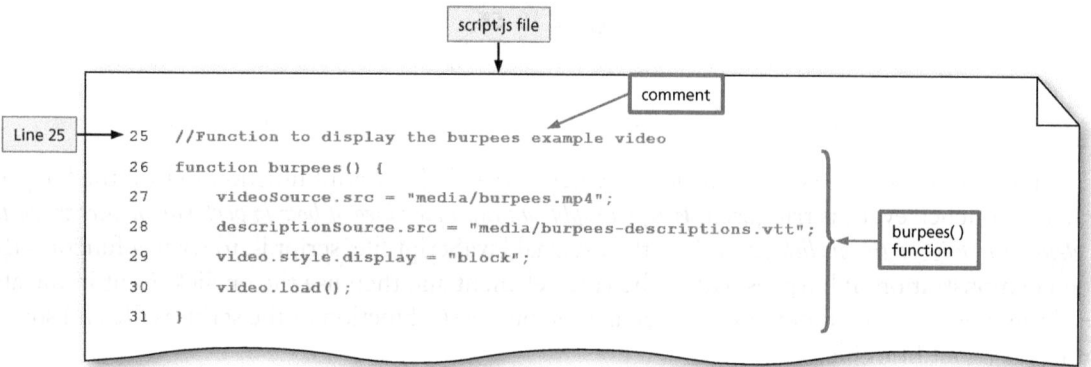

Figure 10–58

Q&A

What is meant by the JavaScript statement **videoSource.src = "media/burpees.mp4";**?
This statement takes the videoSource variable (an object) and sets its src (source) property to the burpees.mp4 video file, located in the media folder. Recall that videoSource is a global variable that is set to the vid-src id in the about.html file. The vid-src id is an attribute within the source element.

What is meant by the JavaScript statement **descriptionSource.src = "media/burpees-descriptions.vtt";**?
This statement takes the descriptionSource variable (an object) and sets its src (source) property to the burpees-descriptions.vtt descriptions file, located in the media folder. Recall that descriptionSource is a global variable that is set to the despsrc id in the about.html file. The despsrc id is an attribute within the track element.

What is meant by the JavaScript statement **video.style.display = "block";**?
This statement takes the video variable (an object) sets its display style (CSS) property to a block to display the video on the page. Recall that video is a global variable that is set to the example id in the about.html file. The example id is an attribute within the video element.

What is meant by the JavaScript statement **video.load();**?
This statement applies the load() method to the video variable (an object) and loads the video on the page.

- Open the about.html file in your text editor to prepare to modify the file.
- On Line 105, place your insertion point before the closing </dd> tag, press the SPACEBAR, and then type **<span class="viewex" onclick="burpees()"> View Example.</span>** to insert a span element the viewex class and an onclick event that calls the burpees() function (Figure 10–59).

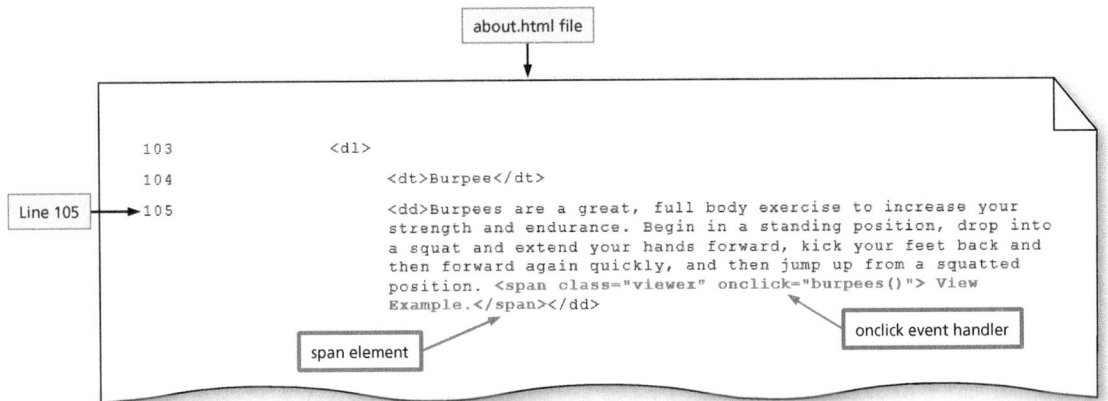

Figure 10–59

4

- If necessary, reopen the styles.css file in your text editor to prepare to modify the file.

- Tap or click at the end of Line 320, press the ENTER key twice to insert new Lines 321 and 322, and then type `.viewex {` to add a new selector.

- Press the ENTER key to insert a new Line 323, increase the indent, and then type `font-weight: bold;` to add a declaration.

- Press the ENTER key to insert a new Line 324, and then type `cursor: pointer;` to add a declaration.

- Press the ENTER key to insert a new Line 325, decrease the indent, and then type `}` to close the style rule (Figure 10–60).

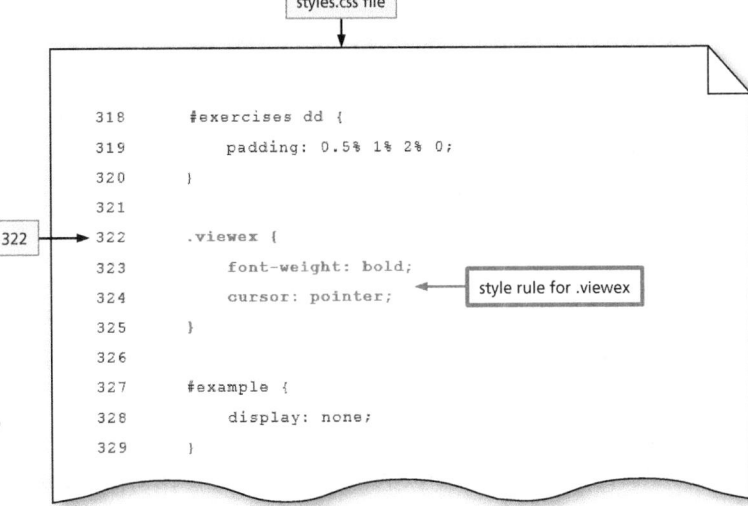

Q&A What is the purpose of the cursor declaration?
This declaration changes the mouse pointer from an arrow to a hand pointer. This visual change lets the user know that the text can be clicked as a link.

Figure 10–60

5

- Save your changes to the script.js, about.html, and styles.css files.

- Refresh or reopen the about.html file in your browser to view the page in a desktop viewport.

- Tap or click the View Example text to display the burpees video (Figure 10–61).

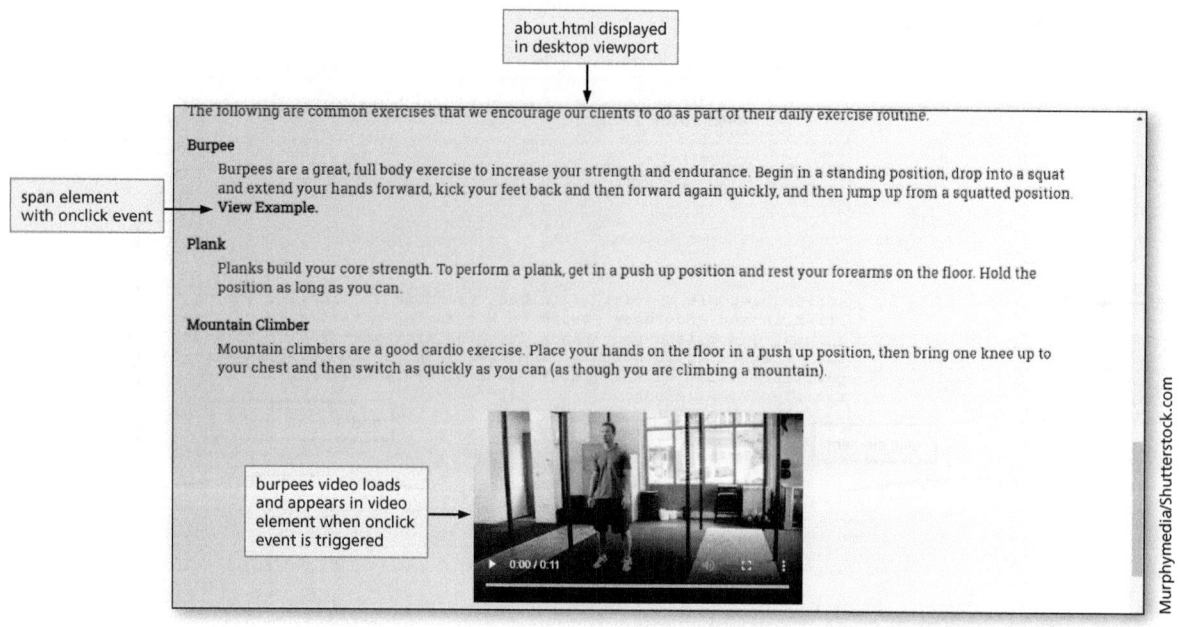

about.html displayed
in desktop viewport

span element
with onclick event

burpees video loads
and appears in video
element when onclick
event is triggered

Murphymedia/Shutterstock.com

Figure 10–61

To Create and Call the plank( ) Function

Next, you need to create a function to load and display the plank.mp4 video within the video element on the About Us page. *Why? Display an example video of how to perform a plank when the user clicks an element to trigger the onclick event.* Use the external JavaScript file, script.js, to write a function that displays a video demonstration of a plank within the video element, and then use the onclick event in the about.html file to call the function. The following steps create the plank( ) function in the script.js file and specify an onclick event in the about.html file.

- If necessary, reopen the script.js file in your text editor to prepare to modify it.

- Tap or click at the end of Line 31, and then press the ENTER key twice to insert new Lines 32 and 33.

- On Line 33, decrease the indent if necessary, and then type `//Function to display the plank example video` to insert a new comment.

- Press the ENTER key to insert a new Line 34, and then type `function plank() {` to begin a new function.

- Press the ENTER key to insert a new Line 35, increase the indent, and then type `videoSource.src = "media/plank.mp4";` to set the src property for the videoSource variable to the plank.mp4 video file.

- Press the ENTER key to insert a new Line 36, and then type `descriptionSource.src = "media/plank-descriptions.vtt";` (including the hyphen in plank-descriptions.vtt) to set the src property for the descriptionSource variable to the plank-descriptions.vtt file.

- Press the ENTER key to insert a new Line 37, and then type `video.style.display = "block";` to set the display style for the video variable to block.

- Press the ENTER key to insert a new Line 38, and then type `video.load();` to apply the load( ) method to the video variable.

- Press the ENTER key to insert a new Line 39, decrease the indent, and then type `}` to close the function (Figure 10–62).

Q&A
What is the purpose of the plank( ) function?
When called, the plank( ) function loads and displays the plank.mp4 video within the example video element on the About Us page.

script.js file

comment

Line 33

```
33    //Function to display the plank example video
34    function plank() {
35        videoSource.src = "media/plank.mp4";
36        descriptionSource.src = "media/plank-descriptions.vtt";
37        video.style.display = "block";
38        video.load();
39    }
```

plank()
function

Figure 10–62

2

- Open the about.html file in your text editor to prepare to modify the file.

- On Line 108, place your insertion point before the closing </dd> tag, press the SPACEBAR, and then type **<span class="viewex" onclick="plank()"> View Example.</span>** to insert a span element the viewex class and an onclick event that calls the plank( ) function (Figure 10–63).

about.html file

```
107              <dt>Plank</dt>
108                  <dd>Planks build your core strength. To perform a plank, get in
                     a push up position and rest your forearms on the floor. Hold the
                     position as long as you can. <span class="viewex"
                     onclick="plank()"> View Example.</span></dd>
```

Line 108

onclick event handler

span element

Figure 10–63

3

- Save your changes to the script.js and about.html files.

- Refresh or reopen the about.html file in your browser to view the page in a desktop viewport.

- Tap or click the View Example text below the Plank term to display the plank video (Figure 10–64).

about.html displayed
in desktop viewport

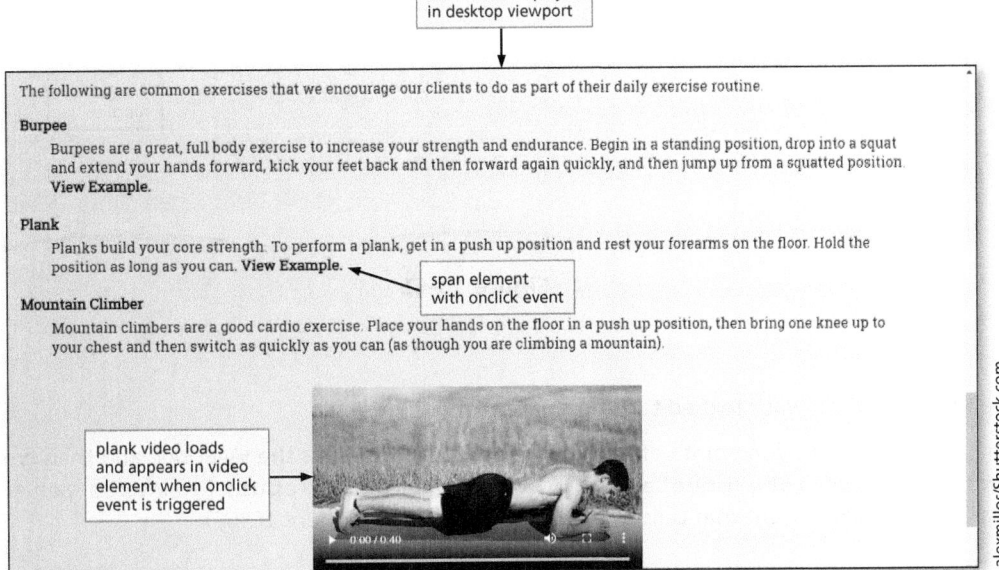

The following are common exercises that we encourage our clients to do as part of their daily exercise routine.

Burpee
Burpees are a great, full body exercise to increase your strength and endurance. Begin in a standing position, drop into a squat and extend your hands forward, kick your feet back and then forward again quickly, and then jump up from a squatted position. **View Example.**

Plank
Planks build your core strength. To perform a plank, get in a push up position and rest your forearms on the floor. Hold the position as long as you can. **View Example.**

span element
with onclick event

Mountain Climber
Mountain climbers are a good cardio exercise. Place your hands on the floor in a push up position, then bring one knee up to your chest and then switch as quickly as you can (as though you are climbing a mountain).

plank video loads
and appears in video
element when onclick
event is triggered

alexmillos/Shutterstock.com

Figure 10–64

To Create and Call the mountain( ) Function

Next, you need to create a function to load and display the mc.mp4 video within the video element on the About Us page. **Why?** *Display an example video of how to perform mountain climbers when the user clicks an element to trigger the onclick event.* Use the external JavaScript file, script.js, to write a function that displays a video demonstration of mountain climbers within the video element, and then use the onclick event in the about.html file to call the function. The following steps create the mountain( ) function in the script.js file and specify an onclick event in the about.html file.

- If necessary, reopen the script.js file in your text editor to prepare to modify it.
- Tap or click at the end of Line 39, and then press the ENTER key twice to insert new Lines 40 and 41.
- On Line 41, decrease the indent if necessary, and then type `//Function to display the mountain climbers example video` to insert a new comment.
- Press the ENTER key to insert a new Line 42, and then type `function mountain() {` to begin a new function.
- Press the ENTER key to insert a new Line 43, increase the indent, and then type `videoSource.src = "media/mc.mp4";` to set the src property for the videoSource variable to the mc.mp4 video file.
- Press the ENTER key to insert a new Line 44, and then type `descriptionSource.src = "media/mountain-descriptions.vtt";` to set the src property for the descriptionSource variable to the mountain-descriptions.vtt file.
- Press the ENTER key to insert a new Line 45, and then type `video.style.display = "block";` to set the display style for the video variable to block.
- Press the ENTER key to insert a new Line 46, and then type `video.load();` to apply the load( ) method to the video variable.
- Press the ENTER key to insert a new Line 47, decrease the indent, and then type `}` to close the function (Figure 10–65).

Q&A

What is the purpose of the mountain( ) function?

When called, the mountain( ) function loads and displays the mc.mp4 video within the example video element on the About Us page.

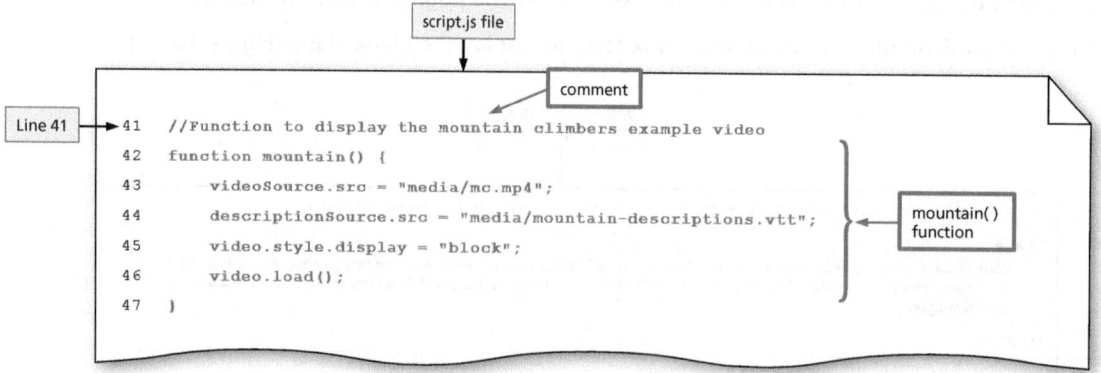

Figure 10–65

- Open the about.html file in your text editor to prepare to modify the file.
- On Line 111, place your insertion point before the closing `</dd>` tag, press the SPACEBAR, and then type `<span class="viewex" onclick="mountain()"> View Example.</span>` to insert a span element the viewex class and an onclick event that calls the mountain( ) function (Figure 10–66).

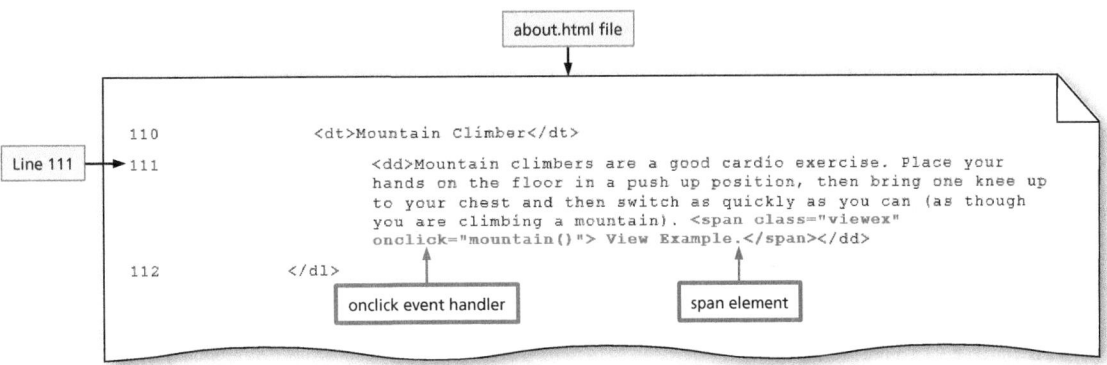

Figure 10–66

3

- Save your changes to the script.js and about.html files.

- Refresh or reopen the about.html file in your browser to view the page in a desktop viewport.

- Tap or click the View Example text below the Mountain Climber term to display the mountain climber video (Figure 10–67).

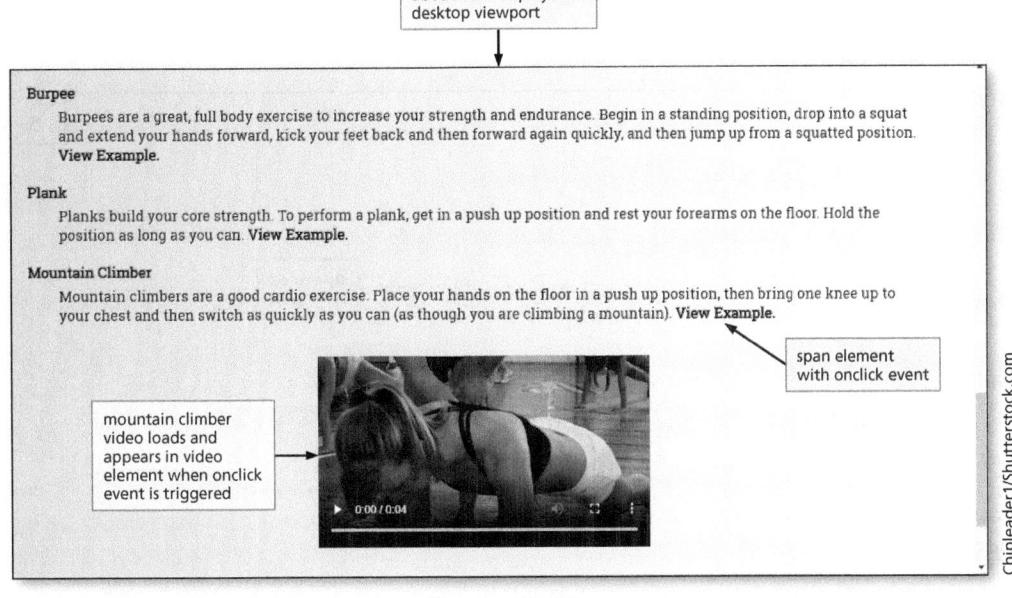

Figure 10–67

BTW
Vue.js
Vue.js is a progressive JavaScript framework used by developers to create user interfaces. To learn more about Vue.js, visit vuejs.org.

To Create and Call the discount( ) Function

1 CREATE CSS TRANSFORM | 2 CREATE CSS ANIMATION | 3 CREATE HAMBURGER MENU
4 CREATE JAVASCRIPT FILE | 5 CREATE & CALL JAVASCRIPT FUNCTIONS

Update the Contact Us page to include an input element for a discount promotional code. Add a new heading 3 element to the contact.html file to entice the user with a special discount promotional code. The user will need to tap or click the heading to view the discount code. *Why? Provide another form of interactivity on the webpage to provide a discount code to the user.* First, add a new heading element to the Contact Us page. Then, insert a new label and input element within the form. Next, use the external JavaScript file, script.js, to write a new function that replaces the text within the heading element and applies a new style. The following steps create and use the discount( ) function.

1

- Open the contact.html file in your text editor to prepare to modify it.

- Tap or click at the end of Line 57, and then press the ENTER key to insert a new Line 58.

- On Line 58, type `<h3 class="offer" onclick="discount()" id="special">View Promo Code</h3>` to insert a new heading 3 element.

- Tap or click at the end of Line 109, and then press the ENTER key twice to insert new Lines 110 and 111.

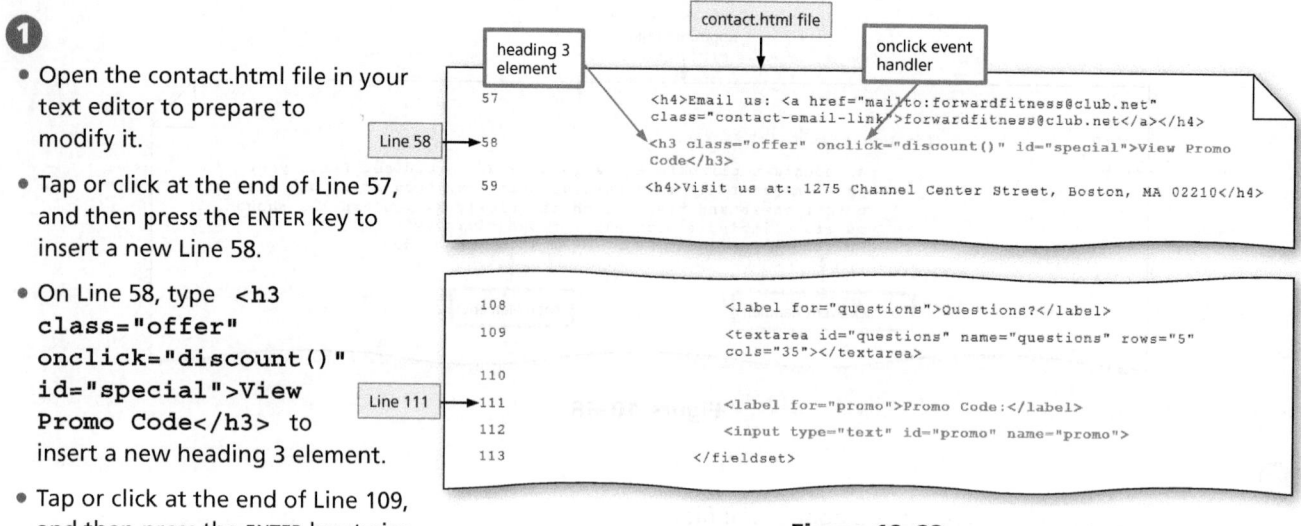

Figure 10–68

- On Line 111, type `<label for="promo">Promo Code:</label>` to insert a new label element.

- Press the ENTER key to insert a new Line 112, and then type `<input type="text" id="promo" name="promo">` to insert a new input element (Figure 10–68).

2

- If necessary, reopen the styles.css file in your text editor to prepare to modify the file.

- Tap or click at the end of Line 470, and then press the ENTER key twice to insert new Lines 471 and 472.

- On Line 472, type `.offer:hover {` to add a new selector.

- Press the ENTER key to insert a new Line 473, increase the indent, and then type `transform: scale(1.25);` to add a declaration.

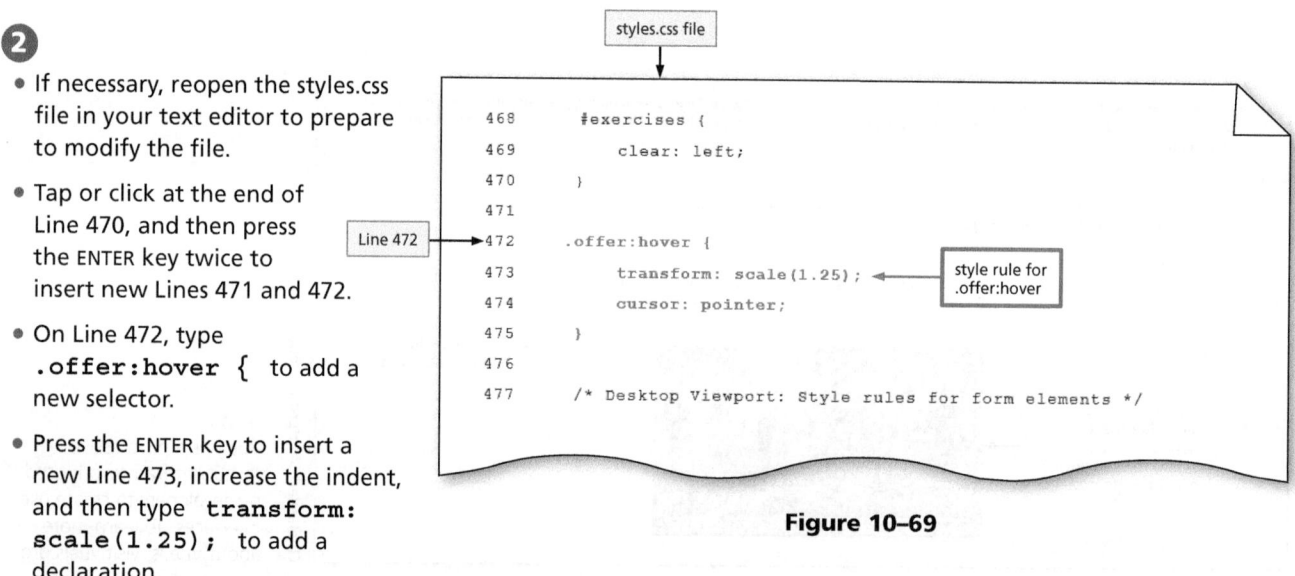

Figure 10–69

- Press the ENTER key to insert a new Line 474, and then type `cursor: pointer;` to add a declaration.

- Press the ENTER key to insert a new Line 475, decrease the indent, and then type `}` to close the style rule (Figure 10–69).

3

- If necessary, reopen the script.js file in your text editor to prepare to modify it.

- Tap or click at the end of Line 47, and then press the ENTER key twice to insert new Lines 48 and 49.

- On Line 49, type `//Function to display a promo code` to insert a new comment.

- Press the ENTER key to insert a new Line 50, and then type `function discount() {` to begin a new function.

- Press the ENTER key to insert a new Line 51, increase the indent, and then type `var promo = document.getElementById("special");` to define a local variable.

- Press the ENTER key to insert a new Line 52, and then type `promo.firstChild.nodeValue = "Promo Code: D25START";` to set the promo variable to the text, Promo Code: D25START.

- Press the ENTER key to insert a new Line 53, and then type `promo.style.color = "#ff0000";` to set the display color for the promo variable to red.

- Press the ENTER key to insert a new Line 54, and then type `promo.style.fontSize = "2em";` to set the font size for the promo variable to 2em.

- Press the ENTER key to insert a new Line 55, decrease the indent, and then type `}` to close the function (Figure 10–70).

Q&A What is the purpose of the statement `promo.firstChild.nodeValue = "Promo Code: D25START";`? This statement takes the first child of the promo variable, which is the text within the heading 3 element, and sets its nodeValue (or value) to the text, Promo Code: D25START.

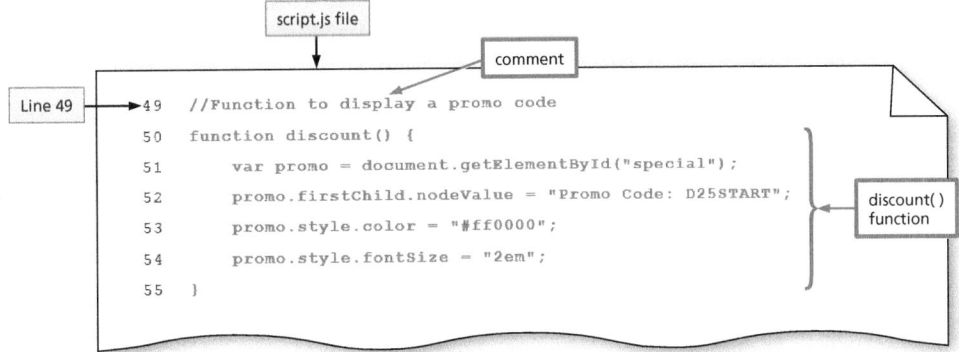

script.js file	
comment	
Line 49	

```
49    //Function to display a promo code
50    function discount() {
51        var promo = document.getElementById("special");
52        promo.firstChild.nodeValue = "Promo Code: D25START";
53        promo.style.color = "#ff0000";
54        promo.style.fontSize = "2em";
55    }
```

discount() function

Figure 10–70

4
- Save your changes to the script.js, contact.html, and styles.css files.
- Open the contact.html file in your browser to view the page in a desktop viewport.
- Tap or click the View Promo Code text to display the promo code (Figure 10–71).

contact.html displayed in desktop viewport

Ready to get started? Contact us today.

(814) 555-9608

Email us: forwardfitness@club.net

new text appears within heading 3 element when onclick event is triggered → Promo Code: D25START

Visit us at: 1275 Channel Center Street, Boston, MA 02210

Figure 10–71

BTW
The jQuery css( ) Method
You can use the jQuery css( ) method to style webpage content. Visit w3schools.com/jquery/jquery_css.asp for a demonstration.

To Validate the Style Sheet

Always run your files through W3C's validator to check the document for errors. If the document has any errors, validating gives you a chance to identify and correct them. Validation is also an effective troubleshooting tool during the development process and adds a valuable level of professionalism to your work. The following steps validate a CSS document.

1 Open your browser and type `http://jigsaw.w3.org/css-validator/` in the address bar to display the W3C CSS Validation Service page.

2 Tap or click the By file upload tab to display the Validate by file upload information.

3 Tap or click the Browse button to display the Choose File to Upload dialog box.

4 Navigate to your css folder to find the styles.css file.

5 Tap or click the styles.css document to select it.

6 Tap or click the Open button to upload the selected file to the W3C CSS validator.

7 Tap or click the Check button to send the document through the validator and display the validation results page.

8 If necessary, correct any errors, save your changes, and run through the validator again to revalidate the page.

To Validate the HTML Files

Every time you create a new webpage or modify an existing webpage, run it through W3C's validator to check the document for errors. If any errors exist, you need to correct them. Validation is also an effective troubleshooting tool during the development process and adds a valuable level of professionalism to your work. The following steps validate an HTML document.

1 Open your browser and type `http://validator.w3.org/` in the address bar to display the W3C validator page.

2 Tap or click the Validate by File Upload tab to display the Validate by File Upload information.

3 Tap or click the Browse button to display the Open dialog box.

4 Navigate to your fitness folder to find the index.html file.

5 Tap or click the index.html document to select it.

6 Tap or click the Open button to upload it to the W3C validator.

7 Tap or click the Check button to send the document through the validator and display the validation results page.

8 If necessary, correct any errors, save your changes, and run through the validator again to revalidate the page.

9 Follow these steps to validate all HTML pages within your fitness folder and correct any errors.

Chapter Summary

In this chapter, you learned how to integrate interactivity using CSS and JavaScript. You learned how to use the CSS transform property. You learned how to create animations with CSS keyframes. You learned how to create a JavaScript file and write JavaScript functions. You also learned how to use event handlers to call JavaScript functions. The items listed below include all the new skills you have learned in this chapter, with the tasks grouped by activity.

Creating Interactivity with CSS
Apply a CSS Transform to a Webpage (HTML 512)
Create Animation with CSS (HTML 515)

Incorporating JavaScript
Create a Hamburger Menu (HTML 519)
Create an External JavaScript File (HTML 536)

Create a Function for the Hamburger Menu (HTML 538)
Call a JavaScript Function (HTML 540)
Add More Functions to a JavaScript File (HTML 543)
Call the New Functions (HTML 543)

How will you use interactivity within your website?
Use these guidelines as you complete the assignments in this chapter and create your own webpages outside of this class.

1. Determine how to integrate animation within your website.

    a) Determine best pages for animation.

    b) Determine which CSS properties to use for animation.

2. Decide how to best integrate JavaScript.

    a) Determine the types of interactivity you wish to use within your website.

    b) Determine what code is needed to accomplish your goal.

3. Decide what pages will use JavaScript.

    a) Determine how many functions will be needed.

    b) Determine the best method for calling JavaScript functions.

4. Determine other forms of interactivity that JavaScript can provide.

    a) Research how to use JavaScript to validate form information.

    b) Research how to use the jQuery JavaScript library.

How should you submit solutions to questions in the assignments identified with a symbol?
Every assignment in this book contains one or more questions identified with a ✳ symbol. These questions require you to think beyond the assigned presentation. Present your solutions to the questions in the format required by your instructor. Possible formats may include one or more of these options: create a document that contains the answer; present your answer to the class; discuss your answer in a group; record the answer as audio or video using a webcam, smartphone, or portable media player; or post answers on a blog, wiki, or website.

CONSIDER THIS

CONSIDER THIS

Apply Your Knowledge

Reinforce the skills and apply the concepts you learned in this chapter.

Using CSS Animation and JavaScript

Note: To complete this assignment, you will be required to use the Data Files. Please contact your instructor for information about accessing the Data Files.

Instructions: In this exercise, you will use your text editor to create animation using CSS. You will also use JavaScript to create a function and set an event handler to call the function. First, you create animation using CSS. Next, use JavaScript to create a function and then specify an event handler to call the function. Work with the index.html file in the apply folder from the Data Files. The completed webpage is shown in Figure 10–72. You will also use professional web development practices to indent, space, comment, and validate your code.

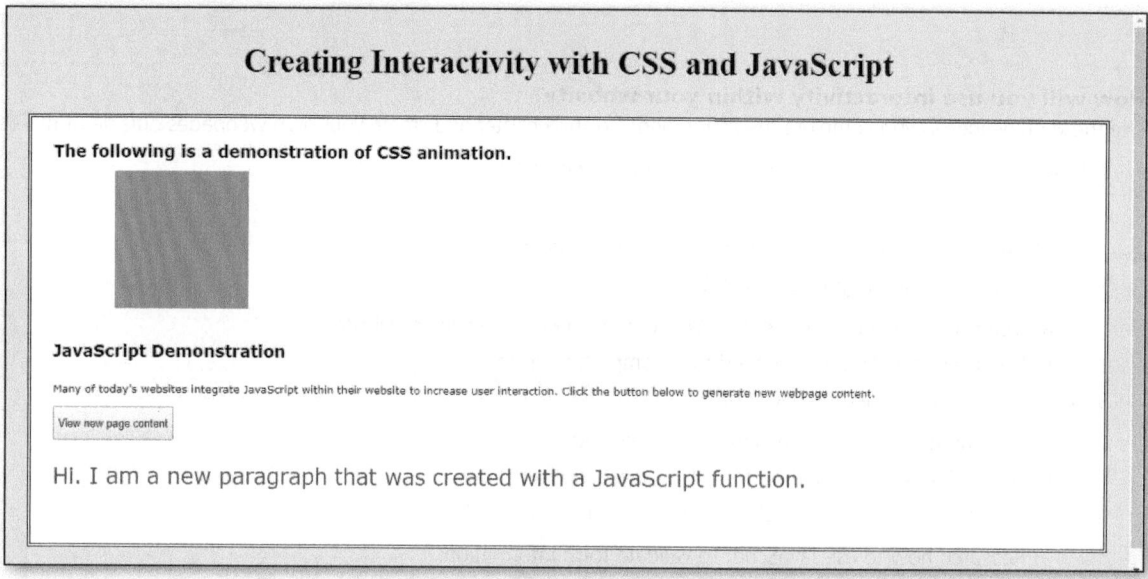

Figure 10–72

Perform the following tasks:

1. Open the index.html file in the chapter10\apply folder from the Data Files in your text editor. Update the comment with your name, the file name, and today's date. Add your name to the paragraph element located within the footer element near the bottom of the page.

2. Open the index.html file in your browser to view the page.

3. Update the CSS link within the head element to use the apply10.css file located within the apply\css folder.

4. Open the apply10.css file from the apply\css folder. Modify the comment at the top of the style sheet to include your name, today's date, and the file name.

5. Add the following comment and @keyframes rules above the footer style rule:

```
/* Animation */
@-webkit-keyframes color {
    from { background-color: #fbdae9; }
    to { background-color: #660b32; }
}
```

```
@keyframes color {
    from { background-color: #fbdae9; }
    to { background-color: #660b32; }
}
```

6. Insert the following declarations to the style rule for the square class selector. For each declaration, you must first include a declaration with the -webkit- prefix, followed by the standard declaration.

   a. Animation name property that specifies the name of the @keyframes rule animation.

   b. Animation duration property with a value of 5 seconds.

7. Create a new style rule for the square class selector with the hover pseudo-class that specifies a transform property with **translate(80px)** as the value.

8. Create a script.js file and save it within the apply\scripts folder. Include a multi-line comment at the top of the page with your name, today's date, and the file name.

9. Add a single line comment with the text **Function to display content**.

10. Create the following function below the comment:

```
function content() {
    var text = document.getElementById("new");
    text.textContent = "Hi. I am a new paragraph that was created with
    a JavaScript function.";
    text.style.color = "#c0145f";
    text.style.fontSize = "2em";
}
```

11. In the index.html file, above the closing body tag, add a script element and specify **script.js** as the src.

12. Add an onclick event handler that calls the content( ) function to the button element in the main section.

13. Save all of your changes and open index.html in your browser. View the animation and click the button to ensure that the content( ) function is called and the new text is displayed.

14. Validate your HTML document and fix any errors that are identified.

15. Submit the files in a format specified by your instructor.

16. ✲ In this exercise, you created animation using CSS. Identify another way to use the @keyframes rule to create animation with the square div element on the page.

Extend Your Knowledge

Extend the skills you learned in this chapter and experiment with new skills. You may need to use additional resources to complete the assignment.

Using jQuery

Note: To complete this assignment, you will be required to use the Data Files. Please contact your instructor for information about accessing the Data Files.

Instructions: In this exercise, you research how to use jQuery to hide and show webpage content. An example of the completed webpage is shown in Figure 10–73. You will also use professional web development practices to indent, space, comment, and validate your code.

Continued >

Extend Your Knowledge *continued*

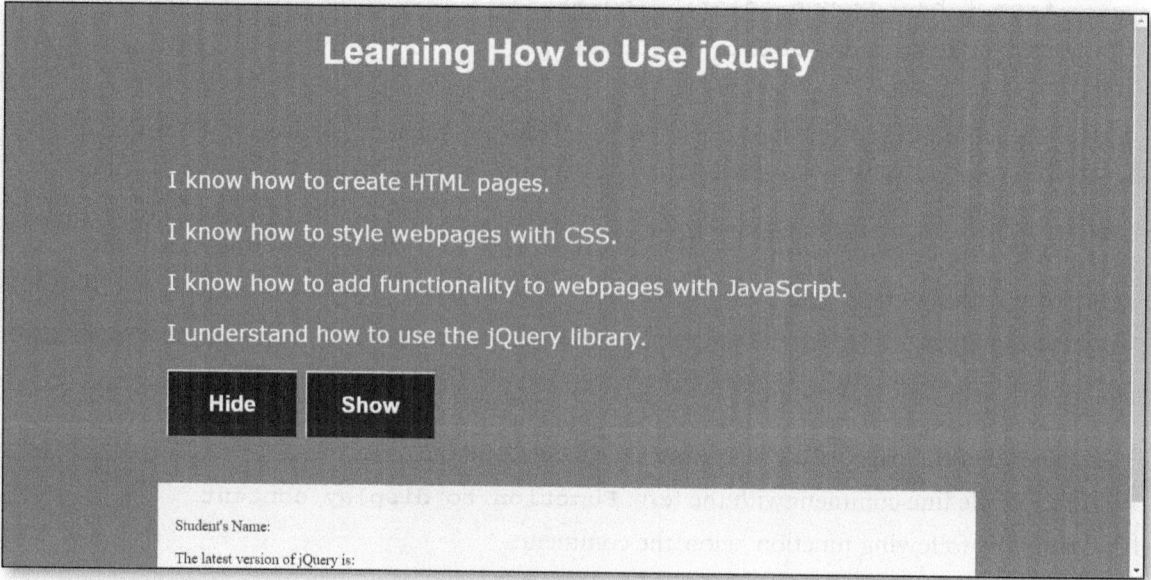

Figure 10–73

Perform the following tasks:

1. In your text editor, open the extend10.html file in the chapter10\extend folder from the Data Files. Update the comment with your name and today's date. Add your name to the paragraph element located within the footer element near the bottom of the page. Add a script element referring to the scripts/script.js file above the closing body tag.

2. Open the extend10.html file in your browser to view the page.

3. In your text editor, open the script.js file in the chapter 10\extend\scripts folder from the Data Files. Update the comment with your name, the file name, and today's date.

4. Obtain the jQuery library and insert a script element in extend10.html with a source attribute to the jQuery library. You can do this by 1) downloading the jQuery library or 2) linking to a jQuery CDN (Content Delivery Network). Use your browser to research and find the jQuery library file and download it or find a jQuery CDN link. If you download the jQuery library, save it in your scripts folder and use the script element to reference the library in your extend10.html file. Otherwise, add a script element to the extend10.html file that includes a jQuery CDN link as the source. Visit jquery.com/download/ or w3schools.com/jquery/jquery_get_started.asp for information the jQuery CDN.

5. Use your browser to research the jQuery hide( ) and show( ) methods. Use the script.js file to write jQuery functions or statements to make the paragraph elements within the article elements hide and show. Use the Hide and Show buttons to call your functions.

6. Update the paragraph elements in the footer to indicate the latest version of jQuery. Also provide the resource that you used to complete this assignment.

7. Submit the document in a format specified by your instructor.

8. ✳ In this exercise, you researched how to use jQuery hide( ) and show( ) methods. Research and discuss another jQuery method and provide a code example.

Analyze, Correct, Improve

Analyze a website, correct all errors, and improve it.

Improving a Webpage with JavaScript

Note: To complete this assignment, you will be required to use the Data Files. Please contact your instructor for information about accessing the Data Files.

Instructions: Work with the analyze10.html file in the analyze folder from the Data Files. The analyze10.html webpage needs JavaScript functions to display larger pictures. First, correct the JavaScript syntax errors on the page. Next, create global variables. Then, use the first function as an example to create a function to display a larger image of the second thumbnail picture within the placeholder figure element. Also use the first function as an example to create a function to display a larger image of the third thumbnail picture within the placeholder figure element. Finally, create new style rules for the figure and img elements. The completed webpage is shown in Figure 10–74. You will also use professional web development practices to indent, space, comment, and validate your code.

Figure 10–74

1. Correct

   a. Open the analyze10.html file in the chapter10\analyze folder from the Data Files in your text editor. Modify the comment at the top of the page to include your name and today's date, and then link the file to styles10.css. Add a title to the page and add your name to the footer element.

   b. Insert a script element above the closing body tag with the script.js file as the source.

   c. In your text editor, open the script.js file in the chapter10\analyze\scripts folder from the Data Files. Modify the comment at the top of the page to include your name and today's date.

   d. Review the pic1( ) function and correct all six syntax errors. Look for missing curly braces, missing quotation marks, missing parentheses, and missing semicolons.

Continued >

Analyze, Correct, Improve *continued*

e. Create the following three global variables above the comment for the pic1( ) function. Begin with a comment that identifies the global variables.

```
var figElement = document.getElementById("placeholder");

var imgSource = document.getElementById("image");

var figCap = document.querySelector("figcaption");
```

f. Add a new comment below the pic1( ) function, followed by a new function named pic2( ). Carefully analyze the pic1( ) function to understand the purpose of the four statements within the function. Use it as a guide to create the pic2( ) function. The pic2( ) function should display the sanjuan.jpg image, use **Elevated view of San Juan coast** for the img alt text, and use **Coast of San Juan** for the figcaption text.

g. Add a new comment below the pic2( ) function, followed by a new function named pic3( ). Use the pic1( ) function as a guide to create the pic3( ) function. The pic3( ) function should display the curacao.jpg image, use **The blue waters of Curacao** for the img alt text, and use **Curacao** for the figcaption text.

h. In the styles10.css file, add your name and today's date to the comment. Above the footer style rule, create a new style rule for the placeholder id that sets the display to none.

2. Improve

a. In the analyze10.html file, add an onclick event handler to the first img element that calls the pic1( ) function.

b. In the analyze10.html file, add an onclick event handler to the second img element that calls the pic2( ) function.

c. In the analyze10.html file, add an onclick event handler to the third img element that calls the pic3( ) function.

d. In the styles10.css file, create a style rule for the figure element to align it center.

e. In the styles10.css file, create a style rule for the img element and specify **1em** of padding.

f. Save all of your changes and open analyze10.html in your browser.

g. Validate your CSS file using the W3C validator found at http://jigsaw.w3.org/css-validator/ and fix any errors that are identified.

h. Validate your HTML webpage using the W3C validator found at validator.w3.org and fix any errors that are identified.

i. ✸ In this exercise, you used JavaScript to view larger images. Use your browser to research how to use JavaScript to create an image gallery and write a summary of your findings.

In the Lab

Labs 1 and 2, which increase in difficulty, require you to create webpages based on what you learned in the chapter; Lab 3 requires you to dive deeper into a topic covered in the chapter.

Lab 1: **Adding Interactivity to the Strike a Chord Website**

Problem: You work for a local music lesson company called Strike a Chord that provides music lessons for piano, guitar, and violin. The company needs a web presence and has hired you to create their website. You have already created the website and now need to add a hamburger menu for a mobile viewport and a transform to create interactivity to the website. Figure 10–75 shows the Lessons page in a mobile viewport. Figure 10–76 shows the Lessons page in a desktop viewport.

Monkey Business Images/Shutterstock.com

Figure 10–75

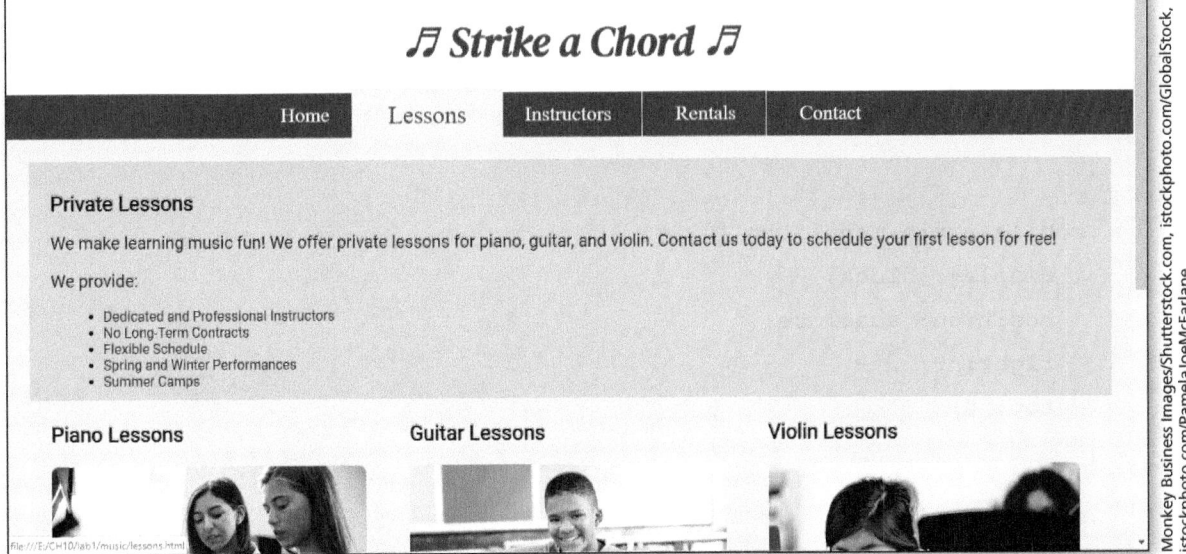

Monkey Business Images/Shutterstock.com, istockphoto.com/GlobalStock, istockphoto.com/PamelaJoeMcFarlane

Figure 10–76

Instructions: Perform the following tasks:

1. Use your text editor to open all the HTML files within your music folder and update the comment with today's date.

2. Add the following comment and nav element above the header element on all HTML files in the music folder.

```
<!-- Mobile Nav -->

<nav class="mobile-nav">

    <div id="menu-links">

        <a href="index.html">Home</a>

        <a href="lessons.html">Lessons</a>
```

Continued >

In the Lab *continued*

```
        <a href="instructors.html">Instructors</a>
        <a href="rentals.html">Rentals</a>
        <a href="contact.html">Contact Us</a>
    </div>
    <a class="menu-icon" onclick="hamburger()">
        <div>&#9776;</div>
    </a>
</nav>
```

3. Apply the tab-desk class to the nav element below the header element for all HTML files in the music folder.

4. Open the styles.css file in your text editor. Add the following style rules below the nav style rule in the mobile style rules section.

```
.mobile-nav a {
    color: #fff;
    text-align: center;
    font-size: 2em;
    text-decoration: none;
    padding: 3%;
    display: block;
}

.mobile-nav a.menu-icon {
    display: block;
    position: absolute;
    right: 0;
    top: 0;
}

.menu-icon div {
    height: 50px;
    width: 50px;
    background-color: #373684;
}
```

5. In the mobile style rules section, move the style rule for the nav ul selector to the tablet media query, below the comment for the tablet nav area style rules.

6. In the mobile style rules section, delete the style rule for the nav li selector.

7. In the mobile style rules section, within the nav li a style rule, delete the padding declaration. Move the remaining declarations to the tablet style rule for the nav li a selector. Delete the empty style rule for the nav li a within the mobile style rule section.

8. In the mobile style rules section, add **#menu-links** as another selector to the .tab-desk style rule with the declaration that sets the display to none.

9. In the mobile style rules section, add the following declarations to the header h1 style rule:

   ```
   font-size: 1.5em;
   padding: 4%;
   margin-right: 15%;
   ```

10. In the tablet media query, add `.mobile-nav` as another selector to the .mobile style rule with the declaration that sets the display to none.

11. In the tablet media query, below the comment, Tablet Viewport: Style rule for header content, add a new style rule for the header h1 selector that sets the margin and padding to `0` and the font size to `2em`.

12. Open your music folder and create a new subfolder named scripts. Create a new JavaScript file named script.js and save it within your scripts folder. Add a multi-line comment to Lines 1 through 5 that includes your name, file name, and today's date.

13. Add a single-line comment on Line 7 with the text `Hamburger menu function`.

14. Create the following function below the comment:

    ```
    function hamburger() {
          var menu = document.getElementById("menu-links");
          if (menu.style.display === "block") {
              menu.style.display = "none";
          } else {
              menu.style.display = "block";
          }
    }
    ```

15. Add a script element with the src attribute that points to the script.js file above the closing body tag in all HTML files within the music folder.

16. In the styles.css file, within the desktop media query, add a new declaration to the nav li a:hover style rule that applies a `transform` with the value `scale(1.2)`.

17. Save all files. Open index.html in Google Chrome's device mode, select a mobile viewport, and test your hamburger icon on each page.

18. Exit the device mode to display a desktop viewport. Hover over the navigation links to view the transform effect.

19. Check your spelling. Validate your HTML file and correct any errors. Save your changes.

20. Submit your assignment in the format specified by your instructor.

21. ✳ In this assignment, you applied a transform to the navigation. Identify another element within the website where you might apply a transform element.

Lab 2: Adding Interactivity to the Wild Rescues Website

Problem: You volunteer at a local wildlife rescue, a nonprofit organization called Wild Rescues. The organization rescues all kinds of wild animals, rehabilitates them, and then releases them back into the wild. Wild Rescues needs a website to help raise awareness about the organization. You have already created the website and now need to add a hamburger menu for a mobile viewport and create other functions to add interactivity to the website. Figure 10–77 shows the home page in a mobile (375px) viewport. Figure 10–78 shows the FAQs page in a desktop viewport.

Continued >

In the Lab *continued*

Figure 10–77

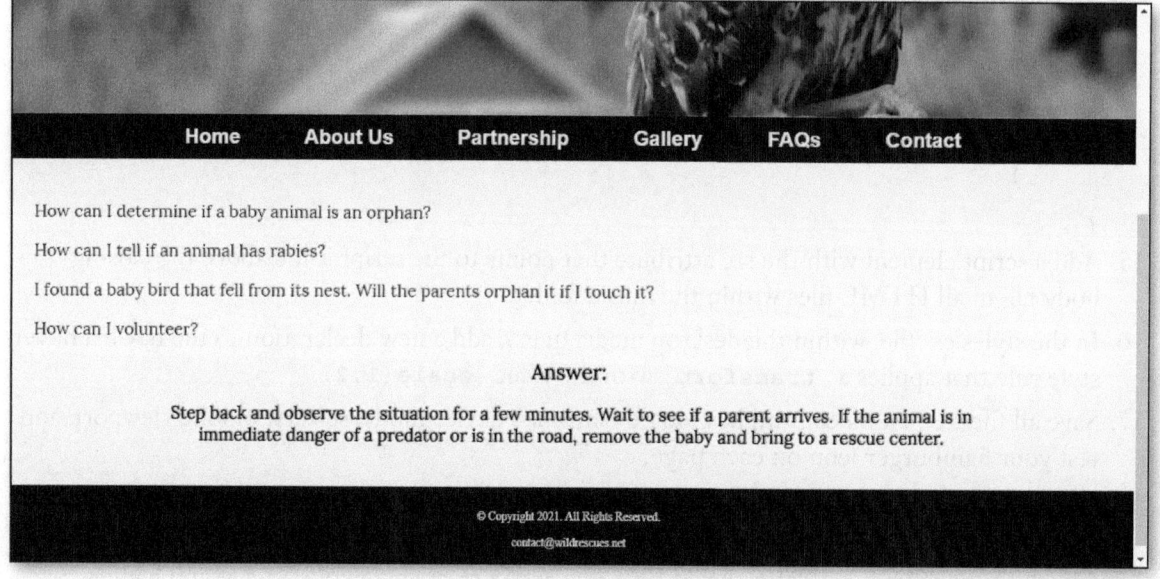

Figure 10–78

Instructions: Perform the following tasks:

1. Open all the HTML files within your rescue folder in your text editor and update the comment with today's date.

2. Add the following comment and nav element above the header element on all HTML files in the rescue folder.

```
<!-- Mobile Nav -->

<nav class="mobile-nav">

    <div id="nav-links">

        <a href="index.html">Home</a>

        <a href="about.html">About Us</a>
```

```
        <a href="partnership.html">Partnership</a>

        <a href="gallery.html">Gallery</a>

        <a href="faqs.html">FAQs</a>

        <a href="contact.html">Contact Us</a>

    </div>

    <a class="nav-icon" onclick="hamburger()">

        <div id="icon">&#9776;</div>

    </a>

</nav>
```

3. Apply the tab-desk class to the nav element below the header element for all HTML files in the rescue folder.

4. Open the styles.css file in your text editor. Add the following style rules below the nav style rule in the mobile style rules section.

```
.mobile-nav a {
    color: #fff;
    text-align: center;
    font-size: 2em;
    text-decoration: none;
    padding: 3%;
    display: block;
}

.mobile-nav a.nav-icon {
    display: block;
    position: absolute;
    left: 0;
    top: 0;
    color: #f6eee4;
    padding: 2%;
}

.nav-icon div {
    height: 40px;
    width: 40px;
    color: #2a1f14;
}
```

5. In the mobile style rules section, move the style rule for the nav ul selector to the tablet media query, below the comment for the tablet nav area style rules.

6. In the mobile style rules section, delete the following declarations for the nav li style rule: display, font size, and border top. Move the declarations for the font family and font weight to the nav li style rule within the tablet media query. Delete the empty style rule for the nav li within the mobile style rule section.

Continued >

In the Lab *continued*

7. In the mobile style rules section, within the nav li a style rule, delete the padding declaration. Move the remaining declarations to the tablet style rule for the nav li a selector. Delete the empty style rule for the nav li a within the mobile style rule section.

8. In the mobile style rules section, add **#nav-links** as another selector to the style rule for .tab-desk and .desktop, with the declaration that sets the display to none.

9. In the mobile style rules section, add the following declaration to the .mobile h1 style rule:

    ```
    margin: 2% 0 0 3%;
    ```

10. In the tablet media query, add **.mobile-nav** as another selector to the .mobile style rule with the declaration that sets the display to none.

11. Open your rescue folder and create a new subfolder named scripts. Create a new JavaScript file named script.js and save it within your scripts folder. Add a multi-line comment to Lines 1 through 5 that includes your name, file name, and today's date.

12. Add a single-line comment on Line 7 with the text, **Hamburger menu function**.

13. Create the following function below the comment:

    ```
    //Hamburger menu function
    function menu() {
        var navlinks = document.getElementById("nav-links");
        var menuicon = document.getElementById("icon");
        if (navlinks.style.display === "block") {
            navlinks.style.display = "none";
            menuicon.style.color = "#2a1f14";
        } else {
            navlinks.style.display = "block";
            menuicon.style.color = "#f6eee4";
        }
    }
    ```

14. Add a script element with the src attribute that points to the script.js file above the closing body tag in all HTML files within the rescue folder.

15. Open the template.html file and use it to create a new webpage with the file name **faqs.html.** Update the comment with the file name and today's date. Update the title to display it as **Wild Rescues: FAQs.**

16. In the main element, add an id attribute to the div element with the value **questions.**

17. Nest the following paragraph elements within the questions div:

    ```
    <p onclick="ans1()">How can I determine if a baby animal is an
    orphan?</p>

    <p onclick="ans2()">How can I tell if an animal has rabies?</p>

    <p onclick="ans3()">I found a baby bird that fell from its nest. Will
    the parents orphan it if I touch it?</p>

    <p onclick="ans4()">How can I volunteer?</p>
    ```

18. Create another div element below the questions div. Assign an id attribute with the value, **answer.** Nest the following elements within the answer div:

    ```
    <h2>Answer:</h2>

    <p></p>
    ```

19. In the styles.css file, in the mobile style rules section, add the following style rules after the .tel-link a style rule:

```
#questions p {
    cursor: pointer;
}

#answer {
    text-align: center;
    font-weight: bold;
    width: 80%;
    margin: 0 auto;
}

#answer h2 {
    display: none;
}
```

20. In the script.js file, add the following comment and global variables above the comment for the hamburger function:

```
//Global variables
var answer = document.querySelector("#answer p");
var heading = document.querySelector("#answer h2");
```

21. Add the following comments and functions below the hamburger function:

```
//Function to display the first answer
function   ans1() {
    heading.style.display = "block";
    answer.textContent = "Step back and observe the situation for a
    few minutes. Wait to see if a parent arrives. If the animal is in
    immediate danger from a predator or is in the road, remove the baby
    and bring to a rescue center.";
}

//Function to display the second answer
function ans2() {
    heading.style.display = "block";
    answer.textContent = "You cannot tell if an animal has rabies
    simply by seeing it. A test must be performed to determine if an
    animal has rabies. Do not approach wildlife that you suspect might
    be rabid. Contact us to have the animal removed.";
}

//Function to display the third answer
function ans3() {
    heading.style.display = "block";
    answer.textContent = "No. This is a myth. The parents will retrieve
    the baby bird and place it back in its nest. If the parents do not
    return, contact us.";
}
```

Continued >

In the Lab *continued*

```
//Function to display the fourth answer
function ans4() {
    heading.style.display = "block";
    answer.textContent = "We need volunteers to help feed animals, care
    for animals, and clean animal pens. We also accept donations.";
}
```

22. Save all files. Open index.html in Google Chrome's device mode, select a mobile viewport, and test your hamburger icon on each page.

23. Exit the device mode to display a desktop viewport. Navigate to the FAQs page, and click each question to test your functions.

24. Check your spelling. Validate your HTML file and correct any errors. Save your changes.

25. Submit your assignment in the format specified by your instructor.

26. ✳ In this exercise, you used an onclick event handler to call each function. Research the addEventListener( ) method, and explain how you would use it instead of an onclick event handler to call the functions.

Lab 3: Adding Interactivity to the Student Clubs and Events Website

Problem: You and several of your classmates have decided to help increase student involvement in school clubs and events by creating a website to promote awareness about the various activities. You have already created the website and now need to add animation, a hamburger menu for a mobile viewport, and create additional functions to add interactivity to the website.

Instructions:

1. As a team, work together to determine how to best integrate the CSS transform property and an @keyframes rule for animation into the website.

2. As a team, work together to add a hamburger menu icon to all pages within your website. Display the hamburger icon for a mobile viewport and hide it for larger viewports.

3. Create an external JavaScript file named script.js and save it within your student\scripts folder. Use the script.js file to create a function to enable your hamburger menu.

4. As a team, work together to create and call at least one other function within your website.

5. Update your style sheet as necessary to style your webpage elements.

6. Add comments throughout your documents to note all changes.

7. Save all files. Test your hamburger menu icon on each page. Test your animation.

8. Check your spelling. Validate your HTML file and correct any errors. Save your changes.

9. Submit your assignment in the format specified by your instructor.

10. ✳ In this exercise, you used CSS animation. Research the CSS transition property and provide a brief overview of this property.

Consider This: Your Turn

Apply your creative thinking and problem-solving skills to design and implement a solution.

1. Adding Interactivity to Your Personal Portfolio Website

Personal

Part 1:   You have already developed a responsive website for your personal portfolio and now need to add interactivity with CSS and JavaScript to the website.

1. Add a hamburger menu icon to your personal portfolio website. Use CSS to display the icon for a mobile viewport and hide it for larger viewports. Create a JavaScript file named script.js and use it to create a function to enable your hamburger menu.

2. Apply and use the CSS transform property within your website.

3. Save all files. Test your hamburger menu and transform effect.

4. Validate and correct your HTML and CSS files.

5. Submit your assignment in the format specified by your instructor.

Part 2:   In this exercise, you used JavaScript to create a function. Research and explain how to use the != operator in JavaScript.

2. Adding Interactivity to the Dog Grooming Website

Professional

Part 1:   You have already created a responsive design website for a dog grooming business, but now need to add interactivity to the website.

1. Add a hamburger menu icon to the dog grooming website. Use CSS to display the icon for a mobile viewport and hide it for larger viewports. Create a JavaScript file named script.js and use it to create a function to enable your hamburger menu.

2. Create and apply an @keyframes rule for animation within your website.

3. Save all files. Test your hamburger menu and animation.

4. Validate and correct your HTML and CSS files.

5. Submit your assignment in the format specified by your instructor.

Part 2:   In this exercise, you created an animation with CSS. Research the jQuery animate( ) method and provide an overview of how to use this method.

3. Adding Interactivity to the Future Technologies Website

Research and Collaboration

Part 1:   You and several of your classmates have been tasked with creating a website that showcases advances in technology. You have already created a responsive design website and now need to add interactivity to the website.

1. As a team, work together to determine how to best integrate the CSS transform property and an @keyframes rule for animation into the website.

2. As a team, work together to add a hamburger menu icon to all pages within your website. Display the hamburger icon for a mobile viewport and hide it for larger viewports.

3. Create an external JavaScript file named script.js and save it within your tech\scripts folder. Use the script.js file to create a function to enable your hamburger menu.

4. As a team, work together to create and call at least one other function within your website.

5. Update your style sheet as necessary to style your webpage elements.

Continued >

Consider This: Your Turn *continued*

6. Add comments throughout your documents to note all changes.

7. Save all files. Test your hamburger menu icon on each page. Test your animation.

8. Check your spelling. Validate your HTML file and correct any errors. Save your changes.

9. Submit your assignment in the format specified by your instructor.

Part 2: 🌼 As a group, research other ways to use JavaScript within your website and summarize your findings.

11 | Publish, Promote, and Maintain a Website

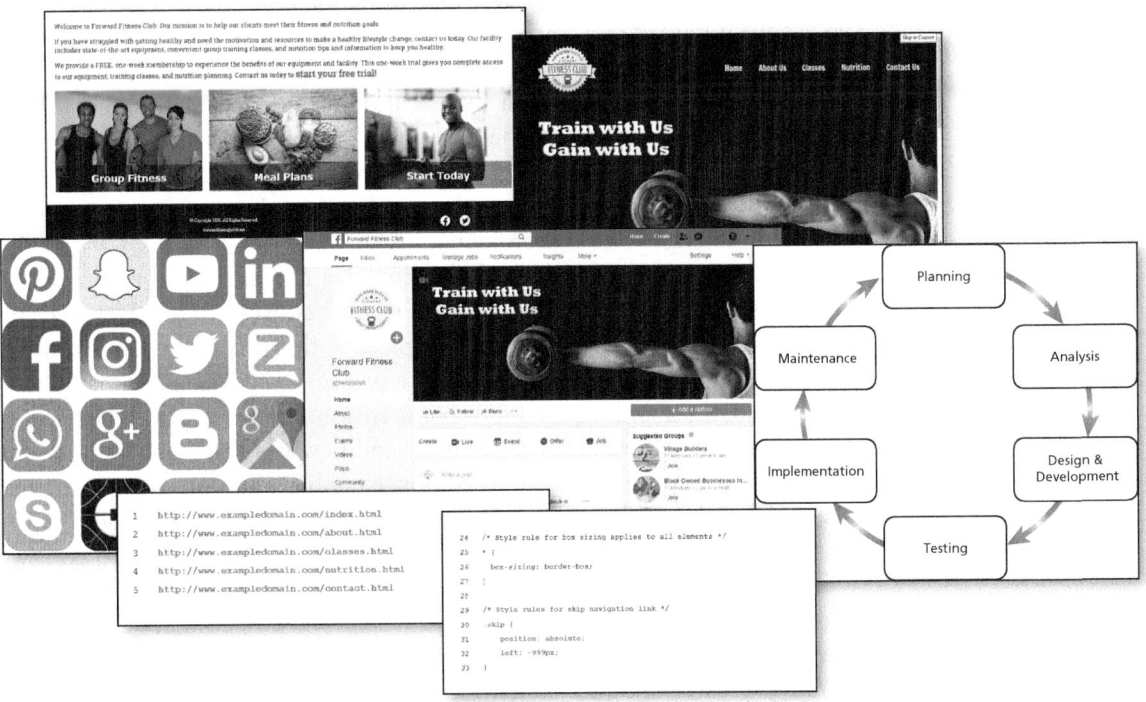

Objectives

You will have mastered the material in this chapter when you can:

- Define, identify, and describe forms of social media
- Describe a blog
- Describe search engines
- Explain search engine optimization (SEO)
- Create description meta tags
- Create a sitemap file
- Describe a domain name and top-level domains
- Explain the role of a web hosting service

- Describe a File Transfer Protocol (FTP) client
- Publish a website with an FTP client
- Explain how to register a website with a search engine
- Describe a website development life cycle
- Add a Skip to Content Link
- Minify a CSS file
- Explain project management for a website
- Define copyright and e-commerce

11 Publish, Promote, and Maintain a Website

Introduction

After you have created, validated, and tested a website, the next step is to publish it on a web server to make it accessible online for customers to access. You then need to take appropriate steps to promote your website so potential customers find it. Word of mouth is one of the best forms of advertisement and happens when a friend or family member recommends a specific product, service, or business to you. This form of advertisement is powerful because most people trust the word of a friend or family member more than a magazine ad or commercial. With the use of social media, word-of-mouth advertising spreads quickly, which is why businesses use social media to interact and engage with customers.

After a website is designed, developed, and launched, the next phase of the website begins: maintenance. A well-polished website involves a continuous maintenance process. As changes take place within a company and within an industry, a web developer must work closely with a project team to ensure that a business website stays fresh and stands out from its competition. Likewise, a web developer must keep up with emerging trends in technology and new ways to reach a target audience.

In this chapter, you will learn how to publish and promote your website. You will learn about the different forms of social media, including Facebook, Twitter, YouTube, Instagram, and Pinterest, and then link your social media pages to your website. You will improve a website for search engine optimization and use the `meta` tag to add a description to a webpage. You will also learn how to connect to a remote server, publish your website, and discover the many ways to promote and market your website. You will create a Skip to Content link to make the website accessible to visually impaired users and minify your CSS file. You also will learn about the development life cycle of a website, and about the project management process, including content and design updates. You will also learn about copyright laws as it pertains to text and media, and how to develop a maintenance plan for a business website. Finally, you will learn more about e-commerce websites.

Project — Publish and Promote a Website

In this chapter, you publish and promote the Forward Fitness Club website to establish an online presence for the business. This chapter provides information for publishing webpages and how to promote a website. This chapter also provides an overview of the popular social media sources available today. The chapter focuses on Facebook, Twitter, YouTube, Instagram, and Pinterest and details how businesses use these social media outlets to interact and engage with their customers. You make the Forward Fitness Club website more engaging by adding social media icons to every page within the website. You will also improve the website for search engine optimization and add improvements to make the website more accessible. You will improve the page load time by minifying the CSS file. This chapter also provides an overview of the website development life cycle, as well as website project management, which are vital when working with very large websites. Finally, this chapter provides a basic introduction to content management systems, frameworks, and electronic commerce.

The project in this chapter involves many steps. First, you add social media icons and link each icon to its respective social media page. Then, you add meta description tags to each webpage. Next, you create a sitemap file. You connect to a remote server, and then use an FTP client to publish your website. Next, you add a Skip to Content link. Finally, you minify a CSS file. Figure 11–1 shows the social media icons added to the home page. You also improve each webpage title element for search engine optimization. Figure 11–2a shows the published home page as displayed on an iPhone X. Figure 11–2b shows the published home page as displayed on an iPad. Figure 11–2c shows the published home page as displayed on a desktop browser. Figure 11–3 shows the Skip to Content link as displayed on a desktop browser.

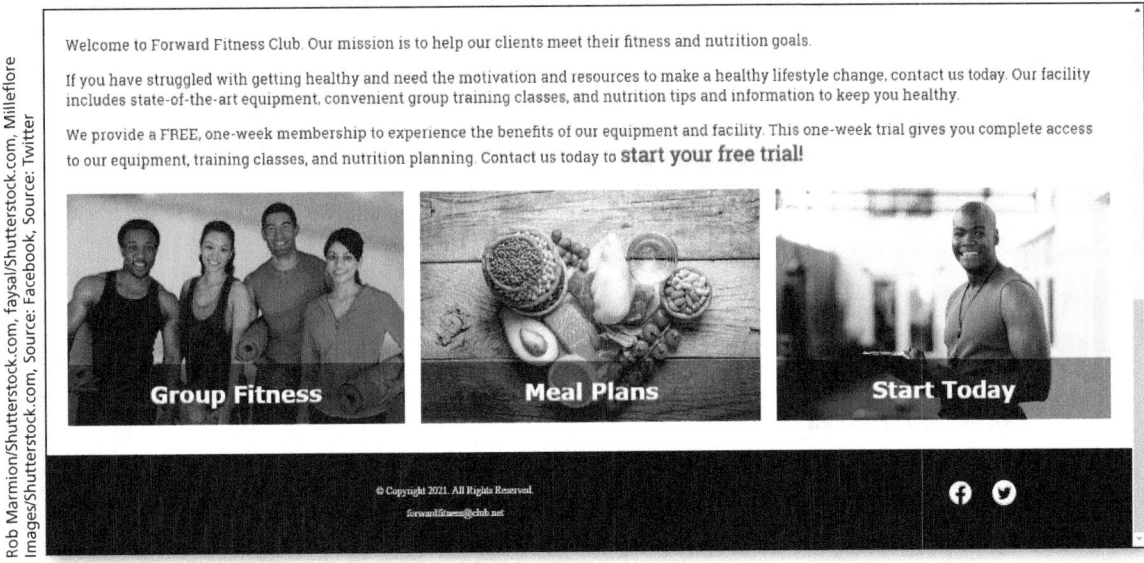

Figure 11–1

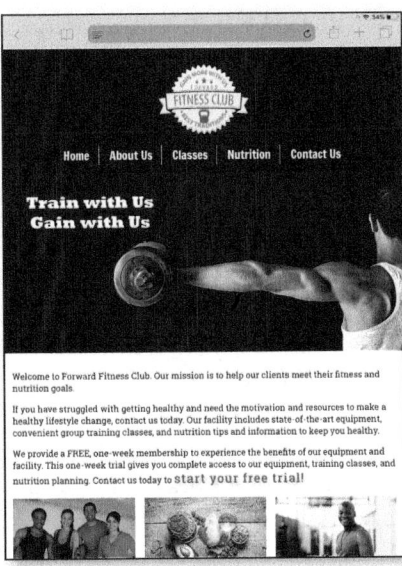

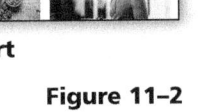

(a) Mobile Viewport

(b) Tablet Viewport

(c) Desktop Viewport

Figure 11–2

Home Page with Skip to Content Link
Figure 11–3

Roadmap

In this chapter, you will learn how to improve and publish the webpages shown in Figures 11–1, 11–2, and 11–3. The following roadmap identifies general activities you will perform as you progress through this chapter:

1. INSERT AND STYLE SOCIAL MEDIA LINKS.
2. MODIFY TITLES AND INSERT a description META TAG.
3. CREATE a SITEMAP FILE.
4. PUBLISH a WEBSITE.
5. CREATE a SKIP TO CONTENT LINK.
6. MINIFY a CSS FILE.

At the beginning of step instructions throughout the chapter, you will see an abbreviated form of this roadmap. The abbreviated roadmap uses colors to indicate chapter progress: gray means the chapter is beyond that activity; blue means the task being shown is covered in that activity, and black means that activity is yet to be covered. For example, the following abbreviated roadmap indicates the chapter would be showing a task in the 4 PUBLISH WEBSITE activity.

1 INSERT & STYLE SOCIAL MEDIA LINKS | 2 MODIFY TITLES & INSERT META TAG | 3 CREATE SITEMAP FILE
4 PUBLISH WEBSITE | 5 CREATE SKIP TO CONTENT LINK | 6 MINIFY CSS FILE

Use the abbreviated roadmap as a progress guide while you read or step through the instructions in this chapter.

Using Social Media

A **social network** is an online community where members post and exchange **social media** content, such as pictures, videos, and music. A social networking site allows members to share information and ideas with fellow online community members, who can view and comment on the shared social media. Social networking is a very popular and powerful medium for advertising your brand and product. As shown in Figure 11–4, the web has many social networking sites, such as Facebook, Twitter, YouTube, Instagram, Pinterest, and LinkedIn.

Social media offers a significant opportunity to market your product to potential customers because it encourages word-of-mouth advertising. Social networking sites allow businesses to immediately connect with their customers and potential customers and instantly engage them with new product information.

Figure 11–4

Facebook

Facebook is a social networking site with more than two billion users, the most users of any social networking site. Users include individuals and businesses. Individuals can exchange comments, share personal updates, and post pictures and video. With so many users, Facebook provides advertising opportunities to businesses to promote their products and services. A business can create a Facebook page and use it to advertise its products and services. Individuals can "like" a business by clicking a button to indicate that they use or approve of a product or service. Businesses can engage with people who have "liked" their page by posting a picture of their latest work, create community events, or provide new product updates. Individuals who like the business's page see the new posts made by the business within their home page feed. Obtaining "likes" is a goal for most businesses, as this increases their presence and positive perception. As shown in Figure 11–5, you can create a Facebook page for your business.

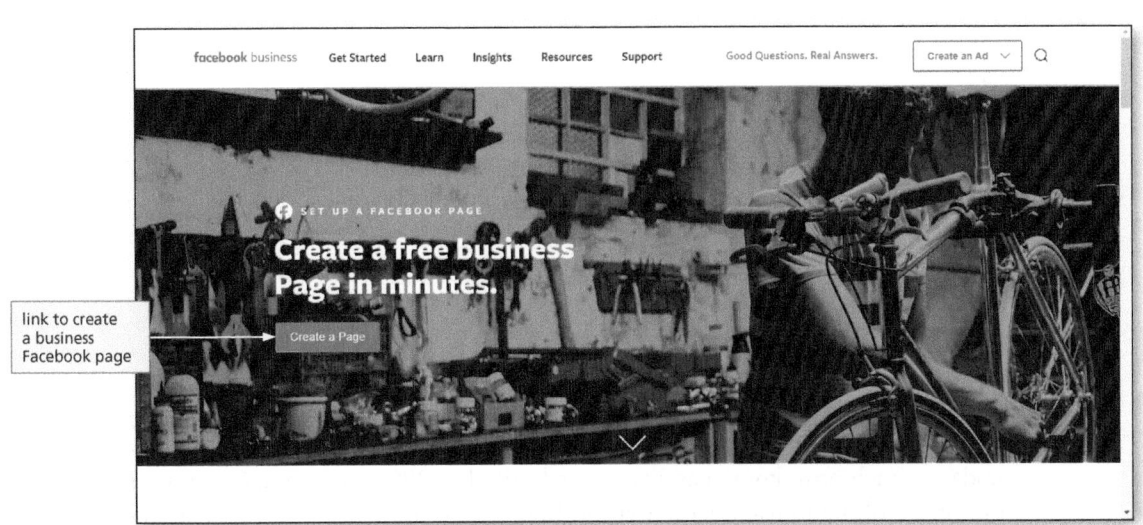

Figure 11–5

A business can create a Facebook page at no cost, and the page allows businesses to instantly connect and engage with customers. Businesses leverage Facebook to increase traffic to their website and increase sales. For a fee, businesses can also create an ad on Facebook to further drive potential customers to their website. Facebook matches a target audience with a company's ad and displays the ad on potential customers' news feed, located on their home page. Facebook provides several tools to measure the success of your ad and your Facebook page.

The following are several key items to consider when creating a Facebook post:

1. Set a positive tone within the first sentence of the status update, which yields interest and engagement.

2. Announce a special offer with a link for more information to drive traffic to your website.

3. Include an image with your posts, as this helps to further engage potential customers.

4. Keep your images mobile-friendly, as many Facebook users use the Facebook app on their mobile device.

5. Positively respond to customer comments to help build relationships.

6. Create a schedule for posts and post consistently.

If you choose to create a Facebook page for your business, visit www.facebook.com /business/pages to learn more about how to create a Facebook page for your business.

CONSIDER THIS

Who can view my business Facebook page?
Once you create a Facebook page for your business, you can control who sees the content on your page.

CONSIDER THIS

Where do I obtain Facebook icon logos to use within my website?
Facebook provides several logo icons, known as brand assets. Visit en.facebookbrand.com to download Facebook brand assets and review Facebook's guidelines before using them.

CONSIDER THIS

How can I incorporate a Facebook Like button into my webpage?
Facebook provides several plug-ins at developers.facebook.com/docs/plugins. Visit this page to obtain a plug-in for the Facebook Like button, Share button, and many more.

Twitter

Twitter is another social networking site used to post short comments or updates. Each post, known as a tweet, is limited to 280 characters. Customers have the option to follow a business on Twitter. Businesses can tweet about special offers or new products to its customers. Twitter's home page is shown in Figure 11–6.

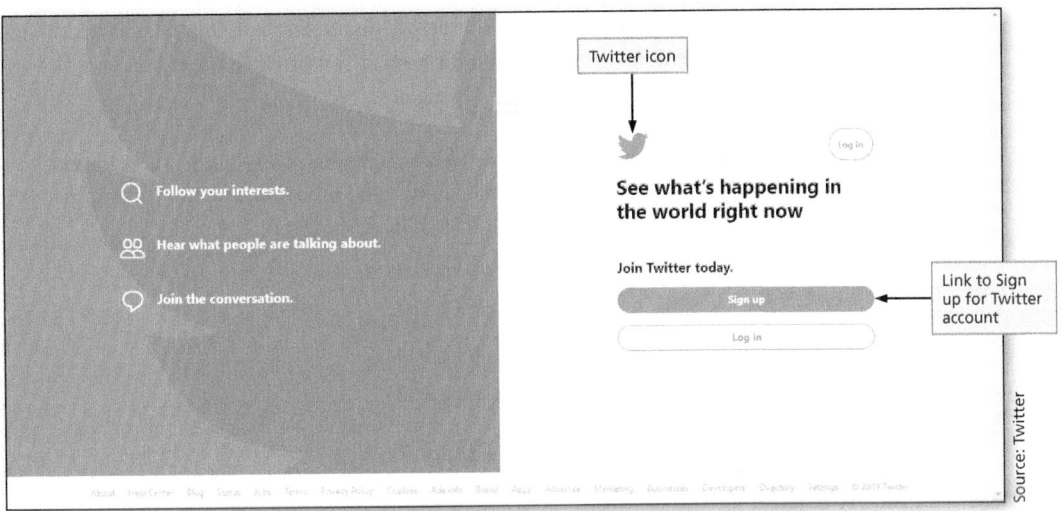

Source: Twitter

Figure 11–6

Creating a business Twitter account is free and allows businesses to instantly connect and engage with their customers. Businesses can follow their competition and learn about special offers made by their competitors. Businesses can also display ads on Twitter for a fee. Twitter provides many marketing opportunities for businesses to help with a content strategy, to engage and obtain more customers, and to measure marketing results in real time. Figure 11–7 shows the Twitter business page (business .twitter.com).

Source: Twitter

Figure 11–7

The following are several key items to consider when creating a tweet.

1. Include a clear call to action.
2. Avoid using abbreviations and all caps.
3. Use links with short URLs.
4. Use facts, images, and questions to drive engagement.
5. Retweet relative content.
6. Use Twitter's tools to schedule tweets and tweet campaigns.

BTW
Bitly.com
Bitly.com is a good resource used to shorten URLs. Twitter statistics show that bitly URLs help generate more retweets.

If you choose to create a Twitter page for your business, visit business.twitter .com to learn more about how to create a Twitter page for your business.

CONSIDER THIS

Do I need to have followers before potential customers can see my tweets?
No. If you use Twitter ads, your tweets or ad will be displayed on pages of potential customers. You can set a budget for Twitter ads and view ad results in real time.

CONSIDER THIS

How can I embed tweets within my webpage?
Twitter provides several embedding options at publish.twitter.com. Visit this page to obtain the required code to embed a tweet, embed a Twitter timeline, and add Twitter buttons.

YouTube

YouTube is a social media website where members can upload and share original videos. YouTube was founded in 2005 and has grown to over two billion users. Every day, YouTube's visitors watch several hundred hours of video and generate billions of views. This provides businesses a good opportunity to advertise and market their products. More than a million people advertise on YouTube, and the bulk of the advertisers are small businesses. YouTube also has a Facebook and Twitter presence.

Businesses can purchase ad space on YouTube to attract its target audience. Business ads can be a banner image that is displayed on the lower part of a video or a full-length commercial that plays before the selected video. Figure 11–8 shows an example of banner ad. Figure 11–9 shows an example of commercial ad that plays before a video.

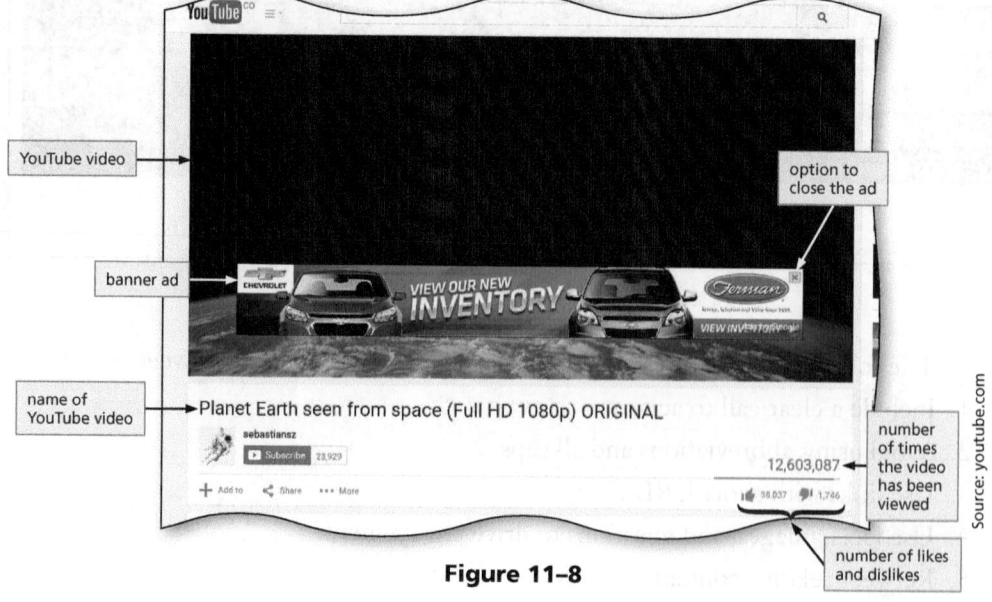

Source: youtube.com

Figure 11–8

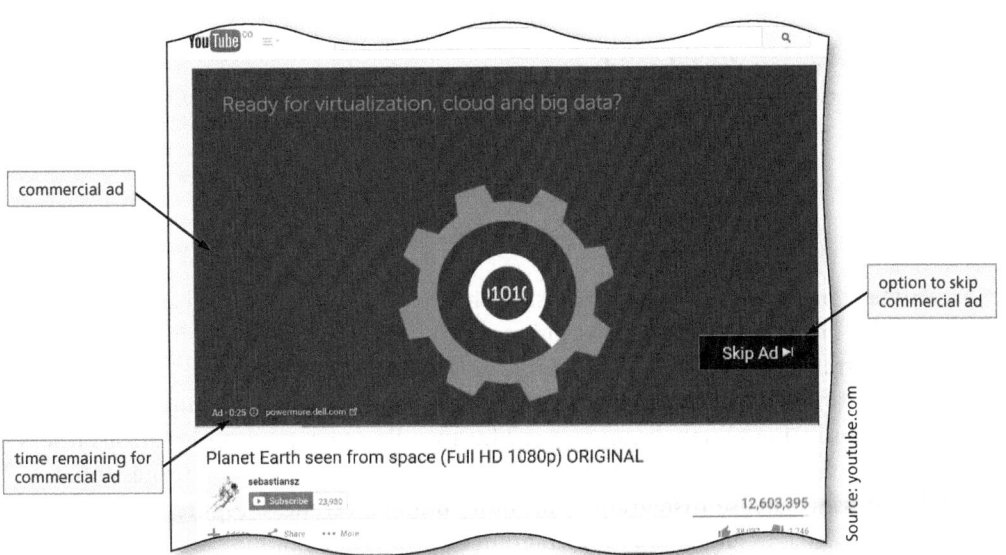

Figure 11–9

Businesses can create their own channel on YouTube and then upload videos to the channel. Users can subscribe to a channel and view the latest video for the business. The Olympics channel video page is shown in Figure 11–10.

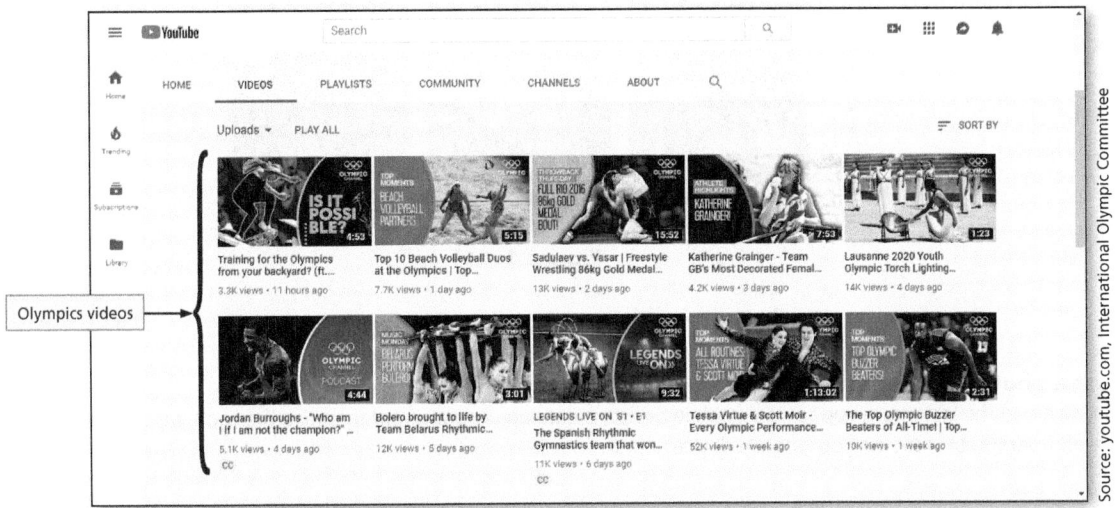

Figure 11–10

The following are several key items to consider when creating and uploading a video to YouTube for your business:

1. Use a clever title to attract your target audience.

2. Use a meaningful name for the video file.

3. Describe your video using keywords to help your customers find your video.

4. Include a call to action and a link to your website.

If you choose to create a YouTube channel for your business, visit support .google.com/accounts and search for "manage brand account" to learn more about how to create a YouTube Brand Account for your business.

BTW

YouTube Founders
YouTube was created in 2005 by Steve Chen, Chad Hurley, and Jawed Karim. Jawed posted the first YouTube video, titled "Me at the zoo," on April 23, 2005. It is just 18 seconds long. Google purchased YouTube in 2006.

What file format do I need to use for my YouTube video?
YouTube accepts the following file formats: .mov, .mpeg4, .mp4, .avi, .wmv, .mpegps, .flv, .webm, 3GPP, DNxHR, ProRes, CineForm, and HEVC.

Instagram

Instagram is a social networking site where members can upload and share photographs, images, and video. Most users view and use Instagram from a mobile device. Instagram is also a free app available at the Apple App Store and Google Play. The creators of Instagram wanted to provide users a unique way to connect and express ideas with captivating visual photography. The app allows users to apply various filters that enhance photographs, images, and video to make them look more professional. Many businesses also use Instagram to promote brand awareness. Figure 11–11 shows how Intel uses images and video on Instagram to promote its brand.

Instagram images posted by Intel

Instagram video posted by Intel

Source: instagram.com/intel

Figure 11–11

How do I post a photograph or video to Instagram?
You must first download the Instagram app to your mobile device, create an account, and then use the tools within the app to edit and post a photograph or video on your mobile device.

Pinterest

BTW
Privacy Policy
Each social networking site has a privacy policy. Be sure to read and review the policy to inform yourself on how each company uses the information you provide on their website.

On **Pinterest**, members browse and "pin" ideas found on the web. Pinterest users search for ideas for just about anything, including recipes, crafts, photography, and do-it-yourself (DIY) projects. Users can follow boards that interest them most and "pin" photos, links, and comments to their own board for future use. Figure 11–12 shows the Pinterest board for Lowe's, which contains several home improvement ideas. Users with an interest in Lowe's content can follow the board and see any new pins made by Lowe's.

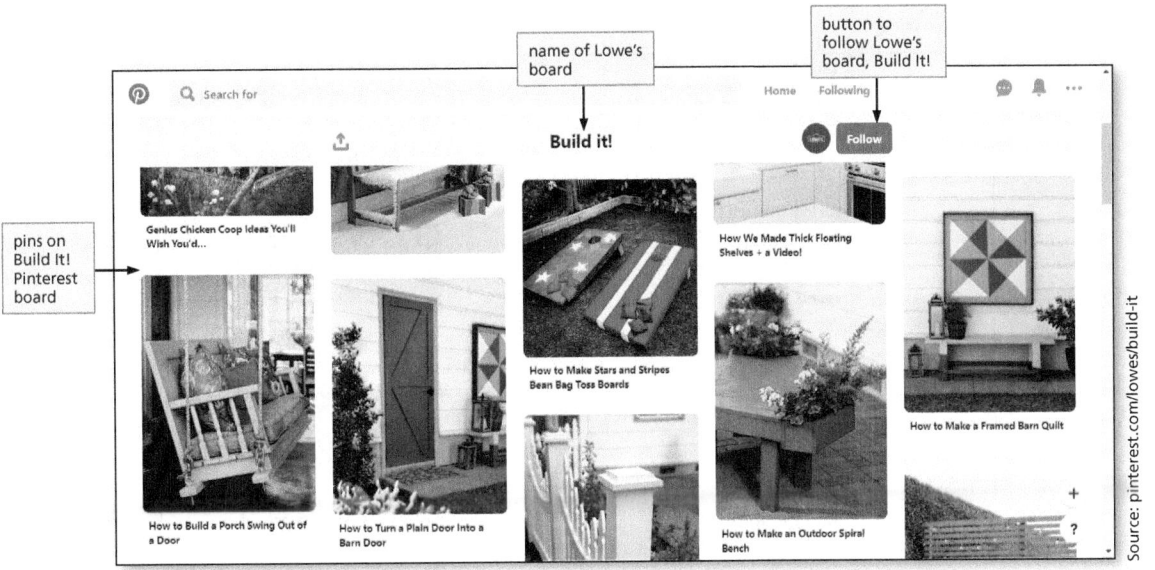

Figure 11–12

Source: pinterest.com/lowes/build-it

Are photographs required for Pinterest?
To place a pin on a Pinterest board, it must include an image, photograph, or video.

Other Social Media Options

Other social media options for your business to explore include LinkedIn, Snapchat, TikTok, Flickr, and many more. The key is to determine which social media outlets are best for your business in attracting new customers. As a business owner, you must also consider the time involved with keeping your social media current and relevant.

Blogs

Many businesses use blogs to promote their business. A **blog** is an online journal, maintained by an individual, group, or a business. The term blog is short for a combination of the words web and log. Businesses use a blog to share new information and to keep their customers engaged. Businesses can also use their blog to discuss current trends or changes in the market. Customers can respond to each blog entry to ask questions or provide feedback. Business owners who maintain a blog should respond to customer comments in a timely manner and keep their blog content fresh. The Apps blog, one of the many blogs available from Tech Crunch, is shown in Figure 11–13.

BTW
Social Media Banned in Certain Countries
Although Facebook has more than two billion users, did you know that Facebook and other forms of social media are banned in several countries? Facebook is banned in China, Iran, and North Korea. Some countries have temporarily banned Facebook when its citizens have posted something derogatory about its government.

How can I start my own blog?
You can use one of many free resources available to start your own blog. If you have a Google account, you can use Google Blogger to create a blog at www.blogger.com. WordPress.org is another popular source for blogs.

Figure 11–13

Adding Facebook and Twitter Links to a Website

Businesses that use social media display social media icons and links on their website. The icons let customers know how to connect with the business on social media. When users click a social media icon, they are redirected to the social media page for the business. Social media links are typically included near the top or bottom of a webpage. Figure 11–14 shows the various social media links near the bottom of the page at noaa.gov.

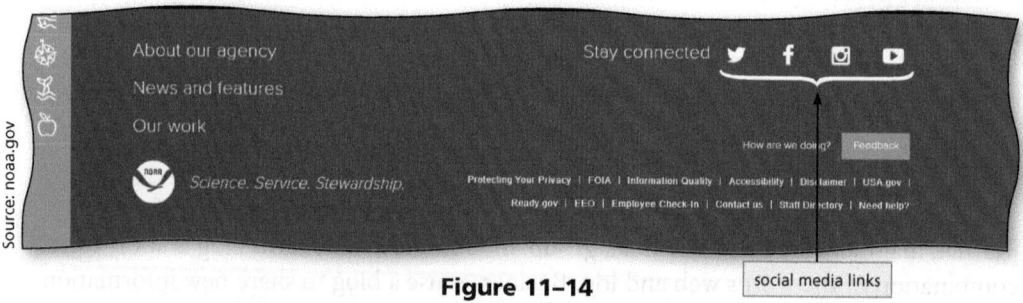

Figure 11–14

The owners of the Forward Fitness Club have decided to promote their business using social media and created a Facebook page, as shown in Figure 11–15, and a Twitter presence, as shown in Figure 11–16.

CONSIDER THIS

Where do I obtain social media icons to use on my website?

Each social media source has a brand or brand assets page, which contains information and guidelines for the use of their icons. Most of these pages include logos available for download.

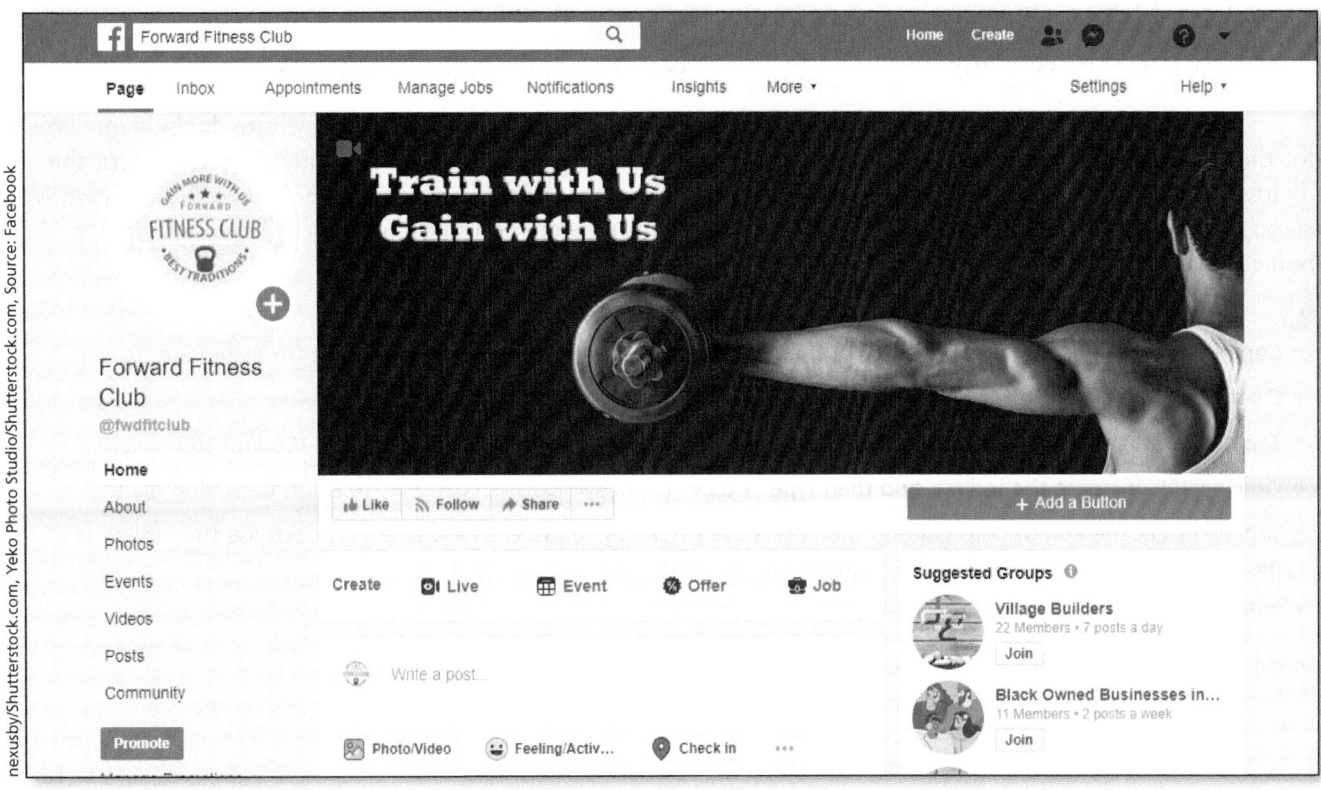

Figure 11–15

Figure 11–16

**I downloaded social media brand assets, but the image dimensions are too large.
How do I change them?**

First, review the brand asset guidelines to determine the minimum dimensions for the icon. You can use a basic image editor, such as Paint, to resize the image dimensions.

To Add Social Media Icons and Links to the Home Page

Add Facebook and Twitter icons to the home page for the Forward Fitness Club website. Include one link for the Facebook icon that links to the Forward Fitness Club's Facebook page, and include another link for the Twitter icon that links to the Forward Fitness Club's Twitter page. *Why? Connecting with customers on social media allows you to connect and engage with your customers.* The following steps add social media icons and links to the home page.

1

- Copy the image files from the chapter11\fitness folder provided with the Data Files to the fitness\images folder.
- Open index.html in your text editor and update the comment with today's date.
- Tap or click at the end of Line 107, and then press the ENTER key twice to insert new Lines 108 and 109.
- On Line 109, increase the indent, and then type `<div class="copyright">` to insert a starting div tag.
- Tap or click at the end of Line 111 and then press the ENTER key to insert a new Line 112, decrease the indent, if necessary, and then type `</div>` to insert an closing div tag.
- Indent Lines 110 and 111 (Figure 11–17).

Q&A What is the purpose of the copyright class?
The copyright class will be formatted in future steps.

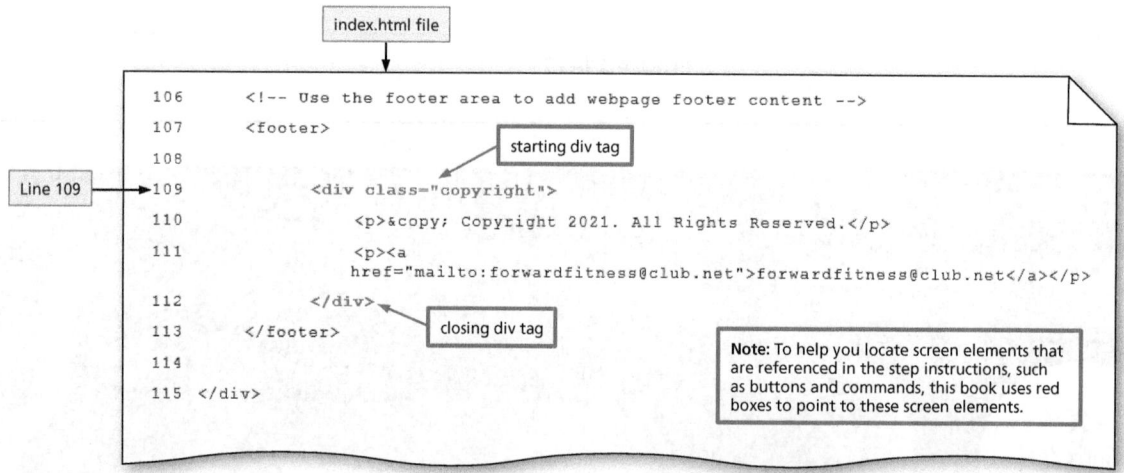

Figure 11–17

2

- Press the ENTER key twice to insert new Lines 113 and 114.
- On Line 114, type `<div class="social">` to insert a starting div tag.
- Press the ENTER key to insert a new Line 115, increase the indent, and then type `<a href="https://www.facebook.com/fwdfitclub" target="_blank"><img src="images/facebook-logo.png" alt="black and white Facebook logo"></a>` to insert an anchor element and an image element.
- Press the ENTER key to insert a new Line 116, and then type `<a href="https://twitter.com/fwdfitclub" target="_blank"><img src="images/twitter-logo.png" alt="black and white Twitter logo"></a>` to insert an anchor element and an image element.
- Press the ENTER key to insert a new Line 117, decrease the indent, and then type `</div>` to insert an ending div tag.
- Press the ENTER key to insert a new, blank Line 118 (Figure 11–18).

Q&A What is the purpose of the social class I just added?
The social class contains the social media icons and links. You will format this class in future steps.

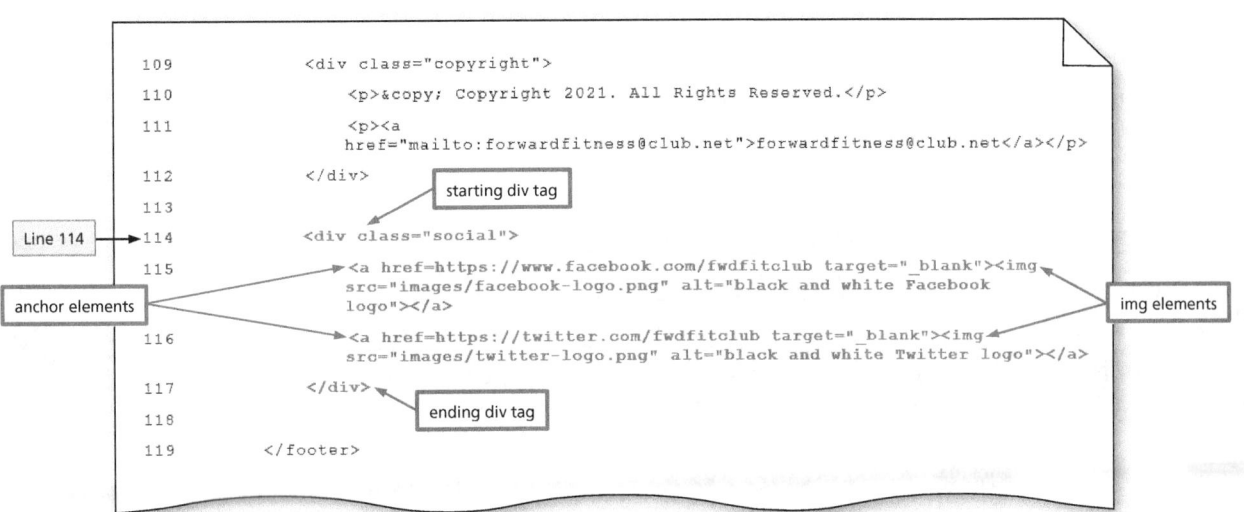

```
109              <div class="copyright">
110                 <p>&copy; Copyright 2021. All Rights Reserved.</p>
111                 <p><a
                    href="mailto:forwardfitness@club.net">forwardfitness@club.net</a></p>
112              </div>
113
114              <div class="social">
115                 <a href=https://www.facebook.com/fwdfitclub target="_blank"><img
                    src="images/facebook-logo.png" alt="black and white Facebook
                    logo"></a>
116                 <a href=https://twitter.com/fwdfitclub target="_blank"><img
                    src="images/twitter-logo.png" alt="black and white Twitter logo"></a>
117              </div>
118          </footer>
119
```

starting div tag

Line 114

anchor elements

img elements

ending div tag

Figure 11–18

3
- Save your changes, open index.html in your browser, adjust the window to the size of a desktop viewport, and then scroll down to view the social media icons (Figure 11–19).

Q&A Why do the Facebook and Twitter icons appear on the left side of the footer?
A style rule has not yet been created to style these elements. You will style them in future steps.

index.html page in desktop viewport

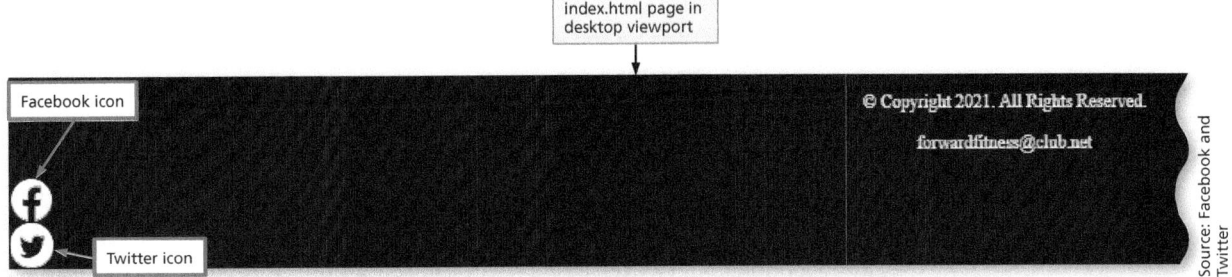

Facebook icon

Twitter icon

© Copyright 2021. All Rights Reserved.

forwardfitness@club.net

Source: Facebook and Twitter

Figure 11–19

4
- Tap or click the Facebook icon to display the Facebook page for the Forward Fitness Club in a new tab (Figure 11–20).

nexusby/Shutterstock.com, Yeko Photo Studio/Shutterstock.com, Facebook

Figure 11–20

● Close the tab.

● Tap or click the Twitter icon to display the Twitter page for the Forward Fitness Club in a new tab (Figure 11–21).

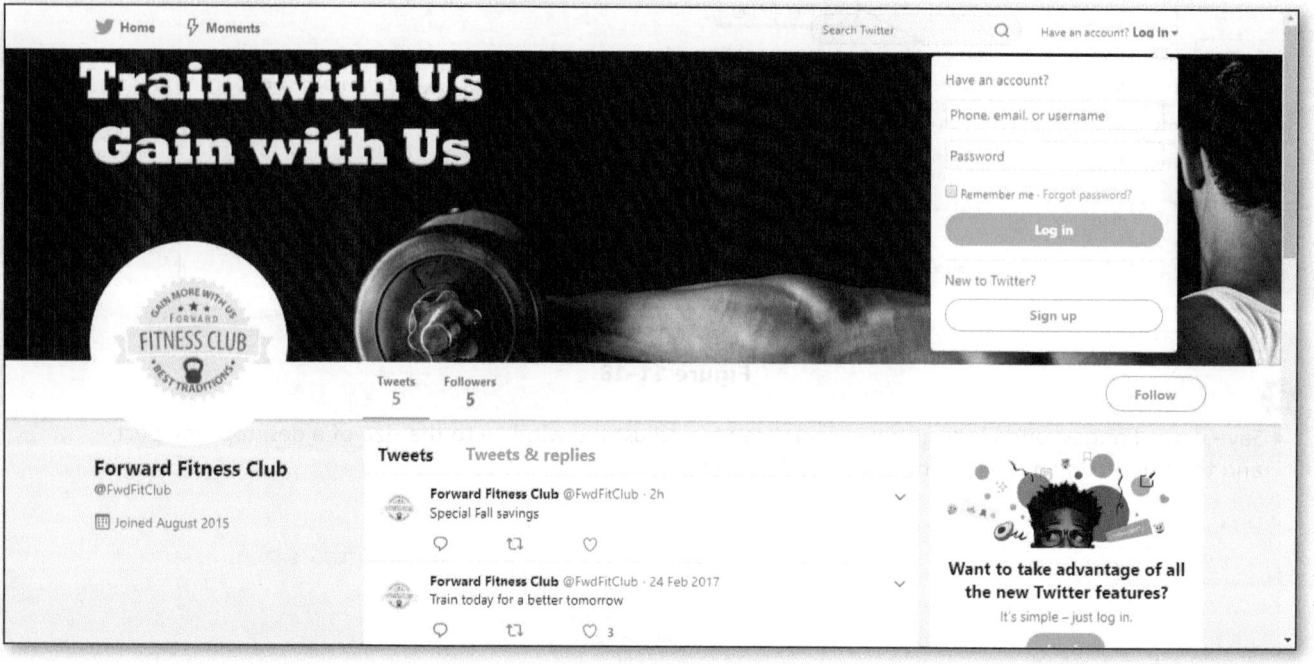

Figure 11–21

To Add Social Media Icons and Links to Webpages

Add Facebook and Twitter icons to all the remaining webpages for the Forward Fitness Club website, including the template. This gives customers access to the social media links from all pages. The following steps add social media icons and links to the About, Classes, Contact, Nutrition, and template webpages for the Forward Fitness Club.

1 Select Lines 107 through 119 on the index.html page, and then press CTRL+C to copy the code.

2 Open about.html, select Lines 127 through 130, and then press CTRL+V to paste the code. Save your changes and close the file.

3 Open classes.html, select Lines 140 through 143, and then press CTRL+V to paste the code. Save your changes and close the file.

4 Open contact.html, select Lines 122 through 125, and then press CTRL+V to paste the code. Save your changes and close the file.

5 Open nutrition.html, select Lines 107 through 110, and then press CTRL+V to paste the code. Save your changes and close the file.

6 Open template.html, select Lines 54 through 57, and then press CTRL+V to paste the code (Figure 11–22).

7 Save your changes and close the file.

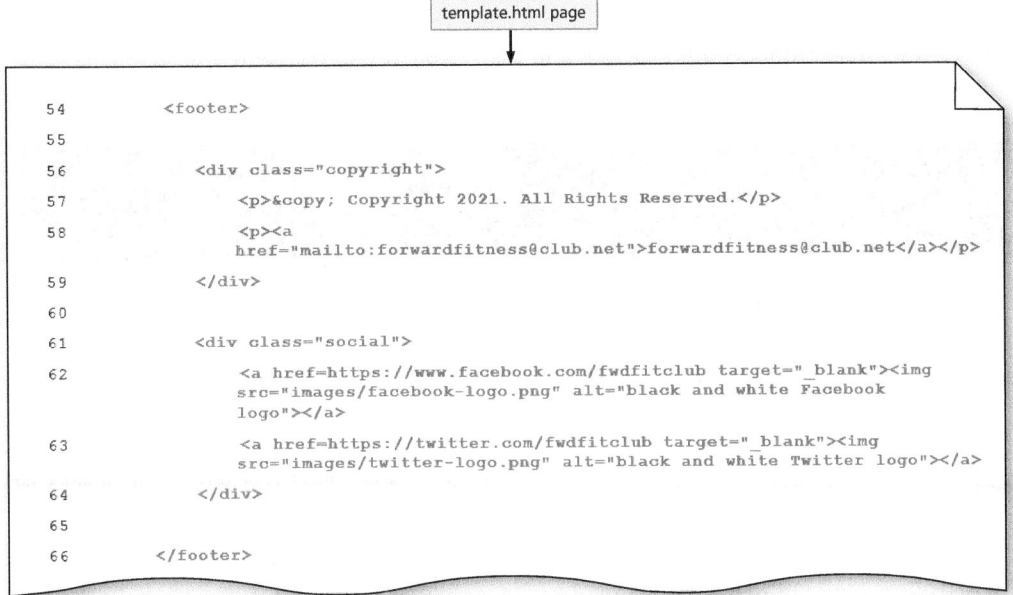

Figure 11–22

To Style the Copyright Class

You created a **div** element with the **copyright** class attribute within the footer, which contains the copyright information and the email address and link. Now you must format this **copyright** class to improve its appearance on the webpage. *Why? Style the copyright class to appear to the left of the social div.* Modify the style rule for the footer p selector. Change the selector from p to .copyright. Modify the padding value declaration. Create a new declaration to float left and specify its width. The following steps modify a style rule for the **copyright** class in the styles.css file.

- Open styles.css in your text editor and update the comment with today's date.
- Locate the style rule for the footer p selector that begins on Line 216. Replace the p selector with the **.copyright** selector.
- On Line 220, change the padding value to **2% 4%**.
- Tap or click at the end of Line 220, and then press the ENTER key to insert a new Line 221.
- On Line 221, type **float: left;** to insert a new declaration.
- Press the ENTER key to insert a new Line 222, and then type **width: 75%;** to insert a new declaration (Figure 11–23).

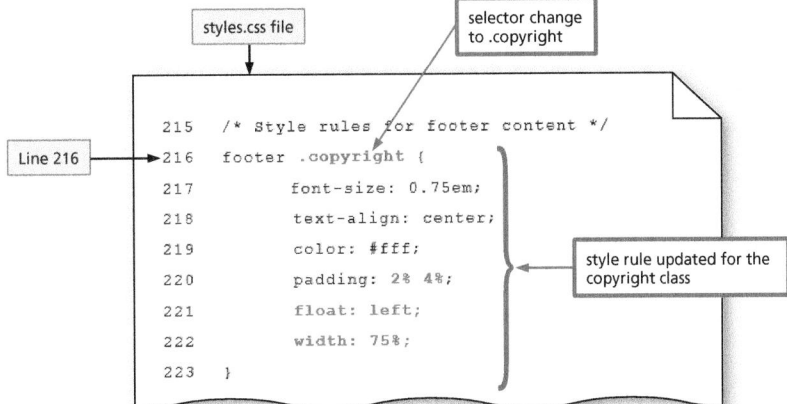

Figure 11–23

• Save your changes, open or refresh index.html in your browser, and then scroll down to view the social media icons (Figure 11–24).

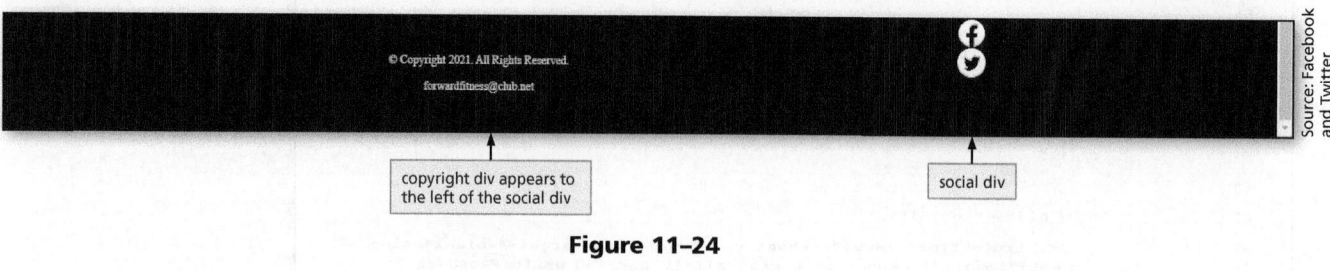

copyright div appears to the left of the social div

social div

Figure 11–24

To Style the Social Class

You created a `div` element with the class value `social` within the footer element. The new div contains the Facebook and Twitter icons and links to social media pages for the Forward Fitness Club. Style the `social` class to float right, specify a width, and apply padding. Style the anchor elements within the `social` class by applying padding and setting the display to an inline-block. *Why? Format the social class and its images to improve their appearance on the webpage.* After you style the `social` class and specify a float property, some content within the footer area will not be visible. To correct this issue, specify an overflow property with a value of auto for the footer element within the desktop media query, as this will prevent the content within the social div element from overflowing. The following steps create two new style rules for within the styles.css file.

• In the styles.css file, tap or click at the end of Line 228, and then press the ENTER key twice to insert new Lines 229 and 230.

• On Line 230, type `.social {` to insert a new selector.

• Press the ENTER key to insert a new Line 231, increase the indent, and then type `float: right;` to insert a declaration.

• Press the ENTER key to insert a new Line 232, and then type `width: 20%;` to insert a declaration.

• Press the ENTER key to insert a new Line 233, and then type `padding: 2%;` to insert a declaration.

• Press the ENTER key to insert a new Line 234, decrease the indent, and then type `}` to close the style rule (Figure 11–25).

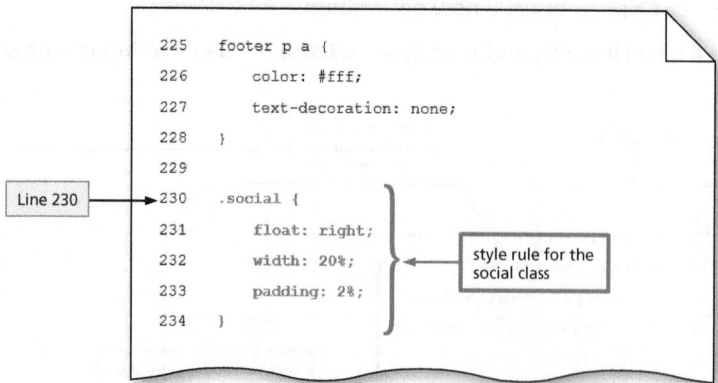

```
225    footer p a {
226        color: #fff;
227        text-decoration: none;
228    }
229
230    .social {
231        float: right;
232        width: 20%;
233        padding: 2%;
234    }
```

Line 230

style rule for the social class

Figure 11–25

2

- Press the ENTER key twice to insert new Lines 235 and 236.
- On Line 236, type `.social img {` to insert a new selector.
- Press the ENTER key to insert a new Line 237, increase the indent, and then type `display: inline-block;` to insert a declaration.
- Press the ENTER key to insert a new Line 238, and then type `padding: 5%;` to insert a declaration.
- Press the ENTER key to insert a new Line 239, decrease the indent, and then type `}` to insert a closing brace (Figure 11–26).

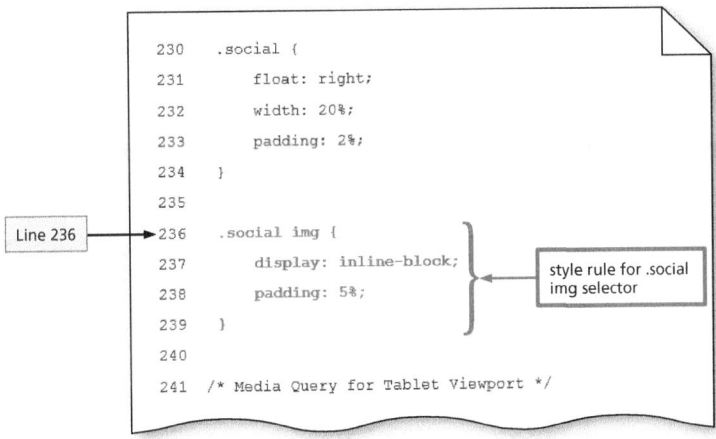

```
230    .social {
231        float: right;
232        width: 20%;
233        padding: 2%;
234    }
235
236    .social img {
237        display: inline-block;
238        padding: 5%;
239    }
240
241    /* Media Query for Tablet Viewport */
```

Line 236 → 236

style rule for .social img selector

Figure 11–26

3

- Save your changes, open or refresh index.html in your browser, and then scroll down to view the social media icons (Figure 11–27).

index.html page in desktop viewport

Welcome to Forward Fitness Club. Our mission is to help our clients meet their fitness and nutrition goals.

If you have struggled with getting healthy and need the motivation and resources to make a healthy lifestyle change, contact us today. Our facility includes state-of-the-art equipment, convenient group training classes, and nutrition tips and information to keep you healthy.

We provide a FREE, one-week membership to experience the benefits of our equipment and facility. This one-week trial gives you complete access to our equipment, training classes, and nutrition planning. Contact us today to **start your free trial!**

© Copyright 2021. All Rights Reserved.
forwardfitness@club.net

Figure 11–27

social media icons

4

- Tap or click the About Us link in the nav area, and then scroll down to view the social media icons.

- Tap or click each page link in the nav area to view all the webpages and to confirm that the social media icons appear at the bottom of each page.

- Use Google Chrome's device mode to display the Contact Us page in a tablet viewport (Figure 11–28).

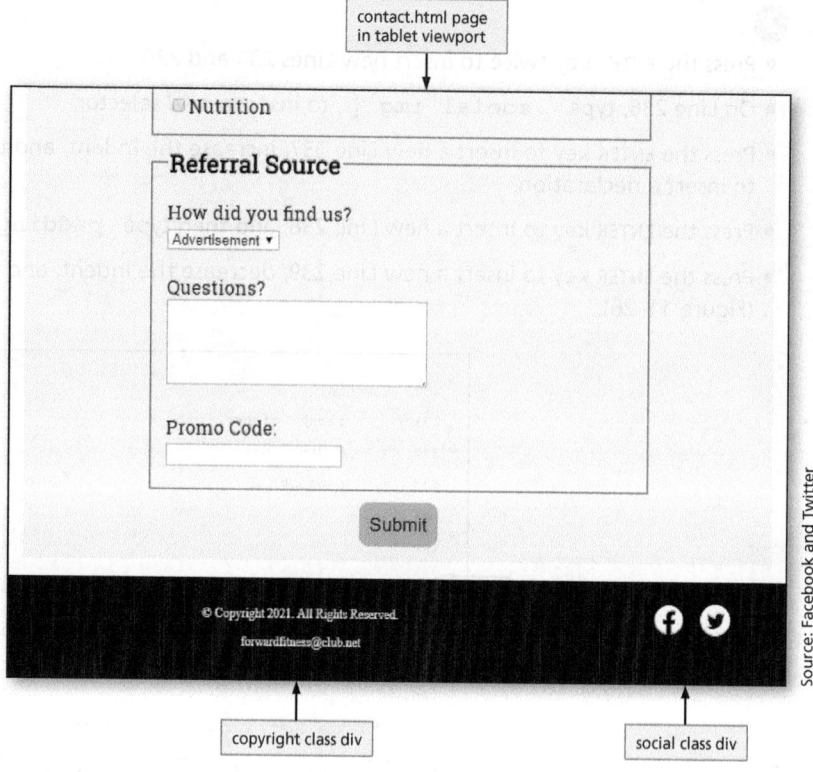

contact.html page
in tablet viewport

copyright class div

social class div

Source: Facebook and Twitter

Figure 11–28

5

- Change the device mode to display a mobile viewport (Figure 11–29).

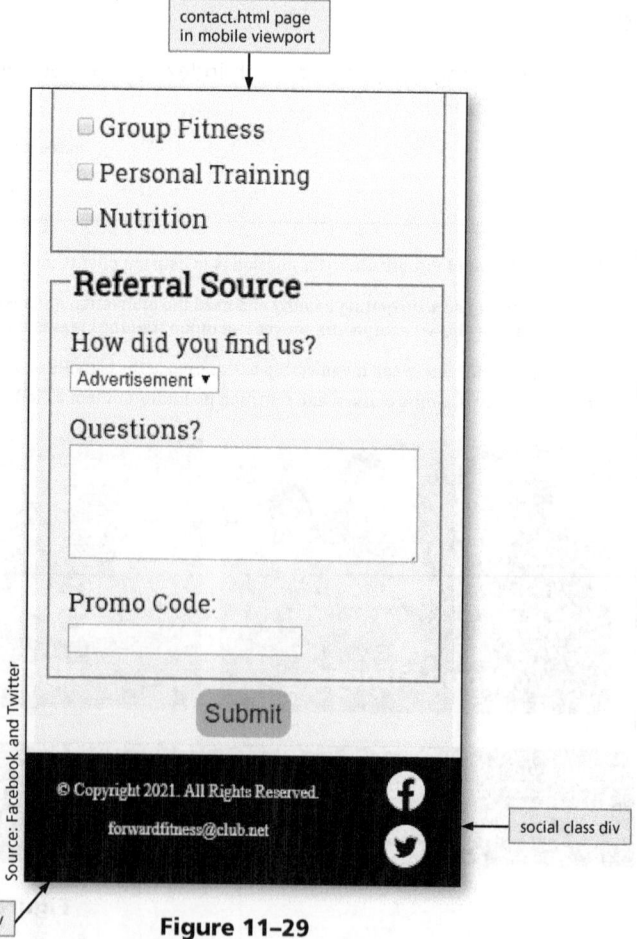

contact.html page
in mobile viewport

social class div

copyright class div

Source: Facebook and Twitter

Figure 11–29

Finding a Website

Finding a website is easy when you know the website address. But how do you locate a website when you do not know the URL? The answer is a search engine.

Search Engines

Many people use a **search engine** to find specific businesses or content on the web. A search engine is an online tool that searches for websites based on keywords users enter. Search engines provide a search form where users type keywords. Search engines use **robots** (also known as bots or spiders), which are programs that run automated tasks on the Internet, to traverse the web in search of the keywords entered by users. As the robots browse the web, they index and organize their findings, which are stored in a database. The robots view and may store webpage titles, meta tag descriptions, and h1 or other heading element content. Popular search engines include Google.com, Bing.com, Ask.com, and Yahoo.com, as shown in Figure 11–30.

(a) Google

(b) Bing

(c) Ask

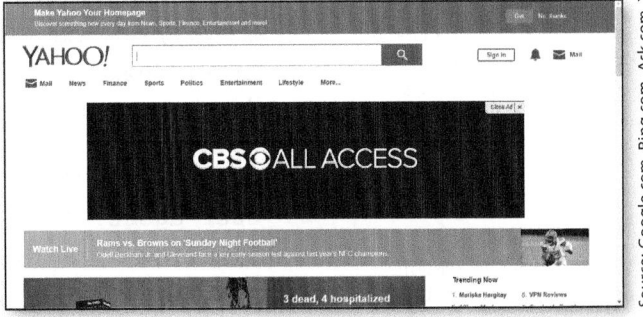

(d) Yahoo!

Source: Google.com, Bing.com, Ask.com, Yahoo.com

Figure 11–30

Google is the most popular search engine used. In fact, according to statcounter .com, Google has over 90 percent worldwide market share when it comes to search engines. Bing is in second place with just over 2 percent market share.

BTW

Baidu Search Engine
Baidu is a popular search engine in China. Baidu often referred to as "China's Google."

Search Engine Optimization

Search engine optimization (SEO) is the process of increasing the amount of traffic to your website by improving the ranking of your site in search engine results pages (SERPs). Your **rank** is the position of your webpage link, as displayed on the SERP.

Each time your webpage link appears in a SERP of a related query, it creates what is called an **impression**. The more impressions you have in a SERP, the higher the chances of a user visiting your website. Many business have learned the art of effective SEO and have significantly boosted the amount of traffic to their websites.

Optimizing a website involves editing the content and HTML code in the webpage to increase its relevant keywords and to remove barriers to the page-indexing functions of search engines.

Effective SEO involves several key tasks. First, brainstorm keywords that describe your business and write them down. Use these keywords within your domain name, page titles, heading elements, and meta description tag. Research your competitors and note keywords used within their website. For example, Forward Fitness Club might brainstorm the keywords fitness, gym, nutrition, fitness equipment, personal training, free trial, and fitness classes. The business should then examine its page titles, heading elements, and meta tags and incorporate these keywords throughout the website pages.

The title element is very important when it comes to SEO. Use unique titles on each page. Begin with the most important keyword for the page, followed by a secondary keyword that pertains to the page content. End with the company or brand name. This helps identify the business name and is commonly displayed in the SERP. Keep your title between 50–60 characters. The following is a suggested title format:

```
First Keyword - Second Keyword | Name of Business or Brand
```

Optimize your images. Because robots cannot read text on images, be sure to use meaningful alt text with your images. Use keywords within your alt text. For example, the Forward Fitness Club uses the fitness and nutrition keywords in some alt text, but the current alt text will be reviewed to maximize its optimization strategy.

Create a sitemap and a robots.txt file. A sitemap instructs the search engine where to find important webpage content. This helps search engine bots or spiders to quickly index your website content. The sitemap file can be a text file (txt) or XML file. The following is an example of a sitemap:

```
http://www.exampledomain.com/index.html
http://www.exampledomain.com/about.html
http://www.exampledomain.com/services.html
```

The robots.txt file lets the search engine robots know which pages it may or may not index. It is a simple text file. The search engine robot will look for this file before it begins indexing the website. The following is an example of a robots.txt file:

```
User-agent: *
Disallow: /login.html
Disallow: /signup.html
```

In this example, the robots.txt file instructs the search engine robot to not index the login.html page or the signup.html page. If a page does not contain helpful content about the website, such as a login page or a sign-up page, the robot does not need to index it. You should also include a robots.txt file if you have a directory that needs to remain private, such as an admin directory. Save your robots.txt file within the website root directory.

BTW

Google Webmaster Guidelines

Google provides webmaster guidelines at support.google .com/webmasters. On this page, search for "webmaster guidelines." The Webmaster Guidelines page includes more information about preparing sitemap and robots.txt files for Google.

BTW

Search Engines

Both Google and Yahoo! provide information about optimizing your websites. Review their webmaster guidelines and resources for ideas on registering with their search engines.

CONSIDER THIS

How does Google generate its results page?
Google uses algorithms to generate its search results page. These algorithms are updated on a regular basis. Some of Google's named algorithms are Panda, Penguin, Hummingbird, Pigeon, Pirate, and Mobile-Friendly.

Meta Tags

The `meta` tag name derives from the word, **metadata**, which is information about data. You already included the following `meta` tag in the initial HTML code that you inserted into every webpage:

```
<meta charset="utf-8">
```

You included this element in all webpages throughout the book. As mentioned earlier, this statement declares the character encoding as UTF-8. The Unicode Transformation Format (UTF) is a compressed format that allows computers to display and manipulate text. When the browser encounters this meta tag, it displays the webpage properly, based on the particular UTF-8 encoding embedded in the tag. UTF-8 is the preferred encoding standard for webpages, email, and other applications.

You have also used a `meta` tag to specify a viewport to support mobile devices.

Besides specifying the character encoding and viewport, the `meta` tag also allows you to specify the author, a description, and keywords for the webpage through the use of the `name` and `content` attributes. The `name` attribute identifies the type of information in the `content` attribute, and the `content` attribute identifies the specific phrases or words that you want to appear as metadata. You must use these two attributes together; the `content` attribute cannot be defined if the `name` attribute is not defined. The following is an example of an author meta tag:

```
<meta name="author" content="Jordan Wells">
```

In this meta tag example, `author` is the value for the `name` attribute. The `content` attribute specifies the name of the author, in this case, Jordan Wells. The following is an example of a description meta tag:

```
<meta name="description" content="Forward Fitness Club is
an elite fitness center dedicated to helping our clients achieve
their fitness and nutrition goals.">
```

In the description meta tag example, `description` is the value for the `name` attribute. The value of the `content` attribute is a descriptive sentence about the Forward Fitness Club. The description is what some search engines add below your webpage URL in the search results to describe the content of the webpage. Google uses the description meta tag and the webpage title to create a snippet of information about the page that displays in the SERP results. An example of a Google SERP list is shown in Figure 11–31. Visitors often read the snippet to determine whether they want to click that particular link (or URL) in the list of URLs in the search engine results.

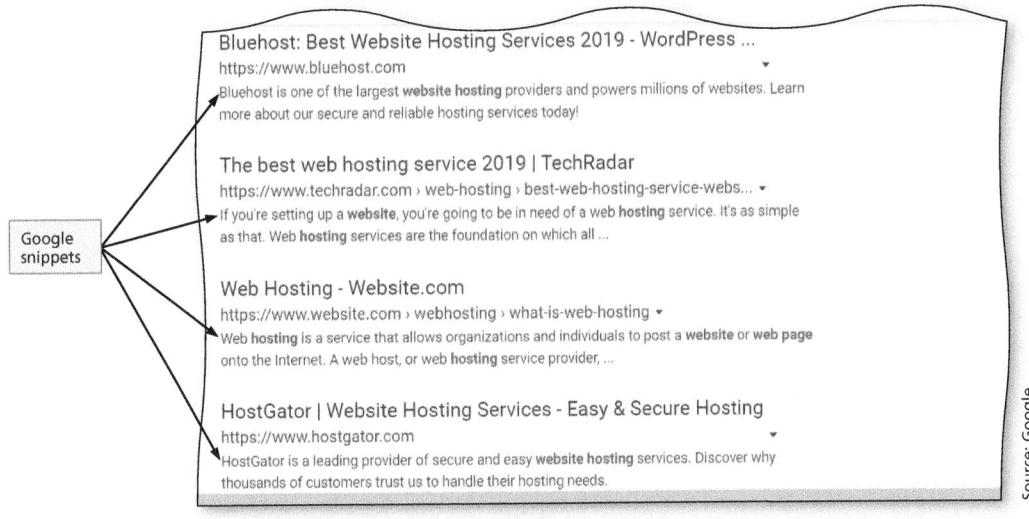

Figure 11–31

Source: Google

The following is an example of a keywords meta tag:

```
<meta name="keywords" content="fitness, gym, group fitness,
nutrition">
```

In this meta tag example, `keywords` is the value for the name attribute. The `content` attribute specifies keywords that describe the website content, in this case, fitness, gym, group fitness, and nutrition. The keywords meta tag used to be a common standard, but it is not heavily used today. Search engine companies discovered that many websites used keywords that did not pertain to its websites. As a result, many search engines, including Google, have stopped using the keywords meta tag in their search algorithms. Give focus to two keywords within your meta description and consistently use these keywords within a description meta tag across your webpages. Your description meta tag should not exceed 160 characters.

The Google Search Console provides several tools to help businesses with its SEO performance. Visit search.google.com/search-console/about for more information.

In this project, you will use the description meta tag to provide search engines information about the content of the Forward Fitness Club website. You will also modify the title elements to be more descriptive and unique for each page within the website. You will also create a sitemap file to aid search engine robots with indexing your webpage content.

To Modify Titles and Add a Description Meta Tag to a Webpage

1 INSERT & STYLE SOCIAL MEDIA LINKS | 2 MODIFY TITLE & INSERT META TAG | 3 CREATE SITEMAP FILE
4 PUBLISH WEBSITE | 5 CREATE SKIP TO CONTENT LINK | 6 MINIFY CSS FILE

To assist with SEO for the Forward Fitness Club website, modify the title element on each page to be descriptive and unique. Also add a description meta tag to the home, About Us, Classes, Nutrition, and Contact Us pages. The description meta tag is placed within the head element and contains several keywords to improve SEO. Each description meta tag describes the purpose of a particular page for the Forward Fitness Club website. Using description meta tags that contain consistent keywords on pages throughout a website helps to improve SERP. *Why? Most search engines use the title element and description meta tag to display information about the website in its search results.* The following steps modify the title element and add a description meta tag to the Forward Fitness Club webpages.

- Open index.html in your text editor, if necessary.

- Tap or click before the word Forward within the title element on Line 5, and then type `Complete Fitness – Free Trial |` to update the title element.

- Tap or click at the end of Line 8, and then press the ENTER key to insert a new Line 9.

- On Line 9, type `<meta name="description" content="The Forward Fitness Club is an elite fitness center dedicated to helping clients achieve their fitness and nutrition goals.">` to insert a new meta tag (Figure 11–32).

Q&A What is the | symbol?
The | is known as the "pipe." It is located with the backslash key on your keyboard.

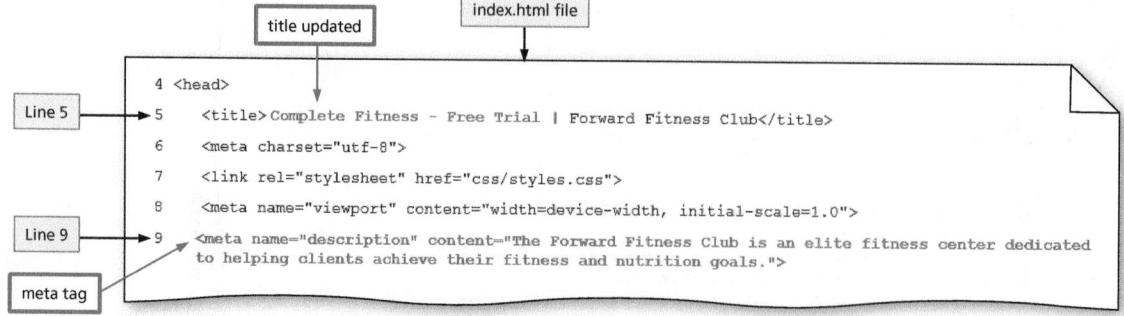

Figure 11–32

2

- Save your changes and close index.html.

- Open about.html in your text editor and update the comment with today's date.

- Tap or click before the word Forward within the title element on Line 5, and then type `Fitness Equipment - Personal Training |` to update the title element.

- Tap or click at the end of Line 8, and then press the ENTER key to insert a new Line 9.

- On Line 9, type `<meta name="description" content="Forward Fitness Club has state-of-the-art fitness equipment and provides personal training.">` to insert a new meta tag (Figure 11–33).

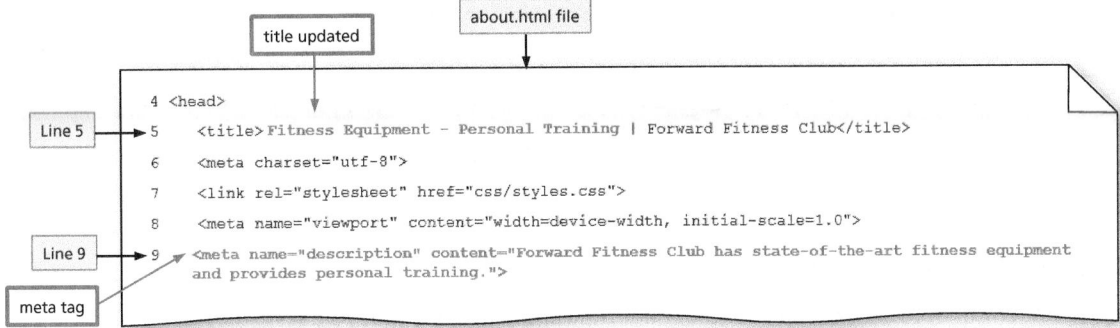

```
                    title updated              about.html file

        4 <head>
Line 5  5     <title>Fitness Equipment - Personal Training | Forward Fitness Club</title>
        6     <meta charset="utf-8">
        7     <link rel="stylesheet" href="css/styles.css">
        8     <meta name="viewport" content="width=device-width, initial-scale=1.0">
Line 9  9     <meta name="description" content="Forward Fitness Club has state-of-the-art fitness equipment
              and provides personal training.">
meta tag
```

Figure 11–33

3

- Save your changes and close about.html.

- Open classes.html in your text editor and update the comment with today's date.

- Tap or click before the word Forward within the title element on Line 5, and then type `Fitness Class Schedule |` to update the title element.

- Tap or click at the end of Line 8, and then press the ENTER key to insert a new Line 9.

- On Line 9, type `<meta name="description" content="Forward Fitness Club has many fitness classes to meet your needs, including boot camp, cardio, kickboxing, spinning, yoga, and Zumba.">` to insert a new meta tag (Figure 11–34).

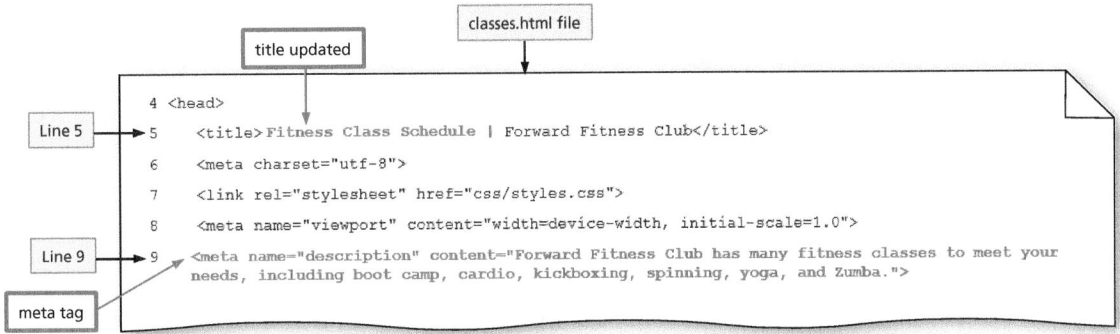

```
                    title updated              classes.html file

        4 <head>
Line 5  5     <title>Fitness Class Schedule | Forward Fitness Club</title>
        6     <meta charset="utf-8">
        7     <link rel="stylesheet" href="css/styles.css">
        8     <meta name="viewport" content="width=device-width, initial-scale=1.0">
Line 9  9     <meta name="description" content="Forward Fitness Club has many fitness classes to meet your
              needs, including boot camp, cardio, kickboxing, spinning, yoga, and Zumba.">
meta tag
```

Figure 11–34

4

- Save your changes and close classes.html.

- Open nutrition.html in your text editor and update the comment with today's date.

- Tap or click before the word Forward within the title element on Line 5, and then type `Nutrition Guidance |` to update the title element.

- Tap or click at the end of Line 8, and then press the ENTER key to insert a new Line 9.

- On Line 9, type `<meta name="description" content="Forward Fitness Club provides nutrition guides and meal planning to help you meet your nutrition goals.">` to insert a new meta tag (Figure 11–35).

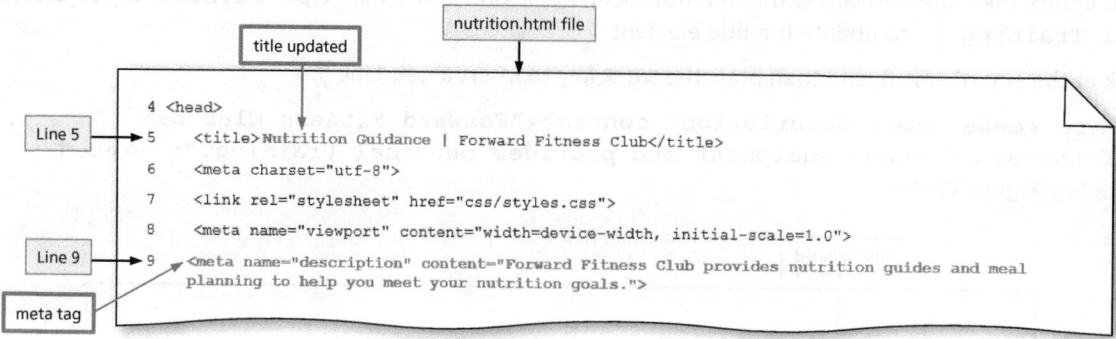

Figure 11–35

- Save your changes and close nutrition.html.

- Open contact.html in your text editor and update the comment with today's date.

- Tap or click before the word Forward within the title element on Line 5, and then type `Contact Us – Location |` to update the title element.

- Tap or click at the end of Line 8, and then press the ENTER key to insert a new Line 9.

- On Line 9, type `<meta name="description" content="Forward Fitness Club provides a complimentary one-week trial membership. Contact us today to learn more.">` to insert a new meta tag.

- Save your changes (Figure 11–36).

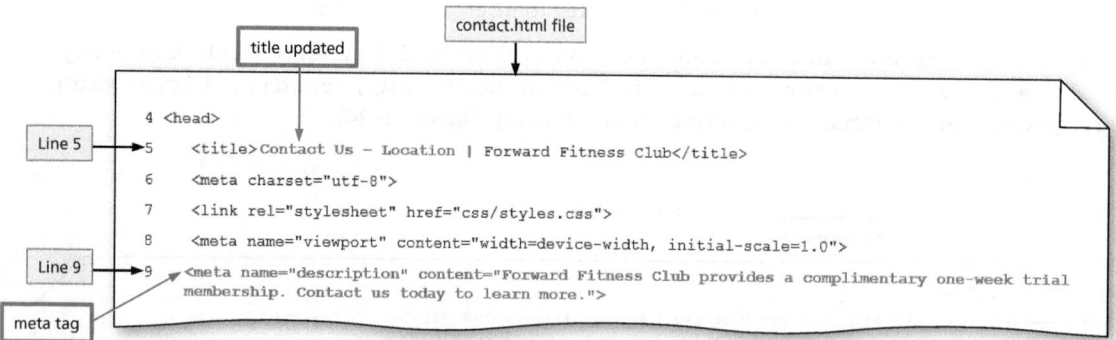

Figure 11–36

To Create a Sitemap File

1 INSERT & STYLE SOCIAL MEDIA LINKS | 2 MODIFY TITLE & INSERT META TAG | **3 CREATE SITEMAP FILE**
4 PUBLISH WEBSITE | 5 CREATE SKIP TO CONTENT LINK | 6 MINIFY CSS FILE

Now that you have improved the Forward Fitness webpages for SEO, the next step is to create a sitemap file. *Why? This file provides search engine robots with information about where to find webpage content.* The following steps create a sitemap file.

- Use your text editor to create a new text file named sitemap.txt. Save it within the fitness folder.

- On Line 1, type `http://www.exampledomain.com/index.html` to specify the location of the home page within the website.

- Press the ENTER key to insert Line 2, and then type `http://www.exampledomain.com/about.html` to specify the location of the About Us page within the website.

- Press the ENTER key to insert Line 3, and then type `http://www.exampledomain.com/classes.html` to specify the location of the Classes page within the website.

- Press the ENTER key to insert Line 4, and then type `http://www.exampledomain.com/nutrition.html` to specify the location of the Nutrition page within the website.

- Press the ENTER key to insert Line 5, and then type `http://www.exampledomain.com/contact.html` to specify the location of the Contact Us page within the website.

- Save your changes (Figure 11–37).

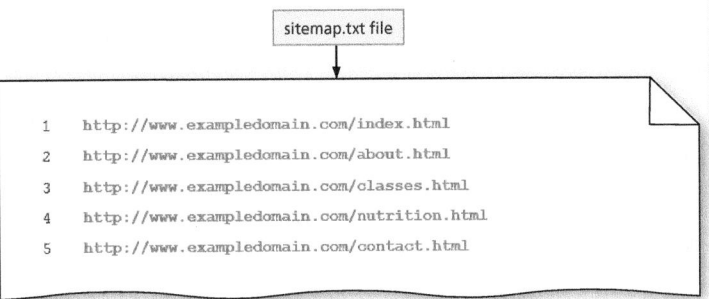

Figure 11–37

Break Point: If you want to take a break, this is a good place to do so. You can exit the text editor now. To resume at a later time, run your text editor, open index.html, and continue following the steps from this location forward.

Publishing a Website

When you finish developing your website, the next step is to register a domain name, determine a web hosting strategy, and then publish the website to make it accessible to everyone with an Internet connection. To do so, you need to select and register a domain name, select a web hosting service, and then transfer the website files to the host's server.

Domain Name

A **domain name** is the server name portion of a URL. You can use the domain name of the server on which you publish your webpages together with a path to your specific pages for your webpage address. However, this webpage address option can result in a URL that is long, hard to remember, and not representative of your website or business.

As an alternative, you can register your own domain name on the Internet for a fee. A unique domain name can make it easier for visitors to find your webpages. The Forward Fitness Club wants to register a unique domain name for their website, as long as you can find a name that is both suitable and available.

When selecting and registering a domain name, make sure it represents your business. Brainstorm and make a list of the top five keywords or phrases that best describe your business. For example, "forwardfitness" or "forwardfitclub" would be an ideal domain name for the Forward Fitness Club. A short and concise domain name makes it more memorable. Long domain names are more difficult to remember. Avoid the use of hyphens within a domain name, as this make the domain name harder to pronounce and less memorable.

The .com top-level domain (TLD) name is preferred for businesses. Many users assume that business websites end with .com, so using that TLD makes it easier for visitors to find your website. However, there are times when the .com TLD you desire is already taken. In this instance, you could consider several open, top-level domain names. An open TLD means that any person or entity can register with the domain name. The .com TLD is not always the best option for every website. For example, most nonprofit organizations use the .org TLD. Likewise, most educational institutions use the .edu TLD. Table 11–1 lists common TLDs and their original purpose.

Table 11–1 Common Top-Level Domains	
Name	**Original Purpose**
.com	Commercial
.biz	Business or commercial
.net	Network-related domains
.co	Business or commercial
.org	Nonprofit organizations
.edu	Educational institutions
.gov	Restricted use by the United States government
.mil	Restricted use by the United States military
.me	Personal website

To determine if the domain name you are considering is available, you can start your search at InterNIC, www.internic.net. InterNIC is a registered service mark of the U.S. Department of Commerce. The InterNIC website is operated by the Internet Corporation for Assigned Names and Numbers (ICANN) to provide information to the public regarding Internet domain name registration services. ICANN is responsible for managing and coordinating the Domain Name System (DNS) so that every Internet address is unique, and so that all users of the Internet can find valid addresses.

CONSIDER THIS

Do domain names expire?

Yes. When you purchase a domain name, note the expiration date. If you do not renew the domain name, it may go to an auction to be sold.

Website Hosting

The next step in publishing your website is to find a hosting service. One popular option is to use a company that charges for website hosting services. Of the thousands of companies that provide web hosting services, most charge a monthly fee, but some offer free web hosting in exchange for advertising on your website. Bluehost .com, as shown in Figure 11–38, is one of many web hosting companies.

Another option is to set up and maintain your own web server. You would have to know enough about the technology to set it up and keep it running.

Whether you choose to use a web hosting service or to set up your own web server, you need to answer the following questions:

• What is the total cost? Compare monthly or annual costs; the highest cost may not always provide the best service.

• How much space is available to you? Assess your current needs (i.e., file sizes, number of graphics and other media) and your future needs (i.e., how much more information you will create).

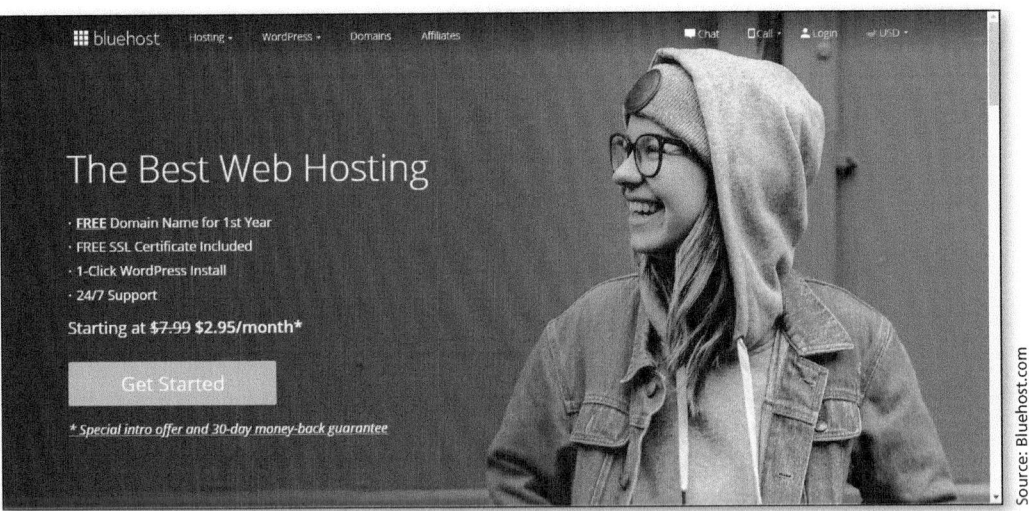

Source: Bluehost.com

Figure 11–38

- How fast is the connection speed? The speed of the connection to the Internet determines how efficiently you can serve your visitors.
- How much total bandwidth transfer is available? The number and size of webpages in your website together with the number and size of graphical images is important to consider. Lack of efficient bandwidth can delay the time it takes for a page to load. Pages must load quickly in order to maintain user interest.
- Is technical support provided? You may occasionally need help, especially when you first publish the site.
- Are tracking services provided? Many hosting companies allow you to see how visitors use your website by viewing a tracking log.

After you have selected a web hosting service, you need to transfer your files to the host's server.

BTW
Free Web Hosting Services
There are several free options for noncommercial web hosting services, including GitHub pages.

Publishing a Website

After you register a domain name and secure a web hosting strategy, the next step is to publish your website so that it is accessible to the world. When you **publish** your website, you transfer your website files to a web server. Visitors can then access the website by typing the domain name into the address bar on a browser. One way to upload files to a web server is to use a File Transfer Protocol (FTP) client program. An **FTP client** is software used to transfer files from one computer to another over the Internet. This is the most common method for transferring website files and folders to a web server. FTP uses one port to communicate over a network, typically port 20, and another port, typically 21, for control commands. For a list of port numbers used on the Internet, visit iana.org/assignments/port-numbers.

BTW
SSH and SFTP
SSH stands for secure shell and is a secure way to move data between two endpoints. SFTP stands for SSH File Transfer Protocol and uses SSH to securely move data between two endpoints.

FTP Clients

Like other types of software, some FTP clients are free and some are for purchase. FileZilla is a free FTP option, available for download at filezilla-project .org. The FileZilla FTP client software is available for several OS platforms, including Windows, macOS, and Linux. Figure 11–39 shows the FileZilla FTP client software. The Quickconnect bar is located near the top of the user interface. Use the Quickconnect bar to enter the name of the host (your domain name), your username

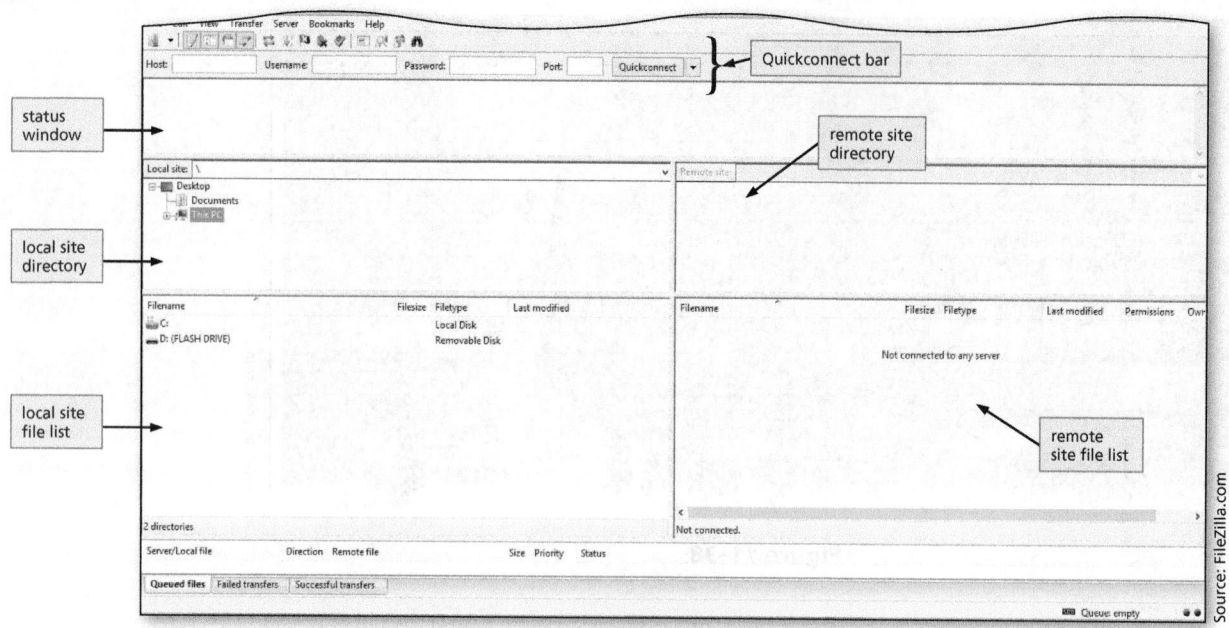

Figure 11–39

and password, as well as the port number. If you paid for a web hosting service, you establish an FTP username and password through your web hosting service provider. Use the local site directory window, located on the left, to navigate folders and files on your local computer. Once you navigate to your website folder, its contents are displayed in the lower-left window, in the local site file list. The remote site directory window, located on the right, displays the root folder for the website on the remote web server. After you publish the website to a remote web server, its folders and files are displayed in the lower-right window. To publish local files to the remote server, select the local folders and files in the local site file list, and then drag them to the remote site file list window or select Transfer on the application menu.

Another popular free FTP client is WinSCP, available for download at winscp .net. WinSCP is for the Windows platform.

TO DOWNLOAD AND INSTALL AN FTP CLIENT

Unless you have direct access to the web hosting server, you will need an FTP client to upload and publish your website files and folders. Ask your instructor if there is a preferred FTP client to use for this course. If no preference is specified, download one of the FTP clients previously discussed. If you wanted to download and install the FileZilla FTP client, you would perform the following steps.

1. Use your browser to access the website for FileZilla at filezilla-project.org.
2. Tap or click the link to download the FileZilla client.
3. Locate the option to install the client for your operating system, and then tap or click the appropriate link to download the installation package.
4. When the download is complete, open the downloaded package to begin the install.
5. Follow the instructions within the wizard window to complete the installation.
6. Run FileZilla when finished.

You need several key pieces of information to publish your website, including a URL or domain name, an FTP username and password, and a port number.

If you secured a web hosting service provider, contact your provider to obtain this information. Many times, you can establish your own FTP username and password by logging into your web hosting service provider's website. Your institution may have web server space available to you as a student. Contact your instructor to request this information. A few web hosting service providers offer free web hosting services. Ask your instructor if there is a preferred, free web hosting service to use.

To Start FileZilla and Connect to a Remote Server

1 INSERT & STYLE SOCIAL MEDIA LINKS | 2 MODIFY TITLE & INSERT META TAG | 3 CREATE SITEMAP FILE
4 PUBLISH WEBSITE | **5 CREATE SKIP TO CONTENT LINK** | **6 MINIFY CSS FILE**

Before you can publish the Forward Fitness Club website, you must use an FTP client to connect to a remote web server. *Why? You need access to a remote server to publish a website.* Before you begin the following steps, ask your instructor if your school has a preferred web hosting provider and request the login information. The following steps start FileZilla, based on a typical installation in Windows 10, and connect to a remote web server.

• Type **filezilla** in the Search text box and watch the Search results appear in the Apps list (Figure 11–40).

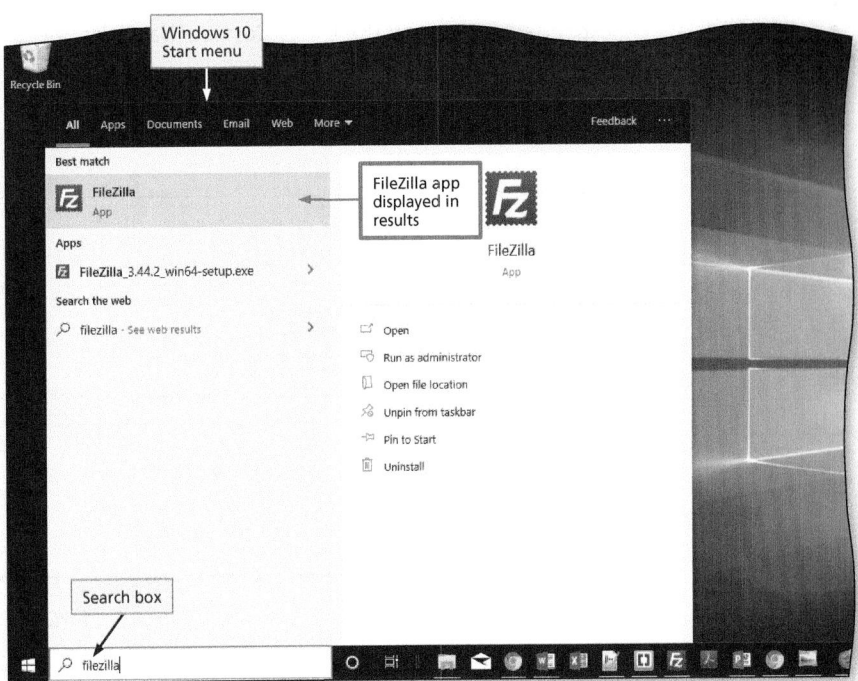

Figure 11–40

2

• Tap or click FileZilla in the search results to start FileZilla.

• In the Host text box on the Quick Connect bar, type the URL of the server to complete the field.

• Type your username in the Username text box to complete the field.

• Type your password in the Password text box to complete the field.

• Type **21** in the Port text box to complete the field (Figure 11–41).

Q&A | Where do I obtain this information?
Ask your instructor for this information.

What if I am required to enter different information from that shown in Figure 11–41?
Your information will be different from that shown in Figure 11–41.

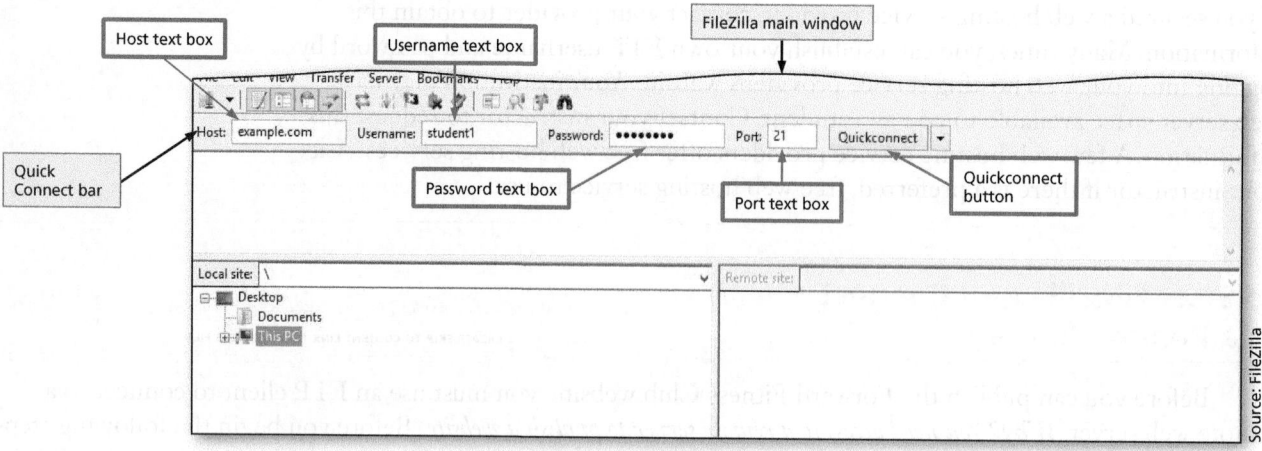

Figure 11–41

3

- Tap or click the Quickconnect button on the Quick Connect bar to connect to the remote server.
- Verify that the status shows Connected in the status window to confirm that you have successfully connected to the remote server (Figure 11–42).

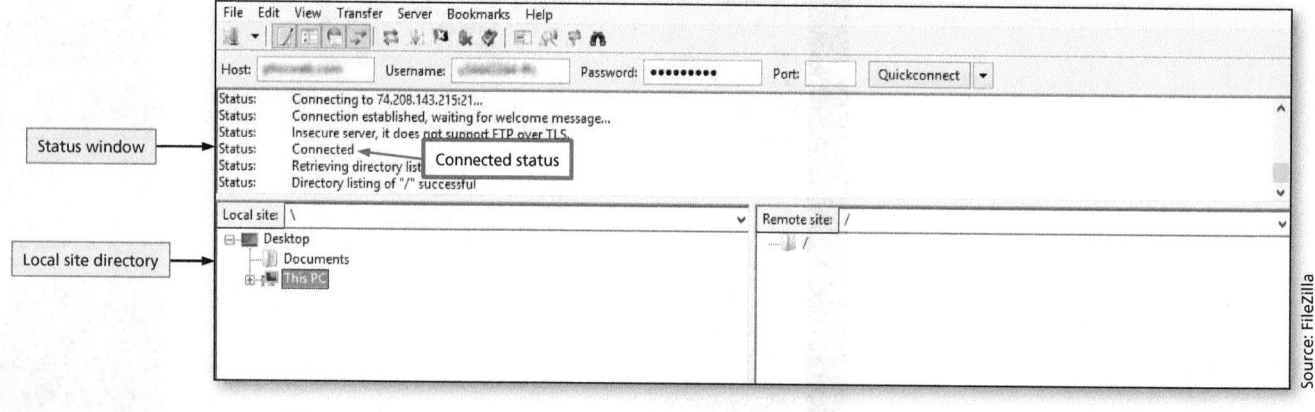

Figure 11–42

To Upload Folders and Files to a Remote Server

1 INSERT & STYLE SOCIAL MEDIA LINKS | 2 MODIFY TITLE & INSERT META TAG | 3 CREATE SITEMAP FILE
4 PUBLISH WEBSITE | 5 CREATE SKIP TO CONTENT LINK | 6 MINIFY CSS FILE

After you connect to a remote server, upload your website folders and files to publish your website. *Why?* *You transfer your website files to a remote server to make the website accessible to everyone with an Internet connection.* The following steps upload your website folders and files to a remote web server.

1

- In the Local site pane of the FileZilla window, navigate to your fitness folder, and then tap or click it to display the fitness folder contents in the Local site file list.
- Tap or click the css folder in the Local site file list to select the folder.
- Press the CTRL+A keys to select all of the folders and files within the fitness folder (Figure 11–43).

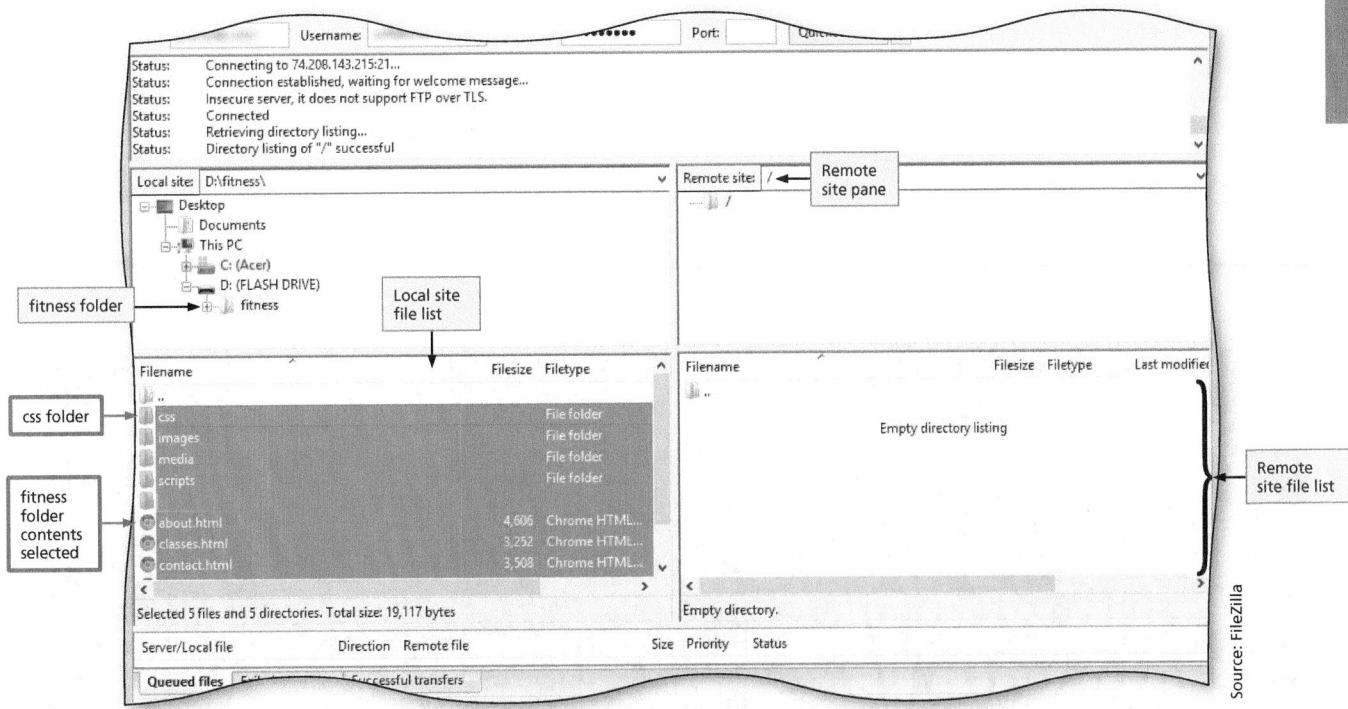

Figure 11–43

2

- Drag the folders and files to the Remote site file list window on the right to upload the folders and files to the remote server (Figure 11–44).

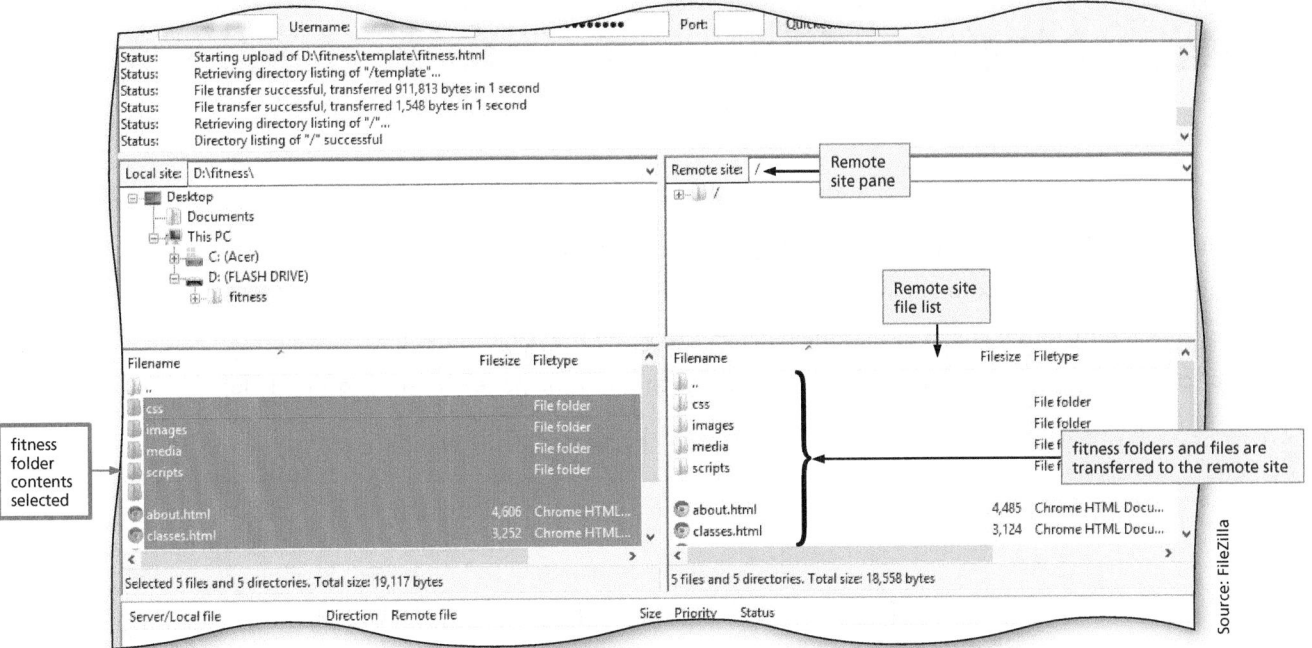

Figure 11–44

To View and Test a Published Website

After successfully publishing your website, view the website on your browser and test all the links. *Why? Verify that the website works as designed and confirm that all pages and content are accessible.* The following steps view the published website in a browser.

- Open your browser, type your URL in the address bar, and then press ENTER to display the home page of the website (Figure 11–45).

Q&A What is my URL?

If your instructor provided you with the remote site login credentials, ask your instructor for the URL. If you published through another web hosting service, view your account information or contact the web hosting service provider.

Figure 11–45

- Tap or click the About Us link to display the page and to verify the page content.
- Tap or click the Classes link to display the page and to verify the page content.
- Tap or click the Nutrition link to display the page and to verify the page content.
- Tap or click the Contact Us link to display the page and to verify the page content (Figure 11–46).

Q&A One or more of my pages is not displayed when I click a link. How do I correct this error?

If one or more pages were not displayed, either the page is not published or the link to the page is incorrect. Verify that your pages are published by confirming that the pages appear in the remote file list window. View all of your local site webpages files in your text editor to verify your page links. If you discover and correct a page link, save your changes, select the file(s) from the local site file list window, and then drag it to the remote site file list window to republish your page(s).

None of my images are displayed. How do I correct this problem?

If one or more images are not displayed, upload your images folder to the remote site.

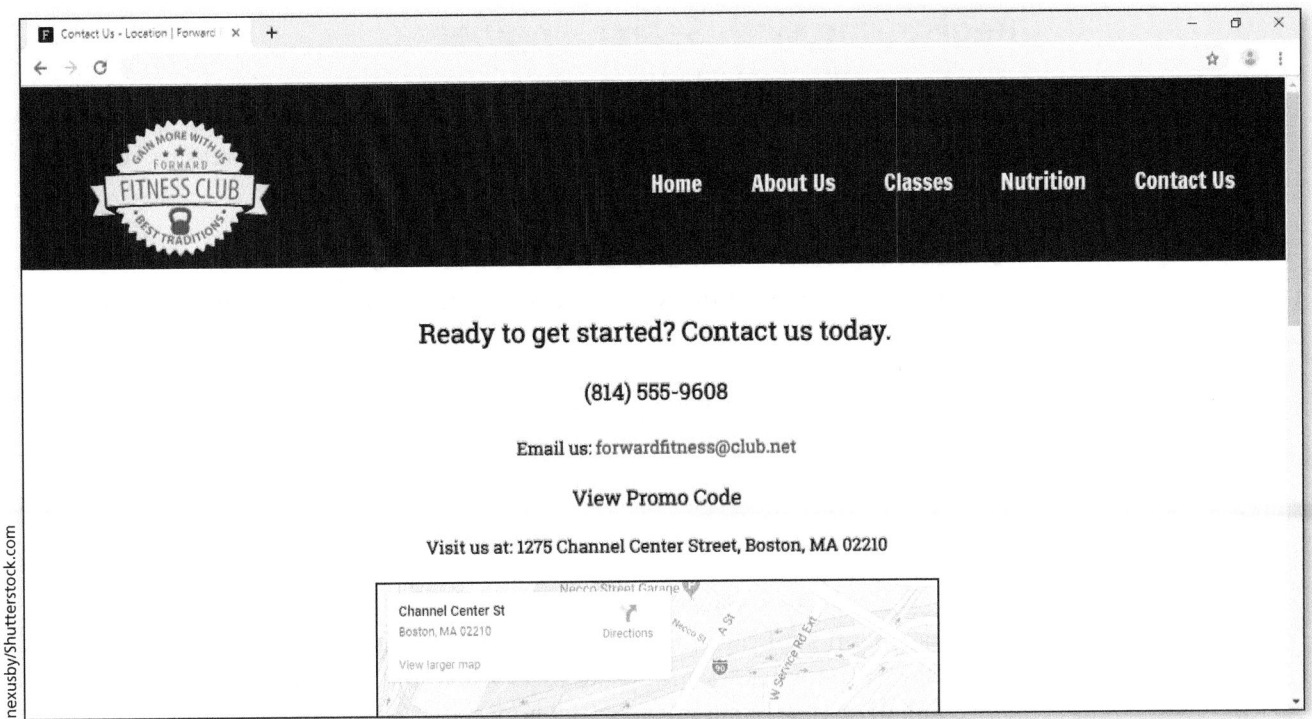

nexusby/Shutterstock.com

Figure 11–46

- If possible, view your published website from a mobile device.
- If possible, view your published website from a tablet device.

Promoting a Website

After you implement SEO for your website, and then publish and test your site, the next step is to promote the website to attract visitors. Develop a comprehensive marketing plan. A website is a passive marketing tool; it serves no purpose if no one knows it is available on the web. To attract customers to your website, take appropriate steps to promote and market it. You can promote and market your website to reach your target audience in the following ways:

- Register your website with search engines.
- Add your business website to Google, Bing, and Yahoo to make it easier for online users to find your business.
- Advertise through various social networking platforms, such as Facebook and Instagram.
- Post social media on a regular basis and respond to comments.
- Write a guest blog.
- Create a Google Ad.
- Add your website to your business cards, company brochures, stationery, and email signature.
- Advertise your website through email marketing.
- Tell people you meet about your website.
- Negotiate reciprocal links in which you agree to link to a website if they agree to link to your website.
- Use newsgroups specific to your industry.

BTW
Website Marketing Services
Many businesses handle all marketing aspects of a website, including social media. Use your favorite search engine to research more about website marketing services.

Registering with Search Engines

Once you have published your website, you can register it with the two most popular search engines, Google and Yahoo! It is also a good idea to register your site with search engines that specialize in subject matter related to your website. You can register your website through Google's Search Console.

TO REGISTER A WEBSITE WITH GOOGLE'S SEARCH CONSOLE

To register your website with Google's Search Console, you would perform the following steps.

1. Open your browser and type search.google.com/search-console/welcome and, if necessary, sign into your Google account. If you do not have a Google account, create one, and then sign in.
2. Type your URL in the Domain text box provided.

After you register your website with Google's Search Console, you can use Google Analytics, a free tool from Google, to learn more about the users that access your website. You can review your website performance and traffic and see the geographic location of your top visitors. Google Analytics also provides data about your webpage content and which pages users visited the most. To get started with Google Analytics, visit analytics.google.com/analytics/web/provision.

Website Development Life Cycle

University and college information technology courses stress the importance of following the systems development life cycle (SDLC) when designing and implementing new software to ensure consistency and completeness. The web development process should follow a similar cycle. Comprehensive planning and analysis ensure that developers will provide what the users want. If you start to code your webpages without thorough planning and analysis, you run the risk of missing pertinent information. It is much less expensive to make corrections to a website in the early phases of project development than it is to alter webpages that are completed.

The web development life cycle outlined in this section is one that can be used for any type or size of web development project. The **web development life cycle** is a process that can be used for developing webpages at any level of complexity. As shown in Figure 11–47, the web development life cycle includes the following phases:

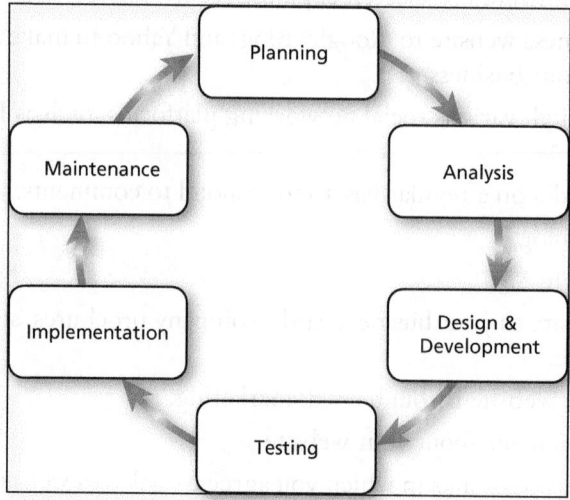

Figure 11–47

planning, analysis, design and development, testing, implementation, and maintenance. Table 11–2 lists several questions that should be asked during each phase in the web development life cycle.

Table 11–2 Web Development Life Cycle	
Web Development Phase	**Questions to Ask**
Planning	What is the purpose of this website?
	Who will use this website?
	What are the users' computing environments?
	Who owns and authors the information on the website?
	Who decides if/where the information goes on the website?
Analysis	What tasks do the users need to perform?
	What information is useful to the users?
	What process considerations must be made?
Design and development	How many webpages will be included in the website?
	How will the webpages be organized?
	What type of website structure is appropriate for the content?
	How can I best present the content for ease of use?
	What file naming convention will be employed for this website?
	What folder structure will be used for the webpage files?
	How do I apply standards throughout the development process?
	What forms of multimedia contribute positively to the website?
	How can accessibility issues be addressed without limiting usability?
	Will there be an international audience?
Testing	Do the webpages pass the World Wide Web Consortium (W3C) validation process as HTML 5 compliant?
	Does the style sheet pass the W3C validation process as CSS compliant?
	Is the website content correct?
	Does the website function correctly?
	Are users able to find the information they need to complete desired tasks?
	Is navigation clear and easy to use?
	Is the website accessible to visually impaired users?
Implementation	How is the website published?
	How can users be attracted to visit and revisit the website?
Maintenance	How is the website updated?
	Who is responsible for content updates?
	Who is responsible for structure updates?
	How will users be notified about updates to the website?
	Will the website be monitored?

Website Planning

Website planning is the first phase of the web development life cycle. As you learned in Chapter 1, it involves identifying the goals or purpose of the website. The first step in the website planning phase is to answer the question "What is the purpose of this website?" As you have learned, individuals and groups design and publish websites for a variety of purposes. Individuals develop websites to share their hobbies, to post résumés, or just to share ideas on personal interests. Organizations create websites to keep members informed of upcoming events or to recruit new members. Businesses create websites to advertise and sell products or to give their customers 24-hour online support. Instructors publish websites or add information to their courses using the school's online learning management system, to inform students of course policies, assignments, and due dates, as well as course requirements. Until you can adequately identify the intended purpose of the website, you should not proceed with the web development project.

In addition to understanding the website's purpose, you should also understand who will use the website and the computing environments of most users. Knowing the makeup of your target audience, including age, gender, general demographic background, and level of computer literacy, will help you design a website appropriate for the target users. Understanding users' computing environments will determine what types of web technologies to use. For example, if most users have low-speed Internet connections, you would not want to create pages with large graphics or multimedia elements.

A final aspect to the website planning phase is to identify the content owners and authors. To determine this, you need to ask the following questions:

- Who owns and authors the information on the website?
- Who decides content placement on the website?

Once you have identified who will provide and authorize the website content, you can include those individuals in all aspects of the web development project.

Website Analysis

During the analysis phase, you make decisions about the website content and functionality. To help define the appropriate website content and functionality, you should first identify the tasks that users need to perform. Answering that question allows you to define necessary content to facilitate those tasks and determine useful information for the users. Extraneous content that does not serve any purpose should be eliminated from the website.

In the analysis phase, consider the processes required to support website features. For example, if you determine that users should be able to order products through the website, then you also need to define the processes or actions to be taken each time an order is submitted. For instance, after an order is submitted, how will that order be processed throughout the back-office business applications such as inventory control and accounts payable? Will users receive email confirmations with details about their orders? The analysis phase is one of the more important phases in the web development life cycle. Clearly understanding and defining the desired content and functionality of the website will direct the type of website that you design and reduce changes during website development.

Website Design and Development

After determining the purpose of the website and defining the content and functionality, you need to consider the website's design. Some key considerations in website design are defining how to organize web page content, selecting the appropriate website structure, determining how to use multimedia, addressing accessibility issues, and designing pages for an international audience. One of the most important aspects of website design is determining the best way to provide navigation on the website. If users cannot easily find the information that they are seeking, they will not return to your website.

You can organize a webpage in many ways, just as you can organize a report or paper in many ways. Table 11–3 lists some organizational standards for creating a webpage that is easy to read and navigate.

Table 11–3 Webpage Organizational Standards

Element	Organizational Standard	Reason
Titles	Use unique titles with primary and secondary keywords to clearly identify the page content.	Titles help users understand the purpose of the page; a good title explains the page in the search engine results lists.
Headings	Use headings to separate main topics.	Headings make a webpage easier to read; simple headlines clearly explain the purpose of the page.
Paragraphs	Use brief paragraphs to help divide large amounts of text.	Paragraphs provide shorter, more readable sections of text.
Lists	Use bulleted or numbered lists when appropriate.	Lists provide organized, easy-to-read text that readers can scan.
Page length	Maintain suitable webpage lengths.	Web users do not always scroll to view information on longer pages; appropriate page lengths increase the likelihood that users will view key information.
Content	Emphasize the most important information by placing it at the top of a webpage.	Web users are quick to peruse a page; placing critical information at the top of the page increases the likelihood that users will view key information.
Contact information	Provide contact information, such as an email address, on the home page.	An email address gives users a way to contact a business with questions.

As a web developer, you must select an appropriate structure for the website and work to balance breadth and depth. Users go to a website looking for information to complete a task. Good design provides ease of navigation, allowing users to find content quickly and easily. In addition to planning the design of the website itself, a web developer should always plan the specifics of the file naming and storage conventions early in the design phase. Once you determine the structure of the website and the approximate number of pages necessary to fulfill the site purpose, then you need to identify what standards to use with file naming and the folder structure. For instance, saving your webpages with names such as page1.html and page2.html does not tell you the purpose of those webpages. A better option would be to file names such as about.html, contact.html, and services.html. These file names tell the current developer, as well as future developers maintaining the website, the purpose of the webpages.

The same principle applies to the folder structure that you use in your web development. It is a best practice to place images in an images folder, audio/video in a media folder, CSS in a css folder, and so on. Larger, more complex websites might also require a folder for webpages pertaining to specific departments. Where you store the files will affect how you access those files in your HTML code. Determining a good folder structure in the planning phase of the web development life cycle is important.

During the design and development phase, you should also consider what, if any, types of multimedia could contribute positively to the website experience. For instance, adding a video to showcase a new product or service might attract buyers, but if the computing environment of your users cannot accommodate video playback, then the video serves no purpose. Use advanced multimedia technologies in a website when it can make a positive contribution to the website experience. Today, more websites are using audio and video content.

Finally, consider accessibility issues and internationalization. A web developer should always design for viewing by a diverse audience, including physically impaired and global users. A key consideration is that the software used by physically impaired individuals does not work with some web features. For instance, if you use graphics on the website, always include alternative text for each graphic. To support an international audience, use generic icons that can be understood globally, avoid slang expressions in the content, and build simple pages that load quickly over lower-speed connections. The W3C provides a list of accessibility evaluation tools at w3.org/WAI/ER/tools.

To help improve a website for keyboard-only users, create a Skip to Content link. This enables keyboard-only users to skip directly to the main content of the webpage, rather than tabbing through the same header or navigation elements on each page.

The design issues just discussed are only a few of the basic webpage design issues that you need to consider. Many good webpage design resources are also available on the Internet.

Website Testing

A website should be tested at various stages of the web design and development processes. The testing process should be comprehensive and include a review of webpage content, functionality, and usability. Websites with broken links, missing graphics, and incorrect content create a poor impression. You want to attract users to your website and maintain their interest. If visitors find that your website is poorly tested and maintained, they will be less likely to return. You cannot get your message out if users do not frequently visit the website. Some basic steps to test content and functionality include:

- Validating each HTML page by running it through the W3C markup validation service.
- Validating your stylesheet by running it through the W3C CSS validation service.
- Proofreading page content and titles to review for accurate spelling and grammar.
- Checking links to ensure they are not broken and are linked correctly.
- Checking graphics to confirm they appear properly and are linked correctly.
- Ensuring that accessibility and internationalization issues are addressed.
- Testing forms and other interactive page elements.
- Testing pages to make sure they load quickly, even over lower-speed connections.
- Printing each page to view how each page looks when printed.

Usability is the measure of how well a product, such as a website, allows a user to accomplish his or her goals. **Usability testing** is a method by which users of a website or other product are asked to perform certain tasks in an effort to measure the website's ease of use and the user's perception of the experience. Usability testing for a website should focus on three key aspects: content, navigation, and presentation.

Usability testing can be conducted in several ways. One effective way is to directly observe visitors using the website. As you observe users, you can track the links they click and record their actions and comments. You can even ask the users to explain what tasks they were trying to accomplish while navigating the site. The information gained by observing users can be invaluable in helping identify potential problem areas in the website. For example, if you observe that users have difficulty finding the webpage that lists store locations and hours of operation, you may want to clarify the link descriptions or make the links more prominent on the home page.

Another way to conduct usability testing is to give users a specific task to complete (such as finding a product price list), and then observe how they navigate the site to complete the task. If possible, ask them to explain why they selected certain links. Both of these observation methods are extremely valuable, but require access to users.

Usability testing can also be completed using a questionnaire or survey. When writing a questionnaire or survey, be sure to write open-ended questions that can give you valuable information. For instance, asking the yes/no question "Is the website visually appealing?" will not gather useful information. If you change that question to use a scaled response, such as, "Rate the visual appeal of this website, using a scale of 1 for low and 5 for high," you can get more valuable input from the users. Make sure, however, that the scale itself is clear and understandable to the users. If you intend that a selection of 1 equates to a "low" rating, but the users think a 1 means "high," then your survey results are questionable. A usability testing questionnaire should always include space for users to write additional explanatory comments.

Table 11–4 provides a questionnaire with sample statements to ask a user.

Table 11–4 Sample Questionnaire for Website Users					
Statement	Strongly Agree	Agree	Neutral	Disagree	Strongly Disagree
The website is easy to navigate.					
The graphics on the website are visually appealing.					
I would recommend this website to family and friends.					
I was able to find what I was looking for.					
The website is intuitive and user-friendly.					
The information on the website is clearly organized.					

The following are additional examples of the types of questions to include in a website usability testing questionnaire.

- If you could change one thing about the website, what would it be?
- What do you like best about the website?
- What do you like least about the website?

You can find additional usability testing tools online.

In addition to content, functionality, and usability testing, there are other types of testing. For a newly implemented or maintained website, two other types of tests should be conducted: compatibility testing and stress testing. **Compatibility testing** is done to verify that the website works with a variety of browsers and browser versions. Initially, test using the browsers that your audience is most likely to use. Different browsers display some aspects of webpages differently, so it is important to test webpages in several different browsers to verify the pages appear correctly in each browser. If you have used technologies that are not supported by older browsers or that require plug-ins, consider changing the content or providing alternative webpages for viewing in older browsers. If your audience uses both Windows and macOS computers, you need to test the webpages using browsers on both platforms. You may also want to test the webpages in several versions of the same browser (usually the two most recent versions), in the event users have not yet upgraded.

Stress testing determines what happens on your website when a significant number of users access the site at the time same. A website with 120 users accessing it simultaneously may be fine. When thousands of users use the website at once, it may operate at an unacceptably slow speed. Stress testing verifies that a website runs at an acceptable speed with many users. In the cases where companies did not effectively stress test their websites, the results have been disastrous, with websites locking up when too many users tried to access the same website function. Especially in the case of websites used for e-commerce, it is imperative for the website to stay online. A crashed or locked-up website will not sell products or services, and the company stands to lose a lot of money. You can find many options for stress testing online.

One way to improve the loading time of webpage is to minify, or apply minification, your website files. HTML, CSS, and JavaScript files can all be minified. When you **minify** a file, you remove any unnecessary white space and characters, such as comments. This can significantly reduce the file size, which helps improve the page load time within a browser window. Many online tools minify files, including minifier. org and cssminifier.com. When you minify a file, keep your original file, as the minified files are not reader-friendly. Save minified files using "min" within the file name, such as styles.min.css. You can use Google's developer tools to analyze your page loading time. Visit developers.google.com/speed/ to get started.

CONSIDER THIS

How can I test my website on multiple browsers?
You can download and install multiple browsers to view and test your website. Several resources are also available online to test websites across multiple browsers, such as browsershots.org.

Implementation

Once website testing is complete and any required changes have been made, the website can be implemented. Implementation of a website involves publishing the webpages to a web server. As discussed earlier, you can use FTP software, such as FileZilla, to publish your webpages to a web server. After you publish a website, you should test the webpages again to confirm they have no obvious errors such as broken links or missing graphics.

Maintenance

After a site is tested and implemented, you need to develop a process to maintain the website. Employees within the business will undoubtedly request changes and timely content will require updates. If it is a large website, the webmaster should meet with webpage content authors to discuss ongoing updates and maintenance plan for the website. This includes refreshing content, possible design changes, marketing promotions, and link checking. You need to ensure, however, that updates to the website do not compromise the site's integrity and consistency. For example, if several people update various webpages on a large website, you might find it difficult to maintain a consistent look on pages across the website. You should plan to update your website on a regular basis to keep content up to date. This could mean hourly, daily, weekly, or less often, depending on the site's purpose. Do not allow your content to become stale, outdated, or include broken links to webpages that no longer exist.

To help manage the task of website maintenance, first determine who is responsible for updates to content, structure, functionality, and so on. Then, limit update responsibilities to specific users. Be sure the implementation is controlled by one or more web developers who can verify that the webpages are tested thoroughly before they are published.

Depending on how large the website is, you may need to create a form for employees of the business to complete in order to request a change to the website. Figure 11–48 shows an example of a website maintenance request form.

As updates and changes are made to a website, consider notifying users through social media and an announcement on the home page, explaining any new features and

Website Maintenance Request Form	
Employee Name:	
Employee Department:	
Employee Email:	
Today's Date:	
Path and Page to Update:	
Priority Level:	High Medium Low
Date Needed by:	
Detailed Change Requested:	

Figure 11–48

how the features will benefit them. This technique not only keeps users informed, but encourages them to come back to the website to see what is new. This also improves SEO for your website.

Finally, website monitoring is another key aspect of maintaining a website. Google Analytics and web hosting service providers offer invaluable data about website usage. A **log** is the file that lists all of the webpages that have been requested from the website. Obtaining and analyzing the logs allow you to determine information such as the number of visitors, browser types and versions, connection speeds, pages most commonly requested, and usage patterns. With this information, you can design a website that is effective for your target audience, providing visitors with a rich and rewarding experience.

Being an Observant Web User

As you embark on your web development career, one useful practice is to be an observant web user. Most people use the web several times a day (or more often) to complete daily tasks. As a web developer, you should review the webpages that you access with an eye on functionality and design. You can bookmark websites you think are effective and ineffective, good and bad, and use them as references for your own web development efforts. Watch for trends on the web as you search for information or make online purchases. For example, the use of Flash used to be very popular on the web, but now other design techniques have taken over. Being an observant web user can help you become a more effective web developer.

The Forward Fitness Club has received feedback about making its content more accessible to keyboard-only users. To improve the website for keyboard-only users, create a Skip to Content link, which skips to the main content on each webpage. Additionally, improve overall site performance by creating and using a minified CSS file.

To Create a Skip to Content Link

Create a Skip to Content link to improve the user experience for keyboard-only users. *Why? The Skip to Content link allows users to skip over navigation links and move to the main content of the webpage.* The following steps create a Skip to Content link within each HTML file.

- Open index.html in your text editor, tap or click at the end of Line 16, and then press the ENTER key twice to insert new Lines 17 and 18.

- On Line 18, type `<!-- Skip to Content Link -->` to insert a comment.

- Press the ENTER key to insert a new Line 19, and then type `<a class="skip" href="#content">Skip to Content</a>` to insert an anchor element (Figure 11–49).

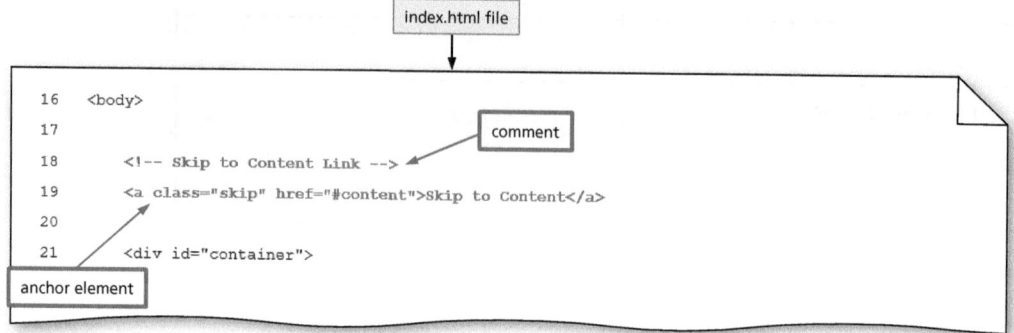

Figure 11–49

- On Line 59, add `id="content"` to the main tag to insert an id attribute.

- Save your changes (Figure 11–50).

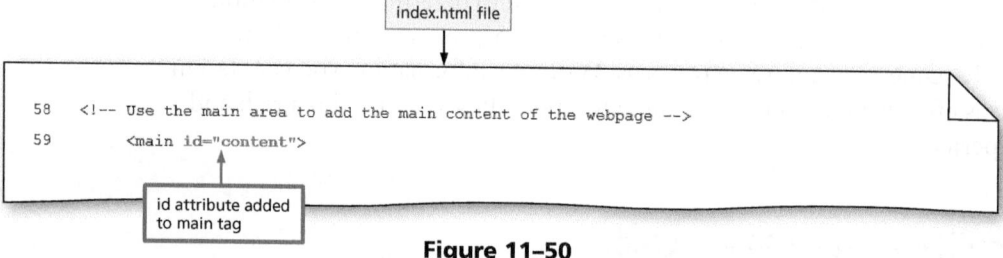

Figure 11–50

- Add the same comment, anchor element, and id attribute to the about.html, classes.html, nutrition.html, contact.html, and template.html files, and then save the changes.

To Style the Skip to Content Link

Create style rules to style the Skip to Content link when the page is loaded and when the link has focus. *Why? The Skip to Content link does not need to be viewed by default. Display the Skip to Content link when a visitor uses the keyboard to access the link or give it focus.* The following steps create two style rules to style the skip to content link.

- Open styles.css in your text editor, tap or click at the end of Line 27, and then press the ENTER key twice to insert new Lines 28 and 29.

- On Line 29, type `/* Style rules for skip navigation link */` to insert a comment.

- Press the ENTER key to insert a new Line 30, and then type `.skip {` to add a selector.

- Press the ENTER key to insert a new Line 31, increase the indent, and then type `position: absolute;` to add a declaration.

- Press the ENTER key to insert a new Line 32, and then type `left: -999px;` to add a declaration.

- Press the ENTER key to insert a new Line 33, decrease the indent, and then type `}` to close the style rule (Figure 11–51).

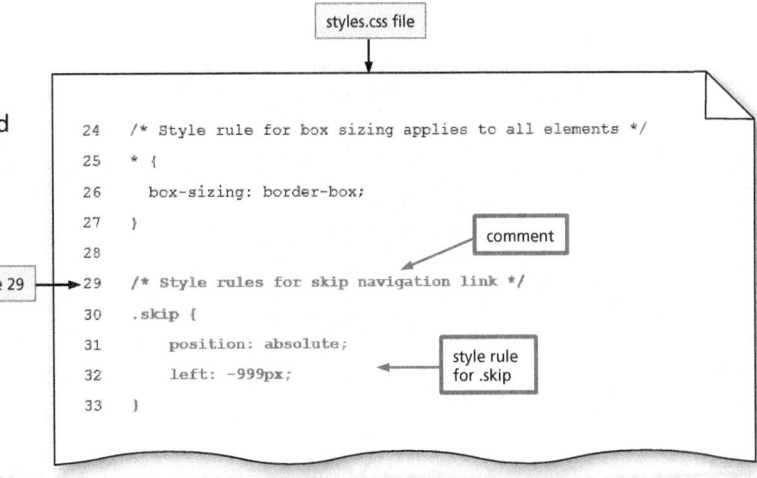

Figure 11–51

2

- Press the ENTER key twice to insert new Lines 34 and 35.

- On Line 35, type `.skip:focus {` to add a selector.

- Press the ENTER key to insert a new Line 36, increase the indent, and then type `color: #000;` to add a declaration.

- Press the ENTER key to insert a new Line 37, and then type `background-color: #fff;` to add a declaration.

- Press the ENTER key to insert a new Line 38, and then type `text-decoration: none;` to add a declaration.

- Press the ENTER key to insert a new Line 39, and then type `padding: 0.5%;` to add a declaration.

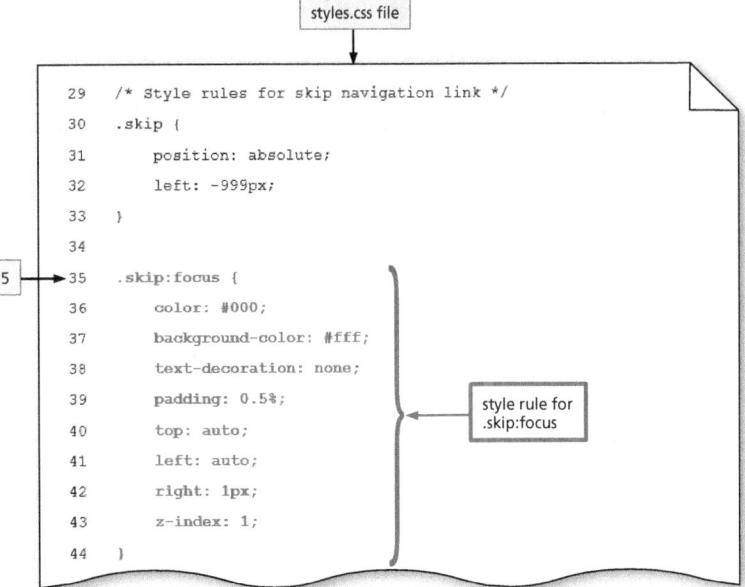

Figure 11–52

- Press the ENTER key to insert a new Line 40, and then type `top: auto;` to add a declaration.

- Press the ENTER key to insert a new Line 41, and then type `left: auto;` to add a declaration.

- Press the ENTER key to insert a new Line 42, and then type `right: 1px;` to add a declaration.

- Press the ENTER key to insert a new Line 43, and then type `z-index: 1;` to add a declaration.

- Press the ENTER key to insert a new Line 44, decrease the indent, and then type `}` to close the style rule (Figure 11–52).

3

- Save your changes, open index.html in your browser, and then display the page in a normal desktop viewport.

- Press the TAB key to give focus to the Skip to Content link and display the link (Figure 11–53).

index.html file

Skip to Content link

Figure 11–53

4

• Press the ENTER key to activate the link to the content id (Figure 11–54).

Skip to Content link takes user to main content

Figure 11–54

5

• Test the Skip to Content link on all other pages within the website to ensure it works correctly.

To Minify a CSS File

Create and link all of your HTML webpages to a minified stylesheet. *Why? Using a minified CSS file can decrease the page load time.* The following steps create a minified stylesheet.

- Open styles.css in your text editor, press CTRL+A to select all the style rules in the document, then press CTRL+C to copy all the style rules.
- Open your web browser to minifier.org, place your insertion point within the code box, and then press CTRL+V to paste the CSS code.
- Tap or click the CSS radio button to select the CSS minify option (Figure 11–55).

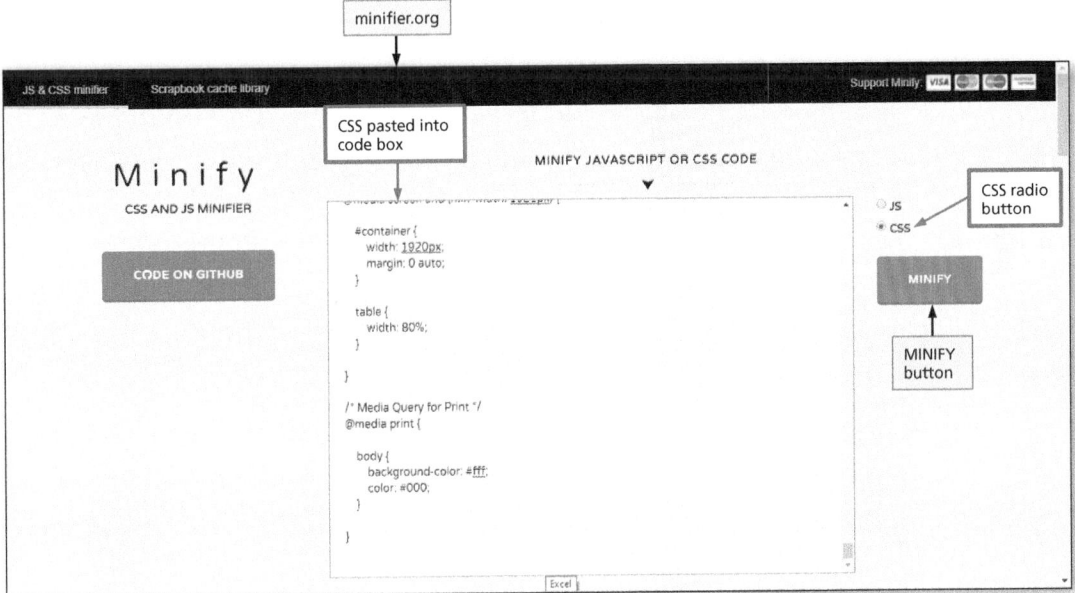

Figure 11–55

2

- Tap or click the MINIFY button to minify the code.
- Press CTRL+C to copy the minified code (Figure 11–56).

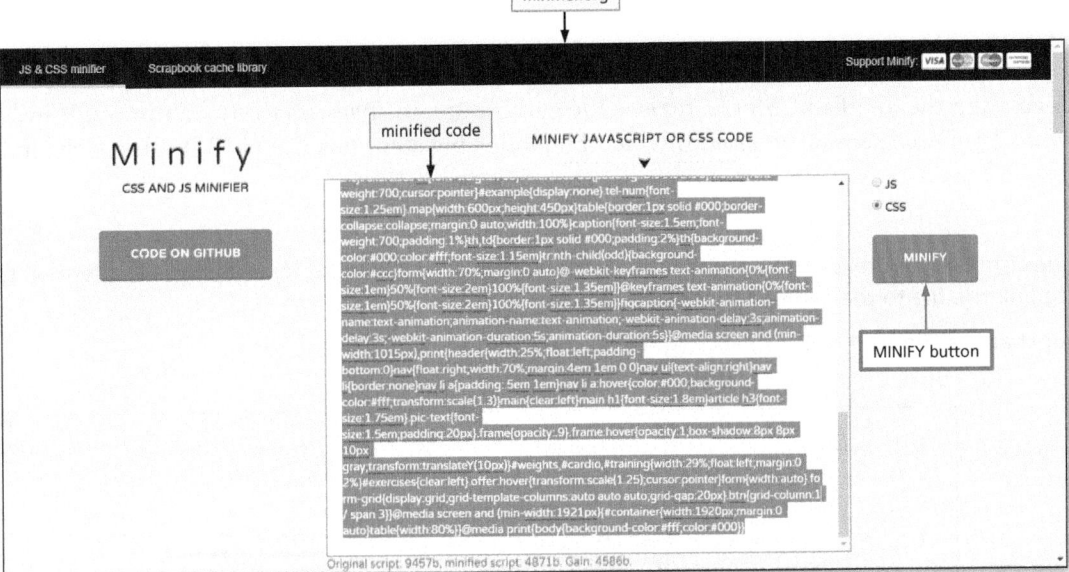

Figure 11–56

- Return to your text editor, select File on the menu bar, and then select New to create a new file.

- Press CTRL+V to paste the minified CSS code into the new file.

- Save the new file as **styles.min.css** within your fitness\css folder (Figure 11–57).

Q&A

Why do I need to create another stylesheet named styles.min.css?
You will link all of your HTML webpages to the styles.min.css stylesheet to improve page load time.

Do I still need the styles.css?
Yes, you still need the styles.css file to make any future design changes, as the styles.css file is much easier to read than the minified CSS file.

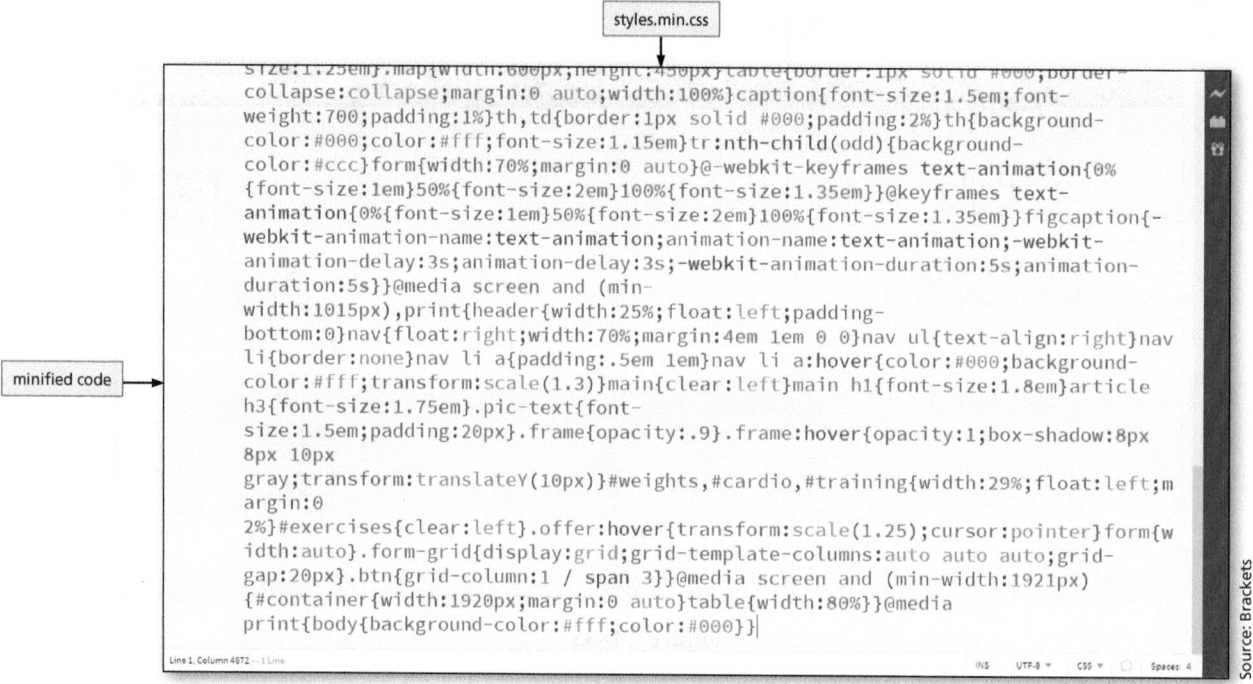

Figure 11–57

To Link HTML Files to the Minified CSS File

1 INSERT & STYLE SOCIAL MEDIA LINKS | 2 MODIFY TITLE & INSERT META TAG | 3 CREATE SITEMAP FILE
4 PUBLISH WEBSITE | 5 CREATE SKIP TO CONTENT LINK | 6 MINIFY CSS FILE

After creating the minified CSS file, replace the current link to styles.css to styles.min.css. *Why? Linking to the minified CSS file can decrease the page load time.* The following steps link the HTML files to the minified stylesheet.

- Open index.html in your text editor, place your insertion point after the word styles on Line 7, and then type **.min** to link the file to the minified stylesheet.

- Save your changes (Figure 11–58).

index.html file

```
4      <head>
5          <title>Complete Fitness - Free Trial | Forward Fitness Club</title>
6          <meta charset="utf-8">
7          <link rel="stylesheet" href="css/styles.min.css">
```

file name changed to styles.min.css

Figure 11–58

- Open about.html in your text editor, place your insertion point after the word styles on Line 7, and then type `.min` to link the file to the minified stylesheet.

- Save your changes.

- Open classes.html in your text editor, place your insertion point after the word styles on Line 7, and then type `.min` to link the file to the minified stylesheet.

- Save your changes.

- Open nutrition.html in your text editor, place your insertion point after the word styles on Line 7, and then type `.min` to link the file to the minified stylesheet.

- Save your changes.

- Open contact.html in your text editor, place your insertion point after the word styles on Line 7, and then type `.min` to link the file to the minified stylesheet.

- Save your changes.

- Open template.html in your text editor, place your insertion point after the word styles on Line 7, and then type `.min` to link the file to the minified stylesheet.

- Save your changes (Figure 11–59).

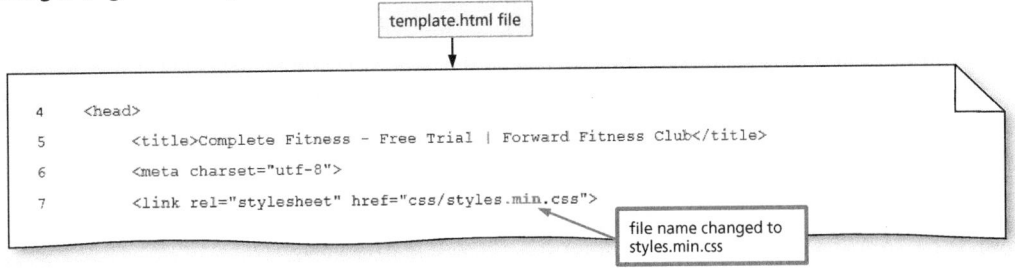

template.html file

```
4      <head>
5          <title>Complete Fitness - Free Trial | Forward Fitness Club</title>
6          <meta charset="utf-8">
7          <link rel="stylesheet" href="css/styles.min.css">
```

file name changed to styles.min.css

Figure 11–59

Project Management

Efficient project management of a website is vital when working with very large websites, such as the National Park Service website at nps.gov. More than 400 parks are listed within the National Park Service, and each has its own webpage. That is a significant number of webpages to maintain. It would be difficult for just one person to design, development, monitor, and update this website.

Larger websites require a project team to design, develop, and maintain a big website. Generally speaking, website project team members include a project manager, website designer, website developer, content specialist, and a webmaster. **Project management** of a website involves the delegation and supervision of website development activities. A website project management team works together to plan, design, develop, publish, and maintain a website.

A **project manager** oversees the entire project and maintains a timeline of project tasks and goals. The project manager creates a project plan, which includes a schedule and project deliverables. The project manager oversees all aspects of the project, delegates tasks, and ensures the final product is quality and timely. The project manager must have exceptional communication and managerial skills.

The **website designer** creates the design for the web design. This includes the planning phase of the web design process. The website designer is responsible for creating a sitemap and wireframe for the new website. The designer creates site concepts for the team to review. Once a concept is determined, it is given to the website developer. The designer role may be divided into two: a user interface (UI) designer and a user experience (UX) designer. The UI designer is responsible for designing the look of the website. The UX designer is responsible for designing the functionality of the website.

The **website developer** develops the webpages for the website. This project team member takes the mock-up webpage concepts and creates the actual webpages. The website developer uses HTML, CSS, JavaScript, and other possible web programming languages to develop the desired webpages. The website developer works closely with the website designer, the content specialist, and the graphic designer.

The **content specialist** develops webpage content that will attract the target audience. Requirements include finding creative ways to brand and message the business. The person in this role needs experience in persuasive writing. The content specialist is also responsible for keeping content fresh, editing content, and copywriting.

The **marketing professional** develops a marketing campaign to drive traffic to the website. The marketing professional may be someone within the business' marketing department or may be outsourced. The marketing professional works closely with the content specialist.

The **server administrator** maintains the web server used to host the website. The server administrator may be someone within the business' information technology (IT) department or may be outsourced. The person in this role is responsible for ensuring that the website is accessible via the Internet and for the hardware, software, and security needed to keep the website running smoothing.

CONSIDER THIS

Who puts a website project team together?
The project manager is typically the person in charge of delegating these tasks. The project manager should use experienced team members and carefully review each team member's portfolio, education, and past experience.

Content Updates

Updating website content is an ongoing process. When a business launches a new product or service, its website content must be updated to reflect the changes. Updating a website regularly can help increase search engine results and improve SEO. The following is a list of tips to keep your content updated and fresh:

- When you have a new product or service, add an image or video to your website to showcase it.
- If your company submits press releases on a regular basis, create a page for press releases, as this shows that your business is active and busy.
- Consider a page for client testimonials to spur potential sales.
- Post social media on regular basis.

Copyright Law

You may find images, audio, and video on a website that fit your needs, but think twice before downloading media to use on your website. The person or business who created the media is its owner. You cannot legally use media content created by someone else without permission. You must be granted permission to use the media on your website. This includes photographs, illustrations, audio, video, and other webpage content.

There are times when it is acceptable to use media created by another source on your website. Students and educators may use online media for educational purposes, such as an academic project. This is known as **fair use**. Fair use pertains to the use of copyrighted material without the need for permission from the creator.

Use of a Creative Commons license provides media content authors the ability to share their work with others, while maintaining ownership of their work. The Creative Commons license specifies appropriate use of the media. For more information about the creative commons license, visit creativecommons.org.

BTW
U.S. Copyright Law
For more information about U.S. copyright law, visit copyright.gov.

CONSIDER THIS

Can I purchase media for use on my website?

Yes. Several online resources provide images, audio, and video for a fee. Some examples of online media resources include gettyimages.com, istockphoto.com, and shutterstock.com.

E-Commerce

The term electronic commerce, or **e-commerce**, describes online businesses that conduct transactions online, including large, retail websites that sell products to consumers. Amazon, shown in Figure 11–60, is a popular e-commerce website that sells an array of products to consumers.

Amazon home page

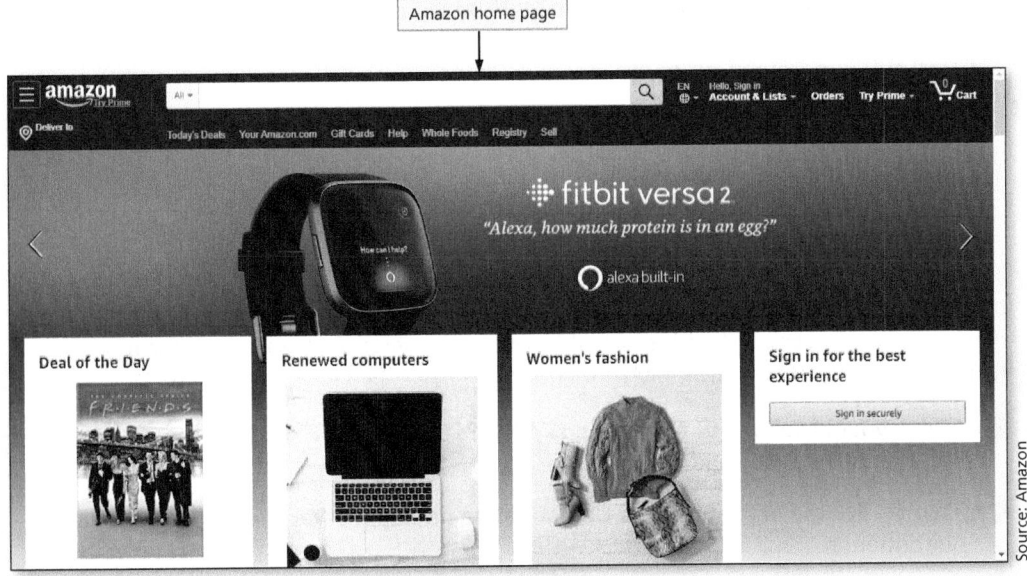

Source: Amazon

Figure 11–60

E-commerce is a booming business. Having an online store that is open 24 hours a day and 7 days a week is an advantage for e-commerce businesses because it allows them the opportunity to sell products anytime. Online customers enjoy purchasing what they want, when they want it. E-commerce also reduces store-front overhead costs because there is no physical store expense.

E-commerce also has its obstacles. With the rise in identity theft and fraud, some consumers are hesitant to make purchases online. An e-commerce business must invest time and money into securing its systems. For enhanced security, an e-commerce site should implement Secure Sockets Layer (SSL) technology to encrypt sensitive customer information.

E-commerce websites must also consider what happens if a server goes down and the site is not accessible to customers. Downtime can result in the loss of sales and make the site seem unreliable to a customer. E-commerce websites must ensure their connections, create and maintain several backups, and have a plan in place to deal with potential technology issues that may arise.

E-commerce websites must have a proven and tested interface to handle orders. This is primarily done through the use of shopping carts. Many online tools can help e-commerce developers create and maintain shopping carts . The websites must also be able to efficiently handle order payments. Common payment methods include a major credit card, PayPal, Bill Me Later, and Google Wallet.

E-commerce is often categorized in four common business models, including business-to-consumer, business-to-business, consumer-to-consumer, and business-to-government.

The business-to-consumer model (B2C) is the most common e-commerce business model. Examples of a B2C e-commerce websites include Amazon and Wayfair.

In the business-to-business (B2B) model, businesses make purchases from other businesses, such as raw material and supplies. An example of a B2B business model is a wholesale glass manufacturer that supplies glass for a window company.

The consumer-to-consumer (C2C) business model takes place between two individuals buying and selling over the Internet. Examples of C2C e-commerce websites include eBay and Etsy.

With the business-to-government (B2G) business model, government agencies make online purchases from a business, such as a government agency purchasing software from an online vendor.

To Validate the HTML Files

Every time you create a new webpage or modify an existing webpage, run it through W3C's validator to check the document for errors. If any errors exist, you need to correct them. Validation is also an effective troubleshooting tool during the development process and adds a valuable level of professionalism to your work. The following steps validate an HTML document.

1 Open your browser and type `http://validator.w3.org/` in the address bar to display the W3C validator page.

2 Tap or click the Validate by File Upload tab to display the Validate by File Upload information.

3 Tap or click the Browse button to display the Choose File to Upload dialog box.

4 Navigate to your fitness folder to find the index.html file.

5 Tap or click the index.html document to select it.

6 Tap or click the Open button to upload it to the W3C validator.

7 Tap or click the Check button to send the document through the validator and display the validation results page.

8 If necessary, correct any errors, save your changes, and run through the validator again to revalidate the page.

9 Follow these steps to validate other pages recently modified and correct any errors.

Chapter Summary

In this chapter, you learned how to add social media icons and links to a webpage. You also learned how to improve SEO for a website by improving page titles, adding description meta tags, and creating a sitemap file. You also learned how to publish and promote a website, make webpages more accessible by creating a Skip to Content link, and improve page loading time by minifying a CSS file. The items listed below include all the new skills you have learned in this chapter, with the tasks grouped by activity.

Using Social Media
Add a Facebook Icon and Link (HTML 582)
Add a Twitter Icon and Link (HTML 582)
Style Social Media Icons (HTML 585)

Improving Webpages for Search Engine Optimization
Modify Title Elements (HTML 592)
Add a Description Meta Tag to a Webpage (HTML 592)
Create a Sitemap File (HTML 594)

Publishing a Website
Start FileZilla and Connect to a Remote Server (HTML 599)
Upload Folders and Files to a Remote Server (HTML 600)
View and Test a Published Website (HTML 602)

Website Development Life Cycle
Planning (HTML 605)
Analysis (HTML 606)
Design and Development (HTML 606)
Testing (HTML 608)
Implementation (HTML 610)
Maintenance (HTML 610)

Improving a Website
Add a Skip to Content Link (HTML 612)
Minify a CSS File (HTML 615)

Project Management
Content Updates (HTML 618)
Copyright Law (HTML 618)

How will you promote your website?
Use these guidelines as you complete the assignments in this chapter and create your own webpages outside of this class.

1. Determine a domain name.

    a) Keep the domain name short and memorable.

    b) Check the domain name availability.

2. Outline a marketing plan to promote your website.

    a) Make a list of keywords.

    b) Determine your SEO strategy.

    c) Use social media.

3. Determine a web hosting service.

    a) Research and compare web hosting service providers.

    b) Determine the best method for accessing and publishing to your remote site.

CONSIDER THIS

How should you submit solutions to questions in the assignments identified with a  symbol?
Every assignment in this book contains one or more questions identified with a symbol. These questions require you to think beyond the assigned presentation. Present your solutions to the questions in the format required by your instructor. Possible formats may include one or more of these options: create a document that contains the answer; present your answer to the class; discuss your answer in a group; record the answer as audio or video using a webcam, smartphone, or portable media player; or post answers on a blog, wiki, or website.

CONSIDER THIS

Apply Your Knowledge

Reinforce the skills and apply the concepts you learned in this chapter.

Adding Social Media Icons and Meta Tags, and Publishing a Webpage

Note: To complete this assignment, you will be required to use the Data Files. Please contact your instructor for information about accessing the Data Files.

Instructions: In this exercise, you will use your text editor to create a webpage. Add a description meta tag to the webpage and then publish the webpage. Work with the apply11.css file in the apply\css folder from the Data Files to style your webpage. The completed webpage is shown in Figure 11–61. You will also use professional web development practices to indent, space, comment, and validate your code.

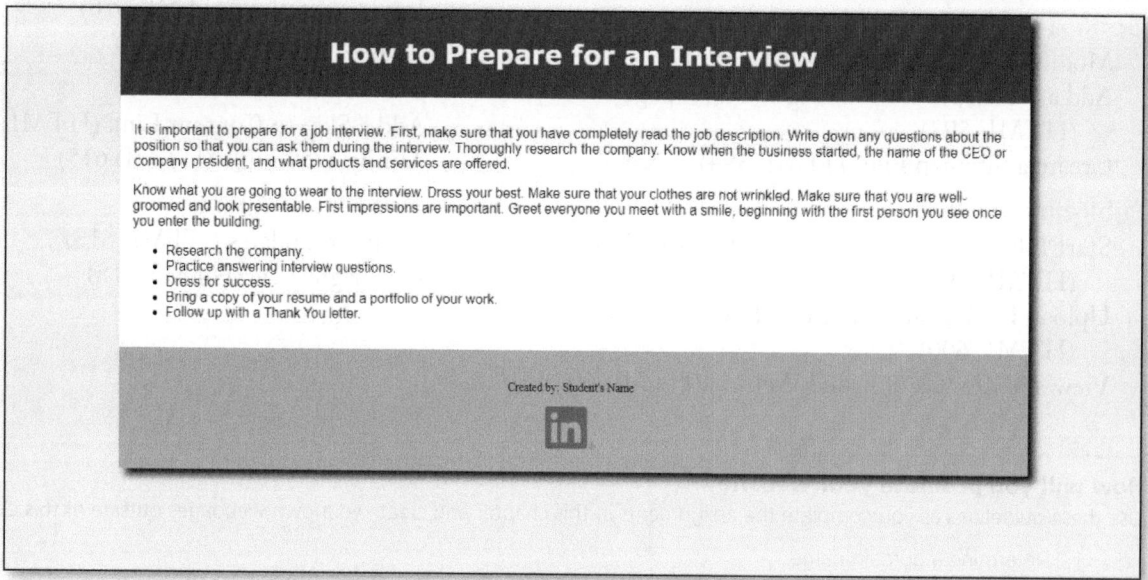

Figure 11–61

Perform the following tasks:

1. Use your text editor to create a new HTML file named index.html. Include a comment with your name and today's date. Save your index.html file in the chapter11\apply folder from the Data Files.

2. Include all necessary HTML 5 elements to create a basic webpage. Link the index.html file to the apply11.css file.

3. Create a title for the page and use `Interview Tips - Prepare` as the webpage title text.

4. Insert a description `meta` tag with a content attribute and use `This website provides helpful tips on how to interview for a job and how to create a resume.` as the value.

5. Create a header element.

6. Nest an `h1` element within the header element and include the text `How to Prepare for an Interview` as the heading text.

7. Create a main element below the header element.

8. Use your browser to research ways to prepare for a job interview. Use two paragraph elements within the main element to summarize your findings.

9. Create an unordered list of at least five tips for preparing for an interview. Place the unordered list below the second paragraph element, but within the main element.

10. Create a footer element that contains your name and the social media icon for LinkedIn. Link the icon to your LinkedIn page or to LinkedIn.com if you do not have a LinkedIn page. LinkedIn icons are provided in the images folder. Determine which icon you will use. Set the link to open in a new tab.

11. Use the apply11.css file to style the social media icons as desired. Modify the style sheet as desired.

12. Save your changes.

13. Publish the website files to a remote server.

14. View your published website in your browser.

15. Submit the project in a format specified by your instructor.

16. ❂ In this exercise, you inserted a social media icon for LinkedIn. Use your browser to research LinkedIn brand assets. Are other LinkedIn logos available for download from LinkedIn?

Extend Your Knowledge

Extend the skills you learned in this chapter and experiment with new skills. You may need to use additional resources to complete the assignment.

Learning More About Google Webmaster Guidelines

Instructions: In this exercise, you research information about Google webmaster guidelines and summarize your findings.

Perform the following tasks:

1. Use your browser to search for Google Webmaster Guidelines.

2. Read the information and use your word processor to summarize your findings.

3. Include the following information in your response.

   a. Identify at least three design guidelines.

   b. Identify at least three technical guidelines.

   c. Identify at least five practices to avoid.

4. Name your file **Extend11.docx** and submit it in a format specified by your instructor.

5. ❂ In this exercise, you learned more about Google webmaster guidelines. Research Bing webmaster guidelines and identify three of its guidelines that coincide with the Google guidelines.

Analyze, Correct, Improve

Analyze a website, correct all errors, and improve it.

Improving SEO for a Webpage

Note: To complete this assignment, you will be required to use the Data Files. Please contact your instructor for information about accessing the Data Files.

Instructions: Work with the index.html file in the analyze folder and the analyze11.css file from analyze/css folder from the Data Files. The index.html webpage needs a page title, a meta description, and heading elements. The image file name and alt text on the page also need to be improved. Use Figure 11–62 as a guide to correct these files.

Continued >

Analyze, Correct, Improve *continued*

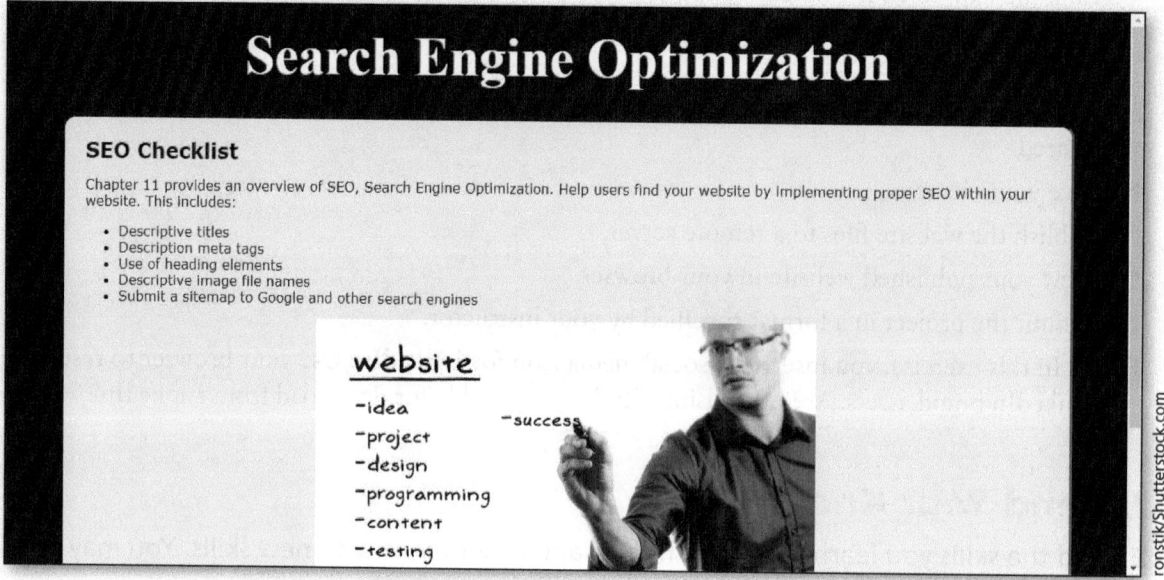

Figure 11–62

1. Correct

a. Open the index.html file in your text editor from the chapter11\analyze folder in the Data Files. Modify the comment at the top of the page to include your name and today's date, and then link the file to analyze11.css.

b. Review the webpage content and insert an appropriate title for this page.

c. Add an appropriate description meta tag to the page.

d. Change paragraph elements to heading elements where appropriate.

2. Improve

a. In the analyze\images folder, review the image file names and modify them for SEO. Update the index.html page to reflect the updated image file names.

b. In the index.html file, review all img alt text attributes and modify them for SEO.

c. Link each social media icon to its respective social network home page. Specify the link to open in a new tab.

d. Add your name to the paragraph element within the footer element.

e. In the analyze11.css file, add your name, current date, and file name to the comment. Create a style rule for the social media icons to provide more space between the icons.

f. Save all of your changes and then open or refresh index.html in your browser.

g. Validate your HTML webpage using the W3C validator found at validator.w3.org, and fix any errors that are identified.

h. ✳ Research and discuss the keywords and author meta tags. Are these meta attributes commonly used? Research to find your answer.

In the Lab

Labs 1 and 2, which increase in difficulty, require you to create webpages based on what you learned in the chapter; Lab 3 requires you to dive deeper into a topic covered in the chapter.

Lab 1: **Publishing the Strike a Chord Website**

Note: To complete this assignment, you will be required to use the Data Files. Please contact your instructor for information about accessing the Data Files.

Problem: You work for a local music lesson company called Strike a Chord that provides music lessons for piano, guitar, and violin. The company needs a web presence and has hired you to create their website. You have already created the website and now need to modify the title element on each page, add a description meta tag to each page, add social media icons to each page, and publish the website. Figure 11–63 shows the social media icons on the published website, as displayed in a desktop browser.

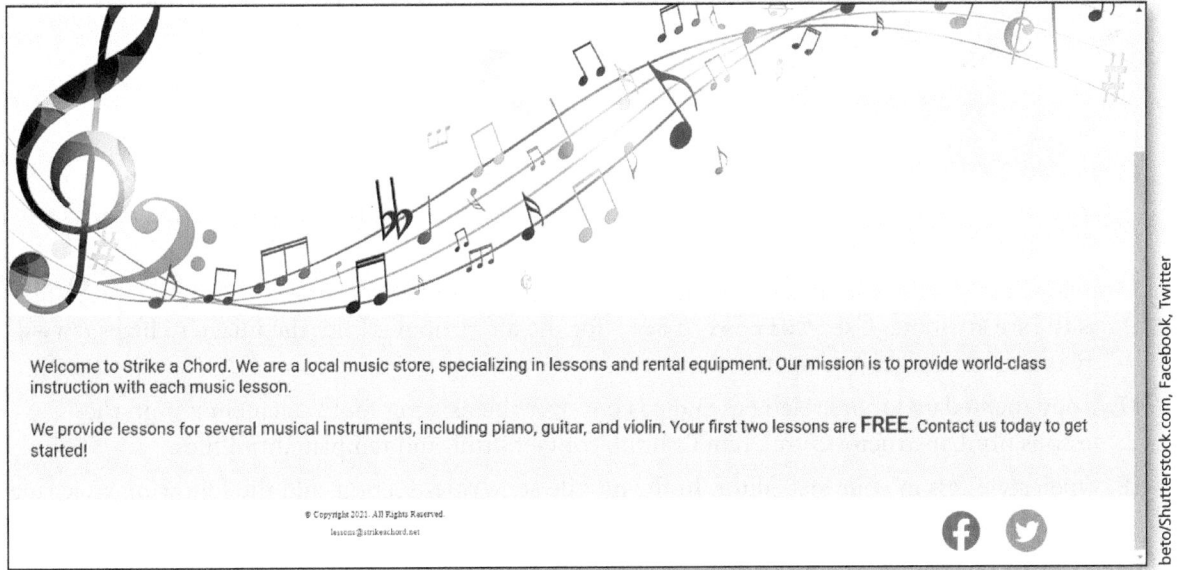

Welcome to Strike a Chord. We are a local music store, specializing in lessons and rental equipment. Our mission is to provide world-class instruction with each music lesson.

We provide lessons for several musical instruments, including piano, guitar, and violin. Your first two lessons are FREE. Contact us today to get started!

© Copyright 2021. All Rights Reserved.
lessons@strikeachord.net

beto/Shutterstock.com, Facebook, Twitter

Figure 11–63

Instructions: Perform the following tasks:

1. Copy the image files in the chapter11\lab1 folder from the Data Files to your music\images folder.

2. Open the index.html file in your text editor and update the comment at the top of the page to include today's date.

3. Change the title element text to `Music Lessons - Rentals | Strike a Chord`.

4. In the head element, below the meta character set tag, insert a description meta tag with a content value of `"Strike a Chord specializes in music lessons and music rental equipment."`.

5. Open lessons.html in your text editor. Change the title element text to: `Piano, Guitar, Violin Lessons | Strike a Chord`.

6. In the head element, below the meta character set tag, insert a description meta tag with a content value of `"We provide music lessons for piano, guitar, electric guitar, bass guitar, ukelele, and the violin. Your first two lessons are free."`.

Continued >

STUDENT ASSIGNMENTS

In the Lab *continued*

7. Open instructors.html in your text editor. Change the title element text to: `Instructors | Strike a Chord`.

8. In the head element, below the meta character set tag, insert a description meta tag with a content value of `"Our instructors are knowledgeable and professional."`

9. Open rentals.html in your text editor. Change the title element text to: `Music Rental Equipment | Strike a Chord`.

10. In the head element, below the meta character set tag, insert a description meta tag with a content value of `"Need music rental equipment? We rent guitars, keyboards, drum kits, microphones, and DJ equipment."`.

11. Open contact.html in your text editor. Change the title element text to: `Location | Strike a Chord`.

12. In the head element, below the meta character set tag, insert a description meta tag with a content value of `"Contact us at (814) 555-9228 or visit us at 1122 Music Lane, Chicago, IL for more information."`.

13. Open index.html in your text editor. In the footer element, wrap the two paragraph elements within a div element that specifies a class attribute value of `copyright`. Indent the two paragraph elements within the div.

14. Below the copyright div, create a new div with the class attribute value of `social`.

15. In the new social div, add an image element and use the `facebook-logo.png` file as the src attribute. Use `Facebook logo` for the alt attribute. Link the image to https://www.facebook.com, and set it to open in a new tab.

16. Below the Facebook logo, add another image element and use the `twitter-logo.png` file as the src attribute. Use `Twitter logo` for the alt attribute. Link the image to https://www.twitter.com and set it to open in a new tab.

17. Copy the updated footer element and paste it over the existing footer element within the lessons.html, instructors.html, rentals.html, contact.html, and template.html files.

18. Open styles.css in your text editor. In the mobile style rules section, add the following style rule below the style rule for footer a:

```
.social img {
    display: inline-block;
    padding: 4%;
}
```

19. In the tablet media query, add the following comment and style rules below the style rule for form:

```
/* Tablet Viewport: Style rules for footer area */
.copyright {
    float: left;
    width: 65%;
}

.social {
    float: right;
    width: 25%;
}
```

20. Save your changes.

21. Publish the website files to a remote server.

22. View your published website in your browser and verify that all webpages and website content is published.

23. Submit the project in a format specified by your instructor.

24. ✹ Research domain name ideas for this website and provide a list of three available domain name options.

Lab 2: **Publishing the Wild Rescues Website**

Note: To complete this assignment, you will be required to use the Data Files. Please contact your instructor for information about accessing the Data Files.

Problem: You volunteer at a local wildlife rescue, a nonprofit organization called Wild Rescues. The organization rescues all kinds of wild animals, rehabilitates them, and then releases them back into the wild. Wild Rescues needs a website to help raise awareness about the organization. You have already created the website and now need to prepare the website for SEO, add a Skip to Content link, and publish it. Figure 11–64 shows the social media icons on the published website, as displayed in a desktop browser.

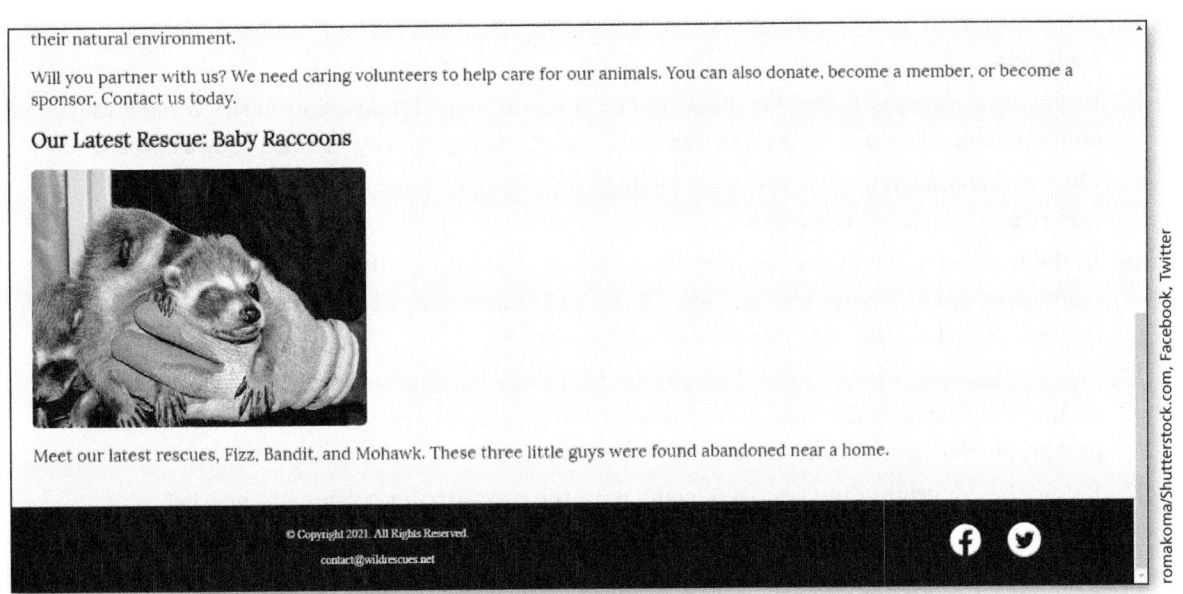

romakoma/Shutterstock.com, Facebook, Twitter

Figure 11–64

Instructions: Perform the following tasks:

1. Copy the image files in the chapter11\lab2 folder from the Data Files to your rescue\images folder.

2. Open your text editor, and then open the index.html document in the rescue folder and update the comment at the top of the page to include today's date.

3. Change the title element text to: `Wildlife Rescue | Wild Rescues`.

Continued >

In the Lab *continued*

4. In the head element, below the meta character set tag, insert a description meta tag with a content value of `"Wild Rescues is a local nonprofit organization dedicated to helping injured, neglected, or orphaned wildlife."`.

5. Open about.html in your text editor. Change the title element text to: `Rescue - Rehabilitate | Wild Rescues`.

6. In the head element, below the meta character set tag, insert a description meta tag with a content value of `"We help rehabilitate local wildlife, such as raccoons, squirrels, fox, birds, deer, horses, pigs, and reptiles."`.

7. Open partnership.html in your text editor. Change the title element text to: `Sponsorship | Wild Rescues`.

8. In the head element, below the meta character set tag, insert a description meta tag with a content value of `"Partner with us. We have several sponsorship opportunities available."`.

9. Open gallery.html in your text editor. Change the title element text to: `Gallery | Wild Rescues`.

10. In the head element, below the meta character set tag, insert a description meta tag with a content value of `"Meet our rescued friends. We have horses, goats, squirrels, pigs, deer, cows, rabbits, birds, turtles, and many more."`.

11. Open faqs.html in your text editor. Change the title element text to: `FAQs | Wild Rescues`.

12. In the head element, below the meta character set tag, insert a description meta tag with a content value of `"Get answers to our most frequently asked questions."`.

13. Open contact.html in your text editor. Change the title element text to: `Contact Us - Location | Wild Rescues`.

14. In the head element, below the meta character set tag, insert a description meta tag with a content value of `"Contact us at (814)555-8989 or visit us at 8989 Rescue Drive, Ocala, FL for more information."`.

15. Open index.html in your text editor. In the footer element, wrap the two paragraph elements within a div element that specifies a class attribute value of `copyright`. Indent the two paragraph elements within the div.

16. Below the copyright div, create a new div with the class attribute value of `social`.

17. In the new social div, add an image element and use the `facebook-logo.png` file as the src attribute. Use `Facebook logo` for the alt attribute. Link the image to https://www.facebook.com and set it to open in a new tab.

18. Below the Facebook logo, add another image element and use the `twitter-logo.png` file as the src attribute. Use `Twitter logo` for the alt attribute. Link the image to https://www.twitter.com and set it to open in a new tab.

19. Copy the updated footer element and paste it over the existing footer element within the about.html, partnership.html, gallery.html, faqs.html, contact.html, and template.html files.

20. Add the following comment and anchor element after the starting body element on every HTML file within the rescue folder:

```
<!-- Skip to Content Link -->
<a class="skip" href="#content">Skip to Content</a>
```

21. Add an id attribute with a value of content to the starting main tag on every HTML file within the rescue folder.

22. Open styles.css in your text editor. Add the following comment and style rules after the style rule for img and video:

```
/* Style rules for skip navigation link */
.skip {
    position: absolute;
    left: -999px;
}

.skip:focus {
    color: #fff;
    background-color: #2a1f14;
    text-decoration: none;
    padding: 0.5%;
    top: auto;
    left: auto;
    right: 1px;
    z-index: 1;
}
```

23. In the mobile style rules section, below the style rule for footer a, create a new style rule for images within the social class that sets the display to an inline block and sets the padding to `4%`.

24. In the tablet media query, below the style rule for form, add a comment with the text `/* Tablet Viewport: Style rules for footer area */`.

25. Below the comment, add a new style rule for the footer that sets the overflow to `auto`. Add another new style rule for the copyright class that specifies a left float and a width of `65%`. Add another new style rule for the social class that specifies a right float and a width of `25%`.

26. Create a sitemap file for the website. Use `www.exampledomain.com` for the domain. Save the sitemap file within the rescue folder.

27. Create a minified version of your stylesheet. Name it `styles.min.css`. Be care not to overwrite your original styles.css file. Update the stylesheet link in each HTML file to use the minified CSS file instead of the original.

28. Save your changes.

29. Publish the website files to a remote server.

30. View your published website in your browser and verify that all webpages and website content is published.

31. Submit the project in a format specified by your instructor.

32. ✳ In this exercise, you minified your stylesheet. What is the difference in file size between the original and the minified file?

Continued >

In the Lab *continued*

Lab 3: **Publishing the Student Clubs and Events Website**

Problem: You and several of your classmates have decided to help increase student involvement in school clubs and events by creating a website to promote awareness about the various activities. You have already created the website and now need to improve the website for SEO, add social media icons and links, create a sitemap, create a Skip to Content link, and minify the CSS file. Work together as a team to complete each task.

Instructions:

1. Review the title element on all pages and update as appropriate.
2. Add a unique description meta tag to every page within the website.
3. Identify and discuss two social networking websites that the website could use to promote student events and activities. Use your browser to search for and download the social media icon logos (brand assets) directly from the social networking company. For example, if you want to download the icons for Facebook, search for Facebook brand assets. If necessary, use basic image editing software, such as Paint, to resize the image. Review the brand asset guidelines to learn the minimum image dimensions.
4. Add two social media icons to the footer element on every page within the website and include a link for both. You may use generic links to the social networking website, such as https://www.facebook.com.
5. Use your style sheet to style the social media icons as desired for each viewport.
6. Create a sitemap file for your website. Use `www.exampledomain.com` as the domain.
7. Create and style a Skip to Content link on each page.
8. Create a new file named `styles.min.css`. Minify your CSS and save it in the styles.min.css file. Be sure to keep your original styles.css file. Update the stylesheet link within every HTML file to use the minified CSS file.
9. Save your changes.
10. Publish your website.
11. Submit your answers in the format specified by your instructor.
12. ✳ In this exercise, you downloaded and added social media icons or brand assets to your website. Research "Facebook brand assets," review their guidelines, and summarize your findings.

Consider This: Your Turn

Apply your creative thinking and problem-solving skills to design and implement a solution.

1. Publishing Your Personal Portfolio Website Design
Personal

Part 1: You have already developed a responsive website for your personal portfolio and now need to modify your HTML files for SEO and publish your website. Complete the following tasks:

1. Review the title element on all pages and update as appropriate.
2. Add a unique description meta tag to every page within the website.
3. Determine at least one social media icon that you can add to your website to promote your skills and experience. Use your browser to search for and download the social media icon logos (brand assets) directly from the social networking company. For example, if you want

to download the icons for Facebook, search for Facebook brand assets. If necessary, use basic image editing software, such as Paint, to resize the image. Review the brand asset guidelines to learn the minimum image dimensions.

4. Add at least one social media icon to the footer element on every page within your website, and include a link to the icon. You may use a generic link to the social networking website, such as https://www.linkedin.com.

5. Use your style sheet to style the social media icon as desired for each viewport.

6. Save your changes.

7. Publish your website.

8. Submit your files in the format specified by your instructor.

Part 2: Use your browser to research the software needed to host your own web server and summarize your findings.

2. Publishing the Dog Grooming Website
Professional

Part 1: You have already developed a responsive website for the dog grooming website and now need to prepare the HTML files for SEO and publish the website. Complete the following tasks:

1. Review the title element on all pages and update as appropriate.

2. Add a unique description meta tag to every page within the website.

3. Identify two social networking websites that you can use to promote the business. Use your browser to search for and download the social media icon logos (brand assets) directly from the social networking company. For example, if you want to download the icons for Facebook, search for Facebook brand assets. If necessary, use basic image editing software, such as Paint, to resize the image. Review the brand asset guidelines to learn the minimum image dimensions.

4. Add two social media icons to the footer element on every page within the website and include a link for both. You may use generic links to the social networking website, such as https://www.facebook.com.

5. Use your style sheet to style the social media icons as desired for each viewport.

6. Create a sitemap file for your website. Use `www.exampledomain.com` as the domain.

7. Minify your CSS and save it with the file name `styles.min.css`. Be sure to keep your original styles.css file. Update the stylesheet link within every HTML file to use the minified CSS file.

8. Save your changes.

9. Publish your website.

10. Submit your files in the format specified by your instructor.

Part 2: Use your browser to research an SEO company and provide a list of their services and costs.

3. Publishing the Future Technologies Website
Research and Collaboration

Part 1: You and several of your classmates have been tasked with creating a website that showcases advances in technology. You have already created a responsive design website and now need to prepare the website for SEO and publish it. Do the following activities as a group:

1. Review the title element on all pages and update as appropriate.

2. Add a unique description meta tag to every page within the website.

Continued >

Consider This: Your Turn *continued*

3. Identify and discuss two social networking websites that the website could use to promote the future technologies website. Use your browser to search for and download the social media icon logos (brand assets) directly from the social networking company. For example, if you want to download the icons for Facebook, search for Facebook brand assets. If necessary, use basic image editing software, such as Paint, to resize the image. Review the brand asset guidelines to learn the minimum image dimensions.

4. Add two social media icons to the footer element on every page within the website and include a link for both. You may use generic links to the social networking website, such as https://www.facebook.com.

5. Use your style sheet to style the social media icons as desired for each viewport.

6. Create a sitemap file for your website. Use `www.exampledomain.com` as the domain.

7. Create and style a Skip to Content link on each page.

8. Create a new file named `styles.min.css`. Minify your CSS and save it in the styles.min .css file. Be sure to keep your original styles.css file. Update the stylesheet link within every HTML file to use the minified CSS file.

9. Save your changes.

10. Publish your website.

11. Submit your files in the format specified by your instructor.

Part 2: ✴ As a group, research how to embed a Twitter feed within your website. Provide an example of how do to this and a link to your resource.

12 | Getting Started with Bootstrap

Objectives

You will have mastered the material in this chapter when you can:

- Describe the Bootstrap framework
- Create a webpage using Bootstrap's starter template
- Create a Bootstrap navbar
- Integrate a Bootstrap hamburger menu
- Style navigation links using Bootstrap
- Define and create a jumbotron
- Explain how to style text using Bootstrap
- Write a jQuery document ready event
- Describe and use the Bootstrap grid system
- Explain how to style images using Bootstrap
- Style a table using Bootstrap
- Describe a content management system

12 | Getting Started with Bootstrap

Introduction

Many of today's modern websites use some type of content management system or web framework. Both tools provide a means to create beautiful, responsive webpages more quickly than a standard text editor.

This chapter provides an introduction to Bootstrap, a popular front-end web framework used to create responsive webpages. You will learn how to create a webpage using Bootstrap's starter template, and then integrate and design a responsive navigation system using the Bootstrap framework. You will learn how to create a hero feature using the Bootstrap framework, to use the Bootstrap grid system to lay out webpage content, and to style text, images, and a table using the Bootstrap framework. Finally, you will learn about content management systems.

Project — Create a Website Using Bootstrap

In Chapters 1–11, you learned how to use HTML, CSS, and JavaScript to create a responsive design website. In Chapter 12, you will learn how to use the Bootstrap framework to create a website.

The project in this chapter recreates the website for the Forward Fitness Club using the Bootstrap framework. To perform these tasks, you create a new webpage using the Bootstrap starter template. Next, you integrate a navigation system using the Bootstrap framework. Then, you create a hero feature with an image in the background and a text overlay. You also use jQuery code to display the hero image the full height of the browser window. Next, you use the Bootstrap grid system to design a three-column and single-column layout for content. Then, you design a footer element using the Bootstrap framework. You also apply Bootstrap classes to existing HTML elements on the About Us page to design the page using the Bootstrap framework. Then, you apply Bootstrap table classes to design a table on the Classes page. Finally, you test the website in each viewport to ensure the website works properly. Figure 12–1 shows the Forward Fitness Club home page in mobile, tablet, and desktop viewports. Figure 12–2 shows the About Us page as displayed in a desktop viewport. Figure 12–3 shows the Classes page as displayed in a desktop viewport.

Roadmap

In this chapter, you will learn how to create the webpages shown in Figures 12–1, 12–2, and 12–3. The following roadmap identifies general activities you will perform as you progress through this chapter:

1. CREATE a BOOTSTRAP WEBPAGE.
2. CREATE a BOOTSTRAP NAVBAR.
3. CREATE a BOOTSTRAP JUMBOTRON.
4. CREATE BOOTSTRAP COLUMNS.

5. CREATE a FOOTER.

6. ADD BOOTSTRAP CLASSES TO the ABOUT US PAGE.

7. ADD BOOSTRAP CLASSES TO the CLASSES PAGE.

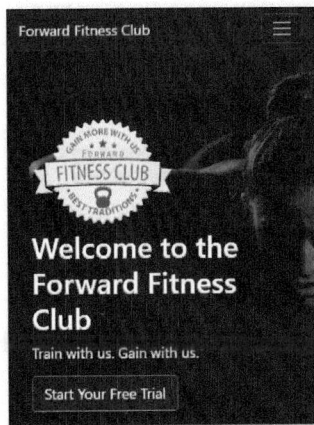

(a) Home Page in Mobile Viewport

(b) Home Page in Tablet Viewport

(c) Home Page in Desktop Viewport

Figure 12–1

About Us Page in Desktop Viewport

Figure 12–2

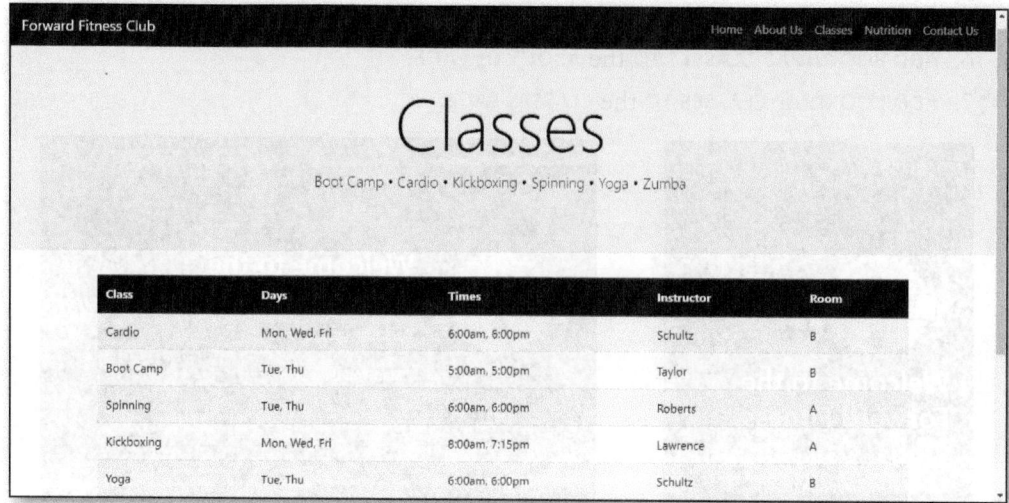

Classes Page in Desktop Viewport

Figure 12–3

At the beginning of step instructions throughout the chapter, you will see an abbreviated form of this roadmap. The abbreviated roadmap uses colors to indicate chapter progress: grey means the chapter is beyond that activity; blue means the task being shown is covered in that activity, and black means that activity is yet to be covered. For example, the following abbreviated roadmap indicates the chapter would be showing a task in the 2 CREATE BOOTSTRAP NAVBAR activity.

1 CREATE BOOTSTRAP WEBPAGE | 2 CREATE BOOTSTRAP NAVBAR | 3 CREATE BOOTSTRAP JUMBOTRON | 4 CREATE BOOTSTRAP COLUMNS

5 CREATE FOOTER | 6 ADD BOOTSTRAP CLASSES TO ABOUT US PAGE | 7 ADD BOOTSTRAP CLASSES TO CLASSES PAGE

Use the abbreviated roadmap as a progress guide while you read or step through the instructions in this chapter.

Exploring Bootstrap

Bootstrap is a popular, mobile-first, front-end, responsive design web framework. A **web framework** is a development tool that consists of HTML, CSS, and JavaScript. It provides a standard foundation on which to build a website and simplifies the coding process by providing access to predefined style sheets and script files. The website for Bootstrap, getbootstrap.com, is shown in Figure 12–4.

Figure 12–4

As of this publication date, Bootstrap 4 is the latest version of Bootstrap. To get started with Bootstrap, you must either download Bootstrap's CSS and script files, or link to the BootstrapCDN. **CDN** is short for content delivery network. A CDN is a network of servers that provides web content based on the user's geographic location. When a user accesses a page that is linked to a CDN, web content from the server closest to the user is provided. This enables webpage content to load more quickly, no matter the geographic location of the user.

To connect to the BootstrapCDN, add the following link into the head element:

```
<link rel="stylesheet" href="https://stackpath.
bootstrapcdn.com/bootstrap/4.3.1/css/bootstrap.min.css"
integrity="sha384-ggOyR0iXCbMQv3Xipma34MD+dH/1fQ784/j6cY/
iJTQUOhcWr7x9JvoRxT2MZw1T" crossorigin="anonymous">
```

This link provides access to a minified version of Bootstrap's CSS file, as noted in the file path, bootstrap.min.css. Note that this link may change from time to time. To ensure you link to the latest BootstrapCDN, visit bootstrapcdn.com.

To view a non-minified version of Bootstrap's CSS file, visit stackpath.bootstrapcdn.com/bootstrap/4.3.1/css/bootstrap.css. This page is shown in Figure 12–5.

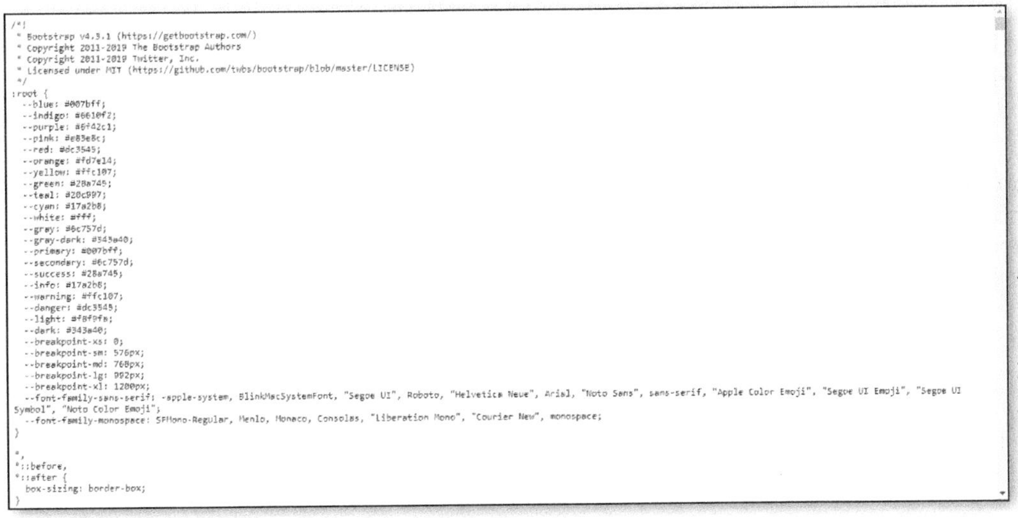

```
/*!
 * Bootstrap v4.3.1 (https://getbootstrap.com/)
 * Copyright 2011-2019 The Bootstrap Authors
 * Copyright 2011-2019 Twitter, Inc.
 * Licensed under MIT (https://github.com/twbs/bootstrap/blob/master/LICENSE)
 */
:root {
  --blue: #007bff;
  --indigo: #6610f2;
  --purple: #6f42c1;
  --pink: #e83e8c;
  --red: #dc3545;
  --orange: #fd7e14;
  --yellow: #ffc107;
  --green: #28a745;
  --teal: #20c997;
  --cyan: #17a2b8;
  --white: #fff;
  --gray: #6c757d;
  --gray-dark: #343a40;
  --primary: #007bff;
  --secondary: #6c757d;
  --success: #28a745;
  --info: #17a2b8;
  --warning: #ffc107;
  --danger: #dc3545;
  --light: #f8f9fa;
  --dark: #343a40;
  --breakpoint-xs: 0;
  --breakpoint-sm: 576px;
  --breakpoint-md: 768px;
  --breakpoint-lg: 992px;
  --breakpoint-xl: 1200px;
  --font-family-sans-serif: -apple-system, BlinkMacSystemFont, "Segoe UI", Roboto, "Helvetica Neue", Arial, "Noto Sans", sans-serif, "Apple Color Emoji", "Segoe UI Emoji", "Segoe UI
Symbol", "Noto Color Emoji";
  --font-family-monospace: SFMono-Regular, Menlo, Monaco, Consolas, "Liberation Mono", "Courier New", monospace;
}

*,
*::before,
*::after {
  box-sizing: border-box;
}
```

Source: stackpath.bootstrapcdn.com

Figure 12–5

When you visit the non-minified Bootstrap CSS file, you will see that it contains hundreds of style rules for HTML elements as well as many classes. Once you have linked your webpage to the BootstrapCDN, these style rules will be applied to your HTML elements. You can apply any of the class selector style rules by adding them as an attribute to your HTML elements. For example, if you want to format an element to use white text, add a class attribute with the value **`text-white`**. If you want to apply rounded corners to an image, add a class attribute with the value **`rounded`** to an img element. Bootstrap has hundreds of predefined classes within its style sheet. For a list of Bootstrap 4 classes, visit www.w3schools.com/bootstrap4/bootstrap_ref_all_classes.asp.

BTW

Internet Explorer and Bootstrap 4

Bootstrap 4 is not supported by Internet Explorer 9 or other legacy versions of Internet Explorer.

Bootstrap provides a starter template at getbootstrap.com/docs/4.3/getting-started/introduction. Figure 12–6 shows the starter template provided on this page.

As shown in Figure 12–6, the Bootstrap Starter template includes all basic HTML elements needed to create an HTML 5 webpage. It also includes the CSS link to the BootstrapCDN. Above the closing body tag, the template includes three script elements that link to three different JavaScript files. The first script element connects to the jQuery JavaScript file. This allows a developer to integrate jQuery if desired.

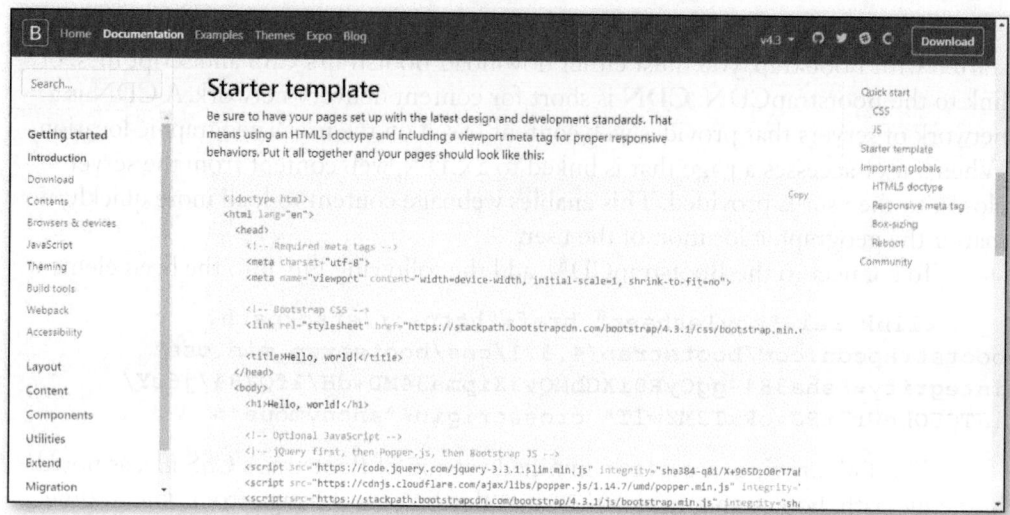

Figure 12–6

The second script connects to Popper.js, which allows a developer to use the Popper .js library. Popper.js is a JavaScript library that helps position elements on a webpage. The third script element connects to the Bootstrap JavaScript file, which enables a developer to use Bootstrap JavaScript functions, such as the hamburger menu.

CONSIDER THIS

How many media queries does Bootstrap use and what breakpoints are used for each media query?
Bootstrap version 4.3 includes several media queries and uses four primary breakpoints within its style sheet: 576 px, 768 px, 992 px, and 1200 px. You can create media queries with these same breakpoints within your custom style sheet in order to style certain elements for specific viewports.

Next, you will get started with your first Bootstrap webpage by using the Bootstrap starter template.

To Create a Bootstrap Webpage

1 CREATE BOOTSTRAP WEBPAGE | 2 CREATE BOOTSTRAP NAVBAR | 3 CREATE BOOTSTRAP JUMBOTRON | 4 CREATE BOOTSTRAP COLUMNS
5 CREATE FOOTER | 6 ADD BOOTSTRAP CLASSES TO ABOUT US PAGE | 7 ADD BOOTSTRAP CLASSES TO CLASSES PAGE

Use the Bootstrap starter template to create a new home page from scratch. *Why? You can learn how to create a Bootstrap page by using the tools provided on the Bootstrap website.* The following steps create a new home page and add the Bootstrap starter template to the page.

1

- Open your text editor, create a new HTML file named `index.html`, and then save it in the fitness-bootstrap folder from the Data Files.
- Open your browser to getbootstrap.com, tap or click the Documentation navigation link, and then scroll down the page to locate the Starter template (Figure 12–7).

Q&A

The Starter template I see is different from Figure 12–7. Why?
The Starter template shown in Figure 12–7 was the template provided at the time of this publication. The Starter template may vary over time.

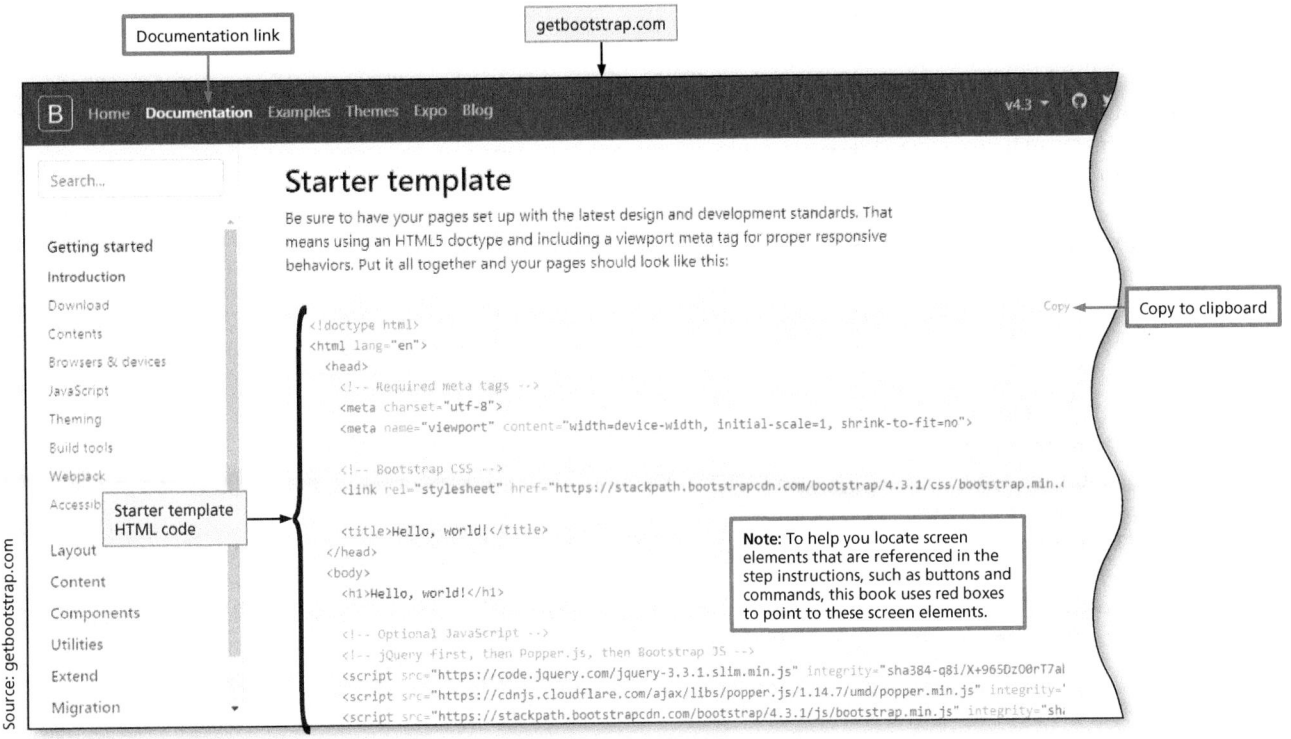

Source: getbootstrap.com

Figure 12–7

2

- Tap or click the Copy link to copy the Starter template code.

- Return to the index.html file in your text editor.

- Tap or click Line 1, and then press CTRL+V to paste the starter template code (Figure 12–8).

Q&A

What is the style sheet link on Line 9?
This is a link to the BootstrapCDN, which provides access to all of the Bootstrap styles.

What are the script elements on Lines 18 through 20?
The first script element connects to the jQuery JavaScript library. This allows a developer to integrate jQuery if desired. The second script connects to Popper.js, which allows a developer to use the Popper JavaScript library. The third script element connects to the Bootstrap JavaScript file, which enables a developer to use Bootstrap JavaScript functions, such as the hamburger menu.

```
10
11        <title>Hello, world!</title>
12      </head>
13      <body>
14        <h1>Hello, world!</h1>
15
16        <!-- Optional JavaScript -->
17        <!-- jQuery first, then Popper.js, then Bootstrap JS -->
18        <script src="https://code.jquery.com/jquery-3.3.1.slim.min.js"
          integrity="sha384-
          q8i/X+965Dz00rT7abK41JStQIAqVgRVzpbzo5smXKp4YfRvH+8abtTE1Pi6jizo"
          crossorigin="anonymous"></script>
19        <script
          src="https://cdnjs.cloudflare.com/ajax/libs/popper.js/1.14.7/umd/popper
          .min.js" integrity="sha384-
          UO2eT0CpHqdSJQ6hJty5KVphtPhzWj9WO1clHTMGa3JDZwrnQq4sF86dIHNDz0W1"
          crossorigin="anonymous"></script>
20        <script
          src="https://stackpath.bootstrapcdn.com/bootstrap/4.3.1/js/bootstrap.mi
          n.js" integrity="sha384-
          JjSmVgyd0p3pXB1rRibZUAYoIIy6OrQ6VrjIEaFf/nJGzIxFDsf4x0xIM+B07jRM"
          crossorigin="anonymous"></script>
21      </body>
22    </html>
```

index.html file

Starter template HTML code

Source: Brackets

Figure 12–8

3

- Save the index.html file.

- Tap or click at the end of Line 1, press the ENTER key to insert a new Line 2, and then type `<!-- Student Name, Current Date -->` to add a comment. Replace Student Name with your name and Current Date with today's date.

- Tap or click at the end of Line 7, press the ENTER key to insert a new Line 8, and then type `<meta name="description" content="The Forward Fitness Club is an elite fitness center dedicated to helping clients achieve their fitness and nutrition goals.">` to insert a new meta tag (Figure 12–9).

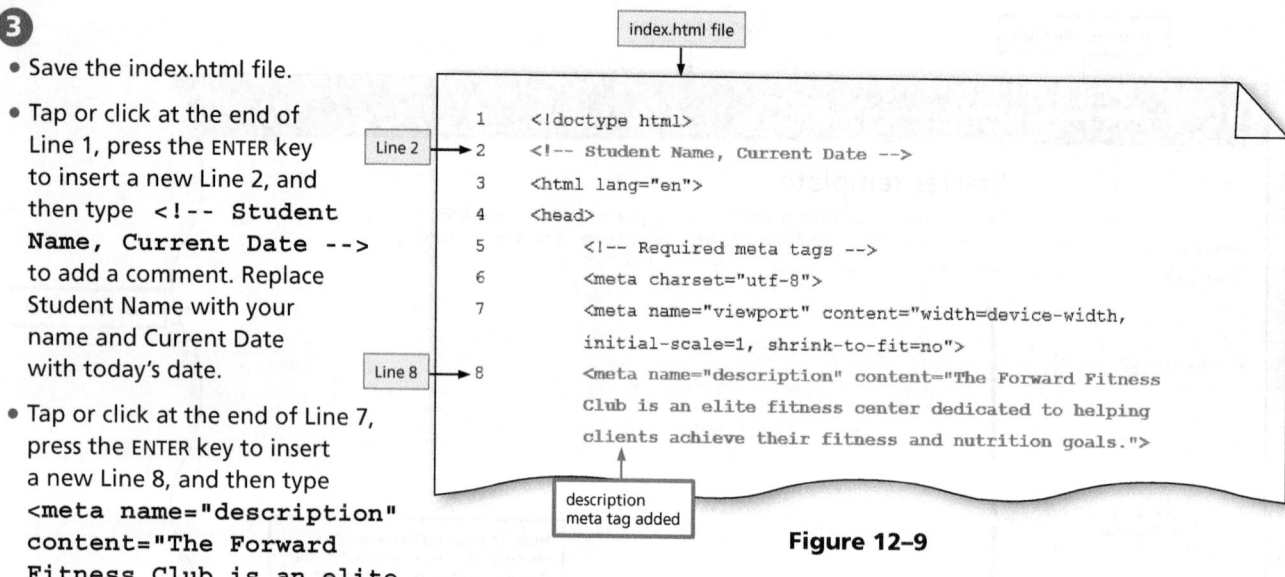

```
                                                index.html file

 1    <!doctype html>
 2    <!-- Student Name, Current Date -->     ← Line 2
 3    <html lang="en">
 4    <head>
 5        <!-- Required meta tags -->
 6        <meta charset="utf-8">
 7        <meta name="viewport" content="width=device-width,
          initial-scale=1, shrink-to-fit=no">
 8        <meta name="description" content="The Forward Fitness   ← Line 8
          Club is an elite fitness center dedicated to helping
          clients achieve their fitness and nutrition goals.">
```

description meta tag added

Figure 12–9

4

- Press the ENTER key twice to insert new Lines 9 and 10.

- On Line 10, type `<!-- Favicon -->` to insert a new comment.

- Press the ENTER to insert a new Line 11, and then type `<link rel="shortcut icon" href="images/favicon.ico">` to add a shortcut icon.

- Press the ENTER to insert a new Line 12, and then type `<link rel="icon" type="image/png" sizes="32x32" href="images/favicon-32.png">` to add a favicon.

- Press the ENTER to insert a new Line 13, and then type `<link rel="apple-touch-icon" sizes="180x180" href="images/apple-touch-icon.png">` to add a favicon.

- Press the ENTER to insert a new Line 14, and then type `<link rel="icon" sizes="192x192" href="images/android-chrome-192.png">` to add a favicon (Figure 12–10).

```
                                                index.html file

 5    <!-- Required meta tags -->
 6    <meta charset="utf-8">
 7    <meta name="viewport" content="width=device-width, initial-
      scale=1, shrink-to-fit=no">
 8    <meta name="description" content="The Forward Fitness Club
      is an elite fitness center dedicated to helping clients
      achieve their fitness and nutrition goals.">
 9
10    <!-- Favicon -->     ← Line 10          comment added
11    <link rel="shortcut icon" href="images/favicon.ico">
12    <link rel="icon" type="image/png" sizes="32x32"
      href="images/favicon-32.png">
13    <link rel="apple-touch-icon" sizes="180x180"
      href="images/apple-touch-icon.png">
14    <link rel="icon" sizes="192x192" href="images/android-
      chrome-192.png">
```

links to favicons

Figure 12–10

● Tap or click at the end of Line 17, and then press the ENTER key twice to insert new Lines 18 and 19.

● On Line 19, type `<!-- My Style Sheet -->` to insert a new comment.

● Press the ENTER to insert a new Line 20, and then type `<link rel="stylesheet" href="css/styles.css">` to add a link to a local style sheet.

● On Line 22, replace the "Hello, world!" title text content with **Complete Fitness - Free Trial | Forward Fitness Club** to update the title element.

● Save your changes (Figure 12–11).

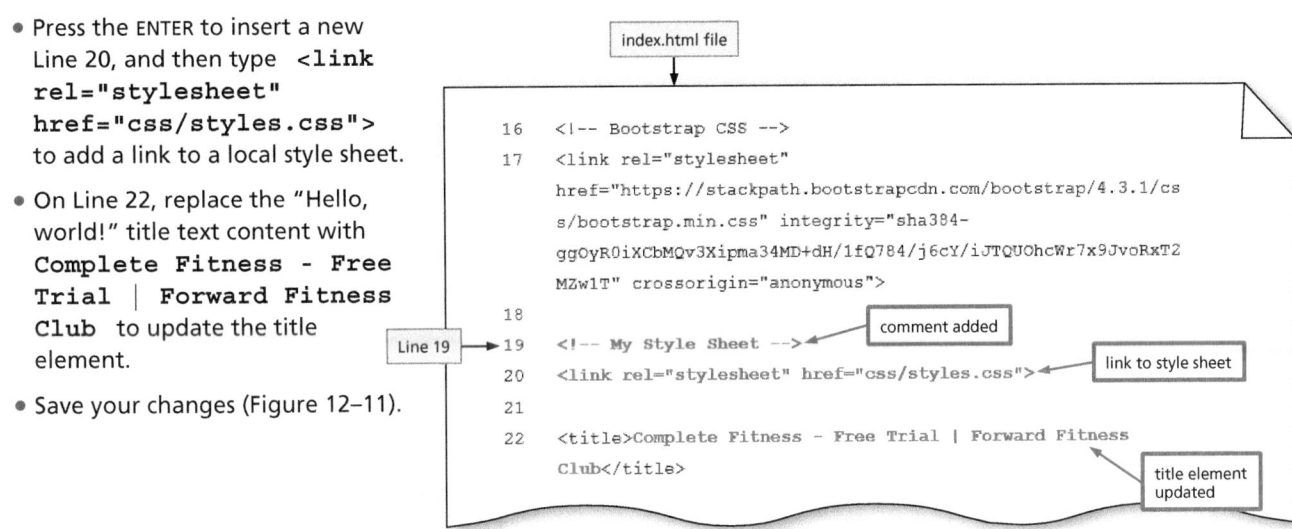

index.html file

```
16    <!-- Bootstrap CSS -->
17    <link rel="stylesheet"
      href="https://stackpath.bootstrapcdn.com/bootstrap/4.3.1/cs
      s/bootstrap.min.css" integrity="sha384-
      ggOyR0iXCbMQv3Xipma34MD+dH/1fQ784/j6cY/iJTQUOhcWr7x9JvoRxT2
      MZw1T" crossorigin="anonymous">
18
19    <!-- My Style Sheet -->
20    <link rel="stylesheet" href="css/styles.css">
21
22    <title>Complete Fitness - Free Trial | Forward Fitness
      Club</title>
```

Line 19

comment added

link to style sheet

title element updated

Figure 12–11

Bootstrap Navigation Bar

The Bootstrap framework provides several options to integrate a navigation bar, or navbar, within a website. Table 12–1 lists several classes that pertain to formatting a Bootstrap navbar.

Table 12–1 Bootstrap Navbar Classes	
Class	**Description**
navbar	Creates a fluid navbar using Bootstrap
navbar-brand	Used to wrap the business name or logo
navbar-collapse	Used to collapse the navbar; a hamburger menu replaces the text navigation links
navbar-dark	Formats navbar text links white
navbar-expand-(sm, md, lg, or lx)	Used to format links vertically for smaller viewports
navbar-light	Formats navbar text links black
navbar-nav	Used to format links within the navbar
navbar-text	Used to vertically center text
navbar-toggler	Used to format the hamburger menu icon

There are several steps in creating a navigation bar with Bootstrap. Step one is to create a nav element that specifies the navbar. The next step is to create a responsive navbar with the **navbar-expand** class, followed by -sm, -md, -lg, or -xl to set the size of the vertical navbar. This will vertically stack links for smaller viewports, or for large viewports, if desired. The following example shows an HTML 5 nav tag with a class attribute that uses the navbar and navbar-expand-sm values.

```
<nav class="navbar navbar-expand-sm">
```

In the above example, the nav element is styled as a Bootstrap navbar and displays links vertically for smaller, mobile viewports.

You can format the background color and link text color for the navbar using Bootstrap as well. Table 12–2 lists Bootstrap background color classes. To apply a dark gray background, use the bg-dark class. To apply a light gray background, use the bg-light class. The navbar-light class formats the navbar text links as black. The navbar-dark formats the navbar text links as white.

Table 12–2 Bootstrap Background Color Classes	
Class	**Description**
bg-danger	Applies a red background color
bg-dark	Applies a dark gray background color
bg-info	Applies a dark teal background color
bg-light	Applies a dark light gray background color
bg-primary	Applies a dark blue background color
bg-secondary	Applies a dark gray background color
bg-success	Applies a dark green background color
bg-warning	Applies a yellow/orange background color

You can also format the navbar to remain at the top of the page, or create a "sticky" navbar, as you scroll by specifying the `fixed-top` class. The following example shows an HTML 5 nav tag with a class attribute that uses the `navbar`, `navbar-expand-sm`, `navbar-dark`, `bg-dark`, and `fixed-top` values.

```
<nav class="navbar navbar-expand-sm navbar-dark bg-dark
fixed-top">
```

Once you have created and formatted the nav element with the desired class attribute values, the next step is to wrap the business name or image within the `navbar-brand` class to style it. This class places the business name or image on the left side of the navbar, as shown in the following example.

```
<a class="navbar-brand" href="index.html">Forward Fitness
Club</a>
```

To integrate a hamburger menu icon using Bootstrap, you wrap a span element within a button element that contains several attributes, as shown in the following example.

```
<button class="navbar-toggler" type="button" data-
toggle="collapse" data-target="#navbarResponsive" aria-
controls="navbarResponsive" aria-expanded="false"
aria-label="Toggle navigation">
        <span class="navbar-toggler-icon"></span>
</button>
```

In this example, the navbar-toggler class is used to style the hamburger menu. The type attribute specifies a button type. The data-toggle attribute uses the Bootstrap collapse.js plug-in to hide content. The data-target attribute is used to assign a CSS selector in which to apply the collapse. The next three attributes all involve ARIA, Accessible Rich Internet Applications, which are attributes used to address accessibility for webpage content. The aria-controls attribute is used with the data-target attribute and refers to the data-target attribute navbarResponsive value. The aria-expanded attribute is set to false because the hamburger menu is collapsed by default. The aria-label attribute is used to specify the label name for accessibility. A span element with a class attribute value of navbar-toggler-icon is wrapped within the button to display the hamburger menu icon.

BTW
ARIA
For more information about ARIA authoring practices, w3.org/TR /wai-aria-practices-1.1.

After you add the code to create the hamburger menu icon, the final step in creating the Bootstrap navigation bar is to create the navbar text links. The following is an example of navbar text links.

```
<div class="collapse navbar-collapse" id="navbarResponsive">

    <ul class="navbar-nav">

        <li class="nav-item">

            <a class="nav-link" href="index.html">Home</a>

        </li>

        <li class="nav-item">

            <a class="nav-link" href="about.html">About Us</a>

        </li>

        <li class="nav-item">

            <a class="nav-link" href="services.html">Services</a>

        </li>

        <li class="nav-item">

            <a class="nav-link" href="contact.html">Contact</a>

        </li>

    </ul>

</div>
```

The collapse class value specifies collapsible content. The navbar-collapse value is used to collapse a navbar when a hamburger menu is displayed. The nav-item class value uses the Bootstrap style rule to style the list item as a nav-item. The nav-link class value uses the Bootstrap style rule to style links within the navbar.

The following is an example of the HTML code used to create a Bootstrap navigation system.

```
<!-- Bootstrap Navigation bar -->

<nav class="navbar navbar-expand-sm navbar-dark fixed-top bg-dark">

    <a class="navbar-brand" href="index.html">Forward
    Fitness Club</a>

    <!-- Hamburger menu icon -->

    <button class="navbar-toggler" type="button" data-toggle="collapse" data-target="#navbarResponsive" aria-controls="navbarResponsive" aria-expanded="false" aria-label="Toggle navigation">

        <span class="navbar-toggler-icon"></span>

    </button>

    <div class="collapse navbar-collapse" id="navbarResponsive">
        <ul class="navbar-nav ml-auto">
            <li class="nav-item">
                <a class="nav-link" href="index.html">Home</a>
            </li>
```

```
                                          <li class="nav-item">
                                           <a class="nav-link" href="about.html">About Us</a>
                                          </li>
                                            <li class="nav-item">
                                           <a class="nav-link" href="classes.html">Classes</a>
                                          </li>
                                            <li class="nav-item">
                                            <a class="nav-link" href="nutrition.
                                           html">Nutrition</a>
                                          </li>
                                          <li class="nav-item">
                                            <a class="nav-link" href="contact.
                                           html">Contact Us</a>
                                          </li>
                                        </ul>
                                      </div>
                                    </nav>
```

BTW

Using the # Symbol for Links

When you are creating a new webpage and need to add links, it is a common practice to use the # symbol for the href value when the page does not yet exist. This allows you to click a link without receiving an error that the page could not be found.

Next, you will integrate a Bootstrap navigation system within the index.html file.

To Create a Bootstrap Navigation Bar

1 CREATE BOOTSTRAP WEBPAGE | 2 CREATE BOOTSTRAP NAVBAR | 3 CREATE BOOTSTRAP JUMBOTRON | 4 CREATE BOOTSTRAP COLUMNS

5 CREATE FOOTER | 6 ADD BOOTSTRAP CLASSES TO ABOUT US PAGE | 7 ADD BOOTSTRAP CLASSES TO CLASSES PAGE

Now that you have created a new home page that uses the Bootstrap framework, integrate a navigation bar that uses Bootstrap. *Why? You use the Bootstrap framework to create a Bootstrap navigation system.* The following steps integrate a Bootstrap navbar on the home page.

1

- Return to index.html in your text editor to prepare to modify the file.
- Delete the heading 1 Hello, world! element on Line 25 to remove it.
- Tap or click at the end of Line 24, and then press the ENTER key twice to insert new Lines 25 and 26.
- On Line 26, type `<!-- Bootstrap Navigation bar -->` to insert a comment.
- Press the ENTER key to insert a new Line 27, and then type `<nav class="navbar navbar-expand-sm navbar-dark fixed-top bg-dark">` to insert a starting nav tag.
- Press the ENTER key twice to insert new Lines 28 and 29, increase the indent, and then type `<a class="navbar-brand" href="index.html">Forward Fitness Club</a>` to insert and anchor element (Figure 12–12).

Q&A What is the purpose of the class values specified for the nav element?

The navbar value is used to specify a Bootstrap navigation bar. The navbar-expand-sm class is used to specify a small vertical navigation link stack for small viewports. The navbar-dark class sets the text color to white. The fixed-top class makes the navbar sticky. The bg-dark class sets the background color to dark gray.

What is the purpose of the navbar-brand class for the anchor element?

The navbar-brand value is used to style the company name or logo.

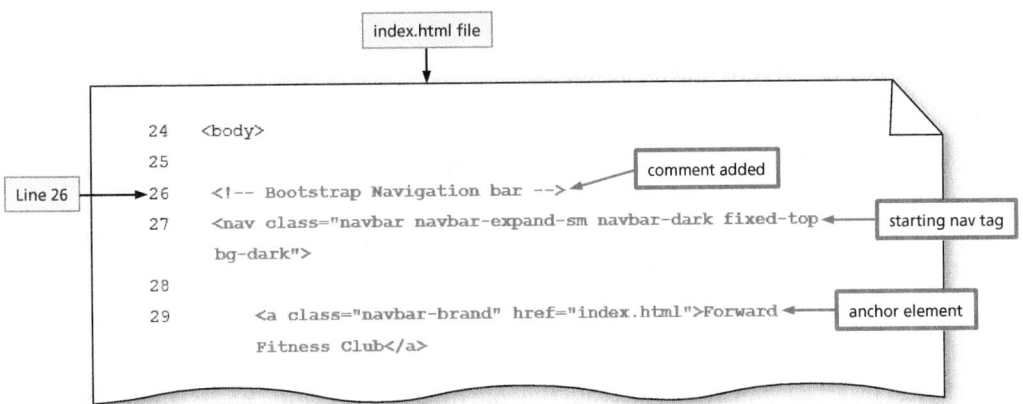

Figure 12–12

2

- Press the ENTER key twice to insert new Lines 30 and 31.

- On Line 31, type `<!-- Hamburger menu icon -->` to insert a comment.

- Press the ENTER key to insert a new Line 32, and then type `<button class="navbar-toggler" type="button" data-toggle="collapse" data-target="#navbarResponsive" aria-controls="navbarResponsive" aria-expanded="false" aria-label="Toggle navigation">` to insert a starting button tag.

- Press the ENTER key to insert a new Line 33, increase the indent, and then type `<span class="navbar-toggler-icon"></span>` to insert a span element.

- Press the ENTER key to insert a new Line 34, decrease the indent, and then type `</button>` to insert an ending button tag (Figure 12–13).

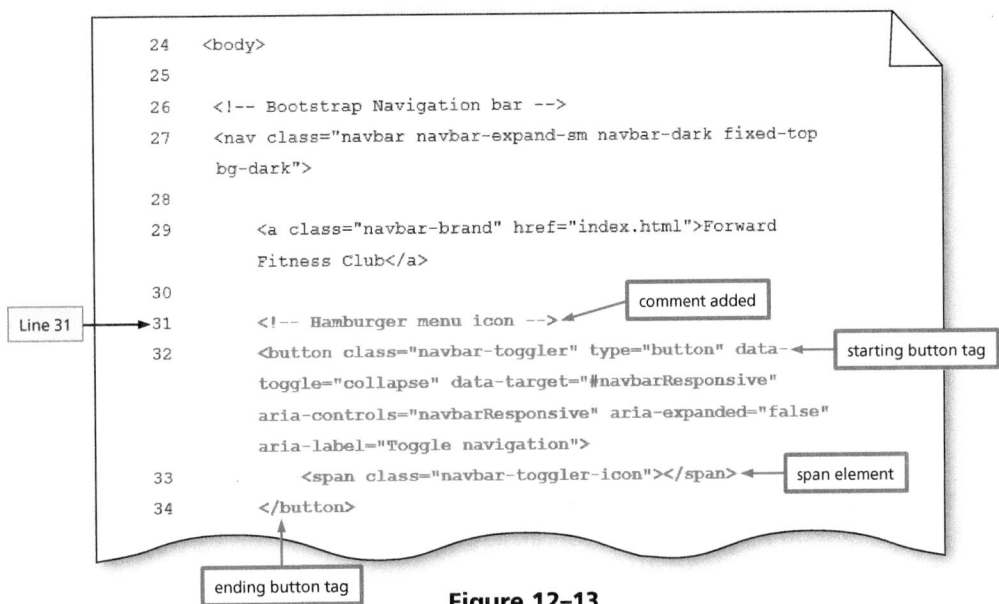

Figure 12–13

Q&A

What is the purpose of the button element and its numerous attributes?
The button element is used to add the hamburger menu icon. The various attributes enable the toggle of the hamburger menu icon.

What is the purpose of the span element?
The span element creates and styles the hamburger menu icon.

- Press the ENTER key twice to insert new Lines 35 and 36.

- On Line 36, type `<!-- Navbar links -->` to insert a comment.

- Press the ENTER key to insert a new Line 37, and then type `<div class="collapse navbar-collapse" id="navbarResponsive">` to insert a starting div tag.

- Press the ENTER key to insert a new Line 38, increase the indent, and then type `<ul class="navbar-nav ml-auto">` to insert a starting unordered list tag.

- Press the ENTER key to insert a new Line 39, increase the indent, and then type `<li class="nav-item">` to insert a starting list item tag.

- Press the ENTER key to insert a new Line 40, increase the indent, and then type `<a class="nav-link" href="index.html">Home</a>` to insert an anchor element.

- Press the ENTER key to insert a new Line 41, decrease the indent, and then type `</li>` to insert a closing list item tag (Figure 12–14).

Q&A

What is the purpose of the div class and id attributes?
The class attributes specify Bootstrap collapsible content. The id attribute specifies the id value used by the button to toggle the navigation list on and off for the hamburger menu.

What is the ml-auto class?
The ml-auto class specifies left margin of auto.

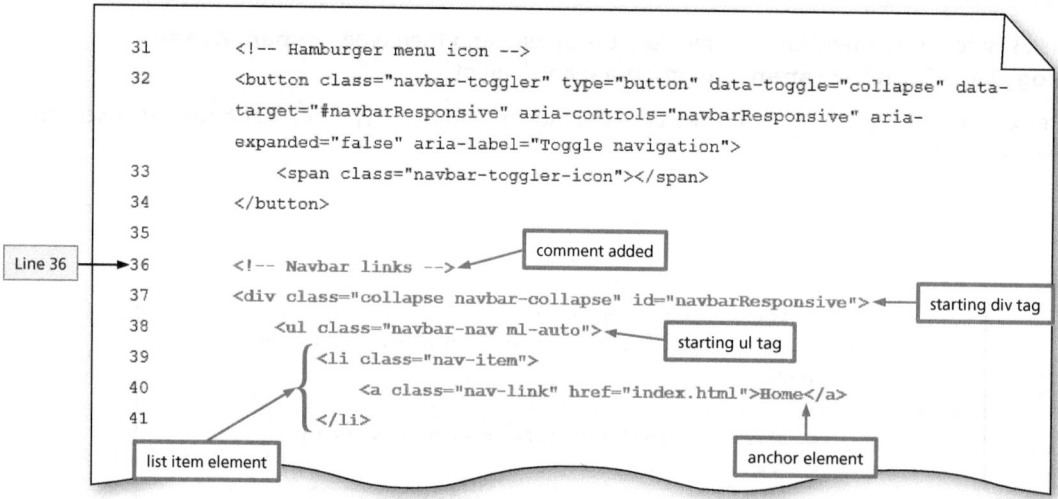

Figure 12–14

- Press the ENTER key to insert a new Line 42, and then type `<li class="nav-item">` to insert a starting list item tag.

- Press the ENTER key to insert a new Line 43, increase the indent, and then type `<a class="nav-link" href="about.html">About Us</a>` to insert an anchor element.

- Press the ENTER key to insert a new Line 44, decrease the indent, and then type `</li>` to insert a closing list item tag.

- Press the ENTER key to insert a new Line 45, and then type `<li class="nav-item">` to insert a starting list item tag.

- Press the ENTER key to insert a new Line 46, increase the indent, and then type `<a class="nav-link" href="classes.html">Classes</a>` to insert an anchor element.

- Press the ENTER key to insert a new Line 47, decrease the indent, and then type `</li>` to insert a closing list item tag (Figure 12–15).

Figure 12–15

5

- Press the ENTER key to insert a new Line 48, and then type `<li class="nav-item">` to insert a starting list item tag.

- Press the ENTER key to insert a new Line 49, increase the indent, and then type `<a class="nav-link" href="nutrition.html">Nutrition</a>` to insert an anchor element.

- Press the ENTER key to insert a new Line 50, decrease the indent, and then type `</li>` to insert a closing list item tag.

- Press the ENTER key to insert a new Line 51, and then type `<li class="nav-item">` to insert a starting list item tag.

- Press the ENTER key to insert a new Line 52, increase the indent, and then type `<a class="nav-link" href="contact.html">Contact Us</a>` to insert an anchor element.

- Press the ENTER key to insert a new Line 53, decrease the indent, and then type `</li>` to insert a closing list item tag.

- Press the ENTER key to insert a new Line 54, decrease the indent, and then type `</ul>` to insert a closing unordered list tag.

- Press the ENTER key to insert a new Line 55, decrease the indent, and then type `</div>` to insert a closing div tag.

- Press the ENTER key twice to insert new Lines 56 and 57, decrease the indent, and then type `</nav>` to insert a closing nav tag (Figure 12–16).

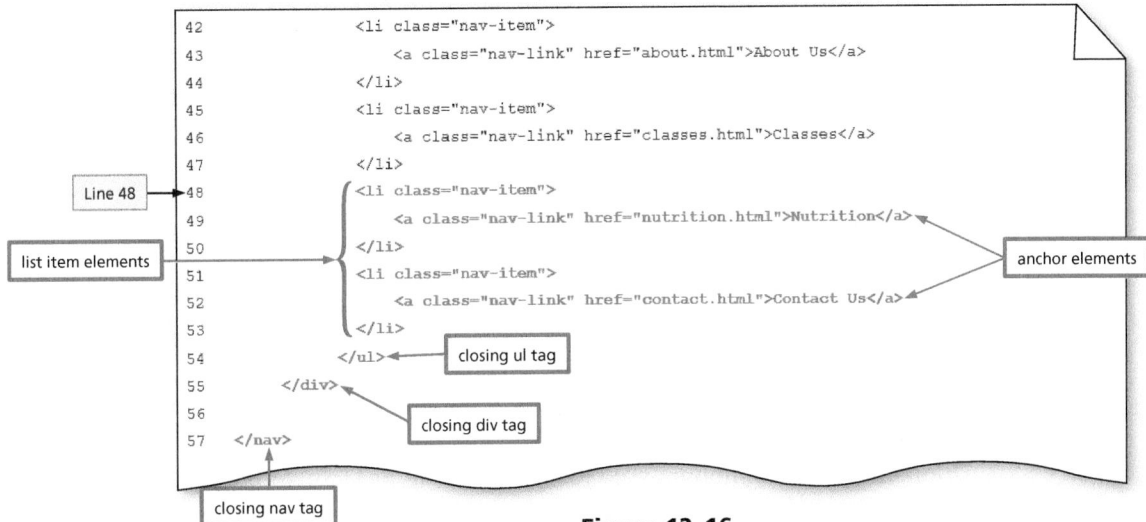

Figure 12–16

- Save your changes.
- Open the index.html file in Chrome and display it in a desktop viewport (Figure 12–17).

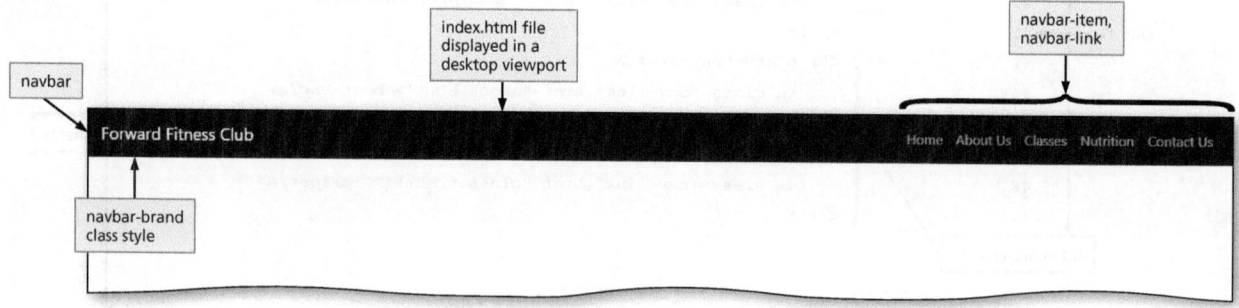

Figure 12–17

- Open Chrome DevTools, and then tap or click the Toggle device toolbar to display the index .html file in a mobile viewport (Figure 12–18).

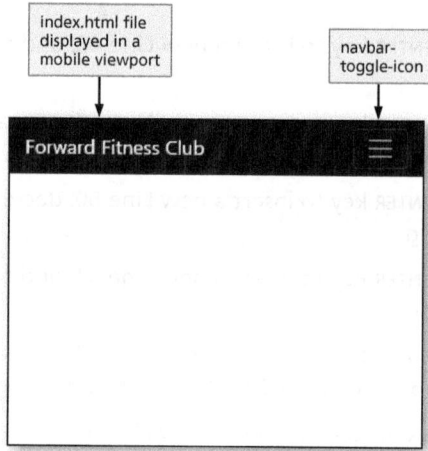

Figure 12–18

Bootstrap Responsive Containers

The Bootstrap framework includes hundreds of predefined style rules for classes. Two important class values are `container` and `container-fluid`. Both classes are used to make an HTML element responsive. The `container` class uses a fixed width, based on the size of the current viewport. The `container-fluid` class sets the width to 100%, using the complete width of the viewport. The following example demonstrates how to apply the `container` class to a `div` element.

```
<div class="container">

</div>
```

Bootstrap Jumbotron

As you develop a webpage, you might want to include a large box of content on the page to grab the user's attention. Bootstrap provides this feature with the **jumbotron**, which is a large, responsive box used to contain webpage information. Jumbotrons are commonly used for hero content near the top of webpage. Figure 12–19 shows an example of a jumbotron from the getbootstrap.com website.

Figure 12–19

To create a jumbotron, you use the `jumbotron` or `jumbotron-fluid` class. The `jumbotron` class includes rounded corners, while the `jumbotron-fluid` class does not use rounded corners and spans the full width of the viewport.

Margins and Padding

Bootstrap makes it easy to add responsive margins and padding to any element using the margin and padding classes listed in Table 12–3.

Table 12–3 Bootstrap Margin and Padding Classes		
Class	**Description**	**Example**
m-	Specifies margin on all sides; can be a number from 0 to 5 or sm, md, lg, or xl	m-3
mt-	Specifies top margin; can be a number from 0 to 5 or sm, md, lg, or xl	mt-2 mt-md
mb-	Specifies bottom margin; can be a number from 0 to 5 or sm, md, lg, or xl	mb-1 mb-sm
ml-	Specifies left margin; can be a number from 0 to 5 or sm, md, lg, or xl	ml-4 ml-lg
mr-	Specifies right margin; can be a number from 0 to 5 or sm, md, lg, or xl	mr-5 mr-xl
my-	Specifies top and bottom margin; can be a number from 0 to 5 or sm, md, lg, or xl	my-4 my-lg
mx-	Specifies left and right margin; can be a number from 0 to 5 or sm, md, lg, or xl	mx-4 mx-lg
mx-auto	Horizontally centers an element	mx-auto

(Continued)

Class	Description	Example
	Table 12–3 Bootstrap Margin and Padding Classes *(Continued)*	
p-	Specifies padding on all sides; can be a number from 0 to 5 or sm, md, lg, or xl	p-3
pt-	Specifies top padding; can be a number from 0 to 5 or sm, md, lg, or xl	pt-2 pt-md
pb-	Specifies bottom padding; can be a number from 0 to 5 or sm, md, lg, or xl	pb-1 pb-sm
pl-	Specifies left padding; can be a number from 0 to 5 or sm, md, lg, or xl	pl-4 pl-lg
pr-	Specifies right padding; can be a number from 0 to 5 or sm, lg, or xl	pr-5 pr-xl
py-	Specifies top and bottom padding; can be a number from 0 to 5 or sm, md, lg, or xl	py-4 py-lg
px-	Specifies left and right padding; can be a number from 0 to 5 or sm, md, lg, or xl	px-4 px-lg

The following example demonstrates how to apply margins and padding using the Bootstrap framework. Here, top and bottom margin of 1 and left and right padding of 3 is applied to a figure element.

```
<figure class="container my-1 px-3">

</figure>
```

Images

As you have learned in Chapters 4 and 5, creating responsive or fluid images is essential for a responsive website. Responsive images allow an image to grow and shrink, depending on the size of the viewport. Recall that to make an image responsive, you need a style rule for the `img` element that sets the max-width to 100%. Bootstrap has already created this style rule with the `img-fluid` class, which also sets the height to auto. To make an image responsive, add the `img-fluid` class to an `img` element. The following example shows an image element that uses the Bootstrap `img-fluid` class.

```
<img src="images/forward-fitness-logo.png" alt="Forward
Fitness Club logo" class="img-fluid">
```

You can also use Bootstrap to apply rounded corners to an image by applying the `rounded` class to an img element. You can make an image a circle by applying the `rounded-circle` class to an img element. You can make an image appear as a thumbnail by applying the `img-thumbnail` class to an img element. The following example shows an image element that uses the Bootstrap `img-fluid` and `rounded` classes.

```
<img src="images/roast-chicken.png" alt="roasted chicken
breast" class="img-fluid rounded">
```

You can align images to the left or right by using the `float-right` and `float-left` classes. The following example shows an image element that uses the Bootstrap `float-right` class.

```
<img src="images/roast-chicken.png" alt="roasted chicken
breast" class="float-right">
```

Bootstrap Colors

The Bootstrap framework uses eight colors to represent specific meanings. Table 12–4 summarizes each color and meaning.

Table 12–4 Bootstrap Colors

Class (Color)	Meaning
primary (blue)	Used to indicate a primary, important information
secondary (medium gray)	Used to indicate secondary information
success (green)	Used to indicate success
info (teal)	Used for information
warning (orange/yellow)	Used to indicate a warning
danger (red)	Used to indicate danger
light (light gray)	Styles with light gray
dark (dark gray)	Styles with dark gray

Styling Buttons

The Bootstrap framework provides many options to style buttons. Table 12–5 summarizes button classes.

Table 12–5 Bootstrap Button Classes

Class	Description
btn	Specifies a basic Bootstrap button; styles a button with a gray background and rounded corners
btn-block	Styles a button as a block element and sets the button width to the size of the parent container
btn-group	Groups buttons together on one line
btn-toolbar	Creates a button toolbar using sets of button groups
btn-lg	Creates a large button
btn-sm	Creates a small button
btn-link	Styles a button to appear as a link
btn-info	Styles a button as teal
btn-light	Styles a button as light gray
btn-dark	Styles a button as dark gray
btn-danger	Styles a button as red
btn-primary	Styles a button as blue
btn-secondary	Styles a button as gray
btn-success	Styles a button as green
btn-warning	Styles a button as orange
btn-outline-dark	Creates an outlined button with a dark gray border
btn-outline-danger	Creates an outlined button with a red border
btn-outline-info	Creates an outlined button with a teal border
btn-outline-light	Creates an outlined button with a light gray border
btn-outline-primary	Creates an outlined button with a blue border
btn-outline-secondary	Creates an outlined button with a gray border
btn-outline-success	Creates an outlined button with a green border
btn-outline-warning	Creates an outlined button with an orange border

The following example shows a button element with three Bootstrap button classes applied.

```
<button class="btn btn-outline-secondary btn-lg">Start Your Free Trial</button>
```

Additionally, you can turn an anchor element into a button by including the role attribute with a value of button. The following example shows the role attribute used within an anchor element to create a button.

```
<a href="contact.html" role="button" class="btn btn-outline-secondary btn-lg">Start Your Free Trial</a>
```

Custom Styles

As you can see, using the Bootstrap framework can significantly reduce the time it takes to create a responsive webpage. It is easy to incorporate Bootstrap's predefined classes where needed. However, as you design, you will likely want to customize certain page elements with your own styles. Despite being connected to Bootstrap's style sheet, you can still create your own custom style sheet and apply it to your website. The key is to list your custom style sheet below the link to the BootstrapCDN.

Next, you will style a header element as a jumbotron and then create a custom style rule that displays an image within the background of the jumbotron. You will use an external style sheet to create custom style rules to style content within the header element. Note that when you created the new home page for the Forward Fitness Club, you added a link to a local style sheet named styles.css, located within the css folder.

BTW

Sass

Sass stands for Syntactically Awesome Style Sheets and is a CSS extension language used to improve efficiency when writing CSS. For more information about Sass, visit sass-lang.com.

To Create a Bootstrap Jumbotron

1 CREATE BOOTSTRAP WEBPAGE | 2 CREATE BOOTSTRAP NAVBAR | 3 CREATE BOOTSTRAP JUMBOTRON | 4 CREATE BOOTSTRAP COLUMNS
5 CREATE FOOTER | 6 ADD BOOTSTRAP CLASSES TO ABOUT US PAGE | 7 ADD BOOTSTRAP CLASSES TO CLASSES PAGE

You have created a new home page that uses the Bootstrap framework and integrated a Bootstrap navbar. Now you need to create a header element for the webpage and add content to it. *Why? Create a header element with content to capture the user's attention.* The following steps create a header element in the index.html file.

1

- Return to index.html in your text editor to prepare to modify the file.
- Tap or click at the end of Line 57, and then press the ENTER key twice to insert new Lines 58 and 59.
- On Line 59, type `<!-- Header and Hero Image -->` to insert a comment.
- Press the ENTER key to insert a new Line 60, and then type `<header class="jumbotron-fluid hero">` to insert a starting header tag.
- Press the ENTER key to insert a new Line 61, increase the indent, and then type `<div class="container welcome text-white">` to insert a starting div element.
- Press the ENTER key to insert a new Line 62, increase the indent, and then type `<img src="images /forward-fitness-logo.png" alt="Forward Fitness Club logo" class="float-left mr-3 img-fluid">` to insert an image element (Figure 12–20).

Q&A

What is the purpose of the container and welcome class values?

The container value is a Bootstrap style that specifies a fixed width, based on the device viewport. The welcome class value will be a custom style rule that you create in future steps.

What is the purpose of the class values specified for the image element?

All of these class values are Bootstrap styles. The float-left specifies a left float. The mr-3 specifies right margin. The img-fluid specifies a fluid or responsive image. The text-white value specifies to use a white font color.

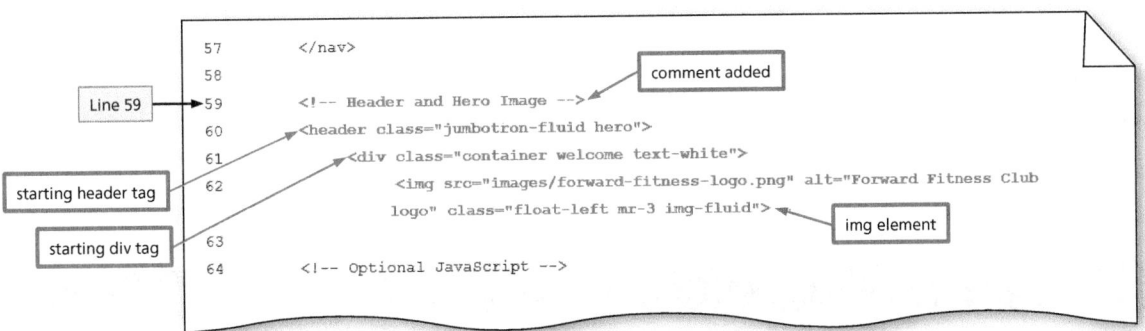

Figure 12–20

2

- Press the ENTER key to insert a new Line 63, and then type `<h1>Welcome to the Forward Fitness Club</h1>` to insert a heading 1 element.

- Press the ENTER key to insert a new Line 64, and then type `<p>Train with us. Gain with us.</p>` to insert a paragraph element.

- Press the ENTER key to insert a new Line 65, and then type `<a href="contact.html" role="button" class="btn btn-outline-secondary btn-lg bg-dark text-white">Start Your Free Trial</a>` to insert an anchor element.

- Press the ENTER key to insert a new Line 66, decrease the indent, and then type `</div>` to insert a closing div element.

- Press the ENTER key to insert a new Line 67, decrease the indent, and then type `</header>` to insert a closing header element (Figure 12–21).

Q&A

What is the purpose of the class values specified for the anchor element?
All of these class values are Bootstrap styles. The btn class specifies a basic Bootstrap button. The btn-outline-secondary class styles the button border. The btn-lg class specifies the button size. The bg-dark class specifies the background color of the button. The text-white value specifies to use white for the font color.

What is the purpose of the role attribute within the anchor element?
The role attribute specifies the anchor element to act as a button.

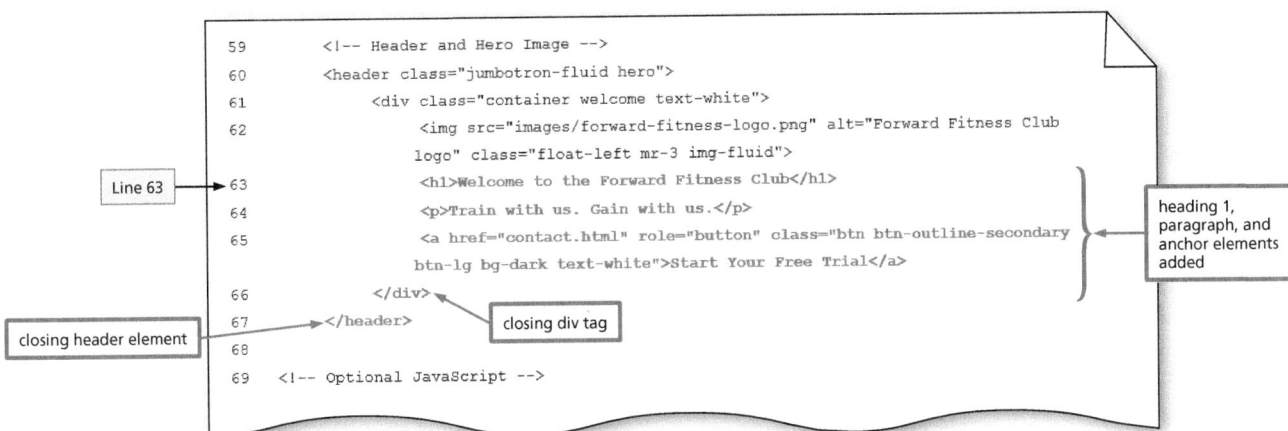

Figure 12–21

- Save your changes.

- Refresh index.html in your browser and display a desktop viewport (Figure 12–22).

Why is the navbar positioned over the header element?
This is due to the current style rules. You will create custom style rules in future steps to correct this.

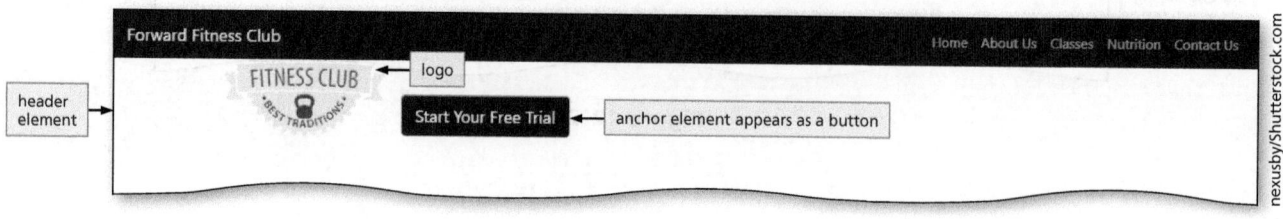

Figure 12–22

To Create Custom Style Rules

1 CREATE BOOTSTRAP WEBPAGE | 2 CREATE BOOTSTRAP NAVBAR | 3 CREATE BOOTSTRAP JUMBOTRON | 4 CREATE BOOTSTRAP COLUMNS
5 CREATE FOOTER | 6 ADD BOOTSTRAP CLASSES TO ABOUT US PAGE | 7 ADD BOOTSTRAP CLASSES TO CLASSES PAGE

You have created a header element and now need to create a custom style rule to set an image as a background. You also need to create custom style rules for the welcome class and elements within the parent of the welcome class. *Why? Create a modern, eye-catching hero image with a text overlay.* The following steps create style rules in the styles.css file.

- Open the styles.css file in your text editor from your fitness-bootstrap\css folder to prepare to modify the file.

- Add your name, file name, and the current date to the comment at the top of the page.

- Tap or click at the end of Line 18, and then press the ENTER key to insert a new Line 19.

- On Line 19, type `.hero {` to insert a selector and opening curly brace.

- Press the ENTER key to insert a new Line 20, increase the indent, and then type `background-image: linear-gradient(rgba(0, 0, 0, 0.5), rgba(0, 0, 0, 0.5)),url(../images /hero-home.jpg);` to insert a declaration.

- Press the ENTER key to insert a new Line 21, and then type `background-size: cover;` to insert a declaration.

- Press the ENTER key to insert a new Line 22, and then type `background-position: center;` to insert a declaration.

- Press the ENTER key to insert a new Line 23, and then type `background-repeat: no-repeat;` to insert a declaration.

- Press the ENTER key to insert a new Line 24, decrease the indent, and then type `}` to close the style rule (Figure 12–23).

Why are there two rgba values for the background image property?
The background image specifies an image with a transparent black gradient overlay used to slightly darken the image.

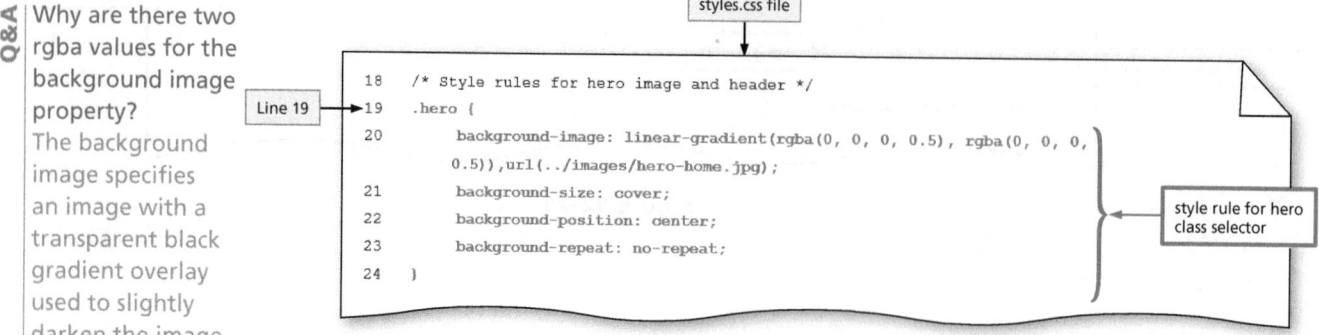

Figure 12–23

2

- Press the ENTER key twice to insert new Lines 25 and 26.

- On Line 26, type `.welcome {` to insert a selector and opening curly brace.

- Press the ENTER key to insert a new Line 27, increase the indent, and then type `position: absolute;` to insert a declaration.

- Press the ENTER key to insert a new Line 28, and then type `top: 20%;` to insert a declaration.

- Press the ENTER key to insert a new Line 29, and then type `margin: auto;` to insert a declaration.

- Press the ENTER key to insert a new Line 30, and then type `padding: 2em;` to insert a declaration.

- Press the ENTER key to insert a new Line 31, decrease the indent, and then type `}` to close the style rule (Figure 12–24).

styles.css file

```
18    /* Style rules for hero image and header */
19    .hero {
20        background-image: linear-gradient(rgba(0, 0, 0, 0.5), rgba(0, 0, 0,
          0.5)),url(../images/hero-home.jpg);
21        background-size: cover;
22        background-position: center;
23        background-repeat: no-repeat;
24    }
25
26    .welcome {
27        position: absolute;
28        top: 20%;
29        margin: auto;
30        padding: 2em;
31    }
```

Line 26

style rule for welcome class selector

Figure 12–24

Q&A | What is the purpose of this style rule?
This style rule positions the div element with the welcome class near the top-left of the header element.

3

- Press the ENTER key twice to insert new Lines 32 and 33.

- On Line 33, type `.welcome p {` to insert a selector and opening curly brace.

- Press the ENTER key to insert a new Line 34, increase the indent, and then type `font-size: 1.25em;` to insert a declaration.

- Press the ENTER key to insert a new Line 35, and then type `width: 70%;` to insert a declaration.

- Press the ENTER key to insert a new Line 36, and then type `line-height: 1.5;` to insert a declaration.

- Press the ENTER key to insert a new Line 37, decrease the indent, and then type `}` to close the style rule (Figure 12–25).

styles.css file

```
26    .welcome {
27        position: absolute;
28        top: 20%;
29        margin: auto;
30        padding: 2em;
31    }
32
33    .welcome p {
34        font-size: 1.25em;
35        width: 70%;
36        line-height: 1.5;
37    }
```

Line 33

style rule for welcome p class selector

Figure 12–25

Q&A | What is the purpose of this style rule?
This style rule styles the paragraph element within the welcome class parent div container.

4

- Save your changes.

- Refresh index.html in your browser (Figure 12–26).

Q&A Why is the background image not displayed?
A little jQuery code is needed to display the hero image.

Figure 12–26

Using jQuery

As you learned in Chapter 11, jQuery is a popular JavaScript library used by developers to quickly add JavaScript functionality to a webpage. To use jQuery, you must either download the jQuery JavaScript file and save it within your scripts folder or use a script element to connect to the jQuery CDN.

Using jQuery, you can select HTML page elements and then use jQuery methods to perform some type of action, such as show or hide. Table 12–6 lists some common jQuery methods. When writing jQuery statements, begin each statement with the $ symbol.

Table 12–6 jQuery Methods		
Method	**Description**	**Example**
hide()	Hides an element	$("p").hide();
show()	Shows an element	$("div").show();
fadeIn()	Fades in an element	$("p").fadeIn();
fadeOut()	Fades out an element	$("div").fadeOut();
slideUp()	Slides an element up	$("p").slideUp();
slideDown()	Slides an element down	$("div").slideDown();
animate()	Animates an element	$("p").animate();

To use jQuery, begin with a document ready event, as shown in the following example.

```
$(document).ready(function(){
    Add jQuery methods here
});
```

nexusby/Shutterstock.com

Add desired methods within the document ready event, as shown in the following example.

```
$(document).ready(function(){
        $('.hero').height($(window).height());
});
```

Next, you will write a jQuery document ready event that uses the height() method to display the hero image the full height of the browser window within the hero class header element.

Add jQuery Code

You have created a header element and now need to display the background image within the full height of the browser window. To do this, you need to write some jQuery code in the script.js file and then connect the script.js file to the index.html file. *Why? Use the jQuery height() method to display the image the extent of the browser window.* The following steps add jQuery code in the script.js file and then add a script element to the index.html file.

- Open the script.js file in your text editor from your fitness-bootstrap\scripts folder to prepare to modify the file.

- Add your name, file name, and the current date to the comment at the top of the page.

- Tap or click at the end of Line 7, and then press the ENTER key to insert a new Line 8.

- On Line 8, type `$(document).ready(function(){` to insert a document ready jQuery event.

- Press the ENTER key to insert a new Line 9, increase the indent, and then type `$('.hero').height($(window).height());` to add the jQuery height() method.

- Press the ENTER key to insert a new Line 10, decrease the indent, and then type `});` to end the event (Figure 12–27).

Q&A | What does this jQuery event do?
The jQuery document ready event is using the height() method to set the height of the hero class to the height of the browser window.

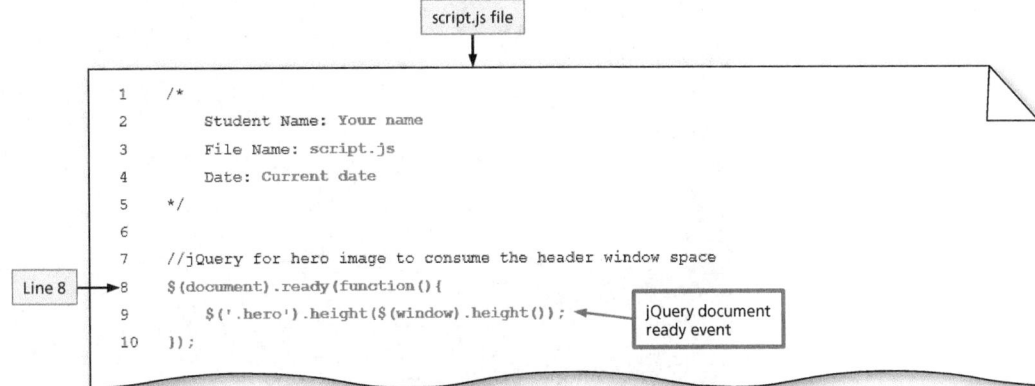

Figure 12–27

2

- Return to index.html in your text editor.

- Tap or click at the end of Line 73, and then press the ENTER key to insert a new Line 74.

- On Line 74, type `<script src="scripts/script. js"></script>` to insert a script element.

- Save your changes (Figure 12–28).

index.html file

```
73        <script
          src="https://stackpath.bootstrapcdn.com/bootstrap/4.3.1/js/bootstrap.min.j
          s" integrity="sha384-
          JjSmVgyd0p3pXB1rRibZUAYoIIy6OrQ6VrjIEaFf/nJGzIxFDsf4x0xIM+B07jRM"
          crossorigin="anonymous"></script>
74        <script src="scripts/script.js"></script>       script element
75      </body>
76    </html>
```

Line 74

Figure 12–28

3

- Refresh index.html in your browser (Figure 12–29).

index.html file displayed in desktop viewport

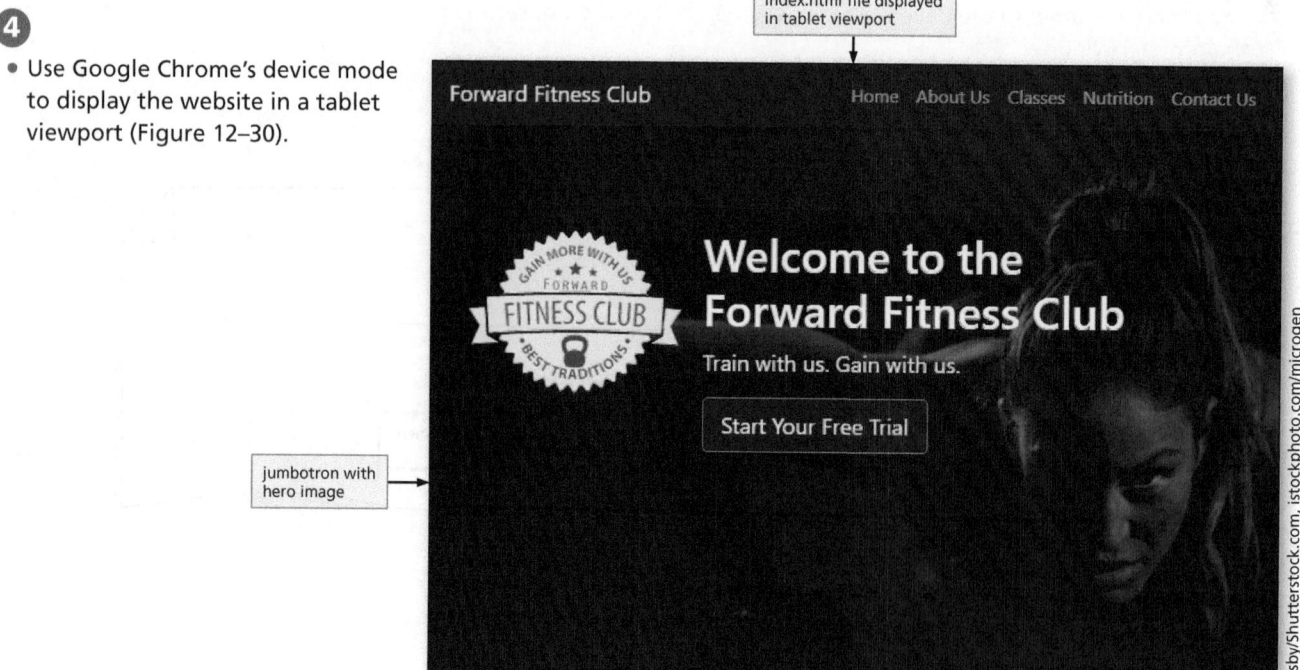

jumbotron with hero image

nexusby/Shutterstock.com, istockphoto.com/microgen

Figure 12–29

4

- Use Google Chrome's device mode to display the website in a tablet viewport (Figure 12–30).

index.html file displayed in tablet viewport

jumbotron with hero image

nexusby/Shutterstock.com, istockphoto.com/microgen

Figure 12–30

5

• Use Google Chrome's device mode to display the website in a mobile viewport (Figure 12–31).

index.html file displayed in mobile viewport

jumbotron with hero image

nexusby/Shutterstock.com, istockphoto.com/microgen

Figure 12–31

Break Point: If you want to take a break, this is a good place to do so. You can exit the text editor now. To resume at a later time, open index.html in your text editor, and continue following the steps from this location forward.

Using the Bootstrap Grid System

Bootstrap uses a grid system that consists of up to 12 columns across a page. To use the grid system, you create a row using the `row` class value, and then specify the number of columns needed for each row. There are five classes that can be used to create rows. Table 12–7 summarizes the Bootstrap grid classes.

Class	Description	Example
Table 12–7 Bootstrap Grid Classes		
col-	Grid column for extra small devices (viewport <576px); is always displayed horizontally on a webpage	<div class="col-6"></div>
col-sm-	Grid column for small devices (viewport >=576px); is displayed vertically on a webpage and then horizontally for larger media query breakpoints	<div class="col-sm-3"></div>
col-md-	Grid column for medium devices (viewport >=768px); is displayed vertically on a webpage and then horizontally for larger media query breakpoints	<div class="col-md-4"></div>
col-lg-	Grid column for large devices (viewport >=992px); is displayed vertically on a webpage and then horizontally for larger media query breakpoints	<div class="col-lg-3"></div>
col-xl-	Grid column for extra-large devices (viewport >=1200px); is displayed vertically on a webpage and then horizontally for larger media query breakpoints	<div class="col-xl-2"></div>

Each grid class scales up to the next media query breakpoint, so if you use col-sm-3, it will scale up for the medium, large, and extra-large device breakpoints.

To use the Bootstrap grid system, begin with an HTML element, such as a div, with a class attribute value of **container** or **container-fluid** to make the element responsive. Next, nest a div element with a class attribute value of **row** to designate a Bootstrap row. Then, nest up to twelve div elements with a **col-sm-*** class attribute value to create the desired number of columns. The following example creates one row with three columns using the Bootstrap grid system.

```
<div class="container">
  <div class="row">
    <div class="col-sm-4">
      Column 1
    </div>
    <div class="col-sm-4">
      Column 2
    </div>
    <div class="col-sm-4">
      Column 3
    </div>
  </div>
</div>
```

Figure 12–32 shows an example of a three-column Bootstrap grid layout with a defined background column and borders when displayed in a browser.

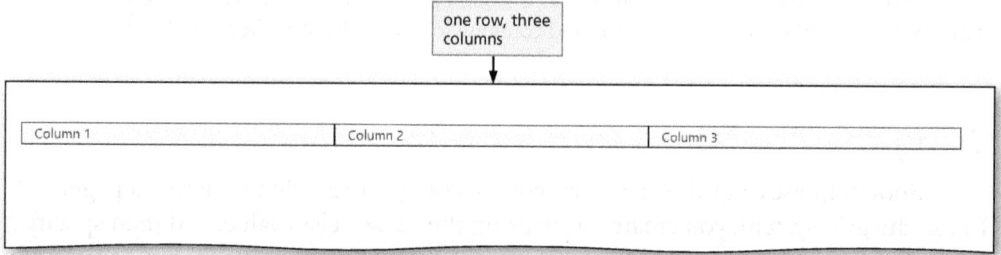

Figure 12–32

Note that the column numbers for each row should total 12. If you want three even columns, use col-sm-4. If you want one large column and one smaller column, use col-sm-8 and col-sm-4 or col-sm-7 and col-sm-5. Figure 12–33 provides an example of a webpage that uses a Bootstrap grid layout with three rows and various column sizes. The column numbers for each row total 12.

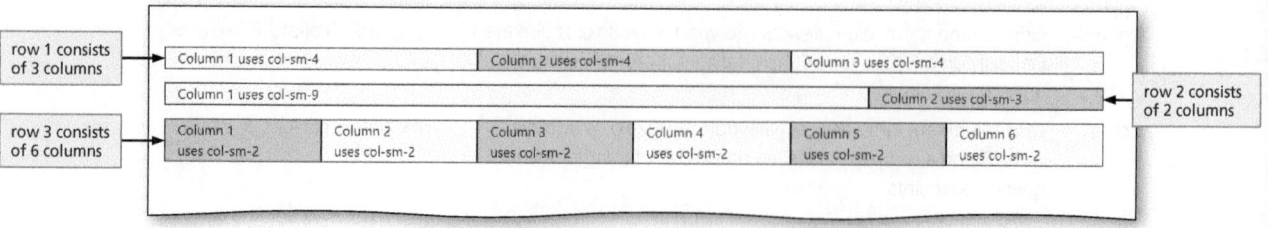

Figure 12–33

Bootstrap Typography Classes

You can style text many ways using Bootstrap classes. Table 12–8 lists several Bootstrap style options for text.

BTW
Bootstrap Typography
More information about Bootstrap typography is available online at getbootstrap.com/docs/4.3 /content/typography.

Table 12–8 Bootstrap Text Classes

Class	Description
font-weight-bold	Applies bold to text
font-italic	Italicizes text
font-weight-light	Applies a lightweight look to text
small	Makes text smaller
lead	Makes a paragraph stand out
display-#	Makes headings stand out; accepts numbers 1 to 4
text-left	Aligns text left
text-right	Aligns text right
text-justify	Justifies text
text-capitalize	Makes text display in all caps
text-lowercase	Makes text display in all lowercase
text-white	Makes text white
text-dark	Makes text dark gray
text-body	Makes text the default body text color
text-muted	Makes text applied grayed out
text-primary	Makes text blue
text-secondary	Makes text medium gray
text-info	Makes text teal
text-success	Makes text green
text-danger	Makes text red
text-light	Makes text light gray
text-warning	Makes text orange/yellow

Next, you will use the Bootstrap grid to lay out the main content on the home page of the Forward Fitness Club.

Add Columns Using Bootstrap

1 CREATE BOOTSTRAP WEBPAGE | 2 CREATE BOOTSTRAP NAVBAR | 3 CREATE BOOTSTRAP JUMBOTRON | **4 CREATE BOOTSTRAP COLUMNS**
5 CREATE FOOTER | 6 ADD BOOTSTRAP CLASSES TO ABOUT US PAGE | 7 ADD BOOTSTRAP CLASSES TO CLASSES PAGE

You have finished creating the header element and hero image. Next, you need to add the main content to the webpage, using the Bootstrap grid system. *Why? Use the Bootstrap grid system to create a single-column layout for a mobile viewport and a three-column layout for tablet and desktop viewports.* The following steps add main content and Bootstrap columns to the index.html file.

- Return to the index.html file in your text editor to prepare to modify the file.
- Tap or click at the end of Line 67, and then press the ENTER key twice to insert new Lines 68 and 69.
- On Line 69, type `<!-- Main Content Area -->` to insert a comment.
- Press the ENTER key to insert a new Line 70, and then type `<main class="container-fluid mt-5">` to add a starting main tag.
- Press the ENTER key twice to insert new Lines 71 and 72, increase the indent, and then type `<div class="row">` to insert a starting div element (Figure 12–34).

What is the purpose of the container-fluid and mt-5 class values?
The container-fluid class value creates a responsive main element. The mt-5 class value specifies top margin.

What is the purpose of the row class value?
The row class value creates a row within a Bootstrap grid layout.

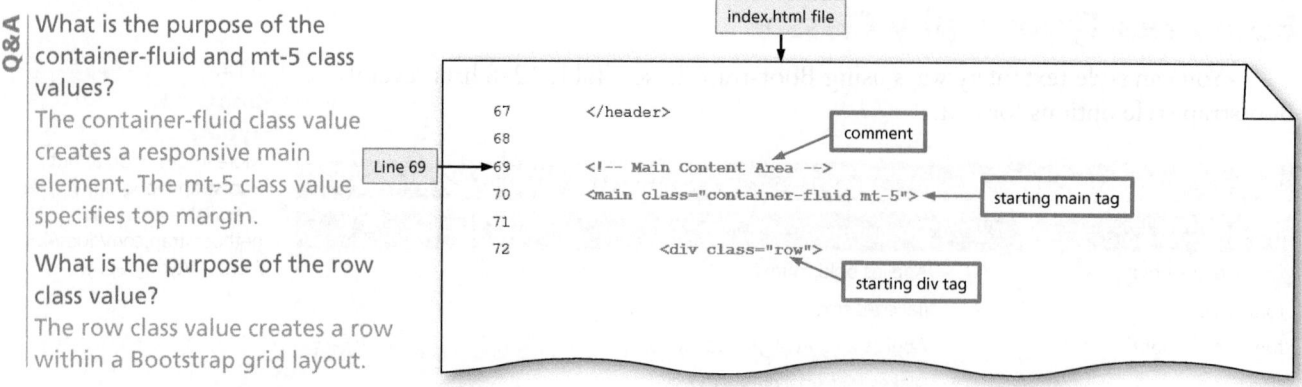

Figure 12–34

 2

- Press the ENTER key twice to insert new Lines 73 and 74, increase the indent, and then type `<div class="col-sm-4">` to insert a starting div element.

- Press the ENTER key to insert a new Line 75, increase the indent, and then type `<figure>` to insert a starting figure element.

- Press the ENTER key to insert a new Line 76, increase the indent, and then type `<a href="classes.html"><img src="images/fitness-group.jpg" alt="group of fitness people" class="img-fluid"></a>` to insert an image element.

- Press the ENTER key to insert a new Line 77, decrease the indent, and then type `</figure>` to insert a closing figure tag.

- Press the ENTER key to insert a new Line 78, and then type `<h1>Group Fitness</h1>` to insert a heading 1 element.

- Press the ENTER key to insert a new Line 79, and then type `<p class="lead">We offer a variety of fitness classes to meet your busy schedule.</p>` to insert a paragraph element.

- Press the ENTER key to insert a new Line 80, decrease the indent, and then type `</div>` to insert a closing div tag (Figure 12–35).

What is the purpose of the col-sm-4 class value?
The col-sm-4 class value creates a column using the Bootstrap grid system.

What is the purpose of the attention and lead class values?
These are both Bootstrap classes used to style text.

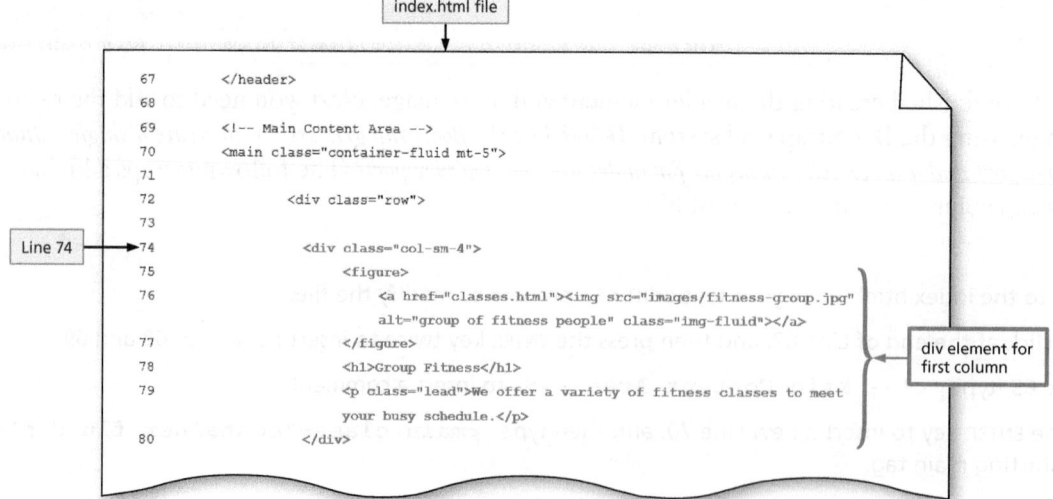

Figure 12–35

3

- Press the ENTER key twice to insert new Lines 81 and 82, and then type `<div class="col-sm-4">` to insert a starting div element.
- Press the ENTER key to insert a new Line 83, increase the indent, and then type `<figure>` to insert a starting figure element.
- Press the ENTER key to insert a new Line 84, increase the indent, and then type `<a href="nutrition.html"><img src="images/food-heart.jpg" alt="group of fitness people" class="img-fluid"></a>` to insert an image element.
- Press the ENTER key to insert a new Line 85, decrease the indent, and then type `</figure>` to insert a closing figure tag.
- Press the ENTER key to insert a new Line 86, and then type `<h1>Nutrition Planning</h1>` to insert a heading 1 element.
- Press the ENTER key to insert a new Line 87, and then type `<p class="lead">We work with you to provide custom nutrition plans to help you reach your goals.</p>` to insert a paragraph element.
- Press the ENTER key to insert a new Line 88, decrease the indent, and then type `</div>` to insert a closing div tag (Figure 12–36).

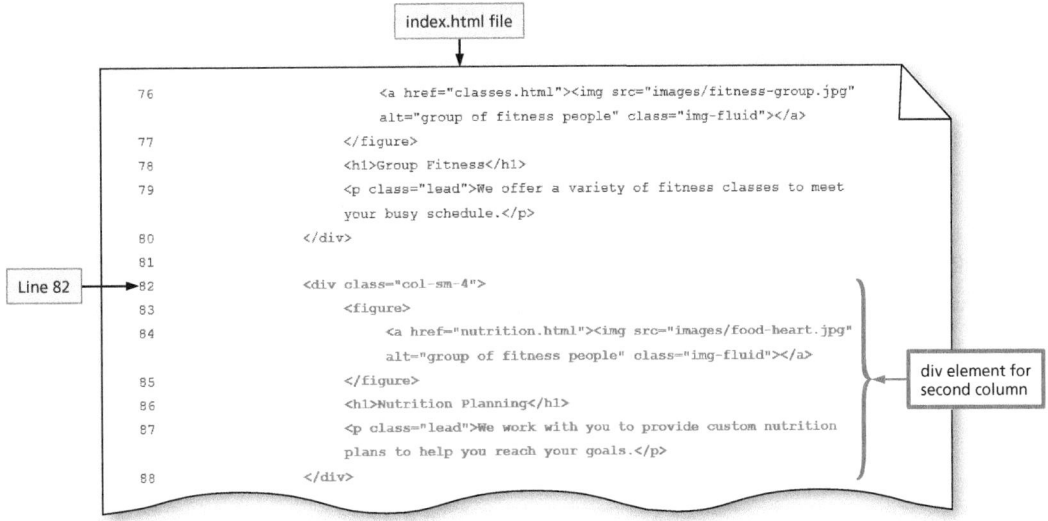

index.html file

```
76              <a href="classes.html"><img src="images/fitness-group.jpg"
                alt="group of fitness people" class="img-fluid"></a>
77          </figure>
78          <h1>Group Fitness</h1>
79          <p class="lead">We offer a variety of fitness classes to meet
            your busy schedule.</p>
80      </div>
81
82      <div class="col-sm-4">
83          <figure>
84              <a href="nutrition.html"><img src="images/food-heart.jpg"
                alt="group of fitness people" class="img-fluid"></a>
85          </figure>
86          <h1>Nutrition Planning</h1>
87          <p class="lead">We work with you to provide custom nutrition
            plans to help you reach your goals.</p>
88      </div>
```

Line 82

div element for second column

Figure 12–36

4

- Press the ENTER key twice to insert new Lines 89 and 90, and then type `<div class="col-sm-4">` to insert a starting div element.
- Press the ENTER key to insert a new Line 91, increase the indent, and then type `<figure>` to insert a starting figure element.
- Press the ENTER key to insert a new Line 92, increase the indent, and then type `<a href="about.html"><img src="images/personal-trainer.jpg" alt="group of fitness people" class="img-fluid"></a>` to insert an image element.
- Press the ENTER key to insert a new Line 93, decrease the indent, and then type `</figure>` to insert a closing figure tag.
- Press the ENTER key to insert a new Line 94, and then type `<h1>Personal Training</h1>` to insert a heading 1 element.
- Press the ENTER key to insert a new Line 95, and then type `<p class="lead">Learn more about personal training and our start-of-the-art equipment.</p>` to insert a paragraph element.

- Press the ENTER key to insert a new Line 96, decrease the indent, and then type `</div>` to insert a closing div tag.

- Press the ENTER key twice to insert new Lines 97 and 98, decrease the indent, and then type `</div>` to insert a closing div tag.

- Press the ENTER key twice to insert new Lines 99 and 100, decrease the indent, and then type `</main>` to insert a closing main tag (Figure 12–37).

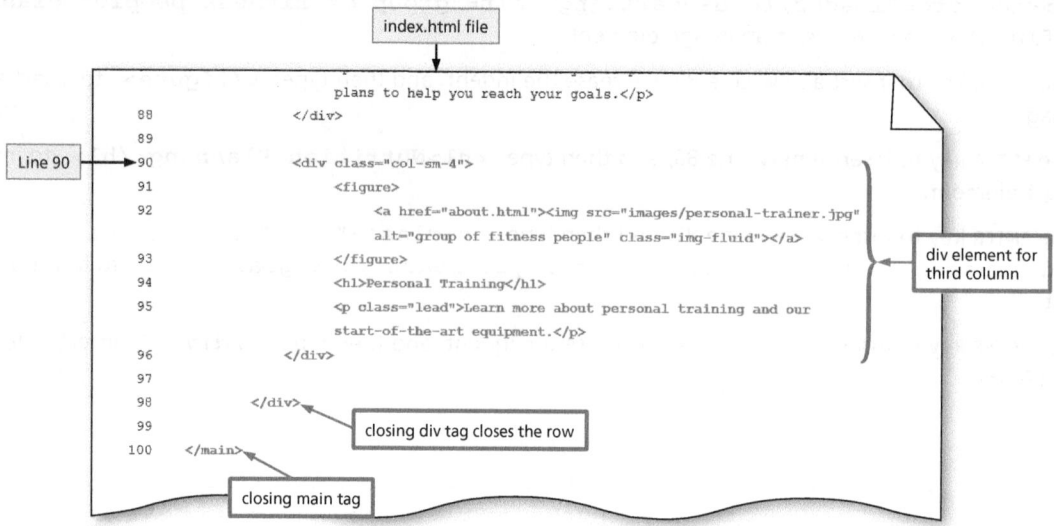

index.html file

```
                              plans to help you reach your goals.</p>
88                   </div>
89
90              <div class="col-sm-4">
91                   <figure>
92                        <a href="about.html"><img src="images/personal-trainer.jpg"
                          alt="group of fitness people" class="img-fluid"></a>
93                   </figure>
94                   <h1>Personal Training</h1>
95                   <p class="lead">Learn more about personal training and our
                     start-of-the-art equipment.</p>
96              </div>
97
98         </div>
99
100    </main>
```

Line 90

div element for third column

closing div tag closes the row

closing main tag

Figure 12–37

5

- Save your changes.

- Open index.html in your browser to display a desktop viewport and scroll down to view the main content area (Figure 12–38).

index.html file displayed in desktop viewport

main content is displayed in three columns

Forward Fitness Club   Home About Us Classes Nutrition Contact Us

Group Fitness
We offer a variety of fitness classes to meet your busy schedule.

Nutrition Planning
We work with you to provide custom nutrition plans to help you reach your goals.

Personal Training
Learn more about personal training and our start-of-the-art equipment.

Figure 12–38

- Use Google Chrome's device mode to display the website in a mobile viewport and scroll down to view the main content area (Figure 12–39).

index.html file displayed in mobile viewport

main content is displayed as single column

Figure 12–39

To Create a Footer Element

1 CREATE BOOTSTRAP WEBPAGE | 2 CREATE BOOTSTRAP NAVBAR | 3 CREATE BOOTSTRAP JUMBOTRON | 4 CREATE BOOTSTRAP COLUMNS
5 CREATE FOOTER | 6 ADD BOOTSTRAP CLASSES TO ABOUT US PAGE | 7 ADD BOOTSTRAP CLASSES TO CLASSES PAGE

You are almost done creating the Bootstrap home page for the Forward Fitness Club website. Next, you need to add a footer element and add content. **Why?** *Complete the HTML page structure by adding a footer element with copyright information, contact information, and social media links.* The following steps add a footer element to the index.html file.

- Return to the index.html file in your text editor to prepare to modify the file.

- Tap or click at the end of Line 100, and then press the ENTER key twice to insert new Lines 101 and 102.

- On Line 102, type `<!-- Footer -->` to insert a comment.

- Press the ENTER key to insert a new Line 103, and then type `<footer class="jumbotron-fluid text-center bg-dark p-5">` to add a starting footer tag.

- Press the ENTER key twice to insert new Lines 104 and 105, increase the indent, and then type `<div class="container text-white">` to insert a starting div tag.

- Press the ENTER key to insert a new Line 106, increase the indent, and then type `<p>&copy; Copyright 2021. All Rights Reserved.</p>` to insert a paragraph element.

- Press the ENTER key to insert a new Line 107, and then type `<p><a href="mailto:forwardfitness@club.net" class="text-white">forwardfitness@club.net</a></p>` to insert a paragraph element (Figure 12–40).

Q&A | What is the purpose of the p-5 class value?
The p-5 class value applies padding on all sides.

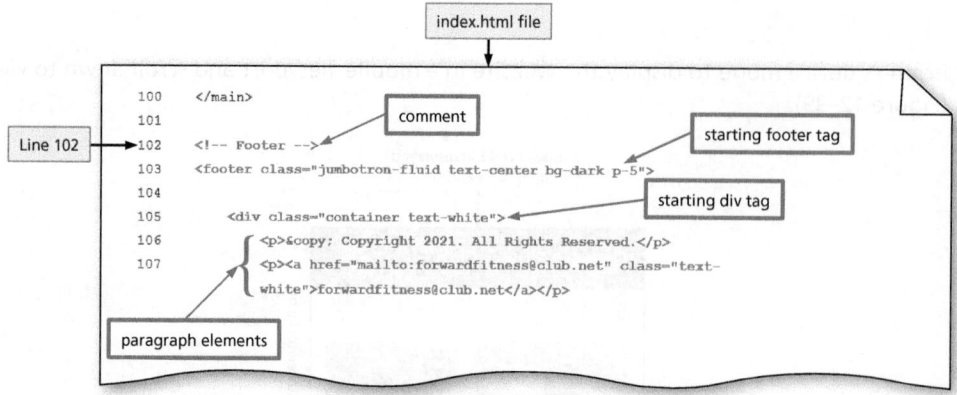

Figure 12–40

- Press the ENTER key to insert a new Line 108, and then type `<a href="https://www.facebook.com/fwdfitclub" target="_blank"><img src="images/facebook-logo.png" alt="black and white Facebook logo" class="pr-4"></a>` to insert an image element wrapped within an anchor element.

- Press the ENTER key to insert a new Line 109, and then type `<a href="https://twitter.com/fwdfitclub" target="_blank"><img src="images/twitter-logo.png" alt="black and white Twitter logo"></a>` to insert an image element wrapped within an anchor element.

- Press the ENTER key to insert a new Line 110, decrease the indent, and then type `</div>` to insert a closing div tag.

- Press the ENTER key twice to insert new Lines 111 and 112, decrease the indent, and then type `</footer>` to insert a closing footer tag (Figure 12–41).

Q&A
What is the purpose of the pr-4 class value?
The pr-4 class value specifies right padding.

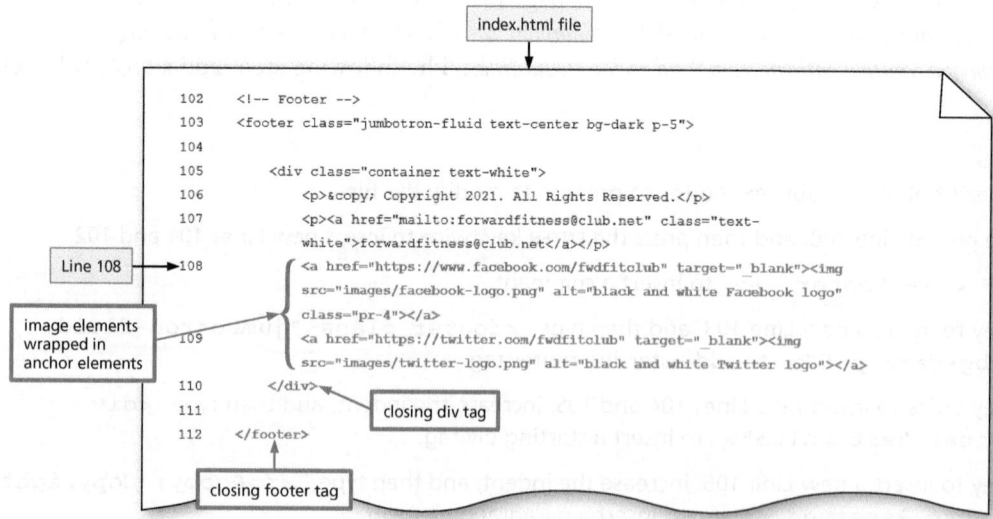

Figure 12–41

• Save your changes.

• Open index.html in your browser to display the page in a desktop viewport and scroll down to view the footer element (Figure 12–42).

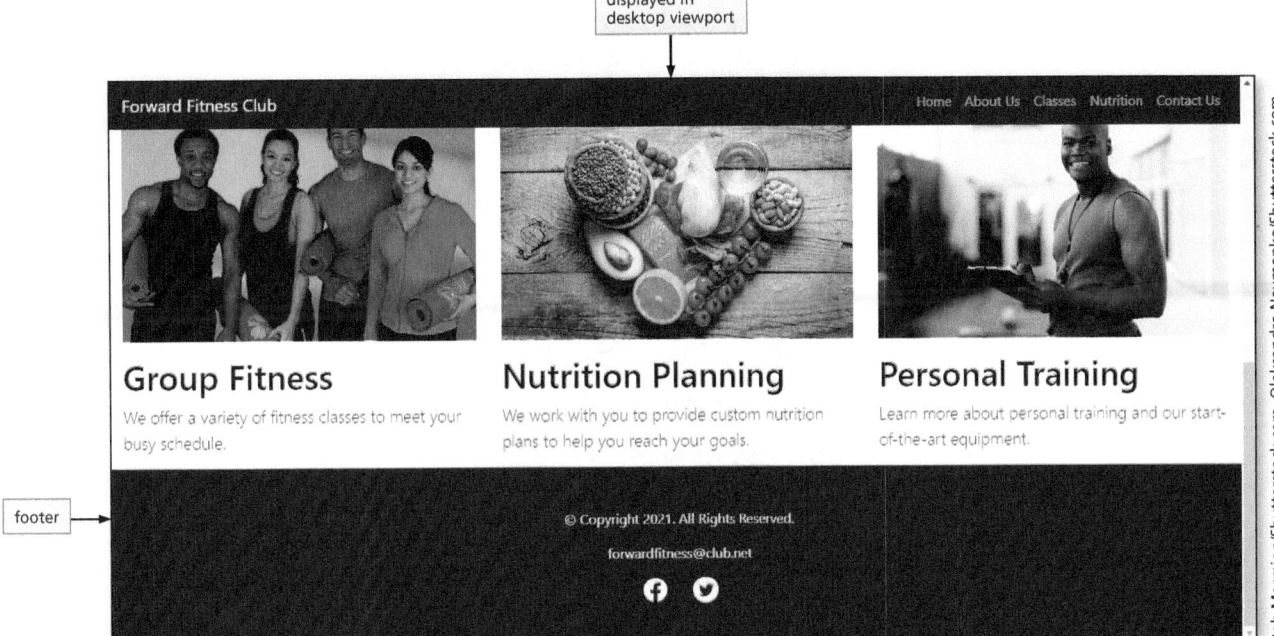

Figure 12–42

• Use Google Chrome's device mode to display the website in a tablet viewport and scroll down to view the footer element (Figure 12–43).

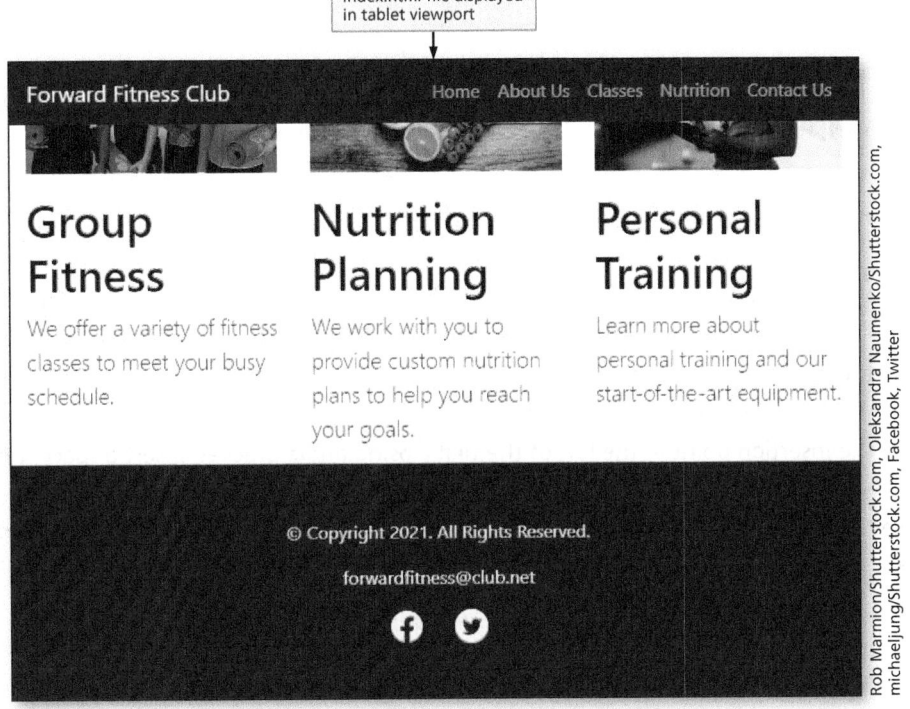

Figure 12–43

- Use Google Chrome's device mode to display the website in a mobile viewport and scroll down to view the footer element (Figure 12–44).

index.html file displayed
in mobile viewport

michaeljung/Shutterstock.com, Facebook, Twitter

Figure 12–44

You have finished creating the new home page using Bootstrap. You now need to improve the appearance of the About Us and Classes pages by adding Bootstrap classes to elements on each page. The Nutrition and Contact Us pages have already been completed.

Add Bootstrap Classes to the About Us Page

1 CREATE BOOTSTRAP WEBPAGE | 2 CREATE BOOTSTRAP NAVBAR | 3 CREATE BOOTSTRAP JUMBOTRON | 4 CREATE BOOTSTRAP COLUMNS
5 CREATE FOOTER | **6 ADD BOOTSTRAP CLASSES TO ABOUT US PAGE** | **7 ADD BOOTSTRAP CLASSES TO CLASSES PAGE**

The About Us page already contains HTML structural elements and a link to the Bootstrap CDN. Add Bootstrap classes to HTML elements on the page to integrate Bootstrap features. **Why?** *Integrate Bootstrap classes to create a Bootstrap page.* The following steps add classes to elements on the about.html file.

- Open the about.html file in your text editor from the Data Files fitness-bootstrap folder to prepare to modify the file.

- On Line 60, place the insertion point to the left of the closing angle bracket, insert a space, and then type `class="jumbotron jumbotron-fluid text-center mt-5"` to add a class attribute to the header tag.

- On Line 61, place the insertion point to the left of the closing angle bracket, insert a space, and then type `class="container"` to add a class attribute to the div tag.

- On Line 62, place the insertion point to the left of the first closing angle bracket, insert a space, and then type `class="display-1"` to add a class attribute to the heading 1 tag.

- On Line 63, place the insertion point to the left of the first closing angle bracket, insert a space, and then type `class="lead"` to add a class attribute to the paragraph tag (Figure 12–45).

Q&A

What are the jumbotron and jumbotron-fluid class values added to the header element?
Using these two class values together creates a full-width, fluid jumbotron without rounded corners.

What is the purpose of the display-1 class value?
The display-1 class value applies a large font to the heading.

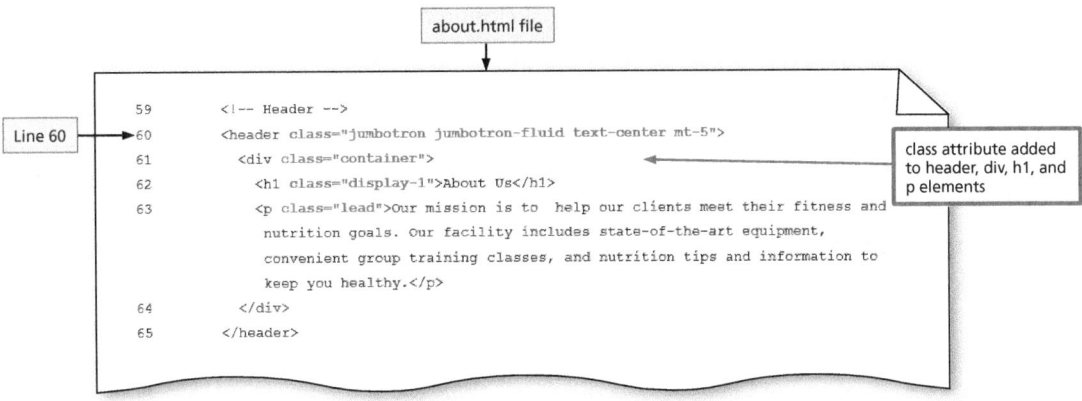

Figure 12–45

2

- Save your changes.
- Open about.html in your browser to display the page in a desktop viewport (Figure 12–46).

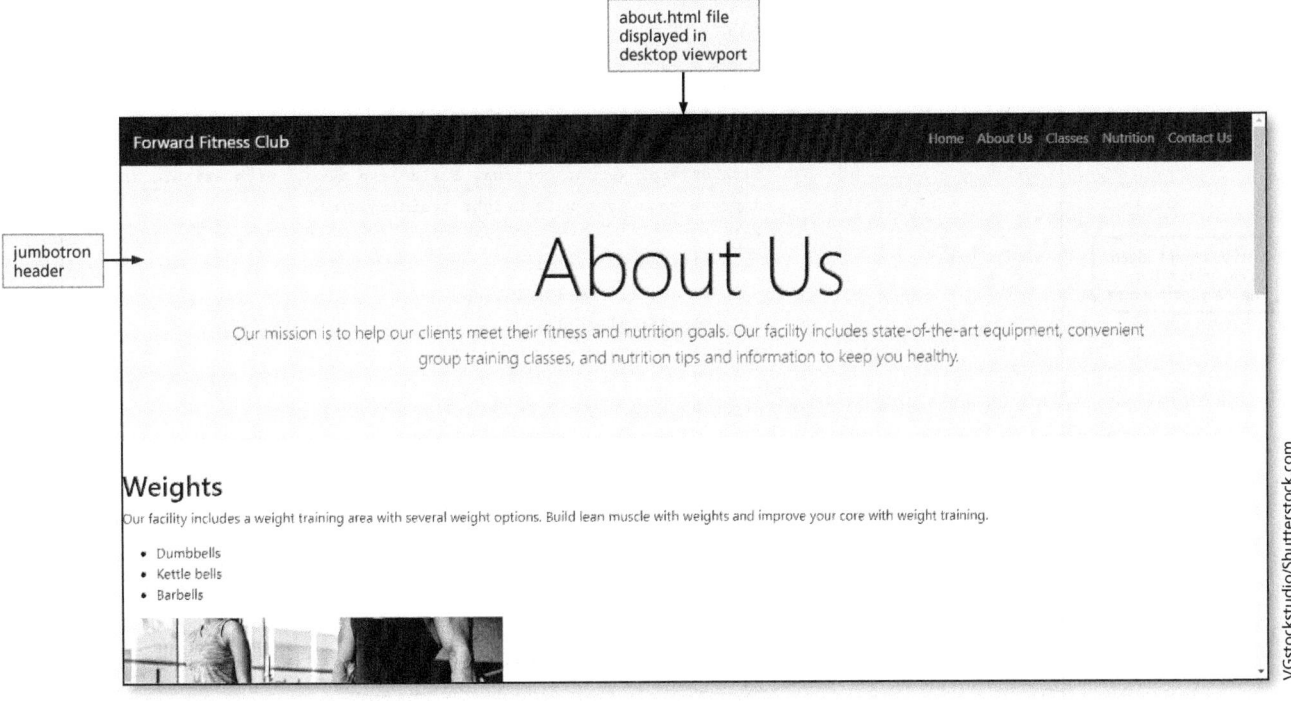

Figure 12–46

3

- Return to the about.html file in your text editor to continue modifying the file.
- On Line 68, place the insertion point to the left of the closing angle bracket, insert a space, and then type `class="container mb-5"` to add a class attribute to the main tag.
- On Line 69, place the insertion point to the left of the closing angle bracket, insert a space, and then type `class="row"` to add a class attribute to the div tag.
- On Line 70, place the insertion point to the left of the closing angle bracket, insert a space, and then type `class="col-md-7"` to add a class attribute to the div tag.

- On Line 71, place the insertion point to the left of the first closing angle bracket, insert a space, and then type `class="display-3"` to add a class attribute to the heading 2 tag.

- On Line 72, place the insertion point to the left of the first closing angle bracket, insert a space, and then type `class="lead"` to add a class attribute to the paragraph tag.

- On Line 79, place the insertion point to the left of the closing angle bracket, insert a space, and then type `class="col-md-5"` to add a class attribute to the div tag.

- On Line 80, place the insertion point to the left of the closing angle bracket, insert a space, and then type `class="img-fluid rounded"` to add a class attribute to the img tag.

- On Line 84, place the insertion point to the left of the closing angle bracket, insert a space, and then type `class="my-5"` to add a class attribute to the thematic break tag (Figure 12–47).

Q&A

What is the purpose of the rounded class value?
The rounded class value rounds the corners on the image.

What is the purpose of the my-5 class value?
The my-5 class value specifies top and bottom margin for the thematic break.

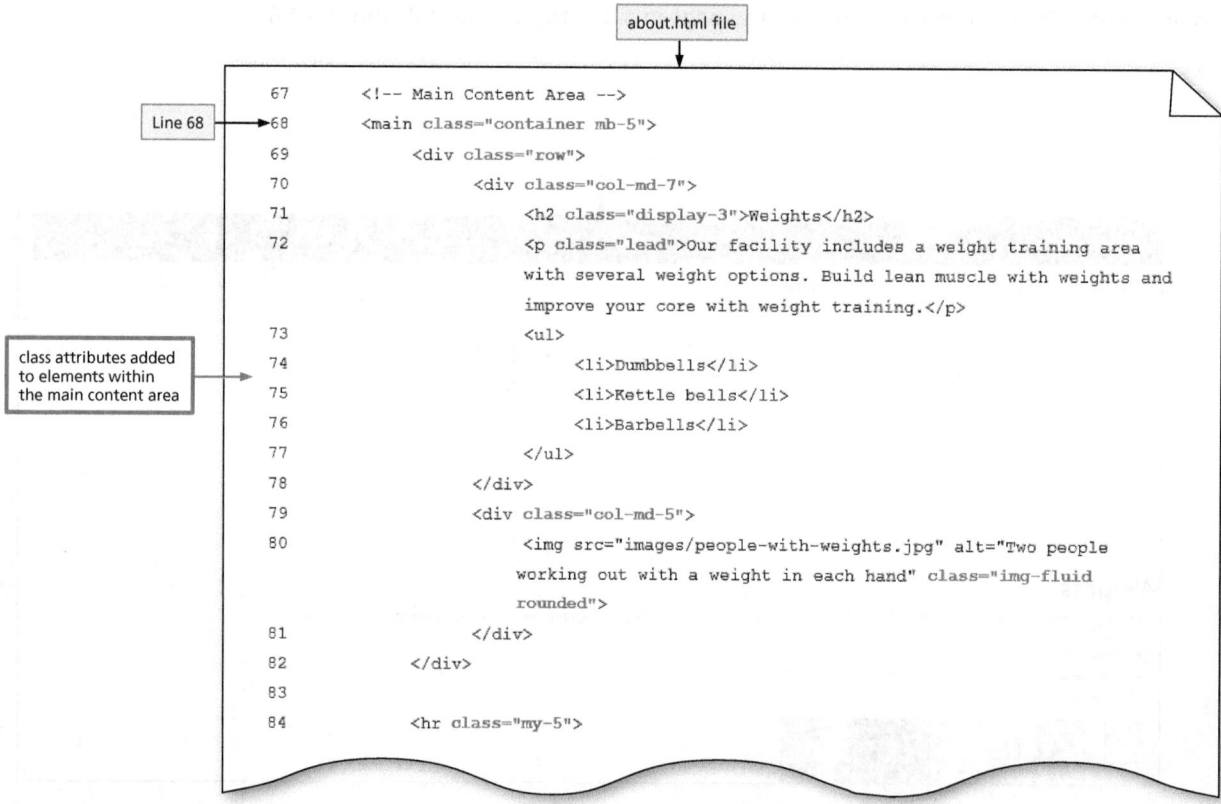

Figure 12–47

- Save your changes.

- Refresh about.html in your browser and scroll down, if necessary, to display the changes (Figure 12–48).

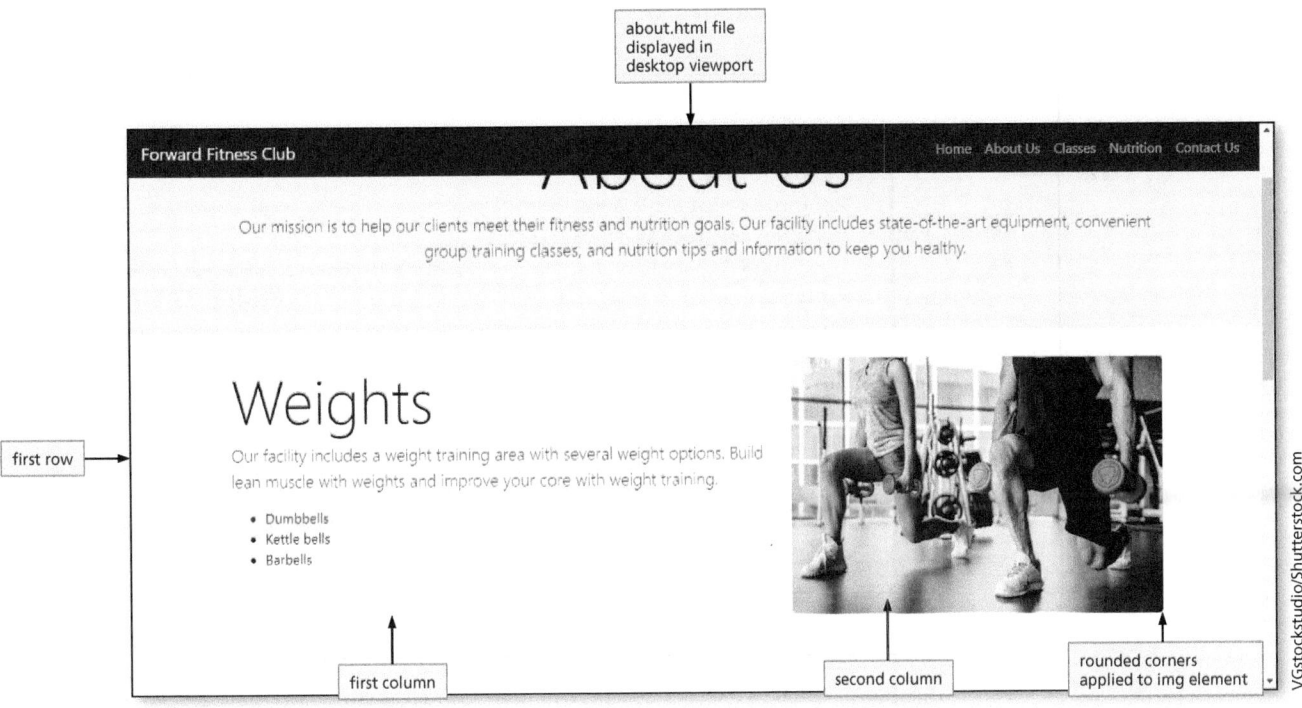

Figure 12–48

- Return to the about.html file in your text editor to continue modifying the file.
- On Line 86, place the insertion point to the left of the closing angle bracket, insert a space, and then type `class="row"` to add a class attribute to the div tag.
- On Line 87, place the insertion point to the left of the closing angle bracket, insert a space, and then type `class="col-md-7 order-2"` to add a class attribute to the div tag.
- On Line 88, place the insertion point to the left of the first closing angle bracket, insert a space, and then type `class="display-3"` to add a class attribute to the heading 2 tag.
- On Line 89, place the insertion point to the left of the first closing angle bracket, insert a space, and then type `class="lead"` to add a class attribute to the paragraph tag.
- On Line 96, place the insertion point to the left of the closing angle bracket, insert a space, and then type `class="col-md-5"` to add a class attribute to the div tag.
- On Line 97, place the insertion point to the left of the closing angle bracket, insert a space, and then type `class="img-fluid rounded"` to add a class attribute to the img tag.
- On Line 101, place the insertion point to the left of the closing angle bracket, insert a space, and then type `class="my-5"` to add a class attribute to the thematic break tag (Figure 12–49).

Q&A What is the purpose of the order-2 class value?
The order-2 class value specifies to display the column as the second column.

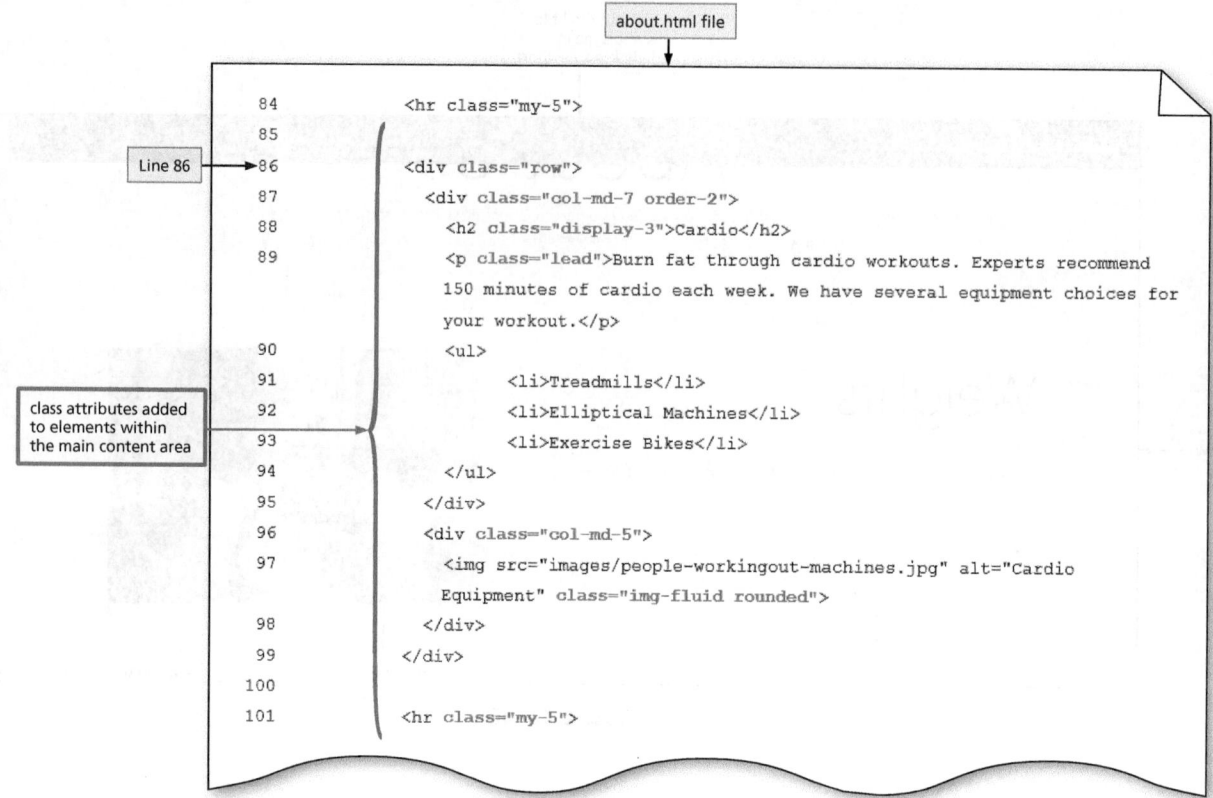

about.html file

```
84                <hr class="my-5">
85
86          <div class="row">
87              <div class="col-md-7 order-2">
88                  <h2 class="display-3">Cardio</h2>
89                  <p class="lead">Burn fat through cardio workouts. Experts recommend
                    150 minutes of cardio each week. We have several equipment choices for
                    your workout.</p>
90                  <ul>
91                      <li>Treadmills</li>
92                      <li>Elliptical Machines</li>
93                      <li>Exercise Bikes</li>
94                  </ul>
95              </div>
96              <div class="col-md-5">
97                  <img src="images/people-workingout-machines.jpg" alt="Cardio
                    Equipment" class="img-fluid rounded">
98              </div>
99          </div>
100
101         <hr class="my-5">
```

Line 86

class attributes added to elements within the main content area

Figure 12–49

6

- On Line 103, place the insertion point to the left of the closing angle bracket, insert a space, and then type **class="row"** to add a class attribute to the div tag.

- On Line 104, place the insertion point to the left of the closing angle bracket, insert a space, and then type **class="col-md-7"** to add a class attribute to the div tag.

- On Line 105, place the insertion point to the left of the first closing angle bracket, insert a space, and then type **class="display-3"** to add a class attribute to the heading 2 tag.

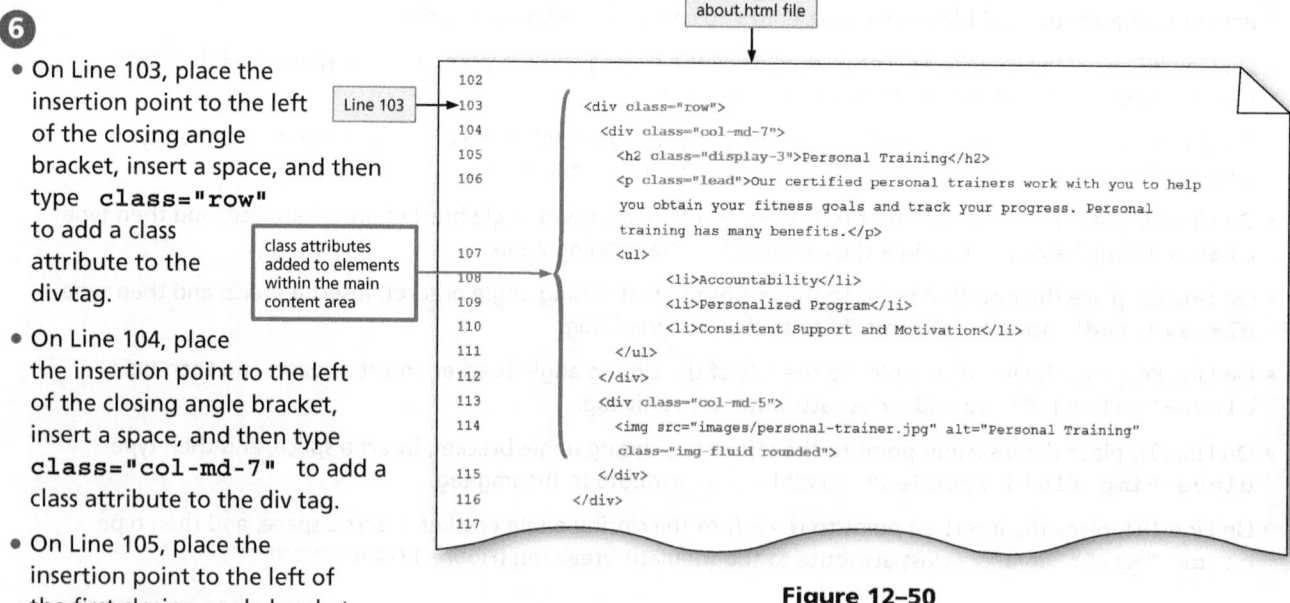

about.html file

```
102
103         <div class="row">
104             <div class="col-md-7">
105                 <h2 class="display-3">Personal Training</h2>
106                 <p class="lead">Our certified personal trainers work with you to help
                    you obtain your fitness goals and track your progress. Personal
                    training has many benefits.</p>
107                 <ul>
108                     <li>Accountability</li>
109                     <li>Personalized Program</li>
110                     <li>Consistent Support and Motivation</li>
111                 </ul>
112             </div>
113             <div class="col-md-5">
114                 <img src="images/personal-trainer.jpg" alt="Personal Training"
                    class="img-fluid rounded">
115             </div>
116         </div>
117
```

Line 103

class attributes added to elements within the main content area

Figure 12–50

- On Line 106, place the insertion point to the left of the first closing angle bracket, insert a space, and then type **class="lead"** to add a class attribute to the paragraph tag.

- On Line 113, place the insertion point to the left of the closing angle bracket, insert a space, and then type **class="col-md-5"** to add a class attribute to the div tag.

- On Line 114, place the insertion point to the left of the closing angle bracket, insert a space, and then type **class="img-fluid rounded"** to add a class attribute to the img tag (Figure 12–50).

- Save your changes.

- Refresh about.html in your browser and scroll down to display the changes (Figure 12–51).

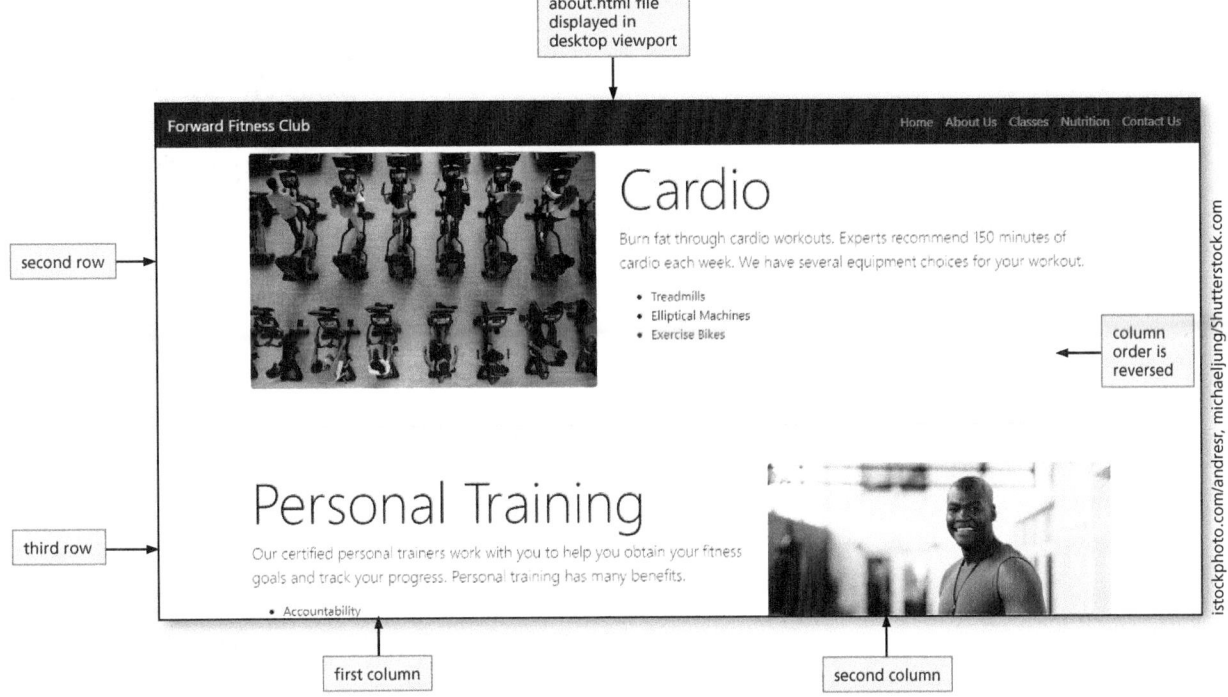

Figure 12–51

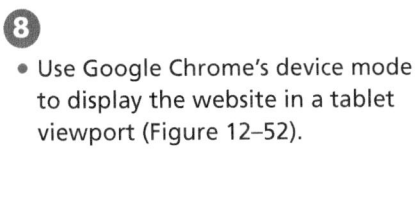

8

- Use Google Chrome's device mode to display the website in a tablet viewport (Figure 12–52).

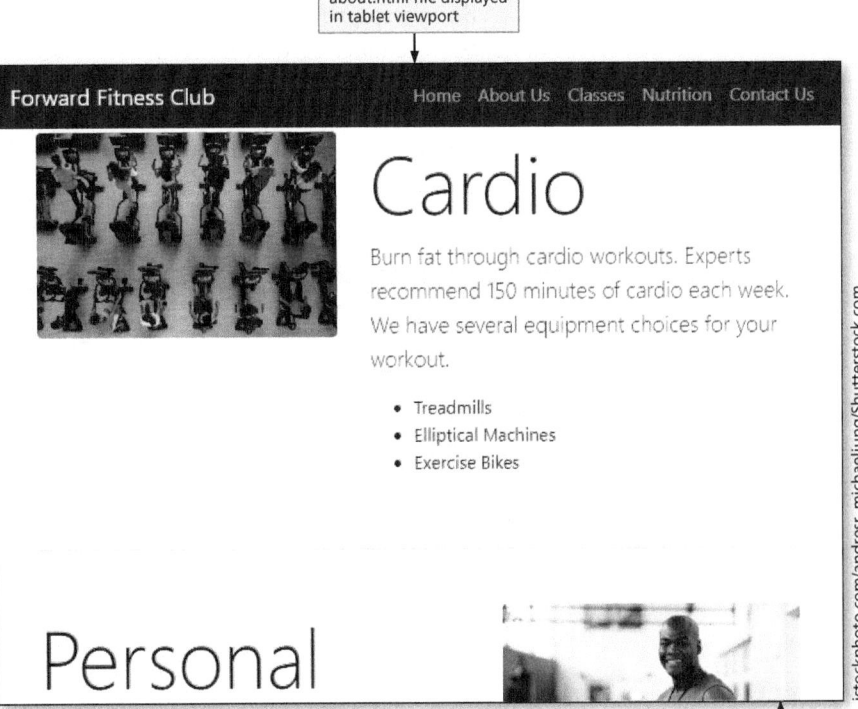

Figure 12–52

• Use Google Chrome's device mode to display the website in a mobile viewport (Figure 12–53).

about.html file displayed in a mobile viewport

single-column layout

istockphoto.com/andresr

Figure 12–53

Styling Tables with Bootstrap

Bootstrap provides many class value options to style a table. To apply a Bootstrap table, add the table class value to the starting table tag, as follows.

```
<table class="table">
```

If you want to style the table to use a dark gray background and white text, apply the **table-dark** class to the starting table tag. Table 12–9 summarizes Bootstrap table classes.

Table 12–9 Bootstrap Text Classes	
Class	**Description**
table	Applies Bootstrap table style rule
table-dark	Applies a dark gray background to the table and white to the text color
table-striped	Applies a light gray background to alternating table rows (zebra-striping) within the body of the table
table-hover	Applies a light gray background to a table row when the mouse pointer is over the row
table-bordered	Applies a border to the table and every cell within the table
table-borderless	Removes all borders from the table
table-sm	Reduces the cell padding
table-responsive	Creates a responsive table, which enable horizontal scrolling for smaller viewports
thead-dark	Applies a dark gray background and white text to cells within the thead element
thead-light	Applies a light gray background and dark gray text to cells within the thead element

Next, you will add table classes to the table element on the classes.html page.

Add Bootstrap Table Classes to the Classes Page

The Classes page already contains HTML structural elements and a link to the Bootstrap CDN. Add Bootstrap table classes to the table elements on the page to integrate Bootstrap features. *Why? Integrate Bootstrap table classes to style the table.* The following steps add classes to table elements in the classes.html file.

- Open the classes.html file in your text editor from the Data Files fitness-bootstrap folder to prepare to modify the file.

- On Line 83, place the insertion point to the left of the closing angle bracket, insert a space, and then type **class= "table table-striped table-hover"** to add a class attribute to the table tag.

- On Line 84, place the insertion point to the left of the closing angle bracket, insert a space, and then type **class="thead-dark"** to add a class attribute to the thead tag (Figure 12–54).

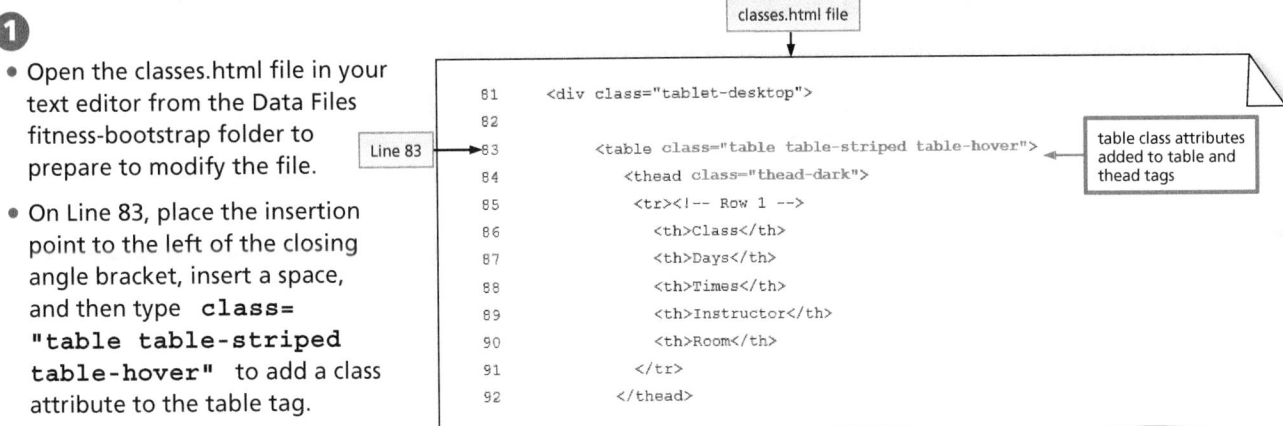

Figure 12–54

Q&A

What is the purpose of the table-striped and table-hover class values?

The table-striped class value applies a light gray background to alternating rows within the tbody element. The table-hover class value applies a light gray background to a row when the mouse pointer is hovering over the row.

What is the purpose of the thead-dark class value?

The thead-dark class value applies a dark gray background and white text to rows within the thead element.

❷

- Save your changes.

- Open classes.html in your browser to display the page and scroll down, if necessary, to view the table in a desktop viewport (Figure 12–55).

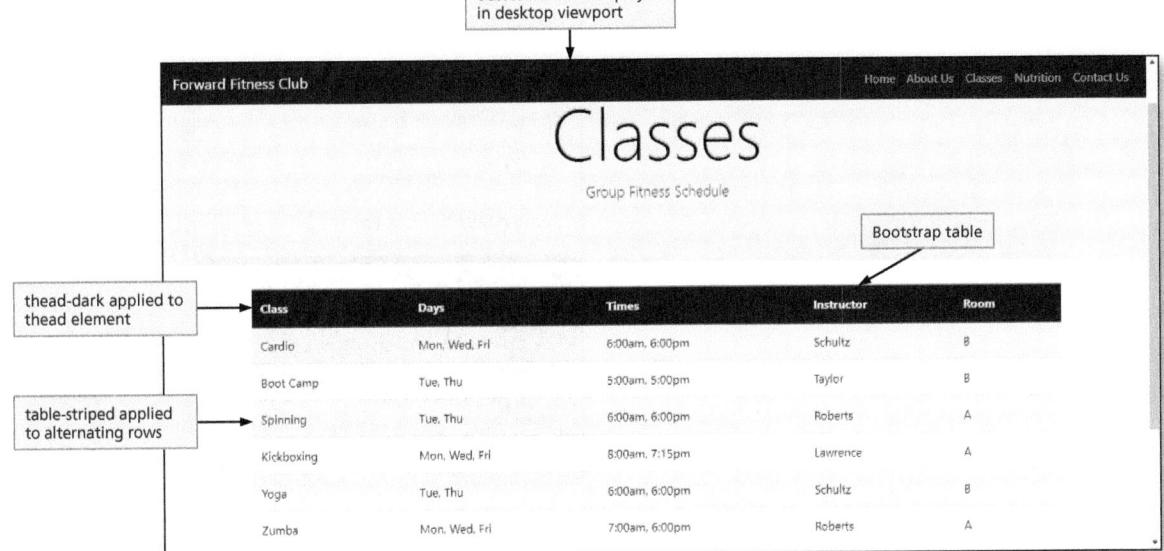

Figure 12–55

• Use Google Chrome's device mode to display the website in a tablet viewport (Figure 12–56).

classes.html file displayed in tablet viewport

Forward Fitness Club   Home   About Us   Classes   Nutrition   Contact Us

table →

Class	Days	Times	Instructor	Room
Cardio	Mon, Wed, Fri	6:00am, 6:00pm	Schultz	B
Boot Camp	Tue, Thu	5:00am, 5:00pm	Taylor	B
Spinning	Tue, Thu	6:00am, 6:00pm	Roberts	A
Kickboxing	Mon, Wed, Fri	8:00am, 7:15pm	Lawrence	A
Yoga	Tue, Thu	6:00am, 6:00pm	Schultz	B
Zumba	Mon, Wed, Fri	7:00am, 6:00pm	Roberts	A

© Copyright 2021. All Rights Reserved.

Figure 12–56

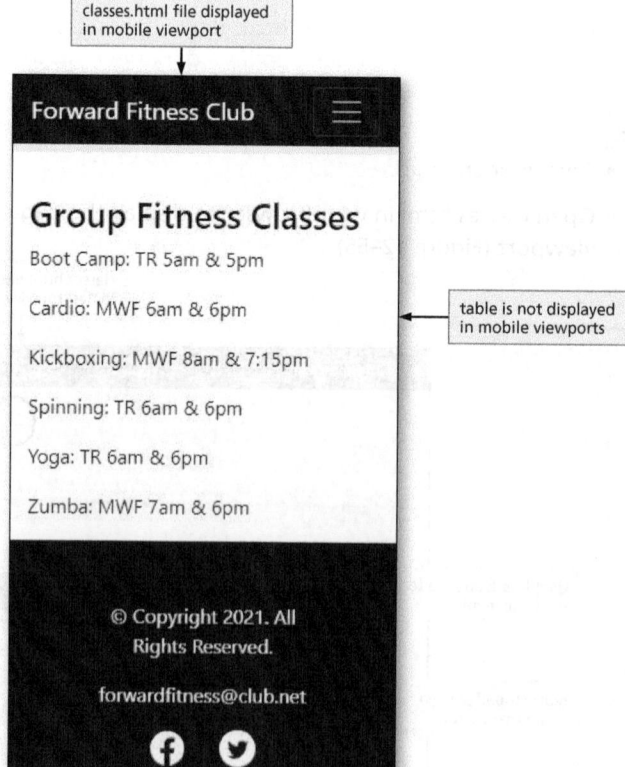

classes.html file displayed in mobile viewport

• Use Google Chrome's device mode to display the website in a mobile viewport and scroll down to view the footer element (Figure 12–57).

Forward Fitness Club

Group Fitness Classes

Boot Camp: TR 5am & 5pm

Cardio: MWF 6am & 6pm

Kickboxing: MWF 8am & 7:15pm

Spinning: TR 6am & 6pm

Yoga: TR 6am & 6pm

Zumba: MWF 7am & 6pm

table is not displayed in mobile viewports

© Copyright 2021. All Rights Reserved.

forwardfitness@club.net

Figure 12–57

To View the Website in a Mobile Viewport

Now that the website is complete, view each page in a mobile viewport. The following steps display each page in a mobile viewport.

1 Open the index.html file in Google Chrome and use Google Chrome's device mode to display the home page in a mobile viewport.

2 Tap or click the hamburger icon and select About Us to view the About Us page in a mobile viewport.

3 Tap or click the hamburger icon and select Classes to view the Classes page in a mobile viewport.

4 Tap or click the hamburger icon and select Nutrition to view the Nutrition page in a mobile viewport.

5 Tap or click the hamburger icon and select Contact Us to view the Contact Us page in a mobile viewport (Figure 12–58).

Figure 12–58

To View the Website in a Tablet Viewport

Now that the website is complete, view each page in a tablet viewport. The following steps display each page in a tablet viewport.

1 Use Google Chrome's device mode to display the Contact Us page in a tablet viewport.

2 Tap or click Home from the navbar to view the Home page in a tablet viewport.

3 Tap or click About Us from the navbar to view the About Us page in a tablet viewport.

4 Tap or click Classes from the navbar to view the Classes page in a tablet viewport.

5 Tap or click Nutrition from the navbar to view the Nutrition page in a tablet viewport (Figure 12–59).

Figure 12–59

To View the Website in a Desktop Viewport

Now that the website is complete, view each page in a desktop viewport. The following steps display each page in a desktop viewport.

1 Exit Google Chrome's device mode to display the Nutrition page in a desktop viewport.

2 Tap or click Contact Us from the navbar to view the Contact Us page in a desktop viewport.

3 Tap or click Classes from the navbar to view the Classes page in a desktop viewport.

4 Tap or click About Us from the navbar to view the About Us page in a desktop viewport.

5 Tap or click Home from the navbar to view the Home page in a desktop viewport (Figure 12–60).

Figure 12–60

Content Management Systems

Content management systems (CMSs) have become increasingly popular with many large, enterprise businesses. A **CMS** is an online system used to manage website content. A typical CMS consists of a content management application (CMA) and a content delivery application (CDA). The CMA provides a webpage author the ability to add, remove, and modify content without knowing HTML. The author can simply make the necessary modifications, and then the CDA compiles the changes and writes the underlying code "behind the scenes." Content management systems provide web developers the means to create a website design and then "lock it down" so that webpage authors can only update content and not modify the webpage design. This is especially helpful and important when it comes to novice users updating webpage content. Using a CMS takes the pressure off a webmaster by allowing multiple authors to update their pages as necessary. It also provides peace of mind to the webmaster, knowing that their hard work in the development phase of the CMS cannot be undone by the person updating page content. Popular content management systems include WordPress, Joomla, and Drupal.

Figure 12–61 shows the home page for WordPress.org. Many businesses use WordPress for their websites and their blogs. In fact, nearly 35% of all websites use WordPress. It has quickly become one of the top-ranked content management systems with over 60% market share, according to w3techs.com Web Technology Surveys.

WordPress.org home page

Source: WordPress.org

Figure 12–61

WordPress offers web developers many tools for building a website. The organization also provides support and functionality for high-traffic e-commerce websites. Clorox is one of the many businesses that use WordPress for its website. Clorox is a global business that makes consumer and commercial cleaning products. Its home page is shown in Figure 12–62.

Clorox home page →

Source: Clorox.com

Figure 12–62

Joomla is an open-source CMS, ideal for experienced web developers who enjoy coding. It is the second most popular CMS. Joomla offers many of the same tools as WordPress for developing a website. Many types of businesses and organizations use Joomla for their website, including e-commerce websites, nonprofit websites, government websites, and other business websites. The home page for Joomla.org is shown in Figure 12–63.

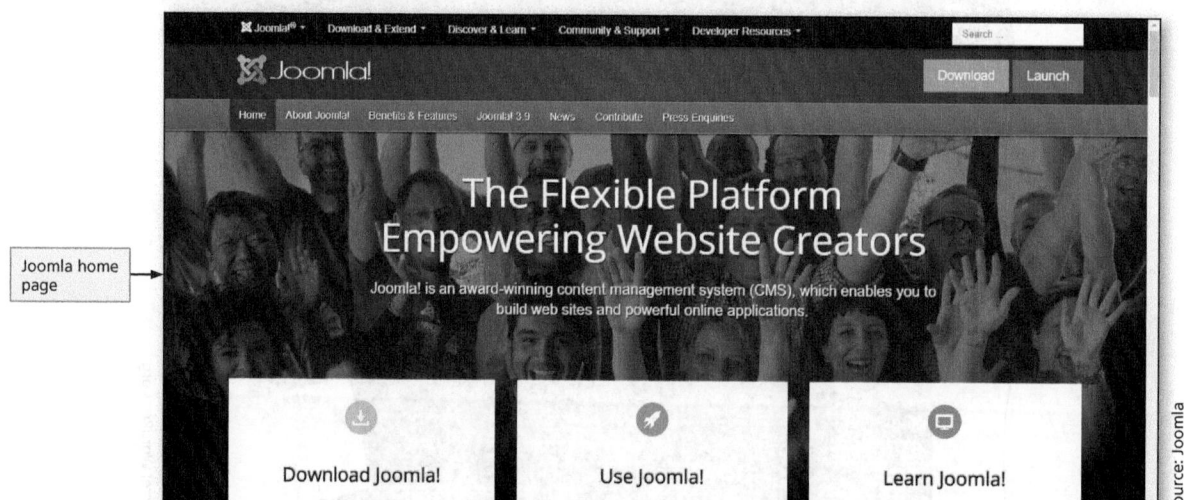

Joomla home page →

Source: Joomla

Figure 12–63

Drupal is another open-source CMS, distributed under the GNU General Public License. It is the third most popular CMS used today. Industries that use Drupal for their website include transportation, sports, healthcare, higher education, and nonprofit organizations. According to w3techs.com, the Drupal CMS is used the most by high-traffic websites. The home page for drupal.org is shown in Figure 12–64.

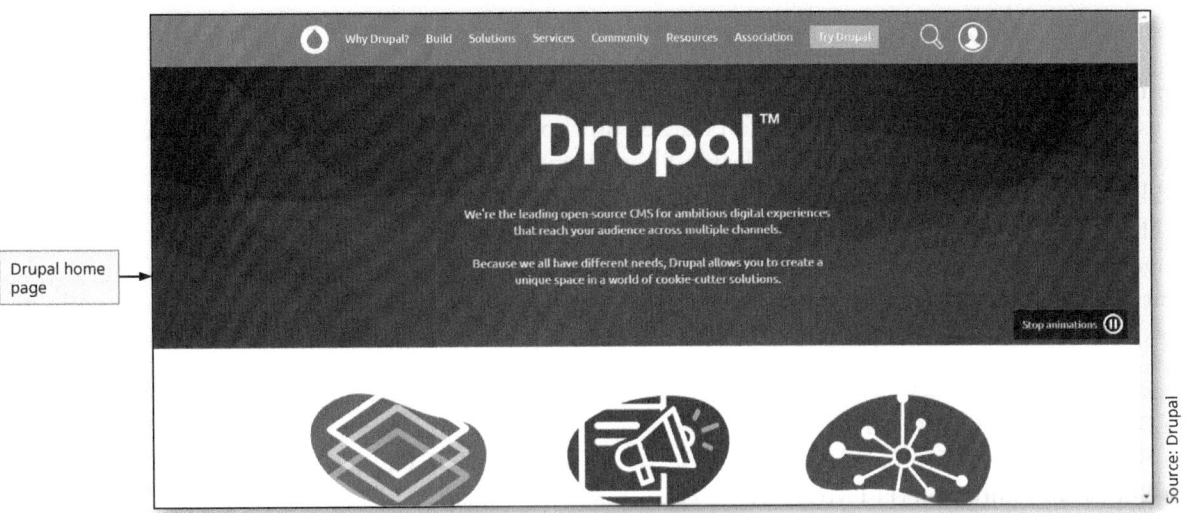

Drupal home
page

Source: Drupal

Figure 12–64

To Validate the HTML Files

Every time you create a new webpage or modify an existing webpage, run it through W3C's validator to check the document for errors. If any errors exist, you need to correct them. Validation is also an effective troubleshooting tool during the development process and adds a valuable level of professionalism to your work. The following steps validate an HTML document.

1 Open your browser and type **http://validator.w3.org/** in the address bar to display the W3C validator page.

2 Tap or click the Validate by File Upload tab to display the Validate by File Upload information.

3 Tap or click the Browse button to display the Open dialog box.

4 Navigate to your fitness folder to find the index.html file.

5 Tap or click the index.html document to select it.

6 Tap or click the Open button to upload it to the W3C validator.

7 Tap or click the Check button to send the document through the validator and display the validation results page.

8 If necessary, correct any errors, save your changes, and run through the validator again to revalidate the page.

9 Follow these steps to validate all HTML pages within your fitness-bootstrap folder and correct any errors.

Chapter Summary

In this chapter, you learned how to create a webpage using the Bootstrap framework. You learned how to obtain and use the Bootstrap starter template. You learned how to create a Bootstrap navbar. You learned how to integrate a Bootstrap hamburger menu. You learned how to style navigation elements using Bootstrap. You learned how to create a Bootstrap jumbotron. You learned how to style text and images using Bootstrap. You learned how to write a jQuery document ready event. You learned how to use the Bootstrap grid system to layout page content. You learned how to style a table using Bootstrap. You also learned about content management systems. The items listed below include all the new skills you have learned in this chapter, with the tasks grouped by activity.

Creating a Bootstrap Webpage

Create a Bootstrap Webpage (HTML 638)
Create a Bootstrap Navigation Bar (HTML 644)
Create a Bootstrap Jumbotron (HTML 652)
Create a Bootstrap Columns (HTML 661)
Create a Footer Using a Jumbotron (HTML 665)

Incorporating Bootstrap Classes on a Webpage

Add Bootstrap Classes to Style the About Us Page (HTML 668)
Add Bootstrap Classes to Style a Table on the Classes Page (HTML 675)

CONSIDER THIS

How will you use Bootstrap to design your website?

Use these guidelines as you complete the assignments in this chapter and create your own webpages outside of this class.

1. Determine which Bootstrap features to use within your website.

   a) Determine the best use of a jumbotron.

   b) Determine how to best integrate a navbar.

   c) Determine a layout for the grid system.

2. Decide how to style elements using Bootstrap classes.

   a) Determine the text color classes and background color classes needed to style your pages.

   b) Determine margin and padding needed to style your page elements.

   c) Determine how to style table elements using Bootstrap classes.

   d) Determine how to style images with Bootstrap.

3. Determine if you need custom style rules.

   a) Determine the custom style rules needed.

   b) Determine media queries and breakpoints needed for your custom style sheet.

4. Determine other Bootstrap components that can be added to your website.

   a) Research other Bootstrap components and their use.

   b) Research examples of integrating other Bootstrap components.

CONSIDER THIS

How should you submit solutions to questions in the assignments identified with a ✳ symbol? Every assignment in this book contains one or more questions identified with a ✳ symbol. These questions require you to think beyond the assigned presentation. Present your solutions to the questions in the format required by your instructor. Possible formats may include one or more of these options: create a document that contains the answer; present your answer to the class; discuss your answer in a group; record the answer as audio or video using a webcam, smartphone, or portable media player; or post answers on a blog, wiki, or website.

Apply Your Knowledge

Reinforce the skills and apply the concepts you learned in this chapter.

Creating a Webpage Using the Bootstrap Framework

Instructions: In this exercise, you will use your text editor to create a webpage using the Bootstrap framework. You will use the Bootstrap starter template and then update it with HTML elements and Bootstrap classes to style the page. First, you copy the Bootstrap starter template. Next, you copy the starter template to a new document in your text editor and save it as an HTML file. Then, you update the webpage and add HTML elements, content, and Bootstrap classes to style the page. The completed webpage is shown in Figure 12–65. You will also use professional web development practices to indent, space, comment, and validate your code.

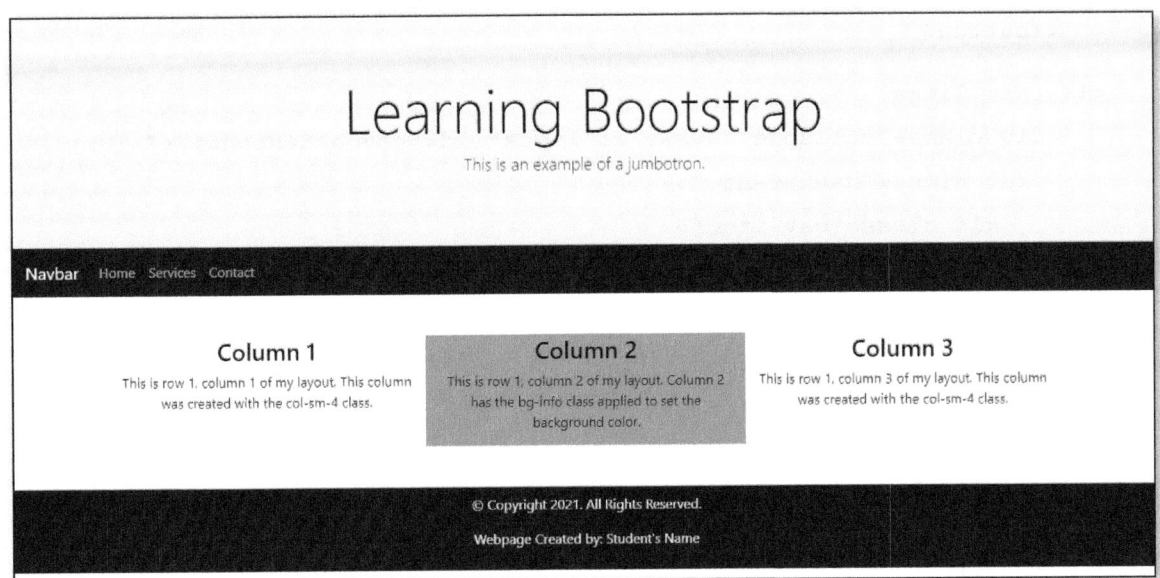

Figure 12–65

Perform the following tasks:

1. Open getbootstrap.com in your browser, navigate to the Documentation page, and then copy the starter template code.

2. Create a new folder named apply. Open a new document in your text editor and paste the Bootstrap starter template code in the file. Save the file as `index.html` within the apply folder.

3. Add a comment on Line 2 that includes your name and today's date. Update the title element with the text `Learning Bootstrap | Apply Your Knowledge 12`.

4. Remove the heading 1 element (Hello, world!) on Line 15.

5. Add the following comment and header jumbotron, starting on Line 16.

```
<!-- Bootstrap Jumbotron -->
<header class="jumbotron jumbotron-fluid text-center mb-0">
   <div class="container">
       <h1 class="display-3">Learning Bootstrap</h1>
       <p class="lead">This is an example of a jumbotron.</p>
   </div>
</header>
```

Continued >

Apply Your Knowledge *continued*

6. Add the following comments, nav element, and navbar after the header element.

```
<!-- Bootstrap Navigation bar -->

<nav class="navbar navbar-expand-sm bg-dark navbar-dark">

    <a class="navbar-brand" href="#">Navbar</a>

    <!-- Hamburger menu -->
    <button class="navbar-toggler" type="button" data-toggle="collapse"
    data-target="#navbarResponsive" aria-controls="navbarResponsive"
    aria-expanded="false" aria-label="Toggle navigation">
        <span class="navbar-toggler-icon"></span>
    </button>

<!-- Nav links -->
    <div class="collapse navbar-collapse" id="navbarResponsive">
      <ul class="navbar-nav">
        <li class="nav-item">
            <a class="nav-link" href="#">Home</a>
        </li>
        <li class="nav-item">
            <a class="nav-link" href="#">Services</a>
        </li>
        <li class="nav-item">
            <a class="nav-link" href="#">Contact</a>
        </li>
      </ul>
    </div>
</nav>
```

7. Add the following comment, main element, Bootstrap columns, and content below the nav element.

```
<!-- Main Content Area -->
<main class="container my-5">

    <div class="row text-center">

        <div class="col-sm-4">
            <h3>Column 1</h3>
            <p>This is row 1, column 1 of my layout. This column was
            created with the col-sm-4 class.</p>
        </div>
        <div class="col-sm-4 bg-info">
            <h3>Column 2</h3>
```

```
    <p>This is row 1, column 2 of my layout. Column 2 has the bg-
       info class applied to set the background color.</p>
  </div>
  <div class="col-sm-4">
    <h3>Column 3</h3>
    <p>This is row 1, column 3 of my layout. This column was
       created with the col-sm-4 class.</p>
  </div>

  </div>

</main>
```

8. Add the following comment, footer element, jumbotron, and content below the main element. Replace "Student's Name" with your name.

```
<!-- Footer -->
<footer class="jumbotron-fluid text-center bg-dark p-2">


  <div class="container text-white">
    <p>&copy; Copyright 2021. All Rights Reserved.</p>
    <p>Webpage Created by: Student's Name</p>
  </div>

</footer>
```

9. Save all your changes and open the index.html in your browser. View the webpage in desktop, tablet, and mobile viewports.

10. Validate your HTML document and fix any errors that are identified.

11. Submit the file in a format specified by your instructor.

12. ✳ In this exercise, you created a navbar using the Bootstrap framework. Research how you can use the Bootstrap framework to incorporate a drop-down menu within the navbar.

Extend Your Knowledge

Extend the skills you learned in this chapter and experiment with new skills. You may need to use additional resources to complete the assignment.

Creating a Carousel Using the Bootstrap Framework

Note: To complete this assignment, you will be required to use the Data Files. Please contact your instructor for information about accessing the Data Files.

Instructions: In this exercise, you research how to add a carousel using the Bootstrap framework. A carousel is a slideshow that lets viewers cycle through images or slides of text. An example of the completed webpage is shown in Figure 12–66. You will also use professional web development practices to indent, space, comment, and validate your code.

Continued >

Extend Your Knowledge *continued*

Figure 12–66

Perform the following tasks:

1. Open the index.html file in the chapter12\extend folder from the Data Files in your text editor. Update the comment with your name and today's date. Add your name to the paragraph element located within the footer element near the bottom of the page.

2. Open the index.html file in your browser to view the page.

3. Use your browser to go to getbootstrap.com and research how to add a Bootstrap Carousel feature within the webpage.

4. Add the carousel within the main element of the index.html file. Use the images provided within the images folder. The carousel should display indicators and previous/next controls.

5. Submit the document in a format specified by your instructor.

6. ✹ In this exercise, you researched how to integrate a Bootstrap carousel. Research and discuss another Bootstrap component that was not discussed in the chapter, summarize its use, and provide a code example.

Analyze, Correct, Improve

Analyze a website, correct all errors, and improve it.

Improving a Webpage with Bootstrap

Note: To complete this assignment, you will be required to use the Data Files. Please contact your instructor for information about accessing the Data Files.

Instructions: Work with the analyze12.html file in the analyze folder from the Data Files. The analyze12.html webpage needs to link to the Bootstrap CDN and then needs Bootstrap classes added to elements. First, link the HTML file to the Bootstrap CDN. Next, add Bootstrap classes to HTML page elements. Then, create an external style sheet and assign your custom style rule to

HTML elements. The completed webpage is shown in Figure 12–67. You will also use professional web development practices to indent, space, comment, and validate your code.

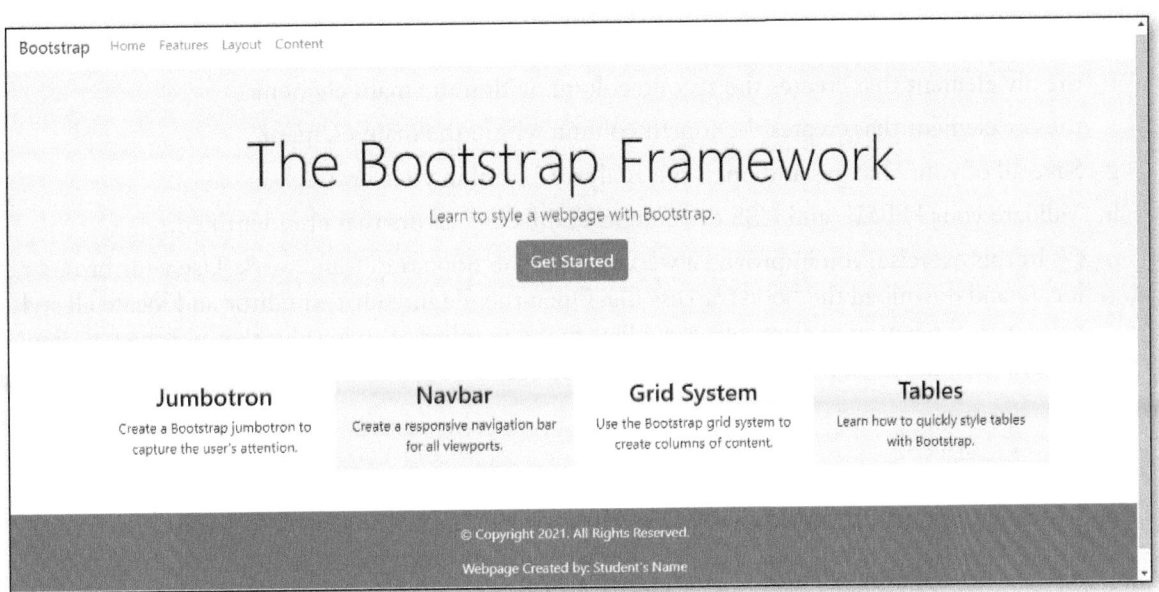

Figure 12–67

1. Correct

a. Open the analyze12.html file in the chapter12\analyze folder from the Data Files in your text editor. Modify the comment at the top of the page to include your name and today's date. Link the file to the Bootstrap CDN, located on at getbootstrap.com. Add your name to the footer element.

b. Add the following classes to the nav element: `navbar navbar-expand-sm navbar-light`.

c. Add the `nav-item` class to each list item element within the navigation. Add `nav-link` to each anchor element wrapped within a list item.

d. Add the following classes to the header element: `jumbotron jumbotron-fluid text-center`.

e. Add the following classes to the anchor element within the header: `btn btn-primary btn-lg`.

f. Add the `role` attribute with a value of `button` to the anchor element within the header.

2. Improve

a. In the analyze12.html file, add the `text-primary` class value to each anchor element wrapped within a list item within the nav element.

b. Change all col-sm-6 class values to `col-sm-3`.

c. Add the `bg-primary` and `p-3` class values to the class within the footer element.

d. Create an external style sheet named styles.css and save it within the css folder. Create a comment that includes your name, file name, and the current date.

e. In the styles.css file, create a style rule for the class selector `bg-light-blue` and add a declaration that sets the background color to `#cce6ff`.

Continued >

Analyze, Correct, Improve *continued*

f. In the analyze12.html file, add a link to the styles.css file below the link to the Bootstrap CDN. Add the `bg-light-blue` class value to the following elements:

header element

the div element that creates the second column within the main element

the div element that creates the fourth column within the main element

g. Save all of your changes and open the analyze12.html in your browser.

h. Validate your HTML and CSS documents and fix any errors that are identified.

i. ✷ In this exercise, you improved a website with the Bootstrap framework. Use your browser locate and download the bootstrap.css file. Open the file in your text editor and locate all style rules with the nav-item class selector. Identify the number of style rules that use the nav-item selector and list all declarations used for this selector.

In the Lab

Labs 1 and 2, which increase in difficulty, require you to create webpages based on what you learned in the chapter; Lab 3 requires you to dive deeper into a topic covered in the chapter.

Lab 1: Creating a Home Page with Bootstrap for the Strike a Chord Website

Note: To complete this assignment, you will be required to use the Data Files. Please contact your instructor for information about accessing the Data Files.

Problem: You work for a local music lesson company called Strike a Chord that provides music lessons for piano, guitar, and violin. The company needs a web presence and has hired you to create their website. You have already created a responsive website and are now considering using the Bootstrap framework. Create a new home page using the Bootstrap framework. Figure 12–68 shows the home page in a mobile viewport. Figure 12–69 shows the home page in a tablet viewport. Figure 12–70 shows the home page in a desktop viewport.

Figure 12–68

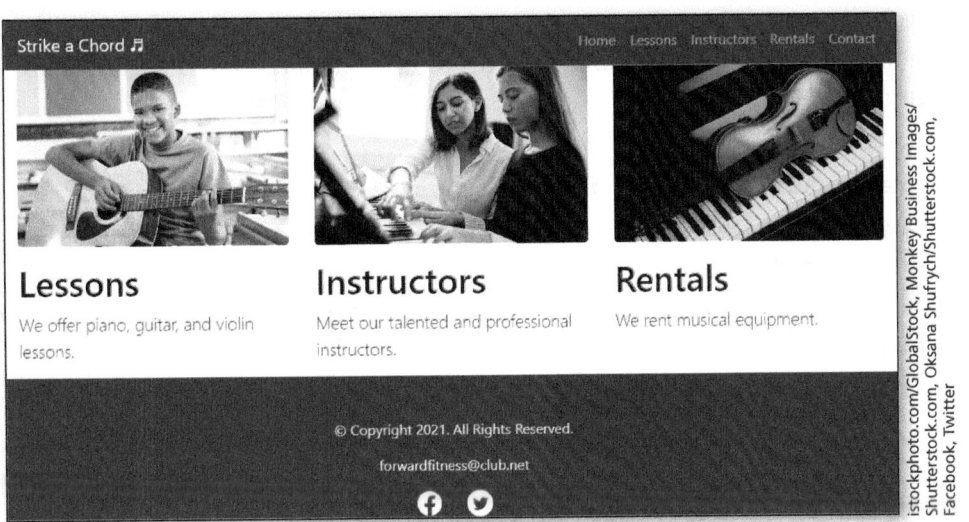

Figure 12–69

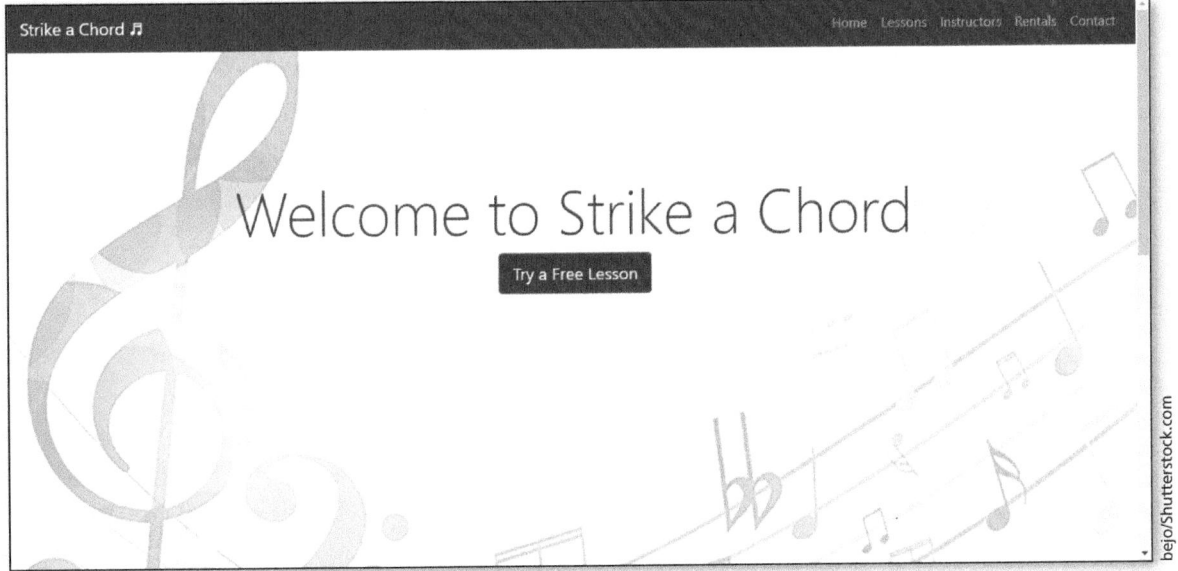

Figure 12–70

Instructions: Perform the following tasks:

1. Open getbootstrap.com in your browser, navigate to the Documentation page, and then copy the starter template code.

2. Create a new document in your text editor and paste the Bootstrap starter template code on the file. Save the file as index.html within the lab1\music-bootstrap folder from the Data Files.

3. Add a comment on Line 2 that includes your name and today's date. Update the title element on Line 12 with the text, `Music Lessons - Rentals | Strike a Chord`.

4. Remove the heading 1 element (Hello, world!) on Line 15.

5. Add the following meta description element after Line 7:

```
<meta name="description" content="Strike a Chord specializes in music
lessons and music rental equipment.">
```

Continued >

In the Lab *continued*

6. Add the following comment and link elements to favicons above the Bootstrap CSS comment:

```
<!-- Favicon -->
<link rel="shortcut icon" href="images/favicon.ico">
<link rel="icon" type="image/png" sizes="32x32" href="images/
favicon-32.png">
<link rel="apple-touch-icon" sizes="180x180" href="images/apple-touch-
icon.png">
<link rel="icon" sizes="192x192" href="images/android-chrome-192.png">
```

7. Add the following comment and style sheet link below the Bootstrap CDN link:

```
<!-- My Style Sheet -->
<link rel="stylesheet" href="css/styles.css">
```

8. Add the following comments, nav element, and navbar after the starting body tag:

```
<!-- Bootstrap Navigation bar -->
<nav class="navbar navbar-expand-sm navbar-dark fixed-top">
    <a class="navbar-brand" href="index.html">Strike a Chord
    &#9836;</a>

    <!-- Hamburger menu icon -->
    <button class="navbar-toggler" type="button" data-
    toggle="collapse" data-target="#navbarResponsive" aria-
    controls="navbarResponsive" aria-expanded="false" aria-
    label="Toggle navigation">
        <span class="navbar-toggler-icon"></span>
    </button>

    <!-- Navbar links -->
    <div class="collapse navbar-collapse" id="navbarResponsive">
        <ul class="navbar-nav ml-auto">
            <li class="nav-item">
                <a class="nav-link" href="index.html">Home</a>
            </li>
            <li class="nav-item">
                <a class="nav-link" href="#.html">Lessons</a>
            </li>
             <li class="nav-item">
                <a class="nav-link" href="#.html">Instructors</a>
            </li>
            <li class="nav-item">
                <a class="nav-link" href="#.html">Rentals</a>
            </li>
```

```
            <li class="nav-item">
                <a class="nav-link" href="#.html">Contact</a>
            </li>
        </ul>
    </div>

</nav>
```

9. Add the following comment and header jumbotron below the nav element:

```
<!-- Header and Hero Image -->
<header class="jumbotron jumbotron-fluid text-center">
    <div class="container">
        <h1 class="display-3">Welcome to Strike a Chord</h1>
        <a href="#.html" role="button" class="btn btn-outline-
        secondary btn-lg text-white">Try a Free Lesson</a>
    </div>
</header>
```

10. Add the following comment, main element, Bootstrap row and columns, and content below the
    header element.

```
<!-- Main Content Area -->
<main class="container-fluid mt-5">

    <div class="row">
        <div class="col-sm-4">
            <figure>
                <a href="#.html"><img src="images/child-guitar.jpg"
                alt="child with a smile holding a guitar" class="img-
                fluid rounded"></a>
            </figure>
            <h1>Lessons</h1>
            <p class="lead">We offer piano, guitar, and violin
            lessons.</p>
        </div>
        <div class="col-sm-4">
            <figure>
                <a href="#.html"><img src="images/piano-lesson.jpg"
                alt="piano teacher and student sitting at a piano"
                class="img-fluid rounded"></a>
            </figure>
            <h1>Instructors</h1>
            <p class="lead">Meet our talented and professional
            instructors.</p>
        </div>
```

Continued >

In the Lab *continued*

```
        <div class="col-sm-4">
            <figure>
                <a href="#.html"><img src="images/violin-on-piano.jpg"
                alt="violin setting on top of piano keys" class="img-
                fluid rounded"></a>
            </figure>
            <h1>Rentals</h1>
            <p class="lead">We rent musical equipment.</p>
        </div>
    </div>

</main>
```

11. Add the following comment, footer element, jumbotron, and content below the main element:

```
<!-- Footer -->
<footer class="jumbotron-fluid text-center p-5">

    <div class="container text-white">
        <p>&copy; Copyright 2021. All Rights Reserved.</p>
        <p><a href=mailto:lessons@strikeachord.net class="text-white"
        >lessons@strikeachord.net</a></p>
        <a href="https://www.facebook.com" target="_blank"><img
        src="images/facebook-logo.png" alt="white Facebook logo"
        class="pr-4"></a>
        <a href="https://twitter.com" target="_blank"><img src="images/
        twitter-logo.png" alt="white Twitter logo"></a>
    </div>

</footer>
```

12. Add the following script element above the closing body tag:

```
<script src="scripts/script.js"></script>
```

13. In the styles.css file, add your name, current date, and the file name to the comment at the top of the file. Add the following style rules:

```
.hero {
    background-image: linear-gradient(rgba(255, 255, 255, 0.7),
    rgba(255, 255, 255, 0.7)),url(../images/music-notes.png);
    background-size: cover;
    background-repeat: no-repeat;
    background-position: left;
}

.welcome {
    margin-top: 10%;
}
```

```
.bg-dark-purple {
    background-color: #373684;
}

.text-dark-purple {
    color: #373684;
}
```

14. In the index.html file, add the following class values to the following elements:

   a. Add the bg-dark-purple class to the nav element.

   b. Add the hero class to the header element.

   c. Add the welcome class to the div element nested within the header element.

   d. Add the text-dark-purple class to the heading 1 element within the header element.

   e. Add the bg-dark-purple class to the anchor element within the header element.

   f. Add the bg-dark-purple class to the footer element.

15. Save all of your changes and open the index.html in your browser. View the webpage in desktop, tablet, and mobile viewports.

16. Validate your HTML document and fix any errors that are identified.

17. Submit the file in a format specified by your instructor.

18. ✷ In this assignment, you created a style sheet to make custom style rules to style the webpage. Use your browser to research Bootstrap themes. Summarize your findings.

Lab 2: Creating a Home Page with Bootstrap for the Wild Rescues Website

Note: To complete this assignment, you will be required to use the Data Files. Please contact your instructor for information about accessing the Data Files.

Problem: You volunteer at a local wildlife rescue, a nonprofit organization called Wild Rescues. The organization rescues all kinds of wild animals, rehabilitates them, and then releases them back into the wild. Wild Rescues needs a website to help raise awareness about the organization. You have already created a responsive website and are now considering using the Bootstrap framework. Create a new home page using the Bootstrap framework. Figure 12–71 shows the home page in a mobile viewport. Figure 12–72 shows the home page in a tablet viewport. Figure 12–73 shows the home page in a desktop viewport.

Courtesy of Jessica Minnick

Figure 12–71

Continued >

In the Lab *continued*

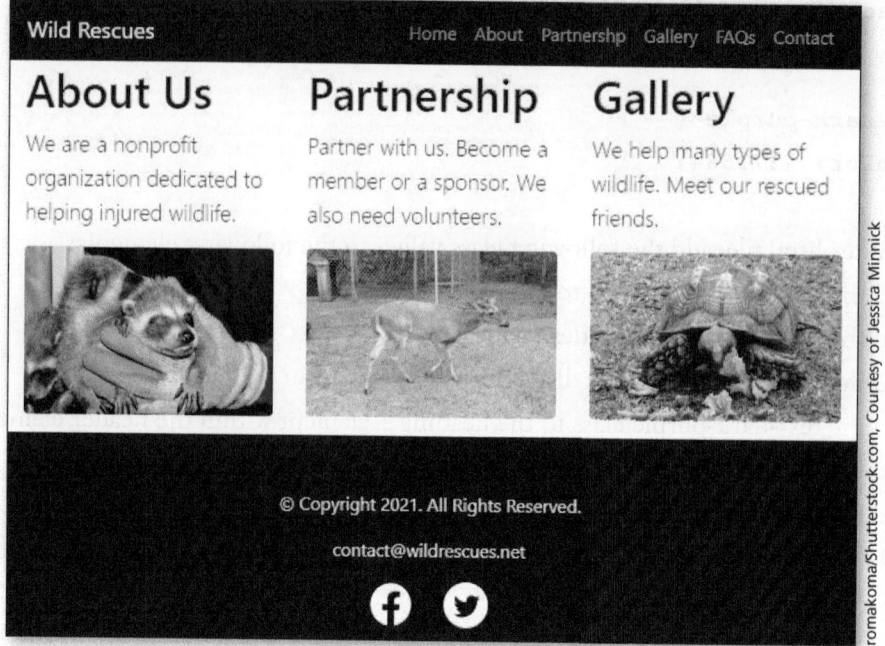

romakoma/Shutterstock.com, Courtesy of Jessica Minnick

Figure 12–72

Courtesy of Jessica Minnick

Figure 12–73

Instructions: Perform the following tasks:

1. Open getbootstrap.com in your browser, navigate to the Documentation page, and then copy the starter template code.

2. Create a new document in your text editor and paste the Bootstrap starter template code in the file. Save the file as index.html within the lab2\rescue-bootstrap folder from the Data Files.

3. Add a comment on Line 2 that includes your name and today's date. Update the title element on Line 12 with the text `Wildlife Rescue | Wild Rescues`.

4. Remove the heading 1 element (Hello, world!) on Line 15.

5. Add the following meta description element after Line 7:

```
<meta name="description" content="Wild Rescues is a local nonprofit
organization dedicated to helping injured, neglected, or orphaned
wildlife.">
```

6. Add the following comment and link elements to favicons above the Bootstrap CSS comment:

```
<!-- Favicon -->

<link rel="shortcut icon" href="images/favicon.ico">

<link rel="icon" type="image/png" sizes="32x32" href="images/
favicon-32.png">

<link rel="apple-touch-icon" sizes="180x180" href="images/apple-touch-
icon.png">

<link rel="icon" sizes="192x192" href="images/android-chrome-192.png">
```

7. Below the Bootstrap CDN link, add a comment and a link to the local style sheet located in the css folder.

8. Add the following comments, nav element, and navbar, after the starting body tag:

```
<!-- Bootstrap Navigation bar -->

<nav class="navbar navbar-expand-sm navbar-dark fixed-top">

    <a class="navbar-brand" href="index.html">Wild Rescues</a>

    <!-- Hamburger menu icon -->

    <button class="navbar-toggler" type="button" data-
    toggle="collapse" data-target="#navbarResponsive" aria-
    controls="navbarResponsive" aria-expanded="false" aria-
    label="Toggle navigation">

        <span class="navbar-toggler-icon"></span>

    </button>

    <!-- Navbar links -->

    <div class="collapse navbar-collapse" id="navbarResponsive">

        <ul class="navbar-nav ml-auto">

          <li class="nav-item">

            <a class="nav-link" href="index.html">Home</a>

          </li>

          <li class="nav-item">

            <a class="nav-link" href="#.html">About</a>

          </li>

          <li class="nav-item">

            <a class="nav-link" href="#.html">Partnership</a>

          </li>

          <li class="nav-item">

            <a class="nav-link" href="#.html">Gallery</a>

          </li>

          <li class="nav-item">
```

Continued >

In the Lab *continued*

```
        <a class="nav-link" href="#.html">FAQs</a>
      </li>
      <li class="nav-item">
        <a class="nav-link" href="#.html">Contact</a>
      </li>
    </ul>
  </div>

</nav>
```

9. Below the nav element, add a comment with the text **Header and Hero Image**. Below the comment, add a header element that includes a class attribute with the following values: `jumbotron jumbotron-fluid`.

10. Nest the following div element within the header element:

```
<div class="container">

    <h1 class="display-1 font-weight-bolder">Wild Rescues</h1>

    <p class="lead font-weight-bold">Rescue. Rehabilitate. Release.</p>

    <a href="#.html" role="button" class="btn btn-outline-secondary
    btn-lg text-white">Partner with Us</a>

</div>
```

11. Below the header element, add a comment with the text **Main Content Area**. Below the comment, add a main element that includes a class attribute with the following values: `container-fluid mt-5`.

12. Next the following div element within the main element:

```
<div class="row">

    <div class="col-sm-4">

        <h1>About Us</h1>

        <p class="lead">We are a nonprofit organization dedicated to
        helping injured wildlife.</p>

        <figure>

            <a href="#.html"><img src="images/baby-raccoons.jpg"
            alt="hands holding three baby raccoons" class="img-fluid
            rounded"></a>

        </figure>

    </div>

    <div class="col-sm-4">

        <h1>Partnership</h1>

        <p class="lead">Partner with us. Become a member or a sponsor.
        We also need volunteers.</p>

        <figure>

            <a href="#.html"><img src="images/blind-deer.jpg"
            alt="blind deer" class="img-fluid rounded"></a>

        </figure>

    </div>
```

```
<div class="col-sm-4">

    <h1>Gallery</h1>

    <p class="lead">We help many types of wildlife. Meet our
    rescued friends.</p>

    <figure>

        <a href="#.html"><img src="images/tortoise.jpg"
        alt="tortoise eating vegetation" class="img-fluid
        rounded"></a>

    </figure>

</div>

</div>
```

13. Below the main element, add a comment with the text **Footer**. Below the comment, add a footer element that includes a class attribute with a value to make a fluid jumbotron, center align text, and padding of 5.

14. Nest the following div element within the footer element:

```
<div class="container text-white">

    <p>&copy; Copyright 2021. All Rights Reserved.</p>

    <p><a href="mailto:contact@wildrescues.net" class="text-
    white">contact@wildrescues.net</a></p>

    <a href="https://www.facebook.com" target="_blank"><img
    src="images/facebook-logo.png" alt="white Facebook logo"
    class="pr-4"></a>

    <a href="https://twitter.com" target="_blank"><img src="images/
    twitter-logo.png" alt="white Twitter logo"></a>

</div>
```

15. Add the following script element above the closing body tag:

```
<script src="scripts/script.js"></script>
```

16. Open the script.js file located in the lab2\rescue-bootstrap\scripts folder. Add your name, file name, and the current date to the comment at the top of the page. Add the following comment and jQuery document ready event to the file:

```
//jQuery for hero image to consume the header window space
    $(document).ready(function(){
    $('.hero').height($(window).height());
});
```

17. In the styles.css file, add your name, current date, and the file name to the comment at the top of the file. Add the following style rule below the comment:

```
.hero {
    background-image: linear-gradient(rgba(255, 255, 255, 0.5),
    rgba(255, 255, 255, 0.5)),url(../images/baby-hawk.jpg);
    background-size: cover;
    background-repeat: no-repeat;
    background-position: right;
}
```

Continued >

In the Lab *continued*

18. In the styles.css file, below the style rule created in Step 17, add the following style rules:

    a. Create a style rule for the welcome class selector that specifies a **position** of **absolute** and a **top** of **40%**.

    b. Create a style rule for the display-1 class selector that sets the font size to **4em**.

    c. Create a style rule for the bg-brown class selector that sets the background color to **#2a1f14**.

19. In the index.html file, add the following class values to the following elements:

    a. Add the bg-brown class to the nav element.

    b. Add the hero class to the header element.

    c. Add the welcome class to the div element nested within the header element.

    e. Add the bg-brown class to the anchor element within the header element.

    f. Add the bg-brown class to the footer element.

20. Save all of your changes and open the index.html in your browser. View the webpage in desktop, tablet, and mobile viewports.

21. Validate your HTML document and fix any errors that are identified.

22. Submit the file in a format specified by your instructor.

23. ✳ In this exercise, you added Facebook and Twitter logos to the footer element. Research how you can use Font Awesome to add social media icons to a webpage and summarize your findings.

Lab 3: Using Bootstrap to Create the Student Clubs and Events Website

Problem: You and several of your classmates have decided to help increase student involvement in school clubs and events by creating a website to promote awareness about the various activities. You have already created a responsive website and are now considering using the Bootstrap framework. Create a new website with a minimum of three pages using the Bootstrap framework.

Instructions:

1. As a team, work together to design a new home page and two other webpages using the Bootstrap framework.

2. As a team, determine which Bootstrap components you will use. At a minimum, use a Bootstrap navbar, jumbotron, and grid system.

3. Create an external style sheet with at least three custom style rules.

4. Use Bootstrap to style text.

5. Use Bootstrap to make all images fluid.

6. Use Bootstrap to specify margins and padding.

7. Use Bootstrap to style a table.

8. Save all files. View your website in mobile, tablet, and desktop viewports.

9. Check your spelling. Validate your HTML and CSS files and correct any errors. Save your changes.

10. Submit your assignment in the format specified by your instructor.

11. ✳ In this exercise, you used the Bootstrap grid system to create a page layout. Research Bootstrap 4 Flex to learn how it is used to create a webpage layout. Summarize your findings.

Consider This: Your Turn

Apply your creative thinking and problem-solving skills to design and implement a solution.

1. Creating Your Personal Portfolio Website with Bootstrap

Personal

Part 1: You have already developed a responsive website for your personal portfolio. Recreate your home page using the Bootstrap framework.

1. Create a new folder named portfolio-bootstrap.

2. Create a new file named index.html and save it within your portfolio-bootstrap folder. Copy the Bootstrap starter template to your index.html file. Add a comment on Line 2 that includes your name and the current date.

3. Add a Bootstrap navbar and jumbotron to your index.html file.

4. Add a main element with your desired home page content. Use Bootstrap classes to style your content.

5. Add your picture and use Bootstrap to make it a fluid image.

6. Save your file and view your new home page in a browser. Display the page in a mobile, tablet, and desktop viewports.

7. Validate and correct your HTML file.

8. Submit your assignment in the format specified by your instructor.

Part 2: ✳ In this exercise, you used the Bootstrap framework to create a new home page for your personal portfolio website. Use your browser to research the Bootstrap Modal. Summarize your findings.

2. Creating the Dog Grooming Website with Bootstrap

Professional

Part 1: You have already developed a responsive website for a dog grooming business. Recreate the home page using the Bootstrap framework.

1. Create a new folder named groom-bootstrap.

2. Create a new file named index.html and save it within your groom-bootstrap folder. Copy the Bootstrap starter template to your index.html file. Add a comment on Line 2 that includes your name and the current date.

3. Integrate a Bootstrap navbar, jumbotron, and grid system to the index.html file.

4. Use Bootstrap to style text.

5. Use Bootstrap to make all images fluid.

6. Use Bootstrap to specify margins and padding.

7. Create an external style sheet with at least three custom style rules. Include a comment with your name, the file name, and the current date.

8. Save your file and view your new home page in a browser. Display the page in mobile, tablet, and desktop viewports.

9. Validate and correct your HTML file.

10. Submit your assignment in the format specified by your instructor.

Part 2: ✳ In this exercise, you created a new home page using the Bootstrap framework, which uses pre-defined style rules. Can you modify these style rules? Explain your answer.

Continued >

Consider This: Your Turn *continued*

3. Creating the Future Technologies Website with Bootstrap
Research and Collaboration

Part 1: You and several of your classmates have been tasked with creating a website that showcases advances in technology. You have already created a responsive website and are now considering using the Bootstrap framework. Create a new website with a minimum of three pages using the Bootstrap framework.

1. As a team, work together to design a new home page and two other webpages using the Bootstrap framework.
2. As a team, determine which Bootstrap components you will use. At a minimum, use a Bootstrap navbar, jumbotron, and grid system.
3. Create an external style sheet with at least three custom style rules.
4. Use Bootstrap to style text.
5. Use Bootstrap to make all images fluid.
6. Use Bootstrap to specify margins and padding.
7. Use a jQuery document ready event.
8. As a team, research other Bootstrap classes that were not discussed in Chapter 12. Use at least one of the classes that you find.
9. Save all files. View your website in mobile, tablet, and desktop viewports.
10. Check your spelling. Validate your HTML and CSS files and correct any errors. Save your changes.
11. Submit your assignment in the format specified by your instructor.

Part 2: ☀ In this exercise, you used the Bootstrap, a front-end framework, to create a website. As a group, research back-end frameworks and list at least three resources that you found and the URL for each.

Appendix A
HTML Quick Reference

Common HTML Elements

HTML uses tags such as <h1> and <p> to structure content into headings, paragraphs, lists, hypertext links, and so on. Many HTML tags have attributes that can be defined in different ways to further structure the content of the webpage. Attributes are the parts of HTML elements that define them. Attributes provide additional information that a browser can use to determine things like how to display an element. As an example, the height and width attributes in the <img> tag describe the size of the image.

As the W3C continually updates the HTML specifications, HTML tags are added to, deleted, and replaced by newer tags. Table A–1 lists HTML tags and their associated attributes. The list provides a brief description of each tag and its values. The default value for each attribute is indicated by bold text in the Description column. The ⑤ icon indicates tags or attributes that were introduced with HTML 5 and are validated successfully with the HTML 5 DOCTYPE. Note that these elements may not work with all browsers.

Global attributes are those that can be used with most HTML tags. HTML 4 had a number of global attributes, and HTML 5 has added some new ones (as indicated in Table A–1). Table A–2 lists the HTML 5 global attributes. This is a comprehensive list of attributes that are common to all HTML 5 elements.

As a web developer, you will most likely inherit a website developed by someone else. Carefully view the code for **deprecated elements** or elements that are no longer supported in HTML 5. Deprecated elements are noted in Table A–3.

For a comprehensive list of HTML tags and attributes, more thorough descriptions, examples of HTML elements, and coding standards, visit the W3C website at w3.org.

Table A–1 Common HTML Elements and Attributes

HTML Tag and Attributes	Description
<!DOCTYPE>	Indicates the version of HTML used
<!-- Comments here -->	Inserts comments that are ignored by browsers
<a>....</a>	Anchor; creates a hyperlink or fragment identifier
href=*URL*	Hyperlink reference that specifies the target URL
media=*media_query* ⑤	Specifies what media/device the target URL is optimized for
id=*text*	Specifies an id for enclosed text, allowing it to be the target of a hyperlink
rel=*relationship*	Indicates the relationship going from the current page to the target
target=_blank, _self, _parent, _top, *framename*	Defines the name of the window or frame in which the linked resource will appear
type=*MIME_type* ⑤	Specifies the MIME type of the target URL

(Continued)

Table A–1 Common HTML Elements and Attributes (Continued)

HTML Tag and Attributes	Description
<abbr> .... </abbr>	Specifies an abbreviation or acronym
<address>....</address>	Used for information such as authorship, email addresses, or addresses; enclosed text appears italicized and indented in some browsers
<area>....</area>	Creates a clickable area, or hotspot, on a client-side image map
alt=*text*	Specifies alternate text for the area
coords=*value1, value2*	Specifies the coordinates that define the edges of the hotspot; a comma-delimited list of values
href=*URL*	Hyperlink reference that specifies the target URL
hreflang=*language_code* 🔲	Specifies the language of the target URL
media=*media query* 🔲	Specifies what media/device the target URL is optimized for
rel=alternate, author, bookmark, help, license, next, nofollow, noreferrer, prefetch, prev, search, tag 🔲	Specifies the relationship between the current page and the target URL
shape=circle, poly, rect	Identifies the shape of the area
target=_blank, _self, _parent, _top, *framename*	Defines the name of the window or frame in which the linked resource will appear
type=*MIME_type* 🔲	Specifies the MIME type of the target URL
<article>...</article> 🔲	Defines an article
<aside>...</aside> 🔲	Defines content aside from the main page content
<audio>...</audio> 🔲	Defines sound content
autoplay=autoplay	Specifies that the audio should start playing as soon as it is ready
controls=controls	Specifies that playback controls should be displayed
loop=loop	Specifies that the audio should start over again, when it is finished
preload=auto, metadata, none	Specifies whether the audio should be loaded when the page loads
src=*URL*	Specifies the URL of the audio to play
....	Specifies text to appear in bold
<base>	Identifies the base in all relative URLs in the document Empty tag
href=*URL*	Specifies the absolute URL used to resolve all relative URLs in the document
target=_blank, _self, _parent, _top, *framename*	Defines the name for the default window (or frame*) in which the hyperlinked pages are displayed
<blockquote>....</blockquote>	Sets enclosed text to appear as a quotation, indented on the right and left
cite=*URL*	Specifies the source of the quotation
<body>....</body>	Defines the start and end of a webpage's content
** **	Inserts a line break Empty tag
<button>....</button>	Creates a button that can be tapped or clicked
<canvas>...</canvas> 🔲	Defines graphics
height=*pixels*	Specifies the height of the canvas
width=*pixels*	Specifies the width of the canvas

(Continued)

Table A–1 Common HTML Elements and Attributes *(Continued)*

HTML Tag and Attributes	Description
<caption>....</caption>	Creates a caption for a table
<cite>....</cite>	Indicates that the enclosed text is a citation; text is usually displayed in italics
<code>....</code>	Indicates that the enclosed text is a code sample from a program; text is usually displayed in fixed width font such as Courier
<col>....</col>	Organizes columns in a table into column groups to share attribute values
span=*number*	Sets the number of columns that span the <col> element
<colgroup>....</colgroup>	Encloses a group of <col> tags and groups the columns to set properties
span=*number*	Sets the number of columns the <col> element spans
<data>....</data>	Links content with a machine-readable value for data processing
value=*number*	Sets the machine-readable value
<datalist>...</datalist> 🖫	Defines a dropdown list
<dd>....</dd>	Indicates that the enclosed text is a definition in the definition list
<del>....</del>	Used to strike through webpage content
cite=*URL*	Includes a URL to a file to explain the reason for the deleted text
datetime=*YYYY-MM-DDThh:mm:ssTZD*	Sets the date and time of the deletion
<details>...</details> 🖫	Defines details of an element
<dfn>....</dfn>	Used to wrap a term when defining a term
<dialog> .... </dialog> 🖫	Specifies a dialog box
<div>....</div>	Defines a block-level structure or division in the HTML document
<dl>....</dl>	Creates a definition list
<dt>....</dt>	Indicates that the enclosed text is a term in the definition list
....	Indicates that the enclosed text should be emphasized; usually appears in italics
<embed>...</embed> 🖫	Defines external interactive content or plugin
height=*pixels*	Specifies the height of the embedded content
src=*URL*	Specifies the URL of the embedded content
type=*MIME_type*	Specifies the MIME type of the embedded content
width=*pixels*	Specifies the width of the embedded content
<fieldset>....</fieldset>	Groups related form controls and labels
disabled=disabled	Specifies that a fieldset should be disabled
form=*form_id*	Specifies one or more forms that a fieldset belongs to
name=*text*	Specifies the name of the fieldset
<figcaption>...</figcaption> 🖫	Defines the caption of a figure element
<figure>...</figure> 🖫	Defines a group of media content and their captions
<footer>...</footer> 🖫	Defines a footer for a section or page
<form>....</form>	Marks the start and end of a webpage form
action=*URL*	Specifies the URL of the application that will process the form; required attribute

(Continued)

Table A–1 Common HTML Elements and Attributes *(Continued)*	
HTML Tag and Attributes	**Description**
autocomplete=on, off 🔲	Specifies whether the form should have autocomplete enabled
enctype=*encoding*	Specifies how the form element values will be encoded
method=get, post	Specifies the method used to pass form parameters (data) to the server
name=*form_name*	Specifies the name for a form
novalidate=novalidate 🔲	If present, the form should not be validated when submitted
target=_blank, _self, _parent, _top, *framename*	Specifies the frame or window that displays the form's results
\<head\>....\</head\>	Delimits the start and end of the HTML document's head
\<header\>...\</header\> 🔲	Defines a header for a section or page
\<hgroup\>...\<hgroup\> 🔲	Defines information about a section in a document
\<h*n*\>....\</h*n*\>	Defines a header level *n*, ranging from the largest (h1) to the smallest (h6)
\<hr\>	Specifies a thematic content change
\<html\>....\</html\>	Indicates the start and the end of the HTML document
manifest=*URL* 🔲	Specifies the URL of the document's cache manifest
\<i\>....\</i\>	Sets enclosed text to appear in italics
\<iframe\>....\</iframe\>	Creates an inline frame, also called a floating frame or subwindow, within an HTML document
height=*pixels*	Sets the frame height to a value in pixels
sandbox=*allow-option* 🔲	Specifies restrictions to the frame content
seamless=seamless 🔲	Specifies that the iframe should be seamlessly integrated
src=*URL*	Defines the URL of the source document that is displayed in the frame
srcdoc=*HTML_code* 🔲	Specifies the HTML of the document showing in the iframe
width=*pixels*	Sets the frame width to a value in pixels
\<img\>....\</img\>	Inserts an image into the current webpage
alt=*text*	Provides a text description of an image if the browser cannot display the image; should always be used
height=*pixels*	Sets the height of the image to a value in pixels (not percentages); should always be used
src=*URL*	Specifies the URL of the image to be displayed; required
usemap=#*mapname*	Specifies the map of coordinates and links that defines the href within this image
width=*pixels*	Sets the width of the image to a value in pixels (not percentages); should always be used
\<input\>....\</input\>	Defines controls used in forms
alt=*text*	Provides a short description of the control or image button; for browsers that do not support inline images
autocomplete=on, off 🔲	Specifies whether the input field should have focus on page load
autofocus=autofocus 🔲	Specifies that the input field should have focus on page load
checked=checked	Sets radio buttons and check boxes to the checked state
disabled=disabled	Disables the control
form=*form_id* 🔲	Specifies one or more forms the input element belongs to

(Continued)

Table A–1 Common HTML Elements and Attributes (*Continued*)

HTML Tag and Attributes	Description
formaction=*URL* 🔲	Overrides the form's action attribute. Defines where to send the data when the form is submitted (for type="submit" and type="image")
formenctype=*encoding* 🔲	Overrides the form's enctype attribute. Defines how form data should be encoded before sending it to the server (for type="submit" and type="image")
formmethod=get, post 🔲	Overrides the form's method attribute. Defines the HTTP method for sending data to the action URL (for type="submit" and type="image")
formnovalidate= formnovalidate 🔲	Overrides the form's novalidate attribute. Defines that the input element should not be validated when submitted
formtarget=_blank, _self, _parent, _top, *framename* 🔲	Overrides the form's target attribute. Defines the target window to use when the form is submitted (for type="submit" and type="image")
height=*pixels, %* 🔲	The height of an input element (for type="image")
list=*datalist_id* 🔲	Refers to a datalist that contains predefined options for the input element
max=*number, date* 🔲	Specifies a maximum value for an input field
maxlength=*number*	Sets a value for the maximum number of characters allowed as input for a text or password control
multiple=*multiple*	If present, the user is allowed more than one value
name=*text*	Assigns a name to the control
pattern=*regexp_pattern* 🔲	Specifies a pattern or format for the input field's value
placeholder=*text* 🔲	Specifies a hint to help users fill out the input field
readonly=readonly	Prevents changes to the control
required=required 🔲	Indicates that the input field's value is required in order to submit the form
size=*number*	Sets the initial size of the control to a value in characters
step=*number* 🔲	Specifies the legal number intervals for the input field
src=*URL*	Identifies the location of the image if the control is set to an image
type=*type*	Defines the type of control
value=*value*	Sets the initial value of the control
<ins>....</ins>	Identifies and displays text as having been inserted in the document in relation to a previous version
cite=*URL*	Specifies the URL of a document that has more information on the inserted text
datetime=*datetime*	Date and time of a change
<kbd>....</kbd>	Sets enclosed text to display as keyboard-like input
<label>....</label>	Creates a label for a form control
for=*element_id*	Indicates the name or ID of the element to which the label is applied
form=*form_id*	Specifies one or more forms the label field belongs to
<legend>....</legend>	Assigns a caption to a fieldset element, as defined by the <fieldset> tags
<li>....</li>	Defines the enclosed text as a list item in a list
value=*value*	Inserts or restarts counting with value

(Continued)

Table A–1 Common HTML Elements and Attributes *(Continued)*

HTML Tag and Attributes	Description
<link>	Establishes a link between the HTML document and another document, such as an external style sheet
href=*URL*	Defines the URL of the linked document
name=*text*	Names the current anchor so that it can be the destination for other links
rel=*relationship*	Indicates the relationship going from the current page to the target
sizes=*heightxwidth, any* 🗲	Specifies sizes (height and width) of the linked resource
type=*MIME_type*	Indicates the data or media type of the linked document (for example, text/css for linked style sheets)
<main> .... </main>	Specifies the main content area of the page
<map>....</map>	Specifies a client-side image map; must enclose <area> tags
name=*text*	Assigns a name to the image map
<mark>...</mark> 🗲	Defines marked text
label=*menulabel*	Specifies a visible label for the menu
type=context, toolbar, list	Specifies which type of menu to display
<meta>	Provides additional data (metadata) about an HTML document Empty tag
charset=*character_set* 🗲	Specifies the character encoding for the HTML document
content=*text*	Specifies the value for the <meta> information; required
http-equiv=content-type, default-style, refresh	Specifies the HTTP-equivalent name for metadata; tells the server to include that name and content in the HTTP header when the HTML document is sent to the client
name=*text*	Assigns a name to metadata
<meter>...</meter> 🗲	Defines measurement within a predefined range
form=*form_id*	Specifies which form this meter belongs to
high=*number*	Specifies at which point the measurement's value is considered a high value
low=*number*	Specifies at which point the measurement's value is considered a low value
max=*number*	Specifies the maximum value; default value is 1.0
min=*number*	Specifies the minimum value; default value is 0
optimum=*number*	Specifies which measurement's value is the best value
value=*number*	Specifies the measurement's current or "measured" value; required
<nav>...</nav> 🗲	Defines navigation links
<noscript>....</noscript>	Provides alternate content for browsers with disabled scripts
<object>....</object>	Includes an external object in the HTML document such as an image, a Java applet, or other external object
data=*URL*	Identifies the location of the object's data
form=*form_id* 🗲	Specifies one or more forms the object belongs to
height=*pixels*	Sets the height of the object to a value in pixels
name=*text*	Assigns a control name to the object for use in forms
type=*MIME_type*	Specifies the content or media type of the object
usemap=#*mapname*	Associates an image map as defined by the <map> element
width=*pixels*	Sets the width of the object to a value in pixels

(Continued)

Table A–1 Common HTML Elements and Attributes *(Continued)*

HTML Tag and Attributes	Description
\<ol\>....\</ol\>	Defines an ordered list that contains numbered list item elements (\<li\>)
reversed=reversed 🗗	Specifies that the list order should be descending
start=*start*	Specifies the start value of an ordered list
type=*option*	Sets or resets the numbering format for the list
\<optgroup\>...\</optgroup\> 🗗	Defines an option group
disabled=disabled	Specifies that an option group should be disabled
label=*text*	Specifies a label for the option group
\<option\>....\</option\>	Defines individual options in a selection list, as defined by the \<select\> element
disabled=disabled	Disables the option items
label=*text*	Provides a shorter label for the option than that specified in its content
selected=selected	Sets the option to be the default or the selected option in a list
value=*text*	Sets a value returned to the server when the user selects the option
\<output\>...\</output\> 🗗	Defines some types of output
for=*element_id*	Specifies one or more elements the output field relates to
form=*form_id*	Specifies one or more forms the output field belongs to
name=*text*	Specifies a name for the object (to use when a form is submitted)
\<p\>....\</p\>	Delimits a paragraph; automatically inserts a blank line between text
\<param\>....\</param\>	Passes a parameter to an object or applet, as defined by the \<object\>
name=*text*	Defines the name of the parameter required by an object
value=*data*	Sets the value of the parameter
\<picture\>....\</picture\>	Parent container used to contain multiple pictures with the source element that specifies a source set
\<pre\>....\</pre\>	Preserves the original format of the enclosed text; keeps line breaks and spacing the same as the original
\<progress\>...\</progress\> 🗗	Defines progress of a task of any kind
max=*number*	Defines the value of completion
value=*number*	Defines the current value of the progress
\<q\>....\</q\>	Sets enclosed text as a short quotation
cite=*URL*	Specifies the source URL of the quote
\<rp\>...\</rp\> 🗗	Used in ruby annotations to define what to show if a browser does not support the ruby element
\<rt\>...\</rt\> 🗗	Defines explanation to ruby annotations
\<ruby\>...\</ruby\> 🗗	Defines ruby annotations, which are used for East Asian typography
\<s\>...\</s\>	Defines text that is no longer correct, accurate, or relevant
\<samp\>....\</samp\>	Sets enclosed text to appear as sample output from a computer program or script; usually appears in a monospace font
\<script\>....\</script\>	Inserts a client-side script into an HTML document

(Continued)

Table A–1 Common HTML Elements and Attributes *(Continued)*

HTML Tag and Attributes	Description
async=async 5	Defines whether the script should be executed asynchronously
defer=defer	Indicates that the browser should defer executing the script
src=*URL*	Identifies the location of an external script
type=*MIME_type*	Specifies the MIME type of the script
<section>...</section> 5	Defines a section
<select>....</select>	Defines a form control to create a multiple-choice menu or scrolling list; encloses a set of <option> tags to define one or more options
autofocus=autofocus 5	Makes the select field focused on page load
disabled=disabled	Disables the selection list
form=form_id	Defines one or more forms the select field belongs to
multiple=multiple	Sets the list to allow multiple selections
name=*text*	Assigns a name to the selection list
size=*value*	Sets the number of visible options in the list
<small>....</small>	Sets enclosed text to appear in a smaller typeface
<source>...</source> 5	Defines media resources
media=*media_query*	Specifies what media/device the media resource is optimized for; default value: all
src=*URL*	The URL of the media
type=*MIME_type*	Specifies the MIME type of the media resource
....	Creates a user-defined container to add inline structure to the HTML document
....	Sets enclosed text to appear with strong emphasis; usually displayed as bold text
<style>....</style>	Encloses embedded style sheet rules for use in the HTML document
media=*media_query*	Identifies the intended medium of the style
scoped=*scoped* 5	If present, the styles should only apply to this element's parent element and its child elements
type=text/css	Specifies the MIME type of the style sheet
_{....}	Sets enclosed text to appear in subscript
<summary>...</summary> 5	Defines the header of a "detail" element
^{....}	Sets enclosed text to appear in superscript
<svg>....</svg>	Container used for SVG graphics
height=*pixels*	Sets the height of the SVG graphic to a value in pixels
width=*pixels*	Sets the width of the SVG graphic to a value in pixels
<table>....</table>	Marks the start and end of a table
sortable=*sortable*	Specifies that the table is sortable
<tbody>....</tbody>	Defines a group of rows in a table body
<td>....</td>	Defines a data cell in a table; contents are left-aligned and normal text by default
colspan=*value*	Defines the number of adjacent columns spanned by the cell
headers=*header_id*	Defines the list of header cells for the current cell
rowspan=*value*	Defines the number of adjacent rows spanned by the cell
<template>....</template>	Used to contain content that does not display on a webpage
<textarea>....</textarea>	Creates a multiline text input area within a form

(Continued)

Table A–1 Common HTML Elements and Attributes *(Continued)*

HTML Tag and Attributes	Description
autofocus=*autofocus* 🔲	Specifies that the text area field should have focus on page load
cols=*value*	Defines the number of columns in the text input area
disabled=disabled	Disables the element
form=*form_id* 🔲	Specifies one or more forms the text area belongs to
maxlength=*number* 🔲	Specifies the maximum number of characters allowed in the text area
name=*text*	Assigns a name to the text area
placeholder=*text* 🔲	Specifies a hint to help users fill out the input field
readonly=readonly	Prevents the user from editing content in the text area
required=required 🔲	Indicates that the input field's value is required in order to submit the form
rows=*value*	Defines the number of rows in the text input area
wrap=hard, soft 🔲	Specifies how the text in the text area is wrapped, and if it should be wrapped when submitted in a form
<tfoot>....</tfoot>	Identifies and groups rows into a table footer
<th>....</th>	Defines a table header cell; contents are bold and center-aligned by default
colspan=*value*	Defines the number of adjacent columns spanned by the cell
headers=*header_id* 🔲	Specifies one or more header cells a cell is related to
rowspan=*value*	Defines the number of adjacent rows spanned by the cell
scope=col, colgroup, row, rowgroup 🔲	Specifies whether a header cell is a header for a column, row, or group of columns or rows
<thead>....</thead>	Identifies and groups rows into a table header
<time>...</time> 🔲	Defines a date/time
datetime=*datetime*	Specifies the date or time for the time element; this attribute is used if no date or time is specified in the element's content
pubdate=*pubdate*	Specifies that the date and time in the <time> element is the publication date and time of the document (or the nearest ancestor article element)
<title>....</title>	Defines the title for the HTML document; should always be used
<tr>....</tr>	Defines a row of cells within a table
<track>....</track>	Used to include a text track for a media element
default=*default*	Enables a track
kind=*captions, chapters, descriptions, metadata, or subtitles*	Defines the type of text track
label=*text*	Provides a title for the text track
src=*URL*	Specifies the URL of the text track file; required
srclang=*language_code*	Specifies the language of the track content
<u>....</u> 🔲	Used to represent text that should be styled different from normal text; previously deprecated in HTML 4, but redefined in HTML 5
<ul>....</ul>	Defines an unordered list that contains bulleted list item elements (<li>)
<var>....</var>	Indicates the enclosed text is a variable's name; used to mark up variables or program arguments

(Continued)

Table A–1 Common HTML Elements and Attributes (Continued)

HTML Tag and Attributes	Description
\<video\>...\</video\> 🔲	Defines a video
autoplay=autoplay	If present, the video will start playing as soon as it is ready
controls=controls	If present, controls will be displayed, such as a play button
height=*pixels*	Sets the height of the video player
loop=loop	If present, the video will start over again, every time it is finished
muted=muted	Specifies the default state of the audio. Currently, only "muted" is allowed
poster=*URL*	Specifies the URL of an image representing the video
preload=auto, metadata, none	Specifies whether the video should be loaded when the page loads
src=*URL*	The URL of the video to play
width=*pixels*	Sets the width of the video player
\<wbr\>...\</wbr\> 🔲	Defines a possible line break

Table A–2 Global Attributes

Attribute	Value	Description
accesskey	*character*	Specifies a shortcut key to access an element
class	*classname*	Refers to a class specified in a style sheet
contenteditable 🔲	true false inherit	Specifies whether a user can edit the content of an element
data-*	*custom*	Used to store custom data
dir	ltr rtl auto	Specifies the text direction for the content in an element
draggable 🔲	true false auto	Specifies whether a user is allowed to drag an element
dropzone 🔲	copy move link	Specifies what happens when dragged items/data are dropped in the element
hidden 🔲	hidden	Specifies that an element should be hidden
id	*id*	Specifies a unique id for an element
lang	*language_code*	Specifies the language of the element's content
spellcheck 🔲	true false	Specifies whether the element must have its spelling and grammar checked
style	*style_definitions*	Specifies an inline style for an element
tabindex	*number*	Specifies the tab order of an element
title	*text*	Specifies extra information about an element
translate 🔲	yes no	Specifies whether content should be translated

Table A–3 Deprecated Elements

Element	Replace with
<acronym>	<abbr>
<applet>	<object>
<basefront>	use CSS
<big>	use CSS
<center>	use CSS
<dir>	<ul>
<font>	use CSS
<frame>	no replacement
<frameset>	no replacement
<noframes>	no replacement
<s>	use CSS
<strike>	use <del> or CSS
<tt>	use CSS
<xmp>	<pre>

Appendix B
CSS Quick Reference

This appendix provides a brief review of Cascading Style Sheets (CSS) concepts and terminology. CSS uses a modularized approach to style sheets, which allows CSS to be updated in a more timely and flexible manner. For a more comprehensive list of CSS properties and values, visit the World Wide Web Consortium at www.w3.org. The W3C site provides the latest information regarding CSS.

CSS Properties

Table B–1 shows units of measurement for web development. Tables B–2 through B–17 show the property names, descriptions, and valid values for various categories of CSS properties. Values listed in bold are the default.

Table B–1 Units of Measurement

Unit	Description
ch	Relative to the width of zero; relative length unit
cm	Centimeters; absolute length unit
em	Relative to the element font size; relative length unit
ex	Relative to the x-height of the current font; relative length unit
in	Inches; absolute length unit
mm	Millimeters; absolute length unit
px	Pixels; absolute length unit
pt	Points; absolute length unit
pc	Picas; absolute length unit
rem	Relative to the root element font size; relative length unit
vw	Relative to 1% of the viewport width; relative length unit
vh	Relative to 1% of the viewport height; relative length unit
vmin	Relative to 1% of the smaller viewport; relative length unit
vmax	Relative to 1% of the larger viewport; relative length unit
%	Relative to the parent element; relative length unit

Table B–2 Animation Properties

Property Name	Description	Values
@keyframes	Specifies the animation	[animationname] [keyframes-selector] [css-styles]
animation	A shorthand property for all the animation properties below, except the animation-play-state property	

(Continued)

Table B–2 Animation Properties *(Continued)*

Property Name	Description	Values
animation-delay	Specifies when the animation will start	[time] initial inherit
animation-direction	Specifies whether the animation should play in reverse on alternate cycles	**normal** alternate
animation-duration	Specifies how many seconds or milliseconds an animation takes to complete one cycle	[time]
animation-fill-mode	Specifies values applied by the animation separate from the time it is executing	**none** forwards backwards both initial inherit
animation-iteration-count	Specifies the number of times an animation should be played	[n] infinite
animation-name	Specifies a name for the @keyframes animation	[keyframename] **none**
animation-play-state	Specifies whether the animation is running or paused	paused **running**
animation-timing-function	Specifies the speed curve of the animation	**ease** ease-in ease-out ease-in-out cubic-bezier linear

Table B–3 Background Properties

Property Name	Description	Values
background	Sets all background properties in one declaration	n/a
background-attachment	Sets the background image to fixed or scrolls with the page	**scroll** fixed
background-clip	Specifies the painting area of the background	**border-box** content-box padding-box
background-color	Sets the background color of an element	**transparent** [color]
background-image	Sets an image as the background	**none** [URL]
background-origin	Specifies the positioning area of the background images	border-box content-box **padding-box**
background-position	Sets the starting position of a background image	[length] [percentage] bottom center left right top

(Continued)

Table B–3 Background Properties (Continued)

Property Name	Description	Values
background-repeat	Sets if/how a background image will be repeated	**repeat** repeat-x repeat-y no-repeat inherit
background-size	Specifies the size of the background images	**auto** contain cover length percentage

Table B–4 Border Properties

Property Name	Description	Values
border	Sets all the border properties in one declaration	n/a
border-collapse	Specifies a single border for table cells	collapse
border-color	Sets the color of the four borders in one declaration; can have from one to four colors	[color] transparent
border-bottom-color border-left-color border-right-color border-top-color	Sets the respective color of the top, right, bottom, and left borders individually	[color]
border-image	Sets all the border-image-*n* properties	url(path/file)
border-image-outset	Specifies the amount by which the border image area extends beyond the border box	[length] [number]
border-image-repeat	Specifies whether the image-border should be repeated, rounded, or stretched	**stretch** repeat round
border-image-slice	Specifies the inward offsets of the image-border	[number] [percentage] fill
border-image-source	Specifies an image to be used as a border	**none** [image]
border-image-width	Specifies the widths of the image-border	[number] [percentage] auto
border-left	Specifies the style of the left border	2px solid #000
border-radius	Sets all the four border-*n*-radius properties	10px
border-bottom-left-radius border-bottom-right-radius border-top-left-radius border-top-right-radius	Sets the shape of the border of the bottom-left, bottom-right, top-left, and top-right corners individually	[percentage] [length]
border-right	Specifies the style of the right border	2px solid #000
border-spacing	Specifies the border spacing for a table	15px
border-style	Sets the style of the four borders in one declaration; can have from one to four styles	**none** dashed dotted double groove inset outset ridge solid

(Continued)

Table B–4 Border Properties *(Continued)*

Property Name	Description	Values
border-bottom-style border-left-style border-right-style border-top-style	Sets the respective style of the top, right, bottom, and left borders individually	**none** dashed dotted double groove inset outset ridge solid
border-width	Sets the width of the four borders in one declaration; can have from one to four values	**medium** [length] thick thin
border-bottom-width border-left-width border-right-width border-top-width	Sets the respective width of the top, right, bottom, and left borders individually	**medium** [length] thick thin

Table B–5 Basic Box Properties

Property Name	Description	Values
box-decoration-break	Sets the behavior of the background and border of an element at page-break, or at line-break for in-line elements	n/a
box-shadow	Attaches one or more drop shadows to the box	[h-shadow] [v-shadow] [blur] [spread] [color] inset **none**
box-sizing	Specifies to include the padding and border within an element's total size	border-box
overflow	Specifies what happens if content overflows into a box element's area	auto hidden scroll **visible**
overflow-x	Specifies whether to clip the left/right edges of the content, if it overflows the element's content area	**visible** hidden scroll auto no-display no-content
overflow-y	Specifies whether to clip the top/bottom edges of the content, if it overflows the element's content area	visible hidden scroll auto no-display no-content

Table B–6 Classification Properties

Property Name	Description	Values
display	Describes how/if an element is displayed on a webpage	**block** inline inline-block none
white-space	Declares how white-space inside the element is handled: the "normal" way (where white-space is collapsed), as *pre* (which behaves like the <pre> element in HTML) or as *nowrap* (where wrapping is done only through elements)	**normal** pre nowrap

Table B–7 Color Properties

Property Name	Description	Values
color	Sets the color of text	[value]
opacity	Sets the opacity level for an element	[value] inherit

Table B–8 Dimension Properties

Property Name	Description	Values
height	Sets the height of an element	**auto** [length] [percentage] inherit
max-height	Sets the maximum height of an element	**none** [length] [percentage] inherit
max-width	Sets the maximum width of an element	**none** [length] [percentage] inherit
min-height	Sets the minimum height of an element	[length] [percentage] inherit
min-width	Sets the minimum width of an element	[length] [percentage] inherit
width	Sets the width of an element	**auto** [length] [percentage] inherit

Table B–9 Flexible Box Properties

Property Name	Description	Values
align-content	Specifies alignment between lines inside flexible container when items do not use all available space	center flex-end flex-start space-around space-between **stretch**
align-items	Specifies alignment for items inside flexible container	baseline center flex-end flex-start **stretch**
align-self	Specifies alignment for specific elements inside flexible container	**auto** baseline center flex-end flex-start
flex	Specifies the length of an element, relative to the other elements	**auto** none
flex-basis	Specifies initial length of a flexible element	**auto**
flex-direction	Specifies direction of the flexible elements	column column-reverse **row** row-reverse
flex-flow	Shorthand property of flex-direction and flex-wrap properties	n/a
flex-grow	Specifies how much an element can grow relative to the other elements	[number]
flex-shrink	Specifies how much an element can shrink relative to the other elements	[number]
flex-wrap	Specifies whether flexible elements can wrap	**nowrap** wrap wrap-reverse
justify-content	Specifies the alignment between elements inside a flexible container when the elements do not use all available space	center flex-end **flex-start** space-around space-between

Table B–10 Font Properties

Property Name	Description	Values
font	Sets font properties in one declaration	n/a
@font-face	A rule that allows websites to use fonts other than the "web-safe" fonts	n/a
font-family	A prioritized list of font-family names and/or generic family names for an element	[family-name] cursive fantasy monospace sans-serif serif
font-feature-settings	Allows control in OpenType font features	n/a
@font-feature-values	Permits web author to give a custom name to a font-variant-alternate for OpenType font features	n/a

(Continued)

Table B–10 Font Properties (*Continued*)

Property Name	Description	Values
font-kerning	Controls the spacing between letters	normal
font-size	Sets the size of a font	[length] [percentage] large larger **medium** small smaller x-large x-small xx-large xx-small inherit
font-size-adjust	Preserves the readability of text when font fallback occurs	[number] **none** inherit
font-stretch	Selects a normal, condensed, or expanded face from a font family	n/a
font-style	Sets the style of a font	**normal** italic oblique
font-variant	Displays text in a small-caps font or a normal font	**normal** small-caps
font-weight	Sets the weight of a font	**normal** bold bolder lighter

Table B–11 Grid Properties

Property Name	Description	Values
grid	Shorthand property for setting grid properties	n/a
grid-area	Used for a grid item name or used as a shorthand property for grid properties	[grid-row-start] [grid-column-start] [grid-row-end] [grid-column-end] [itemname]
grid-auto-columns	Sets the default size of the column	auto fit-content() max-content min-content minmax [length] [percentage]
grid-auto-flow	Used to define how auto-placed items are added to the rid	row column dense row dense column dense
grid-column	Shorthand property for grid-column-start and grid-column-end properties	[grid-column-start] [grid-column-end]
grid-column-end	Identifies where to end the grid item	auto span [n] [column-line]

(Continued)

Table B–11 Grid Properties *(Continued)*

Property Name	Description	Values
grid-column-gap	Used to set the gap between columns	[length]
grid-column-start	Identifies where to start the grid item	auto span [n] [column-line]
grid-template	Shorthand for grid-template-rows, grid-template-columns and grid-areas properties	[grid-template rows] / [grid-template columns] [grid-template-areas]
grid-template-areas	Identifies how to display columns and rows with named grid items	[itemnames]
grid-template-columns	Sets the column size and number of columns for a grid	auto max-content min-content [length]
grid-template-rows	Sets the row size within a grid	auto max-content min-content [length]

Table B–12 List Properties

Property Name	Description	Values
list-style	A shorthand property for setting list-style-image, list-style-position, and list-style-type in one declaration	n/a
list-style-image	Sets an image as the list-item marker	**none** [URL]
list-style-position	Indents or extends a list-item marker with respect to the item's content	**outside** inside
list-style-type	Sets the type of list-item marker	**disc** circle square decimal lower-alpha lower-roman upper-alpha upper-roman

Table B–13 Margin and Padding Properties

Property Name	Description	Values
margin	Sets margin properties in one declaration	n/a
margin-bottom margin-left margin-right margin-top	Sets the top, right, bottom, and left margin of an element individually	[length] [percentage] auto inherit
padding	Sets padding properties in one declaration	n/a
padding-bottom padding-left padding-right padding-top	Sets the top, right, bottom, and left padding of an element individually	[length] [percentage] inherit

Table B–14 Positioning Properties

Property Name	Description	Values
bottom	Specifies the bottom position of a positioned element	**auto** [length] [percentage] inherit
clear	Specifies the sides of an element where other floating elements are not allowed	left right both **none** inherit
clip	Clips an absolutely positioned element	[shape] **auto** inherit
cursor	Specifies the type of cursor to be displayed	[URL] **auto** crosshair default e-resize help move n-resize ne-resize nw-resize pointer progress s-resize se-resize sw-resize text w-resize wait inherit
display	Specifies the type of box an element should generate	none block **inline** inline-block inline-table list-item run-in table table-caption table-cell table-column table-column-group table-footer-group table-header-group table-row table-row-group inherit
float	Specifies whether a box should float	left right **none** inherit
left	Specifies the left position of a positioned element	**auto** [length] [percentage] inherit

(Continued)

Table B–14 Positioning Properties *(Continued)*

Property Name	Description	Values
overflow	Specifies what happens if content overflows an element's box	**visible** hidden scroll auto inherit
position	Specifies the type of positioning method used for an element (static, relative, absolute, or fixed)	**static** absolute fixed relative inherit
right	Specifies the right position of a positioned element	**auto** [length] [percentage] inherit
top	Specifies the top position of a positioned element	**auto** [length] [percentage] inherit
visibility	Specifies whether an element is visible	**visible** hidden collapse inherit
z-index	Sets the stack order of a positioned element	**auto** [number] inherit

Table B–15 Table Properties

Property Name	Description	Values
border-collapse	Specifies whether table borders should be collapsed	collapse **separate** inherit
border-spacing	Specifies the distance between the borders of adjacent cells	[length] inherit
caption-side	Specifies the placement of a table caption	**top** bottom inherit
empty-cells	Specifies whether to display borders and background on empty cells in a table	hide **show** inherit
table-layout	Sets the layout algorithm to be used for a table	**auto** fixed inherit

Table B–16 Text Properties

Property Name	Description	Values
color	Sets the color of text	[color] inherit
direction	Specifies the text direction/writing direction	**ltr** rtl inherit
hanging-punctuation	Specifies whether a punctuation character may be placed outside the line box	none first last allow-end force-end
letter-spacing	Increases or decreases the space between characters	**normal** [length] inherit
line-height	Sets the line height	**normal** [length] [number] [percentage] inherit
punctuation-trim	Specifies whether a punctuation character should be trimmed	none start end allow-end adjacent
text-align	Specifies the horizontal alignment of text	left right center justify inherit
text-align-last	Describes how the last line of a block or a line right before a forced line break is aligned when text-align is "justify"	
text-decoration	Adds decoration to text	**none** blink line-through overline underline inherit
text-indent	Indents the first line of text in an element	[length] [percentage] inherit
text-justify	Specifies the justification method used when text-align is "justify"	**auto** interword interideograph intercluster distribute kashida none
text-overflow	Specifies what should happen when text overflows the containing element	**clip** ellipsis [string]
text-shadow	Adds shadow to text	[h-shadow] [v-shadow] [blur] [color]

(Continued)

Table B–16 Text Properties (Continued)

Property Name	Description	Values
text-transform	Controls text capitalization	**none** capitalize lowercase uppercase inherit
text-wrap	Specifies line breaking rules for text	**normal** none unrestricted suppress
vertical-align	Sets the vertical positioning of text	**baseline** [length] [percentage] bottom middle sub super text-bottom text-top top inherit
white-space	Specifies how white space inside an element is handled	**normal** nowrap pre preline prewrap inherit
word-break	Specifies the line breaking rules for non-CJK scripts	**normal** break-all hyphenate
word-spacing	Increases or decreases the space between words	**normal** [length] inherit
word-wrap	Allows long, unbreakable words to be broken and wrap to the next line	**normal** break-word

Table B–17 Transition Properties

Property Name	Description	Values
transition	Sets the four transition properties in one declaration	n/a
transition-delay	Specifies when the transition effect will start	[time]
transition-duration	Specifies how many seconds or milliseconds a transition effect takes to complete	[time]
transition-property	Specifies the name of the CSS property the transition effect is for	none **all** property
transition-timing-function	Specifies the speed curve of the transition effect	linear **ease** ease-in ease-in-out ease-out cubic-bezier

Appendix C
Symbols Quick Reference

Using Symbols

You can insert symbols onto your HTML page by using a symbol entity code. Tables C–1 and C–2 contain commonly used symbol and mathematical entity codes. You can find a complete list of characters at unicode.org and at w3schools.com. You can also search the web for many other Unicode character map resources.

Table C–1 Commonly Used Characters		
Symbol	Character Reference	Description
&	&amp;	Ampersand
¦	&brvbar;	Broken vertical bar
¢	&cent;	Cent sign
©	&copy;	Copyright sign
¤	&curren;	Currency sign
†	&dagger;	Dagger
‡	&Dagger;	Double dagger
€	&euro;	Euro
>	&gt;	Greater-than sign
«	&laquo;	Left-pointing double angle quotation mark
<	&lt;	Less-than sign
—	&mdash;	Em dash
		Nonbreaking space
–	&ndash;	En dash
¬	&not;	Not sign
¶	&para;	Paragraph sign
£	&pound;	Pound sign
"	&quot;	Quotation mark = APL quote
®	&reg;	Registered mark sign
»	&raquo;	Right-pointing double angle quotation mark
§	&sect;	Section sign
™	&trade;	Trademark sign
¥	&yen;	Yen

Table C–2 Mathematical and Technical Characters

Symbol	Character Reference	Description
$\wedge$	&and;	Logical and
$\angle$	&ang;	Angle
$\approx$	&asymp;	Almost equal to
$\cap$	&cap;	Intersection
$\cup$	&cup;	Union
$^\circ$	&deg;	Degree sign
$\div$	&divide;	Division sign
$\equiv$	&equiv;	Identical to
$\exists$	&exist;	There exists
f	&fnof;	Function
$\forall$	&forall;	For all
$\frac{1}{2}$	&frac12;	Fraction one half
$\frac{1}{4}$	&frac14;	Fraction one quarter
$\frac{3}{4}$	&frac34;	Fraction three quarters
$\geq$	&ge;	Greater-than or equal to
∞	&infin;	Infinity
$\int$	&int;	Integral
$\in$	&isin;	Element of
$\leq$	&le;	Less than or equal to
μ	&micro;	Micro sign
∇	&nabla;	Backward difference
$\neq$	&ne;	Not equal to
$\ni$	&ni;	Contains as a member
∂	&part;	Partial differential
$\perp$	&perp;	Perpendicular
$\pm$	&plusmn;	Plus-minus sign
$\prod$	&prod;	n-ary product
$\propto$	&prop;	Proportional to
$\sqrt{}$	&radic;	Square root
$\sim$	&sim;	Tilde
$\sum$	&sum;	n-ary summation
$\therefore$	&there4;	Therefore

Appendix D
Accessibility Standards for Webpage Developers

Making the Web Accessible

Nearly 15 percent of the world population has some sort of disability, a physical condition that limits the individual's ability to perform certain tasks. The U.S. Congress passed the Rehabilitation Act in 1973, which prohibits discrimination against those with disabilities. In 1998, Congress amended this act to reflect the latest changes in information technology. Section 508 requires that any electronic information developed, procured, maintained, or used by the federal government be accessible to people with disabilities. Disabilities that inhibit a person's ability to use the web fall into four main categories: visual, hearing, motor, and cognitive. This amendment has had a profound effect on how webpages are designed and developed.

Although Section 508 is specific to websites created and maintained by the federal government, all competent web developers adhere to the Section 508 guidelines. It is important to include everyone as a potential user of your website, including those with disabilities. To ignore the needs of nearly 15 percent of our population is just poor practice. However, some portions of Section 508 are not supported by HTML 5. For example, longdesc (§ 1194.22a) and frames (§ 1194.22i) are no longer supported by HTML 5. A web developer would not use those elements, which renders those Section 508 requirements null.

The World Wide Web Consortium (W3C) sponsors its own initiative, called the Web Accessibility Initiative (WAI), that develops guidelines and support materials for accessibility standards. These guidelines, known as the Web Content Accessibility Guidelines (WCAG), cover many of the same issues defined in the Section 508 rules and expand on them relative to superior website design.

Section 508 Guidelines Examples

The 13 parts of the Section 508 guidelines are as follows:

Subpart A—General
- 1194.1 Purpose.
- 1194.2 Application.
- 1194.3 General exceptions.
- 1194.4 Definitions.
- 1194.5 Equivalent facilitation.

Subpart B—Technical Standards

- 1194.21 Software applications and operating systems.
- 1194.22 Web-based intranet and Internet information and applications.
- 1194.23 Telecommunications products.
- 1194.24 Video and multimedia products.
- 1194.25 Self-contained, closed products.
- 1194.26 Desktop and portable computers.

Subpart C—Functional Performance Criteria

- 1194.31 Functional performance criteria.

Subpart D—Information, Documentation, and Support

- 1194.41 Information, documentation, and support.

Web developers should review these guidelines thoroughly. The following sections focus on the specific guidelines for intranet and Internet development.

Subsection **§ 1194.22** of Section 508, **web-based intranet and Internet information and applications**, is the segment of the amendment that impacts web design. There are 16 paragraphs within § 1194.22, which are lettered (a) through (p). These 16 paragraphs describe how each component of a website should be designed to ensure accessibility. The following is a list of the 16 paragraphs:

§ 1194.22 (a) A text equivalent for every non-text element shall be provided (e.g., via "alt", "longdesc", or in element content).

Graphical images that contain webpage content should include a text alternative. For good web development practice, all images should include the alt attribute to describe that image, as shown in Chapter 2. As mentioned earlier, longdesc is not supported by HTML 5.

§ 1194.22 (b) Equivalent alternatives for any multimedia presentation shall be synchronized with the presentation.

Audio clips should contain a transcript of the content; video clips need closed captioning.

§ 1194.22 (c) Web pages shall be designed so that all information conveyed with color is also available without color, for example from context or markup.

Although color is an important component of most webpages, you need to consider those site visitors with forms of color blindness if the color contributes significantly to the website content.

§ 1194.22 (d) Documents shall be organized so they are readable without requiring an associated style sheet.

Style sheets have an important role in web development. Some browser development tools allow a user to turn off the styles or modify the styles for the current browser session. When developing a website using style sheets, ensure that the site maintains its functionality, even if your specified styles have been turned off.

§ 1194.22 (e) Redundant text links shall be provided for each active region of a server-side image map.

and

§ 1194.22 (f) Client-side image maps shall be provided instead of server-side image maps except where the regions cannot be defined with an available geometric shape.

This means that it is preferable for the web developer to use client-side image maps unless the map uses a shape that the client-side will not allow. If the web developer chooses to use server-side image maps, the developer should provide text alternatives for each link on the image map.

§ 1194.22 (g) Row and column headers shall be identified for data tables. *and*

§ 1194.22 (h) Markup shall be used to associate data cells and header cells for data tables that have two or more logical levels of row or column headers.

You should structure your tables so that they appear in a linear fashion. In other words, the table content should be displayed one cell at a time, working from left to right across each row before moving to the next row.

§ 1194.22 (i) Frames shall be titled with text that facilitates frame identification and navigation.

Although frames are not supported by HTML 5, you should understand what the law requires. Nonvisual browsers open frame sites one frame at a time. It is therefore important that the web developer gives a name to each frame, and that the name reflects the contents of that frame. You can use either the title or the id, but because nonvisual browsers differ in which attribute they use, the web developer should use both attributes.

§ 1194.22 (j) Pages shall be designed to avoid causing the screen to flicker with a frequency greater than 2 Hz and lower than 55 Hz.

Animations on a webpage can be irritating to many people. However, they can also be quite harmful to people who have certain cognitive or visual disabilities or seizure disorders. You should therefore ensure that animations fall within the ranges stated, and you should limit the use of animations when possible. You also should make certain that necessary page content is available without the animations.

§ 1194.22 (k) A text-only page, with equivalent information or functionality, shall be provided to make a website comply with the provisions of this part, when compliance cannot be accomplished in any other way. The content of the text-only pages shall be updated whenever the primary page changes.

If you cannot comply with the other 15 guidelines, you should provide a text-only page to display the content of the page. You should also provide an easily accessible link to that text-only web page.

§ 1194.22 (l) When pages utilize scripting languages to display content, or to create interface elements, the information provided by the script shall be identified with functional text that can be read by assistive technology.

Scripts are often used to create a more interesting and dynamic webpage. You should ensure that the functionality of the script is still available for any person using nonvisual browsers.

§ 1194.22 (m) When a web page requires that an applet, plug-in, or other application be present on the client system to interpret page content, the page must provide a link to a plug-in or applet that complies with 1194.21 (a) through (l).

Any applet or plug-in that is used on your webpages should also comply with Section 508. The web developer should provide a link to the applet or plug-in that is compliant with Section 508.

§ 1194.22 (n) When electronic forms are designed to be completed on-line, the form shall allow people using assistive technology to access the information, field elements, and functionality required for completion and submission of the form, including all directions and cues.

Forms need to be accessible to anyone, including those using nonvisual browsers. You should therefore include value attributes or alternative text for buttons, input boxes, and text area boxes on any form included on your web page.

§ 1194.22 (o) A method shall be provided that permits users to skip repetitive navigation links.

As discussed in Chapter 11, it is helpful to provide Skip to Content links at the very top of a webpage so that users of nonvisual browsers can quickly link to the main content of the website.

§ 1194.22 (p) When a timed response is required, the user shall be alerted and given sufficient time to indicate that more time is required.

Users need to be given sufficient time to react to a time-out from inactivity by notifying users that the process will soon time out. The user should then be given a way to easily request additional time.

WAI Guidelines

The WAI includes guidelines for web developers, known as Web Content Accessibility Guidelines (WCAG) 2.0 and 2.1. The WCAG 2.0 and 2.1 document how to make web content more accessible to people with disabilities. WCAG 2.0 was published in December 2008 and the WCAG 2.1 was published in June 2018. WCAG 2.1 extends WCAG 2.0 and is backwards compatible with WCAG 2.0. Both WCAG 2.0 and 2.1 are existing standards and 2.1 does not supersede 2.0. However, if you want to meet both standards, you may refer to the 2.1 standard.

Web **content** generally refers to the information in a webpage or web application, including text, images, forms, sounds, and videos. All web developers should review the information at the official website at w3.org/WAI/standards-guidelines/wcag/ for complete information on these guidelines and should apply the guidelines to their webpage development.

The 12 WCAG 2.0 and 2.1 guidelines are organized under four principles: perceivable, operable, understandable, and robust. Anyone who wants to use the web must have content that is:

Perceivable: Information and user interface components must be presentable to users in ways they can perceive. Users must be able to perceive the information being presented (it can't be invisible to all of their senses).

Operable: User interface components and navigation must be operable. Users must be able to operate the interface (the interface cannot require interaction that a user cannot perform).

Understandable: Information and the operation of the user interface must be understandable. Users must be able to understand the information as well as the operation of the user interface (the content or operation cannot be beyond their understanding).

Robust: Content must be robust enough that it can be interpreted reliably by a wide variety of user agents, including assistive technologies. Users must be able to access the content as technologies advance (as technologies and user agents evolve, the content should remain accessible).

If any of these is not true, users with disabilities will not be able to use the web.

For each guideline, there are testable success criteria, which are at three levels: A, AA, and AAA. For a webpage to conform to WCAG 2.0 and 2.1, all of the following conformance requirements must be satisfied:

- **Level A:** For Level A conformance (the minimum level of conformance), the webpage satisfies all the Level A Success Criteria, or a conforming alternate version is provided.
- **Level AA:** For Level AA conformance, the webpage satisfies all the Level A and Level AA Success Criteria, or a Level AA conforming alternate version is provided.
- **Level AAA:** For Level AAA conformance, the webpage satisfies all the Level A, Level AA, and Level AAA Success Criteria, or a Level AAA conforming alternate version is provided.

Table D–1 contains a summary of the WCAG 2.0 and 2.1 guidelines and the corresponding level of conformance. Note that the following WCAG 2.0 and 2.1 guidelines were current at the time of this publication. For the latest WCAG guidelines, visit w3.org/WAI/standards-guidelines/wcag/.

Table D–1 WCAG 2.0 and 2.1 Guidelines

Item	Level	Added in 2.1
Principle 1: Perceivable—Information and user interface components must be presentable to users in ways they can perceive.		
Guideline 1.1 Text Alternatives: Provide text alternatives for any nontext content so that it can be changed into other forms people need, such as large print, braille, speech, symbols or simpler language.		
1.1.1 Nontext Content: All nontext content that is presented to the user has a text alternative that serves the equivalent purpose.	A	
Guideline 1.2 Time-Based Media: Provide alternatives for time-based media.		
1.2.1 Audio-only and Video-only (Prerecorded): An alternative for time-based media is provided that presents equivalent information for prerecorded audio-only or video-only content.	A	
1.2.2 Captions (Prerecorded): Captions are provided for all prerecorded audio content in synchronized media, except when the media is a media alternative for text and is clearly labeled as such.	A	
1.2.3 Audio Description or Media Alternative (Prerecorded): An alternative for time-based media or audio description of the prerecorded video content is provided for synchronized media, except when the media is a media alternative for text and is clearly labeled as such.	A	
1.2.4 Captions (Live): Captions are provided for all live audio content in synchronized media.	AA	
1.2.5 Audio Description (Prerecorded): Audio description is provided for all prerecorded video content in synchronized media.	AA	
1.2.6 Sign Language (Prerecorded): Sign language interpretation is provided for all prerecorded audio content in synchronized media.	AAA	
1.2.7 Extended Audio Description (Prerecorded): Where pauses in foreground audio are insufficient to allow audio descriptions to convey the sense of the video, extended audio description is provided for all prerecorded video content in synchronized media.	AAA	
1.2.8 Media Alternative (Prerecorded): An alternative for time-based media is provided for all prerecorded synchronized media and for all prerecorded video-only media.	AAA	
1.2.9 Audio-only (Live): An alternative for time-based media that presents equivalent information for live audio-only content is provided.	AAA	
Guideline 1.3 Adaptable: Create content that can be presented in different ways (for example, simpler layout) without losing information or structure.		
1.3.1 Info and Relationships: Information, structure, and relationships conveyed through presentation can be programmatically determined or are available in text.	A	
1.3.2 Meaningful Sequence: When the sequence in which content is presented affects its meaning, a correct reading sequence can be programmatically determined.	A	
1.3.3 Sensory Characteristics: Instructions provided for understanding and operating content do not rely solely on sensory characteristics of components such as shape, size, visual location, orientation, or sound.	A	
1.3.4 Orientation: Content does not restrict its view and operation to a single display orientation, such as portrait or landscape, unless a specific display orientation is essential.	AA	X

(Continued)

Table D–1 WCAG 2.0 and 2.1 Guidelines *(Continued)*

Item	Level	Added in 2.1
1.3.5 Identify Input Purpose: The purpose of each input field collecting information about the user can be programmatically determined when: • The input field serves a purpose identified in the Input Purposes for User Interface Components section; and • The content is implemented using technologies with support for identifying the expected meaning for form input data.	AA	X
1.3.6 Identify Purpose: In content implemented using markup languages, the purpose of User Interface Components, icons, and regions can be programmatically determined.	AAA	X
Guideline 1.4 Distinguishable: Make it easier for users to see and hear content, including separating foreground from background.		
1.4.1 Use of Color: Color is not used as the only visual means of conveying information, indicating an action, prompting a response, or distinguishing a visual element.	A	
1.4.2 Audio Control: If any audio on a web page plays automatically for more than 3 seconds, either a mechanism is available to pause or stop the audio, or a mechanism is available to control the audio volume independently from the overall system volume level.	A	
1.4.3 Contrast (Minimum): The visual presentation of text and images of text has a contrast ratio of at least 4.5:1 (for specific exceptions, refer to w3.org/TR/WCAG).	AA	
1.4.4 Resize Text: Except for captions and images of text, text can be resized without assistive technology up to 200 percent without loss of content or functionality.	AA	
1.4.5 Images of Text: If the technologies being used can achieve the visual presentation, text is used to convey information rather than images of (for specific exceptions, refer to w3.org/TR/WCAG).	AA	
1.4.6 Contrast (Enhanced): The visual presentation of text and images of text has a contrast ratio of at least 7:1 (for specific exceptions, refer to w3.org/TR/WCAG).	AAA	
1.4.7 Low or No Background Audio: For prerecorded audio-only content in which 1) the audio does not contain background sounds, 2) the background sounds can be turned off, or 3) the background sounds are at least 20 decibels lower than the foreground speech content.	AAA	
1.4.8 Visual Presentation: For the visual presentation of blocks of text, a mechanism is available to manipulate the look of the page (e.g., background colors, text size) easily.	AAA	
1.4.9 Images of Text (No Exception): Images of text are only used for pure decoration or where a particular presentation of text is essential to the information being conveyed.	AAA	
1.4.10 Reflow: Content can be presented without loss of information or functionality, and without requiring scrolling in two dimensions for: • Vertical scrolling content at a width equivalent to 320 CSS pixels; • Horizontal scrolling content at a height equivalent to 256 CSS pixels; Except for parts of the content which require two-dimensional layout for usage or meaning.	AA	X
1.4.11 Non-text Contrast: The visual presentation of the following have a contrast ratio of at least 3:1 against adjacent color(s): • **User Interface Components:** Visual information required to identify user interface components and states, except for inactive components or where the appearance of the component is determined by the user agent and not modified by the author; • **Graphical Objects:** Parts of graphics required to understand the content, except when a particular presentation of graphics is essential to the information being conveyed.	AA	X
1.4.12 Text Spacing: In content implemented using markup languages that support the following text style properties, no loss of content or functionality occurs by setting all of the following and by changing no other style property: • Line height (line spacing) to at least 1.5 times the font size; • Spacing following paragraphs to at least 2 times the font size; • Letter spacing (tracking) to at least 0.12 times the font size; • Word spacing to at least 0.16 times the font size. Exception: Human languages and scripts that do not make use of one or more of these text style properties in written text can conform using only the properties that exist for that combination of language and script.	AA	X

(Continued)

Table D–1 WCAG 2.0 and 2.1 Guidelines *(Continued)*

Item	Level	Added in 2.1
1.4.13 Content on Hover or Focus: Where receiving and then removing pointer hover or keyboard focus triggers additional content to become visible and then hidden, the following are true: Hide full description • **Dismissible:** A mechanism is available to dismiss the additional content without moving pointer hover or keyboard focus, unless the additional content communicates an input error or does not obscure or replace other content; • **Hoverable:** If pointer hover can trigger the additional content, then the pointer can be moved over the additional content without the additional content disappearing; • **Persistent:** The additional content remains visible until the hover or focus trigger is removed, the user dismisses it, or its information is no longer valid. Exception: The visual presentation of the additional content is controlled by the user agent and is not modified by the author.	AA	X
Principle 2: Operable—User interface components and navigation must be operable.		
Guideline 2.1 Keyboard Accessible: Make all functionality available from the keyboard.		
2.1.1 Keyboard: All functionality of the content is operable through a keyboard interface without requiring specific timings for individual keystrokes, except where the underlying function requires input that depends on the path of the user's movement and not just the endpoints.	A	
2.1.2 No Keyboard Trap: If keyboard focus can be moved to a component of the page using a keyboard interface, then focus can be moved away from that component using only a keyboard interface, and, if it requires more than unmodified arrow or tab keys or other standard exit methods, the user is advised of the method for moving focus away.	A	
2.1.3 Keyboard (No Exception): All functionality of the content is operable through a keyboard interface without requiring specific timings for individual keystrokes.	AAA	
2.1.4 Character Key Shortcuts: If a keyboard shortcut is implemented in content using only letter (including upper- and lower-case letters), punctuation, number, or symbol characters, then at least one of the following is true: • **Turn off:** A mechanism is available to turn the shortcut off; • **Remap:** A mechanism is available to remap the shortcut to include one or more non-printable keyboard keys (e.g., Ctrl, Alt); • **Active only on focus:** The keyboard shortcut for a user interface component is only active when that component has focus.	A	X
Guideline 2.2 Enough Time: Provide users enough time to read and use content.		
2.2.1 Timing Adjustable: The user should be able to easily change each time limit that is set by the content.	A	
2.2.2 Pause, Stop, Hide: The user should be able to pause, stop, or hide moving, blinking, scrolling, or auto-updating information.	A	
2.2.3 No Timing: Timing is not an essential part of the event or activity presented by the content, except for noninteractive synchronized media and real-time events.	AAA	
2.2.4 Interruptions: Interruptions can be postponed or suppressed by the user, except interruptions involving an emergency.	AAA	
2.2.5 Re-authenticating: When an authenticated session expires, the user can continue the activity without loss of data after re-authenticating.	AAA	
2.2.6 Timeouts: Users are warned of the duration of any user inactivity that could cause data loss, unless the data is preserved for more than 20 hours when the user does not take any actions.	AAA	X
Guideline 2.3 Seizures: Do not design content in a way that is known to cause seizures.		
2.3.1 Three Flashes or Below Threshold: Web pages do not contain anything that flashes more than three times in any one second period, or the flash is below the general flash and red flash thresholds.	A	
2.3.2 Animation from Interactions: Web pages do not contain anything that flashes more than three times in any one second period.	AAA	

(Continued)

Table D–1 WCAG 2.0 and 2.1 Guidelines *(Continued)*		
Item	**Level**	**Added in 2.1**
2.3.3 Three Flashes: Motion animation triggered by interaction can be disabled, unless the animation is essential to the functionality or the information being conveyed.	AAA	X
Guideline 2.4 Navigable: Provide ways to help users navigate, find content, and determine where they are.		
2.4.1 Bypass Blocks: A mechanism is available to bypass blocks of content that are repeated on multiple web pages.	A	
2.4.2 Page Titled: Web pages have titles that describe topic or purpose.	A	
2.4.3 Focus Order: If a Web page can be navigated sequentially and the navigation sequences affect meaning or operation, focusable components receive focus in an order that preserves meaning and operability.	A	
2.4.4 Link Purpose (In Context): The purpose of each link can be determined from the link text alone or from the link text together with its programmatically determined link context, except where the purpose of the link would be ambiguous to users in general.	A	
2.4.5 Multiple Ways: More than one way is available to locate a web page within a set of web pages except where the web Page is the result of, or a step in, a process.	AA	
2.4.6 Headings and Labels: Headings and labels describe topic or purpose.	AA	
2.4.7 Focus Visible: Any keyboard operable user interface has a mode of operation where the keyboard focus indicator is visible.	AA	
2.4.8 Location: Information about the user's location within a set of web pages is available.	AAA	
2.4.9 Link Purpose (Link Only): A mechanism is available to allow the purpose of each link to be identified from link text alone, except where the purpose of the link would be ambiguous to users in general.	AAA	
2.4.10 Section Headings: Section headings are used to organize the content.	AAA	
Principle 3: Understandable—Information and the operation of user interface must be understandable.		
Guideline 3.1 Readable: Make text content readable and understandable.		
3.1.1 Language of Page: The default human language of each web page can be programmatically determined.	A	
3.1.2 Language of Parts: The human language of each passage or phrase in the content can be programmatically determined except for proper names, technical terms, words of indeterminate language, and words or phrases that have become part of the vernacular of the immediately surrounding text.	AA	
3.1.3 Unusual Words: A mechanism is available for identifying specific definitions of words or phrases used in an unusual or restricted way, including idioms and jargon.	AAA	
3.1.4 Abbreviations: A mechanism for identifying the expanded form or meaning of abbreviations is available.	AAA	
3.1.5 Reading Level: When text requires reading ability more advanced than the lower secondary education level after removal of proper names and titles, supplemental content, or a version that does not require reading ability more advanced than the lower secondary education level, is available.	AAA	
3.1.6 Pronunciation: A mechanism is available for identifying specific pronunciation of words where the meaning of the words, in context, is ambiguous without knowing the pronunciation.	AAA	
Guideline 3.2 Predictable: Make web pages appear and operate in predictable ways.		
3.2.1 On Focus: When any component receives focus, it does not initiate a change of context.	A	
3.2.2 On Input: Changing the setting of any user interface component does not automatically cause a change of context unless the user has been advised of the behavior before using the component.	A	

(Continued)

Table D–1 WCAG 2.0 and 2.1 Guidelines *(Continued)*

Item	Level	Added in 2.1
3.2.3 Consistent Navigation: Navigational mechanisms that are repeated on multiple web pages within a set of web pages occur in the same relative order each time they are repeated, unless a change is initiated by the user.	AA	
3.2.4 Consistent Identification: Components that have the same functionality within a set of web pages are identified consistently.	AA	
3.2.5 Change on Request: Changes of context are initiated only by user request or a mechanism is available to turn off such changes.	AAA	
Guideline 3.3 Input Assistance: Help users avoid and correct mistakes.		
3.3.1 Error Identification: If an input error is automatically detected, the item that is in error is identified and the error is described to the user in text.	A	
3.3.2 Labels or Instructions: Labels or instructions are provided when content requires user input.	A	
3.3.3 Error Suggestion: If an input error is automatically detected and suggestions for its correction are known, then the suggestions are provided to the user, unless it would jeopardize the security or purpose of the content.	AA	
3.3.4 Error Prevention (Legal, Financial, Data): For web pages that cause legal commitments or financial transactions for the user to occur, that modify or delete user-controllable data in data storage systems, or that submit user test responses, a mechanism is available for reviewing, confirming, and correcting information before finalizing the submission.	AA	
3.3.5 Help: Context-sensitive help is available.	AAA	
3.3.6 Error Prevention (All): For web pages that require the user to submit information, a mechanism is available for reviewing, confirming, and correcting information before finalizing the submission.	AAA	
Principle 4: Robust—Content must be robust enough that it can be interpreted reliably by a wide variety of user agents, including assistive technologies.		
Guideline 4.1 Compatible: Maximize compatibility with current and future user agents, including assistive technologies.		
4.1.1 Parsing: In content implemented using markup languages, elements have complete start and end tags, elements are nested according to their specifications, elements do not contain duplicate attributes, and any IDs are unique, except where the specifications allow these features.	A	
4.1.2 Name, Role, Value: For all user interface components (including but not limited to: form elements, links, and components generated by scripts), the name and role can be programmatically determined; states, properties, and values that can be set by the user can be programmatically set; and notification of changes to these items is available to user agents, including assistive technologies.	A	
4.1.3 Status Messages: In content implemented using markup languages, status messages can be programmatically determined through role or properties such that they can be presented to the user by assistive technologies without receiving focus.	AA	X

Index

Note:

- Page numbers in bold type indicate definitions.
- Page numbers followed by "t" indicate tables.
- Page numbers followed by "btw" indicate margin notes.
- Page numbers followed by "+t" or "+btw" indicate discussions plus tables or margin notes.

Symbols

client-side scripting language, **HTML 24, HTML 517**
cm (centimeters), unit of measurement, **HTML** 223t
CMS (content management systems), **HTML 679**–681
CMYK (Cyan, Magenta, Yellow, and Black), **HTML** 152BTW
code, **HTML 2, HTML** 3t
codec, **HTML 475**
<code> tag, **APP** 3t
</code> tag, **APP** 3t
<colgroup> tag, **APP** 3t
</colgroup> tag, **APP** 3t
collapsed border, **HTML** 415–416
color(s), **HTML** 19+t
 Bootstrap, **HTML** 651+t
 properties, **HTML** 415t, **APP** 17t
cols, textarea control, **HTML 426,** 437
<col> tag, **APP** 3t
</col> tag, **APP** 3t
column, table, **HTML 402**
column layouts
 exploring, **HTML** 387–388
comments, **HTML** 59–61
 adding for mobile styles, **HTML** 232
 adding in CSS files, **HTML** 193–195
 adding to webpage template, **HTML** 60–61
<!-- Comments here --> tag, **APP** 1t
compatibility testing, **HTML 609**
compression
 lossless, **HTML 87**
 lossy, **HTML 88**
.com top-level domain (TLD), **HTML** 595–596
conformance levels (WCAG guidelines), **APP** 31
consumer-to-consumer (C2C) business model, **HTML** 620
#contact a style rule, **HTML** 262–263
Contact Us webpage, **HTML** 120–121
 adding form, fieldset, labels, and text input controls, **HTML** 432–433
 adding headings and links to, **HTML** 120–121
 check boxes to form, **HTML** 434–435
 design for tablet viewports, **HTML** 295–298
 in desktop viewport, **HTML** 401
 email and tel input controls to form, **HTML** 433–434
 Forward Fitness Club, **HTML** 216–217
 for mobile-first strategy, **HTML** 261–263
 in mobile viewport, **HTML** 401
 modifying, **HTML 262, HTML** 296–297
 navigation link, **HTML** 312
 select element to form, **HTML** 435–437

style rule for id attribute on, **HTML** 182–183
 submit controls to form, **HTML** 438
 in tablet viewport, **HTML** 401
 textarea element to form, **HTML** 437
 validating, **HTML** 126
#container style
 in desktop media query, **HTML** 309
content, webpage, **HTML 62**
 wrapping, **HTML** 62BTW
content attribute, **HTML 591**
contenteditable attribute, **APP** 10t
content specialist, **HTML 618**
controls attribute, **HTML** 476t, **HTML 477**
copyright class attribute, **HTML** 585–586
Corel VideoStudio Ultimate, **HTML 469**
Creative Commons license, **HTML 619**
CSS. *See* Cascading Style Sheets (CSS)
CSS3 gradients, **HTML** 318BTW
CSS files (.css files), **HTML 148**
 adding comments to, **HTML** 193–195
 linking HTML file to minified, **HTML** 616–617
 minify, **HTML** 615–616
 validating, **HTML** 195–197
CSS grid layout, **HTML 347**–348
 grid-template-columns, **HTML** 348
 properties, **HTML** 347+t
 using, **HTML** 347–348
 using in tablet viewports, **HTML** 357–360
CSS reset, **HTML** 188–190
 creating, **HTML** 190
 definition, **HTML 188**
cue text, **HTML 487**
customer feedback form, **HTML** 429BTW
custom fonts, **HTML** 240–247
 integrating custom Google Font, **HTML** 242–247
CyberLink PowerDirector, **HTML 469**

D

data attribute, **HTML** 477
data-* attribute, **APP** 10t
data cell, **HTML 403**
data input control, **HTML 424**
data lines, **HTML 4**
<datalist> tag, **APP** 3t
</datalist> tag, **APP** 3t
<data> tag, **APP** 3t
</data> tag, **APP** 3t
date control, **HTML 426**
date text box, **HTML 424**
<dd> tag, **APP** 3t
</dd> tag, **APP** 3t
dec character code, **HTML 64**

declaration, **HTML 149**
 adding within tablet media query, **HTML** 319
default browsers, **HTML** 70–71+BTW
 displaying home page in, **HTML** 70–71
<del> tag, **APP** 3t
</del> tag, **APP** 3t
deprecated element, **HTML** 147BTW, **APP 1, APP** 11
description lists, **HTML 112**
 adding to About Us webpage, **HTML** 116–118
descriptions file, **HTML 487**–488
desktop layouts design, **HTML** 323
desktop viewports
 About Us page design for, **HTML** 306–307
 About Us page in, **HTML 338, HTML** 634–635
 adding dynamic pseudo-classes to style sheet, **HTML** 316–317
 adding linear gradient, **HTML** 319
 adding new style rules in, **HTML** 360–362
 applying text-shadow, **HTML** 363
 Classes page in, **HTML 401, HTML** 634, **HTML** 636
 Contact Us page in, **HTML** 401
 create media query for, **HTML** 299
 create media query for large, **HTML** 309–310
 create multiple-column layout for, **HTML** 306–307
 designing for, **HTML** 298–312
 determining viewport width for, **HTML** 313–314
 exploring responsive design, **HTML** 218
 form style for, **HTML** 443–444, **HTML 453, HTML** 457
 heading 1 elements within main element style, **HTML** 305
 home page in, **HTML** 338–339, **HTML** 635
 home page wireframe for, **HTML** 351
 layouts design, **HTML** 323
 list item links in navigation area style for, **HTML** 302–303
 main element style, **HTML** 304
 Metropolitan Museum of Art website, **HTML** 221
 navigation style for, **HTML** 300–301
 Nutrition page in, **HTML** 339
 Nutrition page wireframe for, **HTML** 365–366
 personal portfolio styling for, **HTML** 335
 setting new breakpoint for media query, **HTML** 314–315
 Strike a Chord website, **HTML** 390
 styling Dog Grooming website for, **HTML** 335–336